THE
NEW TESTAMENT
OF THE
NEW JERUSALEM BIBLE

THE
NEW TESTAMENT
OF THE
NEW JERUSALEM BIBLE

With Complete Introductions and Notes

DOUBLEDAY
NEW YORK LONDON TORONTO SYDNEY AUCKLAND

PUBLISHED BY DOUBLEDAY
a division of Bantam Doubleday Dell Publishing Group, Inc.
1540 Broadway, New York, New York 10036

DOUBLEDAY and the portrayal of an anchor with
a dolphin are trademarks of Doubleday, a division of
Bantam Doubleday Dell Publishing Group, Inc.

This edition published October 1986
by special arrangement with Doubleday, and
Darton, Longman & Todd, Ltd.

Library of Congress Cataloging-in-Publication Data
Bible, N.T. English. New Jerusalem Bible. 1986.
The New Testament of the New Jerusalem Bible,
with complete introduction and notes.
A retranslation of the New Testament, made directly
from the original Greek.
General editor: Henry Wansbrough.
I. Wansbrough, Henry, 1934–   II. Title.
BS2095.N375   1986   225.5′207   86-11680
ISBN 0-385-23706-5 (pbk.)

GENERAL EDITOR'S FOREWORD

Since its publication in 1966 the Jerusalem Bible has become widely used for liturgical purposes, for study and for private reading. Credit both for the idea of the translation of the French *Bible de Jérusalem* and for the great labours involved in its execution belongs to Alexander Jones; it is sad that he did not live to see the full impact of his work. Both as an intelligible modern translation and as a well laid-out and easily manageable book, the Jerusalem Bible set a new standard for versions of the Bible. However, in 1973 a new edition of the *Bible de Jérusalem* was published, which incorporated progress in scholarship over the two decades since the preparation of its first edition. The introductions and notes were often widely changed to take account of linguistic, archaeological and theological advances, and the text itself in some instances reflected new understanding of the originals.

This 1973 revision was important enough to warrant a completely new edition of the English-language *Jerusalem Bible*. In this new edition the introductions and notes are drawn from that revision, with some additional changes especially in the introductions and notes to the New Testament to take into account further recent advances in scholarship. The biblical text of the first edition was occasionally criticised for following the French translation more closely than the originals. In this edition the translation has been made directly from the Hebrew, Greek or Aramaic. Only where the text admits of more than one interpretation has the option chosen by the *Bible de Jérusalem* been followed, unless permission to adopt another view was granted by the editors of that work. The character of the *Jerusalem Bible* as primarily a study Bible has been kept constantly in mind, and for that reason accuracy of translation has been a prime consideration. Paraphrase has been avoided more rigorously than in the first edition; care has been taken that in parallel passages (for example in the first three gospels) the similarities and differences should be mirrored exactly in the translation. Key terms in the originals, especially those theological key concepts on which there is a major theological note, have been rendered throughout (with very few exceptions) by the same English word, instead of by the variety of words used in the first edition. At the same time the widespread liturgical use of this version has been taken into account; while it is hoped that the translation is fresh and lively, care has been taken to reproduce the dignity of the originals by a certain measured phrasing and avoidance of the colloquial. Considerable efforts have also been made, though not at all costs, to soften or avoid the inbuilt preference of the English language, a preference now found so offensive by some people, for the masculine; the word of the Lord concerns women and men equally.

It has seemed wise to retain the spelling of the proper names traditional in English-speaking lands. Many names in biblical Hebrew have a meaning: for instance 'Adonijah' means 'My Lord is Yah' (Yahweh). Others are given a meaning by a more or less forced pun. Many of these meanings are given in the footnotes. In the rendering of Hebrew words in the footnotes, etc., a more modern system of transliteration is, however, used, thus enabling the reader to come closer to the original sounds. This is often important for onomatopoeia and to understand how textual corruption has occurred.

One acute difficulty was the choice of system when modern equivalents for weights and measures were required. In some English-speaking countries the metric system is rapidly gaining ground, while others, notably the United States, stick firmly to the imperial. Finally it seemed that both systems were needed.

For this edition the alphabetical table of major footnotes has been entirely remade in a way which will, it is hoped, make it more serviceable. Two indexes of proper names have been added, personal and geographical, giving the principal biblical passages in which they occur, as well as important footnotes. The maps have also been completely redesigned.

A list of the original collaborators in the 1966 edition may be found on page 519. In many instances this translation has used their work widely, but they cannot be considered responsible for the resultant version. The initial draft of almost the whole of the Old Testament was prepared by Mr Alan Neame, and credit for the skilful translation must go to him. The publisher's editors, at first Mr W. H. Saumarez-Smith, and for the major part of the work the Revd Cecil Hargreaves, have done far more than their job; especially the latter has been an exciting partner to work with, whose patience, inventiveness and tact have alike been a joy. The linch-pin at the publisher's office, who has co-ordinated all our efforts, has been Mr H. P. Jolowicz; his untiring and painstaking accuracy has ensured the consistency and regularity of this volume. The marginal references throughout the Bible have been reviewed by the Revd David Pope, working under difficult circumstances with impressive patience. A number of consultants who read drafts at an early stage of the work have asked that their names should not be mentioned; to them and even more to the consultants in all five continents who criticised the final drafts, and suggested many improvements, I am most grateful. The names of Professor Kenneth Grayston and Canon Douglas Webster, who worked through the whole Bible, must not go unmentioned. During the whole work my monastic brethren and my students of all ages have provided a constant check and incentive; their criticisms and suggestions have done much to improve both the dignity and the intelligibility of the work. The impatience of the young with obscurity or technicality has been a constant incentive to clarity of thought, while the love and reverence of seniors for the sacred text has helped to keep at bay anything outrageous or slipshod. Over the five years since he asked me to undertake the work, consultation with Père Benoît of the *Ecole biblique* in Jerusalem, whether in our series of letters or in our meetings at Ampleforth, Rome or Jerusalem, has been one of the pleasures of the project; while we have not always agreed, his openness and still youthful enthusiasm have invariably been a stimulus, and his concern to make this volume worthy of the *Bible de Jérusalem* an inspiration to the highest standards.

Ampleforth Abbey
York
November 1984   Henry Wansbrough

CONTENTS

BOOKS OF THE BIBLE IN ALPHABETICAL ORDER OF ABBREVIATIONS

Ac	Acts	Lk	Luke
Am	Amos	Lm	Lamentations
Ba	Baruch	Lv	Leviticus
1 Ch	1 Chronicles	1 M	1 Maccabees
2 Ch	2 Chronicles	2 M	2 Maccabees
1 Co	1 Corinthians	Mi	Micah
2 Co	2 Corinthians	Mk	Mark
Col	Colossians	Ml	Malachi
Dn	Daniel	Mt	Matthew
Dt	Deuteronomy	Na	Nahum
Ep	Ephesians	Nb	Numbers
Est	Esther	Ne	Nehemiah
Ex	Exodus	Ob	Obadiah
Ezk	Ezekiel	1 P	1 Peter
Ezr	Ezra	2 P	2 Peter
Ga	Galatians	Ph	Philippians
Gn	Genesis	Phm	Philemon
Hab	Habakkuk	Pr	Proverbs
Heb	Hebrews	Ps	Psalms
Hg	Haggai	Qo	Ecclesiastes/Qoheleth
Ho	Hosea	Rm	Romans
Is	Isaiah	Rt	Ruth
Jb	Job	Rv	Revelation
Jdt	Judith	1 S	1 Samuel
Jg	Judges	2 S	2 Samuel
Jl	Joel	Sg	Song of Songs
Jm	James	Si	Ecclesiasticus/Ben Sira
Jn	John	Tb	Tobit
1 Jn	1 John	1 Th	1 Thessalonians
2 Jn	2 John	2 Th	2 Thessalonians
3 Jn	3 John	1 Tm	1 Timothy
Jon	Jonah	2 Tm	2 Timothy
Jos	Joshua	Tt	Titus
Jr	Jeremiah	Ws	Wisdom
Jude	Jude	Zc	Zechariah
1 K	1 Kings	Zp	Zephaniah
2 K	2 Kings		

PREFACE

The Hebrew and Greek Bibles

The canon of the Hebrew Bible was fixed by the Palestinian Jews at the beginning of the Christian era and is still maintained by modern Jews. It contains only the Hebrew books, and therefore excludes the books written in Greek and the Greek supplements of Esther and Daniel. It is divided into three parts:

I The Law (the Pentateuch): Genesis, Exodus, Leviticus, Numbers, Deuteronomy

II The Prophets:
a) the 'earlier Prophets': Joshua, Judges, Samuel (1 and 2), Kings (1 and 2)
b) the 'later Prophets': Isaiah, Jeremiah, Ezekiel; the 'Twelve Minor Prophets': Hosea, Joel, Amos, Obadiah, Jonah, Micah, Nahum, Habakkuk, Zephaniah, Haggai, Zechariah, Malachi

III The Writings (Hagiographa): Psalms, Job, Proverbs, Ruth, Song of Songs, Qoheleth (Ecclesiastes), Lamentations, Esther (the last five, read on Jewish feast days, are known as the 'five scrolls'), Daniel, Ezra-Nehemiah, Chronicles

The Hebrew Bible contains twenty-four books, the 'Twelve Minor Prophets' being regarded as one book.

The Greek Bible, the 'Septuagint', or 'LXX', so called because it was supposedly translated by seventy people, was for the use of Jews of the Diaspora. It includes in addition to the text of the Hebrew Bible:

I Judith, Tobit, 1 and 2 Maccabees, Wisdom, Sira (Ecclesiasticus), Baruch (Baruch Chapter 6 is printed under the separate heading of the 'Letter to Jeremiah'). In Daniel the following parts exist only in Greek: Dn 3:24–90; Dn 13 (Susanna); Dn 14 ('Bel and the Dragon'). These books, commonly referred to as deutero-canonical, are generally regarded as part of the Christian canon.

II Books which, although sometimes used by the Fathers and ancient ecclesiastical writers, have not been accepted into the Christian Canon. These 'apocryphal' works are:

Esdras I (in the LXX the canonical Ezra-Nehemiah is entitled Esdras II)
3 and 4 Maccabees
Odes
Psalms of Solomon
In the LXX, 1 and 2 Samuel and 1 and 2 Kings are entitled 'The Four Books of Kingdoms'.

The translation

The translation follows the original Hebrew, Aramaic and Greek texts. For the Old Testament the Massoretic Text is used, that is the text established in the eighth/ninth centuries AD by Jewish scholars who fixed its letters and vowel signs, the text reproduced by most manuscripts. Only when this text presents insuperable difficulties have emendations or the versions of other Hebrew manuscripts or the ancient versions (notably the LXX and Syriac) been used. In such cases the correction made to the Hebrew text, and if possible the sense of the Hebrew, have been given in the notes. For the deutero-canonical books and the New Testament the Greek text established in modern times by critical work on the principal manuscript witnesses to the tradition (also with the help of ancient versions) has been used. When the tradition offers several alternatives, important variants not used in this translation have been indicated in the notes.

Passages considered to be glosses have been put in brackets in the text. In the biblical text this is the only way in which brackets are used.

In this edition an attempt has been made to avoid translating a single term or expression of the original by a variety of renderings. Sometimes it has proved impossible to find a single English equivalent to render all the breadth of meaning and the overtones of a Hebrew or Greek original. Sometimes, also, too literal a translation would, in context, have meant a serious impoverishment of the sense of a phrase or expression. When it has been necessary to make a choice, fidelity to the text has been given preference over a literary quality which the original did not possess.

Verse-numbering

In the Old Testament the division into verses follows the Hebrew except in the few passages where the text is found only in the Septuagint; then the Septuagint numbering is given. Where the numbering of the Vulgate differs from this main verse-numbering, it is given in smaller type. A dot • indicates a verse beginning other than at the start of a line. Occasionally to a verse number is suffixed a letter (e.g. 8:2a; 8:3b; 8:4c) to distinguish earlier or later parts of a verse. In the notes these become 8:2ª; 8:3ᵇ etc.

Italics

Italics are used for two purposes: normally they indicate a quotation from another book of the Bible; in Esther and Daniel, however, they indicate passages of the Septuagint which do not exist in the Hebrew Bible. In some of the New Testament verses shown in italics (as being quotations from the Old Testament) the New Testament writers have given the Old Testament quotations in a wording different from that of the current text of the Old Testament. They were presumably using a different version, current in their own day.

Footnotes and Indexes

The footnotes of the previous edition of the Jerusalem Bible have been revised and brought up to date in the light of recent research.

The footnotes assume that the reader has already read the Introduction to the book (or group of books) concerned. Frequently the notes are interconnected, in which case the reader is referred to other passages where the note provides supplementary explanations. In the case of parallel passages, footnotes are normally given only on the first occurrence of a passage (e.g. in the Synoptic Gospels footnotes explanatory of Mark and Luke are often to be found under the parallel passage in Matthew). A dot • is used in the footnotes to divide separate subjects within the same note.

Transcription of Hebrew

The usual conventions are followed, with these possible exceptions:

> *he* and *het* are represented by *h*
> *zain*   ,,   *z*
> *tet* and *taw*   ,,   *t*
> *kaph*   ,,   *k*
> *samek* and *sin* ,,   *s*
> *zade*   ,,   *tz**
>> *at beginning of a word represented by *z* alone except if doubled – then *tzz*
>
> The presence of *dagesh lene* in the *begadkephat* letters is shown only in the case of *pe*

More abbreviations, together with symbols and terms used in the notes

OT	Old Testament
NT	New Testament

MT	Massoretic text ('massorah' = 'tradition' in Hebrew), the Massoretic text established in the eighth/ninth centuries AD by Jewish scholars who fixed its letters and vowel signs
LXX	the Greek 'Septuagint', the earliest translation into Greek of the Hebrew Old Testament, dating from the last two centuries before Christ
Al.	Codex Alexandrinus, a manuscript of the fifth century AD
Alex.	Alexandrian text, i.e. the type of Greek text of the New Testament that circulated in the Church of Alexandria and in Egypt in early church times
Aq.	Aquila of Pontus, and the Greek text of the Old Testament according to his recension, early second century AD
Arab.	early versions of the Bible in Arabic
Arm.	Armenian
Gk-Luc.	the Greek text of the Old Testament according to the recension or revision of Lucian of Antioch, early fourth century AD
Hebr.	Hebrew
Lat.	Latin
Q	Qumran: this abbreviation is found in various combinations: e.g. '1 Q' = 'material found in Qumran Cave 1': '1 Q p Hab' = 'the commentary (*pesher*) on Habakkuk found in Qumran Cave 1': '1 Q Is^a' = 'the first (a) copy of Isaiah in Qumran Cave 1'
Rec. Luc.	Recension of Lucian (see under 'Gk-Luc.')
Sam.	Samaritan Pentateuch
Sin.	Codex Sinaiticus, a manuscript of the mid-fourth century AD, written in the Alexandrian area but discovered on Mount Sinai
Symm.	Symmachus, and the Greek text of the Old Testament according to his translation or recension, late second century AD
Syr.	Syriac, i.e. the text or rendering of the Syriac versions
Syr. hex.	the Syro-hexaplar version of the Old Testament, from Egypt, early seventh century AD
Targ.	Targum, targums: the ancient Jewish translations into Aramaic of Hebrew writings: they are in fact a combination of text, paraphrase and brief commentary
Text. rec.	*Textus receptus*: or Received text: i.e. the traditional biblical text commonly in use in recent centuries
Theod.	Theodotion, and the Greek text of the Old Testament

	according to his revision or recension, which transmits first-century material, though Theodotion's date is probably late second century
Vat.	Codex Vaticanus: a manuscript of the mid-fourth century AD, from the Alexandrian area
Vet. Lat.	*Vetus Latina*, or Old Latin version(s): i.e. Latin version(s) of the biblical text earlier than the Vulgate
Vulg.	the Latin Vulgate ('popular' version): the revised Latin version of biblical books, made by St Jerome in the late fourth century AD
West.	Western text: a type of Greek text of the New Testament that circulated mainly in the churches of the western Mediterranean and North Africa in early church times
add.	additional words included by some authorities
ch.	chapter
conj.	conjecture or conjectural reading: this may be given in the notes where the original text is uncertain, and especially in the Old Testament where suggested reconstructions of what vowels should be supplied in a Hebrew word may prove helpful
corr.	correction: i.e. a correction of the original text, following an editor or edition of later centuries
dittography	where a copyist has written twice what should have been written once
gloss	an addition to or elaboration of the original text
haplography	where a copyist has written once what should have been written twice
ketib	the Hebrew text as written, and fixed by the consonants
MS, MSS	manuscript(s)
om.	words omitted by some authorities
par.	signifies 'parallel' and points to a passage where other parallels are also indicated
peshitta	'the simple': a fifth-century Syriac version of the Bible, a revision of earlier Syriac versions
qere	the Hebrew text as read, with vowel-provision made by the Massoretes
seq.	and following verse(s)
var.	variant reading
versions	ancient translations of the original biblical language into another language: e.g. into Latin, Coptic

THE SYNOPTIC GOSPELS

INTRODUCTION TO
THE SYNOPTIC GOSPELS

§1 Of the four canonical books that record the 'good news' (*evangelium*, gospel) brought by Jesus Christ, the first three are so alike that they can, in many passages, be placed side by side and viewed as it were at a glance: for this reason they are called 'synoptic' ('at one glance').

Tradition dating from the second century assigns them respectively to St Matthew, St Mark and St Luke. According to the same ecclesiastical tradition Matthew the tax collector, himself one of the apostles (Mt 9:9; 10:3), was the first to write; he wrote his Gospel in Palestine for Christians converted from Judaism. His work, composed in 'the Hebrew idiom', which probably means in Aramaic, was then translated into Greek. John Mark, a disciple from Jerusalem (Ac 12:12) who assisted Paul in his apostolic work (Ac 12:25; 13:5,13; Phm 24; 2 Tm 4:11), and Barnabas his cousin (Ac 15:37,39; Col 4:10) and Peter (1 P 5:13), whose 'interpreter' he was, put Peter's preaching down in writing at Rome. Another disciple, Luke, a medical man (Col 4:14) and, unlike Matthew and Mark, of gentile origin (Col 4:10–14), born at Antioch according to some authorities, accompanied Paul on the latter's second (Ac 16:10seq.) and third (Ac 20:5seq.) missionary journeys and was with him during his two Roman captivities (Ac 27:1seq.; 2 Tm 4:11). For this reason his Gospel, the third to be written, could claim the authority of Paul (*see* perhaps 2 Co 8:18) as that of Mark could claim the authority of Peter. Luke composed also a second work—the 'Acts of the Apostles'. The original language of the second and third Gospels is Greek.

These traditions, though hallowed by age, are not in any way definitive. Their accuracy is disputed by a number of scholars, both Protestant and Catholic. Acceptance of the gospels as authoritative documents, inspired by the Holy Spirit, is not dependent on acceptance that these particular writers were primarily responsible for them. Many would hold that Matthew the tax collector did not write the gospel which bears his name, though he may well have played some part in the formation of the traditions which it incorporates. It is also widely maintained that the tradition radically oversimplifies the relationship of Mark's Gospel to Peter's preaching; at most the connection is remote and tenuous. A third point of doubt is whether the author of the third Gospel and of the Acts of the Apostles was in fact a companion of Paul. But before going on with this, it is necessary to say something about the problem of the literary relations between these gospels, i.e. the 'Synoptic Problem'.

§2 All the many solutions offered so far prove inadequate if taken separately, though each contributes an element of truth to the complete solution. A common oral tradition is inherently probable, if not certain; it would have been written down independently, and consequently with variations, by each of the three Synoptists. But by itself this tradition would never have been able to account for the many striking similarities which exist not only between details in the text but also in the sequence of passages, resemblances which cannot be explained even by the extraordinary memory of people in the ancient Middle East. A *written tradition*, in one or many forms, would be a better explanation. But the theory that the three evangelists merely drew independently on some such written source or sources could never explain passages where these likenesses and divergencies show that the evangelists were aware of one another, as is obvious from the fact that at times they copy or correct one another. There must have been some direct interdependence and it is clear that Luke depends on Mark for most of his direct narrative. But it is much less obvious that, as has long been held, Mark depends on Matthew, for many indications point in the opposite direction. As for the relationship between Matthew and Luke, no direct dependence in either direction can be considered probable, and the non-Markan passages common to these two probably have their common source or sources outside the second Gospel.

Starting from these textual considerations critics have worked out a '*Two-Source Theory*' according to which these sources are: 1 Mark, on whom Matthew and Luke depend for their narrative sections. 2 A source, the existence of which is inferred purely from the textual evidence, and which is called 'Q' (initial of the German word *Quelle*, source). From Q, both the first and third Gospels draw the 'Sayings' or discourses of Jesus ('Logia'), which in Mark are barely represented. In spite of its simplicity, or rather because of it, this very widely accepted theory fails to resolve all problems. Neither Mark in its present form, nor Q as it is commonly reconstructed, can suffice to play the part which is attributed to it.

It is true that Mark generally appears to be more primitive than Matthew and Luke. But contrary instances can be found. Mark sometimes betrays comparatively late traits, such as Paulinisms and adaptations to readers of the Graeco-Roman world, while Matthew and Luke retain some more archaic features such as Semitisms and details of Palestinian origin. The suggestion has been made that Matthew and Luke may have drawn their material from a Mark in an earlier state.

This suggestion is strengthened by another factor. In some places Matthew and Luke present points of agreement against Mark in a way which argues against their common dependence on that Gospel. These agreements are frequent and sometimes striking. Attempts have been made to account for them in a way which leaves the basic theory intact, either as harmonisations by copyists which should be removed by textual criticism, or as corrections by the evangelists themselves who spontaneously and independently refashioned passages of Mark which they considered unsatisfactory. Acceptable as these explanations may be for certain cases, they will not suffice to explain the phenomenon as a whole. All in all the explanation already suggested above is preferable, namely that Matthew and Luke knew and used an earlier version of the Gospel of Mark. The last revision of Mark must have been made after they had already made use of it. This would account for the features which appear late and the cases where Matthew and Luke agree against Mark: they would both reflect an earlier version of his text.

No more satisfactory, at least in the form commonly proposed, is the hypothesis of the source Q. The document suggested is reconstructed by different scholars in ways too diverse for it to have any definable or even intelligible form. Even the idea that it is a single source is disputed. In fact the sayings from which it is made up occur in Matthew and Luke in a way which suggests two sources rather than one, those in the middle (often called 'Peraean') section of Luke (9:51–18:14) contrasting with the other sayings in his Gospel. Although both have equivalents in Matthew, those in the latter category occur in the two gospels in series largely parallel, while those in the former category are grouped in Luke and scattered in Matthew. Everything indicates that Matthew and Luke drew the sayings from two different sources: **1** A collection, called S(ource) by some which Luke has substantially adopted for his Peraean section, while Matthew scattered the elements throughout his discourses, and **2** The Gospel of Matthew in an earlier form.

It seems, indeed, necessary to postulate for Matthew and even for Luke, no less than for Mark, an earlier form than those we now have. Analyses which cannot be reproduced here suggest three stages, at least for Mark and Matthew: a basic document, a first revision and a final revision, which is what we now have. Between these different stages there were interactions in various directions, bringing with them the literary relationships of similarity and difference which we now find in the gospels. Thus, for example, the first revision of Mark will have been influenced by the document which is at the source of Matthew, but in its turn will have exerted an influence on the final revision of Matthew. This lattice-work of interlocking influences, complex though it may seem, is the only solution which adequately explains a complex situation. Any claim to a simple solution of the synoptic problem is illusory.

It is now possible to describe the steps in *the formation of the first three gospels*, although profound differences remain between scholars on many points. The present hypothesis claims only to be one likely solution to the problem.

At the heart of the oral preaching of the apostles lies the *kerygma* proclaiming the redemptive death and resurrection of the Lord. Peter's discourses in the Acts of the Apostles provide us with typical summaries of this apostolic preaching which would in practice have included more detailed narratives: principally the story of the Passion which must have assumed its stereotyped pattern very early, as the close similarity of the four gospel accounts shows, but also many anecdotes taken from the Master's life, and throwing light on his person, his mission and his power, or else illustrating his teaching by means of some well-remembered episode, saying, miracle, pronouncement or parable etc. In addition to the apostles themselves there were professional narrators like the evangelists (those who enjoyed a special *charisma* not limited to the writers of our four gospels; *see* Ac 21:8; Ep 4:11; 2 Tm 4:5), who tended to stereotype the anecdotes by constant repetition. Soon, and particularly when the witnesses who had been in touch with the events themselves began to disappear, measures would have been taken to commit this oral tradition to writing. Episodes originally narrated separately and independently of one another would naturally be grouped together either chronologically (e.g. Mk 1:16–39, the Day at Capernaum) or logically (e.g. Mk 2:1–3:6, the Five Disputes); the groupings would be small at first, but would later grow into more extensive collections. This was the stage at which an author intervened who, according to tradition which there is no reason to doubt, was Matthew the apostle. He was the first to compose a 'gospel' which drew together Christ's deeds and words into a continuous narrative covering the earthly ministry of Jesus from baptism to resurrection. Shortly afterwards a 'Collection', S, of unknown authorship, appeared side by side with this early gospel; its purpose was to preserve other sayings of the Lord, or the same sayings in a different form. This early gospel and this Collection, both written in Aramaic, were soon put into Greek, and eventually various forms of these translations came to exist.

The needs of adaptation to Christians of gentile origin will have led to a new form of that very first Gospel which we have just attributed to Matthew, and this new form constituted a new document on which the Markan tradition was based. Add to these two primitive forms of the Gospel derived respectively from Matthew and the Collection S, another ancient gospel, which can be divined as the source of the accounts of the Passion and Resurrection in Luke and John, and we have four basic documents for the first of the three stages which have already been suggested.

At a second stage these documents were taken up and combined in various ways. From the primitive Matthaean Gospel and its various adaptations, especially the one addressed to Christians of gentile origin, the Markan tradition made a more organised and more complete revision, which was not, however, the final version which we know today. It is this intermediate form of Mark which was known and used by the editors of the canonical Gospels of Matthew and Luke. The Matthaean tradition, for its part, combined the primitive Gospel of Matthew with the Collection S to produce a new revision.

The editor who achieved this combination did so with great delicacy, dividing up the sayings grouped in S to distribute them in the Gospel and thus construct the great discourses. Soon afterwards, an editor of the Gospel of Luke began his work. Having sought out diligently everything which had been written before him (Lk 1:1–4), he used, in a first stage of his work which may be called Proto-Luke, both the document with gentile-Christian tendencies which had formed a basis for Mark and the Gospel of Matthew into which S had already been incorporated; but he also knew S at first hand, and preferred to insert the sayings in large blocks into his middle section, instead of following Matthew who had divided them up. Finally he used, especially in the accounts of the Passion and resurrection, an ancient document used also by the fourth Gospel. This accounts for the numerous contacts of Luke and John against Matthew and Mark in this part of the Gospel. Proto-Luke had no knowledge of Mark, even in its intermediary form; it was only later that he utilised it to complete his Gospel. This brings us to the third stage.

In this final stage the Gospel of the Matthaean tradition was thoroughly remoulded with the help of Mark, though this Mark was not of course in the final state in which we know it, but in the more primitive form which we have assigned to the second stage of the evolution. By a curious criss-crossing, the Gospel of Mark was itself revised in view of the intermediate form of Matthew and perhaps also of Proto-Luke, not without some Pauline influence. As for Luke, this found its final form by the use of Mark in its intermediate form, in the same way as Matthew. Into the course of its first edition (Proto-Luke) were inserted three 'Markan sections' (4:31–6:19; 8:4–9:50; 18:15–21:38). That these insertions occurred only at a late stage of the work is proved by the omission of those Markan elements which he had already adopted in a different literary form from the sources Matthew or S. These latter had been used earlier. It should also be noted that Luke, in the same way as Matthew but to a greater extent, had recourse to special sources discovered by his diligent research (1:3). To these he owes not only his Gospel of the infancy but also many of the fine passages which make his Gospel the indispensable complement of the other two (the good Samaritan, Martha and Mary, the prodigal son, the Pharisee and the tax collector).

§3 The literary process just outlined respects and makes use of the broad data from tradition but is able to fill in details. It does not, however, make it possible, any more than tradition does, to assign an exact *date* to each of the Synoptics with complete certainty: at a guess, though, the interval required for the development of the oral tradition would make it probable that the primitive Gospel and later the Collection S were composed between the years 40 and 50. This early date would be definite if it could be proved that Paul's Letters to the Thessalonians, written about 51–2, made use of the first Gospel's Apocalyptic Discourse. If Mark wrote towards the end of Peter's life (as Clement of Alexandria says) or shortly after Peter's death (as Irenaeus says) the date of his Gospel would be c. 64; in any case it should be dated before 70 as it does not seem from this Gospel that Jerusalem has yet been destroyed. Greek Matthew and Luke are later than Mark but their precise date is more difficult to determine. The existence of Luke's Gospel is presupposed by Acts (Ac 1:1) but the date of Acts, itself uncertain (see p. 220), can provide no criterion. It is true that neither Greek Matthew nor Luke suggests that the destruction of Jerusalem has already taken place (not even Lk 19:42–44; 21:20–24 which employ clichés from the prophetic books to describe an event that cannot have been hard to foresee) but this is not decisive. If neither of them knew of the destruction, then they would have to be put before 70, but if they deliberately aimed at scrupulously preserving the archaic quality of their respective literary sources, then their works might quite well have been composed after the destruction, say about AD 80.

In any case, the apostolic origin, direct or indirect, together with their involved literary formation confirm the *historical value* of the Synoptics, and not only that but at the same time help us to understand the nature of that historical value; since the gospels stem from an oral preaching that goes back to the beginnings of the primitive community, their guarantee in this way would ultimately rest on eye-witness. Neither the apostles themselves, however, nor any of the other preachers of the gospel message and tellers of the gospel story ever aimed at writing or teaching history in the modern technical sense of that word; their concern was missionary and theological: they preached to convert and edify, to infuse faith, to enlighten it and defend it against its opponents. For this purpose they could and did appeal to solid evidence that could be checked, and this appeal was demanded quite as much by their own sincerity as by their anxiety not to leave any loopholes for hostile argument. Those who finally composed the gospels, collecting the evidence and putting it into writing, had the same objective fidelity and equal respect for their sources of information; this is clear from the simple and archaic quality of their work. In this there are no theological developments characteristic of subsequent decades (compare Paul for example); much less is there any trace of the sort of extravagant legends that are frequent in the apocryphal gospels. The three Synoptics may not be history books, but they do set out to give us historical fact.

This does not mean that each of the events or discourses which they record corresponds exactly to what in fact took place. The laws governing witnesses and the spread of evidence warn us against looking for that material sort of precision. Obvious examples can be found in the gospels themselves, where the same events or the same discourses are sometimes recorded in different ways. This is not only true of the content of some episodes, but it is even truer of the order in which these episodes are arranged, which is not the same order in each gospel. This is only to be expected in view of their complex origins. Their component parts, which at first existed separately, were only gradually collected together into groups; and these groups were later joined together or split up, more for reasons of logic or neatness than for anything to do with chronology. In this way many of the gospel events or sayings have been shifted from their original time or place. For this reason it is often impossible to take editorial connective phrases like 'then', 'after this', 'on that day', 'at that time', etc. at their face value.

§4 This process of editing itself took place under the guidance of the Holy Spirit, who directed the community and its spokesmen both in the preservation and in the selection and arrangement of the material. The evangelists are genuine human authors, and the guidance of the Spirit did not override but rather heightened their theological and literary abilities, enabling each to stress different aspects of the rich tradition of the message of Jesus.

§5 The Gospel according to Mark

The *plan* Mark follows is the least complex of the Synoptics. The preaching of John the Baptist plus the baptism and temptation of Jesus make up his prelude (1:1–13); next comes a period of ministry which, according to occasional hints, took place in Galilee (1:14–7:23), then a journey by Jesus and his apostles to the district of Tyre and Sidon, the Decapolis, the neighbourhood of Caesarea Philippi and back to Galilee (7:24–9:50); then the Transfiguration and the final journey through Peraea and Jericho to Jerusalem where the Passion and Resurrection take place (10:1–16:8). Apart from individual sequences of fact, this broad outline itself is possibly artificial since it is likely, and to judge by the fourth Gospel fairly certain, that Jesus visited Jerusalem several times before the last Passover of his life. All the same, this outline, broad as it is, does trace for us an important development which is both factually and theologically significant. The general public received Jesus warmly at first but their enthusiasm waned as they found that his gentle and other-worldly conception of the Messiah did not fulfil their hopes. As a result, Jesus left Galilee to devote himself to the instruction of a small group of faithful followers, and the profession of faith at Caesarea Philippi showed that he had secured their faith. This was a decisive turning-point: after it Jerusalem became the focus of attention, and it was there that further opposition continued mounting, only to end in the drama of the Passion and in the final triumph of the resurrection.

This paradox provides the central interest of this Gospel, i.e. how Jesus, while remaining misunderstood and rejected was at the same time God's triumphant envoy. The Gospel is not particularly concerned with elaborating the Master's teaching, and it records few of his sayings: the real point of its message is the *manifestation of the crucified Messiah*. On the one hand Jesus is the Son of God, acknowledged as such by the Father (1:11; 9:7), by evil spirits (1:24; 3:11; 5:7) and even by men (15:39); he is the Messiah claiming divine rank (14:62), higher than the angels (13:32), taking on himself the forgiveness of sin (2:10), vindicating his power and his mission by miracle (1:31; 4:41; etc.) and by exorcism (1:27; 3:23seq.). On the other hand the Gospel puts great emphasis on his apparent frustration at the hands of many: the mockery or refusal of the public (5:40; 6:2seq.), the antagonism of the religious leaders (2:1–3:6), the lack of understanding even on his disciples' part (4:13b)—all the hostile activities that were to lead to the shame of the cross. It is this 'scandal', this refusal, that the Gospel is intent on explaining. It does this not merely by contrasting the cross with the crowning triumph of the resurrection but also by showing that the hostility was itself an integral part of God's mysterious plan. It was necessary that Christ should suffer and so redeem the human race (10:45; 14:24), since this had been foretold by the scriptures (9:12; 14:21,49). Both for himself (8:31; 9:31; 10:33seq.) and for his own followers (8:34seq.; 9:35; 10:15,24seq., 29seq., 39; 13:9–13) Jesus laid down a way of humility and submission; but the Jews, expecting a victorious warrior-Messiah, were ill-prepared for this answer to their hope; the reason why Jesus wanted silence about his miracles (5:43) and his identity (7:24; 9:30) was to avoid an enthusiasm which would have been as ill-advised as it would have been mistaken. Rather than call himself Messiah, 8:29seq., he used the modest and mysterious expression 'Son of man' (2:10; compare Mt 8:20h). This cautionary measure is what is called 'the messianic secret' (1:34m) and is a basic idea of Mark's Gospel. It was not something Mark invented; it corresponded to that underlying reality in Christ's life of suffering which, in the light of a faith finally and fully established by the Easter event, the evangelist was able to perceive and to place before us for our understanding.

§6 The Gospel according to Matthew

The same light of faith and the same broad outline of Christ's life naturally occur in Matthew as well as in Mark, but with quite a different emphasis. To begin with, the *plan* is not the same and is much more elaborate: Matthew is divided into five books, each consisting of a discourse introduced and prepared by narrative matter; these five books, plus the stories of the infancy and of the Passion, are combined to form a well-knit whole of seven sections. It is possible that this arrangement, which is so clear in Matthew, goes back to the Aramaic gospel; in any case, in Greek Matthew it is unmistakable. As we have already seen, Matthew used his sources with great freedom in order to achieve his carefully mapped-out ensemble. The fact that this Gospel also reports Christ's teaching much more fully than Mark's, and stresses especially the theme of the kingdom of Heaven (4:17f), makes it a *dramatic account in seven acts of the coming of the kingdom of Heaven*. These acts are as follows: **1** The preparation of the kingdom in the person of the child-Messiah, ch. 1–2. **2** The formal proclamation of the charter of the kingdom to the disciples and the public, i.e. the Sermon on the Mount, ch. 5–8. **3** The preaching of the kingdom by missionaries whose credentials (the 'signs', which are to confirm the word) are now hinted at by several miracles done by Jesus himself; the missionaries receive their instructions, ch. 8–10. **4** The obstacles which the kingdom will meet, and which are part of God's design that the kingdom should come without show, as illustrated in the parables of the concluding instruction, 11:1–13:52. **5** Its embryonic existence in the group of disciples with Peter at their head; the rules for this Church in the making are outlined in the concluding instruction on the community, 13:53–18:35. **6** The crisis, provoked by the increasing hostility of the Jewish leaders, which is to prepare the way for the definitive coming of the kingdom and which is the subject of the concluding eschatological instruction, ch. 19–25. **7** Lastly, the coming itself, a coming effected through suffering and triumph, through the Passion and Resurrection, ch. 26–28.

The kingdom of God (of 'the Heavens' in Matthew) is the reassertion that the Law and prophets are 'fulfilled'—a phrase which means that their hopes have been not only realised but also perfected. Matthew applies this to the person of Jesus: he appeals to Old Testament texts for his Davidic descent (1:1–17), for his virgin birth (1:23) at Bethlehem (2:6), for his stay in Egypt and his settling at Capernaum (4:14–16), for his messianic progress into Jerusalem (21:5,16); Matthew applies it also to the work of Jesus: he appeals to Old Testament texts to explain Jesus' cures (11:4–5); and finally he applies it to the teaching of Jesus: this 'fulfils' the Law (5:17) while raising it to further heights (5:21–48; 19:3–9,16–21). Matthew asserts equally strongly that the scriptures are fulfilled also in the lowliness of Jesus' person and in what humanly seems to be the frustration of his work. In this way God's plan contains, and the Old Testament foretells: the massacre of the Innocents (2:17seq.), the hidden life at Nazareth (2:23), the gentle compassion of the 'servant of God' (12:17–21; cf. 8:17; 11:29; 12:7), the disciples' desertion (26:31), the paltry price of betrayal (27:9–10), the arrest (26:54) and the three days' burial (12:40); in this way too the Old Testament foretold the unbelief of the Jews (13:13–15), too tenacious of their man-made traditions (15:7–9), who could be approached only by teaching through the veil of parables (13:14–15,35); Matthew is not the only one of the three Synoptists to make use of arguments from the Old Testament, but he relies so heavily on this argument that he has made it one of the chief characteristics of his Gospel. Matthew's is the most semitic of the gospels: not only does it show great interest in and often refers to the details of Jewish observance, with its Sabbath, phylacteries, tithes and purifications, but also it frequently makes use of the Jewish technique of midrash and other rabbinic methods of argument. Characteristically Jewish also is the preoccupation with the final judgement and retribution and its apocalyptic scenario. This Jewishness accounts for Matthew's concern to show that the new Law of Christ fulfils the old and that the new people of God form the successors to the Israel of the old covenant who were first invited to the messianic feast but refused the invitation (23:34–38, compare 10:5–6, 23; 15:24). In keeping with his concern with fulfilment Matthew often represents Jesus as the new Moses, repeating in his life the story of Moses and the lawgiver of the new covenant. But beyond this, Jesus is somehow endowed with majesty even in his earthly life; he is recognised as God's Son (14:33; 16:16; 22:2; 27:40,43) as well as son of David. From the first announcement of his conception he is known as 'God-with-us'. Another dimension of Matthew's Gospel is that of the community, for one of the discourse chapters (18) is devoted to behaviour within the community, and Matthew stresses the importance of Peter as the foundation-stone of the new Israel (16:18), and of the disciples, consistently toning down or omitting the rebukes to them from Jesus reported by Mark.

§7 The Gospel according to Luke

The third Gospel's distinguishing quality results from the attractive personality of its author which shines through all his work. Luke is at once a most gifted writer and a man of marked sensibility. He set to work in his own way with an eye to exact information and orderly narrative (1:3), but respect for his sources, together with his method of editing them did not lead Luke, any more than Matthew or Mark, to follow a chronological plan. He follows Mark, with some alterations (3:19–20; 4:16–30; 5:1–11; 6:12–19; 22:31–34). Some of these are made in the interests of clarity and logical sequence, some under the influence of other streams of tradition including a tradition traceable also in the fourth Gospel. Other episodes are omitted altogether for various reasons: they were not interesting for Luke's non-Jewish readers (Mk 9:11–13), or they were already to be found in the Collection S (Mk 12:28–34; *see* Lk 10:25–28), or above all (as in the case of Luke's great omission of Mk 6:45–8:26) because Luke regarded it as unnecessarily repetitive. Luke's most obvious difference from Mark is his great intercalation (*see* 9:51–18:14) which, as has been seen, combines Logia or Sayings from the Collection S with information he had found out for himself. This central section uses a journey to Jerusalem for its framework (*see* the reiterated indications, elaborating the datum of Mk 10:1, in Lk 9:51; 13:22; 17:11). But it is not a reminiscence of an actual journey; it is rather a device by which Luke is able to bring out one of his chief theological notions: namely that the Holy City is the predestined stage for the drama of salvation (9:31; 13:33; 18:31; 19:11). Because it is from Jerusalem that the evangelisation of the world must begin (24:47; Ac 1:8), his Gospel had to start there (1:5seq.) and there he will have to bring it to a close (24:52seq.)—the post-resurrection appearances and conversations recorded by Luke do not take place in Galilee (*see* 24:13–51 and compare 24:6 with Mk 16:7; Mt 28:7,16–20).

§8 From a comparison of Luke with his two sources, (a) Mark, the best known, and (b) the sources behind the Matthean passages which are paralleled in Luke. it becomes apparent that Luke has carefully moulded the material he has received. His changes are slight, but through them he gives his work a character peculiarly his own. He avoids or whittles down anything his readers might find offensive (8:43, compare Mk 5:26; he omits Mk 9:43–48; 13:32) or anything they could not be expected to understand (he omits Mt 5:21seq.,33seq.; Mk 15:34; etc.). He omits anything derogatory to the dignity of the apostles (Mk 4:13; 8:32seq.; 9:28seq.; 14:50) and makes excuses for them (Lk 9:45; 18:34; 22:45). He explains obscure phrases (6:15) and clears up points of topography (4:31; 19:28seq.,37; 23:51), etc. One of the most attractive features of Luke is his picture of the gentleness of Christ. He is anxious to stress his Master's love of sinners (15:1seq.,7,10); to record his acts of forgiveness (7:36–50; 15:11–32; 19:1–10; 23:34,39–43); and to contrast his tenderness for the lowly and the poor with his severity towards the proud and towards those who abuse their wealth (1:51–53; 6:20–26; 12:13–21; 14:7–11; 16:15,19–31; 18:9–14). But in spite of this severity, the wicked, however deserving of punishment, will not be condemned till the period set aside for mercy has come to an end (13:6–9; cf. Mk 11:12–14). The one thing necessary is repentance, abdication of self, and on this the gentle, tolerant Luke takes a firm stand, insisting on unflinching and complete detachment (14:25–34), especially from riches (6:34seq.; 12:33; 14:12–14; 16:9–13). Another group of passages which are also found only in the third Gospel is on the necessity of prayer (11:1–8; 18:1–8), of which Jesus sets the example (3:21; 5:16; 6:12; 9:28). Finally, Luke is the only one of the Synoptists to give the Holy Spirit the prominence we find in Paul and in Acts (Lk 1:15,35,41,67; 2:25–27; 4:1,14,18; 10:21; 11:13; 24:49). These qualities, combined with that joy in God and that gratitude to him for his gifts which fill the third Gospel (2:14; 5:26; 10:17; 13:17; 18:43; 19:37; 24:51seq.), are the ones that go to make Luke's achievement such a warm and human work.

§9 Style

Mark's Greek is rough, strongly redolent of Aramaic, and often faulty; but it is fresh, lively and appealing. Matthew's Greek is also rather marked by Aramaic but smoother than Mark's as well as less picturesque and more correct. Luke's is mixed: when writing independently, his Greek is excellent, but out of respect for his sources he incorporates their imperfections—after polishing them a little. Occasionally he goes out of his way to give a good imitation of Septuagint Greek.

§10 This translation

As far as possible this translation preserves stylistic nuances and aims at reproducing the detailed similarities and differences between the three Synoptics, which betray their literary relationships.

THE GOSPEL ACCORDING TO

MATTHEW

I: THE BIRTH AND INFANCY OF JESUS

The ancestry of Jesus

1 **1** Roll of the genealogy of Jesus Christ, son of David, son of Abraham: *

2   Abraham fathered Isaac,
       Isaac fathered Jacob,
       Jacob fathered Judah and his brothers,

3   Judah fathered Perez and Zerah, whose mother was Tamar,
       Perez fathered Hezron,
       Hezron fathered Ram,

4   Ram fathered Amminadab,
       Amminadab fathered Nahshon,
       Nahshon fathered Salmon,

5   Salmon fathered Boaz, whose mother was Rahab,
       Boaz fathered Obed, whose mother was Ruth,
       Obed fathered Jesse;

6   and Jesse fathered King David.

       David fathered Solomon, whose mother had been Uriah's wife,

7   Solomon fathered Rehoboam,
       Rehoboam fathered Abijah,
       Abijah fathered Asa, *

8   Asa fathered Jehoshaphat,
       Jehoshaphat fathered Joram,
       Joram fathered Uzziah,

9   Uzziah fathered Jotham,
       Jotham fathered Ahaz,
       Ahaz fathered Hezekiah,

10   Hezekiah fathered Manasseh,
       Manasseh fathered Amon, *
       Amon fathered Josiah;

11   and Josiah fathered Jechoniah and his brothers.
       Then the deportation to Babylon took place.

12   After the deportation to Babylon:
       Jechoniah fathered Shealtiel,

13 Shealtiel fathered Zerubbabel,
Zerubbabel fathered Abiud,
Abiud fathered Eliakim,
Eliakim fathered Azor,
14 Azor fathered Zadok,
Zadok fathered Achim,
Achim fathered Eliud,
15 Eliud fathered Eleazar,
Eleazar fathered Matthan,
Matthan fathered Jacob;
16 and Jacob fathered Joseph the husband of Mary;
of her was born Jesus *d* who is called Christ.

17 The sum of generations is therefore: fourteen from Abraham to David; fourteen from David to the Babylonian deportation; and fourteen from the Babylonian deportation to Christ.

Joseph adopts Jesus as his son

18 This is how Jesus Christ came to be born. His mother Mary was betrothed to Joseph; *e* but before they came to live together she was found to be with child
19 through the Holy Spirit. ·Her husband Joseph, being an upright man and wanting
20 to spare her disgrace, decided to divorce her informally. *f* ·He had made up his mind to do this when suddenly the angel of the Lord *g* appeared to him in a dream *h* and said, 'Joseph son of David, do not be afraid to take Mary home as your wife,
21 because she has conceived what is in her by the Holy Spirit. ·She will give birth to a son and you must name him Jesus, because he is the one who is to save *i* his
22 people from their sins.' ·Now all this took place to fulfil what the Lord had spoken through the prophet: *j*

23 Look! the virgin is with child and will give birth to a son
whom they will call Immanuel.

24 a name which means 'God-is-with-us'. ·When Joseph woke up he did what the
25 angel of the Lord had told him to do: he took his wife to his home; ·he had not had intercourse with her when she gave birth *k* to a son; and he named him Jesus.

The visit of the Magi

1 2 *a* After Jesus had been born at Bethlehem in Judaea during the reign of King
2 Herod, *b* suddenly some wise men came to Jerusalem from the east *c* ·asking, 'Where is the infant king of the Jews? We saw his star as it rose and have come to
3 do him homage.' ·When King Herod heard this he was perturbed, and so was the
4 whole of Jerusalem. ·He called together all the chief priests and the scribes of the
5 people, *d* and enquired of them where the Christ was to be born. ·They told him, 'At Bethlehem in Judaea, for this is what the prophet wrote:

6 And you, Bethlehem, in the land of Judah,
you are by no means the *least among the leaders of Judah*,
for *from you will come a leader*
who will *shepherd* my people Israel.'

7 Then Herod summoned the wise men to see him privately. He asked them the
8 exact date on which the star had appeared ·and sent them on to Bethlehem with

the words, 'Go and find out all about the child, and when you have found him, let
9 me know, so that I too may go and do him homage.' ·Having listened to what the
king had to say, they set out. And suddenly the star they had seen rising went
10 forward and halted over the place where the child was.ᵉ ·The sight of the star
11 filled them with delight, ·and going into the house they saw the child with his
mother Mary, and falling to their knees they did him homage. Then, opening their
12 treasures, they offered him gifts of gold and frankincense and myrrh.ᶠ ·But they
were given a warning in a dream not to go back to Herod, and returned to their
own country by a different way.

The flight into Egypt. The massacre of the Innocents

13 After they had left, suddenly the angel of the Lord appeared to Joseph in a dream
and said, 'Get up, take the child and his mother with you, and escape into Egypt,
and stay there until I tell you, because Herod intends to search for the child and
14 do away with him.' ·So Joseph got up and, taking the child and his mother with
15 him, left that night for Egypt, ·where he stayed until Herod was dead. This was to
fulfil what the Lord had spoken through the prophet:

> *I called my son out of Egypt.*ᵍ

16   Herod was furious on realising that he had been fooled by the wise men,ʰ and
in Bethlehem and its surrounding district he had all the male children killed who
were two years old or less, reckoning by the date he had been careful to ask the
17 wise men. ·Then were fulfilled the words spoken through the prophet Jeremiah:ⁱ

18   *A voice is heard in Ramah,*
         lamenting and weeping bitterly:
         it is Rachel weeping for her children,
         refusing to be comforted
         because they are no more.

From Egypt to Nazareth

19 After Herod's death, suddenly the angel of the Lord appeared in a dream to
20 Joseph in Egypt ·and said, 'Get up, take the child and his mother with you and go
21 back to the land of Israel, for those who wanted to kill the child are dead.' ·So
Joseph got up and, taking the child and his mother with him, went back to the
22 land of Israel. But when he learnt that Archelausʲ had succeeded his father Herod
as ruler of Judaea he was afraid to go there, and being warned in a dream he
23 withdrew to the region of Galilee.ᵏ ·There he settled in a town called Nazareth. In
this way the words spoken through the prophets were to be fulfilled:

> *He will be called a Nazarene.*ˡ

II: THE KINGDOM OF HEAVEN PROCLAIMED

A: NARRATIVE SECTION

The proclamation of John the Baptist

1 **3** In due courseᵃ John the Baptist appeared; he proclaimed this message in the
2 desert of Judaea,ᵇ ·'Repent,ᶜ for the kingdom of Heavenᵈ is close at hand.'
3 This was the man spoken of by the prophet Isaiah when he said:

A voice of one that cries in the desert,
'Prepare a way for the Lord,
make his paths straight.'

4 This man John wore a garment made of camel-hair with a leather loin-cloth round
5 his waist, and his food was locusts and wild honey. ·Then Jerusalem and all Judaea
6 and the whole Jordan district made their way to him, ·and as they were baptised
7 by him in the river Jordan they confessed their sins. *ᶠ* ·But when he saw a number
of Pharisees *ʲ* and Sadducees *ᵍ* coming for baptism he said to them, 'Brood of
8 vipers, who warned you to flee from the coming retribution? *ʰ* ·Produce fruit in
9 keeping with repentance, ·and do not presume to tell yourselves, "We have
Abraham as our father," because, I tell you, God can raise children for Abraham
10 from these stones. ·Even now the axe is being laid to the root of the trees, so that
11 any tree failing to produce good fruit will be cut down and thrown on the fire. ·I
baptise you in water for repentance, but the one who comes after me is more
powerful than I, and I am not fit to carry his sandals; he will baptise you with the
12 Holy Spirit and fire. *ⁱ* ·His winnowing-fan is in his hand; he will clear his threshing-
floor and gather his wheat into his barn; but the chaff he will burn in a fire that will
never go out.' *ʲ*

Jesus is baptised

13 Then Jesus appeared: he came from Galilee to the Jordan to be baptised by John.
14 John tried to dissuade him, with the words, 'It is I who need baptism from you,
15 and yet you come to me!' ·But Jesus replied, 'Leave it like this for the time being;
it is fitting that we should, in this way, do all that uprightness demands.' *ᵏ* Then
John gave in to him.
16 　　And when Jesus had been baptised he at once came up from the water, and
suddenly the heavens opened *ˡ* and he saw the Spirit of God descending like a dove
17 and coming down on him. *ᵐ* ·And suddenly there was a voice from heaven, 'This is
my Son, the Beloved; my favour rests on him.' *ⁿ*

Testing in the desert *ᵃ*

1 　**4** Then Jesus was led by the Spirit *ᵇ* out into the desert to be put to the test by
2 　　 the devil. *ᶜ* ·He fasted for forty days and forty nights, after which he was
3 hungry, and the tester came and said to him, 'If you are Son of God, *ᵈ* tell these
4 stones to turn into loaves.' ·But he replied, 'Scripture says:

Human beings live not on bread alone
but on every word that comes from the mouth of God.'

5 The devil then took him to the holy city and set him on the parapet of the Temple.
6 'If you are Son of God,' he said, 'throw yourself down; for scripture says:

He has given his angels orders about you,
and *they will carry you in their arms*
in case you trip over a stone.'

7 Jesus said to him, 'Scripture also says:

Do not put the Lord your God to the test.'

8 Next, taking him to a very high mountain, the devil showed him all the kingdoms
9 of the world and their splendour. ·And he said to him, 'I will give you all these, if

10 you fall at my feet and do me homage.' ·Then Jesus replied, 'Away with you, Satan! For scripture says:

> *The Lord your God is the one to whom you must do homage,*
> *him alone you must serve.*'

11 Then the devil left him, and suddenly angels appeared and looked after him.

Return to Galilee

12, 13 Hearing that John had been arrested he withdrew to Galilee, ·and leaving Nazara *
he went and settled in Capernaum, beside the lake, on the borders of Zebulun
14 and Naphtali. ·This was to fulfil what was spoken by the prophet Isaiah:

15
> *Land of Zebulun! Land of Naphtali!*
> *Way of the sea beyond Jordan.*
> *Galilee of the nations!*
16
> *The people that lived in darkness*
> *have seen a great light;*
> *on those who lived in a country of shadow dark as death*
> *a light has dawned.*

17 From then onwards Jesus began his proclamation with the message, 'Repent, for
the kingdom of Heaven *f* is close at hand.'

The first four disciples are called

18 As he was walking by the Lake of Galilee he saw two brothers, Simon, who was
called Peter, and his brother Andrew; they were making a cast into the lake with
19 their net, for they were fishermen. ·And he said to them, 'Come after me and I
20 will make you fishers of people.' ·And at once they left their nets and followed
him.

21 Going on from there he saw another pair of brothers, James son of Zebedee
and his brother John; they were in their boat with their father Zebedee, mending
22 their nets, and he called them. ·And at once, leaving the boat and their father,
they followed him.

Jesus proclaims the message and heals the sick

23 He went round the whole of Galilee teaching in their synagogues, proclaiming the
good news of the kingdom and curing all kinds of disease and illness among the
24 people. *g* ·His fame spread throughout Syria, *h* and those who were suffering from
diseases and painful complaints of one kind or another, the possessed, epileptics,
25 the paralysed, were all brought to him, and he cured them. ·Large crowds followed
him, coming from Galilee, the Decapolis, *i* Jerusalem, Judaea and Transjordan.

B: THE SERMON ON THE MOUNT *a*

The Beatitudes

1 5 Seeing the crowds, he went onto the mountain. *b* And when he was seated his
2 disciples came to him. ·Then he began to speak. This is what he taught them:

3 How blessed *c* are the poor in spirit: *d*

the kingdom of Heaven is theirs.
4 Blessed are *the gentle:* ^f
they shall have the earth as inheritance.
5 Blessed are those who mourn:
they shall be comforted.
6 Blessed are those who hunger and thirst for uprightness:
they shall have their fill.
7 Blessed are the merciful:
they shall have mercy shown them.
8 Blessed are the pure in heart:
they shall see God.
9 Blessed are the peacemakers:
they shall be recognised as children of God.
10 Blessed are those who are persecuted in the cause of uprightness:
the kingdom of Heaven is theirs.

11 'Blessed are you when people abuse you and persecute you and speak all kinds of
12 calumny against you falsely on my account. ·Rejoice and be glad, for your reward
will be great in heaven; this is how they persecuted the prophets before you.*

Salt for the earth and light for the world

13 'You are salt for the earth. But if salt loses its taste, what can make it salty again?
It is good for nothing, and can only be thrown out to be trampled under people's
feet.
14, 15 'You are light for the world. A city built on a hill-top cannot be hidden. ·No
one lights a lamp to put it under a tub; ^g they put it on the lamp-stand where it
16 shines for everyone in the house. ·In the same way your light must shine in people's
sight, so that, seeing your good works, they may give praise to your Father in
heaven.

The fulfilment of the Law

17 'Do not imagine that I have come to abolish the Law or the Prophets. I have come
18 not to abolish but to complete them. ^h ·In truth I tell you, ⁱ till heaven and earth
disappear, not one dot, not one little stroke, is to disappear from the Law until all
19 its purpose is achieved. ·Therefore, anyone who infringes even one of the least of
these commandments and teaches others to do the same will be considered the
least in the kingdom of Heaven; but the person who keeps them and teaches them
will be considered great in the kingdom of Heaven.

The new standard higher than the old

20 'For I tell you, if your uprightness does not surpass that of the scribes and Pharisees,
you will never get into the kingdom of Heaven.
21 'You have heard ^j how it was said to our ancestors, *You shall not kill*; and if
22 anyone does kill he must answer for it before the court. ·But I say this to you,
anyone who is angry with a brother will answer for it before the court; anyone
who calls a brother "Fool" ^k will answer for it before the Sanhedrin; ^l and anyone
23 who calls him "Traitor" ^m will answer for it in hell fire. ·So then, if you are bringing
your offering to the altar and there remember that your brother has something
24 against you, ·leave your offering there before the altar, go and be reconciled with
25 your brother first, and then come back and present your offering. ·Come to terms

with your opponent in good time while you are still on the way to the court with
him, or he may hand you over to the judge and the judge to the officer, and you
26 will be thrown into prison. ·In truth I tell you, you will not get out till you have
paid the last penny.

27, 28   'You have heard how it was said, *You shall not commit adultery*. ·But I say this
to you, if a man looks at a woman lustfully, he has already committed adultery
29 with her in his heart. ·If your right eye should be your downfall, tear it out and
throw it away; for it will do you less harm to lose one part of yourself than to have
30 your whole body thrown into hell. ·And if your right hand should be your downfall,
cut it off and throw it away; for it will do you less harm to lose one part of yourself
than to have your whole body go to hell.

31   'It has also been said, *Anyone who divorces his wife must give her a writ of*
32 *dismissal*. ·But I say this to you, everyone who divorces his wife, except for the
case of an illicit marriage, " makes her an adulteress; and anyone who marries a
divorced woman commits adultery.

33   'Again, you have heard how it was said to our ancestors, *You must not break*
34 *your oath, but must fulfil your oaths to the Lord*. ·But I say this to you, do not
35 swear at all, either by *heaven*, since that is *God's throne*; ·or by *earth*, since that is
36 *his footstool*; or by Jerusalem, since that is *the city of the great King*. ·Do not swear
37 by your own head either, since you cannot turn a single hair white or black. ·All
you need say is "Yes" if you mean yes, "No" if you mean no; ° anything more
than this comes from the Evil One.

38, 39   'You have heard how it was said: *Eye for eye and tooth for tooth*. ·But I say this
to you: offer no resistance to the wicked. ° On the contrary, if anyone hits you on
40 the right cheek, offer him the other as well; ·if someone wishes to go to law with
41 you to get your tunic, ° let him have your cloak as well. ·And if anyone requires
42 you to go one mile, go two miles with him. Give to anyone who asks you, and if
anyone wants to borrow, do not turn away.

43   'You have heard how it was said, *You will love your neighbour* and hate your
44 enemy. ° ·But I say this to you, love your enemies ° and pray for those who persecute
45 you; ° ·so that you may be children of your Father in heaven, for he causes his sun
to rise on the bad as well as the good, and sends down rain to fall on the upright
46 and the wicked alike. ·For if you love those who love you, what reward will you
47 get? Do not even the tax collectors " do as much? ·And if you save your greetings
48 for your brothers, are you doing anything exceptional? ·Do not even the gentiles
do as much? You must therefore set no bounds to your love, just as your heavenly
Father sets none to his.'

Almsgiving in secret

1   **6** 'Be careful not to parade your uprightness ° in public to attract attention;
2   otherwise you will lose all reward from your Father in heaven. ·So when you
give alms, do not have it trumpeted before you; this is what the hypocrites ° do in
the synagogues and in the streets to win human admiration. In truth I tell you,
3 they have had their reward. ·But when you give alms, your left hand must not
4 know what your right is doing; ·your almsgiving must be secret, and your Father
who sees all that is done in secret will reward you.

Prayer in secret

5 'And when you pray, ° do not imitate the hypocrites: they love to say their prayers
standing up in the synagogues and at the street corners for people to see them. In

6 truth I tell you, they have had their reward. ·But when you pray, *go to your private room, shut yourself in, and so pray* to your Father who is in that secret place, and your Father who sees all that is done in secret will reward you.

How to pray. The Lord's Prayer

7 'In your prayers do not babble as the gentiles do, for they think that by using many
8 words they will make themselves heard. ·Do not be like them; your Father knows
9 what you need before you ask him. ·So you should pray like this: *ᵈ*

> Our Father in heaven,
> may your name be held holy,
10 > your kingdom come,
> your will be done,
> on earth as in heaven.
11 > Give us today our daily *ᵉ* bread.
12 > And forgive us our debts,
> as we have forgiven those who are in debt to us.
13 > And do not put us to the test,
> but save us from the Evil One. *ᶠ*

14 'Yes, if you forgive others their failings, your heavenly Father will forgive you
15 yours; ·but if you do not forgive others, your Father will not forgive your failings either.

Fasting in secret

16 'When you are fasting, do not put on a gloomy look as the hypocrites do: they go about looking unsightly to let people know they are fasting. In truth I tell you,
17 they have had their reward. ·But when you fast, put scent on your head and wash
18 your face, ·so that no one will know you are fasting except your Father who sees all that is done in secret; and your Father who sees all that is done in secret will reward you.

True treasures

19 'Do not store up treasures for yourselves on earth, where moth and woodworm
20 destroy them and thieves can break in and steal. ·But store up treasures for yourselves in heaven, where neither moth nor woodworm destroys them and
21 thieves cannot break in and steal. ·For wherever your treasure is, there will your heart be too.

The eye, the lamp of the body

22 'The lamp of the body is the eye. It follows that if your eye is clear, your whole
23 body will be filled with light. ·But if your eye is diseased, your whole body will be darkness. If then, the light inside you is darkened, what darkness that will be! *ᵍ*

God and money

24 'No one can be the slave of two masters: he will either hate the first and love the second, or be attached to the first and despise the second. You cannot be the slave both of God and of money.

Trust in Providence

25 'That is why I am telling you not to worry about your life and what you are to eat,
nor about your body and what you are to wear. Surely life is more than food, and
26 the body more than clothing! ·Look at the birds in the sky. They do not sow or
reap or gather into barns; yet your heavenly Father feeds them. Are you not worth
27 much more than they are? ·Can any of you, however much you worry, add one
28 single cubit to your span of life? ·And why worry about clothing? Think of the
29 flowers growing in the fields; they never have to work or spin; ·yet I assure you
30 that not even Solomon in all his royal robes was clothed like one of these. ·Now if
that is how God clothes the wild flowers growing in the field which are there today
and thrown into the furnace tomorrow, will he not much more look after you, you
31 who have so little faith? ·So do not worry; do not say, "What are we to eat? What
32 are we to drink? What are we to wear?" ·It is the gentiles who set their hearts on
33 all these things. Your heavenly Father knows you need them all. ·Set your hearts
on his kingdom first, and on God's saving justice, and all these other things will be
34 given you as well. ·So do not worry about tomorrow: tomorrow will take care of
itself. Each day has enough trouble of its own.'

Do not judge

1, 2 7 'Do not judge, and you will not be judged; ª ·because the judgements you give
are the judgements you will get, and the standard you use will be the standard
3 used for you. ·Why do you observe the splinter in your brother's eye and never
4 notice the great log in your own? ·And how dare you say to your brother, "Let me
take that splinter out of your eye," when, look, there is a great log in your own?
5 Hypocrite! Take the log out of your own eye first, and then you will see clearly
enough to take the splinter out of your brother's eye.

Do not profane sacred things

6 'Do not give dogs what is holy; ᵇ and do not throw your pearls in front of pigs, or
they may trample them and then turn on you and tear you to pieces.

Effective prayer

7 'Ask, and it will be given to you; search, and you will find; knock, and the door
8 will be opened to you. ·Everyone who asks receives; everyone who searches finds;
9 everyone who knocks will have the door opened. ·Is there anyone among you who
10 would hand his son a stone when he asked for bread? ·Or would hand him a snake
11 when he asked for a fish? ·If you, then, evil as you are, know how to give your
children what is good, how much more will your Father in heaven give good things
to those who ask him!

The golden rule ᶜ

12 'So always treat others as you would like them to treat you; that is the Law and
the Prophets.

The two ways ᵈ

13 'Enter by the narrow gate, since the road that leads to destruction is wide and
14 spacious, ᵉ and many take it; ·but it is a narrow gate and a hard road that leads to
life, and only a few find it.

False prophets

15 'Beware of false prophets[f] who come to you disguised as sheep but underneath
16 are ravenous wolves. ·You will be able to tell them by their fruits. Can people
17 pick grapes from thorns, or figs from thistles? ·In the same way, a sound tree
18 produces good fruit but a rotten tree bad fruit. ·A sound tree cannot bear bad
19 fruit, nor a rotten tree bear good fruit. ·Any tree that does not produce good fruit
20 is cut down and thrown on the fire. ·I repeat, you will be able to tell them by their
fruits.

The true disciple

21 'It is not anyone who says to me, "Lord, Lord," who will enter the kingdom of
22 Heaven, but the person who does the will of my Father in heaven. ·When the day
comes[g] many will say to me, "Lord, Lord, did we not prophesy in your name,
23 drive out demons in your name, work many miracles in your name?" ·Then I shall
tell them to their faces: I have never known you; *away from me, all evil doers!*
24 'Therefore, everyone who listens to these words of mine and acts on them will
25 be like a sensible man who built his house on rock. ·Rain came down, floods rose,
gales blew and hurled themselves against that house, and it did not fall: it was
26 founded on rock. ·But everyone who listens to these words of mine and does not
27 act on them will be like a stupid man who built his house on sand. ·Rain came
down, floods rose, gales blew and struck that house, and it fell; and what a fall it
had!'

The amazement of the crowds

28 Jesus had now finished what he wanted to say, and his teaching made a deep
29 impression on the people ·because he taught them with authority, unlike their
own scribes. [h]

III: THE KINGDOM OF HEAVEN IS PROCLAIMED

A: NARRATIVE SECTION: TEN MIRACLES

Cure of a man with skin-disease

1 ⟨8⟩ After he had come down from the mountain large crowds followed him.
2 ⟨8⟩ Suddenly a man with a virulent skin-disease came up and bowed low in front
3 of him, saying, 'Lord, if you are willing, you can cleanse me.' ·Jesus stretched out
his hand and touched him saying, 'I am willing. Be cleansed.' And his skin-disease
4 was cleansed at once. [a] ·Then Jesus said to him, 'Mind you tell no one, but go and
show yourself to the priest and make the offering prescribed by Moses, as evidence
to them.'

Cure of the centurion's servant

5, 6 When he went into Capernaum a centurion came up and pleaded with him. ·'Sir,'
7 he said, 'my servant is lying at home paralysed and in great pain.' ·Jesus said to
8 him, 'I will come myself and cure him.' ·The centurion replied, 'Sir, I am not
worthy to have you under my roof; just give the word and my servant will be
9 cured. ·For I am under authority myself and have soldiers under me; and I say to
one man, "Go," and he goes; to another, "Come here," and he comes; to my

10 servant, "Do this," and he does it.' ·When Jesus heard this he was astonished and
said to those following him, 'In truth I tell you, in no one in Israel have I found
11 faith *b* as great as this. ·And I tell you that many will come from east and west and
sit down with Abraham and Isaac and Jacob at the feast *c* in the kingdom of
12 Heaven; ·but the children of the kingdom *d* will be thrown out into the darkness
13 outside, where there will be weeping and grinding of teeth.' *e* ·And to the centurion
Jesus said, 'Go back, then; let this be done for you, as your faith demands.' And
the servant was cured at that moment.

Cure of Peter's mother-in-law

14 And going into Peter's house Jesus found Peter's mother-in-law in bed and
15 feverish. ·He touched her hand and the fever left her, and she got up and began to
serve him.

A number of cures

16 That evening they brought him many who were possessed by devils. He drove out
17 the spirits with a command and cured all who were sick. ·This was to fulfil what
was spoken by the prophet Isaiah:

He himself bore our sicknesses away and carried our diseases. *f*

Unconditional commitment

18 When Jesus saw the crowd all about him he gave orders to leave for the other
19 side. *g* One of the scribes then came up and said to him, 'Master, I will follow you
20 wherever you go.' ·Jesus said, 'Foxes have holes and the birds of the air have
nests, but the Son of man *h* has nowhere to lay his head.'
21   Another man, one of the disciples, said to him, 'Lord, let me go and bury my
22 father first.' ·But Jesus said, 'Follow me, and leave the dead to bury their dead.'

The calming of the storm

23. 24 Then he got into the boat followed by his disciples. ·Suddenly a storm broke over
the lake, so violent that the boat was being swamped by the waves. But he was
25 asleep. ·So they went to him and woke him saying, 'Save us, Lord, we are lost!'
26 And he said to them, 'Why are you so frightened, you who have so little faith?'
And then he stood up and rebuked the winds and the sea; and there was a great
27 calm. ·They were astounded and said, 'Whatever kind of man is this, that even
the winds and the sea obey him?'

The demoniacs of Gadara

28 When he reached the territory of the Gadarenes *i* on the other side, two demoniacs
came *j* towards him out of the tombs—they were so dangerously violent that
29 nobody could use that path. ·Suddenly they shouted, 'What do you want with us,
30 Son of God? Have you come here to torture us before the time?' *k* ·Now some
31 distance away there was a large herd of pigs feeding, ·and the devils pleaded with
32 Jesus, 'If you drive us out, send us into the herd of pigs.' ·And he said to them,
'Go then,' and they came out and made for the pigs; and at that the whole herd
33 charged down the cliff into the lake and perished in the water. ·The herdsmen ran
off and made for the city, where they told the whole story, including what had
34 happened to the demoniacs. ·Suddenly the whole city set out to meet Jesus; and
as soon as they saw him they implored him to leave their neighbourhood.

Cure of a paralytic

1, 2 9 He got back in the boat, crossed the water and came to his home town. *ᵃ* ·And suddenly some people brought him a paralytic stretched out on a bed. Seeing their faith, Jesus said to the paralytic, 'Take comfort, my child, your sins are
3 forgiven.'*ᵇ* ·And now some scribes said to themselves, 'This man is being blas-
4 phemous.' ·Knowing what was in their minds Jesus said, 'Why do you have such
5 wicked thoughts in your hearts? ·Now, which of these is easier: to say, "Your sins
6 are forgiven," or to say, "Get up and walk"? ·But to prove to you that the Son of man has authority on earth to forgive sins,'—then he said to the paralytic—'get
7, 8 up, pick up your bed and go off home.' ·And the man got up and went home. ·A feeling of awe came over the crowd when they saw this, and they praised God for having given such authority to human beings. *ᶜ*

The call of Matthew

9 As Jesus was walking on from there he saw a man named Matthew*ᵈ* sitting at the tax office, and he said to him, 'Follow me.' And he got up and followed him.

Eating with sinners

10 Now while he was at table in the house it happened that a number of tax collectors
11 and sinners*ᵉ* came to sit at the table with Jesus and his disciples. ·When the Pharisees saw this, they said to his disciples, 'Why does your master eat with tax
12 collectors and sinners?' ·When he heard this he replied, 'It is not the healthy who
13 need the doctor, but the sick. ·Go and learn the meaning of the words: *Mercy is what pleases me, not sacrifice.*ᶠ And indeed I came to call not the upright, but sinners.'

A discussion on fasting

14 Then John's*ᵍ* disciples came to him and said, 'Why is it that we and the Pharisees
15 fast, but your disciples do not?' ·Jesus replied, 'Surely the bridegroom's attendants cannot mourn as long as the bridegroom*ʰ* is still with them? But the time will
16 come when the bridegroom is taken away*ⁱ* from them, and then they will fast. ·No one puts a piece of unshrunken cloth onto an old cloak, because the patch pulls
17 away from the cloak and the tear gets worse. ·Nor do people put new wine into old wineskins; otherwise, the skins burst, the wine runs out, and the skins are lost. No; they put new wine in fresh skins and both are preserved.'*ʲ*

Cure of the woman with a haemorrhage. The official's daughter raised to life

18 While he was speaking to them, suddenly one of the officials came up, *ᵏ* who bowed low in front of him and said, 'My daughter has just died, but come and lay your
19 hand on her and her life will be saved.' ·Jesus rose and, with his disciples, followed him.
20   Then suddenly from behind him came a woman, who had been suffering from a
21 haemorrhage for twelve years, and she touched the fringe of his cloak, ·for she
22 was thinking, 'If only I can touch his cloak I shall be saved.' ·Jesus turned round and saw her; and he said to her, 'Courage, my daughter, your faith has saved you.' And from that moment the woman was saved.
23   When Jesus reached the official's house and saw the flute-players, with the
24 crowd making a commotion,*ˡ* he said, ·'Get out of here; the little girl is not dead;
25 she is asleep.' And they ridiculed him. ·But when the people had been turned out

26 he went inside and took her by the hand; and she stood up. ·And the news of this spread all round the countryside.

Cure of two blind men

27 As Jesus went on his way two blind men followed him shouting, 'Take pity on us,
28 son of David.' ⁿ ·And when Jesus reached the house the blind men came up with him and he said to them, 'Do you believe I can do this?' They said, 'Lord, we do.'
29 Then he touched their eyes saying, 'According to your faith, let it be done to you.'
30 And their sight returned. Then Jesus sternly warned them, 'Take care that no one
31 learns about this.' ·But when they had gone away, they talked about him all over the countryside.

Cure of a dumb demoniac

32 They had only just left when suddenly a man was brought to him, a dumb
33 demoniac. ·And when the devil was driven out, the dumb man spoke and the
34 people were amazed and said, 'Nothing like this has ever been seen in Israel.' ·But the Pharisees said, 'It is through the prince of devils that he drives out devils.' ⁿ

The distress of the crowds

35 Jesus made a tour through all the towns and villages, teaching in their synagogues, proclaiming the good news of the kingdom and curing all kinds of disease and all kinds of illness.
36   And when he saw the crowds he felt sorry for them because they were harassed
37 and dejected, like sheep without a shepherd. ° ·Then he said to his disciples, 'The harvest is rich but the labourers are few, so ask the Lord of the harvest to send out labourers to his harvest.'

B: INSTRUCTION FOR APOSTLES

The mission of the Twelve

1 **10** He summoned his twelve disciples ° and gave them authority over unclean spirits with power to drive them out and to cure all kinds of disease and all kinds of illness.
2   These are the names of the twelve apostles: ᵇ first, Simon who is known as Peter,
3 and his brother Andrew; James the son of Zebedee, and his brother John; ·Philip and Bartholomew; Thomas, and Matthew the tax collector; James the son of
4 Alphaeus, and Thaddaeus; ·Simon the Zealot and Judas Iscariot, who was also
5 his betrayer. ·These twelve Jesus sent out, instructing them as follows:
    'Do not make your way to gentile territory, and do not enter any Samaritan
6, 7 town; ·go instead to the lost sheep of the House of Israel. ᶜ ·And as you go,
8 proclaim that the kingdom of Heaven is close at hand. ·Cure the sick, raise the dead, cleanse those suffering from virulent skin-diseases, drive out devils. You
9 received without charge, give without charge. ·Provide yourselves with no gold or
10 silver, not even with coppers for your purses, ·with no haversack for the journey or spare tunic or footwear or a staff, for the labourer deserves his keep.
11   'Whatever town or village you go into, seek out someone worthy and stay with
12, 13 him until you leave. ·As you enter his house, salute it, ᵈ ·and if the house deserves it, may your peace come upon it; if it does not, may your peace come back to you.

14 And if anyone does not welcome you or listen to what you have to say, as you
15 walk out of the house or town shake the dust from your feet. ᶜ ·In truth I tell you,
on the Day of Judgement it will be more bearable for Sodom and Gomorrah than
16 for that town. ·Look, I am sending you out like sheep among wolves; so be cunning
as snakes and yet innocent as doves.

Missionaries will be persecuted ᶠ

17 'Be prepared for people to hand you over to sanhedrins ᵍ and scourge you in their
18 synagogues. ·You will be brought before governors and kings for my sake, as
19 evidence to them and to the gentiles. ·But when you are handed over, do not
worry about how to speak or what to say; what you are to say will be given to you
20 when the time comes, ·because it is not you who will be speaking; the Spirit of
your Father will be speaking in you.

21 'Brother will betray brother to death, and a father his child; children will come
22 forward against their parents and have them put to death. ·You will be universally
hated on account of my name; but anyone who stands firm to the end will be
23 saved. ·If they persecute you in one town, take refuge in the next; and if they
persecute you in that, take refuge in another. ʰ In truth I tell you, you will not
have gone the round of the towns of Israel before the Son of man comes. ⁱ
24, 25 'Disciple is not superior to teacher, nor slave to master. ·It is enough for disciple
to grow to be like teacher, and slave like master. If they have called the master of
the house "Beelzebul", how much more the members of his household?

Open and fearless speech

26 'So do not be afraid of them. Everything now covered up will be uncovered, and
27 everything now hidden will be made clear. ·What I say to you in the dark, tell in
the daylight; what you hear in whispers, proclaim from the housetops. ʲ
28 'Do not be afraid of those who kill the body but cannot kill the soul; fear him
29 rather who can destroy both body and soul in hell. ·Can you not buy two sparrows
for a penny? And yet not one falls to the ground without your Father knowing.
30, 31 Why, every hair on your head has been counted. ·So there is no need to be afraid;
you are worth more than many sparrows.
32 'So if anyone declares himself for me in the presence of human beings, I will
33 declare myself for him in the presence of my Father in heaven. ᵏ ·But the one who
disowns me in the presence of human beings, I will disown in the presence of my
Father in heaven.

Jesus, the cause of dissension ˡ

34 'Do not suppose that I have come to bring peace to the earth: it is not peace I have
35 come to bring, but a sword. ·For I have come to set son against *father, daughter*
36 *against mother, daughter-in-law against mother-in-law;* ·*a person's enemies will be*
the members of his own household.

Renouncing self to follow Jesus

37 'No one who prefers father or mother to me is worthy of me. No one who prefers
38 son or daughter to me is worthy of me. ·Anyone who does not take his cross and
39 follow in my footsteps is not worthy of me. ·Anyone who finds his life will lose it;
anyone who loses his life for my sake will find it. ᵐ

Conclusion of the Instruction

40 'Anyone who welcomes you welcomes me; and anyone who welcomes me welcomes the one who sent me.

41 'Anyone who welcomes a prophet because he is a prophet will have a prophet's reward; and anyone who welcomes an upright person because he is upright will have the reward of an upright person. *

42 'If anyone gives so much as a cup of cold water to one of these little ones° because he is a disciple, then in truth I tell you, he will most certainly not go without his reward.'

IV: THE MYSTERY OF THE KINGDOM OF HEAVEN

A: NARRATIVE SECTION

1 **11** When Jesus had finished instructing his twelve disciples he moved on from there to teach and preach in their towns. *

The Baptist's question. Jesus commends him

2 Now John had heard in prison what Christ was doing and he sent his disciples *ᵇ* to
3 ask him, ·'Are you the one who is to come, or are we to expect someone else?' *ᶜ*
4, 5 Jesus answered, 'Go back and tell John what you hear and see; ·the blind see again, and the lame walk, those suffering from virulent skin-diseases are cleansed, and the deaf hear, the dead are raised to life and the good news is proclaimed to
6 the poor; *ᵈ* ·and blessed is anyone who does not find me a cause of falling.'

7 As the men were leaving, Jesus began to talk to the people about John, 'What
8 did you go out into the desert to see? A reed swaying in the breeze? No? ·Then what did you go out to see? A man wearing fine clothes? Look, those who wear
9 fine clothes are to be found in palaces. ·Then what did you go out for? To see a
10 prophet? Yes, I tell you, and much more than a prophet: ·he is the one of whom scripture says:

> Look, I am going to send my messenger in front of you
> to prepare your way before you.

11 'In truth I tell you, of all the children born to women, there has never been anyone greater than John the Baptist; yet the least in the kingdom of Heaven is
12 greater than he. *ᵉ* ·Since John the Baptist came, up to this present time, the kingdom of Heaven has been subjected to violence and the violent are taking it by
13 storm. *ᶠ* ·Because it was towards John that all the prophecies of the prophets and
14 of the Law were leading; ·and he, if you will believe me, is the Elijah who was to
15 return. *ᵍ* ·Anyone who has ears should listen!

Jesus condemns his contemporaries

16 'What comparison can I find for this generation? It is like children shouting to each other as they sit in the market place:

17 > We played the pipes for you,
> and you wouldn't dance;
> we sang dirges,
> and you wouldn't be mourners.

18, 19 'For John came, neither eating nor drinking, and they say, "He is possessed." ·The Son of man came, eating and drinking, and they say, "Look, a glutton and a drunkard, a friend of tax collectors and sinners." Yet wisdom is justified by her deeds.'[h]

Lament over the lake-towns

20 Then he began to reproach the towns in which most of his miracles had been worked, because they refused to repent.

21   'Alas for you, Chorazin! Alas for you, Bethsaida! For if the miracles done in you had been done in Tyre and Sidon, they would have repented long ago in

22 sackcloth and ashes. ·Still, I tell you that it will be more bearable for Tyre and

23 Sidon on Judgement Day than for you. ·And as for you, Capernaum, did you want to be *raised as high as heaven? You shall be flung down to hell.* For if the miracles done in you had been done in Sodom, it would have been standing yet.

24 ·Still, I tell you that it will be more bearable for Sodom on Judgement Day than for you.'

The good news revealed to the simple. The Father and the Son

25 At that time Jesus exclaimed, 'I bless you, Father, Lord of heaven and of earth, for hiding these things[j] from the learned and the clever and revealing them to

26, 27 little children. ·Yes, Father, for that is what it pleased you to do. ·Everything has been entrusted to me by my Father; and no one knows the Son except the Father, just as no one knows the Father except the Son and those to whom the Son chooses to reveal him.[k]

The gentle mastery of Christ

28 'Come to me, all you who labour and are overburdened,[l] and I will give you rest.

29 Shoulder my yoke and learn from me, for I am gentle and humble in heart,[m] *and*

30 *you will find rest for your souls.* ·Yes, my yoke is easy and my burden light.'

Picking corn on the Sabbath

1
2 **12** At that time Jesus went through the cornfields one Sabbath day. His disciples were hungry and began to pick ears of corn and eat them. ·The Pharisees noticed it and said to him, 'Look, your disciples are doing something

3 that is forbidden on the Sabbath.'[a] ·But he said to them, 'Have you not read what

4 David did when he and his followers were hungry——·how he went into the house of God and they ate the loaves of the offering although neither he nor his followers

5 were permitted to eat them, but only the priests? ·Or again, have you not read in the Law that on the Sabbath day the Temple priests break the Sabbath without

6 committing any fault?[b] ·Now here, I tell you, is something greater than the

7 Temple. ·And if you had understood the meaning of the words: *Mercy is what*

8 *pleases me, not sacrifice*, you would not have condemned the blameless. ·For the Son of man is master of the Sabbath.'[c]

Cure of the man with a withered hand

9, 10 He moved on from there and went to their synagogue; ·now a man was there with a withered hand. They asked him, 'Is it permitted to cure somebody on the Sabbath

11 day?' hoping for something to charge him with. ·But he said to them, 'If any one of you here had only one sheep and it fell down a hole on the Sabbath day, would

12 he not get hold of it and lift it out? ·Now a man is far more important than a

13 sheep, so it follows that it is permitted on the Sabbath day to do good.' ·Then he
said to the man, 'Stretch out your hand.' He stretched it out and his hand was
14 restored, as sound as the other one. ·At this the Pharisees went out and began to
plot against him, discussing how to destroy him.

Jesus the 'servant of Yahweh'

15 Jesus knew this and withdrew from the district. Many followed him and he cured
16, 17 them all ·but warned them not to make him known. ·This *d* was to fulfil what was
spoken by the prophet Isaiah:

18   *Look! My servant whom I have chosen,*
            my beloved, in whom my soul delights,
            I will send my Spirit upon him,
            and he will *present* judgement *e* to the nations;
19   *he will not brawl or cry out,*
            his voice is not heard in the streets,
20   *he will not break the crushed reed,*
            or snuff the faltering wick,
21   *until he has made judgement victorious;*
            in him the nations will put their hope.

Jesus and Beelzebul

22 Then they brought to him a blind and dumb demoniac; and he cured him, so that
23 the dumb man could speak and see. ·All the people were astounded and said,
24 'Can this be the son of David?' ·But when the Pharisees heard this they said, 'The
man drives out devils only through Beelzebul, *f* the chief of the devils.'
25   Knowing what was in their minds he said to them, 'Every kingdom divided
against itself is heading for ruin; and no town, no household divided against itself
26 can last. ·Now if Satan drives out Satan, he is divided against himself; so how can
27 his kingdom last? ·And if it is through Beelzebul that I drive devils out, through
28 whom do your own experts *g* drive them out? They shall be your judges, then. ·But
if it is through the Spirit of God that I drive out devils, then be sure that the
kingdom of God has caught you unawares.
29   'Or again, how can anyone make his way into a strong man's house and plunder
his property unless he has first tied up the strong man? Only then can he plunder
his house.
30   'Anyone who is not with me is against me, and anyone who does not gather in
31 with me throws away. ·And so I tell you, every human sin and blasphemy will be
32 forgiven, but blasphemy against the Spirit will not be forgiven. ·And anyone who
says a word against the Son of man will be forgiven; but no one who speaks against
the Holy Spirit will be forgiven either in this world or in the next. *h*

Words betray the heart

33 'Make a tree sound and its fruit will be sound; make a tree rotten and its fruit will
34 be rotten. For the tree can be told by its fruit. ·You brood of vipers, how can your
speech be good when you are evil? For words flow out of what fills the heart.
35 Good people draw good things from their store of goodness; bad people draw bad
36 things from their store of badness. ·So I tell you this, that for every unfounded *i*
37 word people utter they will answer on Judgement Day, ·since it is by your words
you will be justified, and by your words condemned.'

The sign of Jonah

38 Then some of the scribes and Pharisees spoke up. 'Master,' they said, 'we should
39 like to see a sign^j from you.' ·He replied, 'It is an evil and unfaithful^k generation
that asks for a sign! The only sign it will be given is the sign of the prophet Jonah.^l
40 For as Jonah *remained in the belly of the sea-monster for three days and three
nights*, so will the Son of man be in the heart of the earth for three days and
41 three nights.^m ·On Judgement Day the men of Nineveh will appear against this
generation and they will be its condemnation, because when Jonah preached they
42 repented; and look, there is something greater than Jonah here. ·On Judgement
Day the Queen of the South will appear against this generation and be its
condemnation, because she came from the ends of the earth to hear the wisdom of
Solomon; and look, there is something greater than Solomon here.

The return of the unclean spirit

43 'When an unclean spirit goes out of someone it wanders through waterless country
44 looking for a place to rest,ⁿ and cannot find one. ·Then it says, "I will return to
45 the home I came from." But on arrival, finding it unoccupied, swept and tidied, ·it
then goes off and collects seven other spirits more wicked than itself, and they go
in and set up house there, and so that person ends up worse off than before. That
is what will happen to this wicked generation.'

The true kinsfolk of Jesus

46 He was still speaking to the crowds when suddenly his mother and his brothers^o
[47]. 48 were standing outside and were anxious to have a word with him. ^p ·But to the
man who told him this Jesus replied, 'Who is my mother? Who are my brothers?'
49 And stretching out his hand towards his disciples he said, 'Here are my mother
50 and my brothers. ·Anyone who does the will of my Father in heaven is my brother
and sister and mother.'^q

B: DISCOURSE OF PARABLES

Introduction

1. 2 **13** That same day,^a Jesus left the house and sat by the lakeside, ·but such
large crowds gathered round him that he got into a boat and sat there. The
3 people all stood on the shore, ·and he told them many things in parables. ^b

Parable of the sower

4 He said, 'Listen, a sower went out to sow. ·As he sowed, some seeds fell on the
5 edge of the path, and the birds came and ate them up. ·Others fell on patches of
rock where they found little soil and sprang up at once, because there was no
6 depth of earth; ·but as soon as the sun came up they were scorched and, not having
7 any roots, they withered away. ·Others fell among thorns, and the thorns grew up
8 and choked them. ·Others fell on rich soil and produced their crop, some a
9 hundredfold, some sixty, some thirty. ·Anyone who has ears^c should listen!'

Why Jesus speaks in parables

10 Then the disciples went up to him and asked, 'Why do you talk to them in
11 parables?' ·In answer, he said, 'Because to you is granted to understand the
12 mysteries of the kingdom of Heaven, but to them it is not granted. ·Anyone who

has will be given more and will have more than enough; but anyone who has not
13 will be deprived even of what he has. *ᵈ* ·The reason I talk to them in parables is
14 that they look without seeing and listen without hearing or understanding. *ᵉ* ·So in
their case what was spoken by the prophet Isaiah is being fulfilled:

> *Listen and listen, but never understand!*
> *Look and look, but never perceive!*
15 > *This people's heart has grown coarse,*
> *their ears dulled, they have shut their eyes tight*
> *to avoid using their eyes to see, their ears to hear,*
> *their heart to understand,*
> *changing their ways and being healed by me.*

16. 17   'But blessed are your eyes because they see, your ears because they hear! ·In
truth I tell you, many prophets and upright people *ᶠ* longed to see what you see,
and never saw it; to hear what you hear, and never heard it.

The parable of the sower explained

18. 19   'So pay attention to the parable of the sower. ·When anyone hears the word of the
kingdom without understanding, the Evil-One comes and carries off what was
20 sown *ᵍ* in his heart: this is the seed sown on the edge of the path. ·The seed sown
on patches of rock is someone who hears the word and welcomes it at once with
21 joy. ·But such a person has no root deep down and does not last; should some trial
22 come, or some persecution on account of the word and at once he falls away. ·The
seed sown in thorns is someone who hears the word, but the worry of the world
23 and the lure of riches choke the word and so it produces nothing. ·And the seed
sown in rich soil is someone who hears the word and understands it; this is the one
who yields a harvest and produces now a hundredfold, now sixty, now thirty.'

Parable of the darnel

24 He put another parable before them, 'The kingdom of Heaven may be compared
25 to a man who sowed good seed in his field. ·While everybody was asleep his enemy
26 came, sowed darnel all among the wheat, and made off. ·When the new wheat
27 sprouted and ripened, then the darnel appeared as well. ·The owner's labourers
went to him and said, "Sir, was it not good seed that you sowed in your field? If
28 so, where does the darnel come from?" ·He said to them, "Some enemy has done
29 this." And the labourers said, "Do you want us to go and weed it out?" ·But he
said, "No, because when you weed out the darnel you might pull up the wheat
30 with it. ·Let them both grow till the harvest; and at harvest time I shall say to the
reapers: First collect the darnel and tie it in bundles to be burnt, then gather the
wheat into my barn." '

Parable of the mustard seed

31 He put another parable before them, 'The kingdom of Heaven is like a mustard
32 seed which a man took and sowed in his field. ·It is the smallest of all the seeds,
but when it has grown it is the biggest of shrubs and becomes a tree, so that the
birds of the air can come and shelter in its branches.'

Parable of the yeast

33 He told them another parable, 'The kingdom of Heaven is like the yeast a woman
took and mixed in with three measures of flour till it was leavened all through.' *ʰ*

The people are taught only in parables

34 In all this Jesus spoke to the crowds in parables; indeed, he would never speak to
35 them except in parables. ·This was to fulfil what was spoken by the prophet:

> *I will speak to you in parables,*
> *unfold what has been hidden since the foundation of the world.* [i]

The parable of the darnel explained

36 Then, leaving the crowds, he went to the house; and his disciples came to him and
37 said, 'Explain to us the parable about the darnel in the field.' ·He said in reply,
38 'The sower of the good seed is the Son of man. ·The field is the world; the good
39 seed is the subjects of the kingdom; the darnel, the subjects of the Evil One; [j] ·the
enemy who sowed it, the devil; the harvest is the end of the world; the reapers are
40 the angels. ·Well then, just as the darnel is gathered up and burnt in the fire, so it
41 will be at the end of time. ·The Son of man will send his angels and they will gather
42 out of his kingdom all causes of falling and all who do evil, ·and throw them into
43 the blazing furnace, where there will be weeping and grinding of teeth. ·Then the
upright will shine like the sun in the kingdom of their Father. [k] Anyone who has
ears should listen!

Parables of the treasure and of the pearl [l]

44 'The kingdom of Heaven is like treasure hidden in a field which someone has
found; he hides it again, goes off in his joy, sells everything he owns and buys the
field.

45, 46   'Again, the kingdom of Heaven is like a merchant looking for fine pearls; ·when
he finds one of great value he goes and sells everything he owns and buys it.

Parable of the dragnet

47 'Again, the kingdom of Heaven is like a dragnet that is cast in the sea and brings
48 in a haul of all kinds of fish. ·When it is full, the fishermen haul it ashore; then,
sitting down, they collect the good ones in baskets and throw away those that are
49 no use. ·This is how it will be at the end of time: the angels will appear and separate
50 the wicked from the upright, ·to throw them into the blazing furnace, where there
will be weeping and grinding of teeth.

Conclusion

51, 52 'Have you understood all these?' They said, 'Yes.' ·And he said to them, 'Well
then, every scribe who becomes a disciple of the kingdom of Heaven is like a
householder who brings out from his storeroom new things as well as old.' [m]

V: THE CHURCH, FIRST-FRUITS
OF THE KINGDOM OF HEAVEN

A: NARRATIVE SECTION

A visit to Nazareth

53, 54 When Jesus had finished these parables he left the district; ·and, coming to his
home town, [n] he taught the people in their synagogue in such a way that they were

astonished and said, 'Where did the man get this wisdom and these miraculous
55 powers? ·This is the carpenter's son, surely? Is not his mother the woman called
56 Mary, and his brothers James and Joseph and Simon and Jude? ·His sisters, too,
57 are they not all here with us? So where did the man get it all?' ·And they would
not accept him. But Jesus said to them, 'A prophet is despised only in his own
58 country and in his own house,' ·and he did not work many miracles there because
of their lack of faith.

Herod and Jesus

1, 2 **14** At that time Herod the tetrarch heard about the reputation of Jesus ·and
said to his court, 'This is John the Baptist himself; he has risen from the
dead, and that is why miraculous powers are at work in him.'

John the Baptist beheaded

3 Now it was Herod who had arrested John, chained him up and put him in prison
4 because of Herodias, his brother Philip's *a* wife. ·For John had told him, 'It is
5 against the Law for you to have her.' ·He had wanted to kill him but was afraid of
6 the people, who regarded John as a prophet. ·Then, during the celebrations for
Herod's birthday, the daughter of Herodias *b* danced before the company and so
7 delighted Herod ·that he promised on oath to give her anything she asked.
8 Prompted by her mother she said, 'Give me John the Baptist's head, here, on a
9 dish.' ·The king was distressed but, thinking of the oaths he had sworn and of his
10 guests, he ordered it to be given her, ·and sent and had John beheaded in the
11 prison. ·The head was brought in on a dish and given to the girl, who took it to her
12 mother. ·John's disciples came and took the body and buried it; then they went
off to tell Jesus.

First miracle of the loaves *c*

13 When Jesus received this news he withdrew by boat to a lonely place where they
could be by themselves. *d* But the crowds heard of this and, leaving the towns,
14 went after him on foot. *e* ·So as he stepped ashore he saw a large crowd; and he
took pity on them and healed their sick.
15   When evening came, the disciples went to him and said, 'This is a lonely place,
and time has slipped by; so send the people away, and they can go to the villages
16 to buy themselves some food.' ·Jesus replied, 'There is no need for them to go:
17 give them something to eat yourselves.' ·But they answered, 'All we have with us
18, 19 is five loaves and two fish.' ·So he said, 'Bring them here to me.' ·He gave orders
that the people were to sit down on the grass; then he took the five loaves and the
two fish, raised his eyes to heaven and said the blessing. And breaking the loaves
20 he handed them to his disciples, who gave them to the crowds. ·They all ate as
much as they wanted, and they collected the scraps left over, twelve baskets full.
21 Now about five thousand men had eaten, to say nothing of women and children.

Jesus walks on the water and, with him, Peter

22 And at once he made the disciples get into the boat and go on ahead to the other
23 side while he sent the crowds away. ·After sending the crowds away he went up
24 into the hills by himself to pray. *f* When evening came, he was there alone, ·while
the boat, by now some furlongs from land, *g* was hard pressed by rough waves, for
25 there was a head-wind. ·In the fourth watch of the night *h* he came towards them,
26 walking on the sea, ·and when the disciples saw him walking on the sea they were

27 terrified. 'It is a ghost,' they said, and cried out in fear. ·But at once Jesus called
28 out to them, saying, 'Courage! It's me! Don't be afraid.' ·It was Peter' who
answered. 'Lord,' he said, 'if it is you, tell me to come to you across the water.'
29 Jesus said, 'Come.' Then Peter got out of the boat and started walking towards
30 Jesus across the water, ·but then noticing the wind, he took fright and began to
31 sink. 'Lord,' he cried, 'save me!' ·Jesus put out his hand at once and held him.
32 'You have so little faith,' he said, 'why did you doubt?' ·And as they got into the
33 boat the wind dropped. ·The men in the boat bowed down before him and said,
'Truly, you are the Son of God.'

Cures at Gennesaret

34, 35 Having made the crossing, they came to land at Gennesaret. ·When the local
people recognised him they spread the news through the whole neighbourhood
36 and took all that were sick to him, ·begging him just to let them touch the fringe
of his cloak. And all those who touched it were saved.

The traditions of the Pharisees

1, 2 **15** Then Pharisees and scribes from Jerusalem came to Jesus and said, ·'Why
do your disciples break away from the tradition of the elders?ᵃ They eat
3 without washing their hands.'ᵇ ·He answered, 'And why do you break away from
4 the commandment of God for the sake of your tradition? ·For God said, *"Honourᶜ*
your father and your mother" and *"Anyone who curses his father or mother will be*
5 *put to death."* ·But you say, "If anyone says to his father or mother: Anything I
6 might have used to help you is dedicated to God, ·he is rid of his duty to father or
mother."ᵈ In this way you have made God's word ineffective by means of your
7 tradition. ·Hypocrites! How rightly Isaiah prophesied about you when he said:

8 　　　　　*This people honours me only with lip-service,*
　　　　　while their hearts are far from me.
9 　　　　　*Their reverence of me is worthless;*
　　　　　the lessons they teach are nothing but human commandments.'

On clean and uncleanᵉ

10, 11 He called the people to him and said, 'Listen, and understand. ·What goes into
the mouth does not make anyone unclean; it is what comes out of the mouth that
makes someone unclean.'
12 Then the disciples came to him and said, 'Do you know that the Pharisees were
13 shocked when they heard what you said?' ·He replied, 'Any plant my heavenly
14 Father has not planted will be pulled up by the roots. ·Leave them alone. They
are blind leaders of the blind; and if one blind person leads another, both will fall
into a pit.'
15, 16 At this, Peter said to him, 'Explain the parable for us.' ·Jesus replied, 'Even
17 you—don't you yet understand? ·Can't you see that whatever goes into the mouth
18 passes through the stomach and is discharged into the sewer? ·But whatever comes
out of the mouth comes from the heart, and it is this that makes someone unclean.
19 For from the heart come evil intentions: murder, adultery, fornication, theft,
20 perjury, slander. ·These are the things that make a person unclean. But eating
with unwashed hands does not make anyone unclean.'

The daughter of the Canaanite woman healed

21, 22   Jesus left that place and withdrew to the region of Tyre and Sidon. ·And suddenly out came a Canaanite woman from that district *ᶠ* and started shouting, 'Lord, Son

23   of David, take pity on me. My daughter is tormented by a devil.' ·But he said not a word in answer to her. And his disciples went and pleaded with him, saying,

24   'Give her what she wants, *ᵍ* because she keeps shouting after us.' ·He said in reply,

25   'I was sent only to the lost sheep of the House of Israel,' ·But the woman had

26   come up and was bowing low before him. 'Lord,' she said, 'help me.' ·He replied,

27   'It is not fair to take the children's food and throw it to little dogs.' *ʰ* ·She retorted, 'Ah yes, Lord; but even little dogs eat the scraps that fall from their masters'

28   table.' ·Then Jesus answered her, 'Woman, you have great faith. Let your desire be granted.' And from that moment her daughter was well again.

Cures near the lake

29   Jesus went on from there and reached the shores of the Lake of Galilee, and he

30   went up onto the mountain. He took his seat, ·and large crowds came to him bringing the lame, the crippled, the blind, the dumb and many others; these they

31   put down at his feet, and he cured them. ·The crowds were astonished to see the dumb speaking, the cripples whole again, *ⁱ* the lame walking and the blind with their sight, and they praised the God of Israel.

Second miracle of the loaves

32   But Jesus called his disciples to him and said, 'I feel sorry for all these people; they have been with me for three days now and have nothing to eat. I do not want

33   to send them off hungry, or they might collapse on the way.' ·The disciples said to him, 'Where in a deserted place could we get sufficient bread for such a large

34   crowd to have enough to eat?' ·Jesus said to them, 'How many loaves have you?'

35   They said, 'Seven, and a few small fish.' ·Then he instructed the crowd to sit down

36   on the ground, ·and he took the seven loaves and the fish, and after giving thanks he broke them and began handing them to the disciples, who gave them to the

37   crowds. ·They all ate as much as they wanted, and they collected what was left of

38   the scraps, seven baskets full. ·Now four thousand men had eaten, to say nothing

39   of women and children. ·And when he had sent the crowds away he got into the boat and went to the territory of Magadan.

The Pharisees ask for a sign from heaven

1
2   **16**   The Pharisees and Sadducees came, and to put him to the test they asked if he would show them a sign from heaven. ·He replied, 'In the evening you

3   say, "It will be fine; there's a red sky," ·and in the morning, "Stormy weather today; the sky is red and overcast." You know how to read the face of the sky, but

4   you cannot read the signs of the times. *ᵃ* ·It is an evil and unfaithful generation asking for a sign, and the only sign it will be given is the sign of Jonah.' And he left them and went off.

The yeast of the Pharisees and Sadducees

5   The disciples, having crossed to the other side, had forgotten to take any food.

6   Jesus said to them, 'Keep your eyes open, and be on your guard against the yeast

7   of the Pharisees and Sadducees.' ·And they said among themselves, 'It is because

8   we have not brought any bread.' ·Jesus knew it, and he said, 'You have so little

9 faith, why are you talking among yourselves about having no bread? ·Do you still
not understand? Do you not remember the five loaves for the five thousand and
10 the number of baskets you collected? ·Or the seven loaves for the four thousand
11 and the number of baskets you collected? ·How could you fail to understand that
I was not talking about bread? What I said was: Beware of the yeast of the
12 Pharisees and Sadducees.' ·Then they understood that he was telling them to be
on their guard, not against yeast for making bread, but against the teaching of the
Pharisees and Sadducees. *

Peter's profession of faith; his pre-eminence

13 When Jesus came to the region of Caesarea Philippi he put this question to his
14 disciples, 'Who do people say the Son of man is?' ·And they said, 'Some say John
15 the Baptist, some Elijah, and others Jeremiah or one of the prophets.' ' ·'But you,'
16 he said, 'who do you say I am?' ·Then Simon Peter spoke up and said, 'You are
17 the Christ, the Son of the living God.' * ·Jesus replied, 'Simon son of Jonah, you
are a blessed man! Because it was no human agency * that revealed this to you but
18 my Father in heaven. ·So I now say to you: You are Peter * and on this rock I will
build my community. * And the gates of the underworld * can never overpower it.
19 I will give you the keys of the kingdom of Heaven: whatever you bind on earth
will be bound in heaven; whatever you loose on earth will be loosed in heaven.' *
20 Then he gave the disciples strict orders not to say to anyone that he was the Christ.

First prophecy of the Passion

21 From then onwards * Jesus began to make it clear to his disciples that he was
destined to go to Jerusalem and suffer grievously at the hands of the elders and
chief priests and scribes and to be put to death and to be raised up on the third
22 day. ·Then, taking him aside, Peter started to rebuke him. 'Heaven preserve you,
23 Lord,' he said, 'this must not happen to you.' ·But he turned and said to Peter,
'Get behind me, Satan! You are an obstacle * in my path, because you are thinking
not as God thinks but as human beings do.'

The condition of following Christ

24 Then Jesus said to his disciples, 'If anyone wants to be a follower of mine, let him
25 renounce himself and take up his cross and follow me. ·Anyone who wants to save
26 his life will lose it; but anyone who loses his life for my sake will find it. ' ·What,
then, will anyone gain by winning the whole world and forfeiting his life? Or what
can anyone offer in exchange for his life?
27 'For the Son of man is going to come in the glory of his Father with his angels,
28 and then he will reward each one according to his behaviour. * ·In truth I tell you,
there are some standing here who will not taste death before they see the Son of
man coming with his kingdom.' *

The transfiguration *

1 **17** Six days later, Jesus took with him Peter and James and his brother John
2 and led them up a high mountain * by themselves. ·There in their presence
he was transfigured: his face shone like the sun and his clothes became as dazzling
3 as light. ' ·And suddenly Moses and Elijah appeared to them; they were talking
4 with him. ·Then Peter spoke to Jesus. 'Lord,' he said, 'it is wonderful for us to be
here; if you want me to, I will make three shelters here, * one for you, one for
5 Moses and one for Elijah.' ·He was still speaking when suddenly a bright cloud

covered them with shadow, and suddenly from the cloud there came a voice which
6 said, 'This is my Son, the Beloved; he enjoys my favour. Listen to him.' ·When
7 they heard this, the disciples fell on their faces, overcome with fear. ·But Jesus
8 came up and touched them, saying, 'Stand up, do not be afraid.' ·And when they
raised their eyes they saw no one but Jesus.

The question about Elijah

9 As they came down from the mountain Jesus gave them this order, 'Tell no one
10 about this vision until the Son of man has risen from the dead.' ·And the disciples
put this question to him, 'Why then do the scribes say that Elijah must come
11 first?' ·He replied, 'Elijah is indeed coming, and he will set everything right again;
12 however, I tell you that Elijah has come already and they did not recognise him
but treated him as they pleased; and the Son of man will suffer similarly at their
13 hands.' ·Then the disciples understood that he was speaking of John the Baptist.

The epileptic demoniac

14 As they were rejoining the crowd a man came up to him and went down on his
15 knees before him. ·'Lord,' he said, 'take pity on my son: he is demented and in a
16 wretched state; he is always falling into fire and into water. ·I took him to your
17 disciples and they were unable to cure him.' ·In reply, Jesus said, 'Faithless and
perverse generation! How much longer must I be with you? How much longer
18 must I put up with you? Bring him here to me.' ·And when Jesus rebuked it the
devil came out of the boy, who was cured from that moment.
19   Then the disciples came privately to Jesus. 'Why were we unable to drive it
20 out?' they asked. ·He answered, 'Because you have so little faith. *j* In truth I tell
you, if your faith is the size of a mustard seed you will say to this mountain, "Move
from here to there," and it will move; nothing will be impossible for you.'[21] *g*

Second prophecy of the Passion

22 When they were together in Galilee, Jesus said to them, 'The Son of man is going
23 to be delivered into the power of men; ·they will put him to death, and on the
third day he will be raised up again.' And a great sadness came over them.

The Temple tax paid by Jesus and Peter

24 When they reached Capernaum, the collectors of the half-shekel *h* came to Peter
25 and said, 'Does your master not pay the half-shekel?' ·'Yes,' he replied, and went
into the house. But before he could speak, Jesus said, 'Simon, what is your
opinion? From whom do earthly kings take toll or tribute? From their sons *i* or
26 from foreigners?' ·And when he replied, 'From foreigners,' Jesus said, 'Well then,
27 the sons are exempt. ·However, so that we shall not be the downfall of others, go
to the lake and cast a hook; take the first fish that rises, open its mouth and there
you will find a shekel; *j* take it and give it to them for me and for yourself.'

B: THE DISCOURSE ON THE CHURCH

Who is the greatest?

1 **18** At this time the disciples came to Jesus and said, 'Who is the greatest in the
2 kingdom of Heaven?' ·So he called a little child to him whom he set among

3 them. ·Then he said, 'In truth I tell you, unless you change and become like little
4 children you will never enter the kingdom of Heaven. ·And so, the one who makes
himself as little as this little child is the greatest in the kingdom of Heaven.

On leading others astray

5, 6 'Anyone who welcomes one little child like this *c* in my name welcomes me. ·But
anyone who is the downfall of one of these little ones who have faith in me would
be better drowned in the depths of the sea with a great millstone round his neck.
7 Alas for the world that there should be such causes of falling! Causes of falling
indeed there must be, but alas for anyone who provides them!
8   'If your hand or your foot should be your downfall, *b* cut it off and throw it away:
it is better for you to enter into life *c* crippled or lame, than to have two hands or
9 two feet and be thrown into eternal fire. ·And if your eye should be your downfall,
tear it out and throw it away: it is better for you to enter into life with one eye,
than to have two eyes and be thrown into the hell of fire. *d*
10   'See that you never despise any of these little ones, for I tell you that their angels
in heaven are continually in the presence of *e* my Father in heaven.[11]*f*

The lost sheep

12 'Tell me. Suppose a man has a hundred sheep and one of them strays; will he not
13 leave the ninety-nine on the hillside and go in search of the stray? ·In truth I tell
you, if he finds it, it gives him more joy than do the ninety-nine that did not stray
14 at all. ·Similarly, it is never the will of your Father in heaven that one of these
little ones should be lost.

Brotherly correction

15 'If your brother does something wrong, *g* go and have it out with him alone,
16 between your two selves. If he listens to you, you have won back your brother. ·If
he does not listen, take one or two others along with you: *whatever the misdemeanour, the evidence of two or three witnesses is required to sustain the charge.*
17 But if he refuses to listen to these, report it to the community; *h* and if he refuses
to listen to the community, treat him like a gentile or a tax collector. *i*
18   'In truth I tell you, whatever you bind on earth will be bound in heaven;
whatever you loose on earth will be loosed in heaven. *j*

Prayer in common

19 'In truth I tell you once again, if two of you on earth agree to ask anything at all, it
20 will be granted to you by my Father in heaven. ·For where two or three meet in
my name, I am there among them.'

Forgiveness of injuries *k*

21 Then Peter went up to him and said, 'Lord, how often must I forgive my brother if
22 he wrongs me? As often as seven times?' ·Jesus answered, 'Not seven, I tell you,
but seventy-seven times. *l*

Parable of the unforgiving debtor

23 'And so the kingdom of Heaven may be compared to a king who decided to settle
24 his accounts with his servants. ·When the reckoning began, they brought him a
25 man who owed ten thousand talents; *m* ·he had no means of paying, so his master
gave orders that he should be sold, together with his wife and children and all his

26 possessions, to meet the debt. •At this, the servant threw himself down at his
master's feet, with the words, "Be patient with me and I will pay the whole sum."
27 And the servant's master felt so sorry for him that he let him go and cancelled the
28 debt. •Now as this servant went out, he happened to meet a fellow-servant who
owed him one hundred denarii; ^a and he seized him by the throat and began to
29 throttle him, saying, "Pay what you owe me." •His fellow-servant fell at his feet
30 and appealed to him, saying, "Be patient with me and I will pay you." •But the
other would not agree; on the contrary, he had him thrown into prison till he
31 should pay the debt. •His fellow-servants were deeply distressed when they saw
what had happened, and they went to their master and reported the whole affair
32 to him. •Then the master sent for the man and said to him, "You wicked servant,
33 I cancelled all that debt of yours when you appealed to me. •Were you not bound,
34 then, to have pity on your fellow-servant just as I had pity on you?" •And in his
anger the master handed him over to the torturers till he should pay all his debt.
35 And that is how my heavenly Father will deal with you unless you each forgive
your brother from your heart.'

VI: THE APPROACHING ADVENT
OF THE KINGDOM OF HEAVEN

A: NARRATIVE SECTION

The question about divorce

1 **19** Jesus had now finished what he wanted to say, and he left Galilee and came
2 into the territory of Judaea on the far side of the Jordan. •Large crowds
followed him and he healed them there.
3 Some Pharisees approached him, and to put him to the test they said, 'Is it
4 against the Law for a man to divorce his wife on any pretext whatever?' •He
answered, 'Have you not read that the Creator from the beginning *made them*
5 *male and female* •and that he said: *This is why a man leaves his father and mother*
6 *and becomes attached to his wife, and the two become one flesh?* •They are no
longer two, therefore, but one flesh. So then, what God has united, human beings
must not divide.' ^a
7 They said to him, 'Then why did Moses command that a writ of dismissal should
8 be given in cases of divorce?' •He said to them, 'It was because you were so hard-
hearted, that Moses allowed you to divorce your wives, but it was not like this
9 from the beginning. •Now I say this to you: anyone who divorces his wife—I am
not speaking of an illicit marriage ^b—and marries another, is guilty of adultery.'

Continence

10 The disciples said to him, 'If that is how things are between husband and wife, it is
11 advisable not to marry.' •But he replied, 'It is not everyone who can accept what I
12 have said, but only those to whom it is granted. •There are eunuchs born so from
their mother's womb, there are eunuchs made so by human agency and there are
eunuchs who have made themselves so for the sake of the kingdom of Heaven. ^c
Let anyone accept this who can.'

Jesus and the children

13 Then people brought little children to him, for him to lay his hands on them and
14 pray. The disciples scolded them, ·but Jesus said, 'Let the little children alone,
and do not stop them from coming to me; for it is to such as these that the kingdom
15 of Heaven belongs.' ·Then he laid his hands on them and went on his way.

The rich young man

16 And now a man came to him and asked, 'Master, *ᵈ* what good deed must I do to
17 possess eternal life?' ·Jesus said to him, 'Why do you ask me about what is good?
There is one alone who is good. *ᵉ* But if you wish to enter into life, keep the
18 commandments.' ·He said, 'Which ones?' Jesus replied, 'These: *You shall not kill.
You shall not commit adultery. You shall not steal. You shall not give false witness.*
19 *Honour your father and your mother. You shall love your neighbour as* yourself.'
20 The young man said to him, 'I have kept all these.*ᶠ* What more do I need to do?'
21 Jesus said, 'If you wish to be perfect, *ᵍ* go and sell your possessions and give the
money to the poor, and you will have treasure in heaven; then come, follow me.'
22 But when the young man heard these words he went away sad, for he was a man
of great wealth.

The danger of riches

23 Then Jesus said to his disciples, 'In truth I tell you, it is hard for someone rich to
24 enter the kingdom of Heaven. ·Yes, I tell you again, it is easier for a camel to pass
through the eye of a needle than for someone rich to enter the kingdom of Heaven.'
25 When the disciples heard this they were astonished. 'Who can be saved, then?'
26 they said. ·Jesus gazed at them. 'By human resources', he told them, 'this is
impossible; for God everything is possible.'

The reward of renunciation

27 Then Peter answered and said, 'Look, we have left everything and followed you.
28 What are we to have, then?' ·Jesus said to them, 'In truth I tell you, when
everything is made new again *ʰ* and the Son of man is seated on his throne of glory,
29 you yourselves will sit on twelve thrones to judge *ⁱ* the twelve tribes of Israel. ·And
everyone who has left houses, brothers, sisters, father, mother, children*ʲ* or land
for the sake of my name will receive a hundred times as much, and also inherit
eternal life.
30   'Many who are first will be last, and the last, first.'

Parable of the labourers in the vineyard *ᵃ*

1 **20** 'Now the kingdom of Heaven is like a landowner going out at daybreak to
2   hire workers for his vineyard. ·He made an agreement with the workers for
3 one denarius a day and sent them to his vineyard. ·Going out at about the third
4 hour he saw others standing idle in the market place ·and said to them, "You go
5 to my vineyard too and I will give you a fair wage." ·So they went. At about the
6 sixth hour and again at about the ninth hour, he went out and did the same. ·Then
at about the eleventh hour he went out and found more men standing around, and
7 he said to them, "Why have you been standing here idle all day?" ·"Because no
one has hired us," they answered. He said to them, "You go into my vineyard
8 too." ·In the evening, the owner of the vineyard said to his bailiff, "Call the workers
and pay them their wages, starting with the last arrivals and ending with the first."

9 So those who were hired at about the eleventh hour came forward and received
10 one denarius each. ·When the first came, they expected to get more, but they too
11 received one denarius each. ·They took it, but grumbled at the landowner saying,
12 "The men who came last have done only one hour, and you have treated them the
13 same as us, though we have done a heavy day's work in all the heat." ·He answered
one of them and said, "My friend, I am not being unjust to you; did we not agree
14 on one denarius? ·Take your earnings and go. I choose to pay the lastcomer as
15 much as I pay you. ·Have I no right to do what I like with my own? Why should
16 you be envious because I am generous?" ·Thus the last will be first, and the first,
last.' ᵇ

Third prophecy of the Passion

17 Jesus was going up to Jerusalem, and on the road he took the Twelve aside by
18 themselves and said to them, ·'Look, we are going up to Jerusalem, and the Son
of man is about to be handed over to the chief priests and scribes. They will
19 condemn him to death ·and will hand him over to the gentiles to be mocked and
scourged and crucified; and on the third day he will be raised up again.'

The mother of Zebedee's sons makes her request

20 Then the mother of Zebedee's sons came with her sons to make a request of him,
21 and bowed low; ·and he said to her, 'What is it you want?' She said to him,
'Promise that these two sons of mine may sit one at your right hand and the other
22 at your left in your kingdom.' ᶜ ·Jesus answered, 'You do not know what you are
asking. Can you drink the cup ᵈ that I am going to drink?' They replied, 'We can.'
23 He said to them, 'Very well; you shall drink my cup, ᵉ but as for seats at my right
hand and my left, these are not mine to grant; they belong to those to whom they
have been allotted by my Father.' ᶠ

Leadership with service

24, 25 When the other ten heard this they were indignant with the two brothers. ·But
Jesus called them to him and said, 'You know that among the gentiles the rulers
26 lord it over them, and great men make their authority felt. ·Among you this is not
to happen. No; anyone who wants to become great among you must be your
27, 28 servant, ·and anyone who wants to be first among you must be your slave, ·just as
the Son of man came not to be served but to serve, and to give his life as a ransom ᵍ
for many.' ʰ

The two blind men of Jericho

29, 30 As they left Jericho a large crowd followed him. ·And now there were two blind
men sitting at the side of the road. When they heard that it was Jesus who was
31 passing by, they shouted, 'Lord! Have pity on us, son of David.' ·And the crowd
scolded them and told them to keep quiet, but they only shouted the louder,
32 'Lord! Have pity on us, son of David.' ·Jesus stopped, called them over and said,
33 'What do you want me to do for you?' ·They said to him, 'Lord, let us have our
34 sight back.' ·Jesus felt pity for them and touched their eyes, and at once their sight
returned and they followed him.

The Messiah enters Jerusalem

1 **21** When they were near Jerusalem and had come to Bethphage on the Mount
2 of Olives, then Jesus sent two disciples, ·saying to them, 'Go to the village

facing you, and you will at once find a tethered donkey and a colt with her. Untie
3 them and bring them to me. ·If anyone says anything to you, you are to say, "The
4 Master needs them and will send them back at once." ' ·This was to fulfil what
was spoken by the prophet:

5   *Say to the daughter of Zion:*
      Look, your king is approaching,
      humble and riding on a donkey
      and on a colt, the foal of a beast of burden. ᵉ

6, 7 So the disciples went and did as Jesus had told them. ·They brought the donkey
and the colt, then they laid their cloaks on their backs and he took his seat on
8 them. ·Great crowds of people spread their cloaks on the road, while others were
9 cutting branches from the trees and spreading them in his path. ·The crowds who
went in front of him and those who followed were all shouting:

      Hosanna ᵇ to the son of David!
      Blessed is he who is coming in the name of the Lord!
      Hosanna in the highest heavens!

10   And when he entered Jerusalem, the whole city was in turmoil as people asked,
11 'Who is this?' ·and the crowds answered, 'This is the prophet Jesus from Nazareth
in Galilee.'

The expulsion of the dealers from the Temple

12 Jesus then went into the Temple and drove out all those who were selling and
buying there; he upset the tables of the money-changers and the seats of the dove-
13 sellers. ᶜ ·He said to them, 'According to scripture, *my house will be called a house*
14 *of prayer*; but you are turning it into a *bandits' den*.' ·There were also blind and
15 lame people who came to him in the Temple, and he cured them. ·At the sight of
the wonderful things he did and of the children shouting, 'Hosanna to the son of
David' in the Temple, the chief priests and the scribes were indignant and said to
16 him, ·'Do you hear what they are saying?' Jesus answered, 'Yes. Have you never
read this:

      By the mouths of children, babes in arms,
      you have made sure of praise?'

17 With that he left them and went out of the city to Bethany, where he spent the
night.

The barren fig tree withers. Faith and prayer

18, 19 As he was returning to the city in the early morning, he felt hungry. ·Seeing a fig
tree by the road, he went up to it and found nothing on it but leaves. And he said
20 to it, 'May you never bear fruit again,' and instantly the fig tree withered. ᵈ ·The
disciples were amazed when they saw it and said, 'How is it that the fig tree
21 withered instantly?' ·Jesus answered, 'In truth I tell you, if you have faith and do
not doubt at all, not only will you do what I have done to the fig tree, but even if
you say to this mountain, "Be pulled up and thrown into the sea," it will be done.
22 And if you have faith, everything you ask for in prayer, you will receive.'

The authority of Jesus is questioned

23 He had gone into the Temple and was teaching, when the chief priests and the elders of the people came to him and said, 'What authority have you for acting
24 like this?' And who gave you this authority?' ·In reply Jesus said to them, 'And I will ask you a question, just one; if you tell me the answer to it, then I will tell you
25 my authority for acting like this. ·John's baptism, what was its origin, heavenly or human?' And they argued this way among themselves, 'If we say heavenly, he will
26 retort to us, "Then why did you refuse to believe him?"; ·but if we say human, we
27 have the people to fear, for they all hold that John was a prophet.' ·So their reply to Jesus was, 'We do not know.' And he retorted to them, 'Nor will I tell you my authority for acting like this.

Parable of the two sons

28 'What is your opinion? A man had two sons. He went and said to the first, "My
29 boy, go and work in the vineyard today." ·He answered, "I will not go," but
30 afterwards thought better of it and went. ·The man then went and said the same
31 thing to the second who answered, "Certainly, sir," but did not go. ·Which of the two did the father's will?' They said, 'The first.' Jesus said to them, 'In truth I tell you, tax collectors and prostitutes are making their way into the kingdom of God
32 before you. ·For John came to you, showing the way of uprightness, *f* but you did not believe him, and yet the tax collectors and prostitutes did. Even after seeing that, you refused to think better of it and believe in him.

Parable of the wicked tenants *g*

33 'Listen to another parable. There was a man, a landowner, who planted a vineyard; he fenced it round, dug a winepress in it and built a tower; then he leased it to
34 tenants and went abroad. ·When vintage time drew near he sent his servants to
35 the tenants to collect his produce. ·But the tenants seized his servants, thrashed
36 one, killed another and stoned a third. ·Next he sent some more servants, this
37 time a larger number, and they dealt with them in the same way. ·Finally he sent
38 his son to them thinking, "They will respect my son." ·But when the tenants saw the son, they said to each other, "This is the heir. Come on, let us kill him and
39 take over his inheritance." ·So they seized him and threw him out of the vineyard
40 and killed him. ·Now when the owner of the vineyard comes, what will he do to
41 those tenants?' ·They answered, 'He will bring those wretches to a wretched end and lease the vineyard to other tenants who will deliver the produce to him at the
42 proper time.' ·Jesus said to them, 'Have you never read in the scriptures:

> *The stone which the builders rejected*
> *has become the cornerstone;*
> *this is the Lord's doing*
> *and we marvel at it* ?

43 'I tell you, then, that the kingdom of God will be taken from you and given to a people who will produce its fruit.'[44] *h*
45 When they heard his parables, the chief priests and the scribes realised he was
46 speaking about them, ·but though they would have liked to arrest him they were afraid of the crowds, who looked on him as a prophet.

Parable of the wedding feast *

1. 2 **22** Jesus began to speak to them in parables once again, ·'The kingdom of Heaven may be compared to a king who gave a feast for his son's wedding.
3 He sent his servants to call those who had been invited, but they would not come.
4 Next he sent some more servants with the words, "Tell those who have been invited: Look, my banquet is all prepared, my oxen and fattened cattle have been
5 slaughtered, everything is ready. Come to the wedding." ·But they were not
6 interested: one went off to his farm, another to his business, ·and the rest seized
7 his servants, maltreated them and killed them. ·The king was furious. He des-
8 patched his troops, destroyed those murderers and burnt their town. ·Then he said to his servants, "The wedding is ready; but as those who were invited proved
9 to be unworthy, ·go to the main crossroads and invite everyone you can find to
10 come to the wedding." ·So these servants went out onto the roads and collected together everyone they could find, bad and good alike; and the wedding hall was
11 filled with guests. ·When the king came in to look at the guests he noticed one
12 man who was not wearing a wedding garment, ·and said to him, "How did you get
13 in here, my friend, without a wedding garment?" And the man was silent. ·Then the king said to the attendants, "Bind him hand and foot and throw him into the
14 darkness outside, where there will be weeping and grinding of teeth." ·For many are invited but not all are chosen.' *

On tribute to Caesar

15 Then the Pharisees went away to work out between them how to trap him in what
16 he said. ·And they sent their disciples to him, together with some Herodians, ' to say, 'Master, we know that you are an honest man and teach the way of God in all honesty, and that you are not afraid of anyone, because human rank means nothing
17 to you. ·Give us your opinion, then. Is it permissible to pay taxes to Caesar or
18 not?' ·But Jesus was aware of their malice and replied, 'You hypocrites! Why are
19 you putting me to the test? ·Show me the money you pay the tax with.' They
20. 21 handed him a denarius, ·and he said, 'Whose portrait is this? Whose title?' ·They replied, 'Caesar's.' Then he said to them, 'Very well, pay Caesar what belongs to
22 Caesar—and God what belongs to God.' ' ·When they heard this they were amazed; they left him alone and went away.

The resurrection of the dead

23 That day some Sadducees—who deny that there is a resurrection '—approached
24 him and they put this question to him, ·'Master, Moses said that if a man dies childless, his brother is to marry the widow, his sister-in-law, to raise children for
25 his brother. ·Now we had a case involving seven brothers; the first married and
26 then died without children, leaving his wife to his brother; ·the same thing
27 happened with the second and third and so on to the seventh, ·and then last of all
28 the woman herself died. ·Now at the resurrection, whose wife among the seven
29 will she be, since she had been married to them all?' ·Jesus answered them, 'You are wrong, because you understand neither the scriptures nor the power of God.
30 For at the resurrection men and women do not marry; no, they are like the angels
31 in heaven. ·And as for the resurrection of the dead, have you never read what
32 God himself said to you: ·*I am the God of Abraham, the God of Isaac and the God*
33 *of Jacob*? He is God, not of the dead, but of the living.' ' ·And his teaching made a deep impression on the people who heard it.

The greatest commandment of all

34 But when the Pharisees heard that he had silenced the Sadducees they got together
35, 36 and, to put him to the test, one of them *ᵍ* put a further question, ·'Master, which is
37 the greatest commandment of the Law?' ·Jesus said to him, '*You must love the*
38 *Lord your God with all your heart, with all your soul,* and with all your mind. This
39 is the greatest and the first commandment. ·The second resembles it: *You must*
40 *love your neighbour as yourself.* *ʰ* ·On these two commandments hang the whole
Law, and the Prophets too.'

Christ not only son but also Lord of David

41, 42 While the Pharisees were gathered round, Jesus put to them this question, ·'What
43 is your opinion about the Christ? Whose son is he?' They told him, 'David's.' ·He
said to them, 'Then how is it that David, moved by the Spirit, calls him Lord,
where he says:

44
> *The Lord declared to my Lord,*
> *take your seat at my right hand,*
> *till I have made your enemies*
> *your footstool?*

45, 46 'If David calls him Lord, how then can he be his son?' ·No one could think of
anything to say in reply, *ⁱ* and from that day no one dared to ask him any further
questions.

The scribes and Pharisees: their hypocrisy and vanity

1, 2 **23** Then addressing the crowds and his disciples Jesus said, ·'The scribes and
3 the Pharisees occupy the chair of Moses. ·You must therefore do and
observe what they tell you; *ᵃ* but do not be guided by what they do, since they do
4 not practise what they preach. ·They tie up heavy burdens and lay them on people's
5 shoulders, but will they lift a finger to move them? Not they! ·Everything they do
is done to attract attention, like wearing broader headbands and longer tassels, *ᵇ*
6 like wanting to take the place of honour at banquets and the front seats in the
7 synagogues, ·being greeted respectfully in the market squares and having people
call them Rabbi. *ᶜ*

8 'You, however, *ᵈ* must not allow yourselves to be called Rabbi, since you have
9 only one Master, and you are all brothers. ·You must call no one on earth your
10 father, *ᵉ* since you have only one Father, and he is in heaven. ·Nor must you allow
11 yourselves to be called teachers, *ᶠ* for you have only one Teacher, the Christ. ·The
12 greatest among you must be your servant. ·Anyone who raises himself up will be
humbled, and anyone who humbles himself will be raised up.

The sevenfold indictment of the scribes and Pharisees

13 'Alas for you, scribes and Pharisees, you hypocrites! You shut up the kingdom of
Heaven in people's faces, neither going in yourselves nor allowing others to go in *ᵍ*
who want to.[14] *ʰ*
15 'Alas for you, scribes and Pharisees, you hypocrites! You travel over sea and
land to make a single proselyte, *ⁱ* and anyone who becomes one you make twice as
fit for hell as you are.
16 'Alas for you, blind guides! You say, *ʲ* "If anyone swears by the Temple, it has
17 no force; but anyone who swears by the gold of the Temple is bound." ·Fools and

blind! For which is of greater value, the gold or the Temple that makes the gold
18 sacred? ·Again, "If anyone swears by the altar it has no force; but anyone who
19 swears by the offering on the altar, is bound." ·You blind men! For which is of
20 greater worth, the offering or the altar that makes the offering sacred? ·Therefore,
21 someone who swears by the altar is swearing by that and by everything on it. ·And
someone who swears by the Temple is swearing by that and by the One who dwells
22 in it. ·And someone who swears by heaven is swearing by the throne of God and
by the One who is seated there.
23   'Alas for you, scribes and Pharisees, you hypocrites! You pay your tithe of mint
and dill and cummin *k* and have neglected the weightier matters of the Law—
justice, mercy, good faith! These you should have practised, those not neglected.
24 You blind guides, straining out gnats and swallowing camels!
25   'Alas for you, scribes and Pharisees, you hypocrites! You clean the outside of
26 cup and dish and leave the inside full *l* of extortion and intemperance. ·Blind
Pharisee! Clean the inside of cup and dish first so that it and the outside are both
clean.
27   'Alas for you, scribes and Pharisees, you hypocrites! You are like whitewashed
tombs that look handsome on the outside, but inside are full of the bones of the
28 dead and every kind of corruption. ·In just the same way, from the outside you
look upright, but inside you are full of hypocrisy and lawlessness.
29   'Alas for you, scribes and Pharisees, you hypocrites! You build the sepulchres
30 of the prophets and decorate the tombs of the upright, ·saying, "We would never
have joined in shedding the blood of the prophets, had we lived in our ancestors'
31 day." ·So! Your own evidence tells against you! You are the children of those
32 who murdered the prophets! ·Very well then, finish off the work that your ancestors began. *m*

Their crimes and approaching punishment

33   'You serpents, brood of vipers, how can you escape being condemned to hell?
34 This is why—look—I am sending you prophets and wise men and scribes; *n* some
you will slaughter and crucify, some you will scourge in your synagogues and hunt
35 from town to town; ·and so you will draw down on yourselves the blood of every
upright person that has been shed on earth, from the blood of Abel the holy to the
blood of Zechariah son of Barachiah *o* whom you murdered between the sanctuary
36 and the altar. ·In truth I tell you, it will all recoil on this generation.

Jerusalem admonished

37   'Jerusalem, Jerusalem, you that kill the prophets *p* and stone those who are sent to
you! How often *q* have I longed to gather your children together, as a hen gathers
38 her chicks under her wings, and you refused! ·Look! Your house will be deserted, *r*
39 for, I promise, you shall not see me any more until you are saying:

> Blessed is he who is coming in the name of the Lord!' *s*

B: THE END AND THE SECOND COMING *t*

Introduction

1 **24** Jesus left the Temple, and as he was going away his disciples came up to
2 draw his attention to the Temple buildings. ·He said to them in reply, 'You

see all these? In truth I tell you, not a single stone here will be left on another:
3 everything will be pulled down.' ·And while he was sitting on the Mount of Olives
the disciples came and asked him when they were by themselves, 'Tell us, when is
this going to happen, and what sign will there be of your coming *b* and of the end
of the world?'

The beginning of sorrows

4. 5 And Jesus answered them, 'Take care that no one deceives you, ·because many
will come using my name and saying, "I am the Christ," *c* and they will deceive
6 many. ·You will hear of wars and rumours of wars; see that you are not alarmed,
7 for this is something that must happen, but the end will not be yet. ·For nation
will fight against nation, and kingdom against kingdom. There will be famines *d* and
8 earthquakes in various places. *e* ·All this is only the beginning of the birthpangs. *f*
9   'Then you will be handed over to be tortured and put to death; and you will be
10 hated by all nations on account of my name. ·And then many will fall away; people
11 will betray one another and hate one another. ·Many false prophets will arise;
12 they will deceive many, ·and with the increase of lawlessness, love in most people
13 will grow cold; ·but anyone who stands firm to the end will be saved.
14   'This good news of the kingdom will be proclaimed to the whole world *g* as
evidence to the nations. And then the end *h* will come.

The great tribulation of Jerusalem

15 'So when you see *the appalling abomination*, of which the prophet Daniel spoke,
16 set up in the holy place *i* (let the reader understand), ·then those in Judaea must
17 escape to the mountains; ·if anyone is on the housetop, he must not come down to
18 collect his belongings from the house; ·if anyone is in the fields, he must not turn
19 back to fetch his cloak. ·Alas for those with child, or with babies at the breast,
20 when those days come! ·Pray that you will not have to make your escape in winter
21 or on a Sabbath. ·For then there will be *great distress, unparalleled since the world*
22 *began, and such as will never be again. j* ·And if that time had not been shortened,
no human being would have survived; but shortened that time shall be, for the
sake of those who are chosen. *k*
23   'If anyone says to you then, "Look, here is the Christ," or "Over here," do not
24 believe it; ·for false Christs and false prophets will arise and provide great signs
25 and portents, enough to deceive even the elect, if that were possible. ·Look! I
have given you warning.

The coming of the Son of man

26 'If, then, they say to you, "Look, he is in the desert," do not go there; "Look, he
27 is in some hiding place," do not believe it; ·because the coming of the Son of man
28 will be like lightning striking in the east and flashing far into the west. *l* ·Wherever
the corpse is, that is where the vultures will gather. *m*

The universal significance of this coming

29 'Immediately after the distress of those days *n* the sun will be darkened, the moon
will not give its light, the stars will fall from the sky and the powers of the heavens
30 will be shaken. *o* ·And then the sign of the Son of man will appear in heaven; *p*
then, too, all the peoples of the earth will beat their breasts; and they will see the
31 Son of man coming on the clouds of heaven with power and great glory. *q* ·And he

will send his angels with a loud trumpet ' to gather his elect from the four winds, from one end of heaven to the other. '

The time of this coming

32 'Take the fig tree as a parable: as soon as its twigs grow supple and its leaves come
33 out, you know that summer is near. ·So with you when you see all these things:
34 know that he ' is near, right at the gates. ·In truth I tell you, before this generation
35 has passed away, all these things will have taken place. " ·Sky and earth will pass
36 away, but my words will never pass away. ·But as for that day and hour, nobody knows it, neither the angels of heaven, nor the Son, ' no one but the Father alone.

Be on the alert

37. 38 'As it was in Noah's day, so will it be when the Son of man comes. ·For in those days before the Flood people were eating, drinking, taking wives, taking husbands,
39 right up to the day Noah went into the ark, ·and they suspected nothing till the Flood came and swept them all away. This is what it will be like when the Son of
40. 41 man comes. ·Then of two men in the fields, one is taken, one left; ·of two women grinding at the mill, one is taken, one left.
42 'So stay awake, because you do not know the day when your master is coming.
43 You may be quite sure of this, that if the householder had known at what time of the night the burglar would come, he would have stayed awake and would not
44 have allowed anyone to break through the wall of his house. ·Therefore, you too must stand ready because the Son of man is coming at an hour you do not expect.

Parable of the conscientious steward "

45 'Who, then, is the wise and trustworthy servant whom the master placed over his
46 household to give them their food at the proper time? ·Blessed that servant if his
47 master's arrival finds him doing exactly that. ·In truth I tell you, he will put him in
48 charge of everything he owns. ·But if the servant is dishonest and says to himself,
49 "My master is taking his time," ·and sets about beating his fellow-servants and
50 eating and drinking with drunkards, ·his master will come on a day he does not
51 expect and at an hour he does not know. ·The master will cut him off ' and send him to the same fate as the hypocrites, where there will be weeping and grinding of teeth.'

Parable of the ten wedding attendants ᵃ

1 **25** 'Then the kingdom of Heaven will be like this: Ten wedding attendants
2 took their lamps and went to meet the bridegroom. ᵇ ·Five of them were
3 foolish and five were sensible: ·the foolish ones, though they took their lamps,
4 took no oil with them, ·whereas the sensible ones took flasks of oil as well as their
5. 6 lamps. ·The bridegroom was late, and they all grew drowsy and fell asleep. ·But at
7 midnight there was a cry, "Look! The bridegroom! Go out and meet him." ·Then
8 all those wedding attendants woke up and trimmed their lamps, ·and the foolish ones said to the sensible ones, "Give us some of your oil: our lamps are going
9 out." ·But they replied, "There may not be enough for us and for you; you had
10 better go to those who sell it and buy some for yourselves." ·They had gone off to buy it when the bridegroom arrived. Those who were ready went in with him to
11 the wedding hall and the door was closed. ·The other attendants arrived later.
12 "Lord, Lord," they said, "open the door for us." ·But he replied, "In truth I tell

13 you, I do not know you." ·So stay awake, because you do not know either the day or the hour.

Parable of the talents ᶜ

14 'It is like a man about to go abroad who summoned his servants and entrusted his
15 property to them. ·To one he gave five talents, to another two, to a third one,
16 each in proportion to his ability. Then he set out on his journey. ·The man who
had received the five talents promptly went and traded with them and made five
17, 18 more. ·The man who had received two made two more in the same way. ·But the
man who had received one went off and dug a hole in the ground and hid his
19 master's money. ·Now a long time afterwards, the master of those servants came
20 back and went through his accounts with them. ·The man who had received the
five talents came forward bringing five more. "Sir," he said, "you entrusted me
21 with five talents; here are five more that I have made." ·His master said to him,
"Well done, good and trustworthy servant; you have shown you are trustworthy
in small things; I will trust you with greater; come and join in your master's
22 happiness." ᵈ ·Next the man with the two talents came forward. "Sir," he said,
23 "you entrusted me with two talents; here are two more that I have made." ·His
master said to him, "Well done, good and trustworthy servant; you have shown
you are trustworthy in small things; I will trust you with greater; come and join in
24 your master's happiness." ·Last came forward the man who had the single talent.
"Sir," said he, "I had heard you were a hard man, reaping where you had not
25 sown and gathering where you had not scattered; ·so I was afraid, and I went off
26 and hid your talent in the ground. Here it is; it was yours, you have it back." ·But
his master answered him, "You wicked and lazy servant! So you knew that I reap
27 where I have not sown and gather where I have not scattered? ·Well then, you
should have deposited my money with the bankers, and on my return I would
28 have got my money back with interest. ·So now, take the talent from him and give
29 it to the man who has the ten talents. ·For to everyone who has will be given
more, and he will have more than enough; but anyone who has not, will be
30 deprived even of what he has. ·As for this good-for-nothing servant, throw him
into the darkness outside, where there will be weeping and grinding of teeth."

The Last Judgement

31 'When the Son of man comes in his glory, ᵉ escorted by all the angels, then he will
32 take his seat on his throne of glory. ·All nations ᶠ will be assembled before him
and he will separate people one from another as the shepherd separates sheep
33 from goats. ·He will place the sheep on his right hand and the goats on his left.
34 Then the King will say to those on his right hand, "Come, you whom my Father has
blessed, take as your heritage the kingdom prepared for you since the foundation of
35 the world. ᵍ ·For I was hungry and you gave me food, I was thirsty and you gave
36 me drink, I was a stranger and you made me welcome, ·lacking clothes and you
37 clothed me, sick and you visited me, in prison and you came to see me." ʰ ·Then
the upright will say to him in reply, "Lord, when did we see you hungry and feed
38 you, or thirsty and give you drink? ·When did we see you a stranger and make you
39 welcome, lacking clothes and clothe you? ·When did we find you sick or in prison
40 and go to see you?" ·And the King will answer, "In truth I tell you, in so far as
41 you did this to one of the least of these brothers of mine, you did it to me." ·Then
he will say to those on his left hand, "Go away from me, with your curse upon
42 you, to the eternal fire prepared for the devil and his angels. ·For I was hungry

and you never gave me food, I was thirsty and you never gave me anything to
43　drink, ·I was a stranger and you never made me welcome, lacking clothes and you
44　never clothed me, sick and in prison and you never visited me." ·Then it will be
their turn to ask, "Lord, when did we see you hungry or thirsty, a stranger or
45　lacking clothes, sick or in prison, and did not come to your help?" ·Then he will
answer, "In truth I tell you, in so far as you neglected to do this to one of the least
46　of these, you neglected to do it to me." ·And they will go away to eternal
punishment, and the upright to eternal life.'

VII: PASSION AND RESURRECTION

The conspiracy against Jesus

1, 2　**26** Jesus had now finished all he wanted to say, and he told his disciples, ·'It
will be Passover, as you know, in two days' time, and the Son of man will
be handed over to be crucified.'
3　　Then the chief priests and the elders of the people assembled in the palace of
4　the high priest, whose name was Caiaphas, ·and made plans to arrest Jesus by
5　some trick and have him put to death. ·They said, however, 'It must not be during
the festivities; there must be no disturbance among the people.'

The anointing at Bethany *

6　Jesus was at Bethany in the house of Simon, a man who had suffered from a
7　virulent skin-disease, when ·a woman came to him with an alabaster jar of very
8　expensive ointment, and poured it on his head as he was at table. ·When they saw
9　this, the disciples said indignantly, 'Why this waste? ·This could have been sold
10　for a high price and the money given the poor.' ·But Jesus noticed this and said,
'Why are you upsetting the woman? What she has done for me is indeed a good
11　work! *·You have the poor with you always, but you will not always have me.
12, 13　When she poured this ointment on my body, she did it to prepare me for burial. ·In
truth I tell you, wherever in all the world this gospel is proclaimed, what she has
done will be told as well, in remembrance of her.'

Judas betrays Jesus

14　Then one of the Twelve, the man called Judas Iscariot, went to the chief priests
15　and said, 'What are you prepared to give me if I hand him over to you?' They
16　paid him thirty silver pieces,* ·and from then onwards he began to look for an
opportunity to betray him.

Preparations for the Passover supper

17　Now on the first day of Unleavened Bread* the disciples came to Jesus to say,
18　'Where do you want us to make the preparations for you to eat the Passover?' ·He
said, 'Go to a certain man in the city and say to him, "The Master says: My time is
19　near. It is at your house that I am keeping Passover with my disciples." ' ·The
disciples did what Jesus told them and prepared the Passover.

The treachery of Judas foretold

20, 21　When evening came he was at table with the Twelve. ·And while they were eating*
22　he said, 'In truth I tell you, one of you is about to betray me.' ·They were greatly

23 distressed and started asking him in turn, 'Not me, Lord, surely?' ·He answered,
24 'Someone who has dipped his hand into the dish with me will betray me. ·The Son of man is going to his fate, as the scriptures say he will, but alas for that man by whom the Son of man is betrayed! Better for that man if he had never been born!'
25 Judas, who was to betray him, asked in his turn, 'Not me, Rabbi, surely?' Jesus answered, 'It is you who say it.'

The institution of the Eucharist

26 Now as they were eating,*f* Jesus took bread, and when he had said the blessing he broke it and gave it to the disciples. 'Take it and eat,' he said, 'this is my body.'
27 Then he took a cup, and when he had given thanks *g* he handed it to them saying,
28 'Drink from this, all of you, ·for this is my blood, the blood of the *h* covenant,
29 poured out for many for the forgiveness of sins. *i* ·From now on, I tell you, I shall never again drink wine until the day I drink the new wine with you in the kingdom of my Father.'*j*

Peter's denial foretold

30, 31 After the psalms had been sung *k* they left for the Mount of Olives. ·Then Jesus said to them, 'You will all fall away from me tonight, *l* for the scripture says: *I*
32 *shall strike the shepherd and the sheep of the flock will be scattered*, ·but after my
33 resurrection I shall go ahead of you to Galilee.' ·At this, Peter said to him, 'Even
34 if all fall away from you, I will never fall away.' ·Jesus answered him, 'In truth I tell you, this very night, before the cock crows, you will have disowned me three
35 times.' ·Peter said to him, 'Even if I have to die with you, I will never disown you.' And all the disciples said the same.

Gethsemane

36 Then Jesus came with them to a plot of land called Gethsemane; *m* and he said to
37 his disciples, 'Stay here while I go over there to pray.' ·He took Peter and the two sons of Zebedee with him. And he began to feel sadness and anguish.
38 Then he said to them, 'My soul is sorrowful to the point of death. *n* Wait here
39 and stay awake with me.' ·And going on a little further he fell on his face and prayed. 'My Father,' he said, 'if it is possible, let this cup pass me by. Nevertheless,
40 let it be as you, not I, would have it.' *o* ·He came back to the disciples and found them sleeping, and he said to Peter, 'So you had not the strength to stay awake
41 with me for one hour? ·Stay awake, and pray not to be put to the test. The spirit is
42 willing enough, but human nature is weak.' ·Again, a second time, he went away and prayed: 'My Father,' he said, 'if this cup cannot pass by, but I must drink it,
43 your will be done!' ·And he came back again and found them sleeping, their eyes
44 were so heavy. ·Leaving them there, he went away again and prayed for the third
45 time, repeating the same words. ·Then he came back to the disciples and said to them, 'You can sleep on now and have your rest. *p* Look, the hour has come when
46 the Son of man is to be betrayed into the hands of sinners. ·Get up! Let us go! Look, my betrayer is not far away.'

The arrest

47 And suddenly while he was still speaking, Judas, one of the Twelve, appeared, and with him a large number of men armed with swords and clubs, sent by the
48 chief priests and elders of the people. ·Now the traitor had arranged a sign with
49 them saying, 'The one I kiss, he is the man. Arrest him.' ·So he went up to Jesus

50 at once and said, 'Greetings, Rabbi,' and kissed him. ·Jesus said to him, 'My
friend, do what you are here for.'ᶠ Then they came forward, seized Jesus and
51 arrested him. ·And suddenly, one of the followers of Jesus grasped his sword and
52 drew it; he struck the high priest's servant and cut off his ear. ·Jesus then said,
53 'Put your sword back, for all who draw the sword will die by the sword. ·Or do
you think that I cannot appeal to my Father, who would promptly send more than
54 twelve legions of angels to my defence? ·But then, how would the scriptures be
55 fulfilled that say this is the way it must be?' ·It was at this time that Jesus said to
the crowds, 'Am I a bandit, that you had to set out to capture me with swords and
clubs? I sat teaching in the Temple day after day and you never laid a hand on
56 me.' ·Now all this happened to fulfil the prophecies in scripture. Then all the
disciples deserted him and ran away.

Jesus before the Sanhedrin ᵍ

57 The men who had arrested Jesus led him off to the house of Caiaphas the high
58 priest, where the scribes and the elders were assembled. ·Peter followed him at a
distance right to the high priest's palace, and he went in and sat down with the
attendants to see what the end would be.
59 The chief priests and the whole Sanhedrin were looking for evidence against
60 Jesus, however false, on which they might have him executed. ·But they could not
find any, though several lying witnesses came forward. Eventually two came
61 forward ·and made a statement, 'This man said, "I have power to destroy the
62 Temple of God and in three days build it up." 'ʰ ·The high priest then rose and
said to him, 'Have you no answer to that? What is this evidence these men are
63 bringing against you?' ·But Jesus was silent. And the high priest said to him, 'I
put you on oath by the living God to tell us if you are the Christ, the Son of God.'
64 Jesus answered him, 'It is you who say it. But, I tell you that from this time onward
you will see the *Son of man seated at the right hand of the Power* and *coming on the*
65 *clouds of heaven.*'ⁱ ·Then the high priest tore his clothes and said, 'He has
blasphemed.ʲ What need of witnesses have we now? There! You have just heard
66 the blasphemy. ·What is your opinion?' They answered, 'He deserves to die.'
67 Then they spat in his face and hit him with their fists; others said as they struck
68 him, ·'Prophesy to us, Christ! Who hit you then?'ᵏ

Peter's denials

69 Meanwhile Peter was sitting outside in the courtyard, and a servant-girl came up
70 to him saying, 'You, too, were with Jesus the Galilean.' ·But he denied it in front
71 of them all. 'I do not know what you are talking about,' he said. ·When he went
out to the gateway another servant-girl saw him and said to the people there, 'This
72 man was with Jesus the Nazarene.'ˡ ·And again, with an oath, he denied it, 'I do
73 not know the man.' ·A little later the bystanders came up and said to Peter, 'You
74 are certainly one of them too! Why, your accentʲ gives you away.' ·Then he started
cursing and swearing, 'I do not know the man.' And at once the cock crowed,
75 and Peter remembered what Jesus had said, 'Before the cock crows you will have
disowned me three times.' And he went outside and wept bitterly.

Jesus is taken before Pilate

1 **27** When morning came, all the chief priests and the elders of the people met
2 in council to bring about the death of Jesus. ·They had him bound and led
him away to hand him over to Pilate,ᵃ the governor.

The death of Judas

3 When he found that Jesus had been condemned, then Judas, his betrayer, was
filled with remorse and took the thirty silver pieces back to the chief priests and
4 elders ·saying, 'I have sinned. I have betrayed innocent blood.'*ᵇ* They replied,
5 'What is that to us? That is your concern.' ·And flinging down the silver pieces in
6 the sanctuary he made off, and went and hanged himself. ·The chief priests picked
up the silver pieces and said, 'It is against the Law to put this into the treasury; it is
7 blood-money.' ·So they discussed the matter and with it bought the potter's field
8 as a graveyard for foreigners, ·and this is why the field is still called the Field of
9 Blood.*ᶜ* ·The word spoken through the prophet Jeremiah*ᵈ* was then fulfilled: *And
they took the thirty silver pieces, the sum at which the precious One was priced by*
10 *the children of Israel, ·and they gave them for the potter's field, just as the Lord
directed me.*ᵉ

Jesus before Pilate

11 Jesus, then, was brought before the governor, and the governor put to him this
question, 'Are you the king of the Jews?' Jesus replied, 'It is you who say it.'*ᶠ*
12 But when he was accused by the chief priests and the elders he refused to answer
13 at all. ·Pilate then said to him, 'Do you not hear how many charges they have made
14 against you?' ·But to the governor's amazement, he offered not a word in answer
to any of the charges.

15   At festival time it was the governor's practice to release a prisoner for the
16 people, anyone they chose. ·Now there was then a notorious prisoner whose name
17 was Barabbas.*ᵍ* ·So when the crowd gathered, Pilate said to them, 'Which do you
18 want me to release for you: Barabbas, or Jesus who is called Christ?' ·For Pilate
knew it was out of jealousy that they had handed him over.

19   Now as he was seated in the chair of judgement, his wife sent him a message,
'Have nothing to do with that upright man; I have been extremely upset today by
a dream that I had about him.'

20   The chief priests and the elders, however, had persuaded the crowd to demand
21 the release of Barabbas and the execution of Jesus. ·So when the governor spoke
and asked them, 'Which of the two do you want me to release for you?' they said,
22 'Barabbas.' ·Pilate said to them, 'But in that case, what am I to do with Jesus who
23 is called Christ?' They all said, 'Let him be crucified!' ·He asked, 'But what harm
24 has he done?' But they shouted all the louder, 'Let him be crucified!' ·Then Pilate
saw that he was making no impression, that in fact a riot was imminent. So he
took some water, washed his hands*ʰ* in front of the crowd and said, 'I am innocent
25 of this man's blood.*ⁱ* It is your concern.' ·And the people, every one of them,
26 shouted back, 'Let his blood be on us and on our children!'*ʲ* ·Then he released
Barabbas for them. After having Jesus scourged*ᵏ* he handed him over to be
crucified.

Jesus is crowned with thorns

27 Then the governor's soldiers took Jesus with them into the Praetorium*ˡ* and
28 collected the whole cohort round him. ·And they stripped him and put a scarlet
29 cloak round him,*ᵐ* ·and having twisted some thorns into a crown they put this on
his head and placed a reed in his right hand. To make fun of him they knelt to him
30 saying, 'Hail, king of the Jews!'*ⁿ* ·And they spat on him and took the reed and
31 struck him on the head with it. ·And when they had finished making fun of him,

they took off the cloak and dressed him in his own clothes and led him away to crucifixion.

The crucifixion

32 On their way out, they came across a man from Cyrene, called Simon, and enlisted
33 him to carry his cross. ·When they had reached a place called Golgotha, *ᵉ* that is,
34 the place of the skull, ·they gave him wine to drink mixed with gall, *ᵖ* which he
35 tasted but refused to drink. ·When they had finished crucifying him they shared
36 out his clothing by casting lots, *ᵠ* ·and then sat down and stayed there keeping
guard over him.
37 Above his head was placed the charge against him; it read: 'This is Jesus, the
38 King of the Jews.' ·Then two bandits were crucified with him, one on the right and
one on the left.

The crucified Jesus is mocked

39. 40 The passers-by jeered at him; they shook their heads ·and said, 'So you would
destroy the Temple and in three days rebuild it! Then save yourself if you are
41 God's son and come down from the cross!' ·The chief priests with the scribes and
42 elders mocked him in the same way, ·with the words, 'He saved others; he cannot
save himself. He is the king of Israel; let him come down from the cross now, and
43 we will believe in him. ·He has put his trust in God; now let God rescue him if he
44 wants him. For he did say, "I am God's son." ' ·Even the bandits who were
crucified with him taunted him in the same way.

The death of Jesus

45 From the sixth hour there was darkness over all the land until the ninth hour.
46 And about the ninth hour, Jesus cried out in a loud voice, *'Eli, eli, lama sabach-*
47 *thani?'* that is, *'My God, my God, why have you forsaken me?'ˢ* ·When some of
48 those who stood there heard this, they said, 'The man is calling on Elijah,'ᵗ ·and
one of them quickly ran to get a sponge which he filled with vinegarᵘ and, putting
49 it on a reed, gave it him to drink. ·But the rest of them said, 'Wait! And see if
50 Elijah will come to save him.' ·But Jesus, again crying out in a loud voice, yielded
up his spirit.
51 And suddenly, the veil of the Sanctuaryᵛ was torn in two from top to bottom,
52 the earth quaked, the rocks were split,ʷ ·the tombs opened and the bodies of
53 many holy people rose from the dead, ·and these, after his resurrection, came out
54 of the tombs, entered the holy city and appeared to a number of people.ˣ ·The
centurion, together with the others guarding Jesus, had seen the earthquake and
all that was taking place, and they were terrified and said, 'In truth this man was
son of God.'
55 And many women were there, watching from a distance, the same women who
56 had followed Jesus from Galilee and looked after him. ·Among them were Mary
of Magdala, Mary the mother of James and Joseph, and the mother of Zebedee's
sons.

The burial

57 When it was evening, there came a rich man of Arimathaea, called Joseph, who
58 had himself become a disciple of Jesus. ·This man went to Pilate and asked for the
59 body of Jesus. Then Pilate ordered it to be handed over. ·So Joseph took the

60 body, wrapped it in a clean shroud ·and put it in his own new ʸ tomb which he had hewn out of the rock. He then rolled a large stone across the entrance of the tomb
61 and went away. ·Now Mary of Magdala and the other Mary were there, sitting opposite the sepulchre.

The guard at the tomb

62 Next day, that is, when Preparation Day ᶻ was over, the chief priests and the
63 Pharisees went in a body to Pilate ·and said to him, 'Your Excellency, we recall that this impostor said, while he was still alive, "After three days I shall rise
64 again." ·Therefore give the order to have the sepulchre kept secure until the third day, for fear his disciples come and steal him away and tell the people, "He has risen from the dead." This last piece of fraud would be worse than what went
65 before.' ·Pilate said to them, 'You may have your guard; ᵃ go and make all as
66 secure as you know how.' ·So they went and made the sepulchre secure, putting seals on the stone and mounting a guard.

The empty tomb. The angel's message

1 **28** After the Sabbath, ᵃ and towards dawn on the first day of the week, Mary
2 of Magdala and the other Mary ᵇ went to visit the sepulchre. ᶜ ·And suddenly there was a violent earthquake, for an angel of the Lord, descending from heaven,
3 came and rolled away the stone and sat on it. ·His face was like lightning, his robe
4 white as snow. ·The guards were so shaken by fear of him that they were like dead
5 men. ·But the angel spoke; and he said to the women, 'There is no need for you to
6 be afraid. I know you are looking for Jesus, who was crucified. ·He is not here, for
7 he has risen, as he said he would. Come and see the place where he ᵈ lay, ·then go quickly and tell his disciples, "He has risen from the dead and now he is going ahead of you to Galilee; that is where you will see him." Look! I have told you.'
8 Filled with awe and great joy the women came quickly away from the tomb ᵉ and ran to tell his disciples.

Appearance to the women

9 And suddenly, coming to meet them, was Jesus. 'Greetings,' he said. And the
10 women came up to him and, clasping his feet, they did him homage. ·Then Jesus said to them, 'Do not be afraid; go and tell my brothers that they must leave for Galilee; there they will see me.' ᶠ

Precautions taken by the leaders of the people

11 Now while they were on their way, some of the guards went off into the city to tell
12 the chief priests all that had happened. ·These held a meeting with the elders and,
13 after some discussion, handed a considerable sum of money to the soldiers ·with these instructions, 'This is what you must say, "His disciples came during the night
14 and stole him away while we were asleep." ·And should the governor come to hear of this, we undertake to put things right with him ourselves and to see that
15 you do not get into trouble.' ·So they took the money and carried out their instructions, and to this day that is the story among the Jews.

Appearance in Galilee. The mission to the world

16 Meanwhile the eleven disciples set out for Galilee, to the mountain where Jesus
17 had arranged to meet them. ·When they saw him they fell down before him, though
18 some hesitated. ᵍ ·Jesus came up and spoke to them. ʰ He said, 'All authority in

19 heaven and on earth has been given to me. ·Go, therefore, make disciples of all nations; baptise them in the name of the Father and of the Son and of the Holy
20 Spirit, *ⁱ* ·and teach them to observe all the commands I gave you. And look, I am with you always; yes, to the end of time.'

NOTES TO MATTHEW

1 a. Matthew, though stressing the foreign element on the female side, vv. 3,5,6, limits his genealogy to Jesus' Israelitic descent. Its aim is to show how Jesus is connected with the leading recipients of the messianic promises, i.e. with Abraham and David and with the latter's royal line. Luke's genealogy is universal in scope and goes back to Adam, head of the human race. The two lists, from David down to Joseph, have only two names in common. In Mt, moreover, the schematic nature of the genealogy is brought out by the division of Jesus' ancestors into three series of 2 × 7 names (*see* 6:9d), a device which forces the omission of three kings between Joram and Uzziah. It also compels the double reckoning of Jechoniah (vv. 11–12); this is made possible by the fact that the same Greek name can translate the two similar Hebr. names Jehoiakim and Jehoiachin. The lists of both Mt and Lk end with Joseph who was Jesus' legal father only; the reason is that according to ancient mentality legal paternity (adoption, levirate etc.) is sufficient, by itself, to confer all hereditary rights; the rights here are those of the messianic line. The main purpose of this first incident in Mt is to show how Jesus came to be a member of the royal line of David, namely through adoption by Joseph at the prompting of the angel's message.
b. var. 'Asaph'.
c. var. 'Amos'.
d. Several Gk and Lat. authorities, more explicitly, 'Joseph, to whom was betrothed the Virgin Mary who gave birth to Jesus'. It is probably as a result of a misunderstanding of this reading that Syr. Sin. has this text 'Joseph, to whom was betrothed the Virgin Mary, fathered Jesus.'
e. The force of Jewish betrothal was such that the fiancé was already called 'husband' and could release himself from the engagement only by an act of repudiation, v. 19.
f. lit. 'to put her away from him privately'. It is perhaps because Joseph is upright that he does not want to name as his own a child of an unknown father. Another explanation is that he is deterred from proceeding with the marriage by reverence for the mystery of Mary's motherhood and has to be persuaded by means of the angelic message that it is still God's will that he should take her to wife.
g. The 'angel of the Lord' in the early texts (Gn 16:7c) means Yahweh himself. With the development of the doctrine of angels (*see* Tb 5:4b) their distinction from God becomes clearer; they retain their function as heavenly messengers and often appear as such in the narratives of the infancy (Mt 1:20,24; 2:13,19; Lk 1:11; 2:9; *see also* Mt 28:2; Jn 5:4; Ac 5:19; 8:26; 12:7,23).
h. As in the OT, Si 34:1a, God makes his intention known in a dream: Mt 2:12,13,19,22; 27:19; cf. Ac 16:9; 18:9; 23:11; 27:23; and the parallel visions of Ac 9:10seq.; 10:3seq., 11seq.
i. 'Jesus' (Hebr. Jehoshua) means 'Yahweh saves'.
j. This and similar formulae will be frequent in Mt: 2:15,17,23; 8:17; 12:17; 13:35; 21:4; 26:54,56; 27:9; *see also* 3:3; 11:10; 13:14. Already in the OT one of the criteria of a true prophet was that his words were fulfilled, Dt 18:20–22f. In Jesus' view and that of his disciples God had announced his plan either by words or by deeds, and in accordance with the principles of Jewish exegesis of the time, the NT seeks to show that God's plan is fulfilled in Jesus, by pointing out minute and literal correspondence between the life of Jesus and the text of the OT, Jn 2:22; 20:9; Ac 2:23o, 31,34–35; 3:24s; Rm 15:4; 1 Co 10:11; 15:3–4; 2 Co 1:20; 3:14–16.
k. The text is not concerned with the period that followed and, taken by itself, does not assert Mary's perpetual virginity. This is assumed by the remainder of the Gospel and by the tradition of the Church. By naming the child, Joseph accepts it as his own. On the 'brothers' of Jesus, see 12:46o.

2 a. In Ch. 1 Mt introduced the person of Jesus, son of David and son of God; now in Ch. 2 he gives a foretaste of his mission to offer salvation to the gentiles, whose wise men are attracted to his light, vv. 1–12, and to re-live in his own person the suffering undergone by his people: the first exile in Egypt, vv. 13–15, the second captivity, vv. 16–18, the humble return of the little Remnant, vv. 19–23 (*see* v. 23*l*). These midrashic stories, in which the events of Jesus' infancy are recounted in terms which recall the infancy of Moses, use events to teach what Lk teaches by means of the prophetic words of Simeon, *see* Lk 2:34*l*.
b. About 5 or 4 BC. Herod was king of Judaea. Idumaea and Samaria from 37 to 4 BC, *see* Lk 2:2b.
c. A story of this kind demands that the term be left vague and general—the prime place of origin of wise astrologers such as these wise men.
d. Also called 'doctors of the Law', Lk 5:17; Ac 5:34, or 'lawyers', Lk 7:30; 10:25; etc., their function was to interpret the scriptures, especially the Law of Moses, to draw out of it the rules of conduct for Jewish life, *see* Ezr 7:6c; Si 39:2b. This role gained them prestige and influence among the people. Their numbers were drawn primarily but not exclusively from the Pharisees, 3:7f. With the high priests and the elders they constituted the Great Sanhedrin.
e. Obviously the evangelist is thinking of a miraculous star; it is futile to look for a natural explanation, cf. Nb 24:17. The appearance of a star is recorded also at the birth of other great men.
f. The wealth and perfumes of Arabia (Jr 6:20; Ezk 27:22). The Fathers see in them symbols of the royalty (gold), divinity (incense), Passion (myrrh) of Jesus. The adoration of the Magi fulfils the prophecies of the homage paid by the nations to the God of Israel, cf. Nb 24:17; Ps 72:10–15; Is 49:23; 60:5seq., which were accepted as messianic. This recognition of the Messiah by the gentiles stands in contrast to his rejection by the Jews in the person of Herod.
g. Israel, therefore, the 'son' of the prophet's text, prefigured the Messiah.
h. There is an earlier parallel to this story told about Moses in rabbinic literature: after the news of the birth of the child is received, either from visions or from magicians, the Pharaoh has all the new-born male children killed.
i. In its original setting this text means that Rachel, their ancestress, weeps for the people of Ephraim, Manasseh and Benjamin, massacred or deported by the Assyrians. Matthew's application was perhaps suggested to him by a tradition which localised Rachel's tomb in the neighbourhood of Bethlehem (Gn 35:19seq.).

j. Son of Herod by Malthace (like Herod Antipas); ethnarch of Judaea from 4 BC to AD 6.

k. Territory of Herod Antipas, *see* Lk 3:1c.

l. Nazoraios: this is the form used by Mt, Jn and Ac (translated 'Nazarene' throughout this version). Nazarenos ('of Nazareth' in this version) is used by Mk. Lk uses both forms. These two synonyms were current transcriptions of an Aramaic adjective (*nasraya*) itself derived from the name of the town 'Nazareth' (Nasrat). Applied to Jesus, whose origin it indicated (26:69,71), and later to his followers (Ac 24:5), the term became common in the semitic world for the disciples of Jesus; the name 'Christian' (Ac 11:26) prevailed in the Graeco-Roman world. • It is not clear which prophecies Mt alludes to; possibly to the *nazir* of Jg 13:5,7.

3 a. lit. 'in those days'. Stereotyped expression, merely a formula of transition.

b. A desolate hilly region stretching from the central ridge of Palestine to the Jordan Valley and the Red Sea.

c. *Metanoia* or change of heart means a renunciation of sin, repentance. This regret for past conduct is normally accompanied by a 'conversion' by which a person turns back to God and enters upon a new life. The words used for these two complementary aspects of the same movement of heart are often the same, *see* Ac 2:38x; 3:19n. Repentance and conversion are the necessary condition for receiving the salvation which the kingdom of God brings. John the Baptist's call to repentance, cf. Ac 13:24; 19:4, will be taken up by Jesus, Mt 4:17 and par.; Lk 5:32; 13:3,5, by his disciples, Mk 6:12; Lk 24:47, and by Paul, Ac 20:21; 26:20.

d. Instead of 'kingdom of God', *see* 4:17f. The phrase is proper to Mt and reflects the Jewish scruple which substituted metaphor for the divine name.

e. The rite of immersion, symbolic of purification or of renewal, was familiar to ancient religions and to Judaism (baptism of proselytes, Essene purifications). John's baptism, though suggested by these practices, is distinct from them for three main reasons: it is directed to moral, not ritual, purification (3:2,6,8,11; Lk 3:10–14); it takes place once only and for this reason appears as a ceremony of initiation; it has an eschatological value in so far as it enrols its recipients among the number of those who professedly and actively prepare themselves for the imminent coming of the Messiah and who are, therefore, the messianic community in anticipation (3:2,11; Jn 1:19–34). Jesus alone, and not John, will baptise 'in the Holy Spirit' (3:7,10–12). John's baptism continued to be administered by the disciples of Jesus (Jn 4:1–2) until it was absorbed by the new rite which he had instituted (Mt 28:19; Ac 1:5f; Rm 6:4a).

f. A Jewish sect, rigid observers of the Law; but their undue attachment to the oral tradition of their teachers could lead to a conscientious but over-elaborate casuistry. Jesus' independent attitude with regard to the Law and his association with sinners inevitably provoked their opposition, and there are numerous echoes of this in the gospels, especially Mt; *see* 9:11 and par.; 12:2 and par., 14 and par., 24; 15:1 and par.; 16:1 and par., 6 and par.; 19:3 and par.; 21:45; 22:15 and par., 34,41; 23 and par.; Lk 5:21; 6:7; 15:2; 16:14seq.; 18:10seq.; Jn 7:32; 8:13; 9:13seq.; 11:47seq. Nevertheless with certain individuals among them Jesus had friendly relationships, Lk 7:36f; Jn 3:1. His disciples found in them allies against the Sadducees, Ac 23:6–10. It is impossible to deny their zeal, cf. Rm 10:2, or even their uprightness, Ac 5:34seq. Paul himself is proud of his former life as a Pharisee, Ac 23:6; 26:5; Ph 3:5.

g. In opposition to the outlook of the Pharisees, these rejected all tradition not contained in the written Law, *see* Ac 23:8c. They came for the most part from the great priestly families. They were less devout than the Pharisees and more politically minded. They too came into conflict with Jesus, 16:1,6; 22:23seq., and his disciples, Ac 4:1a; 5:17.

h. The retribution of the Day of Yahweh (Am 5:18m), which was to inaugurate the messianic era.

i. In the OT fire, a purifying element more refined and efficacious than water, was already a symbol of God's supreme intervention in history and of his Spirit which comes to purify hearts, *see* Si 2:5; Is 1:25; Zc 13:9; Ml 3:2–3.

j. The fire of Gehenna which for ever goes on consuming what has defied purification (Jdt 16:17; Ps 21:9; Si 7:17; Is 66:24; Zp 1:18).

k. The Baptist's question shows that Jesus' baptism was problematical for the first Christians, because in it the superior is seen to submit himself to the inferior. Jesus' answer shows that it was necessary in order to fulfil God's saving justice, perhaps because by it the Messiah himself enters into the eschatological community, *see* 1:22j; 3:6e.

l. add. 'for him', i.e. before his eyes.

m. The spirit which hovered over the waters at the first creation (Gn 1:2) now appears at the beginning of the new creation. It anoints Jesus for his messianic mission (Ac 10:38) which it is to guide (Mt 4:1seq.; 12:18,28; Lk 4:14,18; 10:21). While in Mk the vision of the dove and the voice from heaven can be understood as an interior personal experience of Jesus, in Mt it must be understood as a public scene: the voice is addressed to the bystanders.

n. The immediate purpose of this sentence is to declare that Jesus is in truth the servant foretold by Isaiah, but the substitution of 'Son' for 'servant' (made possible by the double sense of the Greek word *pais*) underlines the relationship of Jesus with the Father which is that of anointed Son, *see* 4:3d. In Jewish literature a voice from heaven is a means of showing the God-given authority of a teacher.

4 a. Jesus is led into the desert to be put to the test here for forty days, as Israel was for forty years, Dt 8:2,4; *see also* Nb 14:34. There, as the quotations show, he undergoes three similar temptations: seeking nourishment apart from God, Dt 8:3; cf. Ex 16; testing God for the sake of self-indulgence, Dt 6:16; cf. Ex 17:1–7; denying God to follow false gods who serve the powers of this world, Dt 6:13; cf. Dt 6:10–15; Ex 23:23–33. As did Moses, Jesus fasts for forty days and nights, Dt 9:18; *see* Ex 34:28; Dt 9:9. As did Moses, he sees 'all the earth' from a high mountain, Dt 34:1–4. God helps him through his angels, v. 11, as he promised the upright, Ps 91:11–12, and, according to Mk 1:13, protects him from wild beasts, as he does the upright, Ps 91:13, and Israel, Dt 8:15. By means of these biblical allusions Jesus is seen as the new Moses (*see* already 2:16g, 20 and Ex 4:19), who leads the new Exodus, cf. Heb 3:1–4:11; that is the Messiah, as the devil here hints ('if you are the Son of God . . .'), who opens the true way of salvation, not of self-reliance and ease but of obedience to God and self-denial. But in spite of the biblical manner of presentation the episode can have a historical background. Even though free from sin, Jesus can have known external temptations, *see* 16:23. It was necessary that he should be put to the test in order to become our leader, *see* 26:36–46 and par; Heb 2:10,17–18; 4:15; 5:2,7–9. He had to give up the thought of a glorious, political role as Messiah in favour of a spiritual role in total obedience to God, *see* Heb 12:2.

b. The Holy Spirit, 'breath' and creative energy of God, who guided the prophets, Is 11:2c, will guide Jesus himself in the fulfilment of his mission, *see* 3:16n; Lk 4:1b, as he will later guide the beginning and development of the Church, Ac 1:8j.

c. This name, which means Accuser, Calumniator, since his task is to put human beings in the wrong, sometimes translates the Hebr. *satan* (Adversary), Jb 1:6g; *see* Ws 2:24t. The bearer of this name is held responsible for everything which cuts across the work of God and of Christ, 13:39seq.; Jn 8:44; 13:2; Ac 10:38; Ep 6:11; 1 Jn 3:8. His defeat will be the sign of the final victory of God, 25:41; Heb 2:14; Rv 12:9,12; 20:2,10.

d. The biblical title 'Son of God' does not necessarily mean natural sonship but may imply a sonship which is merely adoptive, i.e. which as a result of God's deliberate choice sets up a very intimate relationship between God and his creature. In this sense the title is given to angels (Jb 1:6), to the chosen people (Ex 4:22; Ws 18:13), to individual Israelites (Dt 14:1; Ho 2:1; cf. Mt 5:9,45), to their leaders (Ps 2:7). Where, therefore, it is attributed to the royal Messiah (1 Ch 17:13; Ps 2:7; 89:26) it does not necessarily imply that he is more than human; nor need we suppose that it has any deeper significance when used by Satan (4:3,6) or by the possessed (Mk 3:11; 5:7–8; Lk 4:41), still less when used by the centurion (Mk 15:39; cf. Lk 23:47). By itself the sentence at the baptism (3:17) and at the transfiguration (17:5) suggests no more than the divine predilection for the Messiah-servant, and in all probability the high priest's question (26:63) concerns messiahship only. Nevertheless the title 'Son of God' can bear a further, more profound meaning of sonship. Jesus clearly insinuated this meaning when he spoke of himself as 'the Son' (21:37), ranked above the angels (24:36), having God for his 'Father' in a way others had not (Jn 20:17, and compare 'my Father' in Mt 7:21), enjoying with the Father an altogether singular relationship of knowledge and love (Mt 11:27). These assertions coupled with others that speak of the Messiah's divine rank (22:42–46), of the heavenly origin of the 'Son of man' (8:20h), assertions finally confirmed by the triumph of the resurrection, have endowed the expression 'Son of God' with that strictly divine significance which will later be found, e.g. in Paul (Rm 9:5d). During the lifetime of Jesus, it is true, his disciples had no clear conception of his divinity—the texts of 14:33 and 16:16 which add the title 'Son of God' to the more primitive text of Mk reflect, in all probability, a later stage in the faith's development. The faith that they acquired by the help of the Holy Spirit after Pentecost nevertheless rests on the historical words of the Master, who expressed his consciousness of being the unique Son of the Father.

e. *nazara.* A very rare form attested by excellent authorities, B, Z, Origen k, see Lk 4:16; the great majority of witnesses fall back on the common form 'Nazareth'.

f. The sovereignty of God over the chosen people, and through them over the world, is at the heart of Jesus' preaching as it was of the theocratic ideal of the OT. It implies a kingdom of 'saints' where God will be truly King because they will acknowledge his royal rights by knowing and loving him. This sovereignty, jeopardised by rebellious sin, is to be reasserted by an act of supreme intervention on the part of God and of his Messiah (Dn 2:28h). This is the intervention which Jesus, following John the Baptist (3:2), declares imminent (4:17,23; Lk 4:43). It is to take the form not, as was commonly expected, of a successful nationalist rising (Mk 11:10; Lk 19:11; Ac 1:6) but of a purely spiritual movement (Mk 1:34m; Jn 18:36). The redemptive work of Jesus as 'Son of man' (8:20h) and as 'servant' (8:17f; 20:28g; 26:28i) sets human beings free from Satan's rule which opposes God's (4:8; 8:29k; 12:25–26). Before it achieves its final eschatological realisation when the elect will be with the Father in the joy of the heavenly banquet (8:11c; 13:43; 26:29), the kingdom makes an unimpressive entrance (13:31–33). Its modest beginning is mysterious (13:11) and arouses opposition (13:24–30), it has come unnoticed (12:28; Lk 17:20–21); the development of the kingdom on earth is slow (Mk 4:26–29) and is effected through the community founded by Jesus (Mt 16:18g). By the judgement of God that falls on Jerusalem it is established with power as the kingdom of Christ (16:28; Lk 21:31) and is preached throughout the world by apostolic missionaries (Mt 10:7; 24:14; Ac 1:3d). When the time comes for the final Judgement (13:37–43,47–50; 25:31–46) the return of Christ in glory (16:27; 25:31) will be the final act that establishes the kingdom which Christ will then present to the Father (1 Co 15:24). Until that time the kingdom appears as a free gift of God (20:1–16; 22:9–10; Lk 12:32) accepted by the humble (Mt 5:3; 18:3–4;

19:14,23–24) and the generous (13:44–46; 19:12; Mk 9:47; Lk 9:62; 18:29seq.), refused by the proud and selfish (Mt 21:31–32,43; 22:2–8; 23:13). There is no entering it without the wedding garment which is the new life (22:11–13; Jn 3:3,5) and not everyone is admitted (Mt 8:12; 1 Co 6:9–10; Ga 5:21). One must stay awake so as to be ready when it comes unexpectedly (25:1–13). On Matthew's treatment of the kingdom as the guiding idea of his arrangement, see p. 11.

g. Miraculous cures are the distinctive sign that the messianic age has dawned, see 10:1,7seq.; 11:4seq.

h. The word is not used here in a precise sense and in fact means Galilee with its surrounding districts, cf. Mk 1:28.

i. The Decapolis was a loose federation of ten free towns with their surrounding territories, scattered for the most part on the east side of Jordan and far enough northeast to include Damascus.

5 a. The new spirit of the kingdom of God, 4:17f, is explained in an inaugural sermon absent from Mk. Lk has a different inaugural sermon, 6:20–49, which does not contain the elements concerning Jewish laws and practices, Mt 5:17–6:18, which would be of less interest to his readers. Mt has joined together sayings pronounced on various occasions in order to make a complete picture. In the resulting composite discourse five principal subjects are handled: **1** The spirit in which the children of the kingdom should live, 5:3–48. **2** The way in which they should 'fulfil' the laws and practices of Judaism, 6:1–18. **3** Detachment from wealth, 6:19–34. **4** Attitudes to the neighbour, 7:1–12. **5** Entry to the kingdom by means of a firm decision expressed in action, 7:13–27.

b. One of the hills near Capernaum.

c. The OT employed formulas of congratulation like these occasionally in relation to piety, wisdom, prosperity, Ps 1:1–2; 33:12; 127:5–6; Pr 3:3; Si 31:8. In the spirit of the prophets Jesus here recalls that the poor, too, have a share in these blessings. The first three beatitudes, 5:3–5; Lk 6:20–21, declare that people normally considered wretched and unfortunate are fortunate, since they are fit to receive the blessing of the kingdom. The subsequent beatitudes are concerned more directly with moral attitudes. There are other gospel beatitudes in 11:6; 13:16; 24:46; Lk 11:27–28. See also Lk 1:45; Rv 1:3; 14:13.

d. The word 'poor' is used with the moral connotations already found in Zephaniah, see Zp 2:3d, made explicit by 'in spirit', which is lacking in Lk. Defenceless and oppressed, the 'poor' or the 'lowly' are open to the kingdom, and such is the theme of Mt's beatitudes, cf. Lk 4:18; 7:22 = Mt 11:5; Lk 14:13; Jm 2:5. 'Poverty' goes hand in hand with 'spiritual childhood' required for entrance into the kingdom, 18:1f = Mk 9:33seq.; cf. Mt 11:25seq., and par.; 19:13seq., and par.; Lk 9:46seq.—the mystery revealed to 'little ones', *nepioi,* cf. Lk 12:32; 1 Co 1:26seq. They are the 'poor', *ptochoi,* the 'lowly', *tapeinoi* (18:4; 23:12; Lk 1:48,52; 14:11; 18:14) and both are the 'last' as opposed to the 'first' (Mk 9:35), the 'little ones' as opposed to the 'great' (Lk 9:48; see Mt 19:30 and par.; 20:26 and par.; Lk 17:10). Although the formula of 5:3 stresses the spirit of poverty for the rich as for the poor, Jesus usually has in mind actual poverty, especially for his disciples (6:19seq.; cf. 4:18seq., and par.; 6:25 and par.; Lk 12:33seq.; cf. Lk 5:1seq.) Mt 9:9 and par.; 19:21 and par., 27; cf. Mk 10:28 and par.; see also Ac 2:44seq.; 4:32seq. He himself sets the example of poverty (8:20 and par.; Lk 2:7) and of lowliness (Mt 11:29; 20:28 and par.; 21:5; Jn 13:12seq.; cf. 2 Co 8:9; Ph 2:7seq.). He identifies himself with the little ones and the wretched (25:45; cf. 18:5seq., and par.).

e. Or 'the afflicted'; the word is taken from the LXX version of Psalm 37 and the sense is 'unassuming, undemanding'. v. 4 is possibly only a gloss on v. 3; its omission would reduce the number of 'beatitudes' to 7, see 6:9d.

f. The disciples are the successors of the prophets, cf. 10:41; 13:17; 23:34.

g. lit. 'bushel measure'. In the ancient world a measure was a small receptacle on legs. So it is a question here of hiding the lamp under this receptacle, rather like the bed of Mk 4:21seq., not of extinguishing it by putting the lid on.

h. Jesus comes neither to destroy the Law, Dt 4:8, nor to consecrate it as untouchable, but by his teaching and way of acting to give it a new and definitive form, by which the goal of the Law is fully realised, see Mt 1:22j; Mk 1:15e. This is especially true of uprightness, v. 20, cf. 3:15; Lv 19:15; Rm 1:16i, of which vv. Mt 5:21–48 give several characteristic examples. The old command becomes interior and penetrates right to the secret desires, cf 12:34; 23:25–28. No detail of the Law may be omitted unless it has been brought to fulfilment in this way, vv. 18–19; cf. 13:52. It is less a question of making it lighter than of making it deeper, 11:28. Love, in which the old Law was already summed up, 7:12; 22:34–40 and par., becomes Jesus' new commandment, Jn 13:34, and fulfils the whole Law, Rm 13:8–10; Ga 5:14; cf. Col 3:14.

i. The *amen* which introduces certain sayings, Ps 41:13f; Rm 1:25p, underlines their authority: Mt 6:2,5,16; Jn 1:51.

j. The tradition was taught orally, especially in the synagogues.

k. The Aramaic word *raqa*, transliterated in Mt, translated here, means: 'empty-head', 'nitwit'.

l. Here the Great Sanhedrin which met in Jerusalem, as opposed to the minor courts (vv. 21–22) of the country districts.

m. To the first meaning ('worthless person') of the Greek word, Jewish usage added the much more contemptuous one of 'apostate'.

n. Marriage within the prohibited degrees. See 19:9b.

o. This seemingly well-known formula, see 2 Co 1:17; Jm 5:12, can be understood in various ways: 1 Truthfulness: if something is the case, say it is; if it is not, say it is not. 2 Sincerity: let yes (or no) on the lips correspond to yes (or no) in the heart. 3 Solemnity: the repetition of 'yes' or 'no' as a solemn affirmation or negation so strong that it avoids an oath which invokes the divinity.

p. The examples of vv. 39–40 show that it is harm done to oneself which is at issue. Resistance by way of vengeance (the Jewish law of retribution, v. 38; cf. Ex 21:25; Ps 5:10c) is excluded. The gospel does not forbid reasonable defence against unjust aggression, see Jn 18:22seq., still less opposition to evil in the world.

q. As a surety, cf. Ex 22:25seq.; Dt 24:12seq. It is clear that the sentence is deliberately hyperbolic, cf. 19:24.

r. The second part of this commandment is not found in the law. It is the brusque expression of a language (the original Aramaic) which has few half-tones and is equivalent to, 'There is no obligation to love one's enemy,' cf. Lk 14:26 with its parallel Mt 10:37. Incidentally Si 12:4–7 and the scrolls from Qumran (1 QS 1:10) show a detestation of sinners not far removed from hate, and perhaps Jesus was thinking of this.

s. add. 'do good to those who hate you'.

t. add. 'and for those who treat you badly', cf. Lk 6:27seq.

u. They were employed by the occupying power, and this earned them popular contempt, cf. 9:10.

6 a. lit. 'perform your uprightness' (var. 'perform almsgiving'), i.e. perform good works which make someone upright in the sight of God. For the Jews these works were principally: almsgiving (vv. 2–4), prayer (vv. 5–6), fasting (vv. 16–18).

b. This epithet suggests the false devotees of an artificial and showy piety; in the gospels it applies especially to the Pharisees, cf. 15:7; 22:18; 23:13–15.

c. By his example, 14:23, as well as his introduction Jesus taught his disciples the duty and manner of praying. Prayer should be humble before God, Lk 18:10–14, and

before people, Mt 6:5–6; Mk 12:40 and par. It should come from the heart rather than the lips, 6:7, trusting in God's goodness, 6:8; 7:7–11 and par., and insistent to the point of perseverance, Lk 11:5,8; 18:1–8. Prayer is heard if it is made with faith, 21:22 and par., in the name of Jesus, 18:19–20; Jn 14:13–14; 15:7,16; 16:23–27, asks what is good, 7:11, for instance the Holy Spirit, Lk 11:13, forgiveness, Mk 11:25, the good of persecutors, 5:44 and par.; cf. Lk 23:34, and above all the coming of the kingdom of God and deliverance at the time of the final crisis, 24:20 and par.; 26:41 and par.; Lk 21:36; see Lk 22:31–32; this is the substance of the model prayer taught by Jesus himself, Mt 6:9–15 and par.

d. The Lord's Prayer in its Matthaean form has 7 petitions. The number is a favourite of Matthew's: 2 × 7 generations in the Genealogy (1:17), 7 beatitudes (5:4e), 7 parables (13:3b), forgiveness not 7 but 77 times (18:22), 7 diatribes against the Pharisees (23:13h), 7 sections into which the Gospel is divided (see p. 1605–6).

e. The Greek word is obscure; this traditional rendering is a probable one. Other possibilities: 'necessary for subsistence' or 'for tomorrow'. Whatever the exact translation, the sense is that we must ask God for the sustenance we need in this life but for no more—not for wealth or luxury.

f. Or 'from evil'. • Add. 'For yours is the kingdom and the power and the glory for ever. Amen' (a reading introduced into the text through liturgical influence).

g. According as the eye is clear or diseased it gives or refuses material light; to this light the spiritual light is compared; if this light is itself dimmed the blindness is much worse than physical.

7 a. Do not judge others, in order that you may not be judged by God. Similarly in the next verse, cf. Jm 4:12.

b. Consecrated meat from animals sacrificed in the Temple, see Ex 22:30; Lv 22:14. Similarly the precious teaching of the kingdom must not be set before those who, incapable of receiving it with profit, may even abuse it. The text does not detail who they are: hostile Jews or gentiles (cf. 15:26)?

c. This maxim was well known in the ancient world, especially among the Jews, see Tb 4:15, but in a negative form: Do not to another what you would not have done to yourself. The positive form in which Jesus, and after him Christian literature, puts it, is considerably more demanding.

d. The doctrine of the two ways, good and bad, between which people must choose, is a theme old and widespread in Judaism, see Dt 30:15–20; Ps 1; Pr 4:18–19; 12:28; 15:24; Si 15:17; 33:14. It is expressed in a little treatise on morals which has come down to us via the *Didache* and its Latin translation the *Doctrina Apostolorum*. Its influence has been discerned in 5:14–18; 7:12–14; 19:16–26; 22:34–40 and Rm 12:16–21; 13:8–12.

e. var. 'the gate that leads to perdition is wide, and the road spacious.'

f. Lying teachers who charm the public by their show of piety while pursuing their own selfish ends, see 24:4seq., 24.

g. The Day of Judgement.

h. These always sought support for their teaching in the 'tradition' of the ancients. Add. 'and the Pharisees'.

8 a. By his miracles Jesus shows his power over nature (8:23–27; 14:22–33 and par.), especially over sickness (8:1–4,5–13,14–15; 9:1–8,20–22,27–31; 14:14,36; 15:30; 20:29–34 and par.; Mk 7:32–37; 8:22–26; Lk 14:1–6; 17:11–19; Jn 5:1–16; 9:1–41), over death (Mt 9:23–26 and par.; Lk 7:11–17; Jn 11:1–44), over devils (Mt 8:29k). Jesus' miracles are not elaborate: in this they differ from the fantastic prodigies reported of the hellenistic world and from those attributed to the Jewish rabbis, but they are different most notably by reason of the spiritual and symbolic significance that Jesus attaches to them. They declare the judgements of the messianic age (21:18–22 and par.) as also the privileges it brings (11:5d; 14:13–21; 15:32–39 and par.; Lk 5:4–11; Jn 2:1–11; 21:4–14); they are the first signs of the triumph of the Spirit over Satan's empire (8:29k) and over all the powers of evil, whether sin (9:2b) or disease (8:17f). The motive is sometimes compassion (20:34; Mk 1:41; Lk 7:13) but they are directed principally to the rousing and strengthening of faith (Mt 8:10b; Jn 2:11f). Thus it is only with great deliberation that Jesus works any miracles at all, demanding secrecy for any he does agree to work (Mk 1:34m), and leaving the arousing of faith to be done by his Father in heaven and not by 'flesh and blood' (Mt 16:17). When he sent his apostles to preach the kingdom he gave them his own healing power (10:1,8 and par.) and for this reason Matthew recounts before the Missionary Discourse (ch. 10) a series of ten miracles (ch. 8–9) as signs accrediting the missionary (Mk 16:17seq.; Ac 2:22; see 1:8j).

b. The faith that Jesus asks for from the outset of his public life (Mk 1:15) and throughout his subsequent career, is that act of trust and self-abandonment by which people no longer rely on their own strength and policies but commit themselves to the power and guiding word of him in whom they believe (21:25p,32; Lk 1:20,45). Jesus asks for this faith especially when he works his miracles (8:13; 9:2 and par., 22 and par., 28–29; 15–28; Mk 5:36 and par.; 10:52 and par.; Lk 17:19) which are not merely acts of mercy but also signs attesting his mission and witnessing to the kingdom (Mt 8:3a, see Jn 2:11f); hence he cannot work miracles unless he finds the faith without which the miracles lose their true significance (Mt 12:38–39; 13:58 and par.; 16:1–4). Since faith demands the sacrifice of the whole person, mind and heart, it is not an easy act of humility to perform; many decline it, particularly in Israel (8:10 and par.; 15:28; 27:42 and par.; Lk 18:8), or are half-hearted (Mk 9:24; Lk 8:13). Even the disciples are slow to believe (8:26 and par.; 14:31; 16:8; 17:20 and par.) and are still reluctant after the resurrection (28:17; Mk 16:11–14; Lk 24:11,25,41). When faith is strong it works wonders (17:20 and par.; 21:21 and par.; Mk 16:17) and its appeal is never refused (21:22 and par.; Mk 9:23) especially when it asks for forgiveness of sin (9:2 and par.; Lk 7:50) and for that salvation of which it is the necessary condition (Mk 16:16; Lk 8:12, see Ac 3:16f).

c. Basing their idea on Is 25:6, the Jews often described the joyous messianic era as a banquet (see Mt 22:2–14; 26:29 and par.; Lk 14:15; Rv 3:20; 19:9).

d. That is to say the Jews, natural heirs of the promises. Their place will be taken by the gentiles, who are more worthy.

e. Scriptural image for the dismay and frustration of the wicked at seeing the virtuous rewarded, see Jb 16:9; Ps 37:12; 112:10. In Mt it is used as a description of damnation.

f. As described by Is, the servant 'took' our sorrows on himself in the sense that his own suffering was expiatory. Matthew takes the phrase to mean that Jesus 'took away' these sorrows by his healing miracles. This interpretation, at first sight forced, is in fact profoundly theological. It was to take on himself the expiation of sin that Jesus, the 'servant', came on earth; that is why he could take away the bodily ills which are the consequence and the penalty of sin.

g. The east bank of Lake Tiberias.

h. With the exception of Ac 7:56; Rv 1:13; 14:14 this expression appears in the NT only in the gospels. There is no doubt that Jesus used it as his favourite self-designation. The Aramaic phrase which lies behind it originally meant 'man', compare Ezk 2:1b, but it seems that at the time of Jesus it was frequently used by a speaker to indicate himself, especially to soften a statement which might otherwise seem extravagant or shocking. But in Dn 7:13k the expression is used of a glorious figure who was to receive from God the eschatological kingdom, and this usage occurs also later in the apocalyptic *Book of Enoch*. The evangelists seem to have understood the expression as a title in this sense, 13:13e; 26:64u.

i. The district got its name from the town of Gadara to the southeast of the lake. The var. 'Gerasenes' (Mk, Lk and Vulg. Mt) derives from the name of another town (Gerasa or possibly Chorsia); the var. 'Gergesenes' is the

result of a conjecture of Origen, made because both Gadara and Gerasa are several miles from the lake.

j. In accounts of miracles and cures, the doubling of persons appears to be characteristic of Mt's style: two demoniacs here, where the parallels in Mk and Lk have one; two blind men at Jericho, 20:30; two blind men at Bethsaida, in an incident which appears to be a doublet, 9:27.

k. By his power over demons Jesus destroys the empire of Satan, 12:28 and par.; Lk 10:17–19; cf. Lk 4:6; Jn 12:31i, and inaugurates the messianic kingdom characterised by the Holy Spirit, Is 11:2c; Jl 3:1seq. Demonic possession, 12:43–45,43n, is often accompanied by illness, further evidence of Satan's power, 9:2b, Lk 13:16. Thus the exorcisms of the gospels, which as here often occur as pure exorcisms, see 15:21–28 and par.; Mk 1:23–28 and par.; Lk 8:2, appear frequently also as cures, Mt 9:32–34; 12:22–24 and par.; 17:14–18; Lk 13:10,17. Even if Israel refuses to recognise Jesus, 12:24–32, demons have no doubt about him, here and Mk 1:24 and par.; 3:11 and par.; Lk 4:41; Ac 16:17; 19:15. This power of exorcism is communicated by Jesus to his disciples at the same time as the power of miraculous cures, 10:1,8 and par., which is linked to it, 8:3a; 4:24; 8:16 and par.; Lk 13:32.

9 **a.** Capernaum, see 4:13.

b. Jesus envisages primarily spiritual healing and effects physical healing only with this in view. Nevertheless his words in this verse contain a promise of physical healing since sickness was regarded as the result of a sin committed either by the sufferer or by his parents, see 8:29k; Jn 5:14; 9:2.

c. The power to forgive sins is entrusted to the community, see 18:18, but the plural here may indicate that Matthew is thinking of the ministers who exercise this power.

d. Called Levi by Mk and Lk.

e. Those whose moral conduct or disreputable profession, see 5:46u, rendered them 'unclean' and socially outcast. They were particularly suspect for not observing the numerous culinary laws, whence the problems about eating together, Mk 7:3–4,14–23seq.; Ac 10:15e; 15:20t; Ga 2:12; see also Rm 14; 1 Co 8–9.

f. To the exact performance of the Law's external demands God prefers the inward quality of genuine compassion. It is a favourite theme of the prophets, Am 5:21n.

g. John the Baptist. Like the Pharisees, John's disciples used to observe fasts not prescribed by the Law in the hope that their devotion would hasten the coming of the Day of the Lord.

h. The bridegroom is Jesus. His companions cannot fast because, with his coming, the messianic age has dawned.

i. Jesus' death clearly foretold.

j. The old garment and the old wineskins stand for the elements in Judaism which are to pass away. The new cloth and the new wine represent the new spirit of the kingdom of God. The super additional devotional practices of John's disciples and of the Pharisees, intended to give new life to the old order, in fact are only leading to its downfall. Jesus declines either to add or to patch: his purpose is to produce something quite new—even the spirit of the Law is to be raised to a new plane.

k. The head of the synagogue; called Jairus in Mk and Lk.

l. The loud wailing of the oriental mourner.

m. Messianic title, 2 S 7:1a; cf. Lk 1:32; Ac 2:30; Rm 1:3. As familiar as such to the Jews, Mk 12:35; Jn 7:42, and Matthew in particular emphasises its application to Jesus (Mt 1:1; 12:23; 15:22; 20:30 and par.; 21:9,15) who was hesitant towards the title because it involved a purely human notion of the Messiah, 22:41–46; see also Mk 1:34m He preferred the more obscure expression 'Son of man' 8:20h.

n. Verse omitted by representatives of the Western Text.

o. Familiar biblical metaphor: Nb 27:17; 1 K 22:17; Jdt 11:19; Ezk 34:5.

10 a. Matthew supposes that the reader already knows about the choice of the Twelve; Mark and Luke mention it expressly and distinguish the choice from the mission.

b. The list of the twelve apostles is found in four versions, in Mk, Lk, Mt and Ac. It is normally three groups of four names each, and the groups are headed respectively by Peter, Philip and James the son of Alphaeus. Inside each group, the order varies. In the first group, of the disciples closest to Jesus, Mt and Lk have the order: Peter, Andrew, James, John; but in Mk and Ac, Andrew is given the fourth place as Peter. James and John are seen as equally the intimates of the Lord, see Mk 5:37d. Still later, in Ac, James son of Zebedee is put after his younger brother John who has become more important, see Ac 1:13; 12:2, and already Lk 8:51f; 9:28. In the second group, which seems to have special links with non-Jews, Matthew sinks to last place in the lists of Mt and Ac; only in Mt is he called 'the tax collector. In the third group, those who are the most tenacious of Jewish customs, if Thaddaeus (var. Lebbaeus) in Mt and Mk is the same as Jude (son) of James in Lk and Ac, he moves down in the latter texts from second to third place. Simon the Zealot of Lk and Ac is simply the Gk translation of the Aramaic Simon qan'ana of Mt and Mk. Judas Iscariot the traitor figures always in last place. His name is often interpreted as 'man of Kerioth', cf. Jos 15:25, but it could also derive from the Aramaic sheqarya, 'liar, hypocrite'.

c. Hebraism common in the Bible: the people of Israel. As heirs to the Choice and the Promise, the Jews are to be the first to receive the offer of the Messiah's saving work; but see Ac 8:5; 13:5e.

d. The oriental greeting is a wish of peace. In v. 13 this wish is treated in concrete fashion as an entity which, if it fails to secure its effect, nevertheless remains in being and returns to its original owner.

e. The phrase is Jewish in origin. The dust of any country other than the Holy Land carries; in this passage the impurity attaches to any place that refuses the Word.

f. The instructions of vv. 17–39 clearly suppose a horizon wider than that of this first mission of the Twelve: they must originate at a later date (note their situation in Mk and Lk). Matthew puts them here to complete his missionary's handbook.

g. The small provincial sanhedrins and also the Great Sanhedrin of Jerusalem; cf. 5:21–22.

h. om. 'and if . . . another'.

i. The coming foretold here is not concerned with the world at large but with Israel: it took place at the moment when God 'visited' his now unfaithful people and brought the OT era to an end by the destruction of Jerusalem and of its Temple in c. AD 70, see 24:1a.

j. Jesus' instruction to the crowds was not successful and he turned to instructing his disciples in private. Later on it will be the duty of his disciples to deliver the message in its entirety and without fear. These same words are found in Lk but with an entirely different meaning: the disciples are not to imitate Pharisaic hypocrisy; whatever they may try to hide will certainly come to light eventually; they must therefore speak openly.

k. At the Last Judgement, when the Son will hand over the elect to his Father, see 25:34.

l. Jesus is a 'sign that is rejected', Lk 2:34; his aim is not to provoke dissension, but this becomes inevitable as a result of the demands of the decision he provokes.

m. In Mt this dictum is given in a more archaic form than in Mk or Lk: 'find' covers the idea of 'winning', 'securing for oneself', cf. Gn 26:12; Pr 3:13; 21:21; Ho 12:9. See also 16:25l.

n. 'Prophet' and 'holy (or 'upright') man', see also 13:17 and 23:29, are a familiar biblical pair; here they serve to indicate the missionary and the ordinary Christian.

o. The apostles whom Jesus is sending on their mission, cf. 18:1–6,10,14 and Mk 9:41.

11 a. 'their', i.e. the Jews'.

b. var. 'two of his disciples'.

c. John has been expecting a Messiah who will be the agent of God's 'wrath' or retribution, 3:8,10,12.

d. By this allusion to the prophecies of Isaiah, Jesus shows John that his works do indeed inaugurate the messianic era, but by way of beneficent and saving miracles, not violence and retribution, cf. Lk 4:17–21.

e. Simply because he is a member of the kingdom, whereas John, as the Forerunner, remains at its gates. The sentence contrasts epochs rather than persons. There is no personal slight to John; it is simply that the epoch of the kingdom wholly transcends that which preceded it.

f. Various interpretations have been offered. The 'violence' may be: 1 The praiseworthy violence, the bitter self-sacrifice, of those who would take possession of the kingdom. 2 The misguided violence of those who would establish the kingdom by force (the Zealots). 3 The tyrannical violence of the powers of evil, or of their agents on earth, who seek to maintain their dominion in this world and to thwart the advance of the kingdom of God. 4 A possible translation 'the kingdom of Heaven clears a way for itself by violence,' i.e. is powerfully establishing itself despite all obstacles.

g. John brings the OT era to its close: he carries on where Malachi, the last of the prophets, left off, and fulfils Malachi's last prediction, Ml 3:23.

h. var. 'by her children', see Lk 7:35. Like petulant children who will play none of the games suggested (in this case weddings and funerals) the Jewish leaders reject all God's advances, whether made through the stern penance of John or through the gentle courtesy of Jesus. The different approaches are explained by the different relationships of John and Jesus to the messianic era, cf. 9:14–15; 11:11–13. In spite of human lack of goodwill, God's wise design is justified by the conduct of the Baptist and Jesus. Jesus' 'works' especially, that is, his miracles, either convince or condemn, vv. 6 and 20–24. Jesus is compared to Wisdom also in 11:28–30; 12:42; 23:24 and par.; Jn 6:35k; 1 Co 1:24. Others see here only a proverb which proclaims that the false wisdom of unbelievers, cf. v. 25, will reap its fruit of divine punishment, vv. 20–24.

i. The threats of the prophets had made these towns archetypes of impiety, Is 23; Ezk 26–28; Am 1:9–10; Zc 9:2–4.

j. Vv. 25–27 are not closely connected with the context in which Matthew has placed the passage (compare its different position in Lk). Hence, 'these things' refers not to what precedes but to the 'mysteries of the kingdom', 13:11, which are revealed to the 'little ones'—i.e. to the disciples, cf. 10:42—but hidden from the 'wise'—i.e. from the members and teachers of the Pharisee group.

k. The claim of an intimate connection with God, vv. 26–27, and the call to discipleship, vv. 28–30, recall a number of passages in the Wisdom literature, Pr 8:22–36; Ws 8:3–4; 9:9–18; Si 24:3–9,19–20. Jesus therefore claims the role of Wisdom, see 11:19h, no longer as a personification but as a person, 'the Son', par excellence, of 'the Father', cf. 4:3. With its Johannine flavour, see Jn 1:18; 3:11,35; 6:46; 10:15, this passage expresses, in the most primitive stratum of the synoptic tradition, the same clear awareness in Jesus of his divine sonship as is found in Jn.

l. The burden of the Law and of the additional Pharisaic observances. The 'yoke of the Law' is a current rabbinic metaphor; see also Si 51:26; Jr 2:20; 5:5; Lm 3·27; Zp 3:9 (LXX); cf. Is 14:25.

m. Classic descriptions of the 'Poor' of the OT, see Dn 3:87; Zp 2:3d. Jesus makes their religious attitude his own, and on these grounds claims to be their master in wisdom, as was prophesied of the 'servant', Is 61:1–2;

Lk 4:18; *see also* Mt 12:18–21; 21:5. This attitude to poverty is expressed in the beatitudes and in many other passages of the gospels.

12 a. The disciples' offence is not picking someone else's corn while passing by (Dt 23:26 allowed it) but doing this on the Sabbath. Casuists saw in this a 'work' prohibited by the Law, Ex 34:21.

b. Far from stopping, the work of the priests actually increased on the Sabbath.

c. On this occasion and when he cures on the Sabbath, 12:9–14 and par.; Lk 13:10–17; 14:1–6; Jn 5:1–18; 7:19–24; 9, Jesus affirms that even a custom of divine institution has no absolute value, but must yield to the demands of necessity or love, and that he himself has the right to interpret the Law of Moses authoritatively, *see* 5:17h; 15:1–7 and par.; 19:1–9 and par. This right he has because he proclaims the messianic kingdom, 8:20h, whose new economy, 9:17f, he has the task of establishing already, 9:6. The rabbis did admit of dispensations from the Sabbath law, but only within very scrupulous limits.

d. i.e. his avoidance of publicity for his work of healing.

e. This gives a meaning of the Hebr. term *mishpat* (and of its LXX translation *krisis*), often rendered 'judgement', which signifies the divine statute governing the relationship of God with humanity in so far as it is known through revelation and the religion founded on it.

f. Canaanite divinity. The name means 'Baal the Prince' (not 'Baal of the dunghill' as is sometimes asserted), and so orthodox monotheism naturally interpreted it as 'Prince of devils'. The form 'Beelzebub' (Syr. and Vulg.) is a contemptuous play on words (already found in 2 K 1:2seq.) which makes the name mean 'Baal (Lord) of the flies'.

g. lit. 'your children', a semitism.

h. Not to recognise the Messiah may be excusable, since he is appearing as an ordinary 'son of man', 8:20h; but it is a positive perversity to witness the manifest good works of the Holy Spirit and declare them evil (as in v. 24). By doing this, a person is openly refusing to respond to God; he has 'closed his heart', and so put himself outside the range of forgiveness.

i. i.e. a calumny.

j. A miracle that would prove Jesus had authority and show what sort of authority it was, cf. 5:11seq.; Jn 2:11f. No other sign will be given but the decisive one which is the resurrection, here obscurely foretold.

k. lit. 'adulterous': a common figurative use in the OT, *see* Ho 1:2c.

l. In 16:4 Mt does not define, as he does in v. 40 here, the sense of this 'sign of Jonah', and Lk 11:29seq. understands it as being Jesus' preaching, which is a sign for his contemporaries just as Jonah's was for the men of Nineveh—a sense which lurks beneath v. 41 here. It is, however, less probable, for Jesus' preaching is already taking place and so cannot be announced as still in the future. Further, and more important, Jonah was known in the Jewish tradition for his miraculous deliverance rather than for his preaching to the gentiles, which was not well looked upon. Therefore even if Mt's interpretation in v. 40 is later than Lk's, it reflects Jesus' thought better, for it is a veiled prediction of his final triumph.

m. A ready-made expression borrowed from Jon 2:1 and only approximately indicating the space of time between Jesus' death and resurrection.

n. The ancients thought of desert places as inhabited by demons, *see* 8:28; Lv 16:8b; 17:7d; Is 13:21; 34:14c; Ba 4:35; Rv 18:2. Nevertheless, the devils much prefer to live in human beings, 8:29k.

o. Not necessarily Mary's children but possibly near relations, cousins perhaps, which both Hebr. and Aramaic style 'brothers', *see* Gn 13:8; 14:16; 29:15; Lv 10:4; 1 Ch 23:22seq.

p. V. 47 ('Someone said to him: Your mother and brothers are standing outside and want to speak to you') is omitted by some important textual witnesses. It is probably a restatement of v. 46 modelled on Mk and Lk.

q. The ties of physical relationship yield to those of spiritual relationship, *see* 8:21seq.; 10:37; 19:29.

13 a. A merely transitional cliché of no chronological significance.

b. Making a total of seven, *see* 6:9d, Mt adds five parables to the two he shares with Mk.

c. add. 'to hear'. Similarly 11:15; 13:43.

d. For those of good will, what they have learnt from the old covenant will be added to and perfected by the new, cf. 5:17,20. The ill-disposed will lose even what they have, namely, that Jewish Law which, without the perfection Jesus brings to it, is destined to become obsolete.

e. A deliberate and culpable insensibility which is both the cause and the explanation of the withdrawal of grace. The preceding narratives, all of which throw light on this 'hardening', 11:16–19,20–24; 12:7,14,24–32,34,39,45, prepare the way for the parable discourse. By the use of symbols and images, therefore, Jesus challenges them to reflect and themselves seek to penetrate more deeply into the understanding of the kingdom.

f. The prophets and holy men of the OT. Paul speaks more than once of the time when the 'mystery' was not revealed: Rm 16:25; Ep 3:4–5; Col 1:26; *see also* 1 P 1:11–12.

g. This strange expression is the result of a certain ambiguity in the interpretation of the parable, which identifies human beings sometimes with the ground which receives the Word, sometimes with the seed itself.

h. The kingdom, like the mustard seed and the leaven, is unpretentious in its beginnings but destined for enormous growth.

i. Several authorities omit 'of the world'.

j. lit. 'the children of the kingdom' and 'the children of the Evil One' (semitisms).

k. To the kingdom of the Son (the messianic kingdom) of v. 41 there succeeds the kingdom of the Father to whom the Son commits the elect whom he has saved, *see* 25:34; 1 Co 15:24.

l. No one who discovers the kingdom of Heaven can enter it without leaving all behind, *see* 19:21.

m. The Jewish teacher who becomes a disciple of Christ has at his disposal all the wealth of the Old Testament as well as its completion in the New, v. 12. This picture of a 'scribe who becomes a disciple' sums up the whole ideal of Matthew the evangelist and may well be a self-portrait.

n. Nazareth, where he lived as a child, *see* 2:23.

14 a. om. (Latin text) 'Philip'; the omission is due to the difficulty the name seemed to create. But in fact this Philip is not the tetrarch of Ituraea and Trachonitis, Lk 3:1; he is another son of Herod the Great by Mariamne II and therefore half-brother of Antipas; Josephus himself calls him Herod. Antipas' fault lay not so much in having married his niece as in having taken her from his brother who was still living; moreover, he had repudiated his first wife.

b. According to Josephus, the girl's name was Salome.

c. While Lk 9:10–17 and Jn 6:1–13 have only one multiplication of loaves, Mt 14:13–21; 15:32–39 and Mk 6:30–44; 8:1–10 have two. This duplication, certainly very ancient, *see* 16:9seq., presents the same incident according to two different traditions. The first, more ancient, and of Palestinian origin, seems to situate the incident on the western shore of the lake (see next note) and speaks of twelve baskets, the number of the tribes of Israel and of the apostles, *see* Mk 3:14c. The second, derived from Christians in a gentile milieu, situates it on the eastern, gentile, shore of the lake, *see* Mk 7:31, and speaks of seven baskets, the number of the gentile nations of Canaan, Ac 13:19, and of the hellenist deacons, Ac 6:5; 21:8. Both traditions depict the event in the light of OT precedents, especially the multiplication of oil and bread by Elisha, 2 K 4:1–7,42–44, and the episode of manna and quails, Ex 16; Nb 11. The act of Jesus repeats these gifts of heavenly nourishment with an even greater power. It was, as the earliest tradition already saw, a preparation for the eschatological nourishment of the Eucharist. This aspect is underlined by the literary presentation in the synoptics, *see* 14:19; 15:36 and 26:26, and the discourse on the bread of life, Jn 6.

d. This does not necessarily indicate the eastern shore of the lake. Jesus could have gone along the western shore from north to south or vice versa and so reach 'the other side', v. 22, of the curve made by this shore.

e. On shore the crowd hurried to the place the boat was making for.

f. The evangelists, especially Lk, often note that Jesus prays, in solitude or at night, 14:23 and par.; Mk 1:35; Lk 5:16, at mealtimes, Mt 14:19 and par.; 15:36 and par.; 26:26-27 and par., at the time of important events: at the Baptism, Lk 3:21, before the choice of the Twelve, Lk 6:12, the teaching of the Lord's Prayer, Lk 11:1, *see* Mt 6:5c, the profession of faith at Caesarea, Lk 9:18, the Transfiguration, Lk 9:28-29, in Gethsemane, Mt 26:36-44, on the cross, Mt 27:46 and par.; Lk 23:46. He prays for his executioners, Lk 23:34; for Peter, Lk 22:32, for his disciples and those who will come after them, Jn 17:9-24. He prays also for himself, 26:39 and par., cf. Jn 17:1-5; Heb 5:7. These prayers show that he is in permanent touch with the Father, 11:25-27 and par., who never leaves him on his own, Jn 8:29, and always hears his prayer, Jn 11:22,42; cf. Mt 26:53. Both by this example and by his teaching, Jesus bore in upon his disciples the need and the way to pray, 6:5c. Now in glory he continues to intercede for his own, Rm 8:34; Heb 7:25; 1 Jn 2:1, as he promised, Jn 14:16.

g. Cf. Jn 6:19; var. 'far out on the sea'; cf. Mk 6:47.

h. 3 to 6 am.

i. Matthew deliberately punctuates the narrative section of his 'ecclesiastical book' (13:53-18:35) with three episodes featuring Peter: this passage, 16:16-20 and 17:24-27.

15 a. Oral tradition which, to safeguard the observance of the written Law, made many additions to it. It was held by the rabbis that these additions, being implicit in the Law, were part of the tradition going back through 'the elders' to Moses himself.

b. lit. 'eat bread'.

c. Implying a reverence shown in practical ways.

d. Because property thus made over by vow assumes a sacred character which precludes all claims made by the parents. Such a vow was in fact only a legal fiction involving no sacrifice of ownership; it was no more than a despicable way of escaping the duty of filial piety. Though the rabbis acknowledged its impiety they sustained its validity.

e. The Pharisees had objected to eating with unpurified hands, v. 2, but Jesus passes to the larger question of the legal impurity of certain foods, Lv 11. Legal impurity, he teaches, is secondary to moral, which is the only impurity that really matters, Ac 10:9-16,28; Rm 14:14seq.

f. It is significant that the gentile has to leave gentile territory and come onto the soil of Israel for the cure.

g. Not 'send her away' simply: the Greek verb here means 'let her go with her request granted', as in 18:27; 27:15.

h. Jesus' vocation is primarily to bring salvation to the Jews, 'children' of God and of the promises, before caring for the gentiles who were in the eyes of the Jews, only 'dogs'. The conventional nature of this expression and the diminutive form used lessen the insult of it in Jesus' mouth.

i. om. 'the cripples whole again'.

16 a. om. 'In the evening . . . of the times'. The 'times' are the messianic age; the 'signs' are the miracles worked by Jesus; cf. 11:3-5; 12:38.

b. As leaven ferments the dough, 13:33, but can also make it go bad, cf. 1 Co 5:6; Ga 5:9, so the false doctrine

of the Jewish leaders threatens to misguide those for whom they are responsible, cf. Mt 15:14.

c. Jesus claimed this title of 'prophet' only in a veiled and indirect way, 13:57 and par.; Lk 13:33, but the crowds gave it to him clearly, Mt 16:14 and par.; 21:11,46; Mk 6:15 and par.; Lk 7:16,39; 24:19; Jn 4:19; 9:17. The title had messianic overtones, for the spirit of prophecy, extinct since Malachi, was according to Jewish expectation to return as a sign of the messianic era, either in the person of Elijah, 17:10-11 and par., or in the form of a general outpouring of the Spirit, Ac 2:17-18,33. In fact in Jesus' time there were many (false) prophets, 24:11,24 and par. John the Baptist was truly a prophet, 11:9 and par.; 14:5; 21:26 and par.; Lk 1:76, but as a herald in the spirit of Elijah, Mt 11:10 and par., 14; 17:12 and par. He denied (Jn 1:21) that he was 'the Prophet' foretold by Moses, Dt 18:15, and it is in Jesus alone that Christian faith has recognised this Prophet, Jn 6:14; 7:40; Ac 3:22-26,26s. After Pentecost the spirit of prophecy spread throughout the Church, Ac 11:27m, and this title of Jesus soon yielded to other more specific christological titles.

d. In Mt Peter acknowledges not only that Jesus is the Messiah but also that he is Son of God; this second title is not found in Mk and Lk; compare 14:33 with Mk 6:51seq., *see* 4:3e.

e. lit. 'flesh and blood'. The expression indicates humanity, emphasising a material, limited nature as opposed to that of the spirit world, Si 14:18; Rm 7:5c; 1 Co 15:50; Ga 1:16; Ep 6:12; Heb 2:14; cf. Jn 1:13.

f. Neither the Greek word *petros* nor even, as it seems, its Aramaic equivalent *kepha* ('rock') was used as a personal name before Jesus conferred it on the apostles' leader to symbolise the part he was to play in the foundation of his community. This change of name had possibly been made earlier, *see* Mk 3:16; Lk 6:14; Jn 1:42.

g. The Hebr. *qahal* which the Gk renders *ekklesia* means 'an assembly called together'; it is used frequently in the OT to indicate the community of the chosen people, especially the community of the desert period, cf. Ac 7:38. Certain Jewish groups (among them the Essenes of Qumran) regarded themselves as the chosen remnant of Israel (Is 4:3c) which was to survive in 'the latter days'. These had also used the term that is now adopted to indicate the messianic community, the community of the 'new alliance' sealed with the blood of Jesus, 26:28f; Ep 5:25. By using the term 'community' side by side with that of 'kingdom of Heaven', 4:17f, Jesus shows that this eschatological community (community of the 'end-times') is to have its beginnings here on earth in the form of an organised society whose leader he now appoints; *see* Ac 5:11b; 1 Co 1:2a.

h. Gk: *Hades*; Hebrew: *sheol*, the dwelling-place of the dead, *see* Nb 16:33f. Here, its personified 'gates' suggest the powers of evil which first lead people into that death which is sin and then imprison them once for all in eternal death. The Church's task will be to rescue the elect from death's dominion, from the death of the body and above all from eternal death, so that it may lead them into the kingdom of Heaven, *see* 1 Co 15:26; Col 1:13; Rv 6:8; 20:13. In this the Church follows its Master who died, descended into the underworld, *see* 1 P 3:19h, and rose again, Ac 2:27,31.

i. The City of God, like the City of Death, has its gates too; they grant entrance only to those who are worthy of it. Peter has the keys. It is his function, therefore, to open or close to all who would come to the kingdom of Heaven through the Christian community. • 'bind' and 'loose' are technical rabbinic terms; primarily they have a disciplinary reference; one is 'bound' (condemned to) or 'loosed' (absolved from) excommunication. Their secondary usage is concerned with doctrinal or juridical decisions: an opinion is 'bound' (forbidden) or 'loosed' (allowed). Of the household of God Peter is controller (the keys symbolise this, cf. Is 22:22). In that capacity he is to exercise the disciplinary power of admitting or excluding those he thinks fit; he will also, in his administration of the community, make necessary doctrinal and juridical decisions. The verdicts he delivers and the pronouncements he makes will be ratified by God in heaven. Catholic exegetes maintain that these enduring promises hold good not only for Peter himself but also for Peter's successors. This inference, not explicitly drawn in the text, is considered legitimate because Jesus plainly intends to provide for the future of his community by establishing a structure that will not collapse with Peter's death. • Two other texts, Lk 22:31seq. and Jn 21:15seq., on Peter's primacy emphasise that its operation is to be in the domain of faith; they also indicate that this makes him head not only of the Church after the death of Jesus but of the apostolic group then and there.

j. Jesus has just elicited from his disciples the first explicit profession of faith in him as Messiah. At this crucial moment he tells them for the first time of his coming Passion: he is not only the glorious Messiah, he is also the suffering servant. Within the next few days this teaching method will be pursued in a similar situation: the glorious transfiguration will be followed by an injunction to silence and a prediction of the Passion, 17:1–12. It is Jesus' way of bracing the disciples' faith for the approaching crisis of death and resurrection.

k. By blocking the Messiah's appointed way, Peter becomes an 'obstacle' (primary sense of the Greek *skandalon*) to Christ and becomes, though unwittingly, the tool of Satan, cf. 4:1–10.

l. Paradox. This dictum and those immediately following oscillate between two senses of human 'life': its present stage and its future. The Greek *psyche*, here equivalent to the Hebr. *nephesh*, contains all three senses of 'life', 'soul', 'person'.

m. 'his behaviour'; var. 'his works'.

n. In vv. 27–28 two sayings of Jesus, each dealing with a different event, have been joined together because they have a common reference to the coming of the kingdom of God: v. 27, the kingdom of the Father; v. 28, the kingdom of Christ, *see* 24:1a.

17 a. In Mt's presentation, which differs from those of Mk 9:2 and Lk 9:28f, Jesus appears in his transfiguration above all as the new Moses, *see* Mt 4:1a, meeting God on a new Sinai in the cloud, Mt 17:5; Ex 24:15–18, with his face shining, Mt 17:2; Ex 34:29–35, cf. 2 Co 3:7–4:6, accompanied by two personalities of the OT who received revelations on Sinai, Ex 19:33; 34; 1 K 19:9–13, and personify the Law and the Prophets which Jesus came to bring to perfection, Mt 5:17. The heavenly voice commands that he should be listened to as the new Moses, Dt 18:15; *see also* Ac 3:20–26, and the disciples fall on their faces in reverence of the Master; cf. Mt 28:17. When the vision ends he remains alone, v. 8, for no one else is needed as perfect and definitive teacher of the Law. However, his glory is only transitory, for he is also the 'servant', v. 5; Is 42:1; *see* Mt 3:16–17,17o, who must suffer and die, Mt 16:21; 17:22–23, just like his precursor, Mt 17:9–13, before definitively entering into glory by the resurrection.

b. Tabor, according to the traditional opinion. Some favour Great Hermon.

c. var. 'as snow', *see* 28:3.

d. An alternative translation, 'It is a good thing for us to be here.'

e. The disciples know that the Messiah has already come, 16:16, and have seen him in his glory, 17:1–7; they are therefore surprised that Elijah has not played the part of Precursor assigned to him by Malachi. Jesus replies that Elijah has in fact performed that function, though unrecognised, in the person of the Baptist. *See* Lk 1:17l.

f. var. 'no faith'.

g. add. v. 21 'As for this kind (of devil), it is cast out only by prayer and fasting', cf. Mk 9:29.

h. A yearly tax levied on individuals for the upkeep of the Temple.

i. i.e. 'their subjects', cf. 13:38. Jesus makes a pun on

this semitic metaphorical use of 'son' in order to indicate himself, who is the Son, cf. 3:17; 17:5 and 10:32seq.; 11:25–27, together with his disciples who are his brothers, 12:50, and sons of the same Father, 5:45; *see* 4:3d.

j. This miraculous find of a precious object in a fish's mouth, which is not essential to the episode, has several parallels in Jewish and Gk folk-lore.

18 a. That is to say, one who through the virtue of simplicity becomes a child again, cf. v. 4.

b. lit. 'a snare', according to the primary meaning of the Gk word ('an occasion of falling', *see* 16:23k). • Vv. 8–9 are introduced here by means of this verbal link although they break the sequence of thought. They are already used in 5:29–30.

c. Eternal life.

d. Hebr. Ge-Hinnom, a valley outside Jerusalem once polluted by infant sacrifice, Lv 18:21h. Later the name was used for the place of damnation and punishment of the wicked—what we call 'hell'.

e. An OT expression meaning that the courtier is in the king's presence, cf. 2 S 14:24; 2 K 25:19; Tb 12:15. Here the accent is on the familiarity of the intercourse of the angels with God.

f. add. v. 11 'For the Son of man has come to save what was lost,' cf. Lk 19:10.

g. Many authorities add the specifying phrase 'to you', but it is probably to be omitted. The fault in question is grave and notorious; it has not necessarily been committed against the one whose duty it is to correct it. In v. 21 the case is different.

h. The *ekklesia*, i.e. the *qahal* or gathering of the brethren.

i. Outcasts with whom the pious Jew could not communicate. *see* 5:46u and 9:10e. Compare the excommunication of 1 Co 5:11h.

j. One of the powers conferred on Peter, 16:19, is here conferred also on the community.

k. Imitating God and Jesus, Lk 23:34k, and following the example of the Israelites, Lv 19:18–19; *see* Ex 21:25f, Christians must forgive each other, 5:39; 6:12 and par. (cf. 7:2); 2 Co 2:7; Ep 4:32; Col 3:13. But the 'neighbour' includes everyone, even those to whom one must return good for evil, 5:44–45; Rm 12:17–21; 1 Th 5:15; 1 P 3:9; *see* Ps 5:10c. Love covers over a great number of sins, Pr 10:12, quoted by Jm 5:20; 1 P 4:8.

l. Others render 'seventy-times-seven times', *see* 6:9d. Mt illustrates the lesson by a parable. Many of the parables proper to Mt are concerned with human relationships, illustrated by contrasting characters, *see* 20:1a; 21:28; 22:1a; 24:45w; 25:1a, 31e; Lk 15:11a.

m. Over $60,000,000: the amount is deliberately fantastic.

n. Less than $200.

19 a. Uncompromising assertion of the indissolubility of marriage.

b. In view of the absolute prohibition of the parallel passages, Mk 10:11seq.; Lk 16:18 and 1 Co 7:10seq., it is unlikely that all three have omitted an exceptive clause by Jesus, and more probable that one of the later editors of Mt should have added it in response to a rabbinic problem (a discussion between Hillel and Shammai of the reasons which make divorce legitimate) suggested also by the context, v. 3, which could have concerned the Judaeo-Christian circles for which he was writing. In this case we would have here an ecclesiastical decision of temporary and local application, like the Decree of Jerusalem concerning the district of Antioch, Ac 15:23–29. The meaning of *porneia* points in the same direction. Some take it to mean fornication within marriage, that is adultery, and consider it permissible to divorce in such cases; thus Orthodox and Protestant Churches. But for this sense one would expect another term, *moicheia*. By contrast *porneia* in this context seems to have the technical sense which *zenut* or 'prostitution' has in the rabbinic writings when used of a union incestuous because within the degrees forbidden by the Law, Lv 18. Such unions contracted legally between gentiles or tolerated by the Jews themselves between proselytes must have made difficulties in legalistic Judaeo-Christian circles like that of Mt. when people were converted; hence the instruction to break off such irregular unions which were no true marriages. • Another solution envisages that the freedom granted by the exceptive clause is not to divorce but to separate without remarriage. Such a situation was unknown in Judaism, but on occasion the demands of Jesus did lead to new situations, and this one is clearly presupposed by 1 Co 7:11.

c. Christ invites to perpetual continence as an expression of total consecration to the kingdom of God.

d. var. 'Good Master', see Mk and Lk.

e. i.e. God (explicit in Mk and Lk and Vulg. Mt). Another reading, borrowed from Mk and Lk, is 'Why do you call me good? None is good but God alone.'

f. add. 'from my earliest days', see Mk and Lk.

g. Jesus is not founding a new order of 'perfect disciples', superior to ordinary Christians. The 'perfection' envisaged is that of the new dispensation, which surpasses the old by completing it, see 5:17h. All are called to it equally, see 5:48. But, in order to establish the kingdom, Jesus needs fellow-workers who are especially available; it is from these that he asks radical renunciation of the cares of family life, 18:12, and possessions, 8:19–20.

h. The reference is to the messianic 'renewal of all things' which is to be revealed when the world ends but which, on the spiritual plane, will already have begun when Christ rises from the dead as *Kyrios* in the Church.

i. In the OT sense of 'governors'. The 'twelve tribes' may be regarded as the new Israel, the Church.

j. add. 'wnte'.

20 a. The owner of the vineyard goes on into the evening hiring workmen and yet gives all a full day's pay. He is generous to some without being unjust to the others. So God acts. Into his kingdom he brings late-comers—sinners and gentiles. Those who were called first (the Jewish people who, from Abraham's time, had been privileged with the covenant) have no right to be offended.

b. add. 'For many are called, but few are chosen', probably borrowed from 22:14.

c. The apostles expect Jesus' kingdom to be manifested very shortly and in all its glory, but this is reserved for Christ's second coming, see 4:17f; Ac 1:6h.

d. Biblical metaphor for suffering, see Is 51:17, here referring to the approaching Passion.

e. James son of Zebedee was put to death by Herod Agrippa about the year 44, Ac 12:2. His brother John may not indeed have suffered martyrdom but he had no less a share in his Master's sufferings.

f. Jesus' mission on earth is not to apportion human rewards but to suffer for human salvation, see Jn 3:17; 12:47.

g. By sin human beings incur, as a debt to the divine justice, the punishment of death demanded by the Law, see Rm 8:3–4; 1 Co 15:56; 2 Co 3:7,9; Ga 3:13, with notes. To ransom them from this slavery of sin and death, Rm 3:24j, Jesus is to pay the ransom and discharge the debt with the price of his blood, 1 Co 6:20; 7:23; Ga 3:13; 4:5, with notes. By thus dying in place of the guilty, he fulfils the prophesied function of the 'servant of Yahweh' (Is 53). The Hebr. word translated 'many', Is 53:11seq., 11h, contrasts the enormous crowd of the redeemed with the one Redeemer: it does not imply that the number of redeemed is limited, Rm 5:6–21, see also Mt 26:28i.

h. At this point some authorities insert the following passage, derived probably from some apocryphal gospel 'But as for you, from littleness you seek to grow great and from greatness you make yourselves small. When you are invited to a banquet do not take one of the places of honour, because someone more important than you may arrive and

then the steward will have to say, "Move down lower," and you would be covered with confusion. Take the lowest place, and then if someone less important than you comes in, the steward will say to you, "Move up higher," and that will be to your advantage.' Cf. Lk 14:8–10.

21 a. In thus describing the messianic king's humble mount the prophet had in mind the unpretentious, unwarlike nature of his rule. Jesus, by performing this action, deliberately took to himself both the words of the prophecy and their deeper meaning.

b. A word of Hebr. origin; its first meaning is 'Please, save' but it became a mere shout of acclamation.

c. They provided pilgrims with the coinage and sacrificial victims necessary for oblations: a practice which, however legitimate, lent itself to abuse. Or the expulsion of the traders may simply be seen as part of the messianic gesture of cleansing the Temple and insisting on the primitive purity of its worship.

d. 'It was not the season for figs,' Mk says. But Jesus meant to perform a symbolic action, see Jr 18:1a, in which the fig tree represents Israel punished for its fruitlessness.

e. The unusual events that Jesus has just allowed to take place in the very precincts of the Temple: the messianic ovation, expulsion of the merchants, miraculous cures.

f. An OT expression: John practised and preached that conformity to the will of God makes a person 'upright'.

g. More exactly an 'allegory' because every detail of the story has its own significance: the proprietor is God; the vineyard the chosen people, Israel, see Is 5:1a; the servants the prophets; the son Jesus, put to death outside the walls of Jerusalem; the murderous farmers the faithless Jews; the nation to which the vineyard will be entrusted, the gentiles. Not all these allegorical features are present in Mk's version (e.g. the son's body is thrown out only after his death), but Mt does need to allegorise.

h. add. v. 44 'Anyone who falls on this stone will be dashed to pieces; anyone it falls on will be crushed,' probably a gloss taken from Lk 20:18.

22 a. A parable with allegorical features; in this, as in the lesson it teaches, it resembles the one that precedes it. The king is God; the wedding feast is the happiness of the messianic age and the king's son the Messiah; those sent with invitations are the prophets and the apostles; the invited who ignore them or do them violence are the Jews; those called in from the street are the sinners and the gentiles; the burning of the city is the destruction of Jerusalem. At v. 11 the scene changes to that of the Last Judgement. Matthew, it seems, has combined two parables; one akin to Lk 14:16–24 and another whose concluding verses are found in vv. 11f; these verses explain that the man who accepted the invitation should have been dressed for the occasion—in other words, good works must go with faith, cf. 3:8; 5:20; 7:21seq.; 13:47seq.; 21:28seq.

b. This sentence appears to refer to the first part of the parable rather than to the second. It is a question not of the elect as a whole but of the Jews, the first to be invited. The parable (of vv. 1–10) neither asserts nor denies that some (a 'few') of the Jewish people have accepted the invitation and are 'chosen', see 24:22k.

c. Supporters of the Herodian dynasty, Mk 3:6a, the most suitable people to report to the Roman authorities what they hoped to induce Jesus to say against Caesar.

d. In practice they acknowledge the authority and accept the benefits of Roman government of which this coin is a symbol. Hence it is permissible, indeed it is a duty, for them to pay to that government the tribute of their obedience and of their property so long as this does not encroach on what they owe to the overriding authority of God.

e. This sect, 3:7g, adhered rigidly to the written tradition, especially as contained in the Pentateuch; its members were confident that the doctrine of the resurrection of the body, see 2 M 7:9c, was not to be found in that tradition.

On this point the Pharisees were opposed to the Sadducees. See Ac 4:1a; 23:8c.

f. When God adopts a person (or a people) into that relationship which is called becoming 'his' God, that relationship cannot be so incomplete or so transient that it will allow the person to fall away into nothingness. The necessarily eternal character of God's love was not understood in the earlier ages of the long revelation unfolded in the Bible and the belief continued in 'Sheol', an underworld of shades from which there was no resurrection. Is 38:10-20; Ps 6:5; 88:10-12. To this belief the conservative traditionalism of the Sadducees, Ac 23:8c, claimed to remain faithful. But the progress of Revelation gradually brought a deeper understanding, Ps 16:10-11; 49:15; 73:24, proclaiming a renewal of life. Ws 3:1-9, for everyone; salvation extends even to the body. 2 M 7:9seq.; 12:43-46; 14:46; Dn 12:2-3. It is this last stage of revelation which Jesus approves by showing that in God's plan it was already contained within the old formula of Ex 3:6.

g. add. 'a lawyer', probably borrowed from Lk 10:25.

h. These two commandments of love of God and the neighbour are also associated in the *Didache* 1:2, which could be drawing on a Jewish work on the Two Ways, see 7:13d.

i. The appropriate answer would have been that, though tracing his human origin back to David, see 1:1-17, there would be something divine about the Messiah to set him above David.

23 a. In so far, no doubt, as they hand on the traditional doctrine that goes back to Moses. Jesus in this does not speak of their own interpretations; he has shown elsewhere how these are to be assessed, see 15:1-20; 16:6; 19:3-9.

b. The phylactery is a small receptacle containing the most important words of the Law; the Jews attach it to arm or forehead, carrying out the injunction of Ex 13:9,16; Dt 6:8; 11:18 literally. The four tassels were sewn one at each corner of the cloak, see Nb 15:38c.

c. Aramaic word meaning 'my master', the usual title of the Jewish teacher. Jesus himself was thus addressed by his disciples, 26:25,49.

d. Vv. 8-12, addressed to the disciples only, probably did not belong originally to this discourse.

e. Abba in Aramaic; another title of honour.

f. Perhaps an allusion to the religious leader of the community of Qumran, the 'Teacher of Righteousness'.

g. The exacting casuistry of the rabbis made observance of the Law impossible.

h. add. v. 14 'Alas for you, scribes and Pharisees, you hypocrites! You who devour the property of widows, though you make a show of lengthy prayers. The more severe will be the sentence you receive'—this is an interpolation taken from Mk 12:40; Lk 20:47 and making eight maledictions instead of the deliberate total of seven, see 6:9d.

i. A gentile convert to Judaism. Jewish propaganda was extremely active in the Graeco-Roman world.

j. To release people from injudicious oaths the rabbis used to invoke tortuous reasoning.

k. The Mosaic Law levied tithes on agricultural produce; the rabbis piously applied the precept to the most insignificant of garden herbs.

l. var. 'inside you are full'. • 'intemperance': var. 'iniquity', 'impurity', 'cupidity'.

m. Allusion to Jesus' own death soon to take place, cf. 21:38seq.

n. Terms of Jewish origin but here applied to Christian missionaries, cf. 10:41; 13:52.

o. The one referred to is probably the Zechariah of 2 Ch 24:20-22. His murder is the last one to be described in the Bible (2 Ch being the last book of the Jewish Canon) while Abel's, Gn 4:8, is the first. It is possible that 'son of Berechiah' is the result of confusion with another Zechariah, see Is 8:2 (LXX); Zc 1:1. Alternatively, the words may be a copyist's gloss.

p. *See* 1 K 19:10,14; 2 Ch 24:20-22; Jr 26:20-23;

Ac 7:52; 1 Th 2:15; Heb 11:37; and Jewish apocryphal legends.

q. Allusion to repeated visits to Jerusalem on which the Synoptics are silent but which are reported by Jn.

r. In a little while Jesus will be with them no longer. he is to be rejected by his own people: so also will God abandon Jerusalem and its Temple.

s. In Lk 13:35 Jesus seems to mean that the Jews will not see him again until the entry into Jerusalem on Palm Sunday (Lk 19:28seq.). In Mt's context the words probably refer to a later coming than this, perhaps the triumphant coming at the end of time: the reconciled Jews will acclaim this return, cf. Rm 11:25seq.

24 a. According to the most probable interpretation, this eschatological discourse of Mt combines the announcement of the destruction of Jerusalem with that of the end of the world. Therefore the discourse of Mk, which is concerned only with the former event, is supplemented in three ways: 1 The addition of vv. 26-28,37-41, taken from a discourse on the Day of the Son of man, which Lk also uses, Lk 17:22-37. 2 Alterations which introduce the themes of the *parousia*, vv. 3,27,37,39 (never elsewhere in the gospels, see 24:3b; 1 Co 15:23n), of the 'End of the World', v. 3; cf. 13:39,40,49, and of the 'sign of the Son of man' which affects all nations of the world, v. 30. 3 The addition at the end of the discourse of several parables on watchfulness, 24:42-25:30, which prepare for the return of Jesus and the great final judgement, 25:31-46. Their fusion in this way is a theological expression of truth: though separated in time, these two are inseparable in the sense that the first is the inevitable forerunner and prefiguration of the second. The destruction of Jerusalem marks the end of the old covenant—Christ has thus manifestly returned to inaugurate his kingly rule. Such a decisive intervention in the history of salvation will not occur again until the end of time when God will judge the whole human race, now chosen in Christ, with the same judgement he pronounced (in AD 70) upon the first chosen people.

b. The Greek word is *parousia*; it means 'presence' and in the Graeco-Roman world was used for official visits by royalty. The Christian adopted it as a technical term for the glorious coming of Christ, see 1 Co 15:23n. It is not inevitably linked up with Christ's *final* coming; it can also refer to the power he will display when he comes to establish his messianic kingdom (the Church); see 16:27-28. In this passage Matthew clearly implies that he has combined the two themes.

c. Before the year 70 several impostors posed as messiahs.

d. add. 'plagues', cf. Lk 21:11.

e. Cf. 2 Ch 15:6; Is 8:21seq.; 13:13; 19:2; Jr 21:9; 34:17; Ezk 5:12; Am 4:6-11.

f. Cf. Is 13:8; 26:17; 66:7; Jr 6:24; 13:21; Ho 13:13; Mi 4:9-10. Jewish literature uses this metaphor to describe the coming of the messianic kingdom.

g. The 'inhabited world' (*oikoumene*), i.e. the Graeco-Roman world. All the Jews of the empire are destined to hear the good news before punishment comes to Israel, see Rm 10:18. The earliest 'witness' will be directed against those Jews who refuse to believe, cf. 10:18. Before AD 70 the gospel had already reached the main parts of the Roman empire, cf. Rm 1:5,8; Col 1:6,23; 1 Th 1:8.

h. The fall of Jerusalem.

i. Daniel probably refers to the statue of Zeus set up in Jerusalem by Antiochus Epiphanes (in 167 BC; see 1 M 1:54r). The prophecy is here applied to the siege and capture of the holy city by the gentile armies from Rome, cf. Lk 21:20.

j. Cf Ex 10:14; 11:6; 1 M 9:27; Jr 30:7; Ba 2:2; Dn 12:1; Jl 2:2; Rv 16:18.

k. Those among the Jews who are called to enter the kingdom of God: the 'remnant', see Is 4:3c; Rm 11:5-7.

l. The coming of the Messiah will be as unmistakable as lightning. Lightning is a characteristic phenomenon that goes with divine judgement, see Ps 97:4; Is 29:6; 30:30; Zc 9:14.

m. Perhaps a proverb expressing the same idea of unmistakable manifestation: a corpse, even hidden in the desert, is immediately indicated by the circling vultures.

n. Join with v. 25; vv. 26–28 are a digression.

o. Cf. Jr 4:23–26; Ezk 32:7seq.; Jl 2:10; 3:4; 4:15; Am 8:9; Mi 1:3–4 and especially Is 13:9–10; 34:4; the text repeats the phrases of the last two references. The 'powers of heaven' are the stars and all the other celestial forces.

p. It would be a mistake to look for too exact an interpretation of this sign. The whole passage expresses in highly allusive apocalyptic imagery the certainty that the kingdom will reach its goal in spite of all persecutions and adversity.

q. In these words Daniel foretold the establishment of the messianic kingdom by a Son of man coming on the clouds. The cloud is the usual accompaniment of both OT and NT theophanies: Ex 13:22h; 19:16g; 34:5; Lv 16:2; 1 K 8:10–11; 2 M 2:8; Ps 18:11; 97:2; 104:3; Is 19:1; Jr 4:13; Ezk 1:4; 10:3seq. For NT see 17:5; Ac 1:9,11; 1 Th 4:17; Rv 1:7; 14:14.

r. add. 'and a voice'.

s. lit. 'from the four winds, from the ends of the heavens to their ends', a composite formula from Dt 30:4 and Zc 2:10, texts which treat of the reunion of scattered Israel, cf. Ne 1:9 and Ezk 37:9. See also Is 27:13. Here, therefore, as in vv. 22 and 24, the 'chosen' are those Jews that Yahweh will rescue from the ruin of their nation in order to admit them, along with the gentiles, into his kingdom, v. 30.

t. The Son of man coming to establish his kingdom.

u. This statement refers to the destruction of Jerusalem and not to the end of the world. In the course of his preaching Jesus probably made the distinction between these two things clearer, see 16:28n and 24:1a.

v. om. (many MSS) 'nor the Son'; no doubt for the sake of theological scruples. As man Jesus had no clear knowledge of the details of future history. The evangelists often read back into the lifetime of Jesus the knowledge and understanding of his significance which the disciples later received by the full light of the Holy Spirit, see Jn 1:48dd; Mt 8:20h; 16:16d, and this shows itself in a tendency to make more explicit the details of his predictions of the future, cf. the three formal and detailed prophecies of the Passion and Resurrection, Mk 8:31; 9:31–32; 10:32–34 par., which show a state of knowledge which makes both Jesus' own agony at his approaching Passion, Mk 14:33 par., and the disciples' fear and desertion, Mk 14:50 par.; Mt 26:31l, difficult to understand. Nevertheless the full humanity of Jesus, Ph 2:7g, included the human experiences of learning, Lk 2:52, and of ignorance, compare 26:39o.

w. After the discourse foretelling the destruction of Jerusalem and the visible coming of the messianic reign, Matthew adds three parables dealing with the ultimate fate of individuals. The first presents one of Christ's servants who, like the apostles, is given a task to perform; he is judged on the way he performs it.

x. A word of uncertain meaning; probably to be taken metaphorically: 'he will cut him off', a sort of 'excommunication', cf. 18:17.

25 a. The wedding attendants (lit. 'virgins') represent Christians waiting for Christ. Even if he is slow to come, they must be watchful, i.e. keep their lamps ready.

b. add. 'and the bride'.

c. Christians are servants expected by Jesus, their master, to make full use of any gifts he has given them so that his kingdom may grow on earth; they must give an account of this administration. The parable of the pounds, Lk 19:12–27, has a similar form but a rather different moral.

d. The happiness of the heavenly banquet, 8:11c. • 'I will trust you with greater things' implies an active sharing with Christ in his reign.

e. The perspective changes: it is now a question of Christ's last coming at the end of the world.

f. Every human being of every period of history. The resurrection of the dead does not need to be mentioned, cf. 10:15; 11:22,24; 12:41seq.

g. Christ, the Messiah-King, ushers the elect from his own kingdom into that of his Father, 13:43k.

h. People are judged by their works of mercy (here described in OT terms, cf. Jb 22:6seq.; Si 7:32seq.; Is 58:7) not by their occasional exploits, cf. 7:22seq. In addition to these meritorious acts we find in 10:32seq. the profession of faith.

26 a. In Jn, the woman of this episode is named as Mary, the sister of Lazarus; the event described in Lk 7:36–50 is not the same.

b. The Jews divided 'good works' into 'almsgiving' and 'charitable deeds'; the latter were reckoned superior and included, among other pious acts, the burial of the dead. The woman, therefore, by making provision for Jesus' burial, has performed a 'work' greater than almsgiving. Jesus seems to suggest, v. 12, that some loving instinct has given her a presentiment of the real significance of her action.

c. Thirty shekels—and not thirty denarii as is commonly said. It was the price the Law fixed for a slave's life, Ex 21:32.

d. The 'first day' of the week during which unleavened loaves (azymes) were eaten, see Ex 12:1a; 23:14d, was normally that which followed the Passover supper, i.e. the 15th of Nisan; the Synoptics, however, give this title to the preceding day, thus attesting a wider use of the term. Further, if we take account of Jn 18:28 and of other details connected with the Passion, it seems fairly certain that in this particular year the Passover supper was celebrated on the evening of the Friday (or 'Preparation Day', 27:62; see Jn 19:14,31,42). Christ's Last Supper, which the Synoptics put on the day before, i.e. on the Thursday evening, must therefore be explained in one of two ways: either a whole section of the Jewish people thus anticipated the rite, or (and this is preferable) Christ anticipated it on his own initiative. In this second hypothesis Jesus, unable to celebrate the Passover on the Friday (though, indeed, he celebrated it in his own person on the cross, Jn 19:36u; 1 Co 5:7), instituted his new rite in the course of a supper which, in consequence, became endowed with the characteristics of the old Passover. Nisan 14th (the day of the Passover supper) fell on a Friday in AD 30 and 33; interpreters therefore take one or other of these years as the date of Christ's death according as they assign his baptism to 28 or to 29 and reckon a longer or shorter public ministry.

e. The first course; it preceded the Passover supper properly so called.

f. They have come to the Passover supper itself. The rubrics for this solemn blessing of bread and wine are laid down exactly; onto this ceremony Jesus grafts the sacramental rites of the new religious order of things which he institutes.

g. 'Returned thanks' represents the Greek verb *eucharisto*, the noun from which has been adopted as a name for the whole action which re-creates the Last Supper.

h. add. (some MSS and versions) 'new', cf. Lk 22:20; 1 Co 11:25.

i. As at Sinai, the blood of victims sealed the covenant of Yahweh with his people, Ex 24:4–8c, so on the cross the blood of Jesus, the perfect victim, is about to seal the 'new' covenant, cf. Lk 22:20, between God and humanity—the covenant foretold by the prophets, Jr 31:31l. Jesus takes on himself the task of universal redemption that Isaiah assigns to the 'servant of Yahweh', Is 42:6; 49:6; 53:12, see 41:8f; cf. Heb 8:8; 9:15; 12:24. The idea of a new covenant comes also in Paul in a number of contexts quite apart from 1 Co 11:25, which shows its great importance, 2 Co 3:4–6; Ga 3:15–20; 4:24.

j. Allusion to the eschatological banquet, cf. 8:11;

22:1seq. Jesus and his disciples will never meet at table again.

k. The psalms of the Hallel, Ps 113–18, with which the Passover meal closed.

l. lit. 'be brought down'; it will be an obstacle for their faith when they see the one they believe to be Messiah, 16:16, and whose approaching triumph they expect, 20:21seq., passively yield to his enemies. For a time it will make them lose courage and even faith, cf. Lk 22:31–32.

m. The name means 'oilpress'. It lies in the Kidron valley at the foot of the Mt of Olives.

n. The turn of phrase recalls Ps 42:5 and Jon 4:9.

o. Jesus feels the full force of the human fear of death; he feels the instinctive urge to escape, gives expression to it and then stifles it by his acceptance of the Father's will, see 4:1a.

p. Gently ironical reproach: The hour you should have stayed awake with me has slipped by. Now the testing-time has begun and Jesus must go through it alone; the disciples may go on sleeping if they wish.

q. lit. 'Friend, for what you are here.' Instead of a question ('Why are you here?') or a reproach ('For what purpose are you here!') one may prefer to see in this a stereotyped phrase meaning 'do what you are here for', 'to your work!' Jesus cuts short the empty show of greeting: it is time for action, cf. Jn 13:27.

r. The accounts of Luke and of John enable us to distinguish: a preliminary hearing before Annas, at night time, and a solemn session of the Sanhedrin on the following morning, 27:1. Matthew and Mark describe the night episode in terms of the morning one which was the only formal and decisive meeting. But for an alternative chronology, see 26:17d.

s. Central to Jesus' message was the provisional nature of the Jewish cult, which was to be perfected by his own new covenant. As Jn 2:22i makes clear, the full significance of his statement became clear only after his resurrection. A new Temple was to be substituted for the old one, and this was to be, in the first place, his own body risen after three days, 16:21; 17:23; 20:19; Jn 2:19–22, but beyond that, it was to be the Church, Mt 16:18.

t. var. Some versions presents this as one question 'Do you make no answer to the evidence these men are bringing against you?'

u. 'The Power' is equivalent to 'Yahweh', see 3:2d. The Gospel shows Jesus at this critical moment abandoning his policy of the messianic secret, see Mk 1:34m, and unequivocally accepting the title of Messiah, although making clear that he is Messiah not in the traditional sense of a political liberator, but in the sense of the glorious personage whom Daniel had seen in vision, Dn 7:13k. With this allusion to Dn is combined reference to Ps 110:1, which features so largely in the apostolic preaching, see Ac 2:33t. Since this understanding of the expression 'Son of man' stems probably from the evangelists rather than from Jesus himself, see 8:20h, it is probable also that the evangelists are responsible for this underlining of the significance of this scene: Jesus was rejected and condemned as a messianic claimant although he in fact avoided the title because of its political overtones. It is only in the apostolic preaching after Pentecost that Jesus' disciples explicitly acknowledge him as Messiah.

v. It is difficult to decide precisely what the blasphemy was: not the claim to be Messiah; perhaps the claim to be Son of God though under arrest.

w. Mt's editing is awkward, for, not being blindfolded as in Lk 22:63, Jesus can easily indicate who hit him. The central point is that he is mocked as 'prophet' because of his saying about the Temple, and perhaps more precisely as 'Prophet-Messiah' (this address to Jesus as 'Christ' is unique in the gospel), that is as claimant to be the eschatological High Priest who proposes to found a new Temple.

x. Nazoraios; var. Nazarenos.

y. The Galilean accent.

27 a. var. 'Pontius Pilate', see Lk 3:1b. • In Judaea, as in all the provinces of the Empire, Rome reserved to itself power of life and death; the Jews had to approach this magistrate to gain any legal standing for the decision they had made; they themselves could not pronounce sentence.

b. var. 'upright' blood', cf. 23:35.

c. In Aramaic hakeldama (cf. Ac 1:19). A very ancient tradition locates it in the Valley of Gehinnom.

d. om. 'Jeremiah'. Actually this is a free quotation from Zc 11:12–13 combined with the idea of the purchase of a field, an idea suggested by Jr 32:6–15. This, plus the fact that Jeremiah speaks of potters (Jr 18:2seq.) who lived in the Hakeldama district (Jr 19:1seq.), explains how the whole text could by approximation be attributed to Jeremiah.

e. Yahweh complained that, in the person of his prophet Zechariah, he had received from the Israelites a wage that was nothing but an insult. The sale of Jesus for the same paltry sum appeals to Matthew as a fulfilment of this saying of the prophet.

f. By these words Jesus acknowledges as correct, at least in a sense, what he would never have said on his own initiative. See above 26:25,64; and cf. Jn 18:33–37.

g. Here and in v. 17, var. 'Jesus Barabbas', which would give peculiar point to Pilate's question but appears to have its origin in an apocryphal tradition.

h. The significance of this gesture must have been well understood by the Jews, see Dt 21:6seq.; Ps 26:6; 73:13.

i. var. 'of the blood of this righteous man'.

j. Traditional OT phrase, 2 S 1:16; 3:28–9, cf. Ac 18:6, by which they accept responsibility for the death they demand.

k. In Roman practice the normal prelude to crucifixion.

l. The Praetorium, or residence of the praetor, was probably the former palace of King Herod the Great in which the procurator used to reside whenever he went up from Caesarea to Jerusalem. This palace, situated in the west quarter of the city, was not the family residence of the Hasmonaeans: this was near the Temple and in it Herod Antipas probably received Jesus, sent to him by Pilate, Lk 23:7–12. Some commentators think that the Praetorium was in the fortress called Antonia, to the north of the Temple. But this accords neither with the custom of the procurators as it is known to us from the ancient texts, nor with the usage of the word 'praetorium' which cannot move around like this, nor with the movements of Pilate and the Jewish crowd in the gospel narratives of the Passion, especially that of Jn.

m. The Roman soldier's cloak (sagum); being red it suggested the imperial purple to the mocking soldiery.

n. The Jews had mocked Jesus as 'Prophet', 26:68seq.; the Romans mock him as 'King'. These two scenes well reflect the two aspects, religious and political, of the trial of Jesus.

o. Approximate transliteration of the Aramaic word gulgoltha, 'a place of the skull', in Lat. Calvaria (whence 'Calvary').

p. A narcotic which compassionate Jewish women used to offer the condemned to diminish their sufferings. The wine was mixed with 'myrrh' (cf. Mk 15:23) rather than with 'gall'. The 'gall' in Mt (like the correction of 'wine' to 'vinegar' in the Antiochene recension) is due to a reminiscence of Ps 69:21. Jesus refuses the palliative.

q. add. 'that the saying of the prophet might be fulfilled: they divided my garments between them and for my robe they cast lots' (Ps 22:18), a gloss taken from Jn 19:24.

r. From noon until three in the afternoon.

s. A cry of real distress but not of despair: this lament which Jesus takes from the scriptures is a prayer to God and is followed in the Psalm by an expression of joyful confidence in final victory.

t. Malicious play on words based on the expectation of Elijah as the Messiah's precursor, see 17:10–13e, or on the Jewish belief that he would come to help the upright in their hour of need.

u. Sour drink of the Roman soldier. Probably the gesture was sympathetic, cf. Jn 19:28seq.; the Synoptics regard it as malevolent (Lk 23:36) and describe it in terms that recall Ps 69:21.

v. Either the curtain which hung in front of the Holy Place or, more probably, the one which divided the Holy Place from the Holy of Holies, see Ex 26:31seq. Following Heb 9:12; 10:20, Christian tradition saw in this tearing of the veil the abrogation of the old Mosaic cult and the way opened up by Christ into the messianic sanctuary.

w. The evangelist deliberately describes the circumstances surrounding the crucifixion in terms drawn from prophetic descriptions of the 'Day of Yahweh', see Am 8:9h.

x. This resurrection of the upright is in the OT a sign of the eschatological era (Is 26:19; Ezk 37; Dn 12:2). Freed from Hades by the death of Jesus, see Mt 16:18h, they wait for his resurrection to enter with him the Holy City, that is the Heavenly Jerusalem (Rv 21:2,10; 22:19); this was how the early Fathers understood it. This is the first expression of faith in the liberation of the dead by Christ's descent into hell, see 1 P 3:19h.

y. The fact that the shroud was 'clean' and the tomb 'new' stress that the burial was an act of piety. The latter feature also shows how the burial was possible, for the corpse of an executed man could not be placed in a tomb already in use, where it would have defiled the bones of the upright.

z. Greek *paraskeue* ('preparation') meaning Friday, i.e. the day when preparations were made for the Sabbath.

aa. i.e. either 'Use your own guard', see Lk 22:4c, or 'I put a guard at your disposal', cf. Jn 18:3.

28 a. And not 'On the Sabbath evening' (Vulg.). Since the Sabbath was the day of rest, the 'first day of the (Jewish) week' corresponds to our Sunday (Rv 1:10), *dies dominica*, or the 'day of the Lord' so named in memory of the resurrection. See Ac 20:7k; 1 Co 16:2.

b. 'Mary, mother of James', Mk 16:1; Lk 24:10; cf. Mt 27:56 and 61.

c. In Mt. the tomb is sealed and guarded; the women therefore have not come to anoint the body of Jesus, as in Mk and Lk, but only to 'visit' the tomb.

d. 'he'; var. 'the Lord'.

e. var. 'came quickly out of the tomb', see Mk 16:8.

f. Though they agree in recording the initial apparition of an angel (or angels) to the women (28:5–7; Mk 16:5–7; Lk 24:4–7; Jn 20:12–13), the four gospels show divergencies when it comes to the appearances of Christ. Setting Mark aside (his abrupt conclusion presents a special problem, see Mk 16:8b, and his 'longer ending' recapitulates the data of the other gospels) all the gospels make a clear distinction,

both literary and doctrinal, between: 1 Appearances to individuals that help to prove the fact of the resurrection; to Mary Magdalen, either alone (Jn 20:14–17; cf. Mk 16:9), or accompanied (Mt 28:9–10); to the disciples on the road to Emmaus (Lk 24:13–32; cf. Mk 16:12); to Simon (Lk 24:34); to Thomas (Jn 20:26–29). 2 A collective appearance that is coupled with an apostolic mission (28:16–20; Lk 24:36–49; Jn 20:19–23; see also Mk 16:14–18). As well as this distinction there are two traditions as to where the appearances took place: 1 All in Galilee (28:10,16–20; Mk 16:7). 2 All in Judaea (Lk and Jn 20). By way of appendix, Jn 21 adds an appearance in Galilee which, though it bears the character of an appearance to individuals (it is for Peter and John predominantly), is nevertheless coupled with an apostolic mission (given to Peter). The primitive apostolic preaching that Paul reproduces in 1 Co 15:3–7 lists five appearances (apart from the appearance to Paul himself) which are not easily harmonised with the gospel accounts; in particular he mentions an appearance to James of which the *Gospel to the Hebrews* also speaks. All this gives the impression that different groups, which cannot now be easily identified, have given rise to different strands of tradition. But these very divergencies of tradition are far better witnesses than any artificial or contrived uniformity to the antiquity of the evidence and the historical quality of all these manifestations of the risen Christ.

g. An alternative translation with less grammatical support: 'those who had hesitated'. On the doubts Mt mentions here cf. Mk 16:11,14; Lk 24:11,41; Jn 20:24–29.

h. In these last instructions of Jesus, with the ensuing promise, is contained the apostolic mission of the Church. The glorified Christ wields power on earth just as in heaven, 6:10; cf. Jn 17:2; Ph 2:10; Rv 12:10, limitless power, Mt 7:29; 9:6; 21:23, received from his Father, see Jn 3:35t. His disciples 'therefore' wield this power in his name by baptising and forming Christians. Their mission is universal: after having first been proclaimed to the people of Israel, 10:5f; 15:24, as the divine plan demanded, salvation must then be offered to all nations, 8:11; 21:41; 22:8–10; 24:14,30seq.; 25:32; 26:13; see Ac 1:8i; 13:5e; Rm 1:16h. In this work of universal conversion, however long and laborious, the risen Lord will be present and active with his own.

i. This formula is probably a reflection of the liturgical usage established later in the primitive community. It will be remembered that Ac speaks of baptising 'in the name of Jesus', see Ac 1:5f. The attachment of the baptised person to all three persons of the Trinity will have been made explicit only later. But whatever the variation in formula, the underlying reality remains the same. Baptism attaches a person to Jesus the Saviour; all his work of salvation proceeds from the Father's love and reaches its completion in the outpouring of the Spirit.

THE GOSPEL ACCORDING TO

MARK

I: PRELUDE TO THE PUBLIC MINISTRY OF JESUS

The proclamation of John the Baptist

1, 2 **1** The beginning of the gospel *a* about Jesus Christ, the Son of God. *b* •It is written in the prophet Isaiah:

> *Look, I am going to send my messenger in front of you*
> *to prepare your way before you.*

3   *A voice of one that cries in the desert:*
> *Prepare a way for the Lord,*
> *make his paths straight.*

4 John the Baptist was in the desert, proclaiming a baptism of repentance for the
5 forgiveness of sins. •All Judaea and all the people of Jerusalem made their way to him, and as they were baptised by him in the river Jordan they confessed their
6 sins. John wore a garment of camel-skin, *c* and he lived on locusts and wild honey.
7 In the course of his preaching he said, 'After me is coming someone who is more powerful than me, and I am not fit to kneel down and undo the strap of his sandals.
8 I have baptised you with water, but he will baptise you with the Holy Spirit.'

Jesus is baptised

9 It was at this time that Jesus came from Nazareth in Galilee and was baptised in
10 the Jordan by John. •And at once, as he was coming up out of the water, he saw
11 the heavens torn apart and the Spirit, like a dove, descending on him. •And a voice came from heaven, 'You are my Son, the Beloved; my favour rests on you.'

Testing in the desert *d*

12, 13 And at once the Spirit drove him into the desert •and he remained there for forty days, and was put to the test by Satan. He was with the wild animals, and the angels looked after him.

II: THE GALILEAN MINISTRY

Jesus begins to proclaim the message

14 After John had been arrested, Jesus went into Galilee. There he proclaimed the
15 gospel from God saying, ·'The time is fulfilled, ͨ and the kingdom of God is close
at hand. Repent, and believe the gospel.'

The first four disciples are called

16 As he was walking along by the Lake of Galilee he saw Simon and Simon's brother
17 Andrew casting a net in the lake—for they were fishermen. ·And Jesus said to
18 them, 'Come after me ͟ and I will make you into fishers of people.' ·And at once
they left their nets and followed him.

19   Going on a little further, he saw James son of Zebedee and his brother John;
20 they too were in their boat, mending the nets. At once he called them and, leaving
their father Zebedee in the boat with the men he employed, they went after him.

Jesus teaches in Capernaum and cures a demoniac

21 They went as far as Capernaum, and at once on the Sabbath he went into the
22 synagogue and began to teach. ·And his teaching made a deep impression on them
because, unlike the scribes, he taught them with authority.

23   And at once in their synagogue there was a man with an unclean spirit, ͢ and he
24 shouted, ·'What do you want with us, ͪ Jesus of Nazareth? Have you come ͥ to
25 destroy us? I know who you are: the Holy One of God.' ͫ ·But Jesus rebuked it
26 saying, 'Be quiet! Come out of him!' ·And the unclean spirit threw the man into
27 convulsions and with a loud cry went out of him. ·The people were so astonished
that they started asking one another what it all meant, saying, 'Here is a teaching
that is new, and with authority behind it: he gives orders even to unclean spirits ͪ
28 and they obey him.' ·And his reputation at once spread everywhere, through all
the surrounding Galilean countryside.

Cure of Simon's mother-in-law

29 And at once on leaving the synagogue, he went ͥ with James and John straight to
30 the house of Simon and Andrew. ·Now Simon's mother-in-law was in bed and
31 feverish, and at once they told him about her. ·He went in to her, took her by the
hand and helped her up. And the fever left her and she began to serve them.

A number of cures

32 That evening, after sunset, they brought to him all who were sick and those who
33. 34 were possessed by devils. ·The whole town came crowding round the door, ·and
he cured many who were sick with diseases of one kind or another; he also drove
out many devils, but he would not allow them to speak, because they knew who
he was. ͫ

Jesus quietly leaves Capernaum and travels through Galilee

35 In the morning, long before dawn, he got up and left the house and went off to a
36 lonely place and prayed there. ·Simon and his companions set out in search of
37. 38 him, ·and when they found him they said, 'Everybody is looking for you.' ·He
answered, 'Let us go elsewhere, to the neighbouring country towns, so that I can
39 proclaim the message there too, because that is why I came.' ͫ·And he went all
through Galilee, preaching in their synagogues and driving out devils.

Cure of a man suffering from a virulent skin-disease

40 A man suffering from a virulent skin-disease came to him and pleaded on his
41 knees saying, 'If you are willing, you can cleanse me.' ·Feeling sorry for him, Jesus
stretched out his hand, touched him and said to him, 'I am willing. Be cleansed.'
42. 43 And at once the skin-disease left him and he was cleansed. ·And at once Jesus
44 sternly sent him away and said to him, ·'Mind you tell no one anything, but go and
show yourself to the priest, and make the offering for your cleansing prescribed
45 by Moses as evidence to them.' ·The man went away, but then started freely
proclaiming and telling the story everywhere, so that Jesus could no longer go
openly into any town, but stayed outside in deserted places. Even so, people from
all around kept coming to him.

Cure of a paralytic

1 2 When he returned to Capernaum, some time later word went round that he
2 was in the house; ·and so many people collected that there was no room left,
3 even in front of the door. He was preaching the word to them ·when some people
4 came bringing him a paralytic carried by four men, ·but as they could not get the
man to him through the crowd, they stripped the roof over the place where Jesus
was; and when they had made an opening, they lowered the stretcher on which
5 the paralytic lay. ·Seeing their faith, Jesus said to the paralytic, 'My child, your
6 sins are forgiven.'ᵃ ·Now some scribes were sitting there, and they thought to
7 themselves, ·'How can this man talk like that? He is being blasphemous. Who but
8 God can forgive sins?' ·And at once, Jesus, inwardly aware that this is what they
were thinking, said to them, 'Why do you have these thoughts in your hearts?
9 Which of these is easier to say to the paralytic, "Your sins are forgiven" or to say,
10 "Get up, pick up your stretcher and walk"? ·But to prove to you that the Son of
11 man has authority to forgive sins on earth'—·he said to the paralytic—'I order
12 you: get up, pick up your stretcher, and go off home.' ·And the man got up, and
at once picked up his stretcher and walked out in front of everyone, so that they
were all astonished and praised God saying, 'We have never seen anything like
this.'

The call of Levi

13 He went out again to the shore of the lake;ᵇ and all the people came to him, and
14 he taught them. ·As he was walking along he saw Levi the son of Alphaeus sitting
at the tax office, and he said to him, 'Follow me.' And he got up and followed
him.

Eating with sinners

15 When Jesus was at dinner in his house, a number of tax collectors and sinners
were also sitting at table with Jesus and his disciples; for there were many of them
16 among his followers. ·When the scribes of the Pharisee party saw him eating with
sinners and tax collectors, they said to his disciples, 'Why does he eat with tax
17 collectors and sinners?' ·When Jesus heard this he said to them, 'It is not the
healthy who need the doctor, but the sick. I came to call not the upright, but
sinners.'

A discussion on fasting

18 John's disciples and the Pharisees were keeping a fast, when some people came to
him and said to him, 'Why is it that John's disciples and the disciples of the

19 Pharisees fast, but your disciples do not?' ·Jesus replied, 'Surely the bridegroom's
attendants cannot fast while the bridegroom is still with them? As long as they
20 have the bridegroom with them, they cannot fast. ·But the time will come when
the bridegroom is taken away from them, and then, on that day, they will fast.
21 No one sews a piece of unshrunken cloth on an old cloak; otherwise, the patch
22 pulls away from it, the new from the old, and the tear gets worse. ·And nobody
puts new wine into old wineskins; otherwise, the wine will burst the skins, and the
wine is lost and the skins too. No! New wine into fresh skins!'

Picking corn on the Sabbath

23 It happened that one Sabbath day he was taking a walk through the cornfields,
24 and his disciples began to make a path by plucking ears of corn. ᶜ ·And the
Pharisees said to him, 'Look, why are they doing something on the Sabbath day
25 that is forbidden?' ·And he replied, 'Have you never read what David did in his
26 time of need when he and his followers were hungry—·how he went into the house
of God when Abiathar ᵈ was high priest, and ate the loaves of the offering which
only the priests are allowed to eat, and how he also gave some to the men with
him?'
27　　And he said to them, 'The Sabbath was made for man, not man for the Sabbath; ᵉ
28 so the Son of man is master even of the Sabbath.'

Cure of the man with a withered hand

1 **3** Another time he went into the synagogue, and there was a man present whose
2 hand was withered. ·And they were watching him to see if he would cure him
3 on the Sabbath day, hoping for something to charge him with. ·He said to the man
4 with the withered hand, 'Get up and stand in the middle!' ·Then he said to them,
'Is it permitted on the Sabbath day to do good, or to do evil; to save life, or to
5 kill?' But they said nothing. ·Then he looked angrily round at them, grieved to
find them so obstinate, and said to the man, 'Stretch out your hand.' He stretched
6 it out and his hand was restored. ·The Pharisees went out and began at once to
plot with the Herodians ᵃ against him, discussing how to destroy him.

The crowds follow Jesus

7 Jesus withdrew with his disciples to the lakeside, and great crowds from Galilee
8 followed him. From Judaea, ᵇ ·and from Jerusalem, and from Idumaea and Transjordan and the region of Tyre and Sidon, great numbers who had heard of all he
9 was doing came to him. ·And he asked his disciples to have a boat ready for him
10 because of the crowd, to keep him from being crushed. ·For he had cured so many
11 that all who were afflicted in any way were crowding forward to touch him. ·And
the unclean spirits, whenever they saw him, would fall down before him and shout,
12 'You are the Son of God!' ·But he warned them strongly not to make him known.

The appointment of the Twelve

13 He now went up onto the mountain and summoned those he wanted. So they
14 came to him ·and he appointed twelve; ᶜ they were to be his companions and to be
15, 16 sent out to proclaim the message, ·with power to drive out devils. ·And so he
17 appointed the Twelve, Simon to whom he gave the name Peter, ·James the son of
Zebedee and John the brother of James, to whom he gave the name Boanerges or
18 'Sons of Thunder'; ·Andrew, Philip, Bartholomew, Matthew, Thomas, James the

19 son of Alphaeus, Thaddaeus, Simon the Zealot ·and Judas Iscariot, the man who
was to betray him. *

His family are concerned about Jesus

20 He went home again, and once more such a crowd collected that they could not
21 even have a meal. ·When his relations heard of this, they set out to take charge of
him; they said, ' 'He is out of his mind.'

Allegations of the scribes

22 The scribes who had come down from Jerusalem were saying, 'Beelzebul* is in
23 him,' and, 'It is through the prince of devils that he drives devils out.' ·So he called
24 them to him and spoke to them in parables, ·'How can Satan drive out Satan? If a
25 kingdom is divided against itself, that kingdom cannot last. ·And if a household is
26 divided against itself, that household can never last. ·Now if Satan has rebelled
27 against himself and is divided, he cannot last either—it is the end of him. ·But no
one can make his way into a strong man's house and plunder his property unless
he has first tied up the strong man. Only then can he plunder his house.
28 'In truth I tell you, all human sins will be forgiven, and all the blasphemies ever
29 uttered; ·but anyone who blasphemes against the Holy Spirit will never be
30 forgiven, but is guilty of an eternal sin.' ·This was because they were saying, 'There
is an unclean spirit in him.'

The true kinsmen of Jesus

31 Now his mother and his brothers arrived and, standing outside, sent in a message
32 asking for him. ·A crowd was sitting round him at the time the message was passed
to him, 'Look, your mother and brothers and sisters are outside asking for you.'
33, 34 He replied, 'Who are my mother and my brothers?' ·And looking at those sitting
35 in a circle round him, he said, 'Here are my mother and my brothers. ·Anyone
who does the will of God, that person is my brother and sister and mother.'

Parable of the sower

1 4 Again he began to teach them by the lakeside, but such a huge crowd gathered
round him that he got into a boat on the water and sat there. The whole crowd
2 were at the lakeside on land. ·He taught them many things in parables, and in the
3 course of his teaching he said to them, ·'Listen! Imagine a sower going out to sow.
4 Now it happened that, as he sowed, some of the seed fell on the edge of the path,
5 and the birds came and ate it up. ·Some seed fell on rocky ground where it found
6 little soil and at once sprang up, because there was no depth of earth; ·and when
7 the sun came up it was scorched and, not having any roots, it withered away. ·Some
seed fell into thorns, and the thorns grew up and choked it, and it produced no
8 crop. ·And some seeds fell into rich soil, grew tall and strong, and produced a
9 good crop; the yield was thirty, sixty, even a hundredfold.' ·And he said, 'Anyone
who has ears for listening should listen!'

Why Jesus spoke in parables

10 When he was alone, the Twelve, together with the others who formed his company,
11 asked what the parables meant. ·He told them, 'To you is granted the secret of
the kingdom of God, but to those who are outside everything comes in parables,

12   *so that [a] they may look and look, but never perceive;*
         listen and listen, but never understand;
         to avoid changing their ways and being healed.'

The parable of the sower explained

13 He said to them, 'Do you not understand this parable? Then how will you under-
14, 15 stand any of the parables? [b] ·What the sower is sowing is the word. ·Those on the
edge of the path where the word is sown are people who have no sooner heard it
than Satan at once comes and carries away the word that was sown in them.
16 Similarly, those who are sown on patches of rock are people who, when first they
17 hear the word, welcome it at once with joy. ·But they have no root deep down
and do not last; should some trial come, or some persecution on account of the
18 word, at once they fall away. ·Then there are others who are sown in thorns.
19 These have heard the word, ·but the worries of the world, the lure of riches and
20 all the other passions come in to choke the word, and so it produces nothing. ·And
there are those who have been sown in rich soil; they hear the word and accept it
and yield a harvest, thirty and sixty and a hundredfold.'

Receiving and handing on the teaching of Jesus [c]

21 He also said to them, 'Is a lamp brought in to be put under a tub or under the bed?
22 Surely to be put on the lamp-stand? ·For there is nothing hidden, but it must be
23 disclosed, nothing kept secret except to be brought to light. ·Anyone who has ears
for listening should listen!'

Parable of the measure

24 He also said to them, 'Take notice of what you are hearing. The standard you use
25 will be used for you—and you will receive more besides; ·anyone who has, will be
given more; anyone who has not, will be deprived even of what he has.'

Parable of the seed growing by itself

26 He also said, 'This is what the kingdom of God is like. A man scatters seed on the
27 land. ·Night and day, while he sleeps, when he is awake, the seed is sprouting and
28 growing; how, he does not know. ·Of its own accord the land produces first the
29 shoot, then the ear, then the full grain in the ear. ·And when the crop is ready, at
once he starts to reap because the harvest has come.' [d]

Parable of the mustard seed

30 He also said, 'What can we say that the kingdom is like? What parable can we find
31 for it? ·It is like a mustard seed which, at the time of its sowing, is the smallest of
32 all the seeds on earth. ·Yet once it is sown it grows into the biggest shrub of them
all and puts out big branches so that the birds of the air can shelter in its shade.'

The use of parables

33 Using many parables like these, he spoke the word to them, so far as they were
34 capable of understanding it. ·He would not speak to them except in parables, but
he explained everything to his disciples when they were by themselves.

The calming of the storm

35 With the coming of evening that same day, he said to them, 'Let us cross over to
36 the other side.' ·And leaving the crowd behind they took him, just as he was, in
37 the boat; and there were other boats with him. ·Then it began to blow a great gale

38 and the waves were breaking into the boat so that it was almost swamped. ·But he
39 was in the stern, his head on the cushion, asleep. ·They woke him and said to him,
'Master, do you not care? We are lost!' And he woke up and rebuked the wind
and said to the sea, 'Quiet now! Be calm!' And the wind dropped, and there
40 followed a great calm. ·Then he said to them, 'Why are you so frightened? Have
41 you still no faith?' ' ·They were overcome with awe and said to one another, 'Who
can this be? Even the wind and the sea obey him.'

The Gerasene demoniac

1 5 They reached the territory of the Gerasenes * on the other side of the lake,
2 5 and when he disembarked, a man with an unclean spirit at once came out from
3 the tombs towards him. ·The man lived in the tombs and no one could secure him
4 any more, even with a chain, ·because he had often been secured with fetters and
chains but had snapped the chains and broken the fetters, and no one had the
5 strength to control him. ·All night and all day, among the tombs and in the
6 mountains, he would howl and gash himself with stones. ·Catching sight of Jesus
7 from a distance, he ran up and fell at his feet ·and shouted at the top of his voice,
'What do you want with me, Jesus, son of the Most High God? In God's name do
8 not torture me!' ·For Jesus had been saying to him, 'Come out of the man, unclean
9 spirit.' ·Then he asked, 'What is your name?' He answered, 'My name is Legion,
10 for there are many of us.' ·And he begged him earnestly not to send them out of
11. 12 the district. ·Now on the mountainside there was a great herd of pigs feeding, ·and
13 the unclean spirits begged him, 'Send us to the pigs, let us go into them.' ·So he
gave them leave. With that, the unclean spirits came out and went into the pigs,
and the herd of about two thousand pigs charged down the cliff into the lake, and
14 there they were drowned. ·The men looking after them ran off and told their story
in the city and in the country round about; and the people came to see what had
15 really happened. ·They came to Jesus and saw the demoniac sitting there—the
man who had had the legion in him—properly dressed and in his full senses, and
16 they were afraid. ·And those who had witnessed it reported what had happened
17 to the demoniac and what had become of the pigs. ·Then they began to implore
18 Jesus to leave their neighbourhood. ·As he was getting into the boat, the man
19 who had been possessed begged to be allowed to stay with him. ·Jesus would not
let him but said to him, 'Go home to your people and tell them all that the Lord in
20 his mercy has done for you.' ·So the man went off and proceeded to proclaim in
the Decapolis all that Jesus had done for him. And everyone was amazed.

Cure of the woman with a haemorrhage. The daughter of Jairus raised to life

21 When Jesus had crossed again in the boat to the other side, a large crowd gathered
22 round him and he stayed by the lake. ·Then the president of the synagogue came
23 up, named Jairus, and seeing him, fell at his feet ·and begged him earnestly,
saying, 'My little daughter is desperately sick. Do come and lay your hands on her
24 that she may be saved and may live.' ·Jesus went with him and a large crowd
followed him; they were pressing all round him.
25   Now there was a woman who had suffered from a haemorrhage for twelve years;
26 after long and painful treatment under various doctors, she had spent all she had
27 without being any the better for it; in fact, she was getting worse. ·She had heard
about Jesus, and she came up through the crowd and touched his cloak from
28. 29 behind, thinking, ·'If I can just touch his clothes, I shall be saved.' ·And at once
the source of the bleeding dried up, and she felt in herself that she was cured of

30 her complaint. ·And at once aware of the power that had gone out from him, *
31 Jesus turned round in the crowd and said, 'Who touched my clothes?' ·His disciples
said to him, 'You see how the crowd is pressing round you; how can you ask,
32 "Who touched me?" ' ·But he continued to look all round to see who had done it.
33 Then the woman came forward, frightened and trembling * because she knew what
34 had happened to her, and she fell at his feet and told him the whole truth. ·'My
daughter,' he said, 'your faith has restored you to health; go in peace and be free
of your complaint.'
35   While he was still speaking some people arrived from the house of the president
of the synagogue to say, 'Your daughter is dead; why put the Master to any further
36 trouble?' ·But Jesus overheard what they said and he said to the president of the
37 synagogue, 'Do not be afraid; only have faith.' ·And he allowed no one to go with
38 him except Peter and James and John the brother of James. * ·So they came to the
house of the president of the synagogue, and Jesus noticed all the commotion,
39 with people weeping and wailing unrestrainedly. ·He went in and said to them,
40 'Why all this commotion and crying? The child is not dead, but asleep.' ·But they
ridiculed him. So he turned them all out and, taking with him the child's father
and mother and his own companions, he went into the place where the child lay.
41 And taking the child by the hand he said to her, 'Talitha kum!' * which means,
42 'Little girl, I tell you to get up.' ·The little girl got up at once and began to
walk about, for she was twelve years old. At once they were overcome with
43 astonishment, ·and he gave them strict orders not to let anyone know about it,
and told them to give her something to eat.

A visit to Nazareth

1 **6** Leaving that district, he went to his home town, and his disciples accompanied
2   him. ·With the coming of the Sabbath he began teaching in the synagogue,
and most of them were astonished when they heard him. They said, 'Where did
the man get all this? What is this wisdom that has been granted him, and these
3 miracles that are worked through him? ·This is the carpenter, * surely, the son of
Mary, the brother of James and Joset * and Jude and Simon? His sisters, too, are
4 they not here with us?' And they would not accept him. ·And Jesus said to them,
'A prophet is despised only in his own country, among his own relations and in his
5 own house'; ·and he could work no miracle there, except that he cured a few sick
6 people by laying his hands on them. ·He was amazed at their lack of faith.

The mission of the Twelve

7 He made a tour round the villages, teaching. ·Then he summoned the Twelve and
8 began to send them out in pairs, giving them authority over unclean spirits. ·And
he instructed them to take nothing for the journey except a staff *—no bread, no
9 haversack, no coppers for their purses. ·They were to wear sandals but, he added,
10 'Don't take a spare tunic.' ·And he said to them, 'If you enter a house anywhere,
11 stay there until you leave the district. ·And if any place does not welcome you and
people refuse to listen to you, as you walk away shake off the dust under your feet
12. 13 as evidence to them.' ·So they set off to proclaim repentance; ·and they cast out
many devils, and anointed many sick people with oil and cured them.

Herod and Jesus

14 King Herod had heard about him, since by now his name was well known. Some
were saying, * 'John the Baptist has risen from the dead, and that is why miraculous

15 powers are at work in him.' ·Others said, 'He is Elijah,' others again, 'He is a
16 prophet, like the prophets we used to have.' ·But when Herod heard this he said,
'It is John whose head I cut off; he has risen from the dead.'

John the Baptist beheaded

17 Now it was this same Herod who had sent to have John arrested, and had had him
chained up in prison because of Herodias, his brother Philip's wife whom he had
18 married. ·For John had told Herod, 'It is against the law for you to have your
19 brother's wife.' ·As for Herodias, she was furious with him and wanted to kill
20 him, but she was not able to do so, ·because Herod was in awe of John, knowing
him to be a good and upright man, and gave him his protection. When he had
heard him speak he was greatly perplexed,ᶜ and yet he liked to listen to him.
21   An opportunity came on Herod's birthday when he gave a banquet for the
nobles of his court, for his army officers and for the leading figures in Galilee.
22 When the daughter of this same Herodias came in and danced, she delighted
Herod and his guests; so the king said to the girl, 'Ask me anything you like and I
23 will give it you.' ·And he swore her an oath, 'I will give you anything you ask,
24 even half my kingdom.' ·She went out and said to her mother, 'What shall I ask
25 for?' She replied, 'The head of John the Baptist.' ·The girl at once rushed back to
the king and made her request, 'I want you to give me John the Baptist's head,
26 immediately, on a dish.' ·The king was deeply distressed but, thinking of the oaths
27 he had sworn and of his guests, he was reluctant to break his word to her. ·At once
28 the king sent one of the bodyguard with orders to bring John's head. ·The man
went off and beheaded him in the prison; then he brought the head on a dish and
29 gave it to the girl, and the girl gave it to her mother. ·When John's disciples heard
about this, they came and took his body and laid it in a tomb.

First miracle of the loaves

30. 31 The apostles rejoined Jesus and told him all they had done and taught. ·and he
said to them, 'Come away to some lonely place all by yourselves and rest for a
while'; for there were so many coming and going that there was no time for them
32 even to eat. ·So they went off in the boat to a lonely place where they could be by
33 themselves. ·But people saw them going, and many recognised them; and from
34 every town they all hurried to the place on foot and reached it before them. ·So as
he stepped ashore he saw a large crowd; and he took pity on them because they
were like sheep without a shepherd, and he set himself to teach them at some
35 length. ·By now it was getting very late, and his disciples came up to him and said,
36 'This is a lonely place and it is getting very late, ·so send them away, and they can
go to the farms and villages round about, to buy themselves something to eat.'
37 He replied, 'Give them something to eat yourselves.' They answered, 'Are we to
38 go and spend two hundred denarii on bread for them to eat?' ·He asked, 'How
many loaves have you? Go and see.' And when they had found out they said,
39 'Five, and two fish.' ·Then he ordered them to get all the people to sit down in
40 groups on the green grass, ·and they sat down on the ground in squares of hundreds
41 and fifties. ·Then he took the five loaves and the two fish, raised his eyes to heaven
and said the blessing; then he broke the loaves and began handing them to his
disciples to distribute among the people. He also shared out the two fish among
42. 43 them all. ·They all ate as much as they wanted. ·They collected twelve basketfuls
44 of scraps of bread and pieces of fish. ·Those who had eaten the loaves numbered
five thousand men.

Jesus walks on the water

45 And at once he made his disciples get into the boat and go on ahead to the other
46 side near Bethsaida,ʲ while he himself sent the crowd away. ·After saying good-
47 bye to them he went off into the hills to pray. ·When evening came, the boat was
48 far out on the sea, and he was alone on the land. ·He could see that they were
hard pressed in their rowing, for the wind was against them; and about the fourth
watch of the night he came towards them, walking on the sea. He was going to
49 pass them by, ·but when they saw him walking on the sea they thought it was a
50 ghost and cried out; ·for they had all seen him and were terrified. But at once he
51 spoke to them and said, 'Courage! It's me! Don't be afraid.' ·Then he got into the
boat with them and the wind dropped. They were utterly and completely
52 dumbfounded, ·because they had not seen what the miracle of the loaves meant;
their minds were closed.

Cures at Gennesaret

53 Having made the crossing, they came to land at Gennesaret and moored there.
54, 55 When they disembarked people at once recognised him, ·and started hurrying all
through the countryside and brought the sick on stretchers to wherever they heard
56 he was. ·And wherever he went, to village or town or farm, they laid down the
sick in the open spaces, begging him to let them touch even the fringe of his cloak.
And all those who touched him were saved.

The traditions of the Pharisees

1 7 The Pharisees and some of the scribes who had come from Jerusalem gathered
2   round him, ·and they noticed that some of his disciples were eating with
3 unclean hands, that is, without washing them. ·For the Pharisees, and all the Jews,
keep the tradition of the elders ᵃ and never eat without washing their arms as far
4 as the elbow; ·and on returning from the market place they never eat without first
sprinkling ᵇ themselves. There are also many other observances which have been
handed down to them to keep, concerning the washing of cups and pots and bronze
5 dishes. ·So the Pharisees and scribes asked him, 'Why do your disciples not respect
6 the tradition of the elders but eat their food with unclean hands?' ·He answered,
'How rightly Isaiah prophesied about you hypocrites in the passage of scripture:

> This people honours me only with lip-service,
> while their hearts are far from me.
7 > Their reverence of me is worthless;
> the lessons they teach are nothing but human commandments.

8, 9 You put aside the commandment of God to observe human traditions.' ·And he
said to them, 'How ingeniously you get round the commandment of God in order
10 to preserve your own tradition! ·For Moses said: Honour your father and your
11 mother, and, Anyone who curses father or mother must be put to death. ·But you
say, "If a man says to his father or mother: Anything I have that I might have used
12 to help you is Korban ᶜ (that is, dedicated to God)," ·then he is forbidden from
13 that moment to do anything for his father or mother. ·In this way you make God's
word ineffective for the sake of your tradition which you have handed down. And
you do many other things like this.'

On clean and unclean

14 He called the people to him again and said, 'Listen to me, all of you, and
15 understand. ·Nothing that goes into someone from outside can make that person
unclean; it is the things that come out of someone that make that person unclean.
16 Anyone who has ears for listening should listen!' *d*
17 When he had gone into the house, away from the crowd, his disciples questioned
18 him about the parable. *e* ·He said to them, 'Even you—don't you understand?
Can't you see that nothing that goes into someone from outside can make that
19 person unclean, ·because it goes not into the heart but into the stomach and passes
20 into the sewer?' (Thus he pronounced all foods clean.) *f* ·And he went on, 'It is
21 what comes out of someone that makes that person unclean. ·For it is from within,
22 from the heart, that evil intentions emerge: fornication, theft, murder, ·adultery,
23 avarice, malice, deceit, indecency, envy, slander, pride, folly. ·All these evil things
come from within and make a person unclean.'

III: JOURNEYS OUTSIDE GALILEE

The daughter of the Syro-Phoenician woman healed

24 He left that place and set out for the territory of Tyre. *g* There he went into a
house and did not want anyone to know he was there; but he could not pass
25 unrecognised. ·At once a woman whose little daughter had an unclean spirit heard
26 about him and came and fell at his feet. ·Now this woman was a gentile, *h* by birth
27 a Syro=Phoenician, and she begged him to drive the devil out of her daughter. ·And
he said to her, 'The children should be fed first, because it is not fair to take the
28 children's food and throw it to the little dogs.' ·But she spoke up, 'Ah yes, sir,'
29 she replied, 'but little dogs under the table eat the scraps from the children.' ·And
he said to her, 'For saying this you may go home happy; the devil has gone out of
30 your daughter.' ·So she went off home and found the child lying on the bed and
the devil gone.

Healing of the deaf man

31 Returning from the territory of Tyre, he went by way of Sidon towards the Lake
32 of Galilee, right through the Decapolis territory. ·And they brought him a deaf
man who had an impediment in his speech; and they asked him to lay his hand on
33 him. ·He took him aside to be by themselves, away from the crowd, put his fingers
34 into the man's ears and touched his tongue with spittle. ·Then looking up to
35 heaven he sighed; and he said to him, '*Ephphatha*,' that is, 'Be opened.' ·And his
ears were opened, and at once the impediment of his tongue was loosened and he
36 spoke clearly. ·And Jesus ordered them to tell no one about it, but the more he
37 insisted, the more widely they proclaimed it. ·Their admiration was unbounded,
and they said, 'Everything he does is good, he makes the deaf hear and the dumb
speak.'

Second miracle of the loaves

1 8 And now once again a great crowd had gathered, and they had nothing to eat.
2 So he called his disciples to him and said to them, ·'I feel sorry for all these
3 people; they have been with me for three days now and have nothing to eat. ·If I
send them off home hungry they will collapse on the way; some have come a great

4 distance.' ·His disciples replied, 'Where could anyone get these people enough
5 bread to eat in a deserted place?' ·He asked them, 'How many loaves have you?'
6 And they said to him, 'Seven.' ·Then he instructed the crowd to sit down on the
ground, and he took the seven loaves, and after giving thanks he broke them and
began handing them to his disciples to distribute; and they distributed them among
7 the crowd. ·They had a few small fishes as well, and over these he said a blessing
8 and ordered them to be distributed too. ·They ate as much as they wanted, and
9 they collected seven basketfuls of the scraps left over. ·Now there had been about
10 four thousand people. He sent them away ·and at once, getting into the boat with
his disciples, went to the region of Dalmanutha. *

The Pharisees ask for a sign from heaven

11 The Pharisees came up and started a discussion with him; they demanded of him a
12 sign from heaven, to put him to the test. ·And with a profound sigh he said, 'Why
does this generation demand a sign? In truth I tell you, no sign shall be given to
13 this generation.' *b* ·And, leaving them again, he re-embarked and went away to
the other side.

The yeast of the Pharisees and of Herod

14 The disciples had forgotten to take any bread and they had only one loaf with
15 them in the boat. ·Then he gave them this warning, 'Keep your eyes open; look
16 out for the yeast of the Pharisees and the yeast of Herod.' ·And they said to one
17 another, 'It is because we have no bread.' ·And Jesus knew it, and he said to
them, 'Why are you talking about having no bread? Do you still not understand,
18 still not realise? Are your minds closed? ·Have you *eyes and do not see, ears and*
19 *do not hear?* Or do you not remember? ·When I broke the five loaves for the five
thousand, how many baskets full of scraps did you collect?' They answered,
20 'Twelve.' ·'And when I broke the seven loaves for the four thousand, how many
21 baskets full of scraps did you collect?' And they answered, 'Seven.' ·Then he said
to them, 'Do you still not realise?' *c*

Cure of a blind man at Bethsaida

22 They came to Bethsaida, and some people brought to him a blind man whom they
23 begged him to touch. ·He took the blind man by the hand and led him outside the
village. Then, putting spittle on his eyes and laying his hands on him, he asked,
24 'Can you see anything?' ·The man, who was beginning to see, *d* replied, 'I can see
25 people; they look like trees as they walk around.' ·Then he laid his hands on the
man's eyes again and he saw clearly; he was cured, and he could see everything
26 plainly and distinctly. ·And Jesus sent him home, saying, 'Do not even go into the
village.'

Peter's profession of faith

27 Jesus and his disciples left for the villages round Caesarea Philippi. On the way he
28 put this question to his disciples, 'Who do people say I am?' ·And they told him,
29 'John the Baptist, others Elijah, others again, one of the prophets.' ·'But you,' he
asked them, 'who do you say I am?' Peter spoke up and said to him, 'You are the
30 Christ.' ·And he gave them strict orders not to tell anyone about him.

First prophecy of the Passion

31 Then he began to teach them that the Son of man was destined to suffer grievously, *
and to be rejected by the elders and the chief priests and the scribes, and to be put
32 to death, and after three days to rise again; ·and he said all this quite openly.
33 Then, taking him aside, Peter tried to rebuke him. ·But, turning and seeing his
disciples, he rebuked Peter and said to him, 'Get behind me, Satan! You are
thinking not as God thinks, but as human beings do.'

The condition of following Christ

34 He called the people and his disciples to him and said, 'If anyone wants to be a
follower of mine, let him renounce himself and take up his cross and follow me.
35 Anyone who wants to save his life will lose it; but anyone who loses his life for my
36 sake, and for the sake of the gospel, will save it. ·What gain, then, is it for anyone
37 to win the whole world and forfeit his life? ·And indeed what can anyone offer in
38 exchange for his life? ·For if anyone in this sinful and adulterous generation is
ashamed of me and of my words, the Son of man will also be ashamed of him
when he comes in the glory of his Father with the holy angels.'
1 **9** And he said to them, 'In truth I tell you, there are some standing here who
will not taste death before they see the kingdom of God come with power.'

The Transfiguration *

2 Six days later, Jesus took with him Peter and James and John and led them up
a high mountain on their own by themselves. There in their presence he was
3 transfigured: ·his clothes became brilliantly white, whiter than any earthly bleacher
4 could make them. ·Elijah appeared to them with Moses; and they were talking to
5 Jesus. ·Then Peter spoke to Jesus, 'Rabbi,' he said, 'it is wonderful for us to be
here; so let us make three shelters, one for you, one for Moses and one for Elijah.'
6, 7 He did not know what to say; they were so frightened. ·And a cloud came, covering
them in shadow; and from the cloud there came a voice, 'This is my Son, the
8 Beloved. Listen to him.' ·Then suddenly, when they looked round, they saw no
one with them any more but only Jesus.

The question about Elijah

9 As they were coming down from the mountain he warned them to tell no one what
10 they had seen, until after the Son of man had risen from the dead. ·They observed
the warning faithfully, though among themselves they discussed what 'rising from
11 the dead' could mean. ·And they put this question to him, 'Why do the scribes say
12 that Elijah must come first?' ·He said to them, 'Elijah is indeed first coming to set
everything right again; yet how is it that the scriptures say about the Son of man
13 that he must suffer grievously and be treated with contempt? ·But I tell you that
Elijah has come and they have treated him as they pleased, just as the scriptures
say about him.'

The epileptic demoniac

14 As they were rejoining the disciples they saw * a large crowd round them and some
15 scribes arguing with them. ·At once, when they saw him, the whole crowd were
16 struck with amazement and ran to greet him. ·And he asked them, 'What are you
17 arguing about with them?' ·A man answered him from the crowd, 'Master, I have
18 brought my son to you; there is a spirit of dumbness in him, ·and when it takes

hold of him it throws him to the ground, and he foams at the mouth and grinds his teeth and goes rigid. And I asked your disciples to drive it out and they were
19 unable to.' ·In reply he said to them, 'Faithless generation, how much longer must I be among you? How much longer must I put up with you? Bring him to me.'
20 They brought the boy to him, and at once the spirit of dumbness threw the boy into convulsions, and he fell to the ground and lay writhing there, foaming at the
21 mouth. ·Jesus asked the father, 'How long has this been happening to him?' 'From
22 childhood,' he said, ·'and it has often thrown him into fire and into water, in order
23. 24 to destroy him. ·But if you can do anything, have pity on us and help us.' ·'If you can?' retorted Jesus. 'Everything is possible for one who has faith.' At once the
25 father of the boy cried out, 'I have faith. Help my lack of faith!' ·And when Jesus saw that a crowd was gathering, he rebuked the unclean spirit. 'Deaf and dumb spirit,' he said, 'I command you: come out of him and never enter him again.'
26 Then it threw the boy into violent convulsions and came out shouting, and the
27 boy lay there so like a corpse that most of them said, 'He is dead.' ·But Jesus took
28 him by the hand and helped him up, and he was able to stand. ·When he had gone indoors, his disciples asked him when they were by themselves, 'Why were we
29 unable to drive it out?' ·He answered, 'This is the kind that can be driven out only by prayer.'ᶜ

Second prophecy of the Passion

30 After leaving that place they made their way through Galilee; and he did not want
31 anyone to know, ·because he was instructing his disciples; he was telling them, 'The Son of man will be delivered into the power of men; they will put him to
32 death; and three days after he has been put to death he will rise again.' ·But they did not understand what he said and were afraid to ask him.

Who is the greatest?

33 They came to Capernaum, and when he got into the house he asked them, 'What
34 were you arguing about on the road?' ·They said nothing, because on the road
35 they had been arguing which of them was the greatest. ·So he sat down, called the Twelve to him and said, 'If anyone wants to be first, he must make himself last of
36 all and servant of all.' ·He then took a little child whom he set among them and
37 embraced, and he said to them, ·'Anyone who welcomes a little child such as this in my name, welcomes me; and anyone who welcomes me, welcomes not me but the one who sent me.'

On using the name of Jesus

38 John said to him, 'Master, we saw someone who is not one of us driving out devils
39 in your name, and because he was not one of us we tried to stop him.' ·But Jesus said, 'You must not stop him; no one who works a miracle in my name could soon
40 afterwards speak evil of me. ·Anyone who is not against us is for us.

Generosity shown to Christ's disciples

41 'If anyone gives you a cup of water to drink because you belong to Christ, then in truth I tell you, he will most certainly not lose his reward.

On leading others astray

42 'But anyone who is the downfall of one of these little ones who have faith,ᵈ would
43 be better thrown into the sea with a great millstone hung round his neck. ·And if

your hand should be your downfall, cut it off; it is better for you to enter into life crippled, than to have two hands and go to hell, into the fire that can never be put out. ᵉ ·And if your foot should be your downfall, cut it off; it is better for you to enter into life lame, than to have two feet and be thrown into hell. ·And if your eye should be your downfall, tear it out; it is better for you to enter into the kingdom of God with one eye, than to have two eyes and be thrown into hell where *their worm will never die nor their fire be put out.* ·For everyone will be salted with fire. ᶠ ·Salt is a good thing, but if salt has become insipid, how can you make it salty again? Have salt in yourselves and be at peace with one another.'

The question about divorce

10 After leaving there, he came into the territory of Judaea and Transjordan. And again crowds gathered round him, and again he taught them, as his custom was. ·Some Pharisees approached him and asked, 'Is it lawful for a man to divorce his wife?' They were putting him to the test. ·He answered them, 'What did Moses command you?' ·They replied, 'Moses allowed us to draw up a writ of dismissal in cases of divorce.' ·Then Jesus said to them, 'It was because you were so hard hearted that he wrote this commandment for you. ·But from the beginning of creation *he made them male and female.* *·This is why a man leaves his father and mother,* ᵃ *·and the two become one flesh.* They are no longer two, therefore, but one flesh. ·So then, what God has united, human beings must not divide.' ·Back in the house the disciples questioned him again about this, ·and he said to them, 'Whoever divorces his wife and marries another is guilty of adultery against her. And if a woman divorces her husband ᵇ and marries another she is guilty of adultery too.'

Jesus and the children

People were bringing little children to him, for him to touch them. The disciples scolded them, ·but when Jesus saw this he was indignant and said to them, 'Let the little children come to me; do not stop them; for it is to such as these that the kingdom of God belongs. ·In truth I tell you, anyone who does not welcome the kingdom of God like a little child will never enter it.' ·Then he embraced them, laid his hands on them and gave them his blessing.

The rich young man

He was setting out on a journey when a man ran up, knelt before him and put this question to him, 'Good master, what must I do to inherit eternal life?' ·Jesus said to him, 'Why do you call me good? No one is good but God alone. ·You know the commandments: *You shall not kill; You shall not commit adultery; You shall not steal; You shall not give false witness;* You shall not defraud; *Honour your father and mother.'* ·And he said to him, 'Master, I have kept all these since my earliest days.' ·Jesus looked steadily at him and he was filled with love for him, and he said, 'You need to do one thing more. Go and sell what you own and give the money to the poor, and you will have treasure in heaven; then come, follow me.' But his face fell at these words and he went away sad, for he was a man of great wealth.

The danger of riches

Jesus looked round and said to his disciples, 'How hard it is for those who have riches to enter the kingdom of God!' ·The disciples were astounded by these

words,' but Jesus insisted, 'My children,' he said to them, 'how hard it is to enter
25 the kingdom of God! ·It is easier for a camel to pass through the eye of a needle
26 than for someone rich to enter the kingdom of God.' ·They were more astonished
27 than ever, saying to one another, 'In that case, who can be saved?' ·Jesus gazed at
them and said, 'By human resources it is impossible, but not for God: because for
God everything is possible.'

The reward of renunciation

28 Peter took this up. 'Look,' he said to him, 'we have left everything and followed
29 you.' ·Jesus said, 'In truth I tell you, there is no one who has left house, brothers,
sisters, mother, father, children or land for my sake and for the sake of the gospel
30 who will not receive a hundred times as much, houses, brothers, sisters, mothers,
children and land—and persecutions too—now in this present time and, in the
31 world to come, eternal life. ·Many who are first will be last, and the last, first.'

Third prophecy of the Passion

32 They were on the road, going up to Jerusalem; Jesus was walking on ahead of
them; they were in a daze, and those who followed were apprehensive. Once more
taking the Twelve aside he began to tell them what was going to happen to him,
33 'Now we are going up to Jerusalem, and the Son of man is about to be handed
over to the chief priests and the scribes. They will condemn him to death and will
34 hand him over to the gentiles, ·who will mock him and spit at him and scourge
him and put him to death; and after three days he will rise again.'

The sons of Zebedee make their request

35 James and John, the sons of Zebedee, approached him. 'Master,' they said to
36 him, 'We want you to do us a favour.' ·He said to them, 'What is it you want me
37 to do for you?' ·They said to him, 'Allow us to sit one at your right hand and the
38 other at your left in your glory.' ' ·But Jesus said to them, 'You do not know what
you are asking. Can you drink the cup that I shall drink, or be baptised with the
39 baptism with which I shall be baptised?' ' ·They replied, 'We can.' Jesus said to
them, 'The cup that I shall drink you shall drink, and with the baptism with which
40 I shall be baptised you shall be baptised, ·but as for seats at my right hand or my
left, these are not mine to grant; they belong to those to whom they have been
allotted.'

Leadership with service

41 When the other ten heard this they began to feel indignant with James and John,
42 so Jesus called them to him and said to them, 'You know that among the gentiles
those they call their rulers lord it over them, and their great men make their
43 authority felt. ·Among you this is not to happen. No; anyone who wants to become
44 great among you must be your servant, ·and anyone who wants to be first among
45 you must be slave to all. ·For the Son of man himself came not to be served but to
serve, and to give his life as a ransom for many.'

The blind man of Jericho

46 They reached Jericho; and as he left Jericho with his disciples and a great crowd,
Bartimaeus—that is, the son of Timaeus—a blind beggar, was sitting at the side of
47 the road. ·When he heard that it was Jesus of Nazareth, he began to shout and cry
48 out, 'Son of David, Jesus, have pity on me.' ·And many of them scolded him and

told him to keep quiet, but he only shouted all the louder, 'Son of David, have
49 pity on me,' ·Jesus stopped and said, 'Call him here.' So they called the blind man
50 over. 'Courage,' they said, 'get up; he is calling you.' ·So throwing off his cloak,
51 he jumped up and went to Jesus. ·Then Jesus spoke, 'What do you want me to do
52 for you?' The blind man said to him, 'Rabbuni,ᶠ let me see again.' ·Jesus said to
him, 'Go; your faith has saved you.' And at once his sight returned and he followed
him along the road.

IV: THE JERUSALEM MINISTRY

The Messiah enters Jerusalem

1 **11** When they were approaching Jerusalem, at Bethphage and Bethany, close
2 by the Mount of Olives, he sent two of his disciples ·and said to them, 'Go
to the village facing you, and as you enter it you will at once find a tethered colt
3 that no one has yet ridden. Untie it and bring it here. ·If anyone says to you,
"What are you doing?" say, "The Master needs it and will send it back here at
4 once." ' ·They went off and found a colt tethered near a door in the open street.
5 As they untied it, ·some men standing there said, 'What are you doing, untying
6 that colt?' ·They gave the answer Jesus had told them, and the men let them go.
7 Then they took the colt to Jesus and threw their cloaks on its back, and he mounted
8 it. ·Many people spread their cloaks on the road, and others greenery which they
9 had cut in the fields. ·And those who went in front and those who followed were
all shouting, '*Hosanna! Blessed is he who is coming in the name of the Lord!*
10 Blessed is the coming kingdom of David our father! *Hosanna* in the highest
11 heavens!' ·He entered Jerusalem and went into the Temple; and when he had
surveyed it all, as it was late by now, he went out to Bethany with the Twelve.

The barren fig tree ᵃ

12, 13 Next day as they were leaving Bethany, he felt hungry. ·Seeing a fig tree in leaf
some distance away, he went to see if he could find any fruit on it, but when he
14 came up to it he found nothing but leaves; for it was not the season for figs. ·And
he addressed the fig tree, 'May no one ever eat fruit from you again.' And his
disciples heard him say this.

The expulsion of the dealers from the Temple

15 So they reached Jerusalem and he went into the Temple and began driving out the
men selling and buying there; he upset the tables of the money changers and the
16 seats of the dove sellers. ·Nor would he allow anyone to carry anything through
17 the Temple. ·And he taught them and said, 'Does not scripture say: *My house will
be called a house of prayer for all peoples*?ᵇ But you have turned it into *a bandits'*
18 *den*.' ·This came to the ears of the chief priests and the scribes, and they tried to
find some way of doing away with him; they were afraid of him because the people
19 were carried away by his teaching. ·And when evening came he went out of the
city.

The fig tree withered. Faith and prayer

20 Next morning, as they passed by, they saw the fig tree withered to the roots.
21 Peter remembered. 'Look, Rabbi,' he said to Jesus, 'the fig tree that you cursed

22, 23 has withered away.' •Jesus answered, 'Have faith in God. •In truth I tell you, if
anyone says to this mountain, "Be pulled up and thrown into the sea," with no
doubt in his heart, but believing that what he says will happen, it will be done for
24 him. •I tell you, therefore, everything you ask and pray for, believe that you have
25 it already, and it will be yours. •And when you stand in prayer, forgive whatever
you have against anybody, so that your Father in heaven may forgive your failings
too.' ᶜ[26]

The authority of Jesus is questioned

27 They came to Jerusalem again, and as Jesus was walking in the Temple, the chief
28 priests and the scribes and the elders came to him, •and they said to him, 'What
authority have you for acting like this? Or who gave you authority to act like this?'
29 Jesus said to them, 'And I will ask you a question, just one; answer me and I will
30 tell you my authority for acting like this. •John's baptism, what was its origin,
31 heavenly or human? Answer me that.' •And they argued this way among themselves, 'If we say heavenly, he will say, "Then why did you refuse to believe him?"
32 But dare we say human?'—they had the people to fear, for everyone held that
33 John had been a real prophet. •So their reply to Jesus was, 'We do not know.'
And Jesus said to them, 'Nor will I tell you my authority for acting like this.'

Parable of the wicked tenants

1 **12** He went on to speak to them in parables, 'A man planted a vineyard; he
fenced it round, dug out a trough for the winepress and built a tower; then
2 he leased it to tenants and went abroad. •When the time came, he sent a servant
3 to the tenants to collect from them his share of the produce of the vineyard. •But
4 they seized the man, thrashed him and sent him away empty handed. •Next he
sent another servant to them; him they beat about the head and treated shamefully.
5 And he sent another and him they killed; then a number of others, and they
6 thrashed some and killed the rest. •He had still someone left: his beloved son. He
7 sent him to them last of all, thinking, "They will respect my son." •But those
tenants said to each other, "This is the heir. Come on, let us kill him, and the
8 inheritance will be ours." •So they seized him and killed him and threw him out of
9 the vineyard. •Now what will the owner of the vineyard do? He will come and
10 make an end of the tenants and give the vineyard to others. •Have you not read
this text of scripture:

> *The stone which the builders rejected*
> *has become the cornerstone;*
11 > *this is the Lord's doing,*
> *and we marvel at it?'*

12 And they would have liked to arrest him, because they realised that the parable
was aimed at them, but they were afraid of the crowds. So they left him alone and
went away.

On tribute to Caesar

13 Next they sent to him some Pharisees and some Herodians to catch him out in
14 what he said. •These came and said to him, 'Master, we know that you are an
honest man, that you are not afraid of anyone, because human rank means nothing
to you, and that you teach the way of God in all honesty. Is it permissible to pay
15 taxes to Caesar or not? Should we pay or not?' •Recognising their hypocrisy he

said to them, 'Why are you putting me to the test? Hand me a denarius and let me
16 see it.' ·They handed him one and he said to them, 'Whose portrait is this? Whose
17 title?' ·They said to him, 'Caesar's.' ·Jesus said to them, 'Pay Caesar what belongs
to Caesar—and God what belongs to God.' And they were amazed at him.

The resurrection of the dead

18 Then some Sadducees—who deny that there is a resurrection—came to him and
19 they put this question to him, ·'Master, Moses prescribed for us that if a man's
brother dies leaving a wife but no child, the man must marry the widow to raise up
20 children for his brother. ·Now there were seven brothers; the first married a wife
21 and then died leaving no children. ·The second married the widow, and he too
22 died leaving no children; with the third it was the same, ·and none of the seven
23 left any children. Last of all the woman herself died. ·Now at the resurrection,
when they rise again, whose wife will she be, since she had been married to all
seven?'
24 Jesus said to them, 'Surely the reason why you are wrong is that you understand
25 neither the scriptures nor the power of God. ·For when they rise from the dead,
26 men and women do not marry; no, they are like the angels in heaven. ·Now about
the dead rising again, have you never read in the Book of Moses, in the passage
about the bush, ª how God spoke to him and said: *I am the God of Abraham, the*
27 *God of Isaac and the God of Jacob?* ·He is God, not of the dead, but of the living.
You are very much mistaken.'

The greatest commandment of all

28 One of the scribes who had listened to them debating appreciated that Jesus had
given a good answer and put a further question to him, 'Which is the first of all the
29 commandments?' ·Jesus replied, 'This is the first: *Listen, Israel, the Lord our God*
30 *is the one, only Lord,* ᵇ ·*and you must love the Lord your God with all your heart,*
31 *with all your soul,* with all your mind *and with all your strength.* ·The second is
this: *You must love your neighbour as yourself.* There is no commandment greater
32 than these.' ·The scribe said to him, 'Well spoken, Master; what you have said is
33 true, that *he is one and there is no other.* ·To *love him with all your heart, with all*
your understanding and strength, and to *love your neighbour as yourself*, this is far
34 more important than any burnt offering or sacrifice.' ·Jesus, seeing how wisely he
had spoken, said, 'You are not far from the kingdom of God.' And after that no
one dared to question him any more.

Jesus not only son but also Lord of David

35 While teaching in the Temple, Jesus said, 'How can the scribes maintain that the
36 Christ is the son of David? ·David himself, moved by the Holy Spirit, said:

> *The Lord declared to my Lord,*
> *take your seat at my right hand*
> *till I have made your enemies*
> *your footstool.*

37 David himself calls him Lord; in what way then can he be his son?' And the great
crowd listened to him with delight.

The scribes condemned by Jesus

38 In his teaching he said, 'Beware of the scribes who like to walk about in long
39 robes, to be greeted respectfully in the market squares, ·to take the front seats in
40 the synagogues and the places of honour at banquets; ·these are the men who
devour the property of widows and for show offer long prayers. The more severe
will be the sentence they receive.'

The widow's mite

41 He sat down opposite the treasury and watched the people putting money into the
42 treasury,ᶜ and many of the rich put in a great deal. ·A poor widow came and put
43 in two small coins, the equivalent of a penny. ·Then he called his disciples and
said to them, 'In truth I tell you, this poor widow has put more in than all who
44 have contributed to the treasury; ·for they have all put in money they could spare,
but she in her poverty has put in everything she possessed, all she had to live on.'

The eschatological discourse: Introductionᵃ

1 **13** As he was leaving the Temple oneˉ of his disciples said to him, 'Master,
2 look at the size of those stones! Look at the size of those buildings!' ·And
Jesus said to him, 'You see these great buildings? Not a single stone will be left on
another; everything will be pulled down.'
3 And while he was sitting on the Mount of Olives, facing the Temple, Peter,
4 James, John and Andrew questioned him when they were by themselves, ·'Tell
us, when is this going to happen, and what sign will there be that it is all about to
take place?'

The beginning of sorrows

5. 6 Then Jesus began to tell them, 'Take care that no one deceives you. ·Many will
7 come using my name and saying, "I am he," and they will deceive many. ·When
you hear of wars and rumours of wars, do not be alarmed; this is something that
8 must happen, but the end will not be yet. ·For nation will fight against nation, and
kingdom against kingdom. There will be earthquakes in various places; there will
be famines. This is the beginning of the birth-pangs.
9 'Be on your guard: you will be handed over to sanhedrins; you will be beaten in
synagogues; and you will be brought before governors and kings for my sake, as
10 evidence to them, ·since the gospel must first be proclaimed to all nations.
11 'And when you are taken to be handed over, do not worry beforehand about
what to say; no, say whatever is given to you when the time comes, because it is
12 not you who will be speaking; it is the Holy Spirit. ·Brother will betray brother to
death, and a father his child; children will come forward against their parents and
13 have them put to death. ·You will be universally hated on account of my name;
but anyone who stands firm to the end will be saved.

The great tribulation of Jerusalem

14 'When you see *the appalling abomination* set up where it ought not to be (let
15 the reader understand), then those in Judaea must escape to the mountains; ·if a
man is on the housetop, he must not come down or go inside to collect anything
16 from his house; ·if a man is in the fields, he must not turn back to fetch his cloak.
17 Alas for those with child, or with babies at the breast, when those days come!
18. 19 Pray that this may not be in winter. ·For in those days there will be *great distress,*

20 *unparalleled since* God created the world, and such as will never be again. ·And if the Lord had not shortened that time, no human being would have survived; but he did shorten the time, for the sake of the elect whom he chose.

21   'And if anyone says to you then, "Look, here is the Christ" or, "Look, he is
22 there," do not believe it; ·for false Christs and false prophets will arise and produce
23 signs and portents to deceive the elect, if that were possible. ·You, therefore, must be on your guard. I have given you full warning.

The coming of the Son of man *b*

24 'But in those days, after that time of distress, the sun will be darkened, the moon
25 will not give its light, ·the stars will come falling out of the sky and the powers in
26 the heavens will be shaken. ·And then they will see the Son of man coming in the
27 clouds with great power and glory. ·And then he will send the angels to gather his elect from the four winds, from the ends of the world to the ends of the sky.

The time of this coming

28 'Take the fig tree as a parable: as soon as its twigs grow supple and its leaves come
29 out, you know that summer is near. ·So with you when you see these things
30 happening: know that he is near, right at the gates. ·In truth I tell you, before this
31 generation has passed away all these things will have taken place. ·Sky and earth will pass away, but my words will not pass away.

32   'But as for that day or hour, nobody knows it, neither the angels in heaven, nor the Son; no one but the Father.

Be on the alert

33 'Be on your guard, stay awake, because you never know when the time will come.
34 It is like a man travelling abroad: he has gone from his home, and left his servants in charge, each with his own work to do; and he has told the doorkeeper to stay
35 awake. ·So stay awake, because you do not know when the master of the house is
36 coming, evening, midnight, cockcrow or dawn;ᶜ ·if he comes unexpectedly, he
37 must not find you asleep. ·And what I am saying to you I say to all: Stay awake!'

V: PASSION AND RESURRECTION

The conspiracy against Jesus

1 **14** It was two days before the Passover and the feast of Unleavened Bread, and the chief priests and the scribes were looking for a way to arrest Jesus
2 by some trick and have him put to death. ·For they said, 'It must not be during the festivities, or there will be a disturbance among the people.'

The anointing at Bethany

3 He was at Bethany in the house of Simon, a man who had suffered from a virulent skin-disease; he was at table when a woman came in with an alabaster jar of very costly ointment, pure nard.ᵈ She broke the jar and poured the ointment on his
4 head. ·Some who were there said to one another indignantly, 'Why this waste of
5 ointment? ·Ointment like this could have been sold for over three hundred denarii
6 and the money given to the poor'; and they were angry with her. ·But Jesus said, 'Leave her alone. Why are you upsetting her? What she has done for me is a good

7 work. *b* •You have the poor with you always, and you can be kind to them whenever
8 you wish, but you will not always have me. •She has done what she could: she has
9 anointed my body beforehand for its burial. •In truth I tell you, wherever
throughout all the world the gospel is proclaimed, what she has done will be told
as well, in remembrance of her.'

Judas betrays Jesus

10 Judas Iscariot, one of the Twelve, approached the chief priests with an offer to
11 hand Jesus over to them. •They were delighted to hear it, and promised to give
him money; and he began to look for a way of betraying him when the opportunity
should occur.

Preparations for the Passover supper

12 On the first day of Unleavened Bread, when the Passover lamb was sacrificed, his
disciples said to him, 'Where do you want us to go and make the preparations *c* for
13 you to eat the Passover?' •So he sent two of his disciples, saying to them, 'Go into
14 the city and you will meet a man carrying a pitcher of water. Follow him, •and say
to the owner of the house which he enters, "The Master says: Where is the room
15 for me to eat the Passover with my disciples?" •He will show you a large upper
room furnished with couches, all prepared. Make the preparations for us there.'
16 The disciples set out and went to the city and found everything as he had told
them, and prepared the Passover.

The treachery of Judas foretold

17, 18 When evening came he arrived with the Twelve. •And while they were at table
eating, Jesus said, 'In truth I tell you, one of you is about to betray me, one of you
19 *eating with me.*' •They were distressed and said to him, one after another, 'Not
20 me, surely?' •He said to them, 'It is one of the Twelve, one who is dipping into the
21 same dish with me. •Yes, the Son of man is going to his fate, as the scriptures say
he will, but alas for that man by whom the Son of man is betrayed! Better for that
man if he had never been born.'

The institution of the Eucharist

22 And as they were eating he took bread, and when he had said the blessing he
23 broke it and gave it to them. 'Take it,' he said, 'this is my body.' •Then he took a
cup, and when he had given thanks he handed it to them, and all drank from it,
24 and he said to them, 'This is my blood, the blood of the covenant, poured out for
25 many. •In truth I tell you, I shall never drink wine any more until the day I drink
- the new wine in the kingdom of God.'

Peter's denial foretold

26, 27 After the psalms had been sung they left for the Mount of Olives. •And Jesus said
to them, 'You will all fall away, for the scripture says: *I shall strike the shepherd*
28 *and the sheep will be scattered*; •however, after my resurrection I shall go before
29, 30 you into Galilee.' •Peter said, 'Even if all fall away, I will not.' •And Jesus said to
him, 'In truth I tell you, this day, this very night, before the cock crows twice, you
31 will have disowned me three times.' •But he repeated still more earnestly, 'If I
have to die with you, I will never disown you.' And they all said the same.

Gethsemane

32 They came to a plot of land called Gethsemane, and he said to his disciples, 'Stay
33. 34 here while I pray.' ·Then he took Peter and James and John with him. ·And he
began to feel terror and anguish. And he said to them, 'My soul is sorrowful to the
35 point of death. Wait here, and stay awake.' ·And going on a little further he threw
himself on the ground and prayed that, if it were possible, this hour might pass
36 him by. ·'*Abba*, Father!' *d* he said, 'For you everything is possible. Take this cup
37 away from me. But let it be as you, not I, would have it.' ·He came back and
found them sleeping, and he said to Peter, 'Simon, are you asleep? Had you not
38 the strength to stay awake one hour? ·Stay awake and pray not to be put to the
39 test. The spirit is willing enough, but human nature is weak.' ·Again he went away
40 and prayed, saying the same words. ·And once more he came back and found
them sleeping, their eyes were so heavy; and they could find no answer for him.
41 He came back a third time and said to them, 'You can sleep on now and have your
rest. It is all over. The hour has come. Now the Son of man is to be betrayed into
42 the hands of sinners. ·Get up! Let us go! My betrayer is not far away.'

The arrest

43 And at once, while he was still speaking, Judas, one of the Twelve, came up and
with him a number of men armed with swords and clubs, sent by the chief priests
44 and the scribes and the elders. ·Now the traitor had arranged a signal with them
saying, 'The one I kiss, he is the man. Arrest him, and see he is well guarded when
45 you lead him away.' ·So when the traitor came, he went up to Jesus at once and
46. 47 said, 'Rabbi!' and kissed him. ·The others seized him and arrested him. ·Then
one of the bystanders drew his sword and struck out at the high priest's servant
and cut off his ear.
48   Then Jesus spoke. 'Am I a bandit,' he said, 'that you had to set out to capture
49 me with swords and clubs? ·I was among you teaching in the Temple day after day
50 and you never laid a hand on me. But this is to fulfil the scriptures.' ·And they all
51 deserted him and ran away. ·A young man followed with nothing on but a linen
52 cloth. They caught hold of him, ·but he left the cloth in their hands and ran away
naked. *e*

Jesus before the Sanhedrin

53 They led Jesus off to the high priest; and all the chief priests and the elders and
54 the scribes assembled there. ·Peter had followed him at a distance, right into the
high priest's palace, and was sitting with the attendants warming himself at the
fire.
55   The chief priests and the whole Sanhedrin were looking for evidence against
56 Jesus in order to have him executed. But they could not find any. ·Several, indeed,
57 brought false witness against him, but their evidence was conflicting. ·Some stood
58 up and submitted this false evidence against him, ·'We heard him say, "I am going
to destroy this Temple made by human hands, and in three days build another,
59 not made by human hands."' ·But even on this point their evidence was
60 conflicting. ·The high priest then rose before the whole assembly and put this
question to Jesus, 'Have you no answer to that? What is this evidence these men
61 are bringing against you?' *f* ·But he was silent and made no answer at all. The high
priest put a second question to him saying, 'Are you the Christ, the Son of the
62 Blessed One?' *g* ·'I am,' said Jesus, 'and you will see the *Son of man seated at the*

63 *right hand of the Power and coming with the clouds of heaven.'* ·The high priest
64 tore his robes and said, 'What need of witnesses have we now? ·You heard the
blasphemy. What is your finding?' Their verdict was unanimous: he deserved to
die.
65 Some of them started spitting at his face, hitting him and saying, 'Play the
prophet!'* And the attendants struck him too.

Peter's denials

66 While Peter was down below in the courtyard, one of the high priest's servant-
67 girls came up. ·She saw Peter warming himself there, looked closely at him and
68 said, 'You too were with Jesus, the man from Nazareth.' ·But he denied it. 'I do
not know, I do not understand what you are talking about,' he said. And he went
69 out into the forecourt, and a cock crowed.* ·The servant-girl saw him and again
70 started telling the bystanders, 'This man is one of them.' ·But again he denied it.
A little later the bystanders themselves said to Peter, 'You are certainly one of
71 them! Why, you are a Galilean.' ·But he started cursing and swearing, 'I do not
72 know the man you speak of.' ·And at once the cock crowed for the second time,
and Peter recalled what Jesus had said to him, 'Before the cock crows twice, you
will have disowned me three times.' And he burst into tears.

Jesus before Pilate

1 **15** First thing in the morning, the chief priests, together with the elders and
scribes and the rest of the Sanhedrin, had their plan ready. They had Jesus
bound and took him away and handed him over to Pilate.
2 Pilate put to him this question, 'Are you the king of the Jews?' He replied, 'It is
3 you who say it.' ·And the chief priests brought many accusations against him.
4 Pilate questioned him again, 'Have you no reply at all? See how many accusations
5 they are bringing against you!' ·But, to Pilate's surprise, Jesus made no further
reply.
6 At festival time Pilate used to release a prisoner for them, any one they asked
7 for. ·Now a man called Barabbas was then in prison with the rebels who had
8 committed murder during the uprising. ·When the crowd went up* and began to
9 ask Pilate the customary favour, ·Pilate answered them, 'Do you want me to
10 release for you the king of the Jews?'* ·For he realised it was out of jealousy that
11 the chief priests had handed Jesus over. ·The chief priests, however, had incited
12 the crowd to demand that he should release Barabbas for them instead. ·Then
Pilate spoke again, 'But in that case, what am I to do with the man you call king of
13, 14 the Jews?' ·They shouted back, 'Crucify him!' ·Pilate asked them, 'What harm
15 has he done?' But they shouted all the louder, 'Crucify him!' ·So Pilate, anxious
to placate the crowd, released Barabbas for them and, after having Jesus scourged,
he handed him over to be crucified.

Jesus crowned with thorns

16 The soldiers led him away to the inner part of the palace, that is, the Praetorium,
17 and called the whole cohort together. ·They dressed him up in purple, twisted
18 some thorns into a crown and put it on him. ·And they began saluting him, 'Hail
19 king of the Jews!' ·They struck his head with a reed and spat on him; and they
20 went down on their knees to do him homage. ·And when they had finished making
fun of him, they took off the purple and dressed him in his own clothes.

The way of the cross

21 They led him out to crucify him. ·They enlisted a passer-by, Simon of Cyrene, father of Alexander and Rufus, *c* who was coming in from the country, to carry his
22 cross. ·They brought Jesus to the place called Golgotha, which means the place of the skull.

The crucifixion

23. 24 They offered him wine mixed with myrrh, but he refused it. ·Then they crucified
25 him, and shared out his clothing, casting lots to decide what each should get. ·It
26 was the third hour *d* when they crucified him. ·The inscription giving the charge
27 against him read, 'The King of the Jews'. ·And they crucified two bandits with him, one on his right and one on his left. *e[28]*

The crucified Jesus is mocked

29 The passers-by jeered at him; they shook their heads and said, 'Aha! So you would
30 destroy the Temple and rebuild it in three days! ·Then save yourself; come down
31 from the cross!' ·The chief priests and the scribes mocked him among themselves
32 in the same way with the words, 'He saved others, he cannot save himself. ·Let the Christ, the king of Israel, come down from the cross now, for us to see it and believe.' Even those who were crucified with him taunted him.

The death of Jesus

33 When the sixth hour came there was darkness over the whole land until the ninth
34 hour. ·And at the ninth hour Jesus cried out in a loud voice, '*Eloi, eloi, f lama*
35 *sabachthani?*' which means, '*My God, my God, why have you forsaken me?*' ·When some of those who stood by heard this, they said, 'Listen, he is calling on Elijah.'
36 Someone ran and soaked a sponge in vinegar and, putting it on a reed, gave it to
37 him to drink saying, 'Wait! And see if Elijah will come to take him down.' ·But
38 Jesus gave a loud cry and breathed his last. ·And the veil of the Sanctuary was
39 torn in two from top to bottom. ·The centurion, who was standing in front of him, had seen how he had died, and he said, 'In truth this man was Son of God.' *g*

The women on Calvary

40 There were some women watching from a distance. Among them were Mary of Magdala, Mary who was the mother of James the younger and Joset, and Salome. *h*
41 These used to follow him and look after him when he was in Galilee. And many other women were there who had come up to Jerusalem with him.

The burial

42 It was now evening, and since it was Preparation Day—that is, the day before
43 the Sabbath—·there came Joseph of Arimathaea, a prominent member of the Council, *i* who himself lived in the hope of seeing the kingdom of God, and he
44 boldly went to Pilate and asked for the body of Jesus. ·Pilate, astonished that he should have died so soon, summoned the centurion and enquired if he had been
45 dead for some time. *j* ·Having been assured of this by the centurion, he granted
46 the corpse to Joseph ·who bought a shroud, took Jesus down from the cross, wrapped him in the shroud and laid him in a tomb which had been hewn out of the
47 rock. He then rolled a stone against the entrance to the tomb. ·Mary of Magdala and Mary the mother of Joset took note of where he was laid.

The empty tomb. The angel's message

1 **16** When the Sabbath was over, Mary of Magdala, Mary the mother of James,
2   and Salome, bought spices with which to go and anoint him. •And very
early in the morning on the first day of the week they went to the tomb when the
sun had risen. *
3   They had been saying to one another, 'Who will roll away the stone for us from
4 the entrance to the tomb?' •But when they looked they saw that the stone—which
5 was very big—had already been rolled back. •On entering the tomb they saw a
young man in a white robe seated on the right-hand side, and they were struck
6 with amazement. •But he said to them, 'There is no need to be so amazed. You
are looking for Jesus of Nazareth, who was crucified: he has risen, he is not here.
7 See, here is the place where they laid him. •But you must go and tell his disciples
and Peter, "He is going ahead of you to Galilee; that is where you will see him,
8 just as he told you." ' •And the women came out and ran away from the tomb
because they were frightened out of their wits; and they said nothing to anyone, *
for they were afraid.

Appearances of the risen Christ *

9 Having risen in the morning on the first day of the week, he appeared first to Mary
10 of Magdala from whom he had cast out seven devils. •She then went to those who
had been his companions, and who were mourning and in tears, and told them.
11 But they did not believe her when they heard her say that he was alive and that
she had seen him.
12   After this, he showed himself under another form to two of them as they were
13 on their way into the country. •These went back and told the others, who did not
believe them either.
14   Lastly, he showed himself to the Eleven themselves while they were at table.
He reproached them for their incredulity and obstinacy, because they had refused
15 to believe those who had seen him after he had risen. •And he said to them, 'Go
16 out to the whole world; proclaim the gospel to all creation. •Whoever believes
17 and is baptised will be saved; whoever does not believe will be condemned. •These
are the signs that will be associated with believers: in my name they will cast out
18 devils; they will have the gift of tongues; •they will pick up snakes in their hands
and be unharmed should they drink deadly poison; they will lay their hands on the
sick, who will recover.'
19   And so the Lord Jesus, after he had spoken to them, was taken up into heaven;
20 there at the right hand of God he took his place, •while they, going out, preached
everywhere, the Lord working with them and confirming the word by the signs
that accompanied it.

NOTES TO MARK

1 a. lit. 'good news'. Old English 'god-spel'. Gk *euagge-lion*, is the coming of the kingdom of God, *see* Mt 4:17f. It was prepared for in the OT. Is 40:9; 52:7; 61:1, and is announced by Jesus who 'proclaims' the good news. 1:14 and par.; Mt 4:23; 9:35; Lk 4:43; 8:1; cf. Mk 16:15, and calls for belief in it. Mk 1:15; *see* Mt 8:10b; Rm 1:16h. In his person this kingdom has come. Mt 11:5seq.; Lk 4:18,21. After him, his disciples will bring the good news to the whole world, 16:15; Mt 24:14seq.; 26:13seq.; Ac 5:42q; Ga 2:7. This good news was first proclaimed, then gradually written down, until it took a fixed form in our four canonical gospels, *see* p. 6–7. • The noun, which Lk does not use at all, has always in Mk (and in Mt 26:13) the force of a technical term, used in an absolute sense, and is best translated 'gospel'.

Elsewhere in Mt and always in Lk, who uses the derived verb, Lk 1:19n, the translation 'good news' is preferable.

b. om. 'Son of God'.

c. var. 'John wore a garment of camel-hair with a leather belt round his waist,' cf. Mt 3:4.

d. Mark omits or ignores the detail of the three temptations which Matthew and Luke derive from some other source. The mention of the wild beasts evokes the messianic ideal, announced by the prophets, of a return to the heavenly peace, *see* Is 11:6–9, 6e, associated with the theme of the retreat into the desert, *see* Ho 2;16p. The ministration of the angels expresses the divine protection, cf. Ps 91:11–13, a text made use of by Mt 4:6 and par.

e. Fulfilment implies a continuity between the stages of God's plan, 1 K 8:24; Ws 8:8; Ac 1:7i. When the last of these stages begins, Rm 3:26m; Heb 1:2a, the time is 'fulfilled', Ga 4:4c; cf. 1 Co 10:11; God brings to completion not only the scriptures, Mt 1:22j, and the Law, Mt 5:17h, but also the whole purpose of the old covenant, Mt 9:17; 26:28h; Rm 10:4; 2 Co 3:14–15; Heb 10:1,14. At the end of this last period of history, 1 Co 10:11; 1 Tm 4:1; 1 P 1:5,20; 1 Jn 2:18, which is the 'end of the last age', Heb 9:26, will come another end, the 'end of time', Mt 13:40,49; 24:3; 28:20. This is the Day, 1 Co 15:23n, the Day when he is revealed, 1 Co 1:7c, the Day of his Judgement, Rm 2:6b.

f. Those whom Jesus calls to follow him, 1:20; 2:14seq.; Mt 19:21p, 27–28; Lk 9:57–62; *see also* Dt 13:3,5; 1 K 14:8; 19:20, in order to have a share with him must leave all, Mk 10:21,28 and par.; cf. Jn 12:24–26. For those disciples who will not know the earthly Jesus the same ideas are expressed in terms of 'fellowship', Ph 3:10; 1 Jn 1:3b, or of 'imitation', 2 Th 3:7.

g. This was the name given by Judaism, *see* Zc 13:2, to demons, foreign and even hostile to the religious and moral purity demanded by the service of God; *see also* 3:11,30; Mt 10:1; 12:43; Lk 4:33,36.

h. lit. 'What is there for us and for you?', *see* Jn 2:4d.

i. var. 'You have come'.

j. God is the unique 'Holy One', and all that belongs to him is holy, Lv 17:1a,44f; 19:2; Is 6:3; this is pre-eminently true of Jesus who is God's Son and his chosen Messiah, Mk 1:10seq., the appointed head of 'the nation of saints', Dn 7:18m, i.e. of the company of the elect, the Christian community, Ac 9:13g; cf. Lk 1:35; 4:34; Jn 6:69u; Ac 2:27; 3:14u; 4:17,30; Rv 3:7.

k. Or punctuate 'Here is a teaching that is new; with authority he gives orders even to unclean spirits.'

l. var. 'they went'.

m. Jesus forbids the news that he is the Messiah to be spread by the devils, 1;25,34;3:12, by those he cures, 1:44; 5:43; 7:36; 8:26, even by the apostles, 8:30; 9:9. The silence is not to be broken until after his death, Mt 10:27j. Since the prevailing idea of the Messiah was nationalistic and warlike, in sharp contrast with this own ideal, Jesus had to be very careful, at least on Israelite soil, *see* 5:19, to avoid giving a false and dangerous impression of his mission,*see* Mt 13:13e; Jn 6:15. Some have claimed that this command of silence ('the messianic secret') is an invention of Mark. But it may well have been Jesus' own, to which Mark has given special prominence. With the exception of Mt 9:30, Mt and Lk record the injunction to silence only in passages which are parallel with Mk, frequently omitting it even in those cases.

n. lit. 'came out', i.e. from Capernaum, v. 35. This is the primary sense, but it is possible that another lies behind it, namely the 'coming forth' of Jesus from God, Jn 8:42; 13:3; 16:27seq., 30; cf. Lk 4:43.

2 a. Jesus here claims the divine power to forgive sins, Is 1:18j, which he will exercise frequently in the course of his ministry. He himself connects this power with his death, Mt 20:28g, and with the blood of the covenant, Mt 26:28h. The Christian communities will in their turn attribute this divine power to the risen Christ, e.g. Ac 2:38; 3:19; 10:43; 13:38; Rm 3:21–26,24i; 5:6–9; Ep 1:7; 4:32; Col 1:14; 3:13; Heb 9:26; 1 Jn 1:7; 2:12; Rv 1:5. But Jesus also entrusts this

power to his disciples, promising that God will ratify their decisions, Mt 16:19; 18:18; Jn 20:23.

b. The Sea of Galilee ('Lake of Tiberias').

c. In Mt and Lk the disciples' fault is to pick ears of corn to appease their hunger, but in Mk it is to tear them up in order to make a path. This would have been more intelligible to readers unfamiliar with Jewish casuistry. While it was far from clear that picking ears of corn amounted to 'harvesting', it was obvious that one should not devastate a field in order to cross it! This version sits awkwardly to the rest of the story.

d. The high priest of 1 S 21:1–7 was in fact Ahimelech. Either his son Abiathar is named here because, as high priest in David's reign, 2 S 20:25, he was the better known, or else Mk is following a different tradition according to which Abiathar was Ahimelech's father (2 S 8:17 Hebr.).

e. This verse, lacking in Mt and Lk, must have been added by Mk when the new spirit of Christianity had already reduced the importance of the Sabbath obligation, *see* Lk 5:39f.

3 a. The term signifies not officials of the court of Herod Antipas, tetrarch of Galilee, *see* Lk 3:1c, but politically minded Jews actively supporting his dynasty and enjoying his favour, cf. Mt 22:11c.

b. Punctuation uncertain. 'From Judaea . . . Sidon' may be read with what precedes or with what follows.

c. The new leaders of the chosen people have to be twelve in number, as the tribes of Israel had been. This number is to be re-instituted after Judas' defection, Ac 1:26, to be preserved for ever in heaven, Mt 19:28 and par.; Rv 21:12–14j.

d. Mk has here no discourse like the one given at this point in Mt 5–7 and Lk 6:20–49. The details of Jesus' teaching in relation to the Jewish law would doubtless be seen as less necessary for the readers of the gospel than a record of what Jesus was and did. ..

e. lit. 'because they said'. Others translate 'because it was told (them)'.

f. To attribute to the Evil One what in fact is the work of the Holy Spirit amounts to shutting oneself off from divine grace and the forgiveness that flows from it. In its very nature such an attitude makes salvation impossible. But grace can change this attitude, so that a return to salvation remains possible, *see* 1:23g.

4 a. The conjunction (Mt avoids it) is equivalent to 'in order that the scripture might be fulfilled that says . . .'.

b. The apostles' incomprehension of Jesus' works and words is a recurrent theme of Mk: 6:52; 7:18; 8:17–18,21,33; 9:10,32; 10:38. With the exception of certain parallel places (Mt 15:16; 16:9,23; 20:22; Lk 9:45) and of Lk 18:34; 24:25,45, Mt and Lk often pass over such remarks in silence, or even amend them; compare Mt 14:33 with Mk 6:51–52, and cf. Mt 13:51, *see* Jn 14:26r.

c. Mk, followed by Lk, has collected here, vv. 21–25, four little parables which can be interpreted differently according to the contexts in which they are used; see the applications made by Lk's reduplications and Mt's parallels. In the present context they can all be understood of the teaching of Jesus, a light which must shine out, and for which the recipients are in some way responsible.

d. The kingdom will achieve its full development by virtue of its own hidden intrinsic power.

e. var. 'How is it that you have no faith?'

5 a. var. 'Gadarenes', cf. Mt, or 'Gergesenes'.

b. This power is regarded as a physical emanation that heals, cf. Lk 6:19, by contact; cf. Mk 1:41; 3:10; 6:56; 8:22.

c. Not only from a sense of shame but also because the complaint involved legal impurity, Lv 15:25.

d. These are to be privileged witnesses of the Transfiguration, 9:2, and of the agony, 14:33; cf. 1:29; 13:3.

e. Aramaic; Jesus' native tongue.

6   a. Not 'the carpenter's son', Mt 13:55; Mk's expression accords better with the virgin birth of Jesus.

b. var. 'Jose' or 'Joseph'.

c. In Mt and Lk the staff and sandals are forbidden, but the sense is the same: the complete detachment of the missioners.

d. var. 'He was saying'.

e. var. (Vulg.) 'he did many things'. Alternative, but less probable, translation '. . . gave him his protection. He heard him speak and asked him all kinds of questions and liked to listen to him.'

f. add. 'on the other side', see Mt 14:22.

7   a. The 'tradition of the elders' comprises the injunctions and practices added by the rabbis to the Mosaic Law.

b. var. 'bathing'. Or 'they never eat what comes from the market without having sprinkled it.'

c. *qorban*, Aramaic word meaning an offering, especially to God. See Mt 15:6d.

d. Some versions omit v. 16.

e. 'Parable' in the Hebrew sense of *mashal* which includes even brief enigmatic sayings.

f. lit. 'making all foods clean'; the clause (possibly a gloss) is obscure and variously interpreted.

g. add. 'and Sidon', cf. Mt 15:21.

h. lit. 'a Greek', not racially, since she was a Syro-Phoenician, but culturally, that is to say, gentile in this context; cf. Jn 7:35; Ac 16:1.

8   a. Either a place-name, unidentified like the 'Magadan' of Mt 15:39, or possibly a transliteration of some Aramaic expression.

b. The refusal of any sign in Mk is often considered more primitive than the promise of 'the sign of Jonah' in Mt and Lk. It is, however, also possible that Mk has omitted a biblical allusion which would make no sense to his readers, and that in fact Jesus did promise this sign, in order to foretell the triumph of his final deliverance, as Mt has made explicit, see Mt 12:39l.

c. An invitation to the disciples to forget their materialistic preoccupation and to reflect upon Jesus' mission highlighted by his miracles.

d. Others translate 'raising his eyes'.

e. Peter's profession of faith is the turning point of the plan of Mk, see page 1604. His closest disciples have at last recognised that he is the Messiah; but they still have to learn how the work of the Messiah will be done in a completely unexpected way, cf. 9:32; 10:38.

9   a. While Mt presents the Transfiguration as a proclamation of Jesus as the new Moses, see Mt 17:1a, and Lk emphasises the approaching Passion, see Lk 9:28f, Mk, following the dominant theme of his Gospel, sees in it above all a glorious manifestation of the hidden Messiah. Briefly, the disciples experience the heavenly quality of Jesus, described by means of symbols whose meaning is clear from apocalyptic literature, e.g. Dn 10:5–10.

b. var. 'he rejoined . . . he saw'.

c. var. 'by prayer and fasting'.

d. add. 'in me'.

e. omitting, with the best MSS, vv. 44 and 46 (Vulg.), as repetitions of v. 48.

f. This 'seasoning' fire means either penalties by which the sinner is punished and at the same time preserved, or (preferably) the purifying fire of trials by which the faithful become sacrifices pleasing to God, see Lv 2:13 (to this alludes an add. 'and every victim must be salted with salt'). It appears that v. 50, cf. Mt 5:13, has been inserted here for no other reason than the recurrence of the word 'salt'.

10   a. add. 'and cling to his wife', cf. Gn 2:24 and Mt 19:5.

b. This clause reflects Roman law, for Jewish law permitted only a husband, not a wife, to divorce.

c. Wealth and prosperity were considered signs of

God's favour, see p. 750–1, Intro. to the Wisdom Books (*OT*).

d. When, as Messianic King, your triumph is assured.

e. To drink the cup, cf. 14:36, and to be baptised are symbols of the approaching Passion: Jesus is to be 'immersed' (Gk: *baptizein*) in suffering.

f. Aramaic 'My master' or 'Master'; cf. Jn 20:16.

11   a. The Synoptic Gospels present here a different order which must be explained by the literary evolution of the tradition. On the one hand the entry into Jerusalem and the expulsion of the merchants from the Temple, given by Mt and Lk on the same day, are spread over two days by Mk, and separated by the incident of the cursing of the fig tree. On the other hand, the withered fig tree (and also its curse in Mt) are put by Mk between the expulsion of the merchants and the discussion of Jesus' authority, two incidents which must have come one after the other, see Jn 2:14–22. These divergences are explained if the episode of the fig tree was introduced later into a primitive account (note that it is absent from Lk), and this in two stages: first the curse, then the withering, a later addition intended to draw out of the fulfilment of the curse a lesson on the efficacy of prayer with faith. In Mk alone has this lesson brought with it, by verbal association, a saying on forgiveness which Mt uses after the Lord's Prayer, Mt 6:14.

b. Of the synoptics only Mk quotes, no doubt deliberately, these last four words of Isaiah's text; they foretell the worldwide worship of the messianic age.

c. add. v. 26 'But if you do not forgive, your Father in heaven will not forgive your failings either,' cf. Mt 6:15.

12   a. i.e. in which the burning bush incident is narrated.

b. Monotheism is as uncompromising in the NT as it is in Judaism. Here, on Jesus' lips, it is based on the *shema*, Dt 6:4–5b. Paul will exhort the gentiles to be converted to the one living God, Ac 14:15k; 1 Th 1:9; see also 1 Co 8:4–6c; 1 Tm 2:5. In his view all the work of Jesus Christ comes from God and leads to him, for he makes it contribute to his own glory, Rm 8:28–30; 16:27; 1 Co 1:30; 15:28,57; Ep 1:3–12; 3:11; Ph 2:11; 4:19–20; 1 Tm 2:3–5; 6:15–16; see also Heb 1:1–13; 13:20–21. John's Gospel expresses it differently: Jesus comes from the Father, 3:17,31; 6:46, and goes to the Father, 7:33; 13:3; 14:6d.

c. Evidently the treasure chamber inside the Temple enclosure had an alms box outside.

13   a. By contrast with Mt, who adds the dimension of the end of the world to that of the destruction of Jerusalem and the Temple, see Mt 24:1a, Mk's discourse is limited to the destruction of Jerusalem. Many scholars discern here a little Jewish apocalypse inspired by Daniel, vv. 7–8,14–20,24–27, filled out by sayings of Jesus, vv. 5–6, 9–13, 21–23,28–37. Nothing either in the sayings or in the underlying little Jewish apocalypse foretells anything more than the imminent messianic crisis and the awaited deliverance of the chosen people, which in fact occurred in the resurrection of Christ, his coming in the Church, and the destruction of Jerusalem.

b. In the traditional language of the prophets (see marginal references here and to Mt 24:29–31) cosmic wonders are used to describe powerful interventions of God in history, and in this case the messianic crisis, followed by the final triumph of the chosen people and the Son of man at their head. There is no need to refer them to the end of the world, as is often done because of the context in which Mt has set them, see Mt 24:1a.

· c. The night was divided into these four watches, each of which lasted three hours.

14   a. With Jn 12:3, Mk indicates the quality of the perfume, nard, the extract of an Indian aromatic plant. He alone notes that the woman breaks the jar in order to pour it more abundantly and quickly, a gesture of touching prodigality.

b. 'a good work' may possibly be in a Jewish technical

sense, the works of compassion being ranked as superior to the duty of almsgiving; but it may also be meant in the general sense of 'a beautiful thing'.

c. According to Mt, Jesus sent a message to the man to whose house he invited himself; according to Mk a sign will lead the two appointed disciples to a room which they will find all prepared. Although sign and preparation could have been pre-arranged, their literary presentation, inspired by 1 S 10:2–5, lends a halo of supernatural foreknowledge to the scene. It will further be noted that the structure of the incident closely resembles the preparation for the messianic entry, Mk 11:1–6.

d. *Abba* is an Aramaic word which, on Jesus' lips, expresses the familiarity of Son with Father, cf. Mt 11:25–26 and par.; Jn 3:35; 5:19–20; 8:28–29. It will be placed on the lips of Christians, Rm 8:15; Ga 4:6, for the Spirit, Rm 5:5e makes them children of God, Mt 6:9; 17:25i; Lk 11:2.

e. Detail peculiar to Mk. Some commentators have seen in this young man the evangelist himself.

f. Here, and in Mt 26:62, some translate 'Do you make no reply to the charges these men are bringing against you?'

g. 'The Blessed One' (*see also* 'the Power', v. 62) is a substitute for the name 'Yahweh' which the Jews would not pronounce.

h. 'Spitting in his face', D *Vet Lat* (a f), Caesarean text, Peshitta; 'spitting at him and blindfolding him', the majority, by harmonisation with Lk 22:64. Add. 'Who is it who hit you then?', less good witnesses, by harmonisation with Mt 26:68 and Lk 22:64. If Mk mentions neither blindfold nor question, the scene loses its character of a guessing-game and shows only the outrages to the prophet foretold by Is 50:6.

i. The first cockcrow which does not shake Peter and the partial exit which goes with it are strange and suggest an original account which had only one denial with a cockcrow and exit. The combination of this with two parallel accounts, drawn from other traditions, has produced the traditional figure of three denials: 14:30 and par., 72 and par. *see* Jn 3:38; 21:15–17. This combination of texts, visible in Mk, has been smoothed over in Mt and Lk, who have removed the first cockcrow and diminished (or eliminated, Lk) the first partial exit; it is still discernible in the separation in Jn of the first denial, 18:17, from the other two, 18:25–27.

15 a. This indication implies that the Praetorium was on high ground, which is the case with the Western Hill, where stood the palace previously belonging to Herod the Great.

b. In Mk the crowd comes to the Praetorium to ask for the release of a prisoner without any thought of Jesus. It is Pilate who turns this request to good account by suggesting the release of Jesus in order to save himself from a tricky situation; but his manoeuvre is outplayed by the chief priests, who put forward the name of Barabbas. Mt 27:17 has lost these subtleties by making Pilate himself clumsily put forward the choice between Barabbas and Jesus.

c. Alexander and Rufus were doubtless known to the circle in which Mark wrote his Gospel, *see* Rm 16:13.

d. 9 am, or, more vaguely, sometime between 9 am and noon.

e. add. v. 28 'And the text of scriptures was fulfilled that says, "He was taken for a criminal" ' (Is 53:12), cf. Lk 22:37.

f. This is the Aramaic form *elahi*, transliterated *eloi*, perhaps under the influence of the Hebr. *elohim*. The form *eli*, given by Mt is Hebr.; it is the original text of the Psalm, and better explains the pun of the soldiers.

g. For the Roman officer, this admission would not have its full Christian content, but Mk clearly sees in it an acknowledgement that Jesus was more than a man.

h. Probably the same woman who, in Mt 27:56, is called the mother of Zebedee's sons.

i. i.e. of the Sanhedrin.

j. var. 'if he was already dead'.

16 a. var. 'just as the sun was rising'.

b. According to Mt 28:8; Lk 24:10,22seq.; Jn 20:18, they did in fact tell the news. Mark, too, may have said so in a lost ending of his Gospel (*see* following note); alternatively, he may have deliberately refrained from speaking of it to avoid having to append an account of the appearances which he had made up his mind to omit.

c. The 'longer ending' of Mk, vv. 9–20, is included in the canonically accepted body of inspired scripture, although some important MSS (including Vat. and Sin.) omit it, and it does not seem to be by Mk. It is in a different style, and is little more than a summary of the appearances of the risen Christ, with other material, all of which could be derived from various NT writings. One MS gives instead a shorter ending after v. 8: 'They reported briefly to Peter's companions what they had been told. Then Jesus himself through their agency broadcast from east to west the sacred and incorruptible message of eternal salvation.' Four MSS give the shorter ending and add the longer to it. One MS has the longer ending with the following insertion between vv. 14 and 15: 'And they defended themselves thus, "This age of lawlessness and unbelief is under the sway of Satan, who does not allow those under the yoke of unclean spirits to understand God's truth and power. Now, therefore, reveal your uprightness." This is what they said to Christ, and Christ answered, "The number of years allowed for Satan's authority has been reached, but other terrible things draw near. I was handed over to be killed for those who have sinned, so that they might turn to the truth and sin no more, and so inherit the spiritual and incorruptible glory of uprightness which is in heaven . . ." '

One explanation of this diversity is that Mk's original ending was lost. More probably Mk intended to finish his Gospel at v. 8; but comparison with the other gospels made the first Christian generation feel that this ending was incomplete (and also stylistically somewhat harsh). This led them to add the 'longer ending'.

THE GOSPEL ACCORDING TO
LUKE

Prologue *

1 1 Seeing that many others *b* have undertaken to draw up accounts of the events
2 that have reached their fulfilment among us, ·as these were handed down to
3 us by those who from the outset were eyewitnesses and ministers of the word, ·I in
my turn, after carefully going over the whole story from the beginning, have
4 decided to write an ordered account for you, Theophilus, ·so that your Excellency
may learn how well founded the teaching is that you have received. *c*

I: THE BIRTH AND HIDDEN LIFE

OF JOHN THE BAPTIST AND OF JESUS *d*

The birth of John the Baptist foretold

5 In the days of King Herod of Judaea there lived a priest called Zechariah who
belonged to the Abijah section of the priesthood, and he had a wife, Elizabeth by
6 name, who was a descendant of Aaron. ·Both were upright in the sight of God
and impeccably carried out all the commandments and observances of the Lord.
7 But they were childless: Elizabeth was barren and they were both advanced in
years.
8   Now it happened that it was the turn of his section *e* to serve, and he was
9 exercising his priestly office before God ·when it fell to him by lot, as the priestly
10 custom was, to enter the Lord's sanctuary and burn incense there. *f* ·And at the
hour of incense all the people were outside, praying.
11   Then there appeared to him the angel of the Lord, standing on the right of the
12 altar of incense. ·The sight disturbed Zechariah and he was overcome with fear. *g*
13 But the angel said to him, 'Zechariah, do not be afraid, for your prayer has been
14 heard. Your wife Elizabeth is to bear you a son and you shall name him John. *h* ·He
15 will be your joy and delight and many will rejoice *i* at his birth, ·for he will be great
in the sight of the Lord; he must drink no wine, no strong drink; *j* even from his
16 mother's womb he will be filled with the Holy Spirit, *k* ·and he will bring back
17 many of the Israelites to the Lord their God. ·With the spirit and power of Elijah, *l*
he will go before him *to reconcile fathers to their children* and the disobedient to
the good sense of the upright, preparing for the Lord a people fit for him.'
18 Zechariah said to the angel, '*How can I know this?* *m* I am an old man and my wife

19 is getting on in years.' ·The angel replied, 'I am Gabriel, who stand in God's presence, and I have been sent to speak to you and bring you *ⁿ* this good news.
20 Look! Since you did not believe my words, which will come true at their appointed time, you will be silenced and have no power of speech until this has happened.'
21 Meanwhile the people were waiting for Zechariah and were surprised that he
22 stayed in the sanctuary so long. ·When he came out he could not speak to them, and they realised that he had seen a vision in the sanctuary. But he could only make signs to them *º* and remained dumb.
23, 24   When his time of service came to an end he returned home. ·Some time later
25 his wife Elizabeth conceived and for five months she kept to herself, saying, 'The Lord has done this for me, now that it has pleased him to take away the humiliation I suffered *ᵖ* in public.'

The annunciation *ᵠ*

26 In the sixth month *ʳ* the angel Gabriel was sent by God to a town in Galilee called
27 Nazareth, ·to a virgin betrothed to a man named Joseph, of the House of David;
28 and the virgin's name was Mary. ·He went in and said to her, 'Rejoice, *ˢ* you who
29 enjoy God's favour! The Lord is with you.' ·She was deeply disturbed by these
30 words and asked herself what this greeting could mean, ·but the angel said to her,
31 'Mary, do not be afraid; you have won God's favour. ·Look! You are to conceive
32 in your womb and bear a son, and you must name him Jesus. ·He will be great and will be called Son of the Most High. The Lord God will give him the throne of his
33 ancestor David; ·he will rule over the House of Jacob for ever and his reign will
34 have no end.' *ᵗ* ·Mary said to the angel, 'But how can this come about, since I have
35 no knowledge of man?' *ᵘ* ·The angel answered, 'The Holy Spirit will come upon you, and the power of the Most High will cover you with its shadow. *ᵛ* And so the
36 child will be holy and will be called Son of God. ·And I tell you this too: your cousin Elizabeth also, in her old age, has conceived a son, and she whom people
37, 38 called barren is now in her sixth month, ·*for nothing is impossible to God*.' ·Mary said, 'You see before you the Lord's servant, let it happen to me as you have said.' And the angel left her.

The visitation

39 Mary set out at that time and went as quickly as she could into the hill country to a
40, 41 town in Judah. *ʷ* ·She went into Zechariah's house and greeted Elizabeth. Now it happened that as soon as Elizabeth heard Mary's greeting, the child leapt in her
42 womb and Elizabeth was filled with the Holy Spirit. ·She gave a loud cry and said, 'Of all women you are the most blessed, and blessed is the fruit of your womb.
43, 44 Why should I be honoured with a visit from the mother of my Lord? *ˣ* ·Look, the
45 moment your greeting reached my ears, the child in my womb leapt for joy. ·Yes, blessed is she who believed that the promise made her by the Lord would be fulfilled.' *ʸ*

The Magnificat

46 And Mary *ᶻ* said:

     My soul proclaims the greatness of the Lord
47   and my spirit *rejoices in God my Saviour*;
48   because *he has looked upon the humiliation of his servant*.
     Yes, from now onwards all generations will call me blessed,

49   for the Almighty has done great things for me.
          Holy is his name,
50   and *his faithful love extends age after age to those who fear him.*
51   He has used the power of his arm,
          he has routed the arrogant of heart.
52   *He has pulled down princes* from their thrones *and raised high the lowly.*
53   *He has filled the starving with good things,* sent the rich away empty.
54   *He has come to the help of Israel his servant, mindful of his faithful love*
55   —according to the promise he made to our ancestors—
          of his mercy to Abraham and to his descendants for ever.

56   Mary stayed with her some three months and then went home. *aa*

The birth of John the Baptist and visit of the neighbours

57. 58 The time came for Elizabeth to have her child, and she gave birth to a son; ·and when her neighbours and relations heard that the Lord had lavished on her his faithful love, they shared her joy.

The circumcision of John the Baptist

59 Now it happened that on the eighth day they came to circumcise the child; they
60 were going to call *bb* him Zechariah after his father, ·but his mother spoke up. 'No,'
61 she said, 'he is to be called John.' ·They said to her, 'But no one in your family has
62 that name,' ·and made signs *cc* to his father to find out what he wanted him called.
63 The father asked for a writing-tablet and wrote, 'His name is John.' And they
64 were all astonished. ·At that instant his power of speech returned and he spoke
65 and praised God. ·All their neighbours were filled with awe and the whole affair
66 was talked about throughout the hill country of Judaea. ·All those who heard of it treasured it in their hearts. 'What will this child turn out to be?' they wondered. And indeed the hand of the Lord was with him. *dd*

The Benedictus *ee*

67 His father Zechariah was filled with the Holy Spirit and spoke this prophecy: *ff*

68   *Blessed be the Lord, the God of Israel,*
          for he has visited *gg* his people, he has *set them free,*
69   and he has established for us a saving power *hh*
          in the House of his servant David,
70   just as he proclaimed,
          by the mouth of his holy prophets from ancient times,
71   that he would save us from our *enemies*
          and *from the hands of* all *those who hate us,*
72   and show *faithful love to our ancestors,*
          and so *keep in mind his* holy *covenant.*
73   This was the oath he swore
          to our father Abraham,
74   that he would grant us, free from fear,
          to be delivered from the hands of our enemies,
75   to serve him in holiness and uprightness
          in his presence, all our days.
76   And you, little child,
          you shall be called Prophet of the Most High,

for you will go before *the Lord* [ii]
to prepare a way for him,
77　to give his people knowledge of salvation
through the forgiveness of their sins, [jj]
78　because of the faithful love [kk] of our God
in which the rising Sun has come from on high [ll] to visit us,
79　to give light to *those who live*
in darkness and the shadow dark as death,
and to guide our feet
into *the way of peace*.

The hidden life of John the Baptist

80　Meanwhile the child grew up and his spirit grew strong. [mm] And he lived in the
desert until the day he appeared openly to Israel.

The birth of Jesus and visit of the shepherds

1　2 Now it happened that at this time Caesar Augustus [a] issued a decree that
2　a census should be made of the whole inhabited world. ·This census—the
3　first [b]—took place while Quirinius was governor of Syria, ·and everyone went to
4　be registered, each to his own town. ·So Joseph set out from the town of Nazareth
in Galilee for Judaea, to David's town called Bethlehem, since he was of David's
5　House and line, ·in order to be registered together with Mary, his betrothed, who
6　was with child. ·Now it happened that, while they were there, the time came for
7　her to have her child, ·and she gave birth to a son, her first-born. [c] She wrapped
him in swaddling clothes and laid him in a manger because there was no room for
8　them in the living-space. [d] ·In the countryside close by there were shepherds out in
9　the fields keeping guard over their sheep during the watches of the night. ·An
angel of the Lord stood over them and the glory of the Lord shone round them.
10　They were terrified, ·but the angel said, 'Do not be afraid. Look, I bring you news
11　of great joy, a joy to be shared by the whole people. ·Today in the town of David
12　a Saviour has been born to you; he is Christ the Lord. [e] ·And here is a sign for
you: you will find a baby wrapped in swaddling clothes and lying in a manger.'
13　And all at once with the angel there was a great throng of the hosts of heaven,
praising God with the words:

14　　　　Glory to God in the highest heaven,
　　　　and on earth peace for those he favours. [f]

15　Now it happened that when the angels had gone from them into heaven, the
shepherds said to one another, 'Let us go to Bethlehem and see this event which
16　the Lord has made known to us.' ·So they hurried away and found Mary and
17　Joseph, and the baby lying in the manger. ·When they saw the child they repeated
18　what they had been told about him, ·and everyone who heard it was astonished at
19　what the shepherds said to them. ·As for Mary, she treasured all these things and
20　pondered them in her heart. ·And the shepherds went back glorifying and praising
God [g] for all they had heard and seen, just as they had been told.

The circumcision of Jesus

21　When the eighth day came and the child was to be circumcised, they gave him the
name Jesus, the name the angel had given him before his conception.

Jesus is presented in the Temple

22 And when the day came for them to be purified[k] in keeping with the Law of
23 Moses, they took him up to Jerusalem to present him to the Lord—·observing
what is written in the Law of the Lord: *Every first-born male must be consecrated*
24 *to the Lord*—·and also to offer in sacrifice, in accordance with what is prescribed
25 in the Law of the Lord, *a pair of turtledoves or two young pigeons.*[i] ·Now in
Jerusalem there was a man named Simeon. He was an upright and devout man;
he looked forward to the restoration of Israel and the Holy Spirit rested on him.
26 It had been revealed to him by the Holy Spirit that he would not see death until he
27 had set eyes on the Christ of the Lord.[j] ·Prompted by the Spirit he came to the
Temple; and when the parents brought in the child Jesus to do for him what the
28 Law required, he took him into his arms and blessed God; and he said:

The Nunc Dimittis

29   Now, Master, you are letting your servant go in peace
        as you promised;
30   for my eyes have seen the salvation
31   which you have made ready in the sight of the nations;
32   a light of revelation for the gentiles
        and glory for your people Israel.[k]

The prophecy of Simeon

33 As the child's father and mother were wondering at the things that were being
34 said about him, ·Simeon blessed them and said to Mary his mother, 'Look, he is
destined for the fall and for the rise of many in Israel, destined to be a sign that is
35 opposed[l]—·and a sword will pierce your soul too[m]—so that the secret thoughts of
many may be laid bare.'

The prophecy of Anna

36 There was a prophetess[n], too, Anna the daughter of Phanuel, of the tribe of
Asher. She was well on in years. Her days of girlhood over, she had been married
37 for seven years ·before becoming a widow. She was now eighty-four years old and
38 never left the Temple, serving God night and day with fasting and prayer. ·She
came up just at that moment and began to praise God; and she spoke of the child
to all who looked forward to the deliverance of Jerusalem.[o]

The hidden life of Jesus at Nazareth

39 When they had done everything the Law of the Lord required, they went back to
40 Galilee, to their own town of Nazareth. ·And as the child grew to maturity, he
was filled with wisdom; and God's favour was with him.

Jesus among the doctors of the Law

41. 42 Every year his parents used to go to Jerusalem for the feast of the Passover. ·When
43 he was twelve years old, they went up for the feast as usual. ·When the days of the
feast were over and they set off home, the boy Jesus stayed behind in Jerusalem
44 without his parents knowing it. ·They assumed he was somewhere in the party,
and it was only after a day's journey that they went to look for him among their
45 relations and acquaintances. ·When they failed to find him they went back to
Jerusalem looking for him everywhere.

46   It happened that, three days later,ᵖ they found him in the Temple, sitting among
47   the teachers, listening to them, and asking them questions; ·and all those who
48   heard him were astounded at his intelligence and his replies. ·They were overcome
     when they saw him, and his mother said to him, 'My child, why have you done this
49   to us? See how worried your father and I have been, looking for you.' ·He replied,
     'Why were you looking for me? Did you not know that I must be in my Father's
50   house?'ᵠ ·But they did not understand what he meant.

The hidden life at Nazareth resumed

51   He went down with them then and came to Nazareth and lived under their
52   authority. His mother stored up all these things in her heart. ·And Jesus increased
     in wisdom, in stature, and in favour with God and with people.

II: PRELUDE TO THE PUBLIC MINISTRY OF JESUS

The proclamation of John the Baptist

1   **3** In the fifteenth year of Tiberius Caesar's reign,ᵃ when Pontius Pilateᵇ was
         governor of Judaea, Herodᶜ tetrarch of Galilee, his brother Philipᵈ tetrarch of
2   the territories of Ituraea and Trachonitis, Lysaniasᵉ tetrarch of Abilene, ·and
     while the high-priesthood was held by Annas and Caiaphas,ᶠ the word of God
3   came to John the son of Zechariah, in the desert. ·He went through the whole
4   Jordan area proclaiming a baptism of repentance for the forgiveness of sins, ·as it
     is written in the book of the sayings of Isaiah the prophet:

         A voice of one that cries in the desert:
         Prepare a way for the Lord,
         make his paths straight!
5   *Let every valley be filled in,*
         every mountain and hill be levelled,
         winding ways be straightened
         and rough roads made smooth,
6   *and all humanity will see the salvation of God.* ᵍ

7   He said, therefore, to the crowds who came to be baptised by him, 'Brood of
8   vipers, who warned you to flee from the coming retribution? ·Produce fruit in
     keeping with repentance, and do not start telling yourselves, "We have Abraham
     as our father," because, I tell you, God can raise children for Abraham from these
9   stones. ·Yes, even now the axe is being laid to the root of the trees, so that any
     tree failing to produce good fruit will be cut down and thrown on the fire.'
10, 11   ʰWhen all the people asked him, 'What must we do, then?' ·he answered,
     'Anyone who has two tunics must share with the one who has none, and anyone
12   with something to eat must do the same.' ·There were tax collectors, too, who
13   came for baptism, and these said to him, 'Master, what must we do?' ·He said to
14   them, 'Exact no more than the appointed rate.' ·Some soldiers asked him in their
     turn, 'What about us? What must we do?' He said to them, 'No intimidation! No
     extortion! Be content with your pay!'
15   A feeling of expectancy had grown among the people, who were beginning to
16   wonder whether John might be the Christ, ·so John declared before them all, 'I
     baptise you with water, but someone is coming, who is more powerful than me,

17 and I am not fit to undo the strap of his sandals; he will baptise you with the Holy
Spirit and fire. ·His winnowing-fan is in his hand, to clear his threshing-floor and
to gather the wheat into his barn; but the chaff he will burn in a fire that will never
18 go out.' ·And he proclaimed the good news to the people with many other
exhortations too.

John the Baptist imprisoned

19 But Herod the tetrarch, censured by John for his relations with his brother's wife
20 Herodias and for all the other crimes he had committed, ·added a further crime to
all the rest by shutting John up in prison. *i*

Jesus is baptised

21 Now it happened that when all the people had been baptised and while Jesus after
22 his own baptism was at prayer,*j* heaven opened ·and the Holy Spirit descended on
him in a physical form, like a dove. And a voice came from heaven, '*You are my
Son; today have I fathered you.*' *k*

The ancestry of Jesus *l*

23 When he began, Jesus was about thirty years old, being the son, as it was thought,
24 of Joseph son of Heli, ·son of Matthat, son of Levi, son of Melchi, son of Jannai,
25 son of Joseph, ·son of Mattathias, son of Amos, son of Nahum, son of Esli, son
26 of Naggai, ·son of Maath, son of Mattathias, son of Semein, son of Josech, son of
27 Joda, ·son of Joanan, son of Rhesa, son of Zerubbabel, son of Shealtiel, son of Neri,
28, 29 son of Melchi, son of Addi, son of Cosam, son of Elmadam, son of Er, ·son of
30 Jesus, son of Eliezer, son of Jorim, son of Matthat, son of Levi, ·son of Symeon,
31 son of Judah, son of Joseph, son of Jonam, son of Eliakim, ·son of Melea, son of
32 Menna, son of Mattatha, son of Nathan, son of David, ·son of Jesse, son of Obed,
33 son of Boaz, son of Sala, son of Nahshon, ·son of Amminadab, son of Admin, son
34 of Arni, son of Hezron, son of Perez, son of Judah, ·son of Jacob, son of Isaac,
35 son of Abraham, son of Terah, son of Nahor, ·son of Serug, son of Reu, son of
36 Peleg, son of Eber, son of Shelah, ·son of Cainan, son of Arphaxad, son of Shem,
37 son of Noah, son of Lamech ·son of Methuselah, son of Enoch, son of Jared, son
38 of Mahalaleel, son of Cainan, ·son of Enos, son of Seth, son of Adam, son of
God.

Testing in the desert *a*

1 **4** Filled with the Holy Spirit,*b* Jesus left the Jordan and was led by the Spirit
2 into the desert, ·for forty days being put to the test by the devil. During that
3 time he ate nothing and at the end he was hungry. ·Then the devil said to him, 'If
4 you are Son of God, tell this stone to turn into a loaf.' ·But Jesus replied, 'Scripture
says:

> *Human beings live not on bread alone.*'

5 Then leading him to a height, the devil showed him in a moment of time all the
6 kingdoms of the world ·and said to him, 'I will give you all this power and their
splendour, for it has been handed over to me, for me to give it to anyone I choose. *c*
7, 8 Do homage, then, to me, and it shall all be yours.' ·But Jesus answered him,
'Scripture says:

> *You must do homage to the Lord your God, him alone you must serve.*'

9 Then he led him to Jerusalem and set him on the parapet of the Temple. 'If you

10 are Son of God,' he said to him, 'throw yourself down from here, ·for scripture
says:

> He has given his angels orders about you, to guard you
> and again:

11 　　　　　They will carry you in their arms in case you trip over a stone.'
12 But Jesus answered him, 'Scripture says:

> Do not put the Lord your God to the test.'

13 Having exhausted every way of putting him to the test, *d* the devil left him, until
the opportune moment.

III: THE GALILEAN MINISTRY

Jesus begins to preach

14 Jesus, with the power of the Spirit in him, returned to Galilee; and his reputation
15 spread throughout the countryside. *e* ·He taught in their synagogues and everyone
glorified him. *f*

Jesus at Nazareth

16 He came to Nazara, *g* where he had been brought up, and went into the synagogue
17 on the Sabbath day as he usually did. He stood up to read, *h* ·and they handed him
the scroll of the prophet Isaiah. Unrolling the scroll he found the place where it is
written:

18 　　　　　The spirit of the Lord is on me,
　　　　　for he has anointed me
　　　　　to bring the good news to the afflicted. *i*
　　　　　He has sent me to proclaim liberty to captives,
　　　　　sight to the blind,
　　　　　to let the oppressed go free,
19 　　　　　to proclaim a year of favour from the Lord.

20 He then rolled up the scroll, gave it back to the assistant and sat down. And all
21 eyes in the synagogue were fixed on him. ·Then he began to speak to them, 'This
22 text is being fulfilled today even while you are listening.' ·And he won the approval
of all, and they were astonished by the gracious words that came from his lips.

23 They said, 'This is Joseph's son, surely?' ·But he replied, 'No doubt you will
quote me the saying, "Physician, heal yourself," and tell me, "We have heard all
24 that happened in Capernaum, *j* do the same here in your own country." ' ·And he
went on, 'In truth I tell you, no prophet is ever accepted in his own country.

25 'There were many widows in Israel, I can assure you, in Elijah's day, when
heaven remained shut for three years and six months and a great famine raged
26 throughout the land, ·but Elijah was not sent to any one of these: he was sent *to a*
27 *widow at Zarephath, a town in Sidonia.* ·And in the prophet Elisha's time there
were many suffering from virulent skin-diseases in Israel, but none of these was
cured—only Naaman the Syrian.'

28, 29 When they heard this everyone in the synagogue was enraged. ·They sprang to
their feet and hustled him out of the town; and they took him up to the brow of
30 the hill their town was built on, intending to throw him off the cliff, ·but he passed
straight through the crowd and walked away.

Jesus teaches in Capernaum and cures a demoniac

31 He went down to Capernaum, a town in Galilee, and taught them on the Sabbath.
32 And his teaching made a deep impression on them because his word carried authority.
33   In the synagogue there was a man possessed by the spirit of an unclean devil,
34 and he shouted at the top of his voice, ·'Ha! What do you want with us, Jesus of Nazareth? Have you come to destroy us? I know who you are: the Holy One of
35 God.' ·But Jesus rebuked it, saying, 'Be quiet! Come out of him!' And the devil, throwing the man into the middle, went out of him without hurting him at all.
36 Astonishment seized them and they were all saying to one another, 'What is it in his words? He gives orders to unclean spirits with authority and power and they
37 come out.' ·And the news of him travelled all through the surrounding countryside.

Cure of Simon's mother-in-law

38 Leaving the synagogue he went to Simon's house. Now Simon's mother-in-law was in the grip of a high fever and they asked him to do something for her.
39 Standing over her he rebuked the fever and it left her. And she immediately got up and began to serve them.

A number of cures

40 At sunset all those who had friends suffering from diseases of one kind or another
41 brought them to him, and laying his hands on each he cured them. ·Devils too came out of many people, shouting, 'You are the Son of God.' But he warned them and would not allow them to speak because they knew that he was the Christ.

Dawn departure from Capernaum and travels through Judaea

42 When daylight came he left the house and made his way to a lonely place. The crowds went to look for him, and when they had caught up with him they wanted
43 to prevent him from leaving them, ·but he answered, 'I must proclaim the good news of the kingdom of God to the other towns too, because that is what I was
44 sent to do.' ·And he continued his proclamation in the synagogues of Judaea. *

The first four disciples are called *

1   **5** Now it happened that he was standing one day by the Lake of Gennesaret,
2   with the crowd pressing round him listening to the word of God, ·when he caught sight of two boats at the water's edge. The fishermen had got out of them
3 and were washing their nets. ·He got into one of the boats—it was Simon's *—and asked him to put out a little from the shore. Then he sat down and taught the crowds from the boat.
4   When he had finished speaking he said to Simon, 'Put out into deep water and
5 pay out your nets for a catch.' ·Simon replied, 'Master, we worked hard all night
6 long and caught nothing, but if you say so, I will pay out the nets.' ·And when they had done this they netted such a huge number of fish that their nets began to
7 tear, ·so they signalled to their companions in the other boat to come and help them; when these came, they filled both boats to sinking point.
8   When Simon Peter saw this he fell at the knees of Jesus saying, 'Leave me,
9 Lord; I am a sinful man.' ·For he and all his companions were completely awestruck
10 at the catch they had made; ·so also were James and John, sons of Zebedee, who were Simon's partners. * But Jesus said to Simon, 'Do not be afraid; from now on

11 it is people you will be catching.' ·Then, bringing their boats back to land they left everything and followed him.

Cure of a man suffering from a virulent skin-disease

12 Now it happened that Jesus was in one of the towns when suddenly a man appeared, covered with a skin-disease. Seeing Jesus he fell on his face and implored
13 him saying, 'Sir, if you are willing you can cleanse me.' ·He stretched out his hand, and touched him saying, 'I am willing. Be cleansed.' At once the skin-disease left
14 him. ·He ordered him to tell no one, 'But go and show yourself to the priest and make the offering for your cleansing just as Moses prescribed, as evidence to them.'
15 But the news of him kept spreading, and large crowds would gather to hear him
16 and to have their illnesses cured, ·but he would go off to some deserted place and pray.

Cure of a paralytic

17 Now it happened that he was teaching one day, and Pharisees and teachers of the Law, who had come from every village in Galilee, from Judaea and from Jerusalem, were sitting there. And the power of the Lord⁴ was there so that he should
18 heal. ·And now some men appeared, bringing on a bed a paralysed man whom
19 they were trying to bring in and lay down in front of him. ·But as they could find no way of getting the man through the crowd, they went up onto the top of the house and lowered him and his stretcher down through the tiles⁵ into the middle
20 of the gathering, in front of Jesus. ·Seeing their faith he said, 'My friend, your sins
21 are forgiven you.' ·The scribes and the Pharisees began to think this over. 'Who is
22 this man, talking blasphemy? Who but God alone can forgive sins?' ·But Jesus, aware of their thoughts, made them this reply, 'What are these thoughts you have
23 in your hearts? ·Which of these is easier: to say, "Your sins are forgiven you," or
24 to say, "Get up and walk"? ·But to prove to you that the Son of man has authority on earth to forgive sins,'—he said to the paralysed man—'I order you: get up, and
25 pick up your stretcher and go home.' ·And immediately before their very eyes he got up, picked up what he had been lying on and went home praising God.
26 They were all astounded and praised God and were filled with awe, saying, 'We have seen strange things today.'

The call of Levi

27 When he went out after this, he noticed a tax collector, Levi by name, sitting at
28 the tax office, and said to him, 'Follow me.' ·And leaving everything Levi got up and followed him.

Eating with sinners in Levi's house

29 In his honour Levi held a great reception in his house, and with them at table was
30 a large gathering of tax collectors and others. ·The Pharisees and their scribes complained to his disciples and said, 'Why do you eat and drink with tax collectors
31 and sinners?' ·Jesus said to them in reply, 'It is not those that are well who need
32 the doctor, but the sick. ·I have come to call not the upright but sinners to repentance.'

Discussion on fasting

33 They then said to him, 'John's disciples are always fasting and saying prayers, and
34 the disciples of the Pharisees, too, but yours go on eating and drinking.' ·Jesus
replied, 'Surely you cannot make the bridegroom's attendants fast while the
35 bridegroom is still with them? ·But the time will come when the bridegroom is
taken away from them; then, in those days, they will fast.'

36   He also told them a parable, 'No one tears a piece from a new cloak to put it on
an old cloak; otherwise, not only will the new one be torn, but the piece taken
from the new will not match the old.

37   'And nobody puts new wine in old wineskins otherwise, the new wine will burst
38 the skins and run to waste, and the skins will be ruined. ·No; new wine must be
39 put in fresh skins. ·And nobody who has been drinking old wine wants new. "The
old is good," he says.'ᶠ

Picking corn on the Sabbath

1   **6** It happened that one Sabbath he was walking through the cornfields, and his
disciples were picking ears of corn, rubbing them in their hands and eating
2 them. ·Some of the Pharisees said, 'Why are you doing something that is forbidden
3 on the Sabbath day?' ·Jesus answered them, 'So you have not read what David
4 did when he and his followers were hungry—·how he went into the house of God
and took the loaves of the offering and ate them and gave them to his followers,
5 loaves which the priests alone are allowed to eat?' ·And he said to them, 'The Son
of man is master of the Sabbath.'ᵉ

Cure of the man with a withered hand

6 Now on another Sabbath he went into the synagogue and began to teach, and a
7 man was present, and his right hand was withered. ·The scribes and the Pharisees
were watching him to see if he would cure somebody on the Sabbath, hoping to
8 find something to charge him with. ·But he knew their thoughts; and he said to
the man with the withered hand, 'Get up and stand out in the middle!' And he
9 came forward and stood there. ·Then Jesus said to them, 'I put it to you: is it
permitted on the Sabbath to do good, or to do evil; to save life, or to destroy it?'
10 Then he looked round at them all and said to the man, 'Stretch out your hand.'
11 He did so, and his hand was restored. ·But they were furious and began to discuss
the best way of dealing with Jesus.

The choice of the Twelve

12 Now it happened in those days that he went onto the mountain to pray; and he
13 spent the whole night in prayer to God. ·When day came he summoned his
14 disciples and picked out twelve of them; he called them 'apostles': ᵇ ·Simon whom
he called Peter, and his brother Andrew; James, John, Philip, Bartholomew,
15. 16 Matthew, Thomas, James son of Alphaeus, Simon called the Zealot, ·Judas son
of James,ᶜ and Judas Iscariot who became a traitor.

The crowds follow Jesus

17 He then came down with them and stopped at a piece of level ground where there
was a large gathering of his disciples, with a great crowd of people from all parts
18 of Judaea and Jerusalem and the coastal region of Tyre and Sidon ·who had come
to hear him and to be cured of their diseases. People tormented by unclean spirits

19 were also cured, ·and everyone in the crowd was trying to touch him because power came out of him that cured them all.

The first sermon. *ᵈ* The Beatitudes *ᵉ*

20 Then fixing his eyes on his disciples he said:

> How blessed are you who are poor: the kingdom of God is yours.
21   Blessed are you who are hungry now: you shall have your fill.
> Blessed are you who are weeping now: you shall laugh.

22 'Blessed are you when people hate you, drive you out, abuse you, denounce
23 your name as criminal, on account of the Son of man. ·Rejoice when that day comes and dance for joy, look!—your reward will be great in heaven. This was the way their ancestors treated the prophets.

The curses

24   But alas for you who are rich: you are having your consolation now.
25   Alas for you who have plenty to eat now: you shall go hungry.
> Alas for you who are laughing now: you shall mourn and weep.

26 'Alas for you when everyone speaks well of you! This was the way their ancestors treated the false prophets.

Love of enemies

27 'But I say this to you who are listening: Love your enemies, do good to those who
28, 29 hate you, ·bless those who curse you, pray for those who treat you badly. ·To anyone who slaps you on one cheek, present the other cheek as well; to anyone
30 who takes your cloak from you, do not refuse your tunic. ·Give to everyone who
31, 32 asks you, and do not ask for your property back from someone who takes it. Treat others as you would like people to treat you. ·If you love those who love you,
33 what credit can you expect? Even sinners love those who love them. ·And if you do good to those who do good to you, what credit can you expect? For even
34 sinners do that much. ·And if you lend to those from whom you hope to get money back, what credit can you expect? Even sinners lend to sinners to get back the
35 same amount. ·Instead, love your enemies and do good to them, and lend without any hope of return.*ᶠ* You will have a great reward, and you will be children of the Most High, for he himself is kind to the ungrateful and the wicked.

Compassion and generosity

36, 37 'Be compassionate just as your Father is compassionate. ·Do not judge, and you will not be judged; do not condemn, and you will not be condemned; forgive, and
38 you will be forgiven. ·Give, and there will be gifts for you: a full measure, pressed down, shaken together, and overflowing, will be poured into your lap;*ᵍ* because the standard you use will be the standard used for you.'

Integrity

39 He also told them a parable, 'Can one blind person guide another? Surely both
40 will fall into a pit?*ʰ* ·Disciple is not superior to teacher; but fully trained disciple
41 will be like teacher. ·Why do you observe the splinter in your brother's eye and
42 never notice the great log in your own? ·How can you say to your brother, "Brother, let me take out that splinter in your eye," when you cannot see the

great log in your own? Hypocrite! Take the log out of your own eye first, and then you will see clearly enough to take *ᶦ* out the splinter in your brother's eye.

43 'There is no sound tree that produces rotten fruit, nor again a rotten tree that
44 produces sound fruit. ·Every tree can be told by its own fruit: people do not pick
45 figs from thorns, nor gather grapes from brambles. ·Good people draw what is good from the store of goodness in their hearts; bad people draw what is bad from the store of badness. For the words of the mouth flow out of what fills the heart.

The true disciple

46 'Why do you call me, "Lord, Lord" and not do what I say?
47 'Everyone who comes to me *ʲ* and listens to my words and acts on them—I will
48 show you what such a person is like. ·Such a person is like the man who, when he built a house, dug, and dug deep, and laid the foundations on rock; when the river was in flood it bore down on that house but could not shake it, it was so well built.
49 But someone who listens and does nothing is like the man who built a house on soil, with no foundations; as soon as the river bore down on it, it collapsed; and what a ruin that house became!'

Cure of the centurion's servant

1   7 When he had come to the end of all he wanted the people to hear, he went
2   into Capernaum. ·A centurion there had a servant, a favourite of his, who was
3   sick and near death. ·Having heard about Jesus he sent some Jewish elders *ᵃ* to
4   him to ask him to come and heal his servant. ·When they came to Jesus they
5   pleaded earnestly with him saying, 'He deserves this of you, ·because he is well
6   disposed towards our people; *ᵇ* he built us our synagogue himself.' ·So Jesus went with them, and was not very far from the house when the centurion sent word to him by some friends to say to him, 'Sir, do not put yourself to any trouble because
7   I am not worthy to have you under my roof; ·and that is why I did not presume to
8   come to you myself; let my boy be cured by your giving the word. *ᶜ* ·For I am under authority myself, and have soldiers under me; and I say to one man, "Go," and he goes; to another, "Come here," and he comes; to my servant, "Do this,"
9   and he does it.' ·When Jesus heard these words he was astonished at him and, turning round, said to the crowd following him, 'I tell you, not even in Israel have
10 I found faith as great as this.' ·And when the messengers got back to the house they found the servant in perfect health.

The son of the widow of Nain restored to life *ᵈ*

11 It happened that soon afterwards he went to a town called Nain, accompanied by
12 his disciples and a great number of people. ·Now when he was near the gate of the town there was a dead man being carried out, the only son of his mother, and she
13 was a widow. And a considerable number of the townspeople was with her. ·When
14 the Lord saw her he felt sorry for her and said to her, 'Don't cry.' ·Then he went up and touched the bier and the bearers stood still, and he said, 'Young man, I tell
15 you: get up.' ·And the dead man sat up and began to talk, and Jesus *gave him to*
16 *his mother*. ·Everyone was filled with awe and glorified God saying, 'A great
17 prophet has risen up among us; God has visited his people.' ·And this view of him spread throughout Judaea and all over the countryside.

The Baptist's question. Jesus commends him

18 The disciples of John gave him all this news, and John, summoning two of his
19 disciples, ·sent them to the Lord to ask, 'Are you the one who is to come, or are

20 we to expect someone else?' ·When the men reached Jesus they said, 'John the Baptist has sent us to you to ask, "Are you the one who is to come or are we to
21 expect someone else?" ' ·At that very time he cured many people of diseases and afflictions and of evil spirits, and gave the gift of sight to many who were blind.
22 Then he gave the messengers their answer, 'Go back and tell John what you have seen and heard: the blind see again, the lame walk, those suffering from virulent skin-diseases are cleansed, and the deaf hear, the dead are raised to life, the good
23 news is proclaimed to the poor; ·and blessed is anyone who does not find me a cause of falling.'

24   When John's messengers had gone he began to talk to the people about John,
25 'What did you go out into the desert to see? A reed swaying in the breeze? No! Then what did you go out to see? A man dressed in fine clothes? Look, those who
26 go in magnificent clothes and live luxuriously are to be found at royal courts! ·Then what did you go out to see? A prophet? Yes, I tell you, and much more than a
27 prophet: ·he is the one of whom scripture says:

> Look, I am going to send my messenger innfront of you
> to prepare your way before you.

28   'I tell you, of all the children born to women, there is no one greater than John;
29 yet the least in the kingdom of God is greater than he.' ·All the people who heard him, and the tax collectors too, acknowledged God's saving justice by accepting
30 baptism from John; ·but by refusing baptism from him the Pharisees and the lawyers thwarted God's plan for them.

Jesus condemns his contemporaries

31 'What comparison, then, can I find for the people of this generation? What are
32 they like? ·They are like children shouting to one another while they sit in the market place:

> We played the pipes for you,
> and you wouldn't dance;
> we sang dirges,
> and you wouldn't cry.

33   'For John the Baptist has come, not eating bread, not drinking wine, and you
34 say, "He is possessed." ·The Son of man has come, eating and drinking, and you
35 say, "Look, a glutton and a drunkard, a friend of tax collectors and sinners." ·Yet wisdom is justified by all her children.' '

The woman who was a sinner[f]

36 One of the Pharisees invited him to a meal. When he arrived at the Pharisee's
37 house and took his place at table, ·suddenly a woman came in, who had a bad name in the town. She had heard he was dining with the Pharisee and had brought
38 with her an alabaster jar of ointment. ·She waited behind him at his feet, weeping, and her tears fell on his feet, and she wiped them away with her hair; then she covered his feet with kisses and anointed them with the ointment.
39   When the Pharisee who had invited him saw this, he said to himself, 'If this man were a prophet, he would know who this woman is and what sort of person it is
40 who is touching him and what a bad name she has.' ·Then Jesus took him up and
41 said, 'Simon, I have something to say to you.' He replied, 'Say on, Master.' ·'There was once a creditor who had two men in his debt; one owed him five hundred

42 denarii, the other fifty. ·They were unable to pay, so he let them both off. Which
43 of them will love him more?' ·Simon answered, 'The one who was let off more, I
   suppose.' Jesus said, 'You are right.'
44   Then he turned to the woman and said to Simon, 'You see this woman? I came
   into your house, and you poured no water over my feet, but she has poured out
45 her tears over my feet and wiped them away with her hair. ·You gave me no kiss,
46 but she has been covering my feet with kisses ever since I came in. *·You did not
47 anoint my head with oil, but she has anointed my feet with ointment. ·For this
   reason I tell you that her sins, many as they are, have been forgiven her, because
   she has shown such great love. *It is someone who is forgiven little who shows
48. 49 little love.' ·Then he said to her, 'Your sins are forgiven.' ·Those who were with
   him at table began to say to themselves, 'Who is this man, that even forgives sins?'
50 But he said to the woman, 'Your faith has saved you; go in peace.'

The women accompanying Jesus

1 **8** Now it happened that after this he made his way through towns and villages
      preaching and proclaiming the good news of the kingdom of God. With him
2 went the Twelve, ·as well as certain women who had been cured of evil spirits and
   ailments: Mary surnamed the Magdalene, from whom seven demons had gone
3 out, ·Joanna the wife of Herod's steward Chuza, Susanna, and many others who
   provided for them out of their own resources.

Parable of the sower

4 With a large crowd gathering and people from every town finding their way to
   him, he told this parable:
5   'A sower went out to sow his seed. Now as he sowed, some fell on the edge of
6 the path and was trampled on; and the birds of the air ate it up. ·Some seed fell on
7 rock, and when it came up it withered away, having no moisture. ·Some seed fell
8 in the middle of thorns and the thorns grew with it and choked it. ·And some seed
   fell into good soil and grew and produced its crop a hundredfold.' Saying this he
   cried, 'Anyone who has ears for listening should listen!'

Why Jesus speaks in parables

9. 10 His disciples asked him what this parable might mean, ·and he said, 'To you is
   granted to understand the secrets of the kingdom of God; for the rest it remains in
   parables, so that

> *they may look but not perceive,*
> *listen but not understand.*

The parable of the sower explained

11. 12 'This, then, is what the parable means: the seed is the word of God. ·Those on the
   edge of the path are people who have heard it, and then the devil comes and
   carries away the word from their hearts in case they should believe and be saved.
13 Those on the rock are people who, when they first hear it, welcome the word with
   joy. But these have no root; they believe for a while, and in time of trial they give
14 up. ·As for the part that fell into thorns, this is people who have heard, but as they
   go on their way they are choked by the worries and riches and pleasures of life and
15 never produce any crops. ·As for the part in the rich soil, this is people with a
   noble and generous heart who have heard the word and take it to themselves and
   yield a harvest through their perseverance.

Parable of the lamp

16 'No one lights a lamp to cover it with a bowl or to put it under a bed. No, it is put
17 on a lamp-stand so that people may see the light when they come in. ·For nothing
is hidden but it will be made clear, nothing secret but it will be made known and
18 brought to light. ·So take care how you listen; anyone who has, will be given
more; anyone who has not, will be deprived even of what he thinks he has.'

The true family of Jesus *

19 His mother and his brothers came looking for him, but they could not get to him
20 because of the crowd. ·He was told, 'Your mother and brothers are standing
21 outside and want to see you.' ·But he said in answer, 'My mother and my brothers
are those who hear the word of God and put it into practice.'

The calming of the storm

22 It happened that one day he got into a boat with his disciples and said to them,
23 'Let us cross over to the other side of the lake.' So they set out, ·and as they sailed
he fell asleep. When a squall of wind came down on the lake the boat started
24 shipping water and they found themselves in danger. ·So they went to rouse him
saying, 'Master! Master! We are lost!' Then he woke up and rebuked the wind
25 and the rough water; and they subsided and it was calm again. ·He said to them,
'Where is your faith?' They were awestruck and astounded and said to one another,
'Who can this be, that gives orders even to winds and waves and they obey him?'

The Gerasene demoniac

26 They came to land in the territory of the Gerasenes, *b* which is opposite Galilee.
27 He was stepping ashore when a man from the city who was possessed by devils
came towards him; for a long time the man had been living with no clothes on, not
in a house, but in the tombs.
28   Catching sight of Jesus he gave a shout, fell at his feet and cried out at the top of
his voice, 'What do you want with me, Jesus, son of the Most High God? I implore
29 you, do not torture me.' ·For Jesus had been telling the unclean spirit to come out
of the man. It had seized on him a great many times, and then they used to secure
him with chains and fetters to restrain him, but he would always break the
30 fastenings, and the devil would drive him out into the wilds. ·Jesus asked him,
'What is your name?' He said, 'Legion'—because many devils had gone into him.
31 And these begged him not to order them to depart into the Abyss. *c*
32   Now there was a large herd of pigs feeding there on the mountain, and the
33 devils begged him to let them go into these. So he gave them leave. ·The devils
came out of the man and went into the pigs, and the herd charged down the cliff
into the lake and was drowned.
34   When the swineherds saw what had happened they ran off and told their story
35 in the city and in the country round about; ·and the people went out to see what
had happened. When they came to Jesus they found the man from whom the
devils had gone out sitting at the feet of Jesus, *d* wearing clothes and in his right
36 mind; and they were afraid. ·Those who had witnessed it told them how the man
37 who had been possessed came to be saved. ·The entire population of the Gerasene
territory was in great fear and asked Jesus to leave them. So he got into the boat
and went back.
38   The man from whom the devils had gone out asked to be allowed to stay with

39 him, but he sent him away saying, ·'Go back home and report all that God has done for you.' So the man went off and proclaimed throughout the city all that Jesus had done for him.

Cure of the woman with a haemorrhage. Jairus' daughter raised to life

40 On his return Jesus was welcomed by the crowd, for they were all there waiting
41 for him. ·And suddenly there came a man named Jairus, who was president of the synagogue. He fell at Jesus' feet and pleaded with him to come to his house,
42 because he had an only daughter about twelve years old, who was dying. And the crowds were almost stifling Jesus as he went.

43 Now there was a woman suffering from a haemorrhage for the past twelve years,
44 whom no one had been able to cure. ᶜ ·She came up behind him and touched the
45 fringe of his cloak; and the haemorrhage stopped at that very moment. ·Jesus said, 'Who was it that touched me?' When they all denied it, Peter said, 'Master,
46 it is the crowds round you, pushing.' ·But Jesus said, 'Somebody touched me. I
47 felt that power had gone out from me.' ·Seeing herself discovered, the woman came forward trembling, and falling at his feet explained in front of all the people
48 why she had touched him and how she had been cured at that very moment. ·'My daughter,' he said, 'your faith has saved you; go in peace.'

49 While he was still speaking, someone arrived from the house of the president of the synagogue to say, 'Your daughter has died. Do not trouble the Master any
50 further.' ·But Jesus heard this, and he spoke to the man, 'Do not be afraid, only
51 have faith and she will be saved.' ·When he came to the house he allowed no one to go in with him except Peter and John and James,ᶠ and the child's father and
52 mother. ·They were all crying and mourning for her, but Jesus said, 'Stop crying;
53. 54 she is not dead, but asleep.' ·But they ridiculed him, knowing she was dead. ·But
55 taking her by the hand himself he spoke to her, 'Child, get up.' ·And her spirit returned and she got up at that very moment. Then he told them to give her
56 something to eat. ·Her parents were astonished, but he ordered them not to tell anyone what had happened.

The mission of the Twelve

1 **9** He called the Twelve ᵃ together and gave them power and authority over all
2 devils and to cure diseases, ·and he sent them out to proclaim the kingdom of
3 God and to heal. ·He said to them, 'Take nothing for the journey: neither staff,
4 nor haversack, nor bread, nor money; and do not have a spare tunic. ·Whatever house you enter, stay there; and when you leave let your departure be from there.
5 As for those who do not welcome you, when you leave their town shake the dust
6 from your feet as evidence against them.' ·So they set out and went from village to village proclaiming the good news and healing everywhere.

Herod and Jesus ᵇ

7 Meanwhile Herod the tetrarch had heard about all that was going on; and he was puzzled, because some people were saying that John had risen from the dead,
8 others that Elijah had reappeared, still others that one of the ancient prophets
9 had come back to life. ·But Herod said, 'John? I beheaded him. So who is this I hear such reports about?' And he was anxious to see him.

The return of the apostles. Miracle of the loaves ᶜ

10 On their return the apostles gave him an account of all they had done. Then he took them with him and withdrew towards a town called Bethsaida where they

11 could be by themselves. ·But the crowds got to know and they went after him. He
made them welcome and talked to them about the kingdom of God; and he cured
those who were in need of healing.

12   It was late afternoon when the Twelve came up to him and said, 'Send the
people away, and they can go to the villages and farms round about to find lodging
13 and food; for we are in a lonely place here.' ·He replied, 'Give them something to
eat yourselves.' But they said, 'We have no more than five loaves and two fish,
14 unless we are to go ourselves and buy food for all these people.' ·For there were
about five thousand men. But he said to his disciples, 'Get them to sit down in
15, 16 parties of about fifty.' ·They did so and made them all sit down. ·Then he took the
five loaves and the two fish, raised his eyes to heaven, and said the blessing over
them; then he broke them and handed them to his disciples to distribute among
17 the crowd. ·They all ate as much as they wanted, and when the scraps left over
were collected they filled twelve baskets.

Peter's profession of faith *

18 Now it happened that he was praying alone, and his disciples came to him and he
19 put this question to them, 'Who do the crowds say I am?' ·And they answered,
'Some say John the Baptist; others Elijah; others again one of the ancient prophets
20 come back to life.' ·'But you,' he said to them, 'who do you say I am?' It was
21 Peter who spoke up. 'The Christ of God,' he said. ·But he gave them strict orders
and charged them not to say this to anyone.

First prophecy of the Passion *

22 He said, 'The Son of man is destined to suffer grievously, to be rejected by the
elders and chief priests and scribes and to be put to death, and to be raised up on
the third day.'

The condition of following Christ

23 Then, speaking to all, he said, 'If anyone wants to be a follower of mine, let him
24 renounce himself and take up his cross every day and follow me. ·Anyone who
wants to save his life will lose it; but anyone who loses his life for my sake, will
25 save it. ·What benefit is it to anyone to win the whole world and forfeit or lose his
26 very self? ·For if anyone is ashamed of me and of my words, of him the Son of
man will be ashamed when he comes in his own glory and in the glory of the Father
and the holy angels.

The kingdom will come soon

27 'I tell you truly, there are some standing here who will not taste death before they
see the kingdom of God.'

The transfiguration *

28 Now about eight days after this had been said, he took with him Peter, John and
29 James and went up the mountain to pray. ·And it happened that, as he was
praying, the aspect of his face was changed and his clothing became sparkling
30 white. ·And suddenly there were two men talking to him; they were Moses and
31 Elijah * ·appearing in glory, and they were speaking of his passing which he was to
32 accomplish in Jerusalem. ·Peter and his companions were heavy with sleep, but
33 they woke up * and saw his glory and the two men standing with him. ·As these
were leaving him, Peter said to Jesus, 'Master, it is wonderful for us to be here; so

let us make three shelters, one for you, one for Moses and one for Elijah.' He did
34 not know what he was saying. ·As he was saying this, a cloud came and covered
them with shadow; and when they went into the cloud the disciples were afraid.
35 And a voice came from the cloud saying, 'This is my Son, the Chosen One. *Listen
36 to him.' ·And after the voice had spoken, Jesus was found alone. The disciples
kept silence and, at that time, told no one what they had seen.

The epileptic demoniac

37 Now it happened that on the following day when they were coming down from the
38 mountain a large crowd came to meet him. ·And suddenly a man in the crowd
cried out. 'Master,' he said, 'I implore you to look at my son: he is my only child.
39 A spirit will suddenly take hold of him, and all at once it gives a sudden cry and
throws the boy into convulsions with foaming at the mouth; it is slow to leave him,
40 but when it does, it leaves the boy worn out. ·I begged your disciples to drive it
41 out, and they could not.' ·In reply Jesus said, 'Faithless and perverse generation!
How much longer must I be among you and put up with you? Bring your son
42 here.' ·Even while the boy was coming, the devil threw him to the ground in
convulsions. But Jesus rebuked the unclean spirit and cured the boy and gave him
43 back to his father, ·and everyone was awestruck by the greatness of God.

Second prophecy of the Passion

But while everyone was full of admiration for all he did, he said to his disciples,
44 'For your part, you must have these words constantly in mind: The Son of man is
45 going to be delivered into the power of men.' ·But they did not understand what
he said; it was hidden from them so that they should not see the meaning of it, and
they were afraid to ask him about it.

Who is the greatest?*j*

46, 47 An argument started between them about which of them was the greatest. ·Jesus
knew what thoughts were going through their minds, and he took a little child
48 whom he set by his side ·and then he said to them, 'Anyone who welcomes this
little child in my name welcomes me; and anyone who welcomes me, welcomes
the one who sent me. The least among you all is the one who is the greatest.'

On using the name of Jesus

49 John spoke up. 'Master,' he said, 'we saw someone driving out devils in your
50 name, and because he is not with us we tried to stop him.'*k* ·But Jesus said to him,
'You must not stop him: anyone who is not against you is for you.'

IV: THE JOURNEY TO JERUSALEM*l*

A Samaritan village is inhospitable

51 Now it happened that as the time drew near for him to be taken up,*m* he resolutely
52 turned his face towards Jerusalem ·and sent messengers ahead of him. These set
53 out, and they went into a Samaritan village to make preparations for him, ·but the
54 people would not receive him because he was making for Jerusalem.*n* ·Seeing this,
the disciples James and John said, 'Lord, do you want us to call down fire from

55. 56 heaven to burn them up?'ᵉ •But he turned and rebuked them,ᶠ •and they went on to another village.

Hardships of the apostolic calling

57 As they travelled along they met a man on the road who said to him, 'I will follow
58 you wherever you go.' •Jesus answered, 'Foxes have holes and the birds of the air have nests, but the Son of man has nowhere to lay his head.'
59 Another to whom he said, 'Follow me,' replied,ᶢ 'Let me go and bury my father
60 first.' •But he answered, 'Leave the dead to bury their dead;ʳ your duty is to go and spread the news of the kingdom of God.'
61 Another said, 'I will follow you, sir, but first let me go and say good-bye to my
62 people at home.' •Jesus said to him, 'Once the hand is laid on the plough, no one who looks back is fit for the kingdom of God.'

The mission of the seventy-two disciples ᵃ

1 10 After this the Lord appointed seventy-two ᵇ others and sent them out ahead of himᶜ in pairs, to all the towns and places he himself would be visiting.
2 And he said to them, 'The harvest is rich but the labourers are few, so ask the
3 Lord of the harvest to send labourers to do his harvesting. •Start off now, but
4 look, I am sending you out ɪɪke lambs among wolves. •Take no purse with you, no
5 haversack, no sandals. Salute no one on the road. •Whatever house you enter, let
6 your first words be, "Peace to this house!" •And if a man of peace lives there,ᵈ
7 your peace will go and rest on him; if not, it will come back to you. •Stay in the same house, taking what food and drink they have to offer, for the labourer
8 deserves his wages; do not move from house to house. •Whenever you go into a
9 town where they make you welcome, eat what is put before you. •Cure those in it
10 who are sick, and say, "The kingdom of God is very near to you." •But whenever you enter a town and they do not make you welcome, go out into its streets and
11 say, •"We wipe off the very dust of your town that clings to our feet, and leave it
12 with you. Yet be sure of this: the kingdom of God is very near." •I tell you, on the great Day it will be more bearable for Sodom than for that town.
13 'Alas for you, Chorazin! Alas for you, Bethsaida! For if the miracles done in you had been done in Tyre and Sidon, they would have repented long ago, sitting
14 in sackcloth and ashes. •And still, it will be more bearable for Tyre and Sidon at
15 the Judgement than for you. •And as for you, Capernaum, did you want to be *raised high as heaven? You shall be flung down to hell.*
16 'Anyone who listens to you listens to me; anyone who rejects you rejects me, and those who reject me reject the one who sent me.'

True cause for the apostles to rejoice

17 The seventy-two came back rejoicing. 'Lord,' they said, 'even the devils submit to
18 us when we use your name.' •He said to them, 'I watched Satan fall like lightning
19 from heaven. •Look, I have given you power to tread down serpents and scorpions
20 and the whole strength of the enemy; nothing shall ever hurt you. •Yet do not rejoice that the spirits submit to you; rejoice instead that your names are written in heaven.'

The good news revealed to the simple. The Father and the Son

21 Just at this time, filled with joy by the Holy Spirit, he said, 'I bless you, Father, Lord of heaven and of earth, for hiding these things from the learned and the

clever and revealing them to little children. Yes, Father, for that is what it has
22 pleased you to do. · 'Everything has been entrusted to me by my Father; and no
one knows who the Son is except the Father, and who the Father is except the Son
and those to whom the Son chooses to reveal him.'

The privilege of the disciples

23 Then turning to his disciples he spoke to them by themselves, 'Blessed are the
24 eyes that see what you see, ·for I tell you that many prophets and kings wanted to
see what you see, and never saw it; to hear what you hear, and never heard it.'*

The great commandment

25 And now a lawyer stood up and, to test him, asked, 'Master, what must I do to
26 inherit eternal life?' ·He said to him, 'What is written in the Law? What is your
27 reading of it?' ·He replied, *'You must love the Lord your God with all your heart,
with all your soul, with all your strength*, and with all your mind, *and your neighbour
28 as yourself.'* ·Jesus said to him, 'You have answered right, do this and life is yours.'

Parable of the good Samaritan

29 But the man was anxious to justify himself* and said to Jesus, 'And who is my
30 neighbour?' ·In answer Jesus said, 'A man was once on his way down from
Jerusalem to Jericho and fell into the hands of bandits; they stripped him, beat
31 him and then made off, leaving him half dead. ·Now a priest happened to be
travelling down the same road, but when he saw the man, he passed by on the
32 other side. ·In the same way a Levite who came to the place saw him, and passed
33 by on the other side. ·But a Samaritan* traveller who came on him was moved
34 with compassion when he saw him. ·He went up to him and bandaged his wounds,
pouring oil and wine on them. He then lifted him onto his own mount and took
35 him to an inn and looked after him. ·Next day, he took out two denarii and handed
them to the innkeeper and said, "Look after him, and on my way back I will make
36 good any extra expense you have." ·Which of these three, do you think, proved
37 himself a neighbour to the man who fell into the bandits' hands?' ·He replied,
'The one who showed pity towards him.' Jesus said to him, 'Go, and do the same
yourself.'

Martha and Mary *

38 In the course of their journey he came to a village, and a woman named Martha
39 welcomed him into her house. ·She had a sister called Mary, who sat down at the
40 Lord's feet and listened to him speaking. ·Now Martha, who was distracted with
all the serving, came to him and said, 'Lord, do you not care that my sister is
41 leaving me to do the serving all by myself? Please tell her to help me.' ·But the
Lord answered, 'Martha, Martha,' he said, 'you worry and fret about so many
42 things, ·and yet few are needed, indeed only one.* It is Mary who has chosen the
better part, and it is not to be taken from her.'

The Lord's prayer

1 **11** Now it happened that he was in a certain place praying, and when he had
finished one of his disciples said, 'Lord, teach us to pray, as John taught his
2 disciples.' ·He said to them, 'When you pray, this is what to say: *

Father, may your name be held holy,
your kingdom come;
3   give us each day our daily bread, *b*
and forgive us our sins, *c*
4   for we ourselves forgive each one who is in debt to us.
And do not put us to the test.'

The importunate friend

5 He also said to them, 'Suppose one of you has a friend and goes to him in the
6 middle of the night to say, "My friend, lend me three loaves, ·because a friend of
mine on his travels has just arrived at my house and I have nothing to offer him;"
7 and the man answers from inside the house, "Do not bother me. The door is
bolted now, and my children are with me in bed; I cannot get up to give it to you."
8 ·I tell you, if the man does not get up and give it him for friendship's sake,
persistence will make him get up and give his friend all he wants.

Effective prayer

9 'So I say to you: Ask, and it will be given to you; search, and you will find; knock,
10 and the door will be opened to you. ·For everyone who asks receives; everyone
11 who searches finds; everyone who knocks will have the door opened. ·What father
12 among you, if his son asked for a fish, would hand him a snake? *d* ·Or if he asked
13 for an egg, hand him a scorpion? ·If you then, evil as you are, know how to give
your children what is good, how much more will the heavenly Father give the
Holy Spirit *e* to those who ask him!'

Jesus and Beelzebul

14 He was driving out a devil and it was dumb; and it happened that when the devil
15 had gone out the dumb man spoke, and the people were amazed. ·But some of
them said, 'It is through Beelzebul, the prince of devils, that he drives devils out.'
16, 17 Others asked him, as a test, for a sign from heaven; ·but, knowing what they were
thinking, he said to them, 'Any kingdom which is divided against itself is heading
18 for ruin, and house collapses against house. ·So, too, with Satan: if he is divided
against himself, how can his kingdom last?—since you claim that it is through
19 Beelzebul *f* that I drive devils out. ·Now if it is through Beelzebul that I drive
devils out, through whom do your own sons drive them out? They shall be your
20 judges, then. ·But if it is through the finger of God *g* that I drive devils out, then
21 the kingdom of God has indeed caught you unawares. ·So long as a strong man
22 fully armed guards his own home, his goods are undisturbed; ·but when someone
stronger than himself attacks and defeats him, the stronger man takes away all the
weapons he relied on and shares out his spoil.

No compromise

23 'Anyone who is not with me is against me; and anyone who does not gather in
with me throws away.

Return of the unclean spirit

24 'When an unclean spirit goes out of someone it wanders through waterless country
looking for a place to rest, and not finding one it says, "I will go back to the home
25, 26 I came from." ·But on arrival, finding it swept and tidied, ·it then goes off and

brings seven other spirits more wicked than itself, and they go in and set up house there, and so that person ends up worse off than before.'

The truly blessed

27 It happened that as he was speaking, a woman in the crowd raised her voice and
28 said, 'Blessed the womb that bore you and the breasts that fed you!' ·But he replied, 'More blessed still are those who hear the word of God and keep it!'

The sign of Jonah

29 The crowds got even bigger and he addressed them, 'This is an evil generation; it
30 is asking for a sign. *ʰ* The only sign it will be given is the sign of Jonah. ·For just as Jonah became a sign to the people of Nineveh, so will the Son of man be a sign to
31 this generation. *ⁱ* ·On Judgement Day the Queen of the South will stand up against the people of this generation and be their condemnation, because she came from the ends of the earth to hear the wisdom of Solomon; and, look, there is something
32 greater than Solomon here. ·On Judgement Day the men of Nineveh will appear against this generation and be its condemnation, because when Jonah preached they repented; and, look, there is something greater than Jonah here.

The parable of the lamp repeated

33 'No one lights a lamp and puts it in some hidden place or under a tub; they put it
34 on the lamp-stand so that people may see the light when they come in. ·The lamp of the body is your eye. When your eye is clear, your whole body, too, is filled
35 with light; but when it is diseased your body, too, will be darkened. ·See to it then
36 that the light inside you is not darkness. ·If, therefore, your whole body is filled with light, and not darkened at all, it will be light entirely, as when the lamp shines on you with its rays.' *ʲ*

The Pharisees and the lawyers attacked

37 He had just finished speaking when a Pharisee invited him to dine at his house.
38 He went in and sat down at table. ·The Pharisee saw this and was surprised that
39 he had not first washed before the meal. ·But the Lord said to him, *ᵏ* 'You Pharisees! You clean the outside of cup and plate, while inside yourselves you are
40 filled with extortion and wickedness. ·Fools! Did not he who made the outside
41 make the inside too? ·Instead, give alms from what you have *ˡ* and, look, everything
42 will be clean for you. ·But alas for you Pharisees, because you pay your tithe of mint and rue and all sorts of garden herbs and neglect justice and the love of God!
43 These you should have practised, without neglecting the others. ·Alas for you Pharisees, because you like to take the seats of honour in the synagogues and to
44 be greeted respectfully in the market squares! ·Alas for you, because you are like the unmarked tombs that people walk on without knowing it!' *ᵐ*
45 A lawyer then spoke up. 'Master,' he said, 'when you speak like this you insult
46 us too.' ·But he said, 'Alas for you lawyers as well, because you load on people burdens that are unendurable, burdens that you yourselves do not touch with your fingertips.
47 'Alas for you because you build tombs for the prophets, the people your ances-
48 tors killed! ·In this way you both witness to what your ancestors did and approve it; they did the killing, you do the building. *ⁿ*
49 'And that is why the Wisdom of God *ᵒ* said, "I will send them prophets and
50 apostles; some they will slaughter and persecute, ·so that this generation will have

51 to answer for every prophet's blood that has been shed since the foundation of the world, ·from the blood of Abel to the blood of Zechariah, who perished between the altar and the Temple." Yes, I tell you, this generation will have to answer for it all.

52 'Alas for you lawyers who have taken away the key of knowledge! You have not gone in yourselves and have prevented others from going in who wanted to.'

53 When he left there, the scribes and the Pharisees began a furious attack on him ·

54 and tried to force answers from him on innumerable questions, ·lying in wait to catch him out in something he might say.

Open and fearless speech

1 12 Meanwhile the people had gathered in their thousands so that they were treading on one another. And he began to speak, first of all to his disciples. ·

2 'Be on your guard against the yeast of the Pharisees—their hypocrisy. ·Everything now covered up will be uncovered, and everything now hidden will be made clear.

3 ·For this reason, whatever you have said in the dark will be heard in the daylight, and what you have whispered in hidden places will be proclaimed from the housetops.

4 'To you my friends I say: Do not be afraid of those who kill the body and after
5 that can do no more. ·I will tell you whom to fear: fear him who, after he has
6 killed, has the power to cast into hell. Yes, I tell you, he is the one to fear. ·Can you not buy five sparrows for two pennies? And yet not one is forgotten in God's
7 sight. ·Why, every hair on your head has been counted. There is no need to be afraid: you are worth more than many sparrows.

8 'I tell you, if anyone openly declares himself for me in the presence of human beings, the Son of man will declare himself for him in the presence of God's angels.
9 But anyone who disowns me in the presence of human beings will be disowned in the presence of God's angels.

10 'Everyone who says a word against the Son of man will be forgiven, but no one who blasphemes against the Holy Spirit will be forgiven.

11 'When they take you before synagogues and magistrates and authorities, do not
12 worry about how to defend yourselves or what to say, ·because when the time comes, the Holy Spirit will teach you what you should say.'

On hoarding possessions

13 A man in the crowd said to him, 'Master, tell my brother to give me a share of our
14 inheritance.' ·He said to him, 'My friend, who appointed me your judge, or the
15 arbitrator of your claims?' ·Then he said to them, 'Watch, and be on your guard against avarice of any kind, for life does not consist in possessions, even when someone has more than he needs.'

16 Then he told them a parable, 'There was once a rich man who, having had a
17 good harvest from his land, ·thought to himself, "What am I to do? I have not
18 enough room to store my crops." ·Then he said, "This is what I will do: I will pull down my barns and build bigger ones, and store all my grain and my goods in
19 them, ·and I will say to my soul: My soul, you have plenty of good things laid by
20 for many years to come; take things easy, eat, drink, have a good time." ·But God said to him, "Fool! This very night the demand will be made for your soul;
21 and this hoard of yours, whose will it be then?" ·So it is when someone stores up treasure for himself instead of becoming rich in the sight of God.'

Trust in Providence

22 Then he said to his disciples, 'That is why I am telling you not to worry about your
23, 24 life and what you are to eat, nor about your body and how you are to clothe it. For
life *b* is more than food, and the body more than clothing. ·Think of the ravens.
They do not sow or reap; they have no storehouses and no barns; yet God feeds
25 them. And how much more you are worth than the birds! ·Can any of you,
26 however much you worry, add a single cubit to your span of life? ·If a very small
27 thing is beyond your powers, why worry about the rest? ·Think how the flowers
grow; they never have to spin or weave; *c* yet, I assure you, not even Solomon in
28 all his royal robes was clothed like one of them. ·Now if that is how God clothes a
flower which is growing wild today and is thrown into the furnace tomorrow, how
29 much more will he look after you, who have so little faith! ·But you must not set
30 your hearts on things to eat and things to drink; nor must you worry. ·It is the
gentiles of this world who set their hearts on all these things. Your Father well
31 knows you need them. ·No; set your hearts on his kingdom, and these other things
will be given you as well.
32   'There is no need to be afraid, little flock, for it has pleased your Father to give
you the kingdom.

On almsgiving *d*

33 'Sell your possessions and give to those in need. Get yourselves purses that do not
wear out, treasure that will not fail you, in heaven where no thief can reach it and
34 no moth destroy it. ·For wherever your treasure is, that is where your heart will
be too.

On being ready for the Master's return

35, 36 'See that you have your belts done up *c* and your lamps lit. ·Be like people waiting
for their master to return from the wedding feast, ready to open the door as soon
37 as he comes and knocks. ·Blessed those servants whom the master finds awake
when he comes. In truth I tell you, he will do up his belt, sit them down at table
38 and wait on them. ·It may be in the second watch that he comes, or in the third,
39 but blessed are those servants if he finds them ready. ·You may be quite sure of
this, that if the householder had known at what time the burglar would come, he
40 would not have let anyone break through the wall of his house. ·You too must
stand ready, because the Son of man is coming at an hour you do not expect.'
41, 42   Peter said, 'Lord, do you mean this parable for us, or for everyone?' ·The Lord
replied, 'Who, then, is the wise and trustworthy steward *f* whom the master will
place over his household to give them at the proper time their allowance of food?
43, 44 Blessed that servant if his master's arrival finds him doing exactly that. ·I tell you
45 truly, he will put him in charge of everything that he owns. ·But if the servant says
to himself, "My master is taking his time coming," and sets about beating the
46 menservants and the servant-girls, and eating and drinking and getting drunk, ·his
master will come on a day he does not expect and at an hour he does not know.
The master will cut him off and send him to the same fate as the unfaithful.
47   'The servant who knows what his master wants, but has got nothing ready and
done nothing in accord with those wishes, will be given a great many strokes of
48 the lash. ·The one who did not know, but has acted in such a way that he deserves
a beating, will be given fewer strokes. When someone is given a great deal, a great

deal will be demanded of that person; when someone is entrusted with a great deal, of that person even more will be expected.

Jesus and his Passion

49 'I have come to bring fire *ᵍ* to the earth, and how I wish it were blazing already!
50 There is a baptism I must still receive, and what constraint I am under until it is completed!

Jesus the cause of dissension

51 'Do you suppose that I am here to bring peace on earth? No, I tell you, but rather
52 division. ·For from now on, a household of five will be divided: three against two
53 and two against three; ·*father opposed to son*, son to father, mother to daughter, *daughter to mother*, mother-in-law to daughter-in-law, *daughter-in-law to mother-in-law*.'

On reading the signs of the times *ʰ*

54 He said again to the crowds, 'When you see a cloud looming up in the west you
55 say at once that rain is coming, and so it does. ·And when the wind is from the
56 south you say it's going to be hot, and it is. ·Hypocrites! You know how to interpret the face of the earth and the sky. How is it you do not know how to interpret these times?
57, 58 'Why not judge for yourselves what is upright? ·For example: when you are going to court with your opponent, make an effort to settle with him on the way, or he may drag you before the judge and the judge hand you over to the officer
59 and the officer have you thrown into prison. ·I tell you, you will not get out till you have paid the very last penny.' *ⁱ*

Examples inviting repentance

1 **13** It was just about this time that some people arrived and told him about the Galileans whose blood Pilate had mingled with that of their sacrifices. *ᵃ* At
2 this he said to them, ·'Do you suppose that these Galileans were worse sinners
3 than any others, that this should have happened to them? ·They were not, I tell
4 you. No; but unless you repent you will all perish as they did. ·Or those eighteen on whom the tower at Siloam fell, killing them all? Do you suppose that they were
5 more guilty than all the other people living in Jerusalem? ·They were not, I tell you. No; but unless you repent you will all perish as they did.'

Parable of the barren fig tree *ᵇ*

6 He told this parable, 'A man had a fig tree planted in his vineyard, and he came
7 looking for fruit on it but found none. ·He said to his vinedresser, "For three years *ᶜ* now I have been coming to look for fruit on this fig tree and finding none.
8 Cut it down: why should it be taking up the ground?" ·"Sir," the man replied,
9 "leave it one more year and give me time to dig round it and manure it: ·it may bear fruit next year; if not, then you can cut it down." '

Healing of a crippled woman on the Sabbath

10, 11 One Sabbath day he was teaching in one of the synagogues, ·and there before him was a woman who for eighteen years had been possessed by a spirit that crippled
12 her; she was bent double and quite unable to stand upright. *ᵈ* ·When Jesus saw her

13 he called her over and said, 'Woman, you are freed from your disability,' ·and he
laid his hands on her. And at once she straightened up, and she glorified God.
14 But the president of the synagogue was indignant because Jesus had healed on
the Sabbath, ⸱ and he addressed all those present saying, 'There are six days when
work is to be done. Come and be healed on one of those days and not on the
15 Sabbath.' ·But the Lord answered him and said, 'Hypocrites! Is there one of you
who does not untie his ox or his donkey from the manger on the Sabbath and take
16 it out for watering? ·And this woman, a daughter of Abraham whom Satan has
held bound these eighteen years—was it not right to untie this bond on the Sabbath
17 day?' ·When he said this, all his adversaries were covered with confusion, and all
the people were overjoyed at all the wonders he worked.

Parable of the mustard seed

18 He went on to say, 'What is the kingdom of God like? What shall I compare it
19 with? ·It is like a mustard seed which a man took and threw into his garden: it
grew and became a tree, and the birds of the air sheltered in its branches.'

Parable of the yeast

20, 21 Again he said, 'What shall I compare the kingdom of God with? ·It is like the
yeast a woman took and mixed in with three measures of flour till it was leavened
all through.'

The narrow door; rejection of the Jews, call of the gentiles ͨ

22 Through towns and villages he went teaching, making his way to Jerusalem.
23, 24 Someone said to him, 'Sir, will there be only a few saved?' He said to them, ·'Try
your hardest to enter by the narrow door, because, I tell you, many will try to
enter and will not succeed.
25 'Once the master of the house has got up and locked the door, you may find
yourself standing outside knocking on the door, saying, "Lord, open to us," but
26 he will answer, "I do not know where you come from." ·Then you will start saying,
27 "We once ate and drank in your company; you taught in our streets," ·but he will
reply, "I do not know where you come from; *away from me, all evil doers!*"
28 'Then there will be weeping and grinding of teeth, when you see Abraham and
Isaac and Jacob and all the prophets in the kingdom of God, and yourselves
29 thrown out. ·And people from east and west, from north and south, will come and
sit down at the feast in the kingdom of God.
30 'Look, there are those now last who will be first, and those now first who will be
last.'

Herod the fox

31 Just at this time some Pharisees came up. 'Go away,' they said. 'Leave this place,
32 because Herod ͤ means to kill you.' ·He replied, 'You may go and give that fox
this message: Look! Today and tomorrow I drive out devils and heal, and on the
33 third day ͪ I attain my end. ͥ ·But for today and tomorrow and the next day I must
go on, since it would not be right for a prophet to die outside Jerusalem. ͫ

Jerusalem admonished

34 'Jerusalem, Jerusalem, you that kill the prophets and stone those who are sent to
you! How often have I longed to gather your children together, as a hen gathers
35 her brood under her wings, and you refused! ·Look! Your house will be left to

you. Yes, I promise you, you shall not see me till the time comes when you are saying:

> *Blessed is he who is coming in the name of the Lord!'*

Healing of a dropsical man on the Sabbath

1   **14** Now it happened that on a Sabbath day he had gone to share a meal in the
2 house of one of the leading Pharisees; and they watched him closely. ·Now
3 there in front of him was a man with dropsy, ·and Jesus addressed the lawyers and Pharisees with the words, 'Is it against the law to cure someone on the Sabbath, or
4 not?' ·But they remained silent, so he took the man and cured him and sent him
5 away. ·Then he said to them, 'Which of you here, if his son ᵃ falls into a well, or
6 his ox, will not pull him out on a Sabbath day without any hesitation?' ·And to this they could find no answer.

On choosing places at table

7 He then told the guests a parable, because he had noticed how they picked the
8 places of honour. He said this, ·'When someone invites you to a wedding feast, do not take your seat in the place of honour. A more distinguished person than you
9 may have been invited, ·and the person who invited you both may come and say, "Give up your place to this man." And then, to your embarrassment, you will
10 have to go and take the lowest place. ·No; when you are a guest, make your way to the lowest place and sit there, so that, when your host comes, he may say, "My friend, move up higher." Then, everyone with you at the table will see you
11 honoured. ·For everyone who raises himself up will be humbled, and the one who humbles himself will be raised up.'

On choosing guests to be invited

12 Then he said to his host, 'When you give a lunch or a dinner, do not invite your friends or your brothers or your relations or rich neighbours, in case they invite
13 you back and so repay you. ·No; when you have a party, invite the poor, the
14 crippled, the lame, the blind; ·then you will be blessed, for they have no means to repay you and so you will be repaid when the upright rise again.'

The invited guests who made excuses

15 On hearing this, one of those gathered round the table said to him, 'Blessed is
16 anyone who will share the meal in the kingdom of God!' ·But he said to him, 'There was a man who gave a great banquet, and he invited a large number of
17 people. ·When the time for the banquet came, he sent his servant to say to those
18 who had been invited, "Come along: everything is ready now." ·But all alike started to make excuses. The first said, "I have bought a piece of land and must go
19 and see it. Please accept my apologies." ·Another said, "I have bought five yoke
20 of oxen and am on my way to try them out. Please accept my apologies." ·Yet another said, "I have just got married and so am unable to come."
21   'The servant returned and reported this to his master. Then the householder, in a rage, said to his servant, "Go out quickly into the streets and alleys of the town
22 and bring in here the poor, the crippled, the blind and the lame." ᵇ ·"Sir," said the
23 servant, "your orders have been carried out and there is still room." ·Then the master said to his servant, "Go to the open roads and the hedgerows ᶜ and press
24 people to come in, to make sure my house is full; ·because, I tell you, not one of those who were invited shall have a taste of my banquet." '

Renouncing all that one holds dear

25 Great crowds accompanied him on his way and he turned and spoke to them.
26 'Anyone who comes to me without hating *d* father, mother, wife, *e* children, broth-
27 ers, sisters, yes and his own life too, cannot be my disciple. ·No one who does not
carry his cross and come after me can be my disciple.

Renouncing possessions

28 'And indeed, which of you here, intending to build a tower, would not first sit
29 down and work out the cost to see if he had enough to complete it? ·Otherwise, if
he laid the foundation and then found himself unable to finish the work, anyone
30 who saw it would start making fun of him and saying, ·"Here is someone who
31 started to build and was unable to finish." ·Or again, what king marching to war
against another king would not first sit down and consider whether with ten
thousand men he could stand up to the other who was advancing against him with
32 twenty thousand? ·If not, then while the other king was still a long way off, he
33 would send envoys to sue for peace. ·So in the same way, none of you can be my
disciple without giving up all that he owns. *f*

On loss of enthusiasm in a disciple

34, 35 'Salt is a good thing. But if salt itself loses its taste, what can make it salty again? ·It
is good for neither soil nor manure heap. People throw it away. Anyone who has
ears for listening should listen!'

The three parables of God's mercy

1 **15** The tax collectors and sinners, however, were all crowding round to listen to
2 him, ·and the Pharisees and scribes complained saying, 'This man welcomes
3 sinners and eats with them.' ·So he told them this parable:

The lost sheep

4 'Which one of you with a hundred sheep, if he lost one, would fail to leave the
5 ninety-nine in the desert and go after the missing one till he found it? ·And when
6 he found it, would he not joyfully take it on his shoulders ·and then, when he got
home, call together his friends and neighbours saying to them, " Rejoice with me,
7 I have found my sheep that was lost." ·In the same way, I tell you, there will be
more rejoicing in heaven over one sinner repenting than over ninety-nine upright
people who have no need of repentance.

The lost drachma

8 'Or again, what woman with ten drachmas would not, if she lost one, light a lamp
9 and sweep out the house and search thoroughly till she found it? ·And then, when
she had found it, call together her friends and neighbours, saying to them, "Rejoice
10 with me, I have found the drachma I lost." ·In the same way, I tell you, there is
rejoicing among the angels of God over one repentant sinner.'

The lost son (the 'prodigal') and the dutiful son *a*

11, 12 Then he said, 'There was a man who had two sons. ·The younger one said to his
father, "Father, let me have the share of the estate that will come to me." So the
13 father divided the property between them. ·A few days later, the younger son got
together everything he had and left for a distant country where he squandered his
money on a life of debauchery.

14 'When he had spent it all, that country experienced a severe famine, and now
15 he began to feel the pinch ·so he hired himself out to one of the local inhabitants
16 who put him on his farm to feed the pigs. ·And he would willingly have filled
himself with the husks the pigs were eating but no one would let him have them.
17 Then he came to his senses and said, "How many of my father's hired men have
18 all the food they want and more, and here am I dying of hunger! ·I will leave this
place and go to my father and say: Father, I have sinned against heaven and
19 against you; ·I no longer deserve to be called your son; treat me as one of your
20 hired men." ·So he left the place and went back to his father.

'While he was still a long way off, his father saw him and was moved with pity.
21 He ran to the boy, clasped him in his arms and kissed him. ·Then his son said,
"Father, I have sinned against heaven and against you. I no longer deserve to be
22 called your son." ·But the father said to his servants, "Quick! Bring out the best
23 robe and put it on him; put a ring on his finger and sandals on his feet. ·Bring the
24 calf we have been fattening, and kill it; we will celebrate by having a feast, ·because
this son of mine was dead and has come back to life; he was lost and is found."
And they began to celebrate.

25 'Now the elder son *b* was out in the fields, and on his way back, as he drew near
26 the house, he could hear music and dancing. ·Calling one of the servants he asked
27 what it was all about. ·The servant told him, "Your brother has come, and your
father has killed the calf we had been fattening because he has got him back safe
28 and sound." ·He was angry then and refused to go in, and his father came out and
29 began to urge him to come in; ·but he retorted to his father, "All these years I
have slaved for you and never once disobeyed any orders of yours, yet you never
30 offered me so much as a kid for me to celebrate with my friends. ·But, for this son
of yours, when he comes back after swallowing up your property—he and his loose
women—you kill the calf we had been fattening."

31, 32 'The father said, "My son, you are with me always and all I have is yours. ·But
it was only right we should celebrate and rejoice, because your brother here was
dead and has come to life; he was lost and is found." '

The crafty steward

1   **16** *a*He also said to his disciples, 'There was a rich man and he had a steward
2 who was denounced to him for being wasteful with his property. ·He called
for the man and said, "What is this I hear about you? Draw me up an account of
3 your stewardship because you are not to be my steward any longer." ·Then the
steward said to himself, "Now that my master is taking the stewardship from me,
what am I to do? Dig? I am not strong enough. Go begging? I should be too
4 ashamed. ·Ah, I know what I will do to make sure that when I am dismissed from
office there will be some to welcome me into their homes."

5 'Then he called his master's debtors one by one. To the first he said, "How
6 much do you owe my master?" ·"One hundred measures of oil," he said. The
7 steward said, "Here, take your bond; sit down and quickly write fifty." ·To another
he said, "And you, sir, how much do you owe?" "One hundred measures of
wheat," he said. The steward said, "Here, take your bond and write eighty."

8 'The master praised the dishonest steward for his astuteness. *b* For the children
of this world are more astute in dealing with their own kind than are the children
of light.'

The right use of money

9 'And so I tell you this: use money, tainted as it is, *ᶜ* to win you friends, and thus make sure that when it fails you, they will welcome you into eternal dwellings.
10, 11 Anyone who is trustworthy in little things is trustworthy in great; anyone who is dishonest in little things is dishonest in great. ·If then you are not trustworthy with
12 money, that tainted thing, who will trust you with genuine riches? ·And if you are not trustworthy with what is not yours, *ᵈ* who will give you what is your very own? *ᵉ*
13 'No servant can be the slave of two masters: he will either hate the first and love the second, or be attached to the first and despise the second. You cannot be the slave both of God and of money.'

Against the Pharisees and their love of money

14, 15 The Pharisees, who loved money, heard all this and jeered at him. ·He said to them, 'You are the very ones who pass yourselves off as upright in people's sight, but God knows your hearts. For what is highly esteemed in human eyes is loathsome in the sight of God.

The kingdom stormed

16 'Up to the time of John it was the Law and the Prophets; from then onwards, the kingdom of God has been preached, and everyone is forcing their way into it.

The Law remains

17 'It is easier for heaven and earth to disappear than for one little stroke to drop out of the Law.

Marriage indissoluble

18 'Everyone who divorces his wife and marries another is guilty of adultery, and the man who marries a woman divorced by her husband commits adultery.

The parable of the rich man and Lazarus *ᶠ*

19 'There was a rich man who used to dress in purple and fine linen and feast
20 magnificently every day. ·And at his gate there used to lie a poor man called
21 Lazarus, covered with sores, ·who longed to fill himself with what fell from the
22 rich man's table. *ᵍ* Even dogs came and licked his sores. ·Now it happened that the poor man died and was carried away by the angels into Abraham's embrace. *ʰ* The rich man also died and was buried.
23 'In his torment in Hades he looked up and saw Abraham a long way off with
24 Lazarus in his embrace. ·So he cried out, "Father Abraham, pity me and send Lazarus to dip the tip of his finger in water and cool my tongue, for I am in agony
25 in these flames." ·Abraham said, "My son, remember that during your life you had your fill of good things, just as Lazarus his fill of bad. Now he is being
26 comforted here while you are in agony. ·But that is not all: between us and you a great gulf *ⁱ* has been fixed, to prevent those who want to cross from our side to yours or from your side to ours."
27, 28 'So he said, "Father, I beg you then to send Lazarus to my father's house, ·since I have five brothers, to give them warning so that they do not come to this place of
29 torment too." ·Abraham said, "They have Moses and the prophets, let them listen
30 to them." ·The rich man replied, "Ah no, father Abraham, but if someone comes
31 to them from the dead, they will repent." ·Then Abraham said to him, "If they

will not listen either to Moses or to the prophets, they will not be convinced even if someone should rise from the dead." '

On leading others astray

1 **17** He said to his disciples, 'Causes of falling are sure to come, but alas for the
2 one through whom they occur! ·It would be better for him to be thrown into the sea with a millstone round the neck than to be the downfall of a single one
3 of these little ones. ·Keep watch on yourselves!

Brotherly correction *

'If your brother does something wrong, rebuke him and, if he is sorry, forgive
4 him. ·And if he wrongs you seven times a day and seven times comes back to you and says, "I am sorry," you must forgive him.'

The power of faith

5, 6 The apostles said to the Lord, 'Increase our faith.' ·The Lord replied, 'If you had faith like a mustard seed you could say to this mulberry tree, "Be uprooted and planted in the sea," and it would obey you.

Humble service

7 'Which of you, with a servant ploughing or minding sheep, would say to him when
8 he returned from the fields, "Come and have your meal at once"? ᵇ ·Would he not be more likely to say, "Get my supper ready; fasten your belt and wait on me
9 while I eat and drink. You yourself can eat and drink afterwards"? ·Must he be
10 grateful to the servant for doing what he was told? ·So with you: when you have done all you have been told to do, say, "We are useless ᶜ servants: we have done no more than our duty." '

The ten victims of skin-disease

11 Now it happened that on the way to Jerusalem he was travelling in the borderlands
12 of Samaria and Galilee. ᵈ ·As he entered one of the villages, ten men suffering
13 from a virulent skin-disease came to meet him. They stood some way off ·and
14 called to him, 'Jesus! Master! Take pity on us.' ·When he saw them he said, 'Go and show yourselves to the priests.' Now as they were going away they were
15 cleansed. ·Finding himself cured, one of them turned back praising God at the top
16 of his voice ·and threw himself prostrate at the feet of Jesus and thanked him. The
17 man was a Samaritan. ·This led Jesus to say, 'Were not all ten made clean? The
18 other nine, where are they? ·It seems that no one has come back to give praise to
19 God, except this foreigner.' ·And he said to the man, 'Stand up and go on your way. Your faith has saved you.'

The coming of the kingdom of God

20 Asked by the Pharisees when the kingdom of God was to come, he gave them this
21 answer, 'The coming of the kingdom of God does not admit of observation ·and there will be no one to say, "Look, it is here! Look, it is there!" For look, the kingdom of God is among you.' ᵉ

The Day of the Son of man ᶠ

22 He said to the disciples, 'A time will come when you will long to see one of the
23 days of the Son of man ᵍ and will not see it. ·They will say to you, "Look, it is

24 there!" or, "Look, it is here!" Make no move; do not set off in pursuit; ·for as the
lightning flashing from one part of heaven lights up the other, so will be the Son of
25 man when his Day comes. ·But first he is destined to suffer grievously and be
rejected by this generation.
26. 27   'As it was in Noah's day, so will it also be in the days of the Son of man. *ᵏ* ·People
were eating and drinking, marrying wives and husbands, right up to the day Noah
28 went into the ark, and the Flood came and destroyed them all. ·It will be the same
as it was in Lot's day: people were eating and drinking, buying and selling, planting
29 and building, ·but the day Lot left Sodom, it rained fire and brimstone from
30 heaven and it destroyed them all. ·It will be the same when the day comes for the
Son of man to be revealed.
31   'When that Day comes, no one on the housetop, with his possessions in the
house, must come down to collect them, nor must anyone in the fields turn back.
32. 33 Remember Lot's wife. ·Anyone who tries to preserve his life will lose it; and
34 anyone who loses it will keep it safe. ·I tell you, on that night, when two are in one
35 bed, one will be taken, the other left; ·when two women are grinding corn together,
[36]. 37 one will be taken, the other left.' *ⁱ* ·The disciples spoke up and asked, 'Where,
Lord?' He said, 'Where the body is, there too will the vultures gather.'

The unscrupulous judge and the importunate widow

1 **18** Then he told them a parable about the need to pray continually and never
2   lose heart. *ᵃ* ·'There was a judge in a certain town,' he said, 'who had neither
3 fear of God nor respect for anyone. ·In the same town there was also a widow
who kept on coming to him and saying, "I want justice from you against my
4 enemy!" ·For a long time he refused, but at last he said to himself, "Even though I
5 have neither fear of God nor respect for any human person, ·I must give this
widow her just rights since she keeps pestering me, or she will come and slap me
in the face." '
6. 7   And the Lord said, 'You notice what the unjust judge has to say? ·Now, will
not God see justice done to his elect if they keep calling to him day and night even
8 though he still delays to help them? *ᵇ* ·I promise you, he will see justice done to
them, and done speedily. But when the Son of man comes, will he find any faith
on earth?'

The Pharisee and the tax collector

9 He spoke the following parable to some people who prided themselves on being
10 upright and despised everyone else, ·'Two men went up to the Temple to pray,
11 one a Pharisee, the other a tax collector. ·The Pharisee stood there and said this
prayer to himself, "I thank you, God, that I am not grasping, unjust, adulterous
12 like everyone else, and particularly that I am not like this tax collector here. ·I fast
13 twice a week; I pay tithes on all I get." ·The tax collector stood some distance
away, not daring even to raise his eyes to heaven; but he beat his breast and said,
14 "God, be merciful to me, a sinner." ·This man, I tell you, went home again
justified; the other did not. For everyone who raises himself up will be humbled,
but anyone who humbles himself will be raised up.'

Jesus and the children *ᶜ*

15 People even brought babies to him, for him to touch them; but when the disciples
16 saw this they scolded them. ·But Jesus called the children to him and said, 'Let
the little children come to me, and do not stop them; for it is to such as these that

17 the kingdom of God belongs. ·In truth I tell you, anyone who does not welcome the kingdom of God like a little child will never enter it.'

The rich aristocrat

18 One of the rulers put this question to him, 'Good Master, what shall I do to inherit
19 eternal life?' ·Jesus said to him, 'Why do you call me good? No one is good but
20 God alone. ·You know the commandments: *You shall not commit adultery; You shall not kill; You shall not steal; You shall not give false witness; Honour your*
21 *father and your mother.*' ·He replied, 'I have kept all these since my earliest days.'
22 And when Jesus heard this he said, 'There is still one thing you lack. Sell everything you own and distribute the money to the poor, and you will have treasure in
23 heaven; then come, follow me.' ·But when he heard this he was overcome with sadness, for he was very rich.

The danger of riches

24 Jesus looked at him and said, 'How hard it is for those who have riches to make
25 their way into the kingdom of God! ·Yes, it is easier for a camel to pass through
26 the eye of a needle than for someone rich to enter the kingdom of God.' ·Those
27 who were listening said, 'In that case, who can be saved?' ·He replied, 'Things that are impossible by human resources, are possible for God.'

The reward of renunciation

28, 29 But Peter said, 'Look, we left all we had to follow you.' ·He said to them, 'In truth I tell you, there is no one who has left house, wife, brothers, parents or
30 children for the sake of the kingdom of God ·who will not receive ⁴ many times as much in this present age and, in the world to come, eternal life.'

Third prophecy of the Passion

31 Then taking the Twelve aside he said to them, 'Look, we are going up to Jerusalem, and everything that is written by the prophets ⁴ about the Son of man is to come
32 true. ·For he will be handed over to the gentiles and will be mocked, maltreated
33 and spat on, ·and when they have scourged him they will put him to death; and on
34 the third day he will rise again.' ·But they could make nothing of this; what he said was quite obscure to them, they did not understand what he was telling them.

Entering Jericho: the blind man

35 Now it happened that as he drew near to Jericho there was a blind man sitting at
36 the side of the road begging. ·When he heard the crowd going past he asked what
37, 38 it was all about, ·and they told him that Jesus the Nazarene was passing by. ·So he
39 called out, 'Jesus, Son of David, have pity on me.' ·The people in front scolded him and told him to keep quiet, but he only shouted all the louder, 'Son of David,
40 have pity on me.' ·Jesus stopped and ordered them to bring the man to him, and
41 when he came up, asked him, ·'What do you want me to do for you?' 'Sir,' he
42 replied, 'let me see again.' ·Jesus said to him, 'Receive your sight. Your faith has
43 saved you.' ·And instantly his sight returned and he followed him praising God, and all the people who saw it gave praise to God.

Zacchaeus

1, 2 **19** He entered Jericho and was going through the town ·and suddenly a man whose name was Zacchaeus made his appearance; he was one of the senior

3 tax collectors and a wealthy man. ·He kept trying to see which Jesus was, but he
4 was too short and could not see him for the crowd; ·so he ran ahead and climbed a
5 sycamore tree to catch a glimpse of Jesus who was to pass that way. ·When Jesus
reached the spot he looked up and spoke to him. 'Zacchaeus, come down. Hurry,
6 because I am to stay at your house today.' ·And he hurried down and welcomed
7 him joyfully. ·They all complained when they saw what was happening. 'He has
8 gone to stay at a sinner's house,' they said. ·But Zacchaeus stood his ground and
said to the Lord, 'Look, sir, I am going to give half my property to the poor, and if
9 I have cheated anybody I will pay him back four times the amount.'ᵉ ·And Jesus
said to him, 'Today salvation has come to this house, because this man too is a son
10 of Abraham;ᵇ ·for the Son of man has come to seek out and save what was lost.'

Parable of the pounds ᶜ

11 While the people were listening to this he went on to tell a parable, because he
was near Jerusalem and they thought that the kingdom of God was going to show
12 itself then and there. ·Accordingly he said, 'A man of noble birth went to a distant
13 country to be appointed king and then return. ᵈ ·He summoned ten of his servants
14 and gave them ten pounds, telling them, "Trade with these, until I get back." But
his compatriots detested him and sent a delegation to follow him with this message,
"We do not want this man to be our king."
15   'Now it happened that on his return, having received his appointment as king,
he sent for those servants to whom he had given the money, to find out what profit
16 each had made by trading. ·The first came in, "Sir," he said, "your one pound has
17 brought in ten." ·He replied, "Well done, my good servant! Since you have proved
yourself trustworthy in a very small thing, you shall have the government of ten
18 cities." ·Then came the second, "Sir," he said, "your one pound has made five."
19, 20 To this one also he said, "And you shall be in charge of five cities." ·Next came
the other, "Sir," he said, "here is your pound. I put it away safely wrapped up in a
21 cloth ·because I was afraid of you; for you are an exacting man: you gather in
22 what you have not laid out and reap what you have not sown." ·He said to him,
"You wicked servant! Out of your own mouth I condemn you. So you knew that I
was an exacting man, gathering in what I have not laid out and reaping what I
23 have not sown? ·Then why did you not put my money in the bank? On my return I
24 could have drawn it out with interest." ·And he said to those standing by, "Take
25 the pound from him and give it to the man who has ten pounds." ·And they said
26 to him, "But, sir, he has ten pounds . . ." ·"I tell you, to everyone who has will
be given more; but anyone who has not will be deprived even of what he has.
27   "As for my enemies who did not want me for their king, bring them here and
execute them in my presence." '

V: TEACHING IN JERUSALEM

The Messiah enters Jerusalem

28, 29 When he had said this he went on ahead, going up to Jerusalem. ·Now it happened
that when he was near Bethphage and Bethany, close by the Mount of Olives as it
30 is called, he sent two of the disciples, saying, ·'Go to the village opposite, and as
you enter it you will find a tethered colt that no one has ever yet ridden. Untie it
31 and bring it here. ·If anyone asks you, "Why are you untying it?" you are to say

32 this, "The Master needs it." ' ·The messengers went off and found everything just
33 as he had told them. ·As they were untying the colt, its owners said, 'Why are you
34 untying it?' ·and they answered, 'The Master needs it.'
35   So they took the colt to Jesus and, throwing their cloaks on its back, they lifted
36. 37 Jesus on to it. ·As he moved off, they spread their cloaks in the road, ·and now, as
he was approaching the downward slope of the Mount of Olives, the whole group
of disciples joyfully began to praise God at the top of their voices for all the
38 miracles they had seen. ·They cried out: '

> Blessed is he who is coming
> as King *in the name of the Lord!*
> Peace in heaven
> and glory in the highest heavens!

Jesus defends his disciples for acclaiming him

39, 40 Some Pharisees in the crowd said to him, 'Master, reprove your disciples,' ·but he
answered, 'I tell you, if these keep silence, the stones will cry out.'

Lament for Jerusalem

41, 42 As he drew near and came in sight of the city he shed tears over it ·and said, 'If
you too had only recognised on this day the way to peace! ' But in fact it is hidden
43 from your eyes! ·Yes, a time is coming when your enemies will raise fortifications
44 all round you, when they will encircle you and hem you in on every side; ·they will
dash you and the children inside your walls to the ground; they will leave not one
stone standing on another within you, because you did not recognise the moment
of your visitation.' *

The expulsion of the dealers from the Temple

45 Then he went into the Temple and began driving out those who were busy trading,
46 saying to them, ·'According to scripture, *my house shall be a house of prayer* but
you have turned it into *a bandits' den.*'

Jesus teaches in the Temple

47 He taught in the Temple every day. The chief priests and the scribes, in company
48 with the leading citizens, tried to do away with him, ·but they could not find a way
to carry this out because the whole people hung on his words.

The Jews question the authority of Jesus

1 **20** ª Now it happened that one day while he was teaching the people in the
Temple and proclaiming the good news, the chief priests and the scribes
2 came up, together with the elders, ·and spoke to him. 'Tell us,' they said, 'what
3 authority have you for acting like this? Or who gives you this authority?' ·In reply
4 he said to them, 'And I will ask you a question, just one. Tell me: ·John's baptism:
5 what was its origin, heavenly or human?' ·And they debated this way among
themselves, 'If we say heavenly, he will retort, "Why did you refuse to believe
6 him?"; ·and if we say human, the whole people will stone us, for they are convinced
7 that John was a prophet.' ·So their reply was that they did not know where it came
8 from. ·And Jesus said to them, 'Nor will I tell you my authority for acting like
this.'

Parable of the wicked tenants

9 And he went on to tell the people this parable, 'A man planted a vineyard and
10 leased it to tenants, and went abroad for a long while. ·When the right time came,
he sent a servant to the tenants to get his share of the produce of the vineyard. But
11 the tenants thrashed him, and sent him away empty-handed. ·But he went on to
send a second servant; they thrashed him too and treated him shamefully and sent
12 him away empty-handed. ·He still went on to send a third; they wounded this one
13 too, and threw him out. ·Then the owner of the vineyard thought, "What am I to
14 do? I will send them my own beloved son. Perhaps they will respect him." ·But
when the tenants saw him they put their heads together saying, "This is the heir,
15 let us kill him so that the inheritance will be ours." ·So they threw him out of the
vineyard and killed him.
16   'Now what will the owner of the vineyard do to them? ·He will come and make
an end of these tenants and give the vineyard to others.' Hearing this they said,
17 'God forbid!' ·But he looked hard at them and said, 'Then what does this text in
the scriptures mean:

> *The stone which the builders rejected*
> *has become the cornerstone?*

18 Anyone who falls on that stone will be dashed to pieces; anyone it falls on will be
crushed.'
19   And the scribes and the chief priests would have liked to lay hands on him that
very moment, because they realised that this parable was aimed at them, but they
were afraid of the people.

On tribute to Caesar

20 So they awaited their opportunity and sent agents to pose as upright men, and to
catch him out in something he might say and so enable them to hand him over to
21 the jurisdiction and authority of the governor. ·They put to him this question,
'Master, we know that you say and teach what is right; you favour no one, but
22 teach the way of God in all honesty. ·Is it permissible for us to pay taxes to Caesar
23, 24 or not?' ·But he was aware of their cunning and said, ·'Show me a denarius.
25 Whose portrait and title are on it?' They said, 'Caesar's.' · He said to them, 'Well
then, pay Caesar what belongs to Caesar—and God what belongs to God.'
26   They were unable to catch him out in anything he had to say in public; they
were amazed at his answer and were silenced.

The resurrection of the dead

27 Some Sadducees—those who argue that there is no resurrection—approached him
28 and they put this question to him, ·'Master, Moses prescribed for us, if a man's
married brother dies childless, the man must marry the widow to raise up children
29 for his brother. ·Well then, there were seven brothers; the first, having married a
30, 31 wife, died childless. ·The second ·and then the third married the widow. And the
32 same with all seven, they died leaving no children. ·Finally the woman herself
33 died. ·Now, at the resurrection, whose wife will she be, since she had been married
to all seven?'
34, 35   Jesus replied, 'The children of this world *b* take wives and husbands, ·but those
who are judged worthy of a place in the other world and in the resurrection from
36 the dead *c* do not marry ·because they can no longer die, *d* for they are the same as

37 the angels, and being children of the resurrection ' they are children of God. ·And Moses himself implies that the dead rise again, in the passage about the bush where he calls the Lord *the God of Abraham, the God of Isaac and the God of* 38 *Jacob.* ·Now he is God, not of the dead, but of the living; for to him everyone is alive.'

39, 40 Some scribes' then spoke up. They said, 'Well put, Master.' ·They did not dare to ask him any more questions.

Christ not only son but also Lord of David

41 He then said to them, 'How can people maintain that the Christ is son of David? 42 Why, David himself says in the Book of Psalms:

> *The Lord declared to my Lord,*
> *take your seat at my right hand,*
43 > *till I have made your enemies*
> *your footstool.*

44 David here calls him Lord; how then can he be his son?'

The scribes condemned by Jesus

45, 46 While all the people were listening he said to the disciples, ·'Beware of the scribes who like to walk about in long robes and love to be greeted respectfully in the market squares, to take the front seats in the synagogues and the places of honour 47 at banquets, ·who devour the property of widows, and for show offer long prayers. The more severe will be the sentence they receive.'

The widow's mite

1 **21** Looking up, he saw rich people putting their offerings into the treasury; 2, 3 and he noticed a poverty-stricken widow putting in two small coins, ·and 4 he said, 'I tell you truly, this poor widow has put in more than any of them; ·for these have all put in money they could spare, but she in her poverty has put in all she had to live on.'

Discourse on the destruction of Jerusalem: ' Introduction

5 When some were talking about the Temple, remarking how it was adorned with 6 fine stonework and votive offerings, he said, ·'All these things you are staring at now—the time will come when not a single stone will be left on another; everything 7 will be destroyed.' ·And they put to him this question, 'Master,' they said, 'when will this happen, then, and what sign will there be that it is about to take place?'

The warning signs

8 But he said, 'Take care not to be deceived, because many will come using my name and saying, "I am the one" and "The time is near at hand." Refuse to join 9 them. ·And when you hear of wars and revolutions, do not be terrified, for this is 10 something that must happen first, but the end will not come at once.' ·Then he said to them, 'Nation will fight against nation, and kingdom against kingdom. 11 There will be great earthquakes and plagues and famines in various places; there will be terrifying events and great signs from heaven.

12 'But before all this happens, you will be seized and persecuted; you will be handed over to the synagogues and to imprisonment, and brought before kings 13 and governors for the sake of my name ·—and that will be your opportunity to

14, 15 bear witness. ·Make up your minds not to prepare your defence, ·because I myself *
shall give you an eloquence and a wisdom that none of your opponents will be
16 able to resist or contradict. ·You will be betrayed even by parents and brothers,
17 relations and friends; and some of you will be put to death. ·You will be hated
18, 19 universally on account of my name, ·but not a hair of your head will be lost. ·Your
perseverance will win you your lives.

The siege

20 'When you see Jerusalem surrounded by armies, ᶜ then you must realise that it will
21 soon be laid desolate. ·Then those in Judaea must escape to the mountains, those
inside the city must leave it, and those in country districts must not take refuge in
22 it. ·For this is the time of retribution when all that scripture says ᵈ must be fulfilled.
23 Alas for those with child, or with babies at the breast, when those days come!

The disaster and the age of the gentiles

24 'For great misery will descend on the land and retribution on this people. ·They
will fall by the edge of the sword and be led captive to every gentile country; and
Jerusalem will be trampled down by the gentiles until their time ᵉ is complete.

Cosmic disasters and the glorious appearing of the Son of man

25 'There will be signs in the sun and moon and stars; on earth nations in agony,
26 bewildered by the turmoil of the ocean and its waves; ·men fainting away with
terror and fear at what menaces the world, for the powers of heaven will be
27 shaken. ·And then they will see the Son of man coming in a cloud with power and
28 great glory. ·When these things begin to take place, stand erect, hold your heads
high, because your liberation is near at hand.'

The time of this coming

29, 30 And he told them a parable, 'Look at the fig tree and indeed every tree. ·As soon
31 as you see them bud, you can see for yourselves that summer is now near. ·So
with you when you see these things happening: know that the kingdom of God is
32 near.ᶠ ·In truth I tell you, before this generation has passed away all will have
33 taken place. Sky and earth will pass away, but my words will never pass away.

Be on the alert

34 'Watch yourselves, or your hearts will be coarsened by debauchery and drunken-
35 ness and the cares of life, and that day will come upon you unexpectedly, ·like a
36 trap. For it will come down ᵍ on all those living on the face of the earth. ·Stay
awake, praying at all times for the strength to survive all that is going to happen,
and to hold your ground before the Son of man.'

The last days of Jesus

37 All day long he would be in the Temple teaching, but would spend the night in the
38 open on the hill called the Mount of Olives. ·And from early morning the people
thronged to him in the Temple to listen to him. ʰ

VI: THE PASSION *

The conspiracy against Jesus: Judas betrays him

1 **22** The feast of Unleavened Bread, called the Passover, was now drawing
2 near, ·and the chief priests and the scribes were looking for some way of
doing away with him, because they were afraid of the people. *
3 Then Satan entered into Judas, surnamed Iscariot, who was one of the Twelve.
4 He approached the chief priests and the officers of the guard ʿ to discuss some way
5 of handing Jesus over to them. ·They were delighted and agreed to give him
6 money. ·He accepted and began to look for an opportunity to betray him to them
without people knowing about it.

Preparation for the Passover supper

7 The day of Unleavened Bread came round, on which the Passover had to be
8 sacrificed, ·and he sent Peter and John, saying, 'Go and make the preparations
9 for us to eat the Passover.' ·They asked him, 'Where do you want us to prepare
10 it?' ·He said to them, 'Look, as you go into the city you will meet a man carrying a
11 pitcher of water. Follow him into the house he enters ·and tell the owner of the
house, "The Master says this to you: Where is the room for me to eat the Passover
12 with my disciples?" ·The man will show you a large upper room furnished with
13 couches. Make the preparations there.' ·They set off and found everything as he
had told them and prepared the Passover.

The supper

14, 15 When the time came he took his place at table, and the apostles with him. ·And
he said to them, ᵈ 'I have ardently longed to eat this Passover with you before I
16 suffer; ·because, I tell you, I shall not eat it until it is fulfilled ʿ in the kingdom of
God.'
17 Then, taking a cup, ᶠ he gave thanks and said, 'Take this and share it among
18 you, ·because from now on, I tell you, I shall never again drink wine until the
kingdom of God comes.'

The institution of the Eucharist ᵍ

19 Then he took bread, and when he had given thanks, he broke it and gave it to
20 them, saying, 'This is my body given for you; do this in remembrance of me.' ·He
did the same with the cup after supper, and said, 'This cup is the new covenant in
my blood poured out for you. ʰ

The treachery of Judas foretold

21 'But look, here with me on the table is the hand of the man who is betraying me.
22 The Son of man is indeed on the path which was decreed, but alas for that man by
23 whom he is betrayed! ·And they began to ask one another which of them it could
be who was to do this.

Who is the greatest? ⁱ

24 An argument also began between them about who should be reckoned the greatest;
25 but he said to them, 'Among the gentiles it is the kings who lord it over them, and
26 those who have authority over them are given the title Benefactor. ·With you this
must not happen. No; the greatest among you must behave as if he were the

27 youngest, the leader as if he were the one who serves. •For who is the greater: the one at table or the one who serves? The one at table, surely? Yet here am I among you as one who serves!

The reward promised to the apostles

28. 29 'You are the men who have stood by me faithfully in my trials; •and now I confer
30 a kingdom on you, just as my Father conferred one on me: •you will eat and drink at my table in my kingdom, and you will sit on thrones to judge the twelve tribes of Israel.

Peter's denial and repentance foretold

31. 32 ʲ'Simon, Simon! Look, Satan has got his wish to sift you all like wheat; •but I have prayed for you, Simon, that your faith may not fail, and once you have recovered,
33 you in your turn must strengthen your brothers.'ᵏ •'Lord,' he answered, 'I would
34 be ready to go to prison with you, and to death.' •Jesus replied, 'I∙tell you, Peter, by the time the cock crows today you will have denied three times that you know me.'

A time of crisis

35 He said to them, 'When I sent you out without purse or haversack or sandals,
36 were you short of anything?' •'No, nothing,' they said. He said to them, 'But now if you have a purse, take it, and the same with a haversack; if you have no sword,
37 sell your cloak and buy one,ˡ •because I tell you these words of scripture are destined to be fulfilled in me: *He was counted as one of the rebellious.* Yes, what it
38 says about me is even now reaching its fulfilment.' •They said, 'Lord, here are two swords.' He said to them, 'That is enough!'

The Mount of Olives ᵐ

39 He then left to make his way as usual to the Mount of Olives, with the disciples
40 following. •When he reached the place he said to them, 'Pray not to be put to the test.'
41 Then he withdrew from them, about a stone's throw away, and knelt down ⁿ
42 and prayed. •'Father,' he said, 'if you are willing, take this cup away from me.
43 Nevertheless, let your will be done, not mine.' •Then an angel appeared to him,
44 coming from heaven to give him strength. •In his anguish he prayed even more earnestly, and his sweat fell to the ground like great drops of blood. ᵒ
45 When he rose from prayer he went to the disciples and found them sleeping for
46 sheer grief. •And he said to them, 'Why are you asleep? Get up and pray not to be put to the test.'

The arrest

47 Suddenly, while he was still speaking, a number of men appeared, and at the head of them the man called Judas, one of the Twelve, who went up to Jesus to kiss
48. 49 him. •Jesus said, 'Judas, are you betraying the Son of man with a kiss?' •His followers, seeing what was about to happen, said, 'Lord, shall we use our swords?'
50 And one of them struck the high priest's servant and cut off his right ear. •But at
51 this Jesus said, 'That is enough.' And touching the man's ear he healed him.
52 Then Jesus said to the chief priests and captains of the Temple guard and elders who had come for him, 'Am I a bandit, that you had to set out with swords and

53 clubs? •When I was among you in the Temple day after day you never made a move to lay hands on me. But this is your hour; this is the reign of darkness.'

Peter's denials

54 They seized him then⸍ and led him away, and they took him to the high priest's
55 house. Peter followed at a distance. •They had lit a fire in the middle of the
56 courtyard and Peter sat down among them, •and as he was sitting there by the blaze a servant-girl saw him, peered at him, and said, 'This man was with him
57, 58 too.' •But he denied it, 'Woman, I do not know him,' he said. •Shortly afterwards someone else saw him and said, 'You are one of them too.' But Peter replied, 'I
59 am not, my friend.'ᶜ •About an hour later another man insisted, saying, 'This
60 fellow was certainly with him. Why, he is a Galilean.' •Peter said, 'My friend, I do not know what you are talking about.' At that instant, while he was still speaking,
61 the cock crowed, •and the Lord turned and looked straight at Peter, and Peter remembered the Lord's words when he had said to him, 'Before the cock crows
62 today, you will have disowned me three times.' •And he went outside and wept bitterly.

Jesus mocked by the guards⸍

63, 64 Meanwhile the men who guarded Jesus were mocking and beating him. •They
65 blindfolded him and questioned him, saying, 'Prophesy! Who hit you then?' •And they heaped many other insults on him.

Jesus before the Sanhedrin ⸍

66 When day broke there was a meeting of the elders of the people,⸍ the chief priests
67 and scribes. He was brought before their council, •and they said to him, 'If you
68 are the Christ, tell us.' He replied, 'If I tell you, you will not believe, •and if I
69 question you, you will not answer. •But from now on, the *Son of man* will be ⸍
70 *seated at the right hand* of the Power *of God.'* •They all said, 'So you are the Son
71 of God then?'⸍ He answered, 'It is you who say I am.' •Then they said, 'Why do we need any evidence? We have heard it for ourselves from his own lips.' ⸍

1 **23** The whole assembly then rose, and they brought him before Pilate.

Jesus before Pilate ᵃ

2 They began their accusation by saying, 'We found this man inciting our people to revolt, opposing payment of the tribute to Caesar, and claiming to be Christ, a
3 king.' •Pilate put to him this question, 'Are you the king of the Jews?' He replied,
4 'It is you who say it.' •Pilate then said to the chief priests and the crowd, 'I find no
5 case against this man.' •But they persisted, 'He is inflaming the people with his teaching all over Judaea and all the way from Galilee, where he started, down to
6, 7 here.' •When Pilate heard this, he asked if the man were a Galilean; •and finding that he came under Herod's jurisdiction, he passed him over to Herod, who was also in Jerusalem at that time.

Jesus before Herod ᵇ

8 Herod was delighted to see Jesus; he had heard about him and had been wanting for a long time to set eyes on him; moreover, he was hoping to see some miracle
9 worked by him. •So he questioned him at some length, but without getting any
10 reply. •Meanwhile the chief priests and the scribes were there, vigorously pressing

11 their accusations. ·Then Herod, together with his guards, treated him with contempt and made fun of him; he put a rich cloak ᶜ on him and sent him back to Pilate.
12 And though Herod and Pilate had been enemies before, they were reconciled that same day.

Jesus before Pilate again

13, 14 Pilate then summoned the chief priests and the leading men and the people. ·He said to them, 'You brought this man before me as a popular agitator. Now I have gone into the matter myself in your presence and found no grounds in the man for
15 any of the charges you bring against him. ·Nor has Herod either, since he has sent
16 him back to us. As you can see, the man has done nothing that deserves death, ·so
18 I shall have him flogged and then let him go.' ᵈ[17] ·But as one man they howled,
19 'Away with him! Give us Barabbas!' ·(This man had been thrown into prison because of a riot in the city and murder.)
20, 21 In his desire to set Jesus free, Pilate addressed them again, ·but they shouted
22 back, 'Crucify him! Crucify him!' ·And for the third time ᵉ he spoke to them, 'But what harm has this man done? I have found no case against him that deserves
23 death, so I shall have him flogged and then let him go.' ᶠ ·But they kept on shouting at the top of their voices, demanding that he should be crucified. And their shouts kept growing louder.
24, 25 Pilate then gave his verdict: their demand was to be granted. ·He released the man they asked for, who had been imprisoned because of rioting and murder, and handed Jesus over to them to deal with as they pleased.

The way to Calvary

26 As they were leading him away they seized on a man, Simon from Cyrene, who was coming in from the country, and made him shoulder the cross and carry it
27 behind Jesus. ·Large numbers of people followed him, and women too, ᵍ who
28 mourned and lamented for him. ·But Jesus turned to them and said, 'Daughters of Jerusalem, do not weep for me; weep rather for yourselves and for your
29 children. ·For look, the days are surely coming when people will say, "Blessed are those who are barren, the wombs that have never borne children, the breasts that
30 have never suckled!" ·Then they will begin to *say to the mountains, "Fall on us!"*;
31 *to the hills, "Cover us!"* ·For if this is what is done to green wood, what will be
32 done when the wood is dry?' ʰ ·Now they were also leading out two others, criminals, to be executed with him.

The crucifixion ⁱ

33 When they reached the place called The Skull, there they crucified him and the
34 two criminals, one on his right, the other on his left. ·ʲJesus said, 'Father, forgive them; they do not know what they are doing.' ᵏ Then they cast lots to share out his clothing.

The crucified Christ is mocked

35 The people stayed there watching. As for the leaders, they jeered at him with the words, 'He saved others, let him save himself if he is the Christ of God, the Chosen
36, 37 One.' ·The soldiers mocked him too, coming up to him, offering him vinegar, ·and
38 saying, 'If you are the king of the Jews, save yourself.' ·Above him there was an inscription: 'This is the King of the Jews'.

The good thief

39 One of the criminals hanging there abused him: 'Are you not the Christ?' Save
40 yourself and us as well.' ·But the other spoke up and rebuked him. 'Have you no
41 fear of God at all?' he said. 'You got the same sentence as he did, ·but in our case
we deserved it: we are paying for what we did. But this man has done nothing
42 wrong.' ·Then he said, 'Jesus, remember me when you come into your kingdom.' *
43 He answered him, 'In truth I tell you, today you will be with me in paradise.'

The death of Jesus

44 It was now about the sixth hour and the sun's light failed, so that darkness came
45 over the whole land until the ninth hour. * ·The veil of the Sanctuary was torn
46 right down the middle. ·Jesus cried out in a loud voice saying, 'Father, *into your
hands I commit my spirit.*' With these words he breathed his last.

After the death

47 When the centurion saw what had taken place, he gave praise to God and said,
48 'Truly, this was an upright man.' ·And when all the crowds who had gathered for
the spectacle saw what had happened, they went home beating their breasts.
49   All his friends stood at a distance; so also did the women who had accompanied
him from Galilee and saw all this happen.

The burial

50 And now a member of the Council arrived, a good and upright man named Joseph.
51 He had not consented to what the others had planned and carried out. He came
from Arimathaea, a Jewish town, and he lived in the hope of seeing the kingdom
52, 53 of God. ·This man went to Pilate and asked for the body of Jesus. ·He then took it
down, wrapped it in a shroud and put him in a tomb which was hewn in stone and
54 which had never held a body. ·It was Preparation day and the Sabbath was
beginning to grow light. °
55   Meanwhile the women who had come from Galilee with Jesus were following
behind. They took note of the tomb and how the body had been laid.
56   Then they returned and prepared spices and ointments. And on the Sabbath
day they rested, as the Law required.

VII: AFTER THE RESURRECTION

The empty tomb. The angel's message

1 **24** On the first day of the week, at the first sign of dawn, they went to the
2   tomb with the spices they had prepared. ·They found that the stone had
3 been rolled away from the tomb, ·but on entering they could not find the body of
4 the Lord Jesus. ·As they stood there puzzled about this, two men in brilliant
5 clothes suddenly appeared at their side. ·Terrified, the women bowed their heads
to the ground. But the two said to them, 'Why look among the dead for someone
6 who is alive? ·He is not here; he has risen. Remember what he told you when he
7 was still in Galilee: * ·that the Son of man was destined to be handed over into the
8 power of sinful men and be crucified, and rise again on the third day.' ·And they
remembered his words.

The apostles refuse to believe the women

9 And they returned from the tomb and told all this to the Eleven and to all the
10 others. ·The women were Mary of Magdala, Joanna, and Mary the mother of
11 James. And the other women with them also told the apostles, ·but this story of
theirs seemed pure nonsense, and they did not believe them.

Peter at the tomb

12 ᵇPeter, however, went off to the tomb, running. He bent down and looked in and
saw the linen cloths but nothing else; he then went back home, amazed at what
had happened.

The road to Emmaus

13 Now that very same day, two of them were on their way to a village called Emmaus,
14 seven milesᶜ from Jerusalem, ·and they were talking together about all that had
15 happened. ·And it happened that as they were talking together and discussing it,
16 Jesus himself came up and walked by their side; ·but their eyes were prevented
17 from recognising him. ᵈ ·He said to them, 'What are all these things that you are
discussing as you walk along?' They stopped, their faces downcast. ᵉ
18 Then one of them, called Cleopas, answered him, 'You must be the only person
staying in Jerusalem who does not know the things that have been happening there
19 these last few days.' ·He asked, 'What things?' They answered, 'All about Jesus
of Nazareth,ᶠ who showed himself a prophet powerful in action and speech before
20 God and the whole people; ·and how our chief priests and our leaders handed him
21 over to be sentenced to death, and had him crucified. ·Our own hope had been
that he would be the one to set Israel free. And this is not all: two whole days have
22 now gone by since it all happened; ·and some women from our group have
23 astounded us: they went to the tomb in the early morning, ·and when they could
not find the body, they came back to tell us they had seen a vision of angels who
24 declared he was alive. ·Some of our friendsᵍ went to the tomb and found everything
exactly as the women had reported, but of him they saw nothing.'
25 Then he said to them, 'You foolish men! So slow to believe all that the prophets
26 have said! ·Was it not necessary that the Christ should suffer before entering into
27 his glory?' ·Then, starting with Moses and going through all the prophets, he
explained to them the passages throughout the scriptures that were about himself.
28 When they drew near to the village to which they were going, he made as if to
29 go on; ·but they pressed him to stay with them saying, 'It is nearly evening, and
30 the day is almost over.' So he went in to stay with them. ·Now while he was with
them at table, he took the bread and said the blessing; then he broke it and handed
31 it to them. ·And their eyes were opened and they recognised him; but he had
32 vanished from their sight. ·Then they said to each other, 'Did not our hearts burn
within us as he talked to us on the road and explained the scriptures to us?'
33 They set out that instant and returned to Jerusalem. There they found the
34 Eleven assembled together with their companions, ·who said to them, 'The Lord
35 has indeed risen and has appeared to Simon.' ·Then they told their story of what
had happened on the road and how they had recognised him at the breaking of
bread. ʰ

Jesus appears to the apostles

36 They were still talking about all this when he himself stood among them and said
37 to them, 'Peace be with you!' •In a state of alarm and fright, they thought they
38 were seeing a ghost. •But he said, 'Why are you so agitated, and why are these
39 doubts stirring in your hearts? •See by my hands and my feet that it is I myself.
Touch me and see for yourselves; a ghost has no flesh and bones as you can see I
40. 41 have.' • 'And as he said this he showed them his hands and his feet.ʲ •Their joy was
so great that they still could not believe it, as they were dumbfounded; so he said
42 to them, 'Have you anything here to eat?' •And they offered him a piece of grilled
43 fish, which he took and ate before their eyes.

Last instructions to the apostles

44 Thenᵏ he told them, 'This is what I meant when I said, while I was still with you,
that everything written about me in the Law of Moses, in the Prophets and in the
45 Psalms, was destined to be fulfilled.' •He then opened their minds to understand
46 the scriptures, •and he said to them, 'So it is written that the Christ would suffer
47 and on the third day rise from the dead, •and that, in his name, repentance for the
forgiveness of sins would be preached to all nations, beginning from Jerusalem.
48 You are witnesses to this.
49 'And now I am sending upon you what the Father has promised.ˡ Stay in the
city, then, until you are clothed with the power from on high.'

The ascension

50 Then he took them out as far as the outskirts of Bethany, and raising his hands he
51 blessed them. •Now as he blessed them, he withdrew from them and was carried
52 up to heaven.ᵐ •They worshipped him andⁿ then went back to Jerusalem full of
53 joy; •and they were continually in the Temple praising God.ᵒ

NOTES TO LUKE

1 a. This prologue uses a classical vocabulary and construction; it is similar to the formal prefaces of contemporary Greek historians.

b. Hyperbole: understand 'several'. For the narratives known and used by Lk, *see* p. 12–13.

c. Or possibly 'that has come to your knowledge', in which case Theophilus would be not a Christian to be confirmed in the faith but some distinguished official asking for information.

d. From here till ch. 3 Lk employs the semitising Greek of the Septuagint. Biblical allusions and reminiscences are frequent, and the whole has an archaic colouring. Lk recreates the atmosphere of the circles of the 'Poor', *see* Zp 2:3d. It was in this atmosphere that his characters lived, from here that he derived his information. Lk presents the stories in a series of carefully structured little dramatic episodes, each with its own entries on stage and exits. The stories of John the Baptist and those of Jesus are presented in parallel in order to compare and contrast the two figures, their mission and their importance.

e. Each section was responsible for a week's service, *see* 1 Ch 24:19; 2 Ch 23:8.

f. It was the priest's duty to keep the brazier burning that stood on the altar of incense in front of the Holy of Holies; he would also supply it with fresh incense, once before the morning sacrifice, again after the evening sacrifice; *see* Ex 30:6–8.

g. Lk is fond of mentioning religious fear and awe: 1:29–30,65; 2:9–10; 4:36; 5:8–10,26; 7:16; 8:25,33–37,56; 9:34,43; 24:37; Ac 2:43; 3:10; 5:5,11; 10:4; 19:17.

h. The name means 'Yahweh-is-gracious'.

i. Joy is the keynote of ch. 1–2: 1:28,46,58; 2:10. Cf. *also* 10:17,20seq.; 13:17; 15:7,32; 19:6,37; 24:41,52; Ac 2:46jj.

j. Several OT texts lie behind this remark, especially the law of the nazirite, *see* Nb 6:1a.

k. This expression here, and elsewhere in Lk, does not mean the fullness of sanctifying grace, but the prophetic gift of inspiration, cf. 1:41,67; Ac 2:4; 4:8,31; 7:55; 9:17; 13:9.

l. Ml 3:23 gave rise to the expectation that Elijah would return before the messianic era and pave the way for it. John the Baptist will be 'the Elijah who is to come', *see* 9:30; Mt 17:10–13.

m. Zechariah asks for a 'sign', cf. Gn 15:8; Jg 6:17; Is 7:11; 38:7. But he remains sceptical.

n. First occurrence of a verb beloved of Lk, ten times in the gospel, fifteen in Ac, most often of the good news or 'gospel' of the Kingdom. *see* Ga 1:6d; Mk 1:1a; Ac 5:42q.

o. To give the customary blessing.

p. Barrenness was considered a humiliation. Gn 30:23; 1 S 1:5–8, and even a punishment, 2 S 6:23; Ho 9:11.

q. The presentation of this incident is inspired by several OT passages, notably the angelic promise of a child to Samson's mother, Jg 13:2–7. The dignity of the child is described by means of allusions to OT promises, especially those made to the line of David, 2 S 7:1seq.

r. i.e. of John's conception.

s. 'Rejoice' rather than simply 'hail'. It is an invitation to the joy of the Messiah, an echo of the greetings to the Daughter of Zion, and similarly motivated by the coming of God to his people; cf. Is 12:6; Jl 2:21–27; Zp 3:14–15; Zc 2:14; 9:9. • 'who enjoy God's favour', lit. 'you who have been and remain filled with the divine favour'. Add. 'Of all women you are most blessed' under the influence of 1:42.

t. The angel's words recall several OT passages referring to the Messiah.

u. The virgin Mary is only 'betrothed' (v. 27) and does not have conjugal relations (a semitic sense of 'know'). The seeming opposition between this and the promise of vv. 31–33 calls forth the explanation of v. 35. Nothing in the text suggests a vow of virginity.

v. This expression is used of the bright cloud which is a sign of God's presence, see Ex 13:22h; 19:16g; 24:16f, or of the wings which symbolise God's protective, Ps 17:8; 57:1; 140:7, and creative presence, Gn 1:2, cf. 9:34seq. In the conception of Jesus the power of the Holy Spirit is the only cause.

w. Commonly identified with Ain Karim, about 4 m (about 6.5 km) west of the Old City of Jerusalem.

x. Divine title of the risen Jesus, Ac 2:36w; Ph 2:11p, which Lk gives him already in his earthly life more often than Mt and Mk: 7:13; 10:1,39,41; 11:39.

y. 'the Lord', i.e. God.' • Or 'And blessed are you who have believed, because what has been promised to you by the Lord will be fulfilled.'

z. Not 'Elizabeth', a var. with only slight MS support. • Mary's canticle is reminiscent of Hannah's, 1 S 2:1–10, and of many other OT passages, e.g. Ps 113:7–9. Apart from the main textual similarities noted in the margin there are two characteristic OT ideas: 1 God comes to the help not of the rich and powerful but of the poor and the simple, Zp 2:3d, compare Mt 5:3c. 2 Ever since Abraham received the promises, Gn 15:1a; 17:1a, Israel has been God's favoured one, see Dt 7:6b. Lk must have found this canticle in the circles of the 'Poor' where it was perhaps attributed to the Daughter of Zion. He found it suitable to bring into his prose narrative and put on the lips of Mary.

aa. It would be likely that Mary stayed with Elizabeth until John's birth and circumcision, but Lk's habit is to round off one episode before passing to the next, cf. 1:64 and 67; 3:19–20; 8:37–38.

bb. The name was normally given when the child was circumcised, see 2:21.

cc. Perhaps he is deaf as well as dumb; the same Greek word can be used for either condition.

dd. i.e. protected him: a biblical expression, Jr 26:24; Ac 11:21.

ee. Like the *Magnificat*, this canticle is a poem which Lk has drawn from elsewhere to put on Zechariah's lips, adding vv. 76–77 to adapt it to the context. He has added it after the prose account, v. 64, rather than in the course of it.

ff. In the full sense of the term, because Zechariah not only utters a hymn of thanksgiving (vv. 68–75) but also foresees the future (vv. 76–79).

gg. As often in the OT, Ex 3:16h, God's visitation is understood in the NT uniquely in a favourable sense, 1:78; 7:16; 19:44; 1 P 2:12.

hh. lit. 'a horn of', see Ps 75:4c.

ii. i.e. God, as in 1:16–17, not the Messiah.

jj. Lk depicts the function of the Precursor with the help of texts applied to him by tradition, see 3:4seq.; 7:27seq. He makes his message accord with that of the apostles in Acts, see Ac 2:38; 5:31; 10:43; 13:38; 26:18.

kk. 'faithful love', lit. 'bowels of mercy'. • 'will bring'; var. 'has brought'.

ll. Or 'star that heralds the day', cf. Nb 24:17; Is 60:1; Ml 3:20, and 'Shoot which springs from the stock of David', cf. Jr 23:5; 33:15; Zc 3:8; 6:12.

mm. A kind of refrain: 2:40,52; cf. 1:66.

2 a. Roman emperor from 30 BC to AD 14.

b. The first of a series. The translation sometimes given, 'This census preceded that which was held when Quirinius was governor of Syria' is difficult to justify grammatically. The historical circumstances are little known. Most scholars put the census of Quirinius in AD 6, but the only authority for this is Josephus who is doubtfully reliable in this matter, see Ac 5:37n. The most probable explanation is that the census, which was made with a view to taxation, began in Palestine even before Herod's death, as early as 8–6 BC as part of a general census of the empire, and that Quirinius concluded it in AD 6, as Josephus says. This census, which in fact took place over a considerable period, was then known by the name of this important personality. Jesus was born certainly before Herod's death (4 BC), possibly in 8–6 BC. The 'Christian era', established by Dionysius Exiguus (sixth century), is the result of a false calculation, see 3:1a.

c. In biblical Greek, the term does not necessarily imply younger brothers but emphasises the dignity and rights of the child.

d. Rather than 'inn' (*pandocheion*, 10:34) the Greek word *kataluma* can mean a room, 22:11par.; 1 S 1:18; 9:22, where Joseph's family lived. If Joseph's home was at Bethlehem this would explain why he returned there with his pregnant young wife for the census. The manger where the animals was presumably fixed on a wall of the poor habitation, which was so crowded that there was no better place for the child. A pious legend has embellished this manger with two animals, see Is 1:3; Hab 3:2c.

e. So he is the Messiah awaited; but he will be 'Lord', a title which the OT meticulously reserved for God. A new era is about to begin, see 1:43x.

f. The traditional translation 'peace to men of good will', based on the Vulgate, among other versions, does not render the usual sense of the Greek term. Another version, also less probable is 'peace on earth and God's favour towards men'.

g. A favourite theme of Lk: 1:64; 2:28,38; 5:25–26; 7:16; 13:13; 17:15,18; 18:43; 19:37; 23:47; 24:53. Cf. Ac 2:47ll.

h. Only the mother needed to be purified; the child, however, had to be 'redeemed'. Lk is careful to note that the parents of Jesus, like the Baptist's, observed all that the Law required. The presentation of the child in the sanctuary was not prescribed but was possible, Nb 18:15, and must have seemed fitting to religious people, cf. 1 S 1:24–28. Lk centres his story on the first cultic act of Jesus, in the holy city to which he attaches great importance as the location of the Easter event and the starting-point of the Christian mission. See 2:38o; Ac 1:4e.

i. Offering of the poor.

j. 'the Christ of the Lord' is the one whom the Lord anoints, see Ex 30:22d, i.e. consecrates for a saving mission; the king of Israel, God's chosen prince, is thus consecrated and thus, pre-eminently, the Messiah who is to establish the kingdom of God.

k. Unlike *Magnificat* and *Benedictus* this canticle seems to have been written by Lk himself, using especially texts from Isaiah. After a first triplet about Simeon and his approaching death, a second triplet characterises the universal salvation brought by Jesus the Messiah: light brought to the gentile world which forms one element in the chosen people, and which will bring glory to the chosen people.

l. Jesus' mission of light to the gentile world will bring hostility and persecution from his own people, see Mt 2:1a.

m. As the true Daughter of Zion, Mary will herself

hear the sorrowful destiny of her race. With her Son she will be at the centre of this contradiction, where secret thoughts will be laid bare, for or against Jesus. The symbol of the sword may be inspired by Ezk 14:17, or alternatively Zc 12:10.

n. A woman dedicated to God and the qualified interpreter of his intentions. Cf. Ex 15:20; Jg 4:4; 2 K 22:14.

o. The messianic deliverance of the chosen people. 1:68; 24:21, primarily affected their capital city: cf. Is 40:2; 52:9 (and see 2 S 5:9f). For Lk, Jerusalem is God's chosen centre from which will spread his salvation: 9:31,51,53; 13:22,33; 17:11; 18:31; 19:11; 24:47-49,52; Ac 1:8l.

p. For Lk, the 'finding' of Jesus 'after three days' 'in the house of his Father' may be intended as prefiguring the events of Easter.

q. Alternative translation 'be busy with my Father's affairs'. In either case Jesus affirms, in Joseph's presence, v. 48, that God is his Father, cf. 10:22; 22:29; Jn 20:17, and claims a relationship to him which surpasses human family ties, see Jn 2:4. This is the first manifestation of his consciousness of being 'the Son', see Mt 4:3d.

3 a. Here, as in 1:5 and 2:1-3, Lk dates his narrative by secular events. Tiberius succeeded Augustus, 2:1, on 19 August AD 14. The 15th year, therefore, is from AD 19 August 28 to AD 18 August 29. Alternatively, if the Syrian method of calculating the year of a reign is being followed, the 15th year is from AD Sept.-Oct. 27 to AD Sept.-Oct. 28. At that time, Jesus was at least 33 years old, possibly 35 or 36. The indication of v. 23 is approximate, and perhaps it means only that Jesus was old enough to exercise a public ministry. The mistake in calculating the 'Christian era' results from taking the 'thirty years' of 3:23 as an exact figure: the 15th year of Tiberius was 782 'after the foundation of Rome'; Dionysius Exiguus subtracted 29 full years from this, thus arriving at 753 for the beginning of our era. Actually, it should have been 750 or even 746.

b. Procurator of Judaea (including Idumaea and Samaria) AD 26-36.

c. The Herod referred to is Herod Antipas, son of Herod the Great and Malthace; he was tetrarch of Galilee and Peraea from 4 BC to AD 39.

d. Son of Herod the Great and Cleopatra, tetrarch from 4 BC to AD 34.

e. Known from two inscriptions. Abilene was in Anti-Lebanon.

f. The high priest in office was Joseph, called Caiaphas; he held this position from AD 18-36, and played a leading part in the plot against Jesus, see Mt 26:3; Jn 11:49; 18:14. His father-in-law, Annas, who had been high priest from AD 6 (?) to 15, is associated with him and even named first, see Jn 18:13,24 and Ac 4:6, as if his influence was such that he was high priest in all but name.

g. Mk, followed by Mt, ends the quotation from Is 40 at the end of the third line. Lk continues it to include the specific promise of universal salvation.

h. Vv. 10-14, which are in Lk alone, stress the positive human element in John's message. No profession is excluded from salvation, but justice and charity are essential.

i. Lk finishes with John's ministry before passing to that of Jesus, see 1:56aa. He makes no more than a brief allusion to John's death, 9:7-9.

j. Jesus at prayer is a favourite theme of Lk, see 5:16; 6:12; 9:18,28-29; 11:1; 22:41.

k. The var. 'You are my Son, the beloved; my favour rests on you' is probably a harmonisation with the text of Mk and Mt. The voice from heaven in Lk probably did not originally contain Mt's and Mk's reference to Is 42, but referred to Ps 2:7. Rather than seeing Jesus as the 'servant', it presents him as the King-Messiah of the Ps, enthroned at the Baptism to establish the rule of God in the world.

l. By tracing the ancestry of Jesus further back than Abraham, to Adam, Lk gives his genealogy a more univer-salist character than that of Mt. Descended from Adam and similarly without a human father, 1:35, Jesus inaugurates a new era for the human race. Lk perhaps follows Paul in thinking of the New Adam. Rm 5:12g. For the relation between the two very different genealogies, see Mt 1:1a.

4 a. Lk combines Mk's data (40 days of being put to the test) with Matthew's (three temptations at the end of 40 days' fast). He changes Mt's order so as to end with Jerusalem: see 2:38o. On the nature of this being put to the test, see Mt 4:1a.

b. Lk's interest in the Holy Spirit is evident not only from his first two chapters, 1:15,35,41,67,80; 2:25,26,27, but also from the remainder of the Gospel in which, on several occasions, he adds a mention of the Spirit to the other synoptic passages, 4:1,14,18; 10:21; 11:13. In Ac also Lk very frequently speaks of the Spirit, Ac 1:8j.

c. By bringing into the world sin and its consequence, death, Ws 2:24t; Rm 5:12h, Satan has made the human race his prisoner, Mt 8:29k; Ga 4:3b; Col 2:8d. He has extended over the world, of which he has become the 'Prince', Jn 12:31i, a dominion which Jesus came to overturn by his 'redemption', Mt 20:28g; Rm 3:24j; 6:15g; Col 1:13-14; 2:15m. See also Jn 3:35t; Ep 2:1-6; 6:12d; 1 Jn 2:14; Rv 13:1-8; 19:19-21.

d. Rather than 'finished all the temptations'.

e. One of Lk's recurrent motifs: 4:37; 5:15; 7:17; see, for similar examples, 1:80mm; Ac 2:41cc; 6:7.

f. Another favourite theme of Lk: the people admiring and praising Jesus: 4:22; 8:25; 9:43; 11:27; 13:17; 19:48, related to the previous refrain 4:14e, the theme of praise to God 2:20g, and of religious awe, 1:12g.

g. The crowd's sudden change from admiration, v. 22a, to animosity, v. 22b, 28seq., is astonishing. The anomaly is probably the product of its literary evolution. A first story recounted a visit by Jesus at the beginning of Jesus' ministry, cf. Mk 1:21seq., at Nazareth, cf. Mt 4:13, using the form Nazara, as here in Lk 4:16; this was crowned with success. This story was later taken up again, added to and placed later in Jesus' life, Mt 13:53-58; Mk 6:1-6, to express the misunderstanding and rejection which followed the early acceptance by the people. From this complex text Lk has painted an admirable picture, restrained at the beginning of the ministry, of an inaugural scene in which, with symbolic foreshortening, he depicts Jesus' mission of grace and the rejection by his people.

h. The director of a synagogue could authorise any adult Jew to read and expound the scripture in public.

i. add. 'to heal the broken-hearted', see LXX.

j. i.e. the miracles of which Lk does not speak until after the visit to Nazareth, 4:33. See note g above.

k. Mk reads 'Galilee'. Lk uses 'Judaea' in the wide sense: the land of Israel. Also in 7:17; 23:5; Ac 10:37; 28:21.

5 a. In this narrative, Lk has combined: 1 A topographical note and an incident about Jesus' preaching, vv. 1-3; this section resembles Mk 1:16,19 and 4:1-2. 2 The episode of the miraculous catch, vv. 4-10a, which is like that of Jn 21:1-6. 3. The call of Simon, vv. 10b-11, which is related to Mk 1:17,20. Lk's purpose in placing a period of teaching and miracles before the call of the first disciples was to make their unhesitating response less surprising.

b. In Lk, Simon does not receive the name Peter until 6:14. This is an anticipation. Johannine in character (as the miraculous catch of fish?), for, apart from this instance in Lk and Mt 16:16, the expression 'Simon Peter' occurs only in Jn—17 times.

c. The 'companions' of v. 7. Andrew is not mentioned because he is in Simon's boat (note the plural pronouns in vv. 5,6,7) which is in the centre of Luke's picture.

d. i.e. God, cf. Ac 2:22; 10:38.

e. The Palestinian terrace of Mk 2:4 has become in Lk the roof of a Greco-Roman house.

f. The 'new wine' Jesus provides is not appreciated by those who have drunk the old wine of the Law. This last remark, which comes only in Lk, perhaps reflects the experience of Lk, the disciple of Paul, who knew the difficulties of the mission to the Jews, see Ac 13:5e.

6 **a.** One MS here adds an interesting, but probably spurious, dictum: 'On the same day, seeing a man working on the Sabbath day, he said to him: "Friend, if you know what you are doing, you are blessed; but if you do not know, you are accursed as a breaker of the Law." '

b. Apostle means 'someone sent'. The term, already known in the Jewish and Greek worlds, came in Christianity to mean missionaries 'sent', see Ac 22:21i, as witnesses of Christ, his life, death and resurrection, Ac 1:8k, primarily the Twelve, Mk 3:14c (in Acts the term is used only of them), but also of a wider circle of disciples, see Rm 1:1b, who are mentioned in the first place in the list of charisms, cf. 1 Co 12:28; Ep 4:11. Possibly the *name* of apostle was given to the missionaries only by the earliest community, though Jesus certainly sent his disciples on missions, first to the villages of Galilee, 9:6 and, after his resurrection, to the whole world, 24:47; Ac 1:8; see also Jn 3:11f; 4:34k.

c. lit. 'Judas of James', which could mean 'brother of James' See Mt 10:2b.

d. Luke's form is shorter than Matthew's because he has not filled out the discourse, as Mt has done, with additional sayings on allied subjects; and he has not included much material, notably about the Law, which would not interest non-Jewish readers, see Mt 5:1a.

e. Mt has eight beatitudes, Lk four, and four maledictions. Mt intends them as a pattern of the new life which will bring heavenly rewards; in Lk, the blessings and the curses both speak of material conditions in this life to be reversed in the next, e.g. in 16:25. In Mt, Jesus uses the third person, in Lk he directly addresses his audience.

f. The text is difficult and the translation conj. var. 'driving no one to despair' or 'despairing of no one' or 'not at all despairing'.

g. Folds in the tunic or cloak were used as a pocket or as a bag for provisions.

h. Addressed, in Lk, to the disciples; in Mt 15:14, to the Pharisees. The same applies to vv. 43–45.

i. Or 'and then you will see how to take'.

j. A Johannine expression, see Jn 6:35k.

7 **a.** Local worthies, not to be confused with the Jerusalem 'elders' who were members of the Sanhedrin.

b. Evidently a gentile in sympathy with Judaism, like Cornelius, Ac 10:1–2a.

c. var. 'and my boy will be cured'.

d. Lk only. The episode leads up to the reply of Jesus to John's disciples, 7:22.

e. var. 'by her actions', see Mt 11:19h. The children of Wisdom, i.e., of the all-wise God, appreciate and welcome God's works.

f. Lk only. This episode is not the same as the anointing of the Lord's head at Bethany, Mt 26:6–13 and par., although that incident may well have influenced some of the details of the narrative here. There is no reason to identify the sinful woman with Mary of Magdala, 8:2, and still less with Mary, sister of Martha, 10:39; Jn 11:1,2,5; 12:2–3.

g. var. 'ever since she came in'.

h. In the first part of this verse, love seems to be the cause of forgiveness, in the second its effect. This paradox reflects the composite nature of the pericope. In vv. 37–38, 44–46 the woman's actions express a great love which earns her forgiveness, whence the conclusion 47ª. But in vv. 40–43 a parable has been inserted whose lesson is the opposite: greater forgiveness brings greater love, whence the conclusion 47ᵇ.

8 **a.** Lk has taken this passage out of its context in Mk 3:31–35 to serve as a conclusion to this small section on

the parables; hence he modifies v. 21 (cf. Mk 3:35) to match v. 15.

b. var. 'Gergesenes', 'Gadarenes'.

c. In place of Mark's 'send them out of the district', Mk 5:10. The demons beseech Jesus not to send them back to the depths of the earth, their usual dwelling-place and ultimate home, Rv 9:1,2,11; 11:7; 17:8; 20:1,3.

d. As a disciple sits, see 10:39; Ac 22:3. Lk alone adds this detail.

e. var. 'a woman who, having spent all she had on doctors, could be cured by no one', cf. Mk 5:26.

f. See Mk 5:37d. Here, however, as in 9:28; Ac 1:13, John is named immediately after Peter. This coupling of John with Peter is common to Lk, 22:8; Ac 3:1,3,11; 4:13,19; 8:14, and the fourth gospel, Jn 13:23–26; 18:15–16; 20:3–9; 21:7,20–23.

9 **a.** add. 'apostles'

b. Lk does not record the Baptist's death; instead, he prepares the reader ('he was anxious to see him') for the subsequent meeting of Herod with Jesus, 23:8–12.

c. Lk, as Jn, gives only one multiplication of loaves, while Mt and Mk have two. Possibly Lk has omitted or did not know the whole section Mk 6:45–8:26 which contains the second multiplication. But more probably he is avoiding a reduplication of Mk and Mt, where the two stories of the multiplication of loaves do indeed seem to be parallel versions of the same event, one issuing from a Palestinian milieu (western shore of the lake, see Mt 14:13d; twelve baskets, corresponding to the twelve tribes of Israel), the other issuing from a gentile milieu (eastern shore, see Mk 7:31; seven baskets, corresponding to the seven gentile nations of Canaan before the conquest, Dt 7:1; Ac 13:19); see also Mt 14:13c.

d. Even without the Matthaean addition, 'son of God', see Mt 16:16d, this confession of Peter, speaking in the name of the apostles, is of crucial significance as a turning-point in the earthly career of Jesus. While the crowd cannot grasp his significance and becomes progressively alienated, his disciples recognise for the first time explicitly that he is Messiah, see 2:26j. Henceforth Jesus is going to concentrate on forming this little nucleus of believers and on purifying their faith.

e. This prophecy is to be followed by several others, 9:44; 12:50; 17:25; 18:31–33. Cf. 24:7,25–27. • Lk omits Peter's protest and his rebuke by Jesus, Mk 8:32seq.

f. Certain of the details in this account of the Transfiguration are peculiar to Lk and not found in Mk or Mt. Whereas in Mk it is the revelation of the hidden Messiah as the consummation of the Law and the Prophets, and for Mt it is the manifestation of the new and greater Moses, for Lk the Transfiguration is also a personal experience of Jesus, in the course of earnest prayer, in which he clearly sees the 'passing' (exodus) which he is to accomplish in Jerusalem. These differences have led some commentators to suggest that Lk had a separate and additional tradition to draw on.

g. Since Moses and Elijah are named only to identify the 'two men' mentioned in the first place, it may be that in Lk's source these were two angels, cf. 24:4; Ac 1:10, who were sustaining and strengthening Jesus, cf. Lk 22:43. On the significance of Moses and Elijah in Mt's tradition, see Mt 17:1a.

h. Or 'kept awake'. This irresistible sleep of the disciples occurring only in Lk, recalls that of Gethsemane, 22:45, which is more natural and from which it could be derived.

i. var. 'the Beloved', see Mt and Mk. • The titles 'Chosen One', cf. 23:35; Is 42:1, and 'Son of man' alternate in the *Parables of Enoch*.

j. The answer to this question is given in v. 48ᵇ. The saying which makes up 48ª, is apparently taken from another context, cf. Mt 10:40.

k. var. 'we stopped him'.

l. From 9:51–18:14, Lk deserts Mk. Assembling

material he has found in the Collection (*see* Intro. to Synoptic Gospels, pp. 5–6, 12, which also served Mt. together with information from his own special source. Lk arranges all within the literary framework of a journey to Jerusalem (9:53,57; 10:1; 13:22,33; 17:11; *see* 2:38*o*).

m. lit. 'for his taking up'. This 'assumption' of Jesus, cf. 2 K 2:9–11; Mk 16:19; Ac 1:2,10–11; 1 Tm 3:16, refers to the last days of his suffering life (Passion, death) and the beginning of his glory (resurrection, ascension). Jn, thinking more theologically, uses the word 'glorify' in connection with the whole of this period, Jn 7:39; 12:16,23; 13:31seq.; for him the crucifixion is a 'lifting up', Jn 12:32j.

n. The hatred of the Samaritans for the Jews, Jn 4:9e, would show itself particularly towards those on pilgrimage to Jerusalem; hence it was usual to bypass this territory, cf. Mt 10:5. Only Lk and Jn (4:1–42) mention Jesus' presence in this hostile territory, *see* 17:11,16. It was not long before the primitive Church imitated its Master, Ac 8:5–25.

o. add. 'as Elijah did'. • Allusion to 2 K 1:10–12. James and John are seen here as 'Sons of Thunder' indeed, Mk 3:17.

p. add. 'You do not know what spirit you are made of. The Son of man came not to destroy souls but to save them.'

q. add. 'Lord', cf. Mt 8:21.

r. A play on the two meanings of 'death': physical and spiritual.

10 a. The collection of sayings used by Mt and Lk contained a mission discourse parallel to that of Mk 6:8–11. While Mt has combined both versions in one discourse, 10:7–16, Lk has kept them separate in two discourses addressed respectively to the Twelve, the number of Israel, and to the seventy (or seventy-two) disciples, the traditional number of gentile nations. Compare the case of the two multiplications of loaves, *see* Mt 14:13c.

b. var. 'seventy'.

c. Not, as in 9:52, to arrange for lodgings but to prepare the people for his teaching.

d. lit. 'son of peace', a Hebraism for those who deserve 'peace', i.e. all the spiritual and temporal blessings the word implies. See Jn 14:27s.

e. add. 'and turning to his disciples he said'.

f. Paul emphasises the fact that the 'mystery' was long kept hidden; Rm 16:25l. See also 1 P 1:11–12.

g. For having put the question.

h. The contrast is between the element in Israel most strictly bound to the law of love, and the heretic and stranger, Jn 8:48, see Lk 9:53o, from whom normally only hate could be expected.

i. These two sisters also appear in the story of the raising of Lazarus, Jn 11:1–44.

j. var. 'but only one thing is needed', 'but only a few things are needed', readings which make free with the text and deform the sense. • In his remark Jesus rises from the material plane ('few things are needed', i.e. for the meal) to the 'one thing necessary', which is to listen to the word of God.

11 a. Mt's text has seven petitions, Lk's five. See Mt 6:9d.

b. var. (borrowed, perhaps, from a baptismal liturgy) 'may your Holy Spirit come down on us and cleanse us'.

c. 'Debts' in Mt. Lk is more explicit and less juridical, but he retains 'debts' in the balancing clause that follows.

d. add. 'for bread would hand him a stone', a harmonisation with Mt 7:9.

e. Instead of the 'good things' of Mt 7:11. The Holy Spirit is the best of all 'good things'.

f. var. 'Beezebul' and 'Beelzebub'.

g. On this phrase, see Ex 8:15 and Ps 8:3. This passage and its parallel, Mt 12:28, have combined to provide the title 'finger of God's right hand' for the Holy Spirit.

h. i.e. a miracle as evidence and vindication of Christ's authority, see Jn 2:11f.

i. This interpretation of the 'sign of Jonah' is less prob-

able than that of Mt 12:40, see Mt 12:39l. It is moreover merely the result of the artificial association of originally distinct sayings, 11:29 and par.; Mt 12:38–39 and Lk 11:30–32 and par.; Mt 12:41–42.

j. The textual tradition of vv. 35–36 is confused, and the text is probably corrupt. But the general meaning is clear: Jesus addresses his message to all, and if the mind is 'healthy', i.e. unclouded by selfish prejudice, cf. Jn 3:19–21, it can be understood by all.

k. Lk depends here on the source he shares with Mt; in 20:45–47 he returns to the same theme, this time depending on Mk. Mt has combined both sources in one discourse (ch. 23); see Lk 10:1a; 17:22g.

l. Interpretation difficult. Others translate, 'Instead give alms from what is inside'.

m. Thus contracting ritual impurity, Nb 19:16.

n. Irony. By building the tombs of the prophets they hoped to make amends for their ancestors' sins—yet they have exactly the same mentality as these ancestors.

o. i.e the divine intention as interpreted by Jesus.

p. The attitude of Jesus' enemies continued to harden; Lk traces the process in more detail than Mk; Lk 6:11; 11:53–54; 19:48; 20:19–20; 22:2.

12 a. Or else 'began to say to his disciples: First of all, be on your guard . . .'

b. lit. 'the soul' in the biblical sense, as in v. 19.

c. var. 'work or spin', compare Mt 6:28.

d. That riches are a danger and should be given away in alms is characteristic teaching of Lk; see 3:11; 6:30; 7:5; 11:41; 12:33–34; 14:13–14; 16:9; 18:22; 19:8; Ac 9:36; 10:2,4,31.

e. lit. 'Keep your loins girded'; not by putting on an additional garment, but by tucking up the long skirt which would hinder running.

f. A steward with authority over other servants; Jesus, therefore, is speaking of the apostles (the 'us' of Peter's question).

g. This fire, obviously symbolic, can bear different meanings according to the context: the Holy Spirit, or the fire which will purify hearts and must be lit on the cross. v. 50 points to the latter interpretation, but vv. 51–53 suggest rather the state of spiritual conflict stirred up by Jesus' appearing.

h. The messianic era has arrived, and it is high time to realise this, for judgement is near, vv. 57–59.

i. lit. 'lepton', a Greek coin of very small value. • In Mt 5:25–26 the context gave this saying a community application: how the brethren of the community should be reconciled and settle their differences. In Lk it has an eschatological sense: the judgement of God is near, and putting oneself in order is an urgent necessity.

13 a. There is no other evidence for this incident or for that mentioned in v. 4. The meaning of both is clear: sin is not the immediate cause of this or that calamity (cf. Jn 9:3), but such disasters as these are providential invitations to repentance.

b. The episode of the withered fig tree in Mk 11 may be thought to show Jesus in a hard light; Lk prefers to substitute this parable of his patience.

c. Some have seen this as an allusion to the length of Christ's ministry as described in the fourth gospel.

d. Or 'unable to hold her head erect'.

e. He takes this act of healing for a 'work' forbidden by the Law.

f. The source used by Lk and Mt has here grouped some sayings which Mt has elsewhere separated in his Gospel, see 9:51l. The main idea of this grouping, maintained by Lk, seems to have been the rejection of Israel and the call of the gentiles to salvation. For Israel ties of blood with Jesus will not save them from the exclusion which their conduct deserves, vv. 25–27, cf. 3:7–9 and par.; Jn 8:33seq. So little will they be able to find the way of salvation, vv. 23–24, that the first shall be last, v. 30; cf.

g. Herod Antipas, *see* 3:1c. If, as is possible, he made this threat to rid himself of Jesus, the term 'fox' refers to that sly trick.

h. The expression signifies a short period of time.

i. A word full of meaning, including both his death and the achievement of his perfection: Jesus was made 'perfect' by his suffering and death, Heb 2:10; 5:9. Cf. Jn 19:30.

j. Meaning apparently 'My work will soon be over, but not yet. I have not finished my work of exorcising and healing; this I shall contrive to do on my way to Jerusalem where my destiny lies,' *see* 2:38*o*. Similarly, in Jn 7:30; 8:20 (cf. 8:59; 10:39; 11:54) the enemies of Jesus have no power over him so long as 'his hour has not yet come'.

14 a. 'his son'; var. 'his donkey'.

b. In the scrolls of Qumran, the lame and the blind and cripples are excluded from the eschatological warfare and the banquet which follows it.

c. After the 'streets and alleys of the town' of v. 21, the 'open roads and hedgerows' of v. 23 seem to be outside the town. There appear to be two different categories, on the one hand the poor and 'unclean' of Israel, on the other the gentiles. The 'compulsion' employed to bring in these underprivileged is meant to express only the triumph of grace over their lack of preparation, not violence done to their consciences. But the abuses of such 'compulsion to enter' in the course of history are only too well known.

d. Hebraism. Jesus asks, not for hate, but for total detachment now, cf. 9:57–62.

e. 'wife', peculiar to Lk, illustrating his leaning to asceticism, cf. 1 Co 7. So Lk also, 18:29.

f. Applicable to all disciples—Lk seems to make no distinction; *see* Mk 1:17f.

15 a. Lk has several long parables peculiar to his Gospel. Mk's parables provide teaching on the nature and coming of the kingdom. Many of Mt's proper parables teach a warning about the final judgement, and others are concerned with human relationships. These Lukan parables concern individuals and teach individual morality, often featuring an anti-hero, whose soliloquy is the turning-point of the story, *see* 12:17; 16:3, 24; 18:4,11; Mt 18:22*l*.

b. To the forgiving attitude of the father, symbol of God's forgiveness, is opposed in the elder son the attitude of the Pharisees and scribes who pride themselves on being 'upright' because they do not break any commandments of the Law, v. 29; cf. 18:9seq.

16 a. This chapter is a compilation of two parables and several *logia* of Jesus on the right and wrong use of money. vv. 16,17,18, each with a different theme, interrupt the literary scheme of the chapter.

b. It was the custom for a steward, or responsible servant, to take commission on all sales of his master's goods; this was his only means of making a salary. In the present case the original loan was presumably fifty measures of oil and eighty measures of wheat. In reducing the debtors' bills, he is not depriving his master of anything, but only sacrificing his own immediate interests by forgoing his legitimate commission. It is for this that he is praised as 'astute'; any 'dishonesty' (v. 8) was in his earlier actions for which he is under notice.

c. Money is here called 'tainted' not only because its owner is here presumed to have gained it dishonestly, but because great wealth is rarely acquired without some sharp practice.

d. lit. 'what is outside', i.e. wealth, which is external.

e. 'your very own'; var. 'our very own'. Jesus is speaking of the most intimate possessions anyone can have; these are spiritual.

f. A parable-story without any historical basis.

g. add. 'but no one offered him a thing', cf. 15:16.

h. Jewish figure of speech, the equivalent of the old biblical phrase 'gathered to his fathers', i.e. to the patri-archs, Jg 2:10; cf. Gn 15:15; 47:30; Dt 31:16. 'In the embrace of . . .' implies close intimacy, Jn 1:18, and evokes a picture of the messianic banquet where Lazarus reclines next to Abraham, *see* Mt 8:11c; Jn 13:23.

i. The 'gulf' is a symbol: the destiny of saved and lost is unalterable.

17 a. Lk, apparently, is thinking of a matter that concerns only two of the community; in Mt the offence is more public. Lk does not mention appealing to the community.

b. Contrast this human rule with the gospel paradox 12:37; 22:27; Jn 13:1–6.

c. This adjective hardly fits the context, since the accent is on the state of service itself, *see* the end of the v.; but it is the literal (and traditional) translation of the Greek.

d. Making for the Jordan valley and so down to Jericho, 18:35; from there he goes up to Jerusalem.

e. As something already present and active. The alternative translation, 'within your grasp', is attractive; a third possibility, 'within you', would not furnish as direct an answer to the Pharisees' question.

f. The discourse is proper to Lk, who makes a clear distinction between Jesus prophesying the destruction of Jerusalem, 21:6–24, and Christ's coming in glory at the end of time, 17:22–37. • Some of the passages in this discourse are found in the great eschatological discourse of Mt 24:5–41; there, as elsewhere (*see* Lk 10:1a; 11:39k), Mt has joined together two sources which Lk leaves separate; *see* Mt 24:1a. • 'The Day' of the Lord, adopted by Lk, is a more familiar OT expression than Mt's *parousia* (coming), a term borrowed from the hellenistic world, *see* 1 Co 1:8e.

g. Not to experience again one day of the earthly life of Jesus, nor to see the first day of his glorious coming, but to have the joy of even one of the days that are to follow that coming.

h. i.e. at the time of the coming.

i. add. v. 36 'There will be two men in the fields; one will be taken, the other left,' cf. Mt 24:40.

18 a. A lesson frequently found in Paul's letters: *see* Rm 1:10; 12:12; Ep 6:18; Col 1:3; 1 Th 5:17; 2 Th 1:11 and 2 Co 4:1,16; Ga 6:9; Ep 3:13; 2 Th 3:13.

b. In Si 35:18–19, which seems to have inspired this verse, God will not delay to give their due to the oppressed poor; here, however, he does delay. Perhaps this adaptation reflects concern to explain the delay of the *parousia*. Compare a similar attitude in 2 P 3:9; Rv 6:9–11.

c. Lk here rejoins Mark's narrative which he deserted in 9:50. Cf. 9:51*l*.

d. add. 'in return'.

e. Lk often stresses that the Passion was foretold by the prophets: 24:25,27,44; Ac 2:23*o*; 3:18,24s; 8:32–35; 13:27; 26:22seq. and par.

19 a. Fourfold restitution was imposed by Jewish law (Ex 21:37) for one case only; Roman law demanded it of all convicted thieves. Zacchaeus goes further: he acknowledges the obligation in the case of any injustice for which he may have been responsible.

b. Notwithstanding his despised profession. No social rank excludes 'salvation', cf. 3:12–14. All the Jewish privileges follow from 'sonship of Abraham', cf. 3:8; Rm 4:11seq.; Ga 3:7seq.

c. The parable of the talents, Mt 25:14–30, shows some wide differences, but the two are thought to be based on the same original, treated with great freedom by both the evangelists. Moreover, it seems that in Lk we must distinguish two parables which have been fused into one: that of the pounds, vv. 12–13,15–26, and that of the royal claimant, vv. 12,14,17,19,27.

d. Probably alluding to the journey of Archelaus to Rome in 4 BC to have the will of Herod the Great confirmed in his favour. A deputation of Jews followed him there to thwart the attempt, cf. v. 14.

e. The peace of the messianic age. *see* Is 11:6e;
Ho 2:20s.

f. This whole prophecy is made up of OT references
(especially noticeable in the Greek text for v. 43. *see*
Is 29:3; 37:33; Jr 52: 4–5; Ezk 4:1–3; 21:27 (22): for v. 44;
see Ps 137:9; Ho 10:14; 14:1; Na 3:10) and suggests the
destruction of Jerusalem in 587 BC as much as, and more
than, that of AD 70 of whose distinctive features it says
nothing. It cannot, therefore, be concluded from this text
that the destruction of AD 70 had already taken place, *see*
17:22f; 21:20c.

20 a. From 20:1 to 21:5 Lk follows Mk very closely. He
omits the symbolic episode of the withered fig tree,
Mk 11:12–14,20–25, for which he substitutes the parable of
the barren fig tree, Lk 13:6–9; he also omits here the
discussion on the first commandment of the Law,
Mk 12:28–34, which he has already used, possibly taking it
from another source, Lk 10:25–28.

b. 'children': a semitism for 'those who belong to . . .
Cf. 16:8.

c. Only the resurrection of the just is considered here.
See Ph 3:11h.

d. var. 'they have not to die'.

e. Semitism for those who are actually raised up.

f. The scribes, being Pharisees for the most part,
believed in the resurrection of the dead, *see* Ac 23:6–9.

21 a. In 17:22–37 Lk, following one of his sources, speaks
of the coming of Jesus in glory at the end of time. Here he
follows Mk where two perspectives merge: that of the final
coming and that of the destruction of Jerusalem: *see* 19:44f;
Mt 24:1a.

b. Lk, in this place, assigns to Jesus the role reserved
by 12:12; Mt 10:20; Mk 13:11 to the Spirit of the Father
(Mt), the Holy Spirit (Mk and Lk), Ac 6:10. Cf. Jn
16:13–15.

c. As in 19:43–44, the expressions are biblical and
contain no hint of a description written after the event, *see*
19:44f.

d. Possibly alluding to Dn 9:26,27.

e. i.e. the period during which the gentiles will take
the place of the unfaithful Jewish nation; according to Paul,
Rm 11:11–32, this period will end with the conversion of all
Israel. Thus a period of indeterminate length is introduced
between the ruin of Jerusalem and the end of time.

f. The kingdom has already been inaugurated, 17:21,
but this present verse refers to the period of its triumphant
progress which begins with the destruction of Jerusalem;
cf. 9:27.

g. var. 'for it will come down on you like a snare'.

h. The literary relationship with Jn 8:1–2 is unmistakable. The incident of the adulterous woman, Jn 7:53–8:11,
which so many grounds combine to attribute to Lk, would
fit admirably into this context.

22 a. Throughout the Passion narrative, Lk shows himself
considerably less dependent on Mk than hitherto; on the
other hand, there are many points of contact with Jn. They
probably shared a common source.

b. Lk does not record the anointing at Bethany; he has
already described a similar incident in 7:36–50.

c. Officers of the Temple police. All of these were
Levites; cf. Ac 4:1.

d. In Lk, Christ's discourses at the supper play a more
important part than in Mk and Mt, preparing us for those
of Jn 13:31–17:26. Lk adopts the hellenistic convention of
gathering together at a final meal teachings of the Master
about the future of his disciples. He seems to have thought
of these discourses in the light of the primitive eucharistic
assemblies.

e. The first stage of fulfilment is the Eucharist itself,
the centre of spiritual life in the kingdom founded by Jesus;
the final stage will be at the end of time when the Passover
is to be fulfilled perfectly and in a fashion no longer veiled.

f. Lk distinguishes the Passover and the cup of
vv. 15–18 from the bread and the cup of vv. 19–20 in order
to draw a parallel between the ancient rite of the Jewish
Passover and the new rite of the Christian Eucharist. Some
ancient authorities (including important representatives of
the Latin/Western text), evidently failing to understand this
theological device and, disturbed to find two cups
mentioned, quite mistakenly omitted v. 20, or even v. 20
with the second part of v. 19 (i.e. 'which will be given . . .
of me').

g. Note the affinity between Lk's text and Paul's,
1 Co 11:23–25.

h. Or alternatively 'which has to be given' and 'which
has to be poured out'.

i. By transposing this argument from its place in
Mt 20:25; Mk 10:42, into the context of the institution of
the Eucharist Lk relates it to the dissensions in the early
Church. *See* Ac 6:1; 1 Co 11:17–19; Jm 2:2–4.

j. add. 'And the Lord said'.

k. This saying gives Peter a function in directing faith
with regard to the other apostles. His primacy within the
apostolic college is affirmed more clearly than in
Mt 16:17–19, where he could simply be the spokesman and
representative of the Twelve. *See also* Jn 21:15–17, where
the 'lambs' or 'sheep' whom he is to feed surely include
'these others' whom he surpasses in love.

l. The world which was once sympathetic is now
hostile: the purse and the haversack will be needed, to buy
and to husband the necessities of life which were once freely
provided; the sword will be needed for protection.

m. Lk's account of Jesus' ordeal is far more succinct
than that of Mt and Mk: there is only one prayer. The
accent (vv. 40, 46) is on the need of the disciples to follow
their Master in prayer when they are put to the test.

n. It was normal to stand in prayer, *see* 18:11;
1 K 8:22; Mt 6:5, but also to kneel when prayer was
especially intent or humble, *see* Ps 95:6; Is 45:23; Dn 6:11;
Ac 7:60; 9:40; 20:36; 21:5.

o. Although some good and widely diverse witnesses
omit them, vv. 43–44 should be retained. They are attested
by many witnesses from as early as the second century, and
represent the style and manner of Lk. Their omission is
explained by concern to avoid a humiliation of Jesus which
seemed too human.

p. In Mt and Mk, Jesus is seized immediately after
Judas' greeting; the sword episode follows, and finally the
discourse by Jesus. Lk makes the arrest follow the
discourse, thus emphasising the control Jesus has over what
takes place. *See* for the same emphasis, Jn 10:18j; 18:4–6.

q. lit. 'man'.

r. Occurring during the night's wait, before the session
of the Sanhedrin, and not after it as in Mt and Mk, this
mockery in Lk is the work not of the members of the
Sanhedrin but of the retainers. On all these points Lk's
account may well be more historical than those of Mt and
Mk. Further, in contrast to Mt 26:68; Mk 14:65 (*see* notes)
Jesus is blindfolded, so that the mockery becomes a guessing-game as well known in the ancient world as in any age.

s. Whereas Mk and Mt have two hearings, Lk has
only one, and that in the morning, probably held in the
'Tribunal', a building adjacent to the Temple; *see*
Mt 26:57r.

t. 'elders' here means the whole Sanhedrin, not merely
one of its three component bodies (the elders); of these, Lk
names the two most influential (chief priests and scribes).

u. Lk omits the 'you will see' of Mk and Mt and also
the allusion to Dn. Perhaps he wanted to avoid the suggestion of a *parousia* soon to come which could arise from a
misunderstanding of this saying.

v. Lk distinguishes more clearly than Mt and Mk the
two titles 'Christ', v. 67, and 'son of God', v. 70. Cf.
Jn 10:24–39.

w. Lk has neither false witnesses (but cf. Ac 6:11–14)
nor explicit sentence of death. He certainly seems to use a
different source from Mt and Mk.

23 **a.** Lk's account lies half-way between the less detailed and less dramatic accounts of Mk and Mt, and the prolonged interview in Jn.

b. Lk only. His information might have come from Manaen, 'who had been brought up with Herod the tetrarch', Ac 13:1. It was legally acceptable for a Roman magistrate to refer a prisoner to the ruler of the territory of his origin, in this case Herod Antipas, as tetrarch of Galilee.

c. The ceremonial dress of princes; Herod's gibe at the royal claim of Jesus, v. 3.

d. add. v. 17 'He was under obligation to release one man for them every feast day'; this seems to be an explanatory gloss, cf. Mt 27:15 and par.

e. Lk, like Jn, emphasises Pilate's wish to let Jesus go free, and mentions the procurator's declaration of Christ's innocence three times, cf. Jn 18:38; 19:4,6.

f. Cf. v. 16. Lk does not say what the punishment was; in Mt 27:26–31 and par. it is scourging. Unlike Mk and Mt, but like Jn, Lk regards the punishment as a conciliatory measure designed to avert a sentence not yet pronounced.

g. The Talmud records that noblewomen of Jerusalem were accustomed to give sedative drinks to condemned criminals.

h. If green wood is burnt that is not meant for burning (allusion to Christ's condemnation), what is to happen to dry wood (the truly guilty)?

i. A comparison with Mk and Mt shows how Lk has softened the harshness of the crucifixion: Luke's crowd, vv. 27,35,48, is more inquisitive than hostile, and repents in the end, v. 48; Jesus does not utter the seemingly despairing cry, 'My God, my God, why have you deserted me?'; his ministry of forgiveness goes on to the last, vv. 34,39–43; he dies committing his spirit into the hands of his Father, v. 46.

j. This verse is retained despite its omission by some good and diverse ancient authorities.

k. These words of Jesus recall Is 53:12. The same view of the causes of his death will be repeated, Ac 3:17; 13:27; 1 Co 2:8. Stephen the deacon will pray in the same spirit, Ac 7:60, following the example left by the Master to all his disciples, 1 P 2:23; see Mt 18:21–22k.

l. In the persons of the 'bad thief' and the 'good thief', Jesus is given recognition as Christ, v. 39, and King, v. 42; the titles which were respectively the formal charges in the trial before the Jews and the trial before Pilate.

m. Or else 'in your kingly power', i.e., to establish your kingdom. var. 'when you come with (i.e. in possession of) your kingdom'.

n. Cosmic phenomena which characterise the Day of the Lord, see Mt 27:51x.

o. Or possibly 'was shining'. The Gk word could indicate either sunlight or lamplight.

24 **a.** Lk does not intend to speak of the Galilean apparitions; he therefore modifies Mk 16:7, just as earlier he omitted Mk 14:28.

b. In spite of its omission by several witnesses, this v. is to be retained. In style both Lukan and Johannine, it represents a tradition common to the third and fourth gospels. This is echoed in 24:24 and plainly implies that Peter was not alone in his visit.

c. lit. 'sixty *stadia*' (furlongs); var. (with less support) 'one hundred and sixty'. • The identity of the village is disputed. The story that follows is of a stamp different from the other resurrection appearances, bearing many similarities to the story of Philip and the eunuch in Ac 8:26–40; in each case initial bewilderment is dispersed by instruction, and the stories conclude respectively with a eucharist and a baptism.

d. In the appearances described by Lk and Jn, the disciples do not at first recognise the Lord: they need a word or a sign, 24:30f,35,37,39–43; Jn 20:14,16,20; 21:4,6–7; cf. Mt 28:17. While maintaining its identity, the body of the Risen One is in a new state which modifies its exterior form, Mk 16:12, and transcends the physical limitations of this world, Jn 20:19. On the condition of the risen body, *see* 1 Co 15:44w.

e. var. 'as you walk along and look sad'

f. var. 'the Nazarene'. *See* Mt 2:23*l*.

g. Either, 'Peter' of v. 12 stands for 'the leading apostles'; or else Lk is following the same tradition as Jn 20:3–10 of a visit to the tomb by Peter and the Beloved Disciple.

h. In Ac (2:42gg) Lk uses this as a technical term for the Eucharist; probably it means the same here.

i. In spite of its omission by some good witnesses, this v. should be retained.

j. Writing for Greeks who scoffed at the idea of bodily resurrection, Lk underlines the physical reality of Christ's risen body, cf. v. 43.

k. The impression given is that all these events took place on the same day, the day of resurrection. *See* Mt 28:10f. But Ac 1:1–8 presupposes a period of forty days.

l. That is, the Holy Spirit, *see* Jn 1:33x; Ac 1:1–8; 2:33,39; Ga 3:14,22; 4:6; Ep 1:13.

m. om. 'and was carried up to heaven'. This omission is made by good authorities in the Latin/Western text and in other types of text, but is probably an attempt to avoid an Ascension on the day of Resurrection itself, which seems to clash with that of Ac 1:3,9 forty days later.

n. om. 'They worshipped him, and'.

o. Lk's Gospel ends where it began, in the Temple; its last word is of joy and praise.

THE GOSPEL ACCORDING TO

JOHN

INTRODUCTION TO
THE GOSPEL AND LETTERS OF JOHN

The Gospel

The first ending to the fourth Gospel (20:31) specifies the book's literary form. It is a 'gospel', just as the preaching of the earlier Church was a 'gospel'; i.e. it proclaims that Jesus is Messiah and Son of God, and its teaching, based on 'signs' that Jesus gave, is to bring the reader to believe in the Messiah and so to attain life. The fourth Gospel, therefore, in spite of all indications of its late composition, is not unrelated to the most primitive Christian *kergyma,* or message, and it preserves both the structure and the chief points of this message, e.g. the Holy Spirit descends, as the Baptist testifies, to point out Jesus as Messiah, 1:31–34; Christ's 'glory' is manifested in his work and word, 1:35–12:50; his death, resurrection and subsequent apparitions are described, 13:1–20:20; the apostles are sent out with the gift of the Spirit and the power to forgive sins, 20:21–29. The book claims, moreover, to fulfil the condition that (*see* Ac 1:8k) qualifies a witness as 'apostolic': i.e. it offers an (unnamed) eyewitness for its guarantor, 'the disciple Jesus loved', who took part in the events of the Passion, *see* Jn 13:23; 19:26,35; compare 18:15seq., saw the empty tomb, 20:2seq., and the risen Christ, 21:7,20–24, and was perhaps one of the first two disciples of Jesus, 1:35seq.

There are some features peculiar to the fourth Gospel that mark it off sharply from the Synoptics. In the first place, it is far more concerned than the Synoptics to bring out the *significance* of the events of Christ's life and of all that he did and said. The things Christ did were 'signs': their meaning, hidden at first, could be fully understood only after his glorification, 2:22; 12:16; 13:17. The things he said had a deeper meaning not perceived at the time, *see* 2:20g; it was the business of the Spirit who spoke in the name of the risen Christ, to remind the disciples of what Jesus had said, to deepen their understanding of it, and to 'lead' them 'into the whole truth', *see* 14:26r. The Gospel according to John looks back on the earthly life of Jesus in the light of this completed understanding.

In the second place, the author seems to have been influenced to a considerable extent by ideas current in certain sections of Judaism, ideas that are reflected in the Essene documents of Qumran. In this school of thought the great emphasis laid on 'knowledge' has given its vocabulary the sort of tinge to be found in later Gnostic literature: e.g. the contrasting pairs 'light/darkness', 'truth/lies', 'angel of light/angel of darkness (Beliar)' which all have a dualist flavour. At Qumran—in view of its expectation of an imminent coming of God—a particular stress was laid both on the need for unity and on the necessity for mutual love. All these ideas which recur in the fourth Gospel are characteristic of the Judaeo-Christian *milieu* in which it must have originated.

Moreover, this Gospel is far more interested than the Synoptics in worship and sacraments. It relates the life of Jesus to the Jewish liturgical year and associates his miracles with the principal feasts; the Temple is often given as the setting both for them and for Christ's discourses. Jesus asserts that he himself is the focus of a religion, restored 'in spirit and in truth', 4:24, but a religion also which is expressed and realised in the sacraments. The dialogue with Nicodemus includes all the essentials of a baptismal instruction, 3:1–21, and the narratives of the man born blind and of the paralytic seem to presuppose the ideas of baptism as light, 9:1–39, and new life 5:1–14; 5:21–24. Ch. 6 by itself is a complete collection of teachings on the Eucharist, but the entire Gospel is pervaded by the concept of the Christian Passover, replacing the Jewish Passover, 1:29,36; 2:13; 6:4; 19:36u. Jewish purificatory rites, 2:6; 3:25, give way to a purification of the soul by Word, 15:3, and Spirit, 20:22seq. In this way the life of Christ is seen as directly related to a living liturgical and sacramental Christianity.

The fourth Gospel is a complex work; it is related to the earliest Christian preaching, and yet at the same time it gives us the results of a quest, completed under the guidance of the Holy Spirit, for a deeper and more rewarding apprehension of the mystery of Jesus.

Each of the evangelists has his own approach to Christ's person and mission. For John he is the Word made flesh, come to give life, 1:14, and this, the mystery of the Incarnation, dominates the whole of John's thought. He expresses its theology in concrete terms: Jesus is sent; Jesus bears witness. Christ is God's message, he is the Word sent down to earth by God, to whom he must return when his task is complete, *see* 1:1a. This task of the Word is to declare the hidden things of God; and to be witness to all that he has seen and heard from the Father himself, *see* 3:11e. As credentials God has given him certain works or 'signs' to perform; these demand more than human power and prove that he has been sent by the God who is active in him, *see* 2:11f; through them is glimpsed his glory which will not be revealed fully till the day of his resurrection, *see* 1:14n, when the Son of man is to be 'lifted up' as Isaiah foretold, Is 53:12 (LXX), to return to the Father by way of the cross, *see* Jn 12:32j, and to resume the glory he had with God 'before the world was made', 17:5f,24. This is the glory about which the prophets learned through revelation (*see* 5:27; 12:41; 19:37 and references), and the revealing of this glory is a theophany, or divine self-revelation, that is at once both the culmination and final eclipse of all those other theophanies that had taken place already, whether that given in the act of creation, 1:1, or those given to Moses, 1:17, Jacob, 1:51, Abraham, 8:56, or the prophets. The glory of the 'Day of Yahweh', see Am 5:18m, is identified with the 'Day' of Jesus, Jn 8:56, and more particularly with his Hour, 2:4e, which is the hour of his 'lifting up' and of his glorification. In that hour is revealed the superhuman majesty of him who was 'sent', 8:24g, the majesty of one who came to the world to give life, 3:35t, to all those whose hearts were opened by faith to the saving message he brought, 3:11e. For this 'salvation' and for this alone the Son was 'sent', and in this way his 'sending' was the supreme manifestation of the Father's love for the world, 17:6g.

In the Synoptic Gospels the revelation of Christ's glory is associated primarily with his eschatological 'coming', his return at the end of time, Mt 16:27seq. The basic elements of traditional eschatology: the expectation of the 'Last Day', Jn 6:39seq.; 11:24; 12:48, of the 'coming' of Jesus, 14:3; 21:22seq., of the resurrection of the dead, 5:28seq.; 11:24, and of the last judgement, 3:36; 5:29, are all found in the fourth Gospel, but in it this eschatology receives a new and double emphasis: not only is the End here and now—it is also an inner principle and not an external event. In this way, the 'coming' of the Son of man is interpreted primarily as the 'coming' of Jesus to this world through his Incarnation, his 'lifting up' on the cross, and his return to his own disciples through the Holy Spirit. In the same way the 'judgement' is presented as something already taking place in human hearts, and eternal life (John's counterpart of the synoptic 'kingdom') is made to be something actually present, already in the possession of those who have faith. That these 'last things' should be seen as present is not surprising, since salvation throughout history centres on Christ's historical life and death and resurrection. Beyond the Jews who rejected Jesus looms something more fundamental—the 'world', see 1:9,10,10g, the 'darkness', see 8:12b, which is controlled by Satan, the 'prince of this world', see 1 Jn 2:13seq.; who challenges God and his Anointed. There is no one who is not involved in this dramatic conflict of the spirit: the world, face to face with the Word, suffers its 'judgement', 12:31–32, receives its verdict, and admits defeat, 16:7–11,33. Christ gives his life, see 10:18j, he is 'lifted up' on the cross, but willingly, and only in order to enter into his glory, see 12:32j, a glory that is made visible even in this world to the confusion of unbelievers and ending in the defeat of Satan once and for all. God's victory over evil, his salvation of the world, is already guaranteed by Christ's resurrection in glory; the return of Jesus at the Last Day will be nothing but its confirmation.

It is difficult to determine the precise scheme adopted by John for this great theme. In the first place, the arrangement of the Gospel is not always easy to explain: the sequence of ch. 4, 5, 6, 7:1–24 is awkward; ch. 15–17 are placed after the farewell of 14:31; passages like 3:31–36 and 12:44–50 break into their context. The way the Gospel was both written and edited may be responsible for this. It would seem that we have only the end-stage of a slow process that has brought together not only component parts of different ages, but also corrections, additions and sometimes even more than one revision of the same discourse. Finally all this was published not by the eyewitness himself but by disciples after his death, 21:24. It seems that these disciples had a number of Johannine fragments which they were reluctant to abandon; though uncertain of their place, they worked them into the primitive gospel.

Many ways of dividing the Gospel have been suggested. These all satisfy some of the data but are frequently far too rigidly systematic. It is best to follow such clear indications as are given by the evangelist himself. In the first place there is no doubt that he attaches special importance to the Jewish liturgical feasts which he uses to punctuate his narrative. These are: three feasts of Passover, 2:13; 6:4; 11:55, one unnamed feast, 5:1, one feast of Shelters, 7:2, and one feast of Dedication, 10:22. Secondly, the evangelist on several occasions very deliberately calculates the number of days with a view to dividing the life of Jesus into set periods. Thus we have the first week of Christ's ministry, 1:19–2:11, the week of the feast of Shelters, 7:2, 14, 37, and the week of the Passion, 12:1,12; 19:31,42, which latter is unified by the symbolic burial that begins it, 12:7, and the actual burial with which it ends, 19:38seq; in the same way, 4:45 harks back to the first Passover, *see* 2:13–25, and in this way brackets together a whole section. With the above two points in mind, the following division may be suggested:

A *Prologue,* 1:1–18; 'In the beginning . . .'

B *Jesus' ministry*
  1 Proclamation of the new order, 1:19–4:54; the inaugural week; the events of the first Passover
  2 The second feast: a Sabbath in Jerusalem; the first opposition, 5:1–47
  3 The second Passover, in Galilee; new opposition, 6:1–71
  4 The feast of Shelters: the great messianic revelation; the great rejection, 7:1–10:21
  5 The feast of the Dedication: decision to kill Jesus, 10:22–10:54
  6 Jesus moves towards his death, 11:1–12:50

C *Jesus' Hour. The Passover of the Lamb of God, 13:1–20:31*
  1 Jesus' last meal with the disciples, 13:1–17:26
  2 The Passion, 18–19
  3 The resurrection; commissioning of the disciples, 20:1–29
  4 First ending of the Gospel, 20:30, 31

D *Epilogue,* 21:1–25. The risen Lord teaches the church

The plan of this Gospel thus implies that Jesus fulfilled the institutions of the Jewish religion and in so doing brought them to an end.

Is the fourth Gospel a source of information independent of the three Synoptics? On this problem, and with due caution, the following observations may be made. There are several indications that John was familiar with the traditions embodied in the Synoptics. At times his omissions would be incomprehensible unless he was presuming that the facts would be known from some other source, but there are also times when he seems anxious to fill out the synoptic tradition and add another emphasis. Nevertheless, modern studies continue to provide more and more evidence for the originality and independence of the Johannine tradition. Even when narrating episodes found in the Synoptic Gospels, John remains so much himself that direct literary dependence becomes impossible: the facts must have reached the author by some other route and he must always be considered a source in his own right, an independent witness to the primitive tradition. Between John and Luke the relationship is much closer, close enough to make it possible that when Luke wrote his Gospel he made use not perhaps of the fourth Gospel as it stands but of the traditions that went to its making. This applies especially to the Passion and Resurrection narratives, but the contrary is also possible, namely, that the final editor of the fourth Gospel was influenced by the third.

What then is the historical value of John's Gospel? With the growing scholarly appreciation of the independence of the Johannine tradition there has grown also a recognition of its historical significance. On many points, for example, that have to do with Christ's ministry, John is more precise than the Synoptics; the duration of the ministry and the chronology of the Passion seem to be more exactly defined. Indeed, one of the most exact chronological indications in any of the gospels is to be found in John 2:20, and it is supported by Lk 3:1. Topography in the fourth Gospel is also much more detailed than it is in the Synoptics, and this information has been confirmed more than once by recent discoveries (e.g. the pool with five porticos, 5:2). Moreover, throughout the Gospel we meet with factual detail that displays the author's close familiarity with the Jewish religious practice as also with the rabbinic mind and with the casuistry of the doctors of the law. The portrait of Jesus himself as painted by the evangelist represents him as transcending this world but nevertheless as someone real and entirely human: simple and humble even in his risen glory. Finally it may be remarked that if John had not been convinced of the historical truth of all he wrote, his Gospel would remain an insoluble enigma.

But it is important to realise that 'history' in this context is very different from the concept of modern historians. The absorbing concern of the evangelist is the *meaning* of those historical events which were at once both divine and human, events which were at one and the same time both historical and theological; events which flowered in time but were rooted in eternity. The aim of the evangelist is to make his account a faithful one, something which he intends should be believed; his theme is a supernatural event, played out in human history by Jesus Christ, the Word who became incarnate for the salvation of the human race. With this in mind, the evangelist has selected his material, carefully choosing events which, it seemed to him, could be presented symbolically. In this way he has deepened their meaning and given them new overtones. The miracles he describes are 'signs': they not only manifest Christ's glory, they are also symbolic of the gifts (the new purification, the living bread, light and life) he has brought to the world; even non-miraculous events can be presented in a way that brings out their spiritual meaning, a way that makes them vehicles of the divine mysteries (*see* 2:19–21; 9:7; 11:51seq.; 13:30; 19:31–37 with notes). John can see spiritual depths even in the most material elements of history: when Jesus comes, it is as the light of the world that he comes: his whole life is a battle against darkness; his death is a judgement on the entire world; and in him are realised the types of the Old Testament—he is the lamb of God, 1:29, the new Temple, 2:21, the healing serpent of Moses, 3:14, the bread of life prefigured by manna, 6:35, the perfect shepherd, 10:11, the true vine, 15:1. In John's portrait of him Jesus is presented as divine but it is a portrait filled with the details of Jesus' true humanity: it records the Jesus of history, but Jesus as seen in all his depths as Saviour of the world: John's symbolism, therefore, does not compromise history but presupposes it; for him there is no tension between the symbolic and the factual: his symbols are the real events of history, and his symbolism is inherent in these events; it not only explains the inner meaning of these historic events, but to John, the privileged witness of the incarnate Word, all this symbolism would be useless if these events had not taken place.

As for the *author* of this highly rewarding and complex Gospel, tradition almost unanimously makes him John the apostle, the son of Zebedee. Before 150 AD the fourth Gospel was known and used by Ignatius of Antioch, by the author of the *Odes of Solomon*, by Papias, by Justin, and probably by Clement of Rome, which makes it clear that the work was already considered to have apostolic authority. The first explicit testimony is that of Irenaeus, *c.* 180: 'Last of all John, too, the disciple of the Lord who leant against his breast, himself brought out a gospel while he was in Ephesus.' At about the same time, Clement of Alexandria, Tertullian and the Muratorian Canon expressly attribute the fourth Gospel to John the apostle, though this authorship was denied in about AD 200 by some opponents of the Montanists. These last had used the fourth Gospel to bolster their doctrine of the Spirit, but their opponents' reaction, prompted by theological considerations, has no supporting evidence from tradition.

The matter is, however, not as simple as this. It is today freely accepted that the fourth Gospel underwent a complex development before it reached its final form. Some commentators hold that the evangelist used a variety of sources which he reshaped and expanded to adapt them to his own theology. One has, for example, isolated a 'Sign Source' containing the miracles related in the fourth Gospel, a collection of 'sayings' attributed to Christ, and finally an account of the Passion and Resurrection distinct from that of the Synoptic

Gospels. Following him, several authors have taken steps to work out the nature and scope of this presumed Sign Source. On this hypothesis the attribution of the gospel to the apostle John would become most unlikely: could an eyewitness have used sources to recount his own memories? At best one could suppose that one of the presumed sources was derived from an eyewitness. Other commentators prefer to invoke the hypothesis of a primitive gospel, much simpler than the present one, amplified and developed in several stages during the second half of the first century AD. This hypothesis can appeal for support to the numerous doublets which occur, indications that a single tradition can have evolved along different lines which finally converged in the Gospel as we have it. On this view it is possible to attribute to the apostle John, if not the final editing of the Gospel (which must be the work of his disciples—Jn 21:24), at least the genesis of the primitive gospel. Other indications of this are the topographical and chronological details, which are striking by their precision and coherence.

Must any connection be maintained between the fourth Gospel in whatever form and the apostle John? According to Jn 21:24 it was written by 'the disciple Jesus loved'; should this disciple be identified with the apostle John? An indication that he should is provided by his special friendship with Peter, according to Jn 13:23seq.; 18:15; 20:3–10; 21:20–23. Luke tells us that this was in fact the case with the apostle John (Lk 22:8; Ac 3:1–4; 4:13; 8:14). Nevertheless the argument is not conclusive nor without its difficulties: the apostle John was a fisherman at the Lake of Tiberias; by contrast the 'disciple Jesus loved' lived in or around Jerusalem, since he appears for the first time at Jesus' last supper at Jerusalem (Jn 13:23) and is known to the High Priest (Jn 18:16). In any case, the possibility remains that the attribution of the genesis of the gospel to the apostle John could be the result of a confusion between this John and a certain John the Elder, mentioned by Papias, Bishop of Hierapolis, who was writing *c.* 135 AD. According to Eusebius of Caesarea, this confusion was already made by Irenaeus, *c.* 180 AD.

The Letters

The three letters we have, and which by tradition bear John's name, are so like the gospel in style and doctrine that it is difficult not to accept that they issue from the same school.

For a time the Johannine authorship of the second and third letters was in doubt, and traces of this uncertainty are to be found in Origen, Eusebius of Caesarea and Jerome, while the church of Antioch and the Syrian churches in general refused for a long time to accept them; however, these brief, incidental letters are of little doctrinal import, and it is hard to see how they could have forced their way into the canon had they not in fact been closely related to the Gospel of John.

The third letter was probably written first: it is an attempt to settle the dispute on jurisdiction which had arisen in one of the churches acknowledging the author's jurisdiction; the second letter was written to another church in answer to those who publicly denied the reality of the Incarnation. The first letter, however, is by far the most important: its form is that of an encyclical letter to the Christian communities of Asia, threatened with disintegration under the impact of the early heresies. In this letter the author summarises the entire content of his religious experience. He successively develops the parallel themes of light, 1:5seq.; uprightness, 2:29seq.; love, 4:7–8seq.; and truth, 5:6seq.; and then, taking these as a basis, he goes on to show how we as children of God must necessarily live the life of integrity which, for John, is the only thing which fulfils the twin commandments: faith in Jesus Christ, the son of God, and love of the brethren (*see* notes to 1:3,7). Of the three Johannine letters this is the closest to his Gospel both in style and doctrine; it must have been written about the same time, but whether before or after the Gospel is something that cannot now be determined.

THE GOSPEL ACCORDING TO

JOHN

A: PROLOGUE

1 **1** In the beginning was the Word: [a]
the Word was with God
and the Word was God.

2 He was with God in the beginning.

3 Through him all things came into being,
not one thing came into being except through him.

4 What has come into being [b] in him was life, [c]
life that was the light of men;

5 and light shines in darkness,
and darkness could not overpower it. [d]

6 A man came, sent by God.
His name was John. [e]

7 He came as a witness,
to bear witness to the light,
so that everyone might believe through him.

8 He was not the light,
he was to bear witness to the light.

9 The Word was the real light
that gives light to everyone;
he was coming into the world. [f]

10 He was in the world
that had come into being through him,
and the world did not recognise him. [g]

11 He came to his own
and his own people [h] did not accept him.

12 But to those who did accept him
he gave power to become [i] children of God,
to those who believed in his name [j]

13 who were born not from human stock
or human desire
or human will
but from God himself. [k]

14   The Word became flesh,'
     he lived among us,"
     and we saw his glory,'
     the glory that he has from the Father as only Son of the Father,
     full of grace and truth.°

15   John witnesses to him. He proclaims:
     'This is the one of whom I said:
     He who comes after me
     has passed ahead of me
     because he existed before me.'

16   Indeed, from his fullness we have, all of us, received—
     one gift replacing another,'
17   for the Law was given through Moses,
     grace and truth have come through Jesus Christ.
18   No one has ever seen God;
     it is the only Son,' who is close to the Father's heart,
     who has made him known.

B: JESUS' MINISTRY

I: PROCLAMATION OF THE NEW ORDER

THE MINISTRY OF JESUS

A: THE OPENING WEEK

The witness of John

19   This was the witness of John, when the Jews' sent to him priests and Levites from
20   Jerusalem to ask him, 'Who are you?' ·He declared, he did not deny but declared,
21   'I am not the Christ.' ·So they asked, 'Then are you Elijah?'' He replied. 'I am
22   not.' 'Are you the Prophet?'' He answered, 'No.' ·So they said to him, 'Who are
     you? We must take back an answer to those who sent us. What have you to say
23   about yourself?' ·So he said, 'I am, as Isaiah prophesied:

     A voice of one that cries in the desert:
     Prepare a way for the Lord.
     Make his paths straight!'

24. 25   Now those who had been sent were Pharisees, ·and they put this question to him,
     'Why are you baptising if you are not the Christ, and not Elijah, and not the
26   Prophet?' ·John answered them, 'I baptise with water; but standing among
27   you—unknown to you—·is the one who is coming after me; and I am not fit to
28   undo the strap of his sandal.' ·This happened at Bethany, on the far side of the
     Jordan," where John was baptising.
29   The next day, he saw Jesus coming towards him and said, 'Look, there is the
30   lamb of God' that takes away the sin of the world. ·It was of him that I said,
     "Behind me comes one who has passed ahead of me because he existed before
31   me." ·I did not know him myself, and yet my purpose in coming to baptise with

32 water was so that he might be revealed to Israel.' ·And John declared, 'I saw the
33 Spirit come down on him like a dove *w* from heaven and rest on him. ·I did not
know him myself, but he who sent me to baptise with water had said to me, "The
man on whom you see the Spirit come down and rest is the one who is to baptise
34 with the Holy Spirit." *x* ·I have seen and I testify that he is the Chosen One of
God.' *y*

The first disciples

35 The next day as John stood there again with two of his disciples, Jesus went past,
36, 37 and John looked towards him and said, 'Look, there is the lamb of God.' ·And
38 the two disciples heard what he said and followed Jesus. ·Jesus turned round, saw
them following and said, 'What do you want?' They answered, 'Rabbi'—which
39 means Teacher—'where do you live?' ·He replied, 'Come and see;' so they went
and saw where he lived, and stayed with him that day. It was about the tenth
hour. *z*
40 One of these two who became followers of Jesus after hearing what John had
41 said was Andrew, the brother of Simon Peter. ·The first thing *aa* Andrew did was
to find his brother and say to him, 'We have found the Messiah'—which means
42 the Christ—·and he took Simon to Jesus. Jesus looked at him and said, 'You are
Simon son of John; you are to be called Cephas'—which means Rock.
43 The next day, after Jesus had decided to leave for Galilee, he met Philip and
44 said, 'Follow me.' ·Philip came from the same town, Bethsaida, as Andrew and
45 Peter. ·Philip found Nathanael *bb* and said to him, 'We have found him of whom
Moses in the Law and the prophets wrote, Jesus son of Joseph, from Nazareth.'
46 Nathanael said to him, 'From Nazareth? Can anything good come from that
47 place?' Philip replied, 'Come and see.' ·When Jesus saw Nathanael coming he
said of him, *cc* 'There, truly, is an Israelite in whom there is no deception.'
48 Nathanael asked, 'How do you know me?' Jesus replied, 'Before Philip came to
49 call you, I saw you under the fig tree.' *dd* ·Nathanael answered, 'Rabbi, you are the
50 Son of God, *ee* you are the king of Israel.' ·Jesus replied, 'You believe that just
because I said: I saw you under the fig tree. You are going to see greater things
51 than that.' ·And then he added, 'In all truth I tell you, you will see heaven open
and the angels of God ascending and descending over the Son of man.' *ff*

The wedding at Cana

1 2 On the third day *a* there was a wedding at Cana in Galilee. The mother of Jesus
2, 3 was there, *b* ·and Jesus and his disciples had also been invited. ·And they ran
out of wine, since the wine provided for the feast had all been used, and the
4 mother of Jesus said to him, 'They have no wine.' ·Jesus said, 'Woman, *c* what do
5 you want from me? *d* My hour *e* has not come yet.' ·His mother said to the servants,
6 '*Do whatever he tells you*.' ·There were six stone water jars standing there, meant
for the ablutions that are customary among the Jews: each could hold twenty or
7 thirty gallons. ·Jesus said to the servants, 'Fill the jars with water,' and they filled
8 them to the brim. ·Then he said to them, 'Draw some out now and take it to the
9 president of the feast.' ·They did this; the president tasted the water, and it had
turned into wine. Having no idea where it came from—though the servants who
10 had drawn the water knew—the president of the feast called the bridegroom ·and
said, 'Everyone serves good wine first and the worse wine when the guests are
well wined; but you have kept the best wine till now.'
11 This was the first of Jesus' signs: *f* it was at Cana in Galilee. He revealed his glory,

12 and his disciples believed in him. ·After this he went down to Capernaum with his mother and his brothers and his disciples, but they stayed there only a few days.

B: THE PASSOVER

The cleansing of the Temple

13, 14 When the time of the Jewish Passover was near Jesus went up to Jerusalem, ·and in the Temple he found people selling cattle and sheep and doves, and the money
15 changers sitting there. ·Making a whip out of cord, he drove them all out of the Temple, sheep and cattle as well, scattered the money changers' coins, knocked
16 their tables over ·and said to the dove sellers, 'Take all this out of here and stop
17 using my Father's house as a market.' ·Then his disciples remembered the words
18 of scripture: *I am eaten up with zeal for your house.* ·The Jews intervened and
19 said, 'What sign can you show us that you should act like this?' ·Jesus answered,
20 'Destroy this Temple, and in three days I will raise it up.' ᵉ ·The Jews replied, 'It has taken forty-six years to build this Temple: ʰ are you going to raise it up again
21, 22 in three days?' ·But he was speaking of the Temple that was his body, ⁱ ·and when Jesus rose from the dead, his disciples remembered that he had said this, and they believed the scripture and what he had said.

Jesus in Jerusalem

23 During his stay in Jerusalem for the feast of the Passover many believed in his
24 name when they saw the signs that he did, ·but Jesus knew all people and did not
25 trust himself to them; ·he never needed evidence about anyone; he could tell what someone had in him.

The conversation with Nicodemus

1, 2 **3** There was one of the Pharisees called Nicodemus, a leader of the Jews, ·who came to Jesus by night and said, 'Rabbi, we know that you have come from God as a teacher; for no one could perform the signs that you do unless God were
3 with him.' ·Jesus answered:

> In all truth I tell you,
> no one can see the kingdom of God ᵃ
> without being born from above. ᵇ

4 Nicodemus said, 'How can anyone who is already old be born? Is it possible to go
5 back into the womb again and be born?' ·Jesus replied:

> In all truth I tell you,
> no one can enter the kingdom of God
> without being born through water and the Spirit; ᶜ
6 > what is born of human nature is human;
> what is born of the Spirit is spirit.
7 > Do not be surprised when I say:
> You must be born from above.
8 > The wind ᵈ blows where it pleases;
> you can hear its sound,
> but you cannot tell where it comes from or where it is going.
> So it is with everyone who is born of the Spirit.

9, 10   'How is that possible?' asked Nicodemus. ·Jesus replied, 'You are the Teacher of Israel, and you do not know these things!

       'In all truth I tell you,
11   we speak only about what we know *
       and witness only to what we have seen
       and yet you people reject our evidence. *
12   If you do not believe me
       when I speak to you about earthly things,
       how will you believe me
       when I speak to you about heavenly things? *
13   No one has gone up to heaven *
       except the one who came down from heaven,
       the Son of man;
14   as Moses lifted up the snake in the desert,
       so must the Son of man * be lifted up
15   so that everyone who believes may have eternal life in him. *
16   For this is how God loved the world:
       he gave his only Son,
       so that everyone who believes in him may not perish
       but may have eternal life.
17   For God sent his Son into the world
       not to judge the world,
       but so that through him the world might be saved.
18   No one who believes in him will be judged;
       but whoever does not believe is judged already,
       because that person does not believe
       in the Name of God's only Son. *
19   And the judgement is this:
       though the light has come into the world
       people have preferred
       darkness to the light
       because their deeds were evil.
20   And indeed, everybody who does wrong
       hates the light and avoids it,
       to prevent his actions from being shown up;
21   but whoever does the truth *
       comes out into the light,
       so that what he is doing may plainly appear as done in God.'

Jesus' ministry in Judaea
John bears witness for the last time

22 After this, Jesus went with his disciples into the Judaean countryside and stayed
23 with them there and baptised. * ·John also was baptising at Aenon * near Salim, where there was plenty of water, and people were going there and were being
24 baptised. ·For John had not yet been put in prison.
25   Now a discussion arose between some of John's disciples and a Jew about
26 purification, * ·so they went to John and said, 'Rabbi, the man who was with you on the far side of the Jordan, the man to whom you bore witness, is baptising now,
27 and everyone is going to him.' ·John replied:

'No one can have anything
except what is given him from heaven.

28 'You yourselves can bear me out. I said, "I am not the Christ; I am the one who
has been sent to go in front of him."

'It is the bridegroom who has the bride; *
29 and yet the bridegroom's friend,
who stands there and listens to him,
is filled with joy at the bridegroom's voice.
This is the joy I feel, and it is complete.
30 He must grow greater,
I must grow less.
31 He who comes from above
is above all others; *
he who is of the earth
is earthly himself and speaks in an earthly way.
He who comes from heaven '
32 bears witness to the things he has seen and heard,
but his testimony is not accepted by anybody;
33 though anyone who does accept his testimony
is attesting that God is true,
34 since he whom God has sent
speaks God's own words,
for God gives him the Spirit without reserve. '
35 The Father loves the Son
and has entrusted everything to his hands. '
36 Anyone who believes in the Son has eternal life,
but anyone who refuses to believe in the Son will never see life:
God's retribution hangs over him.'

Jesus among the Samaritans *

1 4 When Jesus * heard that the Pharisees had found out that he was making and
2 baptising more disciples than John—·though in fact it was his disciples who
3, 4 baptised, not Jesus himself—·he left Judaea and went back to Galilee. He had to
5 pass through Samaria. ·On the way he came to the Samaritan town called Sychar *
6 near the land that Jacob gave to his son Joseph. ·Jacob's well was there and Jesus,
7 tired by the journey, sat down by the well. It was about the sixth hour. * ·When a
Samaritan woman came to draw water, Jesus said to her, 'Give me something to
8, 9 drink.' ·His disciples had gone into the town to buy food. ·The Samaritan woman
said to him, 'You are a Jew. How is it that you ask me, a Samaritan, for something
10 to drink?'—Jews, of course, do not associate with Samaritans. * ·Jesus replied to
her:

If you only knew what God is offering
and who it is that is saying to you,
'Give me something to drink,'
you would have been the one to ask,
and he would have given you living water.

11 'You have no bucket, sir,' she answered, 'and the well is deep: how do you get

12 this living water? ·Are you a greater man than our father Jacob, who gave us this
13 well and drank from it himself with his sons and his cattle?' ·Jesus replied:

> Whoever drinks this water
> will be thirsty again;
14 > but no one who drinks the water that I shall give him
> will ever be thirsty again:
> the water that I shall give him
> will become in him a spring of water, welling up for eternal life.

15 'Sir,' said the woman, 'give me some of that water, so that I may never be thirsty
16 or come here again to draw water.' ·'Go and call your husband,' said Jesus to her,
17 'and come back here.' ·The woman answered, 'I have no husband.' Jesus said to
18 her, 'You are right to say, "I have no husband"; ·for although you have had five,
19 the one you now have is not your husband. You spoke the truth there.' ·'I see you
20 are a prophet, sir,' said the woman. ·'Our fathers worshipped on this mountain,*f*
21 though you say that Jerusalem is the place where one ought to worship.'*g* ·Jesus
said:

> Believe me, woman, the hour is coming
> when you will worship the Father
> neither on this mountain nor in Jerusalem.
22 > You worship what you do not know;
> we worship what we do know;
> for salvation comes from the Jews.
23 > But the hour is coming—indeed is already here—
> when true worshippers will worship the Father in spirit and truth: *h*
> that is the kind of worshipper
> the Father seeks.
24 > God is spirit,
> and those who worship *i*
> must worship in spirit and truth.

25 The woman said to him, 'I know that Messiah—that is, Christ—is coming; and
26 when he comes he will explain everything.' ·Jesus said, 'That is who I am, I who
speak to you.'
27 At this point his disciples returned and were surprised to find him speaking to a
woman, though none of them asked, 'What do you want from her?' or, 'What are
28 you talking to her about?' ·The woman put down her water jar and hurried back *j*
29 to the town to tell the people, ·'Come and see a man who has told me everything I
30 have done; could this be the Christ?' ·This brought people out of the town and
they made their way towards him.
31 Meanwhile, the disciples were urging him, 'Rabbi, do have something to eat';
32, 33 but he said, 'I have food to eat that you do not know about.' ·So the disciples said
34 to one another, 'Has someone brought him food?' ·But Jesus said:

> My food
> is to do the will of the one who sent me, *k*
> and to complete his work.
35 > Do you not have a saying:
> Four months and then the harvest?
> Well, I tell you,

> look around you, look at the fields;
> already they are white, ready for harvest! *'*

36   Already ·the reaper is being paid his wages,
> already he is bringing in the grain for eternal life,
> so that sower and reaper can rejoice together.

37   For here the proverb holds true:
> one sows, another reaps;

38   I sent you to reap
> a harvest you have not laboured for.
> Others have laboured for it;
> and you have come into the rewards of their labour. *"*

39   Many Samaritans of that town believed in him on the strength of the woman's
40 words of testimony, 'He told me everything I have done.' ·So, when the Samaritans
came up to him, they begged him to stay with them. He stayed for two days, and
41 many more came to believe on the strength of the words he spoke to them; and
42 they said to the woman, 'Now we believe no longer because of what you told us;
we have heard him ourselves and we know that he is indeed the Saviour of the
world.' *"*

Jesus in Galilee

43, 44 When the two days were over Jesus left for Galilee. ·He himself had declared that
45 a prophet is not honoured in his own home town. ·On his arrival the Galileans
received him well, having seen all that he had done at Jerusalem during the festival
which they too had attended.

Second sign at Cana
The cure of a royal official's son

46 He went again to Cana in Galilee, where he had changed the water into wine.
47 And there was a court official whose son was ill at Capernaum; ·hearing that Jesus
had arrived in Galilee from Judaea, he went and asked him to come and cure his
48 son, as he was at the point of death. ·Jesus said to him, 'Unless you see signs and
49 portents you will not believe!' ·'Sir,' answered the official, 'come down before my
50 child dies.' ·'Go home,' said Jesus, 'your son will live.' The man believed what
51 Jesus had said and went on his way home; ·and while he was still on the way his
52 servants met him with the news that his boy was alive. ·He asked them when the
boy had begun to recover. They replied, 'The fever left him yesterday at the
53 seventh hour.' The father realised that this was exactly the time when Jesus had
said, 'Your son will live'; and he and all his household believed.
54   This new sign, the second, Jesus performed on his return from Judaea to Galilee.

II: THE SECOND FEAST AT JERUSALEM

FIRST OPPOSITION TO REVELATION

The cure of a sick man at the Pool of Bethesda

1, 2   **5** After this there was a Jewish festival, *"* and Jesus went up to Jerusalem. ·Now
in Jerusalem next to the Sheep Pool there is a pool called Bethesda *b* in Hebrew,
3 which has five porticos; ·and under these were crowds of sick people, blind, lame,

5 paralysed. ᶜ ·One man there had an illness which had lasted thirty-eight years, and
6 when Jesus saw him lying there and knew he had been in that condition for a long
7 time, he said, 'Do you want to be well again?' ·'Sir,' replied the sick man. 'I have
no one to put me into the pool when the water is disturbed; and while I am still on
8 the way, someone else gets down there before me.' ·Jesus said, 'Get up, pick up
9 your sleeping-mat and walk around.' ·The man was cured at once, and he picked
up his mat and started to walk around.

10   Now that day happened to be the Sabbath, ·so the Jews said to the man who
had been cured, 'It is the Sabbath; you are not allowed to carry your sleeping-
11 mat.' ·He replied, 'But the man who cured me told me, "Pick up your mat and
12 walk around." ' ·They asked, 'Who is the man who said to you, "Pick up your
13 mat and walk around"? ' ·The man had no idea who it was, since Jesus had
14 disappeared, as the place was crowded. ·After a while Jesus met him in the Temple
and said, 'Now you are well again, do not sin any more, or something worse may
15 happen to you.' ᵈ ·The man went back and told the Jews that it was Jesus who had
16 cured him. ·It was because he did things like this on the Sabbath that the Jews
17 began to harass Jesus. ᵉ ·His answer to them was, 'My Father still goes on working,
18 and I am at work, too.' ᶠ ·But that only made the Jews even more intent on killing
him, because not only was he breaking the Sabbath, but he spoke of God as his
own Father and so made himself God's equal.

19   To this Jesus replied: ᵍ

> In all truth I tell you,
> by himself the Son can do nothing;
> he can do only what he sees the Father doing:
> and whatever the Father does the Son does too.
20 > For the Father loves the Son
> and shows him everything he himself does,
> and he will show him even greater things than these,
> works that will astonish you.
21 > Thus, as the Father raises the dead and gives them life,
> so the Son gives life to anyone he chooses;
22 > for the Father judges ʰ no one;
> he has entrusted all judgement to the Son, ⁱ
23 > so that all may honour the Son
> as they honour the Father.
> Whoever refuses honour to the Son
> refuses honour to the Father who sent him.
24 > In all truth I tell you,
> whoever listens to my words,
> and believes in the one who sent me,
> has eternal life;
> without being brought to judgement
> such a person has passed from death to life.
25 > In all truth I tell you,
> the hour is coming—indeed it is already here—
> when the dead ʲ will hear the voice of the Son of God,
> and all who hear it will live.
26 > For as the Father has life in himself,
> so he has granted the Son also to have life in himself;

27   and, because he is the Son of man,
has granted him power to give judgement.

28   Do not be surprised at this,
for the hour is coming
when the dead will leave their graves
at the sound of his voice:

29   those who did good
will come forth *k* to life;
and those who did evil will come forth to judgement.

30   By myself I can do nothing;
I can judge only as I am told to judge, *l*
and my judging is just,
because I seek to do not my own will,
but the will of him who sent me.

31   Were I to testify on my own behalf,
my testimony would not be true;

32   but there is another witness *m* who speaks on my behalf,
and I know *n* that his testimony is true.

33   You sent messengers to John,
and he gave his testimony to the truth—

34   not that I depend on human testimony;
no, it is for your salvation that I mention it.

35   John was a lamp lit and shining
and for a time you were content to enjoy the light that he gave.

36   But my testimony is greater than John's:
the deeds my Father has given me to perform,
these same deeds of mine
testify that the Father has sent me.

37   Besides, the Father who sent me
bears witness to me himself.
You have never heard his voice,
you have never seen his shape,

38   and his word finds no home in you
because you do not believe
in the one whom he has sent.

39   You pore over *o* the scriptures,
believing that in them you can find eternal life; *p*
it is these scriptures that testify to me, *q*

40   and yet you refuse to come to me to receive life!

41   Human glory means nothing to me.

42   Besides, I know you too well:
you have no love of God in you.

43   I have come in the name of my Father
and you refuse to accept me;
if someone else should come in his own name
you would accept him.

44   How can you believe,
since you look to each other for glory
and are not concerned

with the glory that comes from the one God? '

45 Do not imagine that I am going to accuse you before the Father:
you have placed your hopes on Moses,
and Moses will be the one who accuses you.

46 If you really believed him
you would believe me too,
since it was about me that he was writing;

47 but if you will not believe what he wrote,
how can you believe what I say?

III: THE PASSOVER OF THE BREAD OF LIFE

FURTHER OPPOSITION TO REVELATION

The miracle of the loaves

1, 2 6 After this, Jesus crossed the Sea of Galilee—or of Tiberias— ·and a large
crowd followed him, impressed by the signs he had done in curing the sick.
3, 4 Jesus climbed the hillside and sat down there with his disciples. ·The time of the
Jewish Passover * was near.

5 Looking up, Jesus saw the crowds approaching and said to Philip, 'Where can
6 we buy some bread for these people to eat?' ·He said this only to put Philip to the
7 test; he himself knew exactly what he was going to do. ·Philip answered, 'Two
8 hundred denarii would not buy enough to give them a little piece each.' ·One of
9 his disciples, Andrew, Simon Peter's brother, said, ·'Here is a small boy with five
10 barley loaves and two fish; but what is that among so many?' ·Jesus said to them,
'Make the people sit down.' There was plenty of grass there, and as many as five
11 thousand men sat down. ·Then Jesus took the loaves, gave thanks, and distributed
them to those who were sitting there; he then did the same with the fish, distributing
12 as much as they wanted. ·When they had eaten enough he said to the disciples,
13 'Pick up the pieces left over, so that nothing is wasted.' ·So they picked them up
and filled twelve large baskets with scraps left over from the meal of five barley
14 loaves. ·Seeing the sign that he had done, the people said, 'This is indeed the
15 prophet who is to come into the world.' ·Jesus, as he realised they were about to
come and take him by force and make him king, fled ᵇ back to the hills alone.

Jesus comes to his disciples walking on the waters

16, 17 That evening the disciples went down to the shore of the sea ·and got into a boat
to make for Capernaum on the other side of the sea. It was getting dark by now
18 and Jesus had still not rejoined them. ·The wind was strong, and the sea was
19 getting rough. ·They had rowed three or four miles when they saw Jesus walking
20 on the sea and coming towards the boat. They were afraid, ·but he said, 'It's me.
21 Don't be afraid.' ᶜ ·They were ready to take him into the boat, and immediately it
reached the shore at the place they were making for.

The discourse in the synagogue at Capernaum ᵈ

22 Next day, the crowd that had stayed on the other side saw that only one boat had
been there, and that Jesus had not got into the boat with his disciples, but that the
23 disciples had set off by themselves. ·Other boats, however, had put in from

24 Tiberias, near the place where the bread had been eaten. ᶜ ·When the people saw
that neither Jesus nor his disciples were there, they got into those boats and crossed
25 to Capernaum to look for Jesus. ·When they found him on the other side, they
26 said to him, 'Rabbi, when did you come here?' ·Jesus answered:

> In all truth I tell you,
> you are looking for me
> not because you have seen the signs
> but because you had all the bread you wanted to eat.
27 > Do not work for food that goes bad,
> but work for food that endures for eternal life,
> which the Son of man will give ʲ you,
> for on him the Father, God himself, has set his seal. ᵍ

28   Then they said to him, 'What must we do if we are to carry out God's work?'
29 Jesus gave them this answer, 'This is carrying out God's work: ʰ you must believe
30 in the one he has sent.' ·So they said, 'What sign will you yourself do, the sight of
31 which will make us believe in you? What work will you do? ·Our fathers ate
manna ⁱ in the desert; as scripture says: *He gave them bread from heaven to eat.*'
32   Jesus answered them:

> In all truth I tell you,
> it was not Moses who gave you the bread from heaven,
> it is my Father who gives you the bread from heaven,
> the true bread;
33 > for the bread of God
> is the bread which comes down from heaven
> and gives life to the world.

34, 35 'Sir,' they said, 'give us that bread always.' ·Jesus answered them:

> I am ʲ the bread of life.
> No one who comes to me will ever hunger;
> no one who believes in me will ever thirst. ᵏ
36 > But, as I have told you,
> you can see me and still you do not believe.
37 > Everyone whom the Father gives me will come to me;
> I will certainly not reject
> anyone who comes to me, ˡ
38 > because I have come from heaven,
> not to do my own will,
> but to do the will of him who sent me.
39 > Now the will of him who sent me
> is that I should lose nothing
> of all that he has given to me,
> but that I should raise it up on the last day.
40 > It is my Father's will
> that whoever sees the Son ᵐ and believes in him
> should have eternal life,
> and that I should raise that person up on the last day.

41   Meanwhile the Jews were complaining ⁿ to each other about him, because he
42 had said, 'I am the bread that has come down from heaven.' ·They were saying,

'Surely this is Jesus son of Joseph, whose father and mother we know. How can he
43 now say, "I have come down from heaven?" ' ·Jesus said in reply to them, 'Stop
complaining to each other.

44   'No one can come to me
    unless drawn by the Father who sent me,
    and I will raise that person up on the last day.
45   It is written in the prophets:
    They will all be taught by God;
    everyone who has listened to the Father,
    and learnt from him,
    comes to me.
46   Not that anybody has seen the Father,
    except him who has his being from God:
    he has seen the Father.
47   In all truth I tell you.
    everyone who believes has eternal life.
48   I am the bread of life.
49   Your fathers ate manna in the desert
    and they are dead;
50   but this is the bread which comes down from heaven,
    so that a person may eat it and not die.
51   I am the living bread which has come down from heaven.
    Anyone who eats this bread will live for ever;
    and the bread that I shall give
    is my flesh, *o* for the life of the world.' *p*

52   Then the Jews started arguing among themselves, 'How can this man give us his
53 flesh to eat?' ·Jesus replied to them:

    In all truth I tell you,
    if you do not eat the flesh of the Son of man
    and drink his blood,
    you have no life in you.
54   Anyone who does eat my flesh and drink my blood
    has eternal life,
    and I shall raise that person up on the last day.
55   For my flesh is real food
    and my blood is real drink.
56   Whoever eats my flesh and drinks my blood
    lives in me
    and I live in that person. *q*
57   As the living Father sent me
    and I draw life from the Father,
    so whoever eats me will also draw life from me. *r*
58   This is the bread which has come down from heaven;
    it is not like the bread our ancestors ate: *s*
    they are dead,
    but anyone who eats this bread will live for ever.

59, 60   This is what he taught at Capernaum in the synagogue. ·After hearing it, many
of his followers said, 'This is intolerable language. How could anyone accept it?'

61 Jesus was aware that his followers were complaining about it and said, 'Does this
62 disturb you? ·What if you should see the Son of man ascend to where he was
before?

63   'It is the spirit that gives life,
             the flesh has nothing to offer.
             The words I have spoken to you are spirit
             and they are life. *

64 'But there are some of you who do not believe.' For Jesus knew from the outset
65 who did not believe and who was to betray him. ·He went on, 'This is why I told
66 you that no one could come to me except by the gift of the Father.' ·After this,
many of his disciples went away and accompanied him no more.

Peter's profession of faith

67 Then Jesus said to the Twelve, 'What about you, do you want to go away too?'
68 Simon Peter answered, 'Lord, to whom shall we go? You have the message of
69 eternal life, ·and we believe; we have come to know that you are the Holy One of
70 God.'* ·Jesus replied to them, 'Did I not choose the Twelve of you? Yet one of
71 you is a devil.' ·He meant Judas son of Simon Iscariot, since this was the man, one
of the Twelve, who was to betray him.

IV: THE FEAST OF SHELTERS

Jesus goes up to Jerusalem for the feast and teaches there

1 **7** After this Jesus travelled round Galilee; he could not* travel round Judaea,
      because the Jews were seeking to kill him.
2, 3   As the Jewish feast of Shelters drew near, ·his brothers* said to him, 'Leave this
4 place and go to Judaea, so that your disciples,* too, can see the works you are
5 doing; ·no one who wants to be publicly known acts in secret; if this is what you
   are doing, you should reveal yourself to the world.' ·Not even his brothers had
6 faith in him. Jesus answered, 'For me the right time* has not come yet, but for
7 you any time is the right time. ·The world cannot hate you, but it does hate me,
8 because I give evidence that its ways are evil. ·Go up to the festival yourselves: I
9 am not going* to this festival, because for me the time is not ripe yet.' ·Having
   said that, he stayed behind in Galilee.
10   However, after his brothers had left for the festival, he went up as well, not
11 publicly but secretly. ·At the festival the Jews were on the look-out for him:
12 'Where is he?' they said. ·There was a great deal* of talk about him in the crowds.
13 Some said, 'He is a good man'; others, 'No, he is leading the people astray.' ·Yet
   no one spoke about him openly, for fear of the Jews.
14   When the festival was half over, Jesus went to the Temple and began to teach. *
15 The Jews were astonished and said, 'How did he learn to read? He has not been
16 educated.' ·Jesus answered them:

             'My teaching is not from myself:
             it comes from the one who sent me;
17   anyone who is prepared to do his will,
             will know whether my teaching is from God
             or whether I speak on my own account.

18   When someone speaks on his own account,
    he is seeking honour for himself;
    but when he is seeking the honour of the person who sent him,
    then he is true
    and altogether without dishonesty.
19   Did not Moses give you the Law?
    And yet not one of you keeps the Law!

20 'Why do you want to kill me?' ·The crowd replied, 'You are mad! Who wants to
21. 22 kill you?' ·Jesus answered, 'One work I did, and you are all amazed at it. ·Moses
ordered you to practise circumcision—not that it began with him, it goes back to
23 the patriarchs—and you circumcise on the Sabbath. ·Now if someone can be
circumcised on the Sabbath so that the Law of Moses is not broken, why are you
24 angry with me for making someone completely healthy on a Sabbath?ʰ ·Do not
keep judging according to appearances; let your judgement be according to what
is right.'

The people discuss the origin of the Messiah

25 Meanwhile some of the people of Jerusalem were saying, 'Isn't this the man they
26 want to kill? ·And here he is, speaking openly, and they have nothing to say to
27 him! Can it be true the authoritiesⁱ have recognised that he is the Christ? ·Yet we
all know where he comes from, but when the Christ appears no one will know
where he comes from.'ʲ
28 Then, as Jesus was teaching in the Temple, he cried out:

    You know me and you know where I came from.
    Yet I have not come of my own accord:
    but he who sent me is true;ᵏ
    You do not know him,
29   but I know him
    because I have my being from himˡ
    and it was he who sent me.

30 They wanted to arrest him then, but because his hour had not yet come no one
laid a hand on him.

Jesus foretells his approaching departure

31 There were many people in the crowds, however, who believed in him; they were
saying, 'When the Christ comes, will he give more signs than this man has?'
32 Hearing that talk like this about him was spreading among the people, the
Phariseesᵐ sent the Temple guards to arrest him.
33 Then Jesus said:

    For a short time I am with you still;
    then I shall go back to the one who sent me.
34   You will look for me and will not find me;ⁿ
    where I am
    you cannot come.

35 So the Jews said to one another, 'Where is he intending to go that we shall not
be able to find him? Is he intending to go abroad to the people who are dispersed
36 among the Greeks and to teach the Greeks? ·What does he mean when he says:

> "You will look for me and will not find me;
> where I am,
> you cannot come?" '

The promise of living water

37 On the last day, the great day of the festival, ^e Jesus stood and cried out:

> 'Let anyone who is thirsty come to me! ^f
38 > Let anyone who believes in me come and drink!

As scripture says, "From his heart ^g shall flow streams of living water." '^f
39 He was speaking of the Spirit which those who believed in him were to receive; for there was no Spirit as yet ^s because Jesus had not yet been glorified.

Fresh discussions on the origin of the Messiah

40, 41 Some of the crowd who had been listening said, 'He is indeed the prophet,' ·and some said, 'He is the Christ,' but others said, 'Would the Christ come from
42 Galilee? ·Does not scripture say that the Christ must be descended from David
43 and come from Bethlehem, ⁱ the village where David was?' ·So the people could
44 not agree about him. ·Some wanted to arrest him, but no one actually laid a hand on him.
45 The guards went back to the chief priests and Pharisees who said to them, 'Why
46 haven't you brought him?' ·The guards replied, 'No one has ever spoken like this
47, 48 man.' ·'So,' the Pharisees answered, 'you, too, have been led astray? ·Have any
49 of the authorities come to believe in him? Any of the Pharisees? ·This rabble
50 knows nothing about the Law—they are damned.' ·One of them, Nicodemus—the
51 same man who had come to Jesus earlier—said to them, ·'But surely our Law does not allow us to pass judgement on anyone without first giving him a hearing
52 and discovering what he is doing?' ·To this they answered, 'Are you a Galilean too? Go into the matter, and see for yourself: prophets do not arise in Galilee.'

The adulterous woman ^u

53 They all went home,
1   **8** and Jesus went to the Mount of Olives.
2   At daybreak he appeared in the Temple again; and as all the people came to him, he sat down and began to teach them.
3   The scribes and Pharisees brought a woman along who had been caught commit-
4 ting adultery; and making her stand there in the middle ·they said to Jesus,
5 'Master, this woman was caught in the very act of committing adultery, ·and in the Law Moses has ordered us to stone women of this kind. What have you got to
6 say?' ·They asked him this as a test, looking for an accusation to use against him.
7 But Jesus bent down and started writing on the ground with his finger. ^v ·As they persisted with their question, he straightened up and said, 'Let the one among you
8 who is guiltless be the first to throw a stone at her.' ·Then he bent down and
9 continued writing on the ground. ·When they heard this they went away one by one, beginning with the eldest, until the last one had gone and Jesus was left alone
10 with the woman, who remained in the middle. ·Jesus again straightened up and
11 said, 'Woman, where are they? Has no one condemned you?' ·'No one, sir,' she replied. 'Neither do I condemn you,' said Jesus. 'Go away, and from this moment sin no more.'

Jesus, the light of the world [b]

12 When Jesus spoke to the people again, he said:

> I am the light of the world;
> anyone who follows me will not be walking in the dark,
> but will have the light of life.

A discussion on the testimony of Jesus to himself

13 At this the Pharisees said to him, 'You are testifying on your own behalf; your
14 testimony is not true.' ·Jesus replied:

> Even though I am testifying on my own behalf,
> my testimony is still true,
> because I know
> where I have come from and where I am going;
> but you do not know
> where I come from or where I am going. [c]
15   You judge by human standards; [d]
> I judge [e] no one,
16   but if I judge,
> my judgement will be true,
> because I am not alone:
> the one who sent me is with me;
17   and in your Law it is written
> that the testimony of two witnesses is true.
18   I testify on my own behalf,
> but the Father who sent me testifies on my behalf, too.

19 They asked him, 'Where is your Father then?' Jesus answered:

> You do not know me, nor do you know my Father;
> if you did know me, you would know my Father as well.

20 He spoke these words in the Treasury, while teaching in the Temple. No one
arrested him, because his hour had not yet come.
21 Again he said to them:

> I am going away; you will look for me
> and you will die in your sin. [f]
> Where I am going, you cannot come.

22 So the Jews said to one another, 'Is he going to kill himself, that he says, "Where
23 I am going, you cannot come?" ' ·Jesus went on:

> You are from below;
> I am from above.
> You are of this world;
> I am not of this world.
24   I have told you already: You will die in your sins.
> Yes, if you do not believe that I am He, [g]
> you will die in your sins.

25 So they said to him, 'Who are you?' Jesus answered:

What I have told you from the outset. *

26 About you I have much to say
and much to judge;
but the one who sent me is true,
and what I declare to the world
I have learnt from him.

27, 28 They did not recognise that he was talking to them about the Father. ·So Jesus said:

When you have lifted up the Son of man,
then you will know that I am He '
and that I do nothing of my own accord.
What I say
is what the Father has taught me;
29 he who sent me is with me,
and has not left me to myself,
for I always do what pleases him.

30 As he was saying this, many came to believe in him.

Jesus and Abraham

31 To the Jews who believed in him Jesus said:

If you make my word your home
you will indeed be my disciples;
32 you will come to know the truth, ʲ
and the truth will set you free.

33 They answered, 'We are descended from Abraham and we have never been the
34 slaves of anyone; what do you mean, "You will be set free?" ' ·Jesus replied:

In all truth I tell you,
everyone who commits sin is a slave. *
35 Now a slave has no permanent standing in the household,
but a son belongs to it for ever.
36 So if the Son sets you free,
you will indeed be free.
37 I know that you are descended from Abraham;
but you want to kill me
because my word finds no place in you.
38 What I speak of
is what I have seen at my Father's side,
and you too put into action
the lessons you have learnt from your father.

39 They repeated, 'Our father is Abraham.' Jesus said to them:

If you are Abraham's children,
do as Abraham did. '
40 As it is, you want to kill me,
a man who has told you the truth
as I have learnt it from God;

that is not what Abraham did.

41 You are doing your father's work.

They replied, 'We were not born illegitimate, " the only father we have is God.'
42 Jesus answered:

> If God were your father, you would love me,
> since I have my origin in God and have come from him;
> I did not come of my own accord,
> but he sent me.

43 Why do you not understand what I say?
> Because you cannot bear to listen to my words. "

44 You are from your father, the devil,
> and you prefer to do
> what your father wants.
> He was a murderer from the start;
> he was never grounded ° in the truth;
> there is no truth in him at all.
> When he lies
> he is speaking true to his nature,
> because he is a liar, and the father of lies. °

45 But it is because I speak the truth
> that you do not believe me.

46 Can any of you convict me of sin? °
> If I speak the truth, why do you not believe me?

47 Whoever comes from God
> listens to the words of God;
> the reason why you do not listen
> is that you are not from God.

48 The Jews replied, 'Are we not right in saying that you are a Samaritan and
possessed by a devil?' Jesus answered:

49 I am not possessed;
> but I honour my Father,
> and you deny me honour.

50 I do not seek my own glory;
> there is someone who does seek it and is the judge of it.

51 In all truth I tell you,
> whoever keeps my word
> will never see death.

52 The Jews said, 'Now we know that you are possessed. Abraham is dead, and
the prophets are dead, and yet you say, "Whoever keeps my word will never know
53 the taste of death." ·Are you greater than our father Abraham, who is dead? The
54 prophets are dead too. Who are you claiming to be?' ·Jesus answered:

> If I were to seek my own glory
> my glory would be worth nothing;
> in fact, my glory is conferred by the Father,
> by the one of whom you say, 'He is our God,'
55 although you do not know him.
> But I know him,

and if I were to say, 'I do not know him,'
I should be a liar, as you yourselves are.
But I do know him, and I keep his word.

56   Your father Abraham rejoiced
to think that he would see my Day;ʳ
he saw it and was glad. ˢ

57. 58   The Jews then said, 'You are not fifty yet, and you have seen Abraham!' ·Jesus
replied:

In all truth I tell you,
before Abraham ever was,
I am.

59   At this they picked up stones to throw at him;ᵗ but Jesus hid himself and left the
Temple.

The cure of the man born blind

1, 2   **9** As he went along, he saw a man who had been blind from birth. ·His disciples
asked him, 'Rabbi, who sinned, this man or his parents, that he should have
3   been born blind?' ·'Neither he nor his parents sinned,' Jesus answered, 'he was
born blind so that the works of Godᵃ might be revealed in him.

4   'As long as day lasts
we mustᵇ carry out the work of the one who sent me;
the night will soon be here when no one can work. ᶜ
5   As long as I am in the world
I am the light of the world.' ᵈ

6   Having said this, he spat on the ground, made a paste with the spittle, put this
7   over the eyes of the blind man, ·and said to him, 'Go and wash in the Pool of
Siloamᵉ (the name means 'one who has been sent'). So he went off and washed
and came back able to see.
8   His neighbours and the people who used to see him before (for he was a beggar)
9   said, 'Isn't this the man who used to sit and beg?' ·Some said, 'Yes, it is the same
one.' Others said, 'No, but he looks just like him.' The man himself said, 'Yes, I
10   am the one.' ·So they said to him, 'Then how is it that your eyes were opened?'
11   He answered, 'The man called Jesus made a paste, daubed my eyes with it and
said to me, "Go off and wash at Siloam"; so I went, and when I washed I gained
12   my sight.' ·They asked, 'Where is he?' He answered, 'I don't know.'
13, 14   They brought to the Pharisees the man who had been blind. ·It had been a
15   Sabbath day when Jesus made the pasteᶠ and opened the man's eyes, ·so when the
Pharisees asked him how he had gained his sight, he said, 'He put a paste on my
16   eyes, and I washed, and I can see.' ·Then some of the Pharisees said, 'That man
cannot be from God: he does not keep the Sabbath.' Others said, 'How can a
17   sinner produce signs like this?' And there was division among them. ·So they
spoke to the blind man again, 'What have you to say about him yourself, now that
he has opened your eyes?' The man answered, 'He is a prophet.'
18   However, the Jews would not believe that the man had been blindᵍ without first
19   sending for the parents of the man who had gained his sight and ·asking them, 'Is
this man really the son of yours who you say was born blind? If so, how is it that
20   he is now able to see?' ·His parents answered, 'We know he is our son and we

21 know he was born blind, ·but how he can see, we don't know, nor who opened his
22 eyes. Ask him. * He is old enough: let him speak for himself.' ·His parents spoke
   like this out of fear of the Jews, who had already agreed to ban from the synagogue
23 anyone who should acknowledge Jesus as the Christ. ·This was why his parents
   said, 'He is old enough; ask him.'

24   So the Jews sent for the man again and said to him, 'Give glory to God! ' We are
25 satisfied that this man is a sinner.' ·The man answered, 'Whether he is a sinner I
26 don't know; all I know is that I was blind and now I can see.' ·They said to him,
27 'What did he do to you? How did he open your eyes? ·He replied, 'I have told you
   once and you wouldn't listen. Why do you want to hear it all again? Do you want
28 to become his disciples yourselves?' ·At this they hurled abuse at him, 'It is you
29 who are his disciple, we are disciples of Moses: ·we know that God spoke to
30 Moses, but as for this man, we don't know where he comes from.' ·The man
   replied, 'That is just what is so amazing! You don't know where he comes from
31 and he has opened my eyes! ·We know that God doesn't listen to sinners, but God
32 does listen to men who are devout and do his will. ·Ever since the world began it
33 is unheard of for anyone to open the eyes of a man who was born blind; ʲ ·if this
34 man were not from God, he wouldn't have been able to do anything.' ·They
   retorted, 'Are you trying to teach us, and you a sinner through and through ever
   since you were born!' And they ejected him.

35   Jesus heard they had ejected him, and when he found him he said to him, 'Do
36 you believe in the Son of man?' ·'Sir,' the man replied, 'tell me who he is so that I
37 may believe in him.' ·Jesus said, 'You have seen him; he is speaking to you.' * The
38 man said, 'Lord, I believe,' and worshipped him.
39   Jesus said:

> It is for judgement
> that I have come into this world,
> so that those without sight may see
> and those with sight ' may become blind.

40   Hearing this, some Pharisees who were present said to him, 'So we are blind,
41 are we?' ·Jesus replied:

> If you were blind,
> you would not be guilty,
> but since you say, 'We can see,'
> your guilt remains.

The good shepherd

1 **10** 'In all truth I tell you, anyone who does not enter the sheepfold through
2   the gate, but climbs in some other way, is a thief and a bandit. ·He who
3 enters through the gate is the shepherd of the flock; ·the gatekeeper lets him in,
   the sheep hear his voice, one by one ª he calls his own sheep and leads them out.
4 When he has brought out all those that are his, he goes ahead of them, and the
5 sheep follow because they know his voice. ·They will never follow a stranger, but
   will run away from him because they do not recognise the voice of strangers.'
6   Jesus told them ᵇ this parable but they failed to understand what he was saying
   to them.
7   So Jesus spoke to them again:

In all truth I tell you,
I am the gate of the sheepfold. *

8 All who have come * before me
are thieves and bandits,
but the sheep took no notice of them.

9 I am the gate.
Anyone who enters through me will be safe:
such a one will go in and out
and will find pasture.

10 The thief comes
only to steal and kill and destroy.
I have come
so that they may have life *
and have it to the full.

11 I am the good shepherd: *
the good shepherd lays down his life for his sheep.

12 The hired man, since he is not the shepherd
and the sheep do not belong to him,
abandons the sheep
as soon as he sees a wolf coming, and runs away,
and then the wolf attacks and scatters the sheep;

13 he runs away because he is only a hired man
and has no concern for the sheep.

14 I am the good shepherd;
I know my own
and my own know me, *

15 just as the Father knows me
and I know the Father;
and I lay down my life for my sheep.

16 And there are other sheep I have
that are not of this fold,
and I must lead these too. *
They too will listen to my voice,
and there will be only one flock, *
one shepherd.

17 The Father loves me,
because I lay down my life
in order to take it up again.

18 No one takes it from me;
I lay it down of my own free will, *
and as I have power to lay it down,
so I have power to take it up again;
and this is the command I have received from my Father.

19, 20 These words caused a fresh division among the Jews. ·Many said, 'He is
21 possessed, he is raving; why do you listen to him?' ·Others said, 'These are not
the words of a man possessed by a devil: could a devil open the eyes of the blind?'

V: THE FEAST OF DEDICATION

THE DECISION TO KILL JESUS

Jesus claims to be the Son of God

22, 23 It was the time of the feast of Dedication in Jerusalem. It was winter, •and Jesus
24 was in the Temple walking up and down in the Portico of Solomon. •The Jews
gathered round him and said, 'How much longer are you going to keep us in
25 suspense? If you are the Christ, tell us openly.'[k] •Jesus replied:

I have told you,[l] but you do not believe.
The works I do in my Father's name are my witness;
26 but you do not believe,
because you are no sheep of mine.[m]
27 The sheep that belong to me listen to my voice;
I know them and they follow me.
28 I give them eternal life;
they will never be lost
and no one will ever steal them from my hand.
29 The Father, for what he has given me, is greater than anyone,[n]
and no one can steal[o] anything from the Father's hand.
30 The Father and I are one.[p]

31, 32 The Jews fetched stones to stone him, •so Jesus said to them, 'I have shown you
33 many good works from my Father; for which of these are you stoning me?' •The
Jews answered him, 'We are stoning you, not for doing a good work, but for
34 blasphemy; though you are only a man, you claim to be God.' •Jesus answered:

Is it not written in your Law:
I said, you are gods?[q]
35 So it uses the word 'gods'
of those people to whom the word of God was addressed
—and scripture cannot be set aside.
36 Yet to someone whom the Father has consecrated
and sent into the world you say,
'You are blaspheming'
because I said, 'I am Son of God.'
37 If I am not doing my Father's work,
there is no need to believe me;
38 but if I am doing it,
then even if you refuse to believe in me,
at least believe in the work I do;
then you will know for certain
that the Father is in me and I am in the Father.

39 They again wanted[r] to arrest him then, but he eluded their clutches.

Jesus withdraws to the other side of the Jordan

40 He went back again to the far side of the Jordan to the district where John had
41 been baptising at first and he stayed there. •Many people who came to him said,
42 'John gave no signs, but all he said about this man was true'; •and many of them
believed in him.

VI: JESUS MOVES TOWARDS HIS DEATH

The resurrection of Lazarus

1, 2 **11** There was a man named Lazarus of Bethany, the village of Mary and her sister, Martha, and he was ill. ·It was the same Mary, the sister of the sick man Lazarus, who anointed the Lord with ointment and wiped his feet with her
3, 4 hair. *ª* ·The sisters sent this message to Jesus, 'Lord, the man you love is ill.' ·On receiving the message, Jesus said, 'This sickness will not end in death, but it is for God's glory so that through it the Son of God may be glorified.' *ᵇ*

5, 6 Jesus loved Martha and her sister and Lazarus, ·yet when he heard that he was
7 ill he stayed where he was for two more days ·before saying to the disciples, 'Let
8 us go back to Judaea.' *ᶜ* ·The disciples said, 'Rabbi, it is not long since the Jews
9 were trying to stone you; are you going back there again?' ·Jesus replied:

> Are there not twelve hours in the day?
> No one who walks in the daytime stumbles,
> having the light of this world to see by;
10 > anyone who walks around at night stumbles,
> having no light as a guide.

11 He said that and then added, 'Our friend Lazarus is at rest; I am going to wake
12, 13 him.' ·The disciples said to him, 'Lord, if he is at rest he will be saved.' ·Jesus was speaking of the death of Lazarus, but they thought that by 'rest' he meant 'sleep';
14, 15 so Jesus put it plainly, 'Lazarus is dead; ·and for your sake I am glad I was not
16 there because now you will believe. *ᵈ* But let us go to him.' ·Then Thomas—known as the Twin—said to the other disciples, 'Let us also go to die with him.'
17 On arriving, Jesus found that Lazarus had been in the tomb for four days
18, 19 already. ·Bethany is only about two miles from Jerusalem, ·and many Jews had
20 come to Martha and Mary to comfort them about their brother. ·When Martha heard that Jesus was coming she went to meet him. Mary remained sitting in the
21 house. ·Martha said to Jesus, 'Lord, if you had been here, *ᵉ* my brother would not
22 have died, ·but even now I know that God will grant whatever you ask of him.' *ᶠ*
23, 24 Jesus said to her, 'Your brother will rise again.' ·Martha said, 'I know he will rise
25 again at the resurrection on the last day.' ·Jesus said:

> I am the resurrection. *ᵍ*
> Anyone who believes in me, even though that person dies, will live, *ʰ*
26 > and whoever lives and believes in me
> will never die.
> Do you believe this?

27 'Yes, Lord,' she said, 'I believe that you are the Christ, the Son of God, the one who was to come into this world.'
28 When she had said this, she went and called her sister Mary, saying in a low
29 voice, 'The Master is here and wants to see you.' ·Hearing this, Mary got up
30 quickly and went to him. ·Jesus had not yet come into the village; he was still at
31 the place where Martha had met him. ·When the Jews who were in the house comforting Mary saw her get up so quickly and go out, they followed her, thinking that she was going to the tomb to weep there.
32 Mary went to Jesus, and as soon as she saw him she threw herself at his feet,
33 saying, 'Lord, if you had been here, my brother would not have died.' ·At the sight of her tears, and those of the Jews who had come with her, Jesus was greatly

34 distressed, and with a profound sigh he said, ·'Where have you put him?' They
35, 36 said, 'Lord, come and see.' ·Jesus wept; ·and the Jews said, 'See how much he
37 loved him!' ·But there were some who remarked, 'He opened the eyes of the blind
38 man. Could he not have prevented this man's death?' ·Sighing again, Jesus reached
39 the tomb: it was a cave with a stone to close the opening. ·Jesus said, 'Take the
stone away.' Martha, *i* the dead man's sister, said to him, 'Lord, by now he will
40 smell; this is the fourth day since he died.' ·Jesus replied, 'Have I not told you that
41 if you believe you will see the glory of God?' ·So they took the stone away. Then
Jesus lifted up *j* his eyes and said:

> Father, I thank you for hearing my prayer.
42 > I myself knew that you hear me always,
> but I speak
> for the sake of all these who are standing around me,
> so that they may believe it was you who sent me.

43, 44   When he had said this, he cried in a loud voice, 'Lazarus, come out!' ·The dead
man came out, his feet and hands bound with strips of material, and a cloth over
his face. Jesus said to them, 'Unbind him, let him go free.'

The Jewish leaders decide on the death of Jesus

45 Many of the Jews who had come to visit Mary, and had seen what he did, believed
46 in him, ·but some of them went to the Pharisees to tell them what Jesus had done.
47 Then the chief priests and Pharisees called a meeting. 'Here is this man working
48 all these signs,' they said, 'and what action are we taking? ·If we let him go on in
this way everybody will believe in him, and the Romans will come and suppress
49 the Holy Place *k* and our nation.' ·One of them, Caiaphas, the high priest that
50 year, said, 'You do not seem to have grasped the situation at all; ·you fail to see
that it is to your advantage *l* that one man should die for the people, rather than
51 that the whole nation should perish.' ·He did not speak in his own person, but as
high priest of that year *m* he was prophesying that Jesus was to die for the nation *n*—
52 and not for the nation only, but also to gather together into one the scattered
53, 54 children of God. ·From that day onwards they were determined *o* to kill him. ·So
Jesus no longer went about openly among the Jews, but left the district for a town
called Ephraim, in the country bordering on the desert, and stayed there with his
disciples.

The Passover draws near

55 The Jewish Passover was drawing near, *p* and many of the country people who had
56 gone up to Jerusalem before the Passover *q* to purify themselves ·were looking out
for Jesus, saying to one another as they stood about in the Temple, 'What do you
57 think? Will he come to the festival or not?' ·The chief priests and Pharisees had by
now given their orders: anyone who knew where he was must inform them so that
they could arrest him.

The anointing at Bethany

1 **12** Six days before the Passover, *a* Jesus went to Bethany, where Lazarus was,
2 whom he had raised from the dead. ·They gave a dinner for him there;
3 Martha waited on them and Lazarus was among those at table. ·Mary brought in a
pound of very costly ointment, pure nard, and with it anointed the feet of Jesus,
wiping them with her hair; the house was filled with the scent of the ointment.

4 Then Judas Iscariot—one of his disciples, the man who was to betray him—said,
5 'Why was this ointment not sold for three hundred denarii and the money given to
6 the poor?' ·He said this, not because he cared about the poor, but because he was
a thief; he was in charge of the common fund and used to help himself to the
7 contents. ·So Jesus said, 'Leave her alone; let her keep it for the day of my burial. *
8 You have the poor with you always, you will not always have me.'
9   Meanwhile a large number of Jews heard that he was there and came not only
on account of Jesus but also to see Lazarus whom he had raised from the dead.
10, 11 Then the chief priests decided to kill Lazarus as well, ·since it was on his account
that many of the Jews were leaving them and believing in Jesus.

The Messiah enters Jerusalem

12 The next day the great crowd of people who had come up for the festival heard
13 that Jesus was on his way to Jerusalem. ·They took branches of palm and went out
to receive him, shouting:

> 'Hosanna!
> *Blessed is he who is coming in the name of the Lord,*
> *the king of Israel.'* ^c

14 Jesus found a young donkey and mounted it—as scripture says:

15 > *Do not be afraid, daughter of Zion;*
> *look, your king is approaching,*
> *riding on the foal of a donkey.*

16 At first his disciples did not understand this, but later, after Jesus had been
glorified, they remembered that this had been written about him and that this was
17 what had happened to him. ·The crowd who had been with him when he called
Lazarus out of the tomb and raised him from the dead kept bearing witness to it;
18 this was another reason why the crowd came out to receive him: they had heard
19 that he had given this sign. ·Then the Pharisees said to one another, 'You see, you
are making no progress; look, the whole world has gone after him!'

Jesus foretells his death and subsequent glorification

20, 21 Among those who went up to worship at the festival were some Greeks. * ·These
approached Philip, who came from Bethsaida in Galilee, and put this request to
22 him, 'Sir, we should like to see Jesus.' ·Philip went to tell Andrew, and Andrew
and Philip together went to tell Jesus.
23   Jesus replied to them:

> Now the hour has come
> for the Son of man to be glorified.
24 > In all truth I tell you,
> unless a wheat grain falls into the earth and dies,
> it remains only a single grain;
> but if it dies
> it yields a rich harvest.
25 > Anyone who loves his life loses it;
> anyone who hates his life in this world
> will keep it for eternal life.
26 > Whoever serves me, must follow me,

and my servant will be with me wherever I am. *
If anyone serves me, my Father will honour him.
27 Now my soul is troubled. *
What shall I say:
Father, save me from this hour?
But it is for this very reason that I have come to this hour.
28 Father, glorify your name! *

A voice came from heaven, 'I have glorified it, and I will again glorify it.'
29 The crowd standing by, who heard this, said it was a clap of thunder; others
30 said, 'It was an angel speaking to him.' ·Jesus answered, 'It was not for my sake
that this voice came, but for yours. *

'Now sentence is being passed on this world;
31 now the prince of this world is to be driven out. *
32 And when I am lifted up from the earth, *
I shall draw all people * to myself.' *

33, 34 By these words he indicated the kind of death he would die. ·The crowd
answered, 'The Law has taught us that the Christ will remain for ever. So how can
35 you say, "The Son of man must be lifted up"? Who is this Son of man?' ·Jesus
then said:

The light will be with you only a little longer now.
Go on your way * while you have the light,
or darkness will overtake you,
and nobody who walks in the dark knows where he is going.
36 While you still have the light,
believe in the light
so that you may become children of light.

Having said this, Jesus left them and was hidden from their sight.

Conclusion: the unbelief of the Jews

37 Though they had been present when he gave so many signs, they did not believe
38 in him; ·this was to fulfil the words of the prophet Isaiah:

Lord, who has given credence to what they have heard from us,
and who has seen in it a revelation of the Lord's arm?

39 Indeed, they were unable to believe because, as Isaiah says again:

40 *He has blinded their eyes,*
he has hardened their heart,
to prevent them from using their eyes to see,
using their heart to understand,
changing their ways and being healed by me.

41 Isaiah said this because he saw his glory, * and his words referred to Jesus.
42 And yet there were many who did believe in him, even among the leading men,
but they did not admit it, because of the Pharisees and for fear of being banned
43 from the synagogue: ·they put human glory before God's glory.
44 Jesus declared publicly:

Whoever believes in me
believes not in me
but in the one who sent me,

45   and whoever sees me,
sees the one who sent me.

46   I have come into the world as light,
to prevent anyone who believes in me
from staying in the dark any more.

47   If anyone hears my words and does not keep them faithfully,
it is not I who shall judge such a person,
since I have come not to judge the world,
but to save the world:

48   anyone who rejects me and refuses my words
has his judge already:
the word itself that I have spoken
will be his judge on the last day.

49   For I have not spoken of my own accord;
but the Father who sent me
commanded me what to say and what to speak,

50   and I know that his commands mean eternal life.
And therefore what the Father has told me
is what I speak.

C: JESUS' HOUR COMES

VII: THE PASSOVER OF THE LAMB OF GOD

A: JESUS' LAST MEAL WITH HIS DISCIPLES

The washing of feet

1 **13** Before the festival of the Passover, Jesus, knowing that his hour had come to pass from this world to the Father, *ͨ* having loved *ᵇ* those who were his in the world, loved them to the end. *ͨ*

2 They were at supper, *ᵈ* and the devil had already put it into the mind *ͤ* of
3 Judas Iscariot son of Simon, to betray him. ·Jesus knew that the Father had put everything into his hands, and that he had come from God and was returning to
4 God, and he got up from table, removed his outer garments and, taking a towel,
5 wrapped it round his waist; ·he then poured water into a basin and began to wash the disciples' feet *ᶠ* and to wipe them with the towel he was wearing.

6 He came to Simon Peter, who said to him, 'Lord, are you going to wash my
7 feet?' ·Jesus answered, 'At the moment you do not know what I am doing, but
8 later you will understand.' ·'Never!' said Peter, 'You shall never wash my feet.' Jesus replied, 'If I do not wash you, you can have no share with me.' *ᵍ* Simon Peter
9 said, ·'Well then, Lord, not only my feet, but my hands and my head as well!'
10 Jesus said, 'No one who has had a bath needs washing, *ʰ* such a person is clean all
11 over. *ⁱ* You too are clean, *ʲ* though not all of you are.' ·He knew who was going to betray him, and that was why he said, 'though not all of you are'.

12 When he had washed their feet and put on his outer garments again he went

13 back to the table. 'Do you understand', he said, 'what I have done to you? ·You
14 call me Master and Lord, and rightly; so I am. ·If I, then, the Lord and Master,
15 have washed your feet, you must wash each other's feet. ᵏ ·I have given you an
example so that you may copy what I have done to you.

16   'In all truth I tell you,
          no servant is greater than his master,
          no messenger is greater than the one who sent him.

17, 18   'Now that you know this, blessed are you if you behave accordingly. ·I am not
speaking about all of you: I know the ones I have chosen; but what scripture says
must be fulfilled:

          '*He who shares my table*
          takes advantage ¹ of me.
19   I tell you this now, before it happens,
          so that when it does happen
          you may believe that I am He. ᵐ
20   In all truth I tell you,
          whoever welcomes the one I send, welcomes me,
          and whoever welcomes me, welcomes the one who sent me.'

The treachery of Judas foretold

21 Having said this, Jesus was deeply disturbed and declared, 'In all truth I tell you ,
22 one of you is going to betray me.' ·The disciples looked at each other, wondering
23, 24 whom he meant. ·The disciple Jesus loved was reclining next to Jesus; Simon Peter
25 signed to him and said, 'Ask who it is he means,' ·so leaning back close to Jesus'
26 chest he said, 'Who is it, Lord?' ·Jesus answered, 'It is the one to whom I give the
piece of bread ⁿ that I dip in the dish.' And when he had dipped the piece of bread
27 he gave it to Judas son of Simon Iscariot. ·At that instant, after Judas had taken
the bread, Satan entered him. Jesus then said, 'What you are going to do, do
28, 29 quickly.' ·None of the others at table understood why he said this. ·Since Judas
had charge of the common fund, some of them thought Jesus was telling him,
'Buy what we need for the festival,' or telling him to give something to the poor.
30 As soon as Judas had taken the piece of bread he went out. It was night.

Farewell discourses °

31 When he had gone, Jesus said:

          Now ᵖ has the Son of man been glorified,
          and in him God has been glorified.
32   If God has been glorified in him, ᵠ
          God will in turn glorify him in himself, ʳ
          and will glorify him very soon.
33   Little children,
          I shall be with you only a little longer.
          You will look for me,
          and, as I told the Jews, ˢ
          where I am going,
          you cannot come. ᵗ
34   I give you a new commandment: ᵘ
          love one another;

> you must love one another
> just as I have loved you.

35   It is by your love for one another,
> that everyone will recognise you
> as my disciples.

36   Simon Peter said, 'Lord, where are you going?' Jesus replied, 'Now you cannot
37 follow me where I am going, but later you shall follow me.' ' ·Peter said to him, "
38 'Why can I not follow you now? I will lay down my life for you.' ·'Lay down your
life for me?' answered Jesus. 'In all truth I tell you, before the cock crows you will
have disowned me three times.'

1   **14**   Do not let your hearts be troubled. *
> You trust in God, trust also in me.
2   In my Father's house there are many places to live in;
> otherwise I would have told you. *
> I am going now to prepare a place for you,
3   and after I have gone and prepared you a place,
> I shall return to take you to myself, *
> so that you may be with me
> where I am.
4   You know the way to the place where I am going.

5   Thomas said, 'Lord, we do not know where you are going, so how can we know
6 the way?' ·Jesus said:

> I am the Way; I am Truth and Life. *
> No one can come to the Father except through me.
7   If you know me, * you will know my Father too.
> From this moment you know him and have seen him.

8   Philip said, 'Lord, show us the Father and then we shall be satisfied.' Jesus said
9 to him, ·'Have I been with you all this time, Philip, and you still do not know me?

> 'Anyone who has seen me has seen the Father,
> so how can you say, "Show us the Father"?
10   Do you not believe *
> that I am in the Father and the Father is in me?
> What I say to you I do not speak of my own accord:
> it is the Father, living in me, who is doing his works.
11   You must believe me when I say
> that I am in the Father and the Father is in me;
> or at least believe it on the evidence of these works.
12   In all truth I tell you,
> whoever believes in me
> will perform the same works as I do myself,
> and will perform even greater works,
> because I am going to the Father. *
13   Whatever you ask for in my name I will do,
> so that the Father may be glorified in the Son.
14   If you ask me for anything in my name,
> I will do it.
15   If you love me you will keep my commandments. *

16   I shall ask the Father,
      and he will give you another Paraclete [i]
      to be with you for ever,
17   the Spirit of truth
      whom the world can never accept
      since it neither sees nor knows him;
      but you know him,
      because he is with you, he is in you. [j]
18   I shall not leave you orphans;
      I shall come to you.
19   In a short time the world will no longer see me;
      but you will see that I live
      and you also will live. [k]
20   On that day [l]
      you will know that I am in my Father
      and you in me and I in you. [m]
21   Whoever holds to my commandments and keeps them
      is the one who loves me;
      and whoever loves me will be loved by my Father,
      and I shall love him and reveal myself to him.' [n]

22   Judas [o]—not Judas Iscariot—said to him, 'Lord, what has happened, that you
23   intend to show yourself to us and not to the world?' ·Jesus replied:

      Anyone who loves me will keep my word, [p]
      and my Father will love him,
      and we shall come to him
      and make a home in him.
24   Anyone who does not love me does not keep my words.
      And the word that you hear [q] is not my own:
      it is the word of the Father who sent me.
25   I have said these things to you
      while still with you;
26   but the Paraclete, the Holy Spirit,
      whom the Father will send in my name,
      will teach you everything
      and remind you of all I have said to you. [r]
27   Peace [s] I bequeath to you,
      my own peace I give you,
      a peace which the world cannot give, this is my gift to you.
      Do not let your hearts be troubled or afraid.
28   You heard me say:
      I am going away and shall return.
      If you loved me you would be glad that I am going to the Father,
      for the Father is greater than I. [t]
29   I have told you this now, before it happens,
      so that when it does happen you may believe.
30   I shall not talk to you much longer, [u]
      because the prince of this world is on his way.
      He has no power over me,
31   but the world must recognise that I love the Father

and that I act just as the Father commanded.
Come now, let us go.

The true vine

¹ **15** I am the true vine, *
and my Father is the vinedresser.

² Every branch in me that bears no fruit *
he cuts away,
and every branch that does bear fruit he prunes
to make it bear even more.

³ You are clean * already,
by means of the word that I have spoken to you.

⁴ Remain in me, as I in you.
As a branch cannot bear fruit all by itself,
unless it remains part of the vine,
neither can you unless you remain in me.

⁵ I am the vine,
you are the branches.
Whoever remains in me, with me in him,
bears fruit in plenty;
for cut off from me you can do nothing.

⁶ Anyone who does not remain in me
is thrown away like a branch
—and withers;
these branches are collected and thrown on the fire,
and are burnt.

⁷ If you remain in me
and my words remain in you,
you may ask for whatever you please
and you will get it.

⁸ It is to the glory of my Father that you should bear much fruit,
and be my disciples. *

⁹ I have loved you
just as the Father has loved me.
Remain in my love.

¹⁰ If you keep my commandments
you will remain in my love,
just as I have kept my Father's commandments
and remain in his love.

¹¹ I have told you this
so that my own joy * may be in you
and your joy be complete.

¹² This is my commandment:
love one another,
as I have loved you.

¹³ No one can have greater love
than to lay down his life for his friends.

¹⁴ You are my friends,
if you do what I command you.

¹⁵ I shall no longer call you servants,

because a servant does not know
his master's business;
I call you friends,
because I have made known to you
everything I have learnt from my Father.
16   You did not choose me,
no, I chose you;
and I commissioned you
to go out and to bear fruit,
fruit that will last;
so that the Father will give you
anything you ask him in my name.
17   My command to you
is to love one another.

The disciples and the world*

18   If the world hates you,
you must realise that it hated me before it hated you.
19   If you belonged to the world,
the world would love you as its own;
but because you do not belong to the world,
because my choice of you has drawn you out of the world,
that is why the world hates you.
20   Remember the words I said to you:
A servant is not greater than his master.
If they persecuted me,
they will persecute you too;
if they kept my word,
they will keep yours as well.
21   But it will be on my account that they will do all this to you,
because they do not know the one who sent me.
22   If I had not come,
if I had not spoken to them,
they would have been blameless;
but as it is they have no excuse for their sin.
23   Anyone who hates me hates my Father.
24   If I had not performed such works among them
as no one else has ever done,
they would be blameless;
but as it is, in spite of what they have seen,
they hate both me and my Father.
25   But all this was only to fulfil the words written in their Law:
They hated me without reason.
26   When the Paraclete comes,
whom I shall send to you from the Father,
the Spirit of truth who issues from *the Father,
he will be my witness.
27   And you too will be witnesses,
because you have been with me from the beginning.

16

1   I have told you all this
so that you may not fall away. *

They will expel you from the synagogues,
2   and indeed the time is coming
when anyone who kills you will think he is doing a holy service to God.
3   They will do these things
because they have never known either the Father or me.
4   But I have told you all this,
so that when the time for it comes
you may remember that I told you.

The coming of the Paraclete

I did not tell you this from the beginning,
because I was with you;
5   but now I am going to the one who sent me.
Not one of you asks, 'Where are you going?'
6   Yet you are sad at heart because I have told you this.
7   Still, I am telling you the truth:
it is for your own good that I am going,
because unless I go,
the Paraclete will not come to you;
but if I go,
I will send him to you.
8   And when he comes,
he will show the world how wrong it was, *b*
about sin,
and about who was in the right,
and about judgement:
9   about sin:
in that they refuse to believe in me; *c*
10   about who was in the right:
in that I am going to the Father
and you will see me no more; *d*
11   about judgement:
in that the prince of this world is already condemned. *e*
12   I still have many things to say to you
but they would be too much for you to bear now.
13   However, when the Spirit of truth comes
he will lead you to the complete truth,
since he will not be speaking of his own accord,
but will say only what he has been told;
and he will reveal to you the things to come. *f*
14   He will glorify me,
since all he reveals to you
will be taken from what is mine.
15   Everything the Father has is mine;
that is why I said:
all he reveals to you
will be taken from what is mine. *g*

Jesus to return very soon

16   In a short time you will no longer see me,
        and then a short time later you will see me again. *

17   Then some of his disciples said to one another, 'What does he mean, "In a short
     time you will no longer see me, and then a short time later you will see me again,"
18   and, "I am going to the Father"? ·What is this "short time"? ' We don't know
19   what he means.' ·Jesus knew that they wanted to question him, so he said, 'You
     are asking one another what I meant by saying, "In a short time you will no longer
     see me, and then a short time later you will see me again."

20   'In all truth I tell you,
        you will be weeping and wailing
        while the world will rejoice;
        you will be sorrowful,
        but your sorrow will turn to joy. ʲ

21   A woman in childbirth suffers,
        because her time has come; ᵏ
        but when she has given birth to the child she forgets the suffering
        in her joy that a human being has been born into the world.

22   So it is with you: you are sad now,
        but I shall see you again, and your hearts will be full of joy,
        and that joy no one shall take from you.

23   When that day comes,
        you will not ask me any questions.
        In all truth I tell you,
        anything you ask from the Father
        he will grant in my name.

24   Until now you have not asked anything in my name. ˡ
        Ask and you will receive,
        and so your joy will be complete.

25   I have been telling you these things in veiled language.
        The hour is coming
        when I shall no longer speak to you in veiled language;
        but tell you about the Father in plain words. ᵐ

26   When that day comes
        you will ask in my name;
        and I do not say that I shall pray to the Father ⁿ for you,

27   because the Father himself loves you
        for loving me,
        and believing that I came from God.

28   I came from the Father and have come into the world
        and now I am leaving the world to go to the Father.'

29   His disciples said, 'Now you are speaking plainly and not using veiled language.
30   Now we see that you know everything and need not wait for questions to be put
31   into words; because of this we believe that you came from God.' ·Jesus answered
     them:

        Do you believe at last?
32   Listen; the time will come—indeed it has come already—
        when you are going to be scattered, each going his own way

and leaving me alone.
And yet I am not alone,
because the Father is with me.

33   I have told you all this
so that you may find peace in me.
In the world you will have hardship,
but be courageous:
I have conquered the world.

The prayer of Jesus [a]

1   **17** After saying this, Jesus raised his eyes to heaven and said:

Father, the hour has come:
glorify your Son
so that your Son may glorify you; [b]

2   so that, just as you have given him power over all humanity,
he may give eternal life to all those you have entrusted to him.

3   And eternal life is this:
to know [c] you,
the only true God,
and Jesus Christ whom you have sent. [d]

4   I have glorified you on earth
by finishing the work
that you gave me to do.

5   Now, Father, glorify me
with that glory I had with you [e]
before ever the world existed. [f]

6   I have revealed your name [g]
to those whom you took from the world to give me.
They were yours and you gave them to me,
and they have kept your word.

7   Now at last they have recognised
that all you have given me comes from you;

8   for I have given them
the teaching you gave to me,
and they have indeed accepted it
and know for certain [h] that I came from you,
and have believed that it was you who sent me.

9   It is for them that I pray.
I am not praying for the world
but for those you have given me,
because they belong to you.

10   All I have is yours
and all you have is mine,
and in them I am glorified.

11   I am no longer in the world,
but they are in the world,
and I am coming to you.
Holy Father,
keep those you have given me true to your name, [i]

so that they may be one like us.

12 While I was with them,
I kept those you had given me true to your name.
I have watched over them and not one is lost
except one who was destined to be lost, *j*
and this was to fulfil the scriptures.

13 But now I am coming to you
and I say these things in the world
to share my joy with them to the full.

14 I passed your word on to them,
and the world hated them,
because they belong to the world
no more than I belong to the world.

15 I am not asking you to remove them from the world,
but to protect them from the Evil One. *k*

16 They do not belong to the world
any more than I belong to the world.

17 Consecrate *l* them in the truth;
your word is truth.

18 As you sent me into the world,
I have sent them into the world,

19 and for their sake I consecrate myself *m*
so that they too may be consecrated in truth.

20 I pray not only for these,
but also for those
who through their teaching will come to believe in me. *n*

21 May they all be one,
just as, Father, you are in me and I am in you,
so that they also may be in us,
so that the world may believe it was you who sent me.

22 I have given them the glory you gave to me,
that they may be one as we are one.

23 With me in them and you in me,
may they be so perfected in unity
that the world will recognise that it was you who sent me
and that you have loved them *o* as you loved me.

24 Father,
I want those you have given me
to be with me where I am,
so that they may always see my glory
which you have given me
because you loved me
before the foundation of the world.

25 Father, Upright One,
the world has not known you,
but I have known you,
and these have known
that you have sent me.

26 I have made your name known to them

and will continue to make it known,
so that the love with which you loved me may be in them,
and so that I may be in them.

B: THE PASSION

The arrest of Jesus

1　18 After he had said all this, Jesus left with his disciples and crossed the Kidron valley where there was a garden into which he went with his disciples.
2 Judas the traitor knew the place also, since Jesus had often met his disciples
3 there, ·so Judas brought the cohort * to this place together with guards sent by the chief priests and the Pharisees, all with lanterns and torches and weapons.
4 Knowing everything that was to happen to him, Jesus came forward and said,
5 'Who are you looking for?' ·They answered, 'Jesus the Nazarene.' He said, 'I am
6 he.' Now Judas the traitor was standing among them. ·When Jesus said to them, 'I
7 am he,' they moved back and fell on the ground. ·He asked them a second time,
8 'Who are you looking for?' They said, 'Jesus the Nazarene.' ·Jesus replied, 'I have told you that I am he. If I am the one you are looking for, let these others go.'
9 This was to fulfil the words he had spoken, 'Not one of those you gave me have I lost.'
10 Simon Peter, who had a sword, drew it and struck the high priest's servant,
11 cutting off his right ear. The servant's name was Malchus. ·Jesus said to Peter, 'Put your sword back in its scabbard; am I not to drink the cup that the Father has given me?'

Jesus before Annas and Caiaphas. Peter disowns him

12 The cohort and its tribune and the Jewish guards seized Jesus and bound him.
13 They took him first to Annas, because Annas was the father-in-law of Caiaphas,
14 who was high priest that year. ·It was Caiaphas who had counselled the Jews, 'It is better for one man to die for the people.'
15 Simon Peter, with another disciple, ᵇ followed Jesus. This disciple, who was
16 known to the high priest, went with Jesus into the high priest's palace, ·but Peter stayed outside the door. So the other disciple, the one known to the high priest,
17 went out, spoke to the door-keeper and brought Peter in. ·The girl on duty at the door said to Peter, 'Aren't you another of that man's disciples?' He answered, 'I
18 am not.' ·Now it was cold, and the servants and guards had lit a charcoal fire and were standing there warming themselves; so Peter stood there too, warming himself with the others.
19, 20 The high priest questioned Jesus about his disciples and his teaching. ·Jesus answered, 'I have spoken openly for all the world to hear; I have always taught in the synagogue and in the Temple where all the Jews meet together; I have said
21 nothing in secret. ·Why ask me? Ask my hearers what I taught; they know what I
22 said.' ·At these words, one of the guards standing by gave Jesus a slap in the face,
23 saying, 'Is that the way you answer the high priest?' ·Jesus replied, 'If there is
24 some offence in what I said, point it out; but if not, why do you strike me?' ·Then Annas sent him, bound, to Caiaphas the high priest. ᶜ
25 As Simon Peter stood there warming himself, someone said to him, 'Aren't you
26 another of his disciples?' He denied it saying, 'I am not.' ·One of the high priest's

servants, a relation of the man whose ear Peter had cut off, said, 'Didn't I see you
27 in the garden with him?' ·Again Peter denied it; and at once a cock crew.

Jesus before Pilate

28 They then led Jesus from the house of Caiaphas to the Praetorium. *ᵈ* It was now
morning. They did not go into the Praetorium themselves to avoid becoming
29 defiled *ᵉ* and unable to eat the Passover. ·So Pilate came outside to them and said,
30 'What charge do you bring against this man?' They replied, ·'If he were not a
31 criminal, we should not have handed him over to you.' ·Pilate said, 'Take him
yourselves, and try him by your own Law.' The Jews answered, 'We are not
32 allowed to put a man to death.' *ᶠ* ·This was to fulfil the words Jesus had spoken
indicating the way he was going to die.

33 So Pilate went back into the Praetorium and called Jesus to him and asked him,
34 'Are you the king of the Jews?' ·Jesus replied, 'Do you ask this of your own
35 accord, or have others said it to you about me?' ·Pilate answered, 'Am I a Jew? It
is your own people and the chief priests who have handed you over to me: what
36 have you done?' ·Jesus replied, 'Mine is not a kingdom of this world; if my
kingdom were of this world, my men would have fought to prevent my being
37 surrendered to the Jews. As it is, my kingdom does not belong here.' ·Pilate said,
'So, then you are a king?' Jesus answered, 'It is you who say that I am a king. I
was born for this, I came into the world for this, to bear witness to the truth; and
38 all who are on the side of truth listen to my voice.' ·'Truth?' said Pilate. 'What is
that?' And so saying he went out again to the Jews and said, 'I find no case against
39 him. ·But according to a custom of yours I should release one prisoner at the
40 Passover; would you like me, then, to release for you the king of the Jews?' ·At
this they shouted, 'Not this man,' they said, 'but Barabbas.' Barabbas was a bandit.

1, 2 **19** Pilate then had Jesus taken away and scourged; *ᵃ* ·and after this, the soldiers
twisted some thorns into a crown and put it on his head and dressed him in
3 a purple robe. ·They kept coming up to him and saying, 'Hail, king of the Jews!'
and slapping him in the face.

4 Pilate came outside again and said to them, 'Look, I am going to bring him out
5 to you to let you see that I find no case against him.' ·Jesus then came out wearing
6 the crown of thorns and the purple robe. Pilate said, 'Here is the man.' ·When
they saw him, the chief priests and the guards shouted, 'Crucify him! Crucify him!'
7 Pilate said, 'Take him yourselves and crucify him: I find no case against him.' ·The
Jews replied, 'We have a Law, and according to that Law he ought to be put to
death, because he has claimed to be Son of God.'

8, 9 When Pilate heard them say this his fears increased. ·Re-entering the Praetorium, he said to Jesus, 'Where do you come from?' *ᵇ* But Jesus made no answer.
10 Pilate then said to him, 'Are you refusing to speak to me? Surely you know I have
11 power to release you and I have power to crucify you?' ·Jesus replied, 'You would
have no power over me at all if it had not been given you from above; that is why
the one who handed me over to you has the greater guilt.' *ᶜ*

Jesus is condemned to death

12 From that moment Pilate was anxious to set him free, but the Jews shouted, 'If
you set him free you are no friend of Caesar's; anyone who makes himself king is
13 defying Caesar.' ·Hearing these words, Pilate had Jesus brought out, and seated
him on the chair of judgement at a place called the Pavement, in Hebrew
14 Gabbatha. *ᵈ* ·It was the Day of Preparation, *ᵉ* about the sixth hour. *ᶠ* 'Here is your

15 king,' said Pilate to the Jews. •But they shouted,[g] 'Away with him, away with him,
crucify him.' Pilate said, 'Shall I crucify your king?' The chief priests answered, 'We
16 have no king except Caesar.' •So at that Pilate handed him over to them to be
crucified.

The crucifixion

17 They then took charge of Jesus,[h] •and carrying his own cross he went out to the
18 Place of the Skull or, as it is called in Hebrew, Golgotha, •where they crucified
19 him with two others, one on either side, Jesus being in the middle. •Pilate wrote
out a notice and had it fixed to the cross; it ran 'Jesus the Nazarene, King of the
20 Jews'. •This notice was read by many of the Jews, because the place where Jesus
was crucified was near the city, and the writing was in Hebrew, Latin and Greek.
21 So the Jewish chief priests said to Pilate, 'You should not write "King of the
22 Jews", but that the man said, "I am King of the Jews". ' •Pilate answered, 'What
I have written, I have written.'

Jesus' garments divided

23 When the soldiers had finished crucifying Jesus they took his clothing and divided
it into four shares, one for each soldier. His undergarment was seamless,[i] woven
24 in one piece from neck to hem; •so they said to one another, 'Instead of tearing it,
let's throw dice to decide who is to have it.' In this way the words of scripture were
fulfilled:

They divide my garments among them
and cast lots for my clothes.

That is what the soldiers did.

Jesus and his mother

25 Near the cross of Jesus stood his mother[j] and his mother's sister,[k] Mary the wife
26 of Clopas, and Mary of Magdala. •Seeing his mother and the disciple whom he
27 loved standing near her, Jesus said to his mother, 'Woman, this is your son.' •Then
to the disciple he said, 'This is your mother.'[l] And from that hour the disciple
took her into his home.

The death of Jesus

28 After this, Jesus knew that everything had now been completed and, so that the
scripture should be completely fulfilled, he said:

I am thirsty.

29 A jar full of sour wine stood there; so, putting a sponge soaked in the wine on a
30 hyssop stick,[m] they held it up to his mouth. •After Jesus had taken the wine he
said, 'It is fulfilled';[n] and bowing his head he gave up his spirit.[o]

The pierced Christ

31 It was the Day of Preparation, and to avoid the bodies' remaining on the cross
during the Sabbath—since that Sabbath was a day of special solemnity—the Jews
32 asked Pilate to have the legs broken[p] and the bodies taken away. •Consequently
the soldiers came and broke the legs of the first man who had been crucified with
33 him and then of the other. •When they came to Jesus, they saw[q] he was already
34 dead, and so instead of breaking his legs •one of the soldiers pierced his side with

35 a lance; and immediately there came out blood and water.ʳ ·This is the evidence of one who saw itʹ—true evidence, and heʹ knows that what he says is true—and
36 he gives it so that you may believe as well. ·Because all this happened to fulfil the words of scripture:

> Not one bone of his will be broken;ᵘ

37 and again, in another place scripture says:

> They will look to the one whom they have pierced.ᵛ

The burial

38 After this, Joseph of Arimathaea, who was a disciple of Jesus—though a secret one because he was afraid of the Jews—asked Pilate to let him remove the body of
39 Jesus. Pilate gave permission, so theyʷ came and took it away. ·Nicodemus came as well—the same one who had first come to Jesus at night-time—and he brought
40 a mixture of myrrh and aloes, weighing about a hundred pounds. ·They took the body of Jesus and bound it in linen cloths with the spices, following the Jewish
41 burial custom. ·At the place where he had been crucified there was a garden, and
42 in this garden a new tomb in which no one had yet been buried. ·Since it was the Jewish Day of Preparation and the tomb was nearby, they laid Jesus there.

C: THE DAY OF CHRIST'S RESURRECTION

The empty tomb

1 **20** It was very early on the first day of the weekᵃ and still dark, when Mary of Magdala came to the tomb. She saw that the stone had been moved away
2 from the tomb ·and came running to Simon Peter and the other disciple, the one whom Jesus loved. 'They have taken the Lord out of the tomb,' she said, 'and we don't know where they have put him.'
3, 4 So Peter set out with the other disciple to go to the tomb. ·They ran together,
5 but the other disciple, running faster than Peter, reached the tomb first; ·he bent
6 down and saw the linen cloths lying on the ground, but did not go in.ᵇ ·Simon Peter, following him, also came up, went into the tomb, saw the linen cloths lying
7 on the ground ·and also the cloth that had been over his head; this was not with
8 the linen cloths but rolled up in a place by itself. ·Then the other disciple who had
9 reached the tomb first also went in; he saw and he believed. ·Till this moment
10 they had still not understood the scripture,ᶜ that he must rise from the dead. ·The disciples then went back home.

The appearance to Mary of Magdala

11 But Mary was standing outside near the tomb, weeping. Then, as she wept, she
12 stooped to look inside, ·and saw two angels in white sitting where the body of
13 Jesus had been, one at the head, the other at the feet. ·They said, 'Woman, why are you weeping?' 'They have taken my Lord away,' she replied, 'and I don't
14 know where they have put him.' ·As she said this she turned round and saw Jesus
15 standing there, though she did not realise that it was Jesus.·Jesus said to her, 'Woman, why are you weeping? Who are you looking for?' Supposing him to be the gardener, she said, 'Sir, if you have taken him away, tell me where you have
16 put him, and I will go and remove him.' ·Jesus said, 'Mary!' She turned roundᵈ

17 then and said to him in Hebrew, 'Rabbuni!' '—which means Master. ·Jesus said to
her, 'Do not cling to me,' because I have not yet ascended to the Father. But go
and find my brothers,' and tell them: I am ascending to my Father' and your
18 Father, to my God and your God.' ·So Mary of Magdala told the disciples, 'I have
seen the Lord,' and that he had said these things to her.

Appearances to the disciples

19 In the evening of that same day, the first day of the week, the doors were closed in
the room where the disciples were,' for fear of the Jews. Jesus came and stood
20 among them. He said to them, 'Peace be with you,' ·and, after saying this, he
showed them his hands and his side. The disciples were filled with joy at seeing
21 the Lord, ·and he said to them again, 'Peace be with you.

> 'As the Father sent me,
> so am I sending you.'

22 After saying this he breathed' on them and said:

> Receive the Holy Spirit.
23 > If you forgive anyone's sins,
> they are forgiven;
> if you retain anyone's sins,
> they are retained.

24 Thomas, called the Twin, who was one of the Twelve, was not with them when
25 Jesus came. ·So the other ' disciples said to him, 'We have seen the Lord,' but he
answered, 'Unless I can see the holes that the nails made in his hands and can put
my finger into the holes they made, and unless I can put my hand into his side, I
26 refuse to believe.' ·Eight days later the disciples were in the house again and
Thomas was with them. The doors were closed, but Jesus came in and stood
27 among them. 'Peace be with you,' he said. ·Then he spoke to Thomas, 'Put your
finger here; look, here are my hands. Give me your hand; put it into my side. ' Do
28 not be unbelieving any more but believe.' ·Thomas replied, 'My Lord and my
29 God!' Jesus said to him:

> You believe because you can see me.
> Blessed are those who have not seen and yet believe. ∎

D: FIRST CONCLUSION

30 There were many other signs that Jesus worked in the sight of the disciples, but
31 they are not recorded in this book. ·These are recorded so that you may believe
that Jesus is the Christ, the Son of God, and that believing this you may have life
through his name.

D: EPILOGUE*a*

The appearance on the shore of Tiberias

1 **21** Later on, Jesus revealed himself again to the disciples. It was by the Sea of
2 Tiberias, and it happened like this: ·Simon Peter, Thomas called the Twin,

Nathanael from Cana in Galilee, the sons of Zebedee and two more of his disciples
3 were together. ·Simon Peter said, 'I'm going fishing.' They replied, 'We'll come
with you.' They went out and got into the boat but caught nothing that night.
4 When it was already light, there stood Jesus on the shore, though the disciples
5 did not realise that it was Jesus. ·Jesus called out, 'Haven't you caught anything,
6 friends?' And when they answered, 'No,' ·he said, 'Throw the net out to starboard
and you'll find something.' So they threw the net out and could not haul it in
7 because of the quantity of fish. *ᵇ* ·The disciple whom Jesus loved said to Peter, 'It
is the Lord.' At these words 'It is the Lord,' Simon Peter tied his outer garment
8 round him (for he had nothing on) and jumped into the water. ·The other disciples
came on in the boat, towing the net with the fish; they were only about a hundred
yards from land.
9 As soon as they came ashore they saw that there was some bread there and a
10 charcoal fire with fish cooking on it. ·Jesus said, 'Bring some of the fish you have
11 just caught.' ·Simon Peter went aboard and dragged the net ashore, *ᶜ* full of big
fish, one hundred and fifty-three of them; and in spite of there being so many the
12 net was not broken. ·Jesus said to them, 'Come and have breakfast.' None of the
disciples was bold enough to ask, 'Who are you?' They knew quite well it was the
13 Lord. ·Jesus then stepped forward, took the bread and gave it to them, and the
14 same with the fish. ·This was the third time that Jesus revealed himself to the
disciples after rising from the dead.
15 When they had eaten, Jesus said to Simon Peter, 'Simon son of John, do you
love me more than these others do?' He answered, 'Yes, Lord, you know I love
16 you.' Jesus said to him, 'Feed my lambs.' ·A second time he said to him, 'Simon
son of John, do you love me?' He replied, 'Yes, Lord, you know I love you.' Jesus
17 said to him, 'Look after my sheep.' ·Then he said to him a third time, 'Simon son
of John, do you love me?' Peter was hurt that he asked him a third time, *ᵈ* 'Do you
love me?' *ᵉ* and said, 'Lord, you know everything; you know I love you.' Jesus said
to him, 'Feed my sheep.*ᶠ*

18 In all truth I tell you,
    when you were young
    you put on your own belt
    and walked where you liked;
    but when you grow old
    you will stretch out your hands,
    and somebody else will put a belt round you
    and take you where you would rather not go.'

19 In these words he indicated the kind of death *ᵍ* by which Peter would give glory to
God. After this he said, 'Follow me.' *ʰ*

20 Peter turned and saw the disciple whom Jesus loved following them—the one
who had leant back close to his chest at the supper and had said to him, 'Lord,
21 who is it that will betray you?' ·Seeing him, Peter said to Jesus, 'What about him,
22 Lord?' ·Jesus answered, 'If I want him to stay behind till I come, *ⁱ* what does it
23 matter to you? You are to follow me.' ·The rumour then went out among the
brothers that this disciple would not die. Yet Jesus had not said to Peter, 'He will
not die,' but, 'If I want him to stay behind till I come.' *ʲ*

E: SECOND CONCLUSION

24 This disciple is the one who vouches for these things and has written them down, and we know *k* that his testimony is true.

25 There was much else that Jesus did; if it were written down in detail, I do not suppose the world itself would hold all the books that would be written.

NOTES TO JOHN

1 a. The OT speaks of the Word of God, and of his Wisdom, present with God before the world was made. *see* Pr 8:22e; Ws 7:22i; by it all things were created; it is sent to earth to reveal the hidden designs of God; it returns to him with its work done. Pr 8:22–36; Ws 9:9–12; Si 24:3–22; Is 55:10–11. On its creative role, *see also* Gn 1:3,6; Jdt 16:14; Ps 33:6; Si 42:15; Is 40:8,26; 44:24–28; 48:13; on its mission, *see* Ps 107:20; 147:15–18; Ws 18:14–16. For John, too, 13:3; 16:28, the Word existed before the world in God. vv. 1,2; 8:24g; 10:30p; it has come on earth. vv. 9–14; 3:19; 9:39; 12:46. *see* Mk 1:38n. being sent by the Father. 3:17,34; 5:36,43; 6:29; 7:29; 8:42; 9:7; 10:36; 11:42; 17:3,25. cf. Lk 4:43. to perform a task. Jn 4:34k. namely, to deliver a message of salvation to the world. Jn 1:33x; 3:11e; with its mission accomplished it returns to the Father. Jn 1:18; 7:33; 8:21; 12:35; 13:3; 16:5; 17:11,13; 20:17. The Incarnation enabled the NT, and especially John, to see this separately and eternally existent Word-Wisdom as a person, but this personification is present also in other passages, such as Heb 1:1–2; 1 Jn 1:1–2; Rv 19:13.

b. Alternatively, these words may be joined with what precedes, to give 'and of all that has come to be not one thing had its being except through him'. In that case v. 4 would begin 'In him was life and that life . . .'

c. var. 'is life in him'.

d. The Light (Goodness; the Word) cannot be imprisoned by Darkness (Evil; the powers of evil). cf. 7:33seq.; 8:21; 12:31,32; 14:30; 1 Jn 2:8,14; 4:4; 5:18. Others translate 'could not understand'.

e. Vv. 6–8 form a parenthesis on the mission of John the Baptist. Similarly v. 15; *see* Mt 3:1 and par.

f. Other possible translations: 'The true light, that which enlightens every man, was coming into the world,' or 'He (the Word) was the real light that enlightens every man who comes into the world.'

g. The 'world' variously means: the cosmos or this earth, the human race, those hostile to God who hate Christ and his disciples, 7:7; 15:18,19; 17:14. This last sense coincides with the contemporary Jewish distinction between 'this world', 8:23 and passim, dominated by Satan, 12:31; 14:30; 16:11; 1 Jn 5:19, and 'the world to come' which possibly corresponds to John's 'eternal life', 12:25. The disciples are to remain *in* this world for the present, though not *of* it, 17:11.14seq., compare the pejorative sense of 'earth' in Rv 6:15; 13:3,8; 14:3; 17:2,5,8; *see also* Rm 8:16j.

h. Probably the Jews.

i. var. 'to be called'.

j. 'to those who believe in his name' omitted by many of the Fathers. Those who believe in the Son of God, 3:15j, themselves become children of God, Mt 5:9; 6:9; Rm 8:14; Ga 3:26o; 4:5d; Jm 1:27p; 1 Jn 3:1.

k. The same terms are used in the *Book of Enoch*, 15:4, to describe the birth of the giants, the product of the union of angels with the daughters of men. The original reading may be a shorter one, 'not from human stock or human desire'. • There are strong arguments for reading the verb in the singular, 'who was born', in which case the v. refers to

Jesus' divine origin, not to the virgin birth. We retain the verb in the singular although it is a minority view

l. Even though it is the place of revelation, the 'flesh' considered as frail and mortal denotes humanity, *see* 3:6; 17:2; Gn 6:3; Ps 56:5; Is 40:6. The use of this term, *see* Rm 7:5c, stresses the reality of the coming of Christ in human nature, which Jn constantly brings out. Later the term 'Incarnation' will come into use, *see* 1 Jn 4:2; 2 Jn 7; and in Paul Rm 1:3; Ga 4:4; Ph 2:7; Col 1:19.

m. The Incarnation of the Word makes God personally and visibly present; it is no longer a presence unseen and awe-inspiring as in the Tent and Temple of the old régime. Ex 25:8d; cf. Nb 35:34, nor merely the presence of divine Wisdom enshrined in Israel's Mosaic Law, Si 24:7–22; Ba 3:36–4:4.

n. The 'glory' is the manifestation of God's presence. Ex 24:16f. No one could see its brilliance and live, Ex 33:20i, but the human nature of the Word now screens this glory as the cloud once did. Yet at times it pierces the veil, at the transfiguration, for instance, cf. Lk 9:32,35 (alluded to in Jn 1:14?), and when Jesus works miracles—'signs' that God is active in him, Jn 2:11f; 11:40; cf. 14:24–27 and 15:7; 16:7seq. The resurrection will reveal the glory fully, *see* 17:5f.

o. 'Grace and truth' recalls the 'grace' (or 'love') and 'faithfulness' of God's self-revelation to Moses. Ex 34:6c. *see* Ho 2:16–22, with whom the Word is contrasted. *see* 2:11f; 6:31i.

p. An alternative translation is 'grace upon grace'.

q. var. 'God the only Son'. Jesus is the only Son, vv. 14,18; 3:16–18, beloved of the Father, 15:9; 17:23, in complete reciprocal intimacy with him, 10:30–38p; 14:10–11; 17:21, in knowledge and love, 5:20,30; 10:15; 14:31; cf. Mt 11:27 and par.

r. In Jn this usually indicates the Jewish religious authorities hostile to Jesus, 2:18; 5:10; 7:13; 9:22; 18:12; 19:38; 20:19, but occasionally the Jews as a whole. Cf. v. 11h.

s. On the expected return of Elijah, *see* Ml 3:23–24 and Mk 9:12.

t. From Dt 18:15,18e the Jews argued that the expected Messiah would be another Moses (the prophet *par excellence*, *see* Nb 12:7d) who would repeat on a grand scale the prodigies of the Exodus; *see* Jn 3:14; 6:14,30–31; 7:40,52; 13:1a; Ac 3:22–23; 7:20–44; Heb 3:1–11. *See also* Mt 16:14c.

u. Not the Bethany near Jerusalem, 11:18.

v. One of the most significant of John's symbols of Christ, cf. Rv 5:6,12; etc. It blends the idea of the 'servant' (Is 53), who takes all sin on himself and offers himself as a 'lamb of expiation' (Lv 14), with that of the Passover lamb (Ex 12:1a; *see also* Jn 19:36) in the ritual which symbolises Israel's redemption; cf. Ac 8:31–35; 1 Co 5:7; 1 P 1:18–20.

w. om. 'like a dove'.

x. This phrase sums up the whole purpose of the Messiah's coming, *see* v. 1a, namely, that humanity might be born again in the Spirit; the OT had already foretold it, *see* Ac 2:33u. The Spirit rests on him, 1:33; Is 11:2; 42:1; and so he can confer it on others (baptism in the Spirit, *see* here and Ac 1:5f), but only after his resurrection, 7:39;

16:7,8; 20:22; Ac 2. For Jesus 'came in the flesh'. 1 Jn 4:2; 2 Jn 7, flesh that was corruptible, v. 14*l*, and it is only when he is 'lifted up' and has gone to the Father that his body, glorified now, is fully endowed with divine, life-giving power. Thenceforward the Spirit flows freely to the world from this body as from an inexhaustible spring: 7:37–39; 19:34r; *see* Rm 5:5e. For the water symbolism, *see* 4:1a.

y. var. 'the Son of God'.

z. About 4 pm. Throughout this first week the days are carefully noted: vv. 29, 35, 41, 43; 2:1a.

aa. var. 'early in the morning'.

bb. Perhaps the Bartholomew of the Synoptics, Mt 10:3 and par.; cf. Jn 21:2.

cc. 'of him'; var. 'of Nathanael' or 'to him'.

dd. Jesus' supernatural knowledge of persons and things is one of the features of Jn's portrait of him, *see* 2:24seq.; 4:17–19,29; 6:61,64,71; 13:1,11,27,28; 16:19,30; 18:4; 21:17.

ee. In this passage the phrase implies only that he is Messiah (like 'king of Israel'); *see* Mt 4:3d.

ff. Jacob's dream, Gn 28:10–17, will be fulfilled when the Son of man is 'lifted up', Jn 3:14i.

2 a. i.e. three days after the meeting with Philip and Nathanael. The opening events of the Gospel, therefore, are contained within one week of which almost every day is noticed, *see* 1:39z; it culminates in the manifestation of Christ's glory.

b. Mary is present when Jesus first manifests his glory; she is there again at the cross, 19:25–27. The two descriptions have several details in common, evidently of set purpose.

c. Unusual address from son to mother; the term is used again in 19:26, where its meaning becomes clear as an allusion to Gn 3:15,20; Mary is the new Eve, 'mother of the living'.

d. lit. 'What to me and to thee', a Semitic formula not infrequent in OT, Jg 11:12; 2 S 16:10; 19:23; 1 K 17:18; etc., and in NT, Mt 8:29; Mk 1:24; 5:7; Lk 4:34; 8:28. It is used to deprecate interference or, more strongly, to reject overtures of any kind. The shade of meaning can be deduced only from the context. Here, Jesus objects that his hour has not yet come.

e. The 'hour' of his glorification and of his return to the Father's right hand. Its approach is noted by the evangelist, 7:30; 8:20; 12:23,27; 13:1; 17:1; 19:27. This 'hour' is determined by the Father and cannot be anticipated, though the miracle worked through Mary's intervention is a prophetic symbol of it.

f. For credentials, every true prophet must have 'signs', or wonders worked in God's name, Is 7:11; *see* Jn 3:2; 6:29,30; 7:3,31; 9:16,33; of the Messiah it was expected that he would repeat the Mosaic miracles, Jn 1:21t. Jesus, therefore, works 'signs' in order to stimulate faith in his divine mission, vv. 11,23; 4:48–54; 11:15,42; 12:37; *see also* 3:11e. And indeed his 'works' show that God has sent him, 5:36; 10:25,37, that the Father is within him, 10:30p, manifesting the divine glory in power, 1:14n; it is the Father himself who does the works, 10:38; 14:10. But many refuse to believe, 3:12; 5:38–47; 6:36,64; 7:5; 8:45; 10:25; 12:37, and their sin remains, 9:41; 15:24.

g. In the fourth Gospel, Jesus frequently uses terms which, in addition to their obvious meaning appreciated by the audience, possess a metaphorical and higher sense; *see* v. 20 (Temple); 3:4 (new birth); 4:15 (living water); 6:34 (bread of life); 7:35 (to depart); 11:11 (to awaken); 12:34 (to lift up); 13:9 (to wash); 13:36seq. (to depart); 14:22 (to show oneself). Consequent misapprehensions provide an opportunity for explanatory developments, *see* 3:11e.

h. Reconstruction work on the Temple began in 19 BC. This, therefore, is the Passover of AD 28 or later.

i. One of the great Johannine symbols, *see* Rv 21:22; *see also* Paul, 1 Co 12:12b. The body of the risen Christ is to be the focus of worship in spirit and truth, 4:21seq., the shrine of the Presence, 1:14, the spiritual temple from which living waters flow, 7:37–39; 19:34.

3 a. A phrase common in the Synoptics, Mt 4:17f, but occurring only here (and v. 5) in Jn; its Johannine equivalent is 'life' or 'eternal life'.

b. Here preferred to 'again'

c. Allusion to baptism and its necessity, *see* Rm 6:4a.

d. In Greek, as in Hebr., one word serves for both 'wind' and 'spirit'.

e. Jesus does not speak on his own initiative, 7:17–18; he declares what he has seen 'with the Father', 1:18; 3:11; 8:38; *see* 8:24g; it is the Father's words and teaching that he hands on to us, 3:34; 8:28; 12:49,50; 14:24; 17:8,14; he is himself the Word, 1:1,14. This Word is not idle: it calls all things from nothing, 1:1a, it calls the dead from the tomb, 5:28–29; 11:43,44; it gives life to the soul, 5:24; 6:63; 8:51; it confers the Spirit, the source of immortality, 1:33x; 20:22, and so makes people children of God, 1:12; 10:35. It is required only that someone should have faith in the Word, 1:12, 'dwell' in it, *see* 8:31, 'keep' it, 8:51,55; 12:47; 14:23; 15:20; 17:6, obey its command which is love, 13:34u. Nevertheless, the Word is enigmatic, 2:19g, and difficult, *see* 6:60; 7:36; it makes its way only into humble hearts. Those who hear it, therefore, respond differently, 7:43; 10:19: some believe, 4:41; 7:40seq., 46; 8:30, others go away disappointed, 6:66, in spite of the 'signs', 2:11f; this same rejected Word will judge them at the last day, 12:48.

f. The constant recourse to evidence gives Jn the form of a vast trial, *see* 5:22i. Heralded by the witness of John the Baptist, 1:7–8,15,19; 3:26; 5:33; 10:41, Jesus witnesses to the truth, 18:37, against the world, 7:7, to the Father and to himself as the messenger of the Father, 3:11,31–32; 5:26; 10:25; cf. 1 Tm 6:13; Rv 1:5; 3:14. The climax of the trial comes at Jesus' own trial before Pilate, *see* 18:28d. The Father in his turn bears witness to the Son, 5:31–37; 8:18; and also the Spirit, 15:26; *see* 14:26; Rm 8:16; 1 Jn 5:6–12. To this group of witnesses the apostles, *see* 17:20, join their witness, 15:27; 19:35; Ac 1:8k.

g. 'Believing', *see* Mt 8:10b; Rm 1:16h, consists in Jn in 'accepting' Jesus, 1:12; 5:43, in 'knowing' him, and the Father with him, 10:38; 14:7, in recognising him as the messenger and the Son, 3:16–18; 14:1,10; 17:8,21–25; 20:31, in coming to him, 6:35, in 'seeing' him, 6:36,40; 11:40; 20:8,29. Aroused by signs, 2:11f; 4:53; 20:31, and based on evidence, 3:11f; 10:25, it leads to eternal life, 3:15j; 5:25; 10:26–28m. It is expressed in the love which keeps God's word and commandments. This fundamental attitude towards himself is the criterion on which Jesus judges, 3:17–18, 36; 5:29,44–47.

h. Possibly a denial that any of the revealers renowned in contemporary Jewish literature had in fact ascended into heaven; the only true source of revelation is Jesus who descended from heaven. Possibly an allusion to the ascension, which will both show that Jesus really came from heaven and also establish the Son of man on his glorious throne.

i. The Son of man, *see* Dn 7:13k; Mt 8:20h; 12:32; 24:30, must be lifted up, at the same time on the cross and back into the glory of the Father, 1:51; 8:28; 12:32–34,32j; 13:31–32. To be saved one must 'look on' him 'lifted up' on the cross, 19:37v; Nb 21:8; Zc 12:10f, that is, believe that he is the only Son, Jn 3:18. One will then be cleansed by the water from his pierced side, 19:34; Zc 13:1. In Jn the title shows an insistence on the humanity of Jesus, although his divine origin, stressed in v. 13; 16:62, occasions actions where he anticipates eschatological prerogatives, 5:26–29; 6:27,53; 9:35.

j. var. 'so that everyone who believes in him may receive eternal life'. God, absolute master of life, Gn 9:4–5; Dt 32:39; Ps 36:10, has passed on this mastery to the Son, Jn 5:21; 10:18j; 17:2. The Son is himself life, 11:25; 14:6. He has life in himself and gives life, 5:26, to those who believe in him, 1:4,12; 4:14; 5:24; 6:35; 20:31. This life is signified by water, 4:1a, and nourished by the word, 6:35k. It is often called 'eternal', a word which denotes a quality properly divine which puts this life beyond what is corporeal, beyond time and beyond measure, cf. Gn 21:33; Ps 90:2;

Ws 5:15–16; Is 40:28. It is promised to believers, *see also* 2 Co 4:18, but already given to them, Jn 3:36; 5:24; 6:40, 68; 1 Jn 2:25; it will be completed by the resurrection, 6:39–40,54; 11:25–26; *see also* 7:14; 18:8; 19:16.

k. Semitism: the 'name' is the person.

l. See 1 Jn 3:19g.

m. Presumably a baptism of the same nature as the Baptist's; a baptism of repentance in preparation for the coming of the kingdom.

n. A tradition locates Aenon ('the Springs') in the Jordan valley about 7 miles (12km) south of Scythopolis. Ain Farah is also a possibility.

o. About baptism probably. • a Jew'; var. 'Jews'. The text is corrupt. The reading may have been 'Jesus' or 'the disciples of Jesus'.

p. The OT uses the marriage metaphor to express the relationship between God and Israel, Ho 1:2b. Jesus applies it to himself, Mt 9:15 and par.; 22:1seq.; 25:1seq.; *see also* Paul in 2 Co 11:2; Ep 5:22seq. The Messiah's coming has brought joy to the world, v. 29, cf. 1:29,36–39; 2:1–11, consequently the marriage feast of the Lamb, Rv 19:7; 21:2, has already begun.

q. Or perhaps 'everything'.

r. add. 'is above everything'.

s. Or 'and gives the Spirit without reserve'.

t. By the Father's decree, all things are 'in the hands' (or 'power') of the Son, v. 35; 10:28,29; 13:3; 17:2; cf. 6:37–39; Mt 11:27; 28:18; on this is based the sovereignty, Jn 12:13–15; 18:36–37, that he will assume on the day of his 'lifting up', Jn 12:32j; 19:19; Ac 2:33; Ep 4:8; and on that day, the 'prince of this world' will forfeit his kingdom, Jn 12:31.

4 a. Meetings at a well are a feature of the patriarchal narratives: Gn 25:10seq.; 29:1seq.; Ex 2:15seq. Wells and springs play a significant part in the life and religion of the patriarchal and Exodus periods: Gn 26:14–22; Ex 15:22–27; 17:1–7. In the OT, spring water symbolises the life that God gives, especially that of the messianic age: Ps 36:8–9; Is 12:3–4; 55:1; Jr 2:13; Ezk 47:1seq. (cf. Ps 46:4 and Zc 14:8 and in the NT: Rv 7:16–17; 22:17); it symbolises also the life imparted by divine Wisdom and by the Law, Pr 13:14; Si 15:3; 24:23–29. This symbolism is carried further in the gospel narrative: living (i.e. spring) water signifies the Spirit, *see* 1:33x; 7:37–39.

b. var. 'the Lord'.

c. Either the ancient Shechem (Sichara in Aramaic) or the present village of Askar at the foot of Mt Ebal, about .75 mile (1km) from 'Jacob's Well'. The well is not mentioned in Gn.

d. Noon.

e. Some authorities omit this parenthesis. • The Jews hated the Samaritans, 8:48; Si 50:25–26; Lk 9:52–55, cf. Mt 10:5; Lk 10:33; 17:16, and attributed their origin to the importation of five gentile groups, 2 K 17:24–41, who retained some of their loyalty to their old gods; these may be symbolised by the 'five husbands' of v. 18.

f. i.e. Gerizim; on this mountain the Samaritans had built a rival to the Jerusalem Temple; it was destroyed by John Hyrcanus in 129 BC.

g. var. 'is where one ought to worship'.

h. The Spirit, 14:26r, who makes a person a new creature, 3:5, is also the inspiring principle of the new worship of God. This worship is 'in truth' because it is the only worship that meets the conditions revealed by God through Jesus.

i. var. 'those who worship him', *see* 12:20.

j. Alternatively 'went away'.

k. That Jesus was sent by the Father was taught by Paul and the writers of the Synoptic Gospels, but John stresses this repeatedly, to the point of insistence, 3:17; 5:24,36–38; 8:42; 9:7; 11:42; 17:8,21–25. Jesus has his origin in the Father, 3:31; 6:46; 7:29; 8:42, comes down from the Father, 3:13; 6:38,42. He speaks the words of the Father, 3:34; 7:16; 8:26–28; 12:49–50; 14:24; 17:8,14, he does the will of the Father, 9:4; 10:32,37; 14:10. Faith, 3:12g, consists in recog-

nising him as the envoy of the Father, 7:28–29; 17:21,25; 19:9b. Later the apostles will be similarly sent, 13:20; 17:18; 20:21. *see* 17:20n; Ac 1:26; 22:21i; Rm 1:1b.

l. A harvest of souls: the Samaritans who are coming to Jesus, v. 30, are its first-fruits.

m. The reapers are the disciples, the sowers those who have laboured before them, especially Jesus.

n. Not merely 'King of Israel' as in 1:49. This world-perspective is typical of John, *see* 1:29; 3:16; 11:52; 1 Jn 2:2. Nevertheless, 'salvation comes from the Jews', v. 22.

5 a. var. 'the festival'. Possibly Pentecost.

b. var. 'Bethzatha', 'Bethsaida', 'Belsetha'. 'Bethesda' means 'house of mercy'. • The fifth portico divided the rectangle into two pools; here the water gathered, to be used afterwards in the Temple. Besides these two reservoirs there were other smaller pools attached to a pagan healing sanctuary.

c. Some witnesses add: 'waiting for the water to move;[4] for at intervals the angel of the Lord came down into the pool, and the water was disturbed, and the first person to enter the water after this disturbance was cured of any ailment from which he was suffering.

d. Jesus does not say that the disease was the result of sin, cf. 9:2seq. He warns the man that his cure is a divine favour that must be acknowledged by conversion, cf. Mt 9:2–8; to forget this is to risk something worse than the disease. The miracle is therefore a 'sign' of spiritual resurrection, v. 24.

e. The episode is concluded in 7:19–24. Jesus identifies his own activity with that of the sovereign Judge. Hence the anger of the Jews and the discourse by which Jesus justifies his claim, cf. Lk 6:5, and especially Mt 12:1–8.

f. Jewish theologians reconciled the fact that God 'rested' after the work of creation (the Sabbath was the human counterpart of this 'rest', Gn 2:2seq.) with his unceasing, active government of the world, by distinguishing between God's activity as Creator, which is now at an end, and his activity as judge (or 'governor'), which never ends.

g. The discourse of vv. 19–47 is one of the fullest explanations in Jn of the relationship between Son and Father, and shows in dynamic terms the divine powers of the Son. It falls into two parts: 1 The Father commits lifegiving power to the Son, vv. 19–30. 2 The Father bears witness to the Son: a through the Baptist, b through the works that the Father does through Jesus, c through the scriptures (Moses), vv. 31–47.

h. Power over life and death is the supreme power of the judge, *see* v. 21.

i. Jesus will be the supreme judge at the Last Day, vv. 26–30; 12:48; *see* Mt 25:31–46; Rm 2:6b. This judgement will reveal the outcome of the trial, *see* 3:11f, which began with the coming of the Son, v. 25; 12:31. All people will be judged by faith, 3:12g, given or refused to Jesus, 3:18–21; 16:8–11, Saviour of all who do not reject him, 3:18; 8:15; 12:47. In fact the texts about judgement belong to different phases of editing, the eschatological judgement on the Last Day, and the judgement which has already taken place.

j. Those who are spiritually dead, though *see* vv. 28 and 29.

k. The reference is to the resurrection of the dead at the Last Day, cf. Mt 22:29–32.

l. Jesus listens to the Father.

m. The Father.

n. var. 'you know', wrongly making this verse refer to the Baptist's testimony, v. 33.

o. Alternative translation 'pore over', imperative.

p. The scriptures are the source of life because they transmit to us God's word, *see* Dt 4:1; 8:1,3; 30:15–20; 32:46seq.; Ps 119; Ba 4:1.

q. The scriptures converge on Jesus who is their fulfilment, *see* 1:45; 2:22; 5:39,46; 12:16,41; 19:28; 20:9.

r. var. 'from the Only One'.

6 a. The bread Jesus gives is to be the new Passover.

b. var. 'withdrew'.

c. om. 'Do not be afraid'.

d. Some interpreters hold that a discourse about the Eucharist (vv. 51–58: Jesus nourishing the soul with his flesh and blood, see vv. 51p) has been inserted into the narrative-discourse which may be described as follows: the Jews ask for a 'sign' like that of the manna, vv. 30–31; see 1:21t; Jesus tells them, 'The Father's message, which I pass on (see 3:11e) makes of me true bread, a nourishment that only those with faith can receive,' vv. 32seq.; the Jews do not understand, vv. 60–66; only Peter and the disciples believe, vv. 67–71. More probably vv. 31–58 may be understood as one integral sermon after the Jewish homiletic midrash tradition; v. 31 gives a scriptural text, of which the first part ('bread from heaven') is explained in vv. 32–48, and the second ('to eat') in vv. 49–58. (This doctrine is best understood in the light of Dt 8:3; Pr 8:22–24; 9:1–6; Si 24:3,17–21; Lk 11:29–32.)

e. add. 'after the Lord had given thanks'.

f. var. 'is giving'.

g. The 'seal' that Jesus received at his baptism, namely the Spirit, Mt 3:16n, who is the power of God operative in Christ's 'signs'. Cf. Mt 12:28; Ac 10:38; 2 Co 1:22; Ep 1:13; 4:30.

h. For 'works' in the Jewish sense Jesus substitutes faith in God's representative.

i. The manna of Ex 16, food given by God for the messianic people, Ps 78:23–24; 105:40, was seen by Christians as a figure of the Eucharist, 1 Co 10:3–4. Jesus uses it here as a sign of the true nourishment of faith, vv. 35–50, provided by his flesh and blood, source of eternal life, vv. 51–58; see Mt 4:4; 14:13–21.

j. The Greek phrase *ego eimi* recalls the name that God revealed to Moses, Ex 3:13g, see Jn 8:24g, but here (and frequently elsewhere) it also forms the prelude to the explanation of a parable. In this case the parable is not in words but in action: the gift of the manna and the multiplication of the loaves are explained as parables of Christ's gift of himself, the true bread. See vv. 41,48,51; 8:12; 10:7–11; 11:25; 15:1.

k. As Wisdom invites all people to her table, Pr 9:1seq., so does Jesus. Jn sees him as the Wisdom of God which, in the OT revelation, was already moving towards personification, see 1:1a; Lk 7:35; 1 Co 1:24. This perception springs from Jesus' own teaching already recorded in the Synoptics, Mt 11:19; Lk 11:31 and par., but is given here much more clearly by Jn. Thus, Jesus' origin is mysterious, 7:27–29; 8:14,19; cf. Jb 28:20–28; he alone knows the secrets of God and reveals them, Jn 3:11–12,31–32; cf. Ws 9:13–18; Ba 3:29–38; Mt 11:25–27 and par.; he is the living bread that supremely satisfies, Jn 6:35; cf. Pr 9:1–6; Si 24:19–22.

l. To 'come to' Jesus is to believe in him, as is plainly shown in Mk 2:5; 5:34; etc., where it is accepted as proof of faith without any declaration.

m. 'Seeing' the Son is recognising that he is in truth the Son sent by the Father, cf. 12:45; 14:9; 17:6g.

n. As their ancestors did in the desert, see Ex 16:2seq.; 17:3; Nb 11:1; 14:27; 1 Co 10:10.

o. add. 'that I shall give'; the phrase is, in any case, to be understood. This concise phrase recalls 1 Co 11:24, 'This is my Body which is for you,' cf. Lk 22:19. It is an allusion to the Passion.

p. Jesus is the true bread because he is God's Word, vv. 32seq., and also because he is a victim whose body and blood are offered in sacrifice for the life of the world, vv. 51–58, cf. vv. 22d. The word 'flesh' suggests a connection between Eucharist and Incarnation: the Word made flesh, 1:14, is real food.

q. 'To be in' and even more, 'to live in' are characteristic phrases of this Gospel. The relationship of interior presence thus expressed clearly depends on the nature of the persons or things at issue: one is always greater than the other, especially when it is a divine person. It is particularly remarkable if the relationship is reciprocal, as here, 10:38; 14:10,20; 15:4–7; 17:21–23; 1 Jn 2:24; 3:24; 4:12–16.

r. The life that the Father communicates to the Son passes to the faithful through the Eucharist.

s. add. 'the manna' or 'in the desert'.

t. Jesus' words about the bread from heaven reveal something divine of which only the Spirit, see 1:33x, can supply understanding, see 14:26r, and which is the source of life for all people.

u. i.e. the Messiah, God's chosen representative, consecrated and united in him uniquely, cf. 10:36; 17:19. var. 'you are the Christ, the Son of God' or 'the Son of the living God', cf. Mt 16:16.

7 a. var. 'he did not want to'.

b. In the wide sense: cousins, relations, see Mt 12:46o.

c. Those in Jerusalem and Judaea, cf. 2:23; 3:26; 4:1.

d. i.e. 'my hour', see 2:4e.

e. var. 'I am not going yet'.

f. om. 'a great deal of'.

g. 7:14–52 is made up of separate passages with a common theme—the uncertainty about Jesus' origin. 1 His human origin obscures his divine: he has never been a pupil of the rabbis, what is his knowledge worth? (vv. 14–18); the details of his childhood are known, how can he be the Messiah (vv. 25–30)? 2 His reputed birth at Nazareth shows that he is not the Christ (vv. 40–52). The theme of 'departure', too (vv. 33–36, see 8:21–23) is connected with that of divine origin: the man Jesus departs for the place where (in his divine nature, see vv. 29 and 34) he has always been. • Vv. 19–24 are the conclusion of 5:1–16 and are alien to the present context.

h. The argument is rabbinic in type: circumcision was reckoned the 'healing' of one member; if this 'healing' of one member was allowed on the Sabbath, how much more the healing of the whole person?

i. var. 'the chief priests' or 'the elders' or 'they'.

j. They knew that the Messiah was to be born in Bethlehem, v. 42; Mt 2:5seq., but it was commonly believed that he would stay hidden in some secret place, cf. Mt 24:26, (in heaven, according to some) until the day of his coming. This belief was vindicated, though his audience did not recognise it, by Jesus' heavenly origin.

k. lit. 'he who sent me is true' (var. 'truthful').

l. var. 'because I am at his side'.

m. var. 'Pharisees and chief priests', 'They and the chief priests', 'Chief priests and Pharisees'.

n. Jesus, like God himself, must be sought while there is still time to find him. But the Jews will let his 'time' slip by and instead of coming to them, salvation will come to the gentiles (the 'Greeks'), see 12:20–21,35m; 19:37v.

o. The day, the 7th or perhaps the 8th, celebrating the end of the festival.

p. om. 'to me'. • Jesus' invitation resembles that of divine Wisdom, see 6:35j.

q. From Jesus himself, according to the oldest tradition, though another tradition joins 'anyone who believes in me' with 'from his heart', making the 'streams' flow from the believer.

r. The liturgy of the feast of Shelters ('Tabernacles'), which formed the background of these words, included prayers for rain, the procession to Siloam and the gathering of 'living water', which was then carried back to the Temple for the lustrations. These rites commemorated the Mosaic water-miracle, Ex 17:1–7; cf. 1 Co 10:4, and included readings from biblical passages foretelling lifegiving water for Zion, Ezk 47:1seq.; Zc 14:8; see Jn 4:1a.

s. var. 'the Spirit had not yet been given'.

t. That Jesus was born at Bethlehem was known only to those nearest him.

u. The author of this passage, 7:53–8:11, is not John: it is omitted by the oldest witnesses (MSS, versions, Fathers) and found elsewhere in others; moreover, its style is that of the Synoptics and the author was possibly Luke, see Lk 21:38h. Nevertheless, the passage was accepted in the canon and there are no grounds for regarding it as unhistorical.

8 a. The significance of the gesture is debated.

b. The development in the NT of the light-darkness theme can be traced fairly clearly along three main lines: **1** Just as the sun lights people on their way, so anything that shows them the way to God is 'light': of old it was the Law, the Wisdom and Word of God, Ps 119:105; Pr 4:18–19; 6:23; Qo 2:13; cf. Rm 2:19; now it is Jesus, Jn 1:9; 9:1–39; 12:35; 1 Jn 2:8–11; *see also* 2 Co 4:6, who is compared with the bright cloud that led the Israelites, Jn 8:12; *see also* Ex 13:21seq.; Ws 18:3seq.; it is also his followers from whom the light of God's own perfections shines out, Mt 5:14–16; Lk 8:16; Rv 21:24. **2** Light is symbolic of life, contentment, and joy, as darkness is of death, unhappiness, and misery, Jb 30:26; Is 45:7; hence, enslavement is darkness, the deliverance and salvation of the messianic age is light, Is 8:22–9:1; Mt 4:16; Lk 1:79; Rm 13:11–12. This light shines even on the gentile nations, Lk 2:32; Ac 13:47, through Jesus who is the Light, Jn (*see* texts just quoted); Ep 5:14; it is at its brightest in the kingdom of Heaven, Mt 8:12; 22:13; 25:30; Rv 22:5. **3** The 'light-darkness' contrast came to be used for the mutually hostile worlds of Good and Evil (*see also* the Essene texts of Qumran). Thus in the NT there are two 'empires', Christ the lord of one, Satan of the other, Ac 26:18; 2 Co 6:14–15; Col 1:12–13; 1 P 2:9, each striving for the mastery, Jn 13:29–30; Lk 22:53. People are either 'children of light' or 'children of darkness', 12:36; Lk 16:8; Ep 5:7–9; 1 Th 5:5, according as their life is ruled by the light (Christ) or by darkness (Satan), 1 Th 5:4seq.; 1 Jn 1:6–7; 2:9–10, and what they do shows which they are, Rm 13:12–14; Ep 5:8–11. The coming of the Light makes clear this distinction ('judgement') of one person from another, because this coming forces everyone to declare himself either for or against, 3:19–21; 7:7; 9:39; 12:46; *see* Ep 5:12–13. The perspective remains optimistic: darkness will one day disappear before light, 1:5; Rm 13:12; 1 Jn 2:8.

c. It is enough for the Son to be his own witness since he alone knows the mystery of his heavenly origin, cf. Mt 11:27 and par.

d. The Jews judge by what they can see: a man like themselves, 'in that flesh they fail to see the glory of God's Son shining' (St Augustine).

e. In the semitic sense of the word, i.e. 'condemn'.

f. By rejecting Jesus, the Jews are heading for irremediable loss; they are sinning against the truth, vv. 40,45seq. It is the sin against the Spirit, Mt 12:31 and par., *see* Jn 7:34n.

g. 'I Am' or 'I am He' is the divine name revealed to Moses, Ex 3:13g, 14, it means that the God of Israel is unique, the true God, Dt 32:39. When Jesus appropriates this name, he is claiming to be the one incomparable Saviour, the goal of Israel's faith and hope; *see* vv. 28,58; 13:19 *and also* 6:35; 18:5,8.

h. A very obscure text; it is variously rendered 'Why, in the first place, am I speaking to you?'; 'Why should I speak to you at all?'; 'What I have been telling you from the beginning'; 'Precisely what I am telling you'. Our translation resembles this last but preserves the idea of temporal priority which leads up to the following 'then' of v. 28, thus: as it is, the Jews have the opportunity of knowing Jesus from his words; afterwards, when they know him as one 'lifted up' it will be too late.

i. In the OT the formula 'you shall know that I am', or 'that I am Yahweh', is a declaration of God's power, *see* v. 24g, or else heralds some notable intervention of God in history, *see* Ex 10:2; Is 43:10 (strikingly like John); Ezk 6:7,10,13seq. This verse foretells the glorification of Jesus through his 'lifting up' on the cross, 12:32h, which is to be the reply to the Jews' question (v. 25) but will be also the condemnation of their unbelief; *see* 19:37; Mt 26:64 and par.; 1 Co 2:8; Rv 1:7.

j. Jesus is Truth, the total reality of the gift of the Father and of his saving plan, 14:6; 17:17; *see* Rv 3:7; 19:11. In him the promises of the Law, is 1:17, have been realised. He proclaims the words he has received from the Father who sent him, 3:11e; 8:26,40. Thus he reveals to us the Father whom he knows, 1:18, and invites us to believe in him, 3:12g; 8:45–47. He is the true light, 1:9, and can say 'I am the true

bread,' etc., 6:35. After his glorification, 12:32j, the Spirit of truth, 14:17j, will guide believers to all truth, 16:13. The believer, who 'is of the truth', 18:37; 1 Jn 3:19g; *see also* 2 Th 2:10–12, is sanctified by the truth, 17:17–19; he remains in it, Jn 8:31; walks in it, 2 Jn 4; 3 Jn 4; accomplishes it; Jn 3:21; co-operates with it, 3 Jn 8. He adores the Father in spirit and in truth, 4:23–24. He is saved from lies, vv. 44*o*.

k. add. 'of sin'.

l. var. 'If you were Abraham's children, you would'. Unlike Isaac, the Jews are not 'children' of Abraham because they do not believe; they are merely of his 'race' (like the slave-girl's son, Ishmael, who was cast out, *see* vv. 34–35). On this, *see* Ga 4:30seq. Nevertheless they are not in this sense children of God because they do not believe in Jesus, 1:12j; 3:7–9.

m. The prophets call religious infidelity 'prostitution', *see* Ho 1:2b; here, therefore, the Jews are objecting that they have been faithful to God's covenant.

n. Because they have the devil for master, and he is hostile to the truth. Cf. 18:37.

o. var. 'he has never taken his stand upon the truth'.

p. Or 'father of the liar'. Lying, the opposite of the Word, 1:1a, and of truth, v. 31, is linked to evil, cf. Rm 1:25; 2 Th 2:9–12. The Jews who refuse the truth of Jesus, v. 40, cf. 1 P 2:22, submit to the chief of all the enemies of this truth, *see* Jn 12:31f; 13:2e; 1 Jn 2:14.

q. i.e. of betraying the commission entrusted to him by God.

r. i.e. Jesus' coming. Another example of an expression reserved for God in the OT (the 'Day of Yahweh', *see* Am 5:18m) but adopted for himself by Jesus.

s. Abraham saw Jesus' 'Day' (as Isaiah 'saw his glory', 12:41), but 'from a distance', cf. Nb 24:17; Heb 11:13, because he saw it in the birth of the promised Isaac (at which Abraham 'laughed', Gn 17:17f) which was an event prophetic of Jesus' birth. Jesus claims to be the ultimate fulfilment of this promise made to Abraham; he is Isaac according to the spirit.

t. The claim of Jesus to live on the divine plane (v. 58) is, for the Jews, blasphemy, for which the penalty is stoning, Lv 24:16.

9 a. i.e. 'the signs', *see* 2:11f.

b. var. 'I must'.

c. The life of Jesus is compared to a day's work, 5:17, ending with the night of death, cf. Lk 13:32.

d. Before the miracle takes place its significance is pointed out, *see* v. 37.

e. The water drawn from here during the feast of Shelters ('Tabernacles') symbolised the blessings of the messianic age. Henceforth, the source of these blessings is Jesus himself. • 'The envoy', or 'the one sent', is one of Jn's favourite names for Jesus, *see* 3:17;4:34; 5:36; etc.

f. This was work and forbidden on the Sabbath.

g. var. 'that the man had been blind and had gained his sight'.

h. om. 'ask him'.

i. A biblical phrase putting a person under oath to tell the truth and to make reparation for his insult to the divine majesty, *see* Jos 7:19; 1 S 6:5.

j. There are many points of resemblance between ch. 9 and 3:1–21, and it is probable that to the evangelist's mind the cure of the man born blind is a symbol of the new birth through water and the Spirit, 3:3–7.

k. om. all v. 38 and first two words of v. 39.

l. The complacent who trust to their own 'light', *see* vv. 24,29,34, as opposed to the humble, typified by the blind man, cf. Dt 29:3; Is 6:9seq; Jr 5:21; Ezk 12:2.

10 a. Or possibly 'each by its name'.

b. i.e. to the Pharisees, wilfully blind, 9:40. They fail to realise that the parable refers to them.

c. The gate that gives access to the sheep. Only those who 'go in' by Jesus have authority to guide the flock, 21:15–17.

d. om. 'before me'. The reference is probably to the Pharisees, cf. Mt 23:1–36; Lk 11:39–52 and Mt 9:36; Mk 6:34.

e. Eternal life. Jesus gives it, 3:16,36; 5:40; 6:33,35,48,51; 14:6; 20:31, with abounding generosity, see Mt 25:29; Lk 6:38; Rv 7:17.

f. God, himself the shepherd of his people, was to choose a shepherd for them in the messianic age, cf. Ezk 34:1a. Jesus' assertion that he is the good shepherd is a claim to messiahship.

g. In biblical language, see Ho 2:22v, 'knowledge' is not merely the conclusion of an intellectual process, but the fruit of an 'experience', a personal contact (see Jn 10:14–15 and 14:20; 17:21–22; cf. 14:17; 17:3; 2 Jn 1–2); when it matures, it is love, see Ho 6:6c and 1 Jn 1:3b.

h. Not to take them into the Jewish fold but to gather them into the flock that Jesus 'leads' to eternal life.

i. var. 'one fold' (Vulg.).

j. Jesus has life in himself, 3:35t, and no one can rob him of it, 7:30,44; 8:20; 10:39; he surrenders it of his own will, v. 18; 14:30; 19:11; hence his perfect control and majestic calm in the face of death, 12:27; 13:1–3; 17:19; 18:4–6; 19:28.

k. Not, as hitherto, in the oblique language of parable, see v. 6; 16:25,29. More urgently than before, 2:18; 6:30; 8:25, the Jews press Jesus to say if he is the Messiah. In the Synoptics, the question is put by the high priest before the Passion, Mk 14:61.

l. Jesus' previous statements, in this Gospel, had made it sufficiently clear that he spoke as God's envoy, cf. 2:19; 5:17seq., 39; 6:32seq.; 8:24,28seq.; 56seq.; 9:37.

m. Faith in Jesus implies an inner sympathy with him: one must be 'from above', 8:23, 'of God', 8:47, 'of the truth', 18:37, of his flock, v. 14. Faith presupposes a mind open to truth, 3:17–21, see Ac 13:48jj; Rm 8:29seq.

n. var. 'As for my Father, that which he has given me is greater than all'.

o. var. 'Steal them'.

p. The Son's power is not other than the Father's. The context shows that this is the primary meaning, but the statement is deliberately undefined and hints at a more comprehensive and a profounder unity. The Jews do not miss the implication; they sense a claim to godhead, v. 33; cf. 1:1; 8:24,29; 10:38; 14:9–10; 17:11,21 and 2:11f.

q. The words were addressed to judges whose function made them, in a sense, 'gods' because 'judgement is God's', Ex 21:6; Dt 1:17; 19:17; Ps 58. Jesus' argument is a rabbinic *a fortiori*, the conclusion being that blasphemy is a surprising charge to bring when it is God's consecrated envoy who calls himself Son of God. On this title, 'Son of God', v. 36, cf. 5:25; 11:4,27; 20:17,31; Jesus' fate is henceforth to turn, see 19:7, see also Mt 4:3d.

r. add. 'again'.

11 a. It is unlikely that this is 'the woman who was a sinner' of Lk 7:37.

b. A double meaning here: Jesus will be glorified by the miracle itself, see 1:14n, but the miracle will bring about his death, vv. 46–54, by which also he will be glorified, 12:32h.

c. om. 'back'.

d. The significance of the death of Lazarus includes the strengthening of their faith by a miracle.

e. om. 'Lord'.

f. Martha has faith in Jesus but she stops short as if about to ask an impossibility.

g. om. 'and the life'.

h. The believer has triumphed over death for ever, a victory of which the resurrection of Lazarus is the sign, see 3:11e.

i. om. 'the dead man's sister'.

j. Or 'to heaven', 'up to heaven'.

k. lit. 'our Place'; Jerusalem, the Holy Land, or more probably the holiest of all places, the Temple.

l. var. 'it is better'.

m. om. 'of that year'.

n. Caiaphas means that Jesus must be executed to save the nation from political extinction. The higher, prophetic sense, is that the death of Jesus is necessary for the salvation of the world, see 1:29v.

o. var. 'they plotted'.

p. Jn repeatedly emphasises the connection between the Passover and Christ's death, 13:1; 18:28; 19:14,42.

q. om. 'before the Passover'.

12 a. This last week of Jesus' life is as carefully punctuated as the first, v. 12; 13:1; 18:28; 19:31; see 2:1a. Each of the two weeks culminates in the manifestation of his glory, but the time for 'signs' (see Cana, 2:4,11) is now over: 'the hour has come for the Son of man to be glorified', v. 23; 13:31seq.; 17:1,5.

b. Jesus sees Mary's act as a gesture of respect offered to his dead body before the time; it is a symbol of his actual burial, 19:38seq.

c. The Messiah-King.

d. Not Jews by birth but converts to the monotheism of Israel and adopting certain specific Mosaic observances; they are the 'God-fearers' of Ac 10:2b.

e. In the glory of the Father, cf. 14:3; 17:24.

f. This episode and Gethsemane, Mk 14:32–42, have many details in common: the anguish as the 'hour' draws near, the appeal to the Father's pity, the acceptance of death, the comfort from heaven (cf. Lk). But we should note also the differences: Jesus remains standing, and his cry for mercy remains at the level of a mental struggle (Jn); he 'kneels down' (Lk), 'falls prostrate' (Mt, Mk), see Jn 10:18j; 18:4–6.

g. var. 'your Son'. The Father's 'name' is his person. Jesus worked for the Father's glory; his death, now freely offered, is the completion of that work because it shows how great is the Father's love, 17:6g.

h. Jesus' coming death is thus divinely and publicly sanctioned.

i. Satan (see 14:30; 16:11; 2 Co 4:4; Ep 2:2; 6:12) was lord of the world, 1 Jn 5:19; Jesus' death breaks his dominion over humanity; see Jn 3:35t and Mt 8:29k; Lk 8:31c; Col 1:12–13.

j. om. 'from the earth'. • Allusion both to the 'lifting up' of Jesus on the cross (v. 34) and to his 'lifting up' to heaven, 3:13,14h; 8:28; cf. 6:62, on the day of his resurrection, 20:17h; the two events are two aspects of the same mystery, 13:1a. When Christ is raised to the Father's right hand in glory, v. 23; 17:5e, he will send the Spirit, 7:39, through whom his reign will spread over the world, 16:14; see 3:35t.

k. var. 'every man' or 'all things'.

l. The crucified Jesus will be set before the eyes of the world as its Saviour, cf. 19:37. This is the answer to the Greeks' request to 'see' Jesus, see 6:40m.

m. Jesus urges the Jews to believe in him before it is too late, see 7:34n.

n. var. 'when he saw'. • Alluding to Isaiah's vision in the Temple, Is 6:1–4 and notes, Jn interprets it as a prophetic vision of Christ's glory, see 8:56r.

13 a. According to a Jewish tradition the word 'Passover' (*pesah*: see Ex 12:11f) meant 'a passing, or crossing over', with reference to the crossing of the Sea of Reeds (Red Sea), Ex 14. Jesus (and we with him) will pass from this world, which is enslaved by sin, to the Father's company, the true Promised Land, see 1:21t.

b. Here, for the first time, Jn clearly states that Jesus' life and death are an expression of his love for his disciples. The impression given is one of a secret kept for these final moments, v. 34; 15:9,13; 17:23; Rm 8:35; Ga 2:20; Ep 3:19; 5:2,25; 1 Jn 3:16.

c. lit. 'he loved them to the end', i.e. utterly.

d. var. 'Supper was over'.

e. var. 'the devil having already put in the (his?) heart that Judas Iscariot should betray him', or '. . . having already put in his heart (i.e. made up his mind) . . .', or 'Satan having already entered into the heart of Judas in order that he might betray him'. • Unseen forces are at work in Jesus' Passion: the human agents are tools of the devil; cf. 6:70seq.; 8:44; 12:31; 13:27; 16:11; Lk 22:3; 1 Co 2:8; Rv 12:4,17; 13:2.

f. The dress and duty are those of a slave, see 1 S 25:41.

g. A semitic phrase: Peter is cutting himself off from his Lord and from all share in his ministry and in his glory.

h. add. 'except for the feet'.

i. Peter has understood Jesus' answer, v. 8, superficially, as if a new rite of purification were being instituted. Jesus replies that his sacrifice has already achieved this purification, cf. 15:2–3; Heb 10:22; 1 Jn 1:7. He explains the meaning of his action in vv. 12–15.

j. The same Greek word is used for 'clean' and 'pure'.

k. i.e. serve one another lovingly with complete humility.

l. lit. 'has lifted up his heel against me'.

m. Because it demonstrates Jesus' superhuman knowledge and fulfils the scripture, Judas' betrayal and Christ's death will confirm the disciples' faith.

n. This particular 'morsel' is not the Holy Eucharist; nevertheless, a comparison of 13:2,18 with 6:64,70 seems to show that there was some connection between the institution and Judas' act of treachery, cf. Lk 22:21.

o. The washing of the feet and the exchange which accompanies it form the prelude to a long talk of Jesus with his disciples, compare Lk 22:14d. In their present form ch. 13–17 certainly include teaching given on other occasions. The complex ch. 16 could be another version of Jesus' words in ch. 14. By putting them here John means to show the deepest meaning of the whole of Jesus' life at that moment when he passes from his earthly to his heavenly existence.

p. The Passion has already begun, since Judas has just gone out to do Satan's work: Jesus speaks of his victory as already won, cf. 16:33.

q. om. 'If God has been glorified in him'.

r. 'himself' refers to God the Father who will glorify the Son of man by taking him to himself in glory, cf. 17:5,22,24.

s. Jesus' 'departure' and his glorification are intimately connected. The separation will be, for 'the Jews', final, 8:21; for the disciples, only for a time, 14:2–3.

t. Except by dying, cf. v. 36; 21:19,22seq.

u. Cf. Mt 25:31–46. The reference to Jesus' 'departure', v. 33 (which leads up to the prophecy of Peter's denial, vv. 36–38), makes this command, vv. 34–35, a solemn legacy from him. Though enunciated in the Mosaic Law, this precept of love is 'new' because Jesus sets the standard so high by telling his followers to love one another as he himself loved them, and because love is to be the distinguishing mark of the 'new' era which the death of Jesus inaugurates and proclaims to the world.

v. A veiled prediction of Peter's martyrdom.

w. add. 'Lord'.

14 a. The apostles are perturbed by the predictions of betrayal, of Jesus' departure, and of Peter's denial. Jesus wants to strengthen their faith: this purpose pervades ch. 14.

b. Others translate 'otherwise I would have told you (where I am going)'.

c. This promise keeps the Church's hope alive, cf. 1 Co 4:5; 11:26; 16:22; 1 Th 4:16seq.; 1 Jn 2:28; Rv 22:17,20.

d. Jesus is the Way because he reveals the Father, 12:45; 14:9; he shows us the way to the Father, Ac 9:2b; he alone gives access to the Father, Jn 1:18; 14.4–7. He comes from the Father and returns to the Father, 7:29, 33; 13:3; 16:28, and is one with him, 10:30; 12:45; 14:9; 17:22. He is Truth, 8:32j, and Life 3:15j.

e. var. 'If you had known me, you would have . . .

f. When Philip asks for some marvellous manifestation of the Father, he is falling short of that faith by which alone the Father is seen to be in the Son and the Son in the Father.

g. Jesus brought revelation and salvation; his miracles were 'signs' of these things, 2:11f. The 'works' of the disciples will continue this ministry. The Spirit, from whom mighty

works will proceed, is to be sent by Jesus seated in glory at the Father's right hand, 7:39; 16:7.

h. var. om. 'you will'. Jesus, like God himself, asserts his right to love and obedience.

i. The title 'Paraclete' used in our translation is a transliteration of the Gk word *parakletos*; in English it is difficult to choose between the various meanings: 'advocate', 'intercessor', 'counsellor', 'protector', 'support'. • The parallel between the Spirit's work for the disciples and Jesus' brings out powerfully the personal character of the Spirit, see vv. 26r; 1 Jn 2:1.

j. var. 'will be in you'.

k. The world has seen its last of Jesus, cf. 7:34; 8:21. The disciples, however, will see him in his risen life, not merely with their eyes but with the inward vision of faith, 20:29.

l. Phrase used by the prophets for the occasions when God intervenes notably in human history, see Is 2:17; 4:1seq. The 'day' may indicate a whole epoch; here, it is the post-resurrection era.

m. The relationship between Jesus and his disciples is analogous to that between him and his Father, 6:57; 10:14–15; 15:9.

n. By coming, with the Father, to dwell in him.

o. The 'Judas, brother of James' of Lk 6:16 and Ac 1:13; the Thaddaeus of Mt 10:3 and Mk 3:18.

p. As the world does not: 8:37,43,47.

q. var. 'my word'.

r. In place of the departed Jesus, the faithful will have the Spirit, vv. 16,17; 16:7; see 1:33x. He is the *parakletos*, who intercedes with the Father, cf. 1 Jn 2:1, and whose voice is heard in human courts, 15:26,27; cf. Mt 10:19–20 and par.; Lk 12:11–12; Ac 5:32. He is the Spirit of truth, leading humanity to the very fullness of truth, 16:13, teaching them to understand the mystery of Christ—his fulfilment of the scriptures, 5:39r, the meaning of his words, 2:19g, of his actions, and of his 'signs', v. 16; 16:13; 1 Jn 2:20seq.,27, all hitherto obscure to the disciples, Jn 2:22; 12:16; 13:7; 20:9. In this way the Spirit is to bear witness to Christ, 15:26; 1 Jn 5:6,7, and shame the unbelieving world, Jn 16:8–11.

s. The customary Jewish greeting and farewell, see Lk 10:5 and par.; it means soundness of body but came to be used of the perfect happiness and the deliverance which the Messiah would bring, 2 Th 3:16.

t. Though the Son is the Father's equal, 8:24g; 10:30p, his glory is for the moment veiled, 1:14; his return to the Father will reveal it again, 17:5f, cf. Ph 2:6–9; Heb 1:3.

u. var. 'I will not have much more speech with you.'

15 a. On the vine image, see Is 5:1a; Jr 2:21. In the Synoptics, Jesus uses the vine as a symbol of the kingdom of God, Mt 20:1–8; 21:28–31,33–41 and par., and 'the fruit of the vine' becomes the eucharistic sacrament of the new covenant, Mt 26:29 and par. Here he calls himself the true vine whose fruit, the true Israel, will not disappoint God's expectation.

b. The 'fruit' is that of a life of obedience to the commandments, especially that of love, vv. 12–17, cf. Is 5:7; Jr 2:21.

c. Or 'have been pruned'. The same root denotes in Gk 'pruning' and 'cleansing', cf. 13:10.

d. var. 'and so prove to be my disciples'. In this way the Father is 'glorified in the Son', 14:13, cf. 21:19.

e. The perfect happiness of the messianic era which is communicated by the Son of God.

f. Jesus contrasts the disciples' love for one another with the world's hatred of them. It will be with them as with their Master, and when the world persecutes them, it persecutes Jesus himself, cf. Ac 9:5; Col 1:24.

g. The sending of the Spirit into the world rather than the 'eternal' proceeding from the Father within the Trinity.

16 a. lit. 'so that you may not be tripped'. To preserve their faith from shock, Jesus forewarns the apostles of coming trials, cf. 13:19.

b. The Holy Spirit sent by Jesus will reinforce his witness, 3:11e, so that the rightness of the Saviour's cause stands out in the sight of believers.

c. The world's sin is unbelief, 8:21,24,46; 15:22; the Spirit will expose it.

d. The Spirit will demonstrate the right of Jesus to the title 'Son of God', cf. 10:33; 19:7. The 'passing' of Jesus to the Father will prove that he is God's Son, 13:1; 20:17, because it shows that heaven is his true home, 6:62.

e. The Spirit will reveal the significance of Jesus' death: it is the final sentence pronounced on the prince of this world.

f. The new order of things that is to result from Jesus' death and resurrection.

g. By revealing the hidden depths of the mystery of Jesus, the Spirit makes his glory known. Jesus, in his turn, manifests the glory of the Father, 17:4seq., from whom comes everything he possesses, 3:35; 5:22,26; 13:3; 17:2.

h. A veiled reference to his approaching death and resurrection. • add. 'because I am going to the Father'.

i. add. 'he speaks of'.

j. The happiness of seeing the risen Christ after the sad days of his Passion, cf. 20:20.

k. Traditional biblical metaphor for the sufferings which will herald the new, messianic age, see Mt 24:8f.

l. Because Jesus was not yet glorified, cf. 14:13seq.

m. The resurrection and the coming of the Spirit inaugurate the period of more perfect instruction which is to end in the vision of God 'as he is', 1 Jn 3:2.

n. var. 'and I shall not pray to the Father'. Jesus is still the only mediator, cf. 10:9; 14:6; 15:5; Heb 8:6, but the disciples' faith and love make them one with him and therefore dear to the Father: mediation could not be more perfect.

17 a. The time for the sacrifice draws near: in this prayer Jesus offers himself and intercedes for his disciples.

b. When Jesus asks to be 'glorified' (i.e., shown in glory), it is not for his own sake, cf. 7:18; 8:50, but the glory of the Son and of the Father are one, cf. 12:28; 13:31.

c. Knowledge in its biblical sense, see 10:14g.

d. Hitherto the Mosaic Law had been the instrument of revelation which now comes to all people through Christ.

e. var. 'the glory which was with you' or 'the glory with which I was' or 'the glory with you'.

f. Either the glory he enjoyed as the pre-incarnate Son, or else the glory predestined for him from eternity by the Father, 1:14n.

g. It was Jesus' mission to reveal the 'Name', i.e. the person, of the Father, vv. 3–6,26; 12:28g; 14:7–11; see 3:11e; now love for all people is characteristic of the Father, 1 Jn 4:8,16, and he proves this love by delivering up his only Son, Jn 3:16–18; 1 Jn 4:9,10,14,16; see also Rm 8:32; it follows that all people must believe that Jesus is the Son, Jn 3:18, if they are to appreciate this love, cf. Jn 20:31; 1 Jn 2:23; and thus 'know' the Father.

h. Also translated 'they have given them (the teachings) true welcome because I came from you.'

i. var. 'Keep those in your name whom (var. which) you have given me'. So also in v. 12.

j. This Hebr. expression has either the meaning given in the text, or 'the one who has willingly submitted himself to the power of evil'.

k. Or 'from evil', cf. Mt 6:13.

l. The verb means literally: to set aside for, dedicate to, God; to 'consecrate' (in the original sense of 'dedicate to God'), see Ac 9:13g.

m. Jesus consecrates himself by presenting himself to the Father to be one with him, and to all people as the perfect revelation. He prays that the disciples may live in God's truth, sanctified by faith in the Father he has revealed to them.

n. Finally, vv. 20–26, Jesus prays for the Church of believers gathered by the witness of the apostles, 3:11e; 15:27; see Rm 1:1b, that their unity may foster faith in the mission of Jesus, cf. 1 Jn 1:1–3; 2:24.

o. var. 'that I have loved them'.

18 a. A detachment from the Roman garrison in Jerusalem.

b. Probably the 'disciple' of 20:2seq., 'whom Jesus loved', the evangelist himself, see 19:27l.

c. This is all that John has to say about the Jewish trial because this trial, in fact, runs through the whole Gospel from the Baptist's cross-examination, 1:19, to the decision to kill Jesus, 11:49–53.

d. The Roman procurator's judicial court. 18:28–19:16 may be seen as an elaborately balanced drama in which the Jews demand Jesus' condemnation and eventually obtain it. But in fact Jesus is crowned king (19:2–3) and is seated on the chair of judgement (19:13) while the Jews pronounce their own condemnation by denying that Yahweh is their king (19:15).

e. To enter the house of a gentile was to incur legal impurity, cf. Ac 11:2seq.

f. The Romans had withdrawn from the Sanhedrin the power of life and death. Jesus could have been stoned by the Jews, cf. 8:59; 10:31, but not crucified ('lifted up') by them.

19 a. Mt and Mk put both mockery and scourging of Jesus after his condemnation, while Jn relates both before the condemnation. Scourging was a standard preliminary to crucifixion and presumably followed the sentence, but it is more likely that the mockery filled the delays of the night than that it intruded between sentence and execution.

b. i.e. not 'what district do you come from?' but 'what is the secret of your origin? Who are you?' First, the people of Cana, 2:9, then the Samaritan woman, 4:11, the apostles, the multitude, 6:5, the Jewish leaders, 7:27seq.; 8:14; 9:29seq., and now Pilate, are faced with the mystery of Jesus, 16:28; 17:25, which is the theme of the whole Gospel, 1:13.

c. The Jewish leaders, Caiaphas in particular, 11:51seq.; 18:14, but also Judas who betrayed him to them, 6:71; 13:2,11,21; 18:2,5.

d. Probably meaning 'elevated place', 'mound'.

e. In the course of this day, the Passover supper was made ready (it was to be eaten after sunset, see Ex 12:6c) and everything necessary prepared so that the feast could be celebrated without violating the rest prescribed by the Law.

f. About noon, the time by which all yeast had to be removed from the house; during the Passover unleavened bread ('azymes') was to be eaten, see Ex 12:15seq. It is possible that the evangelist wishes to call attention to this coincidence; cf. 1 Co 5:7.

g. var. 'answered'.

h. add. 'and led him away'. In Jn the chief stress in this passage is on the notice proclaiming Jesus' kingship, Pilate refuses to modify. The royal dignity of Jesus has been stressed throughout Jn's Passion narrative: Jesus controls his arrest (18:4–11); the trial is an assertion of his kingship (18:28d); he carries his cross like a royal banner (19:17). It is truly the hour of his exaltation (3:35t; 12:32j).

i. Possibly allusion to the priesthood of the crucified: the high-priestly robe was without seam.

j. Her presence is mentioned only by John, see 2:1b.

k. Either Salome, mother of the sons of Zebedee (see Mt 27:56 and par.) or else, if the phrase refers to what follows, 'Mary, the wife of Clopas'.

l. The reference to the OT (vv. 24,28,36,37) and the unusual term 'woman' suggest that the evangelist sees more in this than the gesture of a dutiful son: namely, a declaration that Mary, the new Eve, is the spiritual mother of all the faithful, of whom the beloved disciple is the type and representative, cf. 15:10–15.

m. conj. 'on a spear'.

n. i.e. the Father's work: the salvation of the world through the sacrifice of Jesus. Jn does not record the desolate cry of Mt 27:46 and Mk 15:34: it is the calm majesty of Jesus' death that he wishes to emphasise, cf. Lk 23:46; Jn 12:27f.

o. The last breath of Jesus is the first moment of the outpouring of the Spirit, 1:33x; 20:22.

p. To hasten death.

q. var. 'when they found'.

r. var. 'water and blood'. The significance of the incident is brought out by two texts of scripture (vv. 36seq.). The blood shows that the lamb has truly been sacrificed for the salvation of the world, 6:51; the water, symbol of the Spirit, shows that the sacrifice is a rich source of grace. Many of the Fathers interpret the water and blood as symbols of baptism and the Eucharist, and these two sacraments as signifying the Church, which is born like a second Eve from the side of another Adam, cf. Ep 5:23–32.

s. The disciple of v. 26, probably the evangelist himself.

t. Referring either to 'the one who saw' or else to God (or Christ) whom 'the one who saw' calls to witness.

u. Two texts are here combined: one from a Psalm describing how God protects the upright in persecution (cf. Ws 2:18–20), of whom the 'servant of Yahweh' (Is 53) is the ideal example; the other, a ritual instruction for the preparation of the Passover lamb, *see* Jn 1:29v and 1 Co 5:7.

v. 'They will look', in the Johannine sense of 'see and understand'. For Jn, the Roman soldier symbolises the gentiles who will be converted, *see* 12:20–21,32 and notes. Similarly, Mt 27:54 and Mk 15:39j, *see also* Mt 24:30; Lk 23:47,48; Rv 1:7.

w. var. 'he'.

20 a. This was to become 'the Lord's Day', the Christian Sunday; *see* Rv 1:10.

b. The disciple acknowledges that Peter has some title to precedence, cf. 21:15–17.

c. The evangelist does not quote any text. He means to underline the unpreparedness of the disciples for the Easter revelation, despite the scriptures, cf. 2:22; 12:16; Lk 24:27,32,44–45.

d. var. 'She recognised him'.

e. A more solemn address than 'Rabbi', and often used when speaking to God; it is therefore some approximation to Thomas' profession of faith, v. 28.

f. Mary has fallen at the feet of Jesus to embrace them, cf. Mt 28:9.

g. var. 'the brothers'.

h. This assertion does not contradict the account of Ac 1:3seq. Christ 'went up' to the Father, that is to say, his body entered into glory, 3:13; 6:62; Ep 4:10; 1 Tm 3:16; Heb 4:14; 6:19seq.; 9:24; 1 P 3:22; cf. Ac 2:33t, 36w, on the day he rose from the tomb, Jn 20:17; Lk 24:51. The significance of the ascension, 40 days later, Ac 1:2seq., 9–11, is that the time of earthly companionship with Jesus is over, that he is now 'seated at the right hand of God' and will not return before his final coming (the *parousia*).

i. add. 'assembled'.

j. The breath of Jesus is a symbol of the Spirit ('breath' in Hebrew); he sends forth the Spirit who will make all things new, Gn 1:2; 2:7; Ws 15:11; Ezk 37:9. *See* 19:30o and Mt 3:16n.

k. om. 'other'.

l. In the closing words of his Gospel, John again calls the Christian reader's attention to the wound in Christ's side, *see* 19:34r.

m. On the apostles' witness, *see* 17:20–23; *also see* Ac 1:8k.

21 a. Added either by the evangelist or by one of his disciples.

b. This generosity recalls Cana, 2:6, the miracle of the loaves, 6:11seq., the living water, 4:14; 7:37seq., the life which the good shepherd gives, 10:10, and the richness of the Spirit bestowed on Jesus, 3:34.

c. In the Synoptics, this operation is an image of the kingdom's coming, Mt 13:47seq., or of the apostles' task, Mt 4:19 and par. Here, too, it evidently symbolises the apostolic mission under Peter's direction, cf. Jn 21:15–17.

d. It recalls his three denials, 13:38; 18:17,25–27.

e. 'Love' is expressed in the text by two different verbs which denote respectively love and friendship or cherishing. But it is unclear whether this is anything more than a stylistic variation. Similarly with the variation 'lambs'—'sheep'.

f. To the triple profession of love by Peter Jesus replies with a triple investiture. He entrusts to Peter the care of ruling the flock in his name, cf. Mt 16:18; Lk 22:31seq. It is possible that the triple repetition indicates a contract made in due form, according to semitic custom, cf. Gn 23:7–23.

g. Martyrdom.

h. This takes up Jesus' saying to Peter after the washing of the feet, 13:36.

i. A reference perhaps to the Second Coming, cf. 1 Co 11:26; 16:22; Rv 1:7; 22:7,12,17,20.

j. add. 'what does it matter to you?'

k. Possibly the words of a group of John's disciples.

ACTS
OF THE APOSTLES

INTRODUCTION TO
ACTS OF THE APOSTLES

§1 Acts and the third Gospel must originally have been two parts of a book that today we should call 'a history of the rise of Christianity'. About AD 150, when Christians wanted the four gospels bound in one codex, these two parts were separated. The title 'Acts of the Apostles', or 'Acts of Apostles', which may have been given to the second part at this time, follows normal contemporary hellenistic usage as in, e.g., the 'Acts' of Hannibal and the 'Acts' of Alexander, etc. That these two books of the New Testament were once closely associated is suggested: 1 By their Prologues: both are addressed (see Lk 1:1–4) to someone called Theophilus and Ac 1:1, having referred to the Gospel as an 'earlier work', goes on by way of introduction to say why the Gospel was written and to summarise its closing incidents (appearances of the risen Christ, ascension). 2 By their literary affinity: vocabulary, grammar and style are not only consistent all through Acts, showing that it is a literary unity, but they are also characteristic of the third Gospel, which makes it almost certain that both books are by the same author.

The only identification of the author ever suggested by church writers is Luke, and no critic ancient or modern has ever seriously suggested anyone else. This identification was already known to the churches about the year AD 175, as is shown by the Roman canon known as the Muratorian Fragment, by the Anti-Marcionite Prologue, by St Irenaeus, Clement and Origen in Alexandria and by Tertullian; this is supported by internal evidence: the author must have been a Christian of the apostolic age, either a thoroughly hellenised Jew or, more probably, a well-educated Greek very well acquainted with the LXX and with Judaism. The most straightforward (though not the only possible) explanation of the use of the first person plural in some passages of the second part of Acts is that the author accompanied Paul on his journeys. Among Paul's companions tradition has always pointed to Luke, a Syrian from Antioch and a doctor of non-Jewish origin (Col 4:10–14); Paul describes him as a close friend who stuck by him during his captivity in Rome (Col 4:14; Phm 24). To judge from the passages in the first person plural, he accompanied Paul on the second (Ac 16:10seq.) and third (Ac 20:6seq.; cf. perhaps 2 Co 8:18) missionary journeys. The reason why he does not figure in lists like

that of Ac 20:4 is that he compiled these lists himself. Various arguments
have, however, convinced a number of scholars that the author of Acts, and
so also of the third Gospel, cannot have been a companion of Paul, but is a
writer whose identity is otherwise completely unknown. Chief among these
arguments are differences between Acts and Paul's letters in theological
outlook and in the accounts of some incidents; some explanations for these
differences will be suggested below.

There is no clear early tradition about either date or place of writing (Greece,
after Paul's death? Rome, before the end of Paul's trial?), and we have to rely
on internal evidence. Acts ends with Paul's Roman captivity in 61–63, and it
must therefore be later than this, and later also than Mark. A date as late as
80–100, which has been suggested by some critics, is possible, but (as in Luke)
there are no conclusive indications in Acts of a date later than AD 70.

§2 The precise date, however, becomes a secondary consideration once the
book can establish its credentials either as an eyewitness account for the events
that fill a major section or as based on adequate sources at the author's
disposal. Analysis of Acts confirms Lk 1:1–4 (meant as prologue to the
complete work) by suggesting that Luke must have collected a great deal of
detailed evidence from a variety of sources, because in spite of the way Luke
has superimposed his own personality in reworking this material he has not
succeeded in disguising the various sources he has used. Not only does the
flavour of the doctrinal content change according to the context so that in
appropriate sections it seems convincingly primitive, but also there is considerable variation in the literary style. In passages where Luke can control the style,
for example in the travel diary, the Greek is excellent; but in his description of
the early history of the Palestinian community we find that the language
becomes full of semitisms, clumsy and even inaccurate. In some places this is
not only because he is trying to copy Old Testament LXX Greek, but mostly
it is because he is reproducing his various Aramaic sources as closely as
possible. In Luke this can be checked by comparing it with two of its sources,
but unfortunately there are no texts with which to compare Acts; it is possible,
however, to try to determine what kinds of source were used. One suggestion
was that the whole of 1–15:35 is based on a single Aramaic document, but this
is far too sweeping as it does not account for all the editing that Luke has
unmistakably done in these chapters. His sources were more restricted and
more varied than this, and it is not even certain (though probable in some
cases, such as Stephen's speech) that they were in written form. It is rather a
question of oral traditions which he received from various circles. These
provided him with partial accounts which he then combined as best he could
to compose his book. Without being dogmatic about details, it is possible to
classify traditions collected by Luke. 1 Those that relate to the primitive
Jerusalem community, ch. 1–5. 2 Biographical notes about individuals: e.g.
Peter, 9:32–11:18; ch. 12, or Philip, 8:4–40; these details could have been

supplied at first hand by people like Philip, the evangelist whom Luke met at Caesarea, 21:8. **3** Details about the early days of the community in Antioch and its foundation by Hellenists: these were obviously provided by that community, 6:1–8:3; 11:19–30; 13:1–3. **4** Paul's conversion and missionary journeys: these were things Paul himself could have told Luke, 9:1–30; 13:4–14:28; 15:36seq., though places can be found at which Luke's account of an incident differs from the version in Paul's own letters, and it is clear that the lesson he meant to teach was more important to him than literal historicity. **5** For Paul's later journeys Luke seems to have had his own notes, for this is the most straightforward explanation of the 'we' passages which are precisely the sections where the peculiarities of Luke's own style are most concentrated, 11:28; 16:10–17; 20:5–21:18; 27:1–28:16. Luke managed to organise all this material into a single book by sorting it out chronologically as best he could and linking the episodes together with frequent editorial formulae, e.g. 6:7; 9:31; 12:24.

§3 This excellent documentation gives Acts a unique historical worth. Obviously the process of editing has involved a certain amount of anticipation and fusion. Thus the events of ch. 12 should come before the visit of Barnabas and Saul to Jerusalem mentioned in 11:30; 12:25, unless this visit is to be identified with that of ch. 15; though the account of the 'council of Jerusalem' (ch. 15) may itself be a conflation of two quite distinct debates (*see* notes). Slight adjustments like this do not affect the basic reliability of the work, provided that it is understood within its literary type. Like all historians of his time, Luke does not restrict himself to a material exactitude, but rather seeks to draw a theological lesson from events. This concern has its influence on the way he treats his sources. Thus there is a deliberate parallelism between the miracles of Peter and those of Paul: compare 3:1–10 and 14:8–10; 5:15 and 19:12; 5:19 or 12:6–11,17 and 16:23–26,40; 8:15–17 and 19:2–7; 8:18–24 and 13:6–11; 9:36–42 and 20:7–12. In addition, these miracle stories sometimes have parallels in the Gospel: compare 3:6–7 and Lk 4:39; Mk 1:31; compare 9:33–34 and Lk 5:24b–25; 20:10,12 and Lk 8:52–55; it is also clear that the dying words of Stephen (7:59–60) resemble those of Jesus (Lk 23:34,46). Paul's speech at Antioch in Pisidia (13:16–41) is not without analogies with those of Peter at Jerusalem (2:14–36; 3:12–26; 4:8–12; 5:29–32) and at Caesarea (10:34–43). It is therefore reasonable to suppose that Luke did not receive these speeches just as they are, but composed them freely, using the pattern of the first apostolic preaching, with its basic proclamation and its arguments drawn from the scriptures. This pattern he carefully adapted to the various circumstances in which he placed the speeches. A contrast has often been made between the portrait of Paul drawn by Acts and that which appears in the Pauline epistles. It is true that Luke attributes to the apostle a more conciliatory attitude than is shown by the epistles: compare Ac 21:20–26 with Gal 2:12seq.; Ac 16:3 with Ga 2:3; 5:1–12; but due weight must be given to the different interests which inspired these two literary sources. Paul is an advocate who does not shrink from showing unyielding attitudes (but *see also* 1 Co 9:19–23), while Luke is concerned to show the profound unity which existed among the first brethren.

Nevertheless this conciliatory attitude of Acts must not be exaggerated. The Tübingen school thought Acts was a second-century attempt to smooth over the quarrel between Petrine and Pauline factions. Such a radical attack on the objectivity of Acts would not be put forward by any exegete today, if only because the date it suggests is far too late. To what extent, however, is Acts a piece of special pleading? To what extent does it twist the facts that it records? Was Luke's purpose in writing Acts to present a portrait of Paul that would convince the Roman authorities that Paul was not a political criminal? This is certainly one aspect of Acts but not the only one, and in any case such a portrait of Paul need not necessarily be tendentious. The two things he stresses are the exclusively religious nature of Paul's battle with the Jews, and Paul's loyalty to the Roman authorities. However, as has been said, Luke was not merely interested in giving a portrait of Paul to serve as evidence for the Roman courts: what he aimed at was to write the history of the beginnings of Christianity.

§4 This assertion is based on the *structure* of the book as summarised in the words of Christ with which it begins, 'You will be my witnesses not only in Jerusalem but throughout Judaea and Samaria, and indeed to the earth's remotest end,' Ac 1:8. Acts begins with Jerusalem where the faith takes firm root and the first community grows in grace and numbers, ch. 1–5. This community begins to expand, under the stimulus of the world-wide outlook of converts from hellenistic Judaism especially after the martyrdom of Stephen when these converts were expelled, 6:1–8:3. The faith spreads north of Jerusalem to Samaria, 8:4–25, south west to the coast and north again to Caesarea, 8:26–40; 9:32–11:18. The insertion here of Paul's conversion shows that the faith had already reached Damascus and indicates that it was soon to reach Cilicia, 9:1–30. Refrains like the one that closes this section (9:31, which adds Galilee to the list) draw attention repeatedly to the spread of the faith. Acts turns next to the reception of the good news in Antioch, 11:19–26, and shows how Antioch became a missionary headquarters, while keeping in touch with Jerusalem, and how Jerusalem reached a solution to the main problems at Antioch connected with the missions, 11:27–30; 15:1–35. This leads on to the spread of the faith to the gentiles. After his imprisonment following the conversion of Cornelius, Peter goes off to some place that is not named, ch. 12, and from that point Paul takes over the leading part in Luke's story. His first journey takes the faith to Cyprus and Asia Minor, ch. 13–14; his next two journeys take it as far as Macedonia and Greece, 15:36–18:22; 18:23–21:17. After each one he returns to Jerusalem where eventually he is arrested and later imprisoned at Caesarea, 21:18–26:32. This leads him to Rome, where, still a missionary in spite of being a prisoner in chains, Paul preaches the good news, ch. 27–28, and since Rome could be taken as 'the ends of the earth' by anyone who thought of Jerusalem as the centre, Luke has reached a point where he can stop.

One may regret that Luke does not write about what the other apostles did, or describe how the Church was founded, for example, in Rome where it had been established before Paul's arrival (*see* Romans, written during Paul's third journey) or in Alexandria. Luke does not even suggest that Peter had an apostolate outside Palestine: the focus of attention shifts to Paul in ch. 13 as the faith is carried by Hellenists to gentiles, and there is little about developments in Jerusalem. His interest lies in: 1 The spiritual energy inside Christianity that motivates its expansion, and 2 The spiritual doctrine he can deduce from the facts at his disposal.

§5 Here it is possible to list only the main points that we learn from Acts. 1 The *kerygma* of the apostles is centred on faith in Christ, and in Acts this is presented with many slight variations that make it possible for us to recover the history of how this teaching developed; e.g. the earliest Christians are shown as feeling no need to go beyond the stage of contemplating the triumph of the human Jesus who has become the Lord by his resurrection, 2:22–36; but later Paul is made to give him the title 'Son of God', 9:20. 2 From the speeches we know the main scriptural texts that (under the Spirit's guidance) formed the basis both for a systematic Christology and for arguments with the Jews: e.g. the themes of the servant, 3:13,26; 4:27,30; 8:32–33, and the second Moses, 3:22seq.; 7:20seq.; the proof of the resurrection from Ps 16:8–11 (Ac 2:24–32; 13:34–37); and the use of their own history to warn Jews against resisting grace, Ac 7:2–53; 13:16–41. Gentiles, of course, needed a more generalised theological argument, 14:15–17; 17:22–31, and though the apostles are primarily 'witnesses', 1:8k (as such Luke sums up their *kerygma* 2:22h, and records their miraculous 'signs') the most urgent problem facing the new Church was the admission of gentiles, and Acts provides important details about this, without, however, revealing the full extent of the difficulties and disagreements this must have caused within the Christian community, and even between its leaders, *see* Ga 2:11h. The Jerusalem brotherhood led by James remains faithful to the Jewish Law, 15:1,5; 21:20seq.; but the Hellenists, for whom Stephen acts as spokesman, want to break away from Temple worship. In Luke's account, Peter, but even more so Paul, gets the principle of salvation through faith in Christ recognised at the council of Jerusalem. This dispenses the gentiles from the need to be circumcised and from obeying the whole Law of Moses. As it is still true, however, that this salvation comes from Israel, Luke records how Paul always preached to the Jews first, and turned to the gentiles only after his fellow-Jews had rejected him, 13:5e. 3 Acts also provides important details about life in the earliest Christian communities: e.g. the way of prayer and sharing of goods known to the church in Jerusalem; the administration of baptism in water and baptism in Spirit,

Ac 1:5f; celebration of the Eucharist, 2:42gg; early attempts at organisation, e.g. 'prophets' and 'teachers', 13:1a, the separate hierarchy appointed for the Hellenists, *see* 6:5f, the 'elders' who preside in the Jerusalem church, 11:30p, and those who are appointed by Paul in the churches he founds, 14:23. **4** All these developments in community life are attributed to the irresistible guidance of the Spirit. As Lk 4:1b insists on the importance of the Holy Spirit, so Acts (1:8j) attributes the spread of the developing Church to the continuous activity of the Holy Spirit—this is why the book has been called 'the gospel of the Spirit', and why it seems so full of spiritual joy and of wonder at God's works. **5** To this wealth of theology we must add the detailed factual information which we should otherwise lack, the psychological tact with which Luke presents his characters, the shrewdness and the craftsmanship of passages like the speech in the presence of Agrippa, ch. 26, and the pathos of scenes like the farewell to the Ephesian elders, 20:17–38. This book, the only one of its kind in the New Testament, is full of treasures.

§6 The texts of the New Testament have come down to us with a great number of minor variants, and for Acts those in the so-called 'Western' Text (Codex Bezae, the old Latin and old Syriac versions, and early ecclesiastical writers) are the most interesting. Because this Western Text, unlike the Alexandrian recension, was not critically edited in ancient times it contains many corrupt readings, but a number of its concrete and vivid details, absent from the other texts, could be authentic. The most important of these readings have been either mentioned in the footnotes or incorporated in the text.

ACTS
OF THE APOSTLES

Prologue

1 **1** In my earlier work,[a] Theophilus, I dealt with everything Jesus had done and
2 taught from the beginning ·until the day he gave his instructions to the apostles
3 he had chosen through the Holy Spirit,[b] and was taken up to heaven.[c] ·He had
shown himself alive to them after his Passion by many demonstrations: for forty
days he had continued to appear to them and tell them about the kingdom of
4 God.[d] ·While at table with them, he had told them not to leave Jerusalem,[e] but to
wait there for what the Father had promised. 'It is', he had said, 'what you have
5 heard me speak about: ·John baptised with water but, not many days from now,
you are going to be baptised[f] with the Holy Spirit.'

The ascension

6 Now having met together,[g] they asked him, 'Lord, has the time come for you to
7 restore the kingdom to Israel?'[h] ·He replied, 'It is not for you to know times or
8 dates[i] that the Father has decided by his own authority, ·but you will receive the
power of the Holy Spirit which will come on you,[j] and then you will be my
witnesses[k] not only in Jerusalem but throughout Judaea and Samaria, and indeed
to earth's remotest end.'[l]
9 As he said this he was lifted up while they looked on, and a cloud[m] took him
10 from their sight. ·They were still staring into the sky as he went when suddenly
11 two men in white were standing beside them ·and they said, 'Why are you Galileans
standing here looking into the sky? This Jesus[n] who has been taken up from you
into heaven will come back in the same way[o] as you have seen him go to heaven.'

I: THE CHURCH IN JERUSALEM

The group of apostles

12 So from the Mount of Olives, as it is called, they went back to Jerusalem, a short
13 distance away, no more than a Sabbath walk; ·and when they reached the city
they went to the upper room where they were staying; there were Peter and John,
James and Andrew, Philip and Thomas, Bartholomew and Matthew, James son
14 of Alphaeus and Simon the Zealot, and Jude son of James.[p] ·With one heart all
these joined constantly in prayer,[q] together with some women, including Mary
the mother of Jesus, and with his brothers.[r]

Judas is replaced

15 One day Peter stood up to speak to the brothers '—there were about a hundred
16 and twenty people in the congregation, ·'Brothers,' he said, 'the passage of scripture had to be fulfilled in which the Holy Spirit, speaking through David, foretells
17 the fate of Judas, who acted as guide to the men who arrested Jesus— ·after being
18 one of our number and sharing our ministry. ·As you know, he bought a plot of
land with the money he was paid for his crime. He fell headlong and burst open,
19 and all his entrails poured out. ·Everybody in Jerusalem heard about it and the
20 plot came to be called "Bloody Acre", in their language Hakeldama. ' ·Now in the
Book of Psalms it says:

> Reduce his encampment to ruin
> and leave his tent unoccupied.

And again:

> Let someone else take over his office.

21 'Out of the men who have been with us the whole time that the Lord Jesus was
22 living with us, ·from the time when John was baptising until the day when he was
taken up from us—one must be appointed to serve with us as a witness to his
resurrection.'
23 Having nominated two candidates, Joseph known as Barsabbas, whose surname
24 was Justus, and Matthias, ·they prayed, · 'Lord, you can read everyone's heart;
25 show us therefore which of these two you have chosen ·to take over this ministry
26 and apostolate, which Judas abandoned to go to his proper place.' ·They then
drew lots ' for them, and as the lot fell to Matthias, he was listed as one of the
twelve apostles. ·

Pentecost ·

1, 2 **2** When Pentecost day came round, they · had all met together, ·when suddenly
there came from heaven a sound as of a violent wind · which filled the entire
3 house in which they were sitting; ·and there appeared to them tongues as of fire; ·
4 these separated and came to rest on the head of each of them. ·They were all filled
with the Holy Spirit and began to speak different languages as the Spirit gave them
power to express themselves.
5 Now there were devout men · living in Jerusalem from every nation under
6 heaven, ·and at this sound they all assembled, and each one was bewildered to
7 hear these men speaking his own language. ·They were amazed and astonished.
8 'Surely,' they said, 'all these men speaking are Galileans? ·How does it happen
9 that each of us hears them in his own native language? ·Parthians, Medes and
Elamites; people from Mesopotamia, Judaea and Cappadocia, Pontus and Asia,
10 Phrygia and Pamphylia, Egypt and the parts of Libya round Cyrene; residents of
11 Rome—·Jews and proselytes ' alike—Cretans and Arabs; · we hear them preaching
12 in our own language about the marvels of God.' ·Everyone was amazed and
13 perplexed; they asked one another what it all meant. ·Some, however, laughed it
off. 'They have been drinking too much new wine,' they said.

Peter's address to the crowd

14 Then Peter stood up with the Eleven · and addressed them in a loud voice:
'Men of Judaea, and all you who live in Jerusalem, make no mistake about this,
15 but listen carefully to what I say. ·These men are not drunk, as you imagine; why,

16 it is only the third hour of the day.[i] ·On the contrary, this is what the prophet[j] was
saying:

17 In the last days[k]—the Lord declares—
I shall pour out my Spirit on all humanity.
Your sons and daughters shall prophesy,
your young people shall see visions,
your old people dream dreams.
18 *Even on the slaves, men and women,*
shall I pour out my Spirit.
19 *I will show portents in the sky* above
and signs *on the earth* below.
20 *The sun will be turned into darkness*
and the moon into blood
before the day of the Lord comes,[l]
that great and terrible Day.
21 *And all who call on the name of the Lord will be saved.*[m]

22 'Men of Israel, listen to what I am going to say:[n] Jesus the Nazarene was a man
commended to you by God by the miracles and portents and signs that God
23 worked through him when he was among you, as you know. ·This man, who was
put into your power by the deliberate intention[o] and foreknowledge of God, you
24 took and had crucified and killed by men outside the Law.[p] ·But God raised him
to life, freeing him from the pangs of Hades;[q] for it was impossible for him to be
25 held in its power since, ·as David says of him:[r]

I kept the Lord before my sight always,
for with him at my right hand nothing can shake me.
26 *So my heart rejoiced*
my tongue delighted;
my body, too, will rest secure,
27 *for you will not abandon me to Hades*
or allow your holy one to see corruption.
28 *You have taught me the way of life,*
you will fill me with joy in your presence.

29 'Brothers, no one can deny that the patriarch David himself is dead and buried:
30 his tomb is still with us.[s] ·But since he was a prophet, and knew that God *had*
31 *sworn him* an oath *to make one of his descendants succeed him on the throne*, ·he
spoke with foreknowledge about the resurrection of the Christ: he is the one who
32 was *not abandoned to Hades*, and whose body did not *see corruption*. ·God raised
33 this man Jesus to life, and of that we are all witnesses. ·Now raised to the heights
by God's right hand,[t] he has received from the Father the Holy Spirit, who was
34 promised,[u] and what you see and hear is the outpouring of that Spirit. ·For David
himself never went up to heaven,[v] but yet he said:

The Lord declared to my Lord,
take your seat at my right hand,
35 *till I have made your enemies*
your footstool.

36 'For this reason the whole House of Israel can be certain that the Lord and
Christ whom God has made is this Jesus whom you crucified.'[w]

The first conversions

37 Hearing this, they were cut to the heart and said to Peter and the other apostles,
38 'What are we to do, brothers?' ·'You must repent,' *ˣ* Peter answered, 'and every
one of you must be baptised in the name of Jesus Christ *ʸ* for the forgiveness of
39 your sins, and you will receive the gift of the Holy Spirit. ·The promise *ᶻ* that was
made is for you and your children, and for all *those who are far away,* *ᵃᵃ* *for all*
40 *those whom the Lord* our God *is calling to himself.*' ·He spoke to them *ᵇᵇ* for a long
time using many other arguments, and he urged them, 'Save yourselves from this
41 perverse generation.' ·They accepted what he said and were baptised. That very
day about three thousand were added to their number. *ᶜᶜ*

The early Christian community *ᵈᵈ*

42 These remained faithful to the teaching of the apostles, *ᵉᵉ* to the brotherhood, *ᶠᶠ* to
the breaking of bread *ᵍᵍ* and to the prayers. *ʰʰ*
43   And everyone was filled with awe; the apostles worked many signs and
miracles. *ⁱⁱ*
44. 45   And all who shared the faith owned everything in common; ·they sold their
goods and possessions and distributed the proceeds among themselves according
to what each one needed.
46   Each day, with one heart, they regularly went to the Temple but met in their
houses for the breaking of bread; they shared their food gladly *ʲʲ* and generously;
47 they praised God *ᵏᵏ* and were looked up to by everyone. Day by day the Lord
added to their community those destined to be saved. *ˡˡ*

The cure of a lame man

1 3 Once, when Peter and John were going up to the Temple for the prayers at
2 the ninth hour, *ᵃ* ·it happened that there was a man being carried along. He
was a cripple from birth; and they used to put him down every day near the Temple
entrance called the Beautiful Gate *ᵇ* so that he could beg from the people going in.
3 When this man saw Peter and John on their way into the Temple he begged from
4. 5 them. ·Peter, and John too, looked straight at him and said, 'Look at us.' He
6 turned to them expectantly, hoping to get something from them, ·but Peter said,
'I have neither silver nor gold, but I will give you what I have: in the name of Jesus
7 Christ the Nazarene, walk!' *ᶜ* ·Then he took him by the right hand and helped him
8 to stand up. Instantly his feet and ankles became firm, ·he jumped up, stood, and
began to walk, and he went with them into the Temple, walking and jumping and
9. 10 praising God. ·Everyone could see him walking and praising God, and they
recognised him as the man who used to sit begging at the Beautiful Gate of the
Temple. They were all astonished and perplexed at what had happened to him.

Peter's address to the people

11 Everyone came running towards them in great excitement, to the Portico of
12 Solomon, *ᵈ* as it is called, where the man was still clinging to Peter and John. When
Peter saw the people he addressed them. 'Men of Israel, why are you so surprised
at this? Why are you staring at us as though we had made this man walk by our
13 own power or holiness? ·It is *the God of Abraham, Isaac and Jacob, the God of
our ancestors, who has glorified his servant ᵉ* Jesus whom you handed over *ᶠ* and
then disowned *ᵍ* in the presence of Pilate after he had given his verdict to release
14 him. ·It was you who accused *ʰ* the Holy *ⁱ* and Upright *ʲ* One, you who demanded

15 that a murderer should be released to you •while you killed the prince of life.[k]
16 God, however, raised him from the dead, and to that fact we are witnesses; •and it
is the name of Jesus which, through faith in him, has brought back the strength of
this man whom you see here and who is well known to you. It is faith in him that
has restored this man to health, as you can all see.[l]
17 'Now I know, brothers, that neither you nor your leaders had any idea what you
18 were really doing;[m] •but this was the way God carried out what he had foretold,
19 when he said through all his prophets that his Christ would suffer. •Now you must
20 repent and turn to God,[n] so that your sins may be wiped out, •and so that the
Lord may send the time of comfort.[o] Then he will send you the Christ he has
21 predestined, that is Jesus,[p] •whom heaven must keep till the universal restoration[q]
22 comes which God proclaimed, speaking through his holy prophets.[r] •Moses, for
example, said, *"From among your brothers the Lord God will raise up for you a*
23 *prophet like me; you will listen to whatever he tells you. •Anyone who refuses to*
24 *listen to that prophet shall be cut off from the people."* •In fact, all the prophets
that have ever spoken, from Samuel onwards, have predicted these days.[s]
25 'You are the heirs of the prophets, the heirs of the covenant God made with
your ancestors when he told Abraham, *"All the nations of the earth will be blessed*
26 *in your descendants"*. •It was for you in the first place that God raised up[t] his
servant and sent him to bless you[u] as every one of you turns from his wicked
ways.'[v]

Peter and John before the Sanhedrin

1 4 While they were still talking to the people the priests came up to them,
2 accompanied by the captain of the Temple and the Sadducees.[a] •They were
extremely annoyed at their teaching the people the resurrection from the dead by
3 proclaiming the resurrection of Jesus. •They arrested them, and, as it was already
4 late, they kept them in prison till the next day. •But many of those who had
listened to their message became believers; the total number of men had now risen
to something like five thousand.
5 It happened that the next day the rulers, elders and scribes[b] held a meeting in
6 Jerusalem •with Annas the high priest, Caiaphas, Jonathan,[c] Alexander and all
7 the members of the high-priestly families. •They made the prisoners stand in the
middle and began to interrogate them, 'By what power, and by whose name have
8 you men done this?' •Then Peter, filled with the Holy Spirit, addressed them,
9 'Rulers of the people, and elders! •If you are questioning us today about an act of
10 kindness to a cripple and asking us how he was healed, •[d]you must know, all of
you, and the whole people of Israel, that it is by the name of Jesus Christ the
Nazarene, whom you crucified, and God raised from the dead, by this name and
11 by no other that this man stands before you cured. •This is *the stone which* you,
the builders, rejected but which *has become the cornerstone*. Only in him is there
12 salvation; •for of all the names in the world given to men, this is the only one by
which we can be saved.'[e]
13 They were astonished at the fearlessness shown by Peter and John, considering
that they were uneducated laymen; and they recognised them as associates of
14 Jesus; •but when they saw the man who had been cured standing by their side,
15 they could find no answer. •So they ordered them to stand outside while the
16 Sanhedrin had a private discussion. •'What are we going to do with these men?'
they asked. 'It is obvious to everybody in Jerusalem that a notable miracle has
17 been worked through them, and we cannot deny it. •But to stop the whole thing

spreading any further among the people, let us threaten them against ever speaking to anyone in this name again.'

18 So they called them in and gave them a warning*ʲ* on no account to make
19 statements or to teach in the name of Jesus. •But Peter and John retorted, 'You
20 must judge whether in God's eyes it is right to listen to you and not to God. •We
21 cannot stop proclaiming what we have seen and heard.' •The court repeated the
threats and then released them; they could not think of any way to punish them,
22 since all the people were giving glory to God for what had happened. •The man
who had been miraculously cured was over forty years old.

The apostles' prayer under persecution

23 As soon as they were released they went to the community and told them every-
24 thing the chief priests and elders had said to them. •When they heard it they lifted
up their voice to God with one heart. 'Master,' they prayed, 'it is you who made
25 sky and earth and sea, and everything in them; •it is you who said through the
Holy Spirit and speaking through our ancestor David, your servant: *ᵍ*

> *Why this uproar among the nations,*
> *this impotent muttering of the peoples?*
26 > *Kings on earth take up position,*
> *princes plot together*
> *against the Lord and his Anointed.* *ʰ*

27 'This is what has come true: in this very city Herod and Pontius Pilate*ⁱ plotted
together* with the gentile *nations* and the *peoples* of Israel, against your holy servant
28 Jesus whom you *anointed,ʲ* •to bring about the very thing that you in your strength
29 and your wisdom*ᵏ* had predetermined should happen. •And now, Lord, take
note of their threats and help your servants to proclaim your message with all
30 fearlessness, •by stretching out your hand to heal and to work miracles and marvels
31 through the name of your holy servant Jesus.' •As they prayed, the house where
they were assembled rocked. From this time they were all filled with the Holy
Spirit and began to proclaim the word of God fearlessly. *ˡ*

The early Christian community *ᵐ*

32 The whole group of believers was united, heart and soul; no one claimed private
ownership of any possessions, as everything they owned was held in common.
33 The apostles continued to testify to the resurrection of the Lord Jesus with great
power, *ⁿ* and they were all accorded great respect. *ᵒ*
34 None of their members was ever in want, as all those who owned land or houses
35 would sell them, and bring the money from the sale of them, •to present it to the
apostles; it was then distributed to any who might be in need.

The generosity of Barnabas

36 There was a Levite of Cypriot origin called Joseph whom the apostles surnamed
37 Barnabas (which means 'son of encouragement'). *ᵖ* •He owned a piece of land and
he sold it and brought the money and presented it to the apostles.

The fraud of Ananias and Sapphira

1 **5** There was also a man called Ananias. He and his wife, Sapphira, agreed to
2 sell a property; •but with his wife's connivance he kept back part of the price
3 and brought the rest and presented it to the apostles. •Peter said, 'Ananias, how

can Satan have so possessed you that you should lie to the Holy Spirit and keep
4 back part of the price of the land? ·While you still owned the land, wasn't it yours
to keep, and after you had sold it wasn't the money yours to do with as you liked?
What put this scheme into your mind? You have been lying not to men, but to
5 God.' ·When he heard this Ananias fell down dead. And a great fear came upon
6 everyone present. ·The younger men got up, wrapped up the body, carried it out
and buried it.
7   About three hours later his wife came in, not knowing what had taken place.
8 Peter challenged her, 'Tell me, was this the price you sold the land for?' 'Yes,' she
9 said, 'that was the price.' ·Peter then said, 'Why did you and your husband agree
to put the Spirit of the Lord to the test? Listen! At the door are the footsteps of
10 those who have buried your husband; they will carry you out, too.' ·Instantly she
dropped dead at his feet. When the young men came in they found she was dead,
11 and they carried her out and buried her by the side of her husband. *·And a great
fear came upon the whole church *b* and on all who heard it.

The general situation *c*

12 The apostles worked many signs and miracles among the people. One in heart
13 they all *d* used to meet in the Portico of Solomon. ·No one else dared to join them,
14 but the people were loud in their praise ·and the numbers of men and women who
came to believe in the Lord increased steadily. *e* Many signs and wonders were
15 worked among the people at the hands of the apostles ·so that the sick were even
taken out into the streets and laid on beds and sleeping-mats in the hope that at
16 least the shadow of Peter might fall across some of them as he went past. ·People
even came crowding in from the towns round about Jerusalem, bringing with them
their sick and those tormented by unclean spirits, and all of them were cured.

The apostles' arrest and miraculous deliverance

17 Then the high priest *f* intervened with all his supporters from the party of the
18 Sadducees. Filled with jealousy, ·they arrested the apostles and had them put in
the public gaol.
19   But at night the angel of the Lord opened the prison gates and said as he led
20 them out, ·'Go and take up position in the Temple, and tell the people all about
21 this new Life.' *g* ·They did as they were told; they went into the Temple at dawn
and began to preach.

A summons to appear before the Sanhedrin

When the high priest arrived, he and his supporters convened the Sanhedrin—this
22 was the full Senate *h* of Israel—and sent to the gaol for them to be brought. ·But
when the officials arrived at the prison they found they were not inside, so they
23 went back and reported, ·'We found the gaol securely locked and the warders on
24 duty at the gates, but when we unlocked the door we found no one inside.' ·When
the captain of the Temple and the chief priests heard this news they wondered
25 what could be happening. ·Then a man arrived with fresh news. 'Look!' he said,
'the men you imprisoned are in the Temple. They are standing there preaching to
26 the people.' ·The captain went with his men and fetched them—though not by
force, for they were afraid that the people might stone them.
27   When they had brought them in to face the Sanhedrin, the high priest demanded
28 an explanation. ·'We gave you a strong warning', he said, 'not to preach in this
name, *i* and what have you done? You have filled Jerusalem with your teaching,

29 and seem determined to fix the guilt for this man's death on us.' •In reply Peter
30 and the apostles said, 'Obedience to God comes before obedience to men; •it was
the God of our ancestors who raised up Jesus, whom you executed by hanging on
31 a tree.[j] •By his own right hand God has now raised him up to be leader and
32 Saviour,[k] to give repentance and forgiveness of sins through him to Israel. •We
are witnesses to this, we and the Holy Spirit[l] whom God has given to those who
33 obey him.' •This so infuriated them that they wanted to put them to death.

Gamaliel's intervention

34 One member of the Sanhedrin, however, a Pharisee called Gamaliel, who was a
teacher of the Law respected by the whole people,[m] stood up and asked to have
35 the men taken outside for a time. •Then he addressed the Sanhedrin, 'Men of
36 Israel, be careful how you deal with these people. •Some time ago there arose
Theudas. He claimed to be someone important, and collected about four hundred
followers; but when he was killed, all his followers scattered and that was the end
37 of them. •And then there was Judas the Galilean, at the time of the census,
who attracted crowds of supporters; but he was killed too, and all his followers
38 dispersed.[n] •What I suggest, therefore, is that you leave these men alone and let
them go. If this enterprise, this movement of theirs, is of human origin it will
39 break up of its own accord; •but if it does in fact come from God you will be
unable to destroy them. Take care not to find yourselves fighting against God.'[o]

40 His advice was accepted; •and they had the apostles called in, gave orders for
them to be flogged, warned them not to speak in the name of Jesus and released
41 them. •And so they left the presence of the Sanhedrin, glad to have had the honour
of suffering humiliation for the sake of the name.[p]

42 Every day they went on ceaselessly teaching and proclaiming the good news[q] of
Christ Jesus, both in the temple and in private houses.

II: THE EARLIEST MISSIONS

The institution of the Seven

1 6 About this time, when the number of disciples[a] was increasing, the Hellenists
made a complaint against the Hebrews:[b] in the daily distribution their own
2 widows were being overlooked. •So the Twelve called a full meeting of the disciples
and addressed them, 'It would not be right for us to neglect the word of God so as
3 to give out food; •you, brothers, must select[c] from among yourselves seven men
of good reputation,[d] filled with the Spirit and with wisdom, to whom we can hand
4 over this duty. •We ourselves will continue to devote ourselves to prayer and to
5 the service of the word.'[e] •The whole assembly approved of this proposal and
elected Stephen, a man full of faith and of the Holy Spirit, together with Philip,
Prochorus, Nicanor, Timon, Parmenas, and Nicolaus of Antioch, a convert to
6 Judaism.[f] •They presented these to the apostles, and after prayer they laid their
hands on them.[g]

7 The word of the Lord continued to spread:[h] the number of disciples in Jerusalem
was greatly increased, and a large group of priests made their submission to the
faith.

Stephen's arrest

8 Stephen was filled with grace and power and began to work miracles and great
9 signs among the people. ·Then certain people came forward to debate with
Stephen, some from Cyrene and Alexandria who were members of the synagogue
10 called the Synagogue of Freedmen, *and others from Cilicia and Asia. ·They found
they could not stand up against him because of his wisdom, and the Spirit that
11 prompted what he said. ·So they procured some men to say, 'We heard him using
12 blasphemous language against Moses and against God.' ·Having turned the people
against him as well as the elders and scribes, they took Stephen by surprise, and
13 arrested him and brought him before the Sanhedrin. ·There they put up false
witnesses to say, 'This man is always making speeches against this Holy Place and
14 the Law. ·We have heard him say that Jesus, this Nazarene, is going to destroy
15 this Place and alter the traditions that Moses handed down to us.' ·The members
of the Sanhedrin all looked intently at Stephen, and his face appeared to them like
the face of an angel. *

Stephen's speech

1, 2 **7** The high priest asked, 'Is this true?' ·He replied, ª 'My brothers, my fathers,
listen to what I have to say. The God of glory appeared to our ancestor
3 Abraham, while he was in Mesopotamia before settling in Haran, ª ·and *said to*
him, "*Leave your country, your kindred and your father's house for this country*
4 *which I shall show you.*" ·So he left Chaldaea and settled in Haran; and after his
father died God made him leave that place and come to this land where you are
5 living today. ·God did not give him any property in this land or even a foothold,
yet he promised to *give it to him and after him to his descendants, childless* though
6 he was. ·The actual words God used when he spoke to him are that *his descendants*
would be exiles in a land not their own, where they would be enslaved and oppressed
7 *for four hundred years.* ·"*But I will bring judgement on the nation that enslaves*
them," God said, "*and after this they will leave, and worship me in this* place." ª
8 Then he made the *covenant of circumcision* with him: and so when his son Isaac
was born Abraham *circumcised him on the eighth day*; similarly Isaac circumcised
Jacob, and Jacob the twelve patriarchs.
9 'The patriarchs were *jealous of Joseph and sold him into slavery in Egypt.* But
10 *God was with him,* ·and rescued him from all his miseries by making him so wise
that he *won the favour* of Pharaoh king of Egypt, who *made him governor of Egypt*
11 and *put him in charge of his household.* ·*Then a famine set in* that caused much
suffering *throughout Egypt and Canaan*, and our ancestors could find nothing to
12 eat. ·When Jacob *heard that there were supplies in Egypt*, he sent our ancestors
13 there on a first visit; ·and on the second *Joseph made himself known to his brothers*,
14 and Pharaoh came to know his origin. ·Joseph then sent for his father Jacob and
15 his whole family, a total of *seventy-five people.* ·Jacob went down into Egypt and
16 after he and our ancestors had died there, ·their bodies were brought back to
Shechem and buried in the tomb that Abraham had bought for money from the
sons of Hamor, the father of Shechem. *
17 'As the time drew near for God to fulfil the promise he had solemnly made to
18 Abraham, our nation in Egypt *became very powerful and numerous, ·there came*
19 *to power in Egypt a new king who had never heard of Joseph.* ·He took precautions
and wore down our race, forcing our ancestors to expose their babies rather than
20 *letting them live.* ·It was at this time that Moses was born, *a fine child* before God.

21 He was looked after for *three months* in his father's house, ·and after he had been
22 exposed, *Pharaoh's daughter adopted* him and brought him up *like a son*. ·So
Moses was taught all the wisdom of the Egyptians and became a man with power
both in his speech and in his actions.

23, 24 'At the age of forty^e he decided to visit *his kinsmen, the Israelites*. ·When he
saw one of them being ill-treated he went to his defence and rescued the man by
25 *killing the Egyptian*. ·He thought his brothers would realise that through him God
26 would liberate them, but they did not. ·The next day, when he came across some
of them fighting, he tried to reconcile them, and said, "Friends, you are brothers;
27 why are you hurting each other?" ·But *the man who was attacking his kinsman*
pushed him aside, saying, "*And who appointed you to be prince over us and judge?*^f
28, 29 *Do you intend to kill me as you killed the Egyptian yesterday?*" ·Moses fled when
he heard this^g and *he went to dwell in the land of Midian*, where he fathered two
sons.

30 'When forty years were fulfilled, *in the desert near Mount* Sinai, *an angel
31 appeared to him in a flame blazing from a bush* that was on fire. ·Moses was
amazed by what he saw. *As he went nearer to look at it, the voice of the Lord was
32 heard,* ·"I am the God of your ancestors, the God of Abraham, Isaac and Jacob."
33 Moses trembled and *was afraid to look*. ·The Lord said to him, "*Take off your
34 sandals, for the place where you are standing is holy ground. ·I have seen the misery
of my people in Egypt, I have heard them crying for help, and I have come down to
rescue them. So come here; I am sending you into Egypt.*"

35 'It was the same Moses that they had disowned^h when they said, "*Who appointed
you to be our leader and judge?*" whom God sent to be both leader and redeemer
36 through the angel who had appeared to him in the bush. ·It was this man who led
them out, after performing *miracles and signs in Egypt* and at the Red Sea and *in
37 the desert for forty years*. ·It was this Moses who told the sons of Israel, "*From
38 among your own brothers God will raise up a prophet like me.*"ⁱ ·When they held
the assembly^j in the desert it was he who was with our ancestors and the angel
who had spoken to him on Mount Sinai;^k it was he who was entrusted with words
39 of life^l to hand on to us. ·This is the man that our ancestors refused to listen to;
40 they pushed him aside, *went back to Egypt* in their thoughts,^m ·*and said to Aaron,
"Make us a god to go at our head; for that Moses, the man who brought us here
41 from Egypt, we do not know what has become of him.*" ·It was then that *they made
the statue of a calf and offered sacrifice* to the idol. They were perfectly happy with
42 something they had made for themselves. ·God turned away from them and
abandoned them to the worship of the army of heaven,ⁿ as scripture says in the
book of the prophets:

> *Did you bring me sacrifices and oblations
> those forty years in the desert, House of Israel?*
43 > *No, you carried the tent of Moloch on your shoulders
> and the star of the god Rephan,
> the idols you made for yourselves* to adore,
> *and so now I am about to drive you into captivity beyond* Babylon.

44 'While they were in the desert our ancestors possessed the Tent of Testimony
that had been constructed according to the instructions God gave Moses, telling
45 him to *work to the design* he had been shown. ·It was handed down from one
ancestor of ours to another until Joshua brought it into the country that had
belonged to the nations which were driven out by God before us. Here it stayed

46 until the time of David. ·He won God's favour and asked permission *to find a*
47 *dwelling for* the House*⁰* of *Jacob*, ·though it was *Solomon* who actually *built a*
48 *house for God.* ·Even so the Most High does not live in a house that human hands
have built: for as the prophet says:

49   *With heaven my throne*
          and earth my footstool,
          what house could you build me, says the Lord,
          what place for me to rest,
50   *when all these things were made by me?*

51 'You stubborn people, with uncircumcised hearts and ears. You are always
52 resisting the Holy Spirit,*ᵖ* just as your ancestors used to do. ·Can you name a
single prophet your ancestors never persecuted? They killed those who foretold
the coming of the Upright One, and now you have become his betrayers, his
53 murderers. ·In spite of being given the Law through angels, you have not kept it.'
54 They were infuriated when they heard this, and ground their teeth at him.

The stoning of Stephen. Saul as persecutor

55 But Stephen, filled with the Holy Spirit, gazed into heaven and saw the glory of
56 God, and Jesus standing*ᵠ* at God's right hand.*ʳ* ·'Look! I can see heaven thrown
57 open,' he said, 'and the Son of man standing at the right hand of God.' ·All the
members of the council shouted out and stopped their ears with their hands; then
58 they made a concerted rush at him, ·thrust him out of the city and stoned him.*ˢ*
59 The witnesses*ᵗ* put down their clothes at the feet of a young man called Saul. *ᵘ* ·As
they were stoning him, Stephen said in invocation,*ᵛ* 'Lord Jesus, receive my spirit.'
60 Then he knelt down and said aloud, 'Lord, do not hold this sin against them.' And
with these words he fell asleep.

8 *ᵃ*Saul approved of the killing.
That day a bitter persecution started against the church in Jerusalem, and
everyone*ᵇ* except the apostles scattered to the country districts of Judaea and
Samaria.*ᶜ*
2 There were some devout people, however, who buried Stephen and made great
mourning for him.
3 Saul then began doing great harm to the church; he went from house to house
arresting both men and women and sending them to prison.

Philip in Samaria

4 Once they had scattered, they went from place to place preaching the good news.
5,6 And Philip went to a Samaritan town*ᵈ* and proclaimed the Christ to them.*ᵉ* ·The
people unanimously welcomed the message Philip preached, because they had
7 heard of the miracles he worked and because they saw them for themselves. ·For
unclean spirits came shrieking out of many who were possessed, and several
8 paralytics and cripples were cured. ·As a result there was great rejoicing in that
town.

Simon the magician

9 Now a man called Simon had for some time been practising magic arts in the town
and astounded the Samaritan people. He had given it out that he was someone
10 momentous, ·and everyone believed in him; eminent citizens and ordinary people
11 alike had declared, 'He is the divine power that is called Great.'*ᶠ* ·He had this

following because for a considerable period they had been astounded by his
12 wizardry. •But when they came to accept Philip's preaching of the good news
about the kingdom of God and the name of Jesus Christ, they were baptised, both
13 men and women, •and even Simon himself became a believer. After his baptism
Simon went round constantly with Philip and was astonished when he saw the
wonders and great miracles that took place.

14 When the apostles in Jerusalem heard that Samaria had accepted the word of
15 God, they sent Peter and John to them, •and they went down there and prayed for
16 them to receive the Holy Spirit, •for as yet he had not come down on any of them:
17 they had only been baptised in the name of the Lord Jesus. •Then they laid hands
on them, and they received the Holy Spirit.

18 When Simon saw that the Spirit was given through the laying on of the apostles'
19 hands, he offered them money, •with the words, 'Give me the same power so that
20 anyone I lay my hands on will receive the Holy Spirit.' •Peter answered, 'May
your silver be lost for ever, and you with it, for thinking that money could buy
21 what God has given[g] for nothing! •You have no share, no part, in this: God can
22 see how your heart is warped. •Repent of this wickedness of yours, and pray to
23 the Lord that this scheme of yours may be forgiven; •it is plain to me that you are
24 held in the bitterness of gall and the chains of sin.'[h] •Simon replied, 'Pray to the
Lord for me yourselves so that none of the things you have spoken about may
happen to me.'[i]

25 Having given their testimony and proclaimed the word of the Lord, they went
back to Jerusalem, preaching the good news to a number of Samaritan villages.

Philip baptises a eunuch

26 The angel of the Lord[j] spoke to Philip saying, 'Set out at noon[k] and go along the
27 road that leads from Jerusalem down to Gaza, the desert road.' •So he set off on
his journey. Now an Ethiopian[l] had been on pilgrimage to Jerusalem; he was a
eunuch and an officer at the court of the kandake, or queen, of Ethiopia; he was
28 her chief treasurer. •He was now on his way home; and as he sat in his chariot he
29 was reading the prophet Isaiah. •The Spirit said to Philip, 'Go up and join that
30 chariot.' •When Philip ran up, he heard him reading Isaiah the prophet and asked,
31 'Do you understand what you are reading?' •He replied, 'How could I, unless I
32 have someone to guide me?' So he urged Philip to get in and sit by his side. •Now
the passage of scripture he was reading was this:[m]

Like a lamb led to the slaughter-house,
like a sheep dumb in front of its shearers,
he never opens his mouth.
33 *In his humiliation fair judgement was denied him.*
Who will ever talk about his descendants,
since his life on earth has been cut short?

34 The eunuch addressed Philip and said, 'Tell me, is the prophet referring to
35 himself or someone else?' •Starting, therefore, with this text of scripture Philip
proceeded to explain the good news of Jesus to him.

36 Further along the road they came to some water, and the eunuch said, 'Look,
38 here is some water; is there anything to prevent my being baptised?'[n] •He ordered
the chariot to stop, then Philip and the eunuch both went down into the water and
39 he baptised him. •But after they had come up out of the water again Philip was
taken away by the Spirit of the Lord,[o] and the eunuch never saw him again but

40 went on his way rejoicing. ·Philip appeared in Azotus and continued his journey, proclaiming the good news in every town as far as Caesarea.

The conversion of Saul ᵃ

1 9 Meanwhile Saul was still breathing threats to slaughter the Lord's disciples.
2   He went to the high priest ·and asked for letters addressed to the synagogues in Damascus, that would authorise him to arrest and take to Jerusalem any followers of the Way, ᵇ men or women, that he might find. ᶜ
3   It happened that while he was travelling to Damascus and approaching the city,
4 suddenly a light from heaven shone all round him. ·He fell to the ground, and
5 then he heard a voice saying, 'Saul, Saul, ᵈ why are you persecuting me?' ·'Who are you, Lord?' he asked, and the answer came, 'I am Jesus, whom you are
6 persecuting. ᵉ ·Get up and go into the city, and you will be told what you are to do.'
7 The men travelling with Saul stood there speechless, for though they heard the
8 voice they could see no one. ·Saul got up from the ground, but when he opened his eyes he could see nothing at all, and they had to lead him into Damascus by
9 the hand. ·For three days he was without his sight and took neither food nor drink.
10   There was a disciple in Damascus called Ananias, and he had a vision in which
11 the Lord said to him, 'Ananias!' When he replied, 'Here I am, Lord,' ·the Lord said, 'Get up and go to Straight Street and ask at the house of Judas for someone
12 called Saul, who comes from Tarsus. At this moment he is praying, ·and has seen a man called Ananias coming in and laying hands on him to give him back his sight.'
13   But in response, Ananias said, 'Lord, I have heard from many people about this man and all the harm he has been doing to your holy people ᶠ in Jerusalem.
14 He has come here with a warrant from the chief priests to arrest everybody who
15 invokes your name.' ·The Lord replied, 'Go, for this man is my chosen instrument
16 to bring my name before gentiles and kings and before the people of Israel; ʰ ·I
17 myself will show him how much he must suffer for my name.' ·Then Ananias went. He entered the house, and laid his hands on Saul and said, 'Brother Saul, I have been sent by the Lord Jesus, who appeared to you on your way here, so that
18 you may recover your sight and be filled with the Holy Spirit.' ⁱ ·It was as though scales fell away from his eyes and immediately he was able to see again. So he got
19 up and was baptised, ·and after taking some food he regained his strength.

Saul's preaching at Damascus

20 After he had spent only a few days with the disciples in Damascus, ·he began
21 preaching in the synagogues, 'Jesus is the Son of God.' ʲ ·All his hearers were amazed, and said, 'Surely, this is the man who did such damage in Jerusalem to the people who invoke this name, and who came here for the sole purpose of
22 arresting them to have them tried by the chief priests?' ·Saul's power increased steadily, and he was able to throw the Jewish colony at Damascus into complete confusion by the way he demonstrated that Jesus was the Christ.
23, 24   Some time passed, ᵏ and the Jews worked out a plot to kill him, ·but news of it reached Saul. They were keeping watch at the gates day and night in order to kill
25 him, ·but the disciples ˡ took him by night and let him down from the wall, lowering him in a basket.

Saul's visit to Jerusalem ▪

26 When he got to Jerusalem he tried to join the disciples, but they were all afraid of
27 him: they could not believe he was really a disciple. ·Barnabas, however, took
charge of him, introduced him to the apostles, and explained how the Lord had
appeared to him and spoken to him on his journey, and how he had preached
28 fearlessly at Damascus in the name of Jesus. ·Saul now started to go round with
29 them in Jerusalem, preaching fearlessly in the name of the Lord: ·But after he had
spoken to the Hellenists ▪ and argued with them, they became determined to kill
30 him. ·When the brothers got to know of this, they took him to Caesarea and sent
him off from there to Tarsus. ᵒ

A lull

31 The churches ᵖ throughout Judaea, Galilee and Samaria were now left in peace,
building themselves up and living in the fear of the Lord; encouraged by the Holy
Spirit, they continued to grow.

Peter cures a paralytic at Lydda

32 It happened that Peter visited one place after another and eventually came to
33 God's holy people living down in Lydda. ·There he found a man called Aeneas, a
34 paralytic who had been bedridden for eight years. ·Peter said to him, 'Aeneas,
Jesus Christ cures you: get up and make your bed.' Aeneas got up immediately; ᑫ
35 everybody who lived in Lydda and Sharon saw him, and they were converted to
the Lord.

Peter raises a woman to life at Jaffa

36 At Jaffa there was a disciple called Tabitha, or in Greek, Dorcas, ʳ who never tired
37 of doing good or giving to those in need. ·But it happened that at this time she
became ill and died, and they washed her and laid her out in an upper room.
38 Lydda is not far from Jaffa, so when the disciples heard that Peter was there, they
sent two men to urge him, 'Come to us without delay.'
39   Peter went back with them immediately, and on his arrival they took him to the
upper room, where all the widows stood round him in tears, showing him tunics
40 and other clothes Dorcas had made when she was with them. ·Peter sent everyone
out of the room and knelt down and prayed. Then he turned to the dead woman
and said, 'Tabitha, stand up.' She opened her eyes, looked at Peter and sat up.
41 Peter helped her to her feet, then he called in the members of the congregation
42 and widows and showed them she was alive. ·The whole of Jaffa heard about it
and many believed in the Lord.
43   Peter stayed on some time in Jaffa, lodging with a leather-tanner called Simon.

Peter visits a Roman centurion ᵃ

1 **10** One of the centurions of the Italica cohort stationed in Caesarea was called
2 Cornelius. ·He and the whole of his household were devout and God-
fearing, ᵇ and he gave generously to Jewish causes and prayed constantly to God.
3   One day at about the ninth hour he had a vision in which he distinctly saw the
4 angel of God come into his house and call out to him, 'Cornelius!' ·He stared at
the vision in terror and exclaimed, 'What is it, Lord?' The angel answered 'Your
5 prayers and charitable gifts have been accepted by God. ᶜ ·Now you must send
6 some men to Jaffa and fetch a man called Simon, known as Peter, ·who is lodging

7 with Simon the tanner whose house is by the sea.' ·When the angel who said this
8 had gone, Cornelius called two of the slaves and a devout soldier of his staff, ·told
them all that had happened, and sent them off to Jaffa. ·

9 Next day, while they were still on their journey and had only a short distance to
go before reaching the town, Peter went to the housetop at about the sixth hour to
10 say his prayers. ·He felt hungry and was looking forward to his meal, but before it
11 was ready he fell into a trance ·and saw heaven thrown open and something like a
12 big sheet being let down to earth by its four corners; *d* ·it contained every kind of
13, 14 animal, reptile and bird. ·A voice then said to him, 'Now, Peter; kill and eat!' ·But
. Peter answered, 'Certainly not, Lord; I have never yet eaten anything profane or
15 unclean.' ·Again, a second time, the voice spoke to him, 'What God has made
16 clean, you have no right to call profane.' *e* ·This was repeated three times, and
then suddenly the container was drawn up to heaven again.

17 Peter was still at a loss over the meaning of the vision he had seen, when the
men sent by Cornelius arrived. They had asked where Simon's house was and they
18 were now standing at the door, ·calling out to know if the Simon known as Peter
19 was lodging there. ·While Peter's mind was still on the vision, the Spirit *f* told him,
20 'Look! Some men *g* have come to see you. ·Hurry down, and do not hesitate to
21 return with them; it was I who told them to come.' ·Peter went down and said to
22 them, 'I am the man you are looking for; why have you come?' ·They said, 'The
centurion Cornelius, who is an upright and God-fearing man, highly regarded by
the entire Jewish people, was told by God through a holy angel to send for you
23 and bring you to his house and to listen to what you have to say.' ·So Peter asked
them in and gave them lodging.

Next day, he was ready to go off with them, accompanied by some of the
24 brothers from Jaffa. ·They reached Caesarea the following day, and Cornelius
25 was waiting for them. He had asked his relations and close friends to be there, ·and
as Peter reached the house Cornelius went out to meet him, fell at his feet and did
26 him reverence. ·But Peter helped him up. 'Stand up,' he said, ' after all, I am only
27 a man!' ·Talking together they went in to meet all the people assembled there,
28 and Peter said to them, 'You know it is forbidden for Jews to mix with people of
another race and visit them; but God has made it clear to me that I must not call
29 anyone profane or unclean. ·That is why I made no objection to coming when I
30 was sent for; but I should like to know exactly why you sent for me.' ·Cornelius
replied, 'At this time three days ago I was in my house saying the prayers for the
31 ninth hour, *h* when I suddenly saw a man in front of me in shining robes. ·He said,
"Cornelius, your prayer has been heard and your charitable gifts have not been
32 forgotten by God; *i* ·so now you must send to Jaffa and fetch Simon known as
33 Peter who is lodging in the house of Simon the tanner, by the sea." ·So I sent for
you at once, and you have been kind enough to come. Here we all are, assembled
in front of you to hear all the instructions God has given you.'

Peter's address in the house of Cornelius

34 Then Peter addressed them, 'I now really understand', he said, 'that God has no
35 favourites, ·but that anybody of any nationality who fears him and does what is
right is acceptable to him. *j*

36 'God sent his word *k* to the people of Israel, and it was to them that *the good*
37 *news of peace was brought* by Jesus Christ—he is the Lord of all. ·You know what
happened all over Judaea, *l* how Jesus of Nazareth began *m* in Galilee, after John
38 had been preaching baptism. ·*God had anointed him with the Holy Spirit* and with

power, and because God was with him, Jesus went about doing good and curing
39 all who had fallen into the power of the devil. ·Now we are witnesses to everything
he did throughout the countryside of Judaea and in Jerusalem itself: and they
40 killed him by hanging him on a tree, ·yet on the third day God raised him to life "
41 and allowed him to be seen, ·not by the whole people but only by certain witnesses
that God had chosen beforehand. Now we are those witnesses—we have eaten
42 and drunk with him ° after his resurrection from the dead—·and he has ordered us
to proclaim this to his people ° and to bear witness that God has appointed him to
43 judge everyone, alive or dead. ° ·It is to him that all the prophets bear this witness:
that all who believe in Jesus will have their sins forgiven through his name.'

Baptism of the first gentiles

44 While Peter was still speaking the Holy Spirit came down ° on all the listeners.
45 Jewish believers who had accompanied Peter were all astonished that the gift of
46 the Holy Spirit should be poured out on gentiles too, ·since they could hear them
speaking strange languages and proclaiming the greatness of God. Peter himself
47 then said, ·'Could anyone refuse the water of baptism to these people, now they
48 have received the Holy Spirit just as we have?' ·He then gave orders ° for them to
be baptised in the name of Jesus Christ. Afterwards they begged him to stay on
for some days. '

Jerusalem: Peter justifies his conduct

1   The apostles and the brothers in Judaea heard that gentiles too had accepted
2 **11** the word of God, ·and when Peter came up to Jerusalem the circumcised
3 believers protested to him ° ·and said, 'So you have been visiting the uncircumcised
4. 5 and eating with them!' ·Peter in reply gave them the details point by point, ·'One
day, when I was in the town of Jaffa,' he began, 'I fell into a trance as I was
praying and had a vision of something like a big sheet being let down from heaven
6 by its four corners. This sheet came right down beside me. ·I looked carefully into
it and saw four-footed animals of the earth, wild beasts, reptiles, and birds of
7. 8 heaven. ·Then I heard a voice that said to me, "Now, Peter; kill and eat!" ·But I
answered, "Certainly not, Lord; nothing profane or unclean has ever crossed my
9 lips." ·And a second time the voice spoke from heaven, "What God has made
10 clean, you have no right to call profane." ·This was repeated three times, before
the whole of it was drawn up to heaven again.
11   'Just at that moment, three men stopped outside the house where we were
12 staying; they had been sent from Caesarea to fetch me, ·and the Spirit told me to
have no hesitation about going back with them. The six brothers here came with
13 me as well, and we entered the man's house. ·He told us he had seen an angel
standing in his house who said, "Send to Jaffa and fetch Simon known as Peter;
14 he has a message for you that will save you and your entire household."
15   'I had scarcely begun to speak when the Holy Spirit came down on them in the
16 same way as it came on us at the beginning, ·and I remembered that the Lord had
17 said, "John baptised with water, but you will be baptised with the Holy Spirit." ·I
realised then that God ° was giving them the identical gift he gave to us when we
believed in the Lord Jesus Christ; and who was I to stand in God's way?' °
18   This account satisfied them, and they gave glory to God, saying 'God has clearly
granted to the gentiles too the repentance that leads to life.'

Foundation of the church of Antioch

19 Those who had scattered *d* because of the persecution that arose over Stephen travelled as far as Phoenicia and Cyprus and Antioch, *e* but they proclaimed the
20 message only to Jews. ·Some of them, however, who came from Cyprus and Cyrene, went to Antioch where they started preaching also to the Greeks, *f*
21 proclaiming the good news of the Lord Jesus *g* to them. ·The Lord helped them, and a great number believed and were converted to the Lord.
22 The news of them came to the ears of the church in Jerusalem *h* and they sent
23 Barnabas out to Antioch. ·There he was glad to see for himself that God had given grace, and he urged *i* them all to remain faithful to the Lord *j* with heartfelt
24 devotion; ·for he was a good man, filled with the Holy Spirit and with faith. And a large number of people were won over to the Lord.
25, 26 Barnabas then left for Tarsus to look for Saul, ·and when he found him he brought him to Antioch. And it happened that they stayed together in that church *k* a whole year, instructing a large number of people. It was at Antioch that the disciples were first called 'Christians'. *l*

Barnabas and Saul sent as deputies to Jerusalem

27 While they were there some prophets *m* came down to Antioch from Jerusalem, *n*
28 and one of them whose name was Agabus, seized by the Spirit, stood up and predicted that a severe and universal famine was going to happen. This in fact
29 happened while Claudius was emperor. *o* ·The disciples decided to send relief,
30 each to contribute what he could afford, to the brothers living in Judaea. ·They did this and delivered their contributions to the elders *p* through the agency of Barnabas and Saul.

Peter's arrest and miraculous deliverance *a*

1 12 It was about this time that King Herod started persecuting certain members
2, 3 of the church. ·He had James the brother of John beheaded, ·and when he
4 saw that this pleased the Jews he went on to arrest Peter as well. ·As it was during the days of Unleavened Bread that he had arrested him, he put him in prison, assigning four sections of four soldiers each to guard him, meaning to try him in
5 public after the Passover. ·All the time Peter was under guard the church prayed to God for him unremittingly.
6 On the night before Herod was to try him, Peter was sleeping between two soldiers, *b* while guards kept watch at the main entrance
7 to the prison. ·Then suddenly an angel of the Lord stood there, and the cell was filled with light. He tapped Peter on the side and woke him. 'Get up!' he said,
8 'Hurry!'—and the chains fell from his hands. ·The angel then said, 'Put on your belt and sandals.' After he had done this, the angel next said, 'Wrap your cloak
9 round you and follow me.' ·He followed him out, but had no idea that what the
10 angel did was all happening in reality; he thought he was seeing a vision. ·They passed through the first guard post and then the second and reached the iron gate leading to the city. This opened of its own accord; they went through it *c* and had
11 walked the whole length of one street when suddenly the angel left him. ·It was only then that Peter came to himself. And he said, 'Now I know it is all true. The Lord really did send his angel and save me from Herod and from all that the Jewish people were expecting.'
12 As soon as he realised this he went straight to the house of Mary the mother of

13 John Mark,ᵈ where a number of people had assembled and were praying. ·He
14 knocked at the outside door and a servant called Rhoda came to answer it. ·She
recognised Peter's voice and was so overcome with joy that, instead of opening
the door, she ran inside with the news that Peter was standing at the main entrance.
15 They said to her, 'You are out of your mind,' but she insisted that it was true.
16 Then they said, 'It must be his angel!'ᵉ ·Peter, meanwhile, was still knocking.
When they opened the door, they were amazed to see that it really was Peter
17 himself. ·He raised his hand for silence and described to them how the Lord had
led him out of prison. He added, 'Tell Jamesᶠ and the brothers.' Then he left and
went elsewhere.
18   When daylight came there was a great commotion among the soldiers, who
19 could not imagine what had become of Peter. ·Herod put out an unsuccessful
search for him; he had the guards questioned, and before leaving Judaea to take
up residence in Caesarea he gave orders for their execution. ᵍ

The death of the persecutor

20 Now Herod was on bad terms with the Tyrians and Sidonians. Yet they sent
a joint deputation which managed to enlist the support of Blastus, the king's
chamberlain, and through him negotiated a treaty, since their country depended
21 for its food supply on the king's territory. ·A day was fixed, and Herod, wearing
22 his robes of state and seated on a throne, began to make a speech to them. ·The
23 people acclaimed him with, 'It is a god speaking, not a man!' ·and at that moment
the angel of the Lord struck him down, because he had not given the glory to
God. He was eaten away by worms and died. ʰ

Barnabas and Saul return to Antioch

24 The word of God continued to spread and to gain followers.
25   Barnabas and Saul completed their task at Jerusalemⁱ and came back, bringing
John Mark with them.

III: THE MISSION OF BARNABAS AND PAUL
THE COUNCIL OF JERUSALEM

The mission sent out

1 **13** In the church at Antioch the following were prophets and teachers:ᵃ
Barnabas, Simeon called Niger, and Lucius of Cyrene, Manaen, who had
2 been brought up with Herod the tetrarch, and Saul. ·One day while they were
offering worshipᵇ to the Lord and keeping a fast, the Holy Spirit said, 'I want
3 Barnabas and Saul set apart for the work to which I have called them.' ·So it was
that after fasting and prayer they laid their hands on themᶜ and sent them off.

Cyprus: the magician Elymas

4 So these two, sent on their mission by the Holy Spirit, went down to Seleucia and
5 from there set sail for Cyprus. ᵈ·They landed at Salamis and proclaimed the word
of God in the synagogues of the Jews;ᵉ John acted as their assistant.
6   They travelled the whole length of the island, and at Paphos they came in
7 contact with a Jewish magician and false prophet called Bar-Jesus. ·He was one of
the attendants of the proconsul Sergius Paulus who was an extremely intelligent

man. The proconsul summoned Barnabas and Saul and asked to hear the word of
8 God, ·but Elymas the magician (this is what his name means in Greek) tried to
9 stop them so as to prevent the proconsul's conversion to the faith. ·Then Saul,
10 whose other name is Paul,ʲ filled with the Holy Spirit, looked at him intently ·and
said, 'You utter fraud, you impostor, you son of the devil, you enemy of all
11 uprightness, will you not stop twisting the straightforward ways of the Lord? ·Now
watch how the hand of the Lord will strike you: you will be blind, and for a time
you will not see the sun.' That instant, everything went misty and dark for him,
12 and he groped about to find someone to lead him by the hand. ·The proconsul,
who had watched everything, became a believer, being much struck by what he
had learnt about the Lord.

They arrive at Antioch in Pisidia

13 Paul and his companions went by sea from Paphos to Perga in Pamphylia where
14 John left them to go back to Jerusalem. ·The others carried on from Perga till
they reached Antioch in Pisidia. Here they went to synagogue on the Sabbath and
15 took their seats. ·After the passages from the Law and the Prophets had been
read, the presidents of the synagogue sent them a message, 'Brothers, if you would
like to address some words of encouragementᵉ to the congregation, please do so.'
16 Paul stood up, raised his hand ʰ for silence and began to speak:

Paul's preaching before the Jews ⁱ

17 'Men of Israel, and fearers of God,ʲ listen! ·The God of our nation Israel ᵏ chose
our ancestors and made our people great when they were living in Egypt, a land
18 not their own; then by divine power he led them out ·and for about forty years
19 *took care of* ˡ them in the desert. ·*When he had destroyed seven nations in Canaan,*
20 *he put them in possession* of their land ·for about four hundred and fifty years.* ᵐ
21 After this he gave them judges, down to the prophet Samuel. ·Then they demanded
a king, and God gave them Saul son of Kish, a man of the tribe of Benjamin. ⁿ
22 After forty years, ·he deposed him and raised up David to be king, whom he
attested in these words, "*I have found David* son of Jesse, *a man after my own*
23 *heart, who will perform my entire will.*" ·To keep his promise, God has raised up ᵒ
24 for Israel one of David's descendants, Jesus, as Saviour, ·whose coming was
heralded by John when he proclaimed a baptism of repentance for the whole
25 people of Israel. ·Before John ended his course he said, "I am not the one ᵖ you
imagine me to be; there is someone coming after me whose sandal I am not fit to
undo."

26 'My brothers, sons of Abraham's race, and all you godfearers, this message of
27 salvation is meant for you. ᵍ ·What the people of Jerusalem and their rulers did,
though they did not realise it, was in fact to fulfil the prophecies read on every
28 Sabbath. ʳ ·Though they found nothing to justify his execution,ˢ they condemned
29 him and asked Pilate to have him put to death.ᵗ ·When they had carried out
everything that scripture foretells about him they took him down from the tree
30, 31 and buried him in a tomb. ᵘ ·But God raised him from the dead, ·and for many
days he appeared to those who had accompanied him from Galilee to Jerusalem:
and it is these same companions of his who are now his witnesses before our
people. ᵛ

32 'We have come here to tell you the good news that the promise made to our
33 ancestors has come about. ·God has fulfilled it to their children ʷ by raising Jesus
from the dead. As scripture says in the psalms: ˣ *You are my son: today I have*

34 *fathered you.*' ·The fact that God raised him from the dead, never to return to
corruption, is no more than what he had declared: *To you I shall give the holy*
35 *things promised to David which can be relied upon.*ᶻ ·This is also why it says in
36 another text: *You will not allow your Holy One to see corruption.* ·Now when
David in his own time had served God's purposes he died; he was buried with his
37 ancestors and has certainly *seen corruption.* ·The one whom God has raised up,
however, has not *seen corruption.*

38 'My brothers, I want you to realise that it is through him that forgiveness of sins
is being proclaimed to you. Through him justification from all sins from which the
39 Law of Moses was unable to justify ·is being offered to every believer.

40 'So be careful—or what the prophets say will happen to you.

41   *Cast your eyes around you, mockers;*
        be amazed, and perish!
        For I am doing something in your own days
        that you would never believe if you were told of it.' ᵃᵃ

42 As they left they were urged to ᵇᵇ continue this preaching the following Sabbath.
43 When the meeting broke up many Jews and devout converts ᶜᶜ followed Paul and
Barnabas, ᵈᵈ and in their talks with them Paul and Barnabas urged them to remain
faithful to the grace God had given them. ᵉᵉ

Paul and Barnabas preach to the gentiles

44 The next Sabbath almost the whole town assembled to hear the word of God. ᶠᶠ
45 When they saw the crowds, the Jews, filled with jealousy, used blasphemies to
46 contradict everything Paul said. ·Then Paul and Barnabas spoke out fearlessly. ᵍᵍ
'We had to proclaim the word of God to you first, but since you have rejected it,
since you do not think yourselves worthy of eternal life, here and now we turn to
47 the gentiles. ·For this is what the Lord commanded us to do when he said:

        I have made you a light to the nations,
        so that my salvation may reach the remotest parts of the earth.' ʰʰ

48 It made the gentiles very happy to hear this and they gave thanks to the Lord
49 for his message; ⁱⁱ all who were destined for eternal life became believers. ʲʲ ·Thus
the word of the Lord spread through the whole countryside.

50 But the Jews worked on some of the devout women of the upper classes and the
leading men of the city; they stirred up a persecution against Paul and Barnabas
51 and expelled them from their territory. ·So they shook the dust from their feet in
protest against them and went off to Iconium; but the converts were filled with joy
and the Holy Spirit.

Iconium evangelised

1 **14** It happened that at Iconium they went to the Jewish synagogue, in the same
way, ᵃ and they spoke so effectively that a great many Jews and Greeks
became believers. ᵇ
2 (However, the Jews who refused to believe stirred up the gentiles against the
brothers and set them in opposition. ᶜ)
3 Accordingly Paul and Barnabas stayed on for some time, preaching fearlessly in
the Lord; and he attested all they said about his gift of grace, allowing signs and
wonders to be performed by them.
4 The people in the city were divided; ᵈ some supported the Jews, others the

5 apostles, ·but eventually with the connivance of the authorities a move was made
6 by gentiles as well as Jews to make attacks on them and to stone them. ·When
they came to hear of this, they went off for safety to Lycaonia where, in the towns
7 of Lystra and Derbe and in the surrounding country, ᶜ ·they preached the good
news.

Healing of a cripple

8 There was a man sitting there ᶠ who had never walked in his life, because his feet
9 were crippled from birth; ·he was listening to Paul preaching, and Paul looked at
10 him intently and saw that he had the faith to be cured. ᵍ ·Paul said in a loud voice,
'Get to your feet—stand up,' and the cripple jumped up and began to walk.
11 When the crowds saw what Paul had done they shouted in the language of
12 Lycaonia, 'The gods have come down to us in human form.' ·They addressed
Barnabas as Zeus, and since Paul was the principal speaker they called him
13 Hermes. ʰ ·The priests of Zeus-outside-the-Gate, ⁱ proposing that all the people
14 should offer sacrifice with them, brought garlanded oxen to the gates. ·When the
apostles Barnabas and Paul heard what was happening they tore their clothes, ʲ
15 and rushed into the crowd, shouting, ·'Friends, what do you think you are doing?
We are only human beings, mortal like yourselves. We have come with good news
to make you turn from these empty idols to the living God ᵏ who made sky and
16 earth and the sea and all that these hold. ˡ ·In the past he allowed all the nations to
17 go their own way; ·but even then he did not leave you without evidence of himself
in the good things he does for you: he sends you rain from heaven and seasons of
18 fruitfulness; he fills you with food and your hearts with merriment.' ·With this
speech they just managed to prevent the crowd from offering them sacrifice.

End of the mission

19 Then some Jews arrived from Antioch and Iconium and turned the people against
them. They stoned Paul and dragged him outside the town, thinking he was dead.
20 The disciples came crowding round him but, as they did so, he stood up and went
back to the town. The next day he and Barnabas left for Derbe.
21 Having preached the good news in that town and made a considerable number
22 of disciples, they went back through Lystra, Iconium and Antioch. ·They put fresh
heart into the disciples, ᵐ encouraging them to persevere in the faith, saying, 'We
23 must all experience many hardships before we enter the kingdom of God.' ·In
each of these churches they appointed elders, ⁿ and with prayer and fasting they
commended them to the Lord in whom they had come to believe.
24, 25 They passed through Pisidia and reached Pamphylia. ·Then after proclaiming
26 the word ᵒ at Perga they went down to Attalia ·and from there sailed for Antioch,
where they had originally been commended to the grace of God for the work they
had now completed.
27 On their arrival they assembled the church and gave an account of all that God
had done with them, and how he had opened the door of faith ᵖ to the gentiles.
28 They stayed there with the disciples for some time.

Controversy at Antioch

1 **15** ᵍThen some men came down from Judaea ᵇ and taught the brothers, 'Unless
you have yourselves circumcised in the tradition of Moses you cannot be
2 saved.' ·This led to disagreement, and after Paul and Barnabas had had a long
argument with these men it was decided that Paul and Barnabas and others of the

church[c] should go up to Jerusalem and discuss the question with the apostles[d] and
elders.
3 The members of the church saw them off,[e] and as they passed through Phoenicia
and Samaria they told how the gentiles had been converted, and this news was
4 received with the greatest satisfaction by all the brothers. •When they arrived in
Jerusalem they were welcomed by the church and by the apostles and elders, and
gave an account of all that God had done through them.

Controversy at Jerusalem

5 But certain members of the Pharisees' party who had become believers objected,[f]
insisting that gentiles should be circumcised and instructed to keep the Law of
6. 7 Moses.[g] •The apostles and elders[h] met to look into the matter, •and after a long
discussion, Peter stood up[i] and addressed them.

Peter's speech

'My brothers,' he said, 'you know perfectly well that in the early days God made
his choice among you: the gentiles were to learn the good news from me and so
8 become believers. •And God, who can read everyone's heart, showed his approval
9 of them by giving the Holy Spirit to them just as he had to us. •God made no
10 distinction between them and us, since he purified their hearts by faith.[j] •Why do
you put God to the test[k] now by imposing on the disciples the very burden that
11 neither our ancestors nor we ourselves were strong enough to support? •But we
believe that we are saved in the same way as they are: through the grace of the
Lord Jesus.'[l]
12 The entire assembly fell silent,[m] and they listened to Barnabas and Paul describing all the signs and wonders God had worked through them among the gentiles.

James' speech

13 When they had finished it was James[n] who spoke. 'My brothers,' he said, 'listen to
14 me. •Simeon[o] has described how God first arranged to enlist a people for his name
15 out of the gentiles. •This is entirely in harmony with the words of the prophets,
since the scriptures say:[p]

16 *After that I shall return*
and rebuild the fallen hut of David;
I shall make good the gaps in it
and restore it.
17 *Then the rest of humanity,*
and of all the nations once called mine,[q]
will look for the Lord,
18 *says the Lord who made this* •known so long ago.[r]

19 'My verdict is, then,[s] that instead of making things more difficult for gentiles
20 who turn to God, •we should send them a letter telling them merely to abstain
from anything polluted by idols,[t] from illicit marriages,[u] from the meat of strangled
21 animals and from blood.[v] •For Moses has always had his preachers in every town
and is read aloud in the synagogues every Sabbath.'

The apostolic letter

22 Then the apostles and elders, with the whole church, decided to choose delegates
from among themselves to send to Antioch with Paul and Barnabas. They chose

Judas, known as Barsabbas, ^w and Silas, ^x both leading men in the brotherhood,
23 and gave them this letter to take with them:

'The apostles and elders, your brothers, send greetings to the brothers of
24 gentile birth in Antioch, Syria and Cilicia. ·We hear that some people coming
from here, but acting without any authority from ourselves, have disturbed you
25 with their demands and have unsettled your minds; ·and so we have decided
unanimously to elect delegates and to send them to you with our wellbeloved
26 Barnabas and Paul, ·who have committed their lives to the name of our Lord
27 Jesus Christ. ·Accordingly we are sending you Judas and Silas, who will confirm
28 by word of mouth what we have written. ·It has been decided by the Holy Spirit
29 and by ourselves not to impose on you any burden beyond these essentials: ·you
are to abstain from food sacrificed to idols, from blood, from the meat of
strangled animals and from illicit marriages. Avoid these, and you will do what
is right.' Farewell.'

The delegates at Antioch

30 The party left and went down to Antioch, where they summoned the whole
31 community and delivered the letter. ·The community read it and were delighted
32 with the encouragement it gave them. ·Judas and Silas, being themselves prophets,
33 spoke for a long time, encouraging and strengthening the brothers. ·These two
spent some time there, and then the brothers wished them peace and they went
35 back to those who had sent them. ^z ·Paul and Barnabas, however, stayed on in
Antioch, and there with many others they taught and proclaimed the good news,
the word of the Lord.

IV: PAUL'S MISSIONS

Paul separates from Barnabas and recruits Silas

36 On a later occasion Paul said to Barnabas, 'Let us go back and visit the brothers in
all the towns where we preached the word of the Lord, so that we can see how
37.38 they are doing.' ·Barnabas suggested taking John Mark, ·but Paul was not in
favour of taking along the man who had deserted them in Pamphylia and had
refused to share in their work.
39 There was sharp disagreement so that they parted company, and Barnabas
40 sailed off with Mark to Cyprus. ·Before Paul left, he chose Silas to accompany
him and was commended by the brothers to the grace of God. ^{ac}

Lycaonia: Paul recruits Timothy

41 He travelled through Syria and Cilicia, consolidating the churches. ^{ab}
1 **16** From there he went to Derbe, and then on to Lystra, where there was a
disciple called Timothy, ^a whose mother was Jewish and had become a
2 believer; but his father was a Greek. ·The brothers at Lystra and Iconium spoke
3 well of him, ·and Paul, who wanted to have him as a travelling companion, had
him circumcised. This was on account of the Jews in the locality ^b where everyone
knew his father was a Greek.
4 As they visited one town after another, they passed on the decisions reached by
the apostles and elders in Jerusalem, with instructions to observe them. ^c
5 So the churches grew strong in the faith, as well as growing daily in numbers.

The crossing into Asia Minor

6 They travelled through Phrygia and the Galatian country, *d* because they had been
7 told by the Holy Spirit not to preach the word in Asia. ·When they reached the
frontier of Mysia they tried to go into Bithynia, but as the Spirit of Jesus *e* would
8 not allow them, ·they went through *f* Mysia and came down to Troas.

9   One night Paul had a vision: a Macedonian appeared and kept urging him in
10 these words, 'Come across to Macedonia and help us.' ·Once he had seen this
vision we *g* lost no time in arranging a passage to Macedonia, convinced that God
had called us to bring them the good news.

Arrival at Philippi

11 Sailing from Troas we made a straight run for Samothrace; the next day for
12 Neapolis, ·and from there for Philippi, a Roman colony and the principal city of
13 that district of Macedonia. *h* ·After a few days in this city we went outside the gates
beside a river as it was the Sabbath and this was a customary place for prayer. *i* We
14 sat down and preached to the women who had come to the meeting. ·One of these
women was called Lydia, a woman from the town of Thyatira who was in the
purple-dye trade, and who revered God. She listened to us, and the Lord opened
15 her heart to accept what Paul was saying. ·After she and her household had been
baptised *j* she kept urging us, 'If you judge me a true believer in the Lord,' she
said, 'come and stay with us.' And she would take no refusal. *k*

Imprisonment of Paul and Silas

16 It happened one day that as we were going to prayer, we were met by a slave-girl
who was a soothsayer *l* and made a lot of money for her masters by foretelling the
17 future. ·This girl started following Paul and the rest of us and shouting, 'Here are
the servants of the Most High God; they have come to tell you how to be saved!'
18 She did this day after day until Paul was exasperated and turned round and said to
the spirit, 'I order you in the name of Jesus Christ to leave that woman.' The spirit
went out of her then and there.

19   When her masters saw that there was no hope of making any more money out
of her, they seized Paul and Silas and dragged them into the market place before
20 the authorities. ·Taking them before the magistrates they said, 'These people are
21 causing a disturbance in our city. They are Jews ·and are advocating practices
22 which it is unlawful for us as Romans to accept or follow.' *m* ·The crowd joined in
and showed its hostility to them, so the magistrates had them stripped and ordered
23 them to be flogged. ·They were given many lashes and then thrown into prison,
24 and the gaoler was told to keep a close watch on them. ·So, following such
instructions, he threw them into the inner prison and fastened their feet in the
stocks.

The miraculous deliverance of Paul and Silas

25 In the middle of the night Paul and Silas were praying and singing God's praises,
26 while the other prisoners listened. ·Suddenly there was an earthquake that shook
the prison to its foundations. All the doors flew open and the chains fell from all
27 the prisoners. ·When the gaoler woke and saw the doors wide open he drew his
sword and was about to commit suicide, presuming that the prisoners had escaped.
28 But Paul shouted at the top of his voice, 'Do yourself no harm; we are all here.'
29   He called for lights, then rushed in, threw himself trembling *n* at the feet of Paul

30 and Silas, ·and escorted them out, saying, 'Sirs, what must I do to be saved?'
31 They told him, 'Become a believer in the Lord Jesus, and you will be saved, and
32 your household too.' ·Then they preached the word of the Lord *e* to him and to all
33 his household. ·Late as it was, he took them to wash their wounds, and was
34 baptised then and there with all his household. ·Afterwards he took them into his
house and gave them a meal, and the whole household celebrated their conversion
to belief in God.

35   When it was daylight the magistrates sent the lictors with the order: 'Release
36 those men.' *f* ·The gaoler reported the message to Paul, 'The magistrates have
37 sent an order for your release; you can go now and be on your way.' *e* ·'What!'
Paul replied. 'Without trial they gave us a public flogging, though we are Roman
citizens,' and threw us into prison, and now they want to send us away on the
quiet! Oh no! They must come and escort us out themselves.'

38   The lictors reported this to the magistrates, who were terrified when they heard
39 they were Roman citizens. ·They came and urged them to leave the town. *f* ·From
40 the prison they went to Lydia's house where they saw all the brothers and gave
them some encouragement; then they left.

Thessalonica: difficulties with the Jews

1   **17** Passing through Amphipolis and Apollonia, they eventually reached Thes-
2   salonica, where there was a Jewish synagogue. ·Paul as usual went in and
for three consecutive Sabbaths developed the arguments from scripture for them,
3 explaining and proving how it was ordained that the Christ should suffer and rise
from the dead. 'And the Christ', he said, 'is this Jesus whom I am proclaiming to
4 you.' ·Some of them *a* were convinced and joined Paul and Silas, and so did a great
many godfearing people and Greeks, *b* as well as a number of the leading women.
5   The Jews, full of resentment, enlisted the help of a gang from the market place,
stirred up a crowd, and soon had the whole city in an uproar. They made for
6 Jason's house, *c* hoping to bring them before the People's Assembly; ·however,
they found only Jason and some of the brothers, and these they dragged before
the city council, shouting, 'The people who have been turning the whole world
7 upside down have come here now; ·they have been staying at Jason's. They have
8 broken Caesar's edicts by claiming that there is another king, *d* Jesus.' ·Hearing
9 this, the citizens and the city councillors were alarmed, ·and they made Jason and
the rest give security before setting them free.

Fresh difficulties at Beroea

10 When it was dark the brothers immediately sent Paul and Silas away to Beroea, *e*
11 where they went to the Jewish synagogue as soon as they arrived. ·Here the Jews
were more noble-minded than those in Thessalonica, and they welcomed the word
very readily; every day they studied the scriptures to check whether it was true.
12 Many of them became believers, and so did many Greek women of high standing
and a number of the men.
13   When the Jews of Thessalonica came to learn that the word of God was being
preached by Paul in Beroea as well, they went there to make trouble and stir up
14 the people. ·So the brothers arranged for Paul to go immediately as far as the
15 coast, leaving Silas and Timothy behind. ·Paul's escort took him as far as Athens,
and went back with instructions for Silas and Timothy to rejoin Paul as soon as
they could. *f*

Paul in Athens

16 Paul waited for them in Athens and there his whole soul was revolted at the sight
17 of a city given over to idolatry. *⁸* ·In the synagogue he debated with the Jews and
the godfearing, and in the market place he debated every day with anyone whom
18 he met. *ʰ* ·Even a few Epicurean and Stoic philosophers *ⁱ* argued with him. Some
said, 'What can this parrot mean?' *ʲ* And, because he was preaching about Jesus
and Resurrection, *ᵏ* others said, 'He seems to be a propagandist for some outlandish
gods.'
19 They got him to accompany them to the Areopagus, *ˡ* where they said to him,
20 'Can we know what this new doctrine is that you are teaching? ·Some of the things
21 you say seemed startling to us and we would like to find out what they mean.' ·The
one amusement the Athenians and the foreigners living there seem to have is to
discuss and listen to the latest ideas.
22 So Paul stood before the whole council of the Areopagus and made this speech:

Paul's speech before the council of the Areopagus *ᵐ*

'Men of Athens, I have seen for myself how extremely scrupulous you are in all
23 religious matters, ·because, as I strolled round looking at your sacred monuments,
I noticed among other things an altar inscribed: To An Unknown God. *ⁿ* In fact,
the unknown God you revere is the one I proclaim to you.
24 'Since the God who made the world and everything in it is himself Lord of
heaven and earth, he does not make his home in shrines made by human hands.
25 Nor is he in need of anything, that he should be served by human hands; *ᵒ* on the
contrary, it is he who gives everything—including life and breath—to everyone.
26 From one single principle *ᵖ* he not only created the whole human race so that
they could occupy the entire earth, but he decreed the times and limits of their
27 habitation. *ᵠ* ·And he did this so that they might seek the deity *ʳ* and, by feeling
their way towards him, succeed in finding him; and indeed he is not far from any
28 of us, ·since it is in him that we live, and move, and exist, *ˢ* as indeed some of your
own writers *ᵗ* have said:

> We are all his children. *ᵘ*

29 'Since we are the children of God, we have no excuse for thinking that the deity
looks like anything in gold, silver or stone that has been carved and designed by a
man. *ᵛ*
30 'But now, overlooking the times of ignorance, God is telling everyone every-
31 where that they must repent, ·because he has fixed a day when the whole world
will be judged in uprightness *ʷ* by a man he has appointed. And God has publicly
proved this by raising him from the dead.' *ˣ*
32 At this mention of rising from the dead, some of them burst out laughing; others
33 said, 'We would like to hear you talk about this another time.' *ʸ* ·After that Paul
34 left them, ·but there were some who attached themselves to him and became
believers, among them Dionysius the Areopagite *ᶻ* and a woman called Damaris,
and others besides.

Foundation of the church of Corinth

1.2 **18** After this Paul left Athens and went to Corinth, *ᵃ* ·where he met a Jew
called Aquila whose family came from Pontus. He and his wife Priscilla *ᵇ*
had recently left Italy because an edict of Claudius had expelled all the Jews from

3 Rome. ʿ Paul went to visit them, ·and when he found they were tentmakers, of the
4 same trade as himself, he lodged with them, and they worked together. ᵈ ·Every
   Sabbath he used to hold debates in the synagogues, trying to convert Jews as well
   as Greeks.
5   After Silas and Timothy had arrived from Macedonia, ʿ Paul devoted all his time
6 to preaching, declaring to the Jews that Jesus was the Christ. ᶠ ·When they turned
   against him and started to insult him, he took his cloak and shook it out in front of
   them, ᵍ saying, 'Your blood be on your own heads; from now on I will go to the
7 gentiles with a clear conscience.' ·Then he left the synagogue and moved to the
8 house next door that belonged to a worshipper of God called Justus. ʰ ·Crispus,
   president of the synagogue, and his whole household, all became believers in the
   Lord. Many Corinthians who had heard him became believers and were baptised. ⁱ
9 One night the Lord spoke to Paul in a vision, 'Be fearless; speak out and do not
10 keep silence: ·I am with you I have so many people that belong to me in this city
11 that no one will attempt to hurt you.' ·So Paul stayed there preaching the word of
   God among them for eighteen months.

The Jews take Paul to court

12 But while Gallio was proconsul of Achaia, ʲ the Jews made a concerted attack on
13 Paul and brought him before the tribunal, saying, ·'We accuse this man of
14 persuading people to worship God in a way that breaks the Law.' ᵏ ·Before Paul
   could open his mouth, Gallio said to the Jews, 'Listen, you Jews. If this were a
15 misdemeanour or a crime, it would be in order for me to listen to your plea; ·but if
   it is only quibbles about words and names, and about your own Law, then you
   must deal with it yourselves—I have no intention of making legal decisions about
16. 17 these things.' ·Then he began to hustle them out of the court, ·and at once they all
   turned on Sosthenes, ˡ the synagogue president, and beat him in front of the
   tribunal. Gallio refused to take any notice at all.

Return to Antioch and departure for the third journey

18 After staying on for some time, Paul took leave of the brothers and sailed for
   Syria, ᵐ accompanied by Priscilla and Aquila. At Cenchreae he had his hair cut
   off, because of a vow he had made. ⁿ
19   When they reached Ephesus, he left them, but first he went alone to the
20 synagogue to debate with the Jews. ·They asked him to stay longer, but he
21 declined, ·though when he took his leave he said, 'I will come back another time,
   God willing.' Then he sailed from Ephesus.
22   He landed at Caesarea and went up to greet the church. ᵒ Then he came down
23 to Antioch ·where he spent a short time before continuing his journey through the
   Galatian country and then through Phrygia, encouraging all the followers.

Apollos

24 An Alexandrian Jew named Apollos ᵖ now arrived in Ephesus. He was an eloquent
25 man, with a sound knowledge of the scriptures, and yet, ·though he had been
   given instruction in the Way of the Lord and preached with great spiritual fervour
   and was accurate in all the details he taught about Jesus, he had experienced only
26 the baptism of John. ·He began to teach fearlessly in the synagogue and, when
   Priscilla and Aquila heard him, they attached themselves to him and gave him
   more detailed instruction about the Way. ᵠ
27   When Apollos thought of crossing over to Achaia, the brothers encouraged him

and wrote asking the disciples to welcome him. ' When he arrived there he was
28 able by God's grace to help the believers considerably ·by the energetic way he
refuted the Jews in public, demonstrating from the scriptures that Jesus was the
Christ.

The disciples of John at Ephesus

1 **19** It happened that while Apollos was in Corinth, " Paul made his way overland
2 as far as Ephesus, " where he found a number of disciples. ·When he asked,
'Did you receive the Holy Spirit when you became believers?' they answered, 'No,
3 we were never even told there was such a thing as a Holy Spirit.' ' ·He asked,
4 'Then how were you baptised?' They replied, 'With John's baptism.' ·Paul said,
'John's baptism was a baptism of repentance; but he insisted that the people should
5 believe in the one who was to come after him—namely Jesus.' ·When they heard
6 this, they were baptised in the name of the Lord Jesus, ·and the moment Paul had
laid hands on them the Holy Spirit came down on them, and they began to speak
7 with tongues and to prophesy. ·There were about twelve of these men in all.

Foundation of the church of Ephesus '

8 He began by going to the synagogue, where he spoke out fearlessly and argued
9 persuasively about the kingdom of God. He did this for three months, ·till the
attitude of some of the congregation hardened into unbelief. As soon as they
began attacking the Way in public, he broke with them and took his disciples apart
10 to hold daily discussions in the lecture room of Tyrannus. ' ·This went on for two
years, ' with the result that all the inhabitants of Asia, " both Jews and Greeks,
were able to hear the word of the Lord.

The Jewish exorcists

11, 12 So remarkable were the miracles worked by God at Paul's hands ·that handker-
chiefs or aprons which had touched him were taken to the sick, and they were
cured of their illnesses, and the evil spirits came out of them.
13   But some itinerant Jewish exorcists " too tried pronouncing the name of the
Lord Jesus over people who were possessed by evil spirits; they used to say, 'I
14 adjure you by the Jesus whose spokesman is Paul.' ·Among those who did this
15 were seven sons of Sceva, a Jewish chief priest. ·The evil spirit replied, 'Jesus I
16 recognise, and Paul I know, but who are you?' ·and the man with the evil spirit
hurled himself at them and overpowered first one and then another, ' and handled
them so violently that they fled from that house stripped of clothing and badly
17 mauled. ·Everybody in Ephesus, both Jews and Greeks, heard about this episode;
. everyone was filled with awe, and the name of the Lord Jesus came to be held in
great honour.
18   Some believers, too, came forward to admit in detail how they had used spells '
19 and a number of them who had practised magic collected their books and made a
bonfire of them in public. The value of these was calculated to be fifty thousand
silver pieces.
20   In this powerful way the word of the Lord spread more and more widely and
successfully. '

V: THE END OF
PAUL'S MISSIONARY JOURNEYS
A PRISONER FOR CHRIST

Paul's plans

21 When all this was over Paul made up his mind to go back to Jerusalem through Macedonia and Achaia. 'After I have been there,' he said, 'I must go on to see 22 Rome as well.' ·So he sent two of his helpers, Timothy and Erastus, ahead of him to Macedonia, while he remained for a time in Asia.

Ephesus: the silversmiths' riot [1]

23 It was during this time that a serious disturbance broke out in connection with the 24 Way. ·A silversmith called Demetrius, who provided work for a large number of 25 craftsmen making silver shrines of Diana, ·called a general meeting of them with others in the same trade. 'As you know,' he said, 'it is on this industry that we 26 depend for our prosperity. ·Now you must have seen and heard how, not just in Ephesus but nearly everywhere in Asia, this man Paul has persuaded and converted a great number of people with his argument that gods made by hand are not gods 27 at all. ·This threatens not only to discredit our trade, but also to reduce the sanctuary of the great goddess Diana to unimportance. It could end up by taking away the prestige of a goddess venerated all over Asia, and indeed all over the 28 world.' ·This speech roused them to fury, and they started to shout, [m] 'Great is 29 Diana of the Ephesians!' ·The whole town was filled with the uproar and the mob made a concerted rush to the theatre, dragging along two of Paul's Macedonian 30 travelling companions, Gaius and Aristarchus. [n] ·Paul wanted to make an appeal 31 to the people, but the disciples refused to let him; ·in fact, some of the Asiarchs, [o] who were friends of his, sent messages urging him not to take the risk of going into the theatre.

32 By now everybody was shouting different things, till the assembly itself had no idea what was going on; most of them did not even know why they had gathered 33 together. ·Some of the crowd prevailed upon [p] Alexander, whom the Jews pushed forward; he raised his hand for silence with the intention of explaining things to 34 the people. ·As soon as they realised he was a Jew, they all started shouting in unison, 'Great is Diana of the Ephesians!' and they kept this up for two hours. 35 When the town clerk eventually succeeded in calming the crowd, he said, 'Citizens of Ephesus! Is there anybody who does not know that the city of the Ephesians is the guardian of the temple of great Diana and of her statue that fell from heaven? 36 Nobody can contradict this and there is no need for you to get excited or do 37 anything rash. ·These men you have brought here are not guilty of any sacrilege 38 or blasphemy against our goddess. ·If Demetrius and the craftsmen he has with him want to complain about anyone, there are the assizes and the proconsuls; let 39 them take the case to court. ·And if you want to ask any more questions you must 40 raise them in the regular assembly. ·We could easily be charged with rioting for today's happenings: there is no ground for it all, and we can give no justification for this gathering.' When he had finished this speech he dismissed the assembly.

Paul leaves Ephesus

1 **20** When the disturbance was over, [a] Paul sent for the disciples and, after speaking words of encouragement to them, said good-bye and set out for

2 Macedonia. ·On his way through those areas [b] he said many words of encourage-
3 ment to them and then made his way into Greece, ·where he spent three months. [c]
He was leaving by ship for Syria [d] when a plot organised against him by the Jews
4 made him decide to go back by way of Macedonia. ·He was accompanied [e] by
Sopater, son of Pyrrhus, who came from Beroea; Aristarchus and Secundus who
came from Thessalonica; Gaius from Derbe, and Timothy, as well as Tychicus
5 and Trophimus who were from Asia. [f] ·They all went on to Troas where they
6 waited for us. [g] ·We ourselves left Philippi by ship [h] after the days of Unleavened
Bread [i] and joined them five days later at Troas, where we stayed for a week. [j]

Troas: Paul raises a dead man to life

7 On the first day of the week [k] we met for the breaking of bread. Paul was due to
leave the next day, and he preached a sermon that went on till the middle of the
8 night. ·A number of lamps were lit in the upstairs room where we were assembled,
9 and as Paul went on and on, a young man called Eutychus who was sitting on the
window-sill grew drowsy and was overcome by sleep and fell to the ground three
10 floors below. He was picked up dead. ·Paul went down and stooped to clasp the
11 boy to him, saying 'There is no need to worry, there is still life in him.' ·Then he
went back upstairs where he broke the bread and ate and carried on talking till he
12 left at daybreak. ·They took the boy away alive, and were greatly encouraged.

From Troas to Miletus

13 We were now to go on ahead by sea, so we set sail for Assos, where we were to
take Paul on board; this was what he had arranged, for he wanted to go overland.
14 When he rejoined us at Assos we took him aboard and went on to Mitylene. The
15 next day we sailed from there and arrived opposite Chios. The second day we
touched at Samos and, after stopping at Trogyllium, made Miletus the next day.
16 Paul had decided to pass wide of Ephesus so as to avoid spending time in Asia,
since he was anxious to be in Jerusalem, if possible, for the day of Pentecost.

Farewell to the elders of Ephesus

17, 18 From Miletus he sent for the elders of the church of Ephesus. ·When they arrived
he addressed these words to them: [l]
'You know what my way of life has been ever since the first day I set foot among
19 you in Asia, ·how I have served the Lord in all humility, with all the sorrows and
20 trials that came to me through the plots of the Jews. ·I have not hesitated to do
anything that would be helpful to you; I have preached to you and instructed you
21 both in public and in your homes, ·urging both Jews and Greeks to turn to God
and to believe in our Lord Jesus. [m]
22 'And now you see me on my way to Jerusalem in captivity to the Spirit; [n] I have
23 no idea what will happen to me there, ·except that the Holy Spirit, in town after
24 town, has made it clear to me that imprisonment and persecution await me. ·But I
do not place any value on my own life, [o] provided that I complete the mission the
Lord Jesus gave me—to bear witness to the good news of God's grace.
25 'I now feel sure that none of you among whom I have gone about proclaiming
26 the kingdom will ever see my face again. [p] ·And so on this very day I swear that
27 my conscience is clear as far as all of you are concerned, ·for I have without
faltering put before you the whole of God's purpose.
28 'Be on your guard for yourselves and for all the flock of which the Holy Spirit

has made you the overseers, to feed the Church of God ʳ which he bought with the blood of his own Son. ʳ

29 'I know quite well that when I have gone fierce wolves will invade you and will
30 have no mercy on the flock. ·Even from your own ranks there will be men coming forward with a travesty of the truth on their lips to induce the disciples to follow
31 them. ·So be on your guard, remembering how night and day for three years I
32 never slackened in counselling each one of you with tears. ·And now I commend you to God and to the word of his grace that has power ʳ to build you up and to give you your inheritance among all the sanctified.

33, 34 'I have never asked anyone for money or clothes; ·you know for yourselves that these hands of mine earned enough to meet my needs and those of my companions.
35 By every means I have shown you that we must exert ourselves in this way to support the weak, remembering the words of the Lord Jesus, who himself said, "There is more happiness in giving than in receiving." ' ʳ

36, 37 When he had finished speaking he knelt down with them all and prayed. ·By now they were all in tears; they put their arms round Paul's neck and kissed him;
38 what saddened them most was his saying they would never see his face again. Then they escorted him to the ship.

The journey to Jerusalem

1 **21** When we had at last torn ourselves away from them and put to sea, we set a straight course and arrived at Cos; the next day we reached Rhodes, and
2 from there went on to Patara. ʳ ·Here we found a ship bound for Phoenicia, so we
3 went on board and sailed in her. ·After sighting Cyprus and leaving it to port, we
4 sailed to Syria and put in at Tyre, since the ship was to unload her cargo there. ·We sought out the disciples and stayed there a week. Speaking in the Spirit, ᵇ they
5 kept telling Paul not to go on to Jerusalem, ·but when our time was up we set off. Together with the women and children they all escorted us on our way till we were
6 out of the town. When we reached the beach, we knelt down and prayed; ·then, after saying good-bye to each other, we went aboard and they returned home.

7 The end of our voyage from Tyre came when we landed at Ptolemais, where we
8 greeted the brothers and stayed one day with them. ·The next day we left and came to Caesarea. Here we called on Philip the evangelist, one of the Seven, and
9, 10 stayed with him. ·He had four unmarried daughters who were prophets. ·When
11 we had been there several days a prophet called Agabus who arrived from Judaea. ·He came up to us, took Paul's belt and tied up his own feet and hands, ʳ and said, 'This is what the Holy Spirit says, "The man to whom this girdle belongs will be tied up like this by the Jews in Jerusalem and handed over to the gentiles." ' ᵈ
12 When we heard this, we and all the local people urged Paul not to go on to
13 Jerusalem. ·To this he replied, 'What are you doing, weeping and breaking my heart? For my part, I am ready not only to be bound but even to die in Jerusalem
14 for the name of the Lord Jesus.' ·And so, as he would not be persuaded, we gave up the attempt, saying, 'The Lord's will be done.'

Paul's arrival in Jerusalem

15, 16 After this we made our preparations and went on up to Jerusalem. ·Some of the disciples from Caesarea accompanied us and took us to the house of a Cypriot with whom we were to lodge; ʳ he was called Mnason and had been one of the earliest disciples.

17, 18 On our arrival in Jerusalem the brothers gave us a very warm welcome. ·The

19 next day Paul went with usʲ to visit James, and all the elders were present. ·After greeting them he gave a detailed account of all that God had done among the
20 gentiles through his ministry. ·They gave glory to God when they heard this. Then they said, 'You see, brother, how thousands of Jews have now become believers,
21 all of them staunch upholders of the Law;ᵍ ·and what they have heard about you is that you instruct all Jews living among the gentiles to break away from Moses,ʰ authorising them not to circumcise their childrenⁱ or to follow the customary
22 practices. ·What is to be done? A crowd is sure to gather, for they will hear that
23 you have come.ʲ ·So this is what we suggest that you should do; we have four men
24 here who are under a vow; ·take these men along and be purified with them and pay all the expenses connected with the shaving of their heads.ᵏ This will let everyone know there is no truth in the reports they have heard about you, and
25 that you too observe the Law by your way of life. ·About the gentiles who have become believers, we have written giving them our decisionˡ that they must abstain from things sacrificed to idols, from blood, from the meat of strangled animals and from illicit marriages.'
26 So the next day Paul took the men along and was purified with them, and he visited the Temple to give notice of the time when the period of purification would be over and the offering would have to be presented on behalf of each of them.ᵐ

Paul's arrest

27 The seven days were nearly over when some Jews from Asia caught sight of him in
28 the Temple and stirred up the crowd and seized him, ·shouting, 'Men of Israel, help! This is the man who preaches to everyone everywhere against our people, against the Law and against this place.ⁿ He has even profaned this Holy Place by
29 bringing Greeks into the Temple.' ·They had, in fact, previously seen Trophimus the Ephesian in the city with him and thought that Paul had brought him into the Temple.
30 This roused the whole city; people came running from all sides; they seized Paul
31 and dragged him out of the Temple, and the gates were closed behind them. While they were setting about killing him, word reached the tribune of the cohortᵒ that
32 there was tumult all over Jerusalem. ·He immediately called out soldiers and centurions and charged down on the crowd, who stopped beating Paul when they
33 saw the tribune and the soldiers. ·When the tribune came up he took Paul into custody, had him bound with two chains and enquired who he was and what he
34 had done. ·People in the crowd called out different things, and since the noise made it impossible for him to get any positive information, the tribune ordered
35 Paul to be taken into the fortress. ·When Paul reached the steps, the crowd became
36 so violent that he had to be carried by the soldiers; ·and indeed the whole mob was after them, shouting 'Do away with him!'
37 Just as Paul was being taken into the fortress, he asked the tribune if he could
38 have a word with him. The tribune said, 'You speak Greek, then? ·Aren't you the Egyptian who started the recent revolt and led those four thousand cut-throatsᵖ
39 out into the desert?' ·'I?' said Paul, 'I am a Jew and a citizen of the well-known
40 city of Tarsus in Cilicia. Please give me permission to speak to the people.' ·The man gave his consent and Paul, standing at the top of the steps, raised his hand to the people for silence. A profound silence followed, and he started speaking to them in Hebrew.ᵠ

Paul's address to the Jews of Jerusalem *

1 **22** 'My brothers, my fathers, listen to what I have to say to you in my defence.'
2 When they realised he was speaking in Hebrew, the silence was even greater
3 than before. ·'I am a Jew', Paul said, 'and was born at Tarsus in Cilicia. I was
brought up here in this city. It was under Gamaliel that I studied and was taught
the exact observance of the Law of our ancestors. In fact, I was as full of duty
4 towards God as you all are today. ·I even persecuted this Way *b* to the death and
5 sent women as well as men to prison in chains ·as the high priest and the whole
council of elders can testify. I even received letters from them to the brothers in
Damascus, which I took with me when I set off to bring prisoners back from there
to Jerusalem for punishment.
6 'It happened that I was on that journey and nearly at Damascus when in the
7 middle of the day a bright light from heaven suddenly shone round me. ·I fell to
8 the ground and heard a voice saying, "Saul, Saul, why are you persecuting me?" ·I
answered, "Who are you, Lord?" and he said to me, "I am Jesus the Nazarene,
9 whom you are persecuting." ·The people with me saw the light but did not hear
10 the voice which spoke to me. ·I said, "What am I to do, Lord?" The Lord
answered, "Get up and go into Damascus, and there you will be told what you
11 have been appointed to do." ·Since the light had been so dazzling that I was blind,
I got to Damascus only because my companions led me by the hand.
12 'Someone called Ananias, a devout follower of the Law and highly thought of
13 by all the Jews living there, *c* ·came to see me; he stood beside me and said,
"Brother Saul, receive your sight." Instantly my sight came back and I was able to
14 see him. ·Then he said, "The God of our ancestors has chosen you to know his
15 will, to see the Upright One *d* and hear his own voice speaking, ·because you are
to be his witness before all humanity, testifying to what you have seen and heard. *e*
16 And now why delay? Hurry and be baptized and wash away your sins, calling on
his name."
17 'It happened that, when I got back to Jerusalem, *f* and was praying in the
18 Temple, I fell into a trance ·and then I saw him. "Hurry," he said, "leave Jerusalem
19 at once; they will not accept the testimony you are giving about me." *g* ·"Lord," I
answered, "they know that I used to go from synagogue to synagogue, imprisoning
20 and flogging those who believed in you; ·and that when the blood of your witness *h*
Stephen was being shed, I, too, was standing by, in full agreement with his
21 murderers, and in charge of their clothes." ·Then he said to me, "Go! I am sending
you out to the gentiles far away." ' *i*

Paul the Roman citizen

22 So far they had listened to him, but at these words they began to shout, 'Rid the
23 earth of the man! He is not fit to live!' ·They were yelling, waving their cloaks and
24 throwing dust into the air, ·and so the tribune had him brought into the fortress
and ordered him to be examined under the lash, to find out the reason for the
25 outcry against him. ·But when they had strapped him down Paul said to the
centurion on duty, 'Is it legal for you to flog a man who is a Roman citizen and has
26 not been brought to trial?' ·When he heard this the centurion went and told the
tribune; 'Do you realise what you are doing?' he said. 'This man is a Roman
27 citizen.' ·So the tribune came and asked him, 'Tell me, are you a Roman citizen?'
28 Paul answered 'Yes'. ·To this the tribune replied, 'It cost me a large sum to acquire
29 this citizenship.' 'But I was born to it,' said Paul. ·Then those who were about to

examine him hurriedly withdrew, and the tribune himself was alarmed when he realised that he had put a Roman citizen in chains. *j*

His appearance before the Sanhedrin *k*

30 The next day, since he wanted to know for sure what charge the Jews were bringing, he freed Paul and gave orders for a meeting of the chief priests and the entire Sanhedrin; then he brought Paul down and set him in front of them.

1 **23** Paul looked steadily at the Sanhedrin and began to speak, 'My brothers, to this day I have conducted myself before God with a perfectly clear 2 conscience.' *a* ·At this the high priest Ananias *b* ordered his attendants to strike 3 him on the mouth. ·Then Paul said to him, 'God will surely strike you, you whitewashed wall! How can you sit there to judge me according to the Law, and 4 then break the Law by ordering a man to strike me?' ·The attendants said, 'Are 5 you insulting the high priest of God? ·Paul answered, 'Brothers, I did not realise it was the high priest; certainly scripture says, "*You will not curse your people's leader.*" '

6 Now Paul was well aware that one party was made up of Sadducees and the other of Pharisees, so he called out in the Sanhedrin, 'Brothers, I am a Pharisee and the son of Pharisees. It is for our hope in the resurrection of the dead that I 7 am on trial.' ·As soon as he said this, a dispute broke out between the Pharisees 8 and Sadducees, and the assembly was split between the two parties. ·For the Sadducees say there is neither resurrection, nor angel, nor spirit, *c* while the 9 Pharisees accept all three. ·The shouting grew louder, and some of the scribes from the Pharisees' party stood up and protested strongly, 'We find nothing wrong 10 with this man. Suppose a spirit has spoken to him, or an angel?' *d* ·Feeling was running high, and the tribune, afraid that they would tear Paul to pieces, ordered his troops to go down and haul him out and bring him into the fortress.

11 Next night, the Lord appeared to him and said, 'Courage! You have borne witness for me in Jerusalem, now you must do the same in Rome.'

The conspiracy of the Jews against Paul

12 When it was day, the Jews held a secret meeting at which they made a vow *e* not to 13 eat or drink until they had killed Paul. ·More than forty of them entered this pact, 14 and they went to the chief priests and elders and told them, 'We have made a 15 solemn vow to let nothing pass our lips until we have killed Paul. ·Now it is up to you and the Sanhedrin together to apply to the tribune to bring him down to you, as though you meant to examine his case more closely; we, on our side, are prepared to dispose of him before he reaches you.'

16 But the son of Paul's sister heard of the ambush they were laying and made his 17 way into the fortress and told Paul, ·who called one of the centurions and said, 18 'Take this young man to the tribune; he has something to tell him.' ·So the man took him to the tribune, and reported, 'The prisoner Paul summoned me and 19 requested me to bring this young man to you; he has something to tell you.' ·Then the tribune took him by the hand and drew him aside and questioned him in 20 private, 'What is it you have to tell me?' ·He replied, 'The Jews have made a plan to ask you to take Paul down to the Sanhedrin tomorrow, as though they meant to 21 enquire more closely into his case. ·Do not believe them. There are more than forty of them lying in wait for him, and they have vowed not to eat or drink until they have got rid of him. They are ready now and only waiting for your order to

22 be given.' ·The tribune let the young man go with this order, 'Tell no one that you have given me this information.'

Paul transferred to Caesarea

·23 Then he summoned two of the centurions and said, 'Get two hundred soldiers ready to leave for Caesarea by the third hour of the night with seventy cavalry and
24 two hundred auxiliaries; ·provide horses for Paul, and deliver him unharmed to
25 Felix the governor.'*/ ·He also wrote a letter in these terms:

26. 27   'Claudius Lysias to his Excellency the governor Felix, greetings. ·This man had been seized by the Jews and would have been murdered by them, but I came on the scene with my troops and got him away, having discovered that he
28   was a Roman citizen. ·Wanting to find out what charge they were making
29   against him, I brought him before their Sanhedrin. ·I found that the accusation concerned disputed points of their Law, *but that there was no charge deserving
30   death or imprisonment. * ·Acting on information that there was a conspiracy against the man, I hasten to send him to you, and have notified his accusers that they must state their case against him in your presence.' *

31 The soldiers carried out their orders; they took Paul and escorted him by night
32 to Antipatris. ·Next day they left the mounted escort to go on with him and
33 returned to the fortress. ·On arriving at Caesarea the escort delivered the letter to
34 the governor and handed Paul over to him. ·When he had read it, he asked Paul
35 what province he came from. Learning that he was from Cilicia he said, ·'I will hear your case as soon as your accusers are here too.' Then he ordered him to be held in Herod's praetorium.*

The case before Felix

1   **24** Five days later the high priest Ananias came down with some of the elders and an advocate named Tertullus, and they laid information against Paul
2 before the governor. ·Paul was called, and Tertullus opened for the prosecution, 'Your Excellency, Felix, the unbroken peace we enjoy and the reforms this nation
3 owes to your foresight ·are matters we accept, always and everywhere, with all
4 gratitude. ·I do not want to take up too much of your time, but I urge you in your
5 graciousness to give us a brief hearing. ·We have found this man a perfect pest; he stirs up trouble among Jews the world over and is a ringleader of the Nazarene
6 sect. * ·He has even attempted to profane the Temple. We placed him under
[7]. 8 arrest. * ·If you ask him * you can find out for yourself the truth of all our accusations
9 against this man.' ·The Jews supported him, asserting that these were the facts.
10 When the governor motioned him to speak, Paul answered: *

Paul's speech before the Roman governor

'I know that you have administered justice over this nation for many years, and I
11 can therefore speak with confidence in my defence. ·As you can verify for yourself,
12 it is no more than twelve days since I went up to Jerusalem on pilgrimage, * ·and it is not true that they ever found me arguing with anyone or stirring up the mob,
13 either in the Temple, in the synagogues, or about the town; ·neither can they give you any proof of the accusations they are making against me now.
14 'What I do admit to you is this: it is according to the Way, which they describe as a sect, that I worship the God of my ancestors, retaining my belief in all points

15 of the Law and in what is written in the prophets;ᶠ ·and I hold the same hope in God as theyᵍ do that there will be a resurrection of the upright and the wicked
16 alike. ·In these things, I, as much as they, do my best to keep a clear conscience at all times before God and everyone.
17 'After several yearsʰ I came to bring relief-money to my nationⁱ and to make
18 offerings;ʲ ·it was in connection with these that they found me in the Temple; I
19 had been purified, and there was no crowd involved, and no disturbance. ·But some Jews from Asia—these are the ones who should have appeared before you
20 and accused me of whatever they had against me. ·At least let those who are present say what crime they held against me when I stood before the Sanhedrin,
21 unless it were to do with this single claim, when I stood up among them and called out, "It is about the resurrection of the dead that I am on trial before you today." 'ᵏ

Paul's captivity at Caesarea

22 At this, Felix, who was fairly well informed about the Way, adjourned the case, saying, 'When Lysias the tribune comes down I will give judgement about your
23 case.' ·He then gave orders to the centurion that he should be kept under arrest but free from restriction, and that none of his own people should be prevented from seeing to his needs. ˡ
24 Some days later Felix came with his wife Drusilla who was a Jewess. ᵐ He sent
25 for Paul and gave him a hearing on the subject of faith in Christ Jesus. ·But when he began to treat of uprightness, self-control and the coming Judgement, Felix took frightⁿ and said, 'You may go for the present; I will send for you when I find
26 it convenient.' ·At the same time he had hopes of receiving money from Paul, and for this reason he sent for him frequently and had talks with him.
27 When two yearsᵒ came to an end, Felix was succeeded by Porcius Festusᵖ and, being anxious to gain favour with the Jews, ᑫ Felix left Paul in custody.

Paul appeals to Caesar

1 **25** Three days after his arrival in the province,ᵃ Festus went up to Jerusalem
2 from Caesarea. ·The chief priests and leaders of the Jews informed him of
3 the case against Paul,ᵇ ·urgently asking him to support them against him, and to have him transferred to Jerusalem. They were preparing an ambush to murder
4 him on the way. ·But Festus replied that Paul was in custody in Caesarea, and that
5 he would be going back there shortly himself. ·He said, 'Let your authorities come down with me, and if there is anything wrong about the man, they can bring a charge against him.'
6 After staying with them for eight or ten days at the most, he went down to Caesarea and the next day he took his seat on the tribunal and had Paul brought
7 in. ·As soon as Paul appeared, the Jews who had come down from Jerusalem surrounded him, making many serious accusations which they were unable to
8 substantiate. ·Paul's defence was this, 'I have committed no offence whatever
9 against either Jewish law, or the Temple, or Caesar.' ·Festus was anxious to gain favour with the Jews, so he said to Paul, 'Are you willing to go up to Jerusalem
10 and be tried on these charges before me there?'ᶜ ·But Paul replied, 'I am standing before the tribunal of Caesar and this is where I should be tried. I have done the
11 Jews no wrong, as you very well know. ·If I am guilty of committing any capital crime, I do not ask to be spared the death penalty. But if there is no substance in the accusations these persons bring against me, no one has a right to surrender me

12 to them. I appeal to Caesar.' *d* ·Then Festus conferred with his advisers and replied, 'You have appealed to Caesar; to Caesar you shall go.'

Paul appears before King Agrippa

13 Some days later King Agrippa and Bernice *e* arrived in Caesarea and paid their
14 respects to Festus. ·Their visit lasted several days, and Festus put Paul's case before the king, saying, 'There is a man here whom Felix left behind in custody,
15 and while I was in Jerusalem the chief priests and elders of the Jews laid information
16 against him, demanding his condemnation. ·But I told them that Romans are not in the habit of surrendering any man, until the accused confronts his accusers and
17 is given an opportunity to defend himself against the charge. ·So they came here with me, and I wasted no time but took my seat on the tribunal the very next day
18 and had the man brought in. ·When confronted with him, his accusers did not
19 charge him with any of the crimes I had expected; ·but they had some argument or other with him about their own religion and about a dead man called Jesus
20 whom Paul alleged to be alive. ·Not feeling qualified to deal with questions of this sort, I asked him if he would be willing to go to Jerusalem to be tried there on this
21 issue. ·But Paul put in an appeal for his case to be reserved for the judgement of the emperor,*f* so I ordered him to be remanded until I could send him to Caesar.'
22 Agrippa said to Festus, 'I should like to hear the man myself.' *g* He answered, 'Tomorrow you shall hear him.'

23 So the next day Agrippa and Bernice arrived in great state and entered the audience chamber attended by the tribunes and the city notables; and Festus
24 ordered Paul to be brought in. ·Then Festus said, 'King Agrippa, and all here present with us, you see before you the man about whom the whole Jewish community has petitioned me, both in Jerusalem and here, loudly protesting that
25 he ought not to be allowed to remain alive. ·For my own part I am satisfied that he has committed no capital crime, but when he himself appealed to the emperor I
26 decided to send him. ·But I have nothing definite that I can write to his Imperial Majesty *h* about him; that is why I have produced him before you all, and before you in particular, King Agrippa, so that after the examination I may have something to
27 write. ·It seems to me pointless to send a prisoner without indicating the charges against him.'

1 **26** Then Agrippa said to Paul, 'You have leave to speak on your own behalf.' And Paul held up his hand and began his defence:

Paul's speech before King Agrippa *a*

2 'I consider myself fortunate, King Agrippa, in that it is before you I am to answer
3 today all the charges made against me by the Jews, ·the more so because *b* you are an expert in matters of custom and controversy among the Jews. So I beg you to listen to me patiently.

4 'My manner of life from my youth, a life spent from the beginning among my
5 own people and in Jerusalem, is common knowledge among the Jews. ·They have known me for a long time and could testify, if they would, that I followed the
6 strictest party in our religion and lived as a Pharisee. ·And now it is for my hope in
7 the promise made by God to our ancestors that I am on trial, ·the promise that our twelve tribes, constant in worship night and day, hope to attain. *c* For that
8 hope, Your Majesty, I am actually put on trial by Jews! ·Why does it seem incredible to you that God should raise the dead? *d*
9 'As for me, I once thought it was my duty to use every means to oppose the

10 name of Jesus the Nazarene. ·This I did in Jerusalem; I myself threw many of God's holy people into prison, acting on authority from the chief priests, and when

11 they were being sentenced to death I cast my vote against them. ·I often went round the synagogues inflicting penalties, trying in this way to force them to renounce their faith; my fury against them was so extreme that I even pursued them into foreign cities.

12 'On such an expedition I was going to Damascus, armed with full powers and a

13 commission from the chief priests, ·and in the middle of the day as I was on my way, Your Majesty, I saw a light from heaven shining more brilliantly than the

14 sun round me and my fellow-travellers. ·We all fell to the ground, and I heard a voice saying to me in Hebrew, "Saul, Saul, why are you persecuting me? It is hard

15 for you, kicking against the goad. " ' ·Then I said, "Who are you, Lord?" And the

16 Lord answered, "I am Jesus, whom you are persecuting. ·But get up and stand on your feet, for I have appeared to you for this reason: to appoint you as my servant and as witness of this vision in which you have seen me, and of others in which I

17 shall appear to you. ·*I shall rescue you* from the people and from *the nations to*

18 *whom I send you* ·*to open their eyes*, so that they may turn *from darkness to light*,*ᶠ* from the dominion of Satan to God, and receive, through faith in me, forgiveness of their sins *ᵍ* and a share in the inheritance of the sanctified."

19, 20 'After that, King Agrippa, I could not disobey the heavenly vision. ·On the contrary I started preaching, first to the people of Damascus, then to those of Jerusalem and all Judaean territory, and also to the gentiles, urging them to repent

21 and turn to God, proving their change of heart by their deeds. ·This was why the

22 Jews laid hands on me in the Temple and tried to do away with me. ·But I was blessed with God's help, and so I have stood firm to this day, testifying to great and small alike, saying nothing more than what the prophets and Moses himself

23 said would happen: ·that the Christ was to suffer and that, as the first to rise from the dead, he was to proclaim a light for our people and for the gentiles.'

His hearers' reactions

24 He had reached this point in his defence when Festus shouted out, 'Paul, you are

25 out of your mind; all that learning of yours is driving you mad.' *ʰ* ·But Paul answered, 'Festus, your Excellency, I am not mad: I am speaking words of sober

26 truth and good sense. ·The king understands these matters, and to him I now speak fearlessly. I am confident that nothing of all this comes as a surprise to him;

27 after all, these things were not done in a corner. *ⁱ* ·King Agrippa, do you believe in

28 the prophets? I know you do.' ·At this Agrippa said to Paul, 'A little more, and

29 your arguments would make a Christian*ʲ* of me.' ·Paul replied 'Little or much, *ᵏ* I wish before God that not only you but all who are listening to me today would come to be as I am—except for these chains.'

30 At this the king rose to his feet, with the governor and Bernice and those who

31 sat there with them. ·When they had retired they talked together and agreed,

32 'This man is doing nothing that deserves death or imprisonment.' ·And Agrippa remarked to Festus, 'The man could have been set free if he had not appealed to Caesar.'

The departure for Rome

1 **27** When it had been decided that we *ᵃ* should sail to Italy, Paul and some other prisoners were handed over to a centurion called Julius, of the

2 Augustan cohort. ·We boarded a vessel from Adramyttium bound for ports on

the Asiatic coast and put to sea; we had Aristarchus with us, a Macedonian of
3 Thessalonica. ·Next day we put in at Sidon, and Julius was considerate enough to
allow Paul to go to his friends to be looked after.
4 From there we put to sea again, but as the winds were against us we sailed under
5 the lee of Cyprus, ·then across the open sea off Cilicia and Pamphylia, taking a
6 fortnight *b* to reach Myra in Lycia. ·There the centurion found an Alexandrian
ship leaving for Italy and put us aboard.
7 For some days we made little headway, and we had difficulty in making Cnidus.
The wind would not allow us to touch there, so we sailed under the lee of Crete
8 off Cape Salmone ·and struggled along the coast until we came to a place called
Fair Havens, near the town of Lasea.

Storm and shipwreck

9 A great deal of time had been lost, and navigation was already hazardous, since it
10 was now well after the time of the Fast, *c* so Paul gave them this warning, ·'Friends,
I can see this voyage will be dangerous and that we will run considerable risk of
11 losing not only the cargo and the ship but also our lives as well.' ·But the centurion
took more notice of the captain and the ship's owner than of what Paul was saying;
12 and since the harbour was unsuitable for wintering, the majority were for putting
out from there in the hope of wintering at Phoenix—a harbour in Crete, facing
south-west and north-west.
13 A southerly breeze sprang up and, thinking their objective as good as reached,
14 they weighed anchor and began to sail past Crete, close inshore. ·But it was not
long before a hurricane, the 'north-easter' as they call it, burst on them from
15 across the island. ·The ship was caught and could not keep head to wind, so we
16 had to give way to the wind and let ourselves be driven. ·We ran under the lee of a
small island called Cauda and managed with some difficulty to bring the ship's
17 boat under control. ·Having hauled it up they used it to undergird the ship; then,
afraid of running aground on the Syrtis banks, they floated out the sea-anchor and
18 so let themselves drift. ·As we were thoroughly storm-bound, the next day they
19 began to jettison the cargo, ·and the third day they threw the ship's gear overboard
20 with their own hands. ·For a number of days both the sun and the stars were
invisible and the storm raged unabated until at last we gave up all hope of surviving.
21 Then, when they had been without food for a long time, *d* Paul stood up among
the men. 'Friends,' he said, 'you should have listened to me and not put out from
22 Crete. You would have spared yourselves all this damage and loss. ·But now I ask
you not to give way to despair. There will be no loss of life at all, only of the ship.
23 Last night there appeared beside me an angel of the God to whom I belong and
24 whom I serve, ·and he said, "Do not be afraid, Paul. You are destined to appear
25 before Caesar, *e* and God grants you the safety of all who are sailing with you." ·So
26 take courage, friends; I trust in God that things will turn out just as I was told; ·but
we are to be stranded on some island.'
27 On the fourteenth night we were being driven one way and another in the
Adriatic, *f* when about midnight the crew sensed that land of some sort was near.
28 They took soundings and found twenty fathoms; after a short interval they sounded
29 again and found fifteen fathoms. ·Then, afraid that we might run aground somewhere on a reef, they dropped four anchors from the stern and prayed for daylight.
30 When the crew tried to escape from the ship and lowered the ship's boat into the
sea as though they meant to lay out anchors from the bows, Paul said to the

31 centurion and his men, ·'Unless those men stay on board you cannot hope to be
32 saved.' ·So the soldiers cut the boat's ropes and let it drop away.
33   Just before daybreak Paul urged them all to have something to eat. 'For fourteen
34 days', he said, 'you have been in suspense, going hungry and eating nothing. ·I
urge you to have something to eat; your safety depends on it. Not a hair of any of
35 your heads will be lost.' ·With these words he took some bread, gave thanks to
36 God in view of them all, broke it and began to eat. *·They all plucked up courage
37 and took something to eat themselves. ·In all we were two hundred and seventy-
38 six souls on board that ship. ·When they had eaten what they wanted they lightened
the ship by throwing the corn overboard into the sea.
39   When day came they did not recognise the land, but they could make out a bay
40 with a beach; they planned to run the ship aground on this if they could. ·They
slipped the anchors and let them fall into the sea, and at the same time loosened
the lashings of the rudders; then, hoisting the foresail to the wind, they headed for
41 the beach. ·But the cross-currents carried them into a shoal and the vessel ran
aground. The bows were wedged in and stuck fast, while the stern began to break
up with the pounding of the waves.
42   The soldiers planned to kill the prisoners for fear that any should swim off and
43 escape. ·But the centurion was determined to bring Paul safely through and would
not let them carry out their plan. He gave orders that those who could swim should
44 jump overboard first and so get ashore, ·and the rest follow either on planks or on
pieces of wreckage. In this way it happened that all came safe and sound to land.

Waiting in Malta

1   **28** Once we had come safely through, we discovered that the island was called
2   Malta. ·The inhabitants treated us with unusual kindness. They made us all
welcome by lighting a huge fire because it had started to rain and the weather was
3 cold. ·Paul had collected a bundle of sticks and was putting them on the fire when
4 a viper brought out by the heat attached itself to his hand. ·When the inhabitants
saw the creature hanging from his hand they said to one another, 'That man must
be a murderer; he may have escaped the sea, but divine justice *would not let him
5 live.' ·However, he shook the creature off into the fire and came to no harm,
6 although they were expecting him at any moment to swell up or drop dead on the
spot. After they had waited a long time without seeing anything out of the ordinary
happen to him, they changed their minds and began to say he was a god.
7   In that neighbourhood there were estates belonging to the chief man of the
island, whose name was Publius. He received us and entertained us hospitably for
8 three days. ·It happened that Publius' father was in bed, suffering from fever and
dysentery. Paul went in to see him, and after a prayer he laid his hands on the man
9 and healed him. ·When this happened, the other sick people on the island also
10 came and were cured; ·they honoured us with many marks of respect, and when
we sailed they put on board the provisions we needed.

From Malta to Rome

11 At the end of three months we set sail in a ship that had wintered in the island; she
12 came from Alexandria and her figurehead was the Twins. ·We put in at Syracuse
13 and spent three days there; ·from there we followed the coast up to Rhegium.
After one day there a south wind sprang up and on the second day we made
14 Puteoli, *·where we found some brothers and had the great encouragement of
staying a week with them. And so we came to Rome.

15 When the brothers there heard about us they came to meet us, as far as the Forum of Appius and the Three Taverns. When Paul saw them he thanked God

16 and took courage. ·On our arrival in Rome Paul was allowed to stay in lodgings of his own with the soldier who guarded him. *

Paul makes contact with the Roman Jews *

17 After three days he called together the leading Jews. When they had assembled, he said to them, 'Brothers, although I have done nothing against our people or the customs of our ancestors, I was arrested in Jerusalem and handed over to the

18 Romans. ·They examined me and would have set me free, since they found me

19 guilty of nothing involving the death penalty; ·but the Jews lodged an objection, and I was forced to appeal to Caesar, though not because I had any accusation to

20 make against my own nation. * ·That is why I have urged you to see me and have a discussion with me, for it is on account of the hope of Israel that I wear this chain.'

21 They answered, *'We have received no letters from Judaea about you, nor has any of the brothers arrived here with any report or story of anything to your

22 discredit. ·We think it would be as well to hear your own account of your position; all we know about this sect is that it encounters opposition everywhere.'

Paul's declaration to the Roman Jews *

23 So they arranged a day with him and a large number of them visited him at his lodgings. He put his case to them, testifying to the kingdom of God and trying to persuade them about Jesus, arguing from the Law of Moses and the prophets from

24 early morning until evening; ·and some were convinced by what he said, while the

25 rest were sceptical. ·So they disagreed among themselves and, as they went away, Paul had one last thing to say to them, *'How aptly the Holy Spirit spoke when he told your ancestors through the prophet Isaiah:

26   *Go and say to this people:*
         Listen and listen but never understand!
         Look and look but never perceive!
27   *This people's heart is torpid,*
         their ears dulled, they have shut their eyes tight,
         to avoid using their eyes to see, their ears to hear,
         using their heart to understand,
         changing their ways and being healed by me.

28 'You must realise, then, that this salvation of God has been sent to the gentiles; and they will listen to it.' *

Epilogue*

30 He spent the whole of the two years * in his own rented lodging. He welcomed all

31 who came to visit him, ·proclaiming the kingdom of God and teaching the truth about the Lord Jesus Christ with complete fearlessness and without any hindrance from anyone. *

NOTES TO ACTS

1 **a.** The Gospel of Luke

b. This emphasises the part played by the Spirit in the first missionary activities of the apostles, vv. 5,8 and ch. 2, as in the opening of Christ's ministry, Lk 4:1,14,18.

c. One form of the Western text does not mention the ascension here.

d. The kingdom of God, Mt 4:17f, must be the main subject preached by the apostles, see Ac 8:12; 19:8; 20:25; 28:23,31, as it was the main thing preached by Christ, see Mt 3:2d.

e. For Luke, Jerusalem is the predestined centre of the whole saving work of God through Christ, Lk 2:22h, 38o, the place at which the earthly mission of Jesus culminates, and the starting-point for the universal mission of the apostles, 1:8.

f. The baptism of the Spirit foretold by John the Baptist, Mt 3:11 and par., and here promised by Jesus, will be initiated by the outpouring of the Spirit at Pentecost, Ac 2:1–4. Subsequently, the apostles, obedient to Christ's command, Mt 28:19, will continue to make use of baptism by water, Ac 2:41; 8:12,38; 9:18; 10:48; 16:15,33; 18:8; 19:5, as the ritual initiation into the messianic kingdom, see Mt 3:6e, but it will be 'in the name of Jesus', Ac 2:38y, and through belief in Christ as Saviour, see Rm 6:4a, will be able to absolve from sins and to give the Spirit, Ac 2:38. Connected with this Christian baptism by water there is the companion rite of the imposition of hands, 1 Tm 4:14e, the purpose of which is to give the gifts of the Spirit in as manifest a way as that in which they had been given at Pentecost, Ac 8:16–19; 9:17–18; 19:5– 6 (but cf. 10:44–48); this is the origin of the sacrament of confirmation. Side by side with these Christian sacraments the baptism of John was for a time still being administered by certain of the less well-instructed early Christians, 19:3.

g. 1:6 takes up the narrative broken off in Lk 24:49.

h. The apostles still expect the messianic kingdom to be the political restoration of David's dynasty, see Mt 4:17f.

i. Human history is the unfolding of salvation, and it develops through the 'times and dates', see Dn 2:21; 1 Th 5:1, that God has always foreseen (Rm 16:25l; 1 Co 2:7; Ep 1:4; 3:9,11; Col 1:26; 2 Tm 1:9; cf. Mt 25:34): first there are the 'times' of preparation, Heb 1:2; 9:9; 1 P 1:11, and of God's patience, Ac 17:30; Rm 3:26; then follows the appointed time, Ga 4:4c, the moment long foretold for the Messiah to come and begin the era of salvation, Rm 3:26m; after this, the time that is to elapse before the final coming, 2 Co 6:2a; lastly, the great and final 'Day', 1 Co 1:8e (preceded by the 'last days', 1 Tm 4:1a) and the Last Judgement itself, Rm 2:6b. However, in the course of the NT itself, the vividness of this hope in a Second Coming, which is founded on the outlook of Jewish apocalyptic, wanes and gives way to a 'realised eschatology', see 1 Co 1:8e.

j. The Holy Spirit is a favourite theme of Luke (Lk 4:1b); he talks generally about the Holy Spirit as a Power, 1:8; 10:38; Lk 1:35; 24:49; Rm 15:13,19; 1 Co 2:4,5; 1 Th 1:5; Heb 2:4, sent from God by Christ, Ac 2:33, to broadcast the good news. 1 From the Spirit come the gifts, 1 Co 12:4seq., that guarantee the message: the gift of tongues, Ac 2:1a,4, of miracles, 10:38, of prophecy, 11:27m; 20:23; 21:11, of wisdom, 6:3,5,10. 2 The Spirit gives strength to proclaim Jesus as Messiah in spite of persecution, 4:8,31; 5:32; 6:10; cf. Ph 1:19, and to bear witness to him, 1:8; Mt 10:20 and par.; Jn 15:26; 2 Tm 1:7seq., see following note. 3 The Spirit guides the Church in her major decisions: the admission of gentiles, 8:29,40; 10:19,44–47; 11:12–16; 15:8, without obligation to observe the Law, 15:28; Paul's mission to the gentile world, 13:2seq.; 16:6–7; 19:1 (Western text), see Mt 3:16n. Ac also mentions the Spirit as received in baptism and forgiving sins, 2:38; see Rm 5:5e.

k. The primary function of the apostles is to bear witness: not only to Christ's resurrection, 2:32; 3:15; 4:33;

5:32; 13:31; 22:15; Lk 24:48, but also to the whole of his public life, 1:21; 10:39seq.; Lk 1:2; Jn 15:27.

l. Nothing can limit the apostolic mission. Is 45:14h. The progress outlined here follows the geographical plan of Ac: Jerusalem was destined to receive the good news, to be the centre from which it is now spreading, see Lk 2:38o.

m. The cloud is part of theophanies in OT. Ex 13:22h, and in NT. Lk 9:34–35 and par. In particular. Dn 7:13, it marks the coming of the Son of man, v. 11 of this passage; Mt 24:30q; cf. 1 Th 4:17; Rv 1:7; 14:14–16.

n. Thus the Western text. *Text. rec.* 'this Jesus who has been taken up from you into heaven'.

o. The glorious coming, the *parousia*, see notes on Mt 24 and Lk 17:22–37; 21:5–33.

p. 'Son' (of Alphaeus, of James) is not in the Greek. The apostle Jude is not the Jude 'brother' of Jesus, see Mt 13:55; Mk 6:3, and brother of James (Jude 1). Nor is it likely that the apostle James son of Alphaeus was James brother of the Lord, 12:17; 15:13; etc.

q. There are many examples in Acts of the earnest prayer enjoined, Mt 6:5c, and practised, Mt 14:23f, by Jesus. Communal prayer under the apostles is centred on the breaking of bread, Ac 2:42,46; 20:7–11. There is prayer on all important occasions, elections, ordinations and the promulgation of rulings, 1:24; 6:6; 13:3; 14:23, confirmation of the Samaritans, 8:15, on the occasion of persecutions, 4:24–31; 12:5,12. Individuals also are seen praying: Stephen for himself and his executioners, 7:59–60, Paul after his vision of Christ, 9:11, Peter and Paul before their miracles, 9:40; 28:8, Peter when God calls him to Cornelius, 10:9; 11:5, Cornelius himself as a man of prayer, 10:2,4,30–31, Paul and Silas in prison, 16:25, Paul taking leave of his friends at Miletus, 20:36, and at Tyre, 21:5. On most occasions it is a prayer of asking, also to obtain pardon in 8:22–24, prayer of praise, 16:25, thanksgiving, 28:15; finally witness to the faith: 'calling on the name of Jesus' is the hallmark of the Christian, 2:21,38; 9:14,21; 22:16.

r. Close relations of Jesus, see Mt 12:46o.

s. Besides its strict sense the word 'brother' has often in the Bible wider senses, a relation more or less distant, Gn 9:25; 13:8, a compatriot, Gn 16:12; Ex 2:11; Dt 2:4; 15:2; Ps 22:22. From there it passes to a deeper relationship by communion in the covenant. In the NT it very frequently denotes Christians, disciples of Christ, 6:3; 9:30; 11:1; 12:17; Mt 28:10; Jn 20:17; Rm 1:13, who, like him, do the will of the Father, Mt 12:50 and par., children of the Father of whom he is the First-born, Mt 25:40; Rm 8:29; Heb 2:11,17, between whom brotherly love reigns, Rm 12:10; 1 Th 4:9; 1 P 1:22; 1 Jn 3:14.

t. This account of the death of Judas differs from the version in Mt 27:3–10. It is not a death by hanging, like that of Ahithopel, 2 S 17:23, but is after the pattern of the death of the wicked in Ws 4:19, and the pouring out of his entrails mirrors the death of many a criminal in folk legends. The field 'of blood' is named not after the blood of Jesus, but that of Judas. Both traditions recall the fact of a sudden and ignominious end to the life of a traitor, and attach it with more or less success to the Hakeldama, well known in Jerusalem as a place of ill omen.

u. var. 'He nominated' v. 23 and var. 'he prayed' v. 24, to give greater prominence to Peter's role.

v. This archaic way of electing, Ex 33:7e; 1 S 14:41r; Lk 1:9, will soon be replaced in the community by a less mechanical process, see 6:3–6; 13:2–3.

w. 'he was listed as one of the twelve apostles', Western text; see Mk 3:14c.

2 **a.** The phenomenon of Pentecost has elements common to the speaking in tongues experienced by Cornelius (10:46seq.; 11:15) and by the disciples of John at Ephesus (19:6), which Paul discusses in 1 Co 14. In none of these cases is there any question of a continuous speech of instruction, but what happens is praise of God (2:11; 10:46; 1 Co 14:2,16) by ecstatic speech which surprises the listeners (2:13; 1 Co 14:23). Analogous happenings in the ancient contemporary world show that these bursts of praise used words of foreign languages (2:6,11; 1 Co 14:10–11,21). Luke uses this fact to see in this occurrence at the beginning of the Church a foretaste of the preaching which was soon to carry the good news to all the peoples of the world, and thus undo the confusion of languages at the Tower of Babel (Gn 11:6–7). He could have been helped in this by a Jewish tradition which commemorated on the day of Pentecost the theophany at Sinai and which claimed that the voice of God, mediated by flames of fire, was then addressed to all the peoples of the world, but was rejected by all except Israel which accepted the Law. In this new Sinai all the peoples are challenged, and they accept.

b. Not the hundred and twenty, 1:15–26, but the group mentioned in 1:13–14.

c. 'Breath' and 'Spirit' are the same word in Hebrew (and in Greek and Latin). *see* Jn 3:8d.

d. The shape of the flames (Is 5:24; cf. Is 6:6–7) is here associated with the gift of tongues.

e. 'devout men' Sin. Western text 'Now the Jews who were living in Jerusalem were men from every nation under heaven.' The other texts have both 'devout men' and 'Jews'.

f. Gentile converts to Judaism who joined the chosen race by being circumcised. These proselytes are not the same as the God-fearers, 10:2b, who admire the Jewish religion and attend the synagogue but do not accept circumcision or the ritual prescribed by the Law. Jews and proselytes are not here additional classes of people: the terms qualify the nations just enumerated.

g. This list of peoples of the Mediterranean world, which runs roughly from east to west and from north to south, appears to depend on an ancient astrological calendar, known from other sources, in which the peoples were attached to the signs of the zodiac and listed in their order. Luke must have taken it over as a handy description of the inhabited world of his day. The mention of Judaea is hard to explain and has, since ancient times, occasioned many attempts at correction.

h. Peter speaks as leader of the apostolic body, *see* 1:15; 2:37; 3:4,6, 12; 4:8,13; 5:3,8,9,15,29; cf. ch. 10–11. *See* Mt 16:19i; Lk 22:32k. John is often joined to him, but rather as a sort of double, 3:1,3,4,11; 4:13,19; 8:14; cf. Lk 22:8. Peter's speech takes the form of a Jewish sermon, commenting on three texts of scripture in turn and applying them to the present situation. This is a recognised rabbinic technique.

i. About 9 am.

j. add. 'Joel'. • Vv. 17–21 quoted as in Western text; Alexandrian text favours the LXX.

k. The messianic era.

l. The day of the Lord's coming in glory, the 'Day of Yahweh', Am 5:18m. In Christian preaching, this 'Day' is that of Christ's return, Mt 24:1a.

m. The Christians style themselves 'those who invoke the name of the Lord', 9:14,21; 22:16; 1 Co 1:2; 2 Tm 2:22; the title 'Lord' indicates no longer Yahweh but Jesus, *see* Ac 3:16l; Ph 2:11. On Judgement Day people will be accepted or rejected according as to whether they have or have not invoked this name, i.e. acknowledged Jesus as Lord: see 4:12 and Rm 10:9.

n. The content of the earliest apostolic preaching (the *kerygma*) is here summarised for the first time (*see* 2:14–39; 3:12–26; 4:8–12; 5:29–32; 10:34–43; the four discourses of Peter and the discourse of Paul): **1** A witness, 1:8k, to Jesus' death and resurrection, 2:24q, and to his exaltation, 2:33t,36w. **2** It also provides certain details of Jesus' ministry; how it was heralded by John the Baptist, 10:37; 13:24, inaugurated by teaching and miracle, 2:22; 10:38, completed by the appearances of the risen Christ, 10:40,41; 13:31, and by the gift of the Spirit, 2:33; 5:32. **3** It places this story in its wider setting: it appeals to the past, adducing the OT

prophecies, 2:23o,25r, and it surveys the future, the advent of the messianic era, inviting Jews and gentiles to repentance, 2:38x, so that Christ's glorious return may come the sooner, 3:19–21. The gospels, which are developments of the primitive preaching, adopt the same scheme.

o. The OT prophecies demonstrate this divine plan: 3:18; 4:28; 13:29, *see also* 8:32–35; 9:22; 10:43; 17:2–3; 18:5,28; 26:22–23,27; 28:23; Lk 18:31e; 22:22; 24:25–27,44.

p. In this case the Romans. The primitive *kerygma* accused the Jews in the same way, and confronted them with the decisive intervention of God in the raising of Jesus from the dead, 2:32,36; 3:13–17; 4:10; 5:30–31; 7:52; 10:39–40; 13:27–30; 17:31; *see* Rm 1:4c; 1 Th 2:14f.

q. 'of Hades' Western text; 'of death' *Text. rec.*, cf. vv. 27 and 31. 'Hades' in LXX is *sheol*, Nb 16:33f; Mt 16:18h.

r. Quoted according to LXX. In the Hebr. text the psalmist prays only for deliverance from imminent death 'You will not allow your faithful one to see the pit.' Hence the argument presupposes the Greek version which, by translating 'pit' (= grave) as 'corruption', introduces a new idea.

s. On the ancient Mount Sion, at a lower level than the Temple, 1 K 2:10. A wrong interpretation of this verse gave rise to the belief that the tomb of David was at the traditional place of the Last Supper, on the western hill which has been given the name Sion since the early Christian centuries.

t. Words borrowed from Ps 118 (v. 16 LXX 'The right hand of the Lord has raised me up') used in their preaching by the apostles who took it to be messianic: 4:11; Mt 21:9 and par., 42 and par.; 23:39; Lk 13:35; Jn 12:13; Heb 13:6; 1 P 2:7. But it is possible to translate 'Having been raised up to the right hand of God' and to see in this an introduction to the quotation (v. 34) of Ps 110:1, which is another theme of apostolic preaching: 7:55,56; Mt 22:44 and par.; 26:64 and par.; Mk 16:19; Rm 8:34; 1 Co 15:25; Ep 1:20; Col 3:1; Heb 1:3,13; 8:1; 10:12; 12:2; 1 P 3:22.

u. According to the prophets, the gift of the Spirit would characterise the messianic era, Ezk 36:27f. Peter explains the miracle his hearers have witnessed as the 'pouring out' of this Spirit, foretold in Jl 3:1–2, by the risen Christ.

v. The argument is, apparently, that David lies in his tomb and therefore did not ascend into heaven; hence God's summons was addressed not to him but to the one who came out from the tomb.

w. Conclusion of the argument from scripture: it is by his resurrection that Jesus has been constituted the 'Lord' of whom Ps 110 speaks, and the 'Messiah' (Christ) to whom Ps 16 refers. From Ps 2:7 (Son of God), Ac 13:33x; Rm 1:4c; Heb 1:5; 5:5 develop a similar argument. *See also* 5:31 (leader and Saviour); 10:42 and Rm 14:9 (Judge and Lord of living and dead); Ph 2:9–11 (glorified Lord). By his resurrection Jesus entered upon the enjoyment of the divine prerogatives which were his by right of birth.

x. Each of the great apostolic discourses closes with a call to repentance (*see* Mt 3:2c) to obtain forgiveness of sins: 3:19,26; 5:31; 10:43; 13:38; *see also* 17:30; 26:20; Lk 1:77; 3:8; 5:32; 13:3.

y. Baptism is administered 'in the name of Jesus Christ' (*see* 1:5f) and the recipient 'invokes the name of the Lord Jesus' (*see* 2:21m; 3:16l) 8:16; 10:48; 19:5; 22:16; Rm 6:3; 1 Co 1:13,15; 6:11; 10:2; Ga 3:27; cf. Jm 2:7. Such expressions are not necessarily the actual liturgical formulae of baptism, cf. Mt 28:19; they may simply indicate its significance, namely, that the baptised profess their faith in Christ, and Christ adopts those who thenceforth are dedicated to him.

z. The promise is addressed primarily to the Jews, 3:25–26; 13:46; Rm 9:4.

aa. i.e. the gentiles, alluding to Is 57:19 quoted and explained in Ep 2:13–17; *see also* 22:21.

bb. Or 'he bore witness', cf. 8:25; 28:23.

cc. Luke repeatedly and deliberately notes the Church's numerical growth: v. 47; 4:4; 5:14; 6:1,7; 9:31p; 11:21,24; 16:5; cf. 12:24; 13:48–49; 19:20.

dd. Compare this passage with 4:32–35 and 5:12–16.

These three composite editorial 'summaries' paint similar pictures of life in the first Christian community.

ee. Not the proclamation of the good news to non-Christians, cf. 15:35, but instructions for the newly converted in which the scriptures were explained in the light of the Incarnation.

ff. 'Brotherhood' (or 'fellowship'), 1 Co 1:9f. occurs here without further detail, cf. Ga 2:9. It certainly denotes community of goods, v. 44; 4:32–35, which expresses and strengthens community of spirit, v. 46; 4:32, as a result of sharing the gospel and all the benefits received in the apostolic community from God through Jesus Christ. But the sense is not limited to help on the social level, nor to a common ideology or feeling of solidarity.

gg. Cf. v. 46; 20:7,11; 27:35; Lk 24:30,35. In itself the phrase suggests a Jewish meal at which the one who presides pronounces a blessing before dividing the bread. For Christians, however, it implies the Eucharistic service, Lk 22:19 and par.; 24:35h; 1 Co 10:16; 11:24. This, v. 46, was celebrated not in the Temple but in private houses; an ordinary meal would accompany it, cf. 1 Co 11:20–34.

hh. Prayer in common, 1:14,24; 4:24–30; 6:4; 12:5.

ii. add. 'in Jerusalem, and upon all there was great fear.'

jj. Joy is the sequel of faith: 8:8,39; 13:48, 52; 16:34; cf. 5:41; Lk 1:14i; Rm 15:13.

kk. Cf. 3:8,9; 4:21; 13:48; 21:20; Lk 2:20g.

ll. When judgement comes the members of the Christian community are assured of salvation, 2:21m; see also 13:48 and Paul's letters. The Church is thus identified with 'the remnant of Israel', Is 4:3c, cf. Rm 9:27.

3 **a.** The time of evening sacrifice, see 10:3,30; Ex 29:39–42; Lk 1:8–10f. There is a clear parallel between the miracles of Peter and those of Paul, and also those of Jesus, see p. 221.

b. Probably the gate known as 'Corinthian', which, to the east of the Sanctuary, led from the outer court or Court of the Gentiles, to the first inner court, or Court of Women.

c. var. 'get up and walk', cf. Lk 5:23–24, etc.

d. A porch or cloister along the eastern side of the Temple.

e. The Christians see in Jesus the mysterious 'servant' of Is 52:13–53:12 (quoted in part in Ac 8:32–33), see Is 42:1a. See below, v. 26; 4:27,30. His 'glorification' by God is his resurrection, v. 15, see Jn 17:5e.

f. Cf. Is 53:12. Same allusion to the servant song in 7:52; Rm 4:25; 8:32; Ga 2:20; Ep 5:2,25.

g. As they disowned Moses, 7:35, himself a figure of Christ.

h. var. 'disowned'.

i. Cf. 4.27,30: Jesus is the 'holy servant' of God. He is also 'the Holy One of God' and 'the Holy One' par excellence: 2:27; Mk 1:24j; Lk 1:35; 4:34; Jn 6:69; Rv 3:7.

j. See 7:52; 22:14; Is 53:11; see also Mt 27:19; Lk 23:47; 1 P 3:18; 1 Jn 2:1.

k. The one who leads his subjects to full life, imparting his own life to them. This same title of 'leader' is given, 7:27,35, to Moses who prefigures Christ, see 5:31k; Heb 2:10.

l. The 'name', according to the ancients, is inseparable from the person and shares his prerogatives, see Ex 3:13g. By the invocation of the name of Jesus, 2:21m,38y, his power is stirred to action, 3:6; 4:7,10,30; 10:43; 16:18; 19:13; Lk 9:49; 10:17; see also Jn 14:13,14; 15:16; 16:24,26; 20:31. Faith is of course required for this invocation to be effective, cf. 19:13–17; Mt 8:10b.

m. Apparently an allusion to Lk 23:34; cf. 7:60.

n. By 'repentance' a person 'comes back' to God, see Mt 3:2c. The gentiles must return to God by forsaking idols, cf. 14:15; 15:19–20; 26:18,20; 1 Co 10:7,14; Ga 4:9; 1 Th 1:9; the Jews must turn to the Lord by acknowledging Jesus as Lord; see Ac 9:35; 2 Co 3:16. The expression of 11:21, Lk 1:16, cf. 1 P 2:25, is somewhat different, see also Is 6:10, quoted in 28:27; Mt 13:15; Mk 4:12, cf. Jn 12:40.

o. This epoch coincides with that of Christ's coming and of 'the restoration of all things', see 1:7h; Rm 2:6b, a period

which, as the apostles thought, would see the re-establishment of the kingdom in Israel, Ac 1:6–7. Repentance and conversion hasten its coming, cf. 2 P 3:12.

p. Or 'Jesus who has been appointed Christ for you', see 2:36w.

q. The return of the captive and scattered Israelites was proclaimed by the prophets as a prelude to the messianic era, Jr 16:15; 23:8; Ho 11:10–11, when happiness and peace would prevail for ever. Is 11:1–9,7e; 65:17–25; Ho 2:20s; Mi 5:6–8. In the same way, at the due time, God will send Jesus, instituted messianic king at the time of his resurrection, 2:36w, who will inaugurate his definitive reign and the renewal of all creation, see Rm 8:19j; 1 Co 15:24–25.

r. add. 'from ancient times'.

s. The earliest Christian preaching made a point of showing how Jesus fulfilled OT prophecy, including many texts in Psalms which were regarded as prophetic: he was a descendant of David, 2:29–31; 13:34, he appeared as a prophet, Moses' successor, 3:22seq., see Mt 16:14c; Jn 1:21t. He suffered, 2:23o, he was the stone rejected by the builders (the Jews) but now set in a place of honour, 4:11, he rose again, 2:25–31; 13:33–37, and is at God's right hand, 2:34seq.

t. Thus implementing the promise recalled in v. 22, because the Greek verb means both 'to raise up' and 'to raise up again'. God by raising Christ from the dead fulfils the promises made to the ancestors, 13:32–34; 24:14–15; 26:6–8.

u. Cf. 26:23; Ga 3:14; 2 Tm 1:10. Christ by his resurrection brought to the world the blessing promised to Abraham, 3:25.

v. Others translate 'so long as each of you turns from his wicked ways'.

4 **a.** The priestly aristocratic faction opposed the Pharisees who were the pious and popular party, see Mt 3:7f. The Sadducees are always represented as denying the doctrine of resurrection, 23:6–8; Lk 20:27–38 and par. More than once the mutual hostility of these two parties produces an alliance of Pharisees with Christians, see 5:34; 23:8–9; 26:5–8; Lk 20:39.

b. The Great Sanhedrin of Jerusalem, Israel's supreme court.

c. var. 'John'.

d. For vv. 10–12 we follow the Western text.

e. 'Jesus' means 'God saves', Mt 1:21.

f. Apparently a solemn legal warning. In matters of this kind the accused (unless they were rabbis) could not be imprisoned except for a second offence (the case in 5:28).

g. Text corrupt, translation uncertain. The composition of the Psalter as a whole was attributed to David.

h. 'Anointed': the Greek word is 'Christ'; it is explained here, v. 27, according to its etymological sense.

i. Representing respectively the 'kings' and 'princes' of the Psalm. For 'Herod', see Lk 23:6–16.

j. The 'anointing' that has constituted him King Messiah, 'the Christ', see Mt 3:16n.

k. lit. 'your hand and counsel'.

l. A miniature Pentecost, cf. the earlier one, 2:1seq.

m. A summary like that of 2:42–47. The prevailing idea is here the pooling of resources; this preludes two examples: Barnabas, Ananias and Sapphira. The emphasis on sacrificing possessions is characteristic of Luke's religious outlook.

n. A power that showed itself by miracles. See 2:22; 3:12; 4:7; 6:8; 8:13; 10:38; 1 Co 2:4–5; 1 Th 1:5.

o. By the people: see 2:47; 4:21; 5:13.

p. The Greek word means both 'consolation' (often in the strong sense of 'rescue') and 'encouragement' (often in the strong sense of 'support and defend'), see 11:23. • 'Son of', a semitic expression here meaning 'with an aptitude for'. • On Barnabas, see 9:27; 11:22–30; 12:25; ch. 13–15; 1 Co 9:6; Ga 2; Col 4:10.

5 **a.** The fault of Ananias and Sapphira is, out of avarice, to have tried to cheat the apostles and through them the Holy Spirit present in the brethren to whom they lied. The purpose of this disturbing story is probably to show Peter's prophetic authority in the community, compare 2 K 2:23–24.

b. The meaning of this term, adopted from the OT, cf. 7:38, to signify the messianic community, Mt 16:18g, expanded as Christianity developed. It originally indicated the mother church in Jerusalem, 8:1; 11:22; later the individual churches throughout Judaea, Ga 1:22; 1 Th 2:14; cf. Ac 9:31, and among the gentiles, Ac 13:1; 14:23; 15:41; 16:5; Rm 16:1,4; 1 Co 1:2a; Jm 5:14; 3 Jn 9; Rv 1:4; 2:1; referring to their 'gatherings', 1 Co 11:18; 14:23,34; cf. Ac 19:32; Phm 2, or to their location or area, Rm 16:5; 1 Co 16:19; Col 4:15. Lastly, it stands for the Church united under God, 20:28; 1 Co 10:32; 12:27–28; for the Church as Body and Bride of Christ, Ep 5:23–32; Col 1:18e, and for the Church as including the whole cosmos, Ep 1:22–23,23t.

c. This third 'summary' stresses the miraculous power of the apostles, cf. 2:43; 4:33. Vv. 12b–14 interrupt the development of this theme.

d. Here, it seems, not the apostles but all the faithful.

e. Rather than 'More and more joined (the community) as believers in the Lord,' cf. 11:24.

f. var. 'Annas the high priest', cf. 4:6.

g. lit. 'all the words (cf. 10:37) of this life'. This means the same thing as 'the message of salvation', 13:26. The purpose of Christian preaching is the 'salvation', *see* 4:12; 11:14; 15:11; 16:17,30–31, and 'life', *see also* 3:15; 11:18; 13:46,48, promised to those 'who invoke the name of the Lord', 2:21,40,47; 4:12.

h. The terms 'Sanhedrin' and 'Senate' both indicate the same council, the Great Sanhedrin of Jerusalem, *see* Lk 22:66t. • The motif of miraculous release from prison is frequent in Ac, 12:6–11; 16:26–27, and in Jewish literature. It is a sign of God's special protection.

i. Western text ' "Did we not expressly forbid you to preach in that name? And now . . ." Then Peter answered, "Which must we obey? God or man?" "God," he said. And Peter then replied, "The God of our ancestors . . ." '

j. The phrase is repeated in 10:39 (*see* 13:29). It recalls Dt 21:22–23, quoted in Ga 3:13, *see* 1 P 2:24.

k. The title matches 'Prince of life', 3:15k; it also corresponds to 'leader and redeemer' applied to Moses as a prefiguring of Christ, 7:35 (cf. 7:25). *See also* Heb 2:10; 12:2. There is an implicit comparison of Jesus with Moses.

l. Cf. 1:8; Mt 10:20 and par.; Jn 15:26–27.

m. Gamaliel I, Paul's teacher, 22:3, belonged to the school of Hillel and was the leading exponent of the more liberal and humane interpretation of the Law. The policy he urges here is in line with that of the Pharisaic party, *see* 4:1a.

n. Josephus mentions the revolts of Theudas and of Judas the Galilean but the dates he gives seem unreliable. Both must have taken place about the time Jesus was born.

o. A variant introduces the idea of ritual purity '. . . leave them alone and do not dirty your hands. For if . . . God, not only you but kings and tyrants will be powerless to destroy them. Do not therefore touch these men lest you find yourselves at war with God.'.

p. The name for whose sake the apostles suffer, cf. 21:13; 1 P 4:14; 3 Jn 7, the name they preach, 4:10,12,17,18; 5:28,40; cf. 3:6,16; 8:12,16; 9:15,16,27,28, and which the Christians invoke, 2:21; 4:12; 9:14,21; 22:16, is the name, i.e. the person, of Jesus, 3:16l, the name he received at his resurrection, 2:36w, 'the name above all other names'. This name was 'Lord', hitherto reserved to God, Ph 2:9–11,11p.

q. The good news of the Kingdom, Mk 1:1a, preached by the disciples, Ac 8:4,25,40; 14:7,15,21; 16:10, or the 'gospel', 15:7; 20:24, receives its concrete embodiment for primitive Christianity in the person of Jesus, 8:35, raised by God, 13:32seq.; 17:18; *see also* 2:23p; 9:20, and become Son of God in power, *see* Rm 1:1b, Christ, 5:42; 8:12; cf. 9:22, and Lord, 10:36; 11:20; 15:35; *see* 2:36w.

6 a. 'Disciples': a new use of the term, in certain parts of Ac (not before 6:1 nor after 21:16, an indication of the sources used by Luke) to indicate the Christians who are thus associated with the small circle of those first adherents of Jesus who are called by this name in the gospels.

b. 'Hellenists': Jews from outside Palestine; in Jerusalem they had their own synagogues where the Bible was read in Greek. The 'Hebrews' were native Palestinian Jews; their language was Aramaic but in their synagogues the Bible was read in Hebrew. This distinction made its way into the early Church. Missionary initiative was to come from the hellenistic group.

c. var. 'We shall select'.

d. The Twelve represent the number of the tribes of Israel; seven is the number of the gentile 'nations' inhabiting Canaan, Dt 7:1, quoted in Ac 13:19.

e. When the community met for public worship the apostles had two functions: they led prayers and were responsible also for the *katechesis* (the doctrinal elaboration of the good news).

f. Luke does not call the chosen seven 'deacons', and this term may have been given to the Seven as a title or rank because he twice uses the word *diakonia* ('service' v. 4; translated 'distribution' in v. 1) *see* Ph 1:1a; Tt 1:5c. All seven have Greek names; the last is a proselyte, *see* 2:11n. The hellenistic Christians now have their own organisation independent of the Hebrew group. The functions of the Seven overlap those of the Twelve, for they both preach and baptise. It is possible that the author has smoothed over some bigger disagreement between the two elements in the community which led to this institution of a parallel leadership.

g. Possibly a gesture of the community, cf. 13:1–3, more probably (v. 3) of the apostles.

h. A fresh formula, *see also* 12:24; 19:20.

i. Probably the descendants of Jews carried off to Rome by Pompey in 63 BC who were sold into slavery and later released.

j. The 'false witnesses' at the trial of Jesus similarly brought the accusation that he 'would destroy the Temple'. There is also a similarity in the climax of the two trials, 7:56–57; Mt 26:62–66. The allegations concerning Mosaic practice will be made in Paul's case also, 15:1,5; 21:21,28; 25:8; 28:17.

k. The sight of an angel induces religious awe, *see* Jg 13:6. The face of Moses, reflecting the glory of God as he came down from Sinai, produced the same effect, Ex 34:29–35; 2 Co 3:7–18; so also the appearance of Jesus was changed, Mt 17:2; Lk 9:29. The members of the Sanhedrin in their turn witness a 'transfiguration, that of Stephen as he contemplates the glory of God, 7:55–56. • The narrative, interrupted by the insertion of Stephen's discourse, 7:1–54, is resumed in 7:55. On theophanies, see Ex 13:22; 19:16; 33:20; Mt 17:1; 24:26–31 and notes there.

7 a. The speech opens with a summary of the stories of Abraham and Joseph, vv. 2–16; it goes on to expound the history of Moses, vv. 17–43 (*see also* the charge made against Stephen, 6:11). With Moses' divine mission of salvation Stephen contrasts the attitude of Israel: rejection, disobedience, faithlessness—traditional themes (*see* Dt) but here elaborated with the Christian event in mind. When Stephen speaks of Moses he is thinking of Christ whom Moses prefigured: the Jews react now as the Israelites did then. In the history of Israel, Stephen underlines anything which goes against attachment to any particular country, vv. 2–6, against sacrifices, vv. 39–43, and against the construction of a material temple, vv. 44–50, *see* the accusation of 6:13. The spirit of the hellenised Judaism of the Diaspora is discernible.

b. According to Gn 11:31 the apparition took place at Haran. Stephen follows a non-biblical tradition.

c. Mt Horeb, but Stephen says 'this place' (i.e. the Temple) instead.

d. 'father of Shechem': this detail is taken from Gn 33:19. var. 'from the sons of Hemor son of Shechem', 'from the sons of Emmor at Shechem', 'from the sons of

Emmor (inhabitants) of Shechem'. v. 16 follows a non-biblical tradition.

e. According to Jewish traditions.

f. By raising up Jesus from the dead God has appointed him 'prince'. cf. 5:31, and 'judge', cf. 10:42; 17:31.

g. In Ex 2:15 Moses runs away because he is afraid of Pharaoh; here it is because his compatriots reject him.

h. The Bible does not apply this verb to Moses, but in 3:13–14 it is applied to Jesus. Nor does the Bible give the name 'redeemer' to Moses. The image of Christ shades into that of Moses who prefigured him.

i. A messianic text already cited, 3:22. One other than Moses—the Messiah—is to play a similar part. Mt 16:14c; Jn 1:21t.

j. The word also means 'church', see 5:11b; Mt 16:18g. In Dt 4:10 it denoted the assembly of the chosen people in the desert. cf. the sacred assembly. Ex 12:16; Lv 23:3; Nb 29:1. The Church, the new chosen people, 9:13g, is the heir of the old.

k. Moses acted as mediator between 'the angel' and the people. 'The angel of Yahweh' in the earliest texts is identical with Yahweh as manifesting himself, Gn 16:7c, see also Mt 1:20g. Later, a distinction was made between Yahweh and his angel in order to emphasise the divine transcendence. Thus Moses is represented as in immediate touch not with God but with one or several angels. There are traces of this idea in Ga 3:19; Heb 2:2.

l. To obey the Law is to live, Lv 18:5; Dt 4:1; 8:1,3; 30:15–16,19–20; 32:46–47, quoted in Rm 10:5; Ga 3:12; the Law, therefore, is referred to as 'the statutes of life', Ba 3:9; Ezk 33:15. For the Christian, the gospel preaching is the 'word of life', Ph 2:16; cf. Ac 5:20, i.e. 'the word of salvation', Ac 13:26. Since life springs from God's word, this word is itself 'living', cf. Heb 4:12; 1 P 1:23. And Jesus is himself 'the Word of life': 1 Jn 1:1.

m. See Ex 16:3 and Nb 14:3, see also Ezk 20:8–14.

n. Biblical phrase for the stars, often worshipped as gods, see Dt 4:19; 17:3; 2 K 21:3–5; Jr 8:2; 19:13; Zp 1:5.

o. var. 'for the God'.

p. Who spoke through Moses and the prophets.

q. Standing rather than seated as in Lk 22:69seq., perhaps as a witness to the martyr.

r. Stephen's vision is to be related to his transfiguration, 6:15k.

s. What is described is not the end of a judicial process, but a lynching by the crowd. It may be that this is historically accurate and the elements of a formal legal hearing are due to Luke's intention of showing the death of the first martyr as a parallel to that of Jesus.

t. The false witness mentioned in 6:13–14. It was for the hostile witnesses to initiate the execution of the sentence, Dt 17:7.

u. The future apostle Paul, 13:9f.

v. Fine example of 'calling upon the name of the Lord', 2:21m. Luke stresses by two features, vv. 59–60, the similarity between Stephen's death and the Passion of Jesus.

8 a. Vv. 1–4 are made up of a number of brief remarks: Stephen's burial (v. 2), the natural conclusion of the foregoing narrative; Saul's campaign against the Christians (vv. 1ª and 3) which links the account of the stoning of Stephen, see 7:58ᵇ, with what appears to be its sequel, namely Paul's conversion, 9:1–30; finally a note on the Church persecuted and scattered (vv. 1ᵇ–4) which introduces the narrative of Philip's mission, 8:5–40, and that of Peter, 9:32–11:18; v. 4 is picked up again in 11:19. We have here, therefore, a preliminary sketch of the various themes developed in the following chapters up to ch. 12.

b. 'everyone': a very general statement. The persecution in fact seems to have been directed principally against the Hellenists, see 6:1,5, and it was this group, scattered by persecution, that gave the Church its first missionaries, see v. 4; 11:19–20.

c. The second stage of the expansion of the Church, see

1:8. The third will start with the foundation of the church of Antioch, 11:20.

d. var. 'the town of Samaria', 'the town of Caesarea'. The reference is probably not to the town called Samaria, by this time a hellenistic city and known as Sebaste, but to the province: those who are evangelised are the 'Samaritans' in the Jewish sense of the word, i.e. akin in blood and religion but cut off from Israel's community and living in heresy, see Mt 10:5–6c; Jn 4:9e.

e. The Samaritans, too, expected the Messiah, see Jn 4:25.

f. Or, less probably, 'that is called Megalleh' (Aramaic for 'Revealing'). Evidently it was thought that Simon's supernatural power issued from some indwelling force of the high God.

g. The Holy Spirit is the gift of God par excellence, see 2:38; 10:45; 11:17; Lk 11:9,13.

h. 'Simony' (trafficking in sacred things) gets its name from this incident.

i. Western text adds 'and he wept bitterly without ceasing'.

j. Angels, see Tb 5:4b; Ep 1:21s, appear in the gospels several times ministering to Jesus and his mission, Mt 4:11 and par.; 26:53; Jn 1:51. In Ac they often minister to the Christian community, 1:10; 5:19; 10:3; 11:3; 12:7–10,23; 27:23. Here, the rest of the narrative refers to 'the Spirit', vv. 29 and 39.

k. Or 'towards the south'.

l. 'Ethiopia' began beyond the first cataract of the Nile: Nubia or the Sudan. It was ruled by queens bearing the title *kandake*.

m. Quoted from the LXX, here somewhat obscure and deriving from a Hebr. text itself obscure and probably corrupt. On the use of Is 53 in early Christian preaching, see Ac 3:13c.

n. V. 37, omitted here, is a very ancient gloss preserved in the Western text and suggested by the baptismal liturgy 'And Philip said, "If you believe with all your heart, you may." And he replied, "I believe that Jesus Christ is the Son of God." '

o. var. West. 'the Holy Spirit came down on the eunuch and the angel of the Lord carried Philip away.'

9 a. Crucial event in the Church's history. Luke gives three accounts whose discrepancies of detail are explained by their differing literary forms: the second and third accounts are found in Paul's discourses. See also Ga 1:12–17.
• The accounts have echoes of OT vocation narratives (Gn 31:11–13; 1 S 3:4–14), of a theophany (Dn 10:5–9) and of the conversion of another persecutor of God's people (2 M 3:24–40). The incident took place probably in AD 36, about 12 years (14 if we reckon as the ancients did) before the council of Jerusalem, Ga 2:1seq.; see Ac 15, held in 49.

b. The 'Way' was the way of life characteristic of the Christian community. The term is used, by extension, for the community itself. The OT usage, Ps 119:1a, is enriched by the new value of conformity to Christ, Mt 7:13–14; 22:16; 1 Co 4:17; 12:31; Heb 9:8; 10:19–22; 2 P 2:2. Jesus is himself called 'the Way', Jn 14:6d. This unqualified use of the word is peculiar to Ac: 18:25–26; 19:9,23; 22:4; 24:14,22.

c. The Roman authority recognised the high priest's jurisdiction over the members of Jewish communities even outside Palestine; according to 1 M 15:21 this even included right of extradition.

d. Aramaic ('Hebrew', 26:14) form of Saul's name.

e. Whatever is done to the disciples for the sake of the name of Jesus is done to Jesus himself, Mt 10:40.

f. var. 'having had a vision of'. Two corelative revelations, to Paul and to Ananias, see 10:11seq. and 30seq.

g. 'your holy people' lit. 'your holy ones' or 'your consecrated people'. Since God is the Holy One par excellence, Is 6:3, those consecrated to his service are called 'holy', Lv 17:1a. The term, applied originally to the people of Israel, Ex 19:3c,6, and in particular to the community of the messianic era, Dn 7:18m, is especially apt for the Christians who are the new 'holy race', 1 P 2:5,9, called, Rm 1:7; 1 Co 1:2; Ep 1:4; 2 Tm 1:9, by their baptismal consecration, Ep 5:26seq., to a blameless life, 1 Co 7:34; Ep 1:4; 5:3; Col 1:22, which makes them holy as God is holy, 1 P 1:15seq.. see 1 Jn 3:3, and like Jesus himself, 'the Holy One of God', Mk 1:24j. In the early community it becomes the usual term for the Christians, in Palestine first, 9:13,32,41; Rm 15:26,31; 1 Co 16:1,15; 2 Co 8:4; 9:1,12, and then in all the churches, Rm 8:27; 12:13; 16:2, 15; 1 Co 6:1seq.; 14:33; 2 Co 13:12; Ep 1:15; 3:18; 4:12; 6:18; Ph 4:21seq.; Col 1:4; 1 Tm 5:10; Phm 5,7; Heb 6:10; 13:24; Jude 3 (and in the introductory formulae of the letters 2 Co 1:1). In Rv 5:8; 8:3 the phrase 'holy ones' is used more specifically of the Christians who witness by their death. At times its application may be restricted to the leaders, the 'apostles and prophets', Ep 3:5 and Col 1:26; Ep 3:8; 4:12; Rv 18:20. Lastly, as in the OT, Jb 5:1a, it may indicate the angels, 10:22; Mk 8:38; Lk 9:26; Jude 14; Rv 14:10, and in some cases it is doubtful whether the reference is to angels or to the saints in glory. Ep 1:18; Col 1:12; 1 Th 3:13; 2 Th 1:10.

h. Cf. Jr 1:10. Paul's mission is 'to all humanity', 22:15, to the gentiles, 26:17; this agrees with what Paul himself writes in Ga 1:16, cf. Rm 1:5; 11:13; 15:16–18; Ga 2:2,8,9; Ep 3:8; Col 1:27; 1 Tm 2:7. On the 'kings', see 26:2a.

i. Characteristic Lucan phrase, 2:4; 4:8,31; 9:17; Lk 1:15,41,67. see Lk 4:1b.

j. 'Son of God' corresponds to 'Christ' in v. 22, see Mt 4:3d. We meet the title 'Son of God' only once more in Ac, at 13:33. It is characteristic of Pauline Christology, Rm 1:3–4,9; Ga 1:16; 2:20; 4:4,6; 1 Th 1:10; see also Rm 9:5d.

k. Three years, according to Ga 1:17–18; Paul's stay in Arabia belongs to this period. Luke's statement is vague.

l. var. 'his disciples'.

m. Paul mentions this visit, Ga 1:18–19. He observes that at that time the churches in Judaea did not yet know him by sight, but says nothing of the part Barnabas played. He states that, of the apostles, he saw none but Peter, and James the brother of the Lord; Ac, generalising, speaks vaguely of 'the apostles'.

n. var. 'the Greeks' (i.e. the gentiles); same variant in 11:20. The Hellenist Christians (see 6:1b) are the most active proselytisers, just as the Hellenist Jews were the most active opponents of Christian propaganda, 6:9seq.; 7:58; 9:1; 21:27; 24:19.

o. Where Barnabas later finds him, 11:25. Compare this with 22:17–21 and with Ga 1:18–21.

p. 'the churches' Western and Antiochene texts; 'the Church' Alexandrian text.

q. For similar miracles: 3:1–10 (and 4:22); 14:8–10; Lk 5:18–26 and par.; 13:11–13; Jn 5:1–14.

r. i.e. 'gazelle'. • The miracle is told in such a way as to bring out the similarity with Jesus' raising to life of the little girl ('Talitha') in Mk 5:38–41, see p. 221.

10 a. For Luke, Cornelius' conversion has a wide application. Its significance for the Church at large appears from the narrative itself and from its emphasis on the two corelative visions of Peter and of Cornelius (as to Paul and Ananias, 9:10–12), but especially from the way the author deliberately links this incident to the decision of the council of Jerusalem, see 15:7–11,14. There seem to be two separate lessons here. First, God himself has made it clear that the gentiles are to be received into the Church without being forced to obey the Law, cf. 10:34–35,44–48ᵃ; 11:1,15–18; 15:7–11,14; and Ga 2:1–10. Secondly, God himself has shown Peter that he must accept the hospitality of the uncircumcised. The problem of social relations between Christians converted from Judaism and Christians converted from paganism underlies the narrative, cf. 10:10–16,28–29; 11:2–14; and Ga 2:11–21.

b. The expressions 'fearing God', 10:2,22,35; 13:16,26, and 'worshipping God', 13:43,50; 16:14; 17:4,17; 18:7, are

technical terms for admirers and followers of the Jewish religion who stop short of circumcision, see 2:11f.

c. lit. 'has ascended as a memorial before God'. The expression recalls the 'memorial' sacrifice, see Lv 2:2,9,16, to which Tb 12:12 compares prayer.

d. Following Western text.

e. Peter is to throw off his scruples of legal purity, 11:9, cf. Mt 15:1–20 and par; Rm 14:14,17. The application is made in 15:9: by faith, God has cleansed the hearts of the gentiles; although their bodies, being uncircumcised, remain unclean. The immediate practical conclusion is that Peter must not fear contact with the uncircumcised, 10:27–28.

f. The intervention of the Spirit is like that of the angel of the Lord, cf. 8:26,29.

g. var. 'Three men', see 11:11.

h. var. 'I was fasting and praying.'

i. This impersonal mode of expression both shows respect for the majesty of God and also alludes to the ministry of angels, see Tb 12:12; Mt 18:11,14; Rv 5:8; 8:3.

j. The language of sacrifice (see v. 4). The unblemished victim and its offerer are both 'acceptable' to God, Lv 1:3; 19:5; 22:19–27. Isaiah (56:7) had prophesied that when the fullness of time came, the gentiles' sacrifices would be 'acceptable' to God; see Ml 1:10–11, cf. Rm 15:16; Ph 4:18; 1 P 2:5.

k. var. 'The word that God has sent'.

l. Vv. 37–42 sum up the gospel story, see 1:21–22; 2:22n, emphasising the same points as Luke brought out in his own Gospel.

m. var. 'It began'.

n. Stereotyped formula of the Christian preaching and faith. It appears as early as 1 Co 15:4 (a first stage of the creed) with the addition 'according to the scriptures'. The formula echoes Jon 2:1 (see Mt 12:40); see also Ho 6:2. It recurs in Mt 16:21; 17:23; 20:19; 27:64; Lk 9:22; 18:33; 24:7,46.

o. add. (Western text) 'and were his companions for forty days after his resurrection from the dead'.

p. i.e. the chosen people, Israel, 10:2; 21:28.

q. Those still alive at the Second Coming and those who have died before the coming but then rise for judgement. Cf. 1 Th 4:13–5:10. By raising up Jesus, God has solemnly invested him as supreme Judge, 17:31; Jn 5:22,27; 2 Tm 4:1; 1 P 4:5; to proclaim the resurrection is therefore to invite people to repentance, cf. Ac 17:30–31.

r. 'The Pentecost of the gentiles'. As Peter notes, v. 47; 11:15; 15:8, it resembles the first Pentecost.

s. It was not usual for the apostles to administer baptism themselves, see 19:5; 1 Co 1:14,17. See also 1 Jn 4:2.

t. That Peter should lodge with the uncircumcised seems to the Jerusalem 'Hebrews' even more shocking and contrary to the Law than that he should authorise their baptism (11:2–3; cf. 10:28). This same question gave rise to the Antioch incident, Ga 2:11seq.

11 a. Western text 'So after some time Peter determined to set out for Jerusalem. After speaking to the brothers and encouraging them, he set out, delivering many sermons throughout the countryside and instructing the people. When he reached them and told them of the favour God had granted, the circumcised brothers remonstrated with him.'

b. 'God' omitted by Western text (because it is Christ who gives the Spirit).

c. Peter explains why he allowed a gentile to be baptised; he does not answer the objection that he had lodged with the uncircumcised, see v. 3, cf. 10:1a. According to Luke, Peter was considered to have been the first to receive gentiles into the Church, in spite of the episode of the Ethiopian eunuch, 8:26–39, and the date of the evangelisation of Antioch to which Luke does not refer till later, vv. 19seq. Against this background the council of Jerusalem, 15:5–29, appears as a kind of sequel to, or repetition of, the discussion in 11:1–18.

d. V. 19 takes up from 8:1 and 8:4 and then presents the founding of the church at Antioch as an immediate sequel to Stephen's martyrdom from which it has been separated by the insertion of the Acts of Philip, 8:5–40, and of Peter, 9:31–11:18. Nevertheless, the narrative presupposes the story of Saul's conversion, 9:1–30, itself a sequel to Stephen's martyrdom.

e. Antioch on the Orontes, capital of the Roman province of Syria, third city of the empire after Rome and Alexandria.

f. var. 'Hellenists', cf. 9:29. • 'Greeks', as opposed to 'Jews', v. 19, includes all the uncircumcised.

g. Not 'Christ', a title more suited to a Jewish audience with its messianic expectation; in preaching to gentiles (Greeks) Jesus was called 'Lord', see 25:26h.

h. The church in Jerusalem enjoyed right of supervision over the other churches, see 8:14; 11:1, and see Ga 2:2b.

i. Apparently a play on the name 'Barnabas', 'son of exhortation', 4:36.

j. var. 'in the Lord'.

k. Meaning doubtful. Possibly 'they worked together', 'they were received (by the church)', i.e. were guests of the church.

l. i.e. supporters or followers of Christus (or Chrestus). The nickname shows that the gentiles of Antioch took the title of 'Christ' (anointed) for a proper name.

m. Like the OT prophets, Dt 18:18e; Mt 5:12; 2 P 1:21, those of the NT are charismatics, 1 Co 12:1a, who speak in God's name, being inspired by his Spirit. Under the new covenant this charism is bestowed even more generously, 2:17–18, and at times it is enjoyed by the faithful at large, 19:6; 1 Co 11:4–5; 14:26,29–33,37. But particular individuals are so specially endowed with the charisms that they are always referred to as 'prophets', 11:27; 13:1; 15:32; 21:9,10. These normally occupy the second place after the apostles in the order of charisms, 1 Co 12:28–29; Ep 4:11; but see Lk 11:49; Rm 12:6; 1 Co 12:10; this is because they are the appointed witnesses of the Spirit, 1 Th 5:19–20; Rv 2:7, whose 'revelations' they communicate, 1 Co 14:6,26,30; Ep 3:5; Rv 1:1, just as the apostles are witnesses to the risen Christ, Ac 1:8k; Rm 1:1b, and proclaim the *kerygma*, Ac 2:22n. They do not simply foretell the future, 11:28; 21:11, or read hearts, 1 Co 14:24–25; see 1 Tm 1:18. When they 'edify, exhort, console', 1 Co 14:3; see Ac 4:36; 11:23–24, they do so by a supernatural revelation; in this they resemble those who 'speak strange languages', Ac 2:1a,4; 19:6, but their gift is greater because their speech is intelligible, 1 Co 14. Their chief work was evidently to explain the prophecies of scripture under the guidance of the Holy Spirit, especially those of the OT prophets, 1 P 1:10–12, and thus expound the 'mystery' of the divine plan, Rm 16:25*l*; 1 Co 13:2; Ep 3:5. For this reason they are named with the apostles as the foundation of the Church, Ep 2:20s. The Revelation of John is a typical example of this NT 'prophecy', Rv 1:3; 10:11; 19:10; 22:7–10,18–19. For all its dignity, the prophetic charism communicates knowledge that is imperfect and provisional, being bound up with faith, Rm 12:6, which is itself destined to vanish in face of the beatific vision, 1 Co 13:8–12.

n. Western text adds 'and there was great rejoicing. While we were together, one of them . . .' If this reading is correct, this is the first of the 'We-sections', see 16:10.

o. In the reign of Claudius (41–54) famine swept through the empire (49–50), through Greece first, and later Rome. Josephus puts it in the time of Tiberius Alexander as procurator (46–48).

p. The apostles are not mentioned, unlike 15:2; they had perhaps left Jerusalem. According to 9:26; 11:29seq.; 15:2, it would seem that Paul made three journeys to Jerusalem before his two visits to Galatia, 16:6; 18:23. Paul himself, however, in Ga 1:18; 2:1seq.; cf. 4:13, mentions only two. The impression produced by Ac arises perhaps from Luke's method of combining his sources. It may be that the journey of 11:29 is the same as that of 15:2. The 'help' which is the purpose of the journey is probably to be distinguished from that which Paul supplied later, 24:17, when the great collection, made at the appeal of the Jeru-

salem church, was completed, Ga 2:10; cf. Rm 15:31; 1 Co 16:1a; 2 Co 8:4; 9:1,12,13.

12 a. This episode, which 11:30 and 12:25 seem to place at the same time as the visit of Barnabas and Saul to Jerusalem, must in fact have preceded it, for Herod Agrippa I (called 'king' to distinguish him from his uncle Herod Antipas, the tetrarch of the Passion story, and awarded the royal title by Caligula in 37) was not actually king of Judaea and Samaria until 41; he died in 44. The events here described took place, therefore, between 41 and 44. The narrative has been rather clumsily fitted into its present literary context. On miraculous release from prison, see 5:21h.

b. Each one to a soldier on each side.

c. add. 'went down the seven steps'.

d. John Mark is mentioned again in 12:25; 13:5, 13; 15:37,39; he was cousin to Barnabas, Col 4:10. During Paul's captivity in Rome Mark was with him, Col 4:10; Phm 24, and shortly before Paul died he asked for Mark's assistance, 2 Tm 4:11. Mark is also named as an assistant to Peter, 1 P 5:13, and tradition names him as author of the second Gospel.

e. It was popularly believed that guardian angels were a kind of spiritual 'double' of their charges.

f. 'James' without qualification means the 'brother of the Lord'. At the time of Paul's first visit to Jerusalem, Ga 1:19 (i.e. probably in 38–39, see Ac 9:1a) and afterwards, James was leader of the 'Hebrew' section of the Jerusalem Christians. After Peter's departure, he was in charge of the mother church. See 15:13; 21:18; 1 Co 15:7. The Letter of James appears under his name.

g. Soldiers who let their prisoners escape were liable to receive the sentence due to the prisoners, see 16:27; 27:42.

h. The scene of Agrippa's apotheosis is described in splendid detail by Josephus. • var. 'When he had come down from the tribune he became food for worms even while he was still alive; and so he died.' His death resembles that of an earlier persecutor of God's people, 2 M 9:9.

i. var. 'came back from Jerusalem', but this seems to be an attempt to simplify.

13 a. On the 'prophets', see 11:27m. The charism of the teacher, or *didaskalos*, was his ability to instruct others on matters of morality and doctrine, instruction usually based on the scriptures, cf. 1 Co 12–14 and notes. The five prophets and teachers here named represent the governing body of the church of Antioch; compare the list of the Twelve, 1:13, and of the Seven, 6:5. Like the latter, the Antiochene Five are, it seems, Hellenist Jews.

b. Or 'holding a service'; the use of the term for Christian prayer in common puts this on a level with the sacrificial worship of the Old Law, see Rm 1:9g.

c. It seems, to judge by 14:26 (see 15:40), that by this act the community commends to God's grace the new missionaries chosen, v. 2, and sent, v. 4, by the Holy Spirit. The significance of the rite is not, therefore, exactly the same as that of 6:6, by which the Seven receive their commission from the apostles, see 1 Tm 4:14e.

d. Barnabas' native country, 4:36.

e. Paul's regular policy, 17:2, is to approach the Jews first, see 13:14; 14:1; 16:13; 17:10,17; 18:4,19; 19:8; 28:17,23, on the principle that the Jews have first claim, see 3:26; 13:46; Mk 7:27; Rm 1:16; 2:9–10; only after their refusal does Paul turn to the gentiles, see Ac 13:46; 18:6; 28:28.

f. The Jews, and the eastern peoples in general, adopted names familiar in the Graeco-Roman world: John took 'Mark', 12:12, Joseph-Barsabbas took 'Justus', 1:23, Tabitha 'Dorcas', 9:36, Simeon 'Niger', 13:1, etc. Luke has given Paul his Roman name for the first time and does not use 'Saul' again. He also gives prominence now to Paul who is no longer a subordinate of Barnabas but the real missionary leader, v. 13.

g. i.e. a sermon based upon the scriptures, cf. Rm 15:4. The synagogue custom mentioned here was followed also when Christians met for worship; the sermons were preached by the 'prophets' or teachers, *see* 11:23; 14:22; 15:32; 16:40; 20:1,2; 1 Co 14:3,31; 1 Tm 4:13; Heb 13:22.

h. The conventional gesture of the public speaker in the ancient world, to invite attention and call for quiet; the right hand was held up with the thumb and little finger bent and the other three fingers extended, *see* 19:33; 21:40; 26:1.

i. The great inaugural discourse of Paul which Luke offers as typical of the apostle's preaching to the Jews. It falls into two parts: vv. 16–25 are a summary of the history of salvation (compare Stephen's sermon, ch. 7) with an appendix recalling John the Baptist's testimony (he is never mentioned in Paul's own letters); vv. 26–39 claim that Jesus who died and has risen is the expected Messiah (thus closely resembling Peter's discourses, though this discourse ends with a suggestion of the Pauline doctrine of justification by faith). The conclusion, vv. 40–41, is a grave warning taken from the scriptures, *see* 28:26–27.

j. The two classes of listeners: Jews by birth and 'god-fearers', 10:2b.

k. lit. 'the God of this people Israel'.

l. var. 'upheld' (or 'bore with').

m. Western (and Antiochene) text 'For about four hundred and fifty years he gave them judges.' The text is obscure.

n. Paul's own name, and he too was of the tribe of Benjamin, Rm 11:1; Ph 3:5.

o. Or 'raised from the dead'. The Greek verb can mean either, and this ambivalence is exploited in the argument, as in 3:20–26: the 'promise' finds fulfilment in Christ's resurrection, vv. 32–33; *see also* 26:6–8; moreover, it is by his resurrection that Jesus is established as Saviour, cf. 5:31; *see also* 2:21; 4:12; Rm 5:9–10; Ph 3:20. Thus the verb which means 'raise up' in v. 22 unequivocally means 'raise from the dead' from v. 30 onwards. In v. 23 it is transitional and ambiguous.

p. var. 'what'.

q. var. 'for us'.

r. Following Western text. Current text 'For those who live in Jerusalem and their leaders did not recognise him or (understand) the prophecies read on every Sabbath: but they fulfilled the prophecies by condemning him.'

s. A recurring element of the Christian plea: the innocence and unjust condemnation of Jesus, *see* 3:13–14; Mt 27:3–10,19,23–24; Lk 23:14,22,47.

t. 'asked Pilate to have him put to death', alternatively (the textual witnesses vary) 'that (he) should be put to death'; or 'that (they might) put him to death . var. 'handed him over to Pilate that he might be put to death.'

u. Western text '. . . foretells about him, after he had been crucified they asked Pilate for permission to take him down from the tree, and when they received it they took him down and buried him in a tomb.'

v. This appeal to the testimony of the Galilean apostles is a little surprising on Paul's lips. In his own letters he makes no distinction between their testimony and his own, 1 Co 15:3–11. This is one of the differences between the viewpoint of Ac and that of Paul.

w. var. 'for our children'.

x. Western text 'first psalm' (following the ancient custom of reading Ps 1 and 2 as one); var. 'second psalm'.

y. By his resurrection Christ was enthroned as Messiah, and from then on his human nature enjoyed all the privileges of the Son of God, *see* Rm 1:4c.

z. A promise of holiness as a gift kept for the messianic era, stemming from the risen Christ, the new David.

aa. The disbelief and rejection of the Jews (cf. Mt 21:33seq.; 22:1seq., 1a) are a favourite theme of Luke, *see* 13:5e; he uses it again as a conclusion to 28:26–27.

bb. var. 'When they left they felt it appropriate to'.

cc. 'converts' or 'proselytes', here in the wide sense, is equivalent to 'those who feared God' or 'those who worshipped God', *see* 10:2b.

dd. add. 'considering it fitting to accept baptism'.

ee. add (Western text) 'And in this way the word of God spread through the whole town.'

ff. var. 'the word of the Lord', or '(to hear) Paul who spoke for a long time about the Lord'.

gg. The 'courage' and 'confidence' of the apostles has been already stressed, 4:13,29,31; Luke repeatedly attributes these qualities to Paul, 9:27–28; 14:3; 19:8; 26:26; 28:31, and Paul himself lays emphasis on them, 2 Co 3:12; 7:4; Ep 3:12; 6:19–20; Ph 1:20; 1 Th 2:2.

hh. LXX text quoted freely. The words may be taken either as referring to Paul himself (cf. 26:17–18), apostle and teacher of the gentiles (cf. Rm 11:13; Ep 3:8; 1 Tm 2:7) or to the risen Christ (cf. Ac 26:23 which also, it seems, is based on Is 49:6; and, cf. Lk 2:32, dependent on Is 49:6): Christ is the light of the gentiles, but since only the apostles' witness can spread this light, *see* Ac 1:8k, Paul considers this prophecy as a command that he must carry out.

ii. var. 'the word of God'.

jj. 'eternal life', cf. v. 46, i.e. the life of the world to come, cf. 3:15; only those achieve it whose names are 'written in heaven', Lk 10:20, in 'the book of life', Ph 4:3; Rv 20:12i. 'Destined for the life of the world to come' was a common rabbinic expression. In Christian teaching the first prerequisite of this predestination to glory is faith in Christ, *see* Jn 10:26m; Rm 8:28–30, and earlier in Ac 2:39.

14 a. Or 'together'.

b. V. 1 is continued in v. 3.

c. Refusal to believe becomes in a short time active opposition, cf. 19:9; 28:24 and 9:23; 13:45,50; 17:5–8,13; 18:6,13.

d. Continuation of v. 2.

e. Lystra, a Roman colony, Timothy's home town, *see* 16:1–2. The events of vv. 8–19 take place in Lystra; Paul is not in Derbe until v. 20.

f. All the MSS have 'in Lystra' but this is evidently an addition, *see* v. 20b.

g. Others translate 'to be saved'. The condition for the miracle is faith, *see* Mt 8:10b; Mk 2:5; 6:5,6. There is a clear parallelism between Paul's miracles and Peter's, and Jesus', *see* 3:1a and p. 221.

h. Hermes (the Latin 'Mercury') was the messenger of the gods.

i. His temple was outside the walls.

j. Sign of agonised protest, cf. Mt 26:65.

k. In preaching against polytheism it was customary to contrast the true God with the false, the living God with helpless idols, and to make an appeal for conversion. For a summary of Paul's preaching to the gentiles see Ga 4:9 and 1 Th 1:9–10; cf. Ac 15:19–20; 26:18,20.

l. That God creates the universe shows that he is a living God: this proposition is found in Jewish creeds, cf. 4:24; 17:24; Ex 20:11; Ne 9:6; Ps 146:6; Rv 10:6; 14:7.

m. Cf. Lk 22:32; Rm 1:11; 1 Th 3:2,13.

n. Paul seems to have modelled the structure of his communities on that of any normal Diaspora Jewish community. The first elders in new churches are appointed by the apostles; or, at a later stage, by the overseer whom the apostle has commissioned, Tt 1:5.

o. add. 'of the Lord' or 'of God'.

p. Paul uses a similar metaphor, 1 Co 16:9seq.; 2 Co 2:12; Col 4:3.

15 a. The events of this chapter raise several difficulties: 1 Vv. 5–7a repeat vv. 1–2a as if the author, having two different accounts of how the controversy started, decided to give both as they stood. 2 V. 6 gives the impression that the community leaders held a private meeting, but vv. 12,22 suggest the debate took place before the whole Christian assembly. 3 The meeting issues a decree about how Christian converts from paganism must observe purity rites, and it entrusts this decree to Paul, vv. 22seq.; later, however (in 21:25), James seems to assume that Paul was then being informed of this decree for the first time. Paul himself does not speak of the decree either in Ga 2:6 (speaking of the Jerusalem meeting) or in Rm 14; 1 Co 8–10 (discussing similar problems). 4 Though the decree of 15:29 was primarily intended for the churches of Syria and Cilicia, 15:23. Luke has nothing to say about Paul's publishing it when he travelled through those provinces, 15:41. Luke does mention it when speaking about Lycaonia, 16:4, but the terms of 15:19–21; 21:25 suggest that the decree was for all regions. All these difficulties may be explained by supposing that Luke has combined two distinct controversies and their varying solutions (Paul distinguishes them more clearly in Ga 2). One controversy was about the obligations of convert gentiles to observe the Law, and Peter and Paul both took part, *see* Ga 2:1–10; the other controversy which took place later was about the social relations between the groups of Christian converts, those from Judaism and those from paganism, *see* Ga 2:11–14. In this James, in Peter's absence, took the leading part. Any contact with gentiles involved legal impurity for Jews, *see* 15:20u.

b. In Ga 2:12 there are several of them and they come from James.

c. Ga 2:1–3 mentions Titus who had gentile blood.

d. The apostles, who are not mentioned either in 11:30 or in 21:18, are grouped here with the elders, cf. Ga 2:2–9 where Peter and John are grouped with James, 'brother of the Lord', as authorities in the Jerusalem church.

e. Others translate 'provided them with all they needed for the journey', cf. 1 Co 16:11; Tt 3:13.

f. In the current text there seems to be no connection between the Pharisees' intervention at Jerusalem and the events that happened at Antioch. The Western text links them together 'But those who had told them to go up to the elders then stood up . . .

g. According to Ga 2:3–5 they are thinking particularly of Titus who had accompanied Paul to Jerusalem.

h. add. (West.) 'and the assembly', cf. v. 12.

i. add. (West.) '(inspired) by the Spirit'.

j. An interpretation of God's message to Peter, 10:15; 11:9; cf. 10:28; Si 38:10.

k. To put God to the test (*see* 1 Co 10:13f) is to demand from him proof in the form of an intervention or sign, 5:8–10; Ex 17:2,7; Nb 14:22; Dt 6:16; Jdt 8:12–17; Ps 95:9; Is 7:11–12; Mt 4:7seq.; 1 Co 10:9.

l. A straight answer to the assertion in v. 1. The doctrine is that of Rm 11:32; Ga 2:15–21; 3:22–26; Ep 2:1–10. On this score the Jews' position is not privileged, cf. 13:38; Ga 5:6; 6:15.

m. Western text 'When the elders had expressed their agreement with what Peter had said, the entire assembly . . .'

n. Ga 2:9 witnesses to the importance of the part played by James in this matter especially in the controversy over local problems of social relations, *see* 15:1a and 20u.

o. Semitic form of Simon Peter's name, *see* 2 P 1:1.

p. The text is quoted according to the LXX; the argument depends on variants peculiar to that version and probably comes from Hellenist circles, though here it is ascribed to the leader of the 'Hebrew' party.

q. lit. 'on whom my name has been invoked' (or 'over whom . . . pronounced'). To invoke the name of Yahweh over a people, *see* 2 Ch 7:14, or over a place, *see* 2 Ch 6:34, is to consecrate it to him.

r. lit. 'says the Lord who makes these things known from of old', var. 'says the Lord who does these things. From of old the Lord knows his work.'

s. James settles the discussion, and the terms of the apostolic letter are those of his own pronouncement. Ga 2:9 also suggests that James at this period occupied the first place in the Jerusalem church, *see* Ac 12:17f. A variant reduces this impression 'And so, for my part . . .

t. The meat of animals killed for heathen sacrifice, cf. v. 29 and 21:25, *see also* 1 Co 8:10.

u. This word refers to all the irregular marriages listed in Lv 18.

v. Western text omits 'the meat of strangled animals' and adds, after 'blood': 'and not to do to others what one would not have done to oneself' (so also in v. 29). Another omits 'impurity'. The ritual exceptions mentioned by James show clearly the sort of thing that was at issue and answer

the question asked in 11:3 and Ga 2:12–14: what gentile Christians must do for Judaeo-Christians to mix with them without incurring legal impurity. James decides to keep only those prescriptions for purity that have a fundamentally religious meaning: 1 To eat idol-meats implies sharing in sacrilegious worship, *see* 1 Co 8–10. 2 Blood symbolises life, and that belongs to God alone. The severity with which the Law forbids it, Lv 1:5e, explains the Jews' reluctance to dispense gentiles from this prohibition. 3 As blood remains in strangled animals, this is part of the previous prohibition. 4 The mention of irregular marriages is included here only because they involved legal impurity, not by way of moral judgement.

w. Not mentioned elsewhere, *see* 1:23.

x. Silas, missionary companion of Paul, 15:40–18:5, is the same as the Silvanus mentioned in 2 Co 1:19; 1 Th 1:1; 2 Th 1:1; 1 P 5:12.

y. Western text adds 'under the guidance of the Holy Spirit'.

z. Western text adds v. 34 'But Silas decided to stay there'. Several MSS further add 'Judas set out by himself.'

aa. var. 'the grace of the Lord'.

bb. Western text adds 'passing on to them the injunctions of the elders', *see* 16:4.

16 a. Timothy became Paul's constant companion, *see* 17:14seq.; 18:5; 19:22; 20:4; Rm 16:21; 1 Co 4:17; 16:10; 2 Co 1:19; 1 Th 3:2,6. 1 Tm and 2 Tm are 'pastoral epistles' in the form of letters addressed to him.

b. Paul opposed circumcision for converts from the gentiles, Ga 2:3; 5:1–12, but Timothy had a Jewish mother and so, by Jewish law, was an Israelite.

c. This editorial note is consistent with the general impression given in ch. 15 that the decree of the council of Jerusalem was made in the presence of Peter and Paul; but *see* 15:1a.

d. Galatia strictly so called, *see* p. 1856. When he left Iconium, therefore, Paul intended to travel westwards to Ephesus. But the Spirit intervened and he turned north into Phrygia, then in a northwesterly direction to 'Galatian country', where illness kept him for a time, Ga 4:13–15, preached the gospel in these places and returned later to visit the disciples there, Ac 18:23.

e. om. 'of Jesus'.

f. Preferable to 'they skirted'.

g. Sudden transition to first person plural: the first 'We-section' of Ac, but *see* 11:27n, *see* p. 219.

h. Philippi, a town in the principal district of the province of Macedonia; it had become a Roman colony and was a Latin city populated largely by veterans of the army, its administration modelled on that of Rome.

i. The Jews had no synagogue in Philippi; they would meet by the side of the River (for ritual ablutions).

j. Lydia's conversion brought her household to the faith; cf. 10:44; 16:31,34; 18:8; 1 Co 1:16.

k. Unusual for Paul: *see* 20:33–35; 1 Co 9; 1 Th 2:9; 2 Th 3:8, though on a later occasion the Philippians persuaded him to accept help again, *see* Ph 4:10–18. He would have accepted it from no one else; it is the greatest compliment to the charity of Lydia and of the other Philippian Christians.

l. lit. 'who had a Python-spirit', so called from the serpent Python of the ancient Delphic oracle.

m. The practices referred to are Jewish, *see* 6:14; 15:1; 21:21; 26:3; 28:17; Jn 19:40; the accusers make no distinction between Christian and Jew. The precise charge is proselytism: though the Jews were allowed to practise their religion, they had no right to proselytise Romans. Christian propaganda could therefore be against the law.

n. This new fear comes from his realising that he has treated as criminals men who are envoys of God.

o. var. 'the word of God'.

p. var. 'When it was daylight the magistrates met in the market place; remembering the earthquake that had taken place they were afraid and sent the officers to say, "Release the men you arrested yesterday." '

q. add. 'in peace'.

r. The *lex Porcia* forbade (under heavy penalties) the scourging of a Roman citizen.

s. Alex. (and Antiochene) text 'They came to apologise, and when they had taken them out they asked them to leave the town.' Western text 'And going with a number of friends to the prison, they urged them to go out, saying, "We had not realised what you wanted and that you were holy men." When they had taken them out, they begged them, "Get out of this town in case those who shouted against you get another mob together." '

17 a. Aristarchus, one of Paul's most faithful companions, *see* 20:4; Col 4:10, was probably one of them.

b. var. 'Greek worshippers of God'. The reading here preferred distinguishes 'those who worship God', 10:2b, from 'Greeks' not previously influenced by Jewish proselytism. Most of the conversions in Thessalonica were made from the gentiles, *see* 1 Th 1:9–10.

c. Possibly the Jason of Rm 16:21.

d. Actually, the Christians deliberately avoided calling Jesus by the emperor's title *basileus* ('king'); they preferred 'Christ' (Messiah) and 'Lord'.

e. Despite their departure the persecution in Thessalonica went on, cf. 1 Th 2:14.

f. Luke is summarising and simplifying. Timothy must have gone with Paul because Paul later sends him from Athens to Thessalonica, 1 Th 3:1seq.

g. Athens was the intellectual metropolis of Hellenism and to Luke was a symbol. This is evident from the fact that Paul's sermon there, the only sample of his preaching to gentiles, is the only one in which he combats paganism by the use of secular wisdom.

h. The one explicit mention in Ac of this kind of preaching (though cf. 14:7seq.).

i. Representatives of the two prevailing philosophical systems.

j. lit. 'What does this seed-picker want to say?' The local Athenian word *spermologos* was used of birds that peck, crows, etc. It came to mean 'beggar', one who picks up food wherever he can find it, and also a garrulous man who speaks in clichés, parrot-wise.

k. Cf. v. 32. They assume *Ahastasis* ('Resurrection') is the name of a goddess, consort of Jesus.

l. A hill to the south of the Agora. The word means also the Athenian supreme council which held its sessions there. The text may be understood in two ways: either the philosophers lead Paul 'on to (the hill of) the Areopagus', away from the city centre for easier listening, or (preferably) they lead him 'before (the council of) the Areopagus'.

m. After a solemn introduction, vv. 22–23, Paul develops his proclamation of the true God by opposition to gentile conceptions: 1 God created the universe, so one cannot suppose that he lives in a temple or needs the worship he is given, vv. 24–25. 2 God created humans and surrounds them with favours; it is absurd to assimilate him to material objects such as statues, vv. 26–29. The speech ends with a call to repentance in the perspective of judgement, vv. 30–31. Both parts of the speech are aimed against idolatry. Paul draws on the habitual arguments of monotheistic propaganda used in Hellenistic Judaism.

n. The Greeks used to dedicate altars 'to the unknown gods' to placate divinities whose names they did not know. Paul turns the practice to his own purpose and thus parries the biblical sense of ignorance of the heathen who do not acknowledge God, Jb 18:21; Ws 13:1; 14:22; Jr 10:25; 1 Co 15:34; Ga 4:8; Ep 4:17–19; 1 Th 4:5; 2 Th 1:8; 1 P 1:14. He thus avoids the charge of preaching outlandish gods.

o. This idea was common in Greek thought and Hellenistic Judaism; it is a form of the old biblical theme in 1 Ch 29:10seq.; Ps 50:9–13; Am 5:21seq.

p. var. 'of one blood', 'of one nation', 'of one race'.

q. The 'times' suggest primarily the seasons, whose regular return provides nourishment, 14:17; cf. Gn 1:14; Ws 7:18; Si 33:8; the 'limits' of human habitation are probably those which divide the habitable world from the waters of the abyss, Gn 1:9–10; Jb 38:8–11; Ps 104:9; Pr 8:28–29; cf. Ps 74:17; Jr 5:22–24. According to another explanation it is a matter of the times and limits which God has allotted to different nations, Gn 10; Dt 32:8seq. In any case it is a question of order in the universe, which leads to knowledge of God.

r. var. 'God' or 'the Lord'.

s. Expression suggested by the poet Epimenides of Cnossos (sixth c. BC).

t. lit. 'of your people'. var. 'of your poets' or 'of your sages'.

u. Quotation from the *Phainomena* of Aratus, a poet of Cilician origin (third c. BC). Cleanthes the Stoic (third c.) used almost identical language. Jewish monotheistic preaching here invoked the fact that man was created in the image and likeness of God, Gn 1:26–27; Ws 2:23; Si 17:1–8, to highlight the absurdity of idolatry.

v. This form of attack on idolatry has ancient precedent, *see* Is 40:20m.

w. Cf. Ps 9:8; 96:13; 98:9. The apostles set their appeal for repentance against the background of judgement, cf. especially 10:42–43; 1 Th 1:10.

x. Christ's resurrection justifies belief in his coming as judge and Saviour at the end of time, *see* Rm 14:9; 2 Tm 4:1; 1 P 4:5.

y. In the Greek world, even among Christians, the doctrine of the resurrection met stubborn resistance from preconceived ideas, *see* 1 Co 15:12seq. The Jerusalem Sanhedrists condemned and attacked this Christian dogma; the Athenians of the Areopagus were content to mock. Paul's failure in Athens was all but complete; from now on he refuses to use the devices of Greek philosophy, 1 Co 2:1–5.

z. Luke's readers must have known him. He became the subject of legend, especially after the fifth c. when an author (the 'pseudo-Dionysius') published various mystical writings under his name. Later legend identified him with St Denys, first Bishop of Paris (third c.).

18 a. Corinth, rebuilt by Julius Caesar, became capital of the Roman province of Achaia and was a flourishing city with two ports. Its population was largely Roman and Latin-speaking, but brisk trade had attracted people of all nations. It had a considerable Jewish colony. The immorality of Corinth was proverbial.

b. Also called Prisca, Rm 16:3; 1 Co 16:19; 2 Tm 4:19.

c. This edict, mentioned by Suetonius, was issued in 49 or 50. It was in force only for a very short time, cf. 28:17; Rm 16:3.

d. Though Paul acknowledges the missionary's right to sustenance, 1 Co 9:6–14; Ga 6:6; 2 Th 3:7–9; cf. Lk 10:7, he himself always practised a trade, 1 Co 4:12, not wishing to be a burden on anyone, 2 Co 12:13seq.; 1 Th 2:9; 2 Th 3:8, and in order to prove his singleness of purpose, Ac 20:33seq.; 1 Co 9:15–18; 2 Co 11:7–12. Only from the Philippians did he accept help, 2 Co 11:8seq.; Ph 4:10–18; *see also* Ac 16:15k. He recommended his followers to do the same to supply their own needs, 1 Th 4:11seq.; 2 Th 3:10–12, and those of the poor, Ac 20:35; Ep 4:28.

e. It was after this that Paul wrote his two letters to the Thessalonians. They came from Macedon with the subsidy, 2 Co 11:8–9; Ph 4:15, and helped Paul evangelise Corinth, 2 Co 1:19.

f. That Jesus was Messiah was the distinctive theme of the preaching to the Jews, cf. 2:36; 3:18,20; 5:42; 8:5,12; 9:22; 17:3; 18:28; 24:24; 26:23.

g. Symbolically breaking off relations. The following sentence is biblical, cf. Lv 20:9–16; 2 S 1:15–16, and means that the Jews must accept full responsibility for the consequences. Their 'blood', i.e. their punishment, is not Paul's affair; his conscience is clear (lit. 'I am clean').

h. var. 'Titus Justus' or 'Titius Justus'.

i. Western text add. 'believing in God through the name of our Lord Jesus Christ', *see* 8:36n. The converts were therefore gentiles.

j. An inscription from Delphi puts Gallio's proconsulate in 51–2. Paul's arraignment before Gallio must have been towards the end (v. 18) of his eighteen-month stay (v. 11) in Corinth: probably the spring of 52.

k. Ambiguous term capable of meaning the Roman Law, *see* 16:21; 17:7, or the Jewish Law which was itself guaranteed by Roman Law. Gallio chooses to see the charge as a question of the interpretation of Jewish Law (v. 15) in which he claims no competence.

l. Possibly the Sosthenes of 1 Co 1:1.

m. Back to Antioch, his base of operations.

n. The Greek is obscure, but apparently it was Paul, not Aquila, who took the vow. To take a vow was to be *nazir*, *see* Nb 6:1a, for the period it covered, usually thirty days, and among other obligations it meant leaving the hair uncut during that time. It is not known whether the vow was taken by Paul at Cenchreae or whether it expired there, cf. 21:23–27, where Paul and four other Jews perform the rites for the fulfilment of a vow.

o. Perhaps the church of Jerusalem.

p. For further information, *see* 1 Co: when he went to Corinth his enormous popularity soon developed into partisanship, *see* 1 Co 1:12; 3:4–11,22; *see also* Tt 3:13. These remarks about Apollos have something in common with the description of John the Baptist's admirers at Ephesus in the following passage: combining these two descriptions of an imperfectly informed Christianity, we may possibly get some idea of Christianity in the church of Alexandria at this time.

q. add. 'of God'.

r. On the use of letters of reference in the early Christian communities, *see* Rm 16:1; 2 Co 3:1seq.; Col 4:10; 3 Jn 9–10,12.

19 a. An editorial link joining two items of information which are inserted in the account of the journey. The Western text has 'When Paul, pursuing his own plan, wanted to set out for Jerusalem, the Spirit told him to go back to Asia. Consequently, he made his way . . .

b. Ephesus at this time was regarded, with Alexandria, as one of the finest cities in the empire; it was a religious, political and commercial centre of mixed population.

c. They were unaware, not that the Spirit existed (evident from the OT to the most casual reader) but that the messianic promises had been fulfilled and the Spirit given in abundance, cf. 2:17–18,33.

d. Resumption of the narrative interrupted by the remarks about Apollos and the followers of John the Baptist: 19:8 follows on 18:23 and 19:1.

e. Western text adds 'from the fifth to the tenth hour' (11 am to 4 pm).

f. 20:31 says three years. During this stay, Paul wrote the first Letter to the Corinthians, the Letter to the Galatians and, possibly, the Letter to the Philippians. 2 Co 1:8, written soon after his departure, mentions hardships undergone in Asia and a threat of death; but Lk tells us nothing of these here.

g. Not the whole of proconsular Asia (the western half of Asia Minor) but the region centred on Ephesus and including the seven towns of Rv 1:11. Epaphras of Colossae had been appointed by Paul to evangelise his own city, and his mission had spread to Laodicea and Hierapolis, Col 1:7; 4:12–13. Paul was also assisted by Timothy and Erastus, 19:22, Gaius and Aristarchus, 19:29, Titus, whom Ac never mentions, and others, *see* 2 Co 12:18. Luke credits Paul with the achievements of his subordinates.

h. On Jewish exorcisms, *see* Mt 12:27. Jesus himself, and his apostles after him, *see* Ac 5:16; 16:18, frequently exorcised, *see* Mt 8:29k.

i. Or 'both' (two of their number).

j. Occult practices for which Ephesus was well known.

k. Alex. text 'Thus, through the power of the Lord, the word spread even more widely and impressively.'

l. The literary style of this narrative is unusual in Luke; he has taken it from a special source and linked it with his story of the evangelisation of Ephesus.

m. Western text adds 'rushing into the street'.

n. Aristarchus, a native of Thessalonica, 20:4, was a companion of Paul during his imprisonment, 27:2; Col 4:10; Phm 24. This Gaius is probably the one mentioned in 20:4.

o. Members of the 'Asiatic assembly' which supervised the cult of Rome and the emperor on behalf of the cities of Asia.

p. Others translate 'they made him stand away from the crowd'.

20 a. The narrative is resumed from 19:22.

b. From here he sent his second letter to the Christians in Corinth.

c. Paul was therefore able to carry out the proposal of 1 Co 16:5–6. During this period in Corinth he wrote the Letter to the Romans. Western text 'When he had been there for three months and the Jews had plotted against him, he intended to set out for Syria, but the Spirit told him to go back through Macedonia.'

d. To take the proceeds of the collection to Jerusalem, *see* 19:21 and 1 Co 16:1a.

e. add. 'as far as Asia'. • Sopater is perhaps the Jew, Sosipater, of Rm 16:21. • 'Derbe'; var. 'Doberus'.

f. Trophimus was an Ephesian, 21:29, cf. 2 Tm 4:20. Tychicus is mentioned several times in the letters, Ep 6:21; Col 4:7; 2 Tm 4:12; Tt 3:12.

g. Narrative in the first person: this continues from Philippi till Jerusalem, *see* 16:10g.

h. From the port of Neapolis, cf. 16:11.

i. Passover week, *see* Ex 12:1a.

j. On Paul's previous ministry in this town (when on the way from Ephesus to Corinth: vv. 1–2) *see* 2 Co 2:12.

k. The first day of the Jewish week, which had become the Christians' day of assembly, *see* Mt 28:1a; 1 Co 16:2, the 'Lord's day', Rv 1:10. This Sunday meeting was held when the Lord's Day began, i.e. on the Saturday evening, because in the Jewish fashion the day was reckoned as beginning at sunset.

l. The third great discourse of Paul in Ac. The first, ch. 13, exemplified his preaching to the Jews; the second, ch. 17, his preaching to the gentiles; the third, vv. 18–35, is as it were the last testament of the departing pastor, compare 1 S 12:2–5. Many of the details of this third discourse are found in his letters; its tone is that of the Pastoral Letters. After referring to his mission in Asia, vv. 18–21, he speaks of this as a final parting and seems to hint at his death, vv. 22–27. Paul's last advice to the elders of Ephesus (and through them to all the pastors in every church) is vigilance, vv. 28–32, selflessness, charity, vv. 33–35. In all of this Paul appeals to his own example: the discourse therefore draws a faithful portrait of the apostle himself.

m. Summary of Pauline preaching, to be compared with 17:30–31; 1 Co 8:4–6; 1 Th 1:9–10. 'Repent and believe' have been coupled since the first preaching of Jesus, Mk 1:15.

n. On his way to captivity Paul speaks of himself as a prisoner; in his heart he is one already. Others translate 'a prisoner of the Spirit', i.e. morally prisoner.

o. Cf. 15:26; 21:13; Ph 1:21–23; 1 Th 2:8. Others translate 'But I do not count my life of any value, as if it were precious to me.'

p. See v. 38. From Jerusalem Paul intended to visit Spain, Rm 15:23–28. His long imprisonment affected his plans and he may have revisited Ephesus despite the presentiment expressed here.

q. var. 'the Church of the Lord'. • 1 P 2:9–10 speaks of the people which God made his own (following Is 43:21); this people was the 'Congregation (= Church) of God', Ac 5:11b, one of Paul's favourite expressions, *see* 1 Co 1:2; 10:32; 11:22.

r. lit. 'which he acquired for himself by his own blood'. Since this cannot be said of God, either it must mean 'by the blood of his own (i.e. own Son)' or Paul's thought slips from the action of the Father to that of the Son, cf. Rm 8:31–39. For the notion, see Ep 5:25–27; Heb 9:12–14; 13:12.

s. 'to God', var. 'to the Lord'. 'that has power', or 'who has power', referring to God, cf. Rm 16:25.

t. This saying has not come down to us in the gospels.

21 a. add. 'and Myra'.

b. The command does not come from the Spirit, but the Spirit has revealed to them Paul's fate which their love for him seeks to avert.

c. Prophecy in mime like that used by the prophets in the past. see Jr 18:1a.

d. The forecast corresponds only approximately to the narrative of Paul's arrest (see 21:31–33; 28:17) but it resembles the prophecy of Jesus' Passion in Lk 18:31–34; cf. Ph 3:10; Col 1:24.

e. The Western text indicates, perhaps correctly, that this was half-way to Jerusalem.

f. The last 'we' until 27:1 (the departure for Rome): see 16:10g.

g. For its observances by others as well as by themselves, see 11:2; 15:1,5; Ga 2:12; 5:1seq.

h. Paul's doctrine of faith as the one source of justification, see Rm 1:16h; 3:22h, did indeed lead to this, since it meant that the Mosaic Law no longer gave the Jew superiority over the gentile. But Paul's purpose in expounding this principle was to leave converts from paganism free of Jewish observance, see Ga 2:11seq., not to dissuade devout Jews from it.

i. See Rm 2:25–29; 4:9–12; 1 Co 7:17–20.

j. var. 'They are bound to hear that you have come.

k. The discharging of the nazirite vow had to be celebrated with expensive sacrifices, Nb 6:14–15.

l. Western text 'Of the gentiles who have become believers they have nothing to say to you. For our part, we have sent out decisions, namely that they have no observance to practise but that of abstaining from things sacrificed to idols, from blood, and from impurity.'

m. Text obscure: it seems to presuppose before the nazirite sacrifice a period of seven days devoted to certain rites of purification; there is no other evidence for this practice.

n. Cf. the charges against Stephen, 6:11–14, and against Jesus, Mt 26:61; 27:40.

o. A Roman garrison consisting of an auxiliary cohort was stationed in the fortress called Antonia overlooking the Temple area from the northwest corner.

p. Or 'four thousand *sikarioi*'; the term strictly means the extremist nationalist Zealots. This revolt is mentioned by Josephus.

q. i.e. Aramaic: Hebrew was barely spoken after the return from exile.

22 a. After the three discourses which sum up the preaching of Paul, ch. 13; 17; 20, Ac records three apologias: before the Jewish people in Jerusalem, ch. 22, before the procurator Felix, ch. 24, before King Agrippa, ch. 26; each is cleverly adapted to the audience, see 9:1a. Before the people Paul defends his conduct as being that of a devout Jew.

b. The Church, see 9:2b. On Paul's career as persecutor, see 7:58; 8:1,3; 9:1–2,21; 22:19–20; 26:10–11; 1 Co 15:9; Ga 1:13,23; Ph 3:6; 1 Tm 1:13.

c. Paul describes Ananias simply as a pious Jew without adding that he was a Christian, 9:10, or mentioning his vision, 9:10–16.

d. Christ, cf. 3:14; 7:52.

e. See 9:15h. Ananias here speaks in the name of 'the God of our ancestors', like an OT prophet. Paul is to be a witness 'before all humanity', but the gentiles are not explicitly mentioned until v. 21.

f. Paul passes over the three years which elapsed before his return, see 9:23k. The trance he speaks of is not mentioned elsewhere; it is not to be confused with that of 2 Co 12:1–4.

g. It is a main theme of Luke's understanding of Paul's apostolate that he turns to the gentiles because the Jews will not believe him, see 13:46–48; 18:6; 28:25–28. Speaking in the Temple he stresses that it was only under divine duress that he abandoned the Jewish mission.

h. The Greek word, *martyr*, had not yet acquired its restricted meaning but was beginning to, the supreme testimony being that of blood, see Rv 2:13; 6:9; 17:6.

i. Since 'apostle' means 'envoy', Christ's words imply that Paul is in fact an apostle, see 1 Co 9:1; 2 Co 12:11–12; Ga 1:1, and in particular, an apostle of the gentiles, Ga 1:16; 2:7–8, though Ac (with the exception of 14:4, 14) reserves the term 'apostle' to the Twelve.

j. Nevertheless, Paul is left in chains, v. 30; 23:18; 24:27; 26:29. Possibly a distinction is to be made between the heavy chains, a torture in themselves (of which Paul may have been relieved), and the lighter chains to prevent the prisoner from escaping.

k. As Jesus foretold to his disciples, Mk 13:9–10 = Mt 10:17–18; Lk 21:12. Paul is to appear before 'councils' 22:30–23:10, 'governors' (Felix, ch. 24), 'kings' (Agrippa, ch. 25–26).

23 a. The 'clear conscience' is a feature of Paul's moral teaching: 1 Co 4:4; 2 Co 1:12; 1 Tm 1:5,19; 3:9; 2 Tm 1:3; see also Heb 13:18.

b. Ananias son of Nedebaios became high priest about AD 47. He was arrested, sent to Rome and probably deprived of office in 51 or 52, then reinstated; he was assassinated in 66 at the beginning of the Jewish War.

c. The resurrection of the body, see 2 M 7:9, and the doctrine of angels, see Tb 5:4, were not part of Jewish teaching until a comparatively late date. From the text it appears that the Sadducees rejected the latter as well as the former (they certainly denied the doctrine of retribution in the world to come). On both questions Paul and the Pharisees were in agreement, see 4:1 seq., 1a, 4. Paul uses this point of disagreement between his opponents to throw them into confusion.

d. This hypothesis seems to be intended to explain the vision on the road to Damascus.

e. By calling down God's vengeance on themselves should they weaken.

f. Antonius Felix, a freedman, brother of Pallas, Agrippina's favourite; he was procurator of Judaea from 52 to 59 or 60.

g. Western text '. . . points of the Law of Moses, and a man called Jesus'.

h. Luke emphasises such statements which attest Paul's innocence, see v. 9; 25:18,25; 26:31; 28:18, as he did in the case of Jesus, see 3:13; 13:28; Lk 23:14–15,22.

i. add. 'Farewell'.

j. A palace built by Herod the Great which had become the official residence of the Roman procurator.

24 a. The opponents of Christianity see in it only a sect, cf. 5:17, within Judaism, cf. v. 14; 28:22.

b. The Jews claim that this is their affair, see 25:9; Jn 18:31f. Several witnesses add 'intending to judge him according to our Law, [7] • but the tribune Lysias intervened and took him out of our hands by force,[8] • ordering the accusers to appear before you.'

c. 'him' is Paul, according to the short text adopted here; according to the long text (see note b) it could be Lysias.

d. Paul denies the charge of inciting to riot (see v. 5), vv. 11–13. He then explains how being a 'Nazarene' (see v. 5) in no way prevents him from being a faithful Jew, vv. 14–16. He goes on to refute the charge of profaning the Temple, vv. 17–19. Finally he reminds them that it had been found impossible to convict him when he appeared before the Sanhedrin, vv. 20–21.

e. lit. 'to worship', cf. 8:27.

f. Christianity is not a different religion, it is Judaism with its ancient hope fulfilled. If the Jews reject Christ, they reject their own religious tradition. Compare the discourse before Agrippa, ch. 26, the early Christian argument from prophecy, 2:23o; 3:24s, and Paul's own assertions, Rm 1:2; 3:31; 10:4; 16:26; 1 Co 15:3–4; Ga 3.

g. The Pharisees, *see* 23:6 and refs.

h. The visit of 18:22 must have been at least four years earlier and the 'council of Jerusalem' visit eight or nine years earlier.

i. The only allusion in Ac to the real purpose of the journey, namely to deliver in Jerusalem the collection made among the churches in gentile territory, *see* 1 Co 16:1a.

j. Sacrifices, cf. 21:24, 26.

k. A doctrine of the Pharisees: Paul shrewdly implies that Christians and Pharisees have something in common.

l. The same conditions as for Paul's imprisonment in Rome.

m. Youngest daughter of Herod Agrippa I (12:1a). She had left her first husband, the king of Emesa, to marry Felix.

n. Felix was avaricious, cruel and dissolute. Compare the attitude of John the Baptist before Herod Antipas.

o. Roman law prescribed penalties for accusers who failed to follow up their charges, but there is no suggestion that the accused should be released in such a case.

p. Appointed probably in 60, died in 62.

q. 'being anxious to gain favour with the Jews'; Western text 'And he left Paul in prison on account of Drusilla.'

25 a. Or 'after taking office'.

b. Same procedure as in 24:1, cf. 25:15.

c. Festus realises that the dispute is about religious matters, a case not for him but for the Sanhedrin (*see* vv. 19–20). But as a Roman citizen Paul could not be committed to the Sanhedrin without his own consent. To secure this, Festus promises to attend and to preside over the discussion.

d. Since Festus has disclaimed jurisdiction, Paul cannot escape trial before the Sanhedrin except by claiming the Roman citizen's privilege of trial before the imperial tribunal.

e. Agrippa, Bernice and Drusilla (*see* 24:24) were children of Herod Agrippa I, *see* 12:1a. The eldest, later Agrippa II, was born in 27. At this time Bernice was living with her brother and their relationship became matter for gossip; some years later Bernice became the mistress of Titus, the Roman general, later emperor.

f. lit. 'Augustus'; so also in v. 25. The title 'Augustus', like 'Caesar', was borne by the ruling emperor, in this case Nero (54–68).

g. Just as his great-uncle Herod Antipas had wanted to see Jesus, Lk 9:9; 23:8.

h. Term for the emperor considered as a king whose power was absolute and universal, and therefore practically divine.

26 a. A flattering address, vv. 2–3; cf. 24:2–3,10, is followed by Paul's assertion that his Christian faith in bodily resurrection is shared by the Pharisees, vv. 4–8; *see* Mt 3:7f. Paul then describes the circumstances of his conversion, vv. 9–18; cf. 9:1–18; 22:3–16, and ends with a summary of his preaching which presents the Christian faith simply as the fulfilment of the scriptures, vv. 19–23; cf. 13:15–41. Behind the actual point of difference lies the whole question of the relationship between Judaism and Christianity, *see* 24:14f.

b. Others translate 'more than anyone'.

c. The messianic hope takes definite shape in the belief in the resurrection of the upright who are to have their place in the kingdom at the end of time, *see* 2 M 7:9c; Dn 12:1–3. This hope has its initial fulfilment in the resurrection of Christ which is the ground of Christian hope. 1 Co 15:15–22; Col 1:18.

d. var. vv. 7–8 'the promise for which our twelve tribes assiduously worship God day and night in the hope of attaining it; it is for this that I am now arraigned by the Jews: namely, that God raises the dead.'

e. Greek proverb for useless resistance: the ox kicking against the goad succeeds only in wounding itself.

f. Paul's missionary vocation is described here in OT terms used about two great prophetic figures, Jeremiah and the servant of Yahweh.

g. In 9:17–18, Paul, his sight restored, passes from darkness to light; in 22:16 (cf. 9:18) Paul is ordered to wash away his sins by baptism. Thus his own experience is a symbol of his mission to others.

h. Festus is taken aback by Paul's biblical erudition and probably by the Jewish method of argument. Agrippa is silent; he is clearly shaken, *see* his evasive reply in v. 28.

i. The scriptures are being fulfilled by events (v. 23; the passion and death of Christ; the widespread apostolic preaching) which all the world can see.

j. The word is still a nickname, *see* 11:26l. • var. 'In a little while you will persuade me to become a Christian!' or, 'In a little while you will persuade yourself you have made me a Christian!'

k. A play on Agrippa's phrase.

27 a. The narrative in the first person resumes and now continues till Paul reaches Rome, *see* 16:10g. The precision of the narrative suggests a carefully kept diary. Alternatively the author may have used a neutral account of a sea voyage ending in shipwreck, and inserted those passages where the prisoner Paul unexpectedly assumes command, vv. 9b–11, 21–26, 30b–31, 33–36.

b. lit. 'for fifteen days', Western text.

c. Another name for the feast of Expiation, the only fast-day prescribed by the Law, Lv 16:29–31. It was celebrated about the time of the autumn equinox.

d. Paul's second speech (vv. 33seq.) would follow naturally on this observation. This first speech (vv. 21–26) seems to have been rather clumsily introduced into this context and to be partly a doublet of the second.

e. Not before Nero in person but before his tribunal.

f. The name was used for all that part of the Mediterranean between Greece, Italy and Africa.

g. Western text add, 'giving it to us also'. • All Jews said a blessing when about to eat; nevertheless, the terms Luke uses seem to suggest the Eucharist, *see* 2:42g.

28 a. lit. 'justice', *dike*, divine justice personified.

b. Pozzuoli on the Gulf of Naples. There was already a Christian colony in this busy port.

c. Western text (adopted by the Antiochene recension) '. . . Rome, the centurion handed the prisoners over to the commander. But Paul was allowed to live outside the (Praetorian) camp.' This additional information agrees with what in fact must have happened. By the concession of *custodia militaris* the prisoner had his own lodgings, but his right arm was chained to the left of the soldier in charge.

d. Paul wants to establish good relations with the Jews of Rome as soon as possible. He gives a brief account of his trial, and for the last time protests his loyalty to Judaism.

e. Western text add. 'but merely wished to escape death'.

f. The reply is cautious.

g. In Rome also Paul preaches the gospel first to the Jews, *see* 13:5e. The summary of this preaching should be compared with the opening discourse in Pisidian Antioch, 13:15–41.

h. Paul's words are reminiscent of those following his discourse at Antioch, 13:46–47. They constitute the finale of Ac, and sound its predominant note, *see* 13:41aa. They recall the vision of the future offered by Jesus at the end of his discourse in Nazareth, Lk 4:23–27, and in his last words to the apostles, Lk 24:27. The text from Is 6:9–10 (LXX) is also used in Mt 13:14–15 (cf. Mk 4:12 and par.) and, in part, in Jn 12:40. Both theme and text are commonplaces of early Christianity.

i. The Western text (followed by the Antiochene recension) adds v. 29 'And when he had said this, the Jews left, arguing hotly between themselves.'

j. Thus Paul arrived in Rome, which brings one period of evangelisation to a close. *see* 1:8i; Lk 24:47, and is presented as the starting-point for a further advance of Christianity. Before Luke had finished his Gospel he had opened up wide horizons to the apostolic mission; his Book of Acts ends with the same prospect for the future.

k. The same term as in 24:27o. The NT gives no clear indication what happens after this period, though Phm 22 (if it was written now) shows that Paul hoped to be released soon. But Nero was given to occasional acts of clemency and Paul may have benefited from one of these.

l. Western text add, 'saying that this is he, Jesus, the son of God, by whom the whole world is destined to be judged,' *see* 17:31. • On Paul's ministry after his discharge, his second imprisonment, and his death, see page 284.

THE LETTERS
OF PAUL

INTRODUCTION TO
THE LETTERS OF PAUL

§1 CHRONOLOGY

Through the Acts of the Apostles and through his own letters Paul is more familiar to us than any other figure of the New Testament. Even though allowance must be made for Luke's particular method of historical writing and his theological interests, there is no reason to believe that the broad outlines of his presentation of Paul's ministry are unreliable. We can therefore construct a fairly exact chronology of Paul's life by reference to events in secular history whose dates are known, such as Gallio's proconsulate in Corinth, Ac 18:12, and the year Festus succeeded Felix, Ac 24:27–25:1. These give us two fixed points relative to which other dates in the life of the Apostle may be established more or less accurately.

Paul, born at Tarsus in Cilicia, Ac 9:11; 21:39; 22:3, about AD 10—possibly in the first decade of our era—of a Jewish family of the tribe of Benjamin, Rm 11:1; Ph 3:5, was a Roman citizen, Ac 16:37seq.; 22:25–28; 23:27. As a young man he received the thorough grounding in the scriptures of an educated Pharisee, with the all-embracing Law as its basis. According to Acts he received this education in Jerusalem from Gamaliel, one of the most distinguished teachers of his generation. Acts also tells us how Paul persecuted the young Christian Church (Ac 22:4seq.; 26:9–12; Ga 1:13; Ph 3:6), played some part in the martyrdom of Stephen (Ac 7:58; 22:20), and became a bitter persecutor of the Hellenist Christians, who had dissociated themselves from the Judaism centred on the Temple in Jerusalem, Ac 8:3; 22:4; Ga 1:13. But on the road to Damascus, c. AD 34, a vision of the risen Jesus changed his whole life. The risen Lord opened his mind to the truth of the Christian faith and revealed that he had chosen him to be the apostle of the gentiles, Ac 9:3–16 and par.; Ga 1:12, 15seq. From then on, Paul dedicated his life to serving Christ who had personally chosen him as his follower, Ph 3:12. After spending some time in Arabia he returned to Damascus, Ga 1:17, and began his preaching there, Ac 9:20. In about AD 39, after a brief visit to Jerusalem, Ac 9:26–29; Ga 1:18, Paul went to Syria and Cilicia, Ac 9:30; Ga 1:21, till Barnabas fetched him back to Antioch where they preached together, Ac 11:25seq. and cf. 9:27.

During Paul's first missionary journey (45–9) to Cyprus, Pamphilia, Pisidia and Lycaonia, Ac 13–14, he started using his Greek name Paul instead of his Jewish name Saul, Ac 13:9, and, because of his more important role in preaching, he began to take the lead over Barnabas, Ac 14:12. In AD 49, fourteen years after his conversion, he went to Jerusalem, Ga 2:1, and he and Barnabas were recognised as the apostles to the gentiles by the leaders of the church there, who were 'the apostles to the circumcised', Ga 2:90. The dates of his second (AD 50–2; Ac 15:36–18:22) and third missionary journeys (AD 53–8; Ac 18:23–21:17) are discussed later under the letters he wrote at intervals during those journeys. In AD 58, Paul was arrested in Jerusalem, Ac 21:27–23:22, and imprisoned at Caesarea Palestinae until AD 60, Ac 23:23–26:32. In the autumn of AD 60, Festus the procurator sent him to Rome under escort, Ac 27:1–28:16 where he lived for two years, AD 61–3, Ac 28:30. There our certain knowledge of Paul's life ends. Ancient tradition, relying to some extent on the Pastoral Letters (on whose historical value *see* below), teaches that after two years his case was dismissed for lack of evidence, and Paul travelled again in the East, though he may well have made his projected (Rm 15:24, 28) visit to Spain. Tradition also holds that a subsequent imprisonment in Rome ended in martyrdom, in AD 67.

§2 THE CHARACTER OF PAUL

As well as this chronology, it is possible to recover quite a detailed portrait of Paul from his letters and from Acts.

He was a person of great dedication, capable of pursuing an ideal with a complete disregard for the cost. For him, the only thing that mattered was God, and as God's servant, Paul refused any sort of compromise. It was with equally single-minded determination that he had persecuted those he considered God's enemies, *see* Ac 24:5, 14, and later preached Christ as the one, universal Saviour. This Saviour he served passionately and selflessly for the rest of his life. He knew what work he had been given to do, 1 Co 9:16, and he let nothing stop him from doing it: hard work, exhaustion, suffering, poverty, danger of death, 1 Co 4:9–13; 2 Co 4:8seq.; 6:4–10; 11:23–27. Far from letting these things weaken his love for God or Christ, Rm 8:35–39, he welcomed them, since they helped him to grow into the image of his suffering and crucified Master, 2 Co 4:10seq.; Ph 3:10seq. The knowledge that his vocation was unique gave him an enormous ambition, but it did not make him arrogant. It was with holy humility that Paul felt a personal pride in being responsible for so many churches, 2 Co 11:28, compare Col 1:24seq., and claimed to have done more missionary work than others, 1 Co 15:10, compare 2 Co 11:5, and offered himself as a model to his converts, 2 Th 3:7b. He never forgot that, having persecuted the Church of Christ, he was the unworthiest of all the apostles. All the great things he succeeded in doing he attributed to God's grace working through him, 1 Co 15:10; 2 Co 4:7; Ph 4:13; Col 1:29.

Paul had a sensitive temperament that showed itself in his attitude to those he had converted. He had a childlike trust in the converts at Philippi, Ph 1:7seq.; 4:10–20, a deep affection for those at Ephesus, Ac 20:17–38; he was furious with those in Galatia who were on the verge of apostasy, Ga 1:6; 3:1–3, and deeply upset when he thought that the Christians in Corinth had become vain and unstable, 2 Co 12:11–13:10. When he was being ironical with people he considered superficial, 1 Co 4:8; 2 Co 11:7; 12:13, or when he was outspoken, 1 Co 3:1–3; 5:1–2; 6:5; 11:17–22; 2 Co 11:3seq.; Ga 3:1–3; 4:11, it was only for their own good, 2 Co 7: 8–13, and after these outbursts he soon became tender, 2 Co 11:1–2; 12:14seq., and fatherly, 1 Co 4:14seq.; 2 Co 6:13, compare 1 Th 2:11; Phm 10, even motherly, Ga 4:19; 1 Th 2:7, and anxious to restore the earlier affection, 2 Co 7:11–13; Ga 4:12–20.

Paul's fiercest outbursts of indignation were directed against anybody who tried to seduce his converts, whether they were strict Jews, who were bitterly opposed to Hellenist Christianity and opposed him wherever he went, Ac 13:45, 50; 14:2, 19; 17:5, 13; 18:6; 19:9; 21:27, or judaising 'Hebrew' Christians who wanted all followers of Christ to follow the Law, Ga 1:7; 2:4; 6:12seq. He never minced his words with either of these groups, Ga 5:12; Ph 3:2; 1 Th 2:15seq. and, however unprepossessing, he felt himself to be an irresistible weapon wielded by divine power against ambitious, arrogant and unspiritual opponents, 2 Co 10:1–12:12. God's weapon was Paul's selfless sincerity, Ac 18:3d. It has been suggested that the people against whom he inveighs were in fact the senior apostles in Jerusalem, but in fact it seems clear from Ga 2 that Paul respected their authority in the Jewish Christian churches of the Jerusalem region while firmly resisting the influence of some of their followers in the gentile Christian churches that he had founded; he claimed only that he was just as much a witness to Christ as they were, 1 Co 9:1; 15:8–11; Ga 1:11seq. Even after his disagreement with Peter, Ga 2:11–14, his attitude was conciliatory. The collection which he organised for the poor Christians of Jerusalem, Ga 2:10, was intended as the proof that his gentile converts were truly one with the Christians of the mother church, Rm 15:25seq.; 2 Co 8:14; 9:12–13, however coolly it was received, Ac 21:17–25.

§3 PAUL AS PREACHER

What Paul proclaimed was in all essentials the apostolic *kerygma*, Ac 2:22n, i.e. that Christ had been crucified and raised from the dead and that this had been foretold in the scriptures, 1 Co 2:2; 15:3–4; Ga 3:1; what he calls 'his' gospel, Rm 2:16; 16:25, was identical to the faith held by the other apostles, Ga 1:6–9; Col 1:5–7, but he had no reservations about the admission of gentiles, and his first missionary activity, according to Ac 11, was at Antioch among gentile converts of the Hellenists 'scattered in the troubles over Stephen', Ga 1:16; 2:7–9. Paul accepts and sometimes appeals to the apostolic tradition, 1 Co 11:23; 15:3–7, to which he was deeply indebted. Though he probably never met Jesus during his earthly life, *see* 2 Co 5:16g, Paul was familiar with his teaching, Ac 20:35; 1 Co 7:10seq.; 1 Th 4:15, and confidently claimed to have seen the risen Christ, not only on the Damascus road, Ac 9:17; 22:14seq.; 26:16; 1 Co 9:1; 15:8, but on several occasions subsequently, Ac 22:17–21; 26:16. He also had revelations and ecstasies, 2 Co 12:1–4, but everything he had received from apostolic tradition he could also attribute, and justly, to direct communication from the Lord, 1 Co 11:23; Ga 1:12.

These mystical experiences have sometimes been attributed to Paul's excitable and morbid temperament, yet this is hardly likely. The disease that detained him in Galatia, Ga 4:13–15, cannot now be determined, but the 'thorn in my side', 2 Co 12:7, may well be the persistent hostility of Jews, his brothers 'according to the flesh', Rm 9:3. Paul does not seem to have had a very vivid imagination, to judge from his sparing and pedestrian use of imagery: the sportsground, 1 Co 9:24–27; Ph 3:12–14; and the sea. Two images, farming, 1 Co 3:6–8, and building, Rm 15:20; 1 Co 3:10–17, are so basic that he often mixes them, 1 Co 3:9; Col 2:7, compare Col 2:19. His genius was much more intellectual than imaginative, his enthusiasm was never divorced from the rigid logic with which he explains his teaching and adapts it to the needs of his audience. It is to this intellectual need to adapt his teaching to the occasion that we owe the remarkable theological analysis to which he repeatedly submits the *kerygma*. His logic, which is based on the rabbinical method in which he had been trained, may be unfamiliar today (e.g. Ga 3:16; 4:21–31). His genius, however, was never restricted by the tradition he inherited, so that these ancient conventions do not obscure the profundity of his teaching.

Paul was a Jew with a Greek cultural background probably acquired during his boyhood in Tarsus; this influence is obvious not only in his logical method but also in his language and style. He sometimes quotes Greek writers, Ac 17:28; 1 Co 15:33, and was familiar with popular Stoic-based philosophy from which he borrows concepts (e.g. of the soul separated from the body and bound for another world, 2 Co 5:6–8; the cosmic *pleroma* in Col) and clichés (Rm 11:36; 1 Co 8:6). From the Cynics and Stoics he borrowed the rapid question and answer method (*diatribe*), Rm 3:1–9, 27–31, and the rhetorical device of heaping word on word, 2 Co 6:4–10. Even the use of long, packed phrases in wave after wave, Ep 1:3–14; Col 1:9–20, has a precedent in Hellenist religious literature. The Greek that was a second mother tongue to Paul (*see* Ac 21:40), that he was able to use so familiarly with only occasional semitisms, was a cultured form of the *koine*, i.e. the popular Greek of his own day. Paul never attempted Attic elegance, and he deliberately avoided rhetoric, so that his audience would be convinced not by the form but by the content of his message of faith and by the signs the Spirit had promised to provide to confirm it, Rm 15:18; 1 Co 2:4seq.; 1 Th 1:5. This is one reason why his grammar is sometimes wrong and his sentences unfinished, 1 Co 9:15; another is that he sometimes thought too fast or too emotionally; a third is that with rare exceptions, Phm 19, he normally dictated his letters, Rm 16:22 (a common practice at the time), and wrote only the final greeting by way of signature, 1 Co 16:21; Ga 6:11; Col 4:18; 2 Th 3:17. Some passages in his letters were obviously written only after long and careful thought, e.g. Col 1:15–20, but mostly his letters suggest spontaneity and lack of revision. In spite of, or perhaps because of these literary faults, Paul's sentences are dynamic and packed with meaning. He is not easy to read, 2 P 3:16; profound thoughts expressed by an urgent writer never are; however, some passages have an extraordinary religious and literary power.

It is important to remember that Paul's letters were not meant as theological treatises: most of them represent his response to a particular situation in a particular church. They begin according to the usual epistolary convention, Rm 1:1a, but cannot be classed either as private letters, or as literary 'epistles'; they are Pauline instructions intended for a specific circle of readers and, in a general way, for all the faithful. Paul's letters do not give any systematic and exhaustive exposition of his teaching; they presuppose the oral teaching which preceded them, and enlarge and comment only upon certain points of that. This does not detract from their value: the depth and range of his letters give us all the essentials of Paul's message. No matter what the reason was for writing or who the people were to whom he was writing, his basic teaching remained the same: that Christ died and was raised from the dead. The apostle who was all things to all people, 1 Co 9:19–22, adapts this, his one basic doctrine, to the listener; he develops and enriches it. Paul has sometimes been accused of being an eclectic, in the sense of adopting not only different but contradictory opinions according to the circumstances in which he found himself, of being interested less in truth than in persuading people to believe in Christ. He has also been accused of not having an open mind, of being obsessed by the vision that converted him, and of never having allowed his ideas to develop. The truth between these extremes seems to be that Paul's theology remains homogeneous but that it did develop under the guidance of the Spirit, who inspired everything he did as an apostle. To show this development of Paul's thought, his letters have to be read in the order in which they were written; the order, however, in which they are printed here is the traditional one that arranges them in order of diminishing length.

§4 PAUL'S JOURNEYS AND LETTERS

§4a 1 and 2 Thessalonians: AD 50–1

The first letters to be written were to the converts Paul had made in Thessalonica in the summer of AD 50, during his second missionary journey, Ac 17:1–10. As a result of the hostility of some Jews he went on to Beroea, and from there to Athens and Corinth where, it seems, he wrote 1 Th during the winter of 50–1. When he wrote this letter, his companions were Silas and

Timothy. Timothy had paid a second visit to Thessalonica, and brought back the good news of their faith under persecution, whence the affectionate tone of the opening chapters, 1–3; these are followed by a series of practical recommendations, 4:1–12; 5:12–28, including an answer to their questions about the destiny of the dead and about Christ's *parousia*, 4:13–5:11. It was at Corinth a few months later that 2 Th was probably written, making further practical recommendations, 1; 2:13–3:15, and offering fresh instruction on the time of the *parousia* and the signs that were to come before it, 2:1–12.

The literary resemblance between 1 and 2 Th is so close that some critics consider 2 Th a forgery made by one who had absorbed Paul's ideas and style; but it is hard to explain why this should have been done. A more obvious explanation is that when Paul wished to clarify and tidy up his teaching on eschatology, he used a number of expressions from the first letter in writing a second. The two letters are not contradictory but complementary and the earliest authorities accepted them both as written by Paul.

These two letters are particularly important because of their eschatological teaching, but they also introduce many points elaborated in subsequent letters. At this early stage, Paul's ideas were structured around the question of how the resurrection and *parousia* of Christ can bring salvation to his followers whether alive or dead, 1 Th 4:13–18. Paul described this *parousia* in the traditional terms of Jewish and the earliest Christian apocalyptic writings (e.g. the eschatological discourses in the Synoptic Gospels, especially in Mt). At one time he so emphasises, 1 Th 5:1–11, the unpredictable imminence of the coming and the necessity for vigilance, as to give the impression that he and his readers would live to see it, 4:17; at other times (2 Th 2:1–12) he tries to allay the anxiety naturally aroused and reminds his readers that the Day could not come till certain signs had preceded it. What these signs were to be is not as clear to us as it must have been to the first readers. Paul seems to consider the 'Adversary' to be an individual person who had to wait till the end of the age before he could appear; some writers consider that by the phrase 'what is still holding him back', 2 Th 2:6, Paul meant the Roman empire, others that he meant the preaching of the gospel; no certainty is possible.

§4b 1 and 2 Corinthians: AD 57

Paul wrote the letters to Thessalonica during the eighteen months he spent evangelising Corinth, Ac 18:1–18, from the end of AD 50 to the middle of 52. His policy was always to establish the Christian faith in a centre of population, and here he chose the great and populous port of Corinth, so that it could spread from there into the whole of Achaia, 2 Co 1:1; 9:2. The Christian community he established grew strong and was composed mostly of poor people, 1 Co 1:26–28, but Corinth was not only a great centre of Hellenism and a magnet to every sort of philosophy and religion, it was also a notorious centre of immorality; it was a *milieu* that could create awkward problems for the newly converted. It was to the solution of these problems that Paul addressed himself when he wrote his two letters to the Christians of Corinth.

How these two letters came to be written is clear enough, though some details are still disputed. There had been an earlier letter than these two canonical ones, 1 Co 5:9–13, but the date at which this first letter was written is unknown and it has not survived. Before the end of the two and a half years he spent at Ephesus (54–7) on his third missionary journey, Ac 19:1–20:1, a Corinthian delegation arrived to ask Paul certain questions, 1 Co 16:17; and as he had also received news of Corinth from Apollos, Ac 18:27seq.; 1 Co 16:12, and from Chloe's household, 1 Co 1:11, he felt obliged to write a second letter. This is 1 Co, and it was written at some time possibly near Easter, 57 (1 Co 5:7seq.; 16:5–9, compare Ac 19:21). Shortly afterwards, some sort of crisis developed in Corinth, and Paul was forced to pay a brief and painful visit, 2 Co 1:23–2:1; 12:14; 13:1–2. While there, he promised another and a longer visit, 2 Co 1:15–16, which never in fact took place. Instead, Paul sent a representative to whom he delegated his authority, but the only result was a second crisis; Paul's authority, committed to this delegate, had been flouted, 2 Co 2:5–10; 7:12. Paul still did not pay the promised visit, but sent a severe letter written 'in agony of mind', 2 Co 2:3seq., 9; this third letter had the desired effect, 2 Co 7:8–13. This good news that he heard from Titus reached Paul only after he had gone to Macedonia, 2 Co 2:12seq.; 7:5–16, having left Ephesus as a result of serious disturbances of which we know little, Ac 19:23–40; 1 Co 15:32; 2 Co 1:8–10. At this stage, towards the end of AD 57, he wrote 2 Co, or at least part of it, 1:1–6:13; 7:2–16 (*see* below). He must subsequently have travelled via Corinth, Ac 20:1seq., *see* 2 Co 9:5; 12:14; 13:1, 10, to Jerusalem, where he was arrested at Pentecost.

It has however been suggested that 2 Co 6:14–7:1 is a fragment of the lost first letter, and 2 Co 10–13 part of the letter written 'in agony of mind'. It would be hard to prove that they were parts of these two particular letters, but it is quite certain that these two sections are not in their original contexts. The first section reads like an insertion: 2 Co 7:2 follows naturally on 6:13, and the whole passage, 6:14–7:1, has remarkable affinity with some of the Essene literature discovered at Qumran. The vehemence of the second section, 2 Co 10–13, is certainly not in place after the friendly tone of the first nine chapters. To these two dislocations should be added the fact that 9:1 does not make sense after what has been said in ch. 8 about the collection, and is probably part of a completely different note on the subject. These were written on different occasions and were joined together only later when the collection of the apostle's writings was being made.

In these letters to Corinth, even the details about Paul and the way he treated his converts are important doctrinally. In particular, 1 Co contains a great deal of information about urgent problems that faced the church and about the decisions made to meet them: internally there were questions of moral conduct, 1 Co 5:1–13; 6:12–20, of marriage and virginity, 7:1–40, of liturgical and eucharistic meetings, of the charisms, 12:1–14:40; and also matters concerning the Church in the world, questions of appeals to civil courts, 6:1–11, and eating foods sacrificed to idols, ch. 8–10. It was Paul's religious genius to turn what might have remained cases of conscience or liturgical instruction into a vehicle for the profound doctrine of Christian liberty, the sanctification of the body, the supremacy of love, union with Christ. When forced to defend his apostolate, 2 Co 10–13, he writes a magnificent passage about the dignity of the apostle's mission, 2 Co 1:12–6:10; and when he brings up the business of collecting money, 2 Co 8–9, this is illuminated by the ideal of union betwen the churches. The eschatological basis of his doctrine is always present in Paul's mind, and provides the perspective in which he explains the resurrection of the body, 1 Co 15; here, however, the apocalyptic imagery of 1 and 2 Th gives place to a philosophical discussion intended to justify a doctrine that the Greek mind found so unsympathetic. This adaptation of the gospel to the new world which it is entering is seen above all in the contrast between the folly of the cross and Greek wisdom. The apostle's converts at Corinth had split into factions, each proud of its own leader and boasting about his talents; Paul reminded them that there is only one master, Christ, and only one message, the cross, and that there is only one true wisdom, 1 Co 1:10–4:13. Quite naturally, through the way events had developed, without surrendering anything of the primacy of his eschatological thought, the inner development of Paul's ideas led him to the point where he had to stress how the life we lead here and now is already a life of union between Christ and his followers, and that this union is achieved by faith, which is the only way to know him. But Paul was yet to reach a still deeper understanding of the life given by faith, and this time in relation to Judaism, in the wake of the crisis in Galatia.

§4c Galatians, Romans: AD 57–8

The letters Paul wrote to the Christians of Galatia and Rome need to be discussed together, since both letters analyse the same problem. The first was Paul's immediate reaction to a particular situation, but the second is an orderly exposition, both calmer and fuller, of the thinking stimulated by the controversy. The very close relationship between the two letters is really the strongest reason against the early dating of Ga (pre-AD 49, the council of Jerusalem) which some scholars have suggested. They argue that Paul's second visit to Jerusalem, Ga 2:1–10, was the second visit mentioned in Ac 11:30; 12:25, not the third, Ac 15:2–30, since several details here differ from Paul's account, and that, as Paul seems unaware of the decree of the council, Ac 15:20, 29 (*see* Ga 2:6), this letter must have been written before it. All difficulties disappear, it is argued, if it is supposed that the 'Galatians' are the Christians of Lycaonia and Pisidia, evangelised by Paul on his first missionary journey when he returned by the way he had come; this would explain the double visit that Ga 4:13 seems to imply. This hypothesis has little to support it, apart from the fact that Lycaonia and Pisidia had been part of the province of Galatia in 36–25 BC; in the first century AD, however, 'Galatia' normally referred to Galatia properly so called, which lay to the north of Lycaonia and Pisidia, and it is unlikely that the inhabitants of each district were *both* called 'Galatians', Ga 3:1. This hypothesis is in any case quite unnecessary. The second visit of Ga 2:1–10 may much more easily be identified with the third visit mentioned in Ac 15, than with the second visit of Ac 11:30; 10:25. The explanation of any discrepancies is therefore either that Paul considered this intermediate visit so unimportant that he omitted to mention it in Ga, or that the visit is simply the product of a literary duplication by Luke (*see* Introduction to Acts of the Apostles p. 222, and Acts 11:30p). Thus the letter to the Galatians was indeed written well after the council of Jerusalem. The reason why Paul does not mention the decree could, perhaps, be that its date was later than that of Galatians, or that Paul learned about the decree only on his return to Jerusalem in AD 58. This would explain Peter's conduct that Paul says he criticised, Ga 2:11–14. The converts to whom the letter was addressed would then be the inhabitants of the 'Galatian territory' (i.e. North Galatia) through which Paul passed on his second and third journeys, Ac 16:6; 18:23. The letter may have been written at Ephesus, or even in Macedonia, about the year 57.

The letter to the Christians of Rome must, in this case, have been written soon after. In the winter of 57–8 Paul was at Corinth preparing to go to Jerusalem and from there to visit Rome on the way to Spain, Rm 15:22–32; cf. 1 Co 16:3–6; Ac 19:21; 20:3. He had not founded the Roman church, and any information he had about it (from people like Aquila, Ac 18:2) was not considerable: all we learn from occasional allusions in the letter is that it was a mixed community and that there was a danger of Jewish and non-Jewish converts looking down on one another. In view of this danger, Paul thought it would be prudent to pave the way for his visit by sending a letter (through Phoebe the deaconess, Rm 16:1) in which he gave the solution to the problem of the relationship between Judaism and Christianity, developed by him as a result of the Galatian crisis. To do this he takes up again the ideas first expressed in Ga, but in a manner both better arranged and more subtle. While Ga gives the impression of a cry from the heart, in which explanation of his own conduct 1:11–2:21, is joined to theological argument, 3:1–4:31, and forceful admonition 5:1–6:18, Rm is a carefully planned whole; it has only a few main sections, and these are linked harmoniously together by the announcement in the preliminary section of the themes which will subsequently be taken up.

Like Corinthians and Galatians, the authenticity of the letter to Roman Christians is not seriously disputed, though it is suggested that ch. 15 and 16 are later insertions. Ch. 16 has many greetings, and it may quite easily have been a separate note for the church at Ephesus, but in spite of certain MSS ch. 15 cannot be amputated so easily. Critics who keep ch. 16 as part of the original letter suggest that it was quite possible for Paul to have met a great many Christians who, as Jews, had eight years previously been expelled under Claudius and then later gone back to Rome, and that it was diplomatic for him to mention their names in a letter to a church he had not yet visited. The unusual style of the doxology, 16:25–27, certainly suggests that it could be a later insertion, but this in itself is not sufficient argument against the authenticity of the chapter.

The first letter to the Corinthians contrasted Christ as the Wisdom of God with the human wisdom of philosophers, but in the letters to Galatia and Rome, Paul contrasted the uprightness people can achieve by purely human effort with Christ who is the Uprightness of God. There Paul had striven to correct the proud reliance of the Greek mind on reason; now he sets out to correct the Jews' proud reliance on the Law. Judaising Christians who had visited Galatia advised the gentile converts to have themselves circumcised to ensure their salvation. This would have meant adopting all the prescriptions of the Law, Ga 5:2seq., the implications of which, to Paul, made nonsense of Christ's redemptive work, Ga 5:4, and it was for this reason that he opposed the circumcision of his converts so violently. He maintained that the true value of the Law could be appreciated only by seeing its place in the development of God's plan, Ga 3:23–25. The Mosaic Law was good and holy, Rm 7:12, because it revealed God's will to the Jews, but without providing the spiritual power necessary to obey it: all the Law could do was make people aware of sin and of the need they have for God to help them, Rm 3:20; 7:7–13; Ga 3:19–22. All human beings need this help, and it is necessarily a gift from God: it was promised to Abraham long before the Law was formulated, Rm 4; Ga 3:16–18, and has now been given in Jesus Christ: his death and resurrection have destroyed the old humanity which was corrupted by Adam's sin, and created a new humanity of which Christ himself is the prototype, Rm 5:12–21. All human beings, united to Christ by faith, and living a new life by sharing the Spirit of Christ, without any merit on their part, are made upright and enabled to carry out God's will, Rm 8:1–4. This faith must result in 'good works', but these will not be at all the same as those 'good works' commanded by the Law, on which Jews were so proud to rely; they will be works prompted by the presence of the Spirit, Rm 8:5–13; Ga 5:22–25. And they can be done by all who have faith, whether Jews or gentiles, Ga 3:6–9, 14. The preparatory or Mosaic stage of religion is over, and Jews who claim they are continuing to fulfil the Law are in fact putting themselves outside the pale of salvation. God allowed their blindness only to bring the gentiles to salvation. But it is out of the question that they should permanently fail to live up to their original choice, for God is faithful to his promises. Some of them, the 'remnant' foretold by the prophets, have already become believers, and one day all of them will, Rm 9–11. Meanwhile, all converts without exception, whether they are Jews or not, must love and help one another as one family, Rm 12:1–15:13. The general outlines of this thesis were sketched in Ga; the details added in

Rm are much deeper insights into mysteries such as the position of the human race while waiting for salvation, Rm 1:18–3:20; the spiritual struggle of each individual to be saved, Rm 7:14–25; God's gift of salvation, Rm 3:24 and *passim*; what the death and resurrection of Jesus actually achieved, Rm 4:24seq.; 5:6–11, and how Christians share in this by dying and rising by faith and baptism, Rm 6:3–11; Ga 3:26seq.; the vocation of the whole human race to be children of God, Rm 8:14–17; Ga 4:1–7; the love and wisdom of God who, being perfect and faithful to his promises, guides each different stage in the plan of salvation Rm 3:21–26; 8:31–39. Paul's thought is still basically eschatological—we are saved 'in hope', Rm 5:1–11; 8:24—but, as in his letters to Corinth, the stress is on the already present reality of salvation: the Spirit that was promised is already possessed, as 'first-fruits', Rm 8:23, by the Christian who from now on lives in Christ, Rm 6:11, as Christ lives in him, Ga 2:20.

The letter to the Romans is a magnificent synthesis of Paul's theology: it does not, however, exhaust his doctrine. It would be unfortunate if the importance accorded to it by the Lutheran controversy isolated it and led to a failure to complete it by its integration into the larger synthesis provided by the other letters.

§4d Philippians: AD 56–7

The Roman colony of Philippi was one of the principal cities of Macedonia; it had been evangelised by Paul in AD 50, during his second missionary journey, Ac 16:12–40, and he revisited it twice during his third: in the autumn of 57, Ac 20:1–2, and at Passover in AD 58, Ac 20:3–6. His converts there had proved their affection by contributing to his support first at Thessalonica, Ph 4:16, then at Corinth, 2 Co 11:9, and later still had commissioned Epaphroditus to take further contributions to him, Ph 4:10–20. Normally, Paul was afraid of doing anything that might give the impression that he was trying to make money out of his preaching, Ac 18:3d; so, by accepting their gift, he shows that he has a unique confidence in them.

If Philippians is accepted at its face value, as being a single letter, it must be said that at the time of writing, Paul was under arrest, Ph 1:7, 12–17, and for a long time this was assumed to be the first Roman captivity. Rome, however, was so far away that it seems unlikely that communications between Paul (with whom Epaphroditus was staying) and Philippi could have been as frequent or as easy as they appear to have been, 2:25–30. Nor is it clear why, if Paul was under arrest in Rome or in Caesarea, Ac 23:23, the Philippians should say that the contribution brought by Epaphroditus was the first chance they had had since the second missionary journey (*see* the mention of the gifts in Ph 4:10, 16) of helping the apostle, since Paul had visited them twice on his third journey. It is easier to suppose that Paul actually wrote this letter during the third journey, before reaching Philippi, i.e. while he was at Ephesus, the capital of Roman Asia, in 56–7, hoping to visit Macedonia after his liberation (compare Ph 1:26; 2:19–24 and Ac 19:21seq.; 20:1; 1 Co 16:5). The 'praetorium', Ph 1:13, and 'Caesar's household', 4:22, do not necessarily refer to Rome, since there were praetoria in all the major cities and there were most certainly detachments of the praetorian guard in Ephesus. It is true that there is no reference anywhere to an Ephesian captivity; but Luke says very little about Paul's three years there, Ac 19:1–20:1, and Paul himself mentions the very grave trials he underwent there, 1 Co 15:32; 2 Co 1:8–10.

If we accept this hypothesis we shall have to dissociate Ph from Col, Ep and Phm and group it with the 'great letters', notably with 1 Co. The style and content of the letter are quite consistent with this. It is not particularly doctrinal, but is just a friendly letter, giving some news to his converts at Philippi, warning them against the 'bad workmen' who are ruining his work in other places and might turn on them next, and, above all, appealing for the unity of corporate humility. As part of this appeal Paul gives us, Ph 2:6–11, the poem on the humility of the Messiah; and whether he wrote it or is quoting it, this poem is an important witness to developments in the early Christian understanding of the nature of Jesus.

Recently the thesis has gained ground that Ph is, in fact, a collection of three originally separate letters. One of the most satisfactory divisions is as follows: A=4:10–20; B=1:1–3:1 plus 4:2–9, 21–23; C=3:2–4:1. Letter A fits well with the beginning of Paul's stay at Ephesus, for the Philippians would not have delayed long before sending Paul help (4:10), nor he before thanking them. Letter B accords better with a time near the end of his stay there (2:9, compare Ac 19:22; 1 Co 16:10).

§4e Ephesians, Colossians, Philemon: AD 61–3

The letters to the Christians of Ephesus and Colossae (both in Roman Asia) and the letter to Philemon are closely related: the mission on which Onesimus is sent in Col 4:9 is the same as that in Phm 10–12; the same is true of Tychicus in Col 4:7seq. and Ep 6:21seq.; Paul's companions in Col 4:10–14 are the same as in Phm 23–24; Col and Ep are very similar in style and doctrine. The author says that he is in prison, Phm 1, 9seq., 13, 23; Col 4:3, 10, 18; Ep 3:1; 4:1; 6:20. If it is granted that this author is Paul, as tradition has long held, this imprisonment would be the one in Rome (61–3) rather than in Caesarea (58–60) where it would be difficult to account for the presence of Mark and of Onesimus, or in Ephesus (56–7) since there is nothing to suggest that Luke was ever there with Paul. The degree to which Paul's style has changed, and his doctrine developed, suggests some interval between Col, Ep and the 'great letters' Rm, Co, Ga. In the meantime a crisis had occurred and Epaphras, Col 1:7, Paul's delegate, arrived from Colossae (a church Paul had not founded) 1:4; 2:1, with disturbing news. Paul promptly wrote a letter to the Christians there, and gave it to Tychicus to deliver. On the traditional view of the authorship of Ep the inherent dangers of this new situation stimulated Paul to rethink things at a deeper level, and just as Rm had systematised the ideas outlined in Ga, so now, at about the same time as Col, Paul wrote another letter in which he restructured his teaching from the new angle that he had been forced by the recent developments at Colossae to adopt. This new synthesis is referred to as the letter he wrote to the Christians at Ephesus. The title, however, is misleading, and has very scanty MS support, *see* Ep 1:1a. This is a general letter addressed to the whole Church and not just to the church at Ephesus where Paul had spent three years, Ep 1:15; 3:2–4, though it is meant in a special way for Colossae and the other Christian communities of the Lycus valley among whom it is to be circulated, Col 4:16.

The interpretation just outlined respects the tradition which attributes Col and Ep to Paul; it retains considerable probability. But since the middle of the nineteenth century critics have contested the authenticity of these two letters. The heavy and repetitious style, they maintain, is not that of Paul; the theological ideas, notably those concerning the Body of Christ, Christ head of the Body, the universal Church, are different from those of previous letters, the errors opposed are later than Paul's time and belong rather to the gnostic ideas of the second century. These objections deserve serious consideration. They are put forward by numerous scholars, even Catholic ones. Nevertheless, they are not incontestable. In fact, for Col the balance is now in favour of Paul, with good justification. Not only does it retain his basic ideas but the new ideas in it are satisfactorily explained by the circumstances mentioned above. The same may be true of Ep although doubt about it still lingers. Among arguments in favour of Paul are: 1 That Ep is the work not of any derivative thinker, but of someone with a genius for creative thinking. 2 That the leisurely, rich and overloaded style of Col and Ep which contrasts so much with the quick, jerky discussions of earlier letters, can probably be explained by these wide new horizons that Paul was opening for himself. 3 That the style of the earlier letters is not itself wholly consistent, and two early examples of this later contemplative, semi-liturgical manner can be found already in Rm 3:23–26; 2 Co 9:8–14. The only real difficulty springs from the many passages in which Ep seems to borrow phrases from Col in a manner slavish and even awkward; but this might be because Paul was not in the habit of composing every word of his letters, and on this occasion may have allowed a disciple to play a greater part than usual. But it must be admitted that the phenomena noted in these second and third points could be explained more economically on the hypothesis of an author other than Paul, if such could be found, who was at the same time a creative thinker of genius similar to Paul's own, and yet content to borrow slavishly whole phrases from other, Pauline, letters. The difficulty of postulating such a hybrid as author of Ephesians is one of the main factors which has led some scholars to suppose that Colossians too, from which the vast majority of the borrowed phrases are taken, is also non-Pauline.

In the knowledge, then, that the genuine Pauline authorship of these two letters is the strongest but not the only possible hypothesis, we can attempt to reconstruct the genesis of Paul's thought in Col and Ep.

The errors at Colossae opposed by Paul are not yet those of the second-century gnostics, but rather ideas common among the Jewish Essenes. The danger at Colossae was the result of the basically Jewish (Col 2:16) speculations which the Christians at Colossae had taken up about the celestial or cosmic powers. These were the powers thought to be responsible for the regular movement of the cosmos, and the speculations about them, much influenced by Hellenist philosophy, attached an importance to these powers that threatened the supremacy of Christ. The author of the letter accepts these cosmological premises and, far from expressing any doubts about these powers, he associates them with the angels of Jewish tradition, Col 2:15; he is concerned only to show their subordinate place in the scheme of salvation. Their task had been to 'mediate' the Law and to administer it, and that task is now accomplished: *Christos Kyrios*, Christ the Lord, has established a new order of things and he now governs the cosmos. Raised up to heaven, he is above all the cosmic powers and has stripped them of their ancient dignities, Col 2:15. Because he is the Son, the Father's image, he was their Lord already when the world was made; now in the new creation he is their confirmed and absolute Master, for gathered into him is the *pleroma*, the fullness of Being, that is to say the fullness both of God and of all that exists through God's creative power, Col 1:13–20. Christians have been set free from these 'elements of the world', Col 2:8, 20, through being united with their Master and thus sharing in his fullness, 2:9–10, Christians must never again accept their tyranny by submitting to outworn and ineffective observances, Col 2:16–23. United to the risen Christ by baptism, Col 2:11–13, they are parts of his Body and receive a new life from him, as from their life-giving Head, 2:19. Paul's primary interest had always been in the salvation of Christians; the new perspective provoked by the arguments at Colossae embraced the effects of Christ's work on the entire cosmos. Since the human race forms part of the cosmos, the cosmos itself must be influenced by the saving act of the one and only Lord of all creation. In this perspective, a whole new breadth is given to the concept of the 'Body of Christ', which was an idea that, a few years previously, Paul had only touched on. Three aspects of this broader view, which focuses on the function of Christ as Head, are: that the scope of salvation is seen to be cosmic; that Christ, into whom the Church has to structure itself, is the victor who has triumphed over the whole cosmos; and finally that the conception of the future, eschatological, promise as already realised, becomes very much more central, *see* Ep 2:6e.

When the letter we know as Ephesians was written it followed the same lines, but this time the author can assume the conclusions of the previous letter about the subordinate place of the powers, Ep 1:20–22, and give further thought to how the Church as the Body of Christ embraces the whole of the new universe, 'the fullness of him who is filled, all in all', 1:23. This supreme vision forms the high point of the author's work. It forms the new focus round which many Pauline insights are synthesised. In particular the author reconsiders some of the problems he had already dealt with in Rm, the high point of Paul's previous period of thought. In a few phrases he recalls the survey of humanity under the shadow of sin and the central teaching that salvation is a gift given by God through Christ, Ep 2:1–10. Next, he re-examines the problem of Jew and gentile that previously caused Paul so much distress, Rm 9–11; but now in the light of eschatology realised in the exalted Christ, he is aware of the unity of Jews and gentiles, who are now reconciled, since each is equally part of the New Humanity, and who advance towards the Father together, Ep 2:11–22. The opening to the gentiles of the salvation promised to Israel is the great 'mystery', Ep 1:9; 3:3–6, 9; 6:19; Col 1:27; 2:2; 4:3. The author writes about the infinite wisdom of this 'mystery', Ep 3:9seq.; Col 2:3, about how it proves Christ's love to be inexhaustible, Ep 3:17seq., and about how God had made the unexpected choice of him, who was 'the least of all', to proclaim this mystery, Ep 3:2–8. This plan of salvation was revealed gradually, according to God's eternal designs, Ep 1:3–14, and its culmination is the wedding of Christ to the saved humanity constituted by the Church, 5:22–32.

The short letter Paul wrote at about the same time as Col is to tell Philemon of Colossae, v. 18, one of Paul's converts, that Onesimus, a runaway slave belonging to Philemon, and also one of Paul's converts, had returned. It is a very short note, and Paul wrote it in his own handwriting, v. 19. The letter reveals a gentle, affectionate side of the apostle, and also shows how he applies his views on slavery to a particular case, Rm 6:15g: as far as society is concerned, the master still owns his slave, but the two of them should live as brothers serving the same Master, Phm 16; compare Col 3:22; 4:1.

§4f 1 Timothy, Titus, 2 Timothy: AD 65–80

The three letters generally known as the Pastoral Epistles are all closely related in substance, form and historical background; two are addressed to Timothy and one to Titus, and all three have the form of letters from Paul to his most loyal followers, Ac 16:1; 2 Co 2:13d, giving them instruction and advice about the organisation and governing of the communities which he had entrusted to their care. Both 1 Tm and Tt seem to have been written from Macedonia, Timothy being at that time in Ephesus, 1 Tm 1:3, where Paul hoped to join him in the near future, 3:14; 4:13. Titus was in Crete, where he had been left by Paul, Tt 1:5, who planned to winter at Nicopolis in Epirus where Titus was to join him, Tt 3:12. In 2 Tm Paul is represented as a prisoner in Rome, 1:8, 16seq.; 2:9, after visits to Troas, 4:13, and Miletus, 4:20. In this threatening situation, 4:16, he feels that death is not far off, 4:6–8, 18, 4:9–16, 21. These circumstances correspond neither to the Roman captivity of Ac 28 nor to the journey that preceded it. Although Acts has nothing to tell us of any later activities, it is not impossible that at the end of the two years of this captivity he was set free and that he made the journey to the East projected in Phm 22. Tradition places the writing of 1 Tm and Tt on that journey, in AD 65, through Crete, Asia Minor, Macedonia and Greece. Similarly 2 Tm with its background of a new captivity, ending probably in Paul's death, is placed shortly before the traditional date of his martyrdom in AD 67.

The historical difficulties combine, however, with problems of thought and language to suggest that another solution to the question of authorship must be found. There is little reference any more to some of the great mysteries of Christianity on which Paul's thought had hinged (the cross, the Body of Christ, Christ as 'the Son'). The method of arguing has changed radically: no longer does Paul argue against false teaching, he simply condemns it. In addition the fiery, enthusiastic and vivid style has gone, and the confidence in his Christian flock has been replaced by a certain timidity of outlook. There is also considerable difference of vocabulary; many of the words common in the Pauline epistles have disappeared and there is a much higher proportion of words not used elsewhere by Paul, or even not used at all elsewhere in the New Testament. It has been argued that these phenomena can be explained either through a lack of confidence and elasticity in the tired and ageing apostle, or by Paul's leaving greater latitude than he does elsewhere to a secretary. But the historical difficulties remain, and the best explanation may be that the Pastoral Epistles are letters written by a follower of Paul, conscious of inheriting his mantle and seeking to give advice and instruction for the administration of local churches. This adoption of a revered name in such circumstances was a literary convention of the times, and the illusion could, as here, be supported by the mention of persons and places associated with the chosen figure. Some critics believe that in these letters such references, e.g. 2 Tm 1:15–18; 4:9–17, 19–21 and Tt 3:12–14, spring from the incorporation of fragments from genuine Pauline letters.

It must on the other hand be noted that the ecclesiastical hierarchy appears in these letters in a stage of evolution which cannot be very distant from that of Paul's time. The titles of *episkopos* and *presbyteros* are still practically synonymous, Ti 1:5–7, as formerly, Ac 20:17 and 28, in the primitive situation of communities governed by a body of elders, Tt 1:5c. There is as yet no trace of the monarchical 'bishop' of whom Ignatius was to write at the beginning of the second century. Nevertheless this development is not far distant, for Timothy and Titus, those delegates of Paul, although responsible for several communities without being attached to any single one, Tt 1:5, represent this apostolic authority which is being transmitted to fill the gap left by the disappearance of the apostles themselves, and which is soon to come to reside in each community in the bishop—the head of the college of presbyters. This intermediate stage of organisation is an argument against dating the letters later than the years 80–90. The same is true of the errors of doctrine opposed in the letters. One purpose of the letters is to fight dangerous new ideas which were already circulating, 1 Tm 1:19, and would later become important features of the Gnostic teaching which flourished in the second century. But most of the ideas, the idle questions, 1 Tm 6:4, empty problems, 'myths and endless genealogies', 1 Tm 1:4, 'Jewish myths', Tt 1:14, 'disputes about the Law', Tt 3:9, and the various ascetical practices they seemed to involve, 1 Tm 4:3, would all appear to belong to those hellenised and syncretistic ideas affecting Judaism, which formed part of the crisis in Colossae.

§5 Hebrews: AD 70–80

The question of who wrote this letter to the Jewish Christians has, unlike the disputed authorship of the pastoral letters, been a subject of debate from the earliest times. Not that its canonical status was often questioned, but up to the end of the fourth century the Western Church denied that Paul had written it, and the Eastern Church affirmed Pauline authorship only with many reservations about its literary composition (Clement of Alexandria, Origen). Its vocabulary and style have a simplicity and a distinction quite uncharacteristic of Paul; the way in which it quotes and uses the Old Testament is different from Paul's; the usual Pauline greetings and introduction are lacking, and though its doctrine has Pauline overtones, it is so original that its immediate attribution to Paul is difficult. Most critics agree that Paul could not have been its author in the same sense as he was author of the other letters, but he is felt to have had sufficient indirect influence to warrant its inclusion from early times in the *corpus Paulinum*.

No sort of agreement exists as to who actually wrote the letter; Barnabas, Silas, Aristion and others, have been suggested; perhaps the most likely is Apollos, the Alexandrian Jew who is praised by Luke for his eloquence, apostolic zeal and knowledge of the scriptures, Ac 18:24–28. Not only are these qualities reflected in the letter itself, but its language and thought, with their marked affinity with Philo, also suggest Alexandrian culture. The argument of the letter, pleaded with rhetorical skill, is founded entirely on the Old Testament.

The place and date of writing are equally uncertain, and the intended recipients are also unknown. But the author seems to be writing from Italy, 13:24, and he speaks as if the Temple were still open for worship, 8:4seq., warning his readers against the temptation of going back to it; when he emphasises the transitory nature of the Mosaic cult, he makes no reference to the destruction of the Temple which would have made a decisive argument for him. This suggests he was writing before AD 70. On the other hand, he certainly makes use of Paul's letters from prison and therefore wrote after 63. If the crisis behind the author's urgent appeal for unshakable faith, 10:25, is the first threat of the Jewish War, the letter could be dated AD 67.

The title 'to the Hebrews' dates from the second century and is well chosen. The letter clearly assumes not only that its readers are thoroughly familiar with the old covenant but that they are Jewish Christians, perhaps even Jewish priests, cf. Ac 6:7, to judge by the emphasis on public worship and ceremonial. Having become Christians, they seem to have left Jerusalem and gone for shelter to some coastal town like Caesarea or Antioch. They are tired of exile and think longingly of the splendour of Temple worship and of the part they played in it; their new faith is not very strong, and they have not yet properly understood it; persecution discourages them and they are tempted to revert to Judaism.

The letter was written to them to try to prevent this from happening, 10:19–39. To these exiles the author presents Christian life in the perspective of the Exodus, marching to the place of rest, the Promised Land of heaven, an exodus guided not by Moses but by Christ, an incomparably superior leader, 3:1–6, and led by the same light of faith and hope that had guided their ancestors in the Exodus and had illumined all the saints of old, 3:7–4:11; 11 *passim*. Christ himself replaces the old priesthood and being a priest like Melchizedek, he is higher than Aaron, 4:14–5:10; 7. The many ineffectual sacrifices of levitical worship are replaced by the one uniquely efficacious sacrifice of Christ himself, 8:1–10:18. To prove this, the author shows how Jesus Christ, the incarnate Son of God, is, as Leader and Priest, higher than all the angels and is ruler of all things, ch.1–2.

In this letter, strictly theological and exegetical passages alternate with passages of exhortation, but the main themes themselves are interwoven in a very intricate and oriental way, as disconcerting to some modern Western readers as its method of using scripture. For this reason the letter is most illuminating about typology, showing how the earliest Christians conceived the harmony of the Old and New Testaments, and how they understood the redemptive work of Jesus in terms of God's whole plan of salvation. This, and the profound intuitions about the central points of Christian belief, combine to make this unsigned document one of the most important books of the New Testament.

ROMANS

THE LETTER OF PAUL
TO THE CHURCH IN ROME

Address [a]

1, 2 **1** From Paul, a servant of Christ Jesus, called to be an apostle, [b] ·set apart for the service of the gospel that God promised long ago through his prophets in the holy scriptures.

3, 4 This is the gospel concerning his Son who, in terms of human nature ·was born a descendant of David and who, in terms of the Spirit and of holiness was designated Son of God in power by resurrection from the dead: [c] Jesus Christ, our
5 Lord, ·through whom we have received grace and our apostolic mission of winning
6 the obedience of faith [d] among all the nations for the honour of his name. ·You
7 are among these, and by his call you belong to Jesus Christ. ·To you all, God's beloved in Rome, called to be his holy people. Grace and peace from God our Father and the Lord Jesus Christ.

Thanksgiving and prayer

8 First I give thanks to my God through Jesus Christ for all of you because your
9 faith is talked of all over the world. ·God, whom I serve [e] with my spirit [f] in preaching the gospel of his Son, is my witness that I continually mention you in
10 my prayers, ·asking always that by some means I may at long last be enabled to
11 visit you, if it is God's will. ·For I am longing to see you so that I can convey to
12 you some spiritual gift that will be a lasting strength, ·or rather that we may be
13 strengthened together through our mutual faith, yours and mine. ·I want you to be quite certain too, brothers, that I have often planned to visit you—though up to the present I have always been prevented—in the hope that I might work as
14 fruitfully among you as I have among the gentiles elsewhere. ·I have an obligation
15 to Greeks [g] as well as barbarians, to the educated as well as the ignorant, and hence the eagerness on my part to preach the gospel to you in Rome too.

SALVATION BY FAITH

I: JUSTIFICATION

The theme stated

16 For I see no reason to be ashamed of the gospel; it is God's power for the salvation
17 of everyone who has faith[h]—Jews first,[i] but Greeks as well—·for in it is revealed
the saving justice of God: a justice[j] based on faith[k] and addressed to faith. As it
says in scripture: *Anyone who is upright through faith will live.*

A: THE RETRIBUTION OF GOD AGAINST GENTILE AND JEW[l]

God's retribution against the gentiles

18 The retribution[m] of God from heaven is being revealed against the ungodliness
19 and injustice of human beings who in their injustice hold back the truth. ·For what
can be known about God is perfectly plain to them, since God has made it plain to
20 them: ·ever since the creation of the world, the invisible existence of God and his
everlasting power have been clearly seen by the mind's understanding of created
21 things. And so these people have no excuse: ·they knew God[n] and yet they did
not honour him as God or give thanks to him, but their arguments became futile
22 and their uncomprehending minds were darkened. ·While they claimed to be wise,
23 in fact they were growing so stupid ·that *they exchanged the glory* of the immortal
God *for an imitation*, for the image of a mortal human being, or of birds, or
animals, or crawling things.

24 That is why God abandoned them[o] in their inmost cravings to filthy practices of
25 dishonouring their own bodies—·because they *exchanged God's truth* for a lie and
have worshipped and served the creature instead of the Creator, who is blessed
for ever. Amen.[p]

26, 27 That is why God abandoned them to degrading passions: ·why their women
have exchanged natural intercourse for unnatural practices; and the men, in a
similar fashion, too, giving up normal relations with women, are consumed with
passion for each other, men doing shameful things with men and receiving in
themselves due reward for their perversion.

28 In other words, since they would not consent to acknowledge God, God aban-
29 doned them to their unacceptable thoughts and indecent behaviour. ·And so now
they are steeped in all sorts of injustice,[q] rottenness, greed and malice;[r] full of
30 envy, murder, wrangling, treachery and spite, ·libellers, slanderers, enemies of
God,[s] rude, arrogant and boastful, enterprising in evil, rebellious to parents,
31, 32 without brains, honour, love[t] or pity. ·They are well aware of God's ordinance:
that those who behave like this deserve to die—yet they not only do it, but even
applaud others who do the same.[u]

The Jews are not exempt from the retribution of God[a]

1 **2** So no matter who you are, if you pass judgement you have no excuse. It is
yourself that you condemn when you judge others, since you behave in the
2 same way as those you are condemning. ·We are well aware that people who
3 behave like that are justly condemned by God.' ·But you—when you judge those
who behave like this while you are doing the same yourself—do you think you will

4 escape God's condemnation? •Or are you not disregarding his abundant goodness,
tolerance and patience, failing to realise that this generosity of God is meant to
5 bring you to repentance? •Your stubborn refusal to repent is only storing up
retribution for yourself on that Day of retribution when God's just verdicts will be
6, 7 made known. •*He will repay everyone as their deeds deserve.*^b •For those who
aimed for glory and honour and immortality by persevering in doing good, there
8 will be eternal life; •but for those who out of jealousy have taken for their guide
9 not truth but injustice, there will be the fury of retribution. •Trouble and distress
will come to every human being who does evil—Jews first, but Greeks as well;
10 glory and honour and peace will come to everyone who does good—Jews first, but
11 Greeks as well. •*There is no favouritism with God.*

The Law will not save them

12 All those who have sinned without the Law will perish without the Law; and those
13 under the Law who have sinned will be judged by the Law. •For the ones that
God will justify are not those who have heard the Law but those who have kept
14 the Law. •So, when gentiles, not having the Law, still through their own innate
sense^c behave as the Law commands, then, even though they have no Law, they
15 are a law for themselves. •They can demonstrate the effect of the Law engraved
on their hearts, to which their own conscience bears witness; since they are aware
of various considerations, some^d of which accuse them, while others provide them
16 with a defence . . . on the day when,^e •according to the gospel that I preach, God,
through Jesus Christ, judges all human secrets.
17   If you can call yourself a Jew, and you really trust in the Law, and are proud of
18 your God, •and know his will, and tell right from wrong because you have been
19 taught by the Law; •if you are confident that you are a guide to the blind and a
20 beacon to those in the dark, •that you can teach the ignorant and instruct the
21 unlearned because the Law embodies all knowledge and all truth—•so then, in
teaching others, do you teach yourself as well? You preach that there is to be no
22 stealing, but do you steal? •You say that adultery is forbidden, but do you commit
adultery? You detest the worship of objects, but do you desecrate holy things
23 yourself? •If, while you are boasting of the Law, you disobey it, then you are
24 bringing God into contempt. •As scripture says: *It is your fault that the name of
God is held in contempt among the nations.*

Circumcision will not save them

25 Circumcision has its value if you keep the Law; but if you keep breaking the Law,
26 you are no more circumcised than the uncircumcised. •And if an uncircumcised
man keeps the commands of the Law, will not his uncircumcised state count as
27 circumcision? •More, the man who, in his native uncircumcised state, keeps the
Law, is a condemnation of you, who, by your concentration on the letter and on
28 circumcision, actually break the Law. •Being a Jew is not only having the outward
appearance of a Jew, and circumcision is not only a visible physical operation.
29 The real Jew is the one who is inwardly a Jew, and real circumcision is in the
heart, a thing not of the letter but of the spirit. He may not be praised by any
human being, but he will be praised by God.

God's promises will not save them

1 **3** Is there any benefit, then, in being a Jew?^a Is there any advantage in being
2 circumcised? •A great deal, in every way. First of all, it was to the Jews that

3 the message of God was entrusted. ·What if some of them were unfaithful? Do
4 you think their lack of faith could cancel God's faithfulness? ·Out of the question!
God will always be true even if *no human being can be relied on.* As scripture
says: *That you may show your saving justice when you pass sentence and your*
5 *victory may appear when you give judgement.* ·But if our injustice serves to bring
God's saving justice *b* into view, can we say that God is unjust when—to use human
6 terms—he brings his retribution down on us? ·Out of the question! It would mean
7 that God could not be the judge of the world. ·You might as well say that *c* if my
untruthfulness makes God demonstrate his truthfulness, to his greater glory, then
8 I should not be judged to be a sinner at all. ·In this case, the slanderous report
some people are spreading *d* would be true, that we teach that one should do evil
that good may come of it. In fact such people are justly condemned.

All are guilty

9 Well: are we any better off? *e* Not at all: we have already indicted Jews and Greeks
10 as being all alike under the dominion of sin. ·As scripture says:

> *Not one of them is upright, not a single one,*
11 > *not a single one is wise,*
> *not a single one seeks God.*
12 > *All have turned away, all alike turned sour,*
> *not one of them does right, not a single one.*
13 > *Their throats are wide-open graves,*
> *their tongues seductive.*
> *Viper's venom behind their lips;*
14 > *their speech is full of cursing and bitterness.*
15 > *Their feet quick to shed innocent blood,*
16 > *wherever they go there is havoc and ruin.*
17 > *They do not know the way of peace,*
18 > *there is no fear of God before their eyes.*

19 Now we are well aware that whatever the Law says *f* is said for those who are
subject to the Law, so that every mouth may be silenced, and the whole world
20 brought under the judgement of God. ·So then, *no human being can be found
upright at the tribunal* of God by keeping the Law; *g* all that the Law does is to tell
us what is sinful.

B: FAITH AND THE JUDGEMENT OF GOD

The revelation of God's judgement

21 God's saving justice was witnessed by the Law and the Prophets, but now it has
22 been revealed altogether apart from law: ·God's saving justice given through faith
23 in Jesus Christ to all who believe. ·No distinction is made: all have sinned and lack
24 God's glory, *h* ·and all are justified by the free gift of his grace *i* through being set
25 free *j* in Christ Jesus. ·God appointed him as a sacrifice for reconciliation, through
faith, *k* by the shedding of his blood, and so showed his justness; first for the past,
26 when sins went unpunished because he held his hand; *l* ·and now again for the
present age, *m* to show how he is just *n* and justifies everyone who has faith in Jesus.

What faith does

27 So what becomes of our boasts? * There is no room for them. On what principle—
28 that only actions count? No; that faith is what counts, * •since, as we see it, a
29 person is justified by faith and not by doing what the Law tells him to do. •Do you
   think God is the God only of the Jews, and not of gentiles too? Most certainly of
30 gentiles too, •since there is only one God; he will justify the circumcised by their
31 faith, and he will justify the uncircumcised through their faith. •Are we saying that
   the Law has been made pointless by faith? Out of the question; we are placing the
   Law on its true footing. *

C: THE EXAMPLE OF ABRAHAM

Abraham justified by faith

1 **4** Then what do we say about Abraham, * the ancestor from whom we are
2 descended physically? * •If Abraham had been justified because of what he
   had done, then he would have had something to boast about. * But not before
3 God: •does not scripture say: *Abraham put his faith in God and this was reckoned*
4 *to him as uprightness?* * •Now, when someone works, the wages for this are not
5 considered as a favour but as due; •however, when someone, without working,
   puts faith in the one who justifies the godless, it is this faith that is reckoned as
6 uprightness. •David, too, says the same: he calls someone blessed if God attributes
   uprightness to that person, apart from any action undertaken:

7   *How blessed are those whose offence is forgiven,*
     whose sin is blotted out.
8   *How blessed are those to whom the Lord imputes no guilt.*

Justified before circumcision

9 Is this blessing only for the circumcised, or is it said of the uncircumcised as well?
10 Well, we said of Abraham that *his faith was reckoned to him as uprightness*. •Now
   how did this come about? When he was already circumcised, or before he had
   been circumcised? Not when he had been circumcised, but while he was still
11 uncircumcised; •and *circumcision* was given to him later, *as a sign* and a guarantee *
   that the faith which he had while still uncircumcised was reckoned to him as
   uprightness. In this way, Abraham was to be the ancestor of all believers who are
12 uncircumcised, so that they might be reckoned as upright; •as well as the ancestor
   of those of the circumcision who not only have their circumcision but who also
   follow our ancestor Abraham along the path of faith that he trod before he was
   circumcised.

Not justified by obedience to the Law

13 For the promise to Abraham and his descendants that he should inherit the world
14 was not through the Law, but through the uprightness of faith. * •For if it is those
   who live by the Law who will gain the inheritance, faith is worthless and the
15 promise is without force; •for the Law produces nothing but God's retribution,
   and it is only where there is no Law that it is possible to live without breaking the
16 Law. •That is why the promise is to faith, so that it comes as a free gift and is secure
   for all the descendants, not only those who rely on the Law but all those others

17 who rely on the faith of Abraham, the ancestor of us all ·(as scripture says: *I have made you the father of many nations*). Abraham is our father in the eyes of God, in whom he put his faith, and who brings the dead to life and calls into existence what does not yet exist. *

Abraham's faith a model of Christian faith

18 Though there seemed no hope, he hoped and believed that he was to become *father of many nations* in fulfilment of the promise: *Just so will your descendants*
19 *be*. ·Even the thought that his body was as good as dead—he was about a hundred
20 years old—and that Sarah's womb was dead too did not shake his faith. *·Counting on the promise of God, he did not doubt or disbelieve, but drew strength from
21 faith *i* and gave glory to God, ·fully convinced that whatever God promised he has
22 the power to perform. ·This is the faith that was *reckoned to him as uprightness*.
23, 24 And the word 'reckoned' in scripture applies not only to him; ·it is there for our
25 sake too—our faith, too, will be 'reckoned' ·because we believe in him who raised from the dead our Lord Jesus who was *handed over to death for our sins* and raised to life for our justification. *j*

II: SALVATION

Faith guarantees salvation *a*

1 **5** So then, now that we have been justified by faith, we are at peace *b* with God
2 through our Lord Jesus Christ; ·it is through him, by faith, that we have been admitted into God's favour in which we are living, and look forward exultantly to
3 God's glory. *c* ·Not only that; let us exult, too, in our hardships, understanding that
4 hardship develops perseverance, ·and perseverance develops a tested character,
5 something that gives us hope, ·and a hope which will not let us down, because the love of God *d* has been poured into our hearts by the Holy Spirit which has been
6 given to us. *e* ·When we were still helpless, at the appointed time, Christ died for
7 the godless. ·You could hardly find anyone ready to die even for someone upright; though it is just possible that, for a really good person, someone might undertake
8 to die. ·So it is proof of God's own love for us, that Christ died for us while we
9 were still sinners. ·How much more can we be sure, therefore, that, now that we have been justified by his death, we shall be saved through him from the retribution
10 of God. ·For if, while we were enemies, we were reconciled to God through the death of his Son, how much more can we be sure that, being now reconciled, we
11 shall be saved by his life. ·What is more, we are filled with exultant trust in God, through our Lord Jesus Christ, through whom we have already gained our reconciliation.

A: DELIVERANCE FROM SIN AND DEATH AND LAW

Adam and Jesus Christ *f*

12 Well then; it was through one man that sin *came into the world*, and through sin death, *g* and thus death has spread through the whole human race because everyone
13 has sinned. *h* ·Sin already existed in the world before there was any law, even
14 though sin is not reckoned when there is no law. ·Nonetheless death reigned over

all from Adam to Moses, even over those whose sin was not the breaking of a commandment, as Adam's was. He prefigured ⁱ the One who was to come . . .

15 There is no comparison between the free gift and the offence. If death came to many ʲ through the offence of one man, how much greater an effect the grace of God has had, coming to so many and so plentifully as a free gift through the one

16 man Jesus Christ! ·Again, there is no comparison between the gift and the offence of one man. One single offence brought condemnation, but now, after many

17 offences, have come the free gift and so acquittal! ·It was by one man's offence that death came to reign over all, but how much greater the reign in life of those who receive the fullness of grace and the gift of saving justice, through the one

18 man, Jesus Christ. ·One man's offence brought condemnation on all humanity;

19 and one man's good act has brought justification and life to all humanity. ·Just as by one man's disobedience many were made sinners, so by one man's act of justice

20 are many to be made upright. ᵏ ·When law ˡ came on the scene, it was to multiply

21 the offences. But however much sin increased, grace was always greater; ·so that as sin's reign brought death, so grace was to rule through saving justice that leads to eternal life through Jesus Christ our Lord.

Baptism

1 6 What should we say then? Should we remain in sin so that grace may be given

2 the more fully? ·Out of the question! We have died to sin; how could we go on

3 living in it? ·You cannot have forgotten that all of us, when we were baptised into

4 Christ Jesus, were baptised into his death. ·So by our baptism into his death we were buried with him, ᵃ so that as Christ was raised from the dead by the Father's

5 glorious power, we too should begin living a new life. ·If we have been joined to

6 him by dying a death like his, so we shall be by a resurrection like his; ·realising that our former self was crucified with him, so that the self which belonged to sin

7 should be destroyed and we should be freed from the slavery of sin. ᵇ ·Someone who has died, of course, no longer has to answer for sin.

8, 9 But ᶜ we believe that, if we died with Christ, then we shall live with him too. ·We know that Christ has been raised from the dead and will never die again. Death

10 has no power over him any more. ·For by dying, he is dead to sin ᵈ once and for

11 all, and now the life that he lives is life with God. ·In the same way, you must see yourselves as being dead to sin but alive for God in Christ Jesus. ᵉ

Holiness, not sin, to be the master

12 That is why you must not allow sin to reign over your mortal bodies ᶠ and make

13 you obey their desires; ·or give any parts of your bodies over to sin to be used as instruments of evil. Instead, give yourselves to God, as people brought to life from the dead, and give every part of your bodies to God to be instruments of

14 uprightness; ·and then sin will no longer have any power over you—you are living not under law, but under grace.

The Christian is freed from the slavery of sin ᵍ

15 What is the implication? That we are free to sin, now that we are not under law

16 but under grace? Out of the question! ·You know well that if you undertake to be somebody's slave and obey him, you are the slave of him you obey: you can be the slave either of sin which leads to death, or of obedience which leads to saving

17 justice. ·Once you were slaves of sin, but thank God you have given whole-hearted

18 obedience to the pattern of teaching to which you were introduced; ·and so, being

19 freed from serving sin, you took uprightness as your master. ·I am putting it in human terms because you are still weak human beings: as once you surrendered yourselves as servants to immorality and to a lawlessness which results in more lawlessness, now you have to surrender yourselves to uprightness which is to result in sanctification. ⁱ

The reward of sin and the reward of uprightness

20. 21 When you were the servants of sin, you felt no obligation to uprightness, ·and what did you gain from living like that? Experiences of which you are now
22 ashamed, ⁱ for that sort of behaviour ends in death. ·But, now you are set free from sin and bound to the service of God, your gain will be sanctification and the
23 end will be eternal life. ·For the wage paid by sin is death; the gift freely given by God is eternal life in Christ Jesus our Lord.

The Christian is freed from slavery to the Law ᶜ

1 7 As people who are familiar with the Law, brothers, you cannot have forgotten
2 that the law can control a person only during that person's lifetime. ᵇ ·A married woman, for instance, is bound to her husband by law, as long as he lives,
3 but when her husband dies all her legal obligation to him as husband is ended. ·So if she were to have relations with another man while her husband was still alive, she would be termed an adulteress; but if her husband dies, her legal obligation comes to an end and if she then has relations with another man, that does not
4 make her an adulteress. ·In the same way you, my brothers, through the body of Christ have become dead to the Law and so you are able to belong to someone else, that is, to him who was raised from the dead to make us live fruitfully for
5 God. ·While we were still living by our natural inclinations, ᶜ the sinful passions aroused by the Law were working in all parts of our bodies to make us live lives
6 which were fruitful only for death. ·But now we are released from the Law, having died to what was binding us, and so we are in a new service, that of the spirit, and not in the old service of a written code.

The function of the Law ᵈ

7 What should we say, then? That the Law itself is sin? Out of the question! All the same, if it had not been for the Law, I should not have known what sin was; for instance, I should not have known what it meant to covet if the Law had not
8 said: *You are not to covet.* ·But, once it found the opportunity through that commandment, sin produced in me all kinds of covetousness; as long as there is no Law, sin is dead.
9 Once, when there was no Law, I used to be alive; ᵉ but when the commandment
10 came, sin came to life ·and I died. The commandment was meant to bring life but
11 I found it brought death, ·because sin; finding its opportunity by means of the commandment, *beguiled* me and, by means of it, killed me.
12 So then, the Law is holy, and what it commands is holy and upright and good.
13 Does that mean that something good resulted in my dying? Out of the question! But sin, ᶠ in order to be identified as sin, caused my death through that good thing, and so it is by means of the commandment that sin shows its unbounded sinful power.

The inward struggle ᵍ

14 We are well aware that the Law is spiritual: but I am a creature of flesh and blood
15 sold as a slave to sin. ·I do not understand my own behaviour; I do not act as I

16 mean to, but I do things that I hate. •While I am acting as I do not want to, I still
17 acknowledge the Law as good, •so it is not myself acting, but the sin which lives in
18 me. •And really, I know of nothing good living in me—in my natural self, that
19 is—for though the will to do what is good is in me, the power to do it is not: •the
   good thing I want to do, I never do; the evil thing which I do not want—that is
20 what I do. •But every time I do what I do not want to, then it is not myself acting,
   but the sin that lives in me. *

21 So I find this rule: ‘ that for me, where I want to do nothing but good, evil is
22, 23 close at my side. •In my inmost ʲ self I dearly love God's law, ᵏ but •I see that acting
   on my body there is a different law which battles against the law in my mind. So I
   am brought to be a prisoner of that law of sin which lives inside my body.

24 What a wretched man I am! Who will rescue me from this body doomed to
25 death? ˡ •God—thanks be to him—through Jesus Christ our Lord.
   So it is that I myself with my mind ᵐ obey the law of God, but in my disordered
   nature I obey the law of sin. ⁿ

B: THE CHRISTIAN'S SPIRITUAL LIFE

The life of the spirit

1 8 Thus, condemnation will never come to those who are in Christ Jesus, because
2   the law of the Spirit which gives life in Christ Jesus has set you ᵃ free from the
3 law of sin and death. ᵇ •What the Law could not do because of the weakness of
   human nature, ᶜ God did, sending his own Son in the same human nature as any
4 sinner to be a sacrifice for sin, and condemning sin in that human nature. ᵈ •This
   was so that the Law's requirements ᵉ might be fully satisfied in us as we direct our
5 lives not by our natural inclinations but by the spirit. •Those who are living by
   their natural inclinations have their minds on the things human nature desires;
6 those who live in the spirit have their minds on spiritual things. •And human
   nature has nothing to look forward to but death, while the spirit looks forward to
7 life and peace, •because the outlook of disordered human nature is opposed to
8 God, since it does not submit to God's Law, and indeed it cannot, •and those who
9 live by their natural inclinations can never be pleasing to God. •You, however,
   live not by your natural inclinations, but by the spirit, since the Spirit of God has
   made a home in you. Indeed, anyone who does not have the Spirit of Christ does
10 not belong to him. •But when Christ is in you, the body is dead because of sin but
11 the spirit is alive because you have been justified; ᶠ •and if the Spirit of him who
   raised Jesus from the dead has made his home in you, then he who raised Christ
   Jesus from the dead will give life to your own mortal bodies through his Spirit
   living in you. ᵍ

12 So then, my brothers, we have no obligation to human nature to be dominated
13 by it. •If you do live in that way, you are doomed to die; but if by the Spirit you
   put to death the habits originating in the body, you will have life.

Children of God

14, 15 All who are guided ʰ by the Spirit of God are sons of God; •for what you received
   was not the spirit of slavery to bring you back into fear; you received the spirit of
16 adoption, enabling us to cry out, '*Abba*, Father!' ⁱ •The Spirit himself joins with
17 our spirit to bear witness that we are children of God. •And if we are children,

then we are heirs, heirs of God and joint-heirs with Christ, provided that we share his suffering, so as to share his glory.

Glory as our destiny

18 In my estimation, all that we suffer in the present time is nothing in comparison
19 with the glory which is destined to be disclosed for us, ·for the whole creation is
20 waiting with eagerness for the children of God to be revealed.ʲ ·It was not for its own purposes that creation had frustration imposed on it, but for the purposes of
21 him who imposed it—;ᵏ ·with the intention that the whole creation itself might be freed from its slavery to corruption and brought into the same glorious freedom as
22 the children of God. ·We are well aware that the whole creation, until this time,
23 has been groaning in labour pains. ·And not only that: we too, who have the first-fruits of the Spirit, even we are groaning inside ourselves, waiting with eagerness
24 forˡ our bodies to be set free. ·In hope, we already have salvation; in hope, not visibly present, or we should not be hoping—nobody goes on hoping for something
25 which he can already see. ·But having this hope for what we cannot yet see, we are able to wait for it with persevering confidence.
26   And as well as this, the Spirit too comes to help us in our weakness, for, when we do not know how to pray properly, then the Spirit personally makes our
27 petitions for us in groans that cannot be put into words; ·and he who can see into all hearts knows what the Spirit means because the prayers that the Spirit makes for God's holy people are always in accordance with the mind of God. ᵐ

God has called us to share his glory

28 We are well aware that God works with those who love him, those who have been
29 called in accordance with his purpose, and turns everything to their good. ⁿ ·He decided beforehand who were the ones destined to be moulded to the pattern of
30 his Son, ° so that he should be the eldest of many brothers; ·it was those so destined that he called; those that he called, he justified, and those that he has justified he has brought into glory. ᵖ

A hymn to God's love

31, 32 After saying this, what can we add? If God is for us, who can be against us? ·Since he did not spare his own Son, but gave him up for the sake of all of us, then can we
33 not expect that with him he will freely give us all his gifts? ·Who can bring any accusation against those that God has chosen? *When God grants saving justice*
34 *who can condemn?* Are we not sure that it is Christ Jesus, who died—yes and more, who was raised from the dead and is at God's right hand—and who is adding
35 his plea for us? ·Can anything cut us off from the love of Christ—can hardships or
36 distress, or persecution, or lack of food and clothing, or threats or violence; ·as scripture says:

> *For your sake we are being massacred all day long,*
> *treated as sheep to be slaughtered?*

37 No; we come through all these things triumphantly victorious, by the power of
38 him who loved us. ·For I am certain of this: neither death nor life, nor angels, nor principalities, nothing already in existence and nothing still to come, nor any
39 power, ·nor the heights nor the depths, ᵠ nor any created thing whatever, will be able to come between us and the love of God, known to us in Christ Jesus our Lord.

C: THE PLACE OF ISRAEL *

The privileges of Israel

1,2 **9** This is the truth and I am speaking in Christ, without pretence, as my conscience testifies for me in the Holy Spirit; ·there is great sorrow and unremitting
3 agony in my heart: ·I could pray that I myself might be accursed *b* and cut off from
4 Christ, if this could benefit the brothers who are my own flesh and blood. *c* They
are Israelites; it was they who were adopted as children, the glory was theirs and
the covenants; to them were given the Law and the worship of God and the
5 promises. ·To them belong the fathers and out of them, so far as physical descent
is concerned, came Christ who is above all, God, blessed for ever. *d* Amen.

God has kept his promise

6 It is not that God's promise has failed. Not all born Israelites belong to Israel, *e*
7 and not all the descendants of Abraham count as his children, for

Isaac is the one through whom your Name will be carried on.

8 That is, it is not by being children through physical descent that people become
children of God; it is the children of the promise that are counted as the heirs.
9 The actual words of the promise were: *I shall come back to you at this season, and*
10 *Sarah will have a son.* ·Even more to the point is what was said to Rebecca when
11 she was pregnant by our ancestor, Isaac, ·before her children were born, so that
neither had yet done anything either good or bad, but in order that it should be
12 God's choice which prevailed, ·—not human merit, but his call—she was told: *the*
13 *elder one will serve the younger.* ·Or as scripture says elsewhere: *I loved Jacob but*
hated Esau.

God is not unjust

14, 15 What should we say, then? That God is unjust? Out of the question! ·For speaking
to Moses, he said: *I am gracious to those to whom I am gracious and I take pity on*
16 *those on whom I take pity.* ·So it is not a matter of what any person wants or what
17 any person does, but only of God having mercy. ·Scripture says to Pharaoh: *I*
raised you up for this reason, *f* to display my power in you and to have my name
18 talked of throughout the world. ·In other words, if God wants to show mercy on
someone, he does so, and if he wants to harden someone's heart, he does so.
19 Then you will ask me, 'How then can he ever blame anyone, since no one can
20 oppose his will?' *g* ·But you—who do you think you, a human being, are, to answer
back to God? *Something that was made, can it say to its maker: why did you make*
21 *me* this shape? ·A potter surely has the right over his clay to make out of the same
lump either a pot for special use or one for ordinary use.
22 But suppose that *h* God, although all the time he wanted to reveal his retribution
and demonstrate his power, has with great patience gone on putting up with those
23 who are the instruments of his retribution and designed to be destroyed; ·so
that *i* he may make known the glorious riches ready for the people who are the
24 instruments of his faithful love and were long ago prepared for that glory. *j* ·We
are that people, called by him not only out of the Jews but out of the gentiles too.

All has been foretold in the Old Testament

25 Just as he says in the book of Hosea: *I shall tell those who were not my people,*
26 *'You are my people,' and I shall take pity on those on whom I had no pity.* ·*And in
the very place where they were told, 'You are not my people,' they will be told that*
27 *they are 'children of the living God'.* ᵏ ·And about Israel, this is what Isaiah cried
out: ˡ *Though the people of Israel are like the sand of the sea, only a remnant will be*
28 *saved;* ·*for without hesitation or delay the Lord will execute his sentence on the*
29 *earth.* ᵐ ·As Isaiah foretold: *Had the Lord Sabaoth not left us a few survivors, we
should be like Sodom, we should be the same as Gomorrah.*
30 　　What should we say, then? ⁿ That the gentiles, although they were not looking
for saving justice, found it, and this was the saving justice that comes of faith;
31 while Israel, looking for saving justice by law-keeping, did not succeed in fulfilling
32 the Law. ° ·And why? Because they were trying to find it in actions and not in
33 faith, and so they stumbled over the *stumbling-stone*—·as it says in scripture: *Now
I am laying in Zion a stumbling-stone, a rock to trip people up; but he who relies on
this will not be brought to disgrace.*

Israel fails to see that it is God who makes us holy

1　**10** Brothers, my dearest wish and my prayer to God is for them, that they may
2　　　 be saved. ·I readily testify to their fervour for God, but it is misguided. ᵃ
3 Not recognising God's saving justice they have tried to establish their own, instead
4 of submitting to the saving justice of God. ᵇ ·But the Law has found its fulfilment
in Christ so that all who have faith will be justified.

The testimony of Moses

5 Moses writes of the saving justice that comes by the Law and says that *whoever
6 complies with it will find life in it.* ·But the saving justice of faith says this: ᶜ *Do not
7 think in your heart, 'Who will go up to heaven?'*·—that is to bring Christ down; or
'Who will go down to the depths?' ᵈ—that is to bring Christ back from the dead.
8 What does it say, then? *The word is very near to you; it is in your mouth and in
9 your heart,* that is, the word of faith, the faith which we preach, · that if you
declare with your mouth that Jesus is Lord, and if you believe with your heart that
10 God raised him from the dead, ᵉ then you will be saved. ·It is by believing with the
heart that you are justified, and by making the declaration with your lips that you
11 are saved. ·When scripture says: *No one who relies on this will be brought to
12 disgrace,* it makes no distinction between Jew and Greek: the same Lord is the
13 Lord of all, and his generosity is offered to all who appeal to him, ·for *all who call
on the name of the Lord will be saved.*

Israel has no excuse

14 How then are they to call on him if they have not come to believe in him? ᶠ And
how can they believe in him if they have never heard of him? And how will they
15 hear of him unless there is a preacher for them? ·And how will there be preachers
if they are not sent? As scripture says: *How beautiful are the feet of the messenger
of good news.* ᵍ
16 　　But in fact they have not all responded to the good news. As Isaiah says: *Lord,
17 who has given credence to what they have heard from us?* ·But it is in that way faith
comes, from hearing, and that means hearing the word of Christ. ʰ
18 　　Well then, I say, is it possible that they have not heard? Indeed they have: *in the*

19 *entire earth their voice ⁱ stands out, their message reaches the whole world.* ·Well, another question, then: is it possible that Israel did not understand? In the first place Moses said: *I rouse you to jealousy with a non-people, I shall exasperate you*
20 *with a stupid nation.ʲ* ·And Isaiah is even bold enough to say: *I have let myself be found by those who did not seek me; I have let myself be seen by those who did not*
21 *consult me*; ·and referring to Israel, he says: *All day long I have been stretching out my hands to a disobedient and rebellious people.ᵏ*

The remnant of Israel

1 **11** What I am saying is this: is it possible ᵃ that *God abandoned his people?* Out of the question! I too am an Israelite, descended from Abraham, of
2 the tribe of Benjamin. ·God never abandoned his own people to whom, ages ago, he had given recognition. Do you not remember what scripture says about Elijah
3 and how he made a complaint to God against Israel: ·*Lord, they have put your prophets to the sword, torn down your altars. I am the only one left, and now they*
4 *want to kill me?* ·And what was the prophetic answer given? *I have spared* for
5 myself *seven thousand men that have not bent the knee to Baal.* ·In the same way,
6 then, in our own time, there is a remnant, set aside by grace. ·And since it is by grace, it cannot now be by good actions, or grace would not be grace at all!
7 What follows? Israel failed to find what it was seeking; only those who were
8 chosen found it and the rest had their minds hardened; ·just as it says in scripture: *God has infused them with a spirit of lethargy; until today they have not eyes to see*
9 *or ears to hear.* ·David too says: *May their own tableᵇ prove a trap for them,* a
10 pitfall and *a snare; let that be their retribution.* ·*May their eyes grow so dim they cannot see, and their backs be bent for ever.*

The Jews to be restored in the future

11 What I am saying is this: Was this stumbling to lead to their final downfall?ᶜ Out of the question! On the contrary, their failure has brought salvation for the
12 gentiles,ᵈ in order to stir them to envy. ·And if their fall has proved a great gain to the world, and their loss has proved a great gain to the gentiles—how much greater a gain will come when all is restored to them!
13 Let me say then to you gentilesᵉ that, as far as I am an apostle to the gentiles, I
14 take pride in this work of service; ·and I want it to be the means of rousing to envy
15 the people who are my own blood-relations and so of saving some of them. ·Since their rejection meant the reconciliation of the world, do you know what their re-acceptance will mean? Nothing less than life from the dead!ᶠ

The Jews are still the chosen people

16 When the first-fruits are made holy, so is the whole batch;ᵍ and if the root is holy,
17 so are the branches. ·Now suppose that some branches were broken off, and youʰ are wild olive, grafted amongⁱ the rest to share withʲ the others the rich sap of the
18 olive tree; ·then it is not for you to consider yourself superior to the other branches; and if you start feeling proud, think: it is not you that sustain the root, but the root
19 that sustains you. ·You will say, 'Branches were broken off on purpose for me to
20 be grafted in.' True; ·they through their unbelief were broken off, and you are
21 established through your faith. So it is not pride that you should have, but fear: ·if God did not spare the natural branches, he might not spare you either.ᵏ
22 Remember God's severity as well as his goodness: his severity to those who fell, and his goodness to you as long as you persevere in it; if not, you too will be cut

23 off. ·And they, if they do not persevere in their unbelief, will be grafted in; for it
24 is within the power of God to graft them back again. ·After all, if you, cut off
.from what was by nature a wild olive, could then be grafted unnaturally on to a
cultivated olive, how much easier will it be for them, the branches that naturally
belong there, to be grafted on to the olive tree which is their own.

The conversion of the Jews

25 I want you to be quite certain, brothers, of this mystery, to save you from
congratulating yourselves on your own good sense: part of Israel had its mind
26 hardened, but only until the gentiles have wholly come in; [^l] ·and this is how all
Israel will be saved. As scripture says: [^m]

> *From Zion will come the Redeemer,*
> *he will remove godlessness from Jacob.*
27   *And this will be my covenant with them,*
> *when I take their sins away.*

28 As regards the gospel, they are enemies, but for your sake; but as regards those
who are God's choice, [^n] they are still well loved for the sake of their ancestors.
29 There is no change of mind on God's part about the gifts he has made or of his
choice.
30   Just as you were in the past disobedient to God but now you have been shown
31 mercy, through their disobedience; ·so in the same way they are disobedient now,
32 so that through the mercy shown to you they too will receive mercy. ·God has
imprisoned all human beings in their own disobedience only to show mercy to
them all.

A hymn to God's mercy and wisdom

33 How rich and deep are the wisdom and the knowledge of God! We cannot reach
34 to the root of his decisions or his ways. ·*Who has ever known the mind of the*
35 *Lord? Who has ever been his adviser?* ·*Who has given anything to him, so that his*
36 *presents come only as a debt returned?* ·Everything there is comes from him and is
caused by him and exists for him. To him be glory for ever! Amen.

EXHORTATION

Spiritual worship [^a]

1   **12** I urge you, then, brothers, remembering the mercies of God, to offer your
bodies as a living sacrifice, dedicated and acceptable to God; that is the
2 kind of worship for you, as sensible people. [^b] ·Do not model your behaviour on
the contemporary world, but let the renewing of your minds transform you, so
that you may discern for yourselves what is the will of God—what is good and
acceptable and mature.

Humility and charity

3 And through the grace that I have been given, I say this to every one of you:
never pride yourself on being better than you really are, but think of yourself
dispassionately, recognising that God has given to each one his measure of faith. [^c]
4 Just as each of us has various parts in one body, and the parts do not all have the

5 same function: ·in the same way, all of us, though there are so many of us, make up one body in Christ, and as different parts we are all joined to one another. *d*

6 Then since the gifts that we have differ according to the grace that was given to each of us: if it is a gift of prophecy, we should prophesy as much as our faith *e* tells

7 us; ·if it is a gift of practical service, let us devote ourselves to serving; if it is

8 teaching, to teaching; if it is encouraging, to encouraging. When you give, you should give generously from the heart; if you are put in charge, you must be conscientious; if you do works of mercy, let it be because you enjoy doing them.

9, 10 Let love be without any pretence. Avoid what is evil; stick to what is good. ·In brotherly love let your feelings of deep affection for one another come to

11 expression and regard others as more important than yourself. *f* ·In the service of the Lord, work *g* not halfheartedly but with conscientiousness and an eager spirit.

12, 13 Be joyful in hope, persevere in hardship; keep praying regularly; ·share with any of God's holy people who are in need; look for opportunities to be hospitable.

Charity to everyone, including enemies *h*

14, 15 Bless your persecutors; never curse them, bless them. ·Rejoice with others when

16 they rejoice, and be sad with those in sorrow. ·Give the same consideration to all others alike. Pay no regard to social standing, but meet humble people on their

17 own terms. *Do not congratulate yourself on your own wisdom.* ·Never pay back

18 evil with evil, but *bear in mind the ideals that all regard with respect.* ·As much as is

19 possible, and to the utmost of your ability, be at peace with everyone. ·Never try to get revenge: leave that, my dear friends, to the Retribution. *i* As scripture says:

20 *Vengeance is mine—I will pay them back*, the Lord promises. ·And more: *If your enemy is hungry, give him something to eat; if thirsty, something to drink. By this,*

21 *you will be heaping red-hot coals on his head.* *j* ·Do not be mastered by evil, but master evil with good.

Submission to civil authority *a*

1 **13** Everyone is to obey the governing authorities, because there is no authority except from God and so whatever authorities exist have been appointed by

2 God. ·So anyone who disobeys an authority is rebelling against God's ordinance;

3 and rebels must expect to receive the condemnation they deserve. ·Magistrates bring fear not to those who do good, but to those who do evil. So if you want to

4 live with no fear of authority, live honestly and you will have its approval; ·it is there to serve God for you and for your good. But if you do what is wrong, then you may well be afraid; because it is not for nothing that the symbol of authority is the sword: it is there to serve God, too, as his avenger, to bring retribution to

5 wrongdoers. ·You must be obedient, therefore, not only because of this retri-

6 bution, but also for conscience's sake. ·And this is why you should pay taxes, too, because the authorities are all serving God as his agents, even while they are busily

7 occupied with that particular task. ·Pay to each one what is due to each: taxes to the one to whom tax is due, tolls to the one to whom tolls are due, respect to the one to whom respect is due, honour to the one to whom honour is due.

Love and Law

8 The only thing you should owe to anyone is love for one another, for to love the

9 other person is to fulfil the law. *b* ·All these: *You shall not commit adultery, You shall not kill, You shall not steal, c You shall not covet*, and all the other commandments that there are, are summed up in this single phrase: *You must*

10 *love your neighbour*[d] as yourself. ·Love can cause no harm to your neighbour, and so love is the fulfilment of the Law.

Children of the light

11 Besides, you know the time[e] has come; the moment is here for you to stop sleeping and wake up, because by now our salvation is nearer than when we first began to
12 believe. ·The night is nearly over, daylight is on the way; so let us throw off
13 everything that belongs to the darkness and equip ourselves for the light. ·Let us live decently, as in the light of day; with no orgies or drunkenness, no promiscuity
14 or licentiousness, and no wrangling or jealousy. ·Let your armour be the Lord Jesus Christ, and stop worrying about how your disordered natural inclinations may be fulfilled.

Charity towards the scrupulous

1,2 **14** Give a welcome to anyone whose faith is not strong,[a] but do not get into arguments about doubtful points. ·One person may have faith enough to
3 eat any kind of food; another, less strong, will eat only vegetables. ·Those who feel free to eat freely are not to condemn those who are unwilling to eat freely; nor must the person who does not eat freely pass judgement on the one who
4 does— because God has welcomed him. ·And who are you, to sit in judgement over somebody else's servant? Whether he deserves to be upheld or to fall is for his own master to decide; and he shall be upheld, for the Lord has power to uphold
5 him. ·One person thinks that some days are holier than others, and another thinks
6 them all equal. Let each of them be fully convinced in his own mind. ·The one who makes special observance of a particular day observes it in honour of the Lord. So the one who eats freely, eats in honour of the Lord, making his thanksgiving to God; and the one who does not, abstains from eating in honour of the Lord and
7 makes his thanksgiving to God. ·For none of us lives for himself and none of us
8 dies for himself; ·while we are alive, we are living for the Lord, and when we die,
9 we die for the Lord: and so, alive or dead, we belong to the Lord. ·It was for this purpose that Christ both died and came to life again: so that he might be Lord of
10 both the dead and the living. ·Why, then, does one of you make himself judge over his brother, and why does another among you despise his brother? All of us
11 will have to stand in front of the judgement-seat of God:[b] ·as scripture says: *By my own life* says the Lord, *every knee shall bow before me, every tongue shall give*
12 *glory to God.* ·It is to God, then, that each of us will have to give an account of himself.

13 Let us each stop passing judgement, therefore, on one another and decide instead that none of us will place obstacles in any brother's way, or anything that
14 can bring him down. ·I am sure, and quite convinced in the Lord Jesus, that no food is unclean in itself; it is only if someone classifies any kind of food as unclean,
15 then for him it is unclean. ·And indeed,[c] if through any kind of food you are causing offence to a brother, then you are no longer being guided by love. You are not to let the food that you eat cause the ruin of anyone for whom Christ died.
16,17 A privilege[d] of yours must not be allowed to give rise to harmful talk; ·for it is not eating and drinking that make the kingdom of God, but the saving justice, the
18 peace and the joy brought by the Holy Spirit. ·It is the person who serves Christ in
19 these things that will be approved by God and respected by everyone. ·So then, let us be always seeking the ways which lead to peace and the ways in which we
20 can support one another. ·Do not wreck God's work[e] for the sake of food.

Certainly all foods are clean; but all the same, any kind can be evil for someone to
21 whom it is an offence to eat it. *ʲ* ·It is best to abstain from eating any meat, or
drinking any wine, or from any other activity which might cause a brother to fall
away, or to be scandalised, or to weaken.
22 Within yourself, before God, hold on to what you already believe. *ᵏ* Blessed is
23 the person whose principles do not condemn his practice. ·But anyone who eats
with qualms of conscience is condemned, because this eating does not spring from
faith *ʰ*—and every action which does not spring from faith is sin.

1 **15** It is for us who are strong to bear with the susceptibilities of the weaker
2 ones, and not please ourselves. ·Each of us must consider his neighbour's
3 good, so that we support one another. ·Christ did not indulge his own feelings,
either; indeed, as scripture says: *The insults of those who insult you fall on me.*
4 And all these things which were written so long ago were written so that we,
learning perseverance and the encouragement which the scriptures give, should
5 have hope. ·Now the God of perseverance and encouragement give you all the
6 same purpose, *ᵉ* following the example of Christ Jesus, ·so that you may together
give glory to the God and Father of our Lord Jesus Christ with one heart.
7, 8 Accept one another, then, for the sake of God's glory, as Christ accepted you. ·I
tell you that Christ's work was to serve the circumcised, fulfilling the truthfulness
9 of God by carrying out the promises made to the fathers, ·and his work was also
for the gentiles, so that they should give glory to God for his faithful love *ᵇ*; as
scripture says: *For this I shall praise you among the nations and sing praise to your
10, 11 name.* And in another place it says: *Nations, rejoice, with his people,* ·and in
12 another place again: *Praise the Lord, all nations, extol him, all peoples.* ·And in
Isaiah, it says: *The root of Jesse will appear, he who rises up to rule the nations,
and in him the nations will put their hope.*
13 May the God of hope fill you with all joy and peace in your faith, so that in the
power of the Holy Spirit you may be rich in hope. *ᶜ*

EPILOGUE

Paul's ministry

14 My brothers, I am quite sure that you, in particular, are full of goodness, fully
15 instructed and capable of correcting each other. ·But I have special confidence in
writing on some points to you, to refresh your memories, *ᵈ* because of the grace
16 that was given to me by God. ·I was given grace to be a minister of Christ Jesus to
the gentiles, dedicated to offer *ᵉ* them the gospel of God, so that gentiles might
become an acceptable offering, sanctified by the Holy Spirit.
17, 18 So I can be proud, in Christ Jesus, of what I have done for God. ·Of course I
can dare to speak only of the things which Christ has done through me to win the
19 allegiance of the gentiles, using what I have said and done, ·by the power of signs
and wonders, by the power of the Spirit of God. In this way, from Jerusalem and
all round, even as far as Illyricum, *ᶠ* I have fully carried out the preaching of the
20 gospel of Christ; ·and what is more, it has been my rule to preach the gospel only
where the name of Christ has not already been heard for I do not build on another's
21 foundations; ·in accordance with scripture: *Those who have never been told about
him will see him, and those who have never heard about him will understand.*

Paul's plans

22, 23 That is why I have been so often prevented from coming to see you; ·now, however, as there is nothing more to keep me in these parts, *e* I hope, after longing
24 for many years past to visit you, to see you when I am on the way to Spain—·and after enjoying at least something of your company, to be sent on my way with
25 your support. ·But now I have undertaken to go to Jerusalem in the service of the
26 holy people of God there, ·since Macedonia and Achaia have chosen to make a generous contribution to the poor among God's holy people at Jerusalem.
27 Yes, they chose to; not that they did not owe it to them. For if the gentiles have been given a share in their spiritual possessions, then in return to give them help
28 with material possessions is repaying a debt to them. ·So when I have done this, and given this harvest into their possession, *h* I shall visit you on the way to Spain.
29 I am sure that, when I do come to you, I shall come with the fullest blessing of Christ.
30 Meanwhile I urge you, brothers, by our Lord Jesus Christ and by the love of the
31 Spirit, that in your prayers to God for me *i* you exert yourselves to help me; ·praying that I may escape the unbelievers in Judaea, and that the aid I am carrying to
32 Jerusalem will be acceptable to God's holy people. ·Then I shall come to you, if
33 God wills, for a happy time of relaxation in your company. ·The God of peace be with you all. Amen.

Greetings and good wishes

1 16 *a*I commend to you our sister Phoebe, *b* a deaconess of the church at
2   Cenchreae; ·give her, in the Lord, a welcome worthy of God's holy people and help her with whatever she needs from you—she herself has come to the help of many people, including myself.
3, 4 My greetings to Prisca and Aquila, my fellow-workers in Christ Jesus, ·who risked their own necks to save my life; *c* to them, thanks not only from me, but
5 from all the churches among the gentiles; ·and my greetings to the church at their house.
Greetings to my dear friend Epaenetus, the first of Asia's offerings to Christ. *d*
6, 7 Greetings to Mary, who worked so hard for you. ·Greetings to those outstanding apostles, Andronicus and Junias, my kinsmen and fellow-prisoners, *e* who were in
8, 9 Christ before me. ·Greetings to Ampliatus, my dear friend in the Lord. ·Greetings
10 to Urban, my fellow-worker in Christ, and to my dear friend Stachys. ·Greetings to Apelles, proved servant of Christ. Greetings to all the household of Aristobulus.
11 Greetings to my kinsman, Herodion, and greetings to those who belong to the
12 Lord in the household of Narcissus. ·Greetings to Tryphaena and Tryphosa who work hard in the Lord; greetings to my dear friend Persis, also a very hard worker
13 in the Lord. ·Greetings to Rufus, *f* chosen servant of the Lord, and to his mother—a
14 mother to me too. ·Greetings to Asyncritus, Phlegon, Hermes, Patrobas, Hermas,
15 and the brothers who are with them. ·Greetings to Philologus and Julia, Nereus
16 and his sister, and Olympas and all God's holy people who are with them. ·Greet each other with the holy kiss. All the churches of Christ send their greetings. *g*

A warning and first postscript

17 I urge you, brothers, be on your guard against the people who are out to stir up disagreements and bring up difficulties against the teaching which you learnt.
18 Avoid them. *h* ·People of that sort are servants not of our Lord Christ, but of their own greed; and with talk that sounds smooth and reasonable they deceive the

19 minds of the unwary. ·Your obedience has become known to everyone, and I am
   very pleased with you for it; but I should want you to be learned only in what is
20 good, and unsophisticated about all that is evil. ·The God of peace will soon crush
   Satan under your feet. The grace of our Lord Jesus Christ be with you. *i*

Last greetings and second postscript

21 Timothy, who is working with me, sends greetings to you, and so do my kinsmen
22 Lucius, Jason and Sosipater. ·I, Tertius, who am writing this letter, greet you in
23 the Lord. ·Greetings to you from Gaius, my host here, and host of the whole
   church. Erastus, the city treasurer, sends greetings to you, and our brother
   Quartus.

Doxology *j*

And now to him who can make you strong *k*
25 in accordance with the gospel that I preach
   and the proclamation of Jesus Christ,
   in accordance with that mystery *l*
   which for endless ages was kept secret
26 but now (as the prophets wrote) is revealed,
   as the eternal God commanded,
   to be made known to all the nations,
   so that they obey in faith:
27 to him, the only wise *m* God,
   give glory through Jesus Christ
   for ever and ever. Amen. *n*

NOTES TO ROMANS

1 a. Adopting the convention of his time Paul begins letters with an introductory paragraph (names of sender and receiver, good wishes) followed by thanks and a prayer. He colours this, however, in a unique way with a Christian spirit, and often includes theological ideas in it so as to anticipate the principal themes of each letter. In Rm these themes are: God's freedom to choose his people; the connection between faith and justification; salvation through Christ's death and resurrection; the harmony of the two Testaments.

b. 'apostle' corresponds to a Jewish title that means 'envoy', cf. Jn 13:16; 2 Co 8:23; Ph 2:25, sometimes used in the NT for the Twelve chosen by Christ, Mt 10:2; Ac 1:26; 2:37; etc.; 1 Co 15:7; Rv 21:14, to be his witnesses, Ac 1:8k, sometimes in a wider sense for those sent to preach the gospel, Rm 16:7; 1 Co 12:28; Ep 2:20; 3:5; 4:11. Though Paul was not a member of the Twelve, the fact that he had been appointed missionary to the gentiles by God, 11:13; Ac 26:17; 1 Co 9:2; Ga 2:8; 1 Tm 2:7, constitutes him an apostle of Christ, Rm 1:1; 1 Co 1:1; etc., equal to the Twelve, Ac 10:41, because like them he had seen the risen Christ, 1 Co 9:1, and been sent by him, Rm 1:5; Ga 1:16, to be his witness, Ac 26:16seq. In spite of being 'the least of the apostles', 1 Co 15:9, he is their equal, 1 Co 9:5; Ga 2:6–9, because it was not from them that he learnt the gospel that he preaches, Ga 1:1,17,19.

c. For Paul, Christ rose only because God raised him, 4:25; 10:9; Ac 2:24q; 1 Co 6:14; 15:15; 2 Co 4:14; cf. Ga 1:1; 1 Th 1:10; compare 1 P 1:21, thus displaying his 'power', Rm 6:4; 2 Co 13:4; Ep 1:19seq.; Col 2:12; Ph 3:10;

Heb 7:16; and because God raised him to life, Rm 8:11, Christ is established in glory as *Kyrios*, Ph 2:9–11,9f; Ac 2:36; Rm 14:9, deserving anew, this time in virtue of his messianic work, the name he had from eternity, 'Son of God', Ac 13:33, Heb 1:1–5; 5:5. See Rm 8:11g, 9:5d.

d. The obedience implicit in the virtue of faith, rather than the obedience owed to the gospel message. Cf. 6:16–17; 10:16; 15:18; 16:19,26; Ac 6:7; 2 Co 10:5–6; 2 Th 1:8; Heb 5:9; 11:8; 1 P 1:22.

e. lit. 'I offer worship in my spirit.' The apostolic ministry is an act of worship offered to God, see 15:16, like any Christian life in which the ruling motive is the love of others, 12:1; Ac 13:2; Ph 2:17r; 3:3; 4:18; 2 Tm 1:3; 4:6; Heb 9:14; 12:28; 13:15; 1 P 2:5.

f. By spirit (*pneuma*) Paul sometimes means the highest element in a human being, Rm 1:9; 8:16; 1 Co 2:11; 16:18; 2 Co 2:13; 7:13; Ga 6:18; Ph 4:23; Phm 25; 2 Tm 4:22; cf. Mt 5:3; 27:50; Mk 2:8; 8:12; Lk 1:47,80; 8:55; 23:46; Jn 4:23seq.; 11:33; 13:21; 19:30; Ac 7:59; 17:16; 18:25. He distinguishes it from the body (1 Co 5:3seq.; 7:34; cf. Rm 7:24; Jm 2:26) and from the *psyche* also (1 Th 5:23h; cf. Heb 4:12; Jude 19); it bears some relationship to *nous* (Rm 7:25; Ep 4:23). See *also* 'dispositions of the spirit' in 2 Co 12:18; Ga 6:1; Ph 1:27. It is contrasted with 'the flesh', which is human nature without the inspiration of the Spirit of God (1 Co 5:5; 2 Co 7:1; Col 2:5; *see* Mt 26:41par.; Rm 7:5; 1 P 4:6) and by choosing this traditional term (*see* Is 11:2c) instead of the *nous* of the Greek philosophers, the NT can suggest a deep affinity between the human spirit and the Spirit of God that stimulates and guides it, Ac 1:8j; Rm 5:5e. There are many texts where it is hard to tell whether it is the natural or supernatural spirit that is referred to, the personal or the indwelling spirit—*see* e.g. Rm 12:11; 2 Co 6:6; Ep 4:3,23; 6:18; Ph 3:3 var.; Col 1:8; Jude 19.

g. In contrast to 'barbarians', 'Greeks' means the inhabitants of the hellenic world (including the Romans, who had adopted the Greek culture); in contrast to 'Jews' it means the gentiles in general, 1:16; 2:9–10; 3:9; 10:12; 1 Co 1:22–24; etc.

h. Faith, which is the response of a human being to God as truth and goodness and so the one source of salvation, is reliance on the truth of God's promises and on God's faithfulness to them (3:3seq.; 1 Th 5:24; 2 Tm 2:13; Heb 10:23; 11:11) and on his power to implement them (Rm 4:17–21; Heb 11:19). After the long OT period of preparation (Heb 11) God has spoken through his Son (Heb 1:1). We must believe the Son (*see* Mt 8:10b; Jn 3:11seq., 11e) and the *kerygma* or proclamation (Rm 10:8–17; 1 Co 1:21; 15:11,14; *see* Ac 2:22n) of the gospel (Rm 1:16; 1 Co 15:1–2; Ep 1:13; Ph 1:27) made by the apostles (Rm 1:5; 1 Co 3:5; *see* Jn 17:20). The *kerygma* proclaims that God raised Jesus from the dead, made him *Kyrios* (4:24seq.; 10:9; Ac 17:31; 1 P 1:21; cf. 1 Co 15:14,17), and through him offers life to all who believe in him (Rm 6:8–11; 2 Co 4:13seq.; Ep 1:19seq.; Col 2:12; 1 Th 4:14). Faith in the name, or person, of Jesus (3:26; 10:13; cf. Jn 1:12; Ac 3:16; 1 Jn 3:23); who is the Messiah (Ga 2:16; cf. Ac 24:24; 1 Jn 5:1), the Lord (Rm 10:9; 1 Co 12:3; Ph 2:11; cf. Ac 16:31) and Son of God (Ga 2:20; cf. Jn 20:31; Ac 9:20; 1 Jn 5:5) is thus the necessary condition of salvation (Rm 10:9–13; 1 Co 1:21; Ga 3:22; *see* Is 7:9e; Jn 3:15–18; Ac 4:12; 16:31; Heb 11:6). Faith is not only intellectual assent, it is trust and obedience (6:17; 10:16; 16:26; cf. Ac 6:7) to the lifegiving truth (2 Th 2:12seq.). Faith which thus unites a person with Christ (2 Co 13:5; Ga 2:16,20; Ep 3:17) also confers the Spirit on him (Ga 3:2,5,14; cf. Jn 7:38seq.; Ac 11:17), the Spirit of the children of God (Ga 3:26; cf. Jn 1:12). Faith is reliance on God and not on self (3:27; Ep 2:9) and thus contrasts with the old order of the Law (Rm 7:7d) with its vain search (Rm 10:3–4; Ph 3:9) for holiness by works (Rm 3:20,28; 9:31seq.; Ga 2:16; 3:11seq.): only faith can effect true holiness, the saving holiness of God himself (Rm 1:17j; 3:21–26), received as a free gift from him (Rm 3:24; 4:16; 5:17; Ep 2:8; cf. Ac 15:11). Faith relates to the promise made to Abraham (4; Ga 3:6–18) and so makes salvation accessible to everyone, gentiles included (Rm 1:5,16; 3:29seq.; 9:30; 10:11seq.; 16:26; Ga 3:8). It is coupled with baptism (6:4a), calls for public profession (10:10; 1 Tm 6:12), and expresses itself in charity (Ga 5:6; *see* Jm 2:14f). Faith is unsupported by the senses or other proof (2 Co 5:7; Heb 11:1; cf. Jn 20:29), and involves hope as its concomitant (Rm 5:2c). It must be allowed to grow (2 Co 10:15; 1 Th 3:10; 2 Th 1:3) amid struggles and sufferings (Ep 6:16; Ph 1:29; 1 Th 3:2–8; 2 Th 1:4; Heb 12:2; 1 P 5:9), demanding fortitude (1 Co 16:13; Col 1:23; 2:5,7) and tenacity (2 Tm 4:7; cf. 1:14; 1 Tm 6:20) right up to the vision and possession of God (1 Co 13:12; cf. 1 Jn 3:2).

i. In the actual development of salvation-history the Jews come first, either for their glory or for their condemnation: 'salvation comes from the Jews' (Jn 4:22). *See* 2:9–10; Mt 10:5seq.; 15:24; Mk 7:27; Ac 13:5e.

j. Not 'distributive' justice, the recompense for actions, but the saving justice (cf. Is 56:1) of God, *see* Rm 3:26, which fulfils the promise of salvation by grace, Rm 4:25j.

k. Faith is the necessary and only condition of this revelation.

l. By way of antithesis, the subject of the gospel being the revelation of God's saving justice, 1:16–17 (resumed in 3:21seq.), is interrupted to consider what the human race is like before it hears the good news. In it both gentile, 1:18–32, and Jew, 2:1–3:20, are subject to God's 'retribution', which is first shown by the multiplication of sins and which will reach its climax in the Last Judgement, 2:6b; Mt 3:7h.

m. lit. 'anger'. In the OT, though the prophet or psalm-

ist may pray that 'God's anger' (Nb 11:1a) should be averted, it is recognised that it is provoked by sin, Ps 85:5–12; Mi 7:9. Here too (2:5–8; 4:15; 9:22h; Ep 5:6; Col 3:6; cf. Jn 3:36; 1 Th 2:16) but now there is deliverance from 'retribution' through faith in Christ which brings justification from sin, Rm 5:9, cf. 1 Th 1:10; 5:9.

n. To know there is one personal God means to know that one must pray to him and adore him.

o. The biblical formula 'God abandoned them', thrice repeated, emphasises that religious error brings in its train the worst moral and social disorders. Sin produces its own consequences and its own punishment; cf. Ws 11:15–16; 12:23–27; Is 64:6; Ezk 23:28–29. Though Paul judges and condemns gentile society he does not condemn individuals (whose intentions God alone must judge, 2:16; 1 Co 4:5; 5:12–13) since he presupposes, Rm 2, that there are gentiles who obey the natural law written in their hearts 2:14–15. But human beings must admit that they are sinners.

p. The Hebrew word *amen*, see Ps 41:13f, passed into Christian usage, 9:5; 11:36; 1 Co 14:16; Rv 1:6–7; 22:20–21. Used by Jesus for emphasis (translated as 'truly' or 'in truth'), the word is later given to him as a proper name (2 Co 1:20; Rv 3:14) because he is the true witness to God's promises.

q. Here, as he frequently does elsewhere, Paul uses lists of vices taken from current gentile and (even more so) Jewish literature: 13:13; 1 Co 5:10–11; 6:9–10; 2 Co 12:20; Ga 5:19–21; Ep 4:31; 5:3–5; Col 3:5–8; 1 Tm 1:9–10; 6:4; 2 Tm 3:2–5; Tt 3:3. (*See also* Mt 15:19par.; 1 P 4:3; Rv 21:8; 22:15.)

r. add. 'fornication'.

s. Others translate 'hateful to God', but cf. 5:10; 8:7.

t. add. 'loyalty', *see* 2 Tm 3:3.

u. The Latin text tradition reads 'They know that God is just, and yet they did not understand that those who behave like this deserve to die, and not only those who do this but those who encourage them.'

2 a. Here Paul turns to the Jews, vv. 1–16, not actually naming them until 2:17–3:20. He is aware, as he condemns others, that he is condemning himself if he behaves in the way they do, vv. 1–5; 17–24. Nothing can take the place of personal virtue: not the Law, vv. 12–16, not circumcision, vv. 25–29, not even the scriptures, 3:1–8. The Jew as well as the gentile will be individually judged by God, 2:6–11, since both are equally liable to sin, 3:9–20.

b. The prophecy of a 'Day of Yahweh' which will be a day of retribution and salvation, Am 5:18m, will be fulfilled eschatologically in the 'Day of the Lord', when Christ returns in glory, 1 Co 1:8e. On this 'Day of Judgement' (*see* Mt 10:15; 11:22,24; 12:36, 2 P 2:9; 3:7; 1 Jn 4:17) the dead will rise again, 1 Co 15:12–23,51seq.; 1 Th 4:13–18, and the whole human race will be judged in God's court, Rm 14:10, and in Christ's, 2 Co 5:10; cf. Mt 25:31seq. This trial is inescapable, 2:3; Ga 5:10; 1 Th 5:3, and impartial, Rm 2:11; Col 3:25; cf. 1 P 1:17; it is conducted by God, Rm 12:19; 14:10; 1 Co 4:5; cf. Mt 7:1par. Through Christ, v. 16; 2 Tm 4:1; cf. Jn 5:22; Ac 17:31, God will judge 'the living and the dead', 2 Tm 4:1; cf. Ac 10:42; 1 P 4:5. He examines the heart, Rm 2:16; 1 Co 4:5; cf. Rv 2:23, and his trial is by fire, 1 Co 3:13–15; he will treat all people according to their works, 1 Co 3:8; 2 Co 5:10; 11:15; Ep 6:8; cf. Mt 16:27; 1 P 1:17; Rv 2:23; 20:12; 22:12. What has been sown will be reaped, Ga 6:7–9; cf. Mt 13:39; Rv 14:15. Angrily he will destroy, 9:22, evil powers, 1 Co 15:24–26; 2 Th 2:8, and evil people, 2 Th 1:7–10; cf. Mt 13:41; Ep 5:6; 2 P 3:7; Rv 6:17; 11:18. But for the chosen, i.e. those who by grace have done good, there will be freedom, Ep 4:30; cf. Rm 8:23, rest, Ac 3:20; cf. 2 Th 1:7; Heb 4:5–11, reward, *see* Mt 5:12; Rv 11:18, salvation, 1 P 1:5, honour, 1 P 5:6, praise; 1 Co 4:5, and glory, Rm 8:18seq.; 1 Co 15:43; Col 3:4; cf. Mt 13:43.

c. i.e. guided by conscience, not by revealed law. As Jews are meant not to be saved by the Law but to be guided by it to salvation, so the natural law in his conscience can guide any human being.

d. Or 'both what will accuse them and what will excuse them'

e. Anacoluthon: v. 16 follows grammatically on v. 13. Alternative translation 'in the court where God judges . . .', cf. 1 Co 4:3.

3 a. There is one last resort for the Jews: if Israel is the people chosen by God to receive the promise, then how can they have strayed from the way to salvation? Later, ch. 9–11, Paul develops at great length the brief answer he gives here: however much human beings are unfaithful to the pact, this cannot abrogate God's promises; indeed the way human beings behave only makes the promises more remarkable, a fact, however, which does not protect the sinner from God's retribution (v. 6), or absolve his sin (v. 8). The dialogue used here seems as if it may echo some of Paul's debates in the synagogues.

b. The argument compares the group: faithfulness, truth (truthfulness), integrity, with its anti-group: faithlessness, falsehood, sinfulness.

c. var. 'in fact'.

d. By twisting Paul's words as in 5:20; Ga 3:22; cf. Rm 6:1,15.

e. Disputed translation; some prefer 'what excuse then can we offer?' or 'Are we worse off, then?'

f. 'Law' here means all the OT, cf. 1 Co 14:34; Jn 10:34; etc.

g. Since Ps 143 says that no human being would ever be forgiven if God judged everyone by their actions, there must be something else that will account for justification, and Paul finds this in God's promises to save his people: this is the 'saving justice of God' which was promised for the messianic era and which, as Paul says, v. 22, is manifest in Jesus Christ. The Law, which merely regulates behaviour, was meant by God not to eliminate sin but to make sinners aware of the fact, *see* Jn 1:16h; 7:7d.

h. 'Glory' in OT sense, Ex 24:16f, that is to say God as present to human beings and communicating himself to them more and more, a process that can reach its climax only in the messianic era, cf. Ps 84:9; Is 40:5.

i. This word (*charis*) when used with reference to human relationships can either mean the quality that makes a person attractive (Ac 2:47), or it can mean thanks for a gift (Lk 6:32–34; 17:9), or it can mean something given free and unearned (1 Co 16:3; 2 Co 8:6–7,19). This last sense predominates in the NT and especially in Paul (John uses *agape*) who uses the word to describe the way God saves through Jesus: it is a work of spontaneous love to which no one had any claim. It was an act of 'grace' for Jesus to come on earth (Jn 1:14,17; 2 Co 8:9; Tt 2:11) to die (Heb 2:9), for his Father to give him up as a gift to us, a gift that includes all divine favours (Rm 8:32; cf. 1 Co 2:12; Ep 1:6seq.): justification, salvation, and the right to inherit by having faith in him without having to perform the works of the Law (Rm 3:24; 4:4seq.; Ep 2:5,8; Tt 3:7; cf. Ac 15:11); it will also be an act of 'grace' for Christ to come again at the end of the world and for us to receive everlasting glory 2 Tm 1:12; 1 P 1:13. It was by grace that Abraham received the promise (4:16; Ga 3:18) and that a few Israelites were chosen to survive (Rm 11:5seq.). Since grace is God's love for us, it is inexhaustible (Ep 1:7; 2:7; cf. 2 Co 4:15; 9:8,14; 1 Tm 1:14) and it conquers sin (Rm 5:15,17,20–21). The one word 'grace' is so useful and full of meaning that it can be used to indicate the entire messianic era (Rm 5:21) that succeeds the era of the Law (6:14; Ga 2:21; 5:4), the same messianic era that was once proclaimed by the prophets (1 P 1:10) and is now proclaimed as the gospel (Col 1:6; compare Ac 14:3; 20:24,32). The word sums up the gifts of God so well that Paul begins and ends his letters by wishing 'grace' to all his readers (1 Th 1:1 and 5:28; etc.; *see also* 1 P 1:2; 5:10,12; 2 P 1:2; 3:18; 2 Jn 3; Rv 1:4; 22:21). It is by an act of grace that 'the God of all grace' (1 P 5:10) calls all people to salvation (Ga 1:6; 2 Tm 1:9; 1 P 3:7), loads them all with spiritual gifts (1 Co 1:4–7; *see* Ac 6:8; 2 Tm 2:16), makes Paul an apostle of the gentiles (Rm 1:5; 15:15seq.;

1 Co 3:10; Ga 1:15seq.; 2:7–9; Ep 3:1–2,7,8; Ph 1:7) and assigns to each Christian a part in the life of the Church (Rm 12:6; 1 Co 12:1a; 2 Co 8:1; Ep 4:7; 1 P 4:10); similarly, it is a 'grace' to suffer for Christ (Ph 1:29; 1 P 2:19–20). Mary 'found grace' with God (Lk 1:30; cf. Ac 7:46 and LXX *passim*); Jesus himself received the 'grace' of the highest name of all (Ph 2:9; cf. Lk 2:40). For human beings to be agreeable to God depends primarily on God's initiative and secondarily on human response. It is possible to receive grace in vain (2 Co 6:1) to fall from grace (Ga 5:4), to forfeit grace (Heb 12:15), and thus to insult the Spirit of grace (Heb 10:29). Grace obtained must be carefully guarded (5:2; Heb 12:28; 1 P 5:12) and used wisely (1 P 4:10); it is not enough to remain in grace (Ac 13:43; cf. 14:26; 15:40), it must increase (2 P 3:18), to strengthen us (2 Tm 2:1), and help us to persist in our good intentions (Heb 13:9). This divine help is given to the humble (Jm 4:6; 1 P 5:5) and is obtained by prayer, since this is to approach 'the throne of grace' confidently (Heb 4:16). Grace will be granted and will be found sufficient; it is the power of Christ operating in weak human beings (2 Co 12–9; cf. 1 Co 15:10), and this grace of Christ triumphs over unspiritual wisdom (2 Co 1:12). The same word *charis* is also used for thanksgiving (6:17; 7:25; 1 Co 10:30; 15:57; 2 Co 2:14; 8:16; 9:15; Col 3:16; 1 Tm 1:12; 2 Tm 1:3; and compare the verb *eucharistein*), since gratitude to God is the fundamental and necessary disposition for grace. From all these shades of meaning it is clear that the word *charis* is always used to emphasise that the gift is absolutely free; to bring out its power and its inwardness Paul also uses the word *pneuma* (*see* Rm 5:5e). *See* 1:h and the emphasis on holiness as something received as a free gift from God. *See also* p. 1857.

j. Yahweh had 'redeemed' Israel by delivering her from the slavery of Egypt, to provide himself with a nation for his 'inheritance', Dt 7:6b. When the prophets spoke of the 'redemption' from Babylon, Is 41:14g, they hinted at a deliverance more profound and less restricted, the forgiveness that is deliverance from sin, Is 44:22; cf. Ps 130:8. This messianic redemption is fulfilled in Christ, 1 Co 1:30; cf. Lk 1:68; 2:38. God the Father through Christ—and indeed Christ himself—has 'delivered' the new Israel from the slavery of the Law, Ga 3:13; 4:5; and of sin, Ep 1:7; Col 1:14; Heb 9:15, by 'acquiring' her, Ac 20:28, making her his own, Tt 2:14; purchasing her 1 Co 6:20; 7:23; cf. Ga 3:13; 4:5; cf. 2 P 2:1. The price was the blood of Christ, Ac 20:28; Ep 1:7; Heb 9:12; 1 P 1:18seq.; Rv 1:5; 5:9. This redemption, begun on Calvary and guaranteed by the present gift of the Spirit, Ep 1:14; 4:30, will be complete only at the *parousia*, Lk 21:28, when deliverance from death is secured by the resurrection of the body, Rm 8:23.

k. lit. 'whom God put forward as (or: destined to be) a propitiatory through faith by his blood'. For the 'propitiatory', or 'throne of mercy', *see* Ex 25:17h; and compare Heb 9:5. On the Day of Expiation, Lv 16:1a, this was sprinkled with blood, Lv 16:15. The blood of Christ has performed what the ancient ritual could only symbolise: purification from sin. Compare the blood of the covenant, Ex 24:8c; Mt 26:28h.

l. A quasi-forgiveness; God declined to attach guilt (a *paresis* or 'passing over'); such 'non-imputation' would be an idle procedure if positive forgiveness were not to follow, i.e. the utter destruction of sin by justification. Others translate 'with a view to the remission of sins'.

m. This 'present age' is in God's plan of salvation the 'time appointed'. Ac 1:7i, for Christ's redemptive work, Rm 5:6; 11:30; 1 Tm 2:6; Tt 1:3, which comes in the appointed time, Ga 4:4c, once for all, Heb 7:27g, and inaugurates the eschatological era. Cf. Mt 4:17 par.; 16:3 par.; Lk 4:13; 19:44; 21:8; Jn 7:6,8.

n. i.e. exercising his (saving, *see* 1:17j) justice, as he had promised, by justifying humanity.

o. The Gk word expresses the attitude of one who boasts of his own achievements, relies on them, and claims to accomplish his supernatural destiny by his own strength. This attitude is ruled out, since one does not win God's acquittal by superior strength, one receives it as a gift. The act of faith excludes self-sufficiency because in it human beings explicitly attest their radical insufficiency.

p. That is, the principle that consists in believing. Paul contrasts the Law engraved on stone, 2 Co 3:3, with faith, Rm 1:16h, an interior Law, written in human hearts, cf. Jr 31:33, which works through love, Ga 5:6, and is the 'law of the Spirit', Rm 8:2.

q. lit. 'we establish (the) Law': it is only by means of the regime of faith that the Law achieves what it was intended to do, viz: to make people holy, *see* 7:7d.

4 a. var. 'What then shall we say that Abraham has gained?'

b. The recurrence of the fatherhood-of-Abraham theme marks the stages in the argument, vv. 1,12,16–22.

c. Jewish tradition, preoccupied with Abraham's loyalty and his fortitude under trial, had made him the outstanding example of justification by works, 1 M 2:52; Ws 10:5; Si 44:20seq., and cf. especially the *Book of Jubilees*, 11–12; 16:19 seq.; *see also* Jm 2:21j, cf. Rm 2:14c. Paul, however, finds that this justification and these works have their source in Abraham's faith, Gn 12:1a and 15:6c. Cf. Heb 11:8seq.

d. The words themselves are capable of various interpretations: by reason of his faith Abraham was reckoned an upright man by God, though in fact he was not so; or, by reason of his faith Abraham had conferred upon him gratuitously by God an uprightness (or 'justice') that had not been his when he came to believe; or thirdly, in God's eyes (and hence in fact) faith and uprightness are so interdependent as to be inseparable. The first of these interpretations is, however, incompatible with Pauline teaching as a whole; so also, it would seem, is the second; the third is completely consistent with it.

e. This word, *sphragis*, (lit. 'seal' or 'impression of a seal') came very soon to be analogically used of baptism, the sacrament of Christian faith, 2 Co 1:22; Ep 1:13; 4:30; *see* Jn 6:27g; Rv 7:2–8; 9:4.

f. lit. 'the uprightness of faith', i.e. that uprightness which is precisely the act of believing with a living faith. The inheritance is conferred not to reward people for observing the clauses of a contract (a law), but to fulfil a promise. The promises, Gn 12:1a, having been offered to faith, the fulfilment of them can be known and welcomed only by faith in the person and work of Jesus Christ, 9:4–8; 15:8; Jn 8:56; Ac 2:39; 13:23; Ga 3:14–19; Ep 1:13,14; 2:12; 3:6; Heb 11:9–10,13. Compare 3:27.

g. As at the creation; the two striking reminders of God's power prepare the reader (or the hearer) for the reference to Christ's resurrection in v. 25.

h. *Text. rec.* 'His faith was not shaken, nor did he give a thought to his own body that was dead already.'

i. Faith is all-powerful, Mk 9:23. It allows God's power true play in us, *see* 2 Co 12:9–10.

j. Paul never thinks of the death of Jesus in isolation from his resurrection. 'Justification' is the entering into the life of the risen Christ, 6:4; 8:10. The God who in the OT gives saving justice by means of judgement, Ps 9:8, is in the NT expected to be the judge at the Last Day, Rm 2:6; his 'justification' (= acquittal) by Christ is conferred in consideration of faith only, Rm 1:17k, and not 'works' of the Law, Rm 3:27p; 7:7d.

5 a. The theme of the second section, ch. 5–11: for the Christian who has received justification, *see* ch. 1–4, God's love and the gift of the Spirit are a pledge of salvation. After the contrast of 5:12–7:25 this theme is resumed in ch. 8.

b. var. 'let us be at peace'.

c. For a Christian to hope is to be confident of receiving the eschatological gifts: the resurrection of the body, 8:18–23; 1 Th 4:13seq.; cf. Ac 2:26; 23:6; 24:15; 26:6–8, the rich inheritance of the saints, Ep 1:18; cf. 1 P 1:3seq., eternal life, Tt 1:2; cf. 1 Co 15:19, glory, Rm 5:2; in short, salvation, 1 Th 5:8; cf. 1 P 1:3–5, of self and neighbour,

2 Co 1:6seq.; 1 Th 2:19. Though it means primarily this virtue of expectation, 'hope' is used sometimes for the expected gifts themselves, Ga 5:5; Col 1:5; Tt 2:13; Heb 6:18. Of old, this hope was given to Israel, Ep 1:11–12; cf. Jn 5:45; Rm 4:18, and not to the gentiles, Ep 2:12; cf. 1 Th 4:13; but it was a step towards a higher hope, Heb 7:19, offered now to the gentile world also, Col 1:27; Ep 1:18; cf. Mt 12:21; Rm 15:12, through the 'mystery' of Christ, Rm 16:25l. The basis of this hope is God himself, 6:17; 1 P 1:21; 3:5, his love, 2 Th 2:16, his invitation, 1 P 1:13–15; cf. Ep 1:18; 4:4, his power, Rm 4:17–21, truthfulness, Tt 1:2; Heb 6:18, fidelity, Heb 10:23, in implementing the promises declared in the written word, Rm 15:4, and in the gospel message, Col 1:23, promises fulfilled in Christ's person, 1 Tm 1:1; 1 P 1:3,21. The hope is therefore not illusory, 5:5. Since the gifts it expects are in the future, 8:24; Heb 11:1, faith is its prop, Rm 4:18; 5:1seq.; 15:13; Ga 5:5; Heb 6:11seq.; 1 P 1:21; charity is its food, Rm 5:5; 1 Co 13:7; hope and faith and charity, the three theological virtues, are closely allied. Hope's superlative source is the Holy Spirit, cf. Ga 5:5, greatest of all the eschatological gifts and in part already conferred, Rm 5:5e; Ac 1:8j; this enlightens, Ep 1:17seq., and strengthens hope, Rm 15:13, and inspires its prayer, Rm 8:26–27, effecting the unity of the Body, for this hope is common, Ep 4:4. And because hope is built on justification through faith in Christ, 5:1seq.; cf. Ga 5:5, it is rich in confidence, 2 Co 3:12; Heb 3:6, consolation, 2 Th 2:16; Heb 6:18, joy, Rm 12:12; 15:13; 1 Th 2:19, and is a thing to be proud of, Rm 5:2; 1 Th 2:19; cf. Ga 5:5, that tests, Rm 5:4, and fortifies it, 2 Co 1:7.

d. God's love for us; of this the Holy Spirit is a pledge and to this, by his active presence within us, he bears witness: cf. 8:15 and Ga 4:6. In him, we speak to God as a child to his father; love is mutual. In him, too, our love for our brothers is the same love with which the Father loves the Son and loves us, *see* Jn 17:26; 1 Jn 4:7seq.

e. The promised Spirit, Ep 1:13, *see* Ac 2:33u; Ga 3:14, distinctive of the new covenant as contrasted with the old, Rm 2:29; 7:6; Ezk 36:27f; 2 Co 3:6; cf. Ga 3:3; 4:29; is not merely an exhibition of healing or charismatic power, Ac 1:8j; it is also, and especially, an inward principle of new life, a principle that God 'gives', 1 Th 4:8, etc., cf. Lk 11:13; Jn 3:34; 14:16seq.; Ac 1:5; 2:38; etc.; 1 Jn 3:24, 'sends', Ga 4:6; cf. Lk 24:49; Jn 14:26; 1 P 1:12, 'pours out', Rm 5:5; Tt 3:5seq.; cf. Ac 2:33. Received into the Christian by faith, Ga 3:2,14; cf. Jn 7:38seq.; Ac 11:17, and baptism, 1 Co 6:11; Tt 3:5; cf. Jn 3:5; Ac 2:38; 19:2–6, it dwells within the Christian, Rm 8:9; 1 Co 3:16; 2 Tm 1:14; cf. Jm 4:5, in the spirit, Rm 8:16; *see* Rm 1:9e, and even in the body, 1 Co 6:19. This Spirit, the Spirit of Christ, 8:9; Ga 4:6; Ph 1:19; cf. Jn 14:26; 15:26; 16:7,14; Ac 16:7; 2 Co 3:17, makes the Christian a child of God, Rm 8:14–16; Ga 4:6seq., and establishes Christ in the heart, Ep 3:16. For the Christian (as for Christ himself, 1:4c) this Spirit is a principle of resurrection, 8:11g, in virtue of an eschatological gift which even in life acts as with a seal, 2 Co 1:22; Ep 1:13; 4:30, and which is present by way of pledge, 2 Co 1:22; 5:5; Ep 1:14, and of first-fruits, Rm 8:23. It takes the place of the ungodly principle in human beings that is 'the flesh', 7:5c, and becomes a principle of supernatural knowledge, 1 Co 2:10–16; 7:40; 12:8seq.; 14:2seq.; Ep 1:17; 3:16,18; Col 1:9; *see* Jn 14:26r, of love, Rm 5:5; 15:30; Col 1:8, of sanctification, Rm 15:16; 1 Co 6:11; 2 Th 2:13; cf. 1 P 1:2, of moral conduct, Rm 8:4–9,13; Ga 5:16–25, of apostolic courage, Ph 1:19; 2 Tm 1:7seq.; *see* Ac 1:8j, of hope, Rm 15:13; Ga 5:5; Ep 4:4, of prayer, Rm 8:26seq.; cf. Jm 4:3,5; Jude 20. The Spirit must not be quenched, 1 Th 5:19, or grieved, Ep 4:30. It unites human beings with Christ, 1 Co 6:17, and thus secures the unity of his Body, 1 Co 12:13; Ep 2:16,18; 4:4.

f. Sin 'lives in' humanity, 7:14–24. Death, the reward of sin, came into the world as a result of Adam's disobedience, Ws 2:24: from this Paul concludes that sin itself entered into all humanity through that first fall. This is the doctrine of original sin and by introducing it here Paul is able to draw the contrast between the deadly work of the first Adam and the more than sufficient compensation of the 'second Adam', vv. 15–19; 1 Co 15:21seq.,25. It is as the new head of the human race, the image in which God remakes his creation, 8:29n; 2 Co 5:17n, that Christ is Saviour of humanity, see 1 Co 15:22m.

g. Sin makes a division from God. This separation is 'death', death spiritual and eternal; physical death is the symbol of it, see Ws 2:24; Heb 6:1b.

h. The exact meaning is a matter of debate. Perhaps 'everyone has sinned in Adam', i.e. by participation in Adam's sins, or perhaps the reference is to everyone sinning through their personal sins. In this instance, the Gk phrase would be best translated 'by the fact that everyone has sinned', referring to the actual situation by which eternal death has extended to everyone. In fact, in the case of adults (who alone are considered here) the power of sin which entered the world with Adam had its effects through personal sins which in some way ratify Adam's revolt. Alternative translation: 'because of which everyone has sinned'.

i. 'prefigured', see 1 Co 10:6d: the likeness, therefore, is not complete—hence the comparison, begun in v. 12 and interrupted by the long parenthesis of vv. 13 and 14, becomes a contrast in v. 15.

j. The word 'many' means all people, see v. 18; see Mt 20:28h.

k. Not only in the remote future of the Last Judgement (for Paul regards justification as a present condition, see 5:1; etc.) but progressively as each individual becomes reborn in Christ.

l. 'law' without the definite article, i.e. a state of things in which Law is the governing factor.

6 **a.** Baptism is not contrasted with faith but goes with it, Ga 3:26seq.; Heb 10:22, cf. Ac 8:12seq.,37; 16:31–33; 18:8; 19:2–5, and gives it outward expression for this reason Paul ascribes to faith and to baptism the same effects (cf. Rm 6:3–9 and Ga 2:16–20). The sinner is immersed in water (the etymological meaning of 'baptise' is 'dip') and thus 'buried' with Christ, Col 2:12, with whom also the Christian emerges to resurrection, Rm 8:11g, as a 'new creature', 2 Co 5:17n, a 'new person', Ep 2:15n, a member of the one Body animated by the one Spirit, 1 Co 12:13; Ep 4:4seq. This resurrection will not be complete or final until the end of time, 1 Co 15:12 (but see Ep 2:6e), but is already taking place in the form of a new life lived 'in the Spirit', Rm 8:2f,8–11,13; Ga 5:16–24. The death-resurrection symbolism of baptism is particularly Pauline, but this initial rite of the Christian life, Heb 6:2, is also spoken of in the NT as a cleansing bath, Ep 5:26; Heb 10:22; cf. 1 Co 6:11; Tt 3:5, a new birth, Jn 3:5; Tt 3:5; cf. 1 P 1:3; 2:2, an enlightenment, Heb 6:4; 10:32; cf. Ep 5:14. On baptism of water and baptism of the Spirit, cf. Ac 1:5f: these two aspects of the consecration of the Christian are seen as the 'anointing' and the 'seal' of 2 Co 1:21seq. According to 1 P 3:20–21 the ark of Noah is an antetype of baptism.

b. Possibly in the sense of no longer having the means to sin, having lost the 'sinful body', v. 6; being no more 'in the flesh', 8:9, and so freed from sin once and for all, cf. 1 P 4:1. Possibly in the sense that in law the death of the accused cancels legal proceedings. Cf. 7:1.

c. var. 'For'.

d. Christ was sinless, 2 Co 5:21, but having a physical body like our own, Rm 8:3, he belonged to the order of sin; when he became 'spiritual', 1 Co 15:45–46, he belonged only to the divine order. Similarly, the Christian, though remaining 'in the flesh' for a time, already lives by the Spirit.

e. Text. rec. 'Christ Jesus our Lord'. Cf. 14:7seq.; 1 Co 3:23h; 2 Co 5:15; Ga 2:20; 1 P 2:24.

f. Though baptism has destroyed human sin, as long as the body has not been 'clothed with immortality',

1 Co 15:54, sin may still find a way to reassert itself in a 'mortal' body, still open to the natural human inclination.

g. Christ has freed human beings from evil so as to restore them to God. Paul develops the biblical ideas of 'redemption', 3:24j, and of liberation from death, 7:1b, and in order to bring out their implications makes frequent use of a metaphor that his contemporaries would find impressive: the slave redeemed and set free who can be a slave no longer but must serve the new master freely and faithfully. Christ has paid for our redemption with his life, 1 Co 6:20; 7:23; Ga 3:13; 4:5; and he has made us permanently free, Ga 5:1,13. The Christian must be careful not to let himself be caught again by those who once owned him, Ga 2:4seq.; 4:9; 5:1, i.e. by sin, Rm 6:18–22; the Law, Rm 6:14; 8:2; Ga 3:13; 4:5; cf. Rm 7:1seq. with its ritual observance, Ga 2:4; the principles of the world, Ga 4:3,8, see also Col 2:20–22; and corruption, Rm 8:21–23. He is free, 1 Co 9:1, the child of a free mother, i.e. the spiritual Jerusalem, Ga 4:26,31. This liberty is not licence to sin, Ga 5:13; cf. 1 P 2:16; 2 P 2:19–21. It means serving a new master, God, 6:22; cf. 1 Th 1:9; 1 P 2:16, the Lord Christ, Rm 1:1; 14:8; 16:8; Jm 1:1; 2 P 1:1; Jude 1; etc., to whom the Christian now belongs, 1 Co 6:19; 3:23, for whom he lives and dies, Rm 7:1b; this obedient service is prompted by faith and leads to uprightness and holiness, Rm 6:16–19. This is the sort of freedom a son has, Ga 4:7, once he has been set free by 'the law of the Spirit', Rm 8:2; cf. 7:6; 8:14seq.; 2 Co 3:17 (and see Jm 1:25; 2:12), and he must be prepared to surrender it to serve his neighbour in charity, Ga 5:13; cf. 2 Co 4:5, respect for someone else's scruples may require it, Rm 14; 1 Co 10:23–33; cf. 1 Co 6:12–13; 1 Co 9:19. Slavery as a social institution may be tolerated in a society that is, after all, transient, 1 Co 7:20–24,31, it has no real significance in the new order established by Christ, 1 Co 12:13; Ga 3:28; Col 3:11, the Christian slave has been enfranchised by the Lord, Christ, and slave and master are equally servants of Christ, 1 Co 7:22; cf. Ep 6:5–9; Col 3:22–4:1; Phm 16.

h. The holiness proper to God, Lv 17:1a, which he communicated to his people, Ex 19:3c,6, is communicated to those who have faith in Christ, Ac 9:13g; Col 1:12c. If it was formal or ritual, it is no longer so; it is 'being made like Christ, the Holy One of God'. The Christian, sanctified because justified and, by belonging to the holy people, inhabited by the Holy Spirit, 5:5c, has still to live out this holiness in practice and progress in sanctification, v. 22; 1 Th 4:3–7,3c; 2 Th 2:13.

i. Or 'what did you get from actions that now you regret?'

7 **a.** Paul now approaches a subject which has been in his mind for some time, 3:20; 4:15; 5:20; 6:14: the emancipation of the Christian from the Law, and this leads him to explain the role of the Law as God intended it, see 7:d.

b. Elsewhere Paul refers to the liberation of the Christian either biblically as 'redemption', 3:24j or hellenistically as 'enfranchisement', 6:15g. He also describes it frequently as a deliverance through death, since death frees a person from the past with all its tyrannical demands, 6:7; 7:1–3. The Christian, in union with the dead and risen Christ, 8:11g, and by virtue of faith, 1:16h, and baptism, 6:4a, is now dead to sin, 6:2,11, cf. 1 P 4:1, to the Law, Rm 7:6; Ga 2:19l; to the principles of the world, Col 2:20, and so lives under the new order of grace and the Spirit, Rm 8:5–13. Like slaves emancipated and enslaved to a new master, 6:15g, Christians, risen in Christ, live no longer for themselves but for Christ and for God, 6:11–13; 14:7seq.; cf. 2 Co 5:15; Ga 2:20.

c. 1 The primary meaning of 'flesh' is the matter of which the body is made. 1 Co 15:39; cf. Lk 24:39; Rv 17:16; 19:18; it is the opposite of spirit, Rm 1:9e, it is the body with its senses, Col 2:1,5, and especially the medium of sexual union, 1 Co 6:16; 7:28; Ep 5:29,31; cf. Mt 19:5par.; Jn 1:13; Jude 7, by which people become parents and heirs, Rm 4:1; 9:3,5; 11:14; cf. Heb 12:9. Thus 'flesh', like basar in biblical usage, emphasises the weak and perishable side of human beings, 6:19; 2 Co 7:5; 12:7; Ga 4:13seq., cf. Mt 26:41par., and their insignificance in comparison with God, Rm 3:20 and Ga 2:16; 1 Co 1:29; cf. Mt 24:22par.; Lk 3:6; Jn 17:2; Ac 2:17; 1 P 1:24. So, in order to distinguish what belongs to human nature from what belongs to grace, the words 'according to the flesh' are used for the first. 1 Co 1:26; 2 Co 1:17; Ep 6:5; cf. Jn 8:15; Phm 16, 'flesh and blood', 1 Co 15:50; Ga 1:16; Ep 6:12; Heb 2:14; cf. Mt 16:17, and 'fleshly', 1 Co 3:1,3; 9:11; 2 Co 1:12; 10:4. 2 Since the sending of the Spirit is what gives this eschatological age its character, Paul can use the word 'flesh' to signify the old dispensation as opposed to the new, 9:8; Jn 3:6; 6:63; Ga 3:3; 6:12seq.; Ph 3:3seq.; Ep 2:11; cf. Heb 9:10,13, so also the phrase 'according to the flesh', 2 Co 11:18; Ga 4:23,29; cf. Rm 1:3seq.; 2 Co 5:16, and 'fleshly', Heb 7:16; but see 1 Co 10:3seq. 3 For Paul the 'flesh' is especially the sphere in which the passions and sin operate, 7:5,14,18,25; 13:14; 2 Co 7:1; Ga 5:13,19; Ep 2:3; Col 2:13,18,23; cf. 1 P 2:11; 2 P 2:10,18; 1 Jn 2:16; Jude 8,23, condemned to corruption, 1 Co 15:50; Ga 6:8; cf. Ac 2:26–27,31; Jm 5:3, and to death, Rm 8:6,13; 1 Co 5:5; 2 Co 4:11; see 1 P 4:6, so much so that 'flesh' becomes personified as a Power of evil hostile to God, Rm 8:7seq., and to the Spirit, Rm 8:4–9,12seq.; Ga 5:16seq. Christ has defeated this Power by assuming 'sinful flesh', 8:3; cf. Jn 1:14; 1 Tm 3:16; 1 Jn 4:2; 2 Jn 7, and putting it to death on the cross, Rm 8:3; Ep 2:14–16; Col 1:22; cf. Heb 5:7seq.; 10:20; 1 P 3:18; 4:1. Being united with him, Jn 6:51seq., Christians are no longer 'in the flesh', Rm 7:5; 8:9, since they have crucified the flesh, Ga 5:24; cf. 1 P 4:1, and cast it off by baptism, Col 2:11; more precisely, they are still 'in the flesh' as long as they remain in this world, Ph 1:22–24; cf. 1 P 4:2, but are not slaves to the flesh any more, 2 Co 10:3; they are its masters through their union with Christ by faith, Ga 2:20, and suffering, Col 1:24. In this theological note, for the sake of clarity, the term 'flesh' is used throughout; in the translation of the biblical text, however, a variety of terms has been used: 'body', 'human nature', 'human ideals', 'natural inclinations', 'physical descent', to render the various facets of this concept.

d. In itself the Law is holy and good since it expresses God's will, 7:12–25; 1 Tm 1:8; it is the glorious prerogative of Israel, Rm 9:4; but see 2:14seq. And yet it seems to have been a failure: in spite of the Law the Jews are sinners like everyone else, 2:21–27; Ga 6:13; Ep 2:3, and obedience to it even makes them so confident, Rm 2:17–20; 3:27; 4:2,4; 9:31seq.; Ph 3:9; Ep 2:8, that they are shut off by it from the grace of Christ, Ga 6:12; Ph 3:18; cf. Ac 15:1. In short, the Law is powerless to make anyone justified as upright, 3:20; Ga 3:11,21seq.; cf. Heb 7:19. Paul's argument, to which polemic lends a tone of paradox, is that this apparent failure of the Law is due to the nature of the Law itself and to the part it was meant to play in the history of salvation. The Law gives information—it does not give spiritual strength. No law, whether Mosaic or otherwise, not even the primordial command given to Adam, see vv. 9–11, can prevent sin, in fact law makes it worse: 1 Because though law is not the source of sin it becomes the instrument of sin by 'multiplying offences' 7:7seq. 2 Because by informing the mind it increases the fault, which becomes a conscious transgression, 4:15; 5:13. 3 Because the only remedy law can offer is punishment, 4:15, curse, Ga 3:10, condemnation, 2 Co 3:9, death, 2 Co 3:6; hence it can be called 'the law of sin and death', Rm 8:2; cf. Rm 7:13; 1 Co 15:56. Nevertheless God willed this defective system, though as a temporary period of schooling, Ga 3:24, to make people conscious of their sin, Rm 3:19seq.; 5:20; Ga 3:19, and to teach them to look for justification solely to the grace of God, Rm 11:32; Ga 3:22. Since this state of things is only provisional it has to give way before the fulfilment of the promise made, before the Law, to Abraham and his descendants, Ga 3:6–22; Rm 4. Christ has put an end to the Law, Ep 2:15; cf. Rm 10:4, by 'fulfilling', see Mt 3:15; 5:17, all in it that is of positive value, Rm 3:31; 9:31, notably by his death, the supreme expression of his love, Rm 5:8; 8:35,39; Ga 2:20; Ph 2:5–8; and also the satisfaction of the Law's demands over sinners, with whom

he was identifying himself, Rm 8:3c; Ga 3:13e; Col 2:14. He emancipates the sons from the guardianship of the tutor, Ga 3:25seq. With him, they are dead to the Law, 7:4–6; Ga 2:19; cf. Col 2:20, from which he has 'redeemed' them, Ga 3:13, to make them children by adoption, Ga 4:5. Through the promised Spirit, he gives to humanity thus renewed, Ep 2:15n, the inward strength to do all the good things prescribed by the Law, Rm 8:4seq. This order of grace, superseding that of the old Law, may still be termed a law in the sense of a rule, but it is 'the law of faith', 3:27, 'the law of Christ', Ga 6:2, 'the law of the Spirit', Rm 8:2, and love is its essential precept, Rm 13:8–10; Ga 5:14; cf. Jn 13:34; Jm 2:8, a sharing in the love of the Father and the Son, Rm 5:5d; Ga 4:6.

e. Paul speaks in the person of humanity before the Law was given, cf. 5:13.

f. Sin personified, cf. 5:12, here takes the place of the snake of Gn 3:1 and the Devil of Ws 2:24.

g. Paul now speaks in the person of humanity still under the empire of sin and not yet justified, whereas in ch. 8, he speaks in the name of the justified Christian with the gift of the Spirit who, nevertheless, is conscious of an inward struggle while on earth, Ga 5:17seq.

h. Paul is not denying personal responsibility for evil done, any more than for the good, in Ga 2:20.

i. lit. 'law', in the sense of regular experience.

j. This 'inmost self' is the reasoning part of human nature as opposed to the 'outer self', 2 Co 4:16[a], the perishable body. This distinction which has its origin in Greek thought is not the same as that between the 'old' and the 'new' self, Col 3:9–10e, which derives from Jewish eschatology. There are texts, however, where Paul speaks of the 'inmost self' in the Christian sense of the 'new self', 2 Co 4:16[b]; Ep 3:16.

k. var. 'reason's law' as in v. 23.

l. lit. 'from the body of this death'. Paul is concerned with the body and its component members, 12:4; 1 Co 12:12,14seq., that is to say with the human being actually existing, a sentient creature, 1 Co 5:3; 2 Co 10:10, with a sexual life, Rm 4:19; 1 Co 6:16; 7:4; Ep 5:28, because it is in the body that people live morally and religiously. The body, though tyrannised by the 'flesh', 7:5c, by sin, 1:24; 6:12c; 7:23; 8:13; 1 Co 6:18, by death, Rm 8:10, and therefore a 'body of flesh', Col 2:11; cf. a 'body of sin', Rm 6:6, and a 'body of death', 7:24, is not, however, doomed to perish, as Greek philosophy would have it, but, in accordance with the biblical tradition, 2 M 7:9c; Ezk 37:10d, destined to live, Rm 8:13; 2 Co 4:10, through resurrection, Rm 8:11g. The principle of this renewal is the Spirit, 5:5e, which takes the place of the psyche, 1 Co 15:44w, and transforms the body of the Christian into the likeness of the risen body of Christ, Ph 3:21. Until this ultimate deliverance takes place, 8:23, the body of the Christian, provisionally delivered from the 'flesh' by its union with Christ's death, 6:6; 8:3seq., is even now the home of the Holy Spirit, 1 Co 6:19, who produces in it a new life of uprightness and holiness, Rm 6:13,19; 12:1; 1 Co 7:34, which is praiseworthy, 2 Co 5:10, and gives glory to God, 1 Co 6:20; Ph 1:20.

m. The nous, human reason or mind, is a Greek idea very different from the pneuma or supernatural Spirit, 5:5e, and even from the spirit in the biblical sense of the higher self, 1:9e. It is the principle of understanding, 1 Co 14:14,15,19; Ph 4:7; 2 Tm 2:2; cf. Luke 24:45; Rv 13:18; 17:9, and of moral judgement, Rm 14:5; 1 Co 1:10. Usually it is reliable, 7:23,25, but at times it is perverted, 1:28; Ep 4:17–19; 1 Tm 6:5; 2 Tm 3:8; Tt 1:15, by the 'flesh', Col 2:18; see Rm 7:5c, and has to be renewed, Rm 12:2, within the human spirit by the Spirit of God, Ep 4:23seq.; cf. Col 3:10.

n. This sentence, which would come more naturally before v. 24, seems to have been added—perhaps by Paul himself.

8 a. var. 'me', 'us'.

b. Paul contrasts the order of sin and death with the new order of the Spirit. The word 'spirit' here means either the Holy Spirit in person (as it does more clearly in v. 9) or the human spirit made new by its presence, see 5:5e; 1:9f.

c. The Mosaic Law, imposed from without, could not be an inward principle of salvation, 7:7d. Christ alone, who by his death destroyed our unspiritual nature (lit. 'flesh') in his own person, could destroy sin whose domain the 'flesh' was.

d. lit. 'sending his Son in the likeness of sinful flesh, and in that flesh . . .'

e. These requirements of the Law, which can be satisfied only through faith and union with Christ, are summed up in the command of love, cf. 13:10; Ga 5:14, and already Mt 22:40. See 7:7d.

f. Because of sin, 5:12h, the body is doomed to physical death and is the instrument of spiritual death also; but the Spirit is Life, a power of resurrection; see following note.

g. The resurrection of Christians is intimately dependent on that of Christ, 6:5; 1 Co 6:14; 15:20seq.; 2 Co 4:14; 13:4; Col 1:18; 2:12seq.; 1 Th 4:14; 2 Tm 2:11. It is by the same power and the same gift of the Spirit, see Rm 1:4c, that the Father will raise them to life in their turn. This operation is already being prepared: a new life is making the Christians into sons (v. 14) in the likeness of the Son himself, 8:29n, and they are being incorporated into the risen Christ by faith, 1:16h, and baptism, 6:4a.

h. More than just an 'internal guide', the Spirit is the principle of a divine life in Christ, see 5:5e; Ga 5:20.

i. The prayer of Christ in Gethsemane, Mk 14:36.

j. The material world, created for humanity, shares its destiny. It was cursed for sin, Gn 3:17, and is consequently deformed, subject to 'frustration', v. 20, a moral condition resulting from sin, and 'corruption', v. 21, a physical condition. But like the human body, destined to be glorified, it too is to be redeemed, v. 21. For some of the Greek philosophers matter was evil and the spirit must be delivered from it; Christianity regards matter as itself enslaved and to be set free. In other texts also salvation is extended to creatures (especially angels) other than humanity, see Col 1:20; Rv 21:1–5. On the new creation see 2 Co 5:17h.

k. Probably humanity through sin. Alternatively God by way of punishment, or God as Creator.

l. Add. 'adoption as sons (and)' which would here have an eschatological sense, but cf. v. 15.

m. Paul insists on the necessity of constant prayer (12:12; Ep 6:18; Ph 4:6; Col 4:2; 1 Th 5:17; 1 Tm 2:8; 5:5; cf. 1 Co 7:5) taught by Jesus himself (Mt 6:5; 14:23f) and practised by the early Christians (Ac 2:42hh). Paul is always praying for the faithful (1:10; Ep 1:16; Ph 1:4; Col 1:3,9; 1 Th 1:2; 3:10; 2 Th 1:11; Phm 4) and asks them to do the same for him (Rm 15:30; 2 Co 1:11; Ep 6:19; Ph 1:19; Col 4:3; 1 Th 5:25; 2 Th 3:1; Phm 22; Heb 13:18), and for each other (2 Co 9:14; Ep 6:18; on prayer for sinners and the sick, see 1 Jn 5:16; Jm 5:13–16). These prayers must ask for growth in holiness but also for the removal of all external (1 Th 2:18 and 3:10) and internal (2 Co 12:8–9) obstacles to it; we have to pray, too, for the orderly conduct of the country's business (1 Tm 2:1–2). Paul lays special stress on prayers of thanksgiving (2 Co 1:11e; Ep 5:4; Ph 4:6; Col 2:7; 4:2; 1 Th 5:18; 1 Tm 2:1) for every gift of God (Ep 5:20; Col 3:17) and particularly for the food God gives us (Rm 14:6; 1 Co 10:31; 1 Tm 4:3–5); he begins all his own letters with a prayer of thanks (Rm 1:8. etc.) and he wants the spirit of thanksgiving to pervade all the Christians' dealings with each other (1 Co 14:17; 2 Co 1:11; 4:15; 9:11–12). In liturgical gatherings prayers of thanksgiving and praise must predominate (1 Co 11–14) and these sentiments must inspire the hymns that the Christians compose for these occasions (Ep 5:19; Col 3:16). It is the Holy Spirit who inspires the prayer of the Christian, and Paul prefers to emphasise this rather than repeat the traditional Wisdom themes, namely the necessary conditions for prayer and its efficacy (see Jm 1:5–8; 4:2–3; 5:16–18; 1 Jn 3:22; 5:14–16) which Paul guarantees by the presence of the Spirit of Christ within the Christian, enabling the Christian to pray as a child to a father (Rm 8:15,26–27; Ga 4:6; cf. Ep 6:18; Jude 20),

while Christ himself intercedes at the right hand of God (Rm 8:34; cf. Heb 7:25; 1 Jn 2:1). The Father's response is therefore most generous (Ep 3:20). Hence Christians are called 'those who invoke the name of Jesus Christ, 1 Co 1:2; cf. Rm 10:9–13; Ac 2:21m; 9:14,21; 22:16; 2 Tm 2:22; Jm 2:7. On the attitude to be adopted when praying, see 1 Co 11:14–16; 1 Tm 2:8.

n. Some interpretations make 'everything', or 'the Spirit' (following v. 27) the subject of the sentence: e.g., 'for those who love God, . . . everything turns to their good.'

o. Christ, the image of God in the primordial creation, Col 1:14d, cf. Heb 1:3, has now come, by a new creation, 2 Co 5:17n, to restore to fallen humanity the splendour of that image which has been darkened by sin, 5:12h; Gn 1:26m; 3:22–24. He does this by forming humanity in the still more splendid image of a child of God (8:29); thus, true moral judgement is restored to the 'new self', Col 3:10e, as is also the claim to glory which had been forfeited by sin, Rm 3:23h. This glory, which Christ as the image of God possesses by right, 2 Co 4:4, is progressively communicated to the Christians, 2 Co 3:18, until the Christian's body is itself clothed in the image of the 'heavenly' man, 1 Co 15:49.

p. Everything has been directed by God to the glory of his elect: it was for this they were called to faith and justified through baptism; with this, it can be said by anticipation, they are already clothed.

q. The 'principalities', like 'angels' and 'princes' are among the mysterious cosmic or elemental forces which to the mind of antiquity were in general hostile to humanity. see Ep 1:21; 3:18. The 'heights' and 'depths' represent Heaven and Hell, also conceived as powers.

9 a. To expound the theme of justification by faith, Paul founded his argument on the uprightness of Abraham, ch. 4. Similarly, the theme of salvation as the free gift of God through the Spirit demands that he consider the case of Israel, ch. 9–11, a people which has not responded with faith although it was given the promise of salvation. These chapters, then, explore not the predestination of the individual to glory, or even to faith, but the problem of Israel's part in the history of salvation—a problem raised by the statements in the OT.

b. lit. *anathema*, a thing accursed, under a curse of destruction, see Jos 6:17c and Lv 27:28e.

c. Actual descendants of Jacob (called 'Israel', Gn 32:29). All the other privileges derive from this: adoptive sonship, Ex 4:22; see Dt 7:6b; the glory of God, Ex 24:16f, who dwells with his people, Ex 25:8f; Dt 4:7b; see Jn 1:14m; the covenant with Abraham, Gn 15:1a; 15:17f; 17:1a, with Jacob-Israel, Gn 32:29, with Moses, Ex 24:7–8; the worship of one true God; the Law which embodies his will; the messianic promises, 2 S 7:1a, and physical relationship with Christ.

d. The context and the internal development of the sentence show that the doxology is addressed to Christ. Paul rarely gives Jesus the title 'God', though see Tt 2:11–14, or addresses a doxology to him, cf. Heb 13:21, but this is because he usually keeps this title for the Father, see Rm 15:6; etc., and considers the divine persons not so much with an abstract appreciation of their nature as with a concrete appreciation of their functions in the process of salvation. Moreover, he has always in mind the historical Christ in his concrete reality as God made man, see Ph 2:5d; Col 1:15d. For this reason he presents Christ as subordinated to the Father, 1 Co 3:23; 11:3, not only in the work of creation, 1 Co 8:6, but also in that of eschatological renewal, 1 Co 15:27seq.; cf. Rm 16:27; etc. Nevertheless, the title 'Lord', *Kyrios*, received by Christ at his resurrection, Ph 2:9–11; see Ep 1:20–22; Heb 1:3seq., is the title given by the LXX to Yahweh in the OT, Rm 10:9,13; 1 Co 2:16. For Paul, Jesus is essentially 'the Son of God', Rm 1:3–4,9; 5:10; 8:29; 1 Co 1:9; 15:28; 2 Co 1:19; Ga 1:16; 2:20; 4:4,6; Ep 4:13; 1 Th 1:10; see also Heb 4:14, his 'own Son', Rm 8:3,32, 'the Son of his love', Col 1:13, who belongs to the sphere of the divine by right, the sphere from which he came, 1 Co 15:47, being sent by God, Rm 8:3; Ga 4:4. The title 'Son of God' became his in a new way with the resurrection, Rm 1:4c; cf. Heb 1:5; 5:5, but it was not then that he received it since he pre-existed not only as prefigured in the OT, 1 Co 10:4, but ontologically, Ph 2:6; cf. 2 Co 8:9. He is the Wisdom, 1 Co 1:24,30, and the Image, 2 Co 4:4, by which and in which all things were created, Col 1:15–17; cf. Heb 1:2; 1 Co 8:6; and have been re-created, Rm 8:29; cf. Col 3:10; 1:18–20, because into his own person is gathered the fullness of the godhead and of the universe, Col 2:9e. In him God has devised the whole plan of salvation, Ep 1:3seq., and he, no less than the Father, as its accomplishment (cf. Rm 11:36; 1 Co 8:6 and Col 1:16,20). The Father raises to life and judges, so does the Son raise to life (see Rm 1:4c; 8:11g and Ph 3:21) and judge (cf. Rm 2:16 and 1 Co 4:5; Rm 14:10 and 2 Co 5:10). In short, he is one of the three persons enumerated in the trinitarian formulae, 2 Co 13:13e.

e. For example, Ishmaelites, and above all the Edomites, descendants of Esau, Gn 36:1, and in the later OT times the archetypal enemy of Israel, Dt 23:8; Ps 137:7d.

f. Like the OT writers Paul attributes to God as their ultimate cause (stressing the phrase of Ex: 'I raised you up') the good and bad actions of human beings, cf. 1:24seq.

g. If human perversity thus becomes part of God's design, how can anyone be accused of not doing the will of God? Paul replies, as before in a similar case (3:7; 6:1,15), by disallowing the objection. God being the absolute master of what he has made, the question of injustice cannot arise. Cf. Mt 20:15.

h. lit. 'But if', an obscure phrase here, to be interpreted by the context. Paul is explaining how the hardening of Pharaoh's heart then, and the unbelief of Israel now, are not acts of injustice if regarded as elements in the plan of God. God could destroy the Jewish people, as he could have destroyed Pharaoh, but he patiently tolerates them: thus (while allowing time to repent, 2:4) he 'shows his anger' (by permitting sins to multiply, see ch. 1–3, though even this paves the way to conversion); he 'displays his power' by brushing such obstacles aside, v. 17, as the present antagonism of the Jews towards the gospel; but above all he carries out his merciful plan for the gentiles, see 11:11–12, to whom the gospel is preached once the Jews have rejected it, see Ac 13:5e.

i. var. 'and he has disclosed'.

j. In the Greek, vv. 22–24, the sentence is left in the air. Supply 'How, if this supposition is correct, could we speak of injustice in God?' In the long run everything is directed to the salvation of both Jews and gentiles, see 11:32.

k. The failure of an Israel welcomed back by God despite its unfaithfulness thus becomes the antetype of the invitation to the gentiles, who had no claim, to the messianic feast.

l. The texts cited here proclaim both the infidelity of Israel and the return of a 'remnant', see Is 4:3c, in which the promises are safeguarded. They are thus a preparation for ch. 11.

m. One var. (Vulg.) makes the quotation follow the LXX text, which Paul abbreviates.

n. This conclusion introduces the argument of the following chapter where the cause of Israel's infidelity is examined not now as seen in God's plan but as seen in Israel's conduct.

o. Only the Christian can do this, 3:31; 8:4; 10:4; cf. 7:7d; Ac 13:39.

10 a. Like that of Paul before his conversion, Ac 22:3; Ga 1:14; Ph 3:6; cf. 1 Tm 1:13.

b. Uprightness is not something to be won: it is a favour received through faith in Christ, see 1:16h; 7:7d.

c. The argument is odd at first reading, because the passage of Dt is a eulogy of uprightness according to the Law. But Paul sees in this text, which sums up the whole Law in the precept of love and the 'circumcision of the heart', Dt 30:6,16,20, a presentiment of the new law, an equivalent to the gift of Law 'written on the heart', Jr 31:33.

d. Of the sea in Dt 30:13, of Sheol in Paul's applied sense. In connection with this text, already the Targum spoke of the descent of Moses from Sinai and the ascent of Jonah from the depths of the sea.

e. Profession of faith, such as is made at baptism, is the outward expression of the inward commitment of the 'heart'.

f. As in other places, Paul puts himself here into the position of a listener who makes qualifications or criticisms of his argument.

g. lit. 'How beautiful the feet of those who bring good news.'

h. var. 'word of God'.

i. Of those who preach the gospel.

j. This allusion to Israel's jealousy prepares the way for 11:11,14.

k. In the Hebr. both texts (vv. 20 and 21) refer to the Jewish people, but in the first of these the prophet speaks of Israel 'not invoking the name of Yahweh' and therefore no better than the gentiles. Paul's application of v. 20 to the gentiles (ethne) is the more easily made in that the Greek version uses ethnos ('nation') in Is 65:1, and not laos (i.e. Israel, the 'people' of God) as in Is 65:2.

11 a. This phrase, used in 10:18,19 to introduce a denunciation of Israel, now prefaces an announcement of its salvation (so also in v. 11); Israel, though unbelieving, 10:21, is still a chosen people, 11:2. The 'remnant', Is 4:3c, its temporary representative, is the pledge of future restoration.

b. This psalm quotation describes the punishment of those who, because they themselves were sated, had no compassion for the sufferings or thirst of the faithful. There may be a reference (as in the Targum) to sacrificial meals; if so, the prophecy is fulfilled to the letter: the Jews are incapable of acknowledging a suffering Messiah precisely because they are so attached to their formal worship.

c. lit. 'have they stumbled so as to fall (without hope of rising)?'

d. The present unbelief of the Jews is only a false step which God has permitted with a view to the conversion of the gentiles, 9:22; 11:12,19,25,30, and ultimately of the Jews themselves: for their own good God will make them 'envious', 10:19, of the gentiles.

e. i.e. the converts to Christianity from the gentiles. Thus even as apostle of the gentiles Paul is working for the salvation of his own people (lit. his 'flesh').

f. This sentence has been variously interpreted. The meaning seems to be that if a comparison may be drawn between the conversion of the gentiles and 'the reconciliation of the world' (the first stage in the redemptive plan), the conversion of Israel will be such a favour from God that it could be compared only with the final resurrection (the second stage). If this is true, Paul is thinking of the general resurrection at the end of time; but he does not say that this is to take place immediately after Israel's conversion. On the other hand some translate 'life from those who were dead'. To bring back someone from the dead is an extraordinary prodigy of which only the power of God is capable, see 4.17g; 2 Co 1:9. The return of Israel, the prodigal (and, in this case) the elder son, will be no less marvellous, compare Lk 15:24, 32.

g. The future conversion of Israel, vv. 11–15 and more explicitly vv. 25–26, will show that the faithful minority is a true 'remnant' and a reliable 'sign' that the nation will be restored. The unbelieving majority retains some measure of solidarity with the faithful minority and so must to some extent share its holiness, as the handful of dough offered as 'first-fruits' makes the whole baking holy (Nb 15:19–21).

h. The gentile who is now a Christian.

i. Or 'in place of'.

j. Add, 'the root and'.

k. lit. 'perhaps he will not spare you'; var. 'he will not spare you'.

l. Paul is still speaking of peoples, not of individuals: the Jews en masse, and the gentile world as a whole.

m. The OT prophesied that as a result of the Messiah's

coming Israel would be cleansed of all her sins. Paul teaches (calling it, lit., a 'mystery', v. 25) that this prophecy, partially fulfilled already in the conversion of the gentiles, implies the conversion of the Jewish people also.

n. A clear distinction between the two great stages in the history of salvation, traditionally known as 'Election' and 'Gospel'. In this time of the gospel the Jews rejecting Christ have become the enemies of God, and God has permitted this while the gentiles are converted, *see* 9:22h; 11:11c; but in the earlier times of the Fathers, the Jews were the only chosen people.

12 a. The Christian community has taken the place of the Temple in Jerusalem, Ps 2:6b; 40:8c, and the indwelling of the Spirit gives a new intensity to the presence of God among his holy people, 1 Co 3:16–17; 2 Co 6:16; Ep 2:20–22. This is also the inspiration of a new, spiritual cult, Rm 1:9f; 12:1, for believers are members of Christ, 1 Co 6:15–20, who has become, in his crucified and risen body, the dwelling-place of a new presence of God and a new cult, Mt 12:6–7; 26:61 par., 6a; 27:40 par.; Jn 2:19–22,21i; 4:20–21; Ac 6:13–14; 7:48; Heb 10:4–10a; Rv 21:22.

b. Or 'a spiritual kind'; the contrast is with the ritual sacrifices of Jews and gentiles, cf. Ho 6:6; compare Rm 1:9f.

c. 'Faith' is used here to mean the spiritual gifts bestowed by God on the members of the Christian community to ensure its life and growth.

d. The sentence emphasises not so much the identification of Christians with Christ, 1 Co 12:27 as their dependence on one another.

e. Another translation, less likely, is 'according to the rule of faith', that is, the common teaching of the Church, as in 1 Co 12:3, where the 'confession of faith' is the criterion of authentic gifts of the Spirit'.

f. Or 'outdo each other in mutual esteem'.

g. lit. 'Serve the Lord'; var. 'Be ready when opportunity arises' (lit. 'Serve the time').

h. The perspective now, particularly from v. 17 onwards, embraces all humanity.

i. Presumably the indignation of God waiting to punish sin.

j. The Christian takes vengeance on an enemy by doing good. The image of red-hot coals, symbol of burning pain, stands for the remorse which will bring the sinner to repentance.

13 a. Paul here enunciates the principle that all lawful authority derives from God. The Christian religion is not in opposition to civil life, 13:1–7, and the Christian is not absolved from the duties and obligations of a citizen. This principle is still maintained even after the first persecutions, Tt 3:1; 1 Tm 2:1,2.

b. Probably law in general rather than the Law of Moses.

c. Add. 'you shall not bear false witness'.

d. In Lv the 'neighbour' was a fellow countryman, here it is any member of the human family which is made one in Christ, Mt 25:40; Ga 3:28.

e. The thought is a fundamental one in Paul's moral teaching. The 'time' (*kairos*) is the eschatological era or 'Last Days', introduced by Christ's death and resurrection and co-extensive with the age of the Church on earth, the age of salvation, 2 Co 6:2a. It is opposed to the era that preceded it by a difference not so much of time as of nature. The Christian, henceforward a 'child of the day', emancipated from the wicked world, Ga 1:4, and from the empire of darkness, belongs to the kingdom of God and of his Son, Col 1:13, is already a citizen of heaven, Ph 3:20. This entirely new status dominates the whole moral outlook, *see* 6:3seq.

14 a. Christians not yet securely grounded in the faith and therefore without the firm convictions that would give them a sure conscience, vv. 2,5,22. These considered themselves bound to observe certain days, v. 5, and to abstain from meat or from wine, vv. 2,21, perhaps as a permanent obligation,

v. 21. Such ascetical practices were familiar to the gentile world (the Pythagoreans) and the Jewish (the Essenes, John the Baptist). Paul lays down the same general rule as in the similar case of 1 Co 8; 10:14–33: each must act 'for the Lord' as conscience dictates, vv. 5–6, provided it is not a doubtful conscience, v. 23; but above all, charity must govern the conduct of those 'strong' in the faith, vv. 1,15,19–21 and 15:1–13.

b. Who alone knows the secrets of the heart, cf. 2:16; 1 Co 4:3seq.

c. 'And indeed'; var. 'But' or 'Now'.

d. Probably the privilege of Christian liberty of which the 'strong' make use but which may be brought into disrepute, *see* 3:8d.

e. Refers to the weaker brothers, v. 15, or the Christian community, cf. 1 Co 3:9.

f. lit. 'by eating it with a cause of stumbling' *see* v. 13; that is, according to the context (v. 21 deals with the duties of the 'strong'), while giving 'scandal'.

g. var. 'Have you a belief? Hold on to it.' Because such faith is correct it has genuine value before God; but love may be an even higher principle.

h. Here in the sense of right conscience, *see* 14:1a. Other translations 'since he does not act from conviction', or, 'since his action is not prompted by a conviction of faith'.

15 a. i.e. to be thoughtful for one another. Others interpret 'to live in good understanding of one another', 'to live in agreement with one another'.

b. Christ welcomed the gentiles and thus gave glory to God. But by confining his work while on earth to the evangelisation of Israel, cf. Mt 15:24, Christ gave evidence of God's loyalty to his promise, the converted gentiles being living evidence rather of God's mercy. Let these in their turn be merciful to their brothers in the faith, *see* 12:1.

c. This blessing recalls in summary the main themes of Paul's teaching in this letter.

d. Towards the end of this letter, Paul once again gives his claim to write to a church which he has not founded, compare 1:13.

e. The apostolate, even more than the ordinary Christian life, 12:1; cf. Ph 2:17, is a liturgical function, *see* 1:9, the apostle—or rather, through him, Christ, v. 18—makes an offering of the whole human race to God.

f. The two extremes of Paul's missionary journeys at the time of writing; whether he had actually been to Illyricum is disputed.

g. Not that all the gentiles there have been converted, but that Paul's task is to lay foundations; he leaves his disciples to build on them, *see* 1 Co 3:6,10; Col 1:7; etc.

h. lit. 'sealed'.

i. Paul often asks his communities to pray for him, *see* 8:27m. On prayer conceived as a struggle with God, see the examples of Abraham, Gn 18:17seq., Jacob, Gn 32:29, Moses, Ex 32:11–14,30–32; Dt 9:18,25, and the gospel, Mk 7:24–30; Lk 11:1–8.

16 a. This chapter may not have formed part of the original epistle, *see* p. 291.

b. Probably the bearer of the letter.

c. Presumably in Ephesus, either at the time of the riot described in Ac 19:23seq., or during Paul's imprisonment there (*see* v. 7); *see* p. 291.

d. lit. 'the first-fruits of Asia for Christ'. This probably means the first convert in the province of Asia.

e. Paul had been imprisoned several times already, *see* 2 Co 11:23. Andronicus and Junias (var. Julias) are apostles in the wide sense, Rm 1:1b.

f. Possibly the son of Simon of Cyrene, Mk 15:21.

g. This form of greeting, not found elsewhere in Paul's letters, shows special respect for the church in Rome.

h. The curt warning is reminiscent of Ga 6:12–17. It probably refers to judaising preachers, cf. Ga 5:7–12 and particularly Ph 3:18–19.

i. Omit v. 24 'The grace . . .' This formula (add. 'all') is placed by some authorities (Vulg.) after v. 23 or v. 27.

j. Most authorities place this doxology here, but in some it appears at the end of ch. 15 or 14; others omit. A solemn presentation, cf. Ep 3:20; Jude 24–25, of the main points of the letter.

k. Firmly grounded in doctrine and strong in Christian practice cf. 1:11; 1 Co 1:8; 2 Co 1:21; Col 2:7; 1 Th 3:2,13; 2 Th 2:17; 3:3.

l. The idea of a 'mystery' of wisdom, v. 27; 1 Co 2:7; Ep 3:9; Col 2:2–3, long hidden in God and now revealed, Rm.16:25–26; 1 Co 2:7,10; Ep 3:5,9seq.; Col 1:26, is borrowed by Paul from Jewish apocalyptic, Dn 2:18–19,18e, but he enriches the content of the term by applying it to the climax of the history of salvation: the saving cross of Christ, 1 Co 2:8; the call of the gentiles, Rm 11:25;16:26;

Col 1:26–27; Ep 3:6, to this salvation preached by Paul, Rm.16:25; Col 1:23; 4:3; Ep 3:3–12; 6:19, and finally the restoration of all things in Christ as their one head, Ep 1:9–10. *See also* Mt 13:11par.; 1 Co 4:1; 13:2; 14:2; 15:51; Ep 5:32; 2 Th 2:7; 1 Tm 3:9,16; 2 Tm 1:9–10; Rv 1:20; 10:7; 17:5–7.

m. Cf. 11:33–36; 1 Co 1:24; 2:7; Ep 3:10; Col 2:3; Rv 7:12.

n. The NT adopts the blessings and doxologies of Israel, Gn 14:19h; Ps 41:13f; but often calls God Father and associates Jesus Christ with him, 9:5; 11:35–36; 1 Co 8:6; cf. Ga 1:5; Ep 3:21; Ph 4:20; 1 Tm 1:17; 6:16; 2 Tm 4:18; Heb 13:21; 1 P 4:11; 2 P 3:18; Jude 25; Rv 1:6k. Later doxologies commonly name all three 'Persons', *see* 2 Co 13:13e.

1 CORINTHIANS

THE FIRST LETTER OF PAUL
TO THE CHURCH AT CORINTH

INTRODUCTION

Address and greetings. Thanksgiving

1 1 Paul, called by the will of God to be an apostle of Christ Jesus, and Sosthenes,
2 our brother, ·to the church of God *a* in Corinth, to those who have been
consecrated in Christ Jesus and called to be God's holy people, with all those
everywhere who call on the name of our Lord Jesus Christ, their Lord as well as
3 ours. *b* ·Grace to you and peace from God our Father and the Lord Jesus Christ.
4 I am continually thanking God about you, for the grace of God which you have
5 been given in Christ Jesus; ·in him you have been richly endowed in every kind of
6, 7 utterance and knowledge; ·so firmly has witness to Christ taken root in you. ·And
so you are not lacking in any gift as you wait for our Lord Jesus Christ to be
8 revealed; *c* ·he will continue to give you strength till the very end, so that you will
9 be irreproachable *d* on the Day *e* of our Lord Jesus Christ. ·You can rely on God,
who has called you to be partners *f* with his Son Jesus Christ our Lord. *g*

I: DIVISIONS AND SCANDALS

A: FACTIONS IN THE CORINTHIAN CHURCH

Dissensions among the faithful

10 Brothers, I urge you, in the name of our Lord Jesus Christ, not to have factions
among yourselves but all to be in agreement in what you profess; so that you are
11 perfectly united in your beliefs and judgements. ·From what Chloe's people *h* have
been telling me about you, brothers, it is clear that there are serious differences
12 among you. ·What I mean is this: every one of you is declaring, 'I belong to Paul,'
13 or 'I belong to Apollos,' or 'I belong to Cephas,' *i* or 'I belong to Christ.' *j* ·Has
Christ been split up? Was it Paul that was crucified for you, or was it in Paul's
14 name that you were baptised? ·I am thankful I did not baptise any of you, except
15 Crispus and Gaius, ·so that no one can say that you were baptised in my name.
16 Yes, I did baptise the family of Stephanas, too; *k* but besides these I do not think I
baptised anyone.

The true wisdom and the false

17 After all, Christ sent me not to baptise, but to preach the gospel; and not by means of wisdom of language, *l* wise words which would make the cross of Christ
18 pointless. *m* ·The message of the cross is folly for those who are on the way to ruin,
19 but for those of us who are on the road to salvation it is the power of God. ·As scripture says: *I am going to destroy the wisdom of the wise and bring to nothing*
20 *the understanding of any who understand.* *n* ·*Where are the philosophers? Where are the experts?* And where are the debaters of this age? Do you not see how God
21 has shown up human wisdom *o* as folly? ·Since in the wisdom of God the world was unable to recognise God through wisdom, *p* it was God's own pleasure to save
22 believers through the folly of the gospel. ·While the Jews demand miracles and
23 the Greeks look for wisdom, *q* ·we are preaching a crucified Christ: to the Jews an
24 obstacle they cannot get over, to the gentiles foolishness, *r* ·but to those who have been called, whether they are Jews or Greeks, a Christ who is both the power of
25 God and the wisdom of God. ·God's folly is wiser than human wisdom, and God's
26 weakness is stronger than human strength. *s* ·Consider, brothers, how you were called; not many of you are wise by human standards, *t* not many influential, not
27 many from noble families. ·No, God chose those who by human standards are fools to shame the wise; he chose those who by human standards are weak to shame
28 the strong, ·those who by human standards are common and contemptible—indeed those who count for nothing—to reduce to nothing all those that do count for
29, 30 something, ·so that no human being might feel boastful before God. ·It is by him that you exist *u* in Christ Jesus, who for us was made wisdom from God, *v* and
31 saving justice and holiness and redemption. *w* ·As scripture says: *If anyone wants to boast, let him boast of the Lord.*

1 **2** Now when I came to you, brothers, I did not come with any brilliance of
2 oratory or wise argument to announce to you the mystery of God. *a* ·I was resolved that the only knowledge I would have while I was with you was knowledge
3 of Jesus, and of him as the crucified Christ. ·I came among you in weakness, in
4 fear and great trembling *b* ·and what I spoke and proclaimed was not meant to convince by philosophical argument, but to demonstrate the convincing power of
5 the Spirit, *c* ·so that your faith should depend not on human wisdom but on the power of God. *d*
6 But still, to those who have reached maturity, *e* we do talk of a wisdom, not, it is true, a philosophy of this age or of the rulers of this age, *f* who will not last long
7 now. ·It is of the mysterious wisdom *g* of God that we talk, the wisdom that was
8 hidden, which God predestined to be for our glory before the ages began. ·None of the rulers of the age recognised it; for if they had recognised it, they would not
9 have crucified the Lord of glory; *h* ·but it is as scripture says: *i* *What no eye has seen and no ear has heard, what the mind of man cannot visualise; all that God has*
10 *prepared for those who love him,* ·to us, though, God has given revelation through the Spirit, for the Spirit explores the depths of everything, even the depths of
11 God. ·After all, is there anyone who knows the qualities of anyone except his own spirit, within him; and in the same way, nobody knows the qualities of God except
12 the Spirit of God. ·Now, the Spirit we have received is not the spirit of the world but God's own Spirit, so that we may understand the lavish gifts God has given us.
13 And these are what we speak of, not in the terms learnt from human philosophy, but in terms learnt from the Spirit, fitting spiritual language to spiritual things. *j*
14 The natural person *k* has no room for the gifts of God's Spirit; to him they are

folly; he cannot recognise them, because their value can be assessed only in the
15 Spirit. ·The spiritual person, on the other hand, can assess the value of everything,
16 and his own value cannot be assessed by anybody else.¹ ·For: *who has ever known*
the mind of the Lord? Who has ever been his adviser? But we are those who have
the mind of Christ.

1 **3** And so, brothers, I was not able to talk to you as spiritual people; I had to talk
to you as people still living by your natural inclinations,ᵃ still infants in Christ;
2 I fed you with milk and not solid food, for you were not yet able to take it—and
3 even now, you are still not able to, ·for you are still living by your natural
inclinations. As long as there are jealousy and rivalryᵇ among you, that surely
means that you are still living by your natural inclinations and by merely human
4 principles ·While there is one that says, 'I belong to Paul' and another that says, 'I
belong to Apollos' are you not being only too human?

The place of the Christian preacher

5 For what is Apollos and what is Paul? The servants through whom you came to
6 believe, and each has only what the Lord has given him. ·I did the planting,
7 Apollos did the watering, but God gave growth. ·In this, neither the planter nor
8 the waterer counts for anything; only God, who gives growth. ·It is all one who
does the planting and who does the watering, and each will have the proper pay
9 for the work that he has done. ·After all, we do share in God's work;ᶜ you are
God's farm, God's building.

10 By the grace of God which was given to me, I laid the foundations like a trained
master-builder, and someone else is building on them. Now each one must be
11 careful how he does the building. ·For nobody can lay down any other foundation
12 than the one which is there already, namely Jesus Christ. ·On this foundation,
13 different people may build in gold, silver, jewels, wood, hay or straw ·but each
person's handiwork will be shown for what it is. The Day which dawns in fire will
14 make it clear and the fire itself will test the quality of each person's work. ·The
15 one whose work stands up to it will be given his wages; ·the one whose work is
burnt down will suffer the loss of it, though he himself will be saved; he will be
saved as someone might expect to be saved from a fire.ᵈ

16 Do you not realise that you are a templeᵉ of God with the Spirit of God living in
17 you? ·If anybody should destroy the temple of God, God will destroy that person,ᶠ
because God's temple is holy;ᵍ and you are that temple.

Conclusions

18 There is no room for self-delusion. Any one of you who thinks he is wise by
19 worldly standards must learn to be a fool in order to be really wise. ·For the
wisdom of the world is folly to God. As scripture says: *He traps the crafty in the*
20 *snare of their own cunning* ·and again: *The Lord knows the plans of the wise and*
21 *how insipid they are.* ·So there is to be no boasting about human beings: everything
22 belongs to you, ·whether it is Paul, or Apollos, or Cephas, the world, life or death,
23 the present or the future—all belong to you; ·but you belong to Christ and Christ
belongs to God.ʰ

1 **4** People should think of us as Christ's servants, stewards entrusted with the
2 mysteries of God. ·In such a matter, what is expected of stewards is that each
3 one should be found trustworthy. ·It is of no importance to me how you or any
4 other human courtᵃ may judge me: I will not even be the judge of my own self. ·It
is true that my conscience does not reproach me,ᵇ but that is not enough to justify

5 me: it is the Lord who is my judge. ·For that reason, do not judge anything before the due time, until the Lord comes; he will bring to light everything that is hidden in darkness and reveal the designs of all hearts. Then everyone will receive from God the appropriate commendation.

6 I have applied all this to myself and Apollos for your sakes, so that you can learn how the saying, 'Nothing beyond what is written' *c* is true of us: no individual among you must become filled with his own importance and make comparisons,

7 to another's detriment. ·Who made you so important? What have you got that was not given to you? And if it was given to you, why are you boasting as though it

8 were your own? ·You already have everything—you are rich already—you have come into your kingdom, *d* without any help from us! Well, I wish you were kings

9 and we could be kings with you! ·For it seems to me that God has put us apostles on show right at the end, like men condemned to death: we have been exhibited

10 as a spectacle *e* to the whole universe, both angelic and human. ·Here we are, fools for Christ's sake, while you are the clever ones in Christ; we are weak, while you

11 are strong; you are honoured, while we are disgraced. *f* ·To this day, we go short

12 of food and drink and clothes, we are beaten up and we have no homes; ·we earn our living by labouring with our own hands; when we are cursed, we answer with a

13 blessing; when we are hounded, we endure it passively; ·when we are insulted, we give a courteous answer. We are treated even now as the dregs of the world, the very lowest scum. *g*

An appeal

14 I am writing all this not to make you ashamed but simply to remind you, as my

15 dear children; ·for even though you might have ten thousand slaves to look after you *h* in Christ, you still have no more than one father, and it was I who fathered

16 you in Christ Jesus, *i* by the gospel. ·That is why I urge you to take me as your

17 pattern ·and why I have sent you Timothy, a dear and faithful son to me in the Lord, who will remind you of my principles of conduct *j* in Christ, as I teach them everywhere in every church.

18 On the assumption that I was not coming to you, some of you have become

19 filled with your own self-importance; ·but I shall be coming to you soon, the Lord willing, and then I shall find out not what these self-important people say, but

20 what power they have. *k* ·For the kingdom of God consists not in spoken words

21 but in power. ·What do you want then? Am I to come to you with a stick in my hand or in love, and with a spirit of gentleness?

B: INCEST IN CORINTH

1 **5** It is widely reported that there is sexual immorality among you, immorality of a kind that is not found even among gentiles: that one of you is living with his

2 stepmother. *a* ·And you so filled with your own self-importance! It would have been better if you had been grieving bitterly, so that the man who has done this

3 thing were turned out of the community. ·For my part, however distant I am physically, I am present in spirit and have already condemned the man who

4 behaved in this way, just as though I were present in person. ·When you have gathered together in the name of our Lord Jesus, *b* with the presence of my spirit, *c*

5 and in the power of our Lord Jesus, ·hand such a man over to Satan, to be

destroyed as far as natural life is concerned, so that on the Day of the Lord *d* his spirit may be saved.

6   Your self-satisfaction is ill founded. Do you not realise that only a little yeast *e*
7 leavens the whole batch of dough? ·Throw out the old yeast so that you can be the fresh dough, unleavened as you are. For our Passover has been sacrificed, that is,
8 Christ; ·let us keep the feast, then, with none of the old yeast and no leavening of evil and wickedness, but only the unleavened bread of sincerity and truth. *f*
9   In my letter, *g* I wrote to you that you should have nothing to do with people
10 living immoral lives. ·I was not including everybody in this present world who is sexually immoral, or everybody who is greedy, or dishonest or worships false gods—that would mean you would have to cut yourselves off completely from the
11 world. ·In fact what I meant was that you were not to have anything to do with anyone going by the name of brother *h* who is sexually immoral, or is greedy, or worships false gods, or is a slanderer or a drunkard or dishonest; never even have
12 a meal with anybody of that kind. ·It is no concern of mine to judge outsiders. *i* It
13 is for you to judge those who are inside, is it not? ·But outsiders are for God to judge.

You must banish this evil-doer from amòng you.

C: RECOURSE TO THE GENTILE COURTS *a*

1   **6** Is one of you with a complaint against another so brazen as to seek judgement
2   from sinners and not from God's holy people? *b* ·Do you not realise that the holy people of God are to be the judges of the world? *c* And if the world is to be
3 judged by you, are you not competent for petty cases? ·Do you not realise that we
4 shall be the judges of angels?—then quite certainly over matters of this life. ·But when you have matters of this life to be judged, you bring them before those who
5 are of no account in the Church! *d* ·I say this to make you ashamed of yourselves. Can it really be that it is impossible to find in the community one sensible person
6 capable of deciding questions between brothers, ·and that this is why brother goes
7 to law against brother, and that before unbelievers? ·No; it is a fault in you, by itself, that one of you should go to law against another at all: why do you not
8 prefer to suffer injustice, why not prefer to be defrauded? ·And here you are, doing the injustice and the defrauding, and to your own brothers.
9   Do you not realise that people who do evil will never inherit the kingdom of God? Make no mistake—the sexually immoral, idolaters, adulterers, the self-
10 indulgent, sodomites, ·thieves, misers, drunkards, slanderers and swindlers, none
11 of these will inherit the kingdom of God. *e* ·Some of you used to be of that kind: but you have been washed clean, you have been sanctified, and you have been justified in the name of the Lord Jesus Christ and through the Spirit of our God. *f*

D: SEXUAL IMMORALITY

12 'For me everything is permissible'; *g* maybe, but not everything does good. True, for me everything is permissible, but I am determined not to be dominated by
13 anything. ·Foods are for the stomach, and the stomach is for foods; and God will
14 destroy them both. But the body is not for sexual immorality; *h* ·it is for the Lord, and the Lord is for the body. God raised up the Lord and he will raise *i* us up too

15 by his power. ·Do you not realise that your bodies are members of Christ's body; do you think one can take parts of Christ's body and join them to the body of a
16 prostitute? Out of the question! ·Or do you not realise that anyone who attaches himself to a prostitute is one body with her, since *the two*, as it is said, *become one*
17 *flesh*. ·But anyone who attaches himself to the Lord is one spirit with him.*ʲ*
18 Keep away from sexual immorality. All other sins that someone may commit are done outside the body;*ᵏ* but the sexually immoral person sins against his own
19 body. Do you not realise that your body is the temple*ˡ* of the Holy Spirit, who is
20 in you and whom you received from God? ·You are not your own property, then; you have been bought at a price.*ᵐ* So use your body for the glory of God.

II: ANSWERS TO VARIOUS QUESTIONS

A: MARRIAGE AND VIRGINITY*ᵃ*

1 7 Now for the questions about which you wrote. Yes, it is a good thing for a
2 man not to touch a woman;*ᵇ* · yet to avoid immorality every man should have
3 his own wife and every woman her own husband.*ᶜ* ·The husband must give to his
4 wife what she has a right to expect, and so too the wife to her husband. ·The wife does not have authority over her own body, but the husband does; and in the same way, the husband does not have authority over his own body, but the wife does.*ᵈ*
5 You must not deprive each other, except by mutual consent for a limited time, to leave yourselves free for prayer, and to come together again afterwards; otherwise
6 Satan may take advantage of any lack of self-control to put you to the test. ·I am
7 telling you this as a concession,*ᵉ* not an order. ·I should still like everyone to be as I am myself; but everyone has his own gift from God, one this kind and the next something different.*ᶠ*
8 To the unmarried*ᵍ* and to widows I say: it is good for them to stay as they are,
9 like me.*ʰ* ·But if they cannot exercise self-control, let them marry, since it is better to be married than to be burnt up.
10 To the married I give this ruling, and this is not mine but the Lord's: a wife must
11 not be separated from her husband—·or if she has already left him, she must remain unmarried or else be reconciled to her husband—and a husband must not divorce his wife.
12 For other cases these instructions are my own, not the Lord's. If one of the brothers has a wife who is not a believer, and she is willing to stay with him, he
13 may not divorce her; ·and if a woman has a husband who is not a believer and he
14 is willing to stay with her, she may not divorce her husband. ·You see, the unbelieving husband is sanctified through his wife and the unbelieving wife is sanctified through the brother. If this were not so, your children would be unclean,
15 whereas in fact they are holy.*ⁱ* ·But if the unbeliever chooses to leave, then let the separation take place:*ʲ* in these circumstances, the brother or sister is no longer
16 tied. But God has called you*ᵏ* to live in peace: ·as a wife, how can you tell whether you are to be the salvation of your husband; as a husband, how can you tell whether you are to be the salvation of your wife?
17 Anyway let everyone continue in the part which the Lord has allotted to him, as
18 he was when God called him. This is the rule that I give to all the churches. ·If a man who is called has already been circumcised, then he must stay circumcised;
19 when an uncircumcised man is called, he may not be circumcised. ·To be circum-

cised is of no importance, and to be uncircumcised is of no importance; what is
20 important is the keeping of God's commandments. ·Everyone should stay in
21 whatever state he was in when he was called. ·So, if when you were called, you
were a slave, *l* do not think it matters—even if you have a chance of freedom, you
22 should prefer to make full use of your condition as a slave. ·You see, anyone who
was called in the Lord while a slave, is a freeman of the Lord; and in the same
23 way, the man who, when called, was a free man, is a slave of Christ. ·You have
24 been bought at a price; do not be slaves now to any human being. *m* ·Each one of
you, brothers, is to stay before God in the state in which you were called.

25   About people remaining virgin, *n* I have no directions from the Lord, but I give
my own opinion as a person who has been granted the Lord's mercy to be faithful.
26 Well then, because of the stress which is weighing upon us, *o* the right thing seems
27 to be this: it is good for people to stay as they are. ·If you are joined to a wife, do
28 not seek to be released; if you are freed of a wife, do not look for a wife. ·However,
if you do get married, that is not a sin, and it is not sinful for a virgin to enter upon
marriage. But such people will have the hardships consequent on human nature, *p*
and I would like you to be without that.

29   What I mean, brothers, is that the time has become limited, *q* and from now on,
30 those who have wives should live as though they had none; ·and those who mourn
as though they were not mourning; those who enjoy life as though they did not
enjoy it; those who have been buying property as though they had no possessions;
31 and those who are involved with the world as though they were people not
engrossed in it. *r* Because this world as we know it is passing away.

32   I should like you to have your minds free from all worry. The unmarried man
33 gives his mind to the Lord's affairs and to how he can please the Lord; ·but the
man who is married gives his mind to the affairs of this world and to how he can
34 please his wife, and he is divided in mind. ·So, too, the unmarried woman, and
the virgin, gives her mind to the Lord's affairs *s* and to being holy in body and
spirit; but the married woman gives her mind to the affairs of this world and to
35 how she can please her husband. ·I am saying this only to help you, not to put a
bridle on you, but so that everything is as it should be, and you are able to give
your undivided attention to the Lord.

36   If someone with strong passions thinks that he is behaving badly towards his
fiancée and that things should take their due course, he should follow his desires.
37 There is no sin in it; they should marry. ·But if he stands firm in his resolution,
without any compulsion but with full control of his own will, and decides to let her
38 remain as his fiancée, then he is acting well. ·In other words, he who marries his
fiancée *t* is doing well, and he who does not, better still.

39   A wife is tied as long as her husband is alive. But if the husband dies, she is free
40 to marry anybody she likes, only it must be in the Lord. *u* ·She would be happier if
she stayed as she is, to my way of thinking—and I believe that I too have the Spirit
of God.

B: FOOD OFFERED TO FALSE GODS *a*

General principles

1   **8** Now about food which has been dedicated to false gods. We are well aware
that all of us have knowledge; but while knowledge puffs up, love is what

2 builds up. ·Someone may think that he has full knowledge of something and yet
3 not know it as well as he should; ·but someone who loves God is known by God.
4 On the subject of eating foods dedicated to false gods, we are well aware that
none of the false gods exists in reality and that there is no God other than the
5 One. Though there are so-called gods, in the heavens or on earth—and there are
6 plenty of gods and plenty of lords ᵇ—·yet for us there is only one God, the Father
from whom all things come and for whom we exist, and one Lord, Jesus Christ,
through whom all things come and through whom we exist. ᶜ

The claims of knowledge

7 However, not everybody has this knowledge. There are some in whose consciences
false gods still play such a part ᵈ that they take the food as though it had been
8 dedicated to a god; then their conscience being vulnerable, is defiled, ·But of
course food cannot make us acceptable to God; ᵉ we lose nothing by not eating it,
9 we gain nothing by eating it. ·Only be careful that this freedom of yours does not
10 in any way turn into an obstacle to trip those who are vulnerable. ·Suppose
someone sees you, who have the knowledge, sitting eating in the temple of some
false god, do you not think that his conscience, vulnerable as it is, may be
11 encouraged to eat foods dedicated to false gods? ·And then it would be through
your knowledge that this brother for whom Christ died, vulnerable as he is,
12 has been lost. ·So, sinning against your brothers and wounding their vulnerable
13 consciences, you would be sinning against Christ. ·That is why, if food can be the
cause of a brother's downfall, I will never eat meat any more, rather than cause
my brother's downfall.

Paul invokes his own example ᵃ

1 9 Am I not free? Am I not an apostle? Have I not seen Jesus our Lord? Are you
2 not my work in the Lord? ·Even if to others I am not an apostle, to you at any
3 rate I am, for you are the seal of my apostolate in the Lord. ·To those who want to
4 interrogate me, this is my answer. ·Have we not every right to eat and drink? ᵇ
5 And every right to be accompanied by a Christian wife, ᶜ like the other apostles,
6 like the brothers of the Lord, and like Cephas? ·Are Barnabas and I the only ones
7 who have no right to stop working? ·What soldier would ever serve in the army at
his own expense? And who is there who would plant a vineyard and never eat the
8 fruit from it; or would keep a flock and not feed on the milk from his flock? ·Do
not think that this is merely worldly wisdom. Does not the Law say exactly the
9 same? It is written in the Law of Moses: ·*You must not muzzle an ox when it is*
10 *treading out the corn.* Is it about oxen that God is concerned here, ·or is it not said
entirely for our sake? Clearly it was written for our sake, because it is right that
whoever ploughs should plough with the expectation of having his share, and
11 whoever threshes should thresh with the expectation of having his share. ·If we
have sown the seed of spiritual things in you, is it too much to ask that we should
12 receive from you a crop of material things? ·Others have been given such rights
over you and do we not deserve more? In fact, we have never exercised this right;
on the contrary, we have put up with anything rather than obstruct the gospel of
13 Christ in any way. ·Do you not realise that the ministers in the Temple get their
food from the Temple, and those who serve at the altar can claim their share from
14 the altar? ·In the same way, the Lord gave the instruction that those who preach
the gospel should get their living from the gospel.
15 However, I have never availed myself of any rights of this kind; and I have not

written this to secure such treatment for myself; I would rather die than that . . .
16 No one shall take from me this ground of boasting. *d* ·In fact, preaching the gospel
gives me nothing to boast of, for I am under compulsion and I should be in trouble
17 if I failed to do it. ·If I did it on my own initiative I would deserve a reward; but if
18 I do it under compulsion I am simply accepting a task entrusted to me. ·What
reward do I have, then? That in my preaching I offer the gospel free of charge to
avoid using the rights which the gospel allows me.

19 So though I was not a slave to any human being, I put myself in slavery to all
20 people, to win as many as I could. ·To the Jews I made myself as a Jew, to win the
Jews; to those under the Law as one under the Law (though I am not), in order to
21 win those under the Law; ·to those outside the Law as one outside the Law,
though I am not outside the Law but under Christ's law, *e* to win those outside the
22 Law. ·To the weak, I made myself weak, to win the weak. I accommodated myself
to people in all kinds of different situations, so that by all possible means I might
23 bring some to salvation. ·All this I do for the sake of the gospel, that I may share
its benefits with others.

24 Do you not realise that, though all the runners in the stadium take part in the
25 race, only one of them gets the prize?·Run like that—to win. ·Every athlete
concentrates completely on training, and this is to win a wreath that will wither,
26 whereas ours will never wither. ·So that is how I run, not without a clear goal; and
27 how I box, not wasting blows on air. ·I punish my body and bring it under
control, to avoid any risk that, having acted as herald for others, I myself may be
disqualified. *f*

A warning and the lessons of Israel's history *a*

1 **10** I want you to be quite certain, brothers, that our ancestors all had the cloud
2   over them and all passed through the sea. ·In the cloud and in the sea they
3, 4 were all baptised into Moses; ·all ate the same spiritual food ·and all drank the
same spiritual drink, *b* since they drank from the spiritual rock which followed
5 them, *c* and that rock was Christ. ·In spite of this, God was not pleased with most
6 of them, and their corpses *were scattered over the desert.* ·Now these happenings
were examples, *d* for our benefit, so that we should never set our hearts, as they
7 did, on evil things;· nor are you to worship false gods, as some of them did, as it
says in scripture: *The people sat down to eat and drink, and afterwards got up to*
8 *amuse themselves.* ·Nor, again, are we to fall into sexual immorality; some of them
9 did this, and twenty-three thousand met their downfall in one day. ·And we are
not to put the Lord *e* to the test; some of them put him to the test, and they were
10 killed by snakes. ·Never complain; some of them complained, and they were killed
11 by the Destroyer. ·Now all these things happened to them by way of example, and
they were described in writing to be a lesson for us, to whom it has fallen to live in
12 the last days of the ages. ·Everyone, no matter how firmly he thinks he is standing,
13 must be careful he does not fall. ·None of the trials which have come upon you is
more than a human being can stand. You can trust that God will not let you be put
to the test *f* beyond your strength, but with any trial will also provide a way out by
enabling you to put up with it.

Sacrificial feasts. No compromise with idolatry

14 For that reason, my dear friends, have nothing to do with the worship of false
15 gods. ·I am talking to you as sensible people; weigh up for yourselves what I have
16 to say. ·The blessing-cup, *g* which we bless, is it not a sharing in the blood of Christ;

and the loaf of bread which we break, is it not a sharing in the body of Christ?
17 And as there is one loaf, so we, although there are many of us, are one single
18 body, for we all share in the one loaf. ᵏ •Now compare the natural people of Israel: ⁱ
19 is it not true that those who eat the sacrifices share the altar? •What does this
mean? That the dedication of food to false gods amounts to anything? Or that
20 false gods themselves amount to anything? •No, it does not; simply that when
pagans sacrifice, *what is sacrificed by them is sacrificed to demons who are not God*.
21 I do not want you to share with demons. •You cannot drink the cup of the Lord
and the cup of demons as well; you cannot have a share at the Lord's table and the
22 demons' table as well.ʲ •Do we really want to arouse the Lord's jealousy; ᵏ are we
stronger than he is?

Food sacrificed to idols. Practical solutions

23 'Everything is permissible'; maybe so, but not everything does good. True, every-
24 thing is permissible, but not everything builds people up. •Nobody should be
25 looking for selfish advantage, but everybody for someone else's. •Eat anything
that is sold in butchers' shops; there is no need to ask questions for conscience's
26.27 sake, •since *To the Lord belong the earth and all it contains*. •If an unbeliever invites
you to a meal, go if you want to, and eat whatever is put before you; you need not
28 ask questions of conscience first. •But if someone says to you, 'This food has been
offered in sacrifice,' do not eat it, out of consideration for the person that told
29 you, for conscience's sake—•not your own conscience, I mean, but the other
person's. Why should my freedom be governed by somebody else's conscience?ⁱ
30 Provided that I accept it with gratitude, why should I be blamed for eating food
31 for which I give thanks? •Whatever you eat, then, or drink, and whatever else you
32 do, do it all for the glory of God. •Never be a cause of offence, either to Jews or to
33 Greeks or to the Church of God, •just as I try to accommodate everybody in
everything, not looking for my own advantage, but for the advantage of everybody
else, so that they may be saved.
1 **11** Take me as your pattern, just as I take Christ for mine.

C: DECORUM IN PUBLIC WORSHIP

Women's behaviour at services

2 I congratulate you for remembering me so consistently and for maintaining the
3 traditions exactly as I passed them on to you. •But I should like you to understand
that the head of every man is Christ, the head of woman is man, and the head of
4 Christ is God. •For any man to pray or to prophesy with his head covered shows
5 disrespect for his head. ᵃ •And for a woman to pray or prophesy with her head
uncovered shows disrespect for her head; it is exactly the same as if she had her
6 hair shaved off. •Indeed, if a woman does go without a veil, she should have her
hair cut off too; but if it is a shameful thing for a woman to have her hair cut off or
shaved off, then she should wear a veil.
7 But for a man it is not right to have his head covered, since he is the image of
8 God and reflects God's glory; but woman is the reflection of man's glory. •For
9 man did not come from woman; no, woman came from man; •nor was man created
10 for the sake of woman, but woman for the sake of man: •and this is why it is right

for a woman to wear on her head a sign of the authority over her, because of the
11 angels. *ᵇ* ·However, in the Lord, though woman is nothing without man, man is
12 nothing without woman; ·and though woman came from man, so does every man
come from a woman, and everything comes from God.

13　　Decide for yourselves: does it seem fitting that a woman should pray to God
14 without a veil? ·Does not nature itself teach you that if a man has long hair, it is a
15 disgrace to him, ·but when a woman has long hair, it is her glory? After all, her
hair was given to her to be a covering.

16　　If anyone wants to be contentious, I say that we have no such custom, nor do
any of the churches of God.

The Lord's Supper

17 Now that I am on the subject of instructions, I cannot congratulate you on the
18 meetings you hold; they do more harm than good. ·In the first place, I hear that
when you all come together in your assembly, there are separate factions among
19 you, and to some extent I believe it. ·It is no bad thing, either, that there should
be differing groups among you so that those who are to be trusted among you can
20 be clearly recognised. ·So, when you meet together, it is not the Lord's Supper
21 that you eat; ·for when the eating begins, each one of you has his own supper *ᶜ*
22 first, and there is one going hungry while another is getting drunk. ·Surely you
have homes for doing your eating and drinking in? Or have you such disregard for
God's assembly that you can put to shame those who have nothing? What am I to
say to you? Congratulate you? On this I cannot congratulate you.

23　　For the tradition I received from the Lord *ᵈ* and also handed on to you is that on
24 the night he was betrayed, the Lord Jesus took some bread, ·and after he had
given thanks, he broke it, and he said, 'This is my body, which is for you; *ᵉ* do this
25 in remembrance of me.' ·And in the same way, with the cup after supper, saying,
'This cup is the new covenant in my blood. Whenever you drink it, do this as a
26 memorial of me.' *ᶠ* ·Whenever you eat this bread, then, and drink this cup, you
27 are proclaiming the Lord's death until he comes. ·Therefore anyone who eats the
bread or drinks the cup of the Lord unworthily is answerable for the body and
blood of the Lord.

28　　Everyone is to examine himself and only then eat of the bread or drink from the
29 cup; ·because a person who eats and drinks *ᵍ* without recognising the body *ʰ* is
30 eating and drinking his own condemnation. ·That is why many of you are weak
31 and ill and a good number have died. *ⁱ* ·If we were critical of ourselves we would
32 not be condemned, ·but when we are judged by the Lord, we are corrected by the
Lord to save us from being condemned along with the world. *ʲ*

33, 34　　So then, my brothers, when you meet for the Meal, wait for each other; ·anyone
who is hungry should eat at home. Then your meeting will not bring your condemnation. The other matters I shall arrange when I come.

Spiritual gifts *ᵃ*

1, 2　**12** About the gifts of the Spirit, brothers, I want you to be quite certain. ·You
remember that, when you were pagans, you were irresistibly drawn to
3 inarticulate heathen gods. *ᵇ* ·Because of that, I want to make it quite clear to you
that no one who says 'A curse on Jesus' can be speaking in the Spirit of God, and
nobody is able to say, 'Jesus is Lord' except in the Holy Spirit.

The variety and the unity of gifts

4, 5 There are many different gifts, but it is always the same Spirit; ·there are many
6 different ways of serving, but it is always the same Lord. ·There are many different
forms of activity, but in everybody it is the same God who is at work in them all. ᶜ
7 The particular manifestation of the Spirit granted to each one is to be used for the
8 general good. ·To one is given from the Spirit the gift of utterance expressing
wisdom; ᵈ to another the gift of utterance expressing knowledge, ᵉ in accordance
9 with the same Spirit; ·to another, faith, ᶠ from the same Spirit; and to another, the
10 gifts of healing, through this one Spirit; ·to another, the working of miracles; to
another, prophecy; to another, the power of distinguishing spirits; ᵍ to one, the
11 gift of different tongues ʰ and to another, the interpretation of tongues. ·But at
work in all these is one and the same Spirit, distributing them at will to each
individual.

The analogy of the body ⁱ

12 For as with the human body which is a unity although it has many parts—all the
parts of the body, though many, still making up one single body—so it is with
13 Christ. ʲ ·We were baptised into one body in a single Spirit, Jews as well as Greeks,
14 slaves as well as free men, and we were all given the same Spirit to drink. ·And
15 indeed the body consists not of one member but of many. ·If the foot were to say,
'I am not a hand and so I do not belong to the body,' it does not belong to the
16 body any the less for that. ·Or if the ear were to say, 'I am not an eye, and so I do
17 not belong to the body,' that would not stop its belonging to the body. ·If the
whole body were just an eye, how would there be any hearing? If the whole body
were hearing, how would there be any smelling?
18, 19 As it is, God has put all the separate parts into the body as he chose. ·If they
20 were all the same part, how could it be a body? ·As it is, the parts are many but
21 the body is one. ·The eye cannot say to the hand, 'I have no need of you,' and nor
can the head say to the feet, 'I have no need of you.'
22 What is more, it is precisely the parts of the body that seem to be the weakest
23 which are the indispensable ones. ·It is the parts of the body which we consider
least dignified that we surround with the greatest dignity; and our less presentable
24 parts are given greater presentability ·which our presentable parts do not need.
God has composed the body so that greater dignity is given to the parts which
25 were without it, ·and so that there may not be disagreements inside the body but
26 each part may be equally concerned for all the others. ·If one part is hurt, all the
parts share its pain. And if one part is honoured, all the parts share its joy.
27 Now Christ's body is yourselves, each of you with a part to play in the whole.
28 And those whom God has appointed in the Church are, first apostles, secondly
prophets, thirdly teachers ᵏ . . . after them, miraculous powers, then gifts of
29 healing, helpful acts, ˡ guidance, ᵐ various kinds of tongues. ·Are all of them
30 apostles? Or all prophets? Or all teachers? Or all miracle-workers? ·Do all have
the gifts of healing? Do all of them speak in tongues and all interpret them?

The order of importance in spiritual gifts. Hymn to Love ⁿ

31 Set your mind on the higher gifts. And now I am going to put before you the best
way of all.
1 **13** Though I command languages both human and angelic—if I speak without
2 love, ᵒ I am no more than a gong booming or a cymbal clashing. And though
I have the power of prophecy, to penetrate all mysteries and knowledge, and

though I have all the faith necessary to move mountains—if I am without love, I
3 am nothing. ·Though I should give away to the poor all that I possess, and even
give up my body to be burned *b*—if I am without love, it will do me no good
whatever.
4 Love is always patient *c* and kind; love is never jealous; love is not boastful or
5 conceited, ·it is never rude and never seeks its own advantage, it does not take
6 offence or store up grievances. ·Love does not rejoice at wrongdoing, but finds its
7 joy in the truth. ·It is always ready to make allowances, to trust, to hope and to
endure whatever comes.
8 Love never comes to an end. *d* But if there are prophecies, they will be done
away with; if tongues, they will fall silent; and if knowledge, it will be done away
9, 10 with. ·For we know only imperfectly, and we prophesy imperfectly; ·but once
11 perfection comes, all imperfect things will be done away with. ·When I was a
child, I used to talk like a child, and see things as a child does, and think like a
child; but now that I have become an adult, I have finished with all childish ways.
12 Now we see only reflections in a mirror, mere riddles, but then we shall be seeing
face to face. Now, I can know only imperfectly; but then I shall know just as fully
as I am myself known.
13 As it is, these remain: *e* faith, hope and love, the three of them; and the greatest
of them is love.

Spiritual gifts: their respective importance in the community

1 **14** Make love your aim; but be eager, too, for spiritual gifts, and especially for
2 prophesying. ·Those who speak in a tongue speak to God, but not to other
people, because nobody understands them; they are speaking in the Spirit and the
3 meaning is hidden. ·On the other hand, someone who prophesies speaks to other
4 people, building them up and giving them encouragement and reassurance. ·Those
who speak in a tongue may build themselves up, but those who prophesy build up
5 the community. ·While I should like you all to speak in tongues, I would much
rather you could prophesy; since those who prophesy are of greater importance
than those who speak in tongues, unless they can interpret what they say so that
the church is built up by it.
6 Now suppose, brothers, I come to you and speak in tongues, what good shall I
7 do you if my speaking provides no revelation or knowledge or prophecy or
instruction? ·It is the same with an inanimate musical instrument. If it does not
make any distinction between notes, how can one recognise what is being played
8 on flute or lyre? ·If the trumpet sounds a call which is unrecognisable, who is going
9 to get ready for the attack? ·It is the same with you: if you do not use your tongue
to produce speech that can be readily understood, how can anyone know what
10 you are saying? You will be talking to the air. ·However many the languages used
11 in the world, all of them use sound; *a* ·but if I do not understand the meaning of
the sound, I am a barbarian *b* to the person who is speaking, and the speaker is a
12 barbarian to me. ·So with you, as you are eager to have spiritual powers, aim to
be rich in those which build up the community.
13 That is why anybody who speaks in a tongue must pray that he may be given the
14 interpretation. ·For if I pray in a tongue, my spirit may be praying but my mind
15 derives no fruit from it. *c* ·What then? I shall pray with the spirit, but I shall pray
with the mind as well: I shall sing praises with the spirit and I shall sing praises
16 with the mind as well. ·Otherwise, if you say your blessing only with the spirit,
how is the uninitiated person *d* going to answer 'Amen' to your thanksgiving,

17 without understanding what you are saying? ·You may be making your thanks-
18 giving well, but the other person is not built up at all. ·I thank God that I speak
19 with tongues more than any of you; ·all the same, when I am in the assembly I
would rather say five words with my mind, to instruct others as well, than ten
thousand words in a tongue.

20 Brothers, do not remain children in your thinking; infants in
21 wickedness—agreed, but in your thinking grown-ups. ·It says in the written Law:
In strange tongues and in a foreign language I will talk to this nation, and even so
22 *they will refuse to listen,* says the Lord.* ·So then, strange languages are significant
not for believers, but for unbelievers; whereas on the other hand, prophesying is
23 not for unbelievers, but for believers.ʲ ·Suppose that, if the whole congregation
were meeting and all of them speaking in tongues, and some uninitiated people or
unbelievers were to come in, don't you think they would say that you were all
24 raving? ·But if you were all prophesying when an unbeliever or someone uniniti-
25 ated came in, he would find himself put to the test by all and judged by all ·and
the secrets of his heart revealed; and so he would fall down on his face and worship
God, declaring that *God is indeed among you.*

Regulating spiritual gifts

26 Then what should it be like, brothers? When you come together each of you brings
a psalm or some instruction or a revelation, or speaks in a tongue or gives an
interpretation. Let all these things be done in a way that will build up the com-
27 munity. ·If there are to be any people speaking in a tongue, then let there be only
two, or at the most three, and those one at a time, and let one of these interpret.
28 If there is no interpreter, then let each of them be quiet in the assembly, and speak
29 only to himself and God. ·Let two prophets, or three, speak while the rest weigh
30 their words; ·and if a revelation comes to someone else who is sitting by, the
31 speaker should stop speaking. ·You can all prophesy, but one at a time, then all
32 will learn something and all receive encouragement. ·The prophetic spirit is to be
33 under the prophets' control, ᵍ ·for God is a God not of disorder but of peace.
34 As in all the churches of God's holy people, ·women are to remain quiet in the
assemblies, since they have no permission to speak: ʰ theirs is a subordinate part,
35 as the Law itself says. ·If there is anything they want to know, they should ask
their husbands at home: it is shameful for a woman to speak in the assembly.
36 Do you really think that you are the source of the word of God? Or that you are
37 the only people to whom it has come? ⁱ ·Anyone who claims to be a prophet, or to
have any spiritual powers must recognise that what I am writing to you is a
38 commandment from the Lord. ·If anyone does not recognise this, it is because
that person is not recognised himself.ʲ
39 So, my brothers, be eager to prophesy, and do not suppress the gift of speaking
40 in tongues. ·But make sure that everything is done in a proper and orderly fashion.

III: THE RESURRECTION OF THE DEAD*

The fact of the resurrection

1   **15**   I want to make quite clear to you, brothers, what the message of the gospel
2   that I preached to you is; you accepted it and took your stand on it, ·and
you are saved by it, if you keep to the message I preached to you; otherwise your

3 coming to believe was in vain. ·The tradition I handed on to you in the first place, a tradition which I had myself received, *b* was that Christy died for our sins, *c* in
4 accordance with the scriptures, ·and that he was buried; and that on the third day,
5 he was raised to life, in accordance with the scriptures; *d* ·and that he appeared to
6 Cephas; and later to the Twelve; ·and next he appeared to more than five hundred of the brothers at the same time, most of whom are still with us, *e* though some
7 have fallen asleep; *f* ·then he appeared to James, and then to all the apostles. *g*
8 Last of all he appeared to me too, as though I was a child born abnormally. *h*

9 For I am the least of the apostles and am not really fit to be called an apostle,
10 because I had been persecuting the Church of God; ·but what I am now, I am through the grace of God, and the grace which was given to me has not been wasted. Indeed, I have worked harder than all the others—not I, but the grace of
11 God which is with me. ·Anyway, whether it was they or I, this is what we preach and what you believed.

12 Now if Christ is proclaimed as raised from the dead, how can some of you be
13 saying that there is no resurrection of the dead? ·If there is no resurrection of the
14 dead, then Christ cannot have been raised either, *i* ·and if Christ has not been
15 raised, then our preaching is without substance, *j* and so is your faith. ·What is more, we have proved to be false witnesses to God, for testifying against God that he raised Christ to life when he did not raise him—if it is true that the dead are not
16, 17 raised. ·For, if the dead are not raised, neither is Christ; ·and if Christ has not been raised, your faith is pointless and you have not, after all, been released from
18, 19 your sins. *k* ·In addition, those who have fallen asleep in Christ are utterly lost. ·If our hope in Christ has been for this life only, *l* we are of all people the most pitiable.

20 In fact, however, Christ has been raised from the dead, as the first-fruits of all
21 who have fallen asleep. ·As it was by one man that death came, so through one
22 man has come the resurrection of the dead. ·Just as all die in Adam, so in Christ
23 all will be brought to life; *m* ·but all of them in their proper order: Christ the first-
24 fruits, and next, at his coming, *n* those who belong to him. *o* ·After that will come the end, when he will hand over the kingdom to God the Father, having abolished
25 every principality, every ruling force and power. *p* ·For he is to be king *until he has*
26 *made his enemies his footstool*, ·and the last of the enemies to be done away with
27 is death, for *he has put all things under his feet*. ·But when it is said *q* everything is subjected, this obviously cannot include the One who subjected everything to him.
28 When everything has been subjected to him, then the Son himself will be subjected to the One who has subjected everything to him, so that God may be all in all.

29 Otherwise, what are people up to who have themselves baptised on behalf of the dead? *r* If the dead are not raised at all, what is the point of being baptised on
30 their behalf? ·And what about us? Why should we endanger ourselves every hour
31 of our lives? ·I swear by the pride that I take in you, in Christ Jesus our Lord, that
32 I face death every day. ·If I fought wild animals at Ephesus *s* in a purely human
33 perspective, what had I to gain by it? ·If the dead are not going to be raised, then
34 *Let us eat and drink, for tomorrow we shall be dead.* *t* ·So do not let anyone lead you astray, 'Bad company corrupts good ways.' *u* Wake up from your stupor as you should and leave sin alone; some of you have no understanding of God; I tell you this to instil some shame in you.

The manner of the resurrection

35 Someone may ask: How are dead people raised, and what sort of body do they
36 have when they come? ·How foolish! What you sow must die before it is given
37 new life; ·and what you sow is not the body that is to be, but only a bare grain, of
38 wheat I dare say, or some other kind; ·it is God who gives it the sort of body that
he has chosen for it, ʳ and for each kind of seed its own kind of body.

39 Not all flesh is the same flesh: there is human flesh; animals have another kind
40 of flesh, birds another and fish yet another. ·Then there are heavenly bodies and
earthly bodies; the heavenly have a splendour of their own, and the earthly a
41 different splendour. ·The sun has its own splendour, the moon another splendour,
and the stars yet another splendour; and the stars differ among themselves in
42 splendour. ·It is the same too with the resurrection of the dead: what is sown is
43 perishable, but what is raised is imperishable; ·what is sown is contemptible but
what is raised is glorious; what is sown is weak, but what is raised is powerful;
44 what is sown is a natural body, and what is raised is a spiritual body. ˮ

45 If there is a natural body, there is a spiritual body too. ·So the first *man*, Adam,
as scripture says, *became a living soul*;ˣ and the last Adam has become a life-
46 giving spirit. ·But first came the natural body, not the spiritual one; that came
47 only afterwards. ·The first man, being made of earth, is earthly by nature; the
48 second man is from heaven. ·The earthly man is the pattern for earthly people,
49 the heavenly man for heavenly ones. ·And as we have borne the likeness of the
earthly man, so we shall bear the likeness of the heavenly one.ʸ

50 What I am saying, brothers, is that mere human nature cannot inherit the
51 kingdom of God: what is perishable cannot inherit what is imperishable. ·Now I
52 am going to tell you a mystery: we are not all going to fall asleep, ·but we are all
going to be changed, instantly, in the twinkling of an eye, when the last trumpet
sounds.ᶻ The trumpet is going to sound, and then the dead will be raised imperish-
53 able, and we shall be changed,ᵃᵃ ·because this perishable nature of ours must put
on imperishability, this mortal nature must put on immortality.

A hymn of triumph. Conclusion

54 And after this perishable nature has put on imperishability ᵇᵇ and this mortal nature
has put on immortality, then will the words of scripture come true:ᶜᶜ *Death is*
55 *swallowed up in victory.* ·*Death, where is your* victory? *Death, where is your sting?*
56, 57 The sting of death is sin, and the power of sin comes from the Law. ᵈᵈ ·Thank God,
then, for giving us the victory through Jesus Christ our Lord.

58 So, my dear brothers, keep firm and immovable, always abounding in energy
for the Lord's work, being sure that in the Lord none of your labours is wasted. ᵉᵉ

CONCLUSION

Commendations. Greetings

1 **16** Now about the collection for God's holy people;ᵃ you are to do the same as
2 I prescribed for the churches in Galatia. ·On the first day of the week,ᵇ
each of you should put aside and reserve as much as each can spare; do not delay
3 the collection till I arrive. ·When I come, I will send to Jerusalem with letters of
4 introduction those people you approve to deliver your gift; ·if it is worth my going
too, they can travel with me.

5 In any case, I shall be coming to you after I have passed through Macedonia, as
6 I have to go through Macedonia; ·and I may be staying some time with you,
perhaps wintering, so that you can start me on my next journey, wherever I may
7 be going. ·I do not want to make only a passing visit to you, ᶜ and I am hoping to
8 spend quite a time with you, the Lord permitting. ·But I shall remain at Ephesus
9 until Pentecost, ·for a very promising door is standing wide open to me ᵈ and there
are many against us.

10 If Timothy comes, make sure that he has nothing to fear from you; he is doing
11 the Lord's work, just as I am, ·and nobody is to underrate him. Start him off in
12 peace on his journey to come on to me: the brothers and I are waiting for him. ·As
for our brother Apollos, I urged him earnestly to come to you with the brothers,
but he was quite firm that he did not want to go yet, ᵉ and he will come when he
finds an opportunity.

13, 14 Be vigilant, stay firm in the faith, be brave and strong. ·Let everything you do
be done in love.

15 There is something else I must urge you to do, brothers. You know how the
Stephanas family have been the first-fruits of Achaia and have devoted themselves
16 to the service of God's holy people; ·I ask you in turn to put yourselves at the
17 service of people like this and all that work with them in this arduous task. ·I am
delighted that Stephanas and Fortunatus and Achaicus have arrived;ᶠ they have
18 made up for your not being here. ·They have set my mind at rest, just as they did
yours; you should appreciate people like them.

19 The churches of Asia ᵍ send their greetings. Aquila and Prisca send their best
20 wishes in the Lord, together with the church that meets in their house. ·All the
brothers send their greetings. Greet one another with the holy kiss.

21 This greeting is in my own hand—PAUL.

22 If there is anyone who does not love the Lord, a curse on such a one. ʰ Maran
atha. ⁱ

23 The grace of the Lord Jesus Christ be with you.

24 My love is with you all in Christ Jesus.

NOTES TO 1 CORINTHIANS

1 **a.** One of Paul's favourite expressions: 10:32; 11:16,22; 15:9; 2 Co 1:1; Ga 1:13; 1 Th 2:14; 2 Th 1:4; 1 Tm 3:5,15; see also Ac 20:28. Cf. 'the churches of Christ', Rm 16:16. See Mt 16:18g; Ac 5:11b.

b. Alternative translation: 'with all those who in every place, theirs as well as ours, pray in the name of our Lord Jesus Christ.'

c. When the hidden plans of God are to be made known, Rm 16:25–26, 25l, Christ will reveal himself at the end of time, the time of his parousia, 15:23n, and his appearing, 1 Tm 6:14f; Cf. Lk 17:30; 2 Th 1:7; Heb 9:28; 1 P 1:5,7,13; 4:13.

d. Cf. Ep 1:4; Ph 1:10; 2:15seq.; Col 1:22; 1 Th 3:13; 5:23; Jude 24.

e. This 'Day of the Lord', 5:5; 2 Co 1:14; 1 Th 5:2; 2 Th 2:2; cf. 2 P 3:10, called also the 'Day of Christ', Ph 1:6,10; 2:16, or simply the 'Day', 1 Co 3:13; 1 Th 5:4; cf. Heb 10:25, or 'that Day', 2 Th 1:10; 2 Tm 1:12,18; 4:8; cf. Mt 7:22; 24:36; Lk 10:12; 21:34, or 'the Day of the Son of man', Lk 17:22–24; cf. v. 26, or 'the Day of God', 2 P 3:12, or 'the Day of visitation', 1 P 2:12, or 'the great Day', Jude

6; Rv 6:17; 16:14, or 'the last Day', Jn 6:39,40,44,54; 11:24; 12:48, is the fulfilment in the eschatological era, ushered in by Christ, of the 'Day of Yahweh' foretold by the prophets, Am 5:18m. This eschatological imagery of the prophets, so widely used in first-century Judaism, is largely current also in the NT. The fulfilment begins with the first coming of Christ, Lk 17:20–24, and the punishment of Jerusalem, Mt 24:1a; and this final stage in the history of salvation, see Ac 1:7i, will be completed by the glorious second coming, 1 Co 1:7 and notes; 15:23n; 1 Tm 6:14f, of the Sovereign Judge, Rm 2:6b; Jm 5:8–9. A cosmic upheaval and renewal will accompany it (see Am 8:9h), Mt 24:29 and par., 29o Heb 12:26seq.; 2 P 3:10–13; Rv 20:11; 21:1; cf. Mt 19:28; Rm 8:20–22. This Day of light is coming, Rm 13:12; Heb 10:25; Jm 5:8; 1 P 4:7; cf. 1 Th 5:5,8, but exactly when is uncertain, 1 Th 5:1a, meanwhile we must prepare for it, 2 Co 6:2a. But this eschatological imagery also receives a different interpretation in the 'realised eschatology' of Jn, see p. 159, Ep 2:6e.

f. 'Koinonia', frequently translated as 'communion', or as here 'being partners with', which has a basic meaning which, underlying a variety of usages, is the sharing of possessions. Amongst Christians, it is not spiritual possessions alone which are shared. Rm 15:26–27; 2 Co 8:4; 9:13; Ga 6:6; Ph 4:15–17. They must be united in actions and concerns, 2 Co 1:7; 6:14; 2 Jn 9; Rv 1:9. The communion from which all other forms derive is the partnership of grace from God, 9:23; Ph 1:5; Phm 6; it unites us to the Father and his Son Jesus Christ, 1 Co 1:9; 1 Jn 1:3b, 7e; to Christ himself, 1 Co 10:16; Ph 3:10; 1 P 4:13; to the Spirit, 2 Co 13:13e; Ph 2:1. Because Christ is our partner in human nature, we are his in the divine nature, 2 P 1:4g. The word becomes characteristic of the Christian community, Ac 2:42ff.

g. Cf. 10:13; 2 Co 1:18; 1 Th 5:24; 2 Th 3:3; 2 Tm 2:13; Heb 10:23; 11:11.

h. It is not known who this Chloe was; the phrase suggests that she may have been a trader with a staff of slaves or freedmen.

i. Either because Cephas (Peter) had visited the church of Corinth, or because some members of that church paid special allegiance to Peter's authority acknowledged in other churches.

j. Perhaps they claimed to have seen Christ on earth, cf. Ac 1:21seq.; 10:41, and so claimed preference over others, cf. 1 Co 9:1; 2 Co 5:16g; 11:5,23; 12:11.

k. This correction to the previous sentence indicates that Paul is dictating, cf. 16:21.

l. This human wisdom (here philosophical speculation and tricks of rhetoric) will be contrasted with the wisdom of God, v. 24 and 2:6seq.

m. Paul develops this point in 2:1–5.

n. The same point is made in Is 29:14: God promises a people who are being terrorised by the Assyrian threat that the workings of a purely human mind will not be able to save them.

o. Nowhere in this passage does Paul condemn genuine human nature, the gift of God and a means to knowledge of God, v. 21; what he condemns is an arrogant wisdom which fails of its object.

p. That is, in the works of God which make his wisdom known, see Ws 13:1–9; Rm 1:19–20. Other interpretations are possible: by deliberate arrangements of God's wisdom; or, at the time of God's wisdom, that is of the old economy which was under the standard of good sense, as opposed to the new economy where God reveals himself by seemingly senseless paradox.

q. It is 'human' to want a proof, whether miracles guaranteeing the truth of the message, or a logical argument resting on philosophical axioms. This desire is not in itself reprehensible, and the cross of Christ, paradoxically, responds to it, v. 24r. But it is unacceptable if it becomes a condition without which the mind refuses to believe.

r. From the human point of view the cross goes against all the expectations both of Jews and of Greeks; it is a rejection rather than a glorious manifestation, foolishness instead of wisdom. But to the eyes of faith the cross is the climax and overflow of the expectations, the power and wisdom of God.

s. The paradox of God's action (1:18–25) is fulfilled in the choice of the Corinthians (1:26–30) and in Paul's preaching (2:1–5).

t. i.e. from a purely human point of view.

u. You who formerly, in the eyes of the world, did not exist (v. 28) now exist in Jesus Christ, while those who in the eyes of the world exist are reduced to nothing. It is about this new existence in Jesus Christ, and this alone, that you should boast (see vv. 29,31).

v. So Christian wisdom is not the fruit of human effort 'according to the flesh'. It is found in a member of the human race who appeared in 'the fullness of time' (Ga 4:4), Christ, whom we must 'win' (Ph 3:8) in order to find in him all the treasures of wisdom and knowledge (Col 2:3). This wisdom is that of an all-embracing salvation, 'saving justice and holiness and redemption'.

w. These three last concepts form the basic themes of

the future letter to the Romans, which was surely already taking shape in Paul's mind, see Rm 1:17; 6:19,22; 3:24.

2 a. var. 'the witness of God'.

b. 'fear and trembling': a biblical cliché, cf. 2:3; Jg 7:3; Ps 2:11seq.; 55:5; Ezk 12:18; Mk 5:33; 2 Co 7:15; Ph 2:12.

c. An allusion to the miracles and outpouring of the Spirit which went with Paul's preaching (cf. 1:5 and 2 Co 12:12).

d. Words of human wisdom are persuasive by themselves (v. 4). They evoke in their listeners a purely human response (v. 5). It is just this that Paul will not accept. His word is indeed a demonstration (v. 4) but shows the action of the Spirit and demands a response on a different plane, that of the Spirit.

e. The 'mature' or 'perfect' (*teleioi*) are not an exclusive group of initiates but those who have reached maturity in Christian life and thought. Cf. 14:20; Mt 19:21g; Ph 3:15; Col 4:12; Heb 5:14. They are the same as the 'spiritual people' whom Paul contrasts with the 'infants in Christ', 3:1.

f. Perhaps human rulers or governments; more probably, the evil powers or demons that control the world, cf. 15:24–25; Ep 6:12. *See also* Lk 4:6 and Jn 12:31i; but the reference is perhaps to both, the latter using the former as their tools.

g. lit. 'in mystery', not an enigmatic wisdom, but a wisdom whose object is a mystery, the secret of the plan of salvation realised in Christ, Rm 16:25l.

h. The 'glory' is the manifestation of Yahweh's power, Ex 24:16f, the incommunicable attribute of God. The title 'Lord of glory' implies the same dignity for Jesus as that of Yahweh himself.

i. A free combination of Is 64:3 and Jr 3:16, or possibly a quotation from the *Apocalypse of Elijah*.

j. A difficult passage. It can also be understood 'showing how spiritual things fit spiritual people' or 'spiritual things thus fitting spiritual people' or 'allowing spiritual people to judge spiritual things'.

k. *psychikos*: a human being left to his own natural resources. *See* the note on *soma psychikon*, see 15:44w.

l. Possibly a defensive remark: Paul, a 'spiritual' man, is not to be judged by the Corinthians who are 'sensual', 3:1–3. In ch. 14, Paul lays down rules to be obeyed by the 'spiritual'; see also 1 Th 5:19–22.

3 a. lit. 'in the flesh'. For the distinction between 'spirit' and 'flesh', see Rm 1:9f.

b. add. 'and dissension'.

c. Or 'We are God's labourers'.

d. i.e., he will escape 'by the skin of his teeth', as one who has run through the flames. Purgatory is not directly envisaged here, but this text is one of those on the basis of which the Church has made this doctrine explicit.

e. It is the Christian community, the Body of Christ (12:12i), which is the Temple of the new covenant, and the Spirit that lives in it makes a reality of what was prefigured by the Temple of Jerusalem in which lived 'the glory' of God, 1 K 8:10–13; see Jn 2:21i; Rv 21:22; and 1 Co 6:19; 2 Co 6:16.

f. Paul distinguishes three kinds of preachers: those who build solidly (v. 14), those who build in non-resistant materials (v. 15), and those who destroy instead of building (v.17). These last are sacrilegious and should be punished accordingly.

g. i.e. consecrated and reserved to God: to lay hands on it is sacrilege.

h. vv. 21–23 deliberately echo the terms of 1:12 'Every one of you is declaring, "I belong to Paul" or "I belong to Apollos" or "I belong to Cephas." ' It is exactly the opposite, retorts Paul. You do not belong to them; they belong to you as your servants. And they are at your service, as is all creation, so that you may belong to Christ, who in his turn belongs to God the Father.

4 a. lit. 'day'. Paul is being ironical, suggesting that people are making their own 'Day of the Lord', *see* 1:8e, by passing a judgement which only God has a right to make.

b. The word *syneidesis*, *see* 1 S 25:31; Ws 17:11c, acquired a Christian value in Paul. Whatever may be the external norms, human conduct springs only from personal judgement, Ac 23:1; 24:16; Rm 2:14–15; 9:1; 13:5; 2 Co 1:12; but this judgement is subject to God's judgement, 1 Co 8:7–12; 10:25–29; 2 Co 4:2, cf. 1 P 2:19. Conscience is good and pure if it is inspired by faith and love, 1 Tm 1:5; 19, etc.; 1 P 3:16,21, and purified by Christ's blood, Heb 9:14; 10:22.

c. Obscure. Perhaps a citation of a proverb familiar to the Corinthian Jews; perhaps a gloss deprecating some insertion by a copyist.

d. Without any help from us, you are already installed in the kingdom of Heaven and enjoy all its riches to your complete satisfaction.

e. Like the men condemned to death in the arena with wild animals, with spectators crowding to watch as though at a sport.

f. At the end of this passage, vv. 6–10, Paul takes up again, ironically, the themes of ch. 1–2; you are, or claim to be, sensible, strong, honoured; but this is in the eyes not of God but of the world, which considers us foolish, weak and contemptible, and consequently persecutes us (vv. 11–13); the reality, in the eyes of God, is exactly the opposite.

g. The words translated 'dregs' and 'scum' are also used for the unfortunates who were used as expiatory victims in public calamities. Paul often returns to the subject of his sufferings, the persecutions he underwent in his apostolate and the way God enabled him to overcome them: 2 Co 4:7–12; 6:4–10; 11:23–33; 1 Th 3:4; 2 Tm 3:10–11. In his view, the weakness of the apostle shows the power of him by whom he was sent, 2 Co 12:9–10; Ph 4:13, because the greatness of the work done cannot be attributed entirely to the envoy, 2 Co 4:7c.

h. 'slaves'. This refers to a type of slave whose business was to take the child, and later the young man, to his teachers, and to watch over him and keep him within bounds. Since the nuance is pejorative, perhaps the best translation is 'nursemaids' even though the original reference is to males.

i. This spiritual fatherhood corresponds to what Paul says in 3:6, 'I did the planting'; I sowed in you the new life of the Spirit which conforms you to Christ; *see* v. 17; Ga 4:19; Phm 10. Elsewhere it is his tenderness for his converts that Paul likens to that of a father or mother, 1 Th 2:7,11, *see* 2 Co 12:15e.

j. Cf. Ps 119:1; Jn 14:6d; Ac 9:2b.

k. Paul is referring to effects of the power of the Spirit (*see* 2:4; 1 Th 1:5), and especially conversion and life according to the Spirit.

5 a. 'His father's wife'. Marriage to a stepmother was forbidden by the OT (Lv 18:8) and Roman Law, but such a union was tolerated by the majority of rabbis in converted gentiles; and this may explain the indulgence of the Corinthian community, who were not subject to Roman civil law. The council of Jerusalem forbade such unions, Ac 15:20u.

b. var. 'of our Lord Jesus Christ'.

c. Paul is asking the church to confirm a decision he has already taken, and make it a verdict of the whole community in the name of Jesus; cf. Mt 18:18.

d. This is not precisely 'excommunication'; the word does not occur in the Bible (it does not exactly correspond to 'anathema', the curse of destruction 16:22h; Jos 6:17b). Punishment by exclusion was practised in the OT, in Judaism and at Qumran. The NT shows several cases where the motives and ways of carrying it out are different. Sometimes the guilty person is kept temporarily apart from the community, 5:2,9–13; 2 Th 3:6–14; Ti 3:10; cf. 1 Jn 5:16–17; 2 Jn 10; sometimes he is 'handed over', here and 1 Tm 1:20, to Satan, deprived of the support of God's people, the Church, and so left exposed to the power which God allows the Adversary, 2 Th 2:4, *see* Jb 1:6g; even in these extreme cases there is hope of repentance and final salvation, as here

and 2 Th 3:15. Such a discipline presupposes that the Church has a certain degree of power over its members, *see* Mt 18:15–18,18j.

e. Yeast is here a symbol of corruption, as in Mt 16:6 and par.; Ga 5:9, and contrary to Mt 13:33 and par. Unleavened bread is the symbol of purity, v. 8. We have here a typical example of Pauline moral teaching: become what you are already. 'You are pure; purify yourselves.' Do in your lives what Christ did in you when you became Christians; cf. Rm 6:11–12; Col 3:3–5.

f. At Passover time, according to the Jewish ritual, all leavened bread was removed from the house (Ex 12:15), the paschal lamb was sacrificed (Ex 12:6) and unleavened bread was eaten (Ex 12:18–20). These were the symbolic preparations for the Christian mystery. By his sacrifice, Christ, the true paschal lamb, destroys the old leaven of sin and makes possible a life holy and pure, of which unleavened bread is the symbol. It is possible that this imagery was suggested to Paul by the time of year at which he was writing.

g. The 'pre-canonical' letter, *see* p. 289.

h. That is, a member of the Christian community, Ac 1:15s.

i. Those who do not belong to the community, cf. Mk 4:11; Col 4:5; 1 Th 4:12; 1 Tm 3:7. The expression is of Jewish origin, *see* Si, prologue v. 5.

6 a. In the following eight verses, Paul's disapproval of the Christians' recourse to the gentile magistrates is expressed with a sarcastic irony which contrasts with his more sober thoughts on gentile courts in Rm 13:1–7.

b. The gentile magistrates. Not that the Corinthian judges were more corrupt than others but they had not been 'justified' by God through faith in Christ. Hence Paul's play on words: how could they administer 'justice' for those who were 'justified', i.e. the consecrated people, or members of the Christian community?

c. Side by side with Christ, the sovereign judge.

d. That is, gentile judges, compare Mt 5:25; 18:17. Alternative translation: 'If you have matters in this life to be judged, bring them, etc . . .', that is, before more lowly Christians, who are perfectly capable of judging 'petty cases.'

e. Cf. 15:50; Ga 5:21; Ep 5:5; Rv 21:8; 22:15.

f. Note the trinitarian formula, *see* 2 Co 13:13e.

g. This may be one of Paul's own sayings which has been quoted against him.

h. A direct answer to the libertines, who maintained that sexual intercourse was as necessary to the body as food and drink. Paul replies that food and drink are linked to the present world and will disappear with it (v. 13); but, cf. 10:31, sexual conduct touches our belonging to Christ and must be such as to befit a member of Christ, vv. 15–17, *see* Ep 5:21–33,23f.

i. var. 'has raised'. This fits the theology of Col 2:12 better than that of Rm 6:4–8, and seems anachronistic in 1 Co.

j. One would expect 'is one body with him', but Paul is careful to avoid too materialistic an understanding of the physical realism of union to Christ (v. 15).

k. This contrast is fairly familiar to Semitic literature, cf. Mt 12:31; Lk 14:26; Rm 9:13. A debauchee sins more against his own body than one who commits another less physical sin; he turns his body away from its true vocation which is to make a relationship with a life other than his own.

l. *See* 3:16e; Jn 2:21i.

m. *See* Rm 3:24j.

7 a. Paul does not consider marriage and virginity in general, but gives answers, seemingly point by point, to the questions put to him. He considers in turn: married people (the Christian couple, vv. 1–11, marriage between Christian and gentile, vv. 12–16) and unmarried people (virgins, vv. 23–35, engaged couples, vv. 36–38, widows, vv. 39–40). The general principle of solution is given in vv. 17,20,24: Everyone should remain in the condition in which he was when called. But this plan is not inflexible: virginity is often mentioned with regard to marriage and vice versa. In this way Paul suggests that the two conditions are complementary and cannot be understood in isolation.

b. Or 'Now for the questions about which you wrote, namely that it is a good thing for a man not to touch a woman.' In any case Paul recognises the validity of this opinion for the unmarried (it is better that they should remain so, v. 8), but contests its application to married people, for whom he does not recommend continence, vv. 2–5.

c. An invitation to married people to make use of marriage, rather than advice to those who have not received the vocation to celibacy.

d. Every selfish use of marriage is ruled out. What is demanded is the gift of self; in Ep 5:25 it is the example of Christ in his sacrifice which is put before married people.

e. This concession applies to periods of abstinence within marriage. For others the concession is to marry, *see* v. 7.

f. For Paul the distinction of virginity from marriage is not that it is a special gift from God, for both conditions are gifts from God.

g. Paul includes in this category separated couples, *see* v. 11.

h. The expression recalls Gn 2:18 and seems to contradict it, 'It is not good for man to be alone.' But this contradiction is only superficial: for the Christian united to Christ and to his brothers, the solitude of Adam is an impossibility.

i. 'Sanctification' and 'holiness' here, as frequently in the Bible, mean not so much the perfection of life as its precondition—dedication to God and adoption by him, *see* Ac 9:13g. By marrying one of God's people a pagan is brought into a special relationship with the true God and with his Church. The children born of such a marriage are members of the holy people by right. It is to be noted that no mention is made of baptism.

j. The same word as at v. 11, where remarriage is explicitly excluded; but in this case Paul does not explicitly envisage a new marriage.

k. var. 'us'.

l. lit. 'rather make good use'. Some supply 'of the chance', but this does not fit the context.

m. Spiritually, by their point of view and morals.

n. This applies to both sexes.

o. The 'time of troubles' between the first coming of Christ and his return, *see* 2 Co 6:2a.

p. Not the trials of concupiscence, 7:2,9, but the upsets of married life.

q. A technical term: 'time has been put under full sail'. Whatever the interval before the *parousia*, it loses its importance in view of the fact that, in the risen Christ, the world to come is already present.

r. A piece of rhetoric where the overall effect is more important than the individual elements. Paul does not recommend indifference with regard to earthly things, he wishes only to prevent his readers from becoming engrossed in them and forgetting that they have a value only relatively to Christ and his coming Kingdom.

s. var. v. 33: '. . . what pleases his wife; v. 34: And there is a difference between the married and the unmarried woman. The unmarried woman gives her mind to the Lord's affairs.'

t. 'his fiancée', lit. 'his virgin'. • The old interpretation of this text sees in it the dilemma of conscience for a father wondering whether he should dispose of his daughter's hand in marriage. The translation then reads

Still, if there is anyone who feels that it would not be fair to his daughter to let her grow too old for marriage, and that he should do something about it, he is free to do as he likes: he is not sinning if there is a marriage. On the other hand, if someone has firmly made his mind up, without any compulsion and in complete freedom of choice, to keep his daughter as she is, he will be doing a good thing. In other words, the man who sees that his daughter is

married has done a good thing but the man who keeps his daughter unmarried has done something even better.

But this interpretation raises such difficulties that it is progressively being abandoned. It is surely a question not of girls who put their virginity under the protection of a trustworthy man with whom they live in dangerous intimacy, but of fiancées. After speaking of married people and of virgins, and before raising the question of widows, Paul discusses those who were engaged at the time of their conversion, to whom the thrice-repeated principle (vv. 17,20,24) 'Let everyone stay as he was when he received the call' obviously cannot apply. Paul's solution agrees with what he said in vv. 8–9.

u. She should marry a Christian.

8 a. When food, especially meat, was offered to the gods, part of it went to the priests and the donor, and what remained might be eaten at a sacred meal or might be sold in the shops and markets. The Corinthians were divided on this matter: could one eat such food without compromising with idolatry? Paul answers as in Rm 14–15: the Christian is free, but love requires him to respect the susceptibilities of his brothers who have scruples. He does not mention the decree of Jerusalem, Ac 15:20,29, and indeed seems ignorant of it. For a discussion of the problems *see* Ac 15:1a.

b. Paul is simply stating a fact. The 'gods' are the mythical gods of Olympus, the 'lords' are divinised human beings.

c. Or possibly 'only one God, the Father, from whom all things (come) and to whom we (go), and one Lord, Jesus Christ, through whom all things (come) and through whom we (go to the Father).' The parentheses indicate words supplied to make this sentence, devoid of verbs, intelligible. Note the affirmation of the pre-existence of Christ, *see* Ph 2:6f; Col 1:15d.

d. var. 'because of the conception of false gods which they still have'.

e. Or 'bring us to judgement before God'.

9 a. Paul has been showing how, though free to do whatever he thinks best about food dedicated to false gods, a Christian should be guided by love. There follows a fairly long description of how he himself has given up some of his rights as an apostle, out of consideration for others.

b. At the expense of the Christian congregations.

c. Or 'a wife who is a believer'. In any case, for the work of attending to their material welfare, married apostles like Cephas (Peter) presumably took their wives.

d. lit. 'I would rather die than . . . No one shall take away something that I can boast of.' Aposiopesis.

e. In the sense explained in 11:1 and Ga 2:20m.

f. This passage uses the sporting vocabulary of the day. Paul invites 'the strong' to imitate him by sacrificing their rights for love, in order to receive a heavenly reward, just as athletes deprive themselves of everything to win the prize.

10 a. vv. 1–13 are a commentary on 'disqualified', in the previous sentence. The examples from Israel's history show there is a real danger of being rejected. The cause of the disqualification was arrogance and presumption, so the 'strong' should beware of these vices.

b. Paul recalls the cloud and the passing through the Sea of Reeds (or Red Sea), images of baptism, and manna and water from the rock, images of the Eucharist, to spur the Corinthians to prudence and humility. The Hebrews in the desert enjoyed, in some sense, the same privileges as themselves, but nevertheless most of them failed to please God, v. 5.

c. According to a rabbinic tradition, the rock of Nb 20:8 followed Israel in the desert. For Paul this rock symbolises the pre-existent Christ already active in Israel's history.

d. The purpose in the events, intended by God, was to prefigure in the history of Israel the spiritual realities of the messianic age (which are known as 'antitypes', 1 P 3:21, but *see* Heb 9:24). These 'typological' (or less accurately, 'allegorical', Ga 4:24) meanings in the OT narrative, though not consciously intended by the authors, are nevertheless valid and necessary for the understanding of scripture intended by God, the author of scripture as a whole. Typological meanings of OT events are often pointed out by the authors of the NT, as though the sole purpose of Israel's written history had been to provide types for the instruction of Christians. Paul does this, v. 11 and 9:9; Rm 4:23 seq.; 5:14; 15:4; cf. 2 Tm 3:16, and some books like John and Hebrews are based on a typological interpretation of the OT.

e. var. 'Christ'.

f. In the NT, the aim of being put to the test is that the reality behind the appearance may be found. God 'tempts' someone although he knows the heart, 2 Ch 32:31; Jr 11:20, to give that person the chance to reveal the very deepest attitudes, Gn 22:1a; Ex 16:4; Dt 8:12,16; 13:4; Jdt 8:25–27. More often, this testing is initiated by external circumstances, or by the Devil, the 'Tempter', 7:5; Jb 1:8–12; Mt 4:1 and par; 1 Th 3:5; Rv 2:10, or by greed, 1 Tm 6:9; Jm 1:13–14, which gives the word the sense of a seduction, an attraction towards evil, over which, however, the faithful can triumph with God's help, Si 44:20; Mt 6:13seq.; 26:41seq.; Lk 8:13; 1 P 1:6–7. Jesus allowed himself to be tempted in order to emphasise his submission to the will of the Father, Mt 4:1 and par.; 26:39–41 and par.; Heb 2:18; 4:15. Anyone who 'tempts' God, however, is guilty of blasphemy, Ex 17:2,7; Ac 15:10k.

g. i.e. the cup of wine for which we thank God, like Christ at the Last Supper.

h. By sharing in the Body of Christ, Christians are united to Christ and to one another. The Eucharist makes the unity of the Church in Christ a reality, *see* 12:12j.

i. The Israel of history, cf. Rm 7:5, as compared with the Israel 'of God', Ga 6:16, the true Israel, the Christian community.

j. In vv. 16–18, eucharistic communion with Christ is compared with the sacrificial meals of the OT, at which the participants were in communion with the altar. Here the table of the Eucharist is contrasted with the table of the sacred meals which conclude pagan sacrifices. For Paul, the Eucharist can clearly be regarded as a sacrificial meal.

k. The jealousy of God, Ex 20:5; Dt 4:24, which the OT compares with the jealousy of a husband for his wife, Ho 2:21seq., 21u,v, is touched on in several places in the NT. Here the word has its full meaning: worship of the true God must exclude all 'communion' with idolatry, and it implies a loyalty to be preserved at all costs, 2 Co 11:2, and zeal in the service of the faith, Ac 22:3; Rm 10:2; Ga 1:13–14; Ph 3:6.

l. One should not do violence to the erroneous conscience of another, but also not submit to its false judgement.

11 a. That is, Christ, from whom he appears to hide instead of 'reflecting his brightness with his face unveiled', 2 Co 3:18. Paul is playing here on the two meanings of the Greek word *kephale*, 'head' or 'master'. His argument is so directly based on the customs to which he is used (v. 16) that his conclusions must be understood in that context.

b. The guardians of order and decorum in public worship, according to a Jewish interpretation of the end of Dt 23:15 (Qumran).

c. Their 'own supper' is contrasted with the 'Lord's Supper' of v. 20, which demands a common celebration in love rather than a selfish division into groups.

d. Not by a direct revelation, but from a tradition going back to the Lord. Here, as in 15:3–7, *see* 15:3b, Paul is using the technical terminology of the rabbis for the passing on of tradition; he seems to be quoting the earliest Christian tradition about the Eucharist, couched in terms and phrases untypical of Paul.

e. var. 'This is my body, broken for you,' 'given for you'.

f. Paul's text is close to that of Lk 22:19–20.

g. add. 'unworthily'.

h. var. 'The Body of the Lord'. This v. is most naturally taken as referring to failures to recognise Christ's presence and activity in the Eucharist (cf. v. 27). However, the emphasis in this letter on the Church as the Body of Christ suggests that there may be also a reference to selfish individuals who ignore needy fellow-members of the Christian family (cf. vv. 11 and 33).

i. Evidently Paul considers the sickness and death of some Corinthians to have been a punishment for irreverence to 'the body and blood of the Lord'.

j. The punishments are sent as a lesson so that people may reform themselves before the Last Judgement. They would not have been necessary if the guilty person had examined and corrected himself, particularly on the occasions of sharing in the Body of Christ (v. 31).

12 a. Chapters 12 to 14 deal with making the proper use of the gifts of the Spirit (charisms), granted to the community as visible evidence of the presence of the Spirit and to help the young community whose faith had not transformed a mentality shot through with paganism. The Corinthian Christians have been tempted to value and develop the more spectacular gifts, and to exercise them at the assemblies of the church in an undisciplined atmosphere reminiscent of certain pagan ceremonies. Paul's response is to declare that charisms are given for the good of the community; they should never give rise to the forming of rival parties (ch. 12). In fact, Christian love surpasses all other gifts (ch. 13). Finally, he explains that the hierarchy of charisms is established according to the contribution that each of them makes to the building up of the community (ch. 14).

b. There is probably an allusion here to the incoherence and disorderliness which were held to be a sign of the authenticity of certain pagan cults; this is contrasted in v. 3 with the meetings of the Christians, at which the content of the sermon or prophecy, not the mere appearance of being inspired, is the sign of its truth.

c. Note again the triadic formulation, cf. 6:11; 2 Co 13:13e.

d. Probably the gift of preaching the deepest Christian truths about God and God's life in us: this is the 'perfect teaching' of Heb 6:1; *see also* 2 Co 2:6–16.

e. The gift of preaching elementary Christian truths: 'the elementary teaching concerning Christ' of Heb 6:1.

f. An unusually intense faith, cf. 13:2.

g. The gift of knowing if *charismata* were spiritual, natural, or evil.

h. The gift of 'tongues', or glossolalia, is the power of praying, especially praising God, under the action of the Spirit and under the pressure of ecstasy, by making sounds which, though continuous and syllabled, are not intelligible as language. This is what Paul calls 'speaking in tongues' (14:5,6,18,23,39) or 'speaking in a tongue' (14:2,4,9,13, 14,19,26,27). This gift was one of the first visible effects of the outpouring of the Spirit in the primitive Church. *See* Ac 2:3–4; 10:44–46; 11:15; 19:6.

i. Paul uses the classical analogy of society as a single body with many parts, but his concept of the Body of Christ goes back to the memory of his own conversion, *see* Ac 9:4seq.; Ga 1:15seq., to faith in Jesus whose body, raised from the dead and given life by the Spirit, Rm 1:4c, became the 'first-fruits' of a new creation, 1 Co 15:23. The words spoken by the Lord at Paul's conversion, 'I am Jesus, whom you are persecuting,' imply that Christians are identified with the risen Christ. In Paul's writings, Christians are bodily united with the risen body, Rm 8:11, by baptism, 1 Co 12:13; cf. Rm 6:4a, and the Eucharist, 1 Co 10:16seq., which make them parts of Christ's body, 1 Co 6:15, united in such a way that he and they together form the Body of Christ (what is now called 'the mystical body'), 1 Co 12:27; Rm 12:4seq. This wholly realistic teaching of 1 Co is taken up later on and developed in the Letters of the Captivity, where the basic idea remains the same, i.e. human beings are reconciled to God by becoming parts of, Ep 5:30, Christ's body which was physically dead but is now spiritually alive. Ep 2:14–18; Col 1:22. The stress, however, is on the unity of the Body that brings all Christians together in one Spirit, Ep 4:4; Col 3:15, and on the identification of the Body with the Church, Ep 1:22seq.; 5:23; Col 1:18,24. Having thus personified the body, Ep 4:12seq.; Col 2:19, Paul asserts that Christ is its Head, Ep 1:22; 4:15seq.; 5:23; Col 1:18; 2:19 (cf. 1 Co 12:21). This assertion probably developed from the concept of Christ as Head of all Powers, Col 2:10. Eventually, in its widest sense, Paul includes in his concept of the Body the entire cosmos as unified under the Lord Christ, Ep 1:23t; see Jn 2:21i.

j. As the human body gives plurality of its parts, so Christ, the principle of unity in his Church, brings all Christians into the unity of his Body.

k. The regular teachers appointed for each separate church, see Ac 13:1a.

l. lit. 'helpings': possibly those who collected or dispensed grants to the poor; or persons appointed to assist regularly at the meetings.

m. The gift of administering and directing the churches.

n. Three parts: superiority of love (vv. 1–3), its works (vv. 4–7), its never-ending duration (vv. 8–13). It is about love between brothers. Love for God is not directly envisaged, but is present implicitly, especially in v. 13, in connection with faith and hope.

13 a. Love (agape) has no possessiveness and is not a desire for satisfaction: it wants to satisfy the other. The supreme love is God's love for us, 1 Jn 4:19, that made him give his Son so that sinners might be reconciled, Rm 5:8; 8:32–39; 2 Co 5:18–21; Ep 2:4–7; see Jn 3:16seq.; 1 Jn 4:9–10, and become not only God's chosen ones, Ep 1:4, but God's sons, 1 Jn 3:1. This love is attributed to God (the Father), Rm 5:5; 8:39; 2 Co 3:11,13; Ph 2:1; 2 Th 2:16; cf. 1 Jn 2:15, but as it is identical with God's nature, 1 Jn 4:7seq., 16, it is found in the Son, Rm 8:35,37,39; 2 Co 5:14; Ep 3:19; 1 Tm 1:14; 2 Tm 1:13, so the Son loves the Father as the Son is loved by the Father, Ep 1:6; Col 1:13; cf. Jn 3:35; 10:17; 14:31, and as the Father loves us, so the Son loves the human race, Jn 13:1,34; 14:21; 15:9, which he was sent to save, 2 Co 5:14seq.; Ga 2:20; Ep 5:2,25; 1 Tm 1:14seq.; cf. Jn 15:13; 1 Jn 3:16; Rv 1:5. This is the same love that the Holy Spirit, Rm 15:30; Col 1:8, gives Christians, Rm 5:5; cf. Ga 5:22. To love friends and enemies, Mt 5:43–48 and par., is not only the necessary consequence of God's love for us, but actually proves that God loves us, 1 Jn 3:17; 4:20seq., and it is the new commandment laid down by Christ, Jn 13:34seq.; 15:12,17; 1 Jn 3:23; etc., and constantly emphasised by his disciples, Rm 13:8; Ga 5:13seq.; Ep 1:15; Ph 2:2seq.; Col 1:4; 1 Th 3:12; 2 Th 1:3; Phm 5–7; cf. Jm 2:8; 1 P 1:22; 2:17; 4:8; 1 Jn 2:10; 3:10seq., 14; etc. This is how Paul loves the Christians of his own churches, 2 Co 2:4; 12:15; etc., and how they love him, Col 1:18; 1 Th 3:6; etc. Love presupposes sincerity, humility, selflessness and self-sacrifice, vv. 4–7; Rm 12:9seq.; 2 Co 6:6; Ph 2:2seq., service. Ga 5:13; cf. Heb 6:10, mutual help, Ep 4:2; cf. Rm 14:15; 2 Co 2:7seq. Love shows itself in the way we behave, 2 Co 8:8–11,24; cf. 1 Jn 3:18, and the way we obey the Lord's commands, Jn 14:15; 1 Jn 5:2seq.; etc., and give effect to our faith, Ga 5:6; cf. Heb 10:24. Love holds the community together, Col 3:14; cf. 2 P 1:7, and it 'covers up many sins', 1 P 4:8; cf. Lk 7:47. Since love of neighbour springs from love of God, its motive cannot be fear, Rm 8:28–39; cf. 1 Jn 4:17seq. Nor can we be charitable without truth, Ep 4:15–16; cf. 2 Th 2:10, and it is this that enables us to make moral judgements, Ph 1:9, and gives us spiritual understanding of the divine mystery, Col 2:2; cf. 1 Jn 4:7, and spiritual knowledge of the otherwise unknowable love of Christ, Ep 3:17–19; cf. 8:1–3; 13:8–12. Since Christ, Ep 3:17, and the whole Trinity, 2 Co 13:13e; cf. Jn 14:15–23; 1 Jn 4:12, live in the soul that has this love, it fosters the theological virtues. see Rm 1:16h; 5:2c, in any person where it is the dominant characteristic, 1 Co 13:3. Love is the only eternal virtue, v. 8, and will be perfect in

the vision, v. 12; cf. 1 Jn 3:2, only when God gives his lovers the gifts he has promised, 1 Co 2:9; Rm 8:28; Ep 6:24; 2 Tm 4:8; cf. Jm 1:12; 2:5.,

b. var. 'I may give all my goods to the poor so that I can boast of it.'

c. In vv. 4–7, Christian love is defined with the use of a series of fifteen verbal phrases, not abstract nouns, i.e. it is not an abstract quality, but is known by the actions to which it gives rise.

d. When our imperfect (v. 11) and indirect (v. 12) knowledge of God disappears before the direct sight of God, love will remain the same as it was in this life.

e. This association of the three theological virtues, which is found earlier in 1 Th 1:3 and which may well have been in use before Paul's time, recurs frequently in his letters, though the order varies: 13:7,13; Rm 5:1–5; 12:6–12; Ga 5:5seq.; Ep 1:15–18; 4:2–5; Col 1:4–5; 1 Th 5:8; 1 Tm 6:11; Tt 2:2. Cf. Heb 6:10–12; 10:22–24; 1 P 1:3–9,21seq. Faith and love are associated in 1 Th 3:6; 2 Th 1:3; Phm 5, faith and fortitude in 2 Th 1:4, love and fortitude in 2 Th 3:5; cf. 2 Co 13:13.

14 a. Or 'none of them is gibberish'.

b. A barbarian was someone who did not understand Greek.

c. This prayer of ecstatic utterance is so freed by 'the spirit' that it contains nothing limited enough to be grasped by the 'mind'.

d. One who is not granted similar gifts.

e. The quotation is very free.

f. An obscure text: the vv. 23–24 seem to be in contradiction to v. 22.

g. Incoherence in a prophecy would prove that the prophet was a false prophet.

h. The attitude in 11:5 is more positive, which diminishes the importance of this prohibition, linked as it is with the social context of the time.

i. Since the answer is negative, Paul is asking the Corinthians to accept the practice of other churches.

j. Or, he is unnoticed by God who does not acknowledge him as his own; var. 'if he refuses to recognise this, well let him refuse' (Paul losing patience). For a similar way of putting an end to discussion, see 11:16; Ph 3:15seq.

15 a. Some of the Christians at Corinth rejected the resurrection of the dead, v. 12. Greeks found it a materialistic idea, Ac 17:32y, while the Jews had first gradually perceived it, Jb 19:25g; Ps 16:10; Ezk 37:10d, and then taught it explicitly, 2 M 7:9c; Dn 12:2,3c. To combat the Corinthians' error, Paul starts from the fundamental assertion of the gospel proclamation, the paschal mystery of Christ's death and resurrection, vv. 3–4 (cf. Rm 1:4; Ga 1:2–4; 1 Th 1:10), which he develops by enumerating the appearances of the Risen Lord, vv. 5–11; see Ac 1:8k. Starting from there he shows the absurdity of the opinion which he is opposing, vv. 12–34, see v. 13i. Christ is the first-fruits and the effective cause of the resurrection of the dead, vv. 20–28; see Rm 8:11g. Finally Paul answers objections about the mode of resurrection of the dead, vv. 35–53, and ends with a hymn of thanks, vv. 54–57.

b. In the phrases, 'keep it unchanged', 'passed on . . . . 'what I had been taught', Paul is adopting the vocabulary of the rabbinic tradition, cf. 11:23. But in addition, the gospel, unlike this tradition, is announced, vv. 1–2, proclaimed (v. 11); cf. Mt 4:23; etc.; the object of faith, 1 Co 15:2,11, cf. Mk 1:15, and the bringer of salvation, 1 Co 15:2; cf. Ac 11:14; 16:17. In the vv. that follow the vocabulary and turn of phrase are uncharacteristic of Paul, which suggests that he is quoting the most ancient tradition of the Church about the resurrection appearances, formulae that were learnt by new converts, cf. 11:23d.

c. The expiation effected by Christ's death is a part of the gospel proclamation even before Paul; cf. Rm 6:3.

d. These three clauses, which will have a place in the

creeds of the future, seem already to have a fixed formulation.

e. Paul implies that they can still attest what they have seen, and that their faith in Christ's resurrection rests on sure witness.

f. i.e. have died; Paul's usual expression. vv. 18,20,51; 1 Th 4:13g.

g. 'The apostles' apparently comprise a larger group than 'the Twelve' of v. 5.

h. An allusion to the abnormal, sudden and *surgical* nature of Paul's birth into the apostolic family. He makes no distinction in kind between the appearance to himself that took place on the Damascus road and the appearances of Jesus that took place between the resurrection and the ascension.

i. Denial of the resurrection of the dead brings with it denial of the particular case of the resurrection of Christ. Alternatively, the resurrection of Christ makes no sense except as the first-fruits of our resurrection. But this consideration enters only at v. 20.

j. None of the aspects of the Christian message and of the faith which corresponds to it makes sense except in function of the central reality, the risen Christ. Without this, everything collapses.

k. What makes sin disappear is the new life, participation in the life of the risen Christ, *see* Rm 6:8–10; 8:2b.

l. Or 'If in this life we have done nothing but hope in Christ'.

m. Contemporary Jewish thought envisaged two Adams, first a perfect, heavenly model of Adam, and second the earthly, historical Adam. Paul turns this thinking on its head: the historical Adam was the first and Christ, the re-founder of humanity, is the second, perfect, heavenly Adam. He is the perfect fulfilment of the ideal of Adam, and his exaltation reverses the fall of Adam, *see* Rm 5:12f,h; Ph 2:6d.

n. A Greek word adopted by early Christians to indicate the glorious coming of Christ on his 'Day', 1:8e, at the end of time, Mt 24:3b; *see also* 1 Th 2:19; 3:13; 4:15; 5:23; 2 Th 2:1; Jm 5:7,8; 2 P 1:16; 3:4,12; 1 Jn 2:28. In 2 Th 2:8,9 the same word is used to indicate the coming of the Lawless One; *see* the similar terms 'revelation', 1 Co 1:7c, and 'appearing', 1 Tm 6:14f.

o. The perspective is not merely physical and biological, but includes the whole person, spiritual death to sin and risen life in justice and love. Paul's perspective does not include a resurrection of sinners; contrast Jn 5:29; Ac 24:15; cf. Dn 12:2.

p. All the forces hostile to the sovereignty of God, 2:6; Ep 1:21; Col 1:16; 2:15; 1 P 3:22.

q. When the whole cosmos has been subjected to him, Jesus will go to the Father and say his task is complete. The translation '*scripture* says' is incorrect.

r. What this practice is unknown: Paul does not say whether he approved of it or not; he merely says that it is absurd if the dead do not rise again.

s. This must be metaphorical. The event is not otherwise known to us, but *see* 2 Co 11:23–26.

t. Cf. Qo 9:7–10. It is possible to give up material pleasures from purely human motives; Paul has himself just said so, 9:25.

u. Quoted from Menander's *Thaïs*: it may have become a popular proverb.

v. In popular thought germination was a process dependent on the goodwill of the divinity, not a natural phenomenon, cf. 2 M 7:22–23. In the relationship between the present and the glorified body Paul stresses change much more than continuity. No doubt he wishes to answer the objection (v. 35) which rightly refused to take the imagery of Ezk 37:1–10,10d too literally.

w. In Paul, as in the OT, *psyche* (Hebr. *nephesh*; cf. Gn 2:7) is what gives life to animals, to the human body, 1 Co 15:45; or it is the actual 'life' of the body, Rm 16:4; Ph 2:30; 1 Th 2:8; cf. Mt 2:20; Mk 3:4; Lk 12:20; Jn 10:11; Ac 20:10; etc., its 'living soul', 2 Co 1:23. The term can also

mean any human being, Rm 2:9; 13:1; 2 Co 12:15; etc. As it gives only natural life, 2:14; cf. Jude 19, it is less important than *pneuma* by which a human life is divinised by a process that begins through the gift of the Spirit, Rm 5:5e; *see* Rm 1:9e, and is completed after death. Greek philosophers thought of the higher soul (the *nous*) escaping from 'the body', to survive immortally. Christians thought of immortality more in terms of the restoration of the whole person, involving a resurrection of the body effected by the Spirit or divine principle which God withdrew from human beings because of sins, Gn 6:3, but restored to all who are united to the risen Christ, Rm 1:4c; 8:11, who is the 'heavenly' man and life-giving Spirit, 1 Co 45–49. The 'body' is no longer *psychikon* but *pneumatikon*, it is incorruptible, immortal, v. 53, glorious, v. 43; cf. Rm 8:18; 2 Co 4:17; Ph 3:21; Col 3:4, no longer subject to the laws of matter, Jn 20:19,26; it does not even answer the description of matter, Lk 24:16. *Psyche* can be used in a wider sense as the opposite of the body to indicate what it is in a human being that behaves and feels, Ep 6:6; Ph 1:27; Col 3:23; *see* Mt 22:37 and par.; 26:38 and par.; Lk 1:46; Jn 12:27; Ac 4:32; 1 P 2:11; etc., or even to indicate the spiritual and immortal soul, Mt 10:28,39 and par.; Ac 2:27; Jm 1:21; 5:20; 1 P 1:9; Rv 6:9; etc.

x. Something that is alive because it has a *psyche* giving it a merely natural life, subject to decay and corruption.

y. var. 'we would be able to'.

z. Since the time of Sinai, Ex 19:16,19, the trumpet has been among the symbols of God's intervention, Mt 24:31; 1 Th 4:16j. A trumpet will mark the stages in God's plan for the End; cf. the seven trumpets of Rv 8:6–11:19.

aa. i.e. those who are alive at the time, among whom Paul may be included, *see* 1 Th 5:1a.

bb. om. 'because this perishable nature has put on imperishability'.

cc. A free quotation.

dd. The compressed thought of this sentence is made explicit in Rm 5–7.

ee. A reference back to v. 14; this verse marks the end of the instruction which began at that point. The certainty of victory gives the believer the strength to go forward. For Paul there can be no faith without advance in life.

16 a. On this collection *see* Ac 24:17; Rm 15:26–28; 2 Co 8–9; Ga 2:10. God's holy people (*see* 2 Co 8:4) are the Christians in Jerusalem who from the earliest days were in need of help, Ac 11:29–30. Paul was very anxious to have this collection made, since he regarded it as a sign and a pledge of unity between the churches he had founded and those of the Judaeo-Christians.

b. i.e. 'The Lord's Day', cf. Mt 28:1; Ac 20:7; Rv 1:10.

c. It has been thought that this translation suggests a previous short visit and this translation has been conjectured: 'I do not want on this occasion to make this only a passing visit.' But this is unlikely.

d. The same image is used in 2 Co 2:12; it indicates Paul's missionary opportunities, cf. Ac 14:27; Rv 3:8.

e. In case his presence aggravated party feeling among his own supporters, 1:12; 3:4–6; 4:6.

f. Probably these had brought the letter from the Corinthians to Paul, 7:1.

g. The Roman province is meant.

h. 'Let him be *anathema*.' The word usually corresponds to the OT Hebrew word *herem*, Jos 6:17e. In the NT it is used once. Lk 21:5, of votive offerings in the Temple. More often it acknowledges a curse on the speaker himself, should he not keep a solemn promise, Rm 9:3, or it endorses a curse on another person for a serious sin, here, 1 Co 16:22; Ga 1:8,9; *see* 12:3; Rv 22:3.

i. These Aramaic words ('the Lord is coming') had passed into liturgical use: they expressed the hope that the *parousia* would not be long delayed. An alternative reading is *Marana tha* (Lord, come!), Rv 22:20; cf. Rm 13:12; Ph 4:5; Jm 5:8; 1 P 4:7.

2 CORINTHIANS

THE SECOND LETTER OF PAUL
TO THE CHURCH AT CORINTH

INTRODUCTION

Address and greetings. Thanksgiving

1 Paul, by the will of God an apostle of Christ Jesus, and Timothy, our brother, to the church of God in Corinth and to all God's holy people in the whole of
2 Achaia. ·Grace to you and peace from God our Father and the Lord Jesus Christ.
3 Blessed be the God and Father of our Lord Jesus Christ, the merciful Father
4 and the God who gives every possible encouragement;ᵃ ·he supports us in every hardship, so that we are able to come to the support of others, in every hardship of theirs because of the encouragement that we ourselves receive from God.
5 For just as the sufferings of Christ overflow into our lives; so too does the
6 encouragement we receive through Christ. ·So if we have hardships to undergo, this will contribute to your encouragement and your salvation; if we receive encouragement, this is to gain for you the encouragement which enables you to
7 bear with perseverance the same sufferings as we do. ·So our hope for you is secure in the knowledge that you share the encouragement we receive, no less than the sufferings we bear. ᵇ
8 So in the hardships we underwent in Asia,ᶜ we want you to be quite certain, brothers, that we were under extraordinary pressure, beyond our powers of endur-
9 ance, so that we gave up all hope even of surviving. ·In fact we were carrying the sentence of death within our own selves, so that we should be forced to trust not
10 in ourselves but in God, who raises the dead. ·He did save us from such a death
11 and will save usᵈ—we are relying on him to do so. ·Your prayer for us will contribute to this, so that, for God's favour shown to us as the result of the prayers of so many, thanksᵉ too may be given by many on our behalf.'ᶠ

I: SOME RECENT EVENTS REVIEWED

Why Paul changed his plans

12 There is one thing that we are proud of, namely our conscientious conviction that we have always behaved towards everyone, and especially towards you, with that

unalloyed holiness [f] that comes from God, relying not on human reasoning but on
13 the grace of God. ·In our writing, there is nothing that you cannot read clearly
14 and understand; ·and it is my hope that, just as you have already understood us
partially, so you will understand fully that you can be as proud of us as we shall be
of you when the Day of our Lord Jesus comes.
15   It was with this assurance that I had been meaning to come to you first, so that
16 you would benefit doubly; [h] ·both to visit you on my way to Macedonia, and then
to return to you again from Macedonia, so that you could set me on my way to
17 Judaea. [i] ·Since that was my purpose, do you think I lightly changed my mind? Or
that my plans are based on ordinary human promptings and I have in my mind
18 Yes, yes at the same time as No, no? ·As surely as God is trustworthy, [j] what we
19 say to you is not both Yes and No. ·The Son of God, Jesus Christ, who was
proclaimed to you by us, that is, by me and by Silvanus [k] and Timothy, was never
20 Yes-and-No; his nature is all Yes. ·For in him is found the Yes to all God's
promises [l] and therefore it is 'through him' that we answer 'Amen' [m] to give praise
21, 22 to God. ·It is God who gives us, with you, a sure place in Christ ·and has both
anointed us and marked us with his seal, [n] giving us as pledge the Spirit in our
hearts.
23   By my life I call on God to be my witness that it was only to spare you that I did
24 not come to Corinth again. ·We have no wish to lord it over your faith, but to
work with you for your joy; for your stand in the faith is firm.
1   **2** I made up my mind, then, that my next visit to you would not be a painful
2 one [a], ·for if I cause you distress I am causing distress to my only possible source
3 of joy. ·Indeed, I wrote as I did [b] precisely to spare myself distress when I visited
you, from the very people who should have given me joy, in the conviction that
4 for all of you my joy was yours too. ·I wrote to you in agony of mind, not meaning
to cause you distress but to show you how very much love I have for you.
5   If anyone did cause distress, he caused it not to me, but—not to exaggerate—in
6 some degree to all of you. ·The punishment already imposed by the majority was
7 quite enough for such a person; [c] ·and now by contrast you should forgive and
encourage him all the more, or he may be overwhelmed by the extent of his
8 distress. ·That is why I urge you to give your love towards him definite expression.
9 This was in fact my reason for writing, to test your quality and whether you are
10 completely obedient. ·But if you forgive anybody, then I too forgive him; and
whatever I have forgiven, if there is anything I have forgiven, I have done it for
11 your sake in Christ's presence, ·to avoid being outwitted by Satan, whose scheming
we know only too well.

From Troas to Macedonia. The apostolate: its importance

12 When I came to Troas for the sake of the gospel of Christ and a door was opened
13 for me there in the Lord, ·I had no relief from anxiety, not finding my brother
14 Titus [d] there, and I said goodbye to them and went on to Macedonia. ·[e] But,
thanks be to God who always gives us in Christ a part in his triumphal procession, [f]
and through us is spreading everywhere the fragrance of the knowledge of himself.
15 To God we are the fragrance of Christ, both among those who are being saved
16 and among those who are on the way to destruction; ·for these last, the smell of
death leading to death, but for the first, the smell of life leading to life. Who is
17 equal to such a task? ·At least we do not adulterate the word of God, as so many [g]
do, but it is in all purity, as envoys of God and in God's presence, that we speak in
Christ.

1 **3** Are we beginning to commend ourselves to you afresh—as though we needed,
like some others, to have letters of commendation either to you or from you? *

2 You yourselves are our letter, written in our *b* hearts, that everyone can read and

3 understand; ·and it is plain that you are a letter from Christ, entrusted to our care,
written not with ink but with the Spirit of the living God; not on stone tablets but
on the tablets of human hearts. *c*

4, 5 Such is the confidence we have through Christ in facing God; ·it is not that we
are so competent that we can claim any credit for ourselves; all our competence

6 comes from God. ·He has given us the competence to be ministers of a new
covenant, a covenant which is not of written letters, but of the Spirit; for the

7 written letters kill, but the Spirit gives life. *d* ·Now if the administering of death,
engraved in letters on stone, occurred in such glory that the Israelites could not
look Moses steadily in the face, because of its glory, transitory though this glory

8, 9 was, ·how much more will the ministry of the Spirit occur in glory! ·For if it is
glorious to administer condemnation, to administer saving justice is far richer in

10 glory. ·Indeed, what was once considered glorious has lost all claim to glory, by

11 contrast with the glory which transcends it. ·For if what was transitory had any
glory, how much greater is the glory of that which lasts for ever.

12, 13 With a hope like this, we can speak with complete fearlessness; ·not like Moses
who put a veil over his face so that the Israelites should not watch the end of what

14 was transitory. *e* ·But their minds were closed; indeed, until this very day, the same
veil remains over the reading of the Old Testament: it is not lifted, for only in

15 Christ is it done away with. *f* ·As it is, to this day, whenever Moses is read, their

16 hearts are covered with a veil, ·and this veil will not be taken away till they turn to

17 the Lord. ·Now this Lord is the Spirit *g* and where the Spirit of the Lord is, there is

18 freedom. ·And all of us, with our unveiled faces like mirrors reflecting *h* the glory
of the Lord, *i* are being transformed into the image *j* that we reflect in brighter and
brighter glory; this is the working of the Lord who is the Spirit. *k*

1, 2 **4** Such by God's mercy is our ministry, and therefore we do not waver ·but have
renounced all shameful secrecy. *a* It is not our way to be devious, or to falsify
the word of God; instead, in God's sight we commend ourselves to every human

3 being with a conscience by showing the truth openly. ·If our gospel seems to be

4 veiled at all, it is so to those who are on the way to destruction, ·the unbelievers
whose minds have been blinded by the god of this world, *b* so that they cannot see

5 shining the light of the gospel of the glory of Christ, who is the image of God. ·It is
not ourselves that we are proclaiming, but Christ Jesus as the Lord, and ourselves

6 as your servants for Jesus' sake. ·It is God who said, 'Let light shine out of
darkness,' that has shone into our hearts to enlighten them with the knowledge of
God's glory, the glory on the face of Christ.

The hardships and hopes of the apostolate

7 But we hold this treasure in pots of earthenware, so that the immensity of the

8 power is God's and not our own. *c* ·We are subjected to every kind of hardship,

9 but never distressed; *d* we see no way out but we never despair; ·we are pursued

10 but never cut off; knocked down, but still have some life in us; always ·we carry
with us in our body the death of Jesus so that the life of Jesus, too, may be visible

11 in our body. ·Indeed, while we are still alive, we are continually being handed
over to death, for the sake of Jesus, so that the life of Jesus, too, may be visible in

12 our mortal flesh. ·In us, then, death is at work; in you, life.

13 But as we have the same spirit of faith as is described in scripture—*I believed*

14 *and therefore I spoke*—we, too, believe and therefore we, too, speak, ·realising that he who raised up the Lord Jesus will raise us up with Jesus in our turn, and
15 bring us to himself—and you as well. ·You see, everything is for your benefit, so that as grace spreads, so, to the glory of God, thanksgiving may also overflow among more and more people.
16   That is why we do not waver; indeed, though this outer human nature of ours may be falling into decay, at the same time our inner human nature is renewed
17 day by day. ·The temporary, light burden of our hardships is earning us for ever
18 an utterly incomparable, eternal weight of glory, ·since what we aim for is not visible but invisible. Visible things are transitory, but invisible things eternal.

1 5 For we are well aware.ᵉ that when the tent that houses us on earth is folded up, there is a house for us from God, not made by human hands but everlasting,
2, 3 in the heavens. ·And in this earthly state we do indeed groan, ·longing to put on our heavenly home over the present one; if indeed we are to be found clothed
4 rather than stripped bare. ᵇ ·Yes, indeed, in this present tent, we groan under the burden, not that we want to be stripped of our covering, but because we want to be covered with a second garment on top, so that what is mortal in us may be
5 swallowed up by life. ·It is God who designed us for this very purpose, and he has given us the Spirit as a pledge.
6   We are always full of confidence, then, realising that as long as we are at home
7 in the body we are exiled from the Lord, ·guided by faith and not yet by sight;ᶜ
8 we are full of confidence, then, and long instead to be exiled from the body and to
9 be at home with the Lord. ᵈ ·And so whether at home or exiled, we make it our
10 ambition to please him. ·For at the judgement seat of Christ we are all to be seen for what we are, so that each of us may receive what he has deserved in the body, matched to whatever he has done, good or bad.

The apostolate in action

11 And so it is with the fear of the Lord always in mind that we try to win people
12 over. But God sees us for what we are, and I hope your consciences do too. ·Again we are saying this not to commend ourselves to you, but simply to give you the opportunity to take pride in us, so that you may have an answer for those who
13 take pride in appearances and not inner reality. ·If we have been unreasonable, it
14 was for God; if reasonable, for you. ᵉ ·For the love of Christ overwhelms us when
15 we consider that if one man died for all, then all have died;ᶠ ·his purpose in dying for all humanity was that those who live should live not any more for themselves, but for him who died and was raised to life.
16   From now onwards, then, we will not consider anyone by human standards: even if we were once familiar with Christ according to human standards, we do
17 not know him in that way any longer. ᵍ ·So for anyone who is in Christ, there is a
18 new creation:ʰ the old order is gone and a new being is there to see. ⁱ ·It is all God's work; he reconciled us to himself through Christ and he gave us the ministry
19 of reconciliation. ·I mean, God was in Christ reconciling the world to himself, not holding anyone's faults against them, but entrusting to us the message of reconciliation.
20   So we are ambassadors for Christ; it is as though God were urging you through
21 us, and in the name of Christ we appeal to you to be reconciled to God. ·For our sake he made the sinless one a victim for sin,ʲ so that in him we might become the uprightness of God.

1,2 **6** As his fellow-workers, we urge you not to let your acceptance of his grace come to nothing. ·As he said, '*At the time of my favour I have answered you; on the day of salvation I have helped you;*' well, now is the real time of favour,
3 now the day of salvation ᵃ is here. ·We avoid putting obstacles in anyone's way, so
4 that no blame may attach to our work of service; ·but in everything we prove ourselves authentic servants of God; by resolute perseverance in times of hard-
5 ships, difficulties and distress; ·when we are flogged or sent to prison or mobbed;
6 labouring, sleepless, starving; ·in purity, in knowledge, in patience, in kindness;
7 in the Holy Spirit, in a love free of affectation; ·in the word of truth and in the
8 power of God; by using the weapons of uprightness for attack and for defence: ·in times of honour or disgrace, blame or praise; taken for impostors and yet we are
9 genuine; ·unknown and yet we are acknowledged; dying, and yet here we are,
10 alive; scourged but not executed; ·in pain yet always full of joy; poor and yet making many people rich; having nothing, and yet owning everything.

A warning

11,12 People of Corinth, we have spoken frankly and opened our heart to you. ·Any
13 distress you feel is not on our side; the distress is in your own selves. ·In fair exchange—I speak as though to children of mine—you must open your hearts too.
14 ᵇDo not harness yourselves in an uneven team with unbelievers; how can uprightness and law-breaking be partners, or what can light and darkness have in
15 common? ·How can Christ come to an agreement with Beliar and what sharing
16 can there be between a believer and an unbeliever? ·The temple of God cannot compromise with false gods, and that is what we are ᶜ—the temple of the living God. We have God's word for it: *I shall fix my home among them and live among*
17 *them; I will be their God and they will be my people.* ·*Get away from them, purify yourselves,* says the Lord. *Do not touch anything unclean, and then I shall welcome*
18 *you.* ·*I shall be father to you, and* you *will be sons* and daughters *to me,* says the almighty Lord.
1 **7** Since these promises have been made to us, my dear friends, we should wash ourselves clean of everything that pollutes either body or spirit, bringing our sanctification to completion in the fear of God.
2 Keep a place for us in your hearts. ᵈ We have not injured anyone, or ruined
3 anyone, or taken advantage of anyone. ·I am not saying this to condemn anybody; as I have already told you, you are in our hearts—so that together we live and
4 together we die. ·I can speak with the greatest frankness to you; and I can speak with the greatest pride about you: in all our hardship, I am filled with encouragement and overflowing with joy.

Paul in Macedonia; he is joined by Titus

5 Even after we had come to Macedonia, there was no rest for this body of ours. ᵇ Far from it; we were beset by hardship on all sides, there were quarrels all
6 around us and misgivings within us. ·But God, who encourages all those who are
7 distressed, encouraged us through the arrival of Titus; ·and not simply by his arrival only, but also by means of the encouragement that you had given him, as he told us of your desire to see us, how sorry you were and how concerned for us; so that I was all the more joyful.
8 So now, though I did distress you with my letter, ᶜ I do not regret it. Even if I did regret it—and I realise that the letter distressed you, even though not for
9 long—·I am glad now, not because you were made to feel distress, but because

the distress that you were caused led to repentance; your distress was the kind
10 that God approves and so you have come to no kind of harm through us. ·For to
be distressed in a way that God approves leads to repentance and then to salvation
11 with no regrets; it is the world's kind of distress that ends in death. ·Just look at
this present case: at what the result has been of your being made to feel distress in
the way that God approves—what concern, what defence, what indignation and
what alarm; what yearning, and what enthusiasm, and what justice done. *d* In every
12 way you have cleared yourselves of blame in this matter. ·So although I wrote a
letter to you, it was not for the sake of the offender, nor for the one offended, *e*
but only so that you yourselves should fully realise in the sight of God what concern
13 you have for us. ·That is what I have found encouraging.

In addition to all this to encourage us, we were made all the more joyful by
14 Titus' joy, now that his spirit has been refreshed by you all. ·And if I boasted
about you to him in any way, then I have not been made to look foolish; indeed,
15 our boast to Titus has been proved to be as true as anything we said to you. ·His
personal affection for you is all the stronger when he remembers how obedient
16 you have all been, and how you welcomed him with fear and trembling. ·I am glad
that I have every confidence in you.

II: ORGANISATION OF THE COLLECTION *a*

Why the Corinthians should be generous

1 **8** Next, brothers, we will tell you of the grace *b* of God which has been granted
2 to the churches of Macedonia, ·and how, throughout continual ordeals of
hardship, their unfailing joy and their intense poverty have overflowed in a wealth
3 of generosity on their part. ·I can testify that it was of their own accord that they
made their gift, which was not merely as far as their resources would allow, but
4 well beyond their resources; ·and they had kept imploring us most insistently for
5 the privilege of a share in the fellowship of service to God's holy people—·it was
not something that we expected of them, but it began by their offering themselves
6 to the Lord and to us at the prompting of the will of God. ·In the end we urged
Titus, since he had already made a beginning, also to bring this work of generosity
7 to completion among you. ·More, as you are rich in everything—faith, eloquence,
understanding, concern for everything, and love for us too *c*—then make sure that
8 you excel in this work of generosity too. ·I am not saying this as an order, but
9 testing the genuineness of your love against the concern of others. ·You are well
aware of the generosity *d* which our Lord Jesus Christ had, that, although he was
rich, he became poor for your *e* sake, so that you should become rich through his
10 poverty. *f* ·I will give you my considered opinion in the matter; this will be the
right course for you as you were the first, a year ago, not only to take any action
11 but also even to conceive the project. ·Now, then, complete the action as well, so
that the fulfilment may—so far as your resources permit—be proportionate to
12 your enthusiasm for the project. ·As long as the enthusiasm is there, the basis on
13 which it is acceptable is what someone has, not what someone does not have. ·It is
not that you ought to relieve other people's needs and leave yourselves in hardship;
14 but there should be a fair balance—·your surplus *g* at present may fill their deficit,
and another time their surplus *h* may fill your deficit. So there may be a fair balance;
15 as scripture says: *No one who had collected more had too much, no one who
collected less had too little.*

The delegates recommended to the Corinthians

16. 17 Thank God for putting into Titus' heart the same sincere concern for you. ·He certainly took our urging to heart; but greater still was his own enthusiasm, and he
18 went off to you of his own accord. ·We have sent with him the brother *i* who is
19 praised as an evangelist in all the churches ·and who, what is more, was elected by the churches to be our travelling companion in this work of generosity, a work to be administered by us for the glory of the Lord and our complete satisfaction.*j*
20 We arranged it this way so that no one should be able to make any accusation
21 against us about this large sum we are administering. ·And so *we have been careful*
22 *to do right* not only *in the sight of the Lord* but also *in the sight of people*. ·Along with these, we have sent a brother of ours *k* whose eagerness we have tested over and over again in many ways and who is now all the more eager because he has so
23 much faith in you. ·If Titus is in question—he is my own partner and fellow-worker in your interests; and if our brothers—they are the emissaries *l* of the churches and
24 the glory of Christ. ·So then, in full view of all the churches, give proof that you love them, and that we were right to boast of you to them.

1 **9** About the help to God's holy people, there is really no need for me to write to
2 you; *a* ·for I am well aware of your enthusiasm, and I have been boasting of it to the Macedonians that 'Achaia has been ready for a year'; your enthusiasm has
3 been a spur to many others. ·All the same, I have sent the brothers, to make sure that our boast about you may not prove hollow in this respect and that you may be
4 ready, as I said you would be; ·so that if by chance some of the Macedonians came with me and found you unprepared we—to say nothing of yourselves—would not
5 be put to shame by our confidence in you. ·So I have thought it necessary to encourage the brothers to go to you ahead of us and make sure in advance of the gift that you have already promised, so that it is all at hand as a real gift and not an imposition.

Blessings to be expected from the collection

6 But remember: anyone who sows sparsely will reap sparsely as well—and anyone
7 who sows generously will reap generously as well. ·Each one should give as much as he has decided on his own initiative, not reluctantly or under compulsion, for
8 *God loves a cheerful giver*. ·God is perfectly able to enrich you with every grace,
9 so that you always have enough for every ·conceivable need, and your resources overflow in all kinds of good work. As scripture says: *To the needy he gave without stint, his uprightness stands firm for ever*.
10 The one who so freely provides *seed for the sower and food to eat* will provide you with ample store of seed for sowing and make *the harvest of your uprightness*
11 a bigger one: ·you will be rich enough in every way for every kind of generosity
12 that makes people thank God for what we have done. ·For the help provided by this contribution not only satisfies the needs of God's holy people, but also
13 overflows into widespread thanksgiving to God; ·because when you have proved your quality by this help, they will give glory to God for the obedience which you show in professing the gospel of Christ, as well as for the generosity of your
14 fellowship towards them and towards all. ·At the same time, their prayer for you will express the affection they feel for you *b* because of the unbounded grace God
15 has given you. ·Thanks be to God for his gift that is beyond all telling! *c*

III: PAUL'S APOLOGIA ᵃ

Paul's reply to accusations of weakness

1 **10** I urge you by the gentleness and forbearance of Christ—this is Paul now speaking personally—I, the one who is so humble when he is facing you 2 but full of boldness at a distance. ᵇ ·Yes, my appeal to you is that I should not have to be bold when I am actually with you, or show the same self-assurance as I reckon to use when I am challenging those who reckon that we are guided by 3 human motives. ·For although we are human, it is not by human methods that we 4 do battle. ·The weapons with which we do battle are not those of human nature, but they have the power, in God's cause, ᶜ to demolish fortresses. It is ideas that 5 we demolish, ·every presumptuous notion that is set up against the knowledge of 6 God, and we bring every thought into captivity and obedience to Christ; ·once you have given your complete obedience, we are prepared to punish any disobedience. 7 Look at the evidence ᵈ of your eyes. Anybody who is convinced that he belongs to Christ should go on to reflect that we belong to Christ ᵉ no less than he does. 8 Maybe I have taken rather too much pride in our authority, but the Lord gave us that for building you up, not for knocking you down, and I am not going to be 9, 10 shamed ·into letting you think that I can put fear into you only by letter. ᶠ ·Someone said, 'His letters are weighty enough, and full of strength, but when you see him in 11 person, he makes no impression and his powers of speaking are negligible.' ·I should like that sort of person to take note that our deeds when we are present will show the same qualities as our letters when we were at a distance.

His reply to the accusation of ambition

12 We are not venturing to rank ourselves, or even to compare ourselves with certain people who provide their own commendations. By measuring themselves by them- 13 selves and comparing themselves to themselves, they only show their folly. ·By contrast we do not intend to boast beyond measure, ᵍ but will measure ourselves by the standard which God laid down for us, namely that of having come all the 14 way to you. ·We are not overreaching ourselves as we would be if we had not come all the way to you; in fact we were the first to come as far as you with the 15 good news of Christ. ʰ ·So we are not boasting beyond measure, about other men's work; in fact, we hope, as your faith increases, to grow greater and greater by this 16 standard of ours, ⁱ ·by preaching the gospel to regions beyond you, rather than 17 boasting about work already done in someone else's province.ʲ ·*Let anyone who* 18 *wants to boast, boast of the Lord.* ·For it is not through self-commendation that recognition is won, but through commendation.

Paul is driven to sound his own praises

1 **11** I wish you would put up with a little foolishness from me—not that you 2 don't do this already. ᵃ ·The jealousy that I feel for you is, you see, God's own jealousy: I gave you all in marriage to a single husband, a virgin pure for 3 presentation to Christ. ᵇ ·But I am afraid that, just as the snake with his cunning seduced Eve, your minds may be led astray from single-minded ᶜ devotion to 4 Christ. ·Because any chance comer has only to preach a Jesus ᵈ other than the one we preached, or you have only to receive a spirit different from the one you received, or a gospel different from the one you accepted—and you put up with 5 that only too willingly. ·Now, I consider that I am not in the least inferior to the

6 super-apostles.ᵉ ·Even if there is something lacking in my public speaking, this is not the case with my knowledge, as we have openly shown to you at all times and before everyone.ᶠ

7 Have I done wrong, then, humbling myself so that you might be raised up, by 8 preaching the Gospel of God to you for nothing? ·I was robbing other churches, 9 taking wages from them in order to work for you. ·When I was with you and needed money, I was no burden to anybody, for the brothers from Macedonia brought me as much as I needed when they came; I have always been careful not 10 to let myself be a burden to you in any way, and I shall continue to be so. ·And as Christ's truth is in me, this boast of mine is not going to be silenced in the regions 11, 12 of Achaia. ·Why should it be? Because I do not love you? God knows that I do. ·I will go on acting as I do at present, to cut the ground from under the feet of those who are looking for a chance to be proved my equals in grounds for boasting. ᵍ 13 These people are counterfeit apostles, dishonest workers disguising themselves as 14 apostles of Christ. ·There is nothing astonishing in this; even Satan disguises 15 himself as an angel of light. ·It is nothing extraordinary, then, when his servants disguise themselves as the servants of uprightness. They will come to the end appropriate to what they have done.

16 To repeat:ʰ let no one take me for a fool, but if you do, then treat me as a fool, 17 so that I, too, can do a little boasting. ·I shall not be following the Lord's way in what I say now, but will be speaking out of foolishness in the conviction that I 18 have something to boast about. ·So many people boast on merely human grounds 19 that I shall too. ·I know how happy you are to put up with fools, being so wise 20 yourselves; ·and how you will still go on putting up with a man who enslaves you, eats up all you possess, keeps you under his orders and sets himself above you, or 21 even slaps you in the face. ·I say it to your shame; perhaps we have been too weak.

Whatever bold claims anyone makes—now I am talking as a fool—I can make 22 them too.ʲ ·Are they Hebrews? So am I. Are they Israelites? So am I. Are they 23 descendants of Abraham? So am I. ·Are they servants of Christ? I speak in utter folly—I am too, and more than they are: I have done more work, I have been in prison more, I have been flogged more severely, many times exposed to death. 24, 25 Five times I have been given the thirty-nine lashes by the Jews; ·three times I have been beaten with sticks; once I was stoned; three times I have been shipwrecked, 26 and once I have been in the open sea for a night and a day; ·continually travelling, I have been in danger from rivers, in danger from brigands, in danger from my own people and in danger from the gentiles, in danger in the towns and in danger in the open country, in danger at sea and in danger from people masquerading as 27 brothers; ·I have worked with unsparing energy, for many nights without sleep; I have been hungry and thirsty, and often altogether without food or drink; I have 28 been cold and lacked clothing. ·And, besides all the external things, there is, day 29 in day out, the pressure on me of my anxiety for all the churches. ·If anyone weakens, I am weakened as well; and when anyone is made to fall, I burn in agony myself.

30, 31 If I have to boast, I will boast of all the ways in which I am weak. ·The God and Father of the Lord Jesus—who is for ever to be blessed—knows that I am not 32 lying. ·When I was in Damascus, the governor who was under King Aretas put 33 guards round Damascus city to catch me, ·and I was let down in a basket through a window in the wall, and that was how I escaped from his hands.

1 **12** I am boasting because I have to. Not that it does any good, but I will move
2 on to visions and revelations from the Lord. ·I know a man in Christ who
fourteen years ago—still in the body? I do not know; or out of the body? I do not
3 know: God knows—was caught up right into the third heaven.ᵃ ·And I know that
4 this man—still in the body? or outside the body? I do not know, God knows—·was
caught up into Paradise and heard words said that cannot and may not be spoken
5 by any human being. ·On behalf of someone like that I am willing to boast, but I
6 am not going to boast on my own behalf except of my weaknesses; ·and then, if I
do choose to boast I shall not be talking like a fool because I shall be speaking the
truth. But I will not go on in case anybody should rate me higher than he sees and
hears me to be, because of the exceptional greatness of the revelations.

7 Wherefore, so that I should not get above myself, I was given a thorn in the
flesh,ᵇ a messenger from Satan to batter me and prevent me from getting above
8 myself.ᶜ ·About this, I have three times pleaded with the Lord that it might leave
9 me; ·but he has answered me, 'My grace is enough for you: for power is at full
stretch in weakness.' It is, then, about my weaknesses that I am happiest of all to
10 boast, so that the power of Christ may rest upon me; ·and that is why I am glad of
weaknesses, insults, constraints, persecutions and distress for Christ's sake. For it
is when I am weak that I am strong.

11 I have turned into a fool, but you forced me to it. It is you that should have
been commending me; those super-apostles had no advantage over me, even if I
12 am nothing at all. ·All the marks characteristic of a true apostle have been at work
13 among you: complete perseverance, signs, marvels, demonstrations of power. ·Is
there any way in which you have been given less than the rest of the churches,
except that I did not make myself a burden to you? Forgive me for this unfairness!ᵈ
14 Here I am, ready to come to you for the third time and I am not going to be a
burden on you: it is not your possessions that I want, but yourselves. Children are
15 not expected to save up for their parents, but parents for their children, ·and I am
more than glad to spend what I have and to be spent for the sake of your souls. Is
it because I love you so much more, that I am loved the less?ᵉ
16 All right, then; I did not make myself a burden to you, but, trickster that I am, I
17 caught you by trickery. ·Have I taken advantage of you through any of the people
18 I have sent to you? ·Titus came at my urging, and I sent his companion with him.
Did Titus take advantage of you? Can you deny that he and I were following the
guidance of the same Spirit and were on the same tracks?

Paul's fears and anxieties

19 All this timeᶠ you have been thinking that we have been pleading our own cause
before you; no, we have been speaking in Christ and in the presence of God—and
20 all, dear friends, to build you up. ·I am afraid that in one way or another, when I
come, I may find you different from what I should like you to be, and you may
find me what you would not like me to be; so that in one way or the other there
will be rivalry, jealousy, bad temper, quarrels, slander, gossip, arrogance and
21 disorders; ·and when I come again, my God may humiliate me in front of you and I
shall be grieved by all those who sinned in the past and have still not repented of
the impurities and sexual immorality and debauchery that they have committed.

1 **13** This will be the third timeᵃ I have confronted you. *Whatever the misdemeanour, the evidence of two or three witnesses is required to sustain a
2 charge.* ·I gave you notice once, and now, though I am not with you, I give notice
again, just as when I was with you for a second time, to those who sinned before,

and to all others; and it is to this effect, that when I do come next time, I shall
3 have no mercy. ·Since you are asking for a proof that it is Christ who speaks in me;
4 he is not weak with you but his power is at work among you; ·for, though it was
out of weakness that he was crucified, he is alive now with the power of God. We,
too, are weak in him, but with regard to you *b* we shall live with him by the power
of God.

5   Put yourselves to the test to make sure you are in the faith. Examine yourselves.
Do you not recognise yourselves as people in whom Jesus Christ is
6 present?—unless, that is, you fail the test. ·But we, as I hope you will come to
7 recognise, do not fail the test. ·It is our prayer to God that you may do nothing
wrong—not so that we have the credit of passing a test, but because you will be
8 doing what is right, even if we do not pass the test. *c* ·We have no power to resist
9 the truth; only to further the truth; ·and we are delighted to be weak if only you
10 are strong. What we ask in our prayers is that you should be made perfect. ·That
is why I am writing this while still far away, so that when I am with you I shall not
have to be harsh, with the authority that the Lord has given me, an authority that
is for building up and not for breaking down.

CONCLUSION

Recommendations, greetings, final good wishes

11 To end then, brothers, we wish you joy; try to grow perfect; encourage one
another; have a common mind and live in peace, and the God of love and peace
will be with you.
12   Greet one another with the holy kiss. *d* All God's holy people send you their
greetings.
13   The grace of the Lord Jesus Christ, the love of God and the fellowship of the
Holy Spirit be with you all. *e*

NOTES TO 2 CORINTHIANS

1 a. This 'support' is the 'consolation' announced by the prophets and seen as a characteristic of the messianic age, Is 40:1, and brought by the Messiah, Lk 2:25. It consists essentially in an end to trials and the beginning of an era of peace and joy, Is 40:1seq., Mt 5:5. In the NT the new age is present in the old, and the Christian united to Christ is comforted even while his trials continue, 1:4–7; 7:4; cf. Col 1:24. This support is not received passively, but is at once comfort, encouragement, exhortation (the same Greek word, *paraklesis*). Its sole source is God, 1:3,4, through Christ, 1:5, and through the Spirit, Ac 9:31p, and the Christian is to communicate it to others, 2 Co 1:4,6; 1 Th 4:18. Among its causes the NT enumerates: progress in the Christian life, 7:4,6,7, conversion, 7:13, the Scriptures, Rm 15:4. It is the source of hope, Rm 15:4.

b. In 2 Co, Paul frequently emphasises the presence of contradictory or paradoxical realities in Christ, and thus in the apostle and the Christian; here suffering and support or consolation, also 7:4; death and life, 4:10–12; 6:9; poverty and riches, 6:10; 8:9; weakness and strength, 12:9–10. It is the paschal mystery, the presence of the risen Christ in the old world of sin and death, *see* 1 Co 1–2.

c. One of the many trials referred to in 11:23seq.

d. var. 'and saves us still'.

e. Thanksgiving plays an important part in Paul's theology, *see* the beginning of the letters, where he thanks God for the faith of his correspondents, Rm 1:8; 1 Co 1:4; Ph 1:3; Col 1:3; 1 Th 1:2; 2 Th 1:3: Phm 4. It is no empty formula; its absence in Ga is significant, Ga 1:1a. Thanksgiving gives life to all the actions of the Christian done in the name of Christ and taken up by him in his thanksgiving to the Father, Ep 5:20; Col 3:17. It is a duty corresponding to God's will, not only for Christians, 1 Th 5:18, but even for gentiles, Rm 1:21. For thanksgiving 'gives', even though imperfectly, thanks to God (1 Th 3:9, literally). It is therefore the ultimate goal of the prayer that asks for grace, 1:11; 4:15, and of the expression of fraternal love, 9:11–15. Hence its importance in the liturgy, 1 Co 14:16; Ep 5:19seq.; Col 3:16, and in personal prayer, Ph 4:6; 1 Th 5:18.

f. var. 'on your behalf'.

g. var. 'simplicity'.

h. var. 'to give you a double pleasure'.

i. Paul must therefore have changed the plan mentioned in 1 Co 16:5–6.

j. God's faithfulness is primarily his 'firmness'. He is the rock of Israel, Dt 32:4, and provides a wholly secure support. This firmness explains the constancy of his plans, his faithfulness to his promises, Ps 89:1–8,24seq; and, especially in the NT God's faithfulness to his plan of mercy and salvation, 1 Co 1:9f; 10:13; 1 Th 5:24; 2 Th 3:3.

k. Silvanus is the disciple called Silas in Ac.

l. God's promises are seen as waiting for fulfilment until perfect obedience and assent to his will are offered by Jesus Christ. The implication is that Paul 'in Christ' is guided only by the will of God for him, and is not to be thought of as consulting his own wishes or changing his mind on a personal impulse, 1:17–18j.

m. Amen means 'that which is solid, trustworthy'; it is the reply of human faithfulness to God's faithfulness in Jesus Christ. Cf. Rm 1:25p.

n. The anointing and the seal mean either the gift of the Spirit to all believers (possibly with an allusion to initiation rites), see Ep 1:13n; 4:30m; 1 Jn 2:20k,27p; or the special gift of the spirit to the apostolic ministry (making a distinction between the 'us' and 'you' of this verse) by a special gift of the Spirit, which makes the apostle the faithful messenger of God's fidelity in Christ (vv. 17–20). Note the trinitarian formulation of vv. 21–22.

2 a. An allusion to a painful visit which Paul must have made to Corinth before writing 2 Co, see p. 1854.

b. An allusion to the 'severe letter' of 2:3,4,9; 7:8,12; see p. 289.

c. The man who had given offence to Paul or to Paul's representative, see p. 289.

d. A Christian of gentile birth, possibly converted by Paul, Tt 1:4, whom he accompanies on Paul's second journey to Jerusalem, Ga 2:1. He was commissioned by Paul to visit Corinth and to settle its problems; in this he was entirely successful, 7:5–7. Soon afterwards Paul sent him to Corinth to organise the collection. If we are to accept the historical data of the Pastoral Letters as genuine (but see pp. 297–99), he appears again in Crete (63–4) controlling the communities Paul had founded there after his release from the first Roman captivity. It was from there that Paul wrote to Titus asking him to meet him again at Nicopolis in Epirus, Tt 3:12. During Paul's second Roman captivity (66–7) Titus was in Dalmatia, 2 Tm 4:10. Titus with his shrewdness and his strong, well-balanced character, seems to have made an admirable colleague for Paul.

e. The account of events is interrupted by a digression on the apostolic ministry, 2:14–7:4. It continues again in 7:5.

f. Like a victorious general making his solemn entry into Rome. The imagery is taken from the custom familiar to all: incense burns before the victor, his lieutenants are given a place in the procession, and the vanquished leaders are put to death. Cf. Col 2:15.

g. var. 'the others'.

3 a. Presumably Paul has been accused of boastful claims, cf. 5:12, whereas other preachers present letters of commendation from their communities, see Ac 18:27r. His answer is that the churches founded by him and animated by the Spirit make written commendations unnecessary just as the new covenant of the Spirit has made the old covenant 'of written letters' superfluous. There is much more here than a play on words, especially if, as is most likely, Paul's opponents are Judaisers, cf. 11:22.

b. var. 'your'.

c. Besides the reference to the tablets of stone at Sinai, Ex 24:12, there may also be an allusion here to Ezk 36:26.

d. See Rm 7:7d. This is not an observation about the 'letter' as opposed to the 'spirit' of a text: the contrast is between the written external Law of the OT, and the Spirit, the interior law of the NT.

e. Cf. Ex 34:30. The transitory character of the glory which lights up the face of Moses shows, according to Paul, the transitoriness of the old covenant, v. 11.

f. Alternative translation 'nor is it revealed to them that this covenant has been abolished by Christ'.

g. A condensed formula which, without denying the distinction between Christ and the Spirit which is so clearly underlined in the letter, 1:20–23; 13:13e, nevertheless affirms their identity in the work of salvation in both covenants. In the same line, later theology will assert that the works of God are common to the three divine Persons. Another interpretation identifies the Lord of v. 17 with the one of v. 16, namely God; it was when he turned to God that Moses took off his veil, Ex 34:34. Paul means that the Lord to whom Moses turned is already in fact the Holy Spirit to whom Christians turn.

h. Rather than 'contemplate'. The comparison of vv. 7–15 continues. By contrast to Moses, our faces are unveiled and we reflect the divine glory in a permanent rather than transitory way, see 3:13e. The privilege which only Moses enjoyed is granted to all.

i. The 'glory of the Lord' is that of Jesus Christ, for the glory of the Lord is on the face of Christ, 4:6.

j. See Rm 8:29n. A final contrast with Moses, whose glory weakened and disappeared as it shone, vv. 7,13. On the contrary, the Christian is transformed into an increasingly faithful image of God in Christ.

k. Alternative translation 'of the Spirit of the Lord'.

4 a. Presumably the lack of courage which leads to concealment of those elements in the gospel which could provoke opposition or persecution: Mk 8:38 and par.; Rm 1:16; 2 Tm 1:8; cf. Ac 20:27.

b. Satan, cf. Ep 2:2. Cf. Lk 4:6; Jn 12:31; 14:30; 16:11.

c. A favourite theme of Paul's, often stressed in this letter: 3:5–6; 10:1,8; 12:5,9–10; 13:3,4. Cf. 1 Co 1:26; 2:5; 4:13g; Ph 4:13; already present in the OT Jg 7:2; 1 S 14:6; 17:47; 1 M 3:19.

d. These four sentences owe their imagery to the gladiatorial contest.

5 a. 5:1–10 continues the contrast of 4:16–18 between the progressive ruin of the exterior nature and the progress of the interior nature, v. 16, see Rm 7:22j. This interior nature, identical with the new humanity, Col 3:10e, is the pledge of the Spirit, 2 Co 5:5, cf. Rm 8:23, whose fullness will be given at the resurrection, when believers will be clothed with their heavenly habitation, 2 Co 5:2, that is the spiritual body, cf. 1 Co 15:44. Hence the burning longing, 5:2, for this fullness and the desire not to be deprived of it even for a time, by death before the parousia, 5:4, and so to be still alive at the coming of the Lord. But see 5:8d.

b. That is to say, on the supposition that we are still alive when Christ returns in glory. Paul wants to be of the number of those who will live to see the coming of the Lord and whose bodies will be transformed without having to die. Over the 'natural body' they will, as it were, 'put on' the 'spiritual body', 1 Co 15:44,53,54, which will be 'absorbed' by the former. Alternative translation: 'having put it on, we shall not be found bare'.

c. Cf. 1 Co 13:12. Faith is compared to clear vision as the imperfect is to the perfect. This passage is important because it stresses the cognitive aspect of faith.

d. Here and in Ph 1:23 Paul has in mind a union of Christians with Christ on the death of each individual. Without running counter to the OT doctrine of a final general resurrection, Rm 2:6b; 1 Co 15:44w, this expectation of a blessedness for the separated soul shows the influence of Greek thought which was already present in Judaism, cf. Lk 16:22; 23:43; 1 P 3:19h. But see also the texts referring to ecstatic states when the soul is 'out of the body', 12:2seq.; cf. Rv 1:10; 4:2; 17:3; 21:10.

e. An allusion to earlier events. Paul was no doubt 'unreasonable' in his letter written 'with many tears', 2:4, but this was 'for God', to show the uncompromising demands of God. If he is 'reasonable' it is 'for you', to make an impression on his reader, in his desire to 'win people over'. In both cases he is 'compelled' by the love of Christ, 5:14.

f. Christ dies for all, that is, in the name of all, as head representing the whole of humanity. But the value of this death comes from the loving obedience which it shows, the sacrifice of the total gift of life. Rm 5:19*l*; Ph 2:8; cf. Lk 22:42 and par.; Jn 15:13; Heb 10:9–10. Believers participate in this death through baptism, Rm 6:3–6, and must ratify this offering of Christ by their own lives (2 Co 5:15 and Rm 6:8–11).

g. Paul does not claim to have known Jesus personally. He maintains that no one, even those who could have known him ('we') may attribute any importance to any connection 'according to human standards', family relationship, acquaintance, race. *See* Mk 3:31–35 and par. Others consider that Paul is contrasting his present knowledge of Christ, the Lord of Glory, with that which he had before his conversion, when he considered Christ an enemy.

h. God who created all things through Christ, cf. Jn 1:3, has restored his work, deformed by sin, by re-creating it in Christ, Col 1:15–20d. The central figure of this 'new creation', here and Ga 6:15—which extends to the whole universe, Col 1:19f; cf. 2 P 3:13; Rv 21:1—is the 'new humanity' created in Christ, Ep 2:15n, to lead a new life, Rm 6:4, of virtue and holiness, Ep 2:10; 4:24k; Col 3:10e. Cf. the 'new birth' of baptism, Rm 6:4a.

i. var. 'everything is new'.

j. God made Christ one with sinful humanity in order to make the human race one with his obedience and saving justice, *see* 5:14e; Rm 5:19*l*. Perhaps 'victim for sin' should here be taken as meaning 'sin', since the same Hebr. word *hatta't* can have both senses, *see* Lv 4:1–5:13.

6 a. There is an intermediary period, Rm 13:11e, between the time of Christ's coming, Rm 3:26m, and his return, 1 Co 1:8e. This period is the 'day of salvation', a time allowed for conversion, Ac 3:20seq.; it is granted to the 'remnant', Rm 11:5, and to the gentiles, Rm 11:25; Ep 2:12seq.; *see* Lk 21:24; Rv 6:11. Though the duration is uncertain, 1 Th 5:1a, this time of pilgrimage must be regarded as being short, 1 P 1:17; 1 Co 7:26–31; cf. Rv 10:6; 12:12; 20:3, and full of trials, Ep 5:16; 6:13, and sufferings which are a prelude to the glory to come, Rm 8:11. The end is at hand, 1 P 4:7; *see* Rv 1:3e and 1 Co 16:22; Ph 4:5; Jm 5:8, the Day approaches, Rm 13:11, and it is necessary to be on the watch, 1 Th 5:6; cf. Mk 13:33, and to use the time well that remains, Col 4:5; Ep 5:16, for one's own salvation and that of others, Ga 6:10, leaving the final vindication to God, Rm 12:19; 1 Co 4:5.

b. 6:14–7:1 is a warning against the infiltration of gentile practices which would split the church and cut it off from its founder. This section is somewhat alien to the context, *see* p. 1855.

c. var. 'you'. *See* Rm 12:1a; 1 Co 3:16e.

7 a. lit. 'Make room for us', which could also be translated 'you must understand us.'

b. That is, his person considered in its weakness, *see* Rm 7:5c.

c. The 'severe letter'; *see* 2:3b.

d. The feelings and conduct of the Corinthians towards Paul and the offender after his severe letter, *see* 2:5–8.

e. The one offended was probably an envoy of Paul's. On him and the offender, 2:6c; we have no idea what the actual offence was.

8 a. On this collection, particularly dear to Paul, *see* 1 Co 16:1a.

b. Various favourite themes are used by Paul to persuade the Corinthians to be generous: poverty as a source of enrichment to others here and 6:10; following Christ's example, v. 9; the gift of God, v. 1, giving rise to the gift of the Christians, v. 4 and 5; cf. 9:8.

c. var. 'the love towards us which unites us to you'.

d. Or 'grace'.

e. var. 'our'.

f. Christ is seen as stripping himself of the glory and

privileges which were rightly his in order to share to the full our life, our suffering and our death. The theme is the same as Ph 2:6–11, but here the emphasis is on Christ's saving work, enriching us with the privileges he renounced, whereas in Ph 2 it is on his ultimate glorification by the Father.

The exhortation to model Christian conduct on the example of Christ is characteristic of Pauline morality. Cf. Rm 14:8; Ep 5:1; 5:25; Ph 2:5; *see also* 2 Th 3:7b.

g. Paul asks the Corinthians to give only from their surplus, whereas the Christians of Macedonia, in their 'intense poverty' had given 'well beyond their resources', v. 2–3. Cf. Mk 12:44 and par. But by setting before them the example of Christ, v. 9, Paul discreetly invites them to imitate the generosity of their brothers in Macedon.

h. Either material goods in the future when the situations could be reversed, or spiritual goods already now, cf. 9:14; Rm 15:27.

i. Traditionally supposed to be Luke.

j. Alternative translation: 'as evidence of our goodwill' or 'as we desired'.

k. This brother cannot be identified.

l. Greek *apostoloi*, apostles, *see* Rm 1:1b. They are 'the glory of Christ' because they show it by their actions, v. 19, by arousing in Christians conduct like his, v. 9.

9 a. Paul has, however, just done so at length. Ch. 9 may perhaps be a separate note to the churches of Achaia, inserted here later because of its similarity to the exhortation to the church at Corinth in ch. 8. *See* p. 289.

b. Paul puts his teaching of 1 Co 13:5 into practice, for certain members of this community had made life difficult for him, Ga 2:4seq. By this collection he aims to disarm such hostility by showing the deference and support of the churches of gentile origin to the mother Church from which they received their spiritual goods, Rm 15:27.

c. The redemption.

10 a. If 2 Co is a single letter, at least there is here a sudden change of subject and tone; *see* p. 289. One possibility is that there was an interruption in the dictation of the letter, and that after completing Ch. 9, Paul received new information about the Corinthians' state of mind and their feelings towards him; perhaps including the comment quoted in v. 10, and alluded to in 10:1. *See also* 12:16,20.

b. An allusion to the sarcastic reproaches of his enemies, *see* v. 10.

c. Or 'in the eyes of God'.

d. Or 'You look only at appearances'.

e. Either 'Christ's party' as in 1 Co 1:12j or, more likely, believers who claimed to have a monopoly of Christ.

f. Cf. v. 11. The Corinthians are not to think that Paul's severity is confined to words.

g. var. 'Oh no; by measuring ourselves against ourselves and comparing ourselves with our own selves, we shall be doing no unmeasured boasting.'

h. The meaning of vv. 12–14 is: My opponents' sole cause for boasting is the power and the gifts that they claim to possess in themselves, v. 12, whereas I am able to produce the evidence that I have done the work that God set me to do, of founding the church at Corinth, vv. 13–14.

i. Alternative translation 'we are trusting, when your faith has developed, to grow further in your esteem and to continue to grow according to the standard allotted to us.'

j. It was Paul's rule not to build on the foundations of another, Rm 15:20seq.

11 a. Or perhaps 'Go on! Be indulgent to me!' On this foolishness of Paul *see* 5:13e; 11:17; 12:11.

b. Paul, the friend of the bridegroom, presents to him his fiancée. Since Ho 2, the love of Yahweh for his people has been represented by the love of husband for wife: Ex 16:23; Is 49:14–21; 50:1; 54:1–10; 62:4–5; Jr 2:1–7; 3; 31:22; 51:5. The NT takes up the same image: Mt 22:2seq.; 25:1seq.; Jn 3:28–29; Ep 5:25–33; Rv 19:7; 21:2.

c. add 'and pure'.

d. Presumably Jesus presented from an earthly point of view, *see* 5:16g, with less emphasis on the risen Lord, head of the new creation, 5:17h. The phrase can also be understood as a conditional: if this happened you would accept it. In any case the situation seems to be less serious than in Ga 1:6–9; but it could become serious.

e. 'Super-apostles'; the term recurs in 12:11, where it is contrasted with 'true apostles' and the same men are termed 'counterfeit apostles' in 11:13. The use of the word is sarcastic, and it must not be taken to mean the Twelve, whose authority may be implicitly admitted by Paul, Ga 1:17; 2:9. By the time of this Letter, the circle of apostles was wider than the Twelve, 1 Co 15:7g. Paul could also mean those who claimed the title without any right to do so.

f. Or 'in every way'.

g. Paul's opponents, the 'super-apostles' of v. 5, would never dare to challenge the selflessness which is the mark of Paul's apostolic mission.

h. In fact, however, he has never said it—contrast 11:1. Paul writes with such a passion of rhetoric that there is no time for precision. His foolishness (a word that rankles) 11:1,17,19,21,23; 12:11, which is not madness 11:16; 12:6, will consist of boasting on merely human grounds 11:18, that is, of his race, 11:22, his labours and sufferings, 11:23–26, his daily care for the churches, 11:28. He will add a boast of the revelations made to him, 12:1–5. This is to meet his opponents on their own ground. But his real boast is his weakness, 11:30; 12:5,9, because it is that which calls forth the strength of Christ, 12:9, proving that the power which is active in his apostolic work comes not from him but from God, 4:7c.

i. var. 'I say it to our shame.'

j. The needs of controversy several times compelled Paul, as here, to recall his past as a practising Jew, Rm 11:1; Ga 1:13–14; Ph 3:4–6; cf. Ac 22:3seq.; 26–4–5.

12 a. That is, to the highest heaven.

b. Perhaps a disease with severe and unforeseeable attacks; perhaps the resistance of Israel, Paul's brothers by physical descent, to the Christian faith.

c. om. 'and prevent me from getting above myself' (lit. 'so that I should not be too proud'). Possibly also the beginning of v. 7 should be read as the conclusion of v. 6, the clause is awkwardly phrased and the text critically uncertain.

d. A good example of Paul's irony at its heaviest.

e. var. '. . . souls, even if, loving you the more, I must be loved the less'. Paul is often explicit about his love for the Christians in the churches to which he is writing: 2:4;6:12,11:11;12:15; 1 Co 16:24; Ga 4:19; Ph 1:8; 1 Th 2:8, comparing it with mother-love, Ga 4:19; 1 Th 2:8, or paternal love, 1 Co 4:14seq.; 2 Co 6:13. He asks the faithful to give him the same love, 6:13; but in the name of this love, he will unhesitatingly correct and reprove the churches, even though this may cool their feelings of love for him, 7:8; 12:15; Ga 4:16.

f. var. 'Once again

13 a. The first time was at the foundation of the church there, the second formed the 'intermediate visit', *see* p. 288–89.

b. 'Towards you', omitted by some authorities.

c. This test will be the conduct of Paul and the Corinthians at his approaching visit, when Paul will give proof that Christ is acting through him, 13:3seq. This proof will be to the Corinthians' disadvantage, 13:6, unless they change their ways; Paul will triumph through the sanctions he applied, 13:7. But if they do change their ways, Paul will not have to make use of his power, and will give the impression of being weak beside their strength, 13:9; he will appear to fail in the test, 13:7, for they will be able to say that his threats are only a matter of words, *see* 10:9seq. He nevertheless accepts the possibility with joy; it will be humiliating for him but magnificent for his beloved disciples.

d. The kiss of peace, familiar in the liturgy of the Eucharist as the symbol of Christian fellowship and unity, Rm 16:16; 1 Co 16:20; 1 Th 5:26.

e. This trinitarian formula, probably derived from liturgical usage, *see also* Mt 28:19, is echoed in many passages of the epistles where the several functions of the three Persons are referred to as the various contexts suggest: 1:21seq.; Rm 1:4c; 15:16,30; 1 Co 2:10–16; 6:11,14,15,19; 12:4–6; Ga 4:6; Ep 1:3–14; 2:18,22; 4:4–6; Ph 2:1; Tt 3:5seq.; Heb 9:14; 1 P 1:2; 3:18; 1 Jn 4:2; Rv 1:4seq.; 22:1; cf. Ac 10:38; 20:28; Jn 14:16,18,23. Note in 1 Co 6:11; Ep 4:4–6 the triple formulations emphasising the trinitarian thought. *See also* the trio of theological virtues in 1 Co 13:13e.

GALATIANS

THE LETTER OF PAUL
TO THE CHURCH IN GALATIA

Address *

1 **1** From Paul, an apostle appointed not by human beings nor through any human
being but by Jesus Christ and God the Father who raised him from the dead,
2, 3 and all the brothers who are with me, to the churches of Galatia. ·Grace and peace
4 from God the Father and our Lord Jesus Christ ·who gave himself for our sins to
liberate us from this present wicked world, *b* in accordance with the will of our
5 God and Father, ·to whom be glory for ever and ever. Amen.

A warning *c*

6 I am astonished that you are so promptly turning away from the one who called
7 you in the grace of Christ and are going over to a different gospel——·not that it is
another gospel; *d* except that there are trouble-makers among you who are seeking
8 to pervert the gospel of Christ. ·But even if we ourselves or an angel from heaven
preaches to you a gospel other than the one we preached to you, let God's curse
9 be on him. *e* ·I repeat again what we declared before: anyone who preaches to you
10 a gospel other than the one you were first given is to be under God's curse. ·Whom
am I trying to convince now, human beings or God? Am I trying to please human
beings? *f* If I were still *g* doing that I should not be a servant of Christ.

I: PAUL'S APOLOGIA

God's call

11 Now *h* I want to make it quite clear to you, brothers, about the gospel that was
12 preached by me, that it was no human message. ·It was not from any human being
that I received it, and I was not taught it, but it came to me through a revelation of
13, 14 Jesus Christ. *i* ·You have surely heard how I lived in the past, within Judaism, ·and
how there was simply no limit to the way I persecuted the Church of God in my
attempts to destroy it; and how, in Judaism, I outstripped most of my Jewish
15 contemporaries in my limitless enthusiasm for the traditions of my ancestors. ·But
when God, who had set me apart from the time when I was *in my mother's womb,*
16 *called* me through his grace and chose ·to reveal his Son in me, *j* so that I should

17 preach him to the gentiles, I was in no hurry to confer with any human being, ·or
to go up to Jerusalem ᵏ to see those who were already apostles before me. Instead,
18 I went off to Arabia, ˡ and later I came back to Damascus. ·Only after three years
19 did I go up to Jerusalem to meet Cephas. I stayed fifteen days with him ·but did not
20 set eyes on any of the rest of the apostles, only James, ᵐ the Lord's brother. ·I
21 swear before God that what I have written is the truth. ·After that I went to places
22 in Syria and Cilicia; ·and was still unknown by sight to the churches of Judaea
23 which are in Christ, ·they simply kept hearing it said, 'The man once so eager to
24 persecute us is now preaching the faith that he used to try to destroy,' ·and they
gave glory to God for me.

The meeting at Jerusalem

1 2 It was not until fourteen years ᵃ had gone by that I travelled up to Jerusalem
2   again, with Barnabas, and I took Titus with me too. ·My journey was inspired
by a revelation and there, in a private session with the recognised leaders, I
expounded the whole gospel that I preach to the gentiles, to make quite sure that
3 the efforts I was making and had already made should not be fruitless. ᵇ ·Even
then, and although Titus, a Greek, was with me, there was no demand that he
4 should be circumcised; ᶜ ·but because of some false brothers who had secretly
insinuated themselves to spy on the freedom that we have in Christ Jesus, intending
5 to reduce us to slavery—·people we did not ᵈ defer to for one moment, or the truth
6 of the gospel preached to you might have been compromised. . .·but those who
were recognised as important people—whether they actually were important or
not: *There is no favouritism with God*—those recognised leaders, I am saying, had
7 nothing to add to my message. ᵉ ·On the contrary, once they saw that the gospel
for the uncircumcised had been entrusted to me, just as to Peter the gospel for the
8 circumcised ·(for he who empowered Peter's apostolate to the circumcision also
9 empowered mine to the gentiles), ·and when they acknowledged the grace that
had been given to me, then James and Cephas and John, ᶠ who were the ones
recognised as pillars, offered their right hands to Barnabas and to me as a sign of
10 partnership: we were to go to the gentiles and they to the circumcised. ᵍ ·They
asked nothing more than that we should remember to help the poor, as indeed I
was anxious to do in any case.

Peter and Paul at Antioch

11 However, when Cephas came to Antioch, then I did oppose him to his face since
12 he was manifestly in the wrong. ʰ ·Before certain people from James came, he
used to eat with gentiles; ⁱ but as soon as these came, he backed out and kept apart
13 from them, out of fear of the circumcised. ·And the rest of the Jews put on the
same act as he did, so that even Barnabas was carried away by their insincerity.
14   When I saw, though, that their behaviour was not true to the gospel, I said to
Cephas in front of all of them, 'Since you, though you are a Jew, live like the
gentiles and not like the Jews, how can you compel the gentiles to live like the
Jews?'

The gospel as preached by Paul ʲ

15, 16 We who were born Jews and not gentile sinners ᵏ ·have nevertheless learnt that
someone is reckoned as upright not by practising the Law but by faith in Jesus
Christ; and we too came to believe in Christ Jesus so as to be reckoned as upright
by faith in Christ and not by practising the Law: since no human being *can be*

17 *found* upright by keeping the Law. ·Now if we too are found to be sinners on the grounds that we seek our justification in Christ, it would surely follow that Christ
18 was at the service of sin. Out of the question! ·If I now rebuild everything I once
19 demolished, I prove that I was wrong before. ·In fact, through the Law I am dead
20 to the Law *f* so that I can be alive to God. I have been crucified with Christ ·and yet I am alive; yet it is no longer I, but Christ living in me. *m* The life that I am now living, subject to the limitation of human nature, I am living in faith, *n* faith in the
21 Son of God *o* who loved me and gave himself for me. ·I am not setting aside God's grace as of no value; *p* it is merely that if saving justice comes through the Law, Christ died needlessly.

II: DOCTRINAL MATTERS

The Christian experience

1 **3** You stupid people in Galatia! After you have had a clear picture of Jesus Christ crucified, *a* right in front of your eyes, who has put a spell on you?
2 There is only one thing I should like you to tell me: How was it that you received the Spirit—was it by the practice of the Law, or by believing in the message you
3 heard? ·Having begun in the Spirit, can you be so stupid as to end in the flesh? *b*
4 Can all the favours you have received *c* have had no effect at all—if there really
5 has been no effect? ·Would you say, then, that he who so lavishly sends the Spirit to you, and causes the miracles among you, is doing this through your practice of the Law or because you believed the message you heard?

Witness of scripture: faith and the Law

6 *Abraham*, you remember, *put his faith in God*, and this was reckoned to him as
7 uprightness. ·Be sure, then, that it is people of faith who are the children of
8 Abraham. ·And it was because scripture foresaw that God would give saving justice to the gentiles through faith, that it announced the future gospel to
9 Abraham in the words: *All nations will be blessed in you.* ·So it is people of faith who receive the same blessing as Abraham, the man of faith.

The curse brought by the Law

10 On the other hand, all those who depend on the works of the Law are under a curse, since scripture says: *Accursed be he who does not make what is written in the*
11 *book of the Law effective, by putting it into practice.* ·Now it is obvious that nobody
12 is reckoned as upright in God's sight, since *the upright will live through faith*; ·and the Law is based not on faith *d* but on the principle, *whoever complies with it will*
13 *find life in it.* ·Christ redeemed us from the curse of the Law by being cursed for
14 our sake *e* since scripture says: *Anyone hanged is accursed*, ·so that the blessing of Abraham might come to the gentiles in Christ Jesus, and so that we might receive the promised Spirit *f* through faith.

The Law did not cancel the promise

15 To put it in human terms, my brothers: even when a will is only a human one,
16 once it has been ratified nobody can cancel it or add more provisions to it. ·Now the promises were addressed to Abraham *and to his progeny*. The words were not *and to his progenies* in the plural, but in the singular; *and to your progeny*, *g* which

17 means Christ. ·What I am saying is this: once a will had been long ago ratified by
God, the Law, coming four hundred and thirty years later, could not abolish it
18 and so nullify its promise. [h] ·You see, if the inheritance comes by the Law, it no
longer comes through a promise; but it was by a promise that God made his gift to
Abraham.

The purpose of the Law

19 Then what is the purpose of the Law? It was added to deal with crimes [i] until
the '*progeny*' to whom the promise had been made should come; [j] and it was
20 promulgated through angels, [k] by the agency of an intermediary. ·Now there can
21 be an intermediary only between two parties, yet God is one [l]. ·Is the Law contrary,
then, to God's promises? Out of the question! If the Law that was given had been
capable of giving life, then certainly saving justice would have come from the Law.
22 As it is, scripture makes no exception when it says that sin is master everywhere;
so the promise can be given only by faith in Jesus Christ to those who have this
faith. [m]

The coming of faith

23 But before faith came, we were kept under guard by the Law, locked up to wait
24 for the faith which would eventually be revealed to us. ·So the Law was serving as
a slave to look after us, [n] to lead us to Christ, so that we could be justified by faith.
25, 26 But now that faith has come we are no longer under a slave looking after us; ·for
27 all of you [o] are the children of God, through faith, in Christ Jesus, ·since every one
28 of you that has been baptised [p] has been clothed in Christ. ·There can be neither
Jew nor Greek, there can be neither slave nor freeman, there can be neither male
29 nor female—for you are all one in Christ Jesus. [q] ·And simply by being Christ's,
you are that *progeny* of Abraham, [r] the heirs named in the promise.

Sons of God

1 4 What I am saying is this: [a] an heir, during the time while he is still under age, is
2 no different from a slave, even though he is the owner of all the property; ·he
is under the control of guardians and administrators until the time fixed by his
3 father. ·So too with us, as long as we were still under age, we were enslaved to the
4 elemental principles of this world; [b] ·but when the completion of the time [c] came,
5 God sent his Son, born of a woman, born a subject of the Law, ·to redeem the
6 subjects of the Law, so that we could receive adoption as sons. [d] ·As you are sons,
7 God has sent into our hearts the Spirit of his Son crying, '*Abba*, Father'; ·and so
you are no longer a slave, but a son; and if a son, then an heir, by God's own act.
8 But formerly when you did not know God, you were kept in slavery to things
9 which are not really gods at all, ·whereas now that you have come to recognise
God—or rather, be recognised by God— [e] how can you now turn back again to
those powerless and bankrupt elements whose slaves you now want to be all over
10, 11 again? ·You are keeping special days, and months, and seasons and years—·I am
beginning to be afraid that I may, after all, have wasted my efforts on you.

A personal appeal

12 I urge you, brothers,—be like me, [f] as I have become like you. You have never
13 been unfair to me; ·indeed you remember that it was an illness [g] that first gave me
14 the opportunity to preach the gospel to you, ·but though my illness was a trial to
you, you did not show any distaste or revulsion; instead, you welcomed me as a

15 messenger of God, as if I were Christ Jesus himself. •What has happened to the
utter contentment you had then? For I can testify to you that you would have
16 plucked your eyes out, were that possible, and given them to me. •Then have I
17 turned into your enemy simply by being truthful with you? •Their devotion to you
has no praiseworthy motive; they simply want to cut you off from me, so that
18 you may centre your devotion on them. •Devotion to a praiseworthy cause is
19 praiseworthy at any time, ^k not only when I am there with you. •My children, I am
going through the pain of giving birth to you all over again, until Christ is formed
20 in you; •and how I wish I could be there with you at this moment and find the right
way of talking to you: I am quite at a loss with you.

The two covenants: Hagar and Sarah

21 Tell me then, you are so eager to be subject to the Law, have you listened to what
22 the Law says?ⁱ •Scripture says that Abraham had two sons, one by the slave girl
23 and one by the freewoman. •The son of the slave girl came to be born in the way
of human nature;^j but the son of the freewoman came to be born through a
24 promise. •There is an allegory here: these women stand for the two covenants. The
one given on Mount Sinai—that is Hagar, whose children are born into slavery;
25 now Sinai is a mountain in Arabia^k and represents Jerusalem in its present state,
26 for she is in slavery together with her children.^l •But the Jerusalem above is free,
27 and that is the one that is our mother; •as scripture says: *Shout for joy, you barren
woman who has borne no children! Break into shouts of joy, you who were never
in labour. For the sons of the forsaken one are more in number than the sons of the
28. 29 wedded wife.* •Now you, brothers, are like Isaac, children of the promise; •just as
at that time, the child born in the way of human nature persecuted the child born
30 through the Spirit, so now. ^m •But what is it that scripture says? *Drive away that
slave girl and her son; the slave girl's son is not to share the inheritance with the son*
31 of the freewoman. •So, brothers, we are the children not of the slave girl but of
the freewoman.

III: EXHORTATION

Christian liberty

1 **5** Christ set us free, so that we should remain free. Stand firm, then, and do not
let yourselves be fastened again to the yoke of slavery. ^a
2 I, Paul, give you my word that if you accept circumcision, Christ will be of no
3 benefit to you at all. •I give my assurance once again to every man who accepts
4 circumcision that he is under obligation to keep the whole Law; •once you seek to
be reckoned as upright through the Law, then you have separated yourself from
5 Christ, you have fallen away from grace. •We are led by the Spirit to wait in the
6 confident hope of saving justice through faith, ^b •since in Christ Jesus it is not being
circumcised or being uncircumcised that can effect anything—only faith working
through love. ^c
7 You began your race well;^d who came to obstruct you and stop you obeying the
8. 9 truth? •It was certainly not any prompting from him who called you! •A pinch of
10 yeast ferments the whole batch. •But I feel sure that, united in the Lord, you ^e will
not be led astray, and that anyone who makes trouble with you will be condemned,
11 no matter who he is. •And I, brothers—if I were still preaching circumcision, ^f why

should I still be persecuted? For then the obstacle which is the cross would have
12 no point any more. •I could wish that those who are unsettling you would go
further and mutilate themselves. *

Liberty and love *ʰ*

13 After all, brothers, you were called to be free; do not use your freedom as an
14 opening for self-indulgence, but be servants to one another in love, •since the
whole of the Law is summarised in the one commandment: *You must love your*
15 *neighbour as yourself.* *ⁱ* •If you go snapping at one another and tearing one another
to pieces, take care: you will be eaten up by one another.

16   Instead, I tell you, be guided by the Spirit, and you will no longer yield to self-
17 indulgence. *ʲ* •The desires of self-indulgence are always in opposition to the Spirit,
and the desires of the Spirit are in opposition to self-indulgence: they are opposites,
one against the other; that is how you are prevented from doing the things that
18 you want to. •But when you are led by the Spirit, you are not under the Law.
19 When self-indulgence is at work the results are obvious: sexual vice, impurity,
20 and sensuality, •the worship of false gods and sorcery; antagonisms and rivalry,
21 jealousy, bad temper and quarrels, disagreements, •factions and malice, drunkenness, orgies and all such things. And about these, I tell you now as I have told you
in the past, that people who behave in these ways will not inherit the kingdom of
22 God. •On the other hand the fruit of the Spirit is love, joy, peace, patience,
23 kindness, goodness, trustfulness, •gentleness and self-control; *ᵏ* no law can touch
24 such things as these. *ˡ* •All who belong to Christ Jesus have crucified self with all its
passions and its desires.
25, 26   Since we are living by the Spirit, let our behaviour be guided by the Spirit •and
let us not be conceited or provocative and envious of one another.

On kindness and perseverance

1 **6** Brothers, even if one of you is caught doing something wrong, those of you
who are spiritual should set that person right in a spirit of gentleness; and
2 watch yourselves that you are not put to the test in the same way. •Carry each
3 other's burdens; that is how to keep* the law of Christ. • Someone who thinks
4 himself important, when he is not, only deceives himself; •but everyone is to
examine his own achievements, and then he will confine his boasting to his own
5 achievements, not comparing them with anybody else's. •Each one has his own
load to carry.
6   When someone is under instruction in doctrine, he should give his teacher a
7 share in all his possessions. •Don't delude yourself: God is not to be fooled;
8 whatever someone sows, that is what he will reap. •If his sowing is in the field of
self-indulgence, then his harvest from it will be corruption; if his sowing is in the
9 Spirit, then his harvest from the Spirit will be eternal life. •And let us never slacken
10 in doing good; for if we do not give up, we shall have our harvest in due time. •So
then, as long as we have the opportunity *ᵇ* let all our actions be for the good *ᶜ* of
everybody, and especially of those who belong to the household of the faith. *ᵈ*

Postscript

11, 12 Notice what large letters I have used in writing to you with my own hand. *ᵉ* •It is
those who want to cut a figure by human standards who force*ʲ* circumcision on
13 you, simply so that they will not be persecuted for the cross of Christ. •Even
though they are circumcised they still do not keep the Law themselves; they want

you to be circumcised only so that they can boast of your outward appearance. ᵍ
14 But as for me, it is out of the question that I should boast at all, except of the
cross ʰ of our Lord Jesus Christ, through whom the world ⁱ has been crucified to
15 me, and I to the world. ʲ ·It is not being circumcised or uncircumcised that matters;
16 but what matters is a new creation. ·Peace and mercy to all who follow this as
their rule and to the Israel of God. ᵏ
17   After this, let no one trouble me; I carry branded on my body the marks of
Jesus. ˡ
18   The grace of our Lord Jesus Christ be with your spirit, my brothers. Amen.

NOTES TO GALATIANS

1 a. This opening is shorter and less friendly than in any other letter: there is not a single word of praise for the Galatians. In vv. 1 and 4, Paul brings in the two main themes of his letter: 1 He is a true apostle, ch. 1–2. 2 He brings the good news that we are saved through faith in Jesus Christ, and that Christians are therefore free, ch. 3–5.

b. The present world, or present age, as opposed to the 'world to come' of the messianic era. It coincides with the rule of Satan, Ac 26:18, 'god of this world', 2 Co 4:4; cf. Jn 8:12; 12:31i; Ep 2:2; 6:12, and with the rule of sin and Law, Ga 3:19. By dying and rising Christ has freed us from these forces and made us members of his kingdom, of God's kingdom, Rm 14:17; Ep 5:5; Col 1:13, though we shall not be completely freed till we also rise from the dead at the second coming, see Rm 5–8.

c. This warning takes the place of the thanksgiving with which Paul's letters usually begin, Rm 1:1a.

d. There is only one gospel, 2 Co 11:4, preached by all the apostles, 1 Co 15:11, for the service of which Paul has been set apart by God, Rm 1:1; 1 Co 1:17; cf. Ga 1:15,16. As in the gospels, Mk 1:1a, and Acts 5:42q, it is the good news proclaimed by word of mouth and listened to. Its content is the revelation of the Son Jesus Christ, Rm 1:1–4, risen from the dead, 1 Co 15:1-5; 2 Tm 1:10, after his crucifixion, 1 Co 2:2, which has inaugurated for the benefit of all sinners, whether Jewish or gentile, Rm 3:22–24, the time of justification, Rm 1:16h, and salvation, Ep 1:13, announced by the prophets, Rm 16:25,26; 1 P 1:10. 'The gospel' or the 'good news' can refer both to the apostle's vocation and to the message which he preaches, 2 Co 2:12; 8:18; Ph 1:5,12; 4:3,15; 1 Th 3:2; Phm 13. The effective power of the proclamation is from God, 1 Th 1:3 (see also 2:13). As the Word of truth which discloses the grace of God, Ac 14:3; 20:24,32; 2 Co 6:1; Ep 1:13; Col 1:5,6, it brings salvation to those who receive it with faith, Rm 1:16,17k; 3:22; 10:14,15; Ph 1:28, and obey it, Rm 1:5; 10:16; 2 Th 1:8. It bears fruit and grows, Col 1:6, and the ministry of the apostle who 'fully carries it out', Rm 15:19, is the main source of all Christian hope, Col 1:23.

e. lit. *anathema*, see Rm 9:3b. In this context, cursed, see Dt 7:26; 1 Co 5:5d.

f. It appears that the Judaisers accused Paul of trying to make the gentiles' conversion easier by not insisting on circumcision. But on this occasion at least, he retorts, he cannot be suspected of a conciliatory attitude.

g. As formerly, before his conversion, when Paul used to preach circumcision.

h. var. 'But'.

i. Jesus Christ was both source and content of this revelation, v. 16. Paul does not mean that he learnt everything by direct revelation, still less all at once on the road to Damascus; he is thinking of the doctrine of salvation by faith without the works of the Law; this alone is here at issue.

j. Others translate 'reveal his Son to me'. Paul is not denying that his vision was real, 1 Co 9:1; 15:8; see also Ac 9:17; 22:14; 26:16, he is stressing that it was personal to himself, and he relates to this his call to be apostle of the gospel to the gentiles, 2:8,9; Rm 1:1b; Ep 3:2–3; 1 Tm 2:7.

k. var. 'leave for', 'go to'.

l. Probably the kingdom of the Nabataean Arabs to the south of Damascus, 1 M 5:25h, where Paul took refuge from Aretas, 2 Co 11:32.

m. Others translate 'except James'; but to do so presumes that either Paul supposed him to be one of the Twelve or that the term 'apostles' is here used with a less precise meaning, see Rm 1:1b.

2 a. Reckoning from the last meeting with Peter or else, more probably, from Paul's conversion. It is possible that the 'three years' of 1:18 and the 'fourteen' of 2:1 are no more than just over one and twelve respectively, since it was customary to count even the last few days or the first few days of a year as a whole year.

b. lit. 'for fear I was running or had run to no purpose'. Paul is not in any doubt of the truth of his gospel, but the foundation of the churches made it essential that there should be no break of the link to the mother church, here represented by the three 'recognised leaders', the 'pillars' of v. 9; that is why he felt the collection for the 'poor' in Jerusalem to be important, see 1 Co 16:1a; see also v. 10.

c. On another occasion, Paul did have Timothy circumcised; but Timothy's mother was a Jewess, and so he was by definition a Jew, Ac 16:3, cf. 1 Co 9:20.

d. By omitting 'not', the Old Latin version makes Paul admit that he gave way for a moment. Papyrus Beatty has 'yield' rather than 'defer'.

e. lit. 'laid down nothing more for me', see v. 2.

f. 'James, Cephas and John'; var. 'James, Peter and John', 'Peter, James and John' or 'James and John'.

g. Not, as it seems, a racial distinction, but a recognition of different geographical territories. 'The circumcised' (lit. 'the circumcision') refers to the Jews in Palestine; in the territory of 'the gentiles', the resident Jews were always Paul's first concern, Ac 13:5e.

h. In itself, Peter's behaviour could be justified; Paul will do the same in other circumstances, Ac 16:3; 21:26; 1 Co 8:13; Rm 14:21; cf. 1 Co 9:20. But in the present circumstances it implied that only convert Jews who practised the Law were real Christians, and this might produce two distinct communities, separate even in their eucharistic meals. Above all, Peter's conduct was 'insincere', v. 13, precisely when he should have made his principles clear.

i. Gentile converts, so also in v. 14, as opposed to the 'circumcised' of v. 12 and 'the Jews' of v. 13, who are converts from Judaism.

j. This paragraph begins as a continuation of Paul's argument to Peter; but it is in fact addressed to all Judaisers and particularly to those in Galatia.

k. 'gentile sinners' is a technical term, perhaps used with a touch of irony; though of course Paul never doubted that Israel kept a privileged position, Rm 1:16; 3:1; 9:4–5, even though unfaithful for a time, Rm 11:12seq.

l. So laconic as to be obscure; it can be understood in two ways: **1** Christians, crucified with Christ, are dead with Christ and therefore, like Christ, dead to the Mosaic Law, see Rm 7:1seq.—and indeed in virtue of that Law, 3:13; this is why Christians already share the life of the risen Christ, Rm 6:4–10; 7:4–6 with notes. **2** Christians are dead to the Mosaic Law only in obedience to a higher law, the law of faith and of the Spirit, Rm 8:2.

m. By faith, Rm 1:16, Christ becomes in a sense the subject of all the living acts of a Christian, Rm 8:2,10–11,10f; Ph 1:21; cf. Col 3:3.

n. Though still living 'in the flesh', Christians already have the life of the Spirit, Rm 7:5c; cf. Ep 3:17; on this paradox, see Rm 8:18–27.

o. var. 'faith in God and in Christ'.

p. By returning to the Law, see 3:17.

3 a. The foundation of everything Paul teaches is the idea that we are redeemed because Christ died and rose again, see 1:1–4; 6:14; Ac 13:26–39; 1 Co 1:17–25; 2:2; 15:1–4,1a; 1 Th 1:9,10.

b. The immediate reference may be to circumcision which had been urged by Judaising preachers.

c. Others translate 'all the sufferings you have undergone'.

d. The Law demands a whole way of life, v. 10 and 5:3; cf. Jn 2:10, which it is insufficient to produce of itself, cf. Ac 15:10; Rm 7:7d.

e. To free the human race from the curse which it had incurred by disobedience to the Law, Christ made himself answerable for the curse, see Rm 8:3c; 2 Co 5:21; Col 2:14. The curse from Dt 21:23, which is part of the old code of criminal law, is introduced in the rabbinical manner, which permits any isolated quotation, or even a single word, to be adduced from scripture to support an argument; Christ was content to be termed a criminal by the Jews, like the servant of Is 53.

f. lit. 'the promise of the Spirit'. var. 'the blessing of the Spirit'.

g. The use in scripture of a collective capable of indicating an individual enables Paul to illustrate his argument with a play on words.

h. God's promise to the Fathers, Gn 12:1a; 15:1a; Rm 4:13f; Heb 11:8, is here regarded as an unconditional bequest, or will, see Heb 9:16,17, made or 'affirmed' before the Law was 'given'. If, long afterwards, he had made fulfilment of his promise depend on observance of the Law, this would have been to make the promise a promise no longer, but a bilateral contract, v. 20, and God would be contradicting himself. In fact, the Law was given for quite a different purpose, vv. 19,24; namely to unmask sin and lead consciences towards faith in Christ vv. 24–25.

i. 'It was added to deal with crimes.' On the meaning of this terse statement, see note h above, and Rm 7:7d.

j. lit. 'Why then the Law? It was added on account of crimes until that progeny came. . . .' var. 'Why then the law of works? It was added until that progeny came. . . .'

k. In Jewish tradition angels were present at Sinai when the Law was given. The 'intermediary' is Moses, see Ac 7:38k.

l. The Law was given through an intermediary; the promise came directly from God.

m. Saving justice is a free gift; it may not be claimed as a due, or as earned by obedience.

n. The educated slave whose duty was to escort the child to his tutor's, and supplement the teaching as they went. His real work is finished when he has conducted the children to their teacher. This was the function, preparatory and strictly temporary, of the Law, brought to completion by faith in Christ and by grace, Rm 6:14–15g; see Mt 5:17h.

o. All, i.e. not only 'we', who are Jews, but 'you', who are gentiles.

p. Far from being opposed to each other, faith and baptism correspond to each other, see Rm 6:4a.

q. var. 'you are all of Christ Jesus.'

r. Paul returns to the theme of the progeny of Abraham, vv. 6–9. It is no longer Abraham's physical descendants, but it is now constituted by the children of God who believe in Jesus Christ and belong to him, see Ph 3:3.

4 a. A further comparison, again taken from the law courts. Though the Jews are chosen as the heir presumptive, yet they are only slaves, v. 3, to the Law. Any Christian who wants to submit to this slavery is going back to a state of childhood, see v. 9.

b. As elsewhere, Paul is here regarding 'the Law and all its works' as part of the material world, Col 2:8,20; we were, he says, slaves to the elements that make up the physical universe, the field in which the Law operates, v. 10; Col 2:16, and to the spirits which made use of the Law, Ga 3:19k; Col 2:15,18, to dominate the universe.

c. lit. 'the fullness of time'; this phrase refers to the coming of the messianic or eschatological era, which completes the long wait of the centuries, like a measure filled at last; see Mk 1:15 and Ac 1:7i; 1 Co 10:11; Ep 1:10; Heb 1:2; 9:26; 1 P 1:20.

d. The two aspects of redemption: the negative, freedom from slavery, and the positive, adoption as sons. But notice that adoption is not only legal accession to the inheritance, v. 7 (see 3:29), but is first the real gift of new life, in which the three Persons are associated, v. 6 (see 2 Co 13:13e).

e. The Galatians were converted by God who 'knew' them before they 'knew' him.

f. Presumably by putting aside observance of the Law, cf. 1 Co 9:21.

g. This probably prolonged Paul's stay in Galatia, and he took the opportunity to preach the gospel.

h. var. 'Pursue good at any time.'

i. i.e. the witness of the scriptures, see Rm 3:19f; to inherit the promise it is not enough just to be a descendant of Abraham, see Mt 3:9; it is not enough to be descended from Abraham like Ishmael, it is necessary to be descended as the result of promise, like Isaac, Ga 4:23; it is necessary to be a spiritual descendant, not just a genealogical one, Ga 4:29; thus Isaac's birth prefigured the rebirth of Christians, Ga 4:28; cf. Rm 9:6seq. This basic argument is embellished with other more contrived comparisons.

j. lit. 'according to the flesh', i.e. in the ordinary course of nature, see Rm 7:5c, without God's working a miracle to fulfil his promise.

k. 'now Sinai is a mountain in Arabia'; var. 'Hagar stands for Sinai in Arabia' (or 'in Arabic').

l. i.e. enslaved to the Law, as opposed to the messianic Jerusalem, cf. Is 2:2, long barren, now a mother, v. 27; cf. Is 54:1–6; Rv 21:1–3.

m. Having demonstrated the Ishmael-Jews, Isaac-Christians, parallel, Paul makes two observations, vv. 29 and 30. According to some Jewish traditions Ishmael 'persecuted' Isaac, and according to the Bible, Sarah sees Ishmael as her son's rival and demands Hagar's expulsion, Gn 21:9.

5 a. To return to circumcision would be to renounce the freedom brought by faith in Christ, see Rm 6:15g. The Law and faith are mutually exclusive, vv. 2–6.

b. Or else 'The saving justice that was hoped for'.

c. Faith is the principle of the new life, 4:5;5:5, but 'through the Spirit' it is bound up with hope, v. 5, and love; see v. 6, 13–14; Rm 5:5c; 13:8; 1 Co 13:13e. It is the practice of love which shows that faith is a living faith, see 1 Jn 3:23–24.

d. One of Paul's favourite images, see 2:2; 1 Co 9:24–26; Ph 2:16; 3:12–14; 2 Tm 4:7; Heb 12:1.

e. Or else 'I have confidence in the Lord that you'.

f. As Paul's enemies apparently claimed, but *see* 1:10; 2:3c.

g. lit. 'I wish that those who are disturbing you might go even further (than circumcision) and castrate themselves.' Perhaps an allusion to the castration which was practised in the cult of Cybele. For similar sarcasm *see* Ph 3:2.

h. The new life of faith is fulfilled in love, v. 6; Rm 13:8; 1 Co 13:1a, and love is its only 'Law', *see* Rm 7:7d, producing the fruit of the Spirit, v. 22; *see* Rm 5:5e; Ph 1:11, not the works of self-indulgence, Ga 5:19; 6:8; *see also* Rm 13:12.

i. The neighbour is no longer, as in Lv, 'a member of the same people'; all members of the human family are neighbours, cf. Lk 10:29–37, identified with Christ in person. Mt 25:40,45. Thus for Paul the second commandment inescapably includes the first.

j. It is to be noted that in vv. 16–21, in which self-indulgence and Spirit are contrasted, 'self-indulgence' does not mean 'originating in, or limited by the physical body' but it includes the total resources of humanity *without* the Spirit. 'The desires of self-indulgence' does not mean exclusively, or even primarily, the desire for sensual or bodily gratification, vv. 19,20. *See* Rm 7:5c.

k. add. 'chastity'.

l. For the believer united to Christ, there is no longer any external law dictating all his outward behaviour. Though Paul can use the phrase, the 'law of Christ', 6:2; Rm 8:1, it is no more than an indication that the Spirit has completely superseded and replaced the Law.

6 a. var. 'you will keep'.

b. Possibly alluding to the time that still remains before the second coming, *see* Rm 13:11e; 2 Co 6:2a.

c. var. 'all our actions are for the good'.

d. Christian love is first exercised within the community, Rm 14:15; 1 Th 4:9–10; 2 Th 1:3, but it is shown to all, Rm 12:18seq.; 1 Th 5:15, even one's enemies, Rm 12:20, and can serve as a testimony to all people, Rm 12:17.

e. As usual, Paul adds a few words in his own hand, cf. 1 Co 16:21–24; Col 4:18; 2 Th 3:17, and possibly Rm 16:17–20. Large letters were used for emphasis.

f. lit. 'It is those who want to make a fair show in the flesh who force . . .

g. lit. 'glory in your flesh'.

h. Cross, *see* 3:1; crucified, *see* 2:19.

i. This present sinful world, cf. 1:4; 4:5; Jn 1:10g; 1 Co 1:20; 2 Co 4:4; Ep 2:2.

j. add. 'in Christ Jesus'.

k. The Christian community, the true Israel, heir of the promises, cf. 3:6–9, 29; 4:21–31; Rm 9:6–8, as opposed to the natural people of Israel, 1 Co 10:18.

l. The marks of ill-treatment suffered for Christ, *see* 2 Co 6:4–5; 11:23seq.; Col 1:24. In Paul's eyes, these marks are incomparably more glorious than any other fleshly sign could be, vv. 13–14; cf. 2 Co 11:18; Ph 3:7.

EPHESIANS

THE LETTER OF PAUL
TO THE CHURCH AT EPHESUS

Address and greetings

1,2 **1** Paul, by the will of God an apostle of Christ Jesus, to God's holy people, [a] faithful in Christ Jesus. ·Grace and peace to you from God our Father and from the Lord Jesus Christ.

I: THE MYSTERY OF SALVATION AND OF THE CHURCH

God's plan of salvation

3   Blessed be God the Father of our Lord Jesus Christ,
     who has blessed us with all the spiritual blessings of heaven in Christ. [b]
4   Thus he chose us in Christ before the world was made
     to be holy and faultless before him in love, [c]
5   marking us out for himself beforehand, to be adopted sons, [d]
          through Jesus Christ.
     Such was his purpose and good pleasure,
6   to the praise of the glory of his grace, [e]
     his free gift to us in the Beloved,
7   in whom, through his blood, we gain our freedom,
          the forgiveness of our sins. [f]
     Such is the richness of the grace
8   which he [g] has showered on us
     in all wisdom and insight.
9   He has let us know the mystery of his purpose, [h]
     according to his good pleasure which he determined beforehand in Christ,
10   for him to act upon when the times had run their course: [i]
     that he would bring everything together under Christ, as head,
     everything in the heavens and everything on earth. [j]
11   And it is in him [k] that we have received our heritage, [l]
     marked out beforehand as we were,
     under the plan of the One who guides all things
     as he decides by his own will,

12　　　chosen to be,
　　　　　for the praise of his glory,
　　　　　the people who would put their hopes in Christ before he came.
13　　　Now you too, * in him,
　　　　　have heard the message of the truth and the gospel of your salvation,
　　　　　and having put your trust in it
　　　　　you have been stamped with the seal of the Holy Spirit of the Promise, *
14　　　who is the pledge of our inheritance,
　　　　　for the freedom of the people whom God has taken for his own, *
　　　　　for the praise of his glory.

The triumph and the supremacy of Christ

15 That is why I, having once heard about your faith in the Lord Jesus, and your
16 love * for all God's holy people, ·have never failed to thank God for you and to
17 remember you in my prayers. ·May the God of our Lord Jesus Christ, the Father
　　of glory, give you a spirit * of wisdom and perception of what is revealed, to bring
18 you to full knowledge of him. ·May he enlighten the eyes of your mind * so that
　　you can see what hope his call holds for you, how rich is the glory of the heritage
19 he offers among his holy people, ·and how extraordinarily great is the power that
20 he has exercised for us believers; this accords with the strength of his power ·at
　　work in Christ, the power which he exercised in raising him from the dead and
21 enthroning him at his right hand, in heaven, ·far above every principality, ruling
　　force, power or sovereignty, * or any other name that can be named, not only in
22 this age but also in the age to come. ·*He has put all things under his feet*, and made
23 him, as he is above all things, the head of the Church; ·which is his Body, the
　　fullness of him who is filled, all in all. *

Salvation in Christ a free gift

1, 2 **2** And you were dead, through the crimes and the sins ·which used to make up
　　　 your way of life when you were living by the principles of this world, obeying
　　the ruler who dominates the air, * the spirit who is at work in those who rebel.
3 We * too were all among them once, living only by our natural inclinations, obeying
　　the demands of human self-indulgence and our own whim; our nature made us no
4 less liable to God's retribution than the rest of the world. ·But God, being rich in
5 faithful love, through the great love with which he loved us, ·even when we * were
　　dead in our sins, brought us to life with Christ *—it is through grace that you have
6 been saved—·and raised us up with him and gave us a place with him in heaven, in
　　Christ Jesus. *
7 　　This was to show for all ages to come, through his goodness towards us in Christ
8 Jesus, how extraordinarily rich he is in grace. ·Because it is by grace that you have
　　been saved, through faith; not by anything of your own, but by a gift from God;
9, 10 not by anything that you have done, so that nobody can claim the credit. ·We are
　　God's work of art, created in Christ Jesus for the good works which God has
　　already designated to make up our way of life.

Reconciliation of the Jews and the gentiles with each other and with God

11 Do not forget, then, that there was a time when you * who were gentiles by physical
　　descent, termed the uncircumcised by those who speak of themselves as the
12 circumcised by reason of a physical operation, ·do not forget, I say, that you were
　　at that time separate from Christ * and excluded from membership of Israel, aliens

with no part in the covenants of the Promise, *k* limited to this world, without hope
13 and without God. *j* ·But now in Christ Jesus, you that used to be so far off have
14 been brought close, by the blood of Christ. *k* ·For he is the peace between us, and
has made the two into one entity and broken down the barrier which used to keep
15 them apart, *l* by destroying in his own person the hostility, ·that is, the Law of
commandments with its decrees. *m* His purpose in this was, by restoring peace, to
16 create a single New Man *n* out of the two of them, ·and through the cross, to
reconcile them both to God in one Body; *o* in his own person he killed the hostility.
17 He came *p* to bring the good news of *peace to you who were far off and peace to*
18 *those who were near.* ·Through him, then, we both in the one Spirit *q* have free
access to the Father.
19   So you *r* are no longer aliens or foreign visitors; you are fellow-citizens with the
20 holy people of God and part of God's household. ·You are built upon the
foundations of the apostles and prophets, *s* and Christ Jesus himself is the corner-
21 stone. ·Every *t* structure knit together in him grows into a holy temple in the Lord;
22 and you too, in him, are being built up into a dwelling-place of God in the Spirit.

Paul, a servant of the mystery

1 **3** It is because of this that I, Paul, a prisoner of the Lord Jesus on behalf of you
2 gentiles. . . ·You have surely heard the way in which God entrusted me with
3 the grace *a* he gave me for your sake; ·he made known to me by a revelation *b* the
4 mystery I have just described briefly—·a reading of it will enable you to perceive
5 my understanding of the mystery of Christ. ·This mystery, as it is now revealed in
the Spirit to his holy apostles and prophets, was unknown to humanity in previous
6 generations: *c* ·that the gentiles now have the same inheritance *d* and form the same
7 Body and enjoy the same promise in Christ Jesus through the gospel. ·I have been
made the servant of that gospel by a gift of grace from God who gave it to me by
8 the workings of his power. ·I, who am less than the least of all God's holy people,
have been entrusted with this special grace, of proclaiming to the gentiles the
9 unfathomable treasure of Christ ·and of throwing light on the inner workings of
the mystery kept hidden through all the ages in God, the Creator of everything.
10 The purpose of this was, that now, through the Church, the principalities and
11 ruling forces should learn *e* how many-sided God's wisdom is, ·according to the
12 plan which he had formed from all eternity in Christ Jesus our Lord. ·In him we
are bold enough to approach God in complete confidence, through our faith in
13 him; ·so, I beg you, do not let the hardships I go through on your account make
you waver; *f* they are your glory. *g*

Paul's prayer

14, 15 This, then, is what I pray, kneeling before the Father, ·from whom every
16 fatherhood, *h* in heaven or on earth, takes its name. ·In the abundance of his glory
may he, through his Spirit, enable you to grow firm in power with regard to your
17 inner self, ·so that Christ may live in your hearts through faith, and then, planted
18 in love and built on love, ·with all God's holy people you will have the strength to
19 grasp the breadth and the length, the height and the depth; *i* ·so that, knowing the
love of Christ, *j* which is beyond knowledge, *k* you may be filled with the utter
fullness of God. *l*
20   Glory be to him whose power, working in us, can do infinitely more than we can
21 ask or imagine; ·glory be to him from generation to generation in the Church and
in Christ Jesus for ever and ever. Amen.

II: EXHORTATION

A call to unity *

4 I, the prisoner in the Lord, urge you therefore to lead a life worthy of the vocation to which you were called. ·With all humility and gentleness, and with patience, support each other in love. ·Take every care to preserve the unity of the Spirit by the peace that binds you together. ·There is one Body, one Spirit, just as one hope is the goal of your calling by God. ·There is one Lord, one faith, one baptism, ·and one God and Father of all, over all, through all and within all.

On each one of us God's favour * has been bestowed in whatever way Christ allotted it. ·That is why it says:

> He went up to the heights, took captives,
> he gave gifts to humanity. *

When it says, 'he went up', it must mean that he had gone down to the deepest levels of the earth. * ·The one who went down is none other than the one who went up above all the heavens to fill all things. * ·And to some, his 'gift' was that they should be apostles; to some prophets; to some, evangelists; to some, pastors and teachers; * ·to knit God's holy people * together for the work of service to build up the Body of Christ, ·until we all reach unity in faith and knowledge of the Son of God and form the perfect Man * fully mature with the fullness of Christ himself.

Then we shall no longer be children, or tossed one way and another, and carried hither and thither by every new gust of teaching, at the mercy of all the tricks people play and their unscrupulousness in deliberate deception. ·If we live by the truth and in love, we shall grow completely into Christ, who is the head ·by whom the whole Body is fitted and joined together, every joint adding its own strength, for each individual part to work according to its function. So the body grows until it has built itself up in love.

The new life in Christ

So this I say to you and attest to you in the Lord, do not go on living the empty-headed life that the gentiles live. ·Intellectually they are in the dark, and they are estranged from the life of God, because of the ignorance which is the consequence of closed minds. ·Their sense of right and wrong once dulled, they have abandoned all self-control and pursue to excess every kind of uncleanness. * ·Now that is hardly the way you have learnt Christ, ·unless you failed to hear him properly when you were taught what the truth is in Jesus. * ·You were to put aside your old self, which belongs to your old way of life and is corrupted by following illusory desires. ·Your mind was to be renewed in spirit ·so that you could put on the New Man that has been created on God's principles, in the uprightness and holiness of the truth. *

So from now on, there must be no more lies. *Speak the truth to one another*, since we are all parts of one another. ·*Even if you are angry, do not sin*: never let the sun set on your anger ·or else you will give the devil a foothold. ·Anyone who was a thief must stop stealing; instead he should exert himself at some honest job with his own hands so that he may have something to share with those in need. ·No foul word should ever cross your lips; let your words be for the improvement of others, as occasion offers, * and do good to your listeners; ·do not grieve the Holy Spirit of God who has marked you with his seal, ready for the day when we shall

31 be set free. * •Any bitterness or bad temper or anger or shouting or abuse must be
32 far removed from you—as must every kind of malice. •Be generous to one another,
sympathetic, forgiving each other as readily as God forgave you * in Christ.

1, 2 **5** As God's dear children, then, take him as your pattern, •and follow Christ by
loving as he loved you, giving himself up for us *as an offering and a sweet-*
3 *smelling sacrifice to God.* •Among you there must be not even a mention of sexual
vice or impurity in any of its forms, or greed: this would scarcely become the holy
4 people of God! •There must be no foul or salacious talk or coarse jokes—all this is
5 wrong for you; there should rather be thanksgiving. •For you can be quite certain
that nobody who indulges in sexual immorality or impurity or greed—which is
6 worshipping a false god *—can inherit the kingdom of God. •Do not let anyone
deceive you with empty arguments: it is such behaviour that draws down God's
7 retribution on those who rebel against him. •Make sure that you do not throw in
8 your lot with them. •You were darkness once, but now you are light in the Lord;
9 behave as children of light, •for the effects of the light are seen in complete
10 goodness and uprightness and truth. •Try to discover what the Lord wants of you,
11 take no part in the futile works of darkness but, on the contrary, show them up for
12 what they are. •The things which are done in secret are shameful even to speak of;
13, 14 but anything shown up by the light will be illuminated •and anything illuminated is
itself a light. *b* That is why it is said: *c*

> Wake up sleeper,
> rise from the dead,
> and Christ will shine on you. *d*

15 So be very careful about the sort of lives you lead, like intelligent and not like
16, 17 senseless people. •Make the best of the present time, *e* for it is a wicked age. •This
is why you must not be thoughtless but must recognise what is the will of the Lord.
18 *Do not get drunk with wine;* this is simply dissipation; be filled with the Spirit.
19 Sing psalms and hymns and inspired songs among yourselves, singing and chanting
20 to the Lord in your hearts, •always and everywhere giving thanks to God who is
our Father in the name of our Lord Jesus Christ.

The morals of the home

21, 22 Be subject to one another out of reverence for Christ. •Wives should be subject to
23 their husbands as to the Lord, •since, *f* as Christ is head of the Church and saves
24 the whole body, so is a husband the head of his wife; •and as the Church is subject
25 to Christ, so should wives be to their husbands, in everything. •Husbands should
26 love their wives, just as Christ loved the Church and sacrificed himself for her •to
27 make her holy by washing her in cleansing water with a form of words, *g* •so that
when he took the Church to himself she would be glorious, with no speck or
28 wrinkle or anything like that, but holy and faultless. *h* •In the same way, husbands
must love their wives as they love their own bodies; for a man to love his wife is
29 for him to love himself. •A man never hates his own body, but he feeds it and
30 looks after it; and that is the way Christ treats the Church, •because we are parts
31 of his Body. •*This is why a man leaves his father and mother and becomes attached*
32 *to his wife, and the two become one flesh.* •This mystery has great significance, but
33 I am applying it to Christ and the Church. *i* •To sum up: you also, each one of you,
must love his wife as he loves himself; and let every wife respect her husband.

1 **6** Children, be obedient to your parents in the Lord *—that is what uprightness
2 demands. •The first commandment that has a promise attached to it is: *Honour*

3 *your father and your mother*, ·and the promise is: *so that you may have long life*
4 *and prosper in the land.* ·And parents, never drive your children to resentment
but bring them up with correction and advice inspired by the Lord.

5   Slaves, be obedient to those who are, according to human reckoning, your
6 masters, with deep respect and sincere loyalty, as you are obedient to Christ: ·not
only when you are under their eye, as if you had only to please human beings, but
7 as slaves of Christ who wholeheartedly do the will of God. ·Work willingly for the
8 sake of the Lord and not for the sake of human beings. ·Never forget that everyone,
whether a slave or a free man, will be rewarded by the Lord for whatever work he
9 has done well. ·And those of you who are employers, treat your slaves in the same
spirit; do without threats, and never forget that they and you have the same Master
in heaven and there is no favouritism with him.

The spiritual war

10, 11 Finally, grow strong in the Lord, with the strength of his power. ·Put on the full
12 armour of God *b* so as to be able to resist the devil's tactics. ·For it is not against
human enemies that we have *c* to struggle, but against the principalities and the
ruling forces who are masters of the darkness in this world, the spirits of evil in the
13 heavens. *d* ·That is why you must take up all God's armour, or you will not be able
to put up any resistance on the evil day, or stand your ground even though you
exert yourselves to the full.

14   So stand your ground, with *truth a belt round your waist*, and *uprightness a*
15 *breastplate*, ·wearing for shoes on your feet *the eagerness to spread the gospel of*
16 *peace* ·and always carrying the shield of faith so that you can use it to quench the
17 burning arrows of the Evil One. ·And then you must take *salvation as your helmet*
and the sword of the Spirit, that is, the word of God.

18   In all your prayer and entreaty keep praying in the Spirit on every possible
19 occasion. Never get tired of staying awake to pray for all God's holy people, ·and
pray for me to be given an opportunity to open my mouth *e* and fearlessly make
20 known the mystery of the gospel *f* ·of which I am an ambassador in chains; pray
that in proclaiming it I may speak as fearlessly as I ought to.

Personal news and final salutation

21 So that you know, as well, what is happening to me and what I am doing, my dear
22 friend Tychicus, my trustworthy helper in the Lord, will tell you everything. ·I am
sending him to you precisely for this purpose, to give you news about us and
encourage you thoroughly.

23   May God the Father and the Lord Jesus Christ grant peace, love and faith to all
24 the brothers. ·May grace be with all who love our Lord Jesus Christ, in life
imperishable.

NOTES TO EPHESIANS

1 **a.** add. 'who are at Ephesus'. The words 'at Ephesus'
were probably not part of the original text. The words 'who
are' could be part of a very early addition. Some critics think
they are authentic, that they were followed by a blank to be
filled in with the name of whichever church was being sent
the letter.

b. Right from the beginning Paul raises the discussion
onto the heavenly plane where it remains throughout the
letter, 1:20; 2:6; 3:10; 6:12. The 'spiritual blessings' listed in
the following verses belong to heaven from all eternity and
will there be fully realised at the end of time.
    c. First blessing: the call of God's chosen ones to eternal

happiness, already begun in a hidden sort of way by the union of the faithful to the glorified Christ. 'Love' here is primarily the love God has for us, and that leads him to 'choose' us and to call us to be 'holy', cf. Rm 11:28; Col 3:12; 1 Th 1:4; 2 Th 2:13, but does not exclude our love for God that results from and is a response to his own love for us, cf. Rm 5:5.

d. Second blessing: the means of becoming holy, divine sonship, of which Jesus Christ, the only Son, is source and model, cf. Rm 8:29.

e. The word 'grace' (*charis*) as it is used here emphasises not so much the interior gift that makes a human being holy, as the fact that God's favour and the way he manifests his glory, *see* Ex 24:16f, are given freely. These are the two themes that run through this account of God's blessings: their *source* is God's liberality, and their *purpose* is to make his glory appreciated by creatures. Everything comes from him, and everything should lead to him.

f. Third blessing: our redemption by an event in time, i.e. the death of Jesus.

g. God the Father.

h. Fourth blessing: the revelation of the 'mystery'. 3:2–3; Rm 16:25*l*.

i. lit. 'for a dispensation of the times' fullness', *see* Ga 4:4seq.

j. The main theme of this letter is how the whole body of creation, having been cut off from the Creator by sin, is decomposing, and how its rebirth is effected by Christ's reuniting all its parts into an organism with himself as the head, so as to re-attach it to God. The human (Jew and gentile) and the angelic worlds are united in the same salvation, *see* 4:10seq.

k. Christ.

l. Fifth blessing: the choice of Israel to be God's own, a witness in the world of the messianic hope. Paul, being a Jew, here uses 'we'.

m. Sixth blessing: the call of the non-Jews to share the salvation that had, till then, been reserved for the Jews; that they will be saved is proved by the fact that they receive the Spirit as was promised.

n. Paul completes his trinitarian account of God's plan with the Spirit, since the giving of the Spirit shows the plan has reached its final stage. Nevertheless, though this gift has already begun, it is given only in a hidden way while the unspiritual world lasts, and will be given fully only when the kingdom of God is complete and Christ comes in glory, cf. Lk 24:49; Jn 1:33k; 14:26d.

o. lit. 'the setting free of that (enslaved people) which has been acquired' i.e. by God, and at the cost of the life of his Son. This is one of the occasions when Paul widens an OT concept, 'the chosen people' (like 'blessing', 'saint', 'choice', 'adoption', 'share', 'promise') by applying it to the Church as the new Israel and the body of the saved.

p. om. 'and the love that you show'.

q. This gift is what technically would be called (actual) grace.

r. lit. 'heart': used in the Bible for the seat of knowledge and understanding as well as of love, conscience and emotions; sometimes to be translated 'mind'. The moral and spiritual connotations of 'heart' in the OT, Gn 8:21c, persist in the NT. God knows the heart, Lk 16:15; Ac 1:24; Rm 8:27. Human beings love God with their whole heart, Mk 12:29–30 and par. God's gift of the Spirit is put in the human heart, Rm 5:5e; 2 Co 1:22; Ga 4:6. Christ makes his home there, 3:17. Hearts which are simple 6:5; Ac 2:46; 2 Co 11:3; Col 3:22, upright Ac 8:21, pure Mt 5:8; Jm 4:8, are open without reservation to the presence and action of God. The first believers in Jerusalem have one heart and one mind, Ac 4:32.

s. Names of cosmic powers attested in Jewish apocryphal writing. Without any discussion of the mode of existence of these celestial beings, Paul insists that they are under the dominion of Christ, Col 1:16; 2:10. By associating them with the angels of OT tradition who were concerned in the giving of the Law, Ga 3:19k, he sees a place for them in salvation-history, but with an increasingly pejorative moral qualification, Ga 4:3b; Col 2:15m, which finally assimilates them with demonic forces, Ep 2:2a; 6:12d; *see* 1 Co 15:24p.

t. The Church, as the body of Christ, 1 Co 12:12seq., can be called the fullness (*pleroma; see* below 3:19; 4:13) in so far as it includes the whole new creation that shares (since it forms the setting of the human race) in the cosmic rebirth under Christ its ruler and head, *see* Col 1:15–20seq. The adverbial phrase 'all in all' is used to suggest something of limitless size, cf. 1 Co 12:6; 15:28; Col 3:11.

2 **a.** Air is the habitat of demons and of their ruler Satan.

b. Paul writes as a Jew.

c. 'We' here means both the gentiles, *see* vv. 1–2, and the Jews, cf. v. 3. • V. 3 is a parenthesis.

d. 'with Christ'; • var. 'in Christ'. 'it is through grace'; var. (Vulg) 'through whose grace'.

e. Here as in 2:12; 3:1–4 the use of the past tense shows that the resurrection and triumph of Christians in heaven is considered as actually existing, whereas the future tense in Rm 6:3–11; 8:11,17seq., treats it as something that has still to take place. Treating the eschatological reality as already existing is a characteristic of the captivity epistles.

f. The description of this past that Paul now gives is meant to apply to all gentiles in a general way—not specifically to those he is writing to.

g. i.e. you had no Messiah.

h. The successive covenants made by God with Abraham, Isaac, Jacob, Moses, David; *see* Gn 12:1a; 15:1a; Ex 19:1a; Lv 26:42,45; 2 M 8:15; Ws 18:22; Si 44–45; Rm 9:4, which contained the promise of salvation through the Messiah.

i. Hope of a Messiah, which was hitherto confined to Israel, 1:12.

j. The non-Jews had many gods but not the one true God, 1 Co 8:5seq.

k. The crucifixion of Christ that brought together Jews and non-Jews, vv. 14–15, and reconciled both with the Father, vv. 16–18.

l. Visibly symbolised by the wall separating the court of the Jews from the court of the non-Jews in the Temple, cf. Ac 21:28seq.

m. The Mosaic Law gave the Jews a privileged status and separated them from gentiles. Jesus abolished this Law by fulfilling it once for all on the cross, Col 2:14*l*.

n. This New Man is the prototype of the new humanity that God re-created (2 Co 5:17i) in the person of Christ, the second Adam (1 Co 15:45), after the sinfully corrupt race of the first Adam had died in the crucifixion (Rm 5:12seq.; 8:3; 1 Co 15:21). This New Adam has been created in 'the goodness and holiness of the truth', 4:24, and he is unique because in him the boundaries between any one group and the rest of the human race all disappear, Ga 3:27seq.; Col 3:10seq.

o. This 'one Body' is both the physical body of Jesus that was sacrificed on the cross, Col 1:22j, and the Church or 'mystical' body of Christ in which, once they are reconciled, all the parts function in their own places, 1 Co 12:12i,j.

p. Through the apostles who in his name preached the good news of salvation and peace.

q. The one Spirit that gives life to the single Body (of Christ who is one with his Church) is the Holy Spirit. The trinitarian structure of this section is repeated in v. 22.

r. Paul inserts vv. 14–18 (how Christ has united gentiles and Jews) between his contrasting descriptions of gentiles before (vv. 11–13) and after (19–22) conversion.

s. The NT prophets, cf. 3:5; 4:11; Ac 11:27m, together with the apostles, are the witnesses to whom the divine plan was first revealed and who were the first to preach the good news, cf. Mt 10:41; 23:34; Lk 11:49. This is why the Church, as well as being founded on Christ, 1 Co 3:10seq., is also said to be founded on them.

t. 'every'; var. 'the entire'.

3 a. On the grace given to the apostle to empower him to preach to the gentiles, *see* 3:7seq.; Rm 1:5; 15:15seq.; 1 Co 3:10. Notice, however, that 'grace' in this sentence is granted to him for him to dispense, not as a possession.

b. Cf. 2 Co 12:1,7. The immediate reference is to what was revealed to Paul on the way to Damascus, *see* Ac 9:15; 22:21; 26:16–18; Ga 1:16.

c. The NT prophets, *see* 2:20s. The OT prophets had only an obscure and imperfect knowledge of the mystery of the Messiah, cf. Mt 13:17; 1 P 1:10–12.

d. i.e. as the Jewish Christians, *see* 2:19.

e. The evil spirits were unaware of God's plan for salvation and so they persuaded human beings to crucify Christ, 1 Co 2:8, and it is only the existence of the Church that makes them aware of it now; cf. 1 P 1:12.

f. An alternative (and less likely) translation: 'so I pray not to lose confidence'.

g. var. 'our glory'.

h. The Gk word here translated 'fatherhood' has a more concrete sense than this English rendering might imply. It denotes any social group which owes its existence and unity to one ancestor. The origin of every human, or even angelic, grouping is in God.

i. Stoics used this expression to mean the totality of the cosmos. Paul uses it to suggest the cosmic function of Christ in the rebirth of the world. (Notice too the eschatological dimensions of the Temple and Promised Land, Ezk 40–45; Rv 21:9seq.) Here the dimensions may be those of the mystery of salvation, or more probably those of Christ's universal love on which (next verse) the mystery depends. As in the case of Wisdom, they surpass all human standards of measurement, 1:17–19,23; 2:7; 3:8; Jb 11:8–9seq.; Col 2:2seq.

j. This love for us that Christ proved by accepting death, 5:2,25; Ga 2:20, is identical with the love the Father has, 2:4,7; Rm 8:35,37,39; 2 Co 5:14,18–19. *See* 1 Co 13:1a.

k. The love of God cannot be 'grasped' (v. 18, using a philosophical term technical in Greek) but can be 'known' by spiritual awareness of it through love, cf. 1:17seq.; 3:3seq.; Ho 2:22v; Jn 10:14g. This awareness is something deeper than scientific knowledge, *see* 1 Co 13, and is less a matter of knowledge than of awareness of being loved, cf. Ga 4:9. Even awareness of this sort, however, can never 'grasp' this sort of love.

l. lit. 'in order that you may be filled to all the fullness (*pleroma*) of God'. (var. 'in order that all the fullness of God may be filled'.) • Christ who is filled with the divine life fills Christians with it, Col 2:9, and in this way Christian's enter both the Church and the new cosmos which they help to build and which is the fullness of the total Christ, 1:23; 2:22; 4:12–13; Col 2:10f.

4 a. Paul lists three different threats to the Church's unity: arguments between Christians vv. 1–3, diversity of service in the Church vv. 7–11, unorthodox teaching vv. 14–15. These threats are all averted by applying the principle of unity in Christ, vv. 4–6,12–13,16.

b. Charisms or special graces given to individuals for the benefit of the whole community, *see* 1 Co 12:1a.

c. Following rabbinic practice Paul quotes this text for the sake of two phrases: 'he ascended' vv. 9–10, and 'he gave gifts' v. 11 which he interprets as the ascension of Jesus and the descent of the Spirit.

d. The subterranean regions where the realms of the dead were placed; *see* Nb 16:33f, and where Christ descended before his resurrection and ascension 'above the heavens'; *see* 1 P 3:19h. Or, according to others, the death, said to be 'lower' in relation to the heavens.

e. By ascending through all the cosmic spheres Christ takes possession of them all one after another, and becomes the head of the whole *pleroma* or total cosmos 1:10j, and makes the entire universe acknowledge him as 'Lord', *see* 1:20–23; Ph 2:8–11; Col 1:19.

f. Paul limits his list to charisms that relate to teaching; these are the only ones that apply in this context, vv. 13–15.

g. The particular holy people of God Paul mentions here seem to be missionaries and other teachers, cf. 3:5, but may include all the faithful in so far as they all help to build up the Church, *see* Ac 9:13v.

h. This does not refer primarily to the individual Christian. The sense is collective. It can be taken as referring to Christ himself, the New Man, the archetype of all who are reborn 2:15n, or else (and this sense is to be preferred) as referring to the total Christ, i.e. the whole body, 1 Co 12:2i,j; made up of head, Ep 1:22; 4:15; Col 1:18; and the rest of the body, Ep 4:16; 5:30.

i. Or 'sexuality and every kind of indecency and greed'.

j. As in Col 2:6, the true Christ is the historic Jesus, who died and rose again to renew our lives in him.

k. Each human being needs to 'put on the New Man', 2:15n (here, as in v. 22, translated 'self'), so as to be re-created in him, cf. Rm 13:14; Ga 3:27. In some places Paul talks in the same way about the 'new creature', 2 Co 5:17i.

l. lit. 'working the good thing with his own hand'. 'Good' and '(own) hand' are omitted or interchanged in various readings; the original text may have been ambiguous.

m. The one Holy Spirit that keeps the one Body of Christ united, 4:4; 1 Co 12:13, is 'grieved', cf. Ep 4:30; Is 63:10, by anything that harms the unity of the Body.

n. 'you'; var. 'us'. The same in 5:2.

5 a. Uncontrolled desires pay to creatures, especially money, a worship due to God alone and thus turn them into idols.

b. The wrong sort of way to talk about sexual immorality is the way that leaves the subject in a dangerous obscurity, v. 3. To talk about it in such a way, however, that it is recognised for what it is will lead to its being corrected; this sort of light is the light of Christ that puts an end to darkness.

c. This (like 1 Tm 3:16) seems to be an extract from an early Christian hymn. On baptism as an enlightening, *see* Heb 6:4; 10:32 (*see* Rm 6:4a).

d. var. 'and you will touch Christ'.

e. lit. 'redeem the present time'.

f. By drawing a parallel between a marriage and the marriage of Christ to his Church, vv. 23–32, Paul makes these two concepts illumine each other. Christ is the husband of the Church because he is her head and because he loves the Church as man loves his own body when he loves his wife. In its turn, this comparison naturally suggests an ideal for human marriage. The symbol of Israel as the wife of Yahweh is common in the OT, Ho 1:2c.

g. Baptism has no value unless it is accompanied by proclamation of the Word, expressed through evangelisation by the minister and the recipient's profession of faith, 1:13, cf. Mk 16:15seq.; Ac 2:38y; Rm 6:4a; 1 P 1:23m.

h. It was customary in the Middle East, at the time this letter was written, for the 'sons of the wedding' to escort the bride to her husband after she had bathed and dressed. As applied mystically to the Church, Christ washes his bride himself in the bath of baptism, and makes her immaculate (note the mention of a baptismal formula) before taking her to himself. Cf. 1 Th 5:8.

i. Paul finds in this Gn text a prophecy of the marriage of Christ and the Church: a mystery, like that of the salvation of the gentiles, that has been hidden but is now revealed, cf. 1:9f; 3:3seq.

6 a. om. 'in the Lord'.

b. God in the OT arms himself against his enemies, *see* Ws 5:17–23; Is 11:4–5; 59:16–18. These are the arms of Yahweh with which, Paul says, the Christian is to arm himself.

c. var. 'you have'.

d. These are the spirits who were thought to move the stars and, consequently, the universe. They lived in 'the heavens', 1:20seq.; 3:10; Ph 2:10, or in 'the air', Ep 2:2, i.e. the space between the surface of the earth and the heaven where God lives. Some of them are among the 'elemental principles of the world', Ga 4:3. They disobeyed God and want to enslave the human race to themselves in sin, 2:2. We used to be their slaves but Christ came to free us, 1:19–21; Col 1:13; 2:15,20, and if Christians are armed with the power of Christ, they will be able to fight them.

e. Hebraism, cf. Ps 51:15; Ezk 3:27; cf. Col 4:3.
f. om. 'of the gospel'.

PHILIPPIANS

THE LETTER OF PAUL
TO THE CHURCH AT PHILIPPI

Address

1 1 Paul and Timothy, servants of Christ Jesus, to all God's holy people in Christ
2 Jesus at Philippi, together with their presiding elders ^a and the deacons. ·Grace
and peace to you from God our Father and the Lord Jesus Christ.

Thanksgiving and prayer

3, 4 I thank my God whenever I think of you, ·and every time I pray for you all, I
5 always pray with joy ^b ·for your partnership in the gospel ^c from the very first day ^d
6 up to the present. ·I am quite confident that the One who began a good work in
7 you will go on completing it until the Day of Jesus Christ comes. ·It is only right
that I should feel like this towards you all, because you have a place in my heart,
since you have all shared together in the grace that has been mine, both my chains
8 and my work defending and establishing the gospel. ·For God will testify for me
9 how much I long for you all with the warm longing of Christ Jesus; ·it is my prayer
that your love for one another may grow more and more with the knowledge and
10 complete understanding ·that will help you to come to true discernment, ^e so that
you will be innocent and free of any trace of guilt when the Day of Christ comes,
11 entirely filled with the fruits of uprightness through Jesus Christ, for the glory and
praise of God.

Paul's own circumstances

12 Now I want you to realise, brothers, that the circumstances of my present life ^f are
13 helping rather than hindering the advance of the gospel. ·My chains in Christ have
14 become well known not only to all the Praetorium, ^g but to everybody else, ·and
so most of the brothers in the Lord have gained confidence from my chains and
are getting more and more daring in announcing the Message ^h without any fear.
15 It is true that some of them are preaching Christ out of malice and rivalry; but
16 there are many as well whose intentions are good; ·some are doing it out of love,
17 knowing that I remain firm in my defence of the gospel. ·There are others who are
proclaiming Christ out of jealousy, not in sincerity but meaning to add to the
18 weight of my chains. ·But what does it matter? Only that in both ways, whether
19 with false motives or true, Christ is proclaimed, and for that I am happy; ·and I
shall go on being happy, too, because I know that *this is what will save me*, with

20 your prayers and with the support of the Spirit of Jesus Christ; ·all in accordance with my most confident hope and trust that I shall never have to admit defeat, but with complete fearlessness I shall go on, so that now, as always, Christ will be 21 glorified in my body, *i* whether by my life or my death. ·Life to me, of course, is 22 Christ, but then death would be a positive gain. ·On the other hand again, if to be alive in the body gives me an opportunity for fruitful work, I do not know which I 23 should choose. ·I am caught in this dilemma: I want to be gone and to be with 24 Christ, *j* and this is by far the stronger desire—·and yet for your sake to stay alive 25 in this body is a more urgent need. ·This much I know for certain, that I shall stay 26 and stand by you all, *k* to encourage your advance and your joy in the faith, ·so that my return to be among you may increase to overflowing your pride in Jesus Christ on my account.

Fight for the faith

27 But you must always behave in a way that is worthy of the gospel of Christ, *l* so that whether I come to you and see for myself or whether I only hear all about you from a distance, I shall find that you are standing firm and united in spirit, battling, 28 as a team with a single aim, for the faith of the gospel, ·undismayed by any of your opponents. This will be a clear sign, for them that they are to be lost, and for you 29 that you are to be saved. ·This comes from God, for you have been granted the privilege for Christ's sake not only of believing in him but of suffering for him as 30 well; ·you are fighting the same battle which you saw me fighting for him and which you hear I am fighting still. *m*

Preserve unity in humility

1 **2** So if in Christ there is anything that will move you, any incentive in love, *a* any
2 fellowship in the Spirit, *b* any warmth or sympathy—I appeal to you, ·make my joy complete by being of a single mind, one in love, one in heart and one in 3 mind. *c* ·Nothing is to be done out of jealousy or vanity; instead, out of humility of 4 mind everyone should give preference to others, ·everyone pursuing not selfish 5 interests but those of others. ·Make your own the mind of Christ Jesus: *d*

6   Who, being in the form of God, *e*
       did not count equality with God
       something to be grasped. *f*

7   But he emptied himself, *g*
       taking the form of a slave, *h*
       becoming as human beings are; *i*

       and being in every way like a human being, *j*
8   he was humbler yet,
       even to accepting death, death on a cross.

9   And for this God raised him high, *k*
       and gave him the name *l*
       which is above all other names; *m*

10   so that *all beings*
       in the heavens, on earth and in the underworld, *n*
       should bend the knee at the name of Jesus

11   and that *every tongue should acknowledge*°
            Jesus Christ as Lord, ᵖ
            to the glory of God the Father. ᵠ

Work for salvation

12 So, my dear friends, you have always been obedient; your obedience must not be
limited to times when I am present. Now that I am absent it must be more in
13 evidence, so work out your salvation in fear and trembling. •It is God who, for his
14 own generous purpose, gives you the intention and the powers to act. •Let your
15 behaviour be free of murmuring and complaining •so that you remain faultless
and pure, *unspoilt children of God* surrounded by *a deceitful and underhand brood*,
16 shining out among them like bright stars in the world, •proffering to it the Word
of life. Then I shall have reason to be proud on the Day of Christ, for it will not be
17 for nothing that I have run the race and toiled so hard. •Indeed, even if my blood
has to be poured as a libation over your sacrifice and the offering of your faith, ʳ
18 then I shall be glad and join in your rejoicing—•and in the same way, you must be
glad and join in my rejoicing.

The mission of Timothy and Epaphroditus

19 I hope, in the Lord Jesus, to send Timothy to you soon, so that my mind may be
20 set at rest when I hear how you are. •There is nobody else that I can send who is
21 like him and cares as sincerely for your well-being; •they all want to work for
22 themselves, not for Jesus Christ. •But you know what sort of person he has proved
23 himself, working with me for the sake of the gospel like a son with his father. •That
is the man, then, that I am hoping to send to you immediately I can make out
24 what is going to happen to me; •but I am confident in the Lord that I shall come
25 myself, too, before long. •Nevertheless I thought it essential to send to you
Epaphroditus, my brother and fellow-worker and companion-in-arms since he
26 came as your representative to look after my needs; •because he was missing you
27 all and was worrying because you had heard that he was ill. •Indeed he was
seriously ill and nearly died; but God took pity on him—and not only on him but
28 also on me, to spare me one grief on top of another. •So I am sending him back as
promptly as I can so that you will have the joy of seeing him again, and that will be
29 some comfort to me in my distress. •Welcome him in the Lord, then, with all joy;
30 hold people like him in honour, •because it was for Christ's work ˢ that he came so
near to dying, risking his life to do the duty to me which you could not do
yourselves.

1 **3** Finally, brothers, I wish you joy in the Lord. ᵃ

The true way of Christian salvation

To write to you what I have already written before is no trouble to me and to you
2 will be a protection. •Beware of dogs! ᵇ Beware of evil workmen! Beware of self-
3 mutilators! ᶜ •We are the true people of the circumcision since we worship by the
Spirit of God ᵈ and make Christ Jesus our only boast, not relying on physical
4 qualifications, ᵉ •although, I myself could rely on these too. If anyone does claim
5 to rely on them, my claim is better. •Circumcised on the eighth day of my life, I
was born of the race of Israel, of the tribe of Benjamin, a Hebrew born of Hebrew
6 parents. ᶠ In the matter of the Law, I was a Pharisee; •as for religious fervour, I
was a persecutor of the Church; as for the uprightness embodied in the Law, I was

7 faultless. ·But what were once my assets I now through Christ Jesus count as
8 losses. ·Yes, I will go further: because of the supreme advantage of knowing Christ
Jesus my Lord, I count everything else as loss. For him I have accepted the loss of
9 all other things, and look on them all as filth if only I can gain Christ ·and be given
a place in him, with the uprightness I have gained not from the Law, but through
10 faith in Christ, an uprightness from God, based on faith,ᶠ ·that I may come to
know him and the power of his resurrection, and partake of his sufferings by being
11 moulded to the pattern of his death, ·striving towards the goal of resurrection
12 from the dead. ʰ ·Not that I have secured it already, not yet reached my goal, but I
am still pursuing it in the attempt to take hold of the prize for which Christ Jesus
13 took hold of me. ⁱ ·Brothers, I do not reckon myself as having taken hold of it; I
can only say that forgetting all that lies behind me, and straining forward to what
14 lies in front, ·I am racing towards the finishing-point to win the prize of God's
15 heavenly call in Christ Jesus. ·So this is the way in which all of us who are matureʲ
should be thinking,ᵏ and if you are still thinking differently in any way, then God
16 has yet to make this matter clear to you. ·Meanwhile, let us go forward from the
point we have each attained. ˡ

17   Brothers, be united in imitating me. Keep your eyes fixed on those who act
18 according to the example you have from me. ·For there are so many people ᵐ of
whom I have often warned you, and now I warn you again with tears in my eyes,
19 who behave like the enemies of Christ's cross. ·They are destined to be lost; their
god is the stomach;ⁿ they glory in what they should think shameful,ᵒ since their
20 minds are set on earthly things. ·But our homeland is in heaven and it is from
21 there that we are expecting a Saviour, the Lord Jesus Christ, ·who will transfigure
the wretched body of ours into the mould of his glorious body, through the working
of the power which he has, even to bring all things under his mastery.

1 **4** So then, my brothers and dear friends whom I miss so much, my joy and my
crown, hold firm in the Lord, dear friends.

Last advice

2 I urge Euodia, and I urge Syntyche to come to agreement with each other in the
3 Lord; ·and I ask you, Syzygus,ᵃ really to be a 'partner' and help them. These
women have struggled hard for the gospel with me, along with Clement and all my
other fellow-workers, whose names are written in the book of life.

4,5   Always be joyful, then, in the Lord; I repeat, be joyful. ·Let your good sense
6 be obvious to everybody. The Lord is near. ·Never worry about anything; but tell
God all your desires of every kind in prayer and petition shot through with
7 gratitude, ·and the peace of God which is beyond our understanding will guard
8 your hearts and your thoughts ᵇ in Christ Jesus. ·Finally, brothers, let your minds
be filled with everything that is true, ᶜ everything that is honourable, everything
that is upright and pure, everything that we love and admire ᵈ—with whatever is
9 good and praiseworthy. ·Keep doing everything you learnt from me and were told
by me and have heard or seen me doing. Then the God of peace will be with you.

Thanks for help received ᵉ

10 As for me, I am full of joy in the Lord, now that at last your consideration for me
has blossomed again; though I recognise that you really did have consideration
11 before, but had no opportunity to show it. ·I do not say this because I have lacked
12 anything; I have learnt to manage with whatever I have. ·I know how to live
modestly, and I know how to live luxuriously too: in every way now I have

mastered the secret of all conditions: full stomach and empty stomach, plenty and
13, 14 poverty. ·There is nothing I cannot do in the One *f* who strengthens me. ·All the
15 same, it was good of you to share with me in my hardships. ·In the early days of
the gospel, as you of Philippi well know, when I left Macedonia, no church other
than yourselves made common account with me in the matter of expenditure and
16 receipts. *g* You were the only ones; ·and what is more, you have twice sent me
17 what I needed in Thessalonica. ·It is not the gift that I value most; what I value is
18 the interest that is mounting up in your account. ·I have all that I need and more:
I am fully provided, now that I have received from Epaphroditus the offering that
you sent, *a pleasing smell*, the sacrifice which is acceptable and pleasing to God.
19 And my God will fulfil *h* all your needs out of the riches of his glory in Christ Jesus.
20 And so glory be to God our Father, for ever and ever. Amen.

Greetings and final wish

21 My greetings to every one of God's holy people in Christ Jesus. The brothers who
22 are with me send you their greetings. ·All God's holy people *i* send you their
greetings, especially those of Caesar's household. *j*
23 May the grace of the Lord Jesus Christ be with your spirit. *k*

NOTES TO PHILIPPIANS

1 **a.** The word *episkopos* (overseer) has not yet acquired
the meaning 'bishop', *see* Tt 1:5seq. The 'deacons' are their
assistants, Ac 6:1–6; 1 Tm 3:8–13.

b. Joy is one of the chief characteristics of this letter; *see*
vv. 18,25; 2:2,17,28,29; 3:1; 4:1,4,10.

c. Not only by sending money, 4:14–16, but also by their
joining in the work of witness, 1:7; cf. 2:15–16, when they
have suffered as he has for the gospel, 1:29–30.

d. Since the day they were converted, *see* Ac 16:12–40.

e. The fruit, cf. Ho 14:9 and Ga 5:22; Ep 5:9, of growing
love is knowledge and discernment of 'what is important',
Rm 2:18; its rectitude and warmth continue to grow to
maturity, v. 11, transcending the limits of all legislation,
Ga 5:23*l*.

f. i.e. Paul's arrest and imprisonment awaiting trial.

g. If Paul is writing from his house-arrest in Rome, this
must refer to members of the Praetorian Guard (who were
quartered just outside the city wall). If Paul is writing from
Ephesus of Caesarea, he is referring to the staff of the Praetorium which was the name of the official residence of the
governor in each of those cities.

h. add. 'of the Lord'.

i. By baptism and Eucharist a Christian is so closely
united to Christ, *see* 1 Co 6:15–16; 10:17; 12:12seq.,27;
Ga 2:20; Ep 5:30, that his life, sufferings and death can be
attributed mystically to Christ living in him and being
glorified in him, *see* Rm 14:8; 1 Co 6:20. This union would
be particularly close in the case of an apostle like Paul, *see*
2 Co 4:10seq.; Col 1:24.

j. For death as a way of being with Christ, *see* Rm 14:8;
Col 3:3; 1 Th 5:10. Paul does not explain what is the 'something more' that death will bring, nor in what way to be with
Christ in death is 'immeasurably better'; he may possibly be
envisaging a more direct relationship with Christ than is
possible in the body. As in 2 Co 5:8*d*, his words suppose that
the state of being 'with Christ' follows immediately after
death, with no temporal interval of waiting for the general
resurrection.

k. This presentiment (it was no more than that, *see* 2:17)

was not mistaken, *see* Ac 20:1–6, unlike that expressed by
Paul at Miletus, Ac 20:25.

l. The Greek term means primarily 'to lead the life of a
citizen', according to the laws of a city. The new City of the
Kingdom of God has Christ as its King, the gospel as its Law
and Christians as its citizens, *see* 3:20; Ep 2:19.

m. The first reference is to the persecution Paul had to
put up with when he was with them in Philippi, Ac 16:19seq.;
1 Th 2:2; the second is to his present imprisonment.

2 **a.** lit. 'If there is any ground for appeal in Christ, etc',
an affectionate invocation of all that is most sacred.

b. Perhaps to be taken as a trinitarian reference; in this
case 'love' is appropriated to the Father, *see* 2 Co 13:13e.

c. This urgent plea for unity suggests that internal
divisions threatened the peace of the church at Philippi, *see*
1:27; 2:14; 4:2. Note how Paul keeps insisting that he is
addressing all of them, 1:1,4,7,25; 2:17,26; 4:21.

d. Vv. 6–11 are probably an early Christian hymn
quoted by Paul, as Ep 5:14; Col 1:15–20; 2 T 2:11–13 etc. It
has been understood of Christ's *kenosis* in emptying himself
of his divine glory in order to live a human life and undergo
suffering. More probably Jesus is here contrasted as the
second with the first Adam, *see* Rm 5:12f, h; 1 Co 15:22m.
The first Adam, being in the form or image of God,
attempted to grasp equality with God and, by this pride, fell.
By contrast, Jesus, through his humility, was raised up by
God to the divine glory.

e. The contrast is with Adam, who was created 'in the
image of God' but misused this.

f. Adam sought illegitimately to be like God; Jesus
humbled himself.

g. In the traditional but less probable interpretation,
this emptying or *kenosis* expressed Jesus' voluntary self-
deprivation, during his earthly life, of the divine glory. But
this interpretation is not only less scriptural but also anachronistic for the development of christology at this moment
of Paul's thinking.

h. A reference to the 'servant' of Is 52:13–53:12 which contains the same movement of exaltation through humiliation; *see* Is 42:1a.

i. There is probably a reference here to the 'one like a son of man' who receives honour and glory from God in Dn 7:13.

j. lit 'and in fashion found as a human being'.

k. lit. 'super-raised him': by the resurrection and ascension. The resurrection is the prime work of the power of God.

l. Imposition of a name confers a real quality, cf. Ep 1:21; Heb 1:4. This name is 'Lord', v. 11; or more profoundly the unspeakable divine name which, in the triumph of the Risen Christ, is expressed by the title 'Lord'; *see* Ac 2:21m; 3:16*l*.

m. Greater even than the angels, cf. Ep 1:21; Heb 1:4; 1 P 3:22. 'in the underworld' refers to those who dwell in Sheol, Nb 16:33f, rather than to demons.

n. The three cosmic divisions that cover the entire creation, cf. Rv 5:3,13.

o. var. 'and every tongue will acclaim'.

p. om. 'Christ'. This proclamation is the essence of the Christian creed, Rm 10:9; 1 Co 12:3; cf. Col 2:6. The use of Is 45:23 (in which this homage is addressed to Yahweh himself) is a clear indication of the divine character that is meant to be understood by the title *Kyrios*, cf. Jn 20:28; Ac 2:36w. God exalted Jesus, and his glory is therefore increased by the Son's humiliation, 2:7.

q. Vulg. interpretation is 'proclaim that Jesus Christ is in the glory of God the Father'.

r. Libations were common to both Greek and Jewish sacrifices. Paul merely applies this custom metaphorically to the spiritual worship of the new creation, cf. 3:3; 4:18; Rm 1:9g.

s. var. 'the Lord's work', or 'the work'.

3 **a.** This appears to be the conclusion of the letter, interrupted by the verses which follow, and not resumed until 4:4, *see* p. 294.

b. Term of abuse applied by Jews to gentiles, Mt 15:26 (and possibly 7:6) which Paul ironically applies to non-Christian Jews.

c. lit. 'for the gash'. Paul uses this term (*katatomē*) as a contemptuous pun on 'circumcision (*peritomē*), implying a comparison between physical circumcision and the self-inflicted gashes in pagan cults, cf. 1 K 18:28; *see* Ga 5:12.

d. var. 'we who worship God in spirit'.

e. lit. 'the flesh', which stands here for the whole system of the old Law with its physical observances, of which circumcision is a typical example. *See* Rm 7:5c. Paul often recalls his Jewish past, 2 Co 11:21j, but nowhere else in such detail.

f. Of Palestinian stock, Ac 23:6, and speaking the language of his ancestors, Ac 21:40, by contrast to the 'Hellenists', Ac 6:1b.

g. The differences between these two sorts of 'uprightness' form the entire subject of Paul's letters to the Christians of Galatia and Rome.

h. Paul is not referring to the general resurrection of both saved and damned, Jn 5:29, but to the true resurrection of the saints who are separated from the 'spiritually' dead to life with Christ, Lk 20:35c.

i. On the road to Damascus.

j. Christians who are mature, *see* 1 Co 2:6e, but who are not totally perfect, Ph 3:12.

k. 'must all think'; var. 'all think'.

l. var. 'let us be united in our convictions (cf. 2:2) and let us follow the same rule of life,' cf. Ga 6:16.

m. The Judaisers, against whom this whole chapter is a warning.

n. The dietary laws loomed large in the Jewish practice of religion, Lv 11; cf. Mt 15:10–20 and par.; 23:25–26; Ac 15:20; Rm 14:17; 16:18; Ga 2:12; Col 2:16,20seq.

o. Probably an allusion to the circumcised member.

4 **a.** 'Syzygus' means yoke-fellow, partner, second of a pair, colleague, companion; a play on words as in Phm 10–11.

b. var. 'your bodies'.

c. In this verse the ideas commended by Paul are expressed in terms current among the Greek moralists of his time; but in v. 9 he returns to his more usual practice of telling his readers to follow him as their example, 3:17, *see* 2 Th 3:7b.

d. add. 'everything there is of knowledge', or 'of discipline'.

e. At the same time as repeating his gratitude for the gifts he has received, v. 18; 2:25–30, Paul insists on the independence of his mission; the essential element remains the spiritual good of everyone, vv. 17,19; 1:5, cf. 1 Co 9:11.

f. 'the One', var. 'Christ'.

g. Paul was usually unwilling to do anything to leave the impression that he took money for his preaching, 1 Co 9:15; 1 Th 2:5; his acceptance of presents from the Philippians is a mark of his special feeling for them and confidence in their understanding, cf. Ac 16:15; 18:3d; 2 Co 11:8.

h. var. 'may my God fulfil'.

i. All the Christians of the place from which Paul is writing.

j. The 'household' of Caesar was a wide term that covered anybody employed in the service of the emperor, either in Rome or in any of the chief towns of the empire.

k. add. 'Amen'.

COLOSSIANS

THE LETTER OF PAUL
TO THE CHURCH AT COLOSSAE

PREFACE

Address

1,2 **1** From Paul, by the will of God an apostle of Christ Jesus, and from our brother Timothy ·to God's holy people in Colossae, our faithful brothers in Christ. Grace and peace to you from God our Father. *

Thanksgiving and prayer

3 We give thanks for you to God, the Father of our Lord Jesus Christ, continually in
4 our prayers, ·ever since we heard about your faith in Christ Jesus and the love
5 that you show towards all God's holy people ·because of the hope which is stored up for you in heaven. News of this hope reached you not long ago through the
6 word of truth, the gospel ·that came to you in the same way as it is bearing fruit and growing throughout the world. It has had the same effect among you, ever
7 since you heard about the grace of God and recognised it for what it truly is. ·This you learnt from Epaphras, our very dear fellow-worker *b* and a trustworthy deputy
8 for us as Christ's servant, ·and it was he who also told us all about your love in the Spirit.
9 That is why, ever since the day he told us, we have never failed to remember you in our prayers and ask that through perfect wisdom and spiritual understanding
10 you should reach the fullest knowledge of his will ·and so be able to lead a life worthy of the Lord, a life acceptable to him in all its aspects, bearing fruit in every
11 kind of good work and growing in knowledge of God, ·fortified, in accordance
12 with his glorious strength, with all power always to persevere and endure, ·giving thanks with joy to the Father who has made you able to share the lot of God's holy people and with them to inherit the light. *c*
13 Because that is what he has done. It is he who has rescued us from the ruling
14 force of darkness and transferred us to the kingdom of the Son that he loves, ·and in him we enjoy our freedom, the forgiveness of sin.

I: FORMAL INSTRUCTION

Christ is the head of all creation [d]

15   He is the image of the unseen God,
the first-born of all creation,
16   for in him were created all things
in heaven and on earth:
everything visible and everything invisible,
thrones, ruling forces, sovereignties, powers—
all things were created through him and for him.
17   He exists before all things
and in him all things hold together,
18   and he is the Head [e] of the Body,
that is, the Church.

He is the Beginning,
the first-born from the dead,
so that he should be supreme in every way;
19   because God wanted all fullness to be found in him [f]
20   and through him to reconcile all things to him, [g]
everything in heaven and everything on earth, [h]
by making peace through his death on the cross.

The Colossians have their share in salvation

21, 22   You were once estranged and of hostile intent [i] through your evil behaviour; ·now
he [j] has reconciled you, by his death and in that mortal body, to bring you before
23   himself holy, faultless and irreproachable—·as long as you persevere and stand
firm on the solid base of the faith, never letting yourselves drift away from the
hope promised by the gospel, which you have heard, which has been preached to
every creature under heaven, [k] and of which I, Paul, have become the servant.

Paul's labours in the service of the gentiles

24   It makes me happy to be suffering for you now, and in my own body to make up
all the hardships that still have to be undergone by Christ for the sake of his body,
25   the Church, [l] ·of which I was made a servant with the responsibility towards you
26   that God gave to me, that of completing God's message, ·the message which was
a mystery hidden for generations and centuries and has now been revealed to his
27   holy people. ·It was God's purpose to reveal to them how rich is the glory of this
28   mystery among the gentiles; it is Christ among you, your hope of glory: [m] ·this is
the Christ we are proclaiming, admonishing and instructing everyone in all wisdom,
29   to make everyone perfect in Christ. ·And it is for this reason that I labour, striving
with his energy which works in me mightily.

Paul's concern for the Colossians' faith

1   2 I want you to know, then, what a struggle I am having on your behalf and on
behalf of those in Laodicea, and on behalf of so many others who have never
2   seen me face to face. ·It is all to bind them together in love and to encourage their
resolution until they are rich in the assurance of their complete understanding and
3   have knowledge of the mystery of God [a] ·in which [b] all the jewels of wisdom and
knowledge are hidden.

4, 5 I say this to make sure that no one deceives you with specious arguments.[c] •I
may be absent in body, but in spirit I am there among you, delighted to find how
well-ordered you are and to see how firm your faith in Christ is.

II: A WARNING AGAINST SOME ERRORS

Live according to the true faith in Christ, not according to false teaching

6, 7 So then, as you received Jesus as Lord and Christ, now live your lives in him, •be
rooted in him and built up on him, held firm by the faith you have been taught,
and overflowing with thanksgiving.
8 Make sure that no one captivates[d] you with the empty lure of a 'philosophy' of
the kind that human beings hand on, based on the principles of this world and not
on Christ.

Christ alone is the true head of all humanity and the angels

9, 10 In him, in bodily form, lives divinity[e] in all its fullness, •and in him you too find
your own fulfilment, in the one who is the head of every sovereignty and ruling
force.[f]
11 In him you have been circumcised, with a circumcision performed, not by human
hand, but by the complete stripping of your natural self.[g] This is circumcision
12 according to Christ.[h] •You have been buried with him by your baptism; by which,
too, you have been raised up with him through your belief in the power of God
13 who raised him from the dead. •You were dead, because you were sinners and
uncircumcised in body: he[i] has brought you[j] to life with him, he has forgiven us[k]
every one of our sins.
14 He has wiped out the record of our debt to the Law, which stood against us; he
15 has destroyed it by nailing it to the cross;[l] •and he has stripped the sovereignties
and the ruling forces, and paraded them in public, behind him in his triumphal
procession.[m]

Against the false asceticism based on the 'principles of this world'

16 Then never let anyone criticise you for what you eat or drink, or about observance
17 of annual festivals, New Moons or Sabbaths. •These are only a shadow of what
18 was coming: the reality is the body of Christ.[n] •Do not be cheated of your prize by
anyone who chooses[o] to grovel to angels and worship them,[p] pinning every hope
19 on visions received,[q] vainly puffed up by a human way of thinking; •such a person
has no connection to the Head,[r] by which the whole body, given all that it needs
and held together by its joints and sinews, grows with the growth given by God.
20 If you have really died with Christ to the principles of this world, why do you
21 still let rules dictate to you, as though you were still living in the world? •—'Do
22 not pick up this, do not eat that, do not touch the other,' •and all about things
which perish even while they are being used—according to merely *human*
23 *commandments and doctrines!* •In these rules you can indeed find what seems to
be good sense—the cultivation of the will, and a humility which takes no account
of the body; but in fact they have no value against self-indulgence.[s]

Life-giving union with the glorified Christ

1,2 **3** Since you have been raised up to be with Christ, you must look for the things that are above, where Christ is, sitting at God's right hand. ·Let your thoughts
3 be on things above, not on the things that are on the earth, ·because you have
4 died, and now the life you have is hidden with Christ in God. ·But when Christ is revealed—and he is your *a* life—you, too, will be revealed with him in glory. *b*

III: ENCOURAGEMENT

General rules of Christian behaviour

5 That is why you must kill everything in you that is earthly: *c* sexual vice, impurity, uncontrolled passion, evil desires and especially greed, which is the same thing as
6 worshipping a false god; ·it is precisely these things which draw God's retribution
7 upon those who resist. *d* ·And these things made up your way of life when you
8 were living among such people, ·but now you also must give up all these things:
9 human anger, hot temper, malice, abusive language and dirty talk; ·and do not lie
10 to each other. You have stripped off your old behaviour with your old self, ·and you have put on a new self which will progress towards true knowledge the more it
11 is renewed in the image of its Creator; *e* ·and in that image there is no room for distinction between Greek and Jew, between the circumcised and uncircumcised, or between barbarian and Scythian, slave and free. There is only Christ: he is everything and he is in everything. *f*
12 As the chosen of God, then, the holy people whom he loves, you are to be clothed in heartfelt compassion, in generosity and humility, gentleness and
13 patience. ·Bear with one another; forgive each other if one of you has a complaint
14 against another. The Lord has forgiven you; now you must do the same. ·Over all
15 these clothes, put on love, the perfect bond. ·And may the peace of Christ reign in your hearts, because it is for this that you were called together in one body. Always be thankful.
16 Let the Word of Christ, *g* in all its richness, find a home with you. Teach each other, and advise each other, in all wisdom. With gratitude in your hearts sing
17 psalms and hymns and inspired songs to God; *h* ·and whatever you say or do, let it be in the name of the Lord Jesus, in thanksgiving to God the Father through him.

The morals of the home and household *i*

18,19 Wives, be subject to your husbands, as you should in the Lord. ·Husbands, love
20 your wives and do not be sharp with them. ·Children, be obedient to your parents
21 always, because that is what will please the Lord. ·Parents, do not irritate your children or they will lose heart.
22 Slaves, be obedient in every way to the people who, according to human reckoning, are your masters; not only when you are under their eye, as if you had only to please human beings, but wholeheartedly, out of respect for the Master. *j*
23 Whatever your work is, put your heart into it as done for the Lord and not for
24 human beings, ·knowing that the Lord will repay you by making you his heirs. *k* It
25 is Christ the Lord that you are serving. ·Anyone who does wrong will be repaid in kind. For there is no favouritism.
1 **4** Masters, make sure that your slaves are given what is upright and fair, knowing that you too have a Master in heaven.

The apostolic spirit

2, 3 Be persevering in your prayers and be thankful as you stay awake to pray. ·Pray for us especially, asking God to throw open a door for us to announce the message
4 and proclaim the mystery of Christ, *ᵃ* for the sake of which I am in chains; ·pray that I may proclaim it as clearly as I ought.
5, 6   Act wisely with outsiders, making the best of the present time. ·Always talk pleasantly and with a flavour of wit *ᵇ* but be sensitive to the kind of answer each one requires.

Personal news

7 Tychicus will tell you all the news about me. He is a very dear brother, and a
8 trustworthy helper and companion in the service of the Lord. ·I am sending him to you precisely for this purpose: to give you news *ᶜ* about us and to encourage you
9 thoroughly. ·With him I am sending Onesimus, that dear and trustworthy brother who is a fellow-citizen of yours. They will tell you everything that is happening here.

Greetings *ᵈ* and final wishes

10 Aristarchus, who is here in prison with me, sends his greetings, and so does Mark, the cousin of Barnabas—you were sent some instructions about him; if he comes
11 to you, give him a warm welcome—·and Jesus Justus adds his greetings. Of all those who have come over from the circumcision, these are the only ones actually working with me for the kingdom of God. They have been a great comfort to me.
12 Epaphras, your fellow-citizen, sends his greetings; this servant of Christ Jesus never stops battling for you, praying that you will never lapse but always hold
13 perfectly and securely to the will of God. ·I can testify for him that he works hard
14 for you, as well as for those at Laodicea and Hierapolis. ·Greetings from my dear friend Luke, the doctor, and also from Demas.
15   Please give my greetings to the brothers at Laodicea and to Nympha and the
16 church which meets in her house. ·After this letter has been read among you, send it on to be read in the church of the Laodiceans; and get the letter *ᵉ* from Laodicea
17 for you to read yourselves. ·Give Archippus this message, 'Remember the service that the Lord assigned to you, and try to carry it out.'
18   This greeting is in my own hand—PAUL. Remember the chains I wear. Grace be with you. *ᶠ*

NOTES TO COLOSSIANS

1   a. add. 'and the Lord Jesus Christ'.

   b. lit. 'A faithful servant of Christ on behalf of us'; var. 'on behalf of you'.

   c. 'Made you (var. 'us') able to'; var. 'called you (var. 'us') to . . .' • The 'lot of God's holy people' is the salvation once reserved to Israel, to which the gentiles are now called, cf. Ep 1:11–13. The expression 'God's holy people' here can mean either Christians, called to live while still on earth in the light of salvation, Rm 6:19h; 13:11–12e, or it can mean the angels who live with God in the eschatological 'light', *see* Ac 9:13g.

   d. In this poem Paul explains, in the form of a diptych, how Christ is the 'head' of everything that exists: **1** He is the head of creation, of all that exists naturally, vv. 15–17. **2** He

is the head of the new creation and of all that exists supernaturally through redemption, vv. 18–20. The subject of the poem is the pre-existent Christ, but considered as manifested in the unique historic person who is the 'image of God', i.e. his human nature was the visible manifestation of God who is invisible, *see* Rm 8:29n, and it is he who must be said to be a creature, but the First-born in the order of creation, not only in time but also with a causal primacy and a primacy of honour.

   e. On the Church as Christ's body, *see* 1 Co 12:12seq., he is called the 'head' of his own body both in a temporal sense (v. 18, i.e. he was the first to rise from the dead) and by his role as Principal in the order of salvation (v. 20).

   f. The exact meaning of the word *pleroma* (i.e. the thing

that fills up a gap or hole, like a patch, *see* Mt 8:16) is not certain here. Some writers have thought it must mean the same as in 2:9 (the fullness of divinity that filled Jesus), but since vv. 15–18 have already dealt with the divinity of Jesus, it seems likely that the reference here is to the biblical concept of the entire cosmos as filled with the creative presence of God, *see* Ps 24:1; 50:12; 72:19; Ws 1:7; Si 43:27; Is 6:3; Jr 23:24. This concept was also widespread in the Graeco-Roman world because of Stoic pantheism. Paul teaches that the Incarnation and Resurrection make Christ head not only of the entire human race, but of the entire created cosmos, for everything that was involved in the fall is equally involved in salvation, *see* Rm 8:19–22; 1 Co 3:22seq.; 15:20–28; Ep 1:10; 4:10; Ph 2:10seq.; 3:21; Heb 2:5–8; cf. Col 2:9f.

g. i.e. through and for Christ, cf. the parallel 'through him and for him', *see* v. 16. Alternatively, it could read 'God wanted everything . . . to be reconciled to himself, through him who made peace . . .' cf. Rm 5:10; 2 Co 5:18seq.

h. This reconciliation of the whole universe (including angels as well as human beings) means, not the individual salvation of the whole human race but the collective salvation of the world by its return to the right order and peace of perfect submission to God. Any individuals who do not through grace join this new creation will be forced to join it, *see* 2:15; 1 Co 15:24–25 (the heavenly spirits) and Rm 2:8; 1 Co 6:9–10; Ga 5:21; Ep 5:5; 2 Th 1:8–9 (human beings).

i. The context suggests that there is a closer parallel with Ep 4:18seq. (foreigners to God and therefore God's enemies) than with Ep 2:12 (foreigners in Israel).

j. 'he', i.e. the Father. The human, mortal body is that of his Son (lit. 'body of his flesh'); this provides the locus where the reconciliation takes place. Into this body the entire human race is effectively gathered, cf. Ep 2:14–16, because Christ has assumed its sin, 2 Co 5:21. The 'flesh' is the body subject to sin, *see* Rm 7:5c; 8:3; Heb 4:15.

k. That is, to all humanity.

l. Jesus suffered in order to establish the reign of God, and anyone who continues his work must share this suffering. Paul is not claiming to add anything to the redemptive value of the cross (to which in any case nothing is lacking); but he associates himself with the trials of Jesus, by his sufferings in his apostolate, *see* 2 Co 1:5; Ph 1:20i. These are the sufferings predicted for the messianic era, Mt 24:8f; Ac 14:22m; 1 Tm 4:1a, and are all part of the way in which God had always intended the Church to develop; Paul feels that, being the messenger Christ has chosen to send to the gentiles, he has been specially called on to complete these sufferings.

m. Previously, when it had seemed (to the Jews) that gentiles could never be saved, as salvation was restricted to 'Israel', gentiles had seemed to be without a Messiah and consequently to be deprived of all hope, Ep 2:12. The 'mystery' or secret of God that had now been revealed was that the gentiles, too, were called to salvation and the glory of heaven through union to Christ, *see* Ep 2:13–22; 3:3–6.

2 a. var. 'the mystery of Christ', cf. 4:3; Ep 3:4; or 'God's mystery of Christ', or 'the mystery of God the Father of Christ', or 'the mystery of God the Father, and of Christ', etc.

b. 'in which', i.e. in the 'mystery' that revealed what till then had been 'hidden', namely the 'infinite wisdom' of God, *see* Rm 16:25l; 1 Tm 3:16e. That it is Christ who is revealed in the mystery, 1:27, is of course true, and he himself is also the Wisdom of God, 1 Co 1:24,30, and he is also the Mystery, 1 Co 2:7, that is hard to understand, Ep 3:8,19.

c. This will be developed in v. 8seq.

d. To deny Christ after he has liberated them from the tyranny of 'darkness', 1:13seq., by going back to error, would be nothing but a new slavery, cf. Ga 4:8seq.; 5:1.

e. The sense of the word 'fullness' here is clarified by 'bodily' and 'of divinity'. In the risen Christ are united the divine sphere, to which he belongs by his pre-existence and his glory, and the whole created world which, by his incarnation and resurrection, he has taken to himself either directly (human nature) or indirectly (the cosmos). In this way he himself is the *pleroma* of all possible categories of being.

f. A Christian shares this *pleroma* of Christ by being part of it, i.e. part of Christ's body, *see* (text and notes) 1:19; Ep 1:23; 3:19; 4:12–13, and associated thus with the Head of Heavenly Powers, he is superior to them all. The following verses develop these two ideas: disciples of Christ share his triumph, vv. 11–13, even the heavenly powers are submitted to his triumph, vv. 14–15.

g. Surgical circumcision removes only a piece of skin.

h. The 'circumcision' instituted by Christ, i.e. baptism.

i. God the Father. Cf. 1:22.

j. 'you'; var. 'us'.

k. 'us'; var. 'you'.

l. The Law was able to do nothing about a sinner except condemn him to death, Rm 7:7d; this death sentence is what God suppressed by means of the death of his own Son, and it was for this very reason that God's Son was 'made a victim for sin', 2 Co 5:21, 'subject to the Law', Ga 4:4, and 'cursed by the Law', Ga 3:13. In the person of his Son, whom he allowed to be executed, God nailed up and destroyed the document which contained our debt and condemned us.

m. The tradition is that the Law was brought down to Moses by angels, Ga 3:19k, and by honouring them as the lawgivers, *see* Col 2:18, people were distracted from the true Creator. Now that God has brought the régime of that Law to an end, by means of the crucifixion, these angelic Powers have lost the one thing that had given them power, and so they too must acknowledge that Christ has triumphed.

n. lit. 'but the body is Christ'—a pun on the word *soma* ('body') as being both that which is more real than any shadow or reflection, and the body of the risen Christ which is the essential eschatological reality and the seed from which the new universe will grow.

o. Or 'Do not let anyone give himself the pleasure of condemning you.'

p. Dietary and cultic practices, v. 16, attribute too much importance to material things and therefore to the 'spirits' that are supposed to control them, cf. Ga 4:3seq.

q. var. 'which he has not seen'. Paul is explaining where the teachers at Colossae have gone wrong, which is either because they attach a false importance to their 'visions' or, at a more general level, because they base all their religion on visible things.

r. Christ, Ep 4:15.

s. This may mean either that they are of no real value in subduing 'self-indulgence', or else that 'they are of no value and help only to satisfy self-indulgence'.

3 a. var. 'our'.

b. Through union with Christ in baptism, 2:12, his followers already live the identical life he lives in heaven, *see* Ep 2:6e, but this spiritual life is not manifest and glorious as it will be at the *parousia*.

c. At the mystical level of union with the glorified Christ, participation in his death and resurrection is instantaneous and total, 2:12seq.,20; 3:1–4; Rm 6:4e, but at the practical level of life on earth, this union has to be grown into gradually. Already 'dead' in theory, the Christian must still put this death into practice by 'killing' day after day the old, sinful self which still lives in him.

d. The words 'upon those who resist', omitted by some ancient witnesses and several modern editions, are required to explain the literary genesis of Ep 2:2–3 and 5:6, on the basis of this passage of Col.

e. The human race, that was to have been 'the image of God', Gn 1:26m, lost its way trying to locate the 'knowledge of good and evil' outside and apart from the will of God, Gn 2:17j, and became the slave of sin and sinful urges, Rm 5:12g. This is the 'old self' that must die, Rm 6:6; Ep 4:22; the 'new self' is reborn in Christ, Ep 2:15n, who is the true image of God, Rm 8:29n. In this way the human race can both recover its original justice and reach true knowledge of what is right and wrong, 1:9; Heb 5:14.

f. The new creation will not be divided into races and religions and cultures and social classes in the way the present creation has been since the Fall; this unity is based on Christ.

g. var. 'of the Lord' or 'of God'; possibly the text originally read simply 'the Word', cf. Ph 1:14; 2:30.

h. These 'inspired songs' could be charismatic improvisations suggested by the Spirit during liturgical assembly, cf. 1 Co 12:7seq.; 14:26.

i. Paul christens these simple precepts of ordinary morality by introducing his phrase 'in the Lord' which must be taken here as meaning 'according to the Christian way of life'. These Christian applications are further developed in Ep 5:21seq.

j. 'your masters . . . the Master': Paul uses the same word each time, i.e. Christ is the master equally of both slave and slave-owner.

k. That a slave should inherit, cf. Mt 21:35–38; Lk 15:19; Ga 4:1–2, is a striking sign of the new order in Christ, see Rm 8:15–17; Ga 4:3–7; Phm 16.

4 a. var. 'of God', cf. 2:2.

b. lit. 'with a seasoning of salt', a classical Gk cliché, cf. Mk 9:50.

c. var. 'to get your news'.

d. On Aristarchus, see Ac 19:29. On Mark, see Ac 12:12d. 'Jesus Justus' is not mentioned anywhere else; his surname was quite common among Jews and Jewish converts, see Ac 1:23; 18:27. Epaphras, born at Colossae (and therefore not the same person as Epaphroditus, who came from Philippi, Ph 2:25; 4:18) had been sent by Paul to evangelise Colossae, his own native town, Col 1:7. Luke is the evangelist and author of Ac: he had joined Paul towards the end of his third journey, Ac 20:5seq., had been with him till they reached Rome, Ac 27:1seq., and now, with Paul under arrest, he is still by his side, see Phm 24, as he will be again (if the historical data of the Pastoral Epistles are reliable) after Paul has been arrested a second time, 2 Tm 4:11. On Demas, see 2 Tm 4:10; Phm 24. Who the woman was called Nympha (or man, if the correct spelling is Nymphas) is unknown. Archippus, v. 17, is probably a son of Philemon, Phm 2; what the service was the Lord wanted him to do is not known.

e. Paul expected his letters to be read in public to the assembled brothers, 1 Th 5:27, and then passed on to the neighbouring churches, see 2 Co 1:1. The letter that was to be brought back from Laodicea to Colossae was probably the one that Paul wrote to Ephesus.

f. var. add. 'Amen', Ph 4:20, see Ph 4:23.

1 THESSALONIANS

THE FIRST LETTER OF PAUL
TO THE CHURCH IN THESSALONICA

Address

1 **1** Paul, Silvanus and Timothy, to the Church in Thessalonica which is in God the Father and the Lord Jesus Christ. Grace to you and peace. *

Thanksgiving and congratulations

2, 3 We always thank God for you all, mentioning you in our prayers continually. ·We remember before our God and Father how active is the faith, how unsparing the love, how persevering the hope which you have from our Lord Jesus Christ. *
4, 5 We know, brothers loved by God, that you have been chosen, ·because our gospel * came to you not only in words, but also in power and in the Holy Spirit and with great effect. And you observed the sort of life we lived when we were
6 with you, which was for your sake. ·You took us and the Lord as your model, welcoming the word with the joy of the Holy Spirit in spite of great hardship.
7, 8 And so you became an example to all believers in Macedonia and Achaia ·since it was from you that the word of the Lord rang out—and not only throughout Macedonia and Achaia, for your faith in God has spread everywhere. We do not
9 need to tell other people about it: * ·other people tell us how we started the work among you, how you broke with the worship of false gods when you were converted
10 to God and became servants of the living and true God; ·and how you are now waiting for Jesus, his Son, whom he raised from the dead, to come from heaven. It is he who saves us from the Retribution * which is coming.

Paul's example in Thessalonica

1 **2** You know yourselves, my brothers, that our visit to you has not been pointless.
2 Although, as you know, we had received rough treatment and insults at Philippi, God gave us the courage to speak his gospel to you fearlessly, in spite of
3 great opposition. ·Our encouragement to you does not come from any delusion or
4 impure motives or trickery. ·No, God has approved us to be entrusted with the gospel, and this is how we preach, seeking to please not human beings but God
5 who *tests* our *hearts*. ·Indeed, we have never acted with the thought of flattering
6 anyone, as you know, nor as an excuse for greed, God is our witness; ·nor have we ever looked for honour from human beings, either from you or anybody else,

7 when we could have imposed ourselves on you with full weight,* as apostles of Christ.

Instead, we lived unassumingly among you. *b* Like a mother feeding and looking
8 after her children, ·we felt so devoted to you, that we would have been happy to share with you not only the gospel of God, but also our own lives, so dear had you
9 become. ·You remember, brothers, with what unsparing energy we used to work, slaving night and day so as not to be a burden on any one of you while we were
10 proclaiming the gospel of God to you. ·You are witnesses, and so is God, that our
11 treatment of you, since you believed, has been impeccably fair and upright. ·As
12 you know we treated every one of you as a father treats his children, ·urging you, encouraging you and appealing to you to live a life worthy of God, who calls *c* you into his kingdom and his glory.

The faith and the patience of the Thessalonians

13 Another reason why we continually thank God for you is that as soon as you heard the word that we brought you as God's message, you welcomed it for what it really is, not the word of any human being, but God's word *d*, a power that is working *e*
14 among you believers. ·For you, my brothers, have modelled yourselves on the churches of God in Christ Jesus which are in Judaea, in that you have suffered the
15 same treatment from your own countrymen as they have had from the Jews, *f* ·who put the Lord Jesus to death, and the prophets too, and persecuted us also. Their conduct does not please God, and makes them the enemies of the whole human
16 race, ·because they are hindering us from preaching to gentiles to save them. Thus all the time they are *reaching the full extent of* their *iniquity*, but retribution *g* has finally overtaken them.

Paul's anxiety

17 Although we had been deprived of you for only a short time in body but never in affection, brothers, we had an especially strong desire and longing to see you face
18 to face again, ·and we tried hard to come and visit you; I, Paul, tried more than
19 once, but Satan prevented us. ·What do you think is our hope and our joy, and
20 what *our crown of honour* in the presence of our Lord Jesus when he comes? ·You are, for you are our pride and joy.

Timothy's mission to Thessalonica

1 **3** When we could not bear it any longer, we decided it would be best to be left
2 without a companion at Athens, and ·sent our brother Timothy, who is God's helper *a* in spreading the gospel of Christ, to keep you firm and encourage you
3 about your faith ·and prevent any of you from being unsettled by the present
4 hardships. As you know, these are bound to come our way: ·indeed, when we were with you, we warned you that we are certain to have hardships to bear, and
5 that is what has happened now, as you have found out. ·That is why, when I could not bear it any longer, I sent to assure myself of your faith: I was afraid the Tester *b* might have put you to the test, and all our work might have been pointless.

Paul thanks God for good reports of the Thessalonians

6 However, Timothy has returned from you and has given us good news of your faith and your love, telling us that you always remember us with pleasure and
7 want to see us quite as much as we want to see you. ·And so, brothers, your faith has been a great encouragement to us in the middle of our own distress and

8. 9 hardship; ·now we can breathe again, as you are holding firm in the Lord. ·How can we thank God enough for you, for all the joy we feel before our God on your
10 account? ·We are earnestly praying night and day to be able to see you face to face again and make up any shortcomings ᶜ in your faith.

11. 12 May God our Father himself, and our Lord Jesus, ease our path to you. ·May the Lord increase and enrich your love for each other and for all ᵈ, so that it
13 matches ours for you. ·And may he so confirm your hearts in holiness that you may be blameless in the sight of our God and Father when our Lord Jesus comes *with all his holy ones.* ᵉ

Live in holiness and charity

1 4 Finally, brothers, we urge you and appeal to you in the Lord Jesus ᵃ; we instructed you how to live in the way that pleases God, and you are so living; ᵇ
2 but make more progress still. ·You are well aware of the instructions we gave you on the authority of the Lord Jesus.
3 God wills you all to be holy. ᶜ He wants you to keep away from sexual immorality,
4 and each one of you to know how to control his body ᵈ in a way that is holy and
5 honourable, ·not giving way to selfish lust like *the nations who do not acknowledge*
6 *God.* ·He wants nobody at all ever to sin by taking advantage of a brother in these matters; the Lord always *pays back* sins of that sort, as we told you before
7. 8 emphatically. ·God called us to be holy, not to be immoral; ·in other words, anyone who rejects this is rejecting not human authority, but God, *who gives you his* Holy *Spirit.* ᵉ
9 As for brotherly love, there is no need to write to you about that, since you
10 have yourselves learnt from God to love one another, ·and in fact this is how you treat all the brothers throughout the whole of Macedonia. However, we do urge
11 you, brothers, to go on making even greater progress ·and to make a point of living quietly, attending to your own business and earning your living, just as we
12 told you to, ·so that you may earn the respect of outsiders and not be dependent on anyone.

The dead and the living at the time of the Lord's coming ᶠ

13 We want you to be quite certain, brothers, about those who have fallen asleep, ᵍ to make sure that you do not grieve for them, as others do who have no hope.
14 We believe that Jesus died and rose again, and that in the same way God will
15 bring with him those who have fallen asleep in Jesus. ·We can tell you this from the Lord's own teaching, ʰ that we ⁱ who are still alive for the Lord's coming will
16 not have any advantage over those who have fallen asleep. ·At the signal given by the voice of the Archangel and the trumpet of God, the Lord himself will come
17 down from heaven; ʲ those who have died in Christ will be the first to rise, ·and only after that shall we who remain alive ᵏ be taken up in the clouds, together with them, to meet the Lord in the air. This is the way we shall be with the Lord for
18 ever. ˡ ·With such thoughts as these, then, you should encourage one another.

Watchfulness while awaiting the coming of the Lord ᵃ

1. 2 5 About times and dates, brothers, ᵇ there is no need to write to you ·for you are well aware in any case that the Day of the Lord is going to come like a thief in
3 the night. ·It is when people are saying, 'How quiet and peaceful it is' that sudden destruction falls on them, as suddenly as labour pains come on a pregnant woman; and there is no escape.

4   But you, brothers, do not live in the dark, that the Day ᶜ should take you
5   unawares like a thief. ·No, you are all children of light and children of the day: we
6   do not belong to the night or to darkness, ·so we should not go on sleeping, as
7   everyone else does, but stay wide awake and sober. ·Night is the time for sleepers
8   to sleep and night the time for drunkards to be drunk, ·but we belong to the day
    and we should be sober; let us put on faith and love for a *breastplate*, and the hope
9   of *salvation* for a *helmet*. ·God destined us not for his retribution, but to win
10 salvation through our Lord Jesus Christ, ·who died for us so that, awake or
11 asleep, ᵈ we should still live united to him. ·So give encouragement to each other,
    and keep strengthening one another, as you do already.
12 We appeal to you, my brothers, to be considerate to those who work so hard
13 among you as your leaders in the Lord and those who admonish you. ᵉ ·Have the
    greatest respect and affection for them because of their work.
14 Be at peace among yourselves. ·We urge you, brothers, to admonish those who
    are undisciplined, encourage the apprehensive, support the weak and be patient
15 with everyone. ·Make sure that people do not try to repay evil for evil; always aim
16. 17 at what is best for each other and for everyone. ·Always be joyful; ·pray con-
18 stantly; ᶠ ·and for all things give thanks; this is the will of God for you in Christ
    Jesus.
19. 20. 21 Do not stifle the Spirit ᵍ ·or despise the gift of prophecy with contempt; ·test
22 everything and hold on to what is good ·and *shun every* form of *evil*.

Closing prayer and farewell

23 May the God of peace make you perfect and holy; and may your spirit, life and
24 body ʰ be kept blameless for the coming of our Lord Jesus Christ. ·He who has
    called you is trustworthy and will carry it out.
25 Pray for us, my brothers.
26. 27 Greet all the brothers with a holy kiss. ·My orders, in the Lord's name, are that
    this letter is to be read to all the brothers. ⁱ
28 The grace of our Lord Jesus Christ be with you.

NOTES TO 1 THESSALONIANS

1 **a.** add. 'from God our Father and the Lord Jesus Christ',
cf. 2 Th 1:2.

b. Note that faith, hope and love, which Paul
distinguishes in 1 Co 13:13 as the three enduring virtues of
the Christian, are here found at work in the life of the
Church.

c. var. 'the gospel of God', or 'of our God'. The gospel
is more than a proclamation, it is the whole new economy of
salvation.

d. Even allowing for some exaggeration one can discern
that the life of Christians in accordance with the gospel by
itself achieves the spread of their faith; it is one form of the
Word of God.

e. Vv. 9–10 seem to give an extremely condensed
summary of Paul's proclamation. The gospel he preached
revolves round two central themes: a vigorous stress on
monotheism, Mk 12:29b; 1 Co 8:4–6; 10:7.14; Ga 4:8–9,
and a Christology stressing the coming of the risen Lord, *see*
1 Co 1:7; 15:23n. • Note the title 'his Son' applied to Jesus
in the earliest of all Paul's letters.

2 **a.** lit. 'make our weight felt': interpreted morally, this

can mean that Paul could have insisted on his own dignity
and prestige, or that materially he could have expected to
have been fed and kept at their expense, cf. 2:9; 2 Co 11:9;
2 Th 3:8.

b. 'unassumingly'; var. 'as babes'.

c. var. 'called you'. • The Kingdom of God, Ep 5:5;
2 Th 1:5; Mt 4:17; Rv 19:8, and its glory are properly divine
entities, but to them God calls, 4:7; 5:24, and guides his
chosen ones, 1:4.

d. A brief summary of the apostolic tradition, the
message is first 'received', 4:1; 2 Th 3:6; 1 Co 15:1; Ga 1:9;
Ph 4:9; Col 2:6, or 'heard', Rm 10:17h; Ep 1:13; Ac 15:7.
It then penetrates the mind or heart, Rm 10:8–10, where
if it is welcomed, 1 Th 1:6; Mk 4:20; Ac 8:14; 2 Co 11:4;
2 Th 2:10, it proves that the hearer acknowledges that God
has been speaking through his missionary, 1 Th 4:1seq.;
2 Co 3:5; 13:3.

e. Or 'has come to be at work'; God acts through his
message that has been welcomed by the believer, cf. 1:8;
2 Th 3:1.

f. The harsh tone of vv. 15–16 gives a good idea of how
bitter the atmosphere was in Jerusalem. Mt 5:12; 21:33–46;

23:29–37; Ac 2:23o, owing to the way Paul upset the Jewish community by preaching to gentiles. 1 Th 2:16; see Ac 13:5e. Later on Paul was able to take a more balanced attitude than he takes here, by frequent references to the special position of God's chosen people, cf. Rm 9:11; Ga 4:21–31. He tried hard to reconcile convert gentile with Jewish Christian, see 1 Co 16:1a; Ep 2:11–22.

g. add 'from God'.

3 a. om. 'who is God's helper', or var. 'who is God's slave' or 'God's slave and our helper'.

b. 'Tester', i.e. 'Satan' as in 2:18, see Mk 1:13.

c. This would refer to gaps in their knowledge of Christian doctrine, as well as gaps in their code of Christian behaviour, cf. Rm 14:1; 2 Co 10:15; Ph 1:25.

d. Brotherly love of one another in the Christian community is only the beginning of charity; it has to spread to love for the whole human race.

e. add. 'Amen'. • Holiness, 4:3c, begins with brotherly love but will not be perfect till the *parousia*. In this context 'holy ones' can refer to the chosen, the saved or the angels, Ac 9:13g.

4 a. Paul speaks 'in' (v. 1) 'by' (v. 2) or 'in the name of' Christ, cf. 4:15; 2 Th 3:6,12. His doctrine on moral behaviour which is based on the earliest Christian teaching invests ordinary day-to-day life with a new depth: it has the seal of Christ on it, Col 3:18i.

b. om. 'and you are so living'.

c. It is the will of God, cf. Mt 6:10, that makes people holy, 1 Th 4:3,7; 2 Th 2:13; Ep 1:4. It is God who makes them holy, 5:23; 1 Co 6:11; see Jn 17:17; Ac 20:32. Christ has made himself our 'holiness', 1 Co 1:30. The Holy Spirit is involved in making us holy, v. 8; 2 Th 2:13; 1 Co 6:11. Christians, however, must make use of this gift, Rm 6:19h. The title 'the holy ones', is common, Ac 9:13h.

d. Either a man's own body, 5:23, cf. Rm 12:1; 1 Co 6:19, or that of his wife, as in several rabbinic texts and 1 P 3:7.

e. Ezekiel foretold that the Spirit would be given to the messianic people: this reference draws attention to the continuity between the church of Thessalonica and the giving of this gift to the early Christian community, Ac 2:16seq., 33,38; etc. On the gift of the Spirit to the spirit of each believer, see Rm 5:5e.

f. The converts in Thessalonica had obviously been worried about friends and relations who had died and would not be there to see the coming of the Lord. Replying to their questions Paul affirms the fundamental doctrine of the resurrection so as to strengthen their faith and hope.

g. lit. 'we do not wish you to be ignorant, brothers, concerning the sleeping'. The euphemism was common in the OT, the NT and in Greek literature: the natural concomitant was to call the resurrection (to new life or from death) an 'awakening'.

h. See Mt 25:32f. Perhaps it is no more than a recourse to the Lord's authority, see Dn 7:1,13,16.

i. 'us'; Paul includes himself among those who will be present at the *parousia*: more by aspiration, however, than by conviction, see 5:1a.

j. The trumpet, voice and clouds were traditional signs that accompanied manifestations of God, see Ex 13:22h;

19:16g and they were adopted as conventional elements of apocalyptic literature, see Mt 24:30seq.; 2 Th 1:8b.

k. om. 'who remain alive'.

l. Of all the details given here: that the dead will answer the summons by returning to life, that they and the living will be taken to meet the Lord, and that they will accompany him to the judgement with which the eternal kingdom begins, the essential one is the last: eternal life with Christ, see 5:10; 2 Th 2:1. That is to be the 'salvation', the 'glory', the 'kingdom' that Jesus shares among his chosen followers.

5 a. Paul asserts that he has no idea when the Last Day will come, and he merely repeats what the Lord said, Mt 24:36 and par.; Ac 1:7, about having to stay awake till it comes, Mt 24:42 and par., 50; 25:13. The Day of the Lord, 1 Co 1:8e, will come like a thief, cf. Mt 24:43 and par., so it is necessary to stay alert, 1 Th 5:6, cf. Rm 13:11; 1 Co 16:13; Col 4:2; 1 P 1:13; 5:8; Rv 3:2seq.; 16:15. It will come soon, 2 Co 6:2a. At first Paul expected he would live to see the Last Day, 4:17; cf. 1 Co 15:51; he later realised he might die before it, 2 Co 5:3; Ph 1:23, and he warns people it will not come as soon as they thought, 2 Th 2:1seq. More than anything, the prospect of how long it would take to convert the gentiles Rm 11:25, made it certain that the Last Day would not come for a very long time, see Mt 25:19; Lk 20:9; 2 P 3:4,8–10, cf. 1 Co 8:8e.

b. 'about times and dates': a cliché, see Ac 1:7i, underlying which is the idea of God as outside time and yet as controlling it and its divisions, Ac 17:26.

c. Mention of 'the Day' without further qualification, 1 Co 1:8e, helps Paul to introduce the mention of light and day and contrast 'wakefulness' with the dark, night and sleep (in a different sense from 1 Th 4:13seq.), and also make the contrast between Christians (children of light) and others (children of darkness), see Jn 8:12b. A very concise summary of Paul's preaching: God saves us by Christ who died for us.

d. 'Awake or asleep' means 'alive or dead', as in 4:14–17; all the faithful will share in final salvation.

e. We know little of these 'teachers'; their devotion exercised in the name of Christ earns them esteem and love.

f. This brief instruction has had an enormous influence on Christian spirituality, see 1:2; 2:13; Lk 18:1a; Rm 1:10; 12:12; Ep 6:18; Ph 1:3–4; 4:6; Col 1:3; 4:2; 2 Th 1:11; 1 Tm 2:8; 5:5; 2 Tm 1:3.

g. The gift of the Spirit, 4:8, is a feature of the messianic era, and discernment of its inspirations is one of its gifts, 1 Co 12:10; 14:29; 1 Jn 4:1; cf. 2 Th 2:2. See 1 Co 12:1a.

h. This is the only reference made by Paul to a tripartite division of body (see Rm 7:24l), soul (see 1 Co 15:44w) and spirit (which can be taken in two ways: as the divine presence in a human being, giving new life in union with Christ, Rm 5:5e, or more probably as the innermost depths of the human being, open and awake to the Spirit, see Rm 1:9e). The accent is on the totality of the effects of the sanctifying action of God, 3:13; 4:3c, the effect of his fidelity.

i. This is the earliest reference to the public reading of an apostle's letter. Paul wanted to address and teach the whole Church and not merely its appointed leaders, 2 Co 1:1 and Col 4:16 also ask that the letters should be passed on to other churches; but it was not for many years that the apostolic writings were put on the same footing as the gospel and the scriptures, 2 P 3:15–16; see 1 M 12:9c; 1 Tm 5:18–19, 18g.

2 THESSALONIANS

THE SECOND LETTER OF PAUL TO THE CHURCH IN THESSALONICA

Address

1 Paul, Silvanus and Timothy, to the Church in Thessalonica which is in God
2 our Father and the Lord Jesus Christ ·Grace to you and peace from God the Father and the Lord Jesus Christ.

Thanksgiving and encouragement. The Last Judgement

3 We must always thank God for you, brothers; quite rightly, because your faith is growing so wonderfully and the mutual love that each one of you has for all never
4 stops increasing. ·Among the churches of God we take special pride in you for your perseverance and faith under all the persecutions and hardships you have to
5 bear. ·It all shows that God's judgement is just, so that you may be found worthy of the kingdom of God; it is for the sake of this that you are suffering now.
6 For God's justice will surely mean hardship being inflicted on those who are
7 now inflicting hardship on you, ·and for you who are now suffering hardship, relief with us, *c* when the Lord Jesus appears from heaven with the angels of his power.
8 He will come *amid flaming fire* [b]; *he will impose a penalty* on those who *do not*
9 *acknowledge God* and *refuse to accept* the gospel of our Lord Jesus. [c] ·Their punishment is to be lost eternally, excluded *from the presence of the Lord and*
10 *from the glory of his strength* ·*on that day* when he comes *to be glorified among his holy ones* and *marvelled at* by all who believe in him; [d] and you are among those who believed our witness. [e]
11 In view of this we also pray continually that our God will make you worthy of his call, and by his power fulfil all your [f] desires for goodness, and complete all
12 that you have been doing through faith; ·so that the *name* of our Lord Jesus Christ *may be glorified* in you and you in him, by the grace of our God and the Lord Jesus Christ.

The coming of the Lord and the prelude to it [a]

1 About the coming of our Lord Jesus Christ, brothers, and our being gathered
2 to him: ·please do not be too easily thrown into confusion or alarmed by any manifestation of the Spirit or any statement or any letter claiming to come from
3 us, suggesting that the Day of the Lord has already arrived. ·Never let anyone deceive you in any way.

It cannot happen until the Great Revolt *b* has taken place and there has appeared
4 the wicked One, the lost One, ·the Enemy,*c* who *raises himself above every* so-
called *God* or object of worship to *enthrone himself in God's* sanctuary and flaunts
5 the claim that he is God. ·Surely you remember my telling you about this when I
6 was with you? ·And you know, too, what is still holding him back *d* from appearing
7 before his appointed time. ·The mystery of wickedness is already at work,*e* but let
8 him who is restraining it once be removed, ·and the wicked One will appear
openly.*f* The Lord *g* will *destroy him with the breath of his mouth* and will annihilate
him with his glorious appearance at his coming.
9 But the coming of the wicked One will be marked by Satan being at work *h* in all
10 kinds of counterfeit miracles and signs and wonders, ·and every wicked deception
aimed at those who are on the way to destruction because they would not accept
11 the love of the truth and so be saved. ·And therefore God sends on them a power
12 that deludes people so that they believe what is false, ·and so that those who do
not believe the truth and take their pleasure in wickedness may all be condemned. *i*

Encouragement to persevere*j*

13 But we must always thank God for you, brothers whom the Lord loves, because
God chose you from the beginning *k* to be saved by the Spirit who makes us holy
14 and by faith in the truth. ·Through our gospel he called you to this so that you
15 should claim as your own the glory of our Lord Jesus Christ. ·Stand firm, then,
brothers, and keep the traditions that we taught you, whether by word of mouth
16 or by letter.*l* ·May our Lord Jesus Christ himself, and God our Father who has
given us his love and, through his grace, such ceaseless encouragement and such
17 sure hope, ·encourage you and strengthen you in every good word and deed.
1 3 Finally, brothers, pray for us that the Lord's message may spread quickly, and
2 be received with honour as it was among you; ·and pray that we may be
3 preserved from bigoted and evil people, for not everyone has faith. ·You can rely
4 on the Lord, who will give you strength and guard you from the evil One,*a* ·and
we, in the Lord, have every confidence in you, that you are doing and will go on
5 doing all that we tell·you. ·May the Lord turn your hearts towards the love of God
and the perseverance of Christ.

Against idleness and disunity

6 In the name of the Lord Jesus Christ, we urge you, brothers, to keep away from
any of the brothers who lives an undisciplined life, not in accordance with the
tradition you received from us.·
7 You know how you should take us as your model:*b* we were not undisciplined
8 when we were with you, ·nor did we ever accept food from anyone without paying
for it; no, we worked with unsparing energy, night and day, so as not to be a
9 burden on any of you. ·This was not because we had no right to be, but in order to
make ourselves a model for you to imitate.
10 We urged you when we were with you not to let anyone eat if he refused to
11 work.*c* ·Now we hear that there are some of you who are living lives without any
12 discipline, doing no work themselves but interfering with other people's. ·In the
Lord Jesus Christ, we urge and call on people of this kind to go on quietly working
and earning the food that they eat.
13, 14 My brothers, never slacken in doing what is right. ·If anyone refuses to obey
what I have written in this letter, take note of him and have nothing to do with

15 him, so that he will be ashamed of himself, •though you are not to treat him as an enemy, but to correct him as a brother.

Prayer and farewell wishes

16 May the Lord of peace himself give you peace at all times and in every way. The Lord be with you all.
17 This greeting is in my own hand—PAUL. It is the mark of genuineness in every
18 letter; this is my own writing. •May the grace of our Lord Jesus Christ be with you all. *

NOTES TO 2 THESSALONIANS

1 **a.** In such phrases, Paul often reveals his ideal of a solidarity between the churches and himself and his anxiety that the churches should preserve it, *see* 1 Co 4:8; Ph 1:30.
b. Heaven, cf. 1 Th 4:16, the angels, cf. Mt 13:39, 41,49; 16:27 and par.; 24:31; 25:31; Lk 12:8seq. (and probably the 'holy ones' of 1 Th 3:13), the 'fire' of various theophanies, *see* Ex 13:22h; 19:16g, are all conventional elements of apocalyptic literature, *see* 1 Th 4:16f.
c. i.e. both gentiles, 1 Th 4:5, and Jews, Rm 10:16. The condemnation of those who reject the gospel is described in severe and implacable terms perhaps to be explained by a persistent persecution.
d. Paul here seems to be thinking of angels (the 'holy ones', *see* Ac 9:13g) and Christians ('those who believe').
e. Vv. 6–10 form a parenthesis, v. 11 follows on from v. 5.
f. Or 'his'.

2 **a.** In 1 Th 4:13–5:11 Paul avoided suggesting anything that would indicate when the *parousia* would take place, *see* 1 Th 5:1b. Obviously replying to further questions, Paul does not now repeat all he said about what would happen to the living and the dead: all he is concerned with is to emphasise that the coming is not imminent, and that it cannot take place till certain specific signs have preceded it.
b. The way this revolt (*apostasia*) is mentioned here shows that the Thessalonians had already been told something about it. The word is used here in its usual sense of 'secession' or 'defection' but with a specifically religious reference, Ac 5:37; 21:21; Heb 3:12. It seems that the rebels are not only those who have never belonged to Christ but also those who have given up the faith, cf. 1 Tm 4:1; 2 Tm 4:3fseq.
c. The apostasy will be due to a being who is given three names. He is the wicked One (lit. 'man of lawlessness' or 'man of sin'). He is a being destined to be lost (lit. 'son of perdition') vv. 9–10; Jn 17:12; cf. 1 Th 5:5. He is the enemy of God and is described here in terms reminiscent of the description of the Great Rebel in Dn 11:36. Later on in Christian traditions, based on Dn, he is called the Antichrist, cf. 1 Jn 2:18; 4:3; 2 Jn 7. Unlike Satan, whose tool he is, and who is already at work in 'secret' (lit. 'the mystery') v. 7, the lawless One is represented as a person who will be revealed at the 'end of time', and whose power will persecute and seduce Christians. On the final 'test', that will come to an end only with the *parousia* of Christ, cf. Mt 24:24; Rv 13:1–8.
d. Paul does not name the cause that delays the *parousia* of Christ. All he says is that there is something, v./6, or someone, v. 7, that can 'delay' it. This person or power blocks the coming of Christ by preventing the manifestation of the Messiah's enemy who must precede the coming of the Messiah himself. The allusion would have been understood, v. 4, by the community to whom he was writing.
e. Wickedness (lit. 'lawlessness') is going on, but it is underground, secretly preparing for the great revolt. When the obstacle, whatever it is, is removed, lawlessness (or the lawless one) will work unmasked.
f. The revealing of the wicked One, vv. 6–8, is the counterpart of the revealing of Christ, 1:7; 1 Co 1:7, in the same way as his *parousia* is the counterpart of Christ's *parousia*, v. 8. The enemy of God becomes the enemy of Christ, but Christ will conquer his enemy.
g. add. 'Jesus'.
h. The wicked One is the instrument through which Satan works, *see* 1 Th 2:18, and whom he endows with superhuman power rather as Christ endows his followers with his own Spirit. Compare the Dragon and the Beast, Rv 13:2,4.
i. Truth and untruth here have a religious as well as an intellectual reference because they involve the whole of human life and activity, *see* Jn 8:32j, 44p; 1 Jn 3:19g.
j. This passage, 2:13–3:5, is closely linked to the description of the *parousia*. Having corrected the false ideas of the Thessalonians, Paul goes on to describe the positive consequences of his conception. Notice that the thought is firmly trinitarian, 2 Co 13:13e; cf. 1 Th 4:6–8.
k. var. 'as first-fruits'.
l. What Paul taught them when he was in Thessalonica and what he had written to them since he returned from there, 2:2,5; 1 Th 3:4; 4:2,6; 5:27, includes, in the message of the good news, *see* 1 Th 2:13d, the principles by which a Christian should live, cf. 1 Co 11:2,23–25; 1 Th 4:1.

3 **a.** Or perhaps 'from evil'. Christians will be tempted but not beyond their powers of resistance, 1 Co 10:13.
b. By imitating Paul, 1 Co 4:16; Ga 4:12; Ph 3:17, Christians will be imitating Christ, 1 Th 1:6; Ph 2:5; cf. Mt 16:24; Jn 13:15; 1 P 2:21; 1 Jn 2:6, who is himself the one that Paul is imitating, 1 Co 11:1. Christians must also imitate God, Ep 5:1 (cf. Mt 5:48), and they must imitate each other, 1 Th 1:7; 2:14; Heb 6:12. Behind this community of life is the idea of a model of doctrine, Rm 6:17, that has been received by tradition, 2 Th 3:6; 1 Co 11:2; 1 Th 2:13d. The leaders who transmit the doctrine must themselves be 'models' v. 9; Ph 3:17; 1 Tm 1:16; 4:12; Tt 2:7; 1 P 5:3, whose faith and life are to be imitated, Heb 13:7.
c. This rule, which aims only at deliberate refusal to work, comes either from a saying of Jesus, or perhaps simply from a popular saying. It constitutes 'the rule of Christian work'.
d. add. 'Amen', cf. 1 Th 3:13; 5:28.

1 TIMOTHY

THE FIRST LETTER
FROM PAUL TO TIMOTHY

Address

1 1 Paul, apostle of Christ Jesus appointed by the command *ᵃ* of God our Saviour *ᵇ*
2   and of Christ Jesus our hope, ·to Timothy, true child of mine in the faith.
Grace, mercy and peace from God the Father and from Christ Jesus our Lord.

Suppress the false teachers

3 When I was setting out for Macedonia I urged you to stay on in Ephesus to instruct
4 certain people not to spread wrong teaching ·or to give attention to myths and
unending genealogies; *ᶜ* these things only foster doubts instead of furthering God's
5 plan *ᵈ* which is founded on faith. ·The final goal at which this instruction aims is
6 love, issuing from a pure heart, a clear conscience and a sincere faith. ·Some
people have missed the way to these things and turned to empty speculation, trying
7 to be teachers of the Law; ·but they understand neither the words they use nor the
matters about which they make such strong assertions.

The purpose of the Law

8 We are well aware that the Law *ᵉ* is good, but only provided it is used legitimately, *ᶠ*
9 on the understanding that laws are not framed for people who are upright. *ᵍ* On
the contrary, they are for criminals and the insubordinate, for the irreligious and
the wicked, for the sacrilegious and the godless; they are for people who kill
10 their fathers or mothers and for murderers, ·for the promiscuous, homosexuals,
kidnappers, for liars and for perjurers—and for everything else that is contrary to
11 the sound teaching *ʰ* ·that accords with the gospel of the glory of the blessed God,
the gospel that was entrusted to me.

Paul on his own calling

12 I thank Christ Jesus our Lord, who has given me strength. By calling me into his
13 service he has judged me trustworthy, ·even though I used to be a blasphemer and
a persecutor and contemptuous. Mercy, however, was shown me, because while I
14 lacked faith I acted in ignorance; ·but the grace of our Lord filled me with faith
15 and with the love that is in Christ Jesus. ·Here is a saying that you can rely on *ⁱ* and
nobody should doubt: that Christ Jesus came into the world to save sinners. I

16 myself am the greatest of them; ·and if mercy has been shown to me, it is because
Jesus Christ meant to make me the leading example of his inexhaustible patience
17 for all the other people who were later to trust in him for eternal life. ·To the
eternal King, the undying,ʲ invisible and only God, be honour and glory for ever
and ever. Amen.

Timothy's responsibility

18 Timothy, my son, these are the instructions that I am giving you, in accordance
with the words once spoken over you by the prophets,ᵏ so that in their light you
19 may fight like a good soldier ·with faith and a good conscience for your weapons.
20 Some people have put conscience aside and wrecked their faith in consequence. I
mean men like Hymenaeus and Alexander, whom I have handed over to Satanˡ
so that they may learn not to be blasphemous.

Liturgical prayer

1 2 I urgeᵃ then, first of all that petitions, prayers, intercessions and thanksgiving
2 should be offered for everyone, ·for kings and others in authority,ᵇ so that we
3 may be able to live peaceful and quiet lives with all devotion and propriety. ·To
4 do this is right, and acceptable to God our Saviour: ·he wants everyone to be
5 savedᶜ and reach full knowledge of the truth. ᵈ ·For there is only one God, and
there is only one mediator between God and humanity, himself a human being,
6 Christ Jesus,ᵉ ·who offered himself as a ransom for all. This was the witnessᶠ given
7 at the appointed time, ·of which I was appointed herald and apostle and—I am
telling the truth and no lie—a teacher of the gentiles in faith and truth.
8   In every place, then, I want the men to lift their hands up reverently in prayer,
with no anger or argument.

Women in the assembly

9 Similarly, women are to wear suitable clothes and to be dressed quietly and
10 modestly, without braided hair or gold and jewellery or expensive clothes; ·their
adornment is to do the good works that are proper for women who claim to be
11, 12 religious. ·During instruction, a woman should be quiet and respectful. I give no
permission for a woman to teach or to have authority over a man. A woman ought
13, 14 to be quiet, ·because Adam was formed first and Eve afterwards, and it was not
Adam who was led astray but the woman who was led astray and fell into sin.
15 Nevertheless, she will be saved by child-bearing,ᵍ provided she lives a sensible life
and is constant in faith and love and holiness.

The elder-in-charge

1 3 Here is a saying that you can rely on: to want to be a presiding elderᵃ is to
2 desire a noble task. ·That is why the president must have an impeccable
character. Husband of one wife,ᵇ he must be temperate, discreet and courteous,
3 hospitable and a good teacher; ·not a heavy drinker, nor hot-tempered, but gentle
4 and peaceable, not avaricious, ·a man who manages his own household well and
5 brings his children up to obey him and be well-behaved: ·how can any man who
does not understand how to manage his own household take care of the Church of
6 God? ·He should not be a new convert, in case pride should turn his head and he
7 incur the same condemnation as the devil. ·It is also necessary that he be held in
good repute by outsiders, so that he never falls into disrepute and into the devil's
trap.

Deacons

8 Similarly, deacons must be respectable, not double-tongued, moderate in the
9 amount of wine they drink and with no squalid greed for money. ·They must hold
10 to the mystery of the faith with a clear conscience. ·They are first to be examined,
11 and admitted to serve as deacons only if there is nothing against them. ·Similarly,
12 women ' must be respectable, not gossips, but sober and wholly reliable. ·Deacons
must be husbands of one wife and must be people who manage their children and
13 households well. ·Those of them who carry out their duties well as deacons will
earn a high standing for themselves and an authoritative voice in matters
concerning faith in Christ Jesus.

The Church and the mystery of the spiritual life

14. 15 I write this to you in the hope that I may be able to come to you soon; ·but in case
I should be delayed, I want you to know how people ought to behave in God's
household—that is, in the Church of the living God, pillar and support of the
16 truth. ' ·Without any doubt, the mystery of our religion is very deep indeed:

> He ' was made visible in the flesh,
> justified in the Spirit,
> seen by angels,
> proclaimed to the gentiles,
> believed in throughout the world,
> taken up in glory. '

False teachers

1 **4** The Spirit has explicitly said that during the last times ' some will desert the
faith and pay attention to deceitful spirits and doctrines that come from devils,
2 seduced by the hypocrisy of liars whose consciences are branded as though with a
3 red-hot iron: ' ·they forbid marriage and prohibit foods which God created to be
4 accepted with thanksgiving by all who believe and who know the truth. ' ·Everything
God has created is good, and no food is to be rejected, provided it is received with
5. 6 thanksgiving: ·the word of God and prayer make it holy. ·If you put all this to the
brothers, you will be a good servant of Christ Jesus and show that you have really
digested the teaching of the faith and the good doctrine which you have always
7 followed. ·Have nothing to do with godless myths and old wives' tales. Train
8 yourself for religion. ' ·Physical exercise is useful enough, but the usefulness of
religion is unlimited, since it holds out promise both for life here and now and for
9 the life to come; ·that is a saying that you can rely on and nobody should doubt it.
10 I mean that the point of all our toiling and battling is that we have put our trust in
the living God and he is the Saviour of the whole human race but particularly of
11 all believers. ·This is what you are to instruct and teach.
12 Let no one disregard you because you are young, but be an example to all the
believers in the way you speak and behave, and in your love, your faith and your
13 purity. ·Until I arrive, devote yourself to reading to the people, encouraging and
14 teaching. ·You have in you a spiritual gift which was given to you when the
prophets spoke and the body of elders laid their hands on you; ' do not neglect it.
15 Let this be your care and your occupation, and everyone will be able to see your
16 progress. ·Be conscientious about what you do and what you teach; persevere in
this, and in this way you will save both yourself and those who listen to you.

Pastoral practice

1,2 **5** Never speak sharply to a man older than yourself, but appeal to him as you would to your own father; treat younger men as brothers, ·older women as mothers and young women as sisters with all propriety.

Widows

3,4 Be considerate to widows—if they really are widowed.ᵃ ·If a widow has children or grandchildren, they are to learn first of all to do their duty to their own families
5 and repay their debt to their parents, because this is what pleases God. ·But a woman who is really widowed and left on her own has set her hope on God and
6 perseveres night and day in petitions and prayer. ·The one who thinks only of
7 pleasure is already dead while she is still alive: ·instruct them in this, too, so that
8 their lives may be blameless. ·Anyone who does not look after his own relations, especially if they are living with him, has rejected the faith and is worse than an unbeliever.
9 Enrolment as a widow is permissible only for a woman at least sixty years old
10 who has had only one husband. ·She must be a woman known for her good works—whether she has brought up her children, been hospitable to strangers and washed the feet of God's holy people,ᵇ helped people in hardship or been active
11 in all kinds of good work. ·Do not accept young widows because if their natural
12 desires distract them from Christ, they want to marry again, ·and then people
13 condemn them for being unfaithful to their original promise.ᶜ ·Besides, they learn how to be idle and go round from house to house; and then, not merely idle, they learn to be gossips and meddlers in other people's affairs and to say what should
14 remain unsaid. ·I think it is best for young widows to marry againᵈ and have children and a household to look after, and not give the enemy any chanceᵉ to
15 raise a scandal about them; ·there are already some who have turned aside to
16 follow Satan. ·If a woman believer has widowed relatives, she should support them and not make the Church bear the expense but enable it to support those who are really widowed.

The elders

17 Elders who do their work well while they are in charge earn double reward,ᶠ
18 especially those who work hard at preaching and teaching. ·As scripture says: *You must not muzzle an ox when it is treading out the corn*; and again: *The worker*
19 *deserves his wages.*ᵍ ·Never accept any accusation brought against an elder unless
20 it is supported *by two or three witnesses.* ·If anyone is at fault, reprimand him
21 publicly, as a warning to the rest. ·Before God, and before Jesus Christ and the angels he has chosen, I charge you to keep these rules impartially and never to be
22 influenced by favouritism. ·Do not be too quick to lay hands on anyone,ʰ and never make yourself an accomplice in anybody else's sin; keep yourself pure.
23 You should give up drinking only water and have a little wine for the sake of your digestion and the frequent bouts of illness that you have.
24 The faults of some people are obvious long before they come to the reckoning,
25 while others have faults that are not discovered until later. ·Similarly, the good that people do can be obvious; but even when it is not, it cannot remain hidden.

Slaves

1 6 All those under the yoke of slavery must have unqualified respect for their masters, so that the name of God and our teaching are not brought into
2 disrepute. ·Those whose masters are believers are not to respect them less because they are brothers; on the contrary, they should serve them all the better, since those who have the benefit of their services are believers and dear to God. *

The true teacher and the false teacher

3 This is what you are to teach and urge. ·Anyone who teaches anything different and does not keep to the sound teaching which is that of our Lord Jesus Christ,
4 the doctrine which is in accordance with true religion, ·is proud and has no understanding, but rather a weakness for questioning *b* everything and arguing about words. All that can come of this is jealousy, contention, abuse and evil
5 mistrust; ·and unending disputes by people who are depraved in mind and deprived
6 of truth, and imagine that religion is a way of making a profit. ·Religion, of course, does bring large profits, but only to those who are content with what they have.
7, 8 We brought nothing into the world, and we can take nothing out of it; ·but as long
9 as we have food and clothing, we shall be content with that. ·People who long to be rich are a prey to trial; they get trapped into all sorts of foolish and harmful
10 ambitions which plunge people into ruin and destruction. ·'The love of money is the root of all evils' *c* and there are some who, pursuing it, have wandered away from the faith and so given their souls any number of fatal wounds.

Timothy's vocation recalled

11 But, as someone dedicated to God, avoid all that. You must aim to be upright and
12 religious, filled with faith and love, perseverance and gentleness. ·Fight the good fight of faith and win the eternal life to which you were called and for which you
13 made your noble profession of faith *d* before many witnesses. ·Now, before God, the source of all life, and before Jesus Christ, who witnessed to his noble profession
14 of faith before Pontius Pilate, *e* I charge you ·to do all that you have been told, with no faults or failures, until the appearing *f* of our Lord Jesus Christ,

> who at the due time will be revealed
> 15 by God, the blessed and only Ruler of all,
> the King of kings and the Lord of lords,
> 16 who alone is immortal,
> whose home is in inaccessible light,
> whom no human being has seen or is able to see:
> to him be honour and everlasting power. Amen. *g*

Rich Christians

17 Instruct those who are rich in this world's goods that they should not be proud and should set their hopes not on money, which is untrustworthy, but on God who
18 gives us richly all that we need for our happiness. ·They are to do good and be rich
19 in good works, generous in giving and always ready to share—·this is the way they can amass a good capital sum for the future if they want to possess the only life that is real.

Final warning and conclusion

20 My dear Timothy, take great care of all that has been entrusted to you.[h] Turn
away from godless philosophical discussions and the contradictions of the 'knowl-
21 edge' which is not knowledge at all;[i] •by adopting this, some have missed the goal
of faith. Grace be with you.[j]

NOTES TO 1 TIMOTHY

1 **a.** var. 'the promise'.

b. The title 'Saviour', rare in the letters of Paul,
Ep 5:23; Ph 3:20, is in the Pastoral Letters applied to the
Father, 1 Tm 2:3; 4:10; Tt 1:3; 2:10; 3:4. The work of Christ
the Saviour fulfilled the design of the Father.

c. Genealogies of OT patriarchs and heroes constructed
by Jewish writers in the same style as those in the *Book of
Jubilees*.

d. var. 'the building-up of God's house.

e. The 'Law of Moses'.

f. lit. 'Now the Law is good if anyone uses it as a law',
i.e. without asking it to be more than it claims to be.

g. The Law, here, is good not because it gives knowledge of sin, Rm 7:7d,12–14, nor because it prepares for the
coming of Christ, Ga 3:24–25, but because it is necessary for
the correction of sinners.

h. The epithet 'sound' in 'sound teaching' is characteristic of the Pastoral Letters *see* 6:3; 2 Tm 1:13; 4:3; Tt 1:9,13;
2:1,8. It is the apostolic preaching with all its qualities of
soundness, and taken in connection with ethical conduct (*see*
Rm 12:1–2; Ph 4:8–9).

i. This is one of the characteristic phrases of the Pastoral
Letters, *see* 3:1; 4:9; 2 Tm 2:11; Tt 3:8. It is a way of
attracting attention, perhaps of stressing an allusion or
quotation which the readers will recognise.

j. lit. 'incorruptible' or 'imperishable'; var. 'immortal'.
• This solemn doxology may be of liturgical origin. Doxologies are frequent in the Pauline letters, Rm 16:27n.

k. Here and in 4:14 Paul reminds Timothy of the part
played by the 'prophets' when the college of elders laid their
hands on his head, Ac 13:1–3; 11:27m.

l. The penalty of exclusion which will give the guilty a
chance to amend, *see* 1 Co 5:5d.

2 **a.** 'I urge'; var. 'Urge'.

b. On Paul's political loyalty, *see* Rm 13:1–7. The end
of the verse perhaps reflects the apostle's fears for the future.

c. Many theological implications have been drawn from
this statement, and it has been used to interpret or correct
some difficult passages in Romans, Rm 9:18,21. It is
founded, v. 5, on an appeal to the oneness of God, cf.
Mt 12:29; Rm 3:29–30; Ep 4:6, and to the unique position
of Christ as divine and human, cf. Heb 2:17; 8:6b. Paul
received from the Saviour, v. 7, the mission to preach a
salvation offered to all, Ac 9:15h; Rm 1:1b.

d. Salvation is knowledge of the truth, 4:3; 2 Tm 2:25;
3:7; Tt 1:1. But this knowledge entails total commitment,
see Ho 2:22v; Jn 8:32j; 2 Th 2:12.

e. Jesus is mediator precisely as a human being, and it
is this which enables him to be Saviour of all, v. 4, by his
death to ransom them, v. 6. Cf. Heb 2:14–17,15i.

f. Cf. 6:13. By accepting to die for humanity Jesus made
clear to the world God's plan to save all humanity. Witness
to the Father by his whole life, he was supremely so by his
death (later the Gk word for 'witness' comes to be used also
for 'martyr'). *See* Jn 3:11; Rv 1:5; 3:14.

g. Perhaps it was a point made against false teachers
who forbade marriage, 4:3, that the primary vocation of
women was giving life and raising children.

3 **a.** 'Bishop' and 'presbyter' are not mentioned here. *See*
Tt 1:5seq., 5c.

b. This list of qualities, and the one which follows in
vv. 8–12, have nothing specific about them. They draw on
the classic lists of qualities required of those who hold office
in the Church.

c. This instruction is probably intended for deacon-
esses, *see* Rm 16:1, rather than for the wives of deacons.

d. The Church of the living God, Dt 5:26d; 2 Co 6:16,
is his house, that is, both his dwelling and his family, Nb 12:7;
Heb 3:6; 10:21; 1 P 4:17, where the saving gospel is firmly
preserved, v. 16.

e. He, i.e. Christ: many authorities (e.g. Vulg.) read
'It', i.e. the 'mystery', *see* Col 2:3a. There follows a fragment
from a hymn or a liturgical profession of faith, composed of
six brief statements grouped in pairs. Cf. 6:15–16;
2 Tm 2:11–13. Also *see* Ep 1:3–14; Ph 2:6–11; Col 1:15–20.

f. The holiness and divinity of Christ were proved by
the fact that he rose in glory, *see* Rm 1:4c. 'Taken up in
glory', i.e. at the ascension.

4 **a.** On the crisis that will characterise the 'last times' *see*
2 Th 2:3–12; 2 Tm 3:1; 4:3–4; 2 P 3:3; Jude 18. Also *see*
Mt 24:6seq. and par.; Ac 20:29–30. As the 'last times' have
already begun, Rm 3:26m, we are already living in this final
epoch of crisis, cf. 1 Co 7:26; Ep 5:6; 6:13; Jm 5:3;
1 Jn 2:18; 4:1,3; 2 Jn 7.

b. i.e. branded like runaway slaves.

c. The rejection of marriage was to be one of the hall-
marks of Gnosticism; dietary regulations were more specifically Jewish, *see* Col 2:16–23.

d. The word translated 'religion' occurs ten times in the
Pastoral Epistles, 2:2; 3:16; 4:7,8; 6:3,5,6,11; 2 Tm 3:12;
Tt 2:12. It sums up the Christian attitude; connected with
the knowledge of faith which is the core of common life in
Christ Jesus, it has the sense also of devotion and seriousness
for the things of God.

e. Some translate 'the imposition of hands for the office
of presbyter'. The 'imposition of hands' can be the rite for
transmitting grace or a charism, Heb 6:2, or it can be the
gesture used when blessing, Mt 19:15, or curing, Mt 9:18
and par.; Mk 6:5; 7:32; 8:23–25; 16:18; Lk 4:40; 13:13;
Ac 9:12,17; 28:8, or imparting the Holy Spirit to the newly
baptised, Ac 1:5f. It can also be the rite for consecrating a
person for a particular public function, Ac 6:6; 13:3, as in
this passage and 1 Tm 5:22h; 2 Tm 1:6. Since the day on
which he received the imposition of hands, Timothy has had
a permanent charism ('grace-gift') that consecrates him to
his ministry. For the part played by the prophets, *see* 1:18.

5 **a.** Three categories of widow are mentioned here: those
who do not need assistance from the Church since they have
relations to look after them, v. 4; those who are 'true widows'
because they have no one to look after them, and whom
the Church is obliged to help, vv. 3–5,16; and those who
(whether helped by the Church or not) are called by the
Church to fulfil certain official functions. Widows in this third
category have to satisfy quite severe regulations, vv. 9–15.

b. The normal courtesy then shown to guests.

c. i.e. their vow or promise to consecrate themselves to God.

d. The caution expressed here stands in marked contrast to the high ideals put before young widows in 1 Co 7:8.

e. Either a malicious person, hostile to Christians, or, less probably, Satan.

f. Or 'double honour'.

g. Or 'his keep', *see* Mt 10:10. To the quotation from Dt 25:4 is added a saying of Jesus which is known to us only through Lk 10:7. But this does not imply that Luke's Gospel was already completed and recognised as scripture. *See* 2 Tm 3:15d.

h. i.e. to confer a function in the Church, *see* 4:14e. Some commentators have suggested that this refers to the giving of absolution to a sinner.

6 a. Or 'and dear brothers'

b. lit. 'seeking'. With the search for God which in the OT summed up the whole attitude of fidelity to God, Dt 4:29; Ps 27:8b; Jr 29:13–14 and which retains its value in the NT. Mt 6:33; 7:7–8; Ac 17:27 the apostle here contrasts, *see* 1:4; 2 Tm 2:16,23; Tt 3:9, subtle and pointless delvings, unending because indiscreet, an illness fatal to sound teaching, 1 Tm 1:10h; 6:3, because of an inquisitiveness which claims to go further than the mystery of faith, cf. 2 Jn 9.

c. A contemporary proverb.

d. We do not know to what incident in Timothy's life this refers: possibly baptism or consecration for the ministry.

e. The proclamation of his royal messiahship and his office as revealer of Truth, Jn 18:36–37. The mention of Pontius Pilate lends strength to the official tone of this witness, which is exemplary for the Christian's profession of faith at baptism or in the face of persecution.

f. The word 'epiphany' ('appearing', used in 2 Th 2:8 with reference to the Great Rebel) is adopted in the Pastoral Letters in preference to *parousia* ('coming', 1 Co 15:23n), or 'apocalypse' ('revealing', 1 Co 1:7c), as the technical term, 2 Tm 4:1,8; Tt 2:13; Heb 9:28. It is used both for the manifestation of Christ in his triumph at the end of the world, and for his first appearance in the world for the saving action of his life, death and resurrection (2 Tm 1:10; Tt 2:11; 3:4).

g. This impressive doxology may be inspired by a liturgical hymn, cf. 1:17. It comprises seven scriptural phrases transposed into Hellenistic language, the themes being that God is the only object of worship and that no one may claim to fathom the mystery of God.

h. The deposit entrusted is an important theme of the Pastoral Letters, 2 Tm 1:12,14. Its content is that of faith, 4:6; 2 Tm 1:13; Tt 1:9, or tradition, 2 Th 2:15i; 3:6. But the notion is legal in origin and stresses the recipient's duty to keep and hand on intact the deposit which has been entrusted to him. Compare 'Hold on firmly to what you have,' Rv 2:25; 3:11.

i. This pseudo-science is that which will later be refuted by Irenaeus.

j. 'you', plural; var. 'you', singular. add. 'Amen'.

2 TIMOTHY

THE SECOND LETTER
FROM PAUL TO TIMOTHY

Greeting and thanksgiving

1 **1** From Paul, apostle of Christ Jesus through the will of God in accordance with
2 his promise of life in Christ Jesus, ·to Timothy, dear son of mine. Grace,
mercy and peace from God the Father and from Christ Jesus our Lord.
3 Night and day I thank God whom I serve with a pure conscience as my ancestors
4 did. I remember you in my prayers constantly night and day; ·I remember your
5 tears *a* and long to see you again to complete my joy. ·I also remember your sincere
faith, a faith which first dwelt in your grandmother Lois, and your mother Eunice,
and I am sure dwells also in you. *b*

The gifts that Timothy has received

6 That is why I am reminding you now to fan into a flame the gift *c* of God that you
7 possess through the laying on of my hands. ·God did not give us a spirit of timidity,
8 but the Spirit of power and love and self-control. ·So you are never to be ashamed
of witnessing to our Lord, or ashamed of me for being his prisoner; but share in
9 my hardships for the sake of the gospel, relying on the power of God ·who has
saved us and called us to be holy *d*—not because of anything we ourselves had
done but for his own purpose and by his own grace. This grace had already been
10 granted to us, in Christ Jesus, before the beginning of time, ·but it has been
revealed only by the appearing *e* of our Saviour Christ Jesus. He has abolished
11 death, and he has brought to light immortality and life through the gospel; ·in
whose service I have been made herald, apostle and teacher. *f*
12 That is why I am experiencing my present sufferings; *g* but I am not ashamed,
because I know in whom I have put my trust, and I have no doubt at all that he is
able to safeguard until that Day what I have entrusted to him. *h*
13 Keep as your pattern the sound teaching you have heard from me, in the faith
14 and love that are in Christ Jesus. ·With the help of the Holy Spirit who dwells in
us, look after that precious thing given in trust.
15 As you know, Phygelus and Hermogenes and all the others in Asia have deserted
16 me. ·I hope the Lord will be kind to all the family of Onesiphorus, because he has
17 often been a comfort to me and has never been ashamed of my chains. ·On the
contrary, as soon as he reached Rome, he searched hard for me and found me.

18 May the Lord grant him to find the Lord's mercy on that Day. ' You know better than anyone else how much he helped me at Ephesus.

How Timothy should face hardships

1 2 As for you, my dear son, take strength from the grace which is in Christ Jesus.
2 Pass on to reliable people what you have heard from me through many witnesses so that they in turn will be able to teach others. *

3, 4 Bear with your share of difficulties, like a good soldier of Christ Jesus. *·No one on active service involves himself in the affairs of civilian life, because he must win
5 the approval of the man who enlisted him; ·or again someone who enters an athletic contest wins only if he competes in the sports—he can win a prize only if
6 he has competed according to the rules; ·and again, it is the farmer who works
7 hard that has the first claim on any crop that is harvested. ·Think over what I have said, and the Lord will give you full understanding.

8 Remember the gospel that I carry, 'Jesus Christ risen from the dead, sprung
9 from the race of David'; ·it is on account of this that I have to put up with suffering, even to being chained like a criminal. But God's message cannot be chained up.
10 So I persevere for the sake of those who are chosen, so that they, too, may obtain the salvation that is in Christ Jesus with eternal glory.
11 Here is a saying that you can rely on: *

If we have died with him, then we shall live with him.
12 If we persevere, then we shall reign with him.
If we disown him, then he will disown us.
13 If we are faithless, he is faithful still,
for he cannot disown his own self. ·

The struggle against the immediate danger from false teachers

14 Remind them of this; and tell them in the name of God * that there must be no wrangling about words: all that this ever achieves is the destruction of those who
15 are listening. ·Make every effort to present yourself before God as a proven worker who has no need to be ashamed, but who keeps the message of truth on a
16 straight path. ·Have nothing to do with godless philosophical discussions—they
17 only lead further and further away from true religion. ·Talk of this kind spreads
18 corruption like gangrene, as in the case of Hymenaeus and Philetus, ·the men who have gone astray from the truth, claiming that the resurrection has already taken place. * They are upsetting some people's faith.
19 However, God's solid foundation-stone stands firm, and this is the seal on it: 'The Lord knows those who are his own' and 'All who call on the name of the Lord must avoid evil.' *

20 Not all the dishes in a large house are made of gold and silver; some are made
21 of wood or earthenware: the former are held in honour, the latter held cheap. ·If someone holds himself aloof from these faults I speak of, he will be a vessel held in honour, dedicated and fit for the Master, ready for any good work.

22 Turn away from the passions of youth, concentrate on uprightness, faith, love
23 and peace, in union with all those who call on the Lord with a pure heart. ·Avoid these foolish and undisciplined speculations, understanding that they only give
24 rise to quarrels; ·and a servant of the Lord must not engage in quarrels, but must
25 be kind to everyone, a good teacher, and patient. ·He must be gentle when he corrects people who oppose him, in the hope that God may give them a change of

26 mind so that they recognise the truth ·and come to their senses, escaping the trap of the devil who made them his captives and subjected them to his will. ⁱ

The dangers of the last days

1,2 **3** You may be quite sure that in the last days there will be some difficult times. ·People will be self-centred and avaricious, boastful, arrogant and rude;
3 disobedient to their parents, ungrateful, irreligious; ·heartless and intractable; they will be slanderers, profligates, savages and enemies of everything that is good;
4 they will be treacherous and reckless and demented by pride, preferring their
5 own pleasure to God. ·They will keep up the outward appearance of religion ᵃ but will have rejected the inner power of it. Keep away from people like that.
6 Of the same kind, too, are those men who insinuate themselves into families in order to get influence over silly women who are obsessed with their sins and follow
7 one craze after another, ·always seeking learning, but unable ever to come to
8 knowledge of the truth. ·Just as Jannes and Jambres defied Moses, ᵇ so these men
9 defy the truth, their minds corrupt and their faith spurious. ·But they will not be able to go on much longer: their folly, like that of the other two, must become obvious to everybody.
10 You, though, have followed my teaching, my way of life, my aims, my faith, my
11 patience and my love, my perseverance ·and the persecutions and sufferings that came to me in places like Antioch, Iconium and Lystra—all the persecutions I
12 have endured; and the Lord has rescued me from every one of them. ·But anybody
13 who tries to live in devotion to Christ is certain to be persecuted; ·while these wicked impostors will go from bad to worse, deceiving others, and themselves deceived.
14 You must keep to what you have been taught and know to be true; remember
15 who your teachers were, ᶜ ·and how, ever since you were a child, you have known the holy scriptures ᵈ—from these you can learn the wisdom that leads to salvation
16 through faith in Christ Jesus. ·All scripture is inspired by God and useful ᵉ for
17 refuting error, for guiding people's lives and teaching them to be upright. ·This is how someone who is dedicated to God becomes fully equipped and ready for any good work.

A solemn charge ᵃ

1,2 **4** Before God and before Christ Jesus who is to be judge of the living and the dead, ᵇ I charge you, in the name of his appearing and of his kingdom: ·proclaim the message and, welcome or unwelcome, insist on it. Refute falsehood, correct error, give encouragement—but do all with patience and with care to instruct.
3 The time is sure to come when people will not accept sound teaching, but their ears will be itching for anything new and they will collect themselves a whole series
4 of teachers according to their own tastes; ·and then they will shut their ears to the
5 truth and will turn to myths. ·But you must keep steady all the time; put up with suffering; do the work of preaching the gospel; fulfil the service asked of you. ᶜ

Paul in the evening of his life

6 As for me, my life is already being poured away as a libation, ᵈ and the time has
7 come for me to depart. ·I have fought the good fight to the end; I have run the
8 race to the finish; I have kept the faith; ·all there is to come for me now is the crown of uprightness which the Lord, the upright judge, will give to me on that Day; and not only to me but to all those who have longed for his appearing. ᵉ

Final advice

9, 10 Make every effort to come and see me as soon as you can. ·As it is, Demas has deserted me for love of this life and gone to Thessalonica, Crescens has gone to

11 Galatia *f* and Titus to Dalmatia; ·only Luke *g* is with me. Bring Mark *h* with you; I

12, 13 find him a useful helper in my work. ·I have sent Tychicus to Ephesus. ·When you come, bring the cloak I left with Carpus in Troas, and the scrolls, especially the

14 parchment ones. ·Alexander the coppersmith has done me a lot of harm; *the Lord*

15 *will repay him as his deeds deserve.* ·Be on your guard against him yourself, because he has been bitterly contesting everything that we say.

16 The first time I had to present my defence, *i* no one came into court to support

17 me. Every one of them deserted me—may they not be held accountable for it. ·But the Lord stood by me and gave me power, so that through me the message might be fully proclaimed for all the gentiles to hear; and so I was *saved from the lion's*

18 *mouth.* ·The Lord will rescue me from all evil attempts on me, and bring me safely to *j* his heavenly kingdom. To him be glory for ever and ever. *k* Amen.

Farewells and final good wishes

19, 20 Greetings to Prisca and Aquila, and the family of Onesiphorus. ·Erastus stayed

21 behind at Corinth, and I left Trophimus ill at Miletus. ·Make every effort to come before the winter.

Greetings to you from Eubulus, Pudens, Linus, Claudia and all the brothers.

22 The Lord *l* be with your spirit. Grace be with you.

NOTES TO 2 TIMOTHY

1 **a.** Possibly when they parted at Ephesus, 1 Tm 1:3.

b. This verse is a happy complement to Ac 16;1. We have not much evidence in the NT of the benefits of education in the faith in the bosom of a Christian family. Cf. 3: 14–15.

c. The charism had already been received, 1 Tm 4:14e, and Timothy must fan it into a flame with the help of the Spirit.

d. This may be taken in two ways here: the calling of Christians to salvation, cf. Rm 1:6–7; 8:28; 1 Co 1:2,24; Ep 1:18; 4:4; Ph 3:14; Col 3:15, or (by metonymy) the state ('vocation') to which Christians have been called.

e. The 'appearing' ('epiphany'), *see* 1 Tm 6:14f, here refers to the incarnation and redemption.

f. Add 'to the non-Jews', cf. 1 Tm 2:7.

g. A second captivity at Rome.

h. The context suggests that this indicates Christian doctrine kept intact, 1 Tm 6:20h, rather than Paul's good deeds, 4:7–8; 1 Tm 6:19.

i. 'Lord' can be taken in either case as a reference either to the Father or to the Son.

2 **a.** The process of transmission of this 'precious trust', or tradition, is here seen at work, in four successive stages.

b. Vv. 4–6 are three short parables: the soldier, the athlete, the farm labourer.

c. Vv. 11–13 are part of a Christian hymn, *see* 1 Tm 3:16e.

d. var. 'the Lord'.

e. The Greek mind found the resurrection particularly hard to accept, Ac 17:32; 1 Co 15:12. Hymenaeus and Philetus may well have given it a purely spiritual interpretation as the mystical resurrection that occurs in baptism,

Rm 6:4; Ep 2:6e, or as a mystical ascent to God. Paul had put the Corinthians on their guard against too material a conception, 1 Co 15:35–53 and notes.

f. Details about a building were often inscribed on its foundation-stone: as the building here is the Church, the foundation-stone could be either Christ himself, 1 Co 3:11, or the apostles, Ep 2:20; cf. Rv 21:14, or faith in the unbreakable promise of God, cf. 2:13.

g. The scriptural texts complement each other: God looks after those he loves, Nb 16:5, and these must live in uprightness, Nb 16:26; Ps 6:8; Is 26:13; 52:11.

3 **a.** This is reminiscent of the 'false prophets' foretold in Mt 7:15; 24:4–5,24. A fresh outbreak of irreligion is one of the characteristics of the 'last times', *see* 1 Tm 4:1a.

b. The magicians of Egypt in Ex 7:11–13,22 are not named. In Jewish writings Jannes and Jambres (or 'Mambres'), represented as the leaders of the Egyptian magicians, are said to be the disciples (or even sons) of Balaam, Nb 22:2b.

c. These teachers were Lois, Eunice, 1:5, and, above all, Paul himself.

d. This was the name given by hellenistic Jews to the books of the Bible, *see* 1 M 12:9c. The NT often quotes 'the scriptures' or 'scripture' or individual books. Rm 1:2 has 'the holy scriptures'; 2 Co 3:14f has 'the old covenant or Testament' (but the sense is not limited to the books of scripture, *see* 1 Th 5:27i; 2 P 3:16).

e. Or (less probably) 'all scripture that is inspired by God can . . .' (Vulg.). This affirmation about the inspiration of the OT, cf. 2 P 1:21, probably includes some Christian writings also. It is by assiduously studying scripture that the Christian nourishes faith and apostolic zeal, vv. 15–17.

4 **a.** This appeal to a cherished disciple, at the end of the last of the epistles, can be compared, in a different tonality, to the discourse at Miletus, Ac 20:18–36. Dominated by the thought of approaching death and the coming of the Lord, Paul charges Timothy to carry on untiringly the mission he bequeaths to him.

b. Christ will judge all, both those who are alive at his coming and those who will rise again. *see* Mt 25:31e; Jn 5:26–29; 1 Th 4:15–17. This claim surely formed part of the earliest *kerygma*, Ac 10:42; 1 P 4:5, and has been included in the Creed.

c. Vulg. adds 'Be sober'.

d. Libations of wine, water or oil were poured over the victims not only in gentile sacrifices but also in Jewish ones, *see* Ex 29:40; Nb 28:7.

e. Paul is sure that he has fulfilled his mission. With him will be crowned all those who have accepted the gospel, Ph 4:1; 2 Th 1:7,10.

f. var. 'Gaul'. • At that time the name 'Galatia' was used for the Roman province in Asia, which had been settled by Gallic ex-servicemen.

g. Presumably Luke the evangelist, *see* Col 4:14.

h. Presumably Mark the evangelist, Ac 12:12d. His old quarrel with Paul, Ac 15:37–39, seems to have been forgotten.

i. At some recent hearing of his case, which gave the Apostle the chance to proclaim the faith entirely on his own, v. 17; Ac 9:15h.

j. Or 'and keep me safe for'.

k. Note that this doxology is addressed to Christ the Saviour and Redeemer, *see* Rm 16:25*l*; Ga 1:5.

l. Some witnesses add 'Jesus Christ', and (at the end) 'Amen'.

TITUS

THE LETTER FROM PAUL TO TITUS

Address *

1 1 From Paul, servant of God, an apostle of Jesus Christ to bring those whom
God has chosen to faith and to the knowledge of the truth that leads to true
2 religion, ·and to give them the hope of the eternal life that was promised so long
3 ago by God. He does not lie ·and so, in due time, he made known his message by
a proclamation which was entrusted to me by the command of God our Saviour.
4 To Titus, true child of mine in the faith that we share. Grace and peace from God
the Father and from Christ Jesus our Saviour.

The appointment of elders

5 The reason I left you behind in Crete was for you to organise everything that still
6 had to be done *b* and appoint elders *c* in every town, in the way that I told you, that
is, each of them must be a man of irreproachable character, husband of one wife,
and his children must be believers and not liable to be charged with disorderly
7 conduct or insubordination. ·The president has to be irreproachable since he is
God's representative: never arrogant or hot-tempered, nor a heavy drinker or
8 violent, nor avaricious; ·but hospitable and a lover of goodness; sensible, upright,
9 devout and self-controlled; ·and he must have a firm grasp of the unchanging
message of the tradition, so that he can be counted on both for giving encouragement in sound doctrine and for refuting those who argue against it.

Opposing the false teachers

10 And in fact there are many people who are insubordinate, who talk nonsense and
11 try to make others believe it, particularly among those of the circumcision. ·They
must be silenced: people of this kind upset whole families, by teaching things that
12 they ought not to, and doing it for the sake of sordid gain. ·It was one of themselves,
one of their own prophets, who said, *d* 'Cretans were never anything but liars,
13 dangerous animals, all greed and laziness'; ·and that is a true statement. So be
14 severe in correcting them, and make them sound in the faith ·so that they stop
taking notice of Jewish myths and the orders of people who turn away from the
truth.
15 To those who are pure themselves, everything is pure; *e* but to those who have
been corrupted and lack faith, nothing can be pure—the corruption is both in their
16 minds and in their consciences. ·They claim to know God but by their works they

deny him; they are outrageously rebellious and quite untrustworthy for any good work.

Some specific moral instruction

2 1 It is for you, then, to preach the behaviour which goes with healthy doctrine.
2 Older men should be reserved, dignified, moderate, sound in faith and love
3 and perseverance. ·Similarly, older women should behave as befits religious people, with no scandal-mongering and no addiction to wine—they must be the
4 teachers of right behaviour ·and show younger women how they should love their
5 husbands and love their children, ·how they must be sensible and chaste, and how to work in their homes, and be gentle, and obey their husbands, so that the
6 message of God is not disgraced. ·Similarly, urge younger men to be moderate *ⁿ* in
7 everything that they do, ·and you yourself set an example of good works, by sincerity and earnestness, when you are teaching, and by a message sound and
8 irreproachable · so that any opponent will be at a loss, with no accusation to make
9 against us. ·Slaves must be obedient to their masters in everything, and do what is
10 wanted without argument; ·and there must be no pilfering—they must show complete honesty at all times, so that they are in every way a credit to the teaching of God our Saviour.

The basis of the Christian moral life

11. 12 You see, God's grace has been revealed to save the whole human race; *ᵇ* ·it has taught us that we should give up everything contrary to true religion and all our worldly passions; we must be self-restrained and live upright and religious lives in
13 this present world, ·waiting in hope for the blessing which will come with the
14 appearing of the glory of our great God and Saviour Christ Jesus. *ᶜ* ·He offered himself for us in order to ransom us from all our *faults* and *to purify a people to be his very own* and eager to do good.
15 This is what you must say, encouraging or arguing with full authority; no one should despise you.

General instruction for believers

3 1 Remind them to be obedient to the officials in authority; to be ready to do
2 good at every opportunity; ·not to go slandering other people but to be
3 peaceable and gentle, and always polite to people of all kinds. ·There was a time when we too were ignorant, disobedient and misled and enslaved by different passions and dissipations; we lived then in wickedness and malice, hating each other and hateful ourselves.
4 But when the kindness and love of God our Saviour for mankind were revealed,
5 it was not because of any upright actions we had done ourselves; it was for no reason except his own faithful love that he saved us, by means of the cleansing
6 water of rebirth and renewal in the Holy Spirit ·which he has so generously poured
7 over us through Jesus Christ our Saviour; ·so that, justified by his grace, we should
8 become heirs in hope of eternal life. *ᵈ* ·This is doctrine that you can rely on.

Personal advice to Titus

I want you to be quite uncompromising in teaching all this, so that those who now believe in God may keep their minds constantly occupied in doing good works.
9 All this is good, and useful for everybody. ·But avoid foolish speculations, and those genealogies, and the quibbles and disputes about the Law—they are useless

10 and futile. •If someone disputes what you teach,[b] then after a first and a second
11 warning, have no more to do with him: •you will know that anyone of that sort is
warped and is self-condemned as a sinner.

Practical recommendations, farewells and good wishes

12 As soon as I have sent Artemas or Tychicus to you, do your best to join me at
13 Nicopolis, where I have decided to spend the winter. •Help eagerly on their way
14 Zenas the lawyer and Apollos, and make sure they have everything they need. •All
our people must also learn to occupy themselves in doing good works for their
practical needs,[c] and not to be unproductive.

15   All those who are with me send their greetings. Greetings to those who love us
in the faith. Grace[d] be with you all.

NOTES TO TITUS

1 **a.** This address, vv. 1-3, contains a whole theology of salvation and of the apostolate.

b. As usual, Paul had begun the work of evangelisation and then left it to be completed by others, see Rm 15:23g; 1 Co 3:6,10; Col 1:7b.

c. In the earliest days each Christian community was governed by a body of elders ('presbyters', whence English word 'priests') or prominent people. This was the case both in Jerusalem (Ac 11:30; 15:2seq.; 21:18) and in the Dispersion (Ac 14:23; 20:17) and it merely continued both the ancient practice of the OT, Ex 18:13seq.; Nb 11:16; Jos 8:10; 1 S 16:4; Is 9:14; Ezk 8:1,11-12, and the more recent practice of the Jews, Ezr 5:5; 10:14; Jdt 6:16; Lk 7:3; 22:66; Ac 4:5, see Josephus, Philo, etc. These *episkopoi* (supervisors, overseers, watchers, guardians) who are not yet 'bishops' and who are mentioned in connection with the *diakonoi* (servants, attendants, assistants, deputies, ministers: 'deacons': Ph 1:1; 1 Tm 3:1-13; the Apostolic Fathers) seem in some passages, Tt 1:5,7; Ac 20:17,28, to be identical with the elders. The Greek word *episkopos*, taken over from the gentile world probably as an equivalent for a semitic title (cf. the *mebaqqer* of the Essenes, and see Nb 4:16; 31:14; Jg 9:28; 2 K 11:15,18; 12:11) indicated the duty of an officer, while *presbyteros* indicated the status or dignity of the same officer. The *episkopoi* in the college of presbyters may have taken turns to carry out their official duties, cf. 1 Tm 5:17. It is quite certain that Christian *presbyteroi* or *episkopoi* were not merely concerned with the practical side of organising things: they had to teach, 1:9; 1 Tm 3:2; 5:17, and govern, Tt 1:7; 1 Tm 3:5. They were appointed by the apostles, Ac 14:23, or their representatives, Tt 1:5, by the imposition of hands, 1 Tm 5:22, see 1 Tm 4:14e; 2 Tm 1:6; their powers derived from God, Ac 20:28, and were charismatic, 1 Co 12:28. The word *episkopos* eventually replaced analogous titles like *proistamenos* (official), Rm 12:8; 1 Th 5:12, *poimen* (pastor, shepherd), Ep 4:11, *hegoumenos* (guide, leader), Heb 13:7,17,24. These heads of the local community who developed into our priests (*presbyteroi*) and bishops (*episkopoi*) were helped by *diakonoi* (deacons). The transformation of a local assembly ruled by a body of bishops or presbyters, into an assembly ruled by a single bishop set over a number of priests (a stage reached in some churches by the time of Ignatius of Antioch, who died c. AD 107) may have involved the intermediate stage when a single *episkopos* in the community was given the same powers over that local community which had previously been exercised over several communities by the apostles or their representatives like Timothy or Titus.

d. Quotation attributed to the Cretan poet Epimenides of Cnossos (sixth century BC); first half quoted by Callimachus of Alexandria (early third century BC).

e. A proverb which takes on a Christian sense, Mt 15:10-20 par.; Rm 14:14-23; see Jn 13:10i; Heb 9:10.

2 **a.** This instruction to be 'sensible' or 'moderate', here aimed at young people, is characteristic of Greek moral advice, vv. 5,12; 1 Tm 2:9,15; 3:2; 2 Tm 1:7. 'In everything' can alternatively be put at the beginning of v. 7, 'set an example in everything'.

b. Grace, the effective mercy of God, Ho 2:2c, and his goodness, his love for mankind, 3:4, have appeared as a prelude to his 'appearing', v. 13, 1 Tm 6:14f. Again (as vv. 1-3), vv. 11-14 and 3:4-7 are two extremely close-knit treatments of the work of salvation, its demands and effects.

c. A clear statement of the divinity of Christ, see Rm 9:5d. The Saviour is here called also the great God, see 1 Tm 1:1b.

3 **a.** The effects of baptism are: rebirth, free forgiveness by Christ, reception of his Holy Spirit, see Rm 5:5e, and the immediate enjoyment of all rights as heir to eternal life (the presence of the Holy Spirit being a pledge of this, cf. 2 Co 1:22).

b. lit. 'a heretic', etymologically, one who makes a choice. The word occurs only here in the Bible, and is borrowed from the terminology of contemporary philosophical schools. In Christian terminology, cf. 1 Co 11:19; Ga 5:20, 'heresy' is a choice made from among truths of faith, which creates separation and division. For the procedure prescribed by Paul see 1 Co 5:5d.

c. Or 'for urgent needs'.

d. Some witnesses add 'of the Lord' or 'of God' and, at the end, 'Amen'.

PHILEMON

THE LETTER FROM PAUL TO PHILEMON

Address

1 From Paul, a prisoner of Christ Jesus and from our brother Timothy; to our dear
2 fellow worker Philemon, ·our sister*ª* Apphia, our fellow soldier Archippus and
3 the church that meets in your house. ·Grace and the peace of God our Father and
the Lord Jesus Christ.

Thanksgiving and prayer

4, 5 I always thank my God, mentioning you in my prayers, ·because I hear of the love
6 and the faith which you have for the Lord Jesus and for all God's holy people. ·I
pray that your fellowship in faith *ᵇ* may come to expression in full knowledge of all
7 the good we can do for Christ. ·I have received much joy and encouragement by
your love; you have set the hearts of God's holy people at rest.

The request about Onesimus

8 Therefore, although in Christ I have no hesitations about telling you what your
9 duty is, ·I am rather appealing to your love, being what I am, Paul, an old man,
10 and now also a prisoner of Christ Jesus. ·I am appealing to you for a child of mine,
11 whose father I became *ᶜ* while wearing these chains: I mean Onesimus. ·He was of
12 no use to you before, but now he is useful *ᵈ* both to you and to me. ·I am sending
13 him back to you—that is to say, sending you my own heart. ·I should have liked to
keep him with me; he could have been a substitute for you, to help me while I am
14 in the chains that the gospel has brought me. ·However, I did not want to do
anything without your consent; it would have been forcing your act of kindness,
15 which should be spontaneous. ·I suppose you have been deprived of Onesimus for
16 a time, *ᵉ* merely so that you could have him back for ever, ·no longer as a slave,
but something much better than a slave, a dear brother; especially dear to me, but
17 how much more to you, both on the natural plane and in the Lord. *ᶠ* ·So if you
18 grant me any fellowship with yourself, welcome him as you would me; ·if he has
19 wronged you in any way or owes you anything, *ᵍ* put it down to my account. ·I am
writing this in my own hand: I, Paul, shall pay it back—I make no mention of a
20 further debt, that you owe your very self to me! *ʰ* ·Well then, brother, I am
21 counting on you, in the Lord; set my heart at rest, in Christ. ·I am writing with
complete confidence in your compliance, *ⁱ* sure that you will do even more than I
ask.

A personal request. Good wishes

22 There is another thing: will you get a place ready for me to stay in? I am hoping through your prayers to be restored to you.

23, 24 Epaphras, a prisoner with me in Christ Jesus, sends his greetings; •so do my fellow-workers Mark, Aristarchus, Demas and Luke.

25 May the grace of our Lord Jesus Christ be with your spirit. *j*

NOTES TO PHILEMON

a. var. 'our beloved Apphia', or 'our beloved sister Apphia'.

b. That is, the sense of fellowship with Christ and with the brothers in Christ (*see* 1 Co 1:9f), which faith establishes in the hearts of the faithful. From this faith, shot through with love (v. 5), *see* Ga 5:6b, Paul expects practical results.

c. He became his 'father' by converting him, cf. 1 Co 4:15; Ga 4:19.

d. A pun: 'Onesimus' means 'useful', cf. Ph 4:3.

e. 'Deprived' of him by God who allowed the slave to escape only so that everyone might subsequently benefit.

f. To the natural ties 'in the flesh' (such is the literal sense of the Greek, *see* Rm 7:5c) between slave and master

are added ties 'in the Lord'. Without ceasing to be a slave, cf. 1 Co 7:20–24, although Paul does suggest to Philemon that he should set Onesimus free, vv. 14–16,21, Onesimus will henceforth be a brother to Philemon. Before the one heavenly Lord, Ep 6:9, there is neither slave nor free man any more, 1 Co 12:13; Col 3:22–25.

g. It looks as if Onesimus had not only run away but had stolen something from Philemon as well.

h. Since he was one of Paul's converts.

i. To Paul obviously, but more radically to the demands of the faith.

j. add. 'Amen', cf. Ph 4:23.

THE LETTER TO THE

HEBREWS

PROLOGUE

The greatness of the incarnate Son of God

1 ¹ At many moments in the past and by many means, God spoke to our ancestors
2 through the prophets; but ·in our time, the final days, * he has spoken to us in
the person of his Son, * whom he appointed heir of all things ° and through whom
3 he made the ages. ª ·He is the reflection of God's glory and bears the impress of
God's own being, ° sustaining all things by his powerful command; and now that
he has purged sins away, he has taken his seat at the right hand of the divine
4 Majesty on high. ·So he is now as far above the angels as the title which he has
inherited is higher than their own name.

I: THE SON IS GREATER THAN THE ANGELS

Proof from the scriptures

5 To which of the angels, then, has God ever said:

> *You are my Son, today I have fathered you,*

or:

> *I shall be a father to him and he a son to me?*

6 Again, when he brings the First-born into the world, ʲ he says:

> *Let all the angels of God pay him homage.* ᵍ

7 To the angels, he says:

> *appointing the winds his messengers and flames of fire his servants,* ʰ

8 but to the Son he says:

> *Your throne, God, is for ever and ever;*

and:

> the *sceptre of ⁱ* his *kingdom* is *a sceptre of justice*;
> 9 *you love uprightness and detest evil.*

> *This is why God, your God, has anointed you*
> *with the oil of gladness, as none of your rivals.* [j]

10 And again:

> *Long ago, Lord, you laid earth's foundations,*
> *the heavens are the work of your hands.*
11 > *They pass away but you remain,*
> *they all wear out like a garment.*
12 > *Like a cloak you will roll them up, like a garment,*
> *and they will be changed.*
> *But you never alter and your years are unending.*

13 To which of the angels has God ever said:

> *Take your seat at my right hand*
> *till I have made your enemies your footstool?*

14 Are they not all ministering spirits, sent to serve for the sake of those who are to inherit salvation? [k]

An exhortation

1 **2** We ought, then, [a] to turn our minds more attentively than before to what we
2 have been taught, so that we do not drift away. ·If a message that was spoken
through angels [b] proved to be so reliable that every infringement and disobedience
3 brought its own proper punishment, ·then we shall certainly not go unpunished if
we neglect such a great salvation. It was first announced by the Lord himself, and
4 is guaranteed to us by those who heard him; ·God himself confirmed their witness
with signs and marvels and miracles of all kinds, and by distributing the gifts of the
Holy Spirit in the various ways he wills.

Redemption brought by Christ, not by angels

5 It was not under angels that he put the world to come, about which we are
6 speaking. ·Someone witnesses to this somewhere with the words:

> *What are human beings that you spare a thought for them,*
> *a child of Adam that you care for him?*
7 > *For a short while you have made him less than the angels;*
> *you have crowned him with glory and honour,*
8 > *put all things under his feet.*

For in *putting all things under* him he made no exceptions. At present, it is true,
9 we are not able to see that *all things are under him,* [c] ·but we do see Jesus, who
was *for a short while made less than the angels*, now *crowned with glory and honour*
because he submitted to death; [d] so that by God's grace [e] his experience of death
should benefit all humanity.
10 It was fitting that God, for whom and through whom everything exists, should,
in bringing many sons to glory, make perfect through suffering the leader of their
11 salvation. [f] ·For consecrator and consecrated are all of the same stock; [g] that is
12 why he is not ashamed to call them *brothers* ·in the text: *I shall proclaim your*
13 *name to my brothers, praise you in full assembly*; or in the text: ·*I shall put my*
hope in him; followed by *Look, I and the children whom God has given me*.
14 Since all the *children* share the same human nature, he too shared equally in it,

so that by his death he could set aside him who held the power of death, namely
15 the devil, *ᵏ* ·and set free *ⁱ* all those who had been held in slavery all their lives by
16 the fear of death. ·For it was not the angels that he took to himself; he took to
17 himself *the line of Abraham.* ·It was essential that he should in this way be
made completely like his brothers so that he could become a compassionate and
trustworthy high priest for their relationship to God, able to expiate the sins of the
18 people. ·For the suffering he himself passed through while being put to the test
enables him to help others when they are being put to the test.

II: JESUS THE FAITHFUL AND MERCIFUL HIGH PRIEST

Christ higher than Moses

1 3 That is why all you who are holy brothers and share the same heavenly call
should turn your minds to Jesus, the apostle and the high priest *ᵃ* of our
2 profession of faith. ·He was *trustworthy* to the one who appointed him, just like
3 *Moses,* who remained trustworthy *in all his household*; ·but he deserves a greater
glory than Moses, just as the builder of a house is more honoured than the house
4 itself. ·Every house is built by someone, of course; but God built everything that
5 exists. ·It is true that Moses was *trustworthy in the household* of God, as a *servant*
6 is, acting as witness to the things which were yet to be revealed, ·but Christ is
trustworthy as a son is, over his household. And we are his household, as long as
we fearlessly maintain the hope in which we glory. *ᵇ*

How to reach God's land of rest

7 That is why, as the Holy Spirit says:

> *If only you would listen to him today!*
8 > *Do not harden your hearts, as at the rebellion,*
> *as at the time of testing in the desert,*
9 > *when your ancestors challenged me,*
> *and put me to the test, and saw what I could do*
10 > *for forty years.*

That was why

> *that generation sickened me*
> *and I said, 'Always fickle hearts,*
> *that cannot grasp my ways!'*
11 > *And then in my anger I swore*
> *that they would never enter my place of rest.*

12 Take care, brothers, that none of you ever has a wicked heart, so unbelieving as
13 to turn away from the living God. ·Every day, as long as this *today* lasts, keep
14 encouraging one another so that none of you is *hardened* by the lure of sin, ·because
we have been granted a share with Christ only if we keep the grasp of our first
15 confidence firm to the end. ·In this saying: *If only you would listen to him today;*
16 *do not harden your hearts, as at the Rebellion,* ·who was it who *listened* and then
17 *rebelled*? Surely all those whom Moses led out of Egypt. ·And with whom was he
angry for forty years? Surely with those who sinned and whose *dead bodies fell in*
18 *the desert.* ·To whom did he *swear they would never enter his place of rest*? Surely

19 those who would not believe. ·So we see that it was their refusal to believe which prevented them from entering.

1
2 4 Let us beware, then: since the promise never lapses, none of you must think that he has come too late for the promise of *entering his place of rest.* [a] ·We received the gospel exactly as they did; but hearing the message did them no good
3 because they did not share the faith of those who did listen. [b] ·We, however, [c] who have faith, are *entering* a *place of rest*, as in the text: *And then in my anger I swore that they would never enter my place of rest.* Now God's work was all finished at
4 the beginning of the world; ·as one text says, referring to the seventh day: *And*
5 *God rested on the seventh day after all the work he had been doing.* ·And, again,
6 the passage above says: *They will never reach my place of rest.* ·It remains the case, then, that there would be some people who would reach it, and since those who first heard the gospel were prevented from entering by their refusal to believe,
7 God fixed another day, a *Today*, when he said through David in the text already
8 quoted: *If only you would listen to him today; do not harden your hearts.* ·If Joshua had led them into this place of rest, God would not later have spoken of another
9 day. There must still be, therefore, a seventh-day rest reserved for God's people,
10, 11 since to *enter the place of rest* is to *rest after your work*, as God did after his. Let us, then, press forward to *enter this place of rest*, or some of you might copy this example of refusal to believe and be lost.
12 The word of God [d] is something alive and active: it cuts more incisively than any two-edged sword: it can seek out the place where soul is divided from spirit, or
13 joints from marrow; it can pass judgement on secret emotions and thoughts. ·No created thing is hidden from him; everything is uncovered and stretched fully open to the eyes of the one to whom we must give account of ourselves.

Jesus the compassionate high priest

14 Since in Jesus, the Son of God, we have the supreme high priest who has gone
15 through to the highest heaven, [e] we must hold firm to our profession of faith. ·For the high priest we have is not incapable of feeling our weaknesses with us, but has
16 been put to the test in exactly the same way as ourselves, apart from sin. ·Let us, then, have no fear in approaching the throne of grace to receive mercy and to find grace when we are in need of help.

1 5 Every high priest is taken from among human beings and is appointed to act on their behalf in relationships with God, to offer gifts and sacrifices for sins; [a]
2 he can sympathise with those who are ignorant or who have gone astray, because
3 he too is subject to the limitations of weakness. ·That is why he has to make sin
4 offerings for himself as well as for the people. ·No one takes this honour on
5 himself; it needs a call from God, as in Aaron's case. ·And so it was not Christ who gave himself the glory of becoming high priest, but the one who said to him:
6 *You are my Son, today I have fathered you,* ·and in another text: *You are a priest*
7 *for ever, of the order of Melchizedek.* ·During his life on earth, [b] he offered up prayer and entreaty, with loud cries and with tears, to the one who had the power
8 to save him from death, [c] and, winning a hearing by his reverence, [d] ·he learnt
9 obedience, Son though he was, through his sufferings; ·when he had been
10 perfected, [e] he became for all who obey him the source of eternal salvation ·and was acclaimed by God with the title of high *priest of the order of Melchizedek.* [f]

III: THE AUTHENTIC PRIESTHOOD OF JESUS CHRIST

Christian life and theology

11 On this subject we have many things to say, and they are difficult to explain
12 because you have grown so slow at understanding. ·Indeed, when you should by
this time have become masters, you need someone to teach you all over again the
elements of the principles of God's sayings; you have gone back to needing milk,
13 and not solid food. ·Truly, no one who is still living on milk can digest the doctrine
14 of saving justice, ᵍ being still a baby. ·Solid food is for adults with minds trained by
practice to distinguish between good and bad.

The author explains his intention

1 **6** Let us leave behind us then ᵃ all the elementary teaching about Christ and go
on to its completion, without going over the fundamental doctrines again: the
2 turning away from dead actions, ᵇ faith in God, ·the teaching about baptisms ᶜ and
the laying-on of hands, about the resurrection of the dead and eternal judgement.
3 This, God willing, is what we propose to do.
4   As for those people who were once brought into the light, and tasted the gift
5 from heaven, and received a share of the Holy Spirit, ·and tasted the goodness of
6 God's message and the powers of the world to come ·and yet in spite of this have
fallen away ᵈ—it is impossible for them to be brought to the freshness of repentance
a second time, since they are crucifying the Son of God again for themselves, and
7 making a public exhibition of him. ·A field that drinks up the rain that has fallen
frequently on it, and yields the crops that are wanted by the owners who grew them,
8 receives God's blessing; ·but one that grows brambles and thistles is worthless, and
near to being cursed. It will end by being burnt.

Words of hope and encouragement

9 But you, my dear friends—in spite of what we have just said, we are sure you are
10 in a better state and on the way to salvation. ·God would not be so unjust as to
forget all you have done, the love that you have for his name or the services you
11 have done, and are still doing, for the holy people of God. ᵉ ·Our desire is that
every one of you should go on showing the same enthusiasm till the ultimate
12 fulfilment of your hope, ·never growing careless, but taking as your model those
who by their faith and perseverance are heirs of the promises.
13   When God made the promise to Abraham, he *swore by his own self*, since there
14 was no one greater he could swear by: ·*I will shower blessings on you and give you*
15 *many descendants.* ·Because of that, Abraham persevered and received fulfilment
16 of the promise. ·Human beings, of course, swear an oath by something greater
than themselves, and between them, confirmation by an oath puts an end to all
17 dispute. ·In the same way, when God wanted to show the heirs of the promise even
18 more clearly how unalterable his plan was, he conveyed it by an oath ·so that
through two unalterable factors ᶠ in which God could not be lying, we who have
fled to him might have a vigorous encouragement to grasp the hope held out to us.
19 This is the anchor our souls have, ᵍ reaching right through *inside the curtain* ·where
20 Jesus has entered as a forerunner on our behalf, having become a high *priest for*
ever, of the order of Melchizedek.

A: CHRIST'S PRIESTHOOD HIGHER THAN LEVITICAL

PRIESTHOOD

Melchizedek *

1 7 *Melchizedek, king of Salem, a priest of God Most High, came to meet Abraham*
2 *when he returned from defeating the kings*, and *blessed him*; ·and Abraham
gave him *a tenth of everything.* By the interpretation of his name, he is, first, 'king
3 of saving justice' and also *king of Salem*, that is, 'king of peace'; ·he has no father,
mother or ancestry, and his life has no beginning or ending; he is like the Son of
God. He remains a priest for ever.

Melchizedek accepted tithes from Abraham

4 Now think how great this man must have been, if the patriarch *Abraham gave him*
5 *a tenth* of the finest plunder. *ᵇ* ·We know that any of the descendants of Levi who
are admitted to the priesthood are obliged by the Law to take tithes from the
people, that is, from their own brothers although they too are descended from
6 Abraham. ·But this man, who was not of the same descent, took his tithe from
7 Abraham, and he gave his blessing to the holder of the promises. ·Now it is
8 indisputable that a blessing is given by a superior to an inferior. ·Further, in the
normal case it is ordinary mortal men who receive the tithes, whereas in that case
9 it was one who is attested as being alive. ·It could be said that Levi himself, who
10 receives tithes, actually paid tithes, in the person of Abraham, ·because he was
still in the loins of his ancestor when *Melchizedek came to meet him.*

From levitical priesthood to the priesthood of Melchizedek ᶜ

11 Now if perfection had been reached through the levitical priesthood—and this was
the basis of the Law given to the people—why was it necessary for a different kind
of priest to arise, spoken of as being *of the order of Melchizedek* rather than of the
12 order of Aaron? ·Any change in the priesthood must mean a change in the Law as
well.
13 So our Lord, of whom these things were said, belonged to a different tribe, the
14 members of which have never done service at the altar; ·everyone knows he came
from Judah, a tribe which Moses did not mention at all when dealing with priests.

The abrogation of the old law

15 This becomes even more clearly evident if another priest, of the type of Melch-
16 izedek, arises who is a priest ·not in virtue of a law of physical descent, *ᵈ* but in
17 virtue of the power of an indestructible life. ·For he is attested by the prophecy:
18 *You are a priest for ever of the order of Melchizedek.* ·The earlier commandment
19 is thus abolished, because of its weakness and ineffectiveness ·since the Law could
not make anything perfect; but now this commandment is replaced by something
better—the hope that brings us close to God.

Christ's priesthood is unchanging

20, 21 Now the former priests became priests without any oath being sworn, ·but this
one with the swearing of an oath by him who said to him, *The Lord has sworn an*
22 *oath he will never retract: you are a priest for ever*; ᵉ ·the very fact that it occurred
with the swearing of an oath makes the covenant of which Jesus is the guarantee
23 all the greater. ·Further, the former priests were many in number, because death

24 put an end to each one of them; ·but this one, because he remains *for ever*, has a
25 perpetual priesthood. ·It follows, then, that his power to save those who come to
God through him *ʲ* is absolute, since he lives for ever to intercede for them.

The perfection of the heavenly high priest

26 Such is the high priest that met our need, holy, innocent and uncontaminated, set
27 apart from sinners, and raised up above the heavens; ·he has no need to offer
sacrifices every day, as the high priests do, first for their own sins and only then for
28 those of the people; this he did once and for all *ᵍ* by offering himself. ·The Law
appoints high priests who are men subject to weakness; but the promise on oath,
which came after the Law, *ʰ* appointed the Son who is made perfect *for ever*.

B: THE SUPERIORITY OF THE WORSHIP, THE SANCTUARY
AND THE MEDIATION PROVIDED BY CHRIST THE PRIEST

The new priesthood and the new sanctuary

1 **8** The principal point of all that we have said is that we have a high priest of
exactly this kind. He *has taken his seat at the right* of the throne of divine
2 Majesty in the heavens, ·and he is the minister of the sanctuary and of the true
3 *Tent* which *the Lord*, and not any man, *set up.* *ᵃ* ·Every high priest is constituted to
4 offer gifts and sacrifices, and so this one too must have something to offer. ·In
fact, if he were on earth, he would not be a priest at all, since there are others who
5 make the offerings laid down by the Law, ·though these maintain the service only
of a model or a reflection of the heavenly realities; just as Moses, when he had the
Tent to build, was warned by God who said: *See that you work to the design that
was shown you on the mountain.*

Christ is the mediator of a greater covenant

6 As it is, he has been given a ministry as far superior as is the covenant of which he
7 is the mediator, *ᵇ* which is founded on better promises. ·If that first covenant had
8 been faultless, there would have been no room for a second one to replace it. ·And
in fact God does find fault with them; he says:

> *Look, the days are coming, the Lord declares,*
> *when I will make a new covenant*
> *with the House of Israel and the House of Judah,*
9 > *but not a covenant like the one I made with their ancestors,*
> *the day I took them by the hand to bring them out of Egypt,*
> *which covenant of mine they broke,*
> *and I too abandoned them, the Lord declares.*
10 > *No, this is the covenant I will make with the House of Israel,*
> *when those days have come, the Lord declares:*
> *In their minds I shall plant my laws*
> *writing them on their hearts.*
> *Then I shall be their God,*
> *and they shall be my people.*
11 > *There will be no further need for each to teach his neighbour,*
> *and each his brother, saying 'Learn to know the Lord!'*

> No, they will all know me,
> from the least to the greatest,
12   since I shall forgive their guilt
> and never more call their sins to mind.

13 By speaking of a *new* covenant, he implies that the first one is old. And anything old and ageing is ready to disappear.

Christ enters the heavenly sanctuary

1 9 The first covenant also *a* had its laws governing worship and its sanctuary, a
2 sanctuary on this earth. •There was a tent which comprised two compartments: the first, in which the lamp-stand, the table and the loaves of permanent offering
3 were kept, was called the Holy Place; *b* •then beyond the second veil, a second
4 compartment which was called the Holy of Holies •to which belonged the gold altar of incense, *c* and the ark of the covenant, plated all over with gold. In this were kept the gold jar containing the manna, Aaron's branch that grew the buds,
5 and the tablets of the covenant. •On top of it were the glorious winged creatures, overshadowing the throne of mercy. This is not the time to go into detail about this.

6 Under these provisions, priests go regularly into the outer tent to carry out their
7 acts of worship, •but the second tent is entered only once a year, and then only by the high priest who takes in the blood to make an offering for his own and the
8 people's faults of inadvertence. •By this, the Holy Spirit means us to see that as
9 long as the old tent stands, the way into the holy place is not opened up; •it is a symbol for this present time. *d* None of the gifts and sacrifices offered under these
10 regulations can possibly bring any worshipper to perfection in his conscience; •they are rules about outward life, connected with food and drink and washing at various times, which are in force only until the time comes to set things right.
11 But now Christ *e* has come, as the high priest of all the blessings which were to come. *f* He has passed through the greater, the more perfect tent, not made by
12 human hands, that is, not of this created order; •and he has entered the sanctuary *g* once and for all, taking with him not the blood of goats and bull calves, but his
13 own blood, having won an eternal redemption. •The blood of goats and bulls and the ashes of a heifer, sprinkled on those who have incurred defilement, may restore
14 their bodily purity. •How much more will the blood of Christ, who offered himself, blameless as he was, to God through the eternal Spirit, *h* purify our conscience from dead actions so that we can worship the living God.

Christ seals the new covenant with his blood *i*

15 This makes him the mediator of a new covenant, so that, now that a death has occurred to redeem the sins committed under an earlier covenant, those who have
16 been called to an eternal inheritance may receive the promise. •Now wherever a
17 will is in question, the death of the testator must be established; •a testament comes into effect only after a death, since it has no force while the testator is still
18. 19 alive. •That is why even the earlier covenant was inaugurated with blood, •and why, after Moses had promulgated all the commandments of the Law to the people, he took the calves' blood, the goats' blood and some water, and with these he sprinkled the book itself and all the people, using scarlet wool and hyssop;
20 saying as he did so: *This is the blood of the covenant that God has made with you.*
21 And he sprinkled both the tent and all the liturgical vessels with blood in the same

22 way. ·In fact, according to the Law, practically every purification ᶦ takes place by means of blood; and if there is no shedding of blood, there is no remission.
23 Only the copies of heavenly things are purified in this way; the heavenly things
24 themselves have to be purified ᵏ by a higher sort of sacrifice than this. ·It is not as though Christ had entered a man-made sanctuary which was merely a model of the real one; he entered heaven itself, so that he now appears in the presence of
25 God on our behalf. ·And he does not have to offer himself again and again, as the high priest goes into the sanctuary year after year with the blood that is not his
26 own, ·or else he would have had to suffer over and over again since the world began. As it is, he has made his appearance once and for all, ᶦ at the end of the last
27 age, to do away with sin by sacrificing himself. ·Since human beings die only once,
28 after which comes judgement, ·so Christ too, having offered himself only once *to bear the sin of many*, will manifest himself a second time, sin being no more, to those who are waiting for him, to bring them salvation. ⁻

SUMMARY: CHRIST'S SACRIFICE SUPERIOR TO THE SACRIFICES OF THE MOSAIC LAW

The old sacrifices ineffective

1   **10** So, since the Law contains no more than a reflection of the good things which were still to come, and no true image of them, it is quite incapable of bringing the worshippers to perfection, by means of the same sacrifices repeatedly
2 offered year after year. ·Otherwise, surely the offering of them would have stopped, because the worshippers, when they had been purified once, would have
3 no awareness of sins. ·But in fact the sins are recalled year after year in the
4, 5 sacrifices. ·Bulls' blood and goats' blood are incapable of taking away sins, ᵐ ·and that is why he said, on coming into the world:

> *You wanted no sacrifice or cereal offering,*
> *but you gave me a body.*
6 > *You took no pleasure in burnt offering or sacrifice for sin;*
7 > *then I said, 'Here I am, I am coming,'*
> *in the scroll of the book it is written of me,*
> *to do your will, God.*

8 He says first *You did not want* what the Law lays down as the things to be offered, that is: *the sacrifices, the cereal offerings, the burnt offerings and the sacrifices for*
9 *sin*, and *you took no pleasure* in them; ·and then he says: *Here I am! I am coming*
10 *to do your will*. He is abolishing the first sort to establish the second. ·And this *will* was for us to be made holy by the *offering* of the *body* of Jesus Christ made once and for all.

The efficacy of Christ's sacrifice

11 Every priest stands at his duties every day, offering over and over again the same
12 sacrifices which are quite incapable of taking away sins. ·He, on the other hand, has offered one single sacrifice for sins, and then *taken his seat for ever, at the right*
13, 14 *hand of God*, ·where he is now waiting *till his enemies are made his footstool*. ·By

virtue of that one single offering, he has achieved the eternal perfection of all who
15 are sanctified. ·The Holy Spirit attests this to us, for after saying:

16   *No, this is the covenant I will make with them,*
       when those days have come.

the Lord says:

       In their minds I will plant my Laws
       writing them on their hearts,
17   *and I shall never more call their sins to mind,*
       or their offences.

18 When these have been forgiven, there can be no more sin offerings.

IV: PERSEVERING FAITH

The Christian opportunity

19 We have then, brothers, complete confidence through the blood of Jesus in
20 entering the sanctuary,*ᵇ* ·by a new way which he has opened for us, a living
21 opening through the curtain, that is to say, his flesh. ·And we have the *high priest*
22 over all *the sanctuary of God.* ·So as we go in, let us be sincere in heart and filled
   with faith, our hearts sprinkled and free from any trace of bad conscience, and our
23 bodies washed with pure water. ·Let us keep firm in the hope we profess, because
24 the one who made the promise is trustworthy. ·Let us be concerned for each other,
25 to stir a response in love and good works. ·Do not absent yourself from your own
   assemblies, as some do, but encourage each other; the more so as you see the
   Day *ᶜ* drawing near.

The danger of apostasy

26 If, after we have been given knowledge of the truth, we should deliberately commit
27 any sins, then there is no longer any sacrifice for them. *ᵈ* ·There is left only the
   dreadful prospect of judgement and of *the fiery wrath* that is to *devour your*
28 *enemies.* ·Anyone who disregards the Law of Moses is ruthlessly *put to death on*
29 *the word of two witnesses or three;* ·and you may be sure that anyone who tramples
   on the Son of God, and who treats *the blood of the covenant* which sanctified him
   as if it were not holy, and who insults the Spirit of grace, will be condemned to a
30 far severer punishment. ·We are all aware who it was that said: *Vengeance is mine;*
31 *I will pay them back.* And again: *The Lord will vindicate his people.* ·It is a dreadful
   thing to fall into the hands of the living God.

Motives for perseverance

32 Remember the great challenge of the sufferings that you had to meet after you
33 received the light, *ᵉ* in earlier days; ·sometimes by being yourselves publicly
   exposed to humiliations and violence, and sometimes as associates of others who
34 were treated in the same way. ·For you not only shared in the sufferings of those
   who were in prison,*ᶠ* but you accepted with joy being stripped of your belongings,
35 knowing that you owned something that was better and lasting. ·Do not lose your
36 fearlessness now, then, since the reward is so great. ·You will need perseverance
   if you are to do God's will and gain what he has promised.

> Only *a little while now, a very little while,*
37 > *for come he certainly will before too long.*
38 > *My upright person will live through faith*
> *but if he draws back, my soul will take no pleasure in him.*

39 We are not the sort of people who *draw back*, and are lost by it; we are the sort who keep *faith* until our souls are saved.

The exemplary faith of our ancestors

1 **11** Only faith can guarantee the blessings that we hope for, or prove the
2 existence of realities that are unseen. *ᵃ* ·It is for their faith that our ancestors are acknowledged.

3 It is by faith that we understand that the ages were created by a word from God, so that from the invisible the visible world came to be. *ᵇ*

4 It was because of his faith that Abel offered God a better sacrifice than Cain, and for that he was acknowledged as upright when *God* himself made acknowledgement of *his offerings*. Though he is dead, he still speaks by faith.

5 It was because of his faith that Enoch was taken up and did not experience death: *he was no more, because God took him*; because before his assumption he
6 was acknowledged to *have pleased God.* ·Now it is impossible to please God without faith, since anyone who comes to him must believe that he exists and rewards those who seek him. *ᶜ*

7 It was through his faith that Noah, when he had been warned by God of something that had never been seen before, took care to build an ark to save his family. His faith was a judgement on the world, *ᵈ* and he was able to claim the uprightness which comes from faith.

8 It was by faith that Abraham obeyed the call to *set out* for a country that was the inheritance given to him and his descendants, and that *he set out* without knowing
9 where he was going. ·By faith he *sojourned* in the Promised Land as though it were not his, living in tents with Isaac and Jacob, who were heirs with him of the
10 same promise. ·He looked forward to the well-founded city, designed and built by God.

11 It was equally by faith that Sarah, in spite of being past the age, was made able to conceive, because she believed that he who had made the promise was faithful
12 to it. ·Because of this, there came from one man, and one who already had the mark of death on him, descendants *as numerous as the stars of heaven and the grains of sand on the seashore which cannot be counted.*

13 All these died in faith, before receiving any of the things that had been promised, but they saw them in the far distance and welcomed them, recognising that they
14 were only *strangers and nomads on earth.* ·People who use such terms about
15 themselves make it quite plain that they are in search of a homeland. ·If they had meant the country they came from, they would have had the opportunity to return
16 to it; ·but in fact they were longing for a better homeland, their heavenly homeland. That is why God is not ashamed to be called their God, since he has founded the city for them.

17 It was by faith that Abraham, *when put to the test, offered up Isaac.* He offered to sacrifice *his only son* even though he had yet to receive what had been promised,
18 and he had been told: *Isaac is the one through whom your name will be carried on.*
19 He was confident that God had the power even to raise the dead; and so, figuratively speaking, *ᵉ* he was given back Isaac from the dead.

20 It was by faith that this same Isaac gave his blessing to Jacob and Esau for the
21 still distant future. ·By faith Jacob, when he was dying, blessed each of Joseph's
22 sons, *bowed in reverence, as he leant on his staff.* ·It was by faith that, when he was
about to die, Joseph mentioned the Exodus of the Israelites and gave instructions
about his own remains.
23 It was by faith that Moses, when he was born, *was kept hidden by his parents for
three months*; because they *saw* that he was a *fine* child; they were not afraid of the
24 royal edict.*ʲ* ·It was by faith that, *when he was grown up,* Moses refused to be
25 known as the son of Pharaoh's daughter ·and chose to be ill-treated in company
26 with God's people rather than to enjoy the transitory pleasures of sin. ·He
considered that the humiliations offered to the Anointed *ᵍ* were something more
precious than all the treasures of Egypt, because he had his eyes fixed on the
27 reward. ·It was by faith that he left Egypt without fear of the king's anger; he held
28 to his purpose like someone who could see the Invisible. ·It was by faith that he
kept *the Passover* and sprinkled *the blood* to prevent *the Destroyer* from touching
29 any of their first-born sons. ·It was by faith they crossed the Red Sea as easily as
dry land, while the Egyptians, trying to do the same, were drowned.
30 It was through faith that the walls of Jericho fell down when the people had
31 marched round them for seven days. ·It was by faith that Rahab the prostitute
welcomed the spies and so was not killed with the unbelievers.
32 What more shall I say? There is not time for me to give an account of Gideon,
33 Barak, Samson, Jephthah, or of David, Samuel and the prophets. ·These were
men who through faith conquered kingdoms, did what was upright and earned the
34 promises. They could keep a lion's mouth shut, ·put out blazing fires and emerge
unscathed from battle. They were weak people who were given strength to be
35 brave in war and drive back foreign invaders. ·Some returned to their wives from
the dead by resurrection; and others submitted to torture, refusing release so that
36 they would rise again to a better life. ·Some had to bear being pilloried and
37 flogged, or even chained up in prison. ·They were stoned, or sawn in half,*ʰ* or
killed by the sword; they were homeless, and wore only the skins of sheep and
38 goats; they were in want and hardship, and maltreated. ·They were too good for
the world and they wandered in deserts and mountains and in caves and ravines.
39 These all won acknowledgement through their faith, but they did not receive
40 what was promised, since God had made provision for us to have something better,
and they were not to reach perfection except with us. *ⁱ*

The example of Jesus Christ

1 **12** With so many witnesses in a great cloud all around us, we too, then, should
throw off everything that weighs us down and the sin that clings so closely,
2 and with perseverance keep running in the race which lies ahead of us. ·Let us
keep our eyes fixed on Jesus, who leads us in our faith and brings it to perfection:
for the sake of the joy which lay ahead of him, he endured the cross, disregarding
3 the shame of it, and *has taken his seat at the right* of God's throne. ·Think of the
way he persevered against such opposition from sinners *ᵉ* and then you will not
4 lose heart and come to grief. ·In the fight against sin, you have not yet had to keep
fighting to the point of bloodshed.

God's fatherly instruction

5 Have you forgotten that encouraging text in which you are addressed as sons?

> My son, do not scorn correction from the Lord,
> do not resent his training,
6   for the Lord trains those he loves,
> and chastises every son he accepts.

7 Perseverence is part of your *training*;*ᵇ* God is treating you as his *sons*. Has there
8 ever been any *son* whose father did not *train* him? ·If you were not getting this
9 training, as all of you are, then you would be not *sons* but bastards. ·Besides, we
have all had our human fathers who punished us, and we respected them for it; all
10 the more readily ought we to submit to the Father of spirits, and so earn life. ·Our
human fathers were training us for a short life and according to their own lights;
11 but he does it all for our own good, so that we may share his own holiness. ·Of
course, any discipline is at the time a matter for grief, not joy; but later, in those
12 who have undergone it, it bears fruit in peace and uprightness. ·So *steady all weary*
13 *hands and trembling knees* ·and make your crooked paths straight; then the injured
limb will not be maimed, it will get better instead.

Unfaithfulness is punished

14 *Seek peace* with all people, and the holiness without which no one can ever see the
15 Lord. ·Be careful that no one is deprived of the grace of God and that no *root of*
bitterness should begin to grow and make trouble; this can poison a large number.
16 And be careful that there is no immoral person, or anyone worldly minded like
17 Esau,*ᶜ who sold his birthright* for one single meal. ·As you know, when he wanted
to obtain the blessing afterwards, he was rejected and, though he pleaded for it
with tears, he could find no way of reversing the decision.

The two covenants *ᵈ*

18 What you have come to is nothing*ᵉ* known to the senses: not a *blazing fire*, or
19 *gloom* or *total darkness*, or a *storm*; ·or *trumpet-blast* or the *sound of a voice*
speaking which made everyone that heard it beg that no more should be said to
20 them. ·They could not bear the order that was given: *If even a beast touches the*
21 *mountain, it must be stoned*. ·The whole scene was so terrible that Moses said, 'I
22 am afraid and trembling.' ·But what you have come to is Mount Zion and the city
of the living God, the heavenly Jerusalem where the millions of angels have
23 gathered for the festival, ·with the whole Church of first-born sons, enrolled as
citizens of heaven. You have come to God himself, the supreme Judge, and to the
24 spirits of the upright who have been made perfect; ·and to Jesus, the mediator of
a new covenant, and to purifying blood which pleads more insistently than Abel's.
25 Make sure that you never refuse to listen when he speaks. If the people who on
earth refused to listen to a warning could not escape their punishment, how shall
26 we possibly escape if we turn away from a voice that warns us from heaven?*ᶠ* ·That
time his voice made the earth shake, but now he has given us this promise: *I am*
27 *going to shake the earth once more and* not only the earth but *heaven as well*. ·The
words *once more* indicate the removal of what is shaken, since these are created
28 things, so that what is not shaken remains. *ᵍ* ·We have been given possession of an
unshakeable kingdom. Let us therefore be grateful and use our gratitude to
29 worship God in the way that pleases him, in reverence and fear. *ʰ* ·For our *God* is a
consuming fire.

APPENDIX

Final recommendations

13 Continue to love each other like brothers,[a] ·and remember always to welcome strangers, for by doing this, some people have entertained angels without knowing it. ·Keep in mind those who are in prison, as though you were in prison with them; and those who are being badly treated, since you too are in the body. ·Marriage must be honoured by all, and marriages must be kept undefiled, because the sexually immoral and adulterers will come under God's judgement. Put avarice out of your lives and be content with whatever you have; God himself has said: *I shall not fail you or desert you*, ·and so we can say with confidence: *With the Lord on my side, I fear nothing: what can human beings do to me*?

Faithfulness

Remember your leaders,[b] who preached the word of God to you, and as you reflect on the outcome of their lives, take their faith as your model. ·Jesus Christ is the same today as he was yesterday and as he will be for ever.[c] ·Do not be led astray by all sorts of strange doctrines: it is better to rely on grace for inner strength than on food, which has done no good to those who concentrate on it. ·We have our own altar[d] from which those who serve the Tent have no right to eat. ·The bodies of the animals *whose blood is taken into the sanctuary* by the high priest *for the rite of expiation are burnt outside the camp*, ·and so Jesus too suffered outside the gate to sanctify the people with his own blood.[e] ·Let us go to him, then, *outside the camp*, and bear his humiliation. ·There is no permanent city for us here; we are looking for the one which is yet to be. ·Through him, *let us offer God* an unending *sacrifice* of praise, the fruit of the lips of those who acknowledge his name. ·Keep[f] doing good works and sharing your resources, for these are the kinds of sacrifice that please God.

Obedience to religious leaders

Obey your leaders and give way to them; they watch over your souls because they must give an account of them; make this a joy for them to do, and not a grief—you yourselves would be the losers. ·Pray for us; we are sure that our own conscience is clear and we are certainly determined to behave honourably in everything we do. ·I ask you very particularly to pray that I may come back to you all the sooner.

EPILOGUE

News, good wishes and greetings

I pray that the God of peace, *who brought back* from the dead[g] our Lord Jesus, the great *Shepherd of the sheep, by the blood that sealed an eternal covenant*, ·may prepare you to do his will in every kind of good action; effecting in us all whatever is acceptable to himself through Jesus Christ, to whom be glory for ever and ever, Amen.

I urge you, brothers,[k] to take these words of encouragement kindly; that is why I have written to you briefly.

I want you to know that our brother Timothy has been set free. If he arrives in time, he will be with me when I see you. ·Greetings to all your leaders and to all

25 God's holy people. God's holy people in Italy send you greetings. ·Grace be with you all.

NOTES TO HEBREWS

1 **a.** In the fullness of time. Mk 1:15; Ga 4:4c, the last times or the last days begin. Ac 2:17; 1 P 1:20.

b. After the prophets. God sends an envoy who is no longer a mere messenger like the others; he is 'Son', cf. Mk 12:2-6; Rm 1:4c, he is even the Word, Jn 1:1a,14m.

c. To be a son implies having the right to inherit, cf. Mt 21:38; Ga 4:7. Here, however, God is credited with the handing over of the whole creation because the inheritance in question is messianic and eschatological.

d. Hebraism for the whole of creation.

e. These two metaphors are borrowed from the *sophia* and *logos* theologies of Alexandria. Ws 7:25-26; they express both the identity of nature between Father and Son, and the distinction of person. The Son is the brightness, the light shining from its source, which is the bright glory, *see* Ex 24:16f. of the Father ('Light from Light'). He is also the replica, *see* Col 1:15d, of the Father's substance, like an exact impression made by a seal on a clay or wax, cf. Jn 14:9.

f. Either at the incarnation or at his enthronement in glory, cf. v. 3; 2:5; Ep 1:20-21; Ph 2:9-10. 'First-born' is a title of honour, Col 1:15,18; Rv 1:5.

g. The quotation is from Dt 32:43, in 'the Song of Moses'.

h. The author, thinking perhaps of the theophany on Sinai, 2:2b, takes this LXX text as a description of the nature of angels, subtle and changeable and therefore inferior to that of the Son reigning from his eschatological throne.

i. var. 'your', *see* Ps 45:6 LXX.

j. The godhead, attributed in the Psalms to the priest-king by way of hyperbole, is here attributed to Jesus the Messiah as of pre-eminent right, v. 3. The divine Christ enjoys an eternal kingship.

k. Compared with the Son, angels are only servants used to save human beings.

2 **a.** If God speaks to us by a Son who saves us and who is superior to the angels, how can we not take notice of such an initiative?

b. The Law, given through the intermediary of angels, *see* Ga 3:19l, and sanctioned by severe penalties.

c. The first Christians, despised and persecuted, are still waiting for the coming of God's reign on earth, 2 P 3:4. Although Christ has already entered his glory, his reign on earth has to continue in time till he has conquered all his enemies (1:13) before his full and final triumph. 1 Co 15:25; Ep 1:21-22; Ph 3:20-21.

d. Christ was glorified precisely because he suffered, and his triumph seals the redeeming value of his death.

e. 'God's grace'; rare var. 'without God' which may have been a gloss meant to emphasis that the Messiah could suffer only in his human, not in his divine, nature; but it could be an allusion to what Jesus cried out from the cross (Mt 27:46), or it could be taken as meaning that Christ died for all people, but not for God, cf. 1 Co 15:27.

f. By dying and fulfilling the will of God, Christ becomes the one perfect Saviour, responsible for the entry of human beings into the glory of God, 2:17-18; 4:15; 5:2-3. The verb 'makes perfect' comes frequently in the letter to denote the various effects of Christ's work on the relationship of humanity to God, 11:40i.

g. From the context, the translation could read 'form a single whole'. The following verses stress this union in the flesh and blood, v. 14, which the Son of God took upon himself, and so they introduce the central theme of the letter, the high-priesthood of Christ, v. 17.

h. Sin and death are related because both derive from Satan whose reign is the opposite of the reign of Christ.

i. By his resurrection, which is the guarantee to believers that they will rise, Rm 8:11g.

3 **a.** Christ is both 'apostle', i.e. someone 'sent' by God to the human race, *see* Jn 3:17,34; 5:36; 9:7; Rm 1:1b; 8:3; Ga 4:4, and high priest representing the human race before God, *see* Heb 2:17; 4:14; 5:5,10; 6:20; 7:26; 8:1; 9:11; 10:21.

b. add. 'unwavering right till the end', *see* v. 14.

4 **a.** The comparison between Moses and Jesus, 3:1seq., cf. Ac 7:20; Jn 1:21t, now develops into one between Israelites and Christians. The Israelites, who doubted the word of God, did not enter the place of rest which was the Promised Land, 3:17-19. But God's promise cannot remain unfulfilled, so it applies to Christians, invited to enter into the repose of heavenly blessedness, of which the Promised Land was only a type.

b. e.g. Joshua and Caleb, *see* Nb 13-14. • var. 'because (the message) was not accompanied by faith in what they heard'.

c. 'however'; var. 'therefore'. • 'a place of rest', var. 'the place of rest'.

d. The word of God mediated by the prophets and then by the Son, of which an instance has just been given in Ps 95:7-11, is living and active in believers, 1 Th 2:13e. It is this word which judges, cf. Jn 12:48; Rv 19:13, the movements and secret intentions of the heart, in its quest for the 'rest' of God. On soul and spirit, see 1 Th 5:26g.

e. First mention of heaven where, according to the letter, Christ exercises his priestly function. Seated at the right hand of God, 1:3; 8:1, he belongs no less than God to the eternal realities; his sacrifice, accomplished once and for all, 7:26-27g, takes on a perfect and eternal value, 8:1-4a; 9:11-12,11e,23-24. The God of Christian hope is the fulfilment of this salvation in the heavenly city, 9:28; 12:23-24.

5 **a.** The priest's office of sacrificing (*see* Lv 1; 4; 9), connected with Aaron rather than with Moses, is to be the subject of a full development. Sacrifice, related to sin, shows that the priest is in solidarity with believers before God.

b. The emphasis of this section is on humanity: a priest must be human since he represents human beings, and he must share their sufferings since he must feel compassion for them, *see* 2:17-18; 4:15. Jesus suffered in this way all through his life on earth, and especially in his agony and death.

c. Not saved from dying, since that was the whole purpose of his life, Jn 12:27seq., but rescued from death after dying. Ac 2:24seq. God transformed his death by raising him to glory after it, 2:9; Jn 12:27seq.; 13:31seq.; 17:5; Ph 2:9-11.

d. The term implies respect and submission. It was because the prayer of Christ in Gethsemane was a prayer of total submission to the will of his Father, Mt 26:39,42, that it was heard and answered.

e. Perfected in his office of Priest and Victim.

f. This sets off all the themes developed in ch. 6-10.

g. 'The doctrine of saving justice', like 'God's prophecies', can mean either the OT, cf. 2 Tm 3:16, or the whole body of doctrine. Here it seems to mean all that Christ taught

about the saving justice of God as applied to humanity.
Rm 3:21–26, and especially about his own priesthood of
mediation, prefigured by Melchizedek, the 'king of saving
justice' Heb 7:2.

6 a. In spite of the difficulties his readers will have, the
author is going to challenge them by formulating the difficult
doctrine already mentioned in 5:11.

b. Anything done without faith and the divine life is
called a 'dead' action because it is done in the context of sin.
Rm 1:18–3:20, which leads to death, Rm 5:12,21; 6:23; 7:5;
1 Co 15:56; Ep 2:1; Col 2:13; Jm 1:15; cf. Jn 5:24;
1 Jn 3:14.

c. Not only Christian baptism, see Ac 1:5f; Rm 6:4a,
but all the washings, lustrations and purificatory rites then
practised, including the 'baptism of John', Ac 18:25; 19:1–5.

d. The irreparable apostasy of rejecting Christ and
ceasing to believe in the power of his sacrifice to save.

e. The same phrase is used, Rm 15:25,31; 2 Co 8:4;
9:1,12, about a collection for the church in Jerusalem. 'God's
holy people' means all Christians, but especially members of
the mother church at Jerusalem, and in particular the
apostles, see Ac 9:13g.

f. The promise of God and the oath joined to it, see
Gn 12:1a; Rm 4:11e, for God does not deceive, 10:23; 11:11;
2 Tm 2:13; Tt 1:2.

g. Anchor: symbol of stability in the classical world,
adopted in Christian iconography of 2nd century as a symbol
of hope.

7 a. Melchizedek the priest-king: here seen as an OT
type of Christ. Gn 14 is oddly silent about any ancestors or
descendants of Melchizedek and this suggested the idea that
he represented the eternal priesthood, vv. 1–3, cf. vv. 15–17
and Ps 110:4. He was superior to Abraham in so far as
Abraham offered him, Gn 14:20, a tithe of everything that
had been captured, so *a fortiori*, the argument goes, he was
superior to all the descendants of Abraham, including the
Levites, v. 4seq.

b. The tithe paid to levitical priests, Dt 14:22d, was
both the stipend for their ministry at the altar and acknowledgement that as priests they were members of a higher
class than those who paid. Levi (in the person of Abraham)
could have paid his tithe only if Melchizedek were a priest of
an even higher class than himself.

c. The argument here is based on Ps 110:4. The Psalm,
in praise of a Davidic king, is interpreted as a prophecy of
the King-Messiah, declaring that he will not be descended
from Levi and that his priesthood will therefore be 'of the
order of Melchizedek' and eternal. This implies that when
Christ comes, his sort of priesthood will replace the levitical
priesthood, and this in turn will necessitate a new law since
the old one was concerned only with the levitical priesthood,
vv. 12,16seq., 21.

d. The law that restricted the priesthood of Levi to his
physical descendants, see Nb 1:47seq.; 3:5seq.; Dt 10:8seq.;
18:1seq.; 33:8seq.

e. add. 'of the order of Melchizedek'.

f. Christ the eternal priest exercises his office of
mediator and intercessor, see Rm 8:34; 1 Jn 2:1. His
entreaty is analogous to that of the Holy Spirit approaching
God on behalf of the faithful, Rm 8:27.

g. The unique sacrifice of Jesus is the culmination of
salvation-history, Ac 1:7i. It closes a long epoch of preparation, 1:1seq.; cf. Rm 10:4; it occurs at 'the appointed
time', Rm 3:26m; Ga 4:4c, and it begins the eschatological
epoch. Though the Last Day, Rm 2:6b; 1 Co 1:8e, will
follow, 2 Co 6:2a, only at some unspecified, 1 Th 5:1b, time
in the future; salvation for the human race has been in
essence certain from the moment when, in the person of
Jesus, it died to sin and rose to live again. Heb makes a
special point of how the whole of this hope flows from the
unique, unrepeatable sacrifice of Jesus, 7:27; 9:12,26,28;
10:10; cf. Rm 6:10; 1 P 3:18. Being unrepeatable, 10:12–14,
this sacrifice is different from all others in the OT, since these

had to be repeated again and again because they were unable
actually to save anyone.

h. Cf. the promise made before the Law was given,
Ga 3:17.

8 a. The argument so far has been to prove that what
Christ is, i.e. an eternal and perfect priest, is superior to
what the levitical priests are, since they are all mortals and
sinners, ch. 7; now the argument goes on to show that what
Christ does is equally superior to what the levitical priests
do: Christ's sanctuary is better because it is in heaven, 8:1–5,
see 9:11seq., while the one on earth is only a copy of it,
Ex 25:40; and the covenant brought by the mediation of
Christ is a better covenant, Heb 6–13.

b. Technically Christ is the one and only true mediator:
he is truly human and truly divine, Col 2:9, and so the one
and only intermediary, Rm 5:15–19; 1 Tm 2:5; cf.
1 Co 3:22–23; 11:3, between God and the human race. He
unites and reconciles them, 2 Co 5:14–20. Through him
came grace, Jn 1:16–17; Ep 1:7, and complete revelation,
1:1–2. In heaven he continues to intercede for those who are
faithful to him, 7:25f.

9 a. om. 'also'.

b. In the desert Tent-Sanctuary, Ex 25–26 (compare
the Temple of Solomon, 1 K 6) a curtain hung between the
Holy Place and the Holy of Holies, Ex 26:33. Only the high
priest ever went into the Holy of Holies and he did so only
once a year on *yom kippur*, the Day of Expiation, see
Lv 16:1a,2.

c. Ex 30:6; 40:26 says that the incense altar, Ex 30:1a,
was in the Holy of Holies. Heb follows a different liturgical
tradition.

d. The spiritual meaning of this ceremonial arrangement is that under the old covenant the people had no access
to God. Under the new covenant, Christ himself is the way
to the Father, Jn 14:6; see Heb 10:19b. The abrogation of
the old worship can thus be appropriately symbolised by the
Temple curtain splitting wide open at the death of Jesus,
Mt 27:51 and par.

e. The Jewish ceremonial of expiation, v. 7; Lv 16, is
replaced by the unique sacrifice, Heb 7:27g, of Christ's
blood, Heb 9:14; Rm 3:24j, which reopens the way to God,
Heb 10:1f,19; cf. Jn 14:6d; Ep 2:18.

f. var. 'blessings already won'.

g. In his ascension Christ 'passed through' all the
successive heavenly spheres that form the 'Holy Place' of the
celestial Tent, and so came into the presence of God in the
celestial 'Holy of Holies'.

h. var. 'the Holy Spirit', cf. Rm 1:4c.

i. This section is parallel to 8:6–13: it shows that the
death of Christ was essential for him to act as mediator. It
does this by making use of a pun: the Greek word *diatheke*
can mean 'pact', as in vv. 15,18–20, or 'last will and testament', as in vv. 16–17; this makes it possible for the author
to argue that a 'pact' or covenant suggests the death of a
'testator'. All pacts were sealed with the shedding of blood,
Ex 24:6–8. Hence Christ had to die to found the new
covenant, see 7:22; 8:6–10; 12:24; Mt 26:28i.

j. e.g. the altar, Lv 8:15; 16:18–19; the priests,
Lv 8:24–30; the Levites, Nb 8:15; the sinful people,
Lv 9:15–18; a mother, Lv 12:7–8, etc.; one exception, see
Lv 5:11.

k. The 'purification' of the sanctuary, whether the
earthly or the heavenly one, does not necessarily imply any
previous 'impurity': it is a consecratory and inaugural rite.

l. The sacrifice of Christ is unique, 7:27g: being offered
'at the end of the last age' (lit. 'at the completion of the
aeons'), i.e. the end of human history, there is no need for it
to be repeated, since it wipes out sin, not with non-human
('alien') blood, but with Christ's own blood, see 9:12–14, so
its effect is unconditional.

m. The first coming of Christ gave him a direct relationship to sin, Rm 8:3; 2 Co 5:21. The second coming of Christ
will, since the redemption is complete, have no connection

with sin. Christians wait for this *parousia* that will take place at the Judgement. Rm 2:6b; 1 Co 1:8e.

10 a. Going beyond the prophets who called for purity at heart in the cult. Is 1:11-13; Jr 6:20; 11:15; Ho 6:6; Am 5:21n. the letter declares that the old sacrifices were ineffective, *see* 9:13-14. Only Christ's spiritual sacrifice can sanctify mankind, vv. 12-14.

b. Only the high priest could enter the Holy of Holies. i.e. the presence of God, and he could do so only once a year. From now on, all who are faithful will be able to reach God through Christ, *see* 4:14-16; 7:19,25; 9:11; 10:9; Rm 5:2; Ep 1:4; 2:18; 3:12; Col 1:22.

c. When Christ returns at the end of history, *see* 1 Co 1:8e. This verse may refer to the signs preceding the *parousia, see* 2 Th 2:1a.

d. The sin of apostasy or deliberate revolt against God. *see* 6:6d. The fire, v. 27, is the traditional weapon God uses in anger. Is 26:11; Mt 3:11-12; Mk 9:48-49f; Rv 11:5.

e. 'Enlightenment' or 'illumination' in NT, as in patristic writers, always refers to baptism. 6:4; Ep 5:14 (*see* Rm 6:4a).

f. var. 'of my chains', which would be an allusion to Paul's captivity. Ph 1:7; Col 4:18.

11 a. var. 'Faith is the assurance of things hoped for (heaven) and the conviction of things unwanted (hell).' The Jewish Christians to whom the author is writing have been discouraged by persecution, so he emphasises that it is only what is future and what is invisible that concerns hope. This verse was adopted as a theological definition of faith, i.e. the anticipated and assured possession of heavenly realities, *see* 6:5; Rm 5:2; Ep 1:13seq. The examples taken from the lives of OT saints are meant to illustrate how faith is the source of patience and strength.

b. Creation seen with the eye of faith reveals 'unseen reality'; before creation everything real existed in God from whom everything comes.

c. The faith that is essential for salvation has two objects: belief in the existence of one personal God, Ws 13:1, who by his very nature cannot be seen, Jn 1:18; 20:29; Rm 1:20; 2 Co 5:7; Col 1:15; 1 Tm 1:17; 6:16, and belief that God will reward all effort spent in searching for him; cf. Mt 5:12 and par.; 6:4,6,18; 10:41seq., and par.; 16:27; 20:1-16; 25:31-46; Lk 6:35; 14:14; Rm 2:6; 1 Co 3:8,14; 2 Co 5:10; Ep 6:8; 2 Tm 4:8,14; 1 P 1:17; 2 Jn 8; Rv 2:23; 11:18; 14:13; 20:12-13; 22:12. *See also* Ps 62:12e. The absence of all mention of Christ is explained by the fact that Enoch precedes any of the covenants, cf. Jn 17:3; 20:31.

d. Noah's confidence in what God had said 'convicts' a sinner, cf. Ws 4:16; Mt 12:41.

e. lit. 'by a parable'. The saving of Isaac from death prefigures the general resurrection and, according to traditional exegesis, the death and resurrection of Jesus.

f. Some authorities insert the story of the murdered Egyptian here, *see* Ex 2:11-12; Ac 7:24.

g. In the psalm, God's 'Anointed' who is 'insulted' refers to the people of God, v. 25, consecrated to Yahweh. Ex 19:6. The author of Heb applies the text to Christ himself on whose account Moses (through faith, since the Messiah was still in the future) suffered, *see* 10:33; 13:13.

h. Some apocryphal books say this was how King Manasseh had Isaiah executed. • add. 'put to the test'.

i. The eschatological epoch of 'perfection' was inaugurated by Christ, 2:10; 5:9; 7:28; 10:14, and access to the divine life has been made available only by him, 9:11seq.; 10:19seq. The OT saints, who could not be 'perfected' by the Law, 7:19; 9:9; 10:1, had thus to wait until the resurrection of

Christ before they could enter the perfect life of heaven. 12:23; cf. Mt 27:52seq.; 1 P 3:19h.

12 a. lit. 'endured contradictions of sinners against himself'; var. '. . . against themselves'.

b. The trials of life are regarded here as part of the 'correction' or 'punishment' which are the basis of a father's education of his son. according to the OT tradition, particularly in the later books. Jb 5:17; 33:19; Ps 94:12; Si 1:27; 4:17; 23:2. The trials, being sent by God, reveal and prove that he is our Father.

c. This refers to the sin committed by Esau when he surrendered the position that was his by birth, of being heir to the messianic promises.

d. The approach to God. 4:16; 10:22. no longer occurs. v. 18. in an awe-inspiring theophany as on Sinai, but, v. 22, in a city built by God, for which the OT saints yearned, 11:10,16. the heavenly city. 4:14; Rv 21:1a. With the angels are assembled round the triumphant Mediator all Christians. cf. Lk 10:20; Jm 1:18, whom he has sanctified and perfected. Heb 10:14; 11:40i; 12:14.

e. var. 'a mountain'.

f. The contrast is not between Moses and Christ so much as between the beneficiaries of the two covenants. The old covenant regulated life on earth. as a pale shadow of the heavenly life introduced by the new one. Hence to turn away from the latter merits a more severe punishment.

g. Cosmic upheavals are traditional metaphors in apocalypses for the time when God intervenes to introduce a new régime. *see* Am 8:9h; Mt 24:1a; 1 Co 1:8e.

h. This is the real conclusion, and an apt one for a letter that lays such emphasis on the liturgy. The 'unshakeable' kingdom summarises vv. 22-24. God reigns over both his angels and his saints in the Kingdom of Heaven, the eternal and spiritual Jerusalem. From now on Christians are able to enter this kingdom and live there a life that is a eucharistic liturgy.

13 a. For love between the brothers, *see* Rm 12:10; 1 Th 4:9; 1 P 1:22; 2 P 1:7; 1 Jn 3:14-18.

b. The first leaders of the community, responsible for proclaiming the word of God. v. 7, and guiding conduct, v. 17.

c. This declaration, introduced by the mention of the word of God and of faith, v. 7, underlines the central theme of the leaders' preaching. They may change or disappear, but Christ remains, and it is to him that Christians owe their allegiance. The recommendations which follow take up again the themes of the letter, stressing the presence of Jesus and the firm confidence of believers.

d. Not the table used for the Eucharist, but either the cross on which Christ was sacrificed, or Christ himself through whom we offer the sacrifice of prayer to God. Non-Christian Jews who still 'served the tabernacle' cannot participate.

e. On the Day of Expiation the high priest went into the Holy of Holies and sprinkled it with the blood of animals that had been killed, and the bodies of these animals were burnt outside the camp. This prefigured how Jesus as expiatory victim was to be killed outside the walls of Jerusalem. The lesson drawn from this is that Christians should break with Judaism.

f. add. 'therefore'.

g. The resurrection is here mentioned explicitly, but it is always implied when Heb mentions the glorified Christ, 1:3.

h. These last lines form a kind of tail-piece to the letter.

INTRODUCTION TO
THE LETTERS
TO ALL CHRISTIANS

There are seven New Testament letters which are not Pauline and which, in spite of having no other obvious connection, were very soon grouped together. Three of these letters are attributed to John, two to Peter and the other two to James and Jude, but these attributions must in each case be evaluated in the light of the literary convention of the time by which literary works could be attributed to great figures of the past who were not concerned, at any rate directly, with their composition. These letters were already given the title 'universal' or 'catholic' by the end of the second century; it is not certain why, possibly because most are addressed to the whole Christian Church and not to particular communities or individuals.

The *Letter of James* became accepted in the Church only gradually. If its canonicity seems to have been no problem in Egypt, where Origen quotes it as inspired scripture, Eusebius of Caesarea at the beginning of the fourth century recognises that it is still contested by some people. In the Syriac-speaking Churches it was only in the course of the fourth century that it was inserted in the canon of the NT. In Africa Tertullian and Cyprian have no knowledge of it, Mommsen's *Catalogue (c. 360)* still does not include it. At Rome it does not feature in the Canon of Muratori attributed to St Hippolytus (*c.* 200) and it is very doubtful whether Clement of Rome and the Shepherd of Hermas (*see* below) quote it. One may conclude therefore that it was not universally recognised in the Churches of East and West until near the end of the fourth century.

When the Churches do come to accept the canonical nature of this letter, they generally identify its author with the James, 'brother of the Lord', Mt 13:55*o*; cf. 12:46 and par., who played an important part in the earliest Christian community in Jerusalem, Ac 12:17f; 15:13–21; 21:18–26; 1 Co 15:7; Ga 1:19; 2:9,12, and who was put to death by Jews about the year 62 (Josephus, Hegesippus). He is obviously not the apostle James, son of Zebedee, Mt 10:2 and par., martyred by Herod in 44, Ac 12:2, though he could theoretically be identified with the apostle James, son of Alphaeus, Mt 10:3 and par.; even

THE LETTERS
TO ALL CHRISTIANS

early writers, however, were doubtful and most critics nowadays reject author-ship by the apostle. Paul's turn of phrase in Ga 1:19 is ambiguous.

But the real problem is a different one, and deeper. It concerns the ascription itself of the letter to James 'brother of the Lord'. The ascription is not without its difficulties. If the letter had really been written by this outstanding person-ality, the difficulty it had in winning a place in the Church as inspired Scripture is difficult to understand. Further, it was composed in Greek, and with an elegance, wealth of vocabulary and sense of rhetoric (*diatribe*) which are surprising for a Galilaean; certainly James could have secured the help of a disciple of good hellenistic culture, but this is a guess which cannot be proved. Finally, and above all, the letter shows a very marked affinity to writings whose composition is dated to the very end of the first century or the beginning of the second, notably the first letter of Clement of Rome and the Shepherd of Hermas. It has often been claimed that these two letters made considerable use of the letter of James, but recognition is today growing more and more widespread that these affinities are explained by the use of common sources and by the fact that the authors of these different works had to face up to similar problems. Consequently many scholars today place the composition of the letter of James at the end of the first century or the beginning of the second. The archaic character of its Christology would then be due not to the antiquity of its composition but to the fact that it issues from Judaeo-Christian circles, heirs to the thought of James, brother of the Lord, unaffected by the development of early Christian theology.

If, however, the authenticity of the letter is maintained, its composition must be placed before 62, the date of James' death. In this case two hypotheses are possible, according to the view adopted of the relationships between Jm and Ga/Rm on the subject of justification by faith (*see* below). For some scholars it is James who is engaging in polemic against Paul, or rather against Christians who deform the teaching of Paul. For others, less and less numerous, it is Paul who wanted to oppose the ideas of James, whose letter must in this case have been written about the years 45–50; this would explain the archaic character of its Christology. But the observations we have made above make such an early date most unlikely.

The letter is addressed to the 'twelve tribes of the Dispersion', 1:1, i.e. to the Jewish Christians scattered all over the Graeco-Roman world but concen-trated in countries near Palestine like Syria and Egypt. The whole tone of the letter shows that it was intended for Jewish converts and presumes that the readers are familiar with the Old Testament since, unlike Paul and the author of the letter to the Hebrews, James hardly ever makes use of direct quotations but argues from the imprecise and rather general allusions that underlie the whole text. His two chief sources are the Old Testament Wisdom literature, on which he bases his moral lessons, and the teaching found in the gospels. Some critics have thought of the letter as an exclusively Jewish product, but, on the contrary, ideas and even characteristic expressions of Jesus can be detected all through it, not so much by explicit quotations from written texts, as by reference to a living, oral tradition. James is a Judaeo-Christian sage who has rethought the maxims of the Jewish Wisdom tradition in the light of his Master's teachings and is able to re-present them in an original way.

More a sermon than a letter, it probably reflects the regular teaching of Judaeo-Christian assemblies and consists of a series of moral exhortations linked either by a common theme or sometimes by nothing more than verbal assonances. The sort of subjects dealt with are: how to behave in time of trial, Jm 1:1–12; 5:7–11; the origin of temptation, 1:13–18; how to control the tongue, 1:26; 3:1–18; good relations and sympathy with one's neighbour, 2:8,13; 3:13–4:2; 4:11seq.; the power of prayer, 1:5–8; 4:2seq.; 5:13–18 etc. In 5:14seq. is the *locus classicus* on the sacramental anointing of the sick.

There are two main themes. The first praises the poor and threatens the rich, 1:9–11; 1:27–2:9; 4:13–5:6, showing a concern for the lowly, God's favoured ones, that follows an Old Testament tradition but particularly the Beatitudes, Mt 5:3d. The second insists that Christians must do good and not be content with a faith that produces nothing, 1:22–27; 2:10–26; this leads on to a section, 2:14–26, that ridicules the preaching of a faith completely unrelated to good works, and some have seen this as aimed against Paul. Jm and Ga/Rm have many significant points of contact, particularly noticeable in the different ways they interpret Old Testament texts on Abraham. James may be opposing Paul himself or, more probably, certain Christians who drew pernicious conclusions from Paul's teaching. Two points are worth remembering: first, that beneath the clash between their different positions, Paul and James agree on essentials, *see* 2:14f; secondly, that the problem of relating faith to works is inherent in the data of Jewish religion and may have been a traditional topic that James and Paul dealt with independently of each other.

Jude who calls himself 'brother of James', v. 1, is also, it appears, one of the 'brothers of the Lord', Mt 13:55 and par. There is no reason to identify him with the apostle of the same name, Lk 6:16; Ac 1:13; cf. Jn 14:22, especially as he refers to himself as being outside the apostolic body, v. 17. Nor is it likely that an anonymous author would have adopted the name, since Jude was not sufficiently prominent to lend authority to a letter. The letter was accepted as canonical by many of the Churches as early as 200, though its use of two apocryphal sources, the *Book of Enoch* in vv. 6,14seq., and the *Assumption of Moses* in v. 9, had prompted certain hesitations; but to quote contemporary Jewish writings is hardly equivalent to recognising their inspiration.

Jude's purpose in writing this letter is to denounce the false teachers who are a danger to Christian faith. He threatens them with the divine punishments familiar from Jewish tradition, vv. 5–7, and also seems to base his description of their false teaching on the same traditions, v. 11. He nowhere states precisely what these doctrines were, so they cannot be identified with second-century Gnosticism. He accuses them of irreligion and immorality, in particular of blasphemies against the Lord Christ and the angels, vv. 4,8–10. These may have been part of the syncretistic tendencies denounced in Colossians, the Pastoral Letters and Revelation.

The letter must be dated fairly late in the first century: the apostles are quoted as belonging to the past, vv. 17seq.; the faith is now something fixed and 'handed on once for all', v. 3; and the author appears to be acquainted with Paul's letters. It is true that 2 Peter borrows from Jude and is therefore later, but the 'Second Letter of Peter' could have been written after Peter's death (*see below*). It can be firmly dated to the last years of the apostolic age.

Two of these 'universal' letters are attributed to Peter. 1 Peter introduces the name of the apostle in the opening verse, 1:1, and has always been accepted in every part of the Church. Clement of Rome seems to have used it; Polycarp certainly did, and since the time of Irenaeus it has been expressly attributed to Peter. The apostle writes from Rome (Babylon, 5:13), and calls Mark, who is with him, his 'son'. Very little is known about Peter's last years; according to tradition he went to Rome and was martyred there under Nero (in 64 or possibly 67). His letter is addressed to the Christians 'of the Dispersion', and names five provinces, 1:1, which represent practically the whole of Asia Minor. From what he says, 1:14,18; 2:9seq.; 4:3, it seems that most of them were converted pagans, though there may have been some Judaeo-Christians among them. He was obviously obliged to send them a letter in Greek—James had done the same with less reason—and though Peter's Greek is unsophisticated it is too accurate and fluent for a fisherman from Galilee. Unlike the letter from James, the name of a disciple and secretary is mentioned who may have helped: this is Silvanus, 5:12, usually identified with the Silvanus who had been a companion of Paul, Ac 15:22x.

The purpose of the letter is to help its readers' faith in a time of trial. Some critics think this may refer to a persecution under Domitian or Trajan, which would date the letter much later than Peter; but the allusions in the letter are not strong enough to make this conclusion inevitable, since it seems that this 'time of trial' could refer rather to the personal malice and spiteful calumnies caused by the strictly moral life led by converts among those whose sins they no longer shared, 2:12; 3:16; 4:4,12–16.

Another argument against Petrine authorship is based on the liberal use the letter makes of John, Romans and Ephesians, and on the surprisingly little direct use it makes of the gospel. There are, however, many reminiscences of the gospel, but these are so implicit as to constitute an argument against the idea that the author merely wanted to pretend the apostle had written it. There is a tendency perhaps to exaggerate the number of points of contact with James and Paul. Specifically Pauline themes, e.g. the abolition of the Jewish Law, the Body of Christ, etc., do not appear at all, and though some themes appear that are best known from Paul's letters, yet these are themes common to all early Christian theology, e.g. the redemptive nature of the death of Jesus; faith and baptism, etc. Certain formulae and certain Old Testament quotations which were common in the primitive preaching are being increasingly identified by critics, and any early writings could well have drawn on these independently. It is also worth remembering that Silvanus was a disciple of both apostles and that some scholars detect affinities not only between 1 Peter and Paul but also between 1 Peter and two groups of writings whose climate is Petrine: i.e. Mark and the discourses of Peter in Acts.

If the substance of the letter had been in existence before Peter's death in 64 or 67, Silvanus could still have given it its present form some years later, working on Peter's instructions and authority. This hypothesis would be more likely if it could be proved that the letter was made up of fragments. It is suggested that, for example, a baptismal homily, 1:13–4:11, is one such fragment, but these identifications remain very tentative.

Though a very practical letter, it is also a valuable summary of apostolic theology. The dominating theme is fortitude in trial, for which Christ himself is the model, 2:21–25; 3:18; 4:1. Christians must suffer patiently like him when their trials are due to their faith and to their saintly lives, 2:19seq.; 3:14; 4:12–19; 5:9, i.e. if, in return for evil, they offer charity, obedience to civil authority, 2:13–17, and gentleness to all, 3:8–17; 4:7–11,19. There is one obscure passage, 3:19seq., cf. 4:6; the 'preaching' of Christ can be taken as an announcement either of salvation or of punishment; the 'spirits in prison' can be taken either as the wicked who were drowned in the Flood or as the fallen angels of biblical and apocalyptic tradition. On either view, this passage refers the 'preaching' to the moment Jesus died and is the chief source for the doctrine of the Descent into Hell.

The Second Letter of Peter claims to have been written by the apostle himself. He is named in the opening address, 1:1, the prediction of Peter's death is made by Jesus to the author himself, 1:14, who also claims to have witnessed the transfiguration, 1:16–18, and who alludes to a former letter that is obviously meant to be 1 Peter.

The purpose of the letter is twofold: to warn against false teachers, ch. 2, and to allay anxiety due to the delay of the *parousia*, ch. 3. It is possible that both these difficulties existed before Peter's death, but other considerations make Petrine authorship doubtful and suggest a later date. The vocabulary is notably different from that of 1 Peter; the whole of ch. 2 is obviously a free repetition of Jude; an accepted Pauline corpus seems to be already in existence, 3:15seq.; the apostolic body is referred to, with the prophets, as a thing of the past and as if the author did not belong to it. These difficulties caused early writers to hesitate, and there is no sure evidence that the letter was accepted at all before the third century, and some, according to Origen, Eusebius and Jerome, explicitly refused to accept it. Most critics nowadays also reject the Petrine authorship, though the writer may have had some claim to represent Peter: perhaps he belonged to a group of Peter's disciples, perhaps he filled out one of Peter's writings with ideas from the letter of Jude. This is what we should call forgery, but the ancients had different conventions about authorship and pseudonymity.

The letter has been definitely accepted by the Church as canonical, and Christians accept it as an authoritative document from the apostolic age. The doctrine it teaches supports this: note especially the vocation of all Christians to the 'share in the divine nature', 1:4; the way scriptural inspiration is defined, 1:20seq.; the assurance that eventually the *parousia* will come though no one can know when; the prediction of a new world free of all injustice after the old world has been destroyed by fire, 3:3–13.

For the three letters of John *see* the Introduction to the Gospel and Letters of John pp. 163–64.

THE LETTER OF

JAMES

Address and greetings

1 From James, servant of God and of the Lord Jesus Christ. Greetings *a* to the twelve tribes of the Dispersion. *b*

Trials a privilege

2 My brothers, consider it a great joy when trials of many kinds come upon you,
3. 4 for you well know that the testing of your faith produces perseverence, ·and perseverence must complete its work *c* so that you will become fully developed, complete, not deficient in any way.

Prayer with confidence

5 Any of you who lacks wisdom must ask God, who gives to all generously *d* and
6 without scolding; it will be given. ·But the prayer must be made with faith, and no trace of doubt, because a person who has doubts is like the waves thrown up in the
7. 8 sea by the buffeting of the wind. ·That sort of person, in two minds, ·inconsistent in every activity, *e* must not expect to receive anything from the Lord.

The lot of the rich

9 It is right that the brother in humble circumstances should glory in being lifted
10 up, *f* ·and the rich in being brought low. For the rich will last no longer than *the*
11 *wild flower*; ·the scorching sun comes up, *g* and the *grass withers*, its *flower falls*, its beauty is lost. It is the same with the rich: in the middle of a busy life, the rich will wither.

Temptation

12 *Blessed is anyone who perseveres* when trials come. Such a person is of proven worth and will win the prize of life, the crown that the Lord *h* has promised to those who love him. *i*
13 Never, when you are being put to the test, *j* say, 'God is tempting me'; God
14 cannot be tempted by evil, and he does not put anybody to the test . ·Everyone is put to the test by being attracted and seduced by that person's own wrong desire.
15 Then the desire conceives and gives birth to sin, and when sin reaches full growth, it gives birth to death.

Receiving the Word and putting it into practice

16, 17 Make no mistake about this, my dear brothers: ·all that is good, all that is perfect, is given us from above; it comes down[k] from the Father of all light;[l] with him there is no such thing as alteration, no shadow caused by change.

18 By his own choice he gave birth to us by the message of the truth[m] so that we should be a sort of first-fruits of all his creation. [n]

True religion

19 Remember this, my dear brothers: everyone should be *quick to listen* but *slow* to
20 speak and slow to human anger; ·God's saving justice is never served by human
21 anger; · so do away with all impurities and remnants of evil. Humbly welcome the Word which has been planted in you and can save your souls.
22 But you must do what the Word tells you and not just listen to it and deceive
23 yourselves. ·Anyone who listens to the Word and takes no action is like someone
24 who looks at his own features in a mirror and, ·once he has seen what he looks
25 like, goes off and immediately forgets it. ·But anyone who looks steadily at the perfect law of freedom[o] and keeps to it—not listening and forgetting, but putting it into practice—will be blessed in every undertaking.
26 Nobody who fails to keep a tight rein on the tongue can claim to be religious;
27 this is mere self-deception; that person's religion is worthless. ·Pure, unspoilt religion, in the eyes of God our Father,[p] is this: coming to the help of orphans and widows in their hardships, and keeping oneself uncontaminated by the world.

Respect for the poor

1 2 My brothers, do not let class distinction enter into your faith in Jesus Christ,
2 our glorified Lord. [a] ·Now suppose a man comes into your synagogue,[b] well-dressed and with a gold ring on, and at the same time a poor man comes in, in
3 shabby clothes, ·and you take notice of the well-dressed man, and say, 'Come this way to the best seats'; then you tell the poor man, 'Stand over there' or 'You can
4 sit on the floor by my foot-rest.' ·In making this distinction among yourselves have you not used a corrupt standard?
5 Listen, my dear brothers: it was those who were poor according to the world that God chose, to be rich in faith[c] and to be the heirs to the kingdom which he
6 promised to those who love him. ·You, on the other hand, have dishonoured the
7 poor. Is it not the rich who lord it over you? ·Are not they the ones who drag you into court, who insult the honourable name which has been pronounced over
8 you?[d] Well, the right thing to do is to keep the supreme Law of scripture: *you will*
9 *love your neighbour as yourself*; ·but as soon as you make class distinctions, you are committing sin and under condemnation for breaking the Law.
10 You see, anyone who keeps the whole of the Law but trips up on a single point,
11 is still guilty of breaking it all. ·He who said, '*You must not commit adultery*' said also, '*You must not kill.*' Now if you commit murder, you need not commit adultery
12 as well to become a breaker of the Law. ·Talk and behave like people who are
13 going to be judged by the law of freedom. ·Whoever acts without mercy will be judged without mercy[e] but mercy can afford to laugh at judgement.

Faith and good deeds[f]

14 How does it help, my brothers, when someone who has never done a single good
15 act claims to have faith? Will that faith bring salvation? ·If one of the brothers or

16 one of the sisters is in need of clothes and has not enough food to live on, ·and one of you says to them, 'I wish you well; keep yourself warm and eat plenty,' without
17 giving them these bare necessities of life, then what good is that? ·In the same way faith: if good deeds do not go with it, it is quite dead. *
18   But someone may say: * So you have faith and I have good deeds? Show me this faith of yours without deeds, then! It is by my deeds that I will show you my faith.
19 You believe in the one God—that is creditable enough, but even the demons have
20 the same belief, and they tremble with fear. * ·Fool! Would you not like to know
21 that faith without deeds is useless? ·Was not Abraham our father* justified by his
22 deed, because he *offered his son Isaac on the altar?* ·So you can see that his faith
23 was working together with his deeds; his faith became perfect by what he did. * ·In this way the scripture was fulfilled: *Abraham put his faith in God, and this was considered as making him upright*; and he received the name 'friend of God'.
24   You see now that it is by deeds, and not only by believing, that someone is
25 justified. ·There is another example of the same kind: Rahab the prostitute, was she not justified by her deeds because she welcomed the messengers* and showed
26 them a different way to leave? ·As a body without a spirit is dead, so is faith without deeds. *

Uncontrolled language

1   **3** Only a few of you, my brothers, should be teachers, * bearing in mind that we
2   shall receive a stricter judgement. ·For we all trip up in many ways.
     Someone who does not trip up in speech has reached perfection and is able to
3 keep the whole body on a tight rein. * ·Once * we put a bit in the horse's mouth, to
4 make it do what we want, we have the whole animal under our control. ·Or think of ships: no matter how big they are, even if a gale is driving them, they are
5 directed by a tiny rudder wherever the whim of the helmsman decides. ·So the tongue is only a tiny part of the body, but its boasts are great. Think how small a
6 flame can set fire to a huge forest; ·The tongue is a flame too. Among all the parts of the body, the tongue is a whole wicked world;* it infects the whole body;
7 catching fire itself from hell, it sets fire to the whole wheel of creation. * ·Wild animals and birds, reptiles and fish of every kind can all be tamed, and have been
8 tamed, by humans; ·but nobody can tame the tongue—it is a pest that will not keep
9 still, full of deadly poison. ·We use it to bless the Lord and Father, but we also use
10 it to curse people who are made in God's image: ·the blessing and curse come out
11 of the same mouth.* My brothers, this must be wrong—·does any water supply
12 give a flow of fresh water and salt water out of the same pipe? ·Can a fig tree yield olives, my brothers, or a vine yield figs? No more can sea water yield fresh water.

Real wisdom and its opposite

13 Anyone who is wise or understanding among you* should from a good life give
14 evidence of deeds done in the gentleness of wisdom. ·But if at heart you have the bitterness of jealousy, or selfish ambition, do not be boastful or hide the truth
15 with lies; ·this is not the wisdom that comes from above, but earthly, human and
16 devilish. ·Wherever there are jealousy and ambition, there are also disharmony
17 and wickedness of every kind; ·whereas the wisdom that comes down from above is essentially something pure; it is also peaceable, kindly and considerate; it is full of mercy and shows itself by doing good; nor is there any trace of partiality or
18 hypocrisy in it. ·The peace sown by peacemakers brings a harvest of justice.

Disunity among Christians

1 4 Where do these wars and battles between yourselves first start? Is it not
2 precisely in the desires fighting inside your own selves? ·You want something
and you lack it; so you kill. You have an ambition that you cannot satisfy; so you
fight to get your way by force. * It is because you do not pray that you do not
3 receive; ·when you do pray and do not receive, it is because you prayed wrongly,
wanting to indulge your passions.
4 Adulterers!* Do you not realise that love for the world is hatred for God?
5 Anyone who chooses the world for a friend is constituted an enemy of God. ·Can
you not see the point of the saying in scripture, 'The longing of the spirit he sent to
6 dwell in us is a jealous longing.'?* ·But he has given us an even greater grace, as
scripture says: *God opposes the proud but he accords his favour to the humble.*
7 Give in to God, then; resist the devil, and he will run away from you. The nearer
8 you go to God, the nearer God will come to you. Clean your hands, you sinners,
9 and clear your minds, you waverers. ·Appreciate your wretchedness, and weep
for it in misery. Your laughter must be turned to grief, your happiness to gloom. *
10 Humble yourselves before the Lord and he will lift you up.
11 Brothers, do not slander one another. Anyone who slanders a brother, or
condemns one, is speaking against the Law and condemning the Law. But if you
condemn the Law, you have ceased to be subject to it and become a judge over it.
12 There is only one lawgiver *and he is the only judge and has the power to save
or to destroy. Who are you to give a verdict on your neighbour?*

A warning for the rich and self-confident

13 Well now, you who say, 'Today or tomorrow, we are off to this or that town; we
14 are going to spend a year there, trading, and make some money.' ·You never
know what will happen tomorrow: you are no more than a mist that appears for a
15 little while and then disappears. * ·Instead of this, you should say, 'If it is the
16 Lord's will, we shall still be alive to do this or that.' ·But as it is, how boastful and
17 loud-mouthed you are! Boasting of this kind is always wrong. ·Everyone who
knows what is the right thing to do and does not do it commits a sin.

1 5 Well now, you rich! Lament, weep for the miseries that are coming to you.
2,3 Your wealth is rotting, your clothes are all moth-eaten. ·All your gold and
your silver are corroding away, and the same corrosion will be a witness against
you and eat into your body. It is like a fire which you have stored up for the final
4 days. * ·Can you hear crying out against you the wages which you kept back from
the labourers mowing your fields? The cries of the reapers have reached the ears
5 of the Lord Sabaoth. ·On earth you have had a life of comfort and luxury; in the
6 time of slaughter you went on eating to your heart's content. * ·It was you who
condemned the upright and killed them; they offered you no resistance.

The coming of the Lord

7 Now be patient, brothers, until the Lord's coming. Think of a farmer: how
patiently he waits for the precious fruit of the ground until it has had the autumn
8 rains * and the spring rains! ·You too must be patient; do not lose heart, because
9 the Lord's coming will be soon. * ·Do not make complaints against one another,
brothers, so as not to be brought to judgement yourselves; the Judge is already to
10 be seen waiting at the gates. ·For your example, brothers, in patiently putting up
11 with persecution, take the prophets who spoke in the Lord's name; ·remember it
is those who had perseverance that we say are the blessed ones. You have heard

of the perseverance of Job and understood the Lord's purpose, realising that *the Lord is kind and compassionate.*

12 Above all, my brothers, do not swear by heaven or by the earth or use any oaths at all. If you mean 'yes', you must say 'yes'; if you mean 'no', say 'no'. Otherwise you make yourselves liable to judgement.

13 Any one of you who is in trouble should pray; ' anyone in good spirits should
14 sing a psalm. ·Any one of you who is ill should send for the elders of the church, and they must anoint the sick person with oil in the name of the Lord *ʲ* and pray
15 over him. The prayer of faith will save the sick person and the Lord will raise him
16 up again; and if he has committed any sins, he will be forgiven. ·So confess your sins to one another, and pray for one another to be cured; *ᵍ* the heartfelt prayer of
17 someone upright works very powerfully. ·Elijah *ʰ* was a human being as frail as ourselves— he prayed earnestly for it not to rain, and no rain fell for three and a
18 half years; then he prayed again and the sky gave rain and the earth gave crops.

19 My brothers, if one of you strays away from the truth, and another brings him
20 back to it, ·he may be sure *ⁱ* that anyone who can bring back a sinner from his erring ways will be saving his soul from death and *covering over many a sin.*

NOTES TO JAMES

1 a. lit. 'Be joyful' or 'Rejoice', a normal Gk greeting. V. 2 makes a pun with the word.

b. In OT days the 'Dispersion' (*diaspora*) was used to describe the Jews who had emigrated from their country, cf. Jdt 5:19; Ps 147:2; *see also* Jn 7:35. Here the reference is to the Jewish Christians living in the Graeco-Roman world, *see* Ac 2:5–11. The twelve tribes prefigured the new People of God, Ac 26:7; Rv 7:4b.

c. For James, as for Judaism, faith must, for perfection, issue in deeds, 2:14f, cf. 1 Th 1:3. The central message of 2:14–26 is already hinted at.

d. i.e. simply, or unreservedly.

e. This inconsistency contrasts with simplicity of heart, Gn 8:21c, and the firmness of attitudes which results from it.

f. The rich are to share in the exaltation of the poor, 1 S 2:7–8; Ps 72:4,12; 113:7–9; Lk 1:52; *see* Zp 2:3d, but only by humbling themselves with them.

g. Or 'The sun comes up with a scorching wind.'

h. om. 'the Lord'.

i. At the outcome of temptation, vv. 2–4, anyone who loves God will receive a reward, 1 Co 9:25; 1 P 5:4; Rv 2:10.

j. *See* 1 Co 10:13f. One who allows himself to be drawn into evil must not blame the fault on God who cannot desire evil. Sin comes from within, Rm 7:8, and culminates in a state wholly opposed to the crown of life, v. 12; Rm 6:23.

k. om. (*Vet. Lat.*) 'from above'.

l. i.e. the maker of the stars, Gn 1:14–18, and source of spiritual light, cf. 1 P 2:9; 1 Jn 1:5. The imagery following this phrase is suggested by astronomy. • var. 'no such thing as alteration due to the movement of a shadow'.

m. This 'word of truth' is everything God has revealed to the human race, it is also called the law of freedom or the supreme Law, *see* 1:21–25; 2:8.

n. Jm speaks of 'grace' only in 4:6. He mentions here the equivalent of it in the new birth through the Word of God, Jn 1:12j; 3:3; 1 P 1:23, which creates the People of God as its first-born, cf. Dt 18:4; 1 Co 15:20; Rv 8:23; 16:5. This Word is planted in human hearts by the saving preaching of the gospel, v. 21, and the faith which is the acceptance of such preaching, *see* 1 Th 2:13d. There are traces here of baptismal catechesis.

o. Like the word of truth, v. 18, this law is Christian revelation accepted and put into practice, *see* Mt 5:17–19h; 7:24–27; Jn 13:17. It sets people free, 2:12, by the keeping of the commandments. Paul will see in the liberty of the Christian a privilege of the New Law, of faith, Rm 3:27; 6:15g; 7:1; Ga 4:21seq.

p. Cf. Mt 6:9; 1 Co 15:24; Ep 5:20. The OT uses the phrase in Dt 32:6; cf. Ws 2:16; Si 23:1,4; Is 63:16. Worship in the Spirit which is acceptable to God takes a concrete form in right conduct and the service of the weak, *see* Dt 27:19; Is 11:17; Jr 5:28.

2 a. lit. 'our Lord Jesus Christ of glory', *see* 1 Co 2:8h.

b. James is writing to Jewish Christians; it is possible that they may even have still been attending Jewish synagogues, or it may be his word for the Christian 'assembly' for liturgical services.

c. i.e. poor in money, rich in faith, *see* 1:9f.

d. In the OT the name of Yahweh pronounced over someone dedicated that person to the divine protection, Is 43:7; Am 9:12. In the NT the only means of salvation is the name of Jesus invoked, e.g. at baptism, Ac 2:21m. Alternative translation 'the honourable name you bear'.

e. Judgement in the sense of condemnation. Judgement belongs to God alone, author of the Law, 4:11–12; 5:9; cf. Ps 9:8. He will reward the practice of the Law, 1:25; 2:8, which is summed up as being that which mercy requires.

f. The different points of view of James and Paul, Rm 3:20–31; Ga 2:16; 3:2,5,11seq.; Ph 3:9, are not wholly irreconcilable. Paul is anxious to rule out the view that a human being can earn salvation without having faith in Christ, since such a reliance on self-made sanctity would be contradicted by the radical sinfulness of unredeemed humanity, Rm 1:18–3:20; Ga 3:22, and would make faith in Christ superfluous, Ga 2:17; *see* Rm 1:16h. But Paul does not deny that God's chosen one who has been made holy by grace must show faith by actually loving, Ga 5:6; cf. 1 Th 1:3; 2 Th 1:11; Phm 6, and in this way obeying the Law, Rm 8:4, i.e. the Law or commandment of Christ and his Spirit, Rm 8:2; Ga 6.2, which is the commandment to love, Rm 13:8–10; Ga 5:14. It is perfectly true, however, that in order to teach the same truth as Paul, James in a different context and under different circumstances explains the case of Abraham in a completely different way from Paul.

g. lit. 'it is dead by itself'.

h. The same opponents as in vv. 14 and 16.

i. The refusal of the demons to believe in the God they recognise, see Mk 1:24,34, does not prevent them from fearing his future anger.

j. Jewish tradition thought of Abraham as the just man faithful to God, Si 44:19-21k, friend of God, 2 Ch 20:7; Is 41:8, father of believers, cf. Mt 3:8; Jn 8:39. On this point Jm agrees with Paul, Rm 4:1,16.

k. No more than Paul does Jm regard Abraham's faith as a deed, Gn 15:6, quoted v. 23; Rm 4:3; Ga 3:6. But he lays more stress on the deeds to which faith, the perfect law, gives birth, 1:25; 2:8.

l. 'messengers'; var. 'spies'. The story of the two spies sent by Joshua was popular among the Jews, see Heb 11:31.

m. Vv. 17,20,24 all point to the comparison of a body deprived of the breath of life.

3 a. Those who aspire to this respected office, Mt 23:8; Ac 13:1; 1 Co 12:28k, must weigh the responsibility which falls on them. The whole of ch. 3 seems to have been written with them in mind.

b. Several images are going to teach the lesson that control of the tongue is the mark of complete self-control. The theme is a classic one both in the Gk moralists and in the wisdom literature.

c. var. 'Look!', cf. v. 4.

d. Alternative punctuation, 'The tongue is a fire, a whole wicked world in itself.'

e. The expression 'wheel (or cycle) of the created world', appears to have come from the Gk orphic mysteries.

f. The antithesis 'bless-curse' is common in the OT, Gn 12:3; 27:29; Nb 23:11; 24:9; Jos 8:34. But the Christian cannot curse, see Lk 6:28; Rm 12:4; 1 P 3:9.

g. Continuing the writer's advice to those who aspire to be teachers, v. 1. Wisdom is seen in its effects, see 1:22-25; 2:14-26.

4 a. Alternative translation (textual corrections): 'You want something and you lack it; you are envious and jealous and you cannot get it; you fight to get your way by force.' This fight is not the interior struggle in each individual, see Rm 7:23; 1 P 2:11, but dissension and rancour among believers, perhaps real conflicts in which Christians took an active part.

b. The Gk term is feminine and so recalls the imagery of Israel, the unfaithful wife of Yahweh, and is traditional in the OT, Ho 1:2b, cf. 2 Co 11:2.

c. The quotation is hard to identify. On God's jealousy, see Dt 4:24f. Probably these are reminiscences drawn for example from Gn 2:7; 6:3 or Ezk 36:27, cf. 1 Th 4:8. Rm 8:26-27 draws its inspiration from the same source: God has put in us his Spirit which makes us desire what he desires; therefore our requests are granted, see Mt 18:19-20; Jn 14:13.

d. Cf. Is 32:11seq.; Jr 4:13seq.; Mi 2:4; Zc 11:2seq.

e. var. 'There is only one: the lawgiver . . .'

f. Judgement belongs to God alone, 1:12; 2:4; 5:7-8; Mt 7:1 and par.. 1a; cf. Ps 5:10c; 9:8. Whoever judges a neighbour goes against the golden rule of love, 2:8, and usurps the place of divine justice.

g. The wisdom theme of human frailty, Ps 39:5-7,11; 102:3; Ws 2:4; 5:9-14, which obliges a person to submit and trust to God.

5 a. The misfortunes of the rich will be apparent only at the Judgement, 5:7-9. We, however, are living already in the Last Days, cf. 2 Co 6:2a; cf. Is 5:8-10; Am 2:6-7; 8:4-8; Mt 6:19.

b. Perhaps an allusion to the acts of violence with which the rich oppressed the just, v. 6; cf. Ps 44:22; Ws 2:10-20; Jr 2:1-3.

c. 'rains', var. 'fruits'.

d. The expectation of the coming (parousia, 1 Co 15:23n) is the ultimate motive of Christian patience, 1:2-4,12; 1 Th 3:13; 1 P 4:7; 5:10. The comparison with the labourer recalls Mk 4:26-29.

e. The common factor in vv. 13-18 is prayer, with stress on the case of the sick and the sinner; then vv. 16^b-18, on the power of those who pray well.

f. om. 'of the Lord'. • Jm assumes that the practice of which he speaks is well known. In this anointing in the name of the Lord, with prayers said by the 'elders', Ac 11:30p, for the relief of illness and the remission of sins, the Church has seen the earliest form of the sacrament of Anointing of the Sick.

g. This mutual confession and prayer for each other, instead of being recommendations only to the sick, v. 15, are here urged on all Christians. Nothing special, however, may be deduced about sacramental confession.

h. The figure of Elijah was as popular with Christians as with Jews. Jm underlines that this man of prayer was like ourselves.

i. var. 'you can be sure'. • Fraternal love and pardon can bring back those who have strayed, see Mt 18:15,21-22k; 1 Th 5:14, and in return will bring advantage on the Day of Judgement to anyone who exercises them, 1 P 4:8; cf. Ezk 3:19; 33:9; Dn 12:3. So ends the letter, without the normal greeting.

1 PETER

THE FIRST LETTER OF PETER

Address. Greetings

1 Peter, apostle of Jesus Christ, to all those living as aliens *a* in the Dispersion *b* of Pontus, Galatia, Cappadocia, Asia and Bithynia, who have been chosen,
2 in the foresight of God the Father, to be made holy by the Spirit, obedient to Jesus Christ and sprinkled with his blood: *c* Grace and peace be yours in abundance.

Introduction. The inheritance of Christians

3 Blessed be God *d* the Father of our Lord Jesus Christ, who in his great mercy has given us a new birth into a living hope through the resurrection of Jesus Christ
4 from the dead ·and into a heritage that can never be spoilt or soiled and never
5 fade away. It is reserved in heaven for you ·who are being kept safe by God's power through faith until the salvation which has been prepared is revealed at the final point of time. *e*

Faithfulness to Christ and love of Christ

6 This is a great joy to you, even though for a short time yet you must bear all sorts
7 of trials; ·so that the worth of your faith, more valuable than gold, which is perishable even if it has been tested by fire, may be proved—to your praise and
8 honour when Jesus Christ is revealed. ·You have not seen him, yet you love him; and still without seeing him you believe in him and so are already filled with a joy
9 so glorious that it cannot be described; ·and you are sure of the goal of your faith, that is, the salvation of your souls. *f*

The hope of the prophets

10 This salvation was the subject of the search and investigation of the prophets who
11 spoke of the grace you were to receive, ·searching out the time and circumstances for which the Spirit of Christ, *g* bearing witness in them, was revealing the sufferings
12 of Christ and the glories to follow them. ·It was revealed to them that it was for your sake and not their own that they were acting as servants delivering the message which has now been announced to you by those who preached to you the gospel through the Holy Spirit sent from heaven. Even the angels long to catch a glimpse of these things.

The demands of the new life
Holiness of the newly baptised

13 Your minds, then, must be sober and ready for action; put all your hope in the
14 grace brought to you by the revelation of Jesus Christ. ·Do not allow yourselves
15 to be shaped by the passions of your old ignorance, ᵏ ·but as obedient children, be
   yourselves holy in all your activity, ⁱ after the model of the Holy One who calls us,
16, 17 since scripture says, '*Be holy, for I am holy.*' ·And if you address as Father him
   who judges without favouritism according to each individual's deeds, live out the
18 time of your exile here in reverent awe. ·For you know that the price of your
   ransom from the futile way of life handed down from your ancestors was paid, not
19 in anything perishable like silver or gold, ·but in precious blood as of a blameless
20 and spotless lamb, Christ.ʲ ·He was marked out before the world was made, and
21 was revealed at the final point of time for your sake. ·Through him you now have
   faith in God, who raised him from the dead and gave him glory for this very
   purpose—that your faith and hope should be in God. ᵏ

Regeneration by the Word

22 Since by your obedience to the truth you have purified yourselves so that you can
   experience the genuine love of brothers, love each other intensely from the heart; ⁱ
23 for your new birth was not from any perishable seed but from imperishable seed,
24 the living and enduring Word of God. ᵐ ·For *all humanity is grass, and all its beauty*
25 *like the wild flower's. As grass withers, the flower fades, ·but the Word of the Lord*
   remains for ever. And this Word is the Good News that has been brought to you.

1 2 Rid yourselves, then, of all spite, deceit, hypocrisy, envy and carping criticism.
2   Like new-born babies all your longing should be for milk—the unadulterated
3 spiritual milk—which will help you to grow up to salvation,ᵃ ·at any rate if *you*
   have tasted that the Lord is good.

The new priesthood

4 ᵇHe is the living stone, rejected by human beings but chosen by God and precious
5 to him; set yourselves close to him ·so that you, too, may be living stones making
   a spiritual house as a holy priesthood to offer the spiritual sacrifices made accept-
6 able to God through Jesus Christ. ·As scripture says: *Now I am laying a stone in*
   Zion, a chosen, precious cornerstone and *no one who relies on this will be brought*
7 *to disgrace.* ·To you believers it brings honour. But for unbelievers, it is rather a
8 *stone which the builders rejected that became a cornerstone, ·a stumbling stone, a*
   rock to trip people up. They stumble over it because they do not believe in the
   Word; it was the fate in store for them. ᶜ
9   But youᵈ are *a chosen race, a kingdom of priests, a holy nation, a people to be a*
   personal possession to sing the praises of God who called you out of the darkness
10 into his wonderful light. ·Once you were *a non-people* and now you are the People
   of God; once you were *outside his pity*; now you *have received pity.*

The obligations of Christians: towards unbelievers

11 I urge you, my dear friends, as *strangers and nomads,*ᵉ to keep yourselves free
12 from the disordered natural inclinations that attack the soul. ·Always behave
   honourably among gentilesᶠ so that they can see for themselves what moral lives
   you lead, and when the day of reckoning comes, give thanks to God for the things
   which now make them denounce you as criminals.

Towards civil authority

13 For the sake of the Lord, accept the authority of every human institution: *the*
14 emperor, as the supreme authority, ·and the governors as commissioned by him
15 to punish criminals and praise those who do good. ·It is God's will that by your
16 good deeds you should silence the ignorant talk of fools. ·You are slaves of no one
except God, so behave like free people, and never use your freedom as a cover for
17 wickedness. ·Have respect for everyone and love for your fellow-believers; fear
God and honour the emperor.

Towards masters

18 Slaves, you should obey your masters respectfully, not only those who are kind
19 and reasonable but also those who are difficult to please. ·You see, there is merit *
20 if, in awareness of God, you put up with the pains of undeserved punishment; ·but
what glory is there in putting up with a beating after you have done something
wrong? The merit in the sight of God is in putting up with it patiently when you
are punished for doing your duty.
21   This, in fact, is what you were called to do, because Christ suffered *for you and*
22 left an example for you to follow in his steps.* ·He had done nothing wrong, and
23 *had spoken no deceit.* ·He was insulted and did not retaliate with insults; when he
24 was suffering he made no threats but put his trust in the upright judge. ·He was
bearing our sins in his own body on the cross, so that we might die to our sins and
25 live for uprightness; *through his bruises you have been healed.* ·You had *gone*
astray like sheep * but now you have returned to the shepherd and guardian of your
souls.

In marriage

1 **3** In the same way, you wives should be obedient to your husbands. Then if there
are some husbands who do not believe the Word, they may find themselves won
2 over, without a word spoken, by the way their wives behave, ·when they see the
3 reverence and purity of your way of life. ·Your adornment should be not an
4 exterior one, consisting of braided hair or gold jewellery or fine clothing, ·but the
interior disposition of the heart, consisting in the imperishable quality of a gentle
5 and peaceful spirit, so precious in the sight of God. ·That was how the holy
women of the past dressed themselves attractively—they hoped in God and were
6 submissive to their husbands; ·like Sarah, who was obedient to Abraham, and
called him her *lord.* You are now her children, as long as you live good lives free
from fear and worry.
7   In the same way, husbands must always treat their wives with consideration in
their life together, respecting a woman as one who, though she may be the weaker
partner, is equally an heir * to the generous gift of life. This will prevent anything
from coming in the way of your prayers.

Love the brothers

8 Finally: * you should all agree among yourselves and be sympathetic; love the
9 brothers, have compassion and be self-effacing. ·Never repay one wrong with
another, or one abusive word with another; instead, repay with a blessing. That is
10 what you are called to do, so that you inherit a blessing. ·For

>   *Who among you delights in life,*
>   *longs for time to enjoy prosperity?*

Guard your tongue from evil,
your lips from any breath of deceit.

11 *Turn away from evil and do good, seek peace and pursue it.*
12 *For the eyes of the Lord are on the upright,*
his ear turned to their cry.
But the Lord's face is set against those who do evil.

In persecution

13. 14 No one can hurt you if you are determined to do only what is right; ·and blessed
are you if you have to suffer for being upright. *Have no dread of them; have no*
15 *fear.* ᶜ ·Simply *proclaim* ᵈ the Lord ᵉ Christ *holy* in your hearts, and always have
your answer ready for people who ask you the reason for the hope that you have.
16 But give it with courtesy and respect and with a clear conscience, so that those
who slander your good behaviour in Christ may be ashamed of their accusations.
17 And if it is the will of God that you should suffer, it is better to suffer for doing
right than for doing wrong.

The resurrection and the descent into hell ᶠ

18 Christ himself died once and for all for sins, ᵍ the upright for the sake of the guilty,
to lead us to God. In the body he was put to death, in the spirit he was raised to
19. 20 life, ·and, in the spirit, he went to preach to the spirits in prison. ʰ ·They refused to
believe long ago, while God patiently waited to receive them, in Noah's time when
the ark was being built. In it only a few, that is eight souls, were saved through
21 water. ·It is the baptism corresponding to ᶦ this water which saves you now—not
the washing off of physical dirt ʲ but the pledge ᵏ of a good conscience given to God
22 through the resurrection of Jesus Christ, ·who has entered heaven and is at God's
right hand, with angels, ruling forces and powers subject to him. ˡ

The break with sin

1   **4** As Christ has undergone bodily suffering, you too should arm yourselves with
the same conviction, that anyone who has undergone bodily suffering has
2 broken with sin, ·because for the rest of life on earth that person is ruled not by
3 human passions but only by the will of God. ·You spent quite long enough in the
past living the sort of life that gentiles choose to live, behaving in a debauched
way, giving way to your passions, drinking to excess, having wild parties and
4 drunken orgies and sacrilegiously worshipping false gods. ·So people are taken
aback that you no longer hurry off with them to join this flood which is rushing
5 down to ruin, ᵃ and then abuse you for it. ·They will have to answer for it before
6 the judge who is to judge the living and the dead. ·And this was why the gospel was
brought to the dead as well, ᵇ so that, though in their bodies they had undergone the
judgement that faces all humanity, in their spirit they might enjoy the life of God.

The revelation of Christ is close

7 The end of all things is near, ᶜ so keep your minds calm and sober for prayer.
8 Above all preserve an intense love for each other, since *love covers over many a*
9. 10 *sin.* ·Welcome each other into your houses without grumbling. ·Each one of you
has received a special grace, so, like good stewards responsible for all these varied
11 graces of God, put it at the service of others. ᵈ ·If anyone is a speaker, let it be as
the words of God, ᵉ if anyone serves, ᶠ let it be as in strength granted by God; so

that in everything God may receive the glory, through Jesus Christ, since to him alone belong all glory and power for ever and ever. *f* Amen.

Suffering for Christ

12 My dear friends, do not be taken aback at the testing by fire which is taking place
13 among you, as though something strange were happening to you; ·but in so far as you share in the sufferings of Christ, be glad, so that you may enjoy a much greater
14 gladness when his glory is revealed. *h* ·If you are insulted for bearing Christ's name,
15 blessed are you, for *on* you *rests the Spirit of God,* *i* the Spirit of glory. ·None of you should ever deserve to suffer for being a murderer, a thief, a criminal or an
16 informer; ·but if any one of you should suffer for being a Christian, then there
17 must be no shame but thanksgiving to God for bearing this name. ·The time has come for the judgement to begin at the household of God; and if it begins with us,
18 what will be the end for those who refuse to believe God's gospel? *·If it is hard for*
19 *the upright to be saved, what will happen to the wicked and to sinners?* ·So even those whom God allows to suffer should commit themselves to a Creator who is trustworthy, and go on doing good. *j*

Instructions: to the elders

1 **5** I urge the elders *a* among you, as a fellow-elder myself and a witness *b* to the
    sufferings of Christ, and as one who is to have a share in the glory that is to be
2 revealed: *c* ·give a shepherd's care to the flock of God that is entrusted to you: watch over it, not simply as a duty but gladly, as God wants; *d* not for sordid
3 money, but because you are eager to do it. ·Do not lord it over the group which is
4 in your charge, but be an example for the flock. *e* ·When the chief shepherd *f* appears, you will be given the unfading crown of glory.

To the faithful

5 In the same way, younger people, *g* be subject to the elders. Humility towards one another must be the garment you all wear constantly, because *God opposes the*
6 *proud but accords his favour to the humble.* ·Bow down, then, before the power of
7 God now, so that he may raise you up in due time; ·*unload* all *your burden on to*
8 *him,* since he is concerned about you. ·Keep sober and alert, because your enemy
9 the devil *h* is on the prowl like a *roaring lion,* looking for someone to devour. ·Stand up to him, strong in faith and in the knowledge that it is the same kind of suffering
10 that the community of your brothers throughout the world is undergoing. ·You will have to suffer only for a little while: the God of all grace who called you to eternal glory in Christ will restore you, he will confirm, strengthen and support
11 you. ·His *i* power lasts for ever and ever. Amen.

Last words. Greetings

12 I write these few words to you through Silvanus, who is a trustworthy brother, to encourage you and attest that this is the true grace of God. Stand firm in it!
13   Your sister in Babylon, who is with you among the chosen, *j* sends you greetings; so does my son, Mark.
14   Greet one another with a kiss of love.
     Peace to you all who are in Christ.

NOTES TO 1 PETER

1 **a.** The world belongs to God (Ps 24:1); human beings live there as passing aliens (Lv 25:23) because at their death they must leave it (1 Ch 29:10–15; Ps 39:12seq.; 119:19). After the revelation of the resurrection of the dead (2 M 7:9c) this theme receives its complement: our true homeland is in heaven (Ph 3:20; Col 3:1–4; Heb 11:8–16; 13:14). On earth we live in exile (*paroikia*, the word from which 'parish' comes, 1:17; 2 Co 5:1–8) in the midst of a gentile world whose vices we must avoid (1 P 2:11; 4:2–4) just as the Jews of the Dispersion did.

b. Dispersion, *Diaspora*: convert Jews, Jm 1:1b; or simply Christians living among gentiles, 1 P 5:9.

c. Cf. Heb 9:18seq. The people promise to obey God's commandments (v. 7) and, to seal the covenant, Moses sprinkles them with the blood of the victims (v. 8). On the Christian use of this text with reference to the blood of Christ, see Mt 26:28; Heb 9:18seq.

d. The blessing formula inherited from the OT (Gn 14:19–20h; Lk 1:68; Rm 1:25; 2 Co 11:31), has become Christian as in Rm 9:5; 2 Co 1:3; Ep 1:3, and the benefits for which God is thanked with praises are tied to the person of Christ, most prominently his resurrection, Rm 1:4–5c.

e. The last age, the end of history, has begun; it will be completed by the 'appearance', or second coming of Jesus, the *parousia*, vv. 7,13; 4:13; 5:1; see 1 Co 1:7–8e.

f. Amid their persecutions, v. 8; 2:12,19; 3:13–17; 4:12–19, Christians draw from their faith in Christ and their love for him the joyful certainty that God is storing up salvation for them (for souls, i.e. persons, 1:22; 2:11; see 1 Co 15:44w).

g. The role of the prophets was to announce the mystery of Christ, v. 10. Their inspiration is attributed to the Spirit of Christ, see Lk 24:27,44; 1 Co 10:1–11,6d; just as is the preaching of the apostles, v. 12. Thus the unity of the two covenants is highlighted.

h. They had crossed over from ignorance to knowledge of God, Ps 78:6; Jr 10:25; 1 Th 4:5, and their behaviour, 1 P 1:18; Ep 4:17–19, had thereby been completely transformed.

i. All must imitate the holiness of God (Lv 19:2). It is by loving others (cf. Lv 19:15), explains Jesus, that the Christian does that, is distinguished from gentiles, and becomes a child of God (Mt 5:43–48 and par.). But whence comes the strength to do this? The apostolic tradition reverses the situation and understands that it is because we are children of God (1:23m) that we can imitate God (1:14–16; Ep 5:1seq.; 1 Jn 3:2–10), for the God who is love (1 Jn 4:8) becomes the principle of our activity. Paul sees in this imitation of God the restoration of the work of creation (Ep 4.24; Col 3: 10–13).

j. Or 'by the precious blood of the Christ, this spotless lamb'.

k. The redemption, Rm 3:25k, by the blood of Christ (Mt 26:28i; Rv 1:5; 5:9) and the resurrection were the outcome of the eternal plan of the Father, 1 P 1:20, who in this way consecrated his new people, the believers, see 1 Th 1:7; 2:10,13. In 1:13–21 there are hints of a baptismal catechesis or even baptismal liturgy.

l. var. 'from a pure heart'.

m. Or 'the Word of the living and enduring God'. Seed of life, the Word of God is the principle of our divine rebirth and gives us the power to act according to the will of God, 1:22–25; Jn 1:12seq.; Jm 1:18n; cf. 1 P 2:13seq.; 5:18, because it is endowed with power, 1 Co 1:18; 1 Th 2:13; Heb 4:12. For Jm the Word is still the Law of Moses, 1:25; for 1 P it is the gospel-preaching, 1 P 1:25 (cf. Mt 13:18–23p); for Jn it is the Son of God in person, 1:1a. Paul sees in the Spirit the principle which makes us the children of God, Rm 6:4a, but the Spirit is the dynamism of the Word.

2 **a.** Birth, 1:23m, is followed by growth, due also to the Word on which Christians feed so avidly.

b. The allusions are to Ex 19, and the covenant constituting Israel a holy people, at Sinai, though the people were forbidden to go near the mountain itself. The new holy people are founded on another Rock, the living stone, to which they may, as a holy priesthood, come close. Instead of the sacrifices which sealed the old covenant, Ex 24:5–8, Christians offer spiritual sacrifices, 1 P 2:5. • The imagery of growth gives way to that of building. Jesus himself had, Mt 21:42 and par., compared himself to the stone rejected, Ps 118:22, and then chosen by God, Is 28:16. Christians, living stones, v. 5, like Christ, v. 4, are built into a spiritual dwelling, 1 Co 3:16–17; 2 Co 6:16; Ep 2:20–22, where they pay God worship worthy of him, Jn 2:21i; Rm 1:9g; Heb 7:27g.

c. lit. 'to this indeed they were appointed'. By rejecting the gospel the Jews have lost their prerogatives, which have been transferred to Christians, 3:9; Ac 28:26–28; cf. Jn 12:37seq. These texts need to be completed by Rm 11:32; 1 Tm 2:4; and this text does not prove the final, eschatological rejection of the Jews.

d. Another series of biblical allusions gives to the Church the titles of the chosen people, to underline its relationship with God and its responsibility in the world, see Rv 1:6; 5:10; 20:6. By belonging to Christ this nation gains a unity which defies all classification, see Ga 3:28; Rv 5:9.

e. The quotation from Ps 39:12 also occurs in Heb 11:13 and may have been in regular use among early Christian teachers as a conventional reminder that the Christian's life on earth is to be lived as a life of exile. But the reference here may be only to the readers, as living 'in the Dispersion' surrounded by gentiles, see 1:1,17; Ph 3:20; Col 3:1–4.

f. By belonging to another city, 1:1a, Christians are not freed from all earthly obligations. Their condition as children of God, citizens of heaven, imposes on them numerous duties which will gain for them the good opinion of their detractors, vv. 12,15.

g. Or 'every human creature'. In both versions opposition to the gentile idea of the divinised monarch may be perceived. The whole of the following passage, 2:13–3:12, is addressed to various social categories, cf. Ep 5:22–6:9; Col 3:18–4:1; Ti 2:1–10.

h. add. 'in the sight of God', cf. v. 20.

i. var. 'died', cf. 3:18.

j. The 'grace' of putting up with injustice, vv. 19–20, is based on the example of Christ, see Jn 13:15; 1 Co 11:1; Ph 2:5; 2 Th 3:7b. vv. 21–25, with their allusions to Is 53, could come from a hymn. Christians, ill-treated, should remember Jesus crucified for our sins, 3:18; Ac 2:23, innocent and patient, Lk 23:41; Jn 8:46; 2 Co 5:21; Heb 4:15.

k. var. 'you were like stray sheep'. These sheep are now in the flock of which Jesus is the shepherd, 5:2–4; Jn 10, and the *episkopos*, the inspector or overseer, cf. Ti 1:5.

3 **a.** '(she) is equally an heir', var. 'you are equally heirs', 'the generous gift', var. 'the varied and generous gift'. Husband and wife have received the same gift from God which demands mutual respect and devotion in love, cf. Ep 5:33; Col 3:19, and makes shared prayer possible and effective.

b. This last exhortation sums up all the others: brotherhood, 2:17, union of hearts, see Rm 12:9–13; forgiveness of enemies, Mt 5:44 and par.; Rm 12:14,17–21; 1 Th 5:15.

c. om. 'or to worry about them'.

d. lit. 'sanctify'.

e. 'Lord'; var. 'God'. 'hope', add. 'and faith'. • Christians bear witness to their adherence to Christ, cf. Lk 12:11–12; 1 Tm 6:12–15; 2 Tm 4:17, before gentiles who have no hope, Ep 2:12; 1 Th 4:13. The opportunity occurs through local persecutions.

f. This paragraph. 3:18–4:6, contains the elements of an ancient profession of faith: death of Christ, descent to hell, resurrection, enthronement at the right hand of God, and judgement of the living and the dead.

g. om. 'to God'.

h. Probably alludes to the descent of Christ to Hades between his death and resurrection. Mt 12:40; Ac 2:24,31; Rm 10:7; Ep 4:9; Heb 13:20. He went there 'in spirit', or 'according to the Spirit'. Rm 1:4c, his 'flesh' being dead on the cross. Rm 8:3seq. The 'spirits in prison' to whom he 'preached' (or 'proclaimed') salvation are identified by some writers as the chained demons mentioned in the *Book of Enoch* (some texts are corrected so as to make Enoch, and not Christ, preach to them). These spirits have thus been put under the authority of Christ as *Kyrios*, v. 22, cf. Ep 1:21seq.; 4:9; Ph 2:8–10, and this subjection to him is to be confirmed later on, 1 Co 15:24seq. Others interpret this passage of the souls of the dead who, punished at the time of the Flood, are nevertheless called by the 'patience of God' to life, cf. 4:6. Mt 27:52seq. has a similar allusion to Christ's deliverance, between his death and his resurrection, of the 'holy ones', that is the upright who were waiting for him, cf. Heb 11:39seq.; 12:23, to enter the eschatological 'holy city'.

i. lit. '. . . that is the antitype to', the reality prefigured by the 'type' (*see* 1 Co 10:6d). In this case the type is the passing through the waters by means of the ark.

j. As so few were saved from drowning, the Flood is taken to symbolise the OT purificatory rites that were, almost without exception, limited to an *external* 'bodily' purity, whereas the baptism by which a person is reborn can have no limits to its efficacy.

k. The 'pledge' (alternative translation: 'the request') made by a convert at his baptism.

l. 'Ruling forces and powers' referred to civil dignitaries. Lk 12:11; 20:20; Ti 3:1. The court of heaven is compared to an earthly court. Ep 3:10; Col 2:10. These 'ruling forces' had charge especially of judicial matters, which explains the role of accuser which Satan had before God. Jb 1; Zc 3:1–5; Rv 12:7–12. Conversely, Jesus will be called our 'advocate' with God, 1 Jn 2:1–2.

4 a. lit. 'this flood of un-salvation', by contrast to the saving Flood, cf. 3:20. Alternative translation: 'this flood of debauchery'.

b. For the proclamation of the gospel to the dead, *see* 3:19h.

c. The closeness of the *parousia* is a spur to the Christian. 1:5–7; 4:17; 5:10; Mt 24:42; 1 Co 16:22i; Jm 5:8d.

d. All the gifts (lit. 'charismata') are for the service of the Church as a whole, 3:7; 1 Co 12:1–11 and notes; cf. 1 Co 4:1–2.

e. This includes the inspired utterances of prophecy and glossolalia, *see* Ac 2:4g; 11:27m; 1 Co 14:2–19, but also the functions of teaching and exhorting, Rm 12:7–8, and even the preaching or defence of the gospel.

f. Presumably the various forms of help, Rm 12:7, and particularly liturgical service.

g. This doxology is the only one in the NT which is addressed to God *through* Jesus Christ and then *to* Christ himself, *see* Rm 16:27m.

h. Those who through baptism have received a share in the sufferings of Christ, 2 Co 1:5,7; Ph 3:10, are assured also of a share in his glory, 1:11; 5:1; Rm 8:17; 2 Co 4:17; Ph 3:11.

i. add. 'and power'; add. at end of verse '(the Spirit) blasphemed by them but honoured by you'. A new trinitarian formula, 1:2c.

j. Here God is trustworthy, 1 Co 1:9f, as Creator, Gn 1:1a, which implies his omnipotence and his command of events. Persecuted Christians can base their unshakeable hope on this thought, cf. Ps 31:6; Lk 23:46.

5 a. These elders are to be identified with the 'presbyters' of Ti 1:5c, *see* 1 P 5:5g. But the term keeps also its etymological sense, contrasting with the 'younger men' of 5:5.

b. Not necessarily a claim as apostle, 1:1, to have been present at the Passion of Christ; it could also be a claim to have borne witness to Christ by his own sufferings.

c. At the *parousia*, *see* 1:5,13; 4:7,17; 5:10.

d. om. 'watch over it' and 'as God wants'.

e. om. 'over the group which is in your charge'. Jesus had already warned his disciples against the instinct to domineer, Mt 20:25–28 and par.; 23:8; cf. 2 Co 1:24; 4:5; 1 Th 2:7.

f. The figure of the shepherd, for Jesus, is frequent in the later writings in the NT, Jn 10:11f; Heb 13:20; and is used in 1 P 2:25. Only here is he called the chief shepherd, when the work of a shepherd has been defined in a context of service.

g. Possibly young people (often turbulent, especially in groups) as opposed to adults, cf. Ep 6:1–4; Col 3:20–21; 1 Tm 4:12; 5:1; possibly the newly baptised of the body of the faithful as opposed to the 'elders', 5:1.

h. Or the 'Accuser' according to the etymology which corresponds to the role of prosecuting counsel here attributed to the devil, *see* 3:22l; Mt 4:1c; 24:42,45w.

i. add. 'glory and'.

j. The title 'chosen one', in the feminine, *see* 2 Jn 1,13, designates the Church of the chosen, 1:1–2; 2:9. • 'Babylon' designates Rome, *see* Rv 14:8; 16:19; 17:5.

2 PETER

THE SECOND LETTER OF PETER

Greetings

1 Simeon Peter, servant and apostle of Jesus Christ, to those who have received
a faith as precious as our own, given through the saving justice of our God and
2 Saviour Jesus Christ.* ·Grace and peace be yours in abundance through the
knowledge of our Lord. *

The generosity of God

3 By his divine power, he has lavished on us all the things we need for life and for
true devotion, through the knowledge of him who has called us by his own glory
4 and goodness. * ·Through these,* the greatest and priceless promises have been
lavished on us, * that through them* you should share the divine nature * and escape
5 the corruption rife in the world through disordered passion. ·With this in view, do
your utmost to support your faith with goodness, goodness with understanding,
6 understanding with self-control, self-control with perseverance, perseverance with
7 devotion, ·devotion with kindness to the brothers, and kindness to the brothers
8 with love. ·The possession and growth of these qualities will prevent your knowl-
9 edge of our Lord Jesus Christ from being ineffectual or unproductive. ·But without
them, * a person is blind or short sighted, forgetting how the sins of the past were
10 washed away. ·Instead of this, brothers, never allow your choice or calling to
11 waver; then there will be no danger of your stumbling, ·for in this way you will be
given the generous gift of entry to the eternal kingdom * of our Lord and Saviour
Jesus Christ.

The apostolic witness

12 That is why I will always go on recalling the same truths* to you, even though you
13 already know them and are firmly fixed in these truths. ·I am sure it is my duty, as
14 long as I am in this tent, to keep stirring you up with reminders, ·since I know the
time for me to lay aside this tent is coming soon, as our Lord Jesus Christ made
15 clear to me. ·And I shall take great care that after my own departure you will still
have a means to recall these things to mind.
16   When we told you about the power and the coming of our Lord Jesus Christ, we
were not slavishly repeating * cleverly invented myths; no, we had seen his majesty
17 with our own eyes. * ·He was honoured and glorified by God the Father, when a
voice came to him from the transcendent Glory, *This is my Son, the Beloved; he*

18 *enjoys my favour.* ·We ourselves heard this voice from heaven, when we were with him on the holy mountain. *ᵐ*

The value of prophecy

19 So we have confirmation of the words of the prophets; *ⁿ* and you will be right to pay attention to it as to a lamp for lighting a way through the dark, until the dawn
20 comes and the morning star rises in your minds. ·At the same time, we must recognise that the interpretation of scriptural prophecy is never a matter for the
21 individual. ·For no prophecy ever came from human initiative. When people spoke for God it was the Holy Spirit that moved them. *ᵒ*

False teachers *ᵃ*

1 **2** As there were false prophets in the past history of our people, so you too will have your false teachers, who will insinuate their own disruptive views and, by disowning the Lord who bought them freedom, will bring upon themselves speedy
2 destruction. ·Many will copy their debauched behaviour and the Way of Truth
3 will be brought into disrepute on their account. ·In their greed they will try to make a profit out of you with untrue tales. But the judgement made upon them long ago is not idle, and the destruction awaiting them is forever on the watch. *ᵇ*

Lessons of the past

4 When angels sinned, God did not spare them: *ᶜ* he sent them down into the underworld and consigned them to the dark abyss to be held there until the
5 Judgement. ·He did not spare the world in ancient times: he saved only Noah, the preacher of uprightness, along with seven others, when he sent the Flood over a
6 world of sinners. ·He condemned the cities of Sodom and Gemorrah by reducing
7 them to ashes *ᵈ* as a warning to future sinners; ·but rescued Lot, an upright man who had been sickened by the debauched way in which these vile people
8 behaved——·for that upright man, living among them, was outraged in his upright
9 soul by the crimes that he saw and heard every day. ·All this shows that the Lord is well able to rescue the good from their trials, and hold the wicked for their
10 punishment until the Day of Judgement, ·especially those who follow the desires of their corrupt human nature and have no respect for the Lord's authority. *ᵉ*

The punishment to come

Such self-willed people with no reverence are not afraid of offending against the
11 glorious ones, *ᶠ* ·but the angels in their greater strength and power make no
12 complaint or accusation against them in the Lord's presence. ·But these people speak evil of what they do not understand; they are like brute beasts, born only to be caught and killed, and like beasts they will be destroyed, being injured in return
13 for the injuries they have inflicted. ·Debauchery even by day they make their pleasure; *ᵍ* they are unsightly blots, and amuse themselves by their trickery even
14 when they are sharing your table; ·with their eyes always looking for adultery, people with an insatiable capacity for sinning, they will seduce any but the most stable soul. Where greed is concerned they are at their peak of fitness. They are
15 under a curse. ·They have left the right path and wandered off to follow the path of Balaam son of Bosor, *ʰ* who set his heart on a dishonest reward, but soon had
16 his fault pointed out to him: ·a dumb beast of burden, speaking with a human voice, put a stop to the madness of the prophet.
17 People like this are dried-up springs, fogs swirling in the wind, and the gloom of

18 darkness is stored up for them. ·With their high-sounding but empty talk they
tempt back people who have scarcely ' escaped from those who live in error, by
playing on the disordered desires of their human nature and by debaucheries.
19 They may promise freedom ʲ but are themselves slaves to corruption; because if
20 anyone lets himself be dominated by anything, then he is a slave to it; ·and anyone
who has escaped the pollution of the world by coming to know our Lord and
Saviour Jesus Christ, and who then allows himself to be entangled ᵏ and mastered
21 by it a second time, ends up by being worse than he was before. ·It would have
been better for them never to have learnt the way of uprightness, than to learn it
22 and then desert the holy commandment that was entrusted to them. ' ·What they
have done is exactly as the proverb rightly says: *The dog goes back to its vomit*
and: *As soon as the sow has been washed, it wallows in the mud.*

The Day of the Lord; the prophets and the apostles

1 **3** My dear friends, this is the second ᵉ letter I have written to you, trying to
2 awaken in you by my reminders an unclouded understanding. ·Remember
what was said in the past by the holy prophets and the command of the Lord and
Saviour given by your apostles.

False teachers

3 First of all, do not forget ᵇ that in the final days ᶜ there will come sarcastic scoffers
4 whose life is ruled by their passions. ·'What has happened to the promise of his
coming?' they will say, 'Since our Fathers ᵈ died everything has gone on just as it
5 has since the beginning of creation!' ·They deliberately ignore the fact that long
ago there were the heavens and the earth, formed out of water and through water
6 by the Word of God, ᵉ ·and that it was through these same factors that the world
7 of those days was destroyed by the floodwaters. ·It is the same Word which is
reserving the present heavens and earth for fire, keeping them till the Day of
Judgement and of the destruction of sinners.
8 But there is one thing, my dear friends, that you must never forget: that with
9 the Lord, a day is like a thousand years, and *a thousand years are like a day*. ·The
Lord is not being slow in carrying out his promises, as some people think he is;
rather is he being patient with you, wanting nobody to be lost and everybody to be
10 brought to repentance. ᶠ ·The Day of the Lord will come like a thief, and then
with a roar the sky will vanish, the elements will catch fire and melt away, the
earth and all that it contains will be burned up. ᵍ

Fresh call to holiness. Doxology

11 Since everything is coming to an end like this, what holy and saintly lives you
12 should be living ·while you wait for the Day of God to come, and try to hasten its
coming:·on that Day the sky will dissolve in flames and the elements melt in the
13 heat. ·What we are waiting for, relying on his promises, is the new heavens and
14 new earth, where uprightness will be at home. ·So then, my dear friends, while
you are waiting, do your best to live blameless and unsullied lives so that he will
15 find you at peace. ·Think of our Lord's patience as your opportunity to be saved;
our brother Paul, who is so dear to us, told you this when he wrote to you with the
16 wisdom that he was given. ·He makes this point too in his letters as a whole
wherever he touches on these things. In all his letters there are of course some
passages which are hard to understand, ʰ and these are the ones that uneducated
and unbalanced people distort, in the same way as they distort the rest of

17 scripture — to their own destruction. ·Since you have been forewarned about this, my dear friends, be careful that you do not come to the point of losing the firm ground that you are standing on, carried away by the errors of unprincipled people. 18 Instead, continue to grow in the grace and in the knowledge of our Lord and Saviour Jesus Christ. To him be glory, in time and eternity. Amen.

NOTES TO 2 PETER

1 **a.** Or 'of our God and of the Saviour Jesus Christ'.

b. var. 'through knowing God and Jesus (or Jesus Christ) our Lord'. All through this letter it is Christ who is proposed as the object of a Christian's knowledge, 1:3,8; 2:20; 3:18, cf. Ho 2:22v; Jn 17:3; Ph 3:10. This knowledge includes moral discernment and the practice of virtue, vv. 5–6,8.

c. 'glory' here refers to the miracles done by Jesus as a sign of his divinity, see Jn 1:14n, but in particular it refers to the transfiguration, 2 P 1:16–18. 'goodness' could refer to his powers both natural and miraculous. These two divine attributes give all that is needed for a life in accord with the demands of piety, 1 Tm 4:7d.

d. The 'glory' and 'goodness' of Christ, the links between the call received and the promised future, cf. 1 Tm 4:8.

e. 'us', var. 'you'. • What has been promised is the 'Day of the Lord', see 3:4,9–10,12–13.

f. i.e. as a result of the glory and goodness of Christ.

g. An expression of Gk origin, unique in the Bible and surprising by its impersonal tone. The author expresses by it the fullness of divine life in Christ, the communication by God of a life which is his own. For the basic idea see e.g. Jn 1:12; 14:20; 15:4–5; Rm 6:5; 1 Co 1:9f; 1 Jn 1:3b. It is one of the starting-points for the doctrine of 'deification' in the Gk Fathers.

h. This is the same sort of warning against Gnosticism that is given in the Johannine letters, see 1 Jn 1:8f. Gnostics claimed to know God without keeping his commandments.

i. This, like 1:4; 3:4,9–10, looks forward to the *parousia*. The kingdom of Christ is also that of the Father, Ep 5:5; 2 Tm 4:1; Rv 11:15.

j. Cf. 1 P 1:10–12. The reminder concerns the foundations of Christian faith and the *parousia*: Christ and the apostles, vv. 14–18, then the prophets, vv. 19–21.

k. This is another warning against Gnostics who had a doctrine of the *parousia* based not on logical proofs, but on an elaborate mythological system, cf. 3:4seq. Peter and the apostles pass on facts of which they are eyewitnesses, see Lk 1:2; Ac 1:8k; 1 Jn 1:1–3, and which the Father himself has confirmed.

l. At the transfiguration.

m. 'holy mountain' should perhaps be taken as Zion, Ps 2:6; Is 11:9, or as a suggestion that the mountain of transfiguration was the antitype of Sinai.

n. The transfiguration is a preliminary glimpse of scriptural prophecy being fulfilled.

o. The way in which the inspiration of the scriptures by the Spirit, 2 Tm 3:15–16,16e, is mentioned suggests that the reading of scripture also is done under the guidance of the Spirit and the apostolic tradition.

2 **a.** All this passage 2:1 to 3:3 echoes Jude, although the two developments differ in details.

b. These false teachers have already been condemned, see Jude 4.

c. The antediluvian world.

d. om. 'to extinction'.

e. All these events show a stability in God's justice which will remain unchanged at the Last Judgement, vv. 10–22.

f. The angels. These false teachers usurp the right to judge them, which belongs to God alone, Rm 12:19; 1 P 2:23.

g. var. 'happy to give themselves up to debauchery in broad daylight'.

h. var. 'Beor', see Nb 22:5.

i. The reference is to the 'unstable souls' of 2:14; many of them copy the shameful behaviour of the false teachers, 2:2.

j. Faith in Christ begets right conduct and true liberty, Rm 6:15g; Jm 1:25o; 1 P 2:16. By contrast, the heretics, on the plea of liberty, absolve themselves from the moral law, see Jude 4. But sin is a slavery, see Jn 8:34; Rm 6:16–17.

k. This refers to those who have been seduced by the false teachers, not to the teachers themselves.

l. Better never to have known faith, Jude 3, with all its demands, than to abandon it.

3 **a.** Alludes probably to 1 P.

b. The prediction that follows seems to be based more on the teaching of the apostles than on OT prophecy, cf. Ac 20:29; 2 Tm 3:1–5. It fits into Jude 18 better than it fits here.

c. That heretics should exist is itself proof that the Last Days are near, Mt 24:24; Ac 20:29–31; 2 Th 2:3–4,9; 1 Tm 4:1.

d. The Christians of the first generation.

e. God created the world by his Word. His Word will play a similar part in the final catastrophe. God does not need to submit to the so-called laws of the universe.

f. God's mercy is an alternative explanation for the alleged delay of the *parousia*, cf. Ws 11:23seq.; 12:8d.

g. 'burned', corr.; 'uncovered' (Gk). This destruction of the world by fire was, in Graeco-Roman times, a common topic for philosophers, as it was also in Jewish apocalyptic writings and the documents of Qumran. Here all this traditional vocabulary is pressed into the service of the Christian message about the Day, see 1 Co 1:8e.

h. About the *parousia*, presumably, since that is the subject under discussion. But other questions also were debated in the churches where Paul's letters were known.

i. This comparison of the collection of letters, as already formed and known, with the rest of scripture, is one of the first indications that the Christian writings are comparable as scripture to the books of the OT; see 1 M 12:9c; 1 Th 5:27i.

1 JOHN

THE FIRST LETTER OF JOHN

INTRODUCTION

The Incarnate Word and sharing with the Father and the Son

1 **1** Something which has existed since the beginning,
which we have heard,
which we have seen with our own eyes,
which we have watched
and touched with our own hands,
the Word of life *—
this is our theme.

2 That life was made visible;
we saw it and are giving our testimony,
declaring to you the eternal life,
which was present to the Father
and has been revealed to us.

3 We are declaring to you
what we have seen and heard,
so that you too may share *b* our life.
Our life is shared with the Father
and with his Son Jesus Christ.

4 We are writing this to you so that our *c* joy may be complete.

I: TO WALK IN THE LIGHT

5 This is what we have heard from him
and are declaring to you:
God is light, and there is no darkness in him at all.

6 If we say that we share in God's *d* life
while we are living in darkness,
we are lying, because we are not living the truth.

7 But if we live in light,
as he is in light,
we have a share in each other's life, *e*
and the blood of Jesus, his Son,
cleanses us from all sin.

First condition: to break with sin

8   If we say, 'We have no sin,'
    we are deceiving ourselves,
    and truth has no place in us;[f]
9   if we acknowledge our sins,
    he is trustworthy and upright,
    so that he will forgive our sins
    and will cleanse us from all evil.
10   If we say, 'We have never sinned,'
    we make him a liar,
    and his word has no place in us.

2 1   My children, I am writing this to prevent you from sinning;
    but if anyone does sin,
    we have an advocate with the Father,
    Jesus Christ, the upright.
2   He is the sacrifice to expiate our sins,
    and not only ours,
    but also those of the whole world.

Second condition: to keep the commandments, especially that of love

3   In this way we know
    that we have come to know him,[a]
    if we keep his commandments.
4   Whoever says, 'I know him'
    without keeping his commandments,
    is a liar,
    and truth[b] has no place in him.
5   But anyone who does keep his word,
    in such a one God's love truly reaches its perfection.[c]
    This is the proof
    that we are in God.
6   Whoever claims to remain in such a person[d]
    must act as he[e] acted.
7   My dear friends,
    this is not a new commandment I am writing for you,
    but an old commandment
    that you have had from the beginning;
    the old commandment is the message you have heard.
8   Yet in another way, I am writing a new commandment for you[f]
    —and this is true for you, just as much as for him—
    for darkness is passing away
    and the true light is already shining.
9   Whoever claims to be in light
    but hates his brother
    is still in darkness.
10   Anyone who loves his brother remains in light
    and there is in him nothing to make him fall away.
11   But whoever hates his brother is in darkness
    and is walking about in darkness

not knowing where he is going,
because darkness has blinded him.

Third condition: detachment from the world

12   I am writing to you, children,
because your sins have been forgiven through his name.

13   I am writing to you, fathers,
because you have come to know the One who has existed since
     the beginning.
I am writing to you, young people,
because you have overcome the Evil One. *

14   I have written to you, children,
because you have come to know the Father.
I have written to you, parents,
because you have come to know the One who has existed since
     the beginning.
I have written to you, young people,
because you are strong,
and God's word remains in you,
and you have overcome the Evil One.

15   Do not love the world
or what is in the world.
If anyone does love the world,
the love of the Father finds no place in him,

16   because everything there is in the world—
disordered bodily desires,
disordered desires of the eyes,
pride in possession— *
is not from the Father
but is from the world.

17   And the world, with all its disordered desires,
is passing away.
But whoever does the will of God
remains for ever.

Fourth condition: to be on guard against Antichrists

18   Children, this is the final hour;
you have heard that the Antichrist *i* is coming,
and now many Antichrists have already come;
from this we know that it is the final hour.

19   They have gone from among us,
but they never really belonged to us; *j*
if they had belonged to us, they would have stayed with us.
But this was to prove
that not one of them belonged to us.

20   But you have been anointed *k* by the Holy One,
and have all received knowledge. *l*

21   I have written to you
not because you are ignorant of the truth,
but because you are well aware of it,

and because no lie can come from the truth. *

22 Who is the liar,
if not one who claims that Jesus is not the Christ?
This is the Antichrist,
who denies both the Father and the Son. *

23 Whoever denies the Son cannot have the Father either;
whoever acknowledges the Son has the Father too.

24 Let what you heard in the beginning remain in you; *
as long as what you heard in the beginning remains in you,
you will remain in the Son
and in the Father.

25 And the promise he made you himself
is eternal life.

26 So much have I written to you
about those who are trying to lead you astray.

27 But as for you, the anointing you received from him
remains in you,
and you do not need anyone to teach you; *
since the anointing he gave you teaches you everything,
and since it is true, not false,
remain in him just as it has taught you.

28 Therefore remain in him now, children,
so that when he appears we may be fearless,
and not shrink from him in shame
at his coming.

II: TO LIVE AS GOD'S CHILDREN

29 If you know that he is upright
you must recognise that everyone whose life is upright
is a child of his.

1 **3** You must see what great love the Father has lavished on us
by letting us be called God's children—
which is what we are! *
The reason why the world does not acknowledge us
is that it did not acknowledge him.

2 My dear friends, we are already God's children,
but what we shall be in the future has not yet been revealed.
We are well aware that when he appears
we shall be like him,
because we shall see him as he really is.

First condition: to break with sin

3 Whoever treasures this hope of him
purifies himself, to be as pure as he is. *

4 Whoever sins, acts wickedly,
because all sin is wickedness.

5 Now you are well aware that he has appeared
in order to take sins away, *

and that in him there is no sin.

6   No one who remains in him sins, *d*
and whoever sins
has neither seen him nor recognised him.

7   Children, do not let anyone lead you astray.
Whoever acts uprightly is upright,
just as he *e* is upright.

8   Whoever lives sinfully belongs to the devil, *f*
since the devil has been a sinner from the beginning.
This was the purpose of the appearing of the Son of God,
to undo the work of the devil.

9   No one who is a child of God sins
because God's seed *g* remains in him.
Nor can he sin, because he is a child of God.

10   This is what distinguishes
the children of God from the children of the devil:
whoever does not live uprightly
and does not love his brother
is not from God.

Second condition: to keep the commandments, especially that of love

11   This is the message
which you heard from the beginning,
that we must love each other,

12   not to be like Cain, who was from the Evil One
and murdered his brother.
And why did he murder his brother?
Because his own actions were evil and his brother's upright. *h*

13   Do not be surprised, brothers,
if the world hates you.

14   We are well aware that we have passed over from death to life
because we love our brothers.
Whoever does not love, remains in death.

15   Anyone who hates his brother is a murderer,
and you are well aware that no murderer
has eternal life remaining in him.

16   This is the proof of love,
that he laid down his life for us,
and we too ought to lay down our lives for our brothers.

17   If anyone is well off in worldly possessions
and sees his brother in need
but closes his heart to him,
how can the love of God be remaining in him?

18   Children,
our love must be not just words or mere talk,
but something active and genuine.

19   This will be the proof that we belong to the truth, *i*
and it will convince us in his presence,

20   even if our own feelings condemn us,
that God is greater than our feelings and knows all things. *j*

21 My dear friends,
if our own feelings do not condemn us,
we can be fearless before God,
22 and whatever we ask
we shall receive from him,
because we keep his commandments
and do what is acceptable to him.
23 His commandment is this,
that we should believe in the name of his Son Jesus Christ
and that we should love each other
as he commanded us.
24 Whoever keeps his commandments
remains in God, and God in him.
And this is the proof that he remains in us:
the Spirit that he has given us.

Third condition: to be on guard against Antichrists and against the world

1 4 My dear friends,
not every spirit is to be trusted,
but test the spirits to see whether they are from God,
for many false prophets are at large in the world. *
2 This is the proof of the spirit of God:
any spirit which acknowledges Jesus Christ, come in human nature,
is from God,
3 and every spirit which does not acknowledge Jesus *
is not from God,
but is the spirit of Antichrist,
whose coming you have heard of;
he is already at large in the world.
4 Children, you are from God
and have overcome them,
because he who is in you
is greater than he who is in the world.
5 They are from the world,
and therefore the world inspires what they say,
and listens to them.
6 We * are from God;
whoever recognises God listens to us;
anyone who is not from God refuses to listen to us.
This is how we can distinguish
the spirit of truth from the spirit of falsehood. *

III: THE SOURCE OF LOVE AND FAITH

The source of love

7 My dear friends,
let us love each other,
since love is from God
and everyone who loves is a child of God and knows God. *

8 Whoever fails to love does not know God,
because God is love. *ʲ*

9 This is the revelation of God's love for us,
that God sent his only Son into the world
that we might have life through him.

10 Love consists in this:
it is not we who loved God,
but God loved us and sent his Son
to expiate our sins.

11 My dear friends,
if God loved us so much,
we too should love each other.

12 No one has ever seen God, *ᵏ*
but as long as we love each other
God remains in us
and his love comes to its perfection in us.

13 This is the proof that we remain in him
and he in us,
that he has given us a share in his Spirit. *ʰ*

14 We ourselves have seen and testify
that the Father sent his Son
as Saviour of the world.

15 Anyone who acknowledges that Jesus is the Son of God,
God remains in him and he in God.

16 We have recognised for ourselves,
and put our faith in, the love God has for us.
God is love,
and whoever remains in love remains in God
and God in him.

17 Love comes to its perfection in us
when we can face the Day of Judgement fearlessly,
because even in this world
we have become as he is.

18 In love there is no room for fear,
but perfect love drives out fear,
because fear implies punishment
and whoever is afraid has not come to perfection in love. *ⁱ*

19 Let us love, then,
because he first loved us.

20 Anyone who says 'I love God'
and hates his brother,
is a liar,
since whoever does not love the brother whom he can see
cannot love God whom he has not seen.

21 Indeed this is the commandment we have received from him,
that whoever loves God, must also love his brother.

5 1 Whoever believes that Jesus is the Christ
is a child of God,
and whoever loves the father
loves the son. *ᵃ*

2   In this way we know that we love God's children,
     when we love God and keep his commandments.
3   This is what the love of God is:
     keeping his commandments.
     Nor are his commandments burdensome,
4   because every child of God
     overcomes the world.
     And this is the victory that has overcome the world—
     our faith.

The source of faith

5   Who can overcome the world
     . but the one who believes that Jesus is the Son of God? *b*
6   He it is who came by water and blood, *c*
     Jesus Christ,
     not with water alone
     but with water and blood,
     and it is the Spirit that bears witness,
     for the Spirit is Truth.
7   So there are three witnesses, *d*
8   the Spirit, water and blood;
     and the three of them coincide. *e*
9   If we accept the testimony of human witnesses,
     God's testimony is greater,
     for this is God's testimony
     which he gave about his Son.
10   Whoever believes in the Son of God
     has this testimony within him,
     and whoever does not believe
     is making God a liar,
     because he has not believed
     the testimony God has given about his Son.
11   This is the testimony:
     God has given us eternal life,
     and this life is in his Son.
12   Whoever has the Son has life,
     and whoever has not the Son of God has not life.
13   I have written this to you
     who believe in the name of the Son of God
     so that you may know that you have eternal life.

SUPPLEMENTS *f*

Prayer for sinners

14   Our fearlessness towards him consists in this,
     that if we ask anything in accordance with his will
     he hears us.
15   And if we know that he listens to whatever we ask him,

we know that we already possess whatever we have asked of him.

16 If anyone sees his brother commit a sin
that is not a deadly sin,
he has only to pray, and God will give life to this brother
—provided that it is not a deadly sin.
There is sin that leads to death *f*
and I am not saying you must pray about that.

17 Every kind of wickedness is sin,
but not all sin leads to death.

Summary of the letter *h*

18 We are well aware that no one who is a child of God sins,
because he who was born from God protects him,
and the Evil One has no hold over him.

19 We are well aware that we are from God,
and the whole world is in the power of the Evil One.

20 We are well aware also that the Son of God has come,
and has given us understanding
so that we may know the One who is true. *i*
We are in the One who is true
as we are in his Son, Jesus Christ.
He is the true God
and this is eternal life.
Children, be on your guard against false gods. *j*

NOTES TO 1 JOHN

1 a. The Word of God was the source of life. Dt 4:1; 32:47; Mt 4:4; 5:20; Ph 2:16. Here the title of 'Word' is given to the Son of God with whom the apostles lived. 'Word of life' alludes to the wish of 1:3; 5:11–13; see Jn 1:1a,14i.

b. This union, and sharing of life, see 1 Co 1:9f; 2 P 1:4, is the idea most central to John's mysticism. Jn 14:20; 15:1–6; 17:11,20–26; union between all Christians results from the union created by Christ between each Christian and God. This union is referred to in different ways: a Christian 'lives in' God and God 'lives in' him. 2:5,6,24,27; 3:6,24; 4:12,13,15,16; a Christian is begotten by God, has new life from him. 2:29; 3:9; 4:7; 5:1,18; the Christian is from God, is his child. 3:10; 4:4–6; 5:19; the Christian knows God. 2:3,13,14; 3:6; 4:7,8 (on knowledge and presence, cf. Jn 14:17; 2 Jn 1:2). This union with God shows itself in a person's faith and in love for the brothers, see 1:7e; Jn 13:34u. The witness of the apostles is the tool of this union. v. 5; 2:7,24,25; 4:6; Jn 4:38; 17:20n; see Ac 1:8k,21,22.

c. 'our own', var. 'your'.

d. Union and sharing with God, 1:3b, who is light. 1:5; and love, 4:8,16, expresses itself in faith and fraternal love. 2:10,11; 3:10,17,23; 4:8,16.

e. God is in Christians, 1:3b, as the principle of their new life. Since God is light, 1:5, uprightness, 2:29, and love, 4:8,16, whoever lives in union with God must live a life of light, virtue and love, and keep God's commandments, especially the commandment to love all human beings. 2:10,11; 3:10; 4:8,16. Faith and love are thus the visible evidence of true union with God. 1:6,7; 2:3,6; 3:6,10,17,24; 4:6,8,13,16,20.

f. This is possibly an allusion to the sect that called themselves 'spirituals', *pneumatikoi*, and who were the forerunners of the Gnostics of the second century. These looked down on other people as being either *psychikoi* or *hylikoi* (see 1 Co 15:44w). Jn is here speaking of transient failures, although union to God, who has taken sin away. 2:2; 3:5, entails a holy and sinless life. 3:3,6,9; 5:18.

2 a. This knowledge. Ho 2:22v, is faith. Jn 3:12g, and embraces a whole way of life. 3:23, 51, in such a way that conduct is the criterion by which life in Christ may be recognised. v. 5; 3:10; 4:13; 5:2.

b. add. 'of God'.

c. This refers more to God's love for us than to our love for him.

d. 'To be in', 'to remain in' are expressions characteristic of Jn, see Jn 6:56q.

e. lit. 'as that One'; Jesus is repeatedly referred to in this way, 3:3,5,7,16; 4:17; see Jn 2:21; 19:35.

f. This commandment is prepared for in the old Law. Lv 19:18, and was known to Christians from their first initiation, v. 7; 3:11, but it received the special stamp of Jesus Christ, Jn 13:34u.

g. The devil is still the Tempter as in Gn 3:1–6; Jb 1:6g, who incites human beings to wickedness, 1 Jn 3:8d. Christians, however, have 'known' the Son; the Son lives in them. 1:3b, and 'clothes' them in light, virtue and love, 1:7e; and as this protects them from sinning. 1 Jn 3:6,9, it constitutes their victory over the devil, 5:18; Jn 17:15, preventing them from sinning. 1 Jn 2:13–14, and over this transient world.

1 Jn 4:4; 5:4–5; cf. Mt 6:13; Jn 1:9f; 12:31; 14:30; 16:33; Ga 6:14; Jm 4:4.

h. Motives which dominate the 'world', sensuality, the lure of appearances, pride which comes from earthly possessions. The true realities are totally different, *see* 2 Co 4:18; Heb 11:1,3,27.

i. var. 'The Antichrist', 'an Antichrist'. • On this Enemy of the last times, of whom Jn here speaks in the plural, *see* 2 Th 2:3–4a. He sets himself against all authentic faith in Christ, Son of God. v. 22,4:2–3; cf. 5:5; Jn 1:18q.

j. Though they seemed to belong to the community, they lacked the spirit of Christ.

k. This is the Spirit given to the Messiah. Is 11:2c; 61:1, and by him to believers, 3:24; 4:13; cf. 2 Co 1:21, to instruct them in all things. v. 27; Jn 16:13f; cf. 1 Co 2:10,15, in virtue of which the words of Jesus are 'spirit and life', Jn 6:63.

l. var. 'you know all things'.

m. Or 'because you know that the lies cannot have come from truth'.

n. It is not easy to name the heretics envisaged (probably Cerinthus, whose error persisted in a diluted form in Gnosticism). Here the title of Christ is not merely a translation of 'Messiah', but calls for the complete faith of 'Christians' in him who 'has come in human nature'.

o. The apostolic teaching concerning the mystery of Christ.

p. Christians are taught by the apostles, 1:3,5; 2:7,24, but merely hearing what is said is not enough, the message must penetrate them and this it cannot do except through the grace of the Holy Spirit.

3 **a.** om. 'and that is what we are'.

b. Jesus.

c. lit. 'sins'; var. 'our sins'.

d. Jn stylises somewhat. From hope of vision, v. 2, and perfect holiness, v. 3, there now flows by the action of Jesus Christ, v. 5; 2:2, that abstinence from all evil befitting children of God, v. 9; 5:18; cf. Ga 5:16, who have been 'justified', v. 7; 2:29; *see* Rm 3:24–25,24i. This does not in fact exclude the possibility of sin, 1:8–10,9g, which breaks such a union, cf. 2:3–5.

e. *See* note 2:e.

f. Having used expressions like: 'of God', 'from Truth', 'child of God', to show how a Christian lives under the influence of God living in him, John now uses expressions like: 'of the devil', 3:8; 'of the Evil One', 3:12, from, or of, the impermanent world, 2:16; 4:5, 'children of the devil' to indicate those who live under the influence of the devil and allow themselves to be seduced by him.

g. The 'seed' of God could be a reference to Christ, cf. Ga 3:16; 1 Jn 5:18, but some commentators take it as a reference to the Spirit, cf. 2:20–27, or to the seed of divine life introduced into us by God.

h. The antithesis between the children of God who live in truth and love and the world ruled by sin and hate continues until 4:6.

i. In the Johannine writings 'truth', 2:4, has a very wide sense which embraces faith and love, 3:23; 5:1. They 'belong to the truth' who believe, 2:21–22, and who love, 3:18–19. *See* Jn 3:21; 8:32k; 18:37; 2 Jn 4–6; 3 Jn 3–8.

j. The person whose conscience (lit. 'heart') reproaches him, will find that God as a judge is both more acute and more lenient than his conscience, providing (it is understood) that charity has been practised. Another translation could be 'In the presence of God we shall prove to our conscience, if it has been accusing us, that God is greater than our conscience is, and that he knows everything.

4 **a.** One must be certain that those who lay claim to the Spirit of God are not in fact motivated by the spirit of the world. They may be known by their fruits, Mt 7:15–20, by their relationships, cf. 1 Jn 2:3–6,13–14, and especially by

what they say of Christ, vv. 2–3. The apostles are capable of this discernment, v. 6.

b. var., supported by several authorities, 'which dissolves (or breaks, splits, divides) Jesus'.

c. 'we' = the Christian prophets, recognised evangelists and preachers with apostolic authority.

d. The theme of the two spirits is well known in Judaism (e.g. Qumran), and is similar to that of the two ways. Dt 11:26–28; Mt 7:13–14,13d. A human being is situated between two worlds, and belongs to one or the other by partaking of their spirit, 3:8,19. The final victory of believers is certain, v. 4; 2:13–14; 5:4–5.

e. Love is characteristic of the children of God, v. 16.

f. God loved Israel, Is 54:8c. The sending of his only Son as Saviour of the world, v. 9; Jn 3:16; 4:42; cf. Rm 3:24–25,24i; 5:8; etc. makes the love of God visible, v. 7, because God himself is love, v. 16; 3:16, and makes the believer who is the child of God, 1:3b, participate in love, vv. 10,19.

g. This is directed against the *pneumatikoi* who held that by intuition a human being can 'reach' God.

h. This gift of the Spirit promised for the last times, Ac 2:17–21,33, has been poured into our hearts, *see* Rm 5:5e; 1 Th 4:8, and there engenders the inner certainty which the apostles proclaimed exteriorly, 5:6–7; cf. Ac 5:32. Here this concerns divine Sonship, Rm 8:15–16; Ga 4:6.

i. Love presupposes the filial element of religious fear, Dt 6:2a; Pr 1:7a, but it excludes servile fear, the fear of being condemned by God, 3:20, who has in his Son given such proof of love, *see* v. 8f.

5 **a.** Whoever loves God loves also his children. The love of God is expressed in love of neighbour, the criterion of its sincerity, 3:14,17–19; 4:20, and the first of the commandments to which one is committed by the love of God, vv. 2–3; cf. 2:3–5; 3:22–24; Mt 22:26–40 and par.; Jn 13:34 = 15:10–14; Rm 13:9; Ga 5:14. Finally, then, it is faith which judges love, the faith by which a person is born of God, 3:1; Jn 1:12j.

b. This argument is based on two previous ones: whoever believes is begotten by God, v. 1, and to be begotten by God is to be the conqueror of the 'world', v. 4. *see* Rm 1:4c.

c. The water and the blood that came from the side of Jesus when it was opened by the lance.

d. Vulg. vv. 7–8 read as follows: 'There are three witnesses *in heaven: the Father, the Word and the Spirit, and these three are one; there are three witnesses on earth*: the Spirit, the water and the blood.' The words in italics (not in any of the early Gk MSS, or any of the early translations, or in the best MSS of the Vulg. itself) are probably a gloss that has crept into the text.

e. The three testimonies converge. Blood and water join the Spirit, 2:20k,27; Jn 3:5; 4:1, to bear witness, *see* Jn 3:11f, in favour of the mission of the Son who gives life, v. 11; Jn 3:15h.

f. As in the gospel, *see* Jn 21, the conclusion is followed by a postscript.

g. No doubt the recipients of the letter knew what this exceptionally grave sin was. Perhaps the sin against the Spirit, against truth, *see* Mt 12:31–32,32h, or the apostasy of the Antichrists, 2:18–29; Heb 6:4–8.

h. Three sentences beginning 'we know' sum up the great Christian certainties and hopes developed in the letter.

i. God the only true One, Jn 17:3d; cf. 8:31; 1 Th 1:19, and the only One known for what he is in truth, i.e. Life and Love.

j. A last warning, no doubt occasioned by the mention of the only true God. The 'false gods', surely in a metaphorical sense, can denote paganism, or the 'false gods of the heart' (Qumran) which turn people away from faith and love.

2 JOHN

THE SECOND LETTER OF JOHN

1 From the Elder: *a* my greetings to the Lady, the chosen one, *b* and to her children,
whom I love in truth—and I am not the only one, for so do all who have come to
2 know the Truth—·because of the truth that remains in us and will be with us for
3 ever. ·In our life of truth and love, we shall have grace, faithful love *c* and peace
from God the Father and from Jesus Christ, the Son of the Father.

The law of love

4 It has given me great joy to find that children of yours have been living the life of
5 truth *d* as we were commanded by the Father. ·And now I am asking you—dear
lady, not as though I were writing you a new commandment, but only the one
which we have had from the beginning—that we should love each other.
6 To love is to live according to his commandments: this is the commandment
which you have heard since the beginning, *e* to live a life of love.

The enemies of Christ

7 There are many deceivers at large in the world, refusing to acknowledge Jesus
Christ as coming in human nature. They are the Deceiver; they are the Antichrist.
8 Watch yourselves, or all our work *f* will be lost and you will forfeit your full reward.
9 If anybody does not remain in the teaching of Christ *g* but goes beyond it, *h* he
does not have God with him: only those who remain in what he taught can have
10 the Father and the Son with them. ·If anyone comes to you bringing a different
doctrine, you must not receive him into your house or even give him a greeting.
11 Whoever greets him has a share in his wicked activities.
12 There are several things I have to tell you, but I have thought it best not to trust
them to paper and ink. I hope instead to visit you and talk to you in person, so
that our joy *i* may be complete.
13 Greetings to you from the children of your sister, *j* the chosen one.

NOTES TO 2 JOHN

a. The elders were the leaders in each community. *see* Tt 1:5c. Here John the Apostle. the outstanding leader of the communities of Asia Minor is in question.

b. The 'Chosen Lady' or 'Sovereign Lady'. cryptic references to one of the local churches under the jurisdiction of the Elder and threatened by the propaganda of false teachers. We do not know which it was.

c. 'Faithful love' occurs nowhere else in the Johannine writings.

d. lit. 'walk in the truth', through observance of the commandments in love.

e. Or 'you must obey that commandment as you learnt it at the beginning'.

f. var. 'your work'.

g. Teaching either by, or about, Christ.

h. Teaching pure speculation as apostolic doctrine, cf. 2 Tm 2:16; Tt 3:9.

i. var. 'your joy'.

j. The church (perhaps Ephesus) from which the letter is being written.

3 JOHN

THE THIRD LETTER OF JOHN

1, 2 From the Elder: greetings to my dear friend Gaius,ᵃ whom I love in truth. ·My
dear friend, I hope everything is going happily with you and that you are as well
3 physically as you are spiritually. ·It was a great joyᵇ to me when some brothers
4 came and told of your faithfulness to the truth, and of your life in the truth. ·It is
always my greatest joy to hear that my children are living according to the truth.

5 My dear friend, you have done loyal work in helping these brothers, even
6 though they were strangers to you.ᶜ ·They are a proof to the whole Church of
your love and it would be a kindness if you could help them on their journey as
7 God would approve. ·It was entirely for the sake of the nameᵈ that they set out,
8 without depending on the non-believers for anything: ·it is our duty to welcome
people of this sort and contribute our share to their work for the truth.

Beware of the example of Diotrephes ᵉ

9 I have written a noteᶠ for the members of the church, but Diotrephes, who enjoys
10 being in charge of it, refuses to accept us.ᵍ ·So if I come, I shall tell everyone how
he has behaved, and about the wicked accusations he has been circulating against
us. As if that were not enough, he not only refuses to welcome our brothers, but
prevents from doing so other people who would have liked to, and expels them
11 from the church. ·My dear friend, never follow a bad example, but keep following
the good one; whoever does what is right is from God, but no one who does what
is wrong has ever seen God.

Commendation of Demetrius

12 Demetriusʰ has been approved by everyone, and indeed by Truth itself. We too
will vouch for him and you know that our testimony is true.

Epilogue

13 There were several things I had to tell you but I would rather not trust them to
14, 15 pen and ink. ·However, I hope to see you soon and talk to you in person. ·Peace
be with you; greetings from your friends; greet each of our friendsⁱ by name.

a. A fairly common name. The bearer is a faithful disciple to whom the Elder sees fit to address the letter.

b. 'Joy', var. 'privilege'.

c. Probably missionaries sent by 'the Elder' to the communities of Asia Minor.

d. The name of the Lord; see Ac 5:41p, expressing the mystery of his divinity, cf. Ph 2:9; 1 Jn 3:25; 5:13; Jm 2:7.

e. By contrast to Gaius, this leader of a community envisaged by the letter fails in submission to the Elder, and so seems to threaten the faith. The Elder intends to intervene when he visits soon, vv. 10.14.

f. Perhaps 2 Jn.

g. In the persons of the apostle's envoys.

h. Either a leading member of that community or one of the missionaries recommended to Gaius (the bearer of the letter ?).

i. Those who resist Diotrephes because they recognise the authority of the Elder.

THE LETTER OF
JUDE

Address

1 From Jude, servant of Jesus Christ and brother of James; to those who are called,
2 to those who are dear to *a* God the Father and kept safe for Jesus Christ, ·mercy, peace and love be yours in abundance.

The reason for this letter

3 My dear friends, at a time when I was eagerly looking forward to writing to you about the salvation that we all share, I felt that I must write to you encouraging you to fight hard for the faith which has been once and for all entrusted to God's
4 holy people. *b* ·Certain people have infiltrated among you, who were long ago marked down for condemnation on this account; *c* without any reverence they pervert the grace of our God to debauchery and deny all religion, rejecting our only Master and Lord, Jesus Christ. *d*

The false teachers: the certainty of punishment

5 I should like to remind you—though you have already learnt it once and for all *e*— that the Lord *f* rescued the nation from Egypt, but afterwards he still destroyed
6 the people who refused to believe him; ·and the angels who did not keep to the authority they had, but left their appointed sphere, *g* he has kept in darkness in
7 eternal bonds until the judgement of the great Day. ·Sodom and Gemorrah, too, and the neighbouring towns, who with the same sexual immorality pursued unnatural lusts, *h* are put before us as an example since they are paying the penalty of eternal fire.

Their violent language

8 Nevertheless, these people *i* are doing the same: in their delusions they not only
9 defile their bodies and disregard Authority, but abuse the Glories *j* as well. ·Not even the archangel Michael, when he was engaged in argument with the devil about the corpse of Moses, *k* dared to denounce him in the language of abuse; all
10 he said was, '*May the Lord rebuke you.*' ·But these people abuse anything they do not understand; and the only things they do understand—merely by nature *l* like unreasoning animals—will turn out to be fatal to them.

Their vicious behaviour

11 Alas for them, because they have followed Cain; they have thrown themselves into the same delusion as Balaam for a reward; they have been ruined by the same

12 rebellion as Korah—and share the same fate. •They are a dangerous hazard " at your community meals, coming for the food and quite shamelessly only looking after themselves. They are like the clouds blown about by the winds and bringing
13 no rain, or like autumn trees, barren and uprooted and so twice dead; •like wild sea waves with their own shame for foam; or like wandering stars " for whom the
14 gloom of darkness is stored up for ever. •It was with them in mind that Enoch, the seventh patriarch from Adam, made his prophecy when he said, 'I tell you, the
15 Lord will come with his holy ones in their tens of thousands, •to pronounce judgement on all humanity and to sentence the godless for all the godless things they have done, and for all the defiant things said against him by godless sinners.' •
16 •They are mischief-makers, grumblers governed only by their own desires, ª with *mouths full of boastful talk*, ready to flatter others for gain.

A warning

17 But remember, my dear friends, what the apostles of our Lord Jesus Christ
18 foretold. ª •'At the final point of time', they told you, 'there will be mockers who
19 follow nothing but their own godless desires.' ʳ •It is they who cause division, who live according to nature and do not possess the Spirit.

The duties of love

20 But you, my dear friends, must build yourselves up on the foundation of your
21 most holy faith, praying in the Holy Spirit; ª •keep yourselves within the love of
22 God and wait for the mercy of our Lord Jesus Christ to give you eternal life. •To
23 some you must be compassionate because they are wavering; •others you must save by snatching them from the fire; ª to others again you must be compassionate but wary, hating even the tunic stained by their bodies.

Doxology

24 To him who can keep you from falling and bring you safe to his glorious presence,
25 innocent and joyful, •to the only God, our Saviour, through Jesus Christ our Lord, be glory, majesty, authority and power, before all ages, now and for ever. Amen. ª

NOTES TO JUDE

a. 'To those who are', var. 'to the nations who are' • 'dear to'; var. 'made holy by'.

b. No change must be made, v. 5, in the tradition of the faith of the apostles, v. 17, the foundation of the Christian life, v. 20; cf. 1 Co 11:2; 2 Th 2:15*f*; 1 Tm 6:20.

c. var. 'for this sin'.

d. var. 'rejecting God, the only Master and our Lord Jesus Christ'.

e. The faith entrusted 'once and for all', v. 3, to God's holy people must never be changed.

f. God the Father, *see* 2 P 2:4. var. (Vulg.) 'Jesus', i.e. a reference to Christ in his divine pre-existence, cf. 1 Co 10:4.

g. They let themselves be seduced by the 'daughters of men', Gn 6:1–2; the subject is elaborated in the *Book of Enoch*.

h. They lusted not after human beings, but after the strangers who were angels, Gn 19:1–11. The apocryphal *Testament of the Twelve Patriarchs*, like Jude 6–7, also compares the sin of the angels with the sin of the Sodomites.

i. Heretics living at the same time as the writer, who are not deterred by the punishment of the fallen angels, vv. 6–7.

j. 'Authority' var. 'Authorities', i.e. angels, *see* Ep 1:21s; Col 1:16. The Glories would also be such cosmic powers.

k. Almost certainly a reference to the apocryphal *Assumption of Moses*, in which Michael (Dn 10:13b) has an altercation with the devil as to who claims Moses' body after his death.

l. Their lack of knowledge results from the fact that they do not possess the Spirit, they know nothing except what they have learnt through their unaided natural powers, *see* Rm 1:9e; 1 Co 15:44. They were despised by the Gnostics.

m. 'community meals' (*agapai*), var. 'deceits', cf. 2 P 2:13. • So the heretics still participated in the life of the Church; their conduct had only recently been noticed. Whether Jude is referring to the Eucharist or to the *agape* which preceded it, their attitude recalls 1 Co 11:17–22.

n. In Jewish apocrypha, e.g. the *Book of Enoch*, 'stars' often stand for angels'.

o. *Enoch* 1:9, probably quoted from memory.

p. Suggested by *Enoch* 5:5.

q. The apostolic preaching received through the tradition, v. 3.

r. No saying is found in this exact form, but *see* Ac 20:29–31; 1 Tm 4:1; 2 Tm 3:1–5; 4:3, and already Mt 24:24; Mk 13:22.

s. Vv. 20–21 mention the three Persons, cf. 2 Co 13:13, in connection with faith, prayer, love, hope, *see* 1 Co 13:13e.

t. Love dictates different treatment of those who are more or less tainted by the heresy. • var. 'Be kind to some, those who are hesitating; save them, snatch them from the fire.'

u. The solemn doxology, cf. Rm 16:25–27,27n; Ep 3:20; Rv 1:6k, comes perhaps from the liturgy.

THE BOOK OF
REVELATION

INTRODUCTION TO
THE REVELATION
TO JOHN

The Greek title of this book is literally 'The Apocalypse of John' or 'The Revelation of John'. (The word 'apocalypse' is merely a transliteration into English of the Greek word for 'Revelation'.) The title phrase is shown in Rv 1:1 and 2 to mean 'The Revelation to John'. Any writing under the title 'Apocalypse' claims to include a revelation of hidden things, imparted by God, and particularly a revelation of events hidden in the future. It is not easy to draw an exact dividing line between prophecy and apocalypse, and the writers of apocalyptic are in some ways the successors of the prophets; but we can at least make the distinction that the Old Testament prophets characteristically received the message by 'hearing the word of God' and passed it on by word of mouth, whereas the author of a written apocalypse was given his revelation in a vision and passed it on in writing.

The language of apocalyptic writing is richly symbolic, and the importance of the visions which are described is never in their immediate literal meaning. It can be taken as a rule that every element in this kind of writing has symbolic value—persons, places, animals, actions, objects, parts of the body, numbers and measurements, stars, constellations, colours and garments—and if we are not to misunderstand or distort the writer's message, we must appreciate the imagery at its true value and do our best to translate the symbols back into the ideas which he intended them to convey. There are parts of the text in which this will involve our distinguishing a direct allegorical interpretation of the images that are used. There are other parts, however, in which no single interpretation can be confidently adopted, since a single group of images will be found to draw its meaning from various different associations.

Apocalyptic writing became very popular in some Jewish circles (including the Essenes of Qumran) in the two centuries before Christ. The visions of prophets like Ezekiel and Zechariah paved the way, and apocalypse as a literary form was already fully developed by the time of Daniel and in the many apocryphal writings about the beginning of the Christian era. The New Testament includes only one apocalypse; its author says he was called John,

1:9, and that at the time of writing he was an exile for his Christian faith on the island of Patmos. A tradition as early as Justin and widespread by the end of the second century (Irenaeus, Clement of Alexandria, Tertullian, the Canon of Muratori) identified this John with the apostle, author of the fourth Gospel. On the other hand, it is almost certain that the Churches of Syria, Cappadocia and even Palestine did not include The Revelation in the canon of scripture until the fifth century; evidently they did not believe it to be the work of an apostle. At the beginning of the third century a priest of Rome, Caius by name, attributed it to Cerinthus the heretic, though this may have been merely an attempt to justify his attack on it. Internal evidence shows that The Revelation to John has some affinity with the other Johannine writings, but it is so sharply distinguished from them by language, style, and some theological positions, notably its view of the second coming, that it is impossible to identify the author of The Revelation to John as it stands with the author of the rest of the Johannine literature. Nevertheless, it makes use of the Johannine vocabulary of theological thinking, and it must have issued from a church in which the tradition preserved was that of John. As for its date, the most common opinion is that it was written in the reign of Domitian, about AD 95; others, with considerable justification, believe that parts of it, if not all, were composed shortly after Nero's death, between AD 68 and 70.

Whatever its precise date, we cannot understand The Revelation without taking into account the historical conditions that gave birth to it. It is first and foremost a tract for the times, like the apocalypses (particularly Daniel) that preceded it and on which it draws. It was written during a period of disturbance and bitter persecution to increase the hope and determination of the infant Church. Jesus had said, 'Be brave: I have conquered the world,' Jn 16:33; how, therefore, could God permit this mortal attack on his own Church? John's answer begins by recalling the classical themes of the prophets, notably that of the great 'Day of Yahweh' (*see* Am 5:18, note m). When the chosen people had been enslaved to the Assyrians, Chaldaeans, and Greeks, when they had been scattered abroad and nearly annihilated by persecution, the prophets had promised: the day is coming, and soon, when God will liberate his people from their oppressors, and restore their independence, and help them to conquer their enemies, after he has punished them and brought them to the point of extinction. When John wrote The Revelation, the Church, the new chosen race, had just been decimated by persecution, ch. 6:10–11; 13; 16:6; 17:6; Rome and its empire (the Beast) was only a tool, but a tool wielded by Satan, ch. 12; 13:2,4, the great and only real enemy of Christ and his people. In the opening vision John describes God as Emperor, enthroned in heaven; he is Master of human destiny, ch. 4, and to the Lamb he gives the scroll that foretells the doom of the persecutors, ch. 5; the vision then proclaims a foreign invasion (the Parthians) and its familiar concomitants, war, famine, plague, ch. 6. During this, God's faithful will be preserved, 7:1–8; *compare* 14:1–5, and eventually rejoice triumphantly in heaven, 7:9–17;

compare 15:1–5. God, however, wants to save their enemies as well, so instead of destroying them immediately, he warns them, as he had warned Egypt and its Pharaoh, by a series of plagues, ch. 8–9; *compare* 16. The persecutors are only hardened in their evil determination, and God is forced to destroy them, ch. 17. Their aim was to corrupt the world and get it to worship Satan (an allusion to emperor-worship in pagan Rome). After this comes a lament over fallen Babylon (Rome), ch. 18, and hymns of victory in heaven, 19:1–10. There is a second vision of the destruction of the Beast (Rome the persecutor) this time by Christ in glory, 19:11–21, that begins an era of prosperity for the Church, 20:1–6, which is to end in a new assault by Satan 20:7seq., followed by the annihilation of the Enemy, the resurrection and judgement of the dead, 20:11–15, and ultimately by the definitive establishment of the kingdom of perfect happiness in heaven when death itself has been destroyed, 21:1–8. A final vision glances back to the period just before this consummation and describes the beauty of the new Jerusalem, or Church, on earth, 21:9seq.

The significance of The Revelation is wider than this primary, basic meaning derived by historical interpretation: the book portrays the unchanging realities on which faith relies in any period of history. God's promise to be 'with his people', *see* Ex 25:8, note d, protecting them and saving them, had always been the foundation of their confidence in him in the Old Testament, and it is this presence that has now been perfected by the marriage of God and his new chosen people in the person of his Son, Immanuel (God-with-us). The promise of the risen Christ, 'I am with you always; yes, to the end of time,' is what gives life to the Church, Mt 28:20. As a result, those who are faithful to Jesus have nothing to fear: they may suffer a while for him but in the end they will triumph over Satan and his schemes.

In its present state the text of The Revelation presents a certain number of repetitions or even double repetitions, breaks of continuity between the visions, passages seemingly out of context (especially in ch. 20–22). Commentators have tried to explain these anomalies in various ways: compilation from different sources, accidental displacement of certain passages, etc. There is general agreement that the letters to the seven Churches (1:9–3:22) were added at the time of the final edition of the book. As for the strictly prophetic part of the book (ch. 4–22), it could have joined together two distinct apocalypses, written by the same author but at different dates. A more complex solution, using three partially distinct apocalypses, could also be envisaged. Whatever the truth of the matter, it is nevertheless possible to read The Revelation as it has been handed down to us, concentrating on the message of certainty and hope expressed by the complex but powerful imagery of the book. The sacrifice of the Lamb has won the final victory. Whatever evils the Church may undergo, its confidence in God's faithfulness remains unshaken; the Lord will 'soon' come (1:1; 22:20). The Revelation is an epic of Christian hope, the victory song of the persecuted Church.

THE REVELATION
TO JOHN

Prologue

1 A revelation of Jesus Christ *, which God gave him so that he could tell his servants *b* *what is* now *to take place* very soon; he sent his angel to make it
2 known *c* to his servant John, ·and John has borne witness to the Word of God and
3 to the witness of Jesus Christ, everything that he saw. ·Blessed *d* is anyone who reads the words of this prophecy, and blessed those who hear them, if they treasure the content, because the Time *e* is near.

I: THE LETTERS TO THE CHURCHES OF ASIA

Address and greeting *f*

4 John, to the seven churches of Asia: grace and peace to you from him who is, who
5 was, and who is to come, *g* from the seven spirits who are before his throne, ·and from Jesus Christ, *the faithful witness, the First-born* from the dead, *the highest of*
6 *earthly kings.* *h* He loves us and has washed away *i* our sins with his blood, ·and made us a *Kingdom of Priests* to serve *j* his God and Father; to him, then, be glory
7 and power for ever and ever. Amen. *k* ·Look, he *is coming on the clouds*; everyone will see him, even *those who pierced him,* and *all the races of the earth will mourn*
8 *over him.* Indeed this shall be so. Amen. ·'I am the Alpha and the Omega,' *l* says the Lord God, who is, who was, and who is to come, the Almighty.

Preliminary vision

9 I, John, your brother and partner in hardships, in the kingdom and in perseverance in Jesus, was on the island of Patmos *m* on account of the Word of God and of
10 witness to Jesus; ·it was the Lord's Day and I was in ecstasy, and I heard a loud
11 voice behind me, like the sound of a trumpet, saying, ·'Write down in a book all that you see, and send it to the seven churches of Ephesus, Smyrna, Pergamum,
12 Thyatira, Sardis, Philadelphia and Laodicea.' ·I turned round to see who was
13 speaking to me, and when I turned I saw seven golden lamp-stands ·and, in the middle of them, one *like a Son of man,* *n* dressed in a long robe tied at the waist
14 with a *belt of gold.* *·His head* and *his hair were white with the whiteness of wool,*
15 *like snow, his eyes* like a *burning* flame, ·*his feet like burnished bronze* when it has
16 been refined in a furnace, and *his voice like the sound of the ocean.* ·In his

right hand he was holding seven stars, out of his mouth came a sharp sword, double-edged, and his face was like the sun shining with all its force.

17 When I saw him, I fell at his feet as though dead, but he laid his right hand on me and said, 'Do not be afraid; it is I, *the First* and *the Last*; I am the Living One, *

18 I was dead and look—I am alive for ever and ever, and I hold the keys of death

19 and of Hades. * ·Now write down all that you see of present happenings * and *what*

20 *is still to come*. ·The secret of the seven stars you have seen in my right hand, and of the seven golden lamp-stands, is this: the seven stars are the angels * of the seven churches, and the seven lamp-stands are the seven churches themselves.'

1 Ephesus *

1   2 'Write to the angel of the church in Ephesus * and say, "Here is the message of the one who holds the seven stars in his right hand and who lives among the

2 seven golden lamp-stands: ·I know your activities, your hard work and your perseverance. I know you cannot stand wicked people, and how you put to the

3 test those who were self-styled apostles * and found them false. ·I know too that you have perseverance, and have suffered for my name * without growing tired.

4 Nevertheless, I have this complaint to make: you have less love now than formerly.

5 Think where you were before you fell; repent, and behave as you did at first, or else, if you will not repent, I shall come to you and take your lamp-stand from its

6 place. * ·It is in your favour, nevertheless, that you loathe as I do the way the

7 Nicolaitans are behaving. ·Let anyone who can hear, listen to what the Spirit is saying to the churches: * those who prove victorious I will feed *from the tree of life* set *in* God's *paradise*."

2 Smyrna

8 'Write to the angel of the church in Smyrna and say, "Here is the message of *the*

9 *First* and *the Last*, who was dead and has come to life again: ·I know your hardships and your poverty, and —though you are rich *—the slander of the people who

10 falsely claim to be Jews * but are really members of the synagogue of Satan. ·Do not be afraid of the sufferings that are coming to you. Look, the devil will send some of you to prison *to put you to the test*, and you must face hardship for *ten days*. * Even if you have to die, keep faithful, and I will give you the crown of life

11 for your prize. ·Let anyone who can hear, listen to what the Spirit is saying to the churches: for those who prove victorious will come to no harm from the second death."

3 Pergamum

12 'Write to the angel of the church in Pergamum and say, "Here is the message of

13 the one who has the sharp sword, double-edged: ·I know where you live, in the place where Satan is enthroned, and that you still hold firmly to my name, and did not disown your faith in me even when my faithful witness, Antipas, was killed among you, where Satan lives. *

14 "Nevertheless, I have one or two charges against you: some of you are followers of Balaam, who taught Balak to set a trap for the Israelites * so that they committed

15 adultery* by eating food that had been sacrificed to idols; ·and among you too

16 there are some also who follow the teaching of the Nicolaitans. * ·So repent, or I shall soon come to you and attack these people with the sword out of my mouth.

17 Let anyone who can hear, listen to what the Spirit is saying to the churches: to

those who prove victorious I will give some hidden manna and a white stone," with *a new name* written on it, known only to the person who receives it."

4 Thyatira

18 'Write to the angel of the church in Thyatira and say, "Here is the message of the
19 Son of God who has eyes like a burning flame and feet like burnished bronze: ·I know your activities, your love, your faith, your service and your perseverance,
20 and I know how you are still making progress. ·Nevertheless, I have a complaint to make: you tolerate the woman Jezebel° who claims to be a prophetess, and by her teaching she is luring my servants away to commit the adultery of eating food
21 which has been sacrificed to idols. ·I have given her time to repent but she is not
22 willing to repent of her adulterous life. ·Look, I am consigning her to a bed of pain, and all her partners in adultery to great hardship, unless they repent of their
23 practices;ᵖ ·and I will see that her children ᵠ die, so that all the churches realise that
24 it is I who *test motives and thoughts and repay* you *as your deeds deserve.* ·But on the rest of you in Thyatira, all of you who have not accepted this teaching or learnt the deep secrets of Satan,ʳ as they are called, I am not laying any other burden;
25. 26 but hold on firmly to what you already haveˢ until I come. ·To anyone who proves victorious, and keeps working for me until the end, *I will give* the authority over
27 *the nations* ·which I myself have been given by my Father, *to rule them with an iron*
28 *sceptre and shatter them like so many pots.* ·And I will give such a person the
29 Morning Star.ᵗ ·Let anyone who can hear, listen to what the Spirit is saying to the churches."

5 Sardis

1 **3** 'Write to the angel of the church in Sardis and say, "Here is the message of the one who holds the seven spiritsᵉ of God and the seven stars: I know about
2 your behaviour: how you are reputed to be alive and yet are dead. ·Wake up; put some resolve into what little vigour you have left: it is dying fast. So far I have failed to notice anything in your behaviour that my God could possibly call perfect;
3 remember how you first heard the message. Hold on to that. Repent! If you do not wake up, I shall come to you like a thief, and you will have no idea at what
4 hour I shall come upon you. ·There are a few in Sardis, it is true, who have kept
5 their robes unstained, and they are fit to come with me, dressed in white. ·Anyone who proves victorious will be dressed, like these, in white robes;ᵇ I shall not blot that name out of the book of life, but acknowledge it in the presence of my Father
6 and his angels. ·Let anyone who can hear, listen to what the Spirit is saying to the churches."

6 Philadelphia

7 'Write to the angel of the church in Philadelphia and say, "Here is the message of the holy and true one who *has the key of David,* so that *when he opens, no one will*
8 close, and when he closes, no one will open: ·I know about your activities. Look, I have opened in front of you a door that no one will be able to closeᶜ—and I know that though you are not very strong, you have kept my commandments and
9 not disowned my name. ·Look, I am going to make the synagogue of Satan—those who falsely claim to be Jews, but are liars, because they are no such thing—I will
10 make them *come and fall at your feet* and recognize that *I have loved you.* ·Because you have kept my commandment to persevere, I will keep you safe in the time of trial which is coming for the whole world, to put the people of the world to the

11 test. *^d* ·I am coming soon: hold firmly to what you already have, and let no one
12 take your victor's crown away from you. ·Anyone who proves victorious I will
make into a pillar in the sanctuary of my God, and it will stay there for ever; I will
inscribe on it the name of my God *^e* and the name of the city of my God, the new
Jerusalem which is coming down from my God in heaven, and my own new name
13 as well.*^f* ·Let anyone who can hear, listen to what the Spirit is saying to the
churches."

7 Laodicea

14 'Write to the angel of the church in Laodicea and say, "Here is the message of the
15 Amen,*^g* the trustworthy, the true witness, the Principle of God's creation:*^h* ·I
know about your activities: how you are neither cold nor hot. I wish you were one
16 or the other, ·but since you are neither hot nor cold, but only lukewarm, I will spit
17 you out of my mouth. ·You say to yourself: I am rich, I have made a fortune and
have everything I want, never realising that you are wretchedly and pitiably poor,
18 and blind and naked too.*ⁱ* ·I warn you, buy from me the gold that has been tested
in the fire*^j* to make you truly rich, and white robes to clothe you and hide your
19 shameful nakedness, and ointment to put on your eyes to enable you to see.*^k* ·I
20 *reprove* and *train those whom I love*: so repent in real earnest. ·Look, I am standing
at the door, knocking. If one of you hears me calling and opens the door, I will
21 come in to share a meal*^l* at that person's side. ·Anyone who proves victorious I
will allow to share my throne, just as I have myself overcome and have taken my
22 seat with my Father on his throne. ·Let anyone who can hear, listen to what the
Spirit is saying to the churches."'

II: THE PROPHETIC VISIONS

A: THE PRELUDE TO THE GREAT DAY OF GOD

God entrusts the future of the world to the Lamb *^a*

1 **4** Then, in my vision, I saw a door open in heaven and heard the same voice
speaking to me, the voice like a trumpet, saying, 'Come up here: I will show
2 you *what is to take place* in the future.' ·With that, I fell into ecstasy and I saw a
3 throne standing in heaven, and the *One* who was *sitting on the throne*, ·and the
One sitting there looked like a diamond and a ruby. There was a rainbow encircling
4 the throne, and this looked like an emerald.*^b* ·Round the throne in a circle were
twenty-four thrones, and on them twenty-four elders*^c* sitting, dressed in white
5 robes with golden crowns on their heads. ·Flashes of lightning were coming from
the throne, and the sound of peals of thunder,*^d* and in front of the throne there
6 were seven flaming lamps burning, the seven Spirits*^e* of God. ·In front of the
throne was a sea*^f* as transparent as crystal. *In the middle* of the throne and around
7 it,*^g* were *four living creatures*^h* all studded with eyes*, in front and behind. ·*The first*
living creature was like *a lion, the second* like *a bull, the third* living creature had *a*
8 *human face*, and *the fourth* living creature was like a flying *eagle*. ·*Each* of the four
living creatures had *six wings* and *was studded with eyes all the way round* as well
as inside; and day and night they never stopped singing:

> Holy, Holy, Holy
> *is the Lord God, the Almighty*;
> who was, and is and is to come.'*ⁱ*

9 Every time the living creatures glorified and honoured and gave thanks to the One
10 sitting on the throne, *who lives for ever and ever*, ·the twenty-four elders prostrated
themselves before him to worship the One *who lives for ever and ever*, and threw
down their crowns in front of the throne,*ʲ* saying:

> You are worthy, our Lord and God,
11 > to receive glory and honour and power,
> for you made the whole universe;
> by your will, when it did not exist, it was created.

1 **5** I saw that in the right hand of the One sitting on the throne there was *a scroll*
2 *that was written on back and front* and was sealed with seven seals. *ᵃ* ·Then I
saw a powerful angel who called with a loud voice, 'Who is worthy *ᵇ* to open the
3 scroll and break its seals?' ·But there was no one, in heaven or on the earth or
4 under the earth, *ᶜ* who was able to open the scroll and read it. ·I wept bitterly
5 because nobody could be found to open the scroll and read it, ·but one of the
elders said to me, 'Do not weep. Look, *the Lion* of the tribe *of Judah, the Root* of
David, has triumphed, *ᵈ* and so he will open the scroll and its seven seals.'
6 Then I saw, in the middle of the throne with its four living creatures and the
circle of the elders, a Lamb that seemed to have been sacrificed; *ᵉ* it had seven
horns, and it had seven eyes,*ᶠ* which are the seven Spirits that God has *sent out*
7 *over the whole world*. ·The Lamb came forward to take the scroll from the right
8 hand of the One sitting on the throne, ·and when he took it, the four living
creatures prostrated themselves before him and with them the twenty-four elders;
each one of them was holding a harp and had a golden bowl full of incense which
9 are the prayers of the saints. ·They sang a new hymn:

> You are worthy to take the scroll
> and to break its seals,
> because you were sacrificed, and with your blood
> you bought *ᵍ* people for God
> of every race, language, people and nation *ʰ*
10 > and made them *a line of kings and priests for God*,
> to rule the world.

11 In my vision, I heard the sound of an immense number of angels gathered round
the throne and the living creatures and the elders; there were *ten thousand times*
12 *ten thousand of them* and *thousands upon thousands*, ·loudly chanting:

> Worthy is the Lamb that was sacrificed
> to receive power, riches, wisdom,
> strength, honour, glory and blessing.

13 Then I heard all the living things in creation—everything that lives in heaven, and
on earth, and under the earth, and in the sea, crying:

> To the One seated on the throne and to the Lamb,
> be all praise, honour, glory and power,
> for ever and ever.

14 And the four living creatures said, 'Amen'; and the elders prostrated themselves
to worship.

The Lamb breaks the seven seals *

1 6 Then, in my vision, I saw the Lamb break one of the seven seals, and I heard one of the four living creatures shout in a voice like thunder, 'Come!'
2 Immediately I saw a white horse appear, and its rider was holding a bow; he was given a victor's crown and he went away, to go from victory to victory. *

3 When he broke the second seal, I heard the second living creature shout,
4 'Come!' ·And out came another horse, bright red, and its rider was given this duty: to take away peace from the earth and set people killing each other. He was given a huge sword. *

5 When he broke the third seal, I heard the third living creature shout, 'Come!' Immediately I saw a black horse appear, and its rider was holding a pair of scales; *
6 and I seemed to hear a voice shout from among the four living creatures and say, 'A day's wages for a quart of corn, and a day's wages for three quarts of barley, but do not tamper with the oil or the wine.'

7 When he broke the fourth seal, I heard the voice of the fourth living creature
8 shout, 'Come!' ·Immediately I saw another horse appear, deathly pale, and its rider was called Death, * and Hades followed at its heels. *

They were given authority over a quarter of the earth, *to kill by the sword, by famine, by plague and through wild beasts.*

9 When he broke the fifth seal, I saw underneath the altar the souls of all the people who had been killed on account of the Word of God, * for witnessing to it.
10 They shouted in a loud voice, 'Holy, true Master, how much longer will you wait before you pass sentence and take vengeance for our death on the inhabitants of
11 the earth?' ·Each of them was given a white robe, * and they were told to be patient a little longer, until the roll was completed of their fellow-servants and brothers who were still to be killed as they had been.

12 In my vision, when he broke the sixth seal, there was a violent earthquake and the sun went as black as coarse sackcloth; the moon turned red as blood all over,
13 and *the stars of the sky fell* onto the earth *like figs* dropping from a fig tree when a
14 high wind shakes it; ·the *sky disappeared like a scroll rolling up* and all the
15 mountains and islands were shaken from their places. * ·Then all the kings of the earth, the governors and the commanders, the rich people and the men of influence, the whole population, slaves and citizens, *hid in caverns and among the*
16 *rocks of the mountains.* ·*They said to the mountains* and the rocks, '*Fall on us* and hide us away from the One who sits on the throne and from the retribution of the
17 Lamb. ·For *the Great Day of his retribution* has come, *and who can face it?*'

God's servants will be preserved

1 7 Next I saw four angels, standing at *the four corners of the earth*, holding back the four winds of the world to keep them from blowing over the land or the
2 sea or any tree. ·Then I saw another angel rising where the sun rises, carrying the seal of the living God; he called in a powerful voice to the four angels * whose duty
3 was to devastate land and sea, ·'Wait before you do any damage on land or at sea or to the trees, until we have put the *seal on the foreheads* of the servants of our
4 God.' ·And I heard how many had been sealed: a hundred and forty-four thousand, * out of all the tribes of Israel.

5 From the tribe of Judah, twelve thousand had been sealed; from the tribe of
6 Reuben, twelve thousand; from the tribe of Gad, twelve thousand; ·from the tribe of Asher, twelve thousand; from the tribe of Naphtali, twelve thousand; from the

7 tribe of Manasseh, twelve thousand; •from the tribe of Simeon, twelve thousand; from the tribe of Levi, twelve thousand; from the tribe of Issachar, twelve thou-
8 sand; •from the tribe of Zebulun, twelve thousand; from the tribe of Joseph, twelve thousand; and from the tribe of Benjamin, twelve thousand had been sealed.

The rewarding of the saints

9 After that I saw that there was a huge number, impossible for anyone to count, of people from every nation, race, tribe and language; *ᶜ* they were standing in front of the throne and in front of the Lamb, dressed in white robes and holding palms
10 in their hands. *ᵈ* They shouted in a loud voice, •'Salvation to our God, who sits on
11 the throne, and to the Lamb!' •And all the angels who were standing in a circle round the throne, surrounding the elders and the four living creatures, prostrated themselves before the throne, and touched the ground with their foreheads,
12 worshipping God •with these words:

> Amen. Praise and glory and wisdom,
> thanksgiving and honour and power and strength
> to our God for ever and ever. Amen.

13 One of the elders then spoke and asked me, 'Who are these people, dressed in
14 white robes, and where have they come from?' •I answered him, 'You can tell me, sir.' Then he said, *ᵉ* 'These are the people who have been through the great trial; *ᶠ*
15 they have washed their robes white again in the blood of the Lamb. *ᵍ* •That is why they are standing in front of God's throne and serving him day and night in his sanctuary; and the One who sits on the throne will spread his tent over them.
16 *They will never hunger or thirst* again; *sun and scorching wind will never plague*
17 *them,* •because the Lamb who is at the heart of the throne *will be their shepherd and will guide them to springs of living water*; and God *will wipe away all tears from their eyes.' ʰ*

The seventh seal

1 **8** The Lamb then broke the seventh seal, and there was silence in heaven for about half an hour. *ᵃ*

The prayers of the saints bring the coming of the Great Day nearer

2 Next I saw seven trumpets being given to the seven angels who stand in the
3 presence of God. •Another angel, who had a golden censer, *ᵇ* came and stood at the altar. *ᶜ* A large quantity of incense was given to him to offer with the prayers of
4 all the saints on the golden altar that stood in front of the throne; •and so from the angel's hand the smoke of the incense went up in the presence of God and with it
5 the prayers of the saints. •Then the angel took the censer and *filled it from the fire of the altar*, which he then hurled down onto the earth; immediately there came peals of thunder and flashes of lightning, and the earth shook.

The first four trumpets

6 The seven angels that had the seven trumpets now made ready to sound them.
7 The first blew his trumpet and, with that, hail and fire, mixed with blood, were hurled on the earth: a third of the earth was burnt up, and a third of all trees, and
8 every blade of grass was burnt. *ᵈ* •The second angel blew his trumpet, and it was as though a great mountain blazing with fire was hurled into the sea: a third of the

9 sea turned into blood, ·a third of all the living things in the sea were killed, and a
10 third of all ships were destroyed. ·The third angel blew his trumpet, and a huge
star fell from the sky, burning like a ball of fire, and it fell on a third of all rivers
11 and on the springs of water; ·this was the star called Wormwood, and a third of all
water turned to wormwood, so that many people died; the water had become so
12 bitter. ·The fourth angel blew his trumpet, and a third of the sun and a third of the
moon and a third of the stars were blasted, so that the light went out of a third of
them and the day lost a third of its illumination, and likewise the night.
13 In my vision, I heard an eagle, *e* calling aloud as it flew high overhead, 'Disaster,
disaster, disaster, on all the people on earth at the sound of the other three
trumpets which the three angels have yet to blow!'

The fifth trumpet

1 9 Then the fifth angel blew his trumpet, and I saw a star *a* that had fallen from
heaven onto the earth, and the angel was given the key to the shaft leading
2 down to the Abyss. *b* ·When he unlocked the shaft of the Abyss, *smoke rose* out of
the Abyss *like the smoke from a* huge *furnace* so that the sun and the sky were
3 darkened by the smoke from the Abyss, ·and out of the smoke dropped locusts
4 onto the earth: they were given the powers that scorpions have on the earth: *c* ·they
were forbidden to harm any fields or crops or trees *d* and told to attack only those
5 people who were without God's seal on their foreheads. ·They were not to kill
them, but to give them anguish for five months, and the anguish was to be the
6 anguish of a scorpion's sting. ·When this happens, *people will long for death and
not find it anywhere*; they will want to die and death will evade them.
7 These locusts *looked like horses* armoured *for battle*; they had what looked like
8 gold crowns on their heads, and their faces looked human, ·and their hair was
9 like women's hair, and *teeth like lion's teeth*. ·They had body-armour like iron
breastplates, and the noise of their wings sounded like *the racket of chariots with
10 many horses charging*. ·Their tails were like scorpions' tails, with stings, and with
11 their tails they were able to torture people for five months. ·As their leader they
had their emperor, the angel of the Abyss, whose name in Hebrew is Abaddon,
and in Greek Apollyon. *e*
12 That was the first of the disasters; there are still two more to come.

The sixth trumpet

13 The sixth angel blew his trumpet, and I heard a single voice issuing from the four
14 horns of the golden altar *f* in God's presence. ·It spoke to the sixth angel with the
trumpet, and said, 'Release the four angels that are chained up at the great river
15 Euphrates.' *g* ·These four angels had been ready for this hour of this day of this
16 month of this year, and ready to destroy a third of the human race. ·I learnt how
many there were in their army: twice ten thousand times ten thousand mounted
17 men. ·In my vision I saw the horses, and the riders with their breastplates of flame
colour, hyacinth-blue and sulphur-yellow; the horses had lions' heads, and fire,
18 smoke and sulphur were coming from their mouths. ·It was by these three plagues,
the fire, the smoke and the sulphur coming from their mouths, that the one third
19 of the human race was killed. ·All the horses' power was in their mouths and their
20 tails: their tails were like snakes, and had heads which inflicted wounds. ·But the
rest of the human race, who escaped death by these plagues, refused either to
abandon *their own handiwork* or to stop worshipping devils, the *idols made of*

21 *gold, silver, bronze, stone and wood* that can neither see nor hear nor move. ·Nor did they give up their murdering, or witchcraft, or fornication or stealing.

The imminence of the last punishment

1 **10** Then I saw another powerful angel coming down from heaven, wrapped in cloud, with a rainbow over his head; his face was like the sun, and his legs
2 were pillars of fire. ·In his hand he had a small scroll, unrolled;ᵃ he put his right
3 foot in the sea and his left foot on the land ·and he shouted so loud, it was *like a*
4 *lion roaring*. At this, the seven claps of thunder made themselves heardᵇ ·and when the seven thunderclaps had sounded, I was preparing to write, when I heard a voice from heaven say to me, 'Keep the words of the seven thunderclaps secret
5 and do not write them down.'ᶜ ·Then the angel that I had seen, standing on the
6 sea and the land, *raised his right hand to heaven*,ᵈ ·and *swore by him who lives for ever* and ever, *and made heaven and all that it contains*, and *earth and all it contains*,
7 and *the sea and all it contains*, 'The time of waiting is over; ·at the time when the seventh angel is heard sounding his trumpet, the mystery of Godᵉ will be fulfilled, just as he announced in the gospel to *his servants the prophets*.'

The seer eats the small scrollᶠ

8 Then I heard the voice I had heard from heaven speaking to me again. 'Go', it said, 'and take that open scroll from the hand of the angel standing on sea and
9 land.' ·I went to the angel and asked him to give me the small scroll, and he said, 'Take it and eat it; it will turn your stomach sour, but it will taste as sweet as
10 honey.' ·So I took it out of the angel's hand, and *I ate it and it tasted sweet as*
11 *honey*, but when I had eaten it my stomach turned sour.ᵍ ·Then I was told, 'You are to prophesy again, this time against many different nations and countries and languages and kings.'

The two witnesses

1 **11** Then I was given a long cane like a measuring rod,ᵃ and I was told, 'Get up and measure God's sanctuary, and the altar, and the people who worship
2 there;ᵇ ·but exclude the outer court and do not measure it, because it has been handed over to gentiles—they will trample on the holy city for forty-two months.ᶜ
3 But I shall send my two witnesses to prophesy for twelve hundred and sixty days,
4 wearing sackcloth. ·These are the *two olive trees* and the two lamps *in attendance*
5 *on the Lord of the world*.ᵈ ·Fire comes from their mouths and consumes their enemies if anyone tries to harm them; and anyone who tries to harm them will
6 certainly be killed in this way. ·They have the power to lock up the sky so that it does not rain as long as they are prophesying; they have the power to turn water
7 into blood and strike the whole world with any plague as often as they like. ·When they have completed their witnessing, the beast that comes out of the Abyssᵉ *is*
8 *going to make war on them and overcome them* and kill them. ·Their corpses lie in the main street of the great cityᶠ known by the symbolic names Sodom and Egypt,
9 in which their Lord was crucified. ·People of every race, tribe, language and nation
10 stare at their corpses, for three-and-a-half days, not letting them be buried, ·and the people of the world are glad about it and celebrate the event by giving presents to each other, because these two prophets have been a plague to the people of the world.'
11 After the three-and-a-half days, *God breathed life into them and they stood up*
12 *on their feet*, and everybody who saw it happen was terrified; ·then I heardᵍ a loud

13 voice from heaven say to them, 'Come up here,' and while their enemies were watching, they went up to heaven in a cloud. ·Immediately, there was a violent earthquake, and a tenth of the city collapsed; seven thousand persons ʰ were killed in the earthquake, and the survivors, overcome with fear, could only praise the God of heaven.

14 That was the second of the disasters; the third is to come quickly after it. ⁱ

The seventh trumpet

15 Then the seventh angel blew his trumpet, and voices could be heard shouting in heaven, calling, 'The kingdom of the world has become the kingdom of our Lord
16 and his Christ, and he will reign for ever and ever.' ·The twenty-four elders, enthroned in the presence of God, prostrated themselves and touched the ground
17 with their foreheads worshipping God ·with these words, 'We give thanks to you, Almighty Lord God, He who is, He who was, for assuming your great power and
18 beginning your reign. ·*The nations were in uproar* and now the time has come for your retribution, and for the dead to be judged, and for *your servants the prophets*, for the saints and for *those who fear* your name, *small and great alike*, to be rewarded. The time has come to destroy those who are destroying the earth.'
19 Then the sanctuary of God in heaven ʲ opened, and the ark of the covenant could be seen inside it. Then came flashes of lightning, peals of thunder and an earthquake and violent hail.

The vision of the woman and the dragon ᵃ

1   **12** Now a great sign appeared in heaven: a woman, ᵇ robed with the sun,
2   standing on the moon, and on her head a crown of twelve stars. ·She was
3   pregnant, and in labour, crying aloud in the pangs of childbirth. ·Then a second sign appeared in the sky: there was a huge red dragon with seven heads and ten
4   horns, and each of the seven heads crowned with a coronet. ᶜ ·Its tail swept a third of *the stars from the sky and hurled them to the ground*, ᵈ and the dragon stopped in front of the woman as she was at the point of giving birth, so that he could eat
5   the child as soon as it was born. ·The woman *was delivered of a boy*, ᵉ the son who was *to rule all the nations with an iron sceptre*, and the child was taken straight up
6   to God and to his throne, ᶠ ·while the woman escaped into the desert, ᵍ where God had prepared a place for her to be looked after for twelve hundred and sixty days.
7   And now war broke out in heaven, when *Michael* ʰ with his angels attacked the
8   dragon. The dragon fought back with his angels, ·but they were defeated and
9   driven out of heaven. ·The great dragon, the primeval serpent, known as the devil or Satan, who had led all the world astray, was hurled down to the earth and his
10 angels were hurled down with him. ·Then I heard a voice shout from heaven, 'Salvation and power and empire for ever have been won by our God, and all authority for his Christ, now that the accuser, who accused our brothers day and
11 night before our God, has been brought down. ·They have triumphed over him by the blood of the Lamb and by the word to which they bore witness, because even
12 in the face of death they did not cling to life. ·So let the heavens rejoice and all who live there; but for you, earth and sea, disaster is coming—because the devil has gone down to you in a rage, knowing that he has little time left.'
13 As soon as the dragon found himself hurled down to the earth, he sprang in
14 pursuit of the woman, the mother of the male child, ·but she was given a pair of the great eagle's wings to fly away from the serpent into the desert, to the place
15 where she was to be looked after for *a time, two times and half a time*. ⁱ ·So the

serpent vomited water from his mouth, like a river, after the woman, to sweep her
16 away in the current,ʲ ·but the earth came to her rescue; it opened its mouth and
17 swallowed the river spewed from the dragon's mouth. ·Then the dragon was
enraged with the woman and went away to make war on the rest of her children,
who obey God's commandments and have in themselves the witness of Jesus.ᵏ

The dragon delegates his power to the beast ᶦ

18 And I took my stand ᵐ on the seashore.

1 **13** Then I saw *a beast emerge from the sea*: it had seven heads and ten horns,
with a coronet on each of its ten horns, and its heads were marked with
2 blasphemous titles. ·I saw that the beast *was like a leopard*, with paws like *a bear*
and a mouth like *a lion*; the dragon had handed over to it his own power and his
3 throne and his immense authority.ᵃ ·I saw that one of its heads seemed to have
had a fatal wound but that this deadly injury had healed ᵇ and the whole world had
4 marvelled and followed the beast. ·They prostrated themselves in front of the
dragon because he had given the beast his authority; and they prostrated themselves in front of the beast, saying, 'Who can compare with the beast?ᶜ Who can
5 fight against him?' ·The beast was allowed *to mouth its boasts* and blasphemies
6 and to be active for forty-two months; ·and it mouthed its blasphemies against
God, against his name, his heavenly Tent and all those who are sheltered there.
7 It was allowed *to make war against the saints and conquer them, and given power*
8 over every race, people, language and nation; ·and all people of the world will
worship it, that is, everybody whose name has not been written down since the
9 foundation of the world in the sacrificial Lamb's book of life. ·Let anyone who
10 can hear, listen: *Those for captivity to captivity; those for* deathᵈ *by the sword to
death by the sword.* ᵉ This is why the saints must have perseverance and faith.

The false prophet as the slave of the beast

11 Then I saw a second beast, emerging from the ground;ᶠ it had two horns like a
12 lamb, but made a noise like a dragon. ·This second beast exercised all the power
of the first beast, on its behalf making the world and all its people worship the first
13 beast, whose deadly injury had healed. ·And it worked great miracles, even to
14 calling down fire from heaven onto the earth while people watched. ·Through the
miracles which it was allowed to do on behalf of the first beast, it was able to lead
astray the people of the world and persuade them to put up a statue in honour of
15 the beast that had been wounded by the sword and still lived. ·It was allowed to
breathe life into this statue, so that the statue of the beast was able to speak, and
16 to have *anyone who refused to worship the statue* of the beast put to death.ᵍ ·It
compelled everyone—small and great alike, rich and poor, slave and citizen—to
17 be branded on the right hand or on the forehead, ·and made it illegal for anyone
to buy or sell anything unless he had been branded with the name of the beast or
with the number of its name.
18 There is need for shrewdness here: anyone clever may interpret the number of
the beast: it is the number of a human being, the number 666.ʰ

The companions of the Lamb ᵃ

1 **14** Next in my vision I saw Mount Zion, and standing on it the Lamb ᵇ who
had with him a hundred and forty-four thousand people, all with his name
2 and his Father's name written on their foreheads. ·I heard a sound coming out of
heaven like the sound of the ocean or the roar of thunder; it was like the sound of

3 harpists playing their harps. ·There before the throne they were singing a new hymn ᶜ in the presence of the four living creatures and the elders, a hymn that could be learnt only by the hundred and forty-four thousand who had been
4 redeemed from the world. ·These are the sons who have kept their virginity ᵈ and not been defiled with women; they *follow* the Lamb wherever he goes; ᵉ they, out of all people, have been redeemed to be *the first-fruits for God* and for the Lamb.
5 *No lie* was found in their mouths and no fault can be found in them. ᶠ

Angels announce the Day of Judgement ᵍ

6 Then I saw another angel, flying high overhead, sent to announce the gospel of
7 eternity to all who live on the earth, every nation, race, language and tribe. ·He was calling, 'Fear God and glorify him, because the time has come for him to sit in judgement; worship *the maker of heaven and earth and sea* and the springs of water.'
8 A second angel followed him, calling, '*Babylon has fallen, Babylon the Great has fallen,* ʰ Babylon which gave the whole world *the wine of retribution* to drink.' ⁱ
9 A third angel followed, shouting aloud, 'All those who worship the beast and
10 his statue, or have had themselves branded on the hand or forehead, ·will be made to drink the wine of God's fury which is ready, undiluted, in his cup of retribution; in *fire and brimstone* ʲ they will be tortured in the presence of the holy angels and
11 the Lamb ·and *the smoke* of their torture *rise for ever and ever.* There will be no respite, *night or day,* for those who worship the beast or its statue or accept
12 branding with its name.' ·This is why there must be perseverance in the saints who
13 keep the commandments of God and faith in Jesus. ·Then I heard a voice from heaven say to me, 'Write down: Blessed are those who die in the Lord! Blessed indeed, the Spirit says; now they can rest for ever after their work, since their good deeds go with them.'

The harvest and vintage of the gentiles ᵏ

14 Now in my vision I saw a white *cloud* and, *sitting on it, one like a son of man* with a
15 gold crown on his head and a sharp sickle in his hand. ·Then another angel came out of the sanctuary and shouted at the top of his voice to the one sitting on the cloud, '*Ply* your *sickle* and reap: harvest time has come and *the harvest* of the earth
16 *is ripe.*' ·Then the one sitting on the cloud set his sickle to work on the earth, and the harvest of earth was reaped.
17 Another angel, who also carried a sharp sickle, came out of the temple in
18 heaven, ·and the angel in charge of the fire left the altar ˡ and shouted at the top of his voice to the one with the sharp sickle, 'Put your sickle in and harvest the
19 bunches from the vine of the earth; all its grapes are ripe.' ·So the angel set his sickle to work on the earth and harvested the whole vintage of the earth and put it
20 into a huge winepress, the winepress of God's anger, ·outside the city, ᵐ where it was trodden until the blood that came out of the winepress was up to the horses' bridles as far away as sixteen hundred furlongs.

The hymn of Moses and the Lamb ⁿ

1 **15** And I saw in heaven another sign, great and wonderful: seven angels were bringing the seven plagues that are the last of all, because they exhaust the
2 anger of God. ·I seemed to be looking at a sea of crystal suffused with fire, and standing by the lake of glass, those who had fought against the beast and won, and against his statue and the number which is his name. They all had harps from God,

3 and they were singing the hymn of Moses, [b] the servant of God, and the hymn of the Lamb:

> How great and wonderful are all your works,
> Lord God Almighty;
> upright and true are all your ways,
> *King of nations*.

4 *Who does not revere* and *glorify your name, O Lord?*
> For you alone are holy,
> *and all nations will come and adore you*
> for the many acts of saving justice you have shown.

The seven bowls of plagues [c]

5 After this, in my vision, the sanctuary, the tent of the Testimony, opened in
6 heaven, ·and out came the seven angels with the seven plagues, wearing pure
7 white linen, fastened round their waists with belts of gold. ·One of the four living creatures gave the seven angels seven golden bowls filled with the anger of God
8 who lives for ever and ever. ·*The smoke from the glory* and the power *of God filled* the temple so that no one could go into it [d] until the seven plagues of the seven angels were completed.

1 **16** Then I heard a loud voice from the sanctuary calling to the seven angels, 'Go, and empty the seven bowls of God's anger over the earth.'
2 The first angel went and emptied his bowl over the earth; at once, on all the people who had been branded with the mark of the beast and had worshipped its statue, there came disgusting and virulent sores.
3 The second angel emptied his bowl over the sea, and it turned to blood, like the blood of a corpse, and every living creature in the sea died.
4 The third angel emptied his bowl into the rivers and springs of water and they
5 turned into blood. ·Then I heard the angel of water say, 'You are the Upright
6 One, He who is, He who was, the Holy One, for giving this verdict: ·they spilt the blood of the saints and the prophets, and blood is what you have given them to
7 drink; it is what they deserve.' ·And I heard the altar itself say, 'Truly, Lord God Almighty, the punishments you give are true and just.'
8 The fourth angel emptied his bowl over the sun and it was made to scorch people
9 with its flames; ·but though people were scorched by the fierce heat of it, they cursed the name of God who had the power to cause such plagues, and they would not repent and glorify him.
10 The fifth angel emptied his bowl over the throne of the beast [e] and its whole
11 empire was plunged into darkness. People were biting their tongues for pain, ·but instead of repenting for what they had done, they cursed the God of heaven because of their pains and sores.
12 The sixth angel emptied his bowl over the great river Euphrates; all the water
13 dried up so that a way was made for the kings of the East [b] to come in. ·Then from the jaws of dragon and beast and false prophet I saw three foul spirits come; they
14 looked like frogs ·and in fact were demon spirits, able to work miracles, going out to all the kings of the world to call them together for the war of the Great Day of
15 God the Almighty. [c]—·Look, I shall come like a thief. Blessed is anyone who has kept watch, and has kept his clothes on, so that he does not go out naked and
16 expose his shame.—·They called the kings together at the place called, in Hebrew, Armageddon. [d]

17 The seventh angel emptied his bowl into the air, and a great voice boomed out
18 from the sanctuary, ' 'The end has come.' ·Then there were flashes of lightning
and peals of thunder and a violent earthquake, *unparalleled since* humanity *first*
19 *came into existence.* ·The Great City was split into three parts and the cities of the
world collapsed; Babylon the Great was not forgotten: God made her drink
20 the full winecup of his retribution. ·Every island vanished and the mountains
21 disappeared;ᶠ ·and hail, with great hailstones weighing a talent each,ᵍ fell from
the sky on the people. They cursed God for sending a plague of hail; it was the
most terrible plague.

B: THE PUNISHMENT OF BABYLON

The great prostitute

1   One of the seven angels that had the seven bowls came to speak to me, and
17 said, 'Come here and I will show you the punishment of the great prostituteᵃ
2 *who* is *enthroned beside abundant waters,*ᵇ ·with whom all the kings of the earth
have prostituted themselves, and who has made all the population of the world
3 drunk with the wine of her adultery.'ᶜ ·He took me in spirit to a desert,ᵈ and there
I saw a woman riding a scarlet beast which had seven heads and ten hornsᵉ and
4 had blasphemous titles written all over it. ·The woman was dressed in purple and
scarlet and glittered with gold and jewels and pearls, and she was holding a gold
5 winecup filled with the disgusting filth of her prostitution; ·on her forehead was
written a name, a cryptic name: 'Babylon the Great, the mother of all the prosti-
6 tutes and all the filthy practices on the earth.' ·I saw that she was drunk, drunk
with the blood of the saints, and the blood of the martyrs of Jesus;ᶠ and when I saw
7 her, I was completely mystified. ·The angel said to me, 'Do you not understand? I
will tell you the meaning of this woman, and of the beast she is riding, with the
seven heads and the ten horns.

The symbolism of the beast and the prostituteᵍ

8 'The beast you have seen was once alive and is alive no longer; it is yet to come up
from the Abyss, but only to go to its destruction. And the people of the world,
whose names have not been written since the beginning of the world in the book
of life, will be astonished when they see how the beast was once alive and is alive
no longer, and is still to come.
9 —'This calls for shrewdness. The seven heads are the seven hills, on which the
10 woman is sitting. ·The seven heads are also seven emperors.ʰ Five of them have
already gone, one is here now, and one is yet to come; once here, he must stay for
11 a short while. ·The beast, who was alive and is alive no longer, is at the same time
the eighth and one of the seven, and he is going to his destruction.
12 '*The ten horns* which you saw *are ten kings* who have not yet been given their
royal power but will have royal authority only for a single hour and in association
13 with the beast. ·They are all of one mind in putting their strength and their powers
14 at the beast's disposal, ·and they will go to war against the Lamb; but because the
Lamb is *Lord of lords* and *King of kings*, he will defeat them, he and his followers,
the called, the chosen, the trustworthy.'ⁱ
15 The angel continued, 'The waters you saw, beside which the prostitute was
16 sitting, are all the peoples, the populations, the nations and the languages. ·But

the ten horns and the beast will turn against the prostitute, and *tear off her clothes* and leave her stark naked; then they will eat her flesh and burn the remains in the
17 fire. ·In fact, God has influenced their minds to do what he intends, to agree together to put their royal powers at the beast's disposal until the time when God's
18 words shall be fulfilled. ·The woman you saw is the great city which has authority over all the rulers on earth.'

An angel announces the fall of Babylon *

1 **18** After this, I saw another angel come down from heaven, with great author-
2 ity given to him; *the earth shone with his glory*. ·At the top of his voice he shouted, '*Babylon has fallen, Babylon* the Great *has fallen*, and has become *the*
3 *haunt of devils* and a lodging for every foul spirit and dirty, loathsome bird. ·All the nations have drunk deep of the wine of her prostitution; ᵇ every king on the earth has prostituted himself with her, and every merchant grown rich through her debauchery.'

The people of God summoned to flee

4 Another voice spoke from heaven; I heard it say, 'Come out, my people, away from her, so that you do not share in her crimes and have the same plagues to
5 bear. ·Her sins have reached up to the sky, and God has her crimes in mind: *treat*
6 *her as she has treated others.* ·She must be paid double the amount she exacted.
7 She is to have a doubly strong cup of her own mixture. ·Every one of her pomps and orgies is to be matched by a torture or an agony. *I am enthroned as queen, she*
8 *thinks; I am no widow and will never know bereavement.* ·For that, *in one day*, the plagues will fall on her: disease and mourning and famine. She will be burned to the ground. The Lord God who has condemned her is mighty.'

The people of the world mourn for Babylon. ᶜ

9 'There will be mourning and weeping for her by the kings of the earth who have prostituted themselves with her and held orgies with her. They see the smoke as
10 she burns, ·while they keep at a safe distance through fear of her anguish. They will say:

> Mourn, mourn for this great city,
> Babylon, so powerful a city,
> in one short hour your doom has come upon you.

11 'There will be weeping and distress over her among all the traders of the earth
12 when no one is left to buy their cargoes of goods; ·their stocks of gold and silver, jewels and pearls, linen and purple and silks and scarlet; all the sandalwood, every
13 piece in ivory or fine wood, in bronze or iron or marble; ·the cinnamon and spices, the myrrh and ointment and incense; wine, oil, flour and corn; their stocks of cattle, sheep, horses and chariots, their slaves and their human cargo.
14 'All the fruits you had set your hearts on have failed you; gone for ever, never to return again, is your life of magnificence and ease.
15 'The traders who had made a fortune out of her will be standing at a safe distance
16 through fear of her anguish, mourning and weeping. ·They will be saying:

> Mourn, mourn for this great city;
> for all the linen and purple and scarlet that you wore,

for all your finery of gold and jewels and pearls;
17   your huge riches are all destroyed within a single hour.'

All the captains and seafaring men, sailors and all those who make a living from
18   the sea kept a safe distance, ·watching the smoke as she burned, and crying out,
19   'Has there ever been a city as great as this!' ·They threw dust on their heads and
said, with tears and groans:

'Mourn, mourn for this great city
whose lavish living has made a fortune
for every owner of a sea-going ship,
ruined within a single hour.'

20   'Now heaven, celebrate her downfall, and all you saints, apostles and prophets:
God has given judgement for you against her.'
21   Then a powerful angel picked up a boulder like a great millstone, and as he
hurled it into the sea, he said, 'That is how the great city of Babylon is going to be
hurled down, never to be seen again. *

Never again in you
22   will be heard the song of harpists and minstrels,
the music of flute and trumpet;
never again will craftsmen of every skill be found in you
or *the sound of the handmill* be heard;
23   never again will shine *the light of the lamp* in you,
never again will be heard in you
the voices of bridegroom and bride.
Your traders were the princes of the earth,
all the nations were led astray by your sorcery.

24   In her was found the blood of prophets and saints, and all the blood that was ever
shed on earth.'

Songs of victory in heaven *

1
2   **19** After this I heard what seemed to be the great sound of a huge crowd in
heaven, singing, 'Alleluia! * Salvation and glory and power to our God! ·He
judges fairly, he punishes justly, and he has condemned the great prostitute who
corrupted the earth with her prostitution; he has avenged the blood of his servants
3   which she shed.' ·And again they sang, 'Alleluia! *The smoke* of her *will rise for*
4   *ever and ever.*' ·Then the twenty-four elders and the four living creatures threw
themselves down and worshipped God seated on his throne, and they cried,
'Amen, Alleluia.'
5   Then a voice came from the throne; it said, 'Praise our God, you servants of his
6   and *those who fear him, small and great alike.*' ·And I heard what seemed to be
the voices of a huge crowd, like the sound of the ocean or the great roar of thunder,
7   answering, 'Alleluia! The reign of the Lord our God Almighty has begun; ·let us
be glad and joyful and give glory to God, because this is the time for the marriage
8   of the Lamb. * ·His bride is ready, and she has been able to dress herself in dazzling
9   white linen, because her linen is made of the good deeds of the saints.' ·The angel
said, 'Write this, "Blessed are those who are invited to the wedding feast of the
10   Lamb," ' and he added, 'These words of God are true.' ·Then I knelt at his feet to
worship him, but he said to me, 'Never do that: * I am your fellow-servant and the

fellow-servant of all your brothers who have in themselves the witness of Jesus. God alone you must worship.' The witness of Jesus is the spirit of prophecy. *

C: THE DESTRUCTION OF THE UNBELIEVERS

The first eschatological battle *

11 And now I saw heaven open, and a white horse * appear; its rider was called
12 Trustworthy and True; *in uprightness he judges* and makes war. ·His eyes were flames of fire, and he was crowned with many coronets; * the name written on him
13 was known only to himself, ·*his cloak was soaked in blood.* * He is known by the
14 name, The Word of God. * ·Behind him, dressed in linen of dazzling white, rode
15 the armies of heaven * on white horses. ·From his mouth came a sharp sword * with which to strike the unbelievers; he is the one *who will rule them with an iron*
16 *sceptre*, and tread out the wine of Almighty God's fierce retribution. * ·On his cloak and on his thigh a name was written: *King of kings* and *Lord of lords*. *
17 I saw an angel standing in the sun, and he shouted aloud to all the birds that were flying high overhead in the sky, 'Come here. *Gather together at* God's *great*
18 *feast*. ·You will eat the flesh of *kings*, and the flesh of great generals and heroes, the flesh of horses and their riders and of all kinds of people, citizens and slaves, small and great alike.'
19 Then I saw the beast, with all the kings of the earth and their armies, gathered
20 together to fight the Rider and his army. ·But the beast was taken prisoner, together with the false prophet who had worked miracles on the beast's behalf and by them had deceived those who had accepted branding with the mark of the beast and those who had worshipped his statue. * These two were hurled alive into
21 the fiery lake of burning sulphur. ·All the rest were killed by the sword of the Rider, which came out of his mouth, and *all the birds glutted themselves with their flesh*.

The reign of a thousand years

1 **20** Then I saw an angel come down from heaven with the key of the Abyss in his
2 hand and an enormous chain. ·He overpowered the dragon, that primeval
3 serpent which is the devil and Satan, and chained him up for a thousand years. ·He hurled him into the Abyss and shut the entrance and sealed it over him, to make sure he would not lead the nations astray again until the thousand years had passed. At the end of that time he must be released, but only for a short while.
4 Then I saw thrones, where they took their seats, and *on them was conferred the power to give judgement*. I saw the souls of all who had been beheaded for having witnessed for Jesus and for having preached God's word, * and those who refused to worship the beast or his statue and would not accept the brand-mark on their foreheads or hands; they came to life, and reigned with Christ for a thousand
5 years. * ·The rest of the dead did not come to life until the thousand years were
6 over; this is the first resurrection. ·Blessed and holy are those who share in the first resurrection; the second death has no power over them * but they will be priests of God and of Christ and reign with him for a thousand years. *
7, 8 When the thousand years are over, Satan will be released from his prison ·and will come out to lead astray all the nations in the four quarters of the earth, *Gog and Magog*, * and mobilise them for war, his armies being as many as the sands of

9 the sea. ·They came swarming over the entire country and besieged the camp of the saints, which is the beloved City. *f But fire rained down on them from heaven*
10 and consumed them. ·Then the devil, who led them astray, was hurled into the lake of fire and sulphur, where the beast and the false prophet are, and their torture will not come to an end, day or night, for ever and ever.

The Last Judgement

11 Then I saw a great white throne and the One who was sitting on it. *g* In his presence,
12 earth and sky vanished, leaving no trace. ·I saw the dead, great and small alike, standing in front of his throne while *the books lay open.* And another book was opened, which is the book of life, and the dead were judged from what was written in the books, as their deeds deserved. *h*
13. 14 The sea gave up all the dead who were in it; ·Death and Hades were emptied of the dead that were in them; and every one was judged as his deeds deserved. Then Death and Hades were hurled into the burning lake. *i* This burning lake is the
15 second death; ·and anybody whose name could not be found written in the book of life was hurled into the burning lake.

D: THE JERUSALEM OF THE FUTURE

The heavenly Jerusalem *a*

1 **21** Then I saw *a new heaven and a new earth;* *b* the first heaven and the first
2 earth had disappeared now, and there was no longer any sea. *c* ·I saw the holy city, the new Jerusalem, coming down out of heaven from God, prepared as
3 a bride dressed for her husband. *d* ·Then I heard a loud voice call from the throne, 'Look, here God lives among human beings. He will make *his home among them;*
4 *they will be his people,* and he will be their God, *God-with-them.* *e* ·*He will wipe away all tears from their eyes*; there will be no more death, and no more mourning or sadness or pain. The world of the past has gone.'
5 Then the One sitting on the throne spoke. 'Look, I am making the whole of creation new. Write this, "What I am saying is trustworthy and will come true." '
6 Then he said to me, 'It has already happened. I am the Alpha and the Omega, the Beginning and the End. I will give water from the well of life free to anybody who
7 is thirsty; *f* ·anyone who proves victorious will inherit these things; and *I will be his*
8 God and *he will be my son.* *g* ·But the legacy for cowards, for those who break their word, or worship obscenities, for murderers and the sexually immoral, and for sorcerers, worshippers of false gods or any other sort of liars, is the second death *h* in the burning lake of sulphur.'

The messianic Jerusalem *i*

9 One of the seven angels that had the seven bowls full of the seven final plagues came to speak to me and said, 'Come here and I will show you the bride that the
10 Lamb has married.' ·*In the spirit, he carried me to the top of a very high mountain,*
11 and showed me Jerusalem, the holy city, coming down out of heaven from God. ·It had *all the glory of God* and glittered like some precious jewel of crystal-clear
12 diamond. ·Its wall was of a great height and had twelve gates; at each of the twelve gates there was an angel, and over the gates were written the names *of the twelve*
13 *tribes of Israel;* ·*on the east there were three gates, on the north three gates, on the*

14 *south three gates, and on the west three gates.* ·The city walls stood on twelve
foundation stones, each one of which bore the name of one of the twelve apostles
of the Lamb.[j]

15 The angel that was speaking to me was carrying a gold measuring rod to measure
16 the city and its gates and wall. ·The plan of the city is perfectly square, its length
the same as its breadth.[k] He measured the city with his rod and it was twelve
17 thousand furlongs, equal in length and in breadth, and equal in height.[l] ·He
measured its wall, and this was a hundred and forty-four cubits high—by human
18 measurements. ·The wall was built of diamond, and the city of pure gold, like
19 clear glass. ·The foundations of the city wall were faced with all kinds of precious
stone:[m] the first with diamond, the second lapis lazuli, the third turquoise, the
20 fourth crystal, ·the fifth agate, the sixth ruby, the seventh gold quartz, the eighth
malachite, the ninth topaz, the tenth emerald, the eleventh sapphire and the
21 twelfth amethyst. ·The twelve gates were twelve pearls, each gate being made of a
22 single pearl, and the main street of the city was pure gold, transparent as glass. ·I
could not see any temple in the city[n] since the Lord God Almighty and the Lamb
23 were themselves the temple, ·and the city did not need the sun or the moon for
light, since it was lit by the radiant glory of God, and the Lamb was a lighted torch
24 for it. ·*The nations will come to its light* and the kings of the earth will bring it their
25 treasures. ·Its *gates will never be closed by day*—and there will be no night
26 there[o]—·and *the nations will come, bringing their treasure* and their wealth.
27 Nothing unclean may come into it: no one who does what is loathsome or false,
but only those who are listed in the Lamb's book of life.

1 **22** Then the angel showed me the river of life, rising from the throne of God
2 and of the Lamb[a] and flowing crystal-clear. ·Down the middle of the city
street, *on either bank[b] of the river were the trees of life, which bear twelve crops of
fruit in a year, one in each month, and the leaves of which are the cure for the
nations.*
3 *The curse of destruction will be abolished.*[c] The throne of God and of the Lamb
4 will be in the city; his servants will worship him, ·they will see him face to face,
5 and his name will be written on their foreheads. ·And night will be abolished; they
will not need lamplight or sunlight, because the Lord God will be shining on them.
They will reign for ever and ever.
6 The angel said to me,[d] 'All that you have written is sure and will come true: the
Lord God who inspires the prophets has sent his angel to reveal to his servants
7 *what is soon to take place.* ·I am coming soon!' Blessed are those who keep the
prophetic message of this book.
8 I, John, am the one who heard and saw these things. When I had heard and
seen them all, I knelt at the feet of the angel who had shown them to me, to
9 worship him; ·but he said, 'Do no such thing: I am your fellow-servant and the
fellow-servant of your brothers the prophets and those who keep the message of
this book. God alone you must worship.'
10 This, too, he said to me, 'Do not keep the prophecies in this book a secret,
11 because the Time is close. ·Meanwhile let the sinner continue sinning, and the
unclean continue to be unclean; let the upright continue in his uprightness, and
12 those who are holy continue to be holy.[e] ·*Look, I am coming* soon, and my *reward
13 is with* me, *to repay everyone as their deeds deserve.* ·I am the Alpha and the
14 Omega, *the First and the Last*, the Beginning and the End. ·Blessed are those who
will have washed their robes clean, so that they will have the right to feed on the
15 tree of life and can come through the gates into the city.[f] ·Others must stay

outside: dogs, fortune-tellers, and the sexually immoral, murderers, idolaters, and everyone of false speech and false life.'

EPILOGUE

16 I, Jesus, have sent my angel to attest these things to you for the sake of the churches. I am the sprig from the root of David and the bright star of the morning.

17 The Spirit and the Bride ^{g} say, 'Come!' Let everyone who listens answer, 'Come!' ^{h} Then *let all who are thirsty come*: all who want it may *have the water* of life, and have it *free*.

18 This is my solemn attestation to all who hear the prophecies in this book: ^{i} if anyone adds anything to them, God will add to him every plague mentioned in the

19 book; ·if anyone cuts anything out of the prophecies in this book, God will cut off his share of the tree of life and of the holy city, which are described in the book.

20 The one who attests these things says: I am indeed coming soon.
Amen; come, Lord Jesus. ^{j}

21 May the grace of the Lord Jesus be with you all. ^{k} Amen.

NOTES TO REVELATION

1 **a.** Jesus Christ is both author and subject of this revelation.

b. 'His servants' are the prophets in the early Church, *see* 10:7; 11:18; 22:6; Ac 11:27m and Am 3:7; but the same word is regularly used for all followers and disciples of Christ, 2:20; 7:3; 19:2,5; 22:3,6.

c. God sends the angel (messenger) 22:16, *see* Gn 16:7c; Ezk 40:3d, who probably represents Christ himself, in accordance with Rv 1:13 and 14:14,15.

d. The first of the seven 'beatitudes' of Rv, *see* 14:13; 16:15; 19:9; 20:6; 22:7; 22:14.

e. When Jesus returns; *see* 1:7 and 3:11; 22:10,12,20.

f. This section makes use of many OT allusions to suggest the King-Messiah's glorious return, solemn enthronement and future reign over God's people in fulfilment of the promise made to David. This is basically what the whole book is about.

g. A stereotyped expression, 1:8; 4:8; 11:17; 16:5, similar to others in Jewish Literature which develop the name revealed to Moses, interpreted as 'He who is', Ex 3:14.

h. The Messiah is the 'witness' to the promise that was made to David, 2 S 7:1a; Ps 89; Is 55:3–4; Zc 12:8, both in his person and in his work; as he fulfils this promise he is the efficacious Word, God's 'Yes', 3:14; 19:11,13; 2 Co 1:20. Not only is he heir to David, 5:5; 22:16, but by his Resurrection he is the 'First-born', Col 1:18, who will reign over the universe when his enemies have been destroyed, Rv 19:16; Dn 7:14.

i. var. 'released us from'.

j. Those who turn to the Messiah and whose sins he forgives, v. 5, will be a royal line of priests, Ex 19:3c,6; kings because they will rule over all the nations, Is 54:11–17; Dn 7:22,27; Zc 12:1–3; cf. Rv 2:26; 5:10; 20:6; 22:5; priests because in union with Jesus the messianic Priest they will consecrate the universe to God in a sacrifice of praise.

k. The doxologies frequent throughout Rv are plainly echoes of an ancient liturgy. They include precious christological material, for the Lamb is associated with the Father in many ways, *see* 5:6e. At the time, they would certainly

have been read as a protest against the imperial cult of the state and emperor.

l. The first and last letters of the Gk alphabet, 21:6; 22:13; a quality of God, originator of all things, Is 41:4; 44:6, is transferred to Christ, cf. Rv 1:17; 2:8.

m. Presumably deported there for being a Christian.

n. The Messiah as Judge (cf. Dn 7:13, also 10:6). The long robe symbolises his priesthood (*see* Ex 28:4; 29:5; Zc 3:4), the golden cord round the waist his royalty, *see* 1 M 10:89, the white hair his eternity (*see* Dn 7:9), the burning eyes (to probe minds and 'hearts', *see* Rv 2:23) his divine knowledge, the feet of bronze (*see* Dn 2:31–45) his permanence; the brightness of his legs and face, and the strength of his voice symbolise the fear inspired by his majesty. In his power (his 'right hand') he holds the seven churches (the 'stars', *see* v. 20); he is prepared to sentence faithless Christians to death (the 'double-edged sword'), *see* 2:16; 19:15*l*; and Is 49:2; Ep 6:17; Heb 4:12. One or other of his attributes as Judge is used, at the beginning of each of the seven letters, to suggest the situation of the particular church addressed.

o. The one who has life 'in himself', *see* Jn 1:4; 3:15j; 5:21,26. The accent is on the fact that the risen Christ is alive here and now.

p. lit. 'Death and Hades'. Hades was the place of the dead, the Gk word corresponding to the *sheol* of the OT, *see* Nb 16:33f. Christ has the power to release souls from Hades, Jn 5:26–28.

q. 'present happenings' refers to the letters of ch. 2 and 3; 'things that are still to come': the revelations of ch. 4–22.

r. In Jewish thought not only the material world, *see* 7:1; 14:18; 16:5, was ruled by angels, but even individuals and communities, *see* Ex 23:20i. Hence each church is considered to be ruled by an angel responsible for it, to whom the letter is addressed. But the churches are also in the hand of Christ, that is, in his power and under his protection.

2 **a.** The seven letters all follow the same pattern. Statements on the condition of the churches ('I know') are followed by eschatological promises or threats. They are very rich in doctrine especially on Jesus Christ, who is presented throughout as speaking. They also give us a picture of Christian life in the Province of Asia at the end of the first century.

b. Metropolis of the Province of Asia; the other six churches of the letters that follow were located in the same province. Numerous pagan cults flourished there, including that of Artemis. Ac 19:24–40.

c. Probably the Nicolaitans of v. 6. *see* 2:15m, *see also* 2 Co 11:5,13.

d. Allusion to some previous persecution.

e. Ephesus will cease to be the religious capital.

f. This formula, which marks the conclusion of each of the letters to the churches, stresses the role of the Spirit in the relation of Christ with his Church.

g. Smyrna's spiritual wealth contrasts with her material poverty.

h. Henceforth the Church of Christ is the true Israel. *see* Rm 9:8; Ga 6:16.

i. i.e. of short duration.

j. Emperor-worship, and the worship of other false gods, flourished in Pergamum, and are always represented in Rv as the antithesis of faith in Christ.

k. According to one Jewish tradition, *see* Nb 31:16, Balaam suggested to Balak that he should persuade Israel to idolatry with the help of the women of Moab. Nb 25:1–3.

l. The prophets used this as a common figure of speech for idolatry, religious infidelity, *see* Ho 1:2b.

m. This doctrine had some affinity with the errors already attacked by Paul in the Captivity Letters (notably in Col); it heralded the gnostic speculations of the second century, but also tolerated a measure of compromise with heathen cults, e.g. participation in sacred banquets, cf. v. 14.

n. The manna (hidden, together with the ark, by Jeremiah, 2 M 2:4–8 *see also* Heb 9:4) will be brought out as the food of those who are saved in the heavenly kingdom, *see* Jn 6:31,49, compare Rv 15:8d. The white stone (white is the colour of triumph and joy) alludes to various ancient usages (badges of honour, tablets of discharge or admission) and symbolises entry into the kingdom. The 'new name' (3:12f; 19:12) signifies the Christian's spiritual rebirth, *see* Is 1:26n.

o. 'Jezebel'; var. 'your wife Jezebel'. A self-styled prophetess of the Nicolaitan sect; her name is symbolic, cf. 2 K 9:22.

p. var. 'their practices'.

q. Those who follow her teaching.

r. The letter takes issue with vain pretensions to penetrate the mystery of God which led to moral laxity.

s. The true faith in Christ.

t. The morning star is the symbol both of power, Nb 24:17; Is 14:12, and also of the glorification of the Christian by Christ the Lord, 22:16; *see* 1:5h; Ac 2:36w; Rm 1:4c.

3 a. In the letter to Ephesus, the seven stars represented the angels guiding the seven churches.

b. A symbol of purity but also of victory and joy. The robe is the conventional image for the profound reality of something. Is 51:9; 52:1; Rm 13:14; 1 Co 15:53–54; Col 3:9–12.

c. Free exercise of the apostolate, *see* Ac 14:27p.

d. In Rv the world always stands for the gentile world, as 'the world' is hostile in Jn 1:10; 17:9. The servants of God are not counted among its inhabitants, but will be preserved, 7:1seq., from the scourges described in ch. 8–9; 16 (cf. 18:4).

e. Cf. 2:17; 14:1; 19:12,13; and Is 56:5; 62:2; 65:15; *see also* Is 1:26n.

f. Either a name that will not be known until the second coming, or the name 'the Word', cf. 19:13.

g. Reference to Is 65:16 where 'God of truth' is literally 'God of Amen'; *see* 1:5h.

h. Christ is here identified with the creative Word and creative Wisdom. Cf. Pr 8:22; Ws 9:1seq.; Jn 1:3; Col 1:16seq.; Heb 1:2.

i. Unlike Smyrna, 2:9, Laodicea was rich in worldly goods, but spiritually poor.

j. The true riches that are of the spirit.

k. The clothing and the eye ointment are, of course, needed to repair the 'blindness and nakedness' of v. 17; but there may be a special point in this as an allusion to the local products for which Laodicea was known.

l. Intimacy with Jesus, a foretaste of the messianic banquet, *see* Mt 8:11c. Very probably a liturgical allusion.

4 a. God on his throne is glorified by the heavenly court, ch. 4, then the horizon broadens to the whole universe, whose destiny is handed over to the Lamb in the form of a sealed book, ch. 5. There follow great symbolic visions which form a prelude to the 'Great Day' when the retribution of God will fall on the persecuting unbelievers, ch. 17–19.

b. John is careful not to describe God anthropomorphically; he prefers to give an impression of light. The whole scene draws heavily on Ezk 1 and 10; *see also* Is 6.

c. These elders, grouped round the throne of God as elders were grouped round the altar at the Eucharist of a local church, have a priestly and royal function; they praise and adore God, 4:10; 5:9; 11:16,17; 19:4, and offer him the prayers of the faithful; they assist in the government of the world (thrones) and share his royal power (crowns). The number 24 perhaps corresponds to the 24 orders of priests in 1 Ch 24:1–19.

d. Thunder is frequently associated with theophanies, *see* Ex 19:16g; Ezk 1:4,13.

e. Not the sevenfold Spirit of medieval tradition but the seven 'angels of the presence', *see* 3:1a; 8:2; Tb 12: 15. God's messengers, cf. Rv 5:6 and *passim*; Tb 12:15; Zc 4:10; Lk 1:26.

f. Either the 'waters above' of Gn 1:7; Ps 104:3, or the prototype of the 'Sea' in the great Temple, 1 K 7:23–26.

g. The arrangement is difficult to imagine. 'In the middle of the throne and' is possibly a gloss from Ezk 1:5.

h. The symbolism derives from Ezk 1:5–21. The 'animals' are the four angels responsible for directing the physical world. 'Four' symbolises the universe; their many eyes symbolise God's omniscience and providence. They give unceasing glory to God for his creation. The figures of lion, bull, man, eagle suggest all that is noblest, strongest, wisest, swiftest, in the created world. Since Irenaeus, these four creatures have been used as symbols of the four evangelists.

i. The doxology of Isaiah was already in use in synagogue worship and was taken up by the Christian liturgies. Worship on earth is seen to be a participation in worship in heaven.

j. The elders do homage to God for the power which they have received from him, which the kings of the earth will refuse to do, 17:2.

5 a. A roll of papyrus in which God's hitherto secret decrees are written. The contents are made known in ch. 6–9. The presentation of the Lamb at the throne of God, ch. 5, occurs in the course of the eternal liturgy of ch. 4.

b. He alone will be worthy who has shown himself to be such in the testing, 5:9,12.

c. In Hades, 1:18p.

d. Over Satan and the world, *see* Jn 3:35t; 1 Jn 2:13g, 13, 14.

e. Taking over from the messianic titles of v. 5, the title of 'Lamb' which first occurs here will be used of Christ some thirty times in Rv. It is the Lamb sacrificed for the salvation of the chosen people, *see* Jn 1:29v; Is 53:7. He bears the wounds of his passion, but has triumphed and therefore stands erect, cf. Ac 7:55, as victor of death, Rv 1:18, and therefore associated with the Father as master of all humanity, *see* v. 13, etc, cf. ch. 21–22; Rm 1:4c.

f. Symbolising the fullness (number seven) of the Messiah's power (horns) and knowledge (eyes).

g. var. 'you bought us', 'you bought us for God'. The reading 'us' supposes that the elders are human beings, possibly the OT patriarchs. lit. 'you were killed and you bought for God by your blood'.

h. Stereotyped expression for 'the whole world'; *see* Dn 3:4,7,96.

6 a. Ch. 6–9 make a homogeneous whole. As the Lamb unseals the book, 6–8:1, and the trumpets sound, 8:2–9, the vision unfurls of the events which announce and prepare the overthrow of the Roman empire, prototype of God's enemies, cf. Mt 24seq. The four horsemen of this first vision are modelled on Zc 1:8–10 and 6:1–3; but they further symbolise the four scourges with which God, through the prophets, threatened a faithless Israel: wild animals, war, famine, plague, cf. Lv 26:21–26; Dt 32:24; Ezk 5:17; 14:13–21; and also Ezk 6:11–12; 7:14–15; 12:16; 33:27.

b. The rider on the white horse (symbol of victory) represents the Parthians, identified by the bow, their favourite weapon. They were the terror of the Roman world in the first century. These are the 'wild beasts' of v. 8 (i.e. victorious gentile nations, cf. Dt 7:22; Jr 15:2–4; 50:17; Ezk 34:28). The Parthian invasion is described in the vision of 9:13seq. One tradition identified the rider with the Messiah, as in 19:11–16.

c. Symbol of war.

d. Symbol of famine: food is rationed and sold at a prohibitive price.

e. The colour is that of a corpse decomposing, especially as a result of plague.

f. To swallow up the victims.

g. The altar, 8:3; 9:13; 14:18; 16:7, corresponds in this liturgy to the altar of burnt offerings, 1 K 8:64s. The martyrs, witnesses to the Word, are associated with their Master's sacrifice, *see* Ph 2:17r.

h. Symbolising triumphant joy, 3:5b; 7:9,13–14; 19:8.

i. In the prophets, these cosmic events signalise the Day of Yahweh, *see* Am 8:9h. They are to be understood not as physical realities but as symbols of God's retribution, *see* Mt 24:1a.

j. var. 'their retribution'.

7 a. The angels of v. 1.

b. Twelve (the sacred number) squared and multiplied by one thousand represents the totality of all who have been faithful to Christ (the new Israel, cf. Ga 6:16). Marked with God's seal, Rm 4:11e, in the end they will escape the plagues to come, cf. Ex 12:7–14.

c. All the Christian martyrs now in heaven, v. 14.

d. The palms of victory form an allusion to the joyful feast of Shelters, Lv 23:33–34; in v. 15 they will live in God's tent.

e. For this form of dialogue *see* Zc 4:4–13 and 6:4–5.

f. The persecutions, of which Nero's was the prototype.

g. Blood is the symbol of the effectiveness of the death of Jesus, Rm 3:25k; 1 Co 11:25; Ep 1:7. Here the gift is given to those who receive its effects.

h. Common metaphors in the prophetic tradition, used to symbolise eschatological bliss, *see* Is 11:6e; Ho 2:20v; they recur in Rv 21:4.

8 a. As in the prophetic tradition a solemn silence precedes and heralds the coming of the Lord. The decrees contained in the open book are now going to be carried out in a new celestial liturgy, marked by seven trumpet-blasts, ch. 8–9; 11:15–18.

b. This was in the shape of a scoop or shovel, and was also used for carrying the live coals from the altar of burnt offering to the altar of incense.

c. The altar of incense, *see* Ex 30:1; 1 K 6:20–21.

d. For the symbolism of these disasters see 6:1a. In addition they seem to recall the plagues of Egypt, Ex 7–10; Ws 11:5–12:2; cf. 15:5seq.

9 a. One of the fallen angels, perhaps Satan himself, *see* v. 11 and Lk 10:18.

b. Where the fallen angels are imprisoned until their final punishment.

c. The vision of locusts is suggested by Jl 1–2 which, according to Jerome, the Jews interpreted historically: the four armies of locusts being successive invaders, Assyrian, Persian, Greek and Roman; see Jr 51:27. Here the locusts probably indicate the Parthians. Another suggestion is that the locusts symbolise spiritual torments inflicted by demons.

d. Possibly symbols of upright, faithful Christians, *see* 7:1seq.

e. Destruction, or ruin, personified.

f. This is to show that the vengeance on unbelievers follows the prayer of the martyrs described in 6:9,10 (*see* 8:2seq.).

g. The Euphrates was the eastern border of the Roman empire, beyond which were the Parthians, at this time a dreaded enemy and the nightmare of the Roman rulers. The description in v. 19 of the warhorses whose power was in their mouths and in their tails recalls the Parthian mounted archers, who having attacked, turned to retreat and fired a 'Parthian shot'—a salvo over their horses' tails.

10 a. Unlike the sealed book given to the Lamb, 5:2, the one offered to John is small and open.

b. The voice of God, cf. Ps 29:3–9.

c. Keep it secret, cf. Dn 12:4; 2 Co 12:4, because the time of its fulfilment, v. 7, has not yet come. It is used in a different sense in 1:11,19; etc; 22:10.

d. The angel, in contact with air, sea and land, the three regions of the universe, is about to swear by him who made them; cf. Gn 14:22; Ex 20:11; Dt 32:40; Ne 9:6.

e. The definitive establishment of the kingdom; the sign of this is the destruction of the enemies of God's people, 17; 18; 20:7–10. On the 'mystery' or 'secret' of God in the eschatological sense, *see* Rm 11:25; 16:25f; 2 Th 2:6seq.

f. The incident draws on the prophetic call of Ezekiel, Ezk 2:8–3:3, cf. Jr 15:16. It renews the mission of John, 1:1–2,9–20, and defines it more closely.

g. The news is sweet because it announces the Church's victory, bitter because it foretells her suffering, 11:1–13.

11 a. Some MSS insert 'and the angel stood there'.

b. The Temple, centre of the holy city Jerusalem, represents the people of God, 20:9; 21:1a; 1 Co 3:16–17,16e. It is to be 'measured', cf. Jr 31:39; Ezk 40:1–6; Zc 2:5–9. Surrounded by unbelievers, v. 2, those who are faithful to Christ will be spared, *see* 7:4; 14:1–5, like the remnant of Israel, *see* Is 4:3.

c. This period (three-and-a-half years) taken from Dn, had become the symbol for any persecution, cf. Lk 4:25; Jm 5:17. Here it is the Roman persecution (the Beast of 13; 17:10–14).

d. In Zc the two olive trees symbolise Joshua and Zerubbabel, the religious and the civil leaders of the repatriated community who restored Temple and city after the Exile. Here they probably stand for the two champions who are to build up the new Temple, Christ's Church; they are described, vv. 5–6,11–12, by means of the features of Moses and Elijah, cf. Mt 17:3seq.,3e. They can hardly be identified, but Peter and Paul, martyred at Rome under Nero, *see* vv. 7–8, have been suggested.

e. The emperor Nero, type of Antichrist, cf. 13:1,18; 17:8 with notes.

f. The great city here is Babylon, i.e. Rome, *see* 16:19; 17:18; 18:10,16,18,19; it is called Sodom and Egypt for its two great crimes: refusing God's messengers and oppressing the people of Christ, *see* 17:4–6. Here it is identified with Jerusalem which is not only the holy city, 11:1, but which 'killed the prophets', Mt 23:37.

g. var. 'they heard'.

h. The figure symbolises people of all classes of society (seven) and in great numbers (thousands).

i. The second disaster was described (the sixth trumpet) in 9:15–19. The third is to be the fall of Babylon (Rome) in ch. 17–18.

j. As opposed to the Jerusalem Temple referred to in vv. 1 and 2, it contains the ark (Ex 25) of the new covenant, permanent home of God among his people, *see* 2 M 2:5–8; Ws 9:8d.

12 a. This chapter is made up of two separate visions: the attack of the dragon on the woman and her children, vv. 1–6 and 13–17; the attack of Michael on the dragon, vv. 7–12.

b. This scene looks back to Gn 3:15–16. The woman gives birth in pain, v. 2, to a child who will be the Messiah, v. 5. Satan tests her, v. 9, *see* 20:2, persecutes both her and her offspring, vv. 6,13,17. She represents the holy people of the messianic era, Is 54; 60; 66:7; Mi 4:9–10, and so the Church militant. It is possible that the author was thinking also of Mary, the new Eve, the daughter of Zion, who gave birth to the Messiah, *see* Jn 19:25j.

c. The dragon is 'Satan', *see* v. 9 and 20:2, a word which the LXX renders as 'devil'. The Hebr. word means 'accuser', *see* v. 10 and Zc 3:1–2; *see also* Jb 1:6g. In the Jewish tradition the Serpent or Dragon represented the power of evil, hostile to God and his people, and God was to destroy it at the end of time, *see* Jb 3:8e and 7:12f.

d. Allusion to the fall of the angels seduced by Satan.

e. The Messiah considered simultaneously as an individual person and as head or leader of the new Israel, cf. the 'Son of man' of Dn 7:13, and the 'servant of Yahweh' of Is 42:1a.

f. The ascension and the triumph of the Messiah that will result in the dragon's fall. The child's triumph is here described immediately after its birth.

g. Traditional OT refuge for the persecuted, *see* Ex 2:15; 1 K 17:2seq.; 19:3seq.; 1 M 2:29,30. To exist, the Church must depend not on the world but on her own divine life, cf. Ex 16; 1 K 17:4,6; 19:5–8; Mt 4:3–4, 14.13 seq.

h. According to Jewish tradition (Dn 10:12–21; 12:1) he is God's champion. The name means 'Who (is) like God?'

i. lit. 'a time and times and half a time'. Three and a half years, *see* 11:2c.

j. The Roman empire, like a flood let loose by Satan, cf. Is 8:7–8, will try to engulf the Church, *see* Rv 13.

k. Two marks of the faithful, 14:1; cf. 14:12; 20:4; already 1:1, and Rm 8:29.

l. This vision draws on Dn 7 (in the persecution of Antiochus Epiphanes). According to Rv 17:10,12–14, the Beast from the (Mediterranean) sea is the Roman empire, type of all forces in opposition to Christ and the Church, because it claims divine powers (its titles, Rv 1, cf. Dn 11:36; 2 Th 2:4). The seven heads and the ten horns recur in 17:3,7–12.

m. var. 'he stood', which would join v. 18 to the preceding passage.

13 a. It is from Satan, 12:3c, that he receives all his power, cf. Mt 4:8–9; Jn 12:31i; 2 Th 2:9.

b. The allusion may be to the empire recovering after some temporary set-back, or to the expectation of Nero *redivivus*. The risen beast is a caricature of the risen Christ.

c. A parody of the name Michael, 12:7.

d. var. 'he who kills by the sword must die . . .'

e. There are two interpretations of this quotation from Jr 15:2: that persecution is ordained and must be endured; or that the punishment of the persecutors is inevitable and will be inexorable, cf. 14:11–12; Ps 5:10c; Mt 26:52.

f. This beast is later referred to as 'false prophet', 16:13; 19:20; 20:10. Before describing the return of the Son of man, 14:14–20, cf. 19:11seq. and Mt 24:30, the author shows the activity of the false messiahs (first beast) and the false prophets (second beast) foretold in the gospel, Mt 24:24; cf. 2 Th 2:9.

g. The second beast mimics the Spirit who works miracles in the Church to encourage faith in Christ. Similarly, the first beast had imitated the risen Messiah, v. 3. The Dragon, the first beast and the second beast form a caricature of the Trinity.

h. var. '616'. In both Gk and Hebr., letters are used for numbers, the value corresponding to the place in the alphabet; by adding up the values of component letters that total 'number of a person's name' is obtained. In Hebr. the letters of Caesar Nero add up to 666, and in Gk the letters of Caesar-God add up to 616 (the alternative reading).

14 a. The followers of the beast who are branded with his name and number, 13:16–17, are now contrasted with the followers of a Lamb marked with his name and the name of his Father. This is the 'remnant' of the new Israel, Is 4:3c, the faithful Christians who have survived persecution and who are to begin the restoration of God's kingdom when its enemies have been destroyed. Mount Zion is God's throne, *see* 21:1a.

b. var. 'the Lamb'.

c. Moses had celebrated the deliverance from Egypt, Ex 15:1–2i; cf. 15:3–5; the new hymn celebrates the new deliverance of God's people and of the new order introduced by the Lamb that was sacrificed.

d. Metaphorically. In the OT marital infidelity is a metaphor for idolatry, *see* Ho 1:2b, in this case the worship of the beast, *see* 17:1, etc. The hundred and forty-four thousand redeemed, 5:9, have remained faithful and true, and have rejected worship of false gods, and so can be betrothed to the Lamb, *see* 19:9; 21:2; 2 Co 11:2.

e. Just as Israel followed Yahweh at the Exodus, so the new Israel, newly redeemed, follows the Lamb into the desert, cf. Jr 2:2–3, where the marriage rites are renewed (Ho 2:16–25).

f. i.e. they have not invoked false gods, the beast. The vocabulary of vv. 4,5 is that of sacrifices: the first-fruits represent the whole harvest; the acceptable sacrifice is without blemish, Ex 12:5; 1 P 1:19.

g. Before God's vengeance strikes, the angels appear to give a final warning of Judgement; but it goes unheeded, *see* 16:2,9,11,21. *See also* 15:5c.

h. The tense is the prophetic perfect.

i. Corr. 'drink the wine of the anger of her adultery' Gk, as in 17:2; 18:3. The 'wine of anger' is a familiar image, *see* Is 51:17h, for the divine anger especially on worshippers of false gods.

j. The lake of burning sulphur is where the wicked are punished, *see* 19:20; 20:10; 21:8.

k. The destruction of the gentile nations. The fulfilment of this prophecy is described in 19:11seq.

l. From the altar arise the prayers of the saints, 8:3–5; 9:13, which the angel carries to God to ask for justice.

m. The gentiles are to be destroyed outside Jerusalem according to Ezk 38–39; Zc 14:2seq., 12seq.; *see* Lv 4:12c; Heb 13:11.

15 a. The vision of seven cups picks up that of the seven trumpets, 8:2seq. Between vv. 1 and 5 is inserted the hymn sung by the saved to the praise of him who saves them.

b. Like the hymn of Moses, Ex 15, this is a song of deliverance, 14:1. It is woven from biblical allusions and dwells less on the severity of the punishments than on the triumph of the Lord and those who belong to him.

c. Before finally destroying Babylon (Rome), 16:18–19, God sends a series of plagues on the wicked (several are reminiscent of the Egyptian plagues, Ex 7–10). The angels who accomplish them issue from the Tent which is the true Temple in heaven, 11:19. They execute justice within the liturgical framework of a theophany.

d. According to 2 M 2:4–8 the reappearance of the sacred tent and the manifestation of God's glory as in the time of Moses, Ex 40:34–35, and of Solomon, 1 K 8:10, were to herald the coming of the messianic age and the rebirth of the chosen people. The 'glory' (*see* Ex 24:16f) is the sign of God's presence (*compare* the appearance of the ark of the covenant in Rv 11:19).

16 a. Rome, type of all gentile powers hostile to God.

b. If the Euphrates dries up, the Romans lose all defences against the Parthian warriors, 9:14.

c. The work of these evil spirits is foreordained to bring the gentile nations to Judgement.

d. i.e. 'the mountains of Megiddo'. The defeat of King Josiah near this town, 2 K 23:29seq., made the place symbolise disaster for any armies assembling there, cf. Zc 12:11.

e. Add. '(proceeding) from the throne' or 'from God'.

f. These cosmic phenomena symbolise the powers of this world withering under God's anger.

g. About 88 lb (40 kg).

17 a. As Jerusalem will be, 21:9, Babylon is personified by a woman, see 12:1; Dn 4:27k. Here it is Rome the idolatrous, 2:14k; 18:3; Ho 1:2b; see Rv 14:4. After its brilliant career, vv. 3–7, it will suffer the condemnation proclaimed and prepared by the previous visions.

b. A literal description of Babylon, metaphorically explained in v. 15.

c. All gentile nations and their kings who have adopted the imperial cult.

d. Where unclean beasts live, see Lv 26:8b; 17:7c.

e. The seven heads are the seven hills of Rome, v. 9, and the ten horns are subject kings, v. 12, who shake off the yoke of the Empire, v. 16. The beast, vv. 3,7–8, represents an emperor, presumably Nero, whom popular belief expected to return to life and power before the coming of the Lamb, see 2 Th 2:8–9. The beginning of v. 8 is a parody of the titles of God, 1:4, and of Christ, 1:18.

f. Like Jerusalem (Ezk 16:36–38 and 23:37–45) Rome is guilty of a double crime: idolatry, v. 4, and murder, v. 6.

g. In the symbolism of the beast two distinct senses can be discerned, vv. 8–9,15–18, and vv. 10,12–14. The woman who is sitting on it thinks herself powerful, but is riding to her destruction.

h. Seven Roman emperors, of whom the sixth is reigning at the moment. Seven is a number symbolic of totality, and the author does not intend to say anything about the number and chronology of the historical Roman emperors.

i. A reference back to 14:4 and forward to 19:11–21.

18 a. The punishment prophesied in cryptic terms, ch. 17, is now imminent. It will occur when the faithful have been set apart from sinners, v. 4, see 3:10d.

b. 'her prostitution'; var. 'the anger of her prostitution', cf. 14:8.

c. Triple lamentation by the kings of the earth, vv. 9–10, by the merchants of the world, vv. 11–17ª, and by seafarers, vv. 17ᵇ–19. It draws on Jr 50–51 and even more Ezk 26–28.

d. A symbolic gesture after which the lament is taken up again, vv. 22–23; v. 21 is continued in v. 24. The description of 18:1–3 is completed here: Babylon is to be destroyed for its idolatry, see 17:4; and for persecuting Christians, 18:24.

19 a. The prelude of songs of joy in 18:20, contrasting vividly with the laments of ch. 18, was for the fall of Babylon. The first song, vv. 1–4, comes from heaven; in the second, vv. 5–9, join the saints of the whole Church, invited to the wedding of the Lamb.

b. The only uses of the word in the NT are in 19:1,3,4,6; this liturgical acclamation ('Praise God') was already used in Jewish worship, Ps 111:1; 113:1a.

c. The wedding of the Lamb symbolises the beginning of the heavenly kingdom described in 21:9seq. See Ho 1:2b and Ep 5:22–23f.

d. Possibly there is in this incident a warning against the worship of heavenly 'powers', Col 2:18; Heb 1:14; 2:5.

e. The 'witness of Jesus' is the word of God to which Jesus testifies and which is implanted in every Christian, see 1:2; 6:9; 12:17, and which inspires the prophets.

f. After the fall of Babylon prophesied 14:8,14–15, and described 16:19–20; 17:12–14, Christ the faithful witness, 3:14, brings about the Day of Yahweh, Am 5:18m, by anni-

hilating the enemies of the Church. The account, as previous descriptions, 12:5; 14:6–20; 17:14, draws on a variety of prophecies.

g. The colour symbolises victory.

h. Because he is King of kings, see v. 16.

i. Alluding (see v. 15) to Is 63:1. Symbol of the mortal ruin he deals his enemies, see 5:5.

j. The names of the victorious horseman, vv. 12,13,16, express different aspects of his nature. To the transcendent divine name, v. 12, are here added the Word, which indicates that he effectively reveals God, cf. Jn 1:1,14, and, more exactly, that he carries out his judgements, Rv 20:11–12; 22:12; see also Ws 18:14–18.

k. The angels, cf. Mt 26:53, or preferably, following Rv 14:5 and 17:14, the white-robed martyrs, see 3:5,18; 6:11; 16:15; 19:8 and also Mt 22:11seq.

l. Symbol of the destroying Word; cf. Ws 18:16; Is 11:4; and also Rv 1:16; Ho 6:5; 2 Th 2:8; Heb 4:12.

m. The winepress is a common image in prophetic literature for God's destruction of his people's enemies on the Great Day of his revenge; cf. Gn 49:9–12; Is 63:1–6; Jr 25:30; Jl 4:13. On the 'wine of retribution', see Is 51:17h.

n. A title of dignity, see 17:14; Ph 2:9–11, which infinitely surpasses the blasphemous titles of the beast, Rv 13:1; 17:3.

o. This long parenthesis echoes the events described in ch. 13.

20 a. This difficult verse is one of those where traces may remain of different stages and revisions in the editing of this book. Is 20:1–6 another version of 19:11–21? Cf. Mt 19:28; 1 Co 6:23.

b. One interpretation makes this 'resurrection' of the martyrs (cf. Is 26:19; Ezk 37) symbolise the recovery of the Church after the Roman persecution; the 'reign of a thousand years' is then the period of the kingdom of Christ on earth from the end of persecution (the fall of Rome) to the Last Judgement (in 20:11seq.). According to Augustine and others who follow him, the 'reign of a thousand years' is reckoned from Christ's Resurrection, and the 'first resurrection' is baptism cf. Jn 5:25–28; Rm 6:1–11. From the time of the early Church there have been some readers who have taken this as a literal forecast: after a first resurrection, that of the martyrs, Christ would come to reign on earth with his faithful for a thousand years. But this literal interpretation has never won acceptance in the Church.

c. The first death is on earth, the second 'death' is failure to win eternal life.

d. The messianic rule of Christians on earth is foretold in 5:9–10, and under the symbol of the new Jerusalem, in 21:9–22:2 and 22:6–15, although this passage comes after the description of the Last Judgement, 20:13–15.

e. Ezk 38–39 (see notes) mentions 'Gog, king of Magog'; here the two names symbolise all the gentile nations leagued against the Church at the end of time.

f. A new promised land of which Jerusalem is the capital, 21:2d; it withstands the final invasion, cf. Lk 21:24. But it also symbolises the whole Church.

g. After the general resurrection occurs the Judgement, 2:23; 3:5; see 19:13j; Dn 7:10. This created universe is to be replaced by another, wholly new, 21:1a.

h. The first scrolls list human deeds; the scroll of life, the last to be opened, is the list of the predestined, see Dn 7:10i; 12:1a; Ac 13:48jj.

i. After the Last Judgement death itself will lose its power, see 20:10; 21:4 and 20:6.

21 a. The city of the elect, in total contrast with Babylon, ch. 17, is a gift of God. The outlook is an entirely celestial one, as in 7:15–17. The opening draws on Isaiah (especially ch. 51 and 65). Jerusalem, city of David, political and religious centre of Israel, 2 S 5:9f; 24:25; 1 K 6:2; Ps 122, city of God, Ps 46:4, holy city, Is 52:1; Dn 9:24; Mt 4:5, whose heart was the mountain, Ps 2:6b, where the Temple stood, Dt 12:2–3b, was considered in Israel as the destined metropolis of the messianic people. Ps 87:1a; 122; Is 2:1–5; 54:11d; 60; Jr 3:17; Lk 2:38o. It is there that the Holy Spirit founded the Christian Church. Ac 1:4, 8j; 2; 8:1–4. In this passage the city is transferred to heaven where the saving plan of God finds its fulfilment, 3:12; 11:1; 20:9; 22:19; *see also* Ac 2:22–24o; Ga 4:26; Ph 3:20, when the wedding of the Lamb is celebrated. Rv 19:7–8c; cf. Is 61:10; 62:4–5; Ho 1:2b; 2:16.

b. In Is 65:17; 66:22 the phrase is merely a symbol of the new messianic age: the fresh start for which the later prophets long. For Paul the shape of the eventual future has become clearer: all creation will be freed from the dominance of corruption and transformed. Rm 8:19j.

c. The sea, home of the Dragon and symbol of evil, *see* Jb 7:12f, will disappear as at the time of the Exodus, but this time for ever, before the victorious advance of the new Israel. cf. Jb 26:12–13; Ps 74:13,14; Is 27:1; 51:9–10.

d. The new and joyful wedding of Jerusalem and her God has taken place, cf. Is 61:10; 62:4–5; 65:18; the Exodus ideal has at last been achieved, *see* Ho 2:16p.

e. var. 'and God himself will be their God' or 'and God himself will be with them'. This is the classic formula of the covenant. Gn 17:8; Lv 26:11–12; Jr 31:33; Ezk 37:27; cf. 2 Co 6:16. The intimate presence of God is the mark of God's covenant with his people, *see* Ex 25:8d and Jn 1:14m. It will reach its consummation at the end of time. Cf. Is 12:6; Jl 4:17,21; Zp 3:15–17; Zc 2:14.

f. In the OT, fresh water is the regular symbol of life-saving refreshment and is a feature of the messianic age. In the NT, it becomes a symbol of the Spirit, *see* Jn 4:1a.

g. The title 'Son of God' was to be conferred on King-Messiah, David's heir, on the day of his enthronement, 2 S 7:14e; hence Jesus was proclaimed 'Son of God' in virtue of his resurrection. Ac 2:36w; Rm 1:4c. He also extended this title to those who believe in him, Jn 1:12j.

h. Eternal death. The fire, like the water of v. 6, is symbolic.

i. It is the messianic Jerusalem because the gentile nations still exist, 21:24, and can be converted to the true God, 22:2. But it is already the heavenly Jerusalem and awaits only its eternal development. The elements of this description are drawn primarily from Ezk 40–48.

j. All the numbers which are multiples of 12 express the idea of perfection, and the new people of God inherits the total perfection of the old. The twelve apostles, *see* Mt 19:28seq.; Mk 3:14seq.; Ep 2:20, correspond to the twelve tribes of Israel, Rv 7:4–8.

k. The symbol of (terrestrial) perfection. Information

concerning ancient weights and measures will be found in the Tables of measures and money.

l. Symbolic number: twelve (for the new Israel) multiplied by one thousand (for immensity).

m. These precious stones and their colours are intended to give an overall impression of solidity and splendour, the reflection of God's glory (*see* 2 Co 3:18). Cf. Is 54:11–12; Ezk 28:13, and the description of the high priest's pectoral, Ex 28:17–21; 39:10–14.

n. The Temple where God used to reside at the heart of the earthly Jerusalem, 11:19; 14:15–17; 15:5–16:1, has now disappeared. Now the new spiritual worship takes place in the body of Christ sacrificed and raised to life, *see* Jn 2:19–22i; 4:23–24; Rm 12:1a.

o. The risen Christ provides the shadowless light of his holiness, v. 27, on all the assembled nations, 22:5; cf. Jn 8:12b; 2 Co 4:6.

22 a. Allusion to the Trinity, since the river of living water is a symbol of the Spirit (Jn 4:1a), *see* Rv 21:6f.

b. Or punctuate '. . . crystal-clear, down the middle of the street . . . on either side'.

c. Vv. 3–5 follow on directly after 21:4. These vv. are in the future tense, a firm promise of the kingdom and the vision which will never come to an end, cf. 1 Co 13:12; 1 Jn 3:2, of the servants of God and of the Lamb, Rv 3:12; 7:3; 14:1.

d. All the rest of the book is a sort of epilogue. It is a conversation between the Angel (or Jesus) and the seer, a commentary on the visions written down in the book and the use to be made of them.

e. Whatever anyone may do, God's plan will still be accomplished.

f. Jerusalem, as described in 21:9seq.

g. The Church, bride of the Messiah, *see* 21:10.

h. The appeal is addressed to the Messiah; it is 'O Lord, come', *marana tha*, the refrain of the liturgical assemblies, 1 Co 16:22, expressive of the Christians' longing for the Second Coming, *see* 1 Th 5:1a.

i. This very ancient formula, Dt 4:2; 13:1; Pr 30:6; cf. Qo 3:14, is a way of protecting sacred writings against falsification.

j. Jesus confirms in vv. 7,12, and already in 1:3,7, that his coming is near. Thus he responds to the call of the Church and of believers. Their 'Amen', Rm 1:25p, expresses their joyful faith and their yearning.

k. var. 'with the saints' or 'with all the saints .

CHRONOLOGICAL TABLE

The columns to the right of the date column concern Palestinian and biblical history; those to the left concern general history; but this distinction is less strict from the Christian era onwards. In the right-hand column, extra-biblical writings are in *italics*, and (before the Roman period) extra-biblical facts or those not taken from Josephus are also in *italics*.

The names of rulers, kings, governors and high priests are in SMALL CAPITALS or CAPITALS according to their importance. In the list of the kings of Judah the succession is from father to son unless anything different is indicated. The names of prophets, and of biblical books when mentioned at the time of their composition, are in **bold type**; and the most important of other items are also in **bold type**.

	BC	
12–6: SULPICIUS QUIRINIUS as legate of Syria (?), subdues the Homonades of Taurus. Several indications of a census throughout the empire		The census of Lk 2:1seq. See the *lapis Venetus* inscription, undated, giving evidence of a census in Apamaea (Syria) by order of Quirinius, 'legate in Syria'; *see* Lk 2:2b
9: ARETAS IV succeeds his father Obodas II as king of Nabataea and reigns until AD 39		9–8: Herod penetrates into the territory of the Nabataeans to capture the brigands of Trachonitis, given asylum by the minister SYLLAIOS, who complains to Augustus. Temporary disgrace of Herod
9–6: SENTIUS SATURNINUS legate in Syria		
		About the year 7: Herod has Alexander and Aristobulus, his two sons by Mariamne I, strangled
According to Tertullian, it is Saturninus who initiates the census of Judaea		More than 6,000 Pharisees refuse to take the oath to Augustus on the occasion of a census (?) (which continues that of Quirinius)
		7–6 (?): **Birth of** JESUS
6–4: QUINTILIUS VARUS legate in Syria		
		March of the year 4: the affair of the golden eagle in the Temple. Execution of Antipater, eldest son of Herod. Herod's will in favour of the sons of Malthace the Samaritan (Archelaus and Herod Antipas) and the son of Cleopatra (Philip)
		End of March beginning of April 4 BC: **death of Herod** at Jericho. Archelaus takes his body to the Herodion
SABINUS procurator for Augustus' estates in Syria		
ARCHELAUS ethnarch of Judaea and Samaria: 4BC–AD6		
HEROD ANTIPAS tetrarch of Galilee and Peraea: 4BC–AD39		

	BC	
PHILIP tetrarch of Gaulanitis, Batanaea, Trachonitis, Auranitis, and of Paneas (Ituraea): 4BC–AD34		
End of year 4: Augustus confirms Herod's last will, but refuses Archelaus the title of king		4 At the Passover (11 April), Archelaus puts down a rebellion at Jerusalem and then goes to Rome to receive the title of king from Augustus
		Sabinus comes to Jerusalem to make an inventory of the resources of the kingdom of Herod: sharp opposition and trouble throughout the country. At this time, possibly, the rebellion of Judas the Galilean, see Ac 5:37 and of the Pharisee Saddok who urged disobedience to Rome and refusal to pay taxes. (Origin of the Zealots, see Mt 22:17.) Sabinus appeals to Varus who pursues the rebels; 2000 are crucified
		The *Assumption of Moses* (apoc.)
3–2 BC: the successor to Varus is unknown Possibly Quirinius legate now		If Quirinius is legate from 3 to 2, he could have continued the census begun by Sabinus and ordered the census of Apamaea (the undated *lapis Venetus*)
	AD	
AD 1/2–4: Quirinius is counsellor to young GAIUS CAESAR, grandson of Augustus, during his mission to the East	1	Philip the tetrarch builds Julias (Bethsaida). He enriches the shrine of Pan (Paneas, the *Paneion*), which he names Caesarea in honour of Augustus
4–5: VOLUSIUS SATURNINUS legate in Syria		
		Between 5 and 10: birth of Paul at Tarsus; pupil of Gamaliel the Elder, Ac 22:3, compare 5:34
6: Augustus deposes Archelaus who is exiled to Vienne (Gaul)		
6: According to Josephus, Quirinius legate in Syria (?)		6: According to Josephus, Quirinius comes to Judaea to make an inventory of possessions of Archelaus; this could have provoked the rebellion of Judas and Saddok. (But for the year 6 Josephus repeats events he has described for the year 4)
6–8: COPONIUS prefect		
		6 (?)–15: ANNAS son of Seth, High Priest
6–41: Judaea a prefectorial province (with Caesarea as the capital)		
14 (19 August): death of Augustus.		
14–37: TIBERIUS emperor		
		15: Valerius Gratus deposes Annas. Three high priests follow
VALERIUS GRATUS prefect: 15–26		
17–19: GERMANICUS adopted son of Tiberius, in the East		About 17: foundation of Tiberias by Antipas Under Tiberius, LYSANIAS tetrarch of Abilene, Lk 3:1, and *inscriptions*
18: Cappadocia becomes a Roman province		
26–36: PONTIUS PILATE prefect		About 27: Herod Antipas, married to the daughter of Aretas, marries Herodias the wife of his brother Herod (son of Mariamne II)
		The preaching of JOHN THE BAPTIST and the beginning of the ministry of Jesus, see Lk 3:2f
		Easter 28: Jesus at Jerusalem, Jn 2:13. The 46 years of Jn 2:20 begin from 20/19 BC

In the 15th year of Tiberius, Lk 3:1: 19 Aug. 28 or 18 Aug. 29—but according to the Syrian calculation, Sept.–Oct. 27 to Sept.–Oct. 28

AD

'(The) Christ condemned to death by Pontius Pilate under the Emperor Tiberius' (Tacitus, *Annals*)

Easter 30: on the eve of the Passover, i.e. 14 Nisan, a Friday, **death of Jesus**, Jn 19:31seq. (The Passover fell on the Saturday, 8 April in 30 and 4 April in 33: the second date is too late, *see* Jn 2:20.) *See* Mt 26:17c

Pentecost 30: outpouring of the Spirit on the Church, Ac 2. The first community, Ac 2:42, etc.

33–34: Philip dies without an heir, and Tiberius merges his tetrarchy into the province of Syria

Pontius Pilate has difficulties with the Jews; the incident of the standards and shields (Philo). Pilate's aqueduct

Election of the seven Hellenist ministers, Ac 6:1seq.

Martyrdom of Stephen and **dispersion** of the community; conversion of Paul; Paul in Arabia

35–39: L. VITELLIUS legate in Syria, father of the emperor Vitellius. He is given full powers in the East

About 35: Pontius Pilate orders the massacre of the Samaritans at Gerizim

Easter 36: Vitellius in Jerusalem. He replaces Caiaphas by Jonathan son of Annas

Paul returns to Damascus, he escapes from there, 2 Co 11:32seq. and visits the elders of the church, Ga 1:18seq. (Cephas and James, the brother of the Lord), Ac 9:25seq.

Autumn 36: Pontius Pilate leaves for Rome, sent thither by Vitellius to justify his conduct. He dies a violent death

Winter 36–37: Vitellius concentrates the legions at Ptolemais in order to attack Aretas IV

March 37: death of Tiberius. Vitellius breaks off his campaign against Aretas

37: Vitellius, on his way to Petra, stops at Jerusalem. He replaces Jonathan by his brother THEOPHILUS, high priest from 37 to 41

Foundation of the church at Antioch, Ac 11:19seq.

37–41: CALIGULA emperor
MARCELLUS prefect

37: Caligula gives AGRIPPA I son of Aristobulus the tetrarchies of Philip and Lysanias, with title of king (37–44)

38: persecution of the Jews in Alexandria

39–42: P. PETRONIUS legate in Syria

39: the Jewish philosopher Philo ambassador to Rome. He died after 41

39: Caligula exiles Antipas and gives, at the beginning of 40, his tetrarchy to Agrippa I

39: Caligula orders the erection of his statue in the Temple. Thanks to Petronius and Agrippa I the affair drags on until Caligula's assassination

PETER in Samaria (Simon the Magician), in the coastal plain (Cornelius the centurion), and at Jerusalem, Ac 8:14–11:18

41–54: CLAUDIUS emperor. Agrippa I, now in Rome contributes to his success: Claudius concedes him Judaea and Samaria. His brother Herod becomes King of Chalcis (41–48) and marries Berenice (daughter of Agrippa)

Herod the Great's kingdom is reconstituted. Agrippa builds the 3rd wall of Jerusalem, but Claudius has the work discontinued. Many buildings, in particular at Berytus (Beirut)

41: edict and letter from Claudius to the Alexandrians

42–44: VIBIUS MARSIUS legate in Syria

Spring 44: on Herod Agrippa's death, Judaea once again becomes a **prefectorial province**, 44–66

44–46: CUSPIUS FADUS prefect

46–48: TIBERIUS ALEXANDER prefect. Nephew of Philo, but an apostate. At this time, several famines throughout the empire

48–52: VENTIDIUS CUMANUS prefect

48–53: AGRIPPA II son of Agrippa I, king of Chalcis.

49: Claudius 'drives from Rome the Jewish agitators stirred up by Chrestos' (Suetonius), *see* Ac 18:2

50–60: UMMIDIUS QUADRATUS legate in Syria

52 (rather than 51): GALLIO, brother of Seneca, proconsul of Achaia

Agrippa in favour in Rome. Claudius exiles Cumanus

52–60: ANTONIUS FELIX prefect, brother of the freedman Pallas. Marries DRUSILLA sister of Agrippa II, already married to Aziz king of Emesa, *see* Ac 24:24

53: Claudius gives to Agrippa II, in exchange for Chalcis, the tetrarchies of Philip and Lysarias (53–95), and the heptarchy of Varus (North Libya)

54–68: NERO emperor

55: Nero adds a part of Galilee and Peraea to Agrippa's kingdom

---

AD

Before Passover 44: Agrippa orders the beheading of JAMES BROTHER OF JOHN (James the Great); during the feast he imprisons Peter, Ac 12

28 June 45: a rescript of Claudius gives the Jews the custody of the priestly vestments. Herod of Chalcis is named inspector of the Temple, with the right to nominate the high priest. In 47 he nominated Ananias son of Nebadius (47–59), *see* Ac 23:2seq.

Fadus and the false prophet, Theudas, *see* Ac 5:36

Between 45 and 49: **1st mission by Paul**: Antioch, Cyprus, Antioch in Pisidia, Lystra, . . . Antioch, Ac 13:1seq.

About 48: famine in Judaea, worsened by the sabbatical year 47–48. Visit to Jerusalem by HELEN queen of Adiabene, a convert to Judaism; she brings relief to the population, Paul and Barnabas bring help to the communities at Antioch and Jerusalem. The **council of Jerusalem**: gentile Christians exempt from the Law, Ac 15:5seq.; Ga 2:1seq.

49–52: 2nd mission by Paul: Lystra (Timothy), Phrygia, Galatia, Philippi, Thessalonica, Athens (sermon on the Areopagus)

50 Earliest oral tradition of the gospel put in written form

Winter of 50 to summer of 52; Paul in Corinth: the **Letters to the Thessalonians**; and, in the spring of 52, summoned to appear before Gallio

Summer 52; Paul goes to Jerusalem (?) and then to Antioch, Ac 18:22

The Jews in their struggle against the Samaritans are supported by Cumanus. He is sent to Rome by Quadratus, who visits Jerusalem, Passover of 52

Felix checks brigandage

52–59: JONATHAN high priest

53–58: 3rd mission by Paul; APOLLOS at Ephesus, then at Corinth

54–57: after passing through Galatia and Phrygia. Paul stays at Ephesus for 2 years and 3 months

After 56 (?): **Letter to the Philippians**

About Passover 57: **First Letter to the Corinthians**, followed by a quick visit to Corinth, 2 Co 12:14. Return to Ephesus (and **Letter to the Galatians?**)

End of 57: passes through Macedonia. **Second letter to the Corinthians**

Winter 57–58: at Corinth, Ac 20:3, compare 1 Co 16:6; **Letter to the Galatians** (?); **Letter to the Romans**

AD

	Passover 58: at Philippi, Ac 20:6, then, by sea, to Caesarea (Philip and Agabus)
	Summer 58: in Jerusalem. JAMES THE BROTHER OF THE LORD heads the Judaeo-Christian community
	About 58: Felix disbands the followers of the false Egyptian prophet on the Mount of Olives, see Ac 21:28
	Pentecost 58: Paul arrested in the Temple and brought before Ananias and the Sanhedrin. Taken to Caesarea, he is brought before Felix
Between 59 and 67: Agrippa II nominates six high priests, including ANAN SON OF ANNAS (62)	58–60: Paul a captive at Caesarea, the scene of serious troubles between Jews and Syrians
	59: Felix has the former high priest Jonathan assassinated in spite of the fact that he owed his position to Jonathan
60–62: PORCIUS FESTUS prefect	60: Paul appears before Festus and appeals to Caesar. He pleads his cause before Agrippa and his sister Berenice
60–63: CORBULO legate in Syria	
	Autumn of 60: Paul's voyage to Rome, the storm, he winters in Malta
	61–63: Paul in Rome under military guard. His apostolate. **Letters to Colossians, Ephesians, Philemon** and **Philippians**(?)
62–64: LUCCEIUS ALBINUS prefect	62: the High Priest Anan has **James** the brother of the Lord **stoned to death** (after the death of Festus and before the arrival of Albinus). SIMEON, son of Cleopas and of Mary succeeds James as head of the church of Jerusalem (Eusebius)
	Anan deposed by Agrippa II
63–66: CESTIUS GALLUS legate in Syria	63: Paul is set free. Perhaps further journeys, possibly to Spain (Rm 15:24seq.)? Asia Minor? **I Timothy** and **Letter to Titus?**
July 64: burning of Rome and persecution of the Christians	**Gospel of Mark** and **1 Peter** **Letter of James**
64–66: GESSIUS FLORUS prefect. Nominated through the influence of Poppaea, the Jewish wife of Nero	64 (or 67): **martyrdom of Peter** at Rome
66: rising of the Alexandrine Jews. Tiberius Alexander, at that time prefect of Egypt, massacres several thousand of them	Summer 66: in Jerusalem, Florus crucifies some Jews, but a rising compels him to leave the city. Troubles in Caesarea and throughout the country
66–67: spectacular tour of Greece by Nero. He appoints VESPASIAN and his son TITUS to restore order in Palestine	Sept 66: Jerusalem attacked by Cestius Gallius. He retires with heavy losses. Rebel government
	Exodus of people of importance and probably some Christians, see Lk 21:20seq., who take refuge in **Pella** (Eusebius)
67–69: MUCIANUS legate in Syria	67: Vespasian, with 60 000 men, reconquers Galilee (Josephus, its rebel governor, is taken prisoner)
	About 67: Paul, prisoner in Rome, writes **2 Timothy** (?) A little later he is beheaded(?)
	Letter to the Hebrews
March 68: in Gaul the revolt of the legate VINDEX	67–68: the Zealots of JOHN OF GISCHALA, escaped from Galilee, are masters of Jerusalem with the Idumaeans. Anan and the leading people are massacred
April 68: GALBA emperor	

June 68: Nero's suicide

AD

68: Vespasian occupies the maritime plain and the Valley of the Jordan (destruction of Qumran). On Nero's death the siege of Jerusalem is broken off

January 69: OTHO proclaimed Emperor by the Praetorians and VITELLIUS by the legions in Germany

69: SIMON BAR-GIORA and the *sicarii* in Jerusalem. Vespasian subdues the rest of Judaea; the *sicarii* hold out in Jerusalem, and in the Herodion. Masada and Machaerus

July 69: Tiberius Alexander declares his support for Vespasian. His lead is followed by all the East

End of 69: Vespasian in sole command of the empire

Passover 70: Many pilgrims in Jerusalem. **Titus lays siege** to the city with four legions. Tiberius Alexander is second in command

Capture of the 3rd wall, then of the 2nd. Circumvallation. Capture of the Antonia. Famine

Beginning of August, sacrifices cease

29 August 70: capture of the Inner Court and **burning of the Temple** (the 10th of Lous, i.e. the 10th of the 5th month, the day when Nebuzaradan set fire to the first Temple, Jr 52:12 and Josephus)

Sacrifice to the standards, in front of the Temple, cf. Mt 24:15. Titus hailed as Imperator

70, end of the year: Judaea an imperial province; under the rule of the legate of the Xth Legion based in Jerusalem. Caesarea a Roman colony

September 70: capture of the Upper City and the palace of Herod. The inhabitants killed, sold into slavery or condemned to hard labour

Titus in Syria; many Jews killed in the gladiatorial games

71–72: LUCILIUS BASSUS legate in Judaea

Summer 71: triumph of Vespasian and Titus in Rome (with the Temple furnishings): execution of Simon BarGiora. The Arch of Titus

The didrachma formerly subscribed to the Temple is now paid to Jupiter Capitolinus

72: foundation of **Flavia Neapolis** (Nablus)

Capture of the Herodion and Machaerus, by L. Bassus

73: FLAVIUS SILVA legate in Judaea

Passover 73: Siege of **Masada** by F. Silva: Eleazar (descendant of Judas the Galilean) and his *sicarii* kill each other rather than yield

A number of *sicarii* take refuge in Egypt, but are handed over to the Romans. Closing of the temple founded by Onias at Leontopolis

Return to Jerusalem of a group **of Judaeo-Christians** (Epiphanius). Rabbi Eleazar re-opens the synagogue of the Alexandrians

Rabbi Johanan ben-Zakkai founds the **Academy of Jabneh** (Jamnia), successor to the Sanhedrin. GAMALIEL II succeeds him; origins of the Mishnah

Before 70? or about 80: **Gospel of Matthew** in Greek, **Gospel of Luke** and **Acts of Apostles**

The Letter of Jude; IV Esdras (apocryphal)

About 78: *The Jewish War* (Josephus)

79–81: TITUS emperor

81–96: DOMITIAN emperor (brother of Titus)

About 93: *The Antiquities of the Jews* (Josephus)

95: Domitian has his cousin FLAVIUS CLEMENS condemned to death as a Christian and exiles his wife Flavia Domitilla to Pandataria

About 95: Final text of **Revelation**. *Letter of Clement*, bishop of Rome, *to the Corinthians*

96–98: NERVA emperor

Gospel of John, then 1 John (3 John and 2 John are possibly earlier). He opposes Cerinthus and his Docetism

98–117: TRAJAN emperor

2 Peter

The *Didache* (end of first century)

AD 100

106: CORNELIUS PALMA, legate in Syria, occupies the kingdom of Nabataea which becomes the **province of Arabia**, capital: Bostra (Bozrah)

CLAUDIUS ATTICUS HERODES governor of Judaea

107: **martyrdom of Simeon**, 2nd bishop of Jerusalem. From now until the Second Revolt there are 13 other bishops, likewise Judaeo-Christians

About 110: the seven *letters* of IGNATIUS, bishop of Antioch, and his martyrdom at Rome

A little later, the *Letter to the Philippians* of Polycarp, bishop of Smyrna and disciple of John (died in 156)

111–113: PLINY THE YOUNGER legate in Bithynia. His letter on the persecution of the Christians and the **rescript of Trajan**

114–116: annexation of Armenia, Assyria Mesopotamia

The Roman Empire at the height of its power

The Odes of Solomon (apocryphal)

117: **rising of the Jews** throughout the East and revolt of the new provinces. The latter are recaptured by the Moor LUSIUS QUIETUS; he is named legate of Judaea

Quietus erects the statue of Trajan in front of the altar of the Temple (Hippolytus). He is deposed and subsequently put to death by Hadrian

117–138: HADRIAN emperor. Establishes the frontier of the empire on the Euphrates

128–134: Hadrian's second tour of the Empire. At Athens the completion of the Temple of Olympian (or 'Capitoline') Zeus; Antiochus Epiphanes had contributed to its construction. Hadrian claims title 'Olympian' or 'Capitoline'

About 130: the *Letter of Barnabas* (apocryphal). At Hierapolis in Phrygia, the bishop PAPIAS. In Alexandria, the gnostic BASILIDES

TINEIUS RUFUS legate in Judaea and PUBLICIUS MARCELLUS legate in Syria

130: Hadrian in Jerusalem. He decides to rebuild the city (Aelia Capitolina) and the Temple, now dedicated to Jupiter

131–135: **second Jewish rebellion**

SIMEON BEN KOSIBA (*letters of Murabbaat*) seizes Jerusalem; Eleazar high priest. Ben Kosiba acknowledged by RABBI AKIBA as Messiah and as the Star of Nb 24:17, whence his name of Bar Kocheba (Son of the Star). He persecutes the Christians because they refuse to join the revolt

In spite of the reinforcements of Marcellus, Rufus is overrun by the rebels; Hadrian sends them the legate of Britain, JULIUS SEVERUS, and comes in person

Beginning of 134: **capture of Jerusalem**

After the conquest of nearly 50 strongholds, Severus seizes **Bether**, where Bar Kocheba perishes in August 135

AD

The captives are sold at Mamre and Gaza

The province of Judaea becomes the **province of Syria-Palestine**. Jerusalem a Roman colony, forbidden to the Jews

135: Rufus builds Aelia (the temple of Jupiter. Juno and Venus on the site of Calvary and the tomb of Christ). **The Temple is made into a sanctuary of Zeus and Hadrian**

The temple of Zeus Hypsistos at Gerizim and the sacred grove of Adonis around the Cave at Bethlehem

The bishop Mark (about 135–155) and the new Christian community. The Judaeo-Christians. dispersed in Transjordan and Syria. in time form the sect of the **Ebionites** (the 'Poor'). with the *Gospel of the Hebrews*; they do not accept the divinity of Christ and reject the Pauline Letters

LIST OF ORIGINAL COLLABORATORS

There follows a list of those whom the Editor, Alexander Jones, named as his principal collaborators in translation and literary revision of the First Edition of the Jerusalem Bible: Joseph Leo Alston, Florence M. Bennett, Joseph Blenkinsopp, David Joseph Bourke, Douglas Carter, Aldhelm Dean, O.S.B., Illtud Evans, O.P., Kenelm Foster, O.P., Ernest Graf, O.S.B., Prospero Grech, O.S.A., Edmund Hill, O.P., Sylvester Houédard, O.S.B., Leonard Johnston, Anthony J. Kenny, D. O. Lloyd James, James McAuley, Alan Neame, Hubert Richards, Edward Sackville West, Ronald Senator, Walter Shewring, Robert Speaight, J. R. R. Tolkien, R. F. Trevett, Thomas Worden, John Wright, Basil Wrighton.

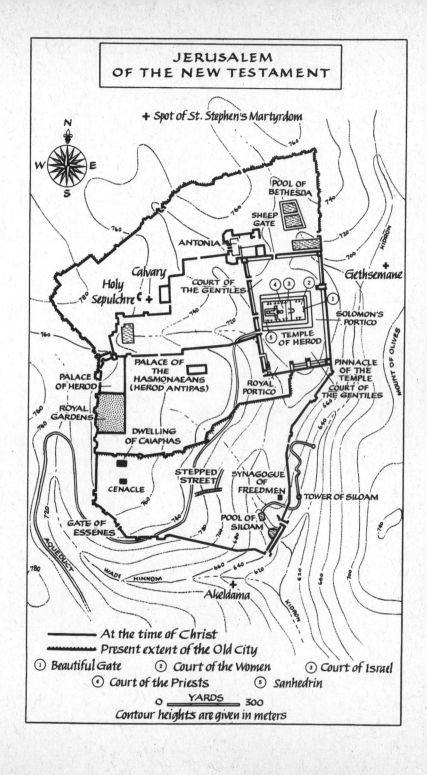

JERUSALEM OF THE NEW TESTAMENT

✝ Spot of St. Stephen's Martyrdom

N · W · E · S

POOL OF BETHESDA

SHEEP GATE

ANTONIA

Calvary

Holy Sepulchre ✝

COURT OF THE GENTILES

Gethsemane ✝

④ ③ ②

①

SOLOMON'S PORTICO

⑤ TEMPLE OF HEROD

MOUNT OF OLIVES

PALACE OF THE HASMONAEANS (HEROD ANTIPAS)

PALACE OF HEROD

ROYAL GARDENS

ROYAL PORTICO

PINNACLE OF THE TEMPLE

COURT OF THE GENTILES

DWELLING OF CAIAPHAS

CENACLE

STEPPED STREET

SYNAGOGUE OF FREEDMEN

TOWER OF SILOAM

POOL OF SILOAM

GATE OF ESSENES

AQUEDUCT

WADI HINNOM

KIDRON

Akeldama ✝

―――――― At the time of Christ
╍╍╍╍╍╍ Present extent of the Old City

① Beautiful Gate   ② Court of the Women   ③ Court of Israel
④ Court of the Priests   ⑤ Sanhedrin

0 ――― YARDS ――― 300

Contour heights are given in meters

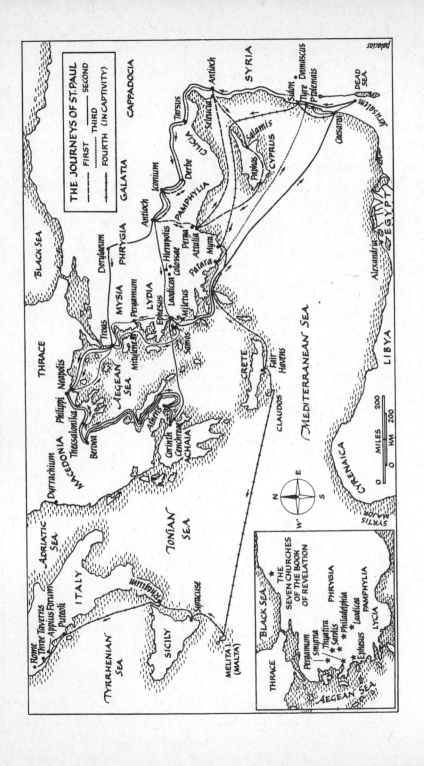

THE JOURNEYS OF ST. PAUL

FIRST ————— SECOND
THIRD ——————— FOURTH (IN CAPTIVITY)

PALESTINE
OF THE
NEW TESTAMENT

MT. HERMON

Caesarea
Philippi

TRACHONITIS

Tyre

SYRO-PHOENICIA

LAKE
SEMECHONITIS

Ptolemais
(Acco, Akka)

Chorazin
Capernaum
Gennesaret
Magdala
Cana (?)

Bethsaida Julias
SEA OF GALILEE
Gergesa

GALILEE

MT.
CARMEL

Cana (?)
Nazareth

Tiberias

R. YARMUK

MT. TABOR

Gadara

Naim

DECAPOLIS

Caesarea

Scythopolis

Pella

SAMARIA

Aenon

Caesaria
Stratonis

MEDITERRANEAN
SEA

Sebaste
(Samaria)

MT. EBAL
MT. GERIZIM
Sychar

RIVER JORDAN

R. JABBOK

Antipatris

PERAEA

Joppa
(Jaffa)

Arimathaea

Philadelphia

Ephraim

Lydda

Jericho

Emmaus (?)

Bethany
Beyond
Jordan

Ain Karim

Jerusalem
Bethany

Qumran

Bethlehem

Ascalon

JUDAEA

Machaerus

Gaza

Hebron

R. ARNON

DEAD

SEA

IDUMAEA

MILES
0   30
0   KM   30

R. ZERED